COURTS AND COMPARATIVE LAW

Courts and Comparative Law

Edited by
MADS ANDENAS
and
DUNCAN FAIRGRIEVE

OXFORD
UNIVERSITY PRESS

OXFORD
UNIVERSITY PRESS

Great Clarendon Street, Oxford, OX2 6DP,
United Kingdom

Oxford University Press is a department of the University of Oxford.
It furthers the University's objective of excellence in research, scholarship,
and education by publishing worldwide. Oxford is a registered trade mark of
Oxford University Press in the UK and in certain other countries

First edition published in 2015
Impression: 1

Published in the United States of America by Oxford University Press
198 Madison Avenue, New York, NY 10016, United States of America

British Library Cataloguing in Publication Data
Data available

Library of Congress Control Number: 2015943516

ISBN 978–0–19–873533–5

Printed and bound by
CPI Group (UK) Ltd, Croydon, CR0 4YY

Contents

List of Abbreviations

ACA-Europe	Association of the Councils of State and the Supreme Administrative Jurisdictions of the Member States of the European Union
Acquis Group	Research Group on existing Community law in the area of general contract law
ACVSB	UK Advisory Committee on Virological Safety of Blood
AG	Attorney General
AIHJA	International Association of Supreme Administrative Jurisdictions (*Association Internationale des Hautes Juridictions Administratives*)
ALI	American Law Institute
AMLA of 2009 (Singapore)	Administration of Muslim Law Act, cap. 3 (No. 27) of 1966, rev. ed., 2009 (Singapore)
ASIL	American Society of International Law
ATS	Alien Tort Statute
BGB	German civil code (*Bürgerliches Gesetzbuch*)
BGBl	Bundesgesetzblatt
BGH	Federal Court of Justice, Germany (*Bundesgerichtshof*)
BNAA	British North America Act of 1867
BVerfGK	Chamber Decisions of the Federal Constitutional Court
CBoR	Canadian Bill of Rights
CEDAW	Convention on the Elimination of All Forms of Discrimination Against Women
CEEP	European Centre of Enterprises with Public Participation
CEOS	Conditions of Employment of Other Servants
CEPEJ	European Commission for the Efficiency of Justice
CERD	International Convention on the Elimination of All Forms of Racial Discrimination
CESL	Common European Sales Law
CFR	Common Frame of Reference
CFREU	Charter of Fundamental Rights of the European Union
Charter	Charter of Fundamental Rights of the European Union
CHRA	Canadian Human Rights Act
CISG	United Nations Convention on Contracts for the International Sale of Goods
CJEU	Court of Justice of the European Union
CMR	Convention on the Contract for the International Carriage of Goods
CPA	Consumer Protection Act 1987
CPR	Constitution of the Portuguese Republic
CRC	Civil Rights Congress
CRDJ	*Centre de recherches et de diffusion juridiques*
CST	EU Civil Service Tribunal
DCFR	Draft Common Frame of Reference

ECHR	European Convention for the Protection of Human Rights and Fundamental Freedoms (European Convention on Human Rights)
ECJ	European Court of Justice
ECtHR	European Court of Human Rights
ECTIL	European Centre of Tort and Insurance Law
EGC	General Court
EIB	European Investment Bank
ELI	European Law Institute
ERPL	European Review of Private Law
ETL	European Tort Law
ETUC	European Trade Union Confederation
EU	European Union
EuGRZ	Europäische Grundrechte-Zeitschrift
FDA	US Food and Drugs Administration
GAAP	generally accepted auditing principles
GG	Grundgesetz, Basic Law
GTC	general terms and conditions
HHL	HIV Haemophiliac Litigation
HRC	UN Human Rights Committee
ICC	International Criminal Court
ICCPR	International Covenant on Civil and Political Rights
ICESCR	International Covenant on Economic, Social and Cultural Rights
ICSID Convention	Convention on the Settlement of Investment Disputes between States and Nationals of Other States
ICTR	International Criminal Tribunal for Rwanda
ICTY	International Criminal Tribunal for the former Yugoslavia
ILC	International Law Commission
ILO	International Law Office
ILOAT	Administrative Tribunal of the International Labour Organization
IULA	International Union of Local Authorities
JCPC	Judicial Committee of the Privy Council
Lando Commission	Commission on European Contract Law
LDIP	Swiss Code on Private International Law
LEC	Spanish Code of Civil Procedure (*Ley de enjuiciamiento civil* 2000)
LGBT	lesbian, gay, bisexual, and transgender
MIB	Brunei Malay Muslim Monarchy (Melayu Islam Beraja)
MTC	OECD Model Tax Convention
NAACP	National Association for the Advancement of Colored People
NANBH	NonA NonB Hepatitis
New York Convention	UN Convention on the Recognition and Enforcement of Foreign Arbitral Awards
NGO	non-governmental organization
NJW	Neue Juristische Wochenschrift

NNC	National Negro Congress
NWO	Netherlands Organisation for Scientific Research
OCR	Office of the Chief Rabbi of the United Hebrew Congregation of the Commonwealth
OECD	Organisation for Economic Co-operation and Development
Oviedo Convention	Convention on Human Rights and Biomedicine
PAP	People's Action Party (Singapore)
PC	Judicial Committee of the Privy Council
PECL	Principles of European Contract Law
PETL	Principles of European Tort Law
PIL	private international law
PLRA	Prison Litigation Reform Act
Rapport	*Rapport de la Cour de cassation*
Rome Statute	Rome Statute of the International Criminal Court
SANE	Society of Americans for National Existence
SCC	Supreme Court of Canada
SECA	Supreme and Exchequer Courts Act
StGB	German Criminal Code
Study Group	Study Group on a European Civil Code
TEU	Treaty on European Union
TFEU	Treaty on the Functioning of the European Union
ThUG	Therapeutic Confinement Act
TOGAs	transnational organizations of government actors
UCLG	United Cities and Local Governments
UDHR	Universal Declaration of Human Rights
UK	United Kingdom
UN	United Nations
UNESCO	General Conference of the UN Educational, Scientific and Cultural Organization
UNICE	Union of Industrial and Employers' Confederations of Europe
UNIDROIT	International Institute for the Unification of Private Law
US	United States of America
USCM	US Conference of Mayors
UTO	United Towns Organisation
VCLT	Vienna Convention on the Law of Treaties
WTO	World Trade Organization
ZEuP	Zeitschrift für Europäisches Privatrecht

List of Contributors

Alexis Albarian Associate Professor of Private Law, Aix-Marseille University, France, Economic Law Center (EA 4224).

Guido Alpa Professore ordinario di diritto civile, Università di Roma 'la Sapienza'; Presidente del Consiglio Nazionale Forense.

Mads Andenas Professor, University of Oslo and Institute of Advanced Legal Studies, University of London. UN Special Rapporteur on Arbitrary Detention.

Annalisa Aschieri PhD Student, University of Turin, Department of Law.

Eirik Bjorge Shaw Foundation Junior Research Fellow, Jesus College, University of Oxford.

Aurélie Bretonneau Maître des Requêtes, Conseil d'Etat, France.

His Honour Judge Michael Brooke QC Judge Brooke died in 2014.

Sir Michael Burton Judge, High Court of England and Wales; President of the Investigatory Powers Tribunal.

Erdem Büyüksagis Priv.-Doz. Dr. at the University of Fribourg in Switzerland and Full-Tenured Aggregate Professor at Antalya International University in Turkey.

Ermanno Calzolaio Professor of Private Comparative Law and Comparative Legal Systems and Dean of the Faculty of Law at the University of Macerata (Italy).

Guy Canivet Member of the Conseil Constitutionnel, France.

Samuel Dahan Cornell Law Clerk, Conseil d'Etat, Cornell University Law School.

Olivier Deparis Président de chambre, Douai Court of Appeal, France.

Olivier Dutheillet de Lamothe Président de la Section Sociale du Conseil d'Etat, France.

Duncan Fairgrieve Senior Fellow in Comparative Law, British Institute of International and Comparative Law, London; Professeur Associé, Université Paris Dauphine PSL.

Bénédicte Fauvarque-Cosson Professor of Law, Université Panthéon-Assas (Paris II), President of the Société de législation comparée.

Richard Fentiman Professor of Private International Law at the University of Cambridge.

Ian Forrester QC White and Case LLP. QC at the Scots Bar.

Martin Gelter Associate Professor, Fordham Law School (US) and Research Associate, European Corporate Governance Institute.

Gianluca Gentili Research Associate in Transnational Constitutional Law, University of Manchester, School of Law (Manchester, UK).

H. Patrick Glenn Peter M. Laing Professor of Law, McGill University. Professor Glenn died in 2014.

Ana Maria Guerra Martins Judge of the Portuguese Constitutional Court; Professor at the Faculty of Law of the University of Lisbon.

Kathleen Gutman Senior Affiliated Researcher at the Institute for European Law, University of Leuven.

Geraint Howells Dean of the School of Law and Chair Professor of Commercial Law, City University of Hong Kong.

Peter M. Huber Justice of the Federal Constitutional Court, Germany.

Thomas Kadner Graziano Professor of Law at the University of Geneva, Faculty of Law.

Galateia Kalouta Legal Researcher, University of Osnabrück.

Rachael Kondak Lawyer, Research Division of the European Court of Human Rights.

Koen Lenaerts Vice-President of the Court of Justice of the European Union and Professor of European Union Law, University of Leuven.

François Lichère Professor of Public law, University of Aix-Marseille.

Romain M. Lorentz Participating Adjunct Professor, University of St Thomas Opus College of Business, St Paul, Minnesota (USA).

Paul Mahoney United Kingdom Judge, European Court of Human Rights.

Elaine Mak Endowed Professor of Empirical Study of Public Law, Erasmus School of Law.

Martha Minow Dean and Jeremiah Smith, Jr. Professor, Harvard Law School.

Marta Otero Crespo Senior Lecturer in Civil Law at Universidad de Santiago de Compostela.

Andreas L. Paulus Justice of the First Senate of the Federal Constitutional Court; Professor, University of Göttingen.

Lucio Pegoraro Full Professor of Comparative Public Law, University of Bologna.

Miguel Prata Roque Professor at the Faculty of Law of the University of Lisbon. Advisor at the Cabinet of Judges of the Portuguese Constitutional Court.

Bernard Rabatel *Procureur general*, Court of Appeals, Fort-de-France, Martinique.

Christa Rautenbach Professor of Law, Faculty of Law, North-West University (Potchefstroom Campus), South Africa.

Marta Requejo Isidro Senior Research Fellow at Max Planck Institute Luxembourg.

Judith Resnik Arthur Liman Professor of Law, Yale Law School.

Geoffrey Samuel Professor of Law, Kent Law School, University of Kent; Professor *affilié*, École de droit, Sciences-Po Paris.

Aldo Sandulli Full Professor of Administrative Law and Dean of the Faculty of Law of the University Suor Orsola Benincasa of Naples.

Mathias Siems Professor of Commercial Law at Durham University (UK) and Research Associate at the Centre for Business Research of the University of Cambridge (UK).

Astrid Stadler University of Konstanz; Erasmus School of Law, Rotterdam.

Kerstin Steiner Senior Lecturer at the Department of Business Law and Taxation, Faculty of Business and Economics, Monash University and Associate of the Asian Law Centre, The University of Melbourne.

Haris Tagaras Professor of Law at the Panteion University of Athens; Former Judge and Chamber President at the European Union Civil Service Tribunal.

Hannes Unberath Professor of Civil Law and Civil Procedure Law at the University of Bayreuth. Professor Unberath died in 2013.

Nicholas Underhill Lord Justice of Appeal, Court of Appeal of England and Wales.

Jeremy Waldron University Professor at New York University School of Law.

Jonathon Watson Wilhelms-Universität Münster, Germany.

PART I

COURTS AND COMPARATIVE LAW

1

Courts and Comparative Law

In Search of a Common Language for Open Legal Systems

Mads Andenas and Duncan Fairgrieve***

I. Current challenges to comparative law and comparative law as a challenge

Comparative law challenges some traditionalists who regard legal method in a dualist paradigm, relying on the autonomy of their legal system. At the same time, the ever more extensive use of comparative law challenges comparative law as an academic discipline and as a method.

In 1965, Otto Kahn-Freund opened his inaugural lecture as Professor of Comparative Law with a paradox his Oxford audience much enjoyed: 'the Professor of Comparative Law suffers from the problem that the subject he professes has by common consent the somewhat unusual characteristic that it does not exist'. He went on to explain that comparative law is 'not a topic but a method', or rather 'the common name for a variety of methods of looking at law, and especially of looking at one's own law'.[1] One of his successors, Sir Basil Markesinis, never enjoyed the paradox, and characterized the great English comparatists of the 20th century as having eventually led their students and successors into an isolated and enclosed intellectual ghetto with little prospect of escape.[2]

In 2004, yet another Oxford professor, and a pupil of Kahn-Freund's, Mark Freedland, added the following: 'One of the main attributes of that heritage is the idea or perception that comparative law is not in any way a separate or ring-fenced area of legal studies; it has open borders, so that legal scholars can enter or leave the state of comparative law without elaborate identity papers.'[3]

Gently self-deprecating comparative law academics, and their academic and less academic opponents, may still query the existence of the academic discipline. At any academic comparative law stage there would be six professors in search of an author, with a focus on the variety more than any common method of looking at law, concluding that methodological problems make practical applications very difficult,

* Professor, University of Oslo and Institute of Advanced Legal Studies, University of London. UN Special Rapporteur on Arbitrary Detention.

** Senior Fellow in Comparative Law, British Institute of International and Comparative Law, London; Professeur Associé, Université Paris Dauphine PSL.

[1] Otto Kahn-Freund, 'Comparative Law as an Academic Subject' (1966) 82 LQR 40, at 40.

[2] Basil Markesinis, *Comparative Law in the Courtroom and the Classroom* (Oxford: Hart Publishing, 2003), at 25–6.

[3] Mark Freedland, 'Introduction', in G Canivet, M Andenas, and D Fairgrieve, *Comparative Law Before the Courts* (London: BIICL, 2004) at xvi.

warning the audience 'Don't Try This at Home'. While some academic comparative lawyers still play in the ghetto (as Markesinis criticized), comparative law has got more than just a helping hand from the courts.

Courts have become the laboratories of comparative law, and try out different methods in their practical work. The forerunner to this book, *Comparative Law Before the Courts*, edited by Guy Canivet, the premier Président of the Cour de cassation of France, with the two of us, was published in 2004 when many courts were restrictive in, or completely excluded, the citation of foreign judgments or other external sources of law.

The seminars leading up to the 2004 book and the book itself were supported by the senior law lord, Lord Bingham, and a predecessor, Lord Goff, who wrote in the Foreword: 'It is heartening to see that comparative law is gaining in utility and relevance in the decisions of the courts.'[4] Canivet, Goff, and Bingham themselves were accomplished comparative law scholars. Their supreme courts were pioneers in their active use of comparative law as a source of law at a time when many courts would not make any reference to comparative law in their judgments, although most of these nonetheless would make use of comparative sources in their preparatory reports and opinions and also encourage parties to make submissions on comparative law points.

The ten years since the book have seen an increased use of comparative law by courts, and in a way which cannot be understood merely as 'a variety of methods of looking at law, and especially of looking at one's own law', in the reductionist manner some have interpreted Sir Otto Kahn-Freund's statement.

International courts have faced particular challenges. The new enforcement mechanisms and the multiplication of enforcement regimes put the international law system's coherence under pressure. Fear of fragmentation made some scholars emphasize the role of international courts in developing substantive law and procedure in a way that made up for the lack of institutional reforms that could remedy the problem. A strong reliance on international law as a system with a hierarchy of norms is provided by 'The Report of the study group on the fragmentation of international law', finalized by Martti Koskenniemi at the 58th session of the United Nation's International Law Commission in 2006. The International Law Commission's Special Rapporteur on the Formation of Custom, Sir Michael Wood, has observed that while:

> [t]he formation and evidence of rules of customary international law in different fields may raise particular issues and it may therefore be for consideration whether, and if so to what degree, different weight may be given to different materials depending on the field in question ... at the same time it should be recalled that, in the words of Judge Greenwood, '[i]nternational law is not a series of fragmented specialist and self-contained bodies of law, each of which functions in isolation from the others; it is a single, unified system of law'.[5]

[4] Lord Goff of Chieveley, 'Foreword', in G Canivet, M Andenas, and D Fairgrieve, *Comparative Law Before the Courts* (London: BIICL, 2004) at vi.

[5] Special Rapporteur Sir Michael Wood, First Report on Formation and Evidence of Customary International Law ILC A/CN.4/663 p 8 [19], citing *Ahmadou Sadio Diallo (Republic of Guinea v Democratic*

For international law to be an effective legal system, the ever-increasing number of bodies with a role to play in international law must take account of one another, and address possible conflicts, as well as those that cannot be resolved, and, in the course of doing so, contribute to the development of general principles and forms of hierarchies of norms and institutions. Such convergence may contribute to the stabilization and promotion of cohesion in the rapidly expanding international legal system.[6]

The International Court of Justice simply did not cite other courts, or national law, but has in recent judgments not only undertaken extensive surveys and analysis of national law and law from other international courts, but relied heavily on them.[7] The European Court of Human Rights has taken its long-standing use of comparative law further, and important judgments sometimes have longer sections under the heading 'Comparative Law'.[8] The European Court of Justice today makes open use of comparative law in the context of its extended tasks concerning fundamental rights and other general principles of EU law.[9]

Most national courts follow the same path of giving comparative law an ever more prominent place as a source of law, as the chapters to this book illustrate, and struggle with the methodological consequences. Comparative law as a source of law still has its opponents, including among judges, but is generally accepted in the different national jurisdictions. The argument today is about the method—how, and not if, courts should make use of the judgments and legal materials from other jurisdictions in reaching a decision. The United States is the exception.[10] The US Supreme Court has become the forum for one of the sharpest discussions on the utility and legitimacy of comparative law. Best known from the debate between Supreme Court Justices on the recourse to sources of foreign and international law that are 'external' to the domestic norms being interpreted, is Justice Scalia's criticism of the majority's use of comparative law as a modern fad and dangerous flirtation with 'alien law' in several opinions.[11] Although some form of comparative law has long been part of the judicial process, in the United States comparison was predominantly undertaken between the states and in the rest of the common law world between common law jurisdictions in different configurations. The inherent characteristics of the common law have perhaps served to mask the fact that it is indeed based on a series of comparative law exercises. Across the national borders dividing the Commonwealth, the seamless nature of the common law, from its origins in English law, through its permutations across to former colonies and beyond, provided a reason and justification for courts to look to each other's jurisprudence, exchange solutions, and thereby create a network of persuasive authority. But there is a long tradition of borrowing from beyond the common law, although often

Republic of the Congo) (Compensation owed by the Democratic Republic of the Congo to the Republic of Guinea), Judgment, 19 June 2012, Declaration of Judge Greenwood [8].

[6] See Mads Andenas and Eirik Bjorge (eds.), *A Farewell to Fragmentation: Reassertion and Convergence in International Law* (Cambridge: Cambridge University Press, 2015).

[7] As described by Eirik Bjorge in Chapter 12 in this book.

[8] See further Paul Mahoney and Rachael Kondak, Chapter 7 in this book.

[9] See further Koen Lenaerts and Kathleen Gutman, Chapter 8 in this book.

[10] See the lively discussion in the US, described by Judith Resnik in Chapter 23.

[11] In *Lawrence et al v Texas*, 539 US 558 (2003), and subsequent cases. See Judith Resnik, Chapter 23 in this book; Martha Minow, Chapter 27 in this book; and J Waldron, Chapter 28 in this book.

conveniently forgotten or at least pushed into the background. The late Lord Bingham, one of the greatest jurists of recent times, was a pioneer in the forensic use of comparative law and a tireless advocate of the idea of 'there is a world elsewhere'. Enjoying the controversy, Lord Bingham often referred to the judicial hero of English commercial lawyers, Lord Mansfield, and how he made good use of Pothier and other French sources in the creation of English commercial law.[12]

The Supreme Court of the United States is much cited internationally. It has had a notable impact on the constitutional law of most jurisdictions, in particular through its due process and freedom of press jurisprudence. Guido Calabresi, sitting as a judge of the Second Circuit of the US Court of Appeals in *US v Manuel Then*, cited the German and Italian constitutional courts, and added that:

> these countries are our 'constitutional offspring', and how they have dealt with problems analogous to ours can be very useful to us when we face difficult constitutional issues. Wise parents do not hesitate to learn from their children.[13]

Justice Sandra Day O'Connor has also extra-judicially restated her support for the use of comparative law:

> I suspect that with time we will rely increasingly on international and foreign law in resolving what now appear to be domestic issues. Doing so may not only enrich our own country's decisions; it will create that all-important good impression. When U.S. courts are seen to be cognizant of other judicial systems, our ability to act as a rule-of-law model for other nations will be enhanced.[14]

Aharon Barak, then the Chief Justice of the Supreme Court of Israel, criticized in 2002 the position of US Supreme Court justices who did not cite foreign judgments: 'They fail to make use of an important source of inspiration, one that enriches legal thinking, makes law more creative, and strengthens the democratic ties and foundations of different legal systems.' Partly as a consequence, the US Supreme Court 'is losing the central role it once had among courts in modern democracies'.[15]

The discussion in the US Supreme Court continues to give rise to interesting scholarship. The case against the use of international and foreign law is set out by, among others, Curtis Bradley and Jack Goldsmith, who challenge the positive foundation in US law for such use.[16]

[12] For instance in Sir Thomas Bingham, 'There is a World Elsewhere: The Changing Perspectives of English Law' (1992) 41 ICLQ 513, reprinted in Bingham, *The Business of Judging* (Oxford: Oxford University Press, 2000) 87. Lord Bingham wrote that 'in showing a new receptiveness to the experience and learning of others, the English courts are not, I think, establishing a new tradition, but reverting to an old and better one', at 527.

[13] *US v Manuel Then*, 2nd Circuit, 56 F.3d 464 (1995).

[14] Remarks by Sandra Day O'Connor, Southern Center for International Studies, Atlanta, Georgia, October 28, 2003, at <http://www.humanrightsfirst.org/wp-content/uploads/pdf/SOUTHERN_CENTER_INTERNATIONAL_STUDIES_Justice_O'Connor.pdf>.

[15] Aharon Barak, 'Foreword: A Judge on Judging: The Role of a Supreme Court in a Democracy' (2002) 116 (2002) Harvard L Rev 16: 97–106.

[16] Curtis A Bradley and Jack L Goldsmith, 'Customary International Law as Federal Common Law: A Critique of the Modern Position' (1997) 110 Harvard L. Rev. 4: 815, at 822.

Judith Resnik in Chapter 23 of this book develops a powerful counter-narrative to the objections made to the use of non-US sources. Pointing out that America is a country of migrants, as is US law, Resnik questions the veracity of labelling law 'domestic' or 'foreign', given that borders are porous and various routes serve to domesticate as well as exile 'foreign' law. Resnik eloquently illustrates the inherent difficulties in avoiding foreign sources in the US system, built as it is on liberal principles. Within the context of legislation effecting prohibitions on the resort to non-domestic law, she analyses the constitutional issues raised by attempts to direct judges as to sources of law, and poses the question whether constitutional principles allow judges to be subject to, or immune from, directions on the sources to consult when rendering judgments. Resnik argues that legislatures cannot try to limit judicial thought-processes by banning consideration of a category of materials, labelled 'foreign.' She ultimately argues that the use of foreign sources is neither exotic nor less intrinsically disciplined than looking at other resources.

Jeremy Waldron provides strong support for the use of foreign law, but opens his chapter in the present book by observing that there is no theory or doctrine which provides a basis either for the use of foreign law or the rejection of such use.[17] He continues by arguing that we should not reject the idea of a theory of the citation of foreign law simply because we see foreign law being cited opportunistically. We should reject it only if we think inconsistent and unprincipled citation is inevitable under the auspices of the theory providing the foundations for such citations. He then goes on to develop a theory that the citation of foreign law can rest on the idea of the law of nations (*ius gentium*). He points to the fact that although the law of nations is often used as a synonym for international law, it once had a broader meaning, comprising something like the common law of mankind. It was not just law on issues between sovereigns but on legal issues generally—on contract, property, crime, and tort. It was a set of principles that had established itself as a sort of consensus among judges, jurists, and lawmakers around the world. Waldron argues for returning the phrase to this broader meaning. He demonstrates the utility of this from both positivist and natural law starting points. He uses an analogy between the law of nations and the established body of scientific findings. Existing science claims neither unanimity among scientists, nor infallibility. Individual scientists could not proceed with their own individual research without taking account of existing science. The law of nations is available to lawmakers and judges as an established body of legal insight, and has a similar function in that it reminds them that their particular problem has been confronted before and 'that they, like scientists, should try to think it through in the company of those who have already dealt with it'. The issues that follow from Waldron's argument are mainly in developing the methodology for establishing and making use of this body of legal insight.

Finally, and following from this argument, Waldron contrasts the positions of those who see law as will, and those who see law as reason. Those who approach the law as a

[17] Jeremy Waldron, Chapter 28 in this book, reprinted from (2005) 119 Harvard L. Rev. 129, and the analysis in John Bell, 'Researching Globalisation: Lessons From Judicial Citations' (2014) Cambridge Journal of International and Comparative Law 22.

matter of will do not, of course, see any reason why expressions of will elsewhere in the world (abroad) should affect expressions of will at home. Those who see law as a matter of reason may well be willing to approach it in 'a scientific spirit that relies not just on our own reasoning but on some rational relation between what we are wrestling with and what others have figured out'.

Martha Minow refers to 'the swirling debate over whether the United States courts should consult international or comparative law' which has puzzled her as a law professor as no one disagrees that US judges have long consulted and referred to materials from other countries as well as international sources. She points out how the evidence of the long-standing practice is undisputed and well forecast by one of the Federalist Papers.[18] Nonetheless, citing foreign and international sources has provoked intense controversy in the course of the last decade. There seems to be a fear of temptation or loss of control. If merely looking at what others are doing causes the worry, the concern seems to be about caving in to peer pressure or being an outlier—some kind of contagion effect.

Minow takes the position that, while not minimizing concerns about peer pressure or influence, one should instead emphasize that 'confidence in who we are, what our values and traditions are, and how we interpret them over time stems from a source deeper than a refusal to look at what others do'.

In her conclusion, Minow points to soft law in the European Union and the complementarity of the International Criminal Court Statute as models for approaching the relationship between national and international legal systems. Her own scholarship on *Brown v Board of Education*[19] has shown the vast impact of US law on other systems from the early days after the *Brown* case to the current judgments of the European Court of Human Rights on discrimination against Roma in European countries.[20]

Our introduction to the 2004 *Comparative Law Before the Courts* had the title 'Finding a Common Language for Open Legal Systems'.[21] Legal systems will not give the same answers to legal questions; they will not even deal with one another in the same manner. The aim of the 2004 book was, as it is of the present book, to examine the use of comparative law by national and international courts, itself a fruitful subject of comparative law scholarship. Both books include authoritative contributions covering both common law and civil law jurisdictions from the viewpoint of practitioners and academic theorists. The starting point is that comparative law is increasingly recognized as an essential reference point for judicial decision-making. The challenge to judges and counsel is considerable. Legal scholarship has an important role in making comparative material available in a systematic manner. At the present stage there is perhaps even more of a need to discuss the role of comparative law in the judicial process. One extension of this discussion of legal method is how legal scholarship can assist. The discussion ranges from jurisprudential questions of the relevance and

[18] Marta Minow, Chapter 27 in this book.

[19] See M Minow, *In Brown's Wake: Legacies of America's Constitutional Landmark* (New York: Oxford University Press, 2010).

[20] Ibid., at 19–25.

[21] Mads Andenas and Duncan Fairgrieve, 'Finding a Common Language for Open Legal Systems', in G Canivet, M Andenas, and D Fairgrieve, *Comparative Law Before the Courts* (London: BIICL, 2004) at xxvii.

weight of comparative law arguments, to the practical aspects of how to present those arguments to a court or where and how to access the source material. Parallel developments in different jurisdictions justify a comparative approach to the use of comparative law. There may be lessons to learn from other jurisdictions.

II. Polycentricity and pluralism

Shedding traditional adherence to 20th-century positivist and national paradigms, domestic courts are deliberately and explicitly making use of comparative law to an unprecedented extent. International courts move freely across the boundaries of the different treaty regimes, searching for and applying the underlying unities, also in relation to domestic law. Many factors can of course be seen as having influenced this process.[22] First amongst these is the breakdown of the traditionally closed and hierarchical national legal systems. Another factor is the increasingly complex issues with which modern courts are required to engage, beyond what follows from the breakdown of the closed national legal systems, whether they be fundamental rights, constitutional review, international law, or emerging areas such as biomedical regulation, in which ethical and moral issues are increasingly prominent. The polycentric nature of these issues poses challenges to the traditional judicial approaches and explains changes in terms procedures, personnel, and outlook.

The complexity of decision-making has heightened the importance of knowing how other jurisdictions have dealt with similar problems. This has opened the door to the use of, and increases in, the utility of comparative law, through the development of formal and informal avenues for judicial dialogues, as well as an increasing engagement with doctrinal literature within the formal decision-making process.

As we will discuss from different perspectives below, and as several of the other contributors to the present book do, comparative law also offers assistance with many of the new issues of method that courts have to resolve in the more open legal systems. The first issue is: how does one deal with comparative law? When is it relevant, what weight should it have, how does one sort out the many practical problems that arise? Comparative law can also assist courts in dealing with other fundamental issues such as international law and European law, and their relationship with national law, or, for that matter, the relationship of courts with the legislatures as parliamentary supremacy (in the sense of the national legislature's supremacy) is eroded.

Comparative law is itself one of several new types of challenges that courts have to deal with. A situation with sources of law with competing claims to legitimacy leaves a whole set of issues to be determined by the courts.[23] The traditional form of a unitary

[22] See more general discussion in Mads Andenas and Duncan Fairgrieve, '"There is a World Elsewhere"—Lord Bingham and Comparative Law', in Mads Andenas and Duncan Fairgrieve (eds.), *Tom Bingham and the Transformation of the Law: A Liber Amicorum* (Oxford: Oxford University Press, 2009 and 2011), and John Bell, 'The Argumentative Status of Foreign Legal Arguments' (2012) 8 Utrecht L. Rev. 8, 17.

[23] What Hart termed the 'secondary rules', representing the constitutional arrangements of any particular society, are undergoing fundamental change. The 'primary rules' are also changing in a way that reflects the change of the secondary rules, developing rights of individuals, harmonizing the laws of European countries over a wide field, etc. See HLA Hart, *The Concept of Law* (Oxford: Oxford University Press, 1961) at 51 about 'secondary rules'.

rule of recognition (if it ever applied fully anywhere)[24] kept the picture simple. The possible recourse to a clear hierarchy, resolving conflicts between norms, seemed to leave the major issues for determination by the legislature. The present, more complex constitutional systems of validity of norms and their hierarchy, leave courts with many new issues. There are certain constitutional issues that traditionally have been left to practice. On the macro or principles level, this applies to the relationship between legal orders. On the micro or rules level, it applies to remedies protecting private parties against the state. These are issues that have come to the fore in most jurisdictions, with courts rapidly developing the law. The macro level developments include, for instance, the role of international and European law in national law, or the role of the case law of one international court before another international court. At the micro level, examples are the intensity of judicial review of administrative action and of legislation, tort liability of administrative authorities, and injunctive remedies against the state.

This opens the way for, and increases the utility of, comparative law. It is not surprising that courts are, to an increasing degree, involved in dialogues with one another across the traditional jurisdictional divides. Our discussion of the cases and typology of current applications of comparative law will illustrate the methodological problems of the use of comparative law in the courts.

Several of the contributors to the present book look at the dialogues between different national and international courts. An international market place for judgments is emerging, where also the form and style of judgments may be influenced by the increased use of comparative law. Courts may wish to explain their judgments not only to parties and the national legal community, but so that they are understood in other jurisdictions. National supreme courts may also consider the review that European and international courts and similar bodies could undertake, and how to explain their position better. In national courts one talks about 'appeal proofing'. This now also applies to supreme courts who may find their judgments reviewed, and to international courts wanting to convince other international courts, or domestic courts, to adopt their views on the law. At a vertical level, the dialogues between the international and national courts are developing and are also formally recognized in a way they were not a few years ago.

One may talk about an international market place for judgments,[25] where the form of judgments may be influenced by the accessibility and increased use of comparative law.[26] In jurisdictions where the form of judgments allows it, judges make open reference to comparative law sources, and in particular to judgments by foreign

[24] See the brief setting out of the case against a universal rule of recognition, or Austin's illimitable and indivisible sovereign, or traditional statehood concepts, in Mads Andenas and John Gardner, 'Introduction: Can Europe have a Constitution' (2001) 12(1) Kings College Law Journal 1.

[25] See Lord Rodger, 'The Form and Language of Judicial Opinion' (2002) 118 Law Quarterly Review 226, 247; and Lord Goff of Chieveley, 'The Future of the Common Law' (1997) 46 International and Comparative Law Quarterly 745, 756–7, on the accessible form of common law judgments, and also Maurice Adams, Jacco Bomhoff, and Nick Huls (eds.), *The Legitimacy of Highest Courts' Rulings* (The Hague: Asser Press, 2008) provides important contributions to this analysis.

[26] There is an increasing access to foreign court judgments and other legal sources in the citations made by courts and in legal scholarship. The court websites that provide translations of important judgments are increasing in number and quality.

courts.[27] We have pointed to the variation between national systems (and sometimes even within them). Where the form of judgments is not open for the citation of foreign law sources, there may be an advocate-general or *rapporteur* who makes direct references, or the use of comparative law sources may be acknowledged in less formal ways.

Comparative law plays a role in resolving fundamental issues such as the relationship between national and international law, in implementing international and European human rights law, in developing constitutional review, in review of administrative action, and in developing effective remedies. Comparative law also plays a role in developing the substantive law in different areas, including in finding normative solutions to questions of a more technical kind. One can hardly expect always to find the ideal solutions to problems of globalization within one's own jurisdiction. Nonetheless, there is still disagreement on when comparative law can be invoked, where it is convenient to do so, and how it should be done.

Similar questions are posed to courts in jurisdictions across the world, but there is much variation in the solutions found. For instance, some courts still find that the autonomy of their legal system prevents them from expressly acknowledging the use of foreign judgments. This is one of the issues where there has been a rapid development in the practice of courts, including the French courts,[28] the Italian *Corte di cassazione*, the International Court of Justice, and the European Court of Justice, which in different ways have relaxed their self-imposed restrictions on citing judgments by courts from other jurisdictions.

Our discussion of the cases and typology of current applications of comparative law will illustrate the methodological problems of the use of comparative law in the courts. There are cases which reflect a general recognition of comparative law as a persuasive authority or source of law, which apply normative models from other jurisdictions where national law is undetermined, and which use comparative law in reviewing factual assumptions about the consequences of legal rules, or assumptions about the universal applicability of rules or principles.

Comparative law has been seen to provide courts with persuasive and non-binding arguments. At the current stage, there is an argument about the consequences of a call for more consistency. One question is whether courts are ever bound to make use of comparative law sources, for instance in certain situations when an authority is based on comparative law sources.

In the new more open legal systems, it is left to courts to weigh and balance ever more complex sources of law. The courts will also have competing claims to legitimacy.

[27] Basil Markesinis and Jorg Fedtke, *Engaging in Foreign Law* (Oxford: Hart Publishing, 2009) is a leading treatise on comparative law method, and deals extensively with comparative law in the courts. See also generally Matthias Reimann and Reinhard Zimmermann, *The Oxford Handbook of Comparative Law* (Oxford: Oxford University Press, 2006), especially the chapter by Stefan Vogenauer, 'Sources of Law and Legal Method in Comparative Law', at 869–98.

[28] See Guy Canivet, 'Variations sur la politique jurisprudentielle: les juges ont-ils un âme?', in Mads Andenas and Duncan Fairgrieve (eds.), *Tom Bingham and the Transformation of the Law: A Liber Amicorum* (Oxford: Oxford University Press, 2009 and 2011) 17, and Bernard Stirn, 'Le Conseil d'Etat, so British', in Mads Andenas and Duncan Fairgrieve (eds.), *Tom Bingham and the Transformation of the Law: A Liber Amicorum* (Oxford: Oxford University Press, 2009 and 2011) 81.

The sources of law may still be supported on a unitary, nationally based, rule of recognition. But the way in which courts deal with the more complex issues of validity of norms and their hierarchy, has one outcome. That is an opening up of the legal system, mainly through the recognition of sources of law from outside the traditionally closed national system.

III. A typology

Courts function within systems of sources of legal authority. The domestic law paradigm remains strong, and the methodological problems in the use of comparative law add to the challenge. The role of comparative law remains open, although ever less controversial (with the prominent exception of the United States). It may be interesting to analyse some of the cases with a view to formulating a typology of the use of comparative law by courts. There are some clear situations that stand out in the recent case law.

The tentative typology is grouped into seven categories, building on our 2012 study included in Pier Giuseppe Monateri's *Methods of Comparative Law.*[29] Comparative law can be used in the following cases:

(1) to provide support for a rule or an outcome;
(2) for normative models in comparative law where national law is undetermined;
(3) to review factual assumptions about the consequences of legal rules;
(4) to review assumptions about the universal applicability of a particular rule;
(5) to overturn authority in domestic law;
(6) to develop principles of domestic law; and
(7) to resolve problems of the application of European and international law, including European Human Rights law.

1. Support for a rule or an outcome

The existence of a solution in other jurisdictions may under certain circumstances provide persuasive arguments for that solution in one's own jurisdictions, if one agrees with Lord Bingham's views on the 'virtue in uniformity of outcome' in *Fairchild*,[30] as set out below, and that '[p]rocedural idiosyncracy is not (like national costume or regional cuisine) to be nurtured for its own sake' in *Dresser*.[31] See also his statement that 'it should be no easier to succeed here than in France or Germany', in *JD v East Berkshire*.[32] But where domestic sources support another rule or outcome, this kind of argument does not seem to have much weight. In practice, comparative law arguments

[29] Mads Andenas, and Duncan Fairgrieve, 'Intent on Making Mischief: Seven Ways of Using Comparative Law', in Pier Giuseppe Monateri (ed.), *Methods of Comparative Law* (London: Edward Elgar Publishing, 2012), Chapter 2, 17–79. See also Martin Bobek, 'Comparative Reasoning in European Supreme Courts' (2013) 245.

[30] *Fairchild v Glenhaven Funeral Services Ltd* [2002] UKHL 22.

[31] *Dresser UK Ltd v Falcongate Ltd* [1992] QB 502, 522.

[32] *JD (FC) (Appellant) v East Berkshire Community Health NHS Trust and others (Respondents) and two other actions (FC)* [2005] UKHL 23, which is quoted more extensively in the text by n 41.

will not often be used where domestic law is clear. There are certain particular situations where comparative law carries more weight.

In *Fairchild*,[33] Lord Bingham states his basic conviction that 'in a shrinking world (in which the employees of asbestos companies may work for those companies in any one or more of several countries) there must be some virtue in uniformity of outcome whatever the diversity of approach in reaching that outcome'.[34] In the same paragraph of the judgment, he also sets out his view on the use of comparative law in the development of the common law:

> Development of the law in this country cannot of course depend on a head-count of decisions and codes adopted in other countries around the world, often against a background of different rules and traditions. The law must be developed coherently, in accordance with principle, so as to serve, even-handedly, the ends of justice. If, however, a decision is given in this country which offends one's basic sense of justice, and if consideration of international sources suggests that a different and more acceptable decision would be given in most other jurisdictions, whatever their legal tradition, this must prompt anxious review of the decision in question.

In the Supreme Court of the United States, Justice Kennedy addressed similar issues in *Roper v Simmons*.[35] The case concerned a very different matter and area of law. But the criteria were not that different. Justice Kennedy states that international and comparative law provides 'respected and significant confirmation' for the majority's view while not controlling the outcome:

> It is proper that we acknowledge the overwhelming weight of international opinion against the juvenile death penalty, resting in large part on the understanding that the instability and emotional imbalance of young people may often be a factor in the crime. See Brief for Human Rights Committee of the Bar of England and Wales et al. as *Amici Curiae* 10–11. The opinion of the world community, while not controlling our outcome, does provide respected and significant confirmation for our own conclusions. It does not lessen our fidelity to the Constitution or our pride in its origins to acknowledge that the express affirmation of certain fundamental rights by other nations and peoples simply underscores the centrality of those same rights within our own heritage of freedom.

In both cases, the courts considered overturning a previous decision. Both courts had good reasons of legal principle and policy for doing so. In *Roper*, Justice Kennedy finds that comparative law provides 'confirmation for our own conclusions'. Lord Bingham reasons along the same lines in *Fairchild*. 'Anxious review' is called for when (1) a national decision offends one's basic sense of justice, and (2) there is a more acceptable decision in most other jurisdictions.

Both courts decided to overturn the previous decision, and the judgments fit into category 5. But the general statements about the role of comparative law also have a bearing on the current category. *Fairchild* was a unanimous decision, whereas the US

[33] *Fairchild v Glenhaven Funeral Services Ltd* [2002] UKHL 22.
[34] At para 31.
[35] *Roper v Simmons* 543 US 551 (2005).

Supreme Court had only a narrow majority for setting aside its previous decision. The *Roper* minority provided arguments against the use of comparative law in US courts in general (with one justice strengthening the argument for comparative law in general but disagreeing with the majority's conclusions in the particular case). The other view in the House of Lords was first expressed in the subsequent decision of *Barker*[36] where an activist panel invented a new concept of 'proportionate liability' to limit the effect of *Fairchild*. These cases will be discussed further in the paragraphs that follow, but what is of particular interest here is the parallel approach that Lord Bingham and Justice Kennedy took in *Fairchild* and *Roper*. In spite of the many differences between the cases, the method used was similar.

Lord Bingham and Justice Kennedy also address the question of whether the use of comparative law is disloyal to the national legal system. Each of them answer no to this, and provide both a principled and practical argument. In *Fairchild*, the issues appear legal and technical, although the outcome would have social implications. Lord Justice Bingham stated in the early 1990s that '[p]rocedural idiosyncracy is not (like national costume or regional cuisine) to be nurtured for its own sake'.[37] In *Fairchild*, Lord Bingham sets out the social and economic issues. Comparative law is of assistance in dealing with both the social and economic issues, but even more so when it comes to the more technical legal solutions. In *Roper*, the question was whether it was unconstitutional to impose capital punishment for crimes committed while under the age of 18. The case went to the core of the question of the extension of constitutional rights protection. On another level, both cases concerned the arguments a court can take into account when it is considering whether to set aside the authority of a previous decision. The question in *Roper* and *Fairchild* is about how comparative law fits into the system of sources of law as the closed and hierarchical national system of legal authority associated with Kelsian (or Hartian) positivist traditions is breaking down.

The discussion in the US Supreme Court has brought out into the open a disagreement about the validity of the general assumption about the virtue of uniformity of outcome. The majority in the line of cases we have already discussed, have based their argument on there being some current connexion between US law and international and foreign law. We have also referred to Justice Scalia's arguments about 'foreign moods, fads or fashions'. The 'US exceptionalism' has counterparts in all countries, where some judges and academics will more or less openly base resistance to comparative law on assumptions about the superiority of their own system. Justice Scalia has counterparts arguing for English, French, German, Norwegian, Icelandic, or Lichtenstein superiority or exceptionalism. Norwegian or Lichtenstein claims are made with no less self-assuredness than Scalia's. Empirically, claims to national superiority are difficult to assess, as are other claims to the autonomy or 'separateness' of legal systems.

[36] *Barker v Corus (UK) plc* [2006] UKHL 20.
[37] *Dresser UK Ltd v Falcongate Ltd* [1992] QB 502, 522.

2. Normative models in comparative law where national law is undetermined

The least complicated situation could be the one where national law does not determine any particular outcome. The judge may be looking for ways of resolving a problem, and finding no solution based on the traditional sources of law, she seeks solutions in rules or normative arguments from other jurisdictions. Here the use of comparative law takes place in a process of developing or interpreting the law without any conflict with domestic law sources. The judge is operating in a field of open discretion or 'policy'.[38] A slight variation is found where national law leaves more than one solution, and foreign law may assist in choosing between them.

Assistance in finding normative solutions to situations where one's own system has none may be found to be useful and is not often controversial. There should not be any strong, or any at all, limitations in the national legal system where it does not proscribe any solution.

3. Comparative law to review factual assumptions about the consequences of legal rules

In the development of the law in different fields, one encounters the 'floodgates' argument. A new rule is considered, for instance giving access to information held by the administration, requiring that some authority has to give reasons for their decisions, giving procedural rights or standing to groups, or giving rights to compensation for breach of rights. The financial, administrative, or behavioural consequences are considered. Some courts will reject the new rule with an assertion that the rule will open the floodgates for claims, with disproportionate consequences of different kinds. The assertions are often made in a seemingly authoritative way. However, judgments in such cases often contain speculations about risks without much foundation.[39] There is practically always a state financial or other interest on the one side, and a particularly weak individual (dyslexic pupil, victim of sexual abuse as a minor) or public interest (environment, human rights) on the other. The acceptance of risks and the different

[38] See the parallel here in *Application of the Convention on the Prevention and Punishment of the Crime of Genocide (Bosnia and Herzegovina v Serbia and Montenegro)* Judgment of 26 February 2007, where the Court of Justice of the European Union (ECJ) cites the International Criminal Tribunal for the former Yugoslavia (ICTY) and the International Criminal Tribunal for Rwanda (ICTR) on the requirement of 'substantiality' in establishing intent, and also the European Court of Human Rights (ECtHR) in the context of accounting for the parties' submissions (but does not rely on or make any further use of the ECtHR references).

[39] Jane Stapleton, 'Benefits of Comparative Tort Reasoning: Lost in Translation', in Mads Andenas and Duncan Fairgrieve (eds.), *Tom Bingham and the Transformation of the Law: A Liber Amicorum* (Oxford: Oxford University Press, 2009), argues that there can be reasons for basing conclusions on risk assessments, and for not requiring too much for establishing them. She also points out that the possibility for misunderstandings when courts and scholars are dealing with judgments from other common law jurisdictions is considerable. When the other jurisdiction belongs to the civil law and judgments are in another language, her view on comparative law is that it is a rather hopeless enterprise, and in particular for courts.

related assertions are more based on values, giving more weight to the interests of the state in balancing these with other interests, than openly admitted to.

Sir Basil Markesinis has compared the arguments of Lord Bingham and Lord Hoffmann, who were two of the most active comparativists in the House of Lords, in a number of cases.[40] In a number of cases Lord Hoffmann had asserted that granting rights or remedies to disadvantaged groups would lead to the opening up of the floodgates and would also have unwanted consequences of other kinds.

Lord Bingham had long rejected this kind of broad assertion. In *JD v East Berkshire*,[41] he sought recourse to comparative law in dealing with similar assertions. If a rule has been applied in another jurisdiction, and has not opened the floodgates there, the court cannot base its conclusions on assertions to the contrary. Lord Bingham dealt with the matter in paragraph 49 of the judgment in *JD*. This passage is interesting also in the extensive way that academic scholarship is used and relied upon.

In the case of *Smith*,[42] Sir Thomas Bingham MR looked at changes in the laws of other European countries, but here he argued that they were too recent for their effect to be evaluated. The case concerned the blanket ban on homosexuals in the armed forces. Sir Thomas Bingham considered different parliamentary materials, and observed that they did consider a less absolute rule, even though since 1991 neither homosexual orientation, nor private homosexual activity, precluded appointments as a civil servant, diplomat, or judge, and very few NATO countries barred homosexuals from their armed forces. This is the case where Sir Thomas Bingham established that the more substantial the interference with human rights, the more the court will require by way of justification before it is satisfied that the decision is reasonable. He nonetheless concluded that the army policy could not be deemed legally irrational, because it was supported by both Houses of Parliament, there was no evidence which plainly invalidated that advice, and because changes elsewhere had been adopted too recently for their effect to be evaluated.[43]

4. Review assumptions about the universal applicability of a particular rule

In *Lawrence*,[44] the use of foreign law in part refuted the claims to universality in *Bowers*[45] (which the *Lawrence* majority used in support of overturning *Bowers*). In *Bowers*, Chief Justice Burger had made 'sweeping references' to the history of Western civilization and to Judeo-Christian moral and ethical standards. He did not take

[40] See in particular Basil Markesinis and Jorg Fedtke, 'Authority or Reason? The Economic Consequences of Liability for Breach of Statutory Duty in a Comparative Perspective' (2007) 18 EBLR 1: 5–75, at 66–7, and also Mads Andenas, 'Introduction' (2007) 18 EBLR 1: at 2.

[41] *JD (FC) (Appellant) v East Berkshire Community Health NHS Trust and others (Respondents) and two other actions (FC)* [2005] UKHL 23.

[42] *R v Ministry of Defence, ex p Smith* [1996] QB 517.

[43] See the extensive discussion in Paul Craig, 'Substance and Procedure in Judicial Review', in Mads Andenas and Duncan Fairgrieve (eds.), *Tom Bingham and the Transformation of the Law: A Liber Amicorum* (Oxford: Oxford University Press, 2009 and 2011) 73.

[44] 539 US 558 (2003).

[45] 478 US 186 (1986).

account of sources pointing in other directions. Legal developments in other countries could then be used to undermine the claims in *Bowers* and to overturn it.

Claims to universality may be challenged by variations in a temporal dimension (for instance in interpreting an old constitutional text), or in a jurisdictional dimension (the case law of another country or international tribunal contradicts the claim). Comparative law may have a role to play in different ways in this context, and may provide powerful arguments against the universality claims made in an authority.

Another feature of *Lawrence* is the way in which Justice Kennedy makes use of the judgment of the European Court of Human Rights in *Dudgeon v United Kingdom*.[46] Justice Kennedy points out how the European Court of Human Rights followed not *Bowers* but its own previous decision in *Dudgeon* in a number of cases after *Bowers*, and that this applies to other countries. This has consequences for the value of the fundamental freedom involved, and for the possible governmental interests in its limitation.

There is a parallel in the European Court of Human Rights in the *Smith* case (the English Court of Appeal decision is discussed in section III.2).[47] The Court placed much weight on the evidence from other countries. The UK government argued that no worthwhile lessons could be gleaned from recent legal changes in those foreign armed forces that now admitted homosexuals. The Court noted that few European countries operated a blanket legal ban on homosexuals in their armed forces. Also, the UK government had to show convincing and weighty reasons to justify their policy in the proportionality review, and had not done so.[48]

5. Additional support to overturn authority in domestic law

Fairchild[49] and *Roper*[50] may be instances of this category. Both cases are based on there being 'some virtue in uniformity of outcome whatever the diversity of approach in reaching that outcome'.[51] They may express a general principle that 'if consideration of international sources suggests that a different and more acceptable decision would be given in most other jurisdictions, whatever their legal tradition, this must prompt anxious review of the decision in question'.[52]

However, in *Fairchild*, the anxious review was also prompted by the fact that the existing authority offended 'one's basic sense of justice'. In *Roper and Simmons*, Justice Kennedy makes it very clear that he had sufficient support in US constitutional law for overturning the previous authority. The dissenting judges disagree between themselves on the use of international and comparative law, but Justice Scalia is highly critical of this way of claiming support for a result which the majority says is also fully supported in domestic law. We have discussed the use of this argument earlier (see text near n 11).

[46] (1983) 5 EHRR. [47] *Smith and Grady v UK* [2000] 29 EHRR 493.

[48] The difference between the Strasbourg Court and the UK courts in *Smith* is better understood when account is taken of the fact that the Convention was not at that time incorporated into UK law. Convention rights were relevant by way of background to the determination of rationality. See Paul Craig, 'Substance and Procedure in Judicial Review', n 43.

[49] *Fairchild v Glenhaven Funeral Services Ltd* [2002] UKHL 22.

[50] *Roper v Simmons* 543 US 551 (2005). [51] *Fairchild*, n. 49, at para 31. [52] Ibid.

The other view in the House of Lords, as expressed in the subsequent decision of *Barker*,[53] is interesting in that the panel's invention of a new concept of 'proportionate liability' to limit the effect of *Fairchild* did not make use of comparative law. It was clearly policy based, in spite of the references to authority and legal principle. It protected a strong economic interest, industrial employers over traditionally weaker applicants, dead or sick workers and their families. *Barker* was overturned by legislation. *Barker* was an 'activist' decision in the sense that it had an outcome based on the kind of reasoning and solution that judicatures typically will concede to legislatures. *Barker* satisfied many of the criteria that English courts have developed for limiting judicial decision-making, in that it concerned allocative and financial matters, social priorities, and a balancing with typical political factors. In the event, it was not unsurprising that it was regarded as an exercise of political discretion that the legislature overturned. Sir Basil Markesinis' criticism that comparative law arguments here deserved consideration, particularly in light of the role that comparative law arguments had played in *Fairchild*, which *Barker* limited, seem well supported.

As mentioned, in *Lawrence*,[54] the use of foreign law in part refuted the claims to universality in *Bowers*[55] which the majority overturned. Comparative law may provide powerful arguments against universality claims of an authority, and support for the overturning of the authority.

The *Lawrence* and *Roper* line of cases has seen the use of comparative law providing support for overturning precedents to strengthen the protection of individual rights. *Fairchild* appears as a technical causation case but has a more complicated background against a case law favouring employers over employees by limiting liability in different ways, and creating a clear tension with fairness and effective remedies. It is not surprising that the disagreement about the role of precedent and comparative law, and the discussion about an American exceptionalism, have to some extent been coloured by the views on the outcome of the cases.

6. Develop principles of domestic law

Comparative law can support the development of principles of domestic law. The minority opinion in *JD v East Berkshire*,[56] as discussed earlier, falls into this category. In this case, Lord Bingham argues for an evolution of tort law, 'analogically and incrementally, so as to fashion appropriate remedies to contemporary problems'. The European Human Rights Convention, as incorporated by the Human Rights Act 1999, provides the assistance in doing so here. The alternative outcome is to leave tort law 'essentially static, making only such changes as are forced upon it, leaving difficult and, in human terms, very important problems to be swept up by the Convention'.[57]

[53] *Barker v Corus (UK) plc* [2006] UKHL 20. [54] 539 US 558 (2003). [55] 478 US 186 (1986).

[56] *JD (FC) (Appellant) v East Berkshire Community Health NHS Trust and others (Respondents) and two other actions (FC)* [2005] UKHL 23. See the quotation from para 49 from this judgment, in text by n 41.

[57] Unfortunately, the majority, not following Lord Bingham, fell into an error which it will take more than a decade to work English law out of.

We discuss *de Freitas v Permanent Secretary of Ministry of Agriculture, Fisheries, Lands and Housing*[58] in section III.7. This judgment also fits in under the present heading in that the Privy Council here used South African, Canadian, United States, Zimbabwean, and German authority to develop the constitutional principles of freedom of expression and proportionality in the constitutional law of Antigua and Barbuda.

7. Resolve problems of applying European and international law, including European human rights law

In *de Freitas*, the Privy Council, drawing on South African, Canadian, and Zimbabwean authority, defined the questions generally to be asked in deciding whether a measure is proportionate.[59] This formulation was built on by the parties in *Huang v Secretary of State for the Home Department*,[60] and the applicants argued in favour of an overriding requirement which featured in a judgment of the Supreme Court of Canada. Dickson CJ in *R v Oakes* had included the need to balance the interests of society with those of individuals and groups.[61] In *Huang*, the House of Lords accepts the argument,[62] and refers to having recognized as much in its previous decision of *R (Razgar) v Secretary of State for the Home Department* (in Lord Bingham's speech).[63]

This is one of a long line of decisions where the House of Lords have made use of Commonwealth authorities in the application of European human rights law. In particular, Canada offers a relevant experience of applying constitutional protection of individual rights in a common law tradition. This may be a surprise in other European jurisdictions, but both counsel and judges have felt comfortable with these judgments. Decisions from other European national courts have been less easily applied.

We also have an opportunity to refer to *Bulmer v Bullinger*,[64] where Lord Denning cites judgments of German and Dutch courts on the application of Article 234 EC on references from national courts to the ECJ.[65]

58 *De Freitas v Permanent Secretary of Ministry of Agriculture, Fisheries, Lands and Housing* [1999] 1 AC 69.

59 Ibid., at 80. They asked whether: (i) the legislative objective is sufficiently important to justify limiting a fundamental right; (ii) the measures designed to meet the legislative objective are rationally connected to it; and (iii) the means used to impair the right or freedom are no more than is necessary to accomplish the objective.

60 *Huang (FC) (Respondent) v Secretary of State for the Home Department (Appellant) and Kashmiri (FC) (Appellant) v Secretary of State for the Home Department (Respondent) (Conjoined Appeals)* [2007] UKHL 11.

61 *R v Oakes* [1986] 1 SCR 103, at 139.

62 In para 19, where it also refers to *de Freitas*. The judgment had the form of an 'Opinion of the Committee', and was not reported as individual 'speeches', as is the tradition. This form, and the general form and content of the opinion, clearly owes much to Lord Bingham.

63 *R (Razgar) v Secretary of State for the Home Department* [2004] UKHL 27, [2004] 2 AC 368, paras 17–20, 26, 27, 60, 77.

64 [1974] Ch 401.

65 See also Lord Goff of Chieveley, 'The Future of the Common Law' (1997) ICLQ 46: 745, 757 on the use of a French judgment to determine whether a question was *acte claire* under the procedure for references to the European Court of Justice.

Another example is provided by *Techna SA*.[66] As noted by Olivier Dutheillet de la Motte in Chapter 13 of this book, the French *Conseil d'Etat* made reference to a decision by the English High Court concerning labelling requirements under EU law, explicitly citing an English case in support of suspending a directive.[67]

IV. Some conclusions and consequences for scholarship

We have looked at some situations where courts make use of comparative law. They illustrate how comparative law is used in a context where domestic law paradigms remain strong. The cases and the typology illustrate some of the many methodological problems in the use of comparative law in the courts. There are cases which reflect a general recognition of comparative law as a persuasive authority or source of law. There are more and perhaps clearer cases of applying normative models from comparative law where national law is undetermined. There are clear cases where comparative law has been given weight, reviewing factual assumptions about the consequences of legal rules, or assumptions about the universal applicability of rules or principles. Arguments based in this kind of analysis have been used to overturn authority in domestic law in a number of cases. Comparative law has also had a further role in developing principles of domestic law. It has a particular role in the application of European and international law, including European human rights law.

We have illustrated how the use and acknowledgement of comparative law sources is on the increase. In some of the cases its use has been criticized as opportunistic. This argument can be turned against the use of comparative law in general, or in favour of the development of a method for the use of comparative law. We have discussed the positions of Justice Scalia[68] and Sir Basil Markesinis, who have used the consistency arguments in these different ways.[69] We pointed out the more general feature that judges make use of the same authorities or sources of law, and legal and factual arguments, and then reach different conclusions. In many cases this will be done without making clear why, for instance, the appellate court disagrees with the first instance court, or one judge with another in the same court. Judgments may also include or exclude sources or arguments, and this discretion may be perceived to be particularly wide when one is dealing with merely persuasive and non-binding authorities or arguments. This may lead to inconsistencies which are unsatisfactory in many instances. At a stage where comparative law provides mostly persuasive authorities or arguments that do not bind, this has often meant that the courts or judges who do not find support for their preferred outcome in comparative law will disregard comparative law arguments in the reasons they give. We find it difficult to disagree with Sir Basil's call for more consistency here. In particular, the call for consistency is powerful in cases

[66] No 260768 *Techna SA* 29 Oct 2003.

[67] Roger Errera, 'The Use of Comparative Law Before the French Administrative Law Courts', in Guy Canivet, Mads Andenas, and Duncan Fairgrieve (eds.), *Comparative Law before the Courts* (London: BIICL, 2004) 153.

[68] For instance, in *Roper v Simmons* 543 US 551 (2005).

[69] Basil Markesinis, 'Judicial Mentality: Mental Disposition or Outlook as a Factor Impeding Recourse to Foreign Law' (2006) Tulane Law Review 80: 1325, at 1361–2 and 1371.

where one judge mentions foreign law. We agree with Sir Basil that reasonable consistency requires that other judges who come to a different conclusion from that which the first judge supported by comparative law, address and counter in a specific manner the first judge's arguments.

Comparative law is no longer an impractical academic discipline. We have discussed how comparative law is more actively used, and its use more openly acknowledged, by courts, and this is also the case in teaching, scholarship, and in statute law reform. This new awakening puts the academic discipline under some pressure. One response is in the growing scholarship on the purposes and methods of comparative law.

A generation ago, there were some disagreements about purpose and method in academic comparative law circles. Looking back, the prevailing impression is nonetheless of an established academic discipline with a high degree of cohesion. There were parallel discourses across jurisdictions, mostly dominated by private lawyers, but with important contributions made by public and criminal lawyers.

Comparative law has lost whatever common language it had as an academic discipline. This is one consequence of the expansion of the discipline: it does not have the coherence of the small academic community that it had a generation ago. It is a current and rather pressing challenge to engage comparative law scholars in a discourse on what can be agreed upon as the core issues. The growing scholarship on the purposes and methods of comparative law is a good beginning,[70] although the present phase demonstrates a wide range of views, some rather fundamentally opposed to one another.[71] There is much to be done before the academic discipline can emerge

[70] Two magisterial volumes provide extensive overviews of the rapidly expanding scholarship, see Matthias Reimann and Reinhard Zimmermann (eds.), *The Oxford Handbook of Comparative Law* (Oxford: Oxford University Press, 2006), and Jan M Smits, (ed.), *Elgar Encyclopedia of Comparative Law* (Cheltenham: Edward Elgar, 2006). See also William Twining, Ward Farnsworth, Stefan Vogenauer, and Fernando Téson, 'The Role of Academics in the Legal System', in Peter Cane and Mark Tushnet (eds.), *The Oxford Handbook of Legal Studies* (Oxford: Oxford University Press, 2003) 920.

[71] See the following authors representing some of the divergence in the current comparative private law scholarship: Pierre Legrand, 'European Systems are not Converging' (1996) 45 ICLQ 52; Mauro Bussani, and Ugo Mattei, 'The Common Core Approach to European Private Law' (1997/98) 3 Columbia Journal of Comparative Law 339; Walter Van Gerven et al, *Tort Law* (Oxford: Oxford University Press, 2000); Basil Markesinis, *Foreign Law and Comparative Methodology: a Subject and a Thesis* (Oxford: Hart Publishing, 1997); Basil Markesinis, *Always on the Same Path: Essays on Foreign Law and Comparative Methodology* (Oxford: Hart Publishing, 2001); Basil Markesinis, *Comparative Law in the Courtroom and Classroom* (Oxford: Hart Publishing, 2003); Basil Markesinis, and Jörg Fedtke, 'Authority or Reason? The Economic Consequences of Liability for Breach of Statutory Duty in a Comparative Perspective' (2007) 18 EBLR 5; Basil Markesinis, 'Judicial Mentality: Mental Disposition or Outlook as a Factor Impeding Recourse to Foreign Law' (2006) 80 Tulane Law Review 1325, 1361–2; Anne Peters and Heine Schwenke, 'Comparative Law beyond Post-Modernism' (2000) 49 ICLQ 800; Horatia Muir Watt, 'La Fonction Subversive du Droit Comparé' (2000) 52 RIDC 503; Alan Rodger, 'Savigny in the Strand' *The Irish Jurist* 28–30 (1995): 1; Rodolfo Sacco, 'Legal Formants: a Dynamic Approach to Comparative Law (I)' (1991) 39 American Journal of Comparative Law and (II) (1991) 39 American Journal of Comparative Law 343; Alan Watson, *Legal Transplants: An Approach to Comparative Law* (Athens, London: University of Georgia Press, 1993); Reinhard Zimmerman, 'Savigny's Legacy: Legal History, Comparative Law, and the Emergence of a European Legal Science' (1996) 112 LQR 576; Konrad Zweigert and Helmut Kotz, *An Introduction to Comparative Law*, 3rd edn (Oxford: Clarendon Press, 1998); Guido Alpa and Vincenzo Zeno-Zencovich, *Italian Private Law* (London: Taylor and Francis (Routledge-Cavendish), 2007); Guido Alpa, et al., *Diritto privato comparato. Istituti e problem* (Rome, Bari: Laterza, 2004); Guido Alpa and Mads Andenas, *Fondamenti del diritto privato europeo* (Milan: Giuffrè, 2005); Mads Andenas et al., *Liber Amicorum Guido Alpa: Private Law Beyond the National Systems* (London: BIICL, 2007); Duncan Fairgrieve, Mads

from this phase with any degree of agreement on what are the fundamental issues in the field, as is required for a critical academic discourse to be meaningful. The active comparative law discourse needs to rediscover at least the core of a common language.[72] It requires this common language for scholarship and comparative law to have full impact on legal scholarship, law making, and legal practice. It needs a mainstream academic discipline to emerge, the academic world now having received more than a helping hand from the courts and their use of comparative law.

Andenas, and John Bell (eds.), *Tort Liability of Public Authorities in Comparative Perspective* (London: BIICL, 2002); Duncan Fairgrieve and Horatia Muir Watt, *Common law et tradition civiliste* (Paris: Presses Universitaires de France, 2006); Martin Siems, *Comparative Law* (2014).

[72] Basil Markesinis and Jorg Fedtke, *Engaging in Foreign Law* (Oxford: Hart Publishing, 2009), makes an important contribution in this respect.

PART II

CONFLICTS AND COMPARISONS

2

Is it Legitimate and Beneficial for Judges to Compare?

*Thomas Kadner Graziano**

I. Introduction

In the early 21st century, it might seem surprising to still ask the question whether it is legitimate for judges to use the comparative method in their reasoning. The experience of teaching comparative law shows, however, that students, i.e. the judges and lawyers of tomorrow, despite the insights and the intellectual pleasure they derive from comparing laws, often doubt whether it is legitimate for courts to use comparative methodology. They also have doubts concerning the benefits they might be able to derive from the comparative method in their future practical life as lawyers.[1] In contrast, they quickly recognize the use of comparative law with regard to legislation, whether on a national or international level, given that national and international legislators regularly rely on comparative studies when preparing legislation. Judges and lawyers[2] in some countries also still question the legitimacy of the use of comparative methodology by the courts.

The following reflections address the question of whether it is *legitimate* for the judge to resort to the comparative method in addition to the classic methods of determining and interpreting domestic law. If it is legitimate, is it *beneficial* for the courts to use the comparative method? And if so, do the benefits of the comparative method justify the sometimes considerable effort that the comparative approach demands?

A practical example serves to illustrate that these questions are far from purely theoretical. The economy of a central European state undertakes privatization. A foreign investor buys one of the largest companies in that country. The company,

* Professor of Law at the University of Geneva, Faculty of Law, <http://www.unige.ch/droit/transnational/professeurs/kadner.html>. This is an extended version of an article first published in European Review of Private Law (ERPL) 2013, 687–716 and reprinted with permission of Kluwer Law International. On this topic by the same author in French: 'Est-il légitime et utile pour le juge de comparer?', *in* M. Faure-Abbad/M. Boudot (eds.), *Obligations, procès et droit savant—Mélanges en l'honneur de Jean Beauchard* (Paris: LGDJ, 2013), 77–101.

[1] Comp. A. Bullier, 'Le droit comparé dans l'enseignement—Le droit comparé est-il un passe-temps inutile?', RDIC [2008] 163 at 164: '*cette matière souffre d'un déficit d'image* . . . . . *Les juristes sont avant tout des internistes. Ils veulent donner des solutions immédiates et tangibles à leurs étudiants ou clients. La spéculation intellectuelle, si elle est appréciée, ne correspond plus à un monde où l'efficacité et le rendement sont considérés comme essentiels et aller voir ailleurs relève de la curiosité intellectuelle comme pour les digressions élégantes et stimulantes de la philosophie ou de la théorie générale du droit.*'

[2] When teaching comparative law to lawyers, it is a frequent experience that their scepticism regarding the use of comparative law usually vanishes only when studying cases in which the courts used this method in their reasoning.

which is of national importance (and too big to fail), risks bankruptcy but is saved by state investment in the region of several billion dollars. The state accuses the foreign investor of not having taken necessary measures to save the company, measures that the investor had been obliged to take under the privatization contract. The state therefore claims damages in the region of several billion dollars for the investments made to save the company.

The case is to be decided on the application of provisions of the civil code of the state concerned. There is little doctrine and no case law interpreting the applicable articles (provisions concerning contractual and tortious liability). That said, in neighbouring countries' codes, there are similar provisions which have been widely commented on and often applied by their courts. These codes served as an inspiration to the state's legislator at the time of codification of its domestic civil law.[3]

In such a case, is it legitimate for the court to take inspiration from foreign statutory law, case law, and legal doctrine when dealing with the issue under the applicable domestic law? Would lawyers be able to use, in the interest of their clients, other legal systems as a source of inspiration and support when proposing a certain interpretation of the law to the judges?

These questions are not limited to Europe. A very animated discussion among judges of the Supreme Court of the United States has helped in putting this issue on the agenda of judges, comparatists, and lawyers.[4]

This contribution firstly analyses the arguments against and for the *legitimacy* of the comparative method when it comes to applying domestic law (section II). Then, the *benefits* that may be derived from comparison by the judge are demonstrated. Numerous decisions of courts in Europe illustrate the *reasons* that lead to the use of comparative methodology and the multiple *aims* that the courts pursue by using this method (section III).

II. Comparative law—a method at the disposal of the courts?

1. Is it legitimate to use comparative law?—Arguments against the use of comparative methodology by courts

Some arguments seem to speak against the use of the comparative method by the courts when interpreting national law.[5]

[3] For more case scenarios, see T. Kadner Graziano, 'Comment enseigner et étudier le droit comparé?—Une proposition', 43 RDUS [2013] 61–87; German language version: 'Rechtsvergleichung lehren und lernen—ein Vorschlag aus Genf', *ZEuP* 2014, 204–23.

[4] The discussion in the USA focuses on the comparative method in constitutional law. In Europe, the legitimacy of judicial comparison has hardly been discussed so far, comp. e.g. C. McCrudden, 'A Common Law of Human Rights? Transnational Judicial Conversations on Constitutional Rights', 20 Oxford J. Leg. Stud. [2000] 499 at 503: a topic 'relatively ignored in the theoretical literature'; R. Reed, 'Foreign Precedents and Judicial Reasoning: the American Debate and British Practice', 124 LQR [2008] 253 at 259: the current discussion in the USA 'has no parallel in the United Kingdom or elsewhere in the common law world'. In the USA, the topic is also regarded as 'under-theorized', R. Hirschl, 'The Question of Case Selection in Comparative Constitutional Law', 53 American J. Comp. L. [2005] 125.

[5] For an emphatic statement against the use of comparative law by US Federal courts, see A. Scalia, 'Keynote Address: Foreign Legal Authority in the Federal courts', in American Society of International Law,

a) A lack of democratic legitimacy

According to a first argument, the judge is bound by the law, but only his domestic law as well as international law in force in his country. Only the national legislator and, where required, an international legislator, would have the necessary democratic legitimacy to guide the judge in his decision. Foreign law failed to respect this democratic legitimacy and would not, in light of this fact, be capable of neither binding, nor convincing, nor even serving as an inspiration to the national judge in the interpretation of his own domestic law.[6]

b) The legal system—a national system

According to a second argument, every domestic legal provision or precedent should be interpreted within its own context, that of a national system.[7] In many continental legal systems, civil law is codified in a coherent system, the system of the national code, whereas in common law countries, case law constitutes a body of jurisprudence with its own coherence. It is claimed that an interpretation that takes inspiration from foreign sources is potentially harmful to national legal systems.

c) Specifics of the national situation

According to another argument, each legal provision as well as each judgment interpreting a provision and applying the law in a specific case is always the result of a weighing of interests. It is argued that this weighting of interests necessarily takes place within the national context, taking into account the specifics of the situation in the country concerned and the cultural context in which the decision will take effect. In this sense, Antonin Scalia, judge of the Supreme Court of the United States, in a judgment concerning US constitutional law, expressed the opinion that looking at foreign law is, at best, of no importance, and, at worst, dangerous. According to him, the Supreme Court of the United States 'should not impose foreign moods, fads or

Proceedings of the 101st Annual Meeting (American Society of International Law), Vol 98 (2004), 305; available also at <http://www.jstor.org/pss/25659941> (last accessed 10.02.2015).

6 A. Scalia, 'Commentary', 40 *St. Louis U. L. J.* [1996] 1119 at 1122: '[we] judges of the American democracies are servants of our peoples, sworn to apply... the laws that those peoples deem appropriate. We are not some international priesthood empowered to impose upon our free and independent citizen supra-national values that contradict their own.' In the USA, some critics have argued that an 'unchecked comparative practice' was 'subversive of the whole concept of sovereignty', see: Appropriate Role of Foreign Judgments in the Interpretation of American Law: Hearing on H.R. Res. 568 before the Subcomm. on the Constitution of the House Comm. on the Judiciary, 108th Cong., 2d Sess. 77 (2004) at 72 (testimony of Prof. Jeremy Rabkin, Cornell Univ.); see also E. Young, 'Foreign Law and the Denominator Problem', 119 Harv. L. Rev. [2005] 148 at 163: '[I]mporting foreign law into the domestic legal system through constitutional interpretation circumvents the institutional mechanism by which the political branches ordinarily control the interaction between the domestic and the foreign'; D. Pfeffer, 'Depriving America of Evolving Its Own Standards of Decency? An Analysis of The Use of Foreign Law In Eighth Amendment Jurisprudence and Its Effect On Democracy', 51 Saint Louis U. L. J. [2007] 855 ff., e.g. at 879; Z. Larsen, 'Discounting Foreign Imports: Foreign Authority in Constitutional Interpretation & the Curb of Popular Sovereignty', 45 Willamette L. Rev. [2009] 767, e.g. at 784.

7 In this sense see A. Scalia, ibid.

fashions on Americans'.[8] In the majority opinion of the Court, Justice Kennedy, who frequently uses the comparative method, had referred to English law and the case law of the European Court of Human Rights. According to Scalia, in his dissenting opinion, such considerations of foreign law would be 'meaningless *dicta*'.[9]

d) Legal science—a largely national science

Over the last few years, certain courts have once again emphasized the fact that, although *comparativa est omnis investigatio* and 'all forms of higher knowledge consist of comparison',[10] the law remains a largely national science. The Federal Supreme Administrative Court of Germany accordingly declared in a 1993 judgment that '*[d]ie Rechtswissenschaft ist eine national geprägte Wissenschaft*'[11] (legal science is a nationally characterized science). A German court of appeal expressly supported this view in a judgment in 2004. This case related to the legitimacy of an agreement reached between a lawyer and his client concerning legal fees calculated according to the final result, *Erfolgshonorare* or contingency fees,[12] valid in US law but prohibited and hitherto deemed contrary to moral and legal standards by German law.

[8] In *Lawrence et al. v Texas* 539 US 558 [2003] 598 (on the constitutionality of a statute of the State of Texas prohibiting certain sexual acts between persons of the same sex; held that this law violates the 'Due Process Clause' of the US Constitution), p. 598: 'The Court's discussion of these foreign views (ignoring, of course, the many countries that have retained criminal prohibitions on sodomy) is therefore meaningless dicta. Dangerous dicta, however, since "this Court... should not impose foreign moods, fads, or fashions on Americans."' With reference to *Foster v Florida*, 537 US 990, note (2002) (J. Thomas): 'Justice Breyer has only added another foreign court to his list while still failing to ground support for his theory in any decision by an American court. Ibid., at 990. While Congress, as a *legislature*, may wish to consider the actions of other nations on any issue it likes, this Court's Eighth Amendment jurisprudence should not impose foreign moods, fads, or fashions on Americans'.

[9] Ibid., p. 573; see also L. Blum, 'Mixed Signals: The Limited Role of Comparative Analysis in Constitutional Adjudication', 39 San Diego L. Rev. [2002] 157 ff., e.g. at 163; B. Lucas, 'Structural Exceptionalism and Comparative Constitutional Law', 96 Virginia L. Rev. [2010] 1965 ff.; E. Young, n. 6, 148 ff. The US Supreme Court has, however, a long tradition when it comes to using the comparative method, see e.g. M. Minow, 'The Controversial Status of International and Comparative Law in the United States', 52 Harv. Int. L. J. Online, 27.08.2010, I.: '[N]o one disagrees that United States judges have long consulted and referred materials from other countries as well as international sources; yet for the past nine or so years, citing foreign and international sources provoked intense controversy'; V. Jackson, 'Constitutional Comparisons: Convergence, Resistance, Engagement', 119 Harv. L. Rev. [2005] 110 ff.; G. Calabresi/S. Dotson Zimdahl, 'The Supreme Court and Foreign Sources of Law: Two Hundred Years of Practice and the Juvenile Death Penalty Decision', William & Mary L. Rev. [2005] 743. See on the debate in the US also A. Barak, 'Comparative Law, Originalism and the Role of a Judge in a Democracy: A Reply to Justice Scalia', *The Fulbright Convention*, 29 January 2006; M. Rosenfeld, 'Le constitutionnalisme comparé en mouvement: d'une controverse américaine sur les références jurisprudentielles au droit étranger', *in* P. Legrand (ed.), *Comparer les droits, résolument* (Paris: PUF, 2009), 561; I. Eisenberger, 'Wer fürchtet sich vor einem Verfassungsrechtsvergleich? Gedanken zur Rechtsvergleichung in der Judikatur des US Supreme Court', *JRP* [2010] 216 at 217: '*Rechtsvergleichung am SC ist beinahe so alt wie die Institution selbst. Ebenso alt wie die Rechtsvergleichungspraxis ist die Kritik daran*'.

[10] M. Freeland, 'Introduction: Comparative and International Law in the Courts', *in* G. Canivet/M. Andenas/D. Fairgrieve (eds.), *Comparative Law before the Courts* (London: BIICL, 2005), p. xvii.

[11] Bundesverwaltungsgericht (BVerwG) (Federal administrative court) 30.06.1992 (on the recognition of a Polish Master of Laws degree), NJW 1993, 276.

[12] OLG Celle (Appellate court of Celle) 26.11.2004, NJW 2005, 2160 et seq.: '*Rechtsvergleichung kann Gemeinsamkeiten und Unterschiede der Rechtsordnungen deutlich machen. Sie kann auch dem Richter eine Auslegungshilfe im Sinne einer "fünften Auslegungsmethode"... sein. Die praktische Bedeutung einer solchen Vorgehensweise ist freilich bislang sehr gering geblieben. Außerhalb des durch Kollisionsnormen bestimmten*

e) Lack of knowledge of foreign law and linguistic barriers

According to yet another argument, it is evident that the national legislator would not expect courts to have knowledge of foreign law. This knowledge would, however, be necessary to correctly employ the comparative method. Given that judges did not know or, at best, only knew a little foreign law, use of the comparative method would open the route to error, to danger of an incorrect understanding and a false interpretation of foreign law.[13] Added to which, there were often also linguistic barriers that made understanding foreign law particularly difficult and multiplied the risks of error.[14] Because of language barriers one US-author (and comparatist) has made the proposal to leave aside 'foreign-language law' when comparing.[15] Last but not least, the judge would simply not have the time and resources necessary to systematically carry out comparative research.[16]

f) The danger of cherry picking

Some have voiced criticism of the courts over selective citing of foreign law. It would always be possible to find support in some countries for a solution that is favoured by the courts. In contrast, diverging solutions in other countries would not always be invoked. In certain cases, the courts relied on the comparative argument, whereas they rejected comparison when the solution found in foreign law differs from that which is preferred by the court. Here the argument in question is that of *cherry picking*. It is used

Bereichs können im Wege der Rechtsvergleichung gewonnene Erkenntnisse nur dort einfließen, wo das eigene Recht "offen" ist und damit Interpretationsspielräume lässt... Auch darf die Bindung des Richters an Recht und Gesetz (Art. 20 III GG) nicht in Frage gestellt werden und muss weiter bedacht werden, dass mit der Übertragung von Rechtsgrundsätzen einer fremden Rechtsordnung, und zwar besonders dann, wenn dieseeiner anderen Rechtsfamilie angehört, in die eigene Rechtsordnung vorsichtig umzugehen ist.'

[13] See on this argument E. Hondius, 'Comparative Law in the Court-Room: Europe and America Compared', in A. Büchler/M. Müller-Chen (eds.), *Festschrift für Schwenzer*, Vol. 1 (Bern: Stämpfli, 2011), 759 at 769: 'The high quality of the [foreign] expert opinions is apparent from the reports on Dutch law. And yet... when reading the expert opinion on Dutch law, I sometimes know almost for certain that a Dutch court would decide differently now'; C. McCrudden, n. 4, at 526; R. Reed, n. 4, at 264.

[14] R. Reed, n. 4, at 264: '[M]any British judges (and counsel) are effectively monolingual, so that decisions must either come from an English-speaking jurisdiction or be translated... [M]ost of the world's case law is in reality inaccessible to most British lawyers'; E. Young, n. 6 at 166: both decision costs and error costs 'seem likely to be high for American courts dealing with foreign materials, given language and cultural barriers and most American lawyers' lack of training in comparative analysis'. See on this issue also J. Bell, 'Le droit comparé au Royaume-Uni', *in* X. Blanc-Jouvan et al., *L'avenir du droit comparé, un défi pour les juristes du nouveau millénaire* (Paris: Société de Législation comparée, 2000), p. 283; B. Markesinis/ J. Fedtke, 'The Judge as Comparatist', 80 Tulane Law Review [2005–06] 11 at 114.

[15] J. Stapleton, 'Benefits of Comparative Tort Reasoning: Lost in Translation', 1 *J. Tort L.* [2007] 6 at 33, introducing the notion of 'comparative foreign-language law': '[T]he general indifference of North American and Australasian courts and practitioners to the tort law of foreign-language jurisdictions seems a wise response from inescapable phenomena. For them there is no more to be reliably derived from foreign-language jurisdictions than from English-speaking ones...: moreover, there are added perils of misinterpretation'; published also *in Liber Amicorum Tom Bingham* (Oxford: Oxford University Press, 2009), p. 773.

[16] See the example given by Hondius, n. 13, p. 759 at 773.

frequently by critics of the comparative approach in recent discussion in the USA and notably by judge Antonin Scalia.[17]

All of these arguments therefore seem to speak against the use of the comparative method by the courts.

2. Widening horizons—Arguments in favour of the use of comparative methodology by the courts

The question thus is, on the one hand, whether, and to what extent these arguments are convincing; and on the other hand, whether there are arguments favouring the use of comparative law by the judge when interpreting and applying domestic law.

a) Cherry picking—an apprehension that has not been confirmed by court practice

The danger of *cherry picking* is not unique to the comparative argument. The risk exists just as well in relation to differing opinions in doctrine and case law that also can be used and cited very selectively by courts.[18] Therefore, provided that the comparative method is used as seriously and balanced as every other method of interpretation, the danger of *cherry picking* does not question the legitimacy of comparison. In fact, numerous examples show that courts choose the jurisdictions for comparison very carefully and do not hesitate to cite foreign law in situations where the solution under foreign law differs from that preferred by the court. In these cases, comparative law is used in order to highlight the specificities of one's own domestic law.[19]

[17] A. Scalia, n. 5, at 309: 'Adding foreign law ... is much like legislative history, which ordinarily contains something for everybody and can be used or not used, used in one part or in another, deemed controlling or pronounced inconclusive, depending upon the result the court wishes to reach ... The Court's reliance has also been selective as to when foreign law is consulted *at all*'; ibid.: 'To invoke alien law when it agrees with one's own thinking, and ignore it otherwise, is not reasoned decision-making but sophistry', dissenting opinion in *Roper v Simmons*, US S.Ct., 543 US 551 [2005] 627; see also Chief Justice of the US S.Ct. John Roberts: 'Foreign law, you can find anything you want. If you don't find it in the decisions of France or Italy, it's in the decisions of Somalia or Japan or Indonesia or wherever. As somebody said in another context, looking at foreign law for support is like looking over a crowd for support and picking out your friends ... And that actually expands the discretion of the judge. It allows the judge to incorporate his or her own personal preferences, cloak them with the authority of precedent ... and use that to determine the meaning of the Constitution', *in* US Senate Judiciary Committee, Hearing on the Nomination of John Roberts to be Chief Justice of the Supreme Court, Transcript, Day Two, Part III, 13.09.2005, at <http://www.washingtonpost.com/wp-dyn/content/article/2005/09/13/AR2005091301210.html> (last accessed: 10.02.2015); see also R. Posner, *Legal Affairs*, July/August 2004, at <http://www.legalaffairs.org/issues/July-August-2004/feature_posner_julaug04.msp> (last accessed: 10.02.2015).

[18] See R. Glensy, 'Which Countries Count? Lawrence v. Texas and the Selection of Foreign Persuasive Authority', 45 Virginia J. Int. L. [2005] 357 at 401 ff.; C. McCrudden, n. 4, at 517: '[T]here are also increasing numbers of judges in particular jurisdictions who appear to consider it important to distinguish judgments of foreign courts if they go against the conclusions that the judge intends to reach'; Stephen Breyer, Judge of the US Supreme Court, *in* 'U.S. Association of Constitutional Law Discussion: Constitutional Relevance of Foreign Court Decisions' (2005), Transcript by Federal News Service, Washington D.C., at <http://www.freerepublic.com/focus/f-news/1352357/posts> (last accessed: 10.02.2015).

[19] For examples and references see section III.2.d). For criteria for choosing the jurisdiction for comparison, see e.g. C. McCrudden, n. 4, at 517 ff.; R. Reed, n. 4, at 264, 271; R. Glensy, n. 18, at 401 ff.;

b) Information on foreign law increasingly accessible

In order to avoid error and misunderstanding as to the content of foreign law, and so that the court has a solid basis for the use of the comparative method, it is effectively essential that the judge is provided with trustworthy, sound, and reliable information on the substance of foreign law.[20]

For numerous points of law, this information is now available. First of all and most obviously, the Internet makes access to information on foreign law as well as access to foreign case law much easier. Moreover, several institutions and research groups and numerous comparatists substantially contribute to the circulation of knowledge on foreign law. To name just some of the particularly active institutions and groups, it is possible to mention the International Institute for the Unification of Private Law (UNIDROIT), the Commission on European Contract Law, the Study Group on a European Civil Code, the Research Group on Existing EC Private Law, the Academy of European Private Lawyers, the Trento Group working on a Common Core of European Private Law, the European Group of Tort Law, the European Centre of Tort and Insurance Law (ECTIL), as well as the Leuven and Maastricht group of researchers working under the leadership of Walter van Gerven on the 'Ius Commune Casebooks for the Common Law of Europe'. Some of these groups count among their members researchers from all European jurisdictions, others researchers from around the world. They seek to make available entire libraries containing reliable and up-to-date information on foreign laws. A large majority of this information is published in English, thus facilitating access.[21] It is also possible to mention the numerous comparative analyses that are published in European law journals, such as the European Review of Private Law (ERPL), the Maastricht Journal of European and Comparative Law, the Columbia Journal of European Law, the Zeitschrift für Europäisches Privatrecht (ZEuP), and the Rivista di diritto pubblico comparato ed europeo, published in English, German, and Italian respectively.

Providing reliable information on foreign and comparative law, in languages easily accessible, is therefore the responsibility of comparatists and researchers using a comparative approach in their publications. English judges have expressly noted that without these publications, comparison would not have been possible for the court.[22]

A. Friedman, 'Beyond Cherry-Picking: Selection Criteria For the Use of Foreign Law in Domestic Constitutional Jurisprudence', 44 Suffolk U. L. Rev. [2011] 873 ff.

[20] C. McCrudden, n. 4, at 527: '(in general) a judge or court in one jurisdiction will not use case law from another jurisdiction unless it is considered to be comparable, and unless the judge or court feels adequately informed about the other jurisdiction'; see also T. Bingham, *Widening Horizons—The Influence of Comparative Law and International Law on Domestic Law* (Cambridge: Cambridge University Press, 2010), p. 5, who reminds us incidentally that 'few human activities are free from the risk of error and judicial decision-making is no exception'.

[21] A reading proficiency in English, French, and German gives access to the law of *nine* European jurisdictions in the original language, and beyond that to further common law jurisdictions as well as to further jurisdictions belonging to the French legal tradition.

[22] See e.g. Lord Goff of Chieveley *in White v Jones* [1995] 2 AC 207, 1 All ER 691 at 705 (House of Lords): '[I]n the present case, thanks to material published in our language by distinguished comparatists, German as well as English, we have direct access to publications which should sufficiently dispel our ignorance of German law and so by comparison illuminate our understanding of our own.'

In a case brought before the court, it is also possible for this comparative research to be carried out on an ad hoc basis by comparative law institutions and lawyers[23] (or their trainees) trained in comparative law.[24] Christopher McCrudden recalls that 'where lawyers appearing before the courts, or clerks assisting the judge, give the judge confidence, then the decisions of foreign systems are more likely to be cited.'[25]

Thanks to this information on foreign law, error and misunderstanding in the substance of foreign law can be avoided. Consequently, this argument does not question the legitimacy and practicability of comparison either.

Ruth Bader Ginsburg, judge at the US Supreme Court, has stated in this respect: '[W]e should approach foreign legal materials with sensitivity to our differences, deficiencies, and imperfect understanding, but imperfection, I believe, should not lead us to abandon the effort to learn what we can from the experience and good thinking foreign sources may convey.'[26]

c) Access to foreign law—the private international law argument

In cross border cases which present closer links with a foreign legal system than with the law of the jurisdiction in which a legal action is brought, the forum's private international law sometimes obliges the court to resolve the case solely on the application of foreign law. The existence of private international law rules clearly shows that the legislators believe it is possible for the national judge to be informed about the substance of foreign law in a reliable and trustworthy way.[27]

d) The comparative methodology—a method of interpretation like the others

It is clear that the national legislator does not expect courts or lawyers to know foreign law as they know domestic law. It is equally clear that judges and lawyers cannot resort to the comparative method in *every* case.

[23] This was the case e.g. in *Tabet v Gett,* [2010] High Court of Australia 12, at <http://www.austlii.edu.au/au/cases/cth/HCA/2010/12.html>, or the English case *A and others v the National Blood Authority* [2001] 3 All ER 289. See also Hein Kötz, 'Alte und neue Aufgaben der Rechtsvergleichung', *JZ* [2002] 257 at 259: lawyers '*sind sich offenbar noch nicht genügend des Umstands bewusst, dass ein für ihre Mandanten günstiger Rechtsstandpunkt sich in vielen Fällen auf rechtsvergleichende Argumente stützen lässt*' (apparently lawyers are not yet sufficiently aware that they can use comparative law in order to further the interests of their clients); E. Hondius, n. 13, p. 759 at 777; for England e.g. Lord Steyn, *Public Law* 1999, 51 at 58: 'Law Lords expect a high standard of research and interpretation from barristers... For example, if the appeal involves a statutory offence we would expect counsel to be familiar with... comparative material from, say, Australia and New Zealand'.

[24] For a method of teaching comparative law that prepares the students for this task, see the author of this contribution, 'Comment enseigner le droit comparé?', n. 3.

[25] C. McCrudden, n. 4, at 526.

[26] R. Bader Ginsburg, 'A Decent Respect to the Opinions of [Human]kind: The Value of a Comparative Perspective in Constitutional Adjudication', 64 Cambridge L. J. [2005] 575 at 580.

[27] In some jurisdictions, such as Switzerland, the judge establishes the content of foreign law *ex officio*, see Art. 16 sect. 1 of the Swiss Code on Private International Law (LDIP); in other jurisdictions, he can require that the parties contribute to the establishment of the content of foreign law or, for certain areas of law, that they establish its content altogether, see *Dicey, Morris & Collins on The Conflict of Laws*, 14th edn. (London: Sweet & Maxwell, 2006), Vol. 1, §§ 9-001 et seq.; see also E. Örücü, 'Comparative Law in Practice: The Courts and the Legislator', *in* E. Örücü/D. Nelken (eds.), *Comparative Law—A Handbook* (Oxford: Hart, 2007) 411 at 414, 418.

In situations where such knowledge is not available or accessible, the court cannot be expected to use the comparative approach. However, in cases where content of foreign law is brought to the attention of the court, the judges are in a position to build on this knowledge and to use the comparative arguments when interpreting domestic law.[28]

The fact that the comparative method can be used in some cases and not in others is not unique to this method. While the literal rule and perhaps also the purposive approach are methods of interpretation that are always available to the court, this is not the case for other methods of statutory interpretation. This is true notably in relation to the historical interpretation, which draws inspiration from the legislative history of the law, and the systematic interpretation, both of which will assist the judge, much like the comparative method, in his search for a solution to specific problems in some cases and not in others.

e) Revival of a European legal science

The argument that legal science is a largely national science is another argument against the use of comparative law that barely convinces. Throughout a large part of the 20th century, in countries such as Germany and France, legal science was effectively a widely national science. However, in other countries, notably the UK as well as some countries in continental Europe, such as the Netherlands, Belgium, Austria, and Switzerland, legal science has never been limited to a single national law. On the contrary, the doctrine in these jurisdictions, and to some extent also the court practice, has a long history of using the comparative approach.[29] In the second half of the 20th century, more and more legal scientists have been arguing in favour of an internationalization (or more accurately, a *re-internationalization*[30]) of legal science.[31] These pleas were eventually successful and we observe today a renaissance of a truly international science of law in Europe. In law, ideas and solutions are circulating across borders again. From a US perspective, Matthias Reimann has observed in this respect: 'In Western Europe, comparative legal studies have... gained a momentum and a significance unprecedented in the last hundred years... From an American perspective, one may... look across the Atlantic with envy these days. Comparative law in Europe is a hot topic. It is practically relevant, self-confident, and enjoys a high profile.'[32]

[28] For the important role that lawyers might play in this respect, see section II.2.b).

[29] References in section III. See also E. Hondius, n. 13, p. 759 at 765: 'It has been suggested that, if one wishes to consider legal research a science, [focusing on domestic developments] is the wrong attitude. Science knows no borders, and legal science is no exception.'

[30] Before the period of the codification of the law started on the continent, legal discourse on the continent was truly European using the same language, Latin; see e.g. R. Zimmermann, *The Law of Obligations. Roman Foundations of the Civilian Tradition* (Oxford: Clarendon Press, 1996); Zimmerman, 'Das römisch-kanonische ius commune als Grundlage europäischer Rechtseinheit', *JZ* 1992, 8; H. Coing, 'Die ursprüngliche Einheit der europäischen Rechtswissenschaft', in Zimmerman, *Gesammelte Schriften*, Vol. II, p. 137; for the situation in private international law, see T. Kadner Graziano, *Gemeineuropäisches Internationales Privatrecht* (Tübingen: Mohr Siebeck, 2002), p. 46–59.

[31] For references see e.g. T. Kadner Graziano, *European Contract Law* (Basingstoke: Palgrave Macmillan, 2009), p. 7 et seq.

[32] M. Reimann, 'The Progress and Failure of Comparative Law in the Second Half of the Twentieth Century', 50 Am. J. Comp. L. [2002] 671 at 691–2.

f) The judge's freedom to choose his methods of determining the law—revival of the idea of justice that transcends borders

Another argument against the use of the comparative method asserts that every law and judgment is the result of a weighing of interests which would necessarily have to take place within each country's own cultural context.[33] This argument overlooks the fact that these days, the national legislators themselves rely on extensive comparative research in practically every important legislative procedure and, at any rate, in matters of private law. To cite just a few recent examples: The recent codifications in the Baltic States have largely taken inspiration from comparative studies. The Estonian legislator has followed the example of the German civil code in his new codification of the law of obligations (and has introduced, for example, a general part in the new Law of Obligations and has, e.g. in torts, codified the essence of a century of German case law). The legislator has also widely taken inspiration from Swiss law, Dutch law, the laws of Quebec and Louisiana, the United Nations Convention on Contracts for the International Sale of Goods (CISG), the Principles of European Contract Law, and the UNIDROIT Principles of International Commercial Contracts.[34] The new Lithuanian Civil Code of 2000 takes inspiration, amongst others, from the codifications and statutes of the Netherlands, Québec, Germany, France, Italy, Switzerland, Sweden, Latvia, Japan, and Russia, as well as from the CISG and the UNIDROIT Principles.[35] Polish law has recently taken inspiration from German and Dutch law, as well as the CISG and the Principles of European Contract Law. In Central and Eastern European countries, the comparative method plays such an important role in modern legislation that it was affirmed that 'the main method used for private law in today's legislative drafting is the comparative method'.[36]

In 2002, the German civil code (the BGB) experienced the most important reform since it came into force in 1900.[37] Initiated by a European Directive, the drafting process of this reform took inspiration from a wide range of European jurisdictions.[38]

In China, important law reforms have taken place over the last 15 years, in particular with the adoption of the Chinese Contract Act of 1999, the Law of Property Act of 2007, and the Tort Law Act of 2010. Among the sources of inspiration for the Contract Act were the codifications of Germany, Japan, and Taiwan, the English Common Law, and US law, as well as the CISG, the UNIDROIT Principles of International Commercial Contracts and the Principles of European Contract Law.[39] The new Law of Property Act drew inspiration from the laws of Germany, France, Japan, and Taiwan

[33] See section III.1.c) with references.

[34] P. Varul, 'Legal Policy Decisions and Choices in the Creation of New Private Law in Estonia', Juridica International [2000] 104 et seq.

[35] S. Selelionyte-Drukteiniene/V. Jurkevicius/T. Kadner Graziano, 'The Impact of the Comparative Method on Lithuanian Private Law', *ERPL* [2013] 959–90.

[36] P. Varul, n. 34, at 107.

[37] Gesetz zur Modernisierung des Schuldrechts, Bundesgesetzblatt 2001, I, 3138.

[38] Compare U. Huber, 'Das geplante Recht der Leistungsstörungen', in W. Ernst/R. Zimmermann (eds.), *Zivilrechtswissenschaft und Schuldrechtsreform* (Tübingen: Mohr Siebeck, 2001), p. 104–7; P. Schlechtriem, 'Das geplante Gewährleistungsrecht', *in* W. Ernst/R. Zimmermann (eds.), ibid., p. 205–24.

[39] L. Huixing, *The Draft Civil Code of the People's Republic of China*, English Translation (Leiden/Boston: Martinus Nijhoff, 2010), p. XIX with examples.

and from some aspects of English and US law.[40] Recently, a draft version of a Chinese Civil Code was presented. The structure of the draft code was inspired by the example of the Pandects and by Dutch law.[41]

These varied examples show that preparing legislation in the field of private law does not take place in a context that is purely specific to each state, but within the context of a European-wide discussion, or, in the case of Chinese law, the CISG and the UNIDROIT Principles, in a worldwide context.

The fact that the legislator himself uses the comparative method in the preparation of domestic law has an important implication for its interpretation: if the legislator takes inspiration from foreign law, because he is inspired by an *idea of justice existing beyond state borders*, the judge must be able to follow this approach when applying the law. In this sense, article 1 section 2 of the Swiss Civil Code expressly states that '*à défaut d'une disposition applicable, le juge prononce selon le droit coutumier et, à défaut d'une coutume, selon les règles qu'il établirait s'il avait à faire acte de législateur*' (in the absence of a provision, the court shall decide in accordance with customary law and, in the absence of customary law, in accordance with the rule that it would make as legislator). This provision expresses a general idea according to which the judge is invited to resort to the same sources of inspiration and methods used by the legislator, notably including the comparative method.[42] This is true, as is explicitly stated in article 1 section 2 of the Swiss Civil Code, in the absence of a legal provision. In many jurisdictions, it is recognized today that this also applies in cases of uncertainty of the law and when interpreting it, since filling gaps in the law and interpreting it are merely two sides of the same coin.[43] The Swiss Federal Court has consequently stated that 'when interpreting the law, all traditional methods of interpretation are to be taken into consideration (systematic, purposive, and historic . . . as well as comparative), all of which are used by the Federal Court in a pragmatic way without giving priority or preference to one of these methods over the others'.[44]

In the same spirit, the highest court in Germany, the Federal Constitutional Court, has repeatedly confirmed that the judge is not bound when it comes to choosing his methods of determining the law. In the 1990s the Constitutional Court held: 'Artikel 20 III of the Fundamental Law [Grundgesetz, i.e. the German Constitution] requires that the judge decides "according to law and justice". The Constitution does not prescribe a particular method of interpretation (or even a purely literal inter-

[40] Ibid., p. XX. [41] Ibid., p. XXII.

[42] Article 1 sect. 2 of the Swiss Civil Code was inspired by the works of the French legal scientist François Gény and thus is itself the fruit of an influence across borders, see F. Gény, *Méthode d'interprétation et sources en droit privé positif*, Vol. 2, 2nd edn. (Paris: Libr. général de droit et de jurisprudence, 1919), p. 326 et seq. no. 204; see also T. Henninger, *Europäisches Privatrecht und Methode* (Tübingen: Mohr Siebeck, 2009), p. 80, with further references.

[43] Konrad Zweigert, 'Rechtsvergleichung als universale Interpretationsmethode', *RabelsZ* [1949] 5 at 9.

[44] Swiss Federal Court 13.01.1998, ATF 124 III 266: '4. . . . *bei der Auslegung [sind] alle herkömmlichen Auslegungselemente zu berücksichtigen (systematische, teleologische und historische . . . ; auch rechtsvergleichende . . .), wobei das Bundesgericht einen pragmatischen Methodenpluralismus befolgt und es ablehnt, die einzelnen Auslegungselemente einer Prioritätsordnung zu unterstellen . . . ;*' French translation in *JdT* 1999 I 414.

pretation).'[45] The court further held that '[t]he courts are bound only by the law and they are not required to follow an opinion that is prevailing in legal doctrine, nor are they obliged to follow the precedents of higher courts; on the contrary, they can follow their own legal opinion and perception of the law... The judge is required to decide according to law and justice (Art. 20 III GG); with respect to the prohibition to render arbitrary decisions, the judge has to give reasons for his decision... In any case, the judge must show that the decision is based on an in depth legal analysis; his view also must not be deprived of objective reasons.'[46] In a 1953 ruling, the Federal Constitutional Court expressly recognized the use of the comparative method by the courts to fill gaps in domestic law and to interpret it.[47]

In other jurisdictions on the continent, legal provisions defining methods of statutory interpretation by the judge are limited to stating general principles, emphasizing the freedom of the judge to interpret and, if necessary, to develop the law.[48]

For common law and mixed jurisdictions, Robert Reed, judge at the Supreme Court of the United Kingdom, has noted with respect to the freedom of judges to choose their sources of inspiration:

> Scottish and English judges have for centuries drawn on ideas developed in other jurisdictions (both common law and civilian)... Judicial reasoning has been seen as a process of rational inquiry, in which there are not in principle any sources of ideas which are off-limit. Judicial reasoning in this country has not been thought of in national terms, with non-national sources of ideas being regarded as suspect: on the contrary, it has long been thought sensible to consider how others, from Ancient Rome onwards, have resolved similar problems. If judges are free to take account of the views of academic lawyers writing in law reviews, whether they are based in Cambridge, England, or Cambridge, Massachusetts, there would seem to be no reason why the opinions of foreign courts should be off-limits.[49]

The courts consequently benefit from a substantial freedom in their choice of the methods they apply to determine the law and they are free with respect to the choice of their sources of inspiration. Numerous examples cited in the third part of this contribution show that in many jurisdictions, judges use the comparative method to fill gaps in domestic law and when interpreting it, without questioning the legitimacy of comparison.[50]

[45] BVerfG 30.03.1993, BVerfGE 88, 145; NJW 1993, 2861 (2863).

[46] BVerfG 19.07.1995, NJW 1995, 2911.

[47] 18.12.1953, BVerfE 3, 225 at 244: '*Im übrigen haben die Gerichte sich der erprobten Hilfsmittel, nämlich der Interpretation und Lückenfüllung, unter Verwertung auch der rechtsvergleichenden Methode bedient.*'

[48] See e.g. §§ 6 et seq. of the Austrian Civil Code (ABGB), Art. 1 et seq. of the Spanish Civil Code (Código civil), Art. 1 et seq. of the Portuguese Civil Code (Código civil), Art. 1 of the introductory provisions of the Italian Civil Code (Codice civile), Art. 6 of the Russian Civil Code, Art. 1.3 et seq. of the Lithuanian Civil Code Art. 4 et seq. of the Latvian Civil Code; see also T. Henninger, n. 42, e.g. p. 437 et seq. with further references.

[49] R. Reed, n. 4, at 261–2; C. McCrudden, n. 4, at 527: 'the decision whether to use foreign judicial decisions seems largely in the realm of judicial discretion'.

[50] For references see section III.

g) *Choice of the most convincing solution while respecting the national legal system*

The argument that the use of the comparative method risks harming the national legal systems is also not convincing. It is true that, in every interpretation of domestic law, the system of the domestic law (be it a national codification or a case law system) must be respected as far as possible. This aim can be achieved through systematic interpretation which is one of the principal methods of interpretation of law. Indeed, like every other method of interpretation, the comparative interpretation must allow an interpretation and development of the law so that, out of the possible solutions, the most convincing is chosen while preserving coherence within the domestic system of law.[51]

h) *The authority of foreign law—a persuasive authority*

It is clear that the judge is bound by domestic law as well as by any provisions of international law in force in his country. Neither foreign statutory law nor foreign case law has democratic legitimacy in the judge's country. In relation to the use of the comparative method, two consequences follow from this:

Firstly, when the text of domestic law in force in the judge's country is clear and its interpretation does not leave any room for doubt, the judge is bound by his country's law. In principle, he cannot deviate from the result prescribed by the law in order to reach another result by using the comparative method; this is even true in cases where the judge finds this other result more adequate, appropriate, and fair, taking into account all the interests at stake.[52] In such a case, it is in principle[53] the role of the

[51] See e.g. G. Canivet, 'The Use of Comparative Law Before the French Courts', in G. Canivet/M. Andenas/D. Fairgrieve (eds.), n. 10, p. 181 at 183 et seq.; K. Zweigert, n. 43, at 16 et seq.; H. Unberath, 'Comparative Law in the German Courts', in G. Canivet/M. Andenas/D. Fairgrieve (eds.), n. 10, p. 307 at 316; see, however, A. Flessner, 'Juristische Methode und Europäisches Vertragsrecht', *JZ* [2002] 14: in a period of a renaissance of a common European legal science and of a European *ius commune*, the systematic interpretation of domestic law should lose its importance when it comes to determining the law.

[52] See e.g. *Bell v Peter Browne & Co.* [1990] 2 QB 495 (Mustill LJ) with respect to the concurrence of liability in contract and tort: 'Other legal systems seem to manage quite well by limiting attention to the contractual obligations which are, after all, the foundation of the relationship between the professional man and his client [citing French law] ... Nevertheless the [English] law is clear and we must apply it'; see for the discussion in the USA, V. Jackson, n. 9, at 125: '[T]he legitimacy of looking to foreign experience will vary with the issue, depending on the specificity and history or our constitutional text, the degree to which the issue is genuinely unsettled, and the strength of other interpretative sources.'

[53] For this rule and its limits, see e.g. the Swiss Federal Court 28.11.2006, ATF 133 III 257 ('parrots' case), 265 cons. 2.4: '*Ergibt die Auslegung eines Bundesgesetzes auf eine Rechtsfrage eine eindeutige Antwort, so ist diese gemäss Art. 19 Bundesverfassung für das Bundesgericht und die anderen rechtsanwendenden Behörden massgebend. Diese dürfen daher nicht mit der Begründung von Bundesrecht abweichen, es ... entspreche nicht dem (künftig) wünschbaren Recht ... Eine Abweichung von einer Gesetzesnorm ist jedoch zulässig, wenn der Gesetzgeber sich offenkundig über gewisse Tatsachen geirrt hat oder sich die Verhältnisse seit Erlass des Gesetzes in einem solchen Masse gewandelt haben, dass die Anwendung einer Rechtsvorschrift rechtsmissbräuchlich wird*' (Translation: If the interpretation of a federal law leads to a clear result, then, according to Art. 19 of the Federal Constitution, the Federal courts and all other law-applying authorities are bound by it. They cannot deviate from federal law arguing that the result under this legal provision is ... undesirable. It is however possible to deviate from a legal provision in cases where the legislator has obviously committed an

legislator (national or international) to solve the problem (if there is a problem). But aren't situations rare where interpretation of domestic law doesn't leave space for doubt or a margin of appreciation for the judge? Numerous uncertainties in domestic law, the demands of interpretation, as well as, in some cases, conflicts between traditional rules of civil law and constitutional values, make the scope of application of the comparative methodology very large.

Secondly, foreign legislation and case law can never *bind* the national judge. The authority of foreign law can only be a *persuasive authority*.[54] The more the values in one country and another are similar or shared, the more important is the persuasive authority of the other country's law.[55] The more a certain issue is politically sensitive, and the more particular circumstances in a given country led to the adoption of a specific rule or result, the less willing will judges be to draw inspiration from foreign law and experience. This is possibly the reason why the use of comparative law in certain constitutional issues before the US Supreme Court has been particularly controversial and disputed over the last years, whereas the use of this same method goes without saying in matters of private law in the USA.[56]

i) Soft harmonization of the law within the context of regional integration

Finally, the use of the comparative method is justified nowadays, in member countries of the European Union, by the membership of these countries in the Union. According to article 3, section 3 of the Treaty on European Union, the Union sets itself the objective, among others, of establishing an internal market and promoting economic cohesion among Member States. The convergence of provisions applicable to economic relations contributes notably to the achievement of this aim, in areas such as contract law, tort law, and, for certain questions, property law. In such matters, a comparative interpretation can result in 'soft harmonization' of the law which constitutes, at least for some matters, an interesting alternative to harmonization through enacting legislation. In relation to this, Walter Odersky, the former President of the German Federal Court, has written:

error or when the circumstances have changed since the enactment of the provision to the point that its application would constitute an abuse of right).

[54] See e.g. P. K. Tripathi, 'Foreign Precedents and Constitutional Law', 57 Columbia L. Rev. [1957] 319 at 346: 'When a judge looks to foreign legal systems for analogies that shed light on any of the new cases before him, he is looking to legal material which he is absolutely free to reject unless it appeals to his reason'; V. Jackson, n. 9, at 114: 'Transnational sources are seen as interlocutors, offering a way of testing and understanding one's own traditions and possibilities by examining them in the reflection of others'; A. Parrish, 'Storm in a Teacup: The U.S. Supreme Court's Use of Foreign Law', U. Illinois L. Rev. [2007] 637 at 674: 'Foreign law is persuasive authority: nothing more, nothing less'; and S. Yeazell, 'When and How U.S. Courts Should Cite Foreign Law', 26 Constitutional Commentary [2009] 59 at 69: '[I]ts persuasiveness has nothing to do with its origin.'

[55] For criteria for choosing the jurisdiction for comparison, see n. 19.

[56] See n. 9. The persuasive authority of the comparative argument loses weight if the fundamental values differ from one jurisdiction to the other, see e.g. A. Scalia, n. 5, p. 310: 'If there was any thought absolutely foreign to the founders of our country, surely it was the notion that we Americans should be governed the way Europeans are. And nothing has changed.'

> The national judge has not only the right to rely on interpretations from other legal systems and courts in his judgment, but also the right, when applying domestic law, and naturally when weighing up all interests and points of view to be taken into consideration in the interpretation and development of the law, to attach a certain importance to the fact that the solution in consideration contributes to the harmonization of European law. Following this reasoning, the judge may, if need be, follow the solution from another legal system as the result of a weighing of interests. With the progressive process of European integration, the judge should use this reasoning more and more often.[57]

According to Christopher McCrudden the impulse to use comparative law 'will be strongest . . . when the integration is set out explicitly as a political programme, with institutional characteristics, such as in Europe. Indeed, the comparative method is there explicitly built into the fabric of judicial decision-making'.[58]

3. Intermediate conclusions

In the search for a fair solution, the judge benefits from substantial freedom to choose his sources of legal knowledge and inspiration. In a large number of countries, judges are nowadays convinced that comparative law is one of the legitimate methods of interpretation of domestic law, and rightly so. The examples cited in the third section of this contribution will show that national courts draw inspiration from foreign solutions when interpreting domestic law. Indeed, important innovations notably in English, German, Austrian, Swiss, and US judicial law have taken inspiration from comparison with solutions that are in force abroad.[59]

In current US discussion, Ruth Bader Ginsburg, judge of the US Supreme Court, has written: 'The US judicial system will be poorer, I believe, if we do not both share our experience with, and learn from, legal systems with values and a commitment to democracy similar to our own . . . [W]e are not so wise that we have nothing to learn from other democratic legal systems newer to judicial review for constitutionality.'[60] Sonia Sotomayor, appointed in 2009 to the US Supreme Court, stated in the year of her appointment: '[T]o the extent that we have freedom of ideas, international law and foreign law will be very important in the discussion of how to think about the unsettled issues of our legal system'.[61] Sandra Day O'Connor expressed the opinion that the judges on the court will 'find [them]selves looking more frequently to the decisions of

[57] W. Odersky, 'Harmonisierende Auslegung und europäische Rechtskultur', *ZEuP* [1994] 3 et seq. (translation from German).

[58] C. McCrudden, n. 4, at 521f (quote on p. 522).

[59] See the references in section III.

[60] R. Bader Ginsburg, n. 26, at 576. Available also at <http://www.supremecourt.gov/publicinfo/speeches/viewspeech/sp_08-02-10> (last accessed: 10.02.2015).

[61] *In* Steven Groves, Questions for Justice Sotomayor on the Use of Foreign and International Law, The Heritage Foundation, July 6, 2009, at <http://www.heritage.org/research/reports/2009/07/questions-for-judge-sotomayor-on-the-use-of-foreign-and-international-law>, note 12 and accompanying text [Transcript of Judge Sotomayor's April 2009 Speech to the American Civil Liberties Union of Puerto Rico].

other constitutional courts... All of these courts have something to teach... about the civilizing functions of constitutional law.'[62]

Following an analysis of the use of the comparative method by courts in Europe, undertaken at the British Institute of International and Comparative Law, Mads Andenas, Duncan Fairgrieve, Guy Canivet (at that time *Premier Président* of the French *Cour de Cassation*), and the English judge of the House of Lords, Lord Goff of Chieveley, have summarized the analysis in relation to the current role of the comparative method before European courts: 'Comparative law is increasingly recognized as an essential reference point for judicial decision-making.'[63] According to Canivet, 'the use of comparative law is essential to the fulfilment of a supreme court's role in a modern democracy'.[64] Andenas and Fairgrieve come to the conclusion that, '[c]ourts make use of comparative law, and make open reference to it, to an unprecedented extent... Comparative law has become a source of law.'[65] Tom Bingham concludes that: 'Judicial horizons have widened and are widening.'[66]

III. Comparative law in court practice

1. Introduction

If it is legitimate to compare, is it beneficial and appropriate for the courts to resort to the comparative method? Do the benefits of the comparative method justify the sometimes considerable effort that the comparative approach demands?

In some countries, judges are nowadays convinced of the benefits of this method. An analysis of around 1500 judgments of the Swiss Federal Court has shown that in around 10 per cent of cases the court refers to one or more foreign legal systems for the purpose of comparison.[67] In matters concerning tort law, over the last few years, the percentage of the Federal Court's judgments that use the comparative approach has exceeded 20 per cent.[68] In other countries on the continent, the courts occasionally resort to the comparative method.[69]

[62] 'Broadening our Horizons: Why American Judges and Lawyers Must Learn About Foreign Law', Int'l. Jud. Observer, June 1997, p. 2. The following judges of the US Supreme Court have favoured the use of the comparative method by the court in recent years: Justices Day O'Connor, Stevens, Souters, Kennedy, Bader Ginsburg, Breyer, and Sotomayor. Have spoken against the use of this method: Chief Justices Rehnquist and Roberts and Justices Scalia, Thomas, and Alito.

[63] In G. Canivet/M. Andenas/D. Fairgrieve (eds.), n. 10, p. v and vii.

[64] In G. Canivet/M. Andenas/D. Fairgrieve (eds.), n. 10, p. 181.

[65] In G. Canivet/M. Andenas/D. Fairgrieve (eds.), n. 10, p. xxvii.

[66] T. Bingham, n. 20, p. 3.

[67] See the excellent analysis by A. Gerber, 'Der Einfluß des ausländischen Rechts in der Rechtsprechung des Bundesgerichts', *in* Institut Suisse de Droit Comparé (ed.), *Perméabilité des ordres juridiques* (Zürich: Schulthess, 1992), p. 141–63.

[68] T. Kadner Graziano, 'Entwicklungstendenzen im schweizerischen ausservertraglichen Haftungs- und Schadensrecht', in P. Jung (ed.), *Aktuelle Entwicklungen im Haftungsrecht* (Zurich: Schulthess, 2007), p. 1 no. 3.

[69] For France see R. Legeais, 'L'utilisation du droit comparé par les tribunaux', 46 Revue Internationale de Droit Comparé [1994] 347; G. Canivet, n. 51, p. 181, in particular p. 190 et seq. Canivet reminds us, however, that the very particular style of reasoning of the French *Cour de cassation* does not allow the judge to reveal his sources of inspiration, p. 187; see also *Cour de cassation*, Bulletin d'information no. 648 du 15/10/2006, Jurisprudence—Arrêts publiés intégralement, Arrêt du 7 juillet 2006 rendu par l'Assemblée

In English law, judgments in which the judges not only cite decisions from other common law jurisdictions, but also the laws, judgments, and doctrine from continental Europe, have multiplied over the last few years.[70] According to a recent study, for the period of 1996 to 2005, between 25 and 33 per cent of House of Lords decisions have included comparative references to other legal systems.[71] Some of the judgments that have benefited from looking beyond borders are among the most prominent cases in English legal history, such as *Hadley v Baxendale*,[72] which concerned the scope of damages for breach of contract. Tom Bingham, former judge of the House of Lords, wrote in relation to this judgment that 'sometimes seen as a fine flowering of common law jurisprudence, the immediate source of the rule [in *Hadley v Baxendale*] were the French Code Civil, Pothier's Treatise on the Law of Civil Obligations, Kent's Commentaries, and Sedgwick's Treatise on Damages, none of them works of indigenous origin.'[73]

plénière. For Spain: J. Canivell, 'Comparative Law before the Spanish Courts', in G. Canivet/M. Andenas/ D. Fairgrieve (eds.), n. 10, p. 211 et seq. For Germany: H. Kötz, 'Der Bundesgerichtshof und die Rechtsvergleichung', in C.-W. Canaris et al. (eds.), *50 Jahre Bundesgerichtshof: Festgabe aus der Wissenschaft*, Vol. II (Munich: C.H. Beck, 2000), p. 825; U. Drobnig, 'The Use of Foreign Law by German Courts', in U. Drobnig/and S. van Erp (eds.), *The Use of Comparative Law by the Courts* (The Hague: Kluwer, 1999), p. 127, with references; for the period from 1950 to 1980, U. Drobnig, 'Rechtsvergleichung in der deutschen Rechtsprechung', 50 RabelsZ [1986], p. 610; H. Unberath, n. 51. For the influence of German law on English, Swiss, and Austrian law, see: K. Schiemann, 'Aktuelle Einflüsse des deutschen Rechts auf die richterliche Fortbildung des englischen Rechts', 1 Europarecht [2003] 17; H. Honsell, 'Rezeption der Rechtsprechung des Bundesgerichtshofs in der Schweiz', *in 50 Jahre Bundesgerichtshof*, Vol. II, p. 927; H. Koziol, 'Rezeption der Rechtsprechung des Bundesgerichtshofs in Österreich', in *50 Jahre Bundesgerichtshof*, Vol. II, p. 943; for Dutch law: E. Hondius, n. 13, p. 764. See also the contributions *in* G. Canivet/ M. Andenas/D. Fairgrieve (eds.), n. 10; T. Koopmans, 'Comparative Law and the Courts', 45 ICLQ [1996], p. 545; B. Markesinis and J. Fedtke, n. 14, p. 11.

[70] See M. Nounckele, 'De la légitimité de la comparaison par les juges—Etude de la jurisprudence de la House of Lords de 1996 à 2005' (study prepared at the University of Louvain-la-Neuve, 2011); E. Örücü, 'Comparative Law in Practice: The Courts and the Legislator', in E. Örücü and D. Nelken (eds.), n. 27, p. 411; E. Örücü, 'Comparative Law in British Courts', in U. Drobnig and S. van Erp (eds.), n. 69, p. 253; K. Schiemann, 'Recent German and French Influences on the Development of English law', in R. Schulze and U. Seif (eds.), *Richterrecht und Rechtsfortbildung in der Europäischen Rechtsgemeinschaft* (Tübingen: Mohr Siebeck, 2003), p. 189. See e.g. the English cases: *Woolwich Building Society v Inland Revenue Commissioners (No. 2)* [1993] AC 70, [1992] 3 All ER 737 (HL): citing German law; *Henderson v Merrett Syndicates Ltd* [1995] 2 AC 145; *White v Jones* [1995] 2 AC 207, 1 All ER 691, comparison with the laws of Germany, New Zealand, California, the USA, France, and the Netherlands; *Antwerp United Diamonds BVBA v Air Europe* [1996] QB 317, [1995] 3 All ER 424, comparison with Dutch and Belgian case law; *Hunter v Canary Wharf Ltd* [1997] AC 655; *Kleinwort Benson Ltd v Lincoln CC* [1999] 2 AC 349; *McFarlane v Tayside Health Board* [2000] 2 AC 59; *Arthur JS Hall & Co v Simons* [2002] 1 AC 615, [2000] 3 All ER 673; *Alfred McAlpine Construction Ltd v Panatown Ltd* [2001] 1 AC 518: comparison with German law; *Greatorex v Greatorex* [2000] 4 All ER 769, [2000] 1 WLR 1970; *A v National Blood Authority* [2001] 3 All ER 289; *Fairchild v Glenhaven Funeral Services Ltd* [2003] 1 AC 32, [2002] UKHL 22, [2002] 3 All ER 305 (HL), damage following exposure to asbestos, comparison with the laws of Germany, Austria, Norway, Canada, Australia, Italy, South Africa, and Switzerland; *Campbell v Mirror Group Newspapers Ltd* [2004] AC 457, [2004] 2 All ER 995, liability for the invasion of personality rights and the violation of a person's privacy, comparison with German and French law; *The Starsin* [2004] 1 AC 715, [2003] 2 All ER 785; *Douglas and others v Hello! Ltd* [2005] [EWCA Civ] 595; *National Westminster Bank plc. v Spectrum Plus Ltd* [2005] UKHL 41, comparison with the laws of the USA, India, Ireland, Canada.

[71] M. Nounckele, n. 70. [72] [1854] 9 Ex Ch 341.

[73] T. Bingham, n. 20, p. 5. See for the USA e.g. M. Minow, n. 9, III. (text following n. 135 and 136). She stresses that *Brown v Board of Education*, 347 US 483 (1954), one of the most famous decisions of the US Supreme Court, has benefited, among others, from foreign input; see also R. Glensy, n. 18, at 361: 'United States Courts have, from the founding of the nation to the present day, referenced foreign legal sources in a

Comparison is no longer limited to private law.[74] An increasing number of public or constitutional law courts have also resorted to the comparative method. In the USA, Justice Scalia, despite being opposed to the comparative approach, has stated:

> In many... cases, opinions for the Court have used foreign law for the purpose of interpreting the Constitution... I expect... that the Court's use of foreign law in the interpretation of the Constitution will continue at an accelerating pace... [U]se of comparative law in our constitutional decisions is the wave of the future.[75]

Based on an international survey Christopher McCrudden, constitutional lawyer at Queen's College, University of Belfast, found:

> It is now commonplace in many jurisdictions as well as for courts to refer extensively to the decisions of foreign jurisdictions when interpreting human rights guarantees.[76]

The Constitution of the Republic of South Africa of 1996 expressly invites courts to use the comparative method in matters concerning fundamental rights. The provision states: 'When interpreting the Bill of Rights, a court, tribunal or forum... (b) must consider international law; and (c) may consider foreign law.'[77] The Constitutional Court of South Africa is consequently today among the most active actors regarding a transnational judicial discourse.[78]

2. Benefits of using the comparative methodology

The reasons to resort to the comparative method, the aims pursued by the courts by comparing, and the assets of this method are plentiful.[79]

variety of different contexts... [E]xamples can be taken from almost every period of this nation's history', with numerous references.

[74] See e.g. C. McCrudden, 'Judicial Comparativism and Human Rights', in E. Örücü and D. Nelken (eds.), n. 27, p. 371: 'Courts are playing an impressive role in the creation of what some see as a "common law of human rights" or, in the context of Europe, "a ius commune of human rights"'; C. McCrudden, n. 4, at 499 ff.; A.-M. Slaughter, 'A Global Community of Courts', 44 Harv. Int. L. J. [2003] 191; P. Häberle, 'Grundrechtsgeltung und Grundrechtsinterpretation im Verfassungsstaat—Zugleich zur Rechtsvergleichung als "fünfter Auslegungsmethode"', *JZ* [1989] 913; S. Baer, 'Verfassungsrechtsvergleichung und reflexive Methode: Interkulturelle und intersubjektive Kompetenz', 64 *Zeitschrift für ausländisches öffentliches Recht und Völkerrecht* [2004] 735; C. Fuchs, 'Verfassungsvergleichung durch den Verfassungsgerichtshof', JRP [2010] 183 (for Austria): '*Dass Verfassungsvergleichung auch für Verfassungsgerichte ein beachtliches Erkenntnispotential bergen kann, ist... heute weithin anerkannt. Der VerfGH zieht rechtsvergleichende Argumente in der—unausgesprochenen—Annahme ihrer grundsätzlichen Zulässigkeit und Leistungsfähigkeit zur Problemlösung heran.*'

[75] A. Scalia, n. 5, p. 307–9; see also Justice Ruth Bader Ginsburg, n. 26, at 591: 'Recognizing that forecasts are risky, I nonetheless believe we will continue to accord "a decent Respect to the Opinions of [Human] kind" as a matter of comity in a spirit of humility.'

[76] C. McCrudden, n. 4, at 506.

[77] Full text: 'When interpreting the Bill of Rights, a court, tribunal or forum (a) must promote the values that underlie an open and democratic society based on human dignity, equality and freedom; (b) must consider international law; and (c) may consider foreign law.'

[78] See C. McCrudden, n. 4, at 506 with references in n. 26.

[79] See A. Gerber, n. 67, p. 150 et seq. ('*Gründe für das Heranziehen ausländischen Rechts*').

a) Positioning the national law in the international legal landscape

In some cases, courts cite foreign and international law in order to show that the national law is fully in line with modern solutions or international trends. This is frequently the case in Central or Eastern European countries that have recently reformed and re-codified their law. An example is the case law of the Lithuanian Supreme Court. The court has frequently referred to the UNIDROIT Principles of International Commercial Contracts, the Principles of European Contract Law, the Principles of European Tort Law, and the Draft Common Frame of Reference, usually with the aim of showing that the new Lithuanian Civil Code is fully in line with these modern soft law principles.[80]

b) Complementary to the historical method of interpretation

Courts often cite foreign law or soft law principles that have served as an inspiration to the national legislator for their own legislation. In these cases the comparative method plays a support role which complements the historical method of interpretation of domestic law.[81]

In two decisions of 2010 and 2011, the Supreme Court of Lithuania has stated that the provisions of the Lithuanian Civil Code which were adopted under the influence of the UNIDROIT Principles shall be interpreted in the light of the Principles.[82]

To cite another example: in a landmark case of 2006, the Federal Court of Switzerland had to rule on the scope of damages for breach of contract. A parrot breeder had bought six parrots for his breeding farm. They were infected with a virus that was subsequently transmitted to the other birds in the breeding farm. As a result, all birds died and the breeder suffered a loss of around two million Swiss francs. He brought a claim for damages against the seller of the infected birds. The claim raised the issue of the scope and the limits of the seller's contractual liability.

The Swiss Federal Court awarded damages and, in defining the scope of contractual liability under article 208, sections 2 and 3 of the Swiss Code of Obligations, drew inspiration from the French author Pothier's Treatise on the Law of Obligations as well as from article 1150 of the French Civil Code, which were already known and had inspired the legislator when the Swiss Code of Obligations was being prepared.[83] The

[80] The Court has referred to the UNIDROIT Principles on International Commercial Contracts in 20 cases, to the Principles of European Contract Law in 11 cases, to the Draft Common Frame of Reference in one case, and to Principles of European Tort Law in three cases explicitly, in others implicitly, see S. Selelionyte-Drukteiniene/V. Jurkevicius/T. Kadner Graziano, n. 35, with references; C. McCrudden, n. 4, at 518, diagnoses a 'pedagogical impulse' in comparative constitutionalism; see also A.-M. Slaughter, 'A Typology of Transjudicial Communication', 29 U. Richmond L. Rev. [1994] 99 at 134: 'The court of a fledgling democracy, for instance, might look to the opinions of courts in older and more established democracies as a way of binding its country to this existing community of states.'

[81] A. Gerber, n. 67, p. 151. See e.g. the Swiss cases TF 03.04.1914, ATF 40 II 249 at 256; TF 05.04.1938, ATF 64 II 121 at 129, or the German cases BGHZ 21, 112 at 119, and BGHZ 24, 214 at 218 f.

[82] See S. Selelionyte-Drukteiniene/V. Jurkevicius/T. Kadner Graziano, n. 35, with references.

[83] TF 28.11.2006, ATF 133 III 257. For the opposite situation, see the Swiss case TF 22.5.2008, ATF 134, 497 c. 4.2.3, 4.3, 4.4.2: Swiss law, notably Art. 418 of the Swiss CO, served as a source of inspiration for Art. 89b of the German Commercial Code (HGB); the Swiss Federal Court then took inspiration from German legal doctrine and case law on Art. 89b HGB when interpreting Art. 418 of the Swiss CO.

most well-known English case concerning the scope of damages for breach of contract, *Hadley v Baxendale*,[84] dating back to 1854, equally takes inspiration from Pothier's Treatise on the Law of Obligations and article 1150 of the French Civil Code. In 1894, the Supreme Court of the United States in turn adopted the principles from *Hadley* for US law.[85]

Pothier's work, article 1150 of the French Civil Code, the English case of *Hadley v Baxendale*, American case law and notably that of the Supreme Court of the United States, and, last but not least, the Swiss Federal Court's judgment in 2006, are thus all based on the same idea of justice concerning the scope of contractual liability, an idea of justice existing well beyond national borders.

c) *Discovering the diversity of solutions from which the court can choose*

Courts use the comparative approach in order to discover and demonstrate the diversity of solutions in force in different jurisdictions and from which the court can choose when interpreting domestic law.[86]

Recent English case law has given, in some cases, an impressive comparative overview. For example, in *Fairchild v Glenhaven*, the House of Lords found inspiration in not only Californian, Canadian, Australian, and South African law, and in the US Restatement of the Law, but also cited German, Greek, Austrian, Dutch, Norwegian, French, Italian, and Swiss law.[87] In *Kleinwort Benson Ltd v Lincoln City Council*, the court referred to US law, and notably, the Restatement of the Law, as well as Canadian, Australian, South African, German, Italian, and French law.[88] In *Arthur Hall v Simons*, the House of Lords compared with US and Canadian law and other continental European legal systems, as well as Australian and New Zealand case law.[89] In *White v Jones*, the House of Lords referred to New Zealand, Australian, US, Canadian, German, French, and Dutch law.[90]

The Supreme Federal Court of Switzerland frequently analyses and cites the laws of countries that border Switzerland, namely, French, German, Austrian, and Italian law.[91]

Sometimes, the comparative overview is established by the court itself. More frequently the courts rely on comparative studies previously published by comparatists. Comparison thus widens the horizon and completes the picture of possible interpretations and solutions that are available to the courts to resolve a specific question. By using the comparative method, judges complete and improve the quality of their reasoning. Anne-Marie Slaughter observed in this respect:

[84] See n. 72. [85] *Primrose v Western Union Tel. Co.*, 154 US 1 [1894].

[86] See also A. Scalia, n. 5, p. 309: 'Adding foreign law to the box of available legal tools is enormously attractive to judges because it vastly increases the scope of their discretion.'

[87] [2003] 1 AC 32. [88] [2002] 2 AC 349.

[89] [2002] 1 AC 615. [90] [1995] 2 AC 207, 1 All ER 691.

[91] Out of numerous examples, see e.g. the cases TF 20.04.1972, ATF 98 II 73 (*Kienast c. Gubler*) (validity of a testament); TF 23.04.2009, ATF 135 III 433, c. 3.3 (contractual penal clauses): change of case law inspired by Italian and German law and legal doctrine.

> For... judges, looking abroad simply helps them to do a better job at home, in the sense that they can approach a particular problem more creatively or with greater insight. Foreign authority... provides a broader range of ideas and experience that makes for better, more reflective opinions. This is the most frequent cited rationale advanced by judges regarding the virtues of looking abroad.[92]

d) *Illustrating the aims and particularities of the domestic solution*

In numerous judgments, courts cite foreign solutions in order to confront them with the solution that they have found for their own domestic law. They hereby illustrate the aims and particularities of their domestic law.[93]

By way of example, it's possible to mention a decision of the Federal Court of Germany (*BGH*) concerning the protection of personality rights and the right to privacy (*Caroline de Monaco*). Here the court compared German and French law, observing that the scope of the right to privacy is more limited in German law than in French law when opposed to the freedom of the press.[94] A German court of appeal provides another illustration in which the court cited US practice with respect to contingency fee agreements (i.e. agreements according to which the lawyer's fees depend on the outcome of the case). The court ultimately sets out that such agreements would be irreconcilable with the role of lawyers in German civil procedure.[95]

In *Kuddus v Chief Constable of Leicestershire Constabulary*, the English House of Lords notes that exemplary or punitive damages do not exist either in continental civil law systems, such as German and French law, nor in mixed legal systems which are influenced by both civil and common laws, such as Scots and South African law. The court therefore observes that, for the matter in question, it is 'unhelpful to look at the position in other jurisdictions'.[96]

In *Awoyomi v Radford*, the Queen's Bench Division of the English High Court refers to case law from the European Court of Justice (ECJ) concerning the immediate or future effects of a change in case law (the question of prospective overruling), before deciding that the case law of the ECJ could be materially distinguished from English law.[97]

[92] A.-M. Slaughter, n. 74, at 201.

[93] Compare A. Gerber, n. 67, p. 154; V. Jackson, n. 9, at 117: '[C]omparison can shed light on the distinctive functioning of one's own system... considering the questions other systems pose may sharpen understanding of how we are different', 128: 'engagement with foreign law... does not necessarily mean adoption, but thoughtful, well-informed consideration'; M. Minow, n. 9, text following n. 56: 'Looking at what others do may sharpen our sense of our differences rather than produce a sense of pressure to conform'; E. Young, n. 6, at 158: 'If American courts were to conclude that only domestic practice is relevant, then their judges might feel pressure to distinguish American mores... from the views they encounter on their European sabbaticals.'

[94] BGH 19.12.1995, BGHZ 131, 332 at 337 (taking inspiration from US law) and at 344 (opposing French law); for this use of the comparative method, see also the Swiss cases TF 04.06.1981, ATF 107 II 105 at 111; TF 18.05.1973, ATF 99 IV 75 at 76.

[95] OLG Celle 26.11.2004, NJW 2005, 2160. See, however, the German case: Constitutional Court 12.12.2006, 1 BvR 2576/04, BVerfGE 117, 163, NJW 2007, 979 (contingency fees admitted under specific circumstances).

[96] [2002] 2 AC 122, [2001] UKHL 29.

[97] [2007] EWHC 1671 (QB) no. 15 (per Lloyd Jones J).

The question of pre-contractual liability was addressed in the case of *Chartbrook v Persimmon Homes*. The House of Lords invoked the Principles of European Contract Law, the UNIDROIT Principles of International Commercial Contracts, and the CISG to highlight that the philosophy on which these regulations are founded differs from English contract law.[98]

It is also possible to mention judgments from the Swiss Federal Court concerning the conditions for the transfer of personal property. The court decided that, in contrast to German law (expressly indicating article 931 of the BGB), in Swiss law the ownership of movables cannot be passed on by the assignment of an action for recovery of the object.[99] The Federal Court therefore demonstrates that another outcome would be possible and practicable, but that there are reasons why it is not favoured by the court.

In another, nowadays classic, case, the Swiss Federal Court explicitly abandoned a solution formerly taken from German law according to which the transfer of ownership is separate from the validity of the contract of sale. The court thus discarded the abstraction principle, a pillar of German property law.[100]

In a case concerning a legal action brought by an environmental protection foundation, the Swiss Federal Court came to the conclusion that French legislation and case law, which was cited by the court of first instance, '*ne se concilient pas avec l'état actuel de notre législation*'[101] (cannot be reconciled with the current state of our legislation).

These examples show that the use of comparative law by courts is not at all limited to situations where the foreign solution is the one favoured by the courts. On the contrary, when the court's solution differs from another country's solution, the comparative approach can cause the court to expose national particularities and historical and cultural divergences that lead the court to favour one solution over another. In these cases, the comparative method contributes to a greater transparency and a better quality of reasoning. McCrudden concludes with respect to this purpose of judicial comparison:

> a use of foreign . . . law does not mean that the approach taken in the other jurisdiction will necessarily be *adopted*, just that it is *considered* . . . Even where the *result* of the foreign judicial approach has not been adopted, it has often been influential in sharpening the understanding of the court's view on domestic law.[102]

[98] *Chartbrook Ltd v Persimmon Homes Ltd* [2009] AC 1101, [2009] UKHL 38, no. 39 (per Lord Hoffmann). See also the case *Agnew v Länsförsäkringsbolagens* [2001] 1 AC 223 (House of Lords): Lord Millet states that with respect to pre-contractual liability there is a fundamental difference between English law on the one hand and French and German law on the other.

[99] TF 02.12.2005, ATF 132 III 155, c. 6.1.1 et 6.1.3: '*Das deutsche Recht . . . anerkennt die Abtretung des Herausgabeanspruchs als Ersatz für eine Übergabe. . . . [Für das schweizerische Recht ist] festzuhalten, dass durch eine Abtretung des Herausgabeanspruchs das Eigentum an einer Fahrnissache nicht übertragen werden kann, da dies mit dem Traditionsprinzip nicht zu vereinbaren ist.*'

[100] 29.11.1929 (*Grimm c. Masse en faillite Näf-Ackermann*), ATF 55 II 302.

[101] TF 20.02.2004, 4C.317/2002/ech (*La Fondation X. c. La Masse en faillite de feu A*, ou '*Gypaète barbu République V*').

[102] C. McCrudden, n. 4, at 512.

e) Countering the argument that a certain solution will lead to harmful results

The experiences in other jurisdictions are frequently cited by courts to counter the argument that a certain solution or interpretation of the law would have harmful or disastrous results.

Illustrations of this use of the comparative method are particularly common in English and US case law. For example, according to an old common law rule, someone who makes a payment following a mistake of law rather than a mistake of fact cannot seek restitution of the payment. In *Kleinwort Benson Ltd v Lincoln City Council*, the House of Lords abandoned this solution. The comparative approach was used to counter the argument that a right to restitution would result in a flood of litigation.[103]

In the English case *Arthur Hall v Simons*, the court considered the question of immunity of legal professionals for conduct during legal procedures. The court referred to the experiences of other countries in order to show that such immunity is not justified by practical needs, and the court subsequently abandoned the immunity.[104]

This use of the comparative method has furthermore been considered legitimate even by those who are in general opposed to the use of comparative law by the courts. In this respect, Justice Scalia has written:

> I suppose foreign statutory and judicial law can be consulted in assessing the argument that a particular construction of an ambiguous provision in a federal statute would be disastrous. If foreign courts have long been applying precisely the rule argued against, and disaster has not ensued, unless there is some countervailing factor at work, the argument can safely be rejected.[105]

f) Legal support for value judgments of the court

Often references to foreign law also play a role in highlighting that the solution favoured by the court is already recognized by other legal systems as being unbiased and fair, even if the legal approach to reaching this solution may differ from one country to another. This use of the comparative argument is particularly common and useful for the court when the decision is based on value judgments. In these situations, references to foreign legislation and case law provide *legal* support for the court's balancing of conflicting values.[106] In the English case *Alfred McAlpine Construction*

[103] [2002] 2 AC 349, 375 C (per Lord Goff): 'For the present purpose, however, the importance of this comparative material is to reveal that, in civil law systems, a blanket exclusion of recovery of money paid under a mistake of law is not regarded as necessary. In particular, the experience of these systems assists to dispel the fears expressed in the early English cases that a right of recovery on the ground of mistake of law may lead to a flood of litigation'.

[104] *Arthur JS Hall & Co v Simons* [2002] 1 AC 615 (see the opinions of Lord Bingham and Lord Hope).

[105] A. Scalia, n. 5, p. 306, see also p. 307: '[T]he argument is sometimes made that a particular holding will be disastrous. Here . . . I think it entirely proper to point out that other countries have long applied the same rule without disastrous consequences.'

[106] See e.g. A. Barak, 'Constitutional Human Rights and Private Law', 3 Review of Constitutional Studies [1996] 218 at 242: Comparative law 'grants comfort to the judge and gives him the feeling that he is treading on safe ground, and it also gives legitimacy to the chosen solution'; A.-M. Slaughter, n. 74, at 201: 'Evidence of like-minded foreign decisions could enhance the legitimacy of a particular opinion on the domestic constituency that a particular court seeks to persuade'; V. Jackson, n. 9, at 119.

Ltd v Panatown Ltd, Lord Goff of Chieveley stated in this sense: 'I find it comforting (though not surprising) to be told that in German law the same conclusion would be reached as I have myself reached on the facts of the present case.'[107]

Here it is possible to refer once again to the famous English case of *Fairchild v Glenhaven Funeral Services Ltd.* In this case, the court discussed liability of employers following the exposure of their employees to asbestos.[108] Inhaling asbestos fibres caused the employees to develop cancer. However, they had worked consecutively for several employers who had all exposed them to asbestos. This resulted in uncertainty as to where they had contracted the illness. According to traditional rules, the claim would have been rejected because the employees could not prove causation with the probability which is traditionally required. While searching for a solution that was favourable to the claim, the House of Lords found support in numerous foreign jurisdictions. In relation to this litigation, Lord Bingham observed:

> Development of the law . . . cannot of course depend on a head-count of decisions and codes adopted in other countries of the world, often against a background of different rules and traditions. The law must be developed coherently, in accordance with principles so as to serve, even-handedly, the ends of justice. If, however, a decision . . . offends one's basic sense of justice, and if consideration of international sources suggests that a different and more acceptable decision would be given in most other jurisdictions, whatever their legal tradition, this must prompt anxious review of the decision in question. In a shrinking world . . . there must be some virtue of uniformity of outcome whatever the diversity of approach in reaching that outcome.[109]

This use of the comparative method can also be found in a recent judgment of the Swiss Federal Court which concerned the capacity of beneficiaries of a will. The court found confirmation for its solution in three out of four of its bordering countries' legal systems (German, Austrian, and Italian law, in contrast with French law).[110]

[107] *Alfred McAlpine Construction Ltd v Panatown Ltd* [2001] 1 AC 518 (per Lord Goff of Chieveley). For other recent examples of this use of the comparative method, see the English cases *Robinson v Jones (Contractors) Ltd* [2012] QB 44, [2011] EWCA Civ 9, nos. 49 and 78 (LJ Jackson); *D v East Berkshire Community Health NHS Trust MAK v Dewsbury Healthcare NHS Trust, RK v Oldham NHS Trust* [2005] 2 AC 373, [2005] UKHL 23: same outcome in Australian law (no. 89, Lord Nicholls) and the law of New Zealand (no. 113 and 114, Lord Rodger), dissenting opinion by Lord Bingham who refers to French and German law (no. 49): 'no flood of claims in these countries'. See, on this use of the comparative method, and criticizing it, A. Scalia, n. 5, p. 309: 'It will seem much more like a real legal opinion if one can cite authority to support the philosophic, moral, or religious conclusions pronounced. Foreign authority can serve that purpose'. See for Switzerland A. Gerber, n. 67, p. 157.

[108] [2003] 1 AC 32. On this and the following cases T. Bingham, n. 20, p. 9 et seq.

[109] *Fairchild v Glenhaven Funeral Services Ltd* [2003] 1 AC 32, [2002] UKHL 22, [2002] 3 All ER 305 at 334.

[110] 06.02.2006, ATF 132 III 305: '*Auch in ausländischen Rechtsordnungen wird . . . die rechtswidrige Beeinträchtigung des freien Erlasserwillens als Erbunwürdigkeit erfasst (z.B. in § 2339 des deutschen BGB, in § 542 des österreichischen ABGB und in Art. 463 des italienischen Codice civile, nicht hingegen in den Art. 727 ff. des französischen Code civil).*' For other examples of the use of the comparative method for the same purpose, see A. Gerber, n. 67, p. 155 et seq.

g) Legal support when changing an established case law or when confronting new problems

In some of the most famous examples of comparison in case law, courts have resorted to the comparative method in order to justify fundamental changes to domestic case law or to confront new problems and to introduce new institutions or remedies.

It is possible to mention many cases where courts have used the comparative method to justify changes to the law: we have already referred to the case *Kleinwort Benson Ltd v Lincoln City Council*,[111] in which the House of Lords abandoned the common law rule according to which it was only possible to claim restitution of money paid following a mistake in fact as opposed to a mistake of law. Here the court also found support in several foreign jurisdictions for overturning the precedent.

In *White v Jones*, the court considered the question of contractual or tortious liability of a solicitor in relation to pure economic losses suffered by the claimant following the solicitor's professional negligence. The House of Lords observed that despite the conceptual difficulties, in many jurisdictions (the court cited German, French, Dutch, Canadian, US, Australian, and New Zealand law), it is possible to find a favourable solution for the claimant in either the law of contract or the law of tort ('Many jurisdictions have found a remedy in the situation in which the present plaintiffs find themselves'). The court subsequently introduced liability for negligence of legal professionals in English tort law.[112]

In two landmark cases, the Supreme Court of Austria consecutively allowed, in Austrian law, liability for nervous shock and damages for immaterial harm following the loss of a close relation (damages for bereavement).[113] The court cited, as sources of inspiration and to support overruling previous case law, Swiss, French, Italian, Spanish, Scots, Greek, Yugoslavian, Belgian, and Turkish law. The court found information on these laws in the writings of comparatists. It seems that the desire to avoid isolation and to support majority trends in Europe was not the least of motivations for the Austrian Supreme Court.

In some decisions, foreign solutions are cited *obiter dictum* to draw attention to new problems that have not yet been dealt with by the national legislator or by domestic case law. In these situations, the aim is to encourage the legislator and doctrine to examine the problem and to work out a solution.[114]

More commonly, the court itself will introduce a new solution. A well-known illustration can be found in decisions in Germany that recognized personality rights and the right to privacy as an absolute right, protected by the means of tort liability (§ 823, section 1 of the BGB and article 2, section 1 of the Basic Law for the Federal Republic of Germany). The Federal Court of Germany[115] as well as the German

[111] [2002] 2 AC 349.

[112] *White v Jones* [1995] 2 AC 207, 1 All ER 691, see the opinion of Lord Goff of Chieveley.

[113] OGH, ZVR 1995/46 and OGH 16.05.2001, JBl. 2001, 660.

[114] See A. Gerber, n. 67, p. 152 and e.g. the cases TF 10.05.1932, ATF 58 II 151 at 156 (company law); 20.01.1981, ATF 107 II 57 at 66 (copyright); 21.12.1982, ATF 108 II 475 at 484 s.

[115] BGH 05.03.1963, BGHZ 39, 124 at 132; BGH 19.12.1995, BGHZ 131, 332 (*Caroline de Monaco*): protection of privacy, reference to US law. For further examples, see H. Kötz, n. 69, p. 832 et seq.

Constitutional Court[116] found support in foreign laws when introducing a protection of personality rights and of privacy ('*Allgemeines Persönlichkeitsrecht*').[117]

In an English case in 1991 the court still stated that '[i]t is well known that in English law there is no right to privacy'.[118] If the judgments of the Court of Appeal and the House of Lords, notably in *Douglas and others v Hello! Ltd*[119] and *Naomi Campbell v Mirror Group Newspapers Ltd*,[120] were to change the law, it would be largely thanks to the case law of the European Court of Human Rights and—last but not least—the influence of comparative law.[121]

Another example is provided by the decisions concerning claims brought by parents, and indeed children, against doctors for damages following an unwanted birth. The issue of medical malpractice for 'wrongful life', 'wrongful birth', or 'wrongful pregnancy' has been considered by the courts in many jurisdictions over the last few years.

In Germany, the landmark case in this matter, published in the official collection under the English title 'wrongful life', drew inspiration from the case law of the English Court of Appeal as well as US law.[122] The Swiss Federal Court took inspiration from German and Dutch case law, distinguishing itself from case law of the English House of Lords and the Supreme Court of Austria.[123] In another landmark decision, the Supreme Court of Austria in turn took inspiration from French, Italian, Scots, and Danish law, while distinguishing German, Dutch, Belgian, and Spanish law.[124] Dutch case law took German law into consideration, and in turn, exerted an influence on Scots law.[125] In France, on the initiative of the judges of the *Cour de Cassation*, the case '*Perruche*' was preceded by comparative studies on liability for wrongful life and wrongful birth, from which it drew inspiration.[126] In truth, judgments relating to this issue that have not referred to foreign case law are very rare.

In Germany, an important procedural innovation, namely the publication of dissenting opinions of judges in the Federal Constitutional Court's judgments, has drawn inspiration from Anglo-Saxon law.[127]

h) Legal discourse on an international scale and 'soft harmonization'

It is possible to identify an eighth and final effect (and perhaps also a final objective) of comparison by the courts. In the aforementioned decisions, as well as in many others,

[116] BVerfG 14.02.1973, BVerfGE 34, 269 at 289, 291.

[117] See H. Ehmann, 'Das Allgemeine Persönlichkeitsrecht—Zur Transformation unmoralischer in unerlaubte Handlungen', *in* C.-W. Canaris et al. (eds.), n. 69, p. 613 at 628 n. 81 and at 640.

[118] *Kaye v Robertson* [1991] FSR 62 (Glidewell, LJ).

[119] [2005] EWCA Civ 595. [120] [2002] EWCA Civ 1373.

[121] Starting with the case *Von Hannover c l'Allemagne*, no. 59320/00, CEDH 2004-VI.

[122] 18.01.1983 ('wrongful life'), BGHZ 86, 240 at 249–51.

[123] 20.12.2005, ATF 132 III 359; case note: J. Essebier, '"Wrongful birth" in der Schweiz', *ZEuP* [2007] 888.

[124] 14.09.2006, 6 Ob 101/06f; see also OGH 25.05.1999, 1Ob 91/99k (comparison with German law).

[125] E. Hondius, n. 13, p. 764.

[126] Cour de Cassation 17.11.2000, D. 2001, 332: report of the 'avocat général' Pierre Sargos, JCP 2000 II No. 10438, p. 2302; conclusions de l'avocat général Jerry Sainte Rose, JCP 2000 II, No. 10438, 2308 et seq.; G. Canivet, *supra* n. 52, p. 190 et seq.; Cour de Cassation 19.11.2002 (*Epoux Brachot c. Banque Worms*), JCP 2002 II No. 10201, and avocat général Jerry Sainte Rose, JCP 2002 II No. 10201.

[127] P. Egbert, 'Für und Wider das Minderheitsvotum', *Die Öffentliche Verwaltung* [1968] 513.

courts draw inspiration from the laws of jurisdictions sharing the same values. In some cases, the courts adopt in their case law a truly European or even a global perspective. By demonstrating such open-mindedness, judges pave the way for discussion of legal problems on a European, or indeed a global, scale, thus creating a genuine European or even global community of lawyers who are able to comfortably discuss with each other.[128] In situations where this discussion leads to shared beliefs and solutions, comparison contributes to 'soft harmonization' of the law on a supranational scale.[129]

IV. Conclusions

From these reflections, a number of conclusions can be drawn:

1. If the applicable domestic law is clear and does not lend itself to interpretation, the judge is bound and can only with great difficulty and exceptionally deviate from the result prescribed by his domestic law by using the comparative approach.
2. None of the arguments against the legitimacy of the comparative approach are convincing. For the numerous cases in which domestic law has gaps or lends itself to interpretation, the comparative method is at the disposal of judges who may use it to find inspiration when interpreting domestic law.
3. Nowadays, it is possible that the comparative method constitutes (as it already does in a certain number of countries) a *fifth method of interpretation*, alongside the classical methods of interpretation, namely the literal, historical, systematic, and purposive approaches (or, depending on the country, alongside interpretation in conformity with principles of the national constitution or EU law also).
4. Neither foreign legislation nor foreign case law binds the judge when interpreting his country's law. Consequently, foreign law is only a *persuasive authority* and may only guide the judge as such.

[128] With regard to transnational judicial comparison in the field of human rights A.-M. Slaughter, n. 80, at 121 f.: 'courts around the world [are] in colloquy with each other'; Slaughter, n. 74, at 193: with respect to certain questions she observes a 'constitutional cross-fertilization' and an 'emerging global jurisprudence'; ibid. at 202: 'The practice of citing foreign decisions reflects a spirit of genuine transjudicial deliberation within a newly self-conscious transnational community'; see in Europe: C. Witz, 'Plaidoyer pour un code européen des obligations', in *Recueil Dalloz* 2000, Chroniques, p. 79 at 81.

[129] See e.g. *Cheah v Equiticorp Finance Group Ltd* [1992] 1 AC 472, [1991] 4 All ER 989 (Lord Browne-Wilkinson): 'It is manifestly desirable that the law on this subject should be the same in all common law jurisdictions'; *Attorney General v Sport Newspapers Ltd* [1992] 1 All ER 503 (High Court, QBD); *Smith v Bank of Scotland* [1997] SC 111 (120) (HL); E. Örücü, n. 27, pp. 415, 421, 425.

5. The aforementioned case law bears witness to the fact that courts, and notably supreme courts, pursue several objectives when using the comparative approach. Courts use the comparative approach:
   - in order to demonstrate that the domestic law is fully in line with modern international trends;
   - to complement the historical method of interpretation of domestic law;
   - to discover and demonstrate the diversity of solutions from which the courts may choose;
   - to benefit from experiences made abroad and to avoid reinventing the wheel again and again;
   - to sharpen one's own understanding of certain legal problems and to compare the national solution with differing foreign solutions in order to highlight the particularities of the domestic law;
   - to counter arguments that a given solution will lead to harmful or disastrous results;
   - to find legal support for a value judgment by the court; and finally,
   - to justify changes to domestic case law or to confront new problems, introduce new institutions or remedies.
6. Insofar as judges agree to take inspiration from foreign law or international principles derived from comparison, the comparative method will also become an important tool for lawyers who wish to use it in court in the interest of their clients.
7. So that the court has a solid base for use of the comparative method, it is essential to provide judges with reliable, solid, and trustworthy information as to the content of foreign law. This responsibility falls with the researchers and comparatists who use the comparative approach in their publications. Regarding a case before the court, this comparative research could also be undertaken, and information provided, on an ad hoc basis by comparative law institutions or by lawyers or their staff trained in comparative law.
8. With the progressive programme of European integration, and notably in matters affecting economic relationships, the judge could use the comparative interpretation while pursuing the aim of soft harmonization which provides an alternative to legislative harmonization ('bottom up' instead of 'top down' approach to harmonization).
9. By using the comparative method, courts contribute to the establishment of a legal discourse that transcends borders. They hereby contribute to the creation of a genuine European or even global community of lawyers who are able to comfortably communicate with each other about topical legal issues.

Thus, the widespread belief in the judiciary of the legitimacy and the multiple benefits of judicial comparison is well founded. With respect to this topic, Thomas Bingham has most aptly made the following point:

> In no other field of intellectual endeavour—be it science, medicine, philosophy, literature, architecture, art, music, engineering or sociology—would ideas or insights

> be rejected simply because they were of foreign origin... [I]t would be strange if [in the field of law] alone practitioners and academics were obliged to ignore developments elsewhere, or at least to regard them as of no practical consequence. Such an approach can only impoverish our law; it cannot enrich it.[130]

[130] T. Bingham, *Widening Horizons*, n. 20, p. 6; in the same sense e.g. Aharon Barak, judge of the Supreme Court of Israel, 'A Judge on Judging: The Role of a Supreme Court in a Democracy', 116 Harv. L. Rev. [2002], 16 at 111: 'Indeed, the importance of comparative law lies in extending the judge's horizons'; Martha Minow, Dean of Harvard Law School, n. 9, III. Reclaiming the Chance to Learn: 'Neglecting development in international and comparative law could vitiate the vitality, nimbleness, and effectiveness of American law or simply leave us without the best tools and insights as we design and run institutions, pass legislation, and work to govern ourselves.'

3

Comparative Law and the Courts

What Counts as Comparative Law?

*Geoffrey Samuel**

Do common law judges make use of comparative law in their decision-making and judgments? The question is not such an easy one because much depends upon what one means by 'comparative law'. In the past the expression tended to be used in a somewhat loose sense without much thought as to its epistemological implications, but over the past couple of decades the literature devoted to comparative law theory has intensified to a considerable degree. This, in short, has provoked the question as to what actually counts as 'comparative law'.

I. Introduction: identifying the difficulties

The use of comparative law in national and international courts is a topic fraught with difficulties. These difficulties stem primarily from the notion of 'comparative law' itself—that is to say its definition, its scope, and its context—but they also stem from the relationship between any given legal system and the various historical, geographical, and intellectual contexts of the given system itself. Thus just because the judges in, say, an English or a French court, during a particular epoch, might never refer to, or seemingly interest themselves in, a foreign case, piece of legislation, or doctrinal work, it does not follow that comparative law, for the epoch in question, has no relevance or even role with regard to these courts. For comparative law is concerned with two fundamental questions. What is 'comparison'? And what is 'law'?

These questions immediately indicate that the mere citing of foreign material in a judgment, report, or argument does not amount in itself to the use of comparative law by a court. One might draw an analogy with the law school. To provide students with a definition of comparative law that is adequate enough to locate the precise boundaries between the subject of the definition and a range of associate subjects such as legal history, legal theory, sociology of law, Roman law, European Contract Law, and the like is probably impossible.[1] What can be done is to state what comparative law is not. Thus it is not, for example, an introduction to French law or to German law, since such subjects do not have at their heart knowledge obtained about law through comparison. Moreover, an introduction to a foreign legal system will not necessarily enlighten

* Professor of Law, Kent Law School, University of Kent; Professor *affilié*, École de droit, Sciences-Po Paris.

[1] See eg K Zweigert and H Kötz, *An Introduction to Comparative Law* (Oxford University Press, 3rd edn, 1998; trans T Weir), pp 2–12.

students about the epistemological issues that surround the 'law' question.[2] No doubt a study of a foreign system could broaden the student's mind about what amounts to legal knowledge. Yet there is the danger that it might also have the opposite effect, in as much as it could consolidate a view that legal knowledge is simply a matter of rules.[3] Of course, the citing of foreign material in a national court is not exactly analogous to the introduction of courses on foreign law in a law faculty, but it does go some way in stressing that great care must be taken when one talks of comparative law in the courts. Often one is not actually talking of comparative law. What is meant is that foreign material is being considered by the court which may, or may not, draw conclusions obtained through methods that can properly be described as comparative. And even if the comparative method is adopted, this will not necessarily in itself mean that comparative law is in play. A true comparatist needs continually to be reflecting on the nature of legal knowledge itself.[4]

II. What is 'law'?

When one turns to this 'law' question, a whole range of issues start to emerge out of the fuzzy image that comparative law as a title seemingly creates. The first concerns the relationship in general between a specific national legal system and what Professor Legrand calls 'the other'.[5] This relationship can be of a great many kinds depending on the systems in play. However, when the national system is the English common law and the 'other' is the civil law tradition, the relationship turns out, possibly, to be rather asymmetrical. Just as equity cannot be properly defined or understood without a thorough knowledge of the common law and its history (the reverse being perhaps not quite so true),[6] so English law cannot today be properly comprehended without a reasonable understanding of aspects of the civil law. In other words the relationship between English law and continental law is probably rather different from the relationship between a civil law system, as a national system, and the common law as 'other'. The reason for this is the common law's complex intellectual relationship with, above all, civilian doctrine which has functioned, particularly during the 19th century, at the level both of theory—one thinks of John Austin and, later, the whole analytical tradition[7]—and of practice.

At the practical level the relationship between the common law and the civil law is, for example, of importance in understanding a number of modern categories of law.[8] The law of contract was virtually an import,[9] citations to foreign material being particularly in evidence between 1850 and 1880, and the language of Roman law was

[2] This point is developed in more depth in G Samuel, *An Introduction to Comparative Law Theory and Method* (Hart, 2014), pp 121–51.

[3] See eg R Perrot, *Institutions judiciaires* (Montchrestien, 14th edn, 2010), para 228.

[4] P Legrand, *Le droit comparé* (Presses Universitaires de France, 3rd edn, 2009), pp 34–49.

[5] Ibid., pp 27–9.

[6] Or at least the reverse being different.

[7] P Stein, *Legal Evolution: The Story of an Idea* (Cambridge University Press, 1980), p 70ff.

[8] J Gordley, *The Jurists: A Critical History* (Oxford University Press, 2013), pp 21–7.

[9] AB Simpson, 'Innovation in Nineteenth Century Contract Law' (1975) 91 Law Quarterly Review 247; Gordley, ibid., pp 251–4.

often extended to torts.[10] In the great case of *Taylor v Caldwell*,[11] much of Blackburn J's judgment is taken up with a detailed consideration of Roman and French materials. And while one cannot talk here of transplantation as such, since Blackburn J skilfully translated the civilian notions into the more home-grown idea of an implied term,[12] it does show that the use of continental ideas in English cases is not some new phenomenon. It would be much more accurate to talk in terms of a longer-term relationship between English case law and the civil law tradition that stretches back to the beginning of the 19th century.[13]

III. Hidden comparative law

This long-term relationship gives rise to what might be called a hidden comparative law, the expression embracing the idea of an unconscious as well as a conscious aspect. Cases such as *White v Jones*[14] and *Fairchild v Glenhaven Funeral Services Ltd*[15] are of course well known for their open and conscious references to civilian material, and both indeed may actually be cases where it would be justified to talk of comparative law (however strong or weak). Lord Goff in *Jones* certainly uses German law to construct a model of possible liability even if, in the end, he abandons everything in the pursuit of a typically English 'practical justice'. In *Fairchild* the foreign material was used, not as a source of law in any positive sense, but as a guide to where a just solution might be found.[16] It is arguable, given these attitudes to justice, that the judges were reflecting, even if only unconsciously, on the nature of law and this in itself might raise the use of foreign material out of the category of descriptive foreign law towards some idea of comparative law as an active tool in decision-making. This reflection, it should be added, at least in the case of *Fairchild*, was not necessarily just vague philosophizing on the nature of justice. There was a real epistemological issue about how social facts were to be comprehended (methodological individualism versus holism) and this in turn can be referred back to deep-level epistemological problems in the social sciences in general.[17]

This open use of foreign material does at first sight seem to set cases like *White*, *Fairchild*, and one or two other decisions[18] apart from the normal run of weekly reports. Yet hidden, or at least relatively hidden, comparative law is to be found in a whole range of other cases where the foreign element might not at first sight seem evident. No doubt most restitution lawyers, even those not familiar with either Roman law or the codes, are more or less aware that the foundation and independence of their subject owes much to civilian thinking.[19] And the same could be said *mutatis mutandis*

[10] G Samuel, *Law of Obligations* (Edward Elgar, 2010), pp 8–9 and references therein.

[11] (1863) 122 ER 309.

[12] D Ibbetson, *A Historical Introduction to the Law of Obligations* (Oxford University Press, 1999), p 224.

[13] Gordley, n 8, p 27.

[14] [1995] 2 AC 207.

[15] [2003] 1 AC 32.

[16] See Lord Bingham, para 32.

[17] G Samuel, *Epistemology and Method in Law* (Ashgate, 2003), pp 295–329.

[18] See eg *Greatorex v Greatorex* [2000] 1 WLR 1970.

[19] Samuel, *Law of Obligations*, n 10, pp 10–11, 387–91. Thus cases such as *Fibrosa etc v Fairbairn etc* [1943] AC 32, especially Lord Wright's judgment, could be said to have a comparative law element.

for the debate surrounding the existence of public and private law[20] or of a doctrine of abuse of rights.[21] Yet there are many less dramatic areas where a relationship between common law and civil law is to be found beneath the surface of judgments. For example, Professor Beale has drawn attention in France to an English decision of the Court of Appeal[22] that raises an issue that is of some relevance to civil lawyers, namely the problem of *imprévision* in contract law.[23] The problem is traditionally of conceptual importance to French lawyers because of a difference of approach between the public and the private law courts.[24] Now Professor Beale makes the point that if one adopts a functional approach to comparative law, an English court would appear to have arrived at the same solution as German law might have done utilizing the doctrine of *Wegfall der Geschäftsgrundlage*. Thus comparative methodology, when applied to an ordinary case of contractual interpretation (ordinary in the sense that there are no specific references to continental cases or texts), can suddenly reveal beneath the surface of the case a hidden depth. Yet Professor Beale's example proves to be even richer when one looks at Lord Denning's judgment in the *Staffordshire Waterworks* case. For the then Master of the Rolls appeared to be formulating a doctrine of change of circumstances when he indicated, at the end of his judgment, that the court could determine the agreement in such a way as to put the parties under an obligation to renegotiate the price. Of course the other two judges were not prepared to support him on this point, but the comparatist will not be slow to observe that Lord Denning's thesis has found acceptance at both a European and an international level.[25]

The idea of comparative law in the national courts is not, then, confined simply to cases where foreign materials are cited and considered. Comparative law—at least in the sense of borrowing—is omnipresent in a whole range of decisions.[26] Lord Diplock's adoption of the distinction between public and private law is one of the more famous examples;[27] but any decision that lends itself to analysis through the use of comparative methodology is, arguably, an illustration of the existence of comparative law in a national court.[28] Perhaps this point can be developed a little further in respect of legal reasoning. In a case of 1964 the victim of a gas explosion brought an action against the public utility supplier,[29] but, because the claimant could not prove fault, the action was framed in nuisance and under the rule of *Rylands v Fletcher*.[30] The Court of Appeal

[20] See generally JWF Allison, *A Continental Distinction in the Common Law: A Historical and Comparative Perspective on English Public Law* (Oxford University Press, 1996).

[21] M Taggart, *Private Property and Abuse of Rights in Victorian England* (Oxford University Press, 2002).

[22] *Staffs Area Health Authority v South Staffs Waterworks Co* [1978] 1 WLR 1387.

[23] H Beale, 'La Commission Lando: le point de vue d'un "common-law lawyer"', in C Jamin and D Mazeaud (eds.), *L'harmonisation du droit des contrats en Europe* (Economica, 2001) 127, p 129.

[24] See Samuel, *Law of Obligations*, n 10, pp 378–9.

[25] Principles of European Contract Law art 6.111; Unidroit Principles for International Commercial Contracts art 6.2.3.

[26] Gordley, n 8, p 252.

[27] *O'Reilly v Mackman* [1983] 2 AC 237.

[28] The point must be stressed that one is not suggesting that any use in the courts of comparative methodology is necessarily sophisticated; often it might just be at the level of borrowing.

[29] *Dunne v NW Gas Board* [1964] 2 QB 806.

[30] *Rylands v Fletcher* (1866) LR 1 Ex 265 (Ex); (1868) LR 3 HL 330 (HL).

rejected the claim. In justifying the refusal to recognize an absolute liability, Sellers LJ said that the supply of gas, water, and electricity 'are well-nigh a necessity of modern life' and thus it 'would seem odd that facilities so much sought after by the community and approved by their legislators should be actionable at common law because they have been brought to places where they are required and have escaped without negligence by an unforeseen sequence of mishaps'.[31] In saying this, the judge was following the comments of an earlier Law Lord who had observed in a case of damage resulting from escaping water that the supply of water was recognized 'as being so desirable in the interests of the community that in some form or other it is usually made obligatory in civilised countries'. However, this common lawyer had equally gone on to assert that it 'would be unreasonable for the law to regard those who install or maintain such a system of supply as doing so at their own peril, with an absolute liability for any damage resulting from its presence even when there has been no negligence'.[32] This statement is pregnant with comparative law possibilities, since it not only raises the activity in issue, the supply of a public benefit, into an international realm ('civilised countries') but also frames its reasoning around the notion of the 'community interest'.

The key point here for the comparatist is the notion of an interest. This is a concept that transgresses national law to play a role in all Western legal systems and, in doing this, it has the capacity to act as a 'master-key' allowing access to legal thinking in a range of legal systems.[33] Accordingly the comparatist, furnished with this key, can compare the reasoning employed in the English gas and water cases with the kind of reasoning that might be employed in a civilian court faced with similar facts. And, with respect to France if not elsewhere, the exercise proves interesting in that the same reasoning starting point—the community interest—would result in solutions completely opposite to those arrived at in the two English decisions. In France the supply of gas or water, because it benefits the community, is, in cases where there is 'an unforeseen sequence of mishaps', subject to 'an absolute liability for any damage resulting from its presence even when there has been no negligence' (to borrow the words of the common law judges). Sellers LJ was of course of the opinion that such liability would seem odd, yet the French view is that if the community benefits from an activity then the community should equally shoulder the burdens. Why should one individual have to shoulder a risk that arises out of a community benefit? In order to achieve the equality of burdens the community, that is to say the state, will automatically pay compensation to the injured citizens.[34]

This gas explosion case might seem like a good example of the non-use of comparative law in the English courts. However, it is not quite the last word on the approach of the common law. In *Dennis v Ministry of Defence*, a judge had to decide whether noise from RAF Harrier jets constituted a nuisance to those living on a neighbouring estate,

[31] *Dunne v NW Gas Board* [1964] 2 QB 806, 832.

[32] Lord Moulton in *Rickards v Lothian* [1913] AC 263, 281–2.

[33] F Ost, *Droit et intérêt: volume 2: Entre droit et non-droit: l'intérêt* (Facultés universitaires Saint-Louis, Bruxelles, 1990), p 10.

[34] L Neville-Brown and J Bell, *French Administrative Law* (Oxford University Press, 5th edn, 1998), pp 193–200.

the defendants arguing that the activity was in the 'public interest' and thus could not constitute a nuisance. Buckley J responded to this defence argument by saying that the 'problem with putting the public interest into the scales when deciding whether a nuisance exists, is simply that if the answer is no, not because the claimant is being over sensitive, but because his private rights must be subjugated to the public interest, it might well be unjust that he should suffer the damage for the benefit of all.'[35] The judge took the view that if the activity was in the public interest then the public should pay and that such payment could be achieved by holding the defendants liable in nuisance. 'The principles or policy underlying these considerations', he said, 'are that public interest should be considered and that selected individuals should not bear the cost of the public benefit.'[36]

It has to be said at once that Buckley J does not refer to any French cases as such. He seems to have regarded the decision as being squarely based upon the ('flexible') common law. Nevertheless his reference to justice suggests a similar approach to the one adopted by the Law Lords in *Fairchild*; comparative law, even unexpressed, can inform legal reasoning.[37] These English cases concerning what were then public utilities are, accordingly, just as relevant to the comparatist as *White v Jones* or the *Fairchild* decision. Moreover, this relevance can be located at several levels. At the level of concepts the comparatist can focus upon the role of an 'interest', and thus the escaping water case becomes a decision in which comparative law is present because community interest is used as a premise for arriving at one conclusion in one country and another conclusion in another country. This is not to suggest that 'interest' necessarily has the same cultural meaning in both systems. Yet the possibility of *mentalité* and cultural difference, or even the possibility of similarity, is exactly the kind of issue that will be of concern to comparative law. The 'comparison' and the 'law' elements of comparative law are of sufficient epistemological sophistication as to engage these kinds of practical problems in all their practical and theory complexity. Yet the point of entry remains the notion of an interest.

IV. Comparing facts and receiving ideas

Another level of comparison is the schematic analysis of the facts.[38] If one envisages society as nothing more than a collection of individual participants each having his or her own individual interests to protect and to pursue, then it is likely that collective interests might well be endowed with a certain structural weakness vis-à-vis the individual.[39] The fact that an 'individual' will include the largest and wealthiest of corporations will of course mean that in reality the community interest and the

35 [2003] EWHC 793, at para 46. 36 Ibid., at para 47.

37 Again the point must be stressed that one is not necessarily talking of a sophisticated use of comparative law.

38 Samuel, *An Introduction to Comparative Law Theory and Method*, n 2, pp 147–50.

39 R Boudon and R Fillieule, *Les méthodes en sociologie* (Presses Universitaires de France, 12th edn, 2002), pp 41–90.

individual interest are often completely distorted.[40] Such a weakness is perhaps evident in some of the public utility cases. The community interest is treated as only a very weak reasoning *unité*[41] quite incapable of effecting a transformation from fault to strict liability; the court thus 'rewards' the community of professionals and *commerçants* by treating them as if they were private individuals pursuing everyday activities.[42] In France the community interest is a much stronger *unité* partly because it is closely interwoven with the power of the state through the constitutional principle of *égalité*. Yet it is also stronger because Republicanism as a political ideal means that the community has an ontological existence that is missing in England. Community interest in France is, accordingly, more than capable of effecting a transformation away from the fault principle. This said, the *Dennis* case indicates that at the level of legal reasoning the situation can sometimes be more complex.

This ontological (and ideological) foundation of community interest can be equally important with regard to what might be called the 'reception' of certain civilian ideas. Here one is not always talking in terms of a hidden or unconscious comparative law, although some relevant cases will not necessarily openly display any European or foreign law dimension. The emphasis is on the circulation and incorporation of concepts from the 'other' and the vehicle is often European Community law. Sometimes such concepts or ideas can be assimilated without, seemingly at any rate, too many problems, and perhaps one such example is proportionality. This clearly is now part of English public law.[43] Yet it may well have a role in private law because it is an idea that can function very easily at the level of the law of actions, and so not only has it proved useful as a means of directly controlling the granting or withholding of certain remedies,[44] but it has the capability of acting as a new rationalizing vehicle for understanding a range of traditional cases.[45] Other concepts are more difficult. The leading example here is good faith, which, as Professor Teubner has observed, is very much context dependent.[46] English courts may think that they can absorb this classic civilian notion,[47] but the recent case law tells a rather different story. The rejection of a general pre-contractual duty to take into consideration the interests of the other party is of course well known.[48] But two relatively recent implied term cases are particularly revealing in that had they occurred in France the plaintiffs would probably have succeeded on the basis that the employers were under a good faith duty to provide

[40] This distortion might perhaps be evident in the House of Lords' attitude towards the relationship between an individual and a bank. The individual is expected to be fully aware of the bank's financial interests: *Director General of Fair Trading v First National Bank plc* [2002] 1 AC 481.

[41] To borrow (and perhaps distort a little) Professor Atias' expression: see C Atias, *Épistémologie juridique* (Dalloz, 2002), para 186ff.

[42] See Samuel, *Law of Obligations*, n 10, p 497.

[43] *Gough v Chief Constable of Derbyshire Constabulary* [2002] QB 459 (DC); [2002] QB 1213 (CA).

[44] *Lock plc v Beswick* [1989] 1 WLR 1268.

[45] Thus cases such as *Hong Kong Fir Shipping Co Ltd v Kawasaki Kisen Kaisha Ltd* [1962] 2 QB 26 could be seen as proportionality decisions. But cf Beale, n 23, p 131, who suggests that the case might be seen as one of abuse of rights.

[46] G Teubner, 'Legal Irritants: Good Faith in British Law or How Unifying Law Ends Up in New Divergences' (1998) 61 Modern Law Review 11.

[47] See eg *Director General of Fair Trading v First National Bank plc* [2002] 1 AC 481.

[48] *Walford v Miles* [1992] 2 AC 128.

the information that formed the focal point of the dispute.[49] The reason for this difference is again one of community interest. However, here one is not talking of the wider community, but of the contracting parties; a contract is a community enterprise between the two parties and good faith needs to be understood within this 'nouvelle philosophie'.[50] Put another way, to what *persona* does the interest notion attach? Is a court envisaging a social reality that consists simply of individuals—'there is no such thing as society'—or a social reality that is made up of co-operating sub-groups themselves capable of being envisaged as a *unité*?

V. Beyond superficiality: structuralism versus functionalism

Good faith is valuable to the question of comparative law and the courts for another reason. It illustrates how easy it is for judges and jurists to indulge in what might be called superficial comparative law. One has heard many times the assertion that courts in different systems, although employing quite different conceptual models or methods, usually end up arriving at the same solutions. This can sometimes be true; yet equally it can often be untrue as the gas, water, and implied term cases so clearly indicate. Moreover, merely putting the emphasis on the actual outcome of cases can be superficial in itself, even where outcomes, as between cases in two different systems, are the same. This is not to suggest that functionalism as a method is superficial; indeed this is not the case. But functionalism, despite an assertion to the contrary by one of the leading textbooks on comparative law,[51] is not the only method in comparative law. The structural scheme is of equal importance on occasions because it can reveal things that the functional scheme cannot.[52] Structuralism can reveal how a legal system operates in terms of a model of elements and relations and how these elements and relations are, in turn, embedded in the law's perception of social reality.

Take, for example, the following problem. A treasure hunter using a metal detector discovered a medieval brooch in his local park and the coroner's court adjudged it not to be treasure trove, thus allowing the finder to keep possession of the article. He was sued by his local authority who claimed that they were entitled to the brooch since it was found in a park of which they were the freeholder and in which the public were not permitted to use metal detectors. Auld LJ, delivering the main judgment in the Court of Appeal, having observed early on that 'the English law of ownership and possession, unlike that of Roman Law, is not a system of identifying absolute entitlement but of priority of entitlement',[53] went on to adjudge that the local authority had a better entitlement than the finder. Now it might well be that a civilian court could reach the

[49] *Reid v Rush & Tompkins Plc* [1990] 1 WLR 212; *University of Nottingham v Eyett* [1999] 2 All ER 437.

[50] F Gendron, *L'interprétation des contrats* (Wilson & Lafleur Itée, 2002), p 148.

[51] See eg Zweigert and Kötz, n 1, p 34.

[52] Cf D Gerber, 'Sculpting the Agenda of Comparative Law: Ernst Rabel and the Facade of Language', in A Riles (ed), *Rethinking the Masters of Comparative Law* (Hart, 2001) 190, 205–7. For a discussion of the structural scheme in law see Samuel, *Epistemology and Method in Law*, n 17, pp 36–308; and Samuel, *An Introduction to Comparative Law Theory and Method*, n 2, pp 79–95. See also G Samuel, 'Dépasser le fonctionnalisme', in P Legrand (ed), *Comparer les droits, résolument* (Presses Universitaires de France, 2009) 405.

[53] *Waverley BC v Fletcher* [1996] QB 334, 345.

same result, but for a comparatist it is unlikely that this would be why the English case is of interest. What is of interest is the structure of the model used by Auld LJ and how this structure compares with the Romanist one to be found in the civil law systems. In Roman law, as the judge pointed out, the structure is one of an absolute relation between person and thing,[54] and the starting point would be a remedy *in rem* that would in turn raise a simple question. Who is the owner of the brooch? However, if one looks in more depth at the English case, not only does the whole question of ownership appear largely irrelevant—for personal property entitlement is based on a better right to possession[55]—but the actual remedy in issue is the tort of conversion which, being a tort, is an action that is categorized in the law of obligations. The implications of this structural difference are quite startling for comparatists dreaming of a European Civil Code, since all of the great European national codes are based on the Roman model of a rigid distinction between the law of property and the law of obligations—between, in other words, real and personal rights.

Functionalism cannot bring out this structural aspect to legal systems.[56] It cannot reveal how the finder loses the brooch to the local authority not because he lacks a direct right *in rem*, but, inter alia, because he was a trespasser in the park. Status, obligation, remedy, and property are all intermixed in the English model and in a manner that must make all thought of harmonizing personal property law a fantasy. Possession as a legal and an empirical concept is so deeply rooted in common law thinking that it transgresses the relation between *persona* and *res* (property) to exert such a major influence in the law of obligations (bailment, conversion, trespass) that, at times, *owning* and *owing* merge within the notion of entitlement. Once one functions at the level of entitlement all rights become the same; they are simply entitlements and thus a person with a mere contractual right to enter property is considered on occasions to have just as good entitlement to a proprietary (possessory) remedy as the actual possessor.[57] The point here, it must be stressed, is not to criticize English law. The point is simply to indicate how the structural models used by different legal systems can be of fundamental importance to the comparatist because it is the differences between these models that give rise to serious epistemological obstacles when it comes to harmonization of legal systems.[58] Emphasizing the functional outcomes of cases is only one aspect of comparative law.[59]

Indeed this more philosophical (epistemological) implication that attaches to a structural view of comparative law is in evidence in a relatively recent case concerning the interpretation of a contract.[60] The question before the House of Lords was whether pre-contractual negotiations could be admitted for consideration by the court and reference was made to the fact that the civil law systems permits such admission.

[54] Well expressed in the *Code civil* art 544.

[55] T Weir, *Tort Law* (Oxford University Press, 2nd edn, 2006), p 168.

[56] This point is developed in much more depth in Samuel, *An Introduction to Comparative Law Theory and Method*, n 2, pp 79–81, 96–107.

[57] *Manchester Airport Plc v Dutton* [2000] 1 QB 133.

[58] This point is discussed in a little more depth in G Samuel, 'English Private Law in the Context of the Codes', in M van Hoecke and F Ost (eds.), *The Harmonisation of European Private Law* (Hart, 2000) 47.

[59] See generally Gerber, n 52.

[60] *Chartbrook Ltd v Persimmon Homes Ltd* [2009] 1 AC 1101.

Indeed the various European and international contract codes provide that the 'common intention of the parties' is to be discovered by examining such prior negotiations.[61] However, Lord Hoffmann's reaction to this argument was to assert that 'these instruments reflect the French philosophy of contractual interpretation, which is altogether different from that of English law.' He then referred to an article by a leading comparatist, Catherine Valcke, to make the point that in French law there is 'a sharp distinction between the ascertainment of [the parties'] intentions and the application of legal rules which may, in the interests of fairness to other parties or otherwise, limit the extent to which those intentions are given effect.' Lord Hoffmann contrasted this approach to the one adopted by English law which, in contrast to French law, 'mixes up the ascertainment of intention with the rules of law by depersonalising the contracting parties and asking, not what their intentions actually were, but what a reasonable outside observer would have taken them to be.' And he concluded that one 'cannot... simply transpose rules based on one philosophy of contractual interpretation to another, or assume that the practical effect of admitting such evidence under the English system of civil procedure will be the same as that under a continental system.'[62] Lord Hoffmann offers as a justification for this difference of philosophy 'the more general interest of economy and predictability in obtaining advice and adjudicating disputes.'[63]

What is interesting about this case is that if a comparatist reverts to a functional approach the position becomes more complex in that English law might offer a Chancery remedy which permits a court to examine the pre-contractual negotiations. If a written contract does not reflect what was actually agreed by the parties, an aggrieved contractor can seek rectification in equity.[64] Thus, as Lord Hoffmann admits, the exclusionary rule at common law 'does not exclude the use of such evidence for other purposes: for example, to establish that a fact which may be relevant as background was known to the parties, or to support a claim for rectification or estoppel.' But these 'exceptions' are not, said Lord Hoffmann, actual exceptions since they 'operate outside' the common law rule.[65] Now a French comparatist using the functional method is likely to conclude that the philosophy is not as different as Lord Hoffmann suggests; one can simply avoid the exclusionary rule by turning to Equity. Yet this would perhaps miss the structural point that Equity is offering its remedy because the common law notion of contract is not founded—as in the civil law—on agreement (*conventio*) but on objective promise.[66] As Lord Atkin made clear in *Bell v Lever Brothers*,[67] a promise once legally made becomes an objective contract subject to the idea that 'it is of paramount importance that contracts should be observed, and that if parties honestly comply with the essentials of the formation of contracts ie, agree in the same terms on the same subject-matter they are bound, and must rely on the

[61] See *Principles of European Contract Law* art 5:102 (a); *Draft Common Frame of Reference* art II-8:102 (a); *Common European Sales Law (proposed)* art 59 (a).

[62] *Chartbrook Ltd v Persimmon Homes Ltd* [2009] 1 AC 1101, at para 39.

[63] Ibid., at para 41.

[64] See now *Daventry DC v Daventry & District Housing Ltd* [2012] 1 WLR 1333.

[65] [2009] 1 AC 1101, at para 42.

[66] Samuel, *Law of Obligations*, n 10, pp 93–9.

[67] [1932] AC 161.

stipulations of the contract for protection from the effect of facts unknown to them.'[68] One is dealing with rather a different creature than in France and this is one reason why *contrat* and contract are not synonymous.[69] Of course Lord Hoffmann does not make this point as such, but his comparative reference to the contract codes and to French legal thinking can certainly be regarded as an example of comparative law being used in the courts.

VI. Concluding remarks: danger and promise

Yet some of these comparative references made in the courts are not always so useful. When judges like Lord Diplock and Lord Goff talk in terms of an English 'law of obligations' they are not just indulging in comparative law.[70] They are, with respect, indulging in a rather superficial version of it. This is because a 'law of obligations' makes structural sense only when it is placed within the civilian institutional scheme and this scheme, which has its origins in the *Institutes of Gaius*, is nowhere reflected in the original forms of action model that acted as the foundation of the common law.[71] Of course much has changed since the early days, and the abolition of the forms of action during the 19th century certainly opened up English legal thinking to new ideas, new models, and new concepts. Yet the absence of a history of institutional learning (Blackstone excepted) means that, viewed in historical perspective, the content of English law is very much more 'open-plan' than is the case with civil law systems where constitutional and code texts have erected solid and often impenetrable walls. Such an open plan architecture does allow judges to erect their own walls and demolish existing ones erected by their predecessors. But when they do this, they may well be indulging in an exercise of hidden or unconscious comparative law.[72] One reason for this is that for well over a century, Roman law was a requirement for the Bar and so all barristers trained before 1970 would have an outline of the Roman blueprint somewhere in their subconscious. Today it is European Union (and to an extent human rights) law that is compulsory.

This subject is—or these subjects are—no substitute, of course, for Roman law in the sense that it, or they, will not directly endow the student with a knowledge of ownership, possession, actions *in rem*, actions *in personam*, obligations, quasi-contract, and so on. Yet they may stimulate another kind of thinking. They may lead to a generation of judges for whom the law is not a matter of national systems each with their own specific concepts, relations, and symmetries (or asymmetries). Law, for them, might be a mélange of ideas, of schemes of intelligibility, of structures, of sub-systems and the like.[73] Comparative law in such an intellectual environment will not necessarily

[68] Ibid., at p 224.

[69] But cf Diplock LJ's judgment in *UDT v Eagle Aircraft Services Ltd* [1968] 1 WLR 74.

[70] See *Moschi v Lep Air Services Ltd* [1973] AC 331, 346; *Henderson v Merrett Syndicates Ltd* [1995] 2 AC 145, 184.

[71] J Hackney, 'More than a Trace of the Old Philosophy', in P Birks (ed), *The Classification of Obligations* (Oxford University Press, 1997) 123.

[72] One rather obvious example is Lord Atkin's use of a term such as *culpa* in *Donoghue v Stevenson* [1932] AC 562.

[73] Samuel, *Epistemology and Method in Law*, n 17, pp 295–329.

be rendered irrelevant. Indeed, the opposite might be true. Comparative law will be the subconscious, if not the conscious, source of this kind of complex knowledge given its epistemological focus on comparison and on law. In addition, it will surely have its role, at the European level, of stimulating the new thinking that one comparatist has suggested is so essential to all national systems acting within the European meta-legal system.[74] On further reflection, and on an historical examination of legal argumentation in the common law of the kind undertaken by Professor Waddams,[75] perhaps, after all, one is not talking about some possible future. Perhaps one is talking of the common law of the here-and-now, perhaps even of the then-and-now. In which case, the whole question of the use of comparative law in common law courts is truly a most complex and subtle one and is an issue that stretches far beyond the citation of a few foreign cases and texts.[76]

[74] C Joerges, 'European Challenges to Private Law: On False Dichotomies, True Conflicts and the Need for a Constitutional Perspective' (1998) 18 Legal Studies 121.

[75] See S Waddams, 'Johanna Wagner and the Rival Opera Houses' (2001) 117 Law Quarterly Review 431; S Waddams, *Dimensions of Private Law: Categories and Concepts in Anglo-American Legal Reasoning* (Cambridge University Press, 2003).

[76] See further Gordley, n 8, pp 195–274.

4

Foreign Law before the French Courts

A Unique Procedural Treatment

*Bénédicte Fauvarque-Cosson**

The question of how foreign law is pleaded and proved before national courts is a crucial one, and, at first sight, it seems to be one of the questions where the difference between common law and civil law countries is most drastic.[1] Some authors even advocate for European regulations of conflict of laws for 'an enormous diversity reigns in Europe, in theory as well as in practice'.[2] While in English law this question tends to be treated as a procedural matter, in most civil law countries it lies at the conceptual core of private international law. While in English law, the rule is that the law must be pleaded and proved as a matter of fact to the satisfaction of the judge by expert evidence (or sometimes by other means). In most civil law countries, the rule is that foreign law should be treated as law. This usually implies that judges should apply it *ex officio*, in other words even if the parties have not pleaded and proved it. Yet, if this is true in most countries which have recently codified their conflict of law rules, the situation is different in France, where there has been no such codification. Major private international law questions such as pleading and proof of foreign law are settled by the French Cour de cassation, the Supreme Civil Court.[3]

* Professor of Law, Université Panthéon-Assas (Paris II), President of the Société de législation comparée, Vice-president of the International Academy of Comparative Law.

[1] For a comparative survey, see Carlos Esplugues Mota, José Luis Iglesias Buhigues, and Guillermo Palao Moreno (eds.), *Application of Foreign Law* (Sellier Law Publishers, 2011); for a report on the current state of French law, see, in this book, Fulli-Lemaire, Rojas Tamayo, France, p. 185; also, Trevor C. Hartley, 'Pleading and Proof of Foreign Law: The Major European Systems Compared', *International and Comparative Quarterly Law Review* (1997), 271; T. M. de Boer, 'Facultative Choice of Law, The Procedural Status of Choice-of-Law Rules and Foreign Law', *Recueil des cours,* 257 (1996), 223–447; M. Reimann, *Conflict of Laws in Western Europe, A Guide through the Jungle* (Irvington, NY, Transnational Publishers, Inc. 1995), 159 et seq.; for an English perspective, R. Fentiman, *Foreign Law in English Courts* (Oxford University Press, 1998); and for a French perspective, B. Fauvarque-Cosson, 'Le juge français et le droit étranger', *Recueil Dalloz* (2000), 125; P. Mayer, 'Les procédés de preuve de la loi étrangère', in *Etudes offertes à Jacques Ghestin* (Paris, LGDJ, 2001), 617 et seq.; H. Muir Watt, 'Loi étrangère', in *Répertoire Dalloz de droit international* (Paris, Dalloz, 2010); A. Bolze, 'Cent ans d'application de la loi étrangère par le juge français', in *Le Monde du droit. Écrits rédigés en l'honneur de Jacques Foyer* (Paris, Economica, 2008), 87.

[2] O. Remien, 'European Private International Law, the European Community and its Emerging Area of Freedom, Security and Justice', CML Rev. (2001), 78.

[3] As a sign of its importance, it should be noted that this question was dealt with three times in the Annual Reports of the French Cour de cassation in less than ten years: A. Ponsard, 'L'office du juge et l'application du droit étranger', *Rapport de la Cour de cassation* (*Rapport*), La documentation française, 1989, p. 11; J. Lemontey and J.-P. Rémery, 'La loi étrangère dans la jurisprudence actuelle de la Cour de cassation', *Rapport* 1993, p. 81; J.-P. Ancel, 'Le juge français et la mise en oeuvre du droit étranger', *Rapport* 1997, p. 33.

In fact, the English and French approaches to foreign law are not as different as they may seem. In English law, foreign law is a question of fact of a particular kind. Conversely, in French law, it is a question of law (as decided by the Cour de cassation in 1993[4]), but a question of law of a particular kind. It benefits from a specific treatment, which is not easy to define. At the end of the 20th century, a series of cases of the French Cour de cassation have completely reshaped French law's approach to foreign law. The case law has had its twists and turns and there have been numerous important decisions of the Cour de cassation. The position now seems to be settled. The French solution is quite unique in Europe and most probably in the world.

In order to simplify matters, most French authors refer to the application *ex officio* of foreign law. In reality, this is not strictly accurate. In fact, there are two different questions which should always be clearly dissociated. First, is the judge bound to apply *ex officio* the choice of law rule? Second, if this rule designates a foreign law, who is to determine the content of this law and how? By referring to pleading and proof of foreign law, English law also dissociates these two stages.

Under French law, three separate questions must be distinguished, although they are so interrelated that they are not always dealt with separately by the courts. The questions are as follows:

- Should the French choice of law rule be applied *ex officio*?
- When the choice of law rule designates a foreign law, is it for the parties or for the judges to determine the exact content of the applicable law and how is this accomplished?
- To what extent can the parties agree to the application of the *lex fori* and, in so doing, prevent the judge from applying *ex officio* the choice of law rule which designates a foreign law (accord procédural)?

I. Should the French choice of law rule be applied *ex officio* by the judge?

For a long time, the following principle prevailed in French law: the choice of law rule was not applicable *ex officio* by the courts. The principle was established in 1959 by the famous 'arrêt *Bisbal*'[5] and, although much criticized, lasted until 1988.

In October 1988, the rule was reversed and the opposing principle was put forward: a judge must always apply the choice of law rule, even *ex officio*.[6] This strict approach for French judges was based upon article 12 of the Civil Procedure Code ('le juge tranche le litige conformément aux règles de droit qui lui sont applicables').

[4] Civ. 1ère, 13 janvier 1993, *Coucke*, *Rev. crit.* 1994.78, note B. Ancel.

[5] Civ. 1ère, 12 mai 1959, *Bisbal*, *Rev. crit.*, 1960.62, note Batiffol, Journal du dr. int. priv. 1960.810, note Sialelli, *D.* 1960.610, note Malaurie, *J.C.P.* 1960. II. 11733, note Motulsky, B. Ancel and Y. Lequette, *Grands arrêts de la jurisprudence française de droit international privé* (Paris, Dalloz, 5th edn., 2006), no. 32.

[6] Civ. 1ère, 11 oct. 1988, *Rebouh*, *Rev. crit* 1989.368, Journal du dr. int. priv. 1989.349, note D. Alexandre and chr. D. Bureau, 1990.317, *J.C.P.*, 1989.II. 21327 note Courbe, *Rép. Defrenois* 1989.310, obs. Massip, Ancel and Lequette, n. 5, no. 74; Civ. 1ère, 18 oct. 1988, *Schule*, *Rev. crit.* 1989.368, Journal du dr. int. priv. 1989.349, note D. Alexandre and chr. D. Bureau, 1990.317, *J.C.P.*, 1989.II. 21259, note J. Prévault, Ancel and Lequette, n. 5, ibid., no. 75.

The great majority of French commentators applauded this important overruling. However, it was itself overruled, two years later, on 4 December 1990, in a case called *Coveco*.[7] This case reaffirmed the *Bisbal* principle: French judges are not bound to apply choice of law rules *ex officio*. Yet it introduced two exceptions which, in practice, deprived the principle of nearly all its substance.

The first of these exceptions was founded upon the origin of the choice of law rule: if it originates in an international convention (for instance, the Rome convention), French judges should apply it *ex officio*. This exception was based upon the idea that once the French government has ratified an international convention, it is bound to apply it and its responsibility may be engaged if it does not do so. True as this may be, this assertion does not explain why, from a mere procedural point of view, international choice of law rules should benefit from a greater authority than mere internal rules. Either judges must apply *ex officio* their own choice of law rules, and in this case, all of them should be so applied; or alternatively they are not bound to do so, and there is no reason why choice of law rules which originate from an international treaty should receive different treatment (unless the treaty itself so decides, although the Hague conventions are silent on this point). This exception was abandoned in 1999.[8]

The second exception, is based upon the nature of the parties' rights (droits disponibles v droits indisponibles). The Cour de cassation decided that judges must apply choice of law rules *ex officio* when the parties do not have 'the libre disposition de leurs droits'. This expression is difficult to translate, as it is hard to know exactly what it means in French. Basically, it refers to matters, such as family law matters, where parties cannot freely dispose of their rights (with some exceptions, such as divorce where parties' autonomy is promoted by European regulations and national codifications). On the other hand, the rights of the parties to a contract are 'disponibles'. Richard Fentiman translates these words by using the expression the parties' 'indefeasible rights'.[9] He also refers to the concept of 'inalienable rights' and has given new keys in order to understand the use of the French distinction, but not its content: 'the distinction mirrors that between fact and law. Where inalienable rights are in question, questions of foreign law are treated in a "legal" fashion. But where the rights are alienable the treatment of foreign law resembles (to common law eyes), the treatment of facts'.[10]

Some authors have referred to the distinction between 'available and unavailable rights',[11] and I will use this terminology.

[7] Civ. 1ère, 4 décembre 1990, *Société Coveco*, Journal du dr. int. priv. 1991.373, note D. Bureau, *Rev. crit.* 1991.558, note M.-L. Niboyet-Hoegy, Ancel and Lequette, n. 5, no. 76.

[8] Civ. 1, 26 mai 1999, *Mutuelles du Mans, Bull. Civ.* I, no. 172, p. 113, *JCP* 1999.IV.2325, *Rev. crit.* 1999.7O7, note H. Muir Watt; B. Fauvarque-Cosson, 'Le juge français et le droit étranger', n. 1. However, a distinction, based upon the European origin of the choice of law rule could be necessary if national judges were obliged to apply *ex officio* European Community Law. On this debate, Marie-Laure Niboyet and Geouffre de la Pradelle, *Droit international privé* (Paris, LGDJ, 3rd edn., 2011), par. 627; G. Canivet and J.-G. Huglo, 'L'obligation pour le juge judiciaire national d'appliquer d'office le droit communautaire au regard des arrêts Jeroen Van Schijndel et Peterbroeck', *Europe,* avril 1996.1., sp. p. 3.

[9] R. Fentiman, *Foreign Law in English Courts,* n. 1, 1998, p. 285.

[10] See, Chapter 5 in this volume, R. Fentiman, 'Foreign Law in National Courts'.

[11] Fulli-Lemaire Rojas Tamayo, n. 1, p. 187: 'There is no perfect translation for the phrase *droits disponibles*, or, more exactly, several are conceivable, some aiming at literal translation, others more specific

Until 1995, the divide between 'available and unavailable rights' was the main key to understanding the French system, which does not treat all questions of foreign law equally. It explained its originality and complexity, especially as it applied to the second question, related to the charge of determining the content of the foreign law. This, however, changed in 1995 and the distinction, which has been regularly confirmed for the first stage of the process (*ex officio* application of the choice of law rule),[12] is no longer relevant at the second stage, that is to say when deciding who should determine the content of the foreign law and how this should be done.

II. Who is in charge of determining the content of the foreign law and how?

From a conceptual point of view, the question of the application *ex officio* of French choice of law rules is distinguished from the problem of who bears the burden of proving the foreign law. However, from a practical point of view, it would seem rather logical to apply similar principles to solve this problem.

For this reason, the French Cour de cassation first adopted the following solutions:[13]

- Where the parties' rights are unavailable, the judge is bound to apply *ex officio* the French choice of law rule. Consequently, he must also determine its content. In this respect, he must examine all relevant sources of law: case law, statute law, custom, etc. If he does not do so, his decision can be quashed by the Cour de cassation, on the basis of article 3 of the Code civil.
- Where the parties' rights are not available, the burden of proof rests upon the party who is pleading that the applicable foreign law is different from the *lex fori*. This eases the identification of 'false conflicts'.

However, in practice, it soon appeared that the line was not so clear-cut, for several reasons.

- Firstly, when the judge must determine for himself the content of the foreign law, the judge's duty amounts to a mere 'obligation de moyens'[14] (best efforts). In other words, if the judge encounters too many obstacles (such as inability to ascertain the exact content of the foreign law), he can turn back to the *lex fori*, as long as he justifies his decision. Moreover, in order to ascertain the content of the foreign law, he can ask for the parties' help. In fact, he may even reject the party's claim if the latter does not help him (art. 11, Civil Procedure Code).

to particular uses of the distinction: rights the parties can freely dispose of, available rights, waivable rights, or defeasible rights.'

[12] See for instance Cass. Civ. 1re, 20 Oct. 2010, no. 08-17033 (available right, succession); 6 Jan. 2010, no. 08-14278 (unavailable right, incapacity), 27 May 2010 (unavailable right, filiation); 9 June 2009, no. 08-11872, rev. crit. *dr. int. priv.* 2010.353, note H. Muir-Watt, (unavailable right, divorce).

[13] Com. 16 nov. 1993, *Amerford, Rev. crit.* 1994.332, note P. Lagarde, Journal du dr. int. priv. 1994.98, note J.-B. Donnier; Ancel and Lequette, n. 5, no. 82.

[14] Ancel and Lequette, n. 5, no. 82.

- Secondly, when the burden of proof rests upon the parties, the judge is not completely freed from all investigation. Proof of the foreign law is usually made by means of 'certificats de coutume' and the judge must check that these documents properly reflect the state of the foreign law.
- Thirdly, if the judge, in spite of not being bound to do so, decides to apply *ex officio* the French choice of law rule, he must also determine the content of the relevant foreign law.

All these elements showed the inappropriateness of the distinction between available and unavailable rights, at least concerning the burden of proving the foreign law. Besides, in actual practice, the party who has an interest in proving the content of the foreign law will most of the time do so.

Gradually, the Cour de cassation took some liberties with its own precedent. Finally, in 1995, it abandoned the distinction between available and unavailable rights regarding the question of ascertaining the content of foreign laws.[15]

In two cases decided on 28 June 2005, one involving available rights and the second unavailable rights,[16] the Cour de cassation ruled that when the judge has acknowledged that a foreign law is applicable, either because he has applied *ex officio* the choice of law rule or a party has pleaded foreign law, he must establish its content, with the assistance of the parties and through personal research if necessary. The nature of the rights is irrelevant: the judge is always in charge of ascertaining the foreign law and the burden of proof ultimately rests on him. This rule has been reaffirmed on several occasions.[17] The formula according to which the judge must ascertain the content of the foreign law, if necessary with the help of the parties, has become a 'ritual' one.[18]

Foreign law can be ascertained by any means.[19] In practice, the judge will request the parties' collaboration in this undertaking.[20] Most of the time the parties supply, at their own costs, some *certificats de coutume*[21] established by official bodies, for instance a public or consular authority, or more often by lawyers. These memorandums may be biased and this explains why certified copies of foreign statutes, judgments, or academic works are sometimes used.[22] The other party may challenge the elements of proof brought to the debate and, ultimately, it is for the judge to make up his own mind and, if needed, to conduct his own research.[23] Since foreign law is not a mere fact, the judge may not be bound by an agreement between the parties on the content of foreign law.[24]

[15] Civ. 1, 18 juin 2002, 18 sept. 2002, 22 oct. 2002, *Rev. crit.* 2003.86, note H. Muir Watt.

[16] C.Cass., commercial chamber, 28.6.2005, *Itraco*, C.Cass., first civil chamber, 28.6.2005, *Aubin*, Ancel and Lequette, n. 5, no. 83, p. 721, *Rev.crit.dr.int.priv.* (2005), p. 645, note B. Ancel and H. Muir Watt. *D.* 2005, p. 2853, and D. 2006, pan. 1495, obs. Courbe and Jault-Seseke.

[17] See, for ex., C.Cass., first civil chamber, 11.2.2009 (2 decisions), *Bull. Civ. I* no. 125 and 127, *JCP* G 2009.II.10065, D. 2009.565, obs. Egéa.

[18] P. Mayer and V. Heuzé, *Droit international privé* (Paris, Montchrestien, 2001), p. 140, footnote (50).

[19] C.Cass., first civil chamber, 13.11.2003, *JDI* 2004, p. 520, *Rev.crit.dr.int.priv.* 2004, p. 95.

[20] Muir Watt, 'Loi étrangère', n. 1, nos. 91 to 93, p. 21.

[21] See Muir Watt, 'Loi étrangère', n. 1, nos. 102 to 105, p. 23; D. Bureau and H. Muir Watt, *Droit international privé*, Vol. I (Paris, PUF, 2nd edn., 2010), no. 442, pp. 472–3.

[22] Muir Watt, 'Loi étrangère', n. 1, nos. 106 and 107, p. 24.

[23] Muir Watt, 'Loi étrangère', n. 1, no. 100, pp. 22–3; Fulli-Lemaire and Rojas Tamayo, n. 1.

[24] Mayer and Heuzé, *Droit international privé*, n. 18, no. 190, p. 143; C.Cass., civil chamber, 30.03.1966, *Rev.crit.dr.int.priv.* 1967, p. 705.

The judge himself can prove foreign law.[25] He may make use of his personal knowledge of the applicable foreign law.[26] He may also use the mechanisms provided for by the Code of civil procedure on preparatory inquiries and ask for a consultation or an expert's report.[27] He may also ask foreign judicial authorities about their respective national laws, as provided for by the international conventions to which France is a party, notably the London Convention on Information on Foreign Law.[28] Nowadays, the Department of European and International affairs (*Service des affaires européennes et internationales*) of the Ministry of Justice has its own network of correspondents and liaison magistrates (*magistrats de liaison*),[29] and these liaison magistrates have been asked for information concerning foreign law.

When applying the foreign law the judge should apply it in its entirety, including all foreign sources (case law, practice, etc).[30] If the foreign legal system gives no solution to the question at stake—no court has decided the issue or differing lines of authority coexist—the judge must interpret the foreign sources (statutes or case law), as the foreign courts would, with the foreign rules of construction. In the absence of a definite answer, he is then allowed to conclude that the content of foreign law could not be established with sufficient certainty, and apply French law by default.[31] In practice, 'First instance and Court of appeal judges, because of the pivotal role they have been granted in establishing the content of foreign law, seem to find themselves under increasing pressure to justify their failure to do so, notably by detailing the steps taken and the reasons why they were unsuccessful.'[32]

[25] On the ways foreign law can be proved before the judge, see Mayer, 'Les procédés de preuve de la loi étrangère', n. 1, pp. 617–36.

[26] C.Cass., first civil chamber, 2.3.1960, *C.A.C.B.*, Ancel and Lequette, n. 5, no. 33, p. 285. This solution is one of the key particularities of the procedural regime of foreign law with respect to the procedural regime of fact.

[27] Muir Watt, 'Loi étrangère', n. 1, no. 111, p. 24, This, however, is not at all frequent, see Mayer and Heuzé, *Droit international privé*, n. 18, no. 189, p. 142.

[28] Fulli-Lemaire and Rojas Tamayo, n. 1, p. 186. These authors note that France is also party to its Additional Protocol, as well as to 31 bilateral mutual judicial assistance conventions, which can be accessed at <http://www.doc.diplomatie.gouv.fr/pacte/index.html> (last accessed June 2010). These instruments are of very little use, see Bureau and Muir Watt, *Droit international privé*, n. 21, no. 442, p. 473; in practice, the number of requests from French tribunals is less than ten per year, Mayer and Heuzé, *Droit international privé*, n.18, no. 189, p. 143.

[29] On the creation of this new network, in 1993, see Fulli-Lemaire, Rojas Tamayo, n. 1, p.189: 'The process was formalised by a Joint Action of the European Union of 22.4.1996, concerning a framework for the exchange of liaison magistrates to improve judicial cooperation between the Member States of the European Union (96/277/JHA). The functions of liaison magistrate are twofold: facilitate bilateral relations and bring the ministries of justice closer in order to draft shared projects; help French magistrates or prosecutors in civil or criminal matters in order to obtain the best cooperation from their counterparts.' For an illustration, see C.Cass., first civil chamber, 21.11.2006, *Bull. Civ. I* no. 500, *Rev.crit.dr.int.priv.* 2007, p. 575. Expressing doubts as to the reliability of this mechanism, see Mayer and Heuzé, *Droit international privé*, n. 18, no. 189, p. 143.

[30] Regarding this issue, see Mayer and Heuzé, *Droit international privé*, n. 18, no. 191–193, pp. 142–4.

[31] C.Cass., first civil chamber, 21.11.2006, *Bull. Civ. I* no. 500, *Rev.crit.dr.int.priv.* 2007, p. 575, note Muir-Watt: 'The French judge who rules that a foreign law is applicable but finds it impossible to obtain the proof of its content can... apply French law by default.'

[32] Fulli-Lemaire, Rojas Tamayo, prec. note 1, p. 186; Muir Watt, 'Loi étrangère', n. 1, nos. 96–99, p. 22; Bureau and Muir Watt, *Droit international privé*, n. 21, no. 441, p. 472; Mayer and Heuzé, *Droit international privé*, n. 18, no. 184, p. 138.

The judge's freedom to interpret the foreign law is not totally unrestricted: the Cour de cassation acknowledges that lower courts 'interprètent souverainement' the foreign law, subject to the 'contrôle de dénaturation'. This means that it does not control the interpretation given by lower cases, except in those exceptional cases where the foreign law was so badly applied that it amounts to a 'dénaturation' (this happens very rarely and only for statutory provisions).

The new regime concerning the ascertainment of foreign law is yet another argument in favour of abandoning the distinction between available and unavailable rights as far as the ex officio application of the choice of rule is concerned.[33] Indeed, the current state of the law is only coherent for unavailable rights: in such a case, the judge must apply the choice of law rule (even if parties have remained silent) and he must ascertain the content of the foreign law. For available rights, there is an unjustified contrast between the fact that the judge has the power not to apply *ex officio* the choice of law rule and the fact that if he freely choses to do so, he then is bound to ascertain the foreign law (this may deter the judge from raising the issue).[34]

This distinction should therefore be rejected when defining the judges' duties, not only as far as proving foreign law is concerned, but also as regards the *ex officio* application of the choice of law rule. Indeed, the French choice of law rule is a rule of law, as any other rule of law and, as such, it should receive the same procedural treatment, based upon article 12 of the Civil Procedure Code. It would seem better, therefore, to abandon this distinction and to turn back to a single regime, according to which French judges would be under a double duty: first to apply, *ex officio*, the choice of law rules and, second, to determine the content of the foreign law.

It is true that some flexibility is needed and that too much rigidity may lead to dilatory manoeuvres, especially in countries such as France where the cost of litigation is not very high. This has become a major concern, as testified by the recent evolution of the judge and the parties in internal litigation. Traditionally, parties were supposed to establish all factual elements, while judges had the duty to apply the relevant rules of law. Nowadays, parties must not only raise the facts, but they must also at least make some suggestions regarding the applicable rules of law. Apart from specific instances where the judge is obliged to raise, *ex officio*, a 'moyen de droit', the judge has no duty to do this. However, he is obliged to requalify a wrong qualification. In actual practice, the distinction between these two operations (requalification/changing the legal basis) is rather blurred.[35]

Turning back to private international law, it is indeed inadvisable that, after the case has been heard twice (at first instance and on appeal), a litigant should be allowed to go before the Cour de cassation and ask for the lower court's decision to be reversed because it had not applied *ex officio* the choice of law rule which designated a foreign law. In the vast majority of cases, if this litigant failed to plead and prove foreign law,

[33] Compare position developed by author advocating the abandonment of such a distinction (at both stages of the process) in "Foreign Law before the French Courts" in M. Andenas and D. Fairgrieve, *Comparative Law before the Courts* (London , BIICL, 2004), pp. 6–9.

[34] Mayer and Heuzé, *Droit international privé*, n. 18, no. 186–187, pp. 141.

[35] S. Guinchard, F. Ferrand, and C. Chainais, *Procédure civile, droit interne et droit commuautaire* (Paris, Dalloz, 30th edn., 2010), no. 533 s.

this was not out of sheer ignorance, but because he knew or at least assumed that the result would be identical. Yet, in my opinion, this does not constitute a sufficient argument to justify the use of the distinction between available and unavailable rights.[36]

The Cour de cassation has found several ways of preventing litigants from using dilatory tactics.

A drastic solution to this problem would be to resort to the doctrine of *estoppel*, which is becoming increasingly popular in France, particularly in the context of arbitration. At the latest stage of the proceedings (i.e. before the Cour de cassation), one should be *estopped* from invoking the application of a foreign law.[37] Such a general solution is not admissible as in most cases it would overturn the obligation to apply *ex officio* the choice of law rule and, consequently, the possibility for the Cour de cassation to quash a decision which does not comply with this obligation.

Another less radical device has been adopted by the Cour de cassation. It is known as the 'théorie of équivalence'. When the two laws in conflict are identical or lead to similar results, the Cour de cassation sometimes allows first instance or appellate judges not to specify in their judgments which law they apply, in spite of their duty to apply *ex officio* the choice of law rule.[38] For the Cour de cassation, the application of the 'théorie of équivalence' is more demanding than the doctrine of *estoppels* as it implies some investigation of the content of the foreign law and not only an appreciation of the parties' procedural behaviour. In fact, the extent to which the Cour de cassation may use this doctrine is not very clear: in principle, our 'Cour régulatrice' is not supposed to engage in such investigations.

The theory of equivalence in many ways resembles the doctrine of the *Antikiesregel*, which was first adopted and then rejected by the *Bundesgerichthof*.[39] According to this doctrine, when all laws lead to a similar result, the judge is not obliged to choose between them. In condemning this doctrine, the *Bundesgerichthof* referred to the parties' interest in knowing which law is applicable, especially as regards the question of the control of the interpretation of the law by the Supreme Court (for there is no control of the interpretation of foreign laws). Moreover, in countries where the doctrine of precedent is particularly important, it is essential to know whether judges have based their decision upon their own law or upon a foreign law. The theory of equivalence is also reminiscent of some American doctrines, based upon the notion of false conflicts, or 'non-conflicts'.[40]

The theory of equivalence could be rooted in the famous presumption of similarity between the foreign law and the *lex fori*, which is traditionally the case in most common law countries, in order to justify the application of the *lex fori*. In all common

[36] For a different view on this point, see Niboyet and De La Pradelle, *Droit international privé*, n. 8, par. 628.

[37] For a comparative perspective on the doctrine of *Estoppel*, see B. Fauvarque-Cosson, 'L'*estoppel* du droit anglais', in '*L'interdiction de se contredire au détriment d'autrui* (Paris, Economica, 2001), p. 3.

[38] Civ. 1, 13 avril 1999, *Rev. crit. dr. int. priv.* 1999.698, note H. Muir Watt, Journal dr. int. priv. 2000.315, note B. Fauvarque-Cosson; 3 avril 2001, *Rev. crit* 2001.513, note H. Muir Watt. Niboyet and La Pradelle call it the 'tempérament ambigü de l'équivalence', *Droit international privé*, n. 8, par. 628.

[39] 3 May 1988, *IPRax* 1988.231.

[40] A. Ehrenzweig, *Private International Law* (General Part, 1967), Sijthoff-Leyden, Dobbs Ferry, N.Y. Oceana publ. inc., section 36, p. 86.

law countries, however, this presumption has been criticized as being a mere fiction.[41] Moreover, it has never been treated as a universal rule: thus, English judges have sometimes refused to apply it when the foreign law does not belong to a common law country. Some authors have said that this mode of reasoning is yet more inappropriate when the *lex fori* has been modified by statute. All these criticisms could lead to question the idea, which was once put forward in comparative law, that there is a general *praesumptio similitudinis* between the conflicting laws, that is to say a presumption that the practical results are similar.[42]

The theory of equivalence is a useful device. However, it should be used carefully and narrowly construed. Otherwise, it would seriously undermine the principles and the equilibrium established by the Cour de cassation over the last 25 years.

III. The parties' right to agree upon the application of the *lex fori (accord procédural)*

During their litigation, the parties whose rights are available, may agree upon the application of the *lex fori*. In so doing, they will prevent the judge from applying the choice of law rule which designated a foreign law. This possibility granted to the parties is called 'accord procédural'; it has emerged as a major topic over the last 25 years and it is not certain whether or not it could be applied in favour of a foreign law.[43]

The accord procédural is sometimes presented as yet another technique, based upon the parties' agreement, not to apply the foreign law. At first sight, it could be compared to the doctrine of *estoppel* or to the theory of equivalence, for it leads to the same result: it is used in order not to quash lower courts' decisions which have not applied the applicable foreign law. Yet, its justification is different and more solid: it is founded upon the parties' freedom of action when their rights are available ('disponibles').[44]

The debate on the 'accord procédural' is clearly linked to the solutions adopted by the Cour de cassation as regards the judge's duty to apply or not apply *ex officio* the choice of law rule. If the judge is not under a duty to do so, he most probably will not do so and, therefore, it is less necessary for the parties to make an agreement aimed at preventing him from applying *ex officio* the choice of law rule (although still advisable if they do not want a foreign law to apply). This may be the reason why the parties' right to agree upon the application of the *lex fori* was not asserted by the French Cour de cassation until 1988, at the same time it overruled the long-lasting *Bisbal* case, and decided instead that judges were bound to apply *ex officio* the French choice of law rule.[45]

[41] R. Fentiman, n. 1, pp. 147 and 148, questioning the 'plausibility of equating English and foreign law'.

[42] K. Zweigert 'Méthodologie du droit comparé', *Mélanges offerts à J. Maury*, t. 2 (Paris, Dalloz-Sirey, 1960), p. 579; K. Zweigert and H. Kötz, *Introduction to Comparative Law* (Oxford, Clarendon Press, 3rd edn., 1998), p. 40. Comp. Fentiman, questioning the 'plausibility of equating English and foreign law', n. 1, p. 148.

[43] B. Fauvarque-Cosson, 'L'accord procédural à l'épreuve du temps', in *Le droit international privé: esprit et méthodes, Mélanges en l'honneur de Paul Lagarde* (Paris, Dalloz, 2005), pp. 263–84.

[44] Niboyet and De La Pradelle, *Droit international privé*, n. 8. par. 631.

[45] Civ. 1, 19 avril 1988, *Roho c. Caron, Rev. crit.* 1989.68, note H. Batiffol, *D.* 1988, *Somm.* 345, obs. B. Audit; 6 mai 1997, *Hannover International*, Journal du dr. int. priv. 1997. 804, note D. Bureau, *Rev. crit.*

The parties' agreement has been called 'accord procédural'[46] because such an agreement is not aimed at choosing the applicable law, but at putting aside the foreign law which is normally applicable. As indicated by its name, it is made during the procedure and must therefore be distinguished from a choice of law based upon parties' autonomy in contract matters (by contrast, this agreement is named 'accord de fond'). Its effects are limited to the matters which are being discussed; if, for instance, it intervenes between two parties to a contract, it does not concern the whole contract but only the precise issues which are being litigated.

Originally, an accord procédural was subject to three conditions:

- it had to occur once the litigation had begun before the courts;
- it could only be valid if the parties' rights were available ('disponibles');
- it had to be express.

While the first two conditions have been constantly reaffirmed by the Cour de cassation, the third one is less stringent. In some cases, the Cour de cassation held that a mere failure to plead the application of foreign law amounted to an implied procedural agreement in favour of the *lex fori*. The Cour de cassation has so decided in contract matters, at a time when judges were obliged to apply the choice of law rule *ex officio* because it originated in the Rome Convention. In fact, it has done so in order to save some judgments which had not applied the choice of law rule *ex officio*. On the other hand, the Cour de cassation ruled that if the case is complex, the 'accord procedural' necessitates an agreement not only between all parties but also between all those implied in the case, the reason being that such an agreement should not prejudice third parties.[47]

There is some inconsistency in stating, first, that judges may apply *ex officio* the choice of law rule when the parties' rights are available and subsequently admitting that the parties can impliedly prevent the same judges from doing so, thanks to an 'accord procédural'.[48] In practice, the parties' so-called 'accord procédural' may result from pure ignorance or deliberate manoeuvres of one party; in that case, it is not the expression of an agreement between parties whose interests are in conflict. Unless there is a true case of false conflict, one of these parties is interested in the application of the foreign law. In the French inquisitorial system, the judge should always have the duty to inform this party that, by virtue of the French choice of law rules, a foreign law is applicable. This is why, as already explained, he should be under a duty to apply *ex officio* the choice of law rule, even when the parties' rights are available. The question would thus be on the table and the parties could, knowingly, agree to put aside the choice of law rule which designates a foreign law.

1997. 514 et la note, Ancel and Lequette, n. 5, no. 84; Civ. 1, 1er juillet 1997, *Sté Karl Ibold GMBH, Rev. crit.* 1998.60, 2me esp., note P. Mayer. On this evolution, see B. Fauvarque-Cosson, *Libre disponibilité des droits et conflits de lois* (Paris, LGDJ, 1996), préf. Y. Lequette.

46 The first person to use this terminology was Professor Paul Lagarde, in his comment of Civ. 1, 4 oct. 1989, *de Baat, Rev. crit.* 1990, p. 316.

47 Cass. Civ. 1re, 22 febr. 2005, *Rev. crit.* 2005, note P. Lagarde; Niboyet and La Pradelle, *Droit international privé*, n. 8, par. 631.

48 Mayer and Heuzé, *Droit international privé*, n. 18, no. 147, p. 118.

The same types of concerns arose in the specific context of the exclusion, by the parties, of the Vienna Convention on International Sale of Goods (CISG, art. 6) and the Cour de cassation, has changed its position several times. After having decided that this Convention constitutes French law and must, as such, be applied *ex officio*, the Cour de cassation has ruled that the parties' silence as to this Convention amounts to an agreement to exclude it and to choose internal French rules of contract law.[49] It then modified this line of authorities to adopt another approach, more respectful of the CISG: there must be, if not an express agreement, at least a clear consciousness of the international character of the sales and a clear willingness to choose French internal law.[50]

If an accord procédural can be inferred from the mere silence of the parties, the French system is not very far from the English principle according to which, in the absence of pleading and proof of foreign law, the court will apply the *lex fori.* In fact, it even comes very close to this solution. The only difference is that, under French law, the parties' rights must be 'disponibles' (available) for such an agreement to be implied, while, in English law, such a requirement is irrelevant.

In his book, R. Fentiman demonstrated that English law's treatment of foreign law is not always within the parties' 'untrammelled control'. Conversely, in countries such as France, where foreign law is in principle treated as a matter of law and where the judge should consequently be under a duty to apply it *ex officio*, this is not always so. Various means exist in order to alleviate this duty. Two of them are particularly important: the equivalence theory, aimed at tracking false conflicts; and the parties' agreement (accord procédural) to turn back to the *lex fori.* The extent of the judges' duties depends on the use, moderate or otherwise, which the courts will make of such devices.

The question of the application of foreign law should not only be limited to that of pleading and proof before the courts. Non-judicial authorities may be involved in international situations.[51] For instance, notaries (*notaires*) or registrars of civil status (*officiers de l'état civil*) face such questions and, when applying foreign law, they usually follow the same rules (subject to some differences).[52]

IV. Conclusion

Neither in England, in France, nor in any other legal system, can foreign law be considered as mere fact or as pure law. Its real nature is hybrid and its procedural treatment depends on various factors as well as on the circumstances of the case. Some flexibility is needed and all legal systems have their solutions for this.

[49] Civ. 1, 26 juin 2001, *Rev. crit.* 2002.93, note H. Muir Watt, Journal du dr. int. priv. 2001.1121, note A. Huet, *D. 2001*.3607, note Cl. Witz.

[50] Civ. 1, 25 oct. 2005, no. 99-12879.

[51] For an overview, see Mayer and Heuzé, *Droit international privé*, n. 18, nos. 465–468, pp. 462–5 and Pamboukis, 'Acte public étranger'. It should be underlined that French legal doctrine has tended to focus on the recognition in France of acts from a foreign non-judicial authority, rather than on how French non-judicial authorities apply foreign law.

[52] For more details, see Fulli-Lemaire, Rojas Tamayo, n. 1 p. 196.

In France, the distinction between available and non available rights (*disponibles* and *indisponibles*) has been put to the forefront and has developed in order to alleviate the judges' duty. This distinction has lost part of its importance since it has become irrelevant in ascertaining the content of the foreign law. In my opinion, this criterion should not be used at all to define the judge's role and there should be one general principle: the judge is under a duty to apply *ex officio* the choice of law rule. Some flexibility could, however, be brought in by several means: the possibility of asking the parties to cooperate in the process of ascertaining the content of the applicable law; limited recognition of the 'théorie de l'équivalence'; admission of the 'accord procédural' when the parties' rights are available.

In the world, due to the ongoing process of internationalization and regionalization, not all laws are as foreign as others. For instance, Belgian law (strongly influenced by the French Civil Code) is not as 'foreign' as Korean law. To what extent should this be taken into account? In all the fields which have been harmonized *via* directives or regulations, one can wonder whether it is still possible to treat the law of a Member State who belongs to the European Union as 'foreign law'. Another question relates to the procedural status of European choice of law rules.[53] As shown by this study, Member States have different regimes and there is, currently no harmonization on this point, in spite of the ongoing Europeanization of private international law. This means that the procedural treatment of a choice of law rule which originates in a European regulation depends on the national legal framework of each Member State. A European model is envisaged. It could become part of a European code of private international law, with general principles on these issues.[54]

In this book dedicated to the use of comparative law before national and international courts, I will conclude with some observations as regard the relationship between the study of foreign laws and conflicts of laws.[55] The discipline of conflict of laws depends to a large extent on comparisons between various legal systems and thus grants practical legitimacy to comparative law. This is particularly true in countries such as Germany, Italy, Switzerland, Austria, and, to a lesser extent, France, where judges are required to apply foreign law *ex officio.* Although this is not comparative law in the strict sense, as rightly noted by Mr Fentiman, it also 'truly raises a question of comparative law', for it is not merely a 'matter of knowledge, but of understanding'.[56] In fact, even if judges eventually turn back to the *lex fori*, the part played by the comparative method in the process of applying a choice of law rule is considerable. For indeed, even before reaching the final step which raises the questions of pleading and proof of foreign law, various comparative insights may be needed. Devices such as characterization, adaptation, and public policy require the review of some foreign

[53] On this debate, Niboyet and de La Pradelle, *Droit international privé*, n. 8, par. 627.

[54] Marc Fallon, Paul Lagarde, and Sylvaine Poillot Peruzzetto (eds.), *Quelle architecture pour un code européen de droit international privé?* (Peter Lange edn., 2011).

[55] B. Fauvarque-Cosson, 'Comparative Law and Conflict of Laws: Allies or Enemies? New Perspectives on an Old Couple', 49 American Journal of Comparative Law (2001) 407.

[56] See Chapter 5 in this volume, R. Fentiman, 'Foreign Law in National Courts'. On this informational role of comparative law, see also M. Reimann, 'Parochialism in American Conflicts law', 49 American Journal of Comparative Law (2001) 369 et seq., 371.

internal rules; the doctrine of renvoi implies reference to the choice-of-law rules of another jurisdiction. Last but not least, the development of true content-oriented choice-of-law rules[57] have made comparative investigations occasionally necessary at a preliminary stage, that is to say in order to apply the forum's conflicts rules.[58]

[57] As to the development of such choice-of-law rules in codified private international law systems, see S. Symeonides, *Private International Law at the End of the Twentieth century: Progress or regress?* (Kluwer Law International, 1998), 37 et seq., 48.

[58] See A.T. Von Mehren, 'The Contribution of Comparative Law to The Theory and Practice of Private International Law', in W.E. Butler (ed.), *International Law in Comparative Perspective* (Sijthoff and Noordhoff, 1980), 153, 159 (topic of 10th Congress of Comp. Law, Budapest, 1978).

5

Foreign Law in National Courts

A Common Law Perspective

*Richard Fentiman**

Courts sometimes resort to foreign law for guidance, or illumination, or to supply a useful analogy. But the hardest conceptual and practical problems arise where one country's courts are required to apply another country's laws.[1] In such cases, reference to foreign law is not merely interesting, or ornamental, but concerns the rights and liabilities of the parties.

The need to apply foreign law arises whenever the rules for choice of law provide that the law governing an issue is foreign. Alpha may sue Beta in England for a tort committed in France. Or Gamma may sue Delta in Germany under a contract expressly governed by English law. In the first case, the law of the place of the tort will doubtless govern; in the second, the law chosen by the parties is likely to be applied. But the application of foreign law begs questions of much difficulty and practical importance. These belong to private international law, or perhaps to the law of international civil procedure. But they also speak to the most fundamental of all questions of comparative law: what may we truly know of the laws of another country?

As this implies, the essential problem of applying foreign law is not one of procedure. Even if a court's procedures are defective, they can always be made more efficient. Nor is it one of information. Courts in contested cases seldom want for evidence of foreign law, and if they do the difficulties are contingent not inherent. Rather the problem is one of adjudication—a problem which arises however effective the procedures for applying foreign law, and even if the information before a court is plentiful. How may a court in one country meaningfully determine a contested question of foreign law? To what extent may a judge in one country participate in the thought processes of a foreign judge? To what extent can a judge adopt an 'internal point of view' when applying foreign law?[2] For, as one commentator has said:[3]

> Like a language, foreign law is difficult to learn by anyone who has not been born and bred in the social environment in which it is used... Most judges dealing with foreign

* Professor of Private International Law at the University of Cambridge.

[1] It is convenient to speak of courts applying foreign law, although whether they truly do so, as distinct from applying norms derived from evidence of foreign law, begs the question with which this chapter is largely concerned.

[2] Borrowing Hart's terminology: HLA Hart, *The Concept of Law* (2nd edn., Oxford, 1994), esp. 86ff. As Postema explains: 'The law, like other similar social practices, is constituted not only by intricate patterns of behavioural interactions, but also by the beliefs, activities, judgments and understandings of participants. The practice has an "inside," the "internal point of view" of participants': GJ Postema, 'Jurisprudence as Practical Philosophy' (1998) 4 *Legal Theory* 32.

[3] TM De Boer, 'Facultative Choice of Law: the Procedural Status of Choice-of-Law, Rules and Foreign Law' (1996) 257 Recueil des Cours 222, 305.

law in a conflicts case are unaccustomed to its vernacular, unaware of its various layers of meaning, insensitive to its subtleties, ignorant of its usage, oblivious to its context. Small wonder that they are apt to make mistakes that their colleagues abroad would avoid instinctively.

As this suggests, the foreign law problem is not, or is not significantly, a practical problem. English lawyers, for example, tend not to doubt the efficacy of the process of proving foreign law. It is rather a problem of principle. But this does not make it irrelevant or tangential. Indeed, whether the courts of one country may truly apply the laws of others begs two questions which could hardly be more fundamental. For if this cannot be achieved, is not the very purpose of the choice-of-law process undermined? And if it cannot, how can justice be done in cases subject to foreign law?

Two contrasting responses to the foreign law problem are evident. Some see the effective application of foreign law as all but impossible, thereby challenging the objectives of the choice-of-law process, and preventing the just resolution of disputes.[4] Their concern is that a judge in one country cannot assume the role of a judge elsewhere. More precisely, perhaps, it is that no mechanism can guarantee that this is achieved. Others, however, take the opposite view, relying on the principle that foreign laws are merely facts, and asserting that the only standard by which the application of foreign law can be judged is that the evidence has been properly assessed.[5]

As we shall see, neither of these extreme positions withstands scrutiny. Instead, principle suggests that the process of applying foreign law is domesticated, in the sense that it can only be controlled by the court applying foreign law. It can only rest on evidence, and the inherent legal expertise of a judge. That expresses the truth in the pragmatic view. But equally it is not sufficient to assert that foreign laws are merely facts. Respect for the choice-of-law process requires a court to aspire to apply foreign law as a foreign court would. This depends, however, on a proper understanding of what it means to decide a question of foreign law. In particular, it means avoiding the fallacy that there can be a right answer to a contested question of law, domestic or foreign.

I. The foreign law problem

1. An English perspective

It is fruitless to consider the foreign law problem in the abstract. For that reason, to anchor the discussion, the following analysis takes English law as its starting point.[6]

[4] See, F Juenger, 'General Course on Private International Law' (1995) 193 Recueil des Cours, 203–5; P Hay, O Lando, and RD Rotunda, 'Conflict of Laws as a Technique for Legal Integration', in M Cappelletti, M Seccombe, and JHH Weiler, eds., *Integration Through Law: Europe and the American Federal Experience. Book 1* (Berlin: 1986), 170; O Lando, 'Lex Fori in Foro Proprio' (1995) 2 Maastricht J. of European and Comp. L. 359, 367–71.

[5] A view expressed by the majority in *Neilson v Overseas Projects Corporation of Victoria Ltd* [2005] HCA 54, [1], [17], [118]; considered in A Briggs, 'The Meaning and Proof of Foreign Law' (2006) 1 LMCLQ 1.

[6] For a full account of English law, see R Fentiman, *International Commercial Litigation* (Oxford, 2nd ed, 2015), Ch 20. For comparative treatments, see TC Hartley, 'Pleading and Proof of Foreign Law: the Major European Systems Compared' (1996) 45 ICLQ 283; S Geeroms, *Foreign Law in Civil Litigation: A Comparative and Functional Analysis* (Oxford, 2004).

But different legal systems inevitably have different experiences of applying foreign law. In some systems, typically those where the parties have no responsibility to supply evidence of foreign law, the difficulty may lie in obtaining sufficient information, or a proper understanding of the rival arguments. Again, judges in some countries have expressed concern about the effectiveness of relying on party-led experts.[7]

The English experience is different. English lawyers and commentators retain confidence in the process of taking evidence from the parties' experts, and it is commonly accepted that this approach, although costly, is the best means of acquiring and presenting information about contested foreign law questions.[8] Again, disputes concerning foreign law before the English courts typically involve strongly contested questions, in disputes concerning substantial sums, as to which the evidence before the court is plentiful. This reflects the adversarial nature of the system, in which each party will seek to argue its case strenuously, aided by as much evidence as possible. But it also reflects the predominantly commercial nature of cross-border disputes in the English courts, in which the scale, complexity, and difficulty of the disputes reflect their monetary value. For that reason, the problem for the court is normally how to answer a novel question of foreign law in circumstances where the evidence is plentiful and conflicting, and no clear guidance is offered by courts or commentators in the relevant foreign system.

2. A problem of adjudication

The rights and duties of the parties may sometimes depend upon a law other than that of the forum. In such cases foreign law must be established, and (as difficult an issue) applied. This process is the very object, the terminus of the choice of law process, yet it is fraught with difficulty, and in the eyes of some may be impossible. Sometimes the difficulties are practical, concerning access to information concerning foreign law, or the identification of suitable experts. And the process of establishing foreign law may be notoriously costly and cumbersome. But we are presently concerned with a more pressing, and in practice more common problem: how is a court to establish the content of foreign law, assuming that the evidence before it is adequate? In this sense the foreign law problem is not a problem of information, or cost, or convenience, but a problem of adjudication.

The problem of adjudicating disputed questions of foreign law may be illustrated by contrasting two English cases: *The Spirit of Independence*,[9] and *City of Gotha and the Federal Republic of Germany v Sotheby's and Cobert Finance SA*.[10]

3. *The Spirit of Independence*

The Spirit of Independence, a cross-Channel ferry, was arrested in Boulogne on the instructions of a shipyard which had not been paid by the charterer for repairs to the

[7] See *Bodum United States Inc v La Cafetiere Inc* (2010) 621 F.3d 624 (7th Cir (US)), 633, per Posner J.

[8] R Fentiman, *Foreign Law in English Courts* (Oxford, 1998), 298–308.

[9] [1999] 1 Lloyd's Rep 43.

[10] 9 September 1998 (unreported).

vessel. The charterer was insolvent. The question was whether the owners were entitled to release of their vessel from arrest without assuming liability for the charterer's debts. There was agreement that the question was one of French maritime law. But the answer under French law was profoundly unclear. The relevant legislation supplied no clear guidance. And both courts and commentators were divided. So the parties deployed expert evidence in support of their rival positions. Both sides employed experts of acknowledged eminence, both of whom supplied lengthy reports, and were examined and cross-examined at length.

Because the point was a novel one, as yet unresolved in French law, Rix J clearly felt himself in some difficulty. He remarked on 'how invidious a position this Court finds itself in, having to resolve what appears to be a crux of the French law of arrest'.[11] Nonetheless, Rix J surveyed the *jurisprudence*, the *doctrine*, and the expert testimony with consummate care and skill, essaying the evidence in a tautly reasoned judgment of some 20 pages. But this impressive forensic exercise led in the end to a profoundly awkward conclusion. The evidence was tied. Although diametrically opposed, the rival positions adopted by each of the parties were equally plausible and compelling. Neither was obviously wrong, neither obviously right. Nor was one more persuasive than the other. How then was the court to resolve the impasse? Rix J's solution is both striking and revealing. He concluded that French law dictated no result either way. More creatively, he judged (without evidence) that a French court in such a case would favour whichever result was more just—which here meant releasing the vessel from arrest without penalizing the shipowner.

The Spirit of Independence provides a lesson in the proof of foreign law. Distinguished experts offered comprehensive, impartial evidence to a judge sensitive to the foreign law problem, who ultimately achieved a just result. But a nagging doubt remains: was French law really applied? In reality, the evidence of French law was inconclusive, and Rix J reached his final decision not by applying French law (other than notionally), but by doing what justice required.

More precisely, the case is revealing for four reasons. First, it highlights the cost and complexity of establishing foreign law.[12] In one sense the point is an obvious one. The protracted examination and cross-examination of experts is a costly, time-consuming process. And in one sense it need cause no particular concern—litigation is expensive, and complex litigation is more expensive still. But the point acquires added meaning if we accept that in *The Spirit of Independence*, French law was never applied at all, save in a notional sense. For it is rightly a matter of concern if so intensive, and so expensive, a process ultimately yields no result. And the cost of establishing foreign law creates a further problem. It is not so much that it exposes the parties—or the losing party—to substantial costs. It is that the potential expense may deter litigants from pursuing or defending claims, and thus discourage or deny access to justice.

[11] At 65.

[12] Concerns about the cost and inefficiency involved often surface in common law jurisdictions in cases involving the doctrine of *forum non conveniens*; see further, R Fentiman, 'Foreign Law and the Forum Conveniens', in S Symeonides and JAR Nafziger, eds., *Law and Justice in a Multistate World: Essays in Honor of Arthur T. von Mehren* (New York, 2002), 275.

Secondly, *The Spirit of Independence* suggests that in some cases the difficulty in applying foreign law is not a matter of knowledge, but of understanding. It shows that a court, however well-informed about foreign law, may be unable to adopt the legal methods and habits of thought of a foreign lawyer. None could doubt the quality and comprehensiveness of the expert evidence in *The Spirit of Independence*. Rix J thought himself 'fortunate to have had the assistance of such experts, and grateful for the wealth of analysis and citation which they provided'.[13] But he also recognized the unreality of the task in which he was engaged, in so far as he was required to approach French law using the methods of the English lawyer. There is no reason why foreign canons of interpretation, and foreign legal methods, cannot themselves be proved (or agreed) in an English court. But in *The Spirit of Independence* both parties had presented the relevant French case law as they might have relied upon English cases in a purely English dispute. They did so even though the craft of reconciling and distinguishing cases, and the doctrine of precedent, are unknown (in the English sense) in France. As Rix J was aware, this inevitably distorted his enquiry into French law. As he said: 'to derive my decision from the material presented to me is to do something which a French Court would be unlikely to do'.[14]

Similar problems of method were also encountered by Hirst J in *The Nile Rhapsody*,[15] a case concerning the staying of actions which turned partly on the difficulty of applying Egyptian law in England. The difficulty lay not in the content of Egyptian law, so much as in the techniques necessary to establish it. An amalgam of French civil law, 'custom, the principles of Islamic law, and the principles of natural law and equity',[16] Hirst J clearly considered Egyptian law to be especially inaccessible to those not familiar with its principles, and the hierarchy existing between its various sources. The problem was compounded by the difficulty to an English judge of giving appropriate weight to juristic writing, case law (in a system without precedent), and the decision of the Court of Cassation (not being a true court of appeal).[17] Such difficulties of approach meant that the issues in dispute 'were pre-eminently more suitable for decision in Egypt than here'.[18]

Thirdly, *The Spirit of Independence* highlights the uncomfortable truth that in some cases foreign law may be beyond proof. More precisely, it suggests that some hard cases[19] cannot be resolved except by a court with a deep, perhaps instinctive grasp of something more than the letter of the law. Some questions can only be answered by reference to underlying principles, which may remain unstated (and so beyond proof); or by recourse to techniques of analysis which can only be learned by long experience (and not merely by hearing evidence). The problem is only hinted at in Rix J's unease about applying English legal methods to a question of French law. It is perhaps best revealed in his (forgivable) inability to resolve the impasse in the evidence before him—other than by juridical sleight of hand. For it is at such a juncture in any legal system that the process of adjudication depends upon experience and the exercise of informed judgment—matters not readily amenable to the process of proof.

[13] At 47. [14] At 66. [15] [1992] 2 Lloyd's Rep 399.
[16] At 411. [17] At 413. [18] At 412.
[19] In Professor Dworkin's sense. See further, R Dworkin, *Taking Rights Seriously* (London, 1977), ch 4.

In this respect *The Spirit of Independence* recalls *Du Pont de Nemours v Agnew*,[20] which contains a classic statement of the foreign law problem. Famously, the case concerned the effect of public policy on a contract of insurance governed by English law. Asked whether a court in England or in Illinois was the most appropriate forum in which to resolve the dispute, Lord Bingham CJ alluded to the problems that a foreign court would encounter in handling the English doctrine of public policy. As he concluded:

> This Court is necessarily better placed than any other to rule on that question ... There is no decided authority in English law which denies them an indemnity. If English public policy is to be held to deny the right to indemnity in these circumstances, then this Court and no other must so hold. I do not regard this as a question capable of fair resolution in any foreign court, however distinguished and well instructed ... that is a question which I do not think any foreign Judge could conscientiously resolve with any confidence that he was reaching a correct answer.[21]

Fourthly, *The Spirit of Independence* illustrates how difficult it is to handle those cases (however rare) in which foreign law cannot meaningfully be applied. What was Rix J to do, given the impasse presented by the tied evidence of the rival experts? In most cases English law admits of only two alternatives.[22] A court may in principle apply English law by default, a result sometimes justified by reference to the perplexing fiction that English and foreign law are deemed to be the same unless the contrary is proved. More commonly, a court can disregard the expert testimony, and look for a solution in any legislation, commentaries, or decided cases relied upon by the experts.[23]

In *The Spirit of Independence*, however, the documentary evidence clearly offered no solution. It too was divided. Nor was it a case in which it would have been possible for the court to apply English law by default. For under English law arrest founds jurisdiction on the merits, and successful claims on the merits can always be executed against the arrested vessel. Whether or not a shipowner may secure release by giving security for a charterer's liabilities is therefore never an issue. As Rix J said, 'the ultimate question which exercises the parties in the present case under French law ... simply does not arise under English law'.[24] As this suggests, it was always going to be necessary to find a novel solution to the problem of a failure in proof. But, however subtle that novel solution, it is hard to escape the conclusion that resort to such devices is always a signal of failure. It is not a means to apply foreign law, but an admission that the application of foreign law is impossible.

4. *City of Gotha v Sotheby's*

This is not to say that foreign law can never be applied satisfactorily. Indeed, the nature of the foreign law problem comes into sharper focus if we examine a case in which the

[20] [1987] 2 Lloyd's Rep 585, at 596 (CA). [21] At 595.

[22] Where the issue goes to full trial; where questions of foreign law arise in interlocutory proceedings several provisional solutions are possible: *The Polessk* [1996] 2 Lloyd's Rep 40.

[23] *Bumper Developments Corpn v Commissioner of Police* [1991] 1 WLR 1362 (CA).

[24] At 52–3.

proof of foreign law was apparently successful. Consider *City of Gotha v Sotheby's*,[25] which repays study in so far as it represents at first sight a counterweight to *The Spirit of Independence*.

City of Gotha turned on a difficult question of German law, on the effect of § 221 of the *Bürgerliches Gesetzbuch*. The dispute concerned title to a painting, originally owned by the ducal family of Saxe-Coburg-Gotha, which disappeared in the closing days of the Second World War. The City of Gotha and the German Government claimed title to the work when it was put up for auction at Sotheby's. The success of the claim depended upon whether the 30-year limitation period in German law had expired. This in turn depended on § 221, which governs the limitation of proprietary actions in the event that a third party acquires possession. The effect of § 221 had never been considered by a German court. But it was a matter of much debate amongst German commentators. Following a comprehensive and supple treatment of the academic sources, and the evidence of the parties' experts, Moses J found that the city's action was not time-barred.

The case appears to be a model of how foreign law should be applied. And so it is. But the reason is worth exploring. It was a case where all that was involved was the interpretation of foreign legislation, assisted by expert opinion and academic commentary. Matters of idiom and conceptual differences aside, the proof of German law depended simply on assessing on their face the strength of the competing views. But this did not involve issues about the relationship between unfamiliar legal sources. Nor were any arcane principles or any peculiarities of German legal method involved. No more was needed than the judge's own skill at weighing the rationality and persuasiveness of the arguments—matters within his inherent knowledge and expertise. Moses J had a clear view of the correct methodology to be adopted under German law, a methodology which was far from being foreign. As he said, in a revealing passage:

> There is no dispute as to the approach the German court would take to issues in respect of which there is no judicial precedent. It would have regard to commentaries on the German Civil Code ('BGB'). It would not feel bound by the mere fact that the majority of commentators took a particular view or by the most recent statement of opinion. It would take into account the quality of the arguments, the consistency of the statements and the reputation of the authors.[26]

Admittedly, in one respect German legal method differed from that of English law. As Moses J noted 'German Courts adopt a teleological approach'. But such an approach is far from being unfamiliar to an English court, and is easily comprehensible. It is a universally understood form of reasoning, not an impenetrable aspect of foreign legal method.

As *City of Gotha*, together with *The Spirit of Independence*, confirms, the problem of foreign law is at root a problem of legal reasoning. To what extent can one court adopt the internal perspective of the courts in a foreign system?

[25] 9 September 1998 (unreported).

[26] Para I.2.

5. A problem stated

As *City of Gotha*, confirms even the hardest questions of foreign law (or the most novel) are sometimes capable of resolution. Like *The Spirit of Independence*, the case involved a novel question of foreign law which admitted of competing solutions. But *City of Gotha* is different in two telling ways. It was clear, as it was not in *The Spirit of Independence*, how a foreign court would approach the problem. And, decisively, that approach depended upon universal methods of adjudication, not any distinctive methodology. Although formally a matter of foreign law, it was within the knowledge and expertise of the English judge.

As this suggests, the problem of applying foreign law is not procedural. There was no complaint about process in *The Spirit of Independence*. Nor is it a problem of information. The difficulty was not a lack of information, but one of adjudication. How may a court in one country meaningfully determine a contested question of foreign law? To what extent may a judge in one country share in the thought processes of a foreign judge? To what extent can a judge assume the necessary internal point of view?

II. Practical responses

All legal systems have developed strategies for responding to the foreign law problem—for addressing those hard cases in which a court is required to resolve a contested question of foreign law, in which the problem is not one of information, but of adjudication. Four responses are possible.

One is to improve the process of taking and assessing evidence. In common law systems this is often achieved by allowing more flexibility into the process than is typical where the assessment of facts is concerned. Certainly, any successful regime is likely to be eclectic, offering a variety of mechanisms for establishing foreign law, each appropriate to the circumstances. Perhaps the American approach offers the best example. Certainly, Rule 44.1 of the Federal Rules of Civil Procedure permits resort to any available means to establish foreign law. Interestingly (but less obviously), English law also offers a range of evidential options. Undeniably, foreign law is almost always proved by reference to the evidence of the parties' experts. But English courts have been prepared to employ several other means.[27] They have, for example, construed foreign legislation without expert assistance.[28] And in principle the rules of procedure permit a court to appoint an independent expert in addition to, or instead of, those of the parties.[29]

Again, any successful regime for establishing foreign law (whatever its origin) is likely to recognize that the conceptual character of foreign law is not immutable, but depends upon the circumstances. Thus, most legal systems have tended to characterize foreign laws as either facts or laws for all purposes. But the reality may be different. Some issues of foreign law may have a 'legal' character, in so far as they resemble questions of domestic law. To treat them as facts (or merely as facts) may be a serious

[27] R Fentiman, *Foreign Law in English Courts* (Oxford, 1998), Chs 7, 8.
[28] Ibid., 257–62. [29] Ibid., 211–18; 232–8.

and misleading distortion. It obscures the reality that all laws have a certain common character, and that, idiom and convention aside, the basic requirements of rational legal discourse are universal. It ignores the extent to which a court may meaningfully employ its legal expertise in handling questions of foreign law. This is especially so when the laws of a cognate legal system are involved, as perhaps when an English court is required to apply the laws of another common law jurisdiction.[30]

A second response to the foreign law problem is to exclude from the start difficult or impossible questions of foreign law. At one time English courts simply declined jurisdiction over foreign laws.[31] Modern common law jurisdictions adopt a more calibrated approach. The doctrine of *forum non conveniens* permits a court to stay proceedings where it considers another forum to be the most appropriate court to hear a dispute.[32] Sometimes jurisdiction will be declined on grounds of efficiency, because the proof of foreign law would be unacceptably costly and time-consuming, by comparison with a trial in the relevant foreign court. And sometimes (if rarely), a case will be excluded because the accurate application of foreign law is impossible.[33] The English courts have responded in like fashion when English law would have to be applied in a foreign court. As we have seen, the Court of Appeal has held that the courts of England are better placed to apply English public policy than those of Illinois.[34]

A third response is to leave the parties free to decide for themselves whether or not to plead and prove foreign law.[35] By this means the foreign law problem is made to disappear at the outset. And some would say that any adverse consequences in establishing foreign law may be laid at the parties' door, since the decision to introduce foreign law is theirs. The market-orientated solution has considerable and obvious benefits, and has traditionally been favoured in many common law jurisdictions, where the parties are normally free to advance their claim or defence under local law as an alternative to doing so under any relevant foreign law.[36]

A fourth strategy is to accept that the proof of foreign law may fail, and design an appropriate response in the event that foreign law is not established.[37] This has attracted less discussion in common law jurisdictions than elsewhere. No doubt this is because the possibility of staying proceedings, and the greater freedom parties enjoy to avoid pleading foreign law, ensures that the problem arises less often. But it may also owe something to the logic of an adversarial approach, in which each party's case

[30] See, e.g. *A-G for New Zealand v Ortiz* [1984] 1 AC 41 (HL)(New Zealand law); *MCC Proceeds Inc. v Bishopsgate Investment Trust plc* [1999] CLC 417 (CA) (US law).

[31] AN Sack, 'Conflicts of Law in the History of English Law', in A Reppy, ed., *Law: A Century of Progress 1835–1935* (New York, 1937), 342, 381.

[32] R Fentiman, 'Foreign Law and the Forum Conveniens', in S Symeonides and JAR Nafziger, eds., *Law and Justice in a Multistate World: Essays in Honor of Arthur T. von Mehren* (New York, 2002), 275.

[33] *The Nile Rhapsody* [1992] 2 Lloyd's Rep 399.

[34] *Du Pont de Nemours v Agnew* [1987] 1 Lloyd's Rep 585 (CA).

[35] See further, R Fentimam, 'Foreign Law in English Courts' (1992) 108 LQR 142; TM De Boer, 'Facultative Choice of Law' (1996) Recueil des Cours, vol. 257, 227.

[36] Party autonomy as a means to diminish the foreign law problem has, however, been recognized in recent EU instruments governing aspects of choice of law. See, Regulation 593/2008 on the law applicable to contractual obligations (Rome I), art. 3(2); Regulation 864/2007 on the law applicable to non-contractual obligations (Rome II), art. 14.

[37] R Fentiman, *Foreign Law in English Courts* (Oxford, 1998), 182ff.

depends upon the strength of its own expert's evidence. In such a system, whatever the correctness of the court's findings, it will generally be possible to say that one expert's argument is the more convincing, or one expert's credentials are more impressive. But, as we have seen, an English court may in principle apply English law by default, although this seldom (if ever) appears to happen. More commonly, an English court will disregard the expert evidence, and make its own findings based upon any documentary evidence of foreign law relied upon by the experts.[38]

In other jurisdictions a failure to establish foreign law may be more common. This is not because their approach to foreign law is inferior. In systems which regard foreign laws as laws it is perhaps harder to adopt a purely 'evidential' solution to the problem, by declaring that the burden of proving foreign law has not been discharged, or by finding that one expert is better qualified, or gave more compelling testimony, than another. In such systems a number of other solutions have been canvassed, which seek to respect the legal character of foreign law.[39] One possibility is to appeal to comparative law, by seeking an answer based upon the solutions adopted in legal systems related to that of the law in question.[40]

To the uninitiated, however, a further solution to the foreign law problem may seem obvious. Why not remit contested questions of foreign law to the courts whose law is disputed? This approach was attempted in English law, but without success. The British Law Ascertainment Act 1859 allows an English court to remit contested questions of foreign law to the courts of other Commonwealth countries. But it has seldom been employed, no doubt because of the delay, increased cost, and unpredictability inherent in such a process.[41] It is perhaps indicative of the unattractiveness of this mechanism to litigants that a parallel statute, the Foreign Law Ascertainment Act 1861, intended to apply in cases involving non-Commonwealth states, was never employed before its repeal in 1973. Again, some legal systems favour enhanced judicial co-operation between courts, so that one court may remit questions of foreign law to the foreign court concerned.[42] Here too, however, it is unlikely that such an approach offers a realistic solution, or a preferable alternative to resolving the matter before the court seised of the substantive dispute.

These are, at best, but partial solutions to the foreign law problem, each of which has inevitable limitations. Consider the machinery for establishing foreign law. However varied the range of techniques, however intensive the forensic process, cases may arise such as *The Spirit of Independence*, where no mechanism is likely to have worked. Again, the flaw in the *forum conveniens* route is that it may be more compelling in principle than in practice. Certainly, it may not always be easy to determine in preliminary proceedings how difficult a question of foreign law may be. Or it may

[38] See, e.g. *Buerger v New York Life Assurance Co.* (1927) 96 LJKB 930 (CA); *Bumper Developments Corpn. v Commissioner of Police* [1991] 1 WLR 1362 (CA).

[39] R Fentiman, *Foreign Law in English Courts* (Oxford, 1998), 281–3.

[40] As in Germany: C von Bar, *Internationales Privatrecht*, vol. II (Munich, 1987–), 329; and see, M Cappelletti, 'Mandatory Ex-Officio Application of Foreign Law: The Comparative Method as a Solution Where the Foreign Law Cannot be Ascertained' (1970) 3 CILSA 60.

[41] For analysis, see, R Fentiman, *Foreign Law in English Courts* (Oxford, 1998), 238–9.

[42] See the New South Wales Uniform Civil Procedure Rules 2005 (NSW) Div. 9 rr.6.42–6.45; considered, JJ Spigelman, 'Proof of Foreign Law by Reference to the Foreign Court' (2011) 127 LQR 291.

not be easy to do so without in effect attempting to prove foreign law in interlocutory proceedings, which itself may be a lengthy, costly, and unsatisfactory process.[43]

Nor is it enough to privatize the problem and leave it to the parties to decide whether to rely upon foreign law. In some cases such a choice is unreal, as when the very basis of a claim or defence depends upon foreign law. In some cases it may also be inappropriate to allow the parties such freedom. Even in English law, the most voluntarist of systems, the courts have qualified the principle of party autonomy in matters of foreign law. They have come to doubt the appropriateness of assuming in every case that English and foreign law can be the same.[44] And in some cases it is arguable that the relevant rules for choice of law are mandatory, leaving no room for party choice.[45]

Nor is it easy to see how any default rule, for use in hard cases, can offer a true solution to the foreign law problem. Some means to avoid deadlock is clearly required, for a court can scarcely declare a draw. And each of the proffered default rules no doubt supplies the courts with an answer. But they are merely devices to avoid an impasse, and secure a result. They are not a means to apply foreign law. Indeed, they are an admission that no solution to the foreign law problem is possible. Most importantly, what may appear to be the most obvious solution is of little value. To suggest that issues of foreign law should be remitted to the relevant foreign court for determination is impractical.

As this suggests, no procedural mechanism can remove the difficulty which ultimately besets any procedure for applying foreign law: how can the courts of one country be expected to engage meaningfully with the laws of foreign countries—at least in those hard cases where the evidence is plentiful and conflicting? Such devices may improve the efficiency of the process of proof, and improve a court's access to information about foreign law. But they cannot solve the problem of deciding questions of foreign law, a problem not of process, or information, but of adjudication.

III. Theoretical responses

1. Two responses

The procedures for establishing foreign law, in whatever the legal system, cannot guarantee that the courts of one country can accurately apply another country's laws. The enterprise of applying foreign law is not always difficult, nor does it always fail. But the risk exists. And the strategies for addressing the problem offer at best partial solutions.

In response, some commentators are drawn to a sceptical vision of the process of applying foreign law, and of the choice of law process which it supports. They would

[43] R Fentiman, 'Foreign Law and the Forum Conveniens', in S Symeonides and JAR Nafziger, eds., *Law and Justice in a Multistate World: Essays in Honor of Arthur T. von Mehren* (New York, 2002), 275, 291–3.

[44] See, e.g. *Shaker v Al-Bedrawi* [2002] 4 All ER 835 (CA); see also *Damberg v Damberg* [2001] NSWCA 87.

[45] See, R Fentiman, *Foreign Law in English Courts* (Oxford, 1998), 80–97.

count the conflicts process a failure, undermined by doubt that one country's courts can truly apply another country's laws.[46] But others take a more robust and pragmatic view. They see such concerns as resting on a mistake about the process of establishing foreign law. They see the process not as one of law-applying (which is bound to fail), but as of fact-finding, which requires only that a court fairly assesses the evidence of foreign law.

2. The sceptical view

Some see the task of effectively applying foreign law as hopeless. More precisely, they may regard the process as inherently flawed because it cannot guarantee the effective application of foreign law.

Presumably none could deny that foreign law can sometimes be applied efficiently, and with accuracy. In some cases foreign law is applied without dispute, where the parties are in agreement as to its content. In others the dispute can be resolved because the evidence in favour of one conclusion is clearly stronger. In others the question resolves itself into little more than a question of statutory construction which a court may resolve with relative ease and confidence of success. Moreover, there are cases, such as *City of Gotha*, in which an English court has answered difficult questions of foreign law with conspicuous success. But the fact that foreign law can be successfully applied offers little comfort to the sceptical. They might suggest that the very existence of cases where the process of proof cannot work (or work effectively) is an indictment of the process. And they might argue that the true nature of the problem is concealed. They would suggest that the risk that the proof of foreign law will fail is always present. They might argue that the very existence of such a risk may deter those with a legitimate claim or defence from pursuing it in court—deterring access to justice by legitimate litigants. Or they might argue that, for those who do proceed, the true nature of the problem will only emerge too late, once the evidence has been heard at considerable expense.

Sceptics might also say that cases where foreign law appears to have been satisfactorily applied are (or are often) an illusion. Hard cases where the evidence is balanced are in their nature those which require of a court uncommon complicity in the thought processes of a foreign lawyer—something which in some cases may be impossible even if the court appears to apply foreign law. Alternatively, they are cases in which a court is likely to resolve the difficulty by resorting to strategies which owe nothing to the foreign law. To favour one view of foreign law over another because one expert was better qualified or more convincing than the other is not in the end to apply foreign law. Such devices are means to untie a knot in the evidence, not to discern the truth about foreign law.

[46] See, F Juenger, 193 *Recueil des Cours*, 203–5 (1995); P Hay, O Lando, and RD Rotunda, 'Conflict of Laws as a Technique for Legal Integration', in M Cappelletti, M Seccombe, and JHH Weiler, eds., *Integration Through Law: Europe and the American Federal Experience. Book 1* (Berlin, 1986), 170; O Lando, 'Lex Fori in Foro Proprio' (1995) 2 Maastricht J. of European and Comp. L. 359, 367–71.

But this apocalyptic view rests on two mistakes. First, it ignores the necessarily domesticated nature of the process. Secondly, it assumes that a court can somehow arrive at a 'right' answer to a question of foreign law.

a) *A domesticated process*

It is perhaps self-evident, though may easily be forgotten, that the proof of foreign law is solely a matter for the court seized of the substantive dispute. Lacking knowledge of the foreign legal system in question, a court is reliant on evidence of foreign law, and sometimes on its inherent legal expertise. But it is neither proper, given that the court has accepted jurisdiction, and has assumed responsibility for the issue, nor practical, given a court's inevitable ignorance of foreign law, for a court to do more than decide such cases using the local tools available.

b) *Of rightness and authenticity*

Some are concerned that courts apply foreign law wrongly.[47] And some adduce statistics to establish the propensity of courts to apply foreign law incorrectly.[48] But this raises two issues. First, it cannot presumably be significant that courts occasionally apply foreign law in a way that the relevant foreign law would not. It can only be material if courts regularly do so or, more importantly, if this is attributable to inherent features of the process. Secondly, what does it mean to conclude that foreign law is wrongly applied? This may rest upon an assumption about the nature of adjudication which most theorists would discount. It may rest upon the philosophical notion that in contested cases there can indeed be a 'right' answer to a question of law—whether local or foreign. Of course there may be in undisputed cases. But beyond that most would now accept that there can be no single right answer, as distinct from a range of possible, plausible answers.[49]

Jurisprudentially this is trite learning. But it has an important consequence here. It suggests that we cannot expect too much of any process of adjudication—and that we should not expect more of the proof of foreign law than of adjudication in general. But this begs a question. What then can we expect of the process of adjudication, and thus of the proof of foreign law? To deny that the outcome of legal disputes can be correct in any objective sense does not mean that adjudication in hard cases cannot be subjected to standards of correctness. Adjudication in hard cases may not be concerned with the excavation of legal truth. But it must (at least) comply with general standards of rationality, with the requirements of coherence, relevance, and lack of bias; it must be consistent with the substantive principles underlying the area in question, and

[47] See further, R Fentiman, *Foreign Law in English Courts* (Oxford, 1998), 308–10.

[48] Reference is often to made to Rheinstein's conclusion that foreign law was misapplied in 32 of 40 US cases surveyed: K Zweigert, 'Some Reflections on the Sociological Dimensions of Private International Law' (1973) 44 Colorado LR 283, 298.

[49] See further, R Dworkin, *Taking Rights Seriously* (London, 1977), Ch 4; AD Woozley, 'No Right Answer' (1979) The Philosophical Quarterly 25.

immanent in the legal system itself; and it must employ the conventions of legal method accepted in the system concerned.

Viewed in these terms, whether foreign law can be satisfactorily applied is not a matter of a court's ability to discern 'the truth' about another country's laws. It is a matter of whether it is possible to replicate the foreign process of adjudication, the process appropriate to elucidating the best answer available. The question is not whether, say, an English court can arrive at the right answer under French law; it is whether it is possible to reproduce the conditions under which questions of French law are answered in France.[50] What matters is whether adequate information can be provided concerning the substance of the matter in dispute, and (of equal importance) whether it is possible to reproduce the legal method, and habits of thought, employed in the country whose laws are in question. The test is not whether the answer is right; it is whether the process of adjudication is authentic. We cannot expect an English court to arrive at the 'right' answer under French law, any more than we could expect a French court to do so. But we can expect both to arrive at an answer which is true to French law.

Here the problem suggested by *The Spirit of Independence* is again revealed. As we have seen, the difficulty there did not concern the quality or the quantity of the evidence, but the authenticity of the evidential process. Rix J himself was concerned that it was inauthentic to approach the French jurisprudence in an English fashion. And it is far from clear that his preferred method of resolving the evidential conflict—doing the just thing—was in fact how a French court would have proceeded. Indeed, it is possible (even likely) that a French judge would have been able to avoid arriving at the position where the competing views seemed evenly balanced.

This perspective, like *The Spirit of Independence*, also suggests the line that must be drawn between cases in which the accurate application of foreign law is possible, and those where it is not. The former category includes those in which the evidence in favour of one solution is compelling. But it also includes at least two situations involving more difficult cases where the evidence is conflicting. In some cases a court may resolve any conflict by appealing either to legal techniques shared with the country whose law is in question—as where an English court is required to apply the law of another common law jurisdiction. In others it may be able to employ ubiquitous standards of sound reasoning—as perhaps in *City of Gotha*, where the idiom was foreign, but the issue turned merely on which of two arguments was soundest on its face. By contrast, the latter category comprises (at least) two types of case: those where everything turns on an understanding of underlying legal principles which cannot readily be communicated by evidence; and those where a grasp of distinctive legal methods, or habits of thought, is required.

It is not sufficient, however, to recognize that such a category of hard cases exists. Two questions remain. How can we tell that a case belongs to this category? More precisely, how can we tell before it is too late, before substantial costs are incurred, and before a court is forced to resort to some technical device to resolve the matter? More

[50] R Fentiman, *Foreign Law in English Courts* (Oxford, 1998), 20–1, 308–11.

troubling, what (if anything) can be done when such cases arise? How can we respond to the uncomfortable conclusion that foreign law cannot always be applied? This, for the conflicts lawyer, is the challenge.

As this suggests, the apocalyptic conclusion that the process of establishing foreign law is doomed to failure may depend on a false expectation as to what the process may achieve. All that we can legitimately expect is that the process is authentic, by capturing the reasoning of the relevant foreign court. There is no meaningful sense in which we can expect a 'right' answer to a question of foreign law. There is, however, a sense in which we can expect a court to achieve an authentic answer under foreign law, and in which the evidential process should strive for this objective.

As this suggests, there remains in principle a category of case in which even authenticity is possible—in which, in a modified sense, there is no right answer. Importantly, however, the existence of such cases is no argument against the process of establishing foreign law. The compulsion to achieve an authentic answer is an important aspiration. And, even it fails in a given case, the process is not subverted. As we have seen, the process is inevitably domesticated. It can only be judged by standards appropriate to one court applying a *foreign* law. In the end, the proper measure is always that the foreign law question was properly addressed according to principles of due process.

3. The pragmatic view

For some, by contrast, no foreign law problem exists because there is no sense in which one country's courts can or should 'apply' foreign law. There is no sense in which one court should replicate the adjudicatory process of another court. And there is no sense in which it matters if it fails to do so. According to this view, what matters is not that one court should mimic the decision-making of a foreign court. All that matters is that the process of establishing foreign law is fair. More precisely, all that matters is that it rests on a fair assessment of the evidence.

According to this approach, the process is perceived as purely evidential, and is in no sense legal—a matter of fact-finding, not law-applying. This evidential-factual approach is revealed in the decision of the High Court of Australia in *Neilson v Overseas Projects Corporation of Victoria Ltd.*[51]

In *Neilson,* Gleeson CJ, with Gummow and Hayne JJ, adopted a view which confirmed the status of issues of foreign law as issues of fact. They emphasized the adversarial nature of common law adjudication, and that establishing foreign law was simply a matter of evidence. The ascertainment of foreign law was a matter of fact, and of evidence, subject to the vicissitudes of the adversarial process. It was not a matter of applying foreign law, so inaccuracy in the application of foreign law could be tolerated.

Neilson concerned the law of China, although the evidence of Chinese law was scant, consisting of the text of the relevant legislation, and remarks by one party's expert concerning its meaning. That it was difficult to establish the true content of Chinese

[51] [2005] HCA 54.

law was for Gleeson CJ no difficulty. Any concern was eased by the constraints of the adversarial process. It is the court's duty to decide on the evidence, which it is the parties' responsibility to supply. As he said:

> It is possible, perhaps even likely, that the evidence of foreign law was incomplete. Nevertheless, it was necessary for the trial judge to decide the issues raised by the parties on the evidence which they presented. This is adversarial litigation, and the outcome of such litigation is commonly influenced by the way in which the parties have chosen to conduct their respective cases.[52]

Similarly, for Hayne and Gummow JJ, the risk of inaccuracy in establishing foreign law was tolerable, and followed from the status of foreign law as fact: 'The trial is not an inquisition into the content of relevant foreign law any more than it is an inquisition into other factual issues that the parties tender for decision by the court.'[53] Gleeson CJ was, however, sensitive to the risk that a court might find itself applying foreign law, if not incorrectly, then in a way which was manifestly absurd. He was prepared to act on what little evidence of Chinese law was available because the view proposed was not 'inherently implausible'.[54] He was also aware that comity might be offended were a court to apply foreign law inaccurately. He was satisfied, however, that the outcome would cause no offence in China: 'The Chinese authorities are totally unaffected by the outcome of the litigation, no Chinese interests are involved, and there appears to be no reason of policy for a Chinese court to resist the proposition.'[55]

This pragmatic, evidential-factual perspective sets at its lowest the benchmark for measuring the success of the foreign-law process. It suggests that there will be few, if any, cases in which the application of foreign law can be said to fail. This robust approach does not, however, withstand scrutiny, for two reasons. First, it obscures the inherently legal character of issues of foreign law. Secondly, the pragmatic response to the foreign law problem ignores its role in the choice-of-law process.

a) *The legal character of foreign law*

It is possible to cleave adamantly to first principles and insist (as some common lawyers might) that issues of foreign law are simply issues if fact, or (as some civil lawyers might) that they are invariably issues of law. But the matter is more complex. Such issues have a legal dimension in two distinct senses. First, to establish the content of foreign law is to establish the legal norms according to which the parties' rights and duties are judged. Justice demands that those norms should be properly determined. In that sense, the process is concerned with a normative question, with standards by which the case is adjudicated. Unlike the process of establishing other facts, it is not merely concerned with establishing the data in accordance with which those standards are applied. It sits at the heart of the case. Secondly, the legal nature of such questions introduces an element absent when the proof of other facts is required. A court may, at least sometimes, bring its own legal expertise to bear on resolving the question.

[52] At [1]. [53] At [118]. [54] At [17]. [55] At [17].

The legal, or at least hybrid, character of foreign law issues is reflected in the approach of some legal systems. Notably, in US federal practice such issues are issues neither of fact nor of law, but issues to be resolved by any feasible means available to the court.[56] This implies an answer to the underlying epistemological question. In some cases, if not all, a court cannot engage with foreign law, so issues of foreign law must be treated objectively as issues of fact to be established, not issues of law to be known. But in others a court can engage with foreign law, and so can treat such issues essentially as questions of law.

In English law also, the trend has been to adopt a mixed approach. Some issues of foreign law cannot be assimilated to English law, and so must be treated evidentially as issues of fact. But in respect of others a court may proceed effectively as if the issue were one of English law.

English law begins with the proposition that issues of foreign law are issues of fact.[57] The importance of this classification is that English courts cannot generally take judicial notice of facts. They are thus deemed to lack knowledge of foreign law. This affects both the means by which information concerning foreign law is supplied to the court, and the way in which a court establishes foreign law. It means that the parties must supply evidence of foreign law, and that a court cannot rely upon information concerning foreign law apart from that tendered in evidence. Foreign law is proved in the same manner as other (opinion-based) facts. Foreign law is normally established in substantive proceedings after receiving reports from party-led experts, on which the experts are examined and cross-examined. The decision is not one on foreign law, but on evidence of foreign law. Any conflict in the evidence may be resolved by disregarding expert opinion, but not by reference to materials not put in evidence by the parties.

But in two particular respects the legal character of foreign law is evident from the treatment of foreign law in English practice. First, foreign law is approximated to English law for appeal purposes. Although technically raising a question of fact, an appeal on a point of foreign law is permitted,[58] and an appeal court will revisit any issue of foreign law just as it would a question of law.[59]

Secondly, and more significantly, the distinction between fact and law weakens in so far as the answer to a question of foreign law is a matter of interpretation, not knowledge, and within the province of an English judge, by virtue of the judge's legal expertise. Several cases suggest that English courts recognize the 'legal' element in the application even of foreign law in such cases. They suggest that issues of foreign law are not immutably either issues of fact or law. Rather the treatment of such issues (and thus the evidential means used) varies with the nature of the issue. As has been said, of a judge's role in resolving questions of foreign law:[60]

> He is entitled and indeed bound to bring that part of his qualifications to bear on the issue which he has to decide, notwithstanding that it is an issue of foreign law. There is

[56] Rule 44.1 of the Federal Rules of Civil Procedure permits resort to any available means to establish foreign law.

[57] *Bumper Development Corp Ltd v Metropolitan Commissioner of Police* [1991] 1 WLR 1362, 1367 et seq.

[58] *MCC Proceeds Inc v Bishopsgate Investment Trust plc* [1999] CLC 417; *Morgan Grenfell & Co Ltd v SACE* [2001] EWCA Civ 1932.

[59] [1999] CLC 417 (CA).

[60] *MCC Proceeds v Bishopsgate Investment Trust plc* [1999] CLC 417 (CA).

a legal input from him, in addition to the judicial task of assessing the weight of the evidence given.[61]

In so deciding, the Court of Appeal has resolved the long-standing tension between the 'constructionist' and 'factual' tendencies in the authorities by favouring the former. Previously, some judges had insisted on taking a strictly evidential ('factual') view which excluded any role for the court's legal expertise.[62]

The courts have further recognized that the proper treatment of foreign law may depend upon the circumstances, and indeed may vary from issue to issue in a given case. The correct approach 'varies according to the nature of the issue which arises in the particular case'.[63] This variable approach may be illustrated by contrasting two cases. *MCC Proceeds Inc v Bishopsgate Investment Trust plc*[64] concerned the interpretation of the New York Uniform Commercial Code. The nature of the question in *Bishopsgate*, concerning the interpretation of a statute written in English from a common law jurisdiction, made it appropriate to handle it as if it were a question of English law. It is implicit that in other cases it might be appropriate to treat the question more strictly as one of fact, where the conceptual fabric of the foreign system is clearly different.

In *Morgan Grenfell & Co Ltd v SACE*[65] somewhat different questions of foreign law were involved, concerning an insured party's duty of disclosure to an insurer under Italian law. The law in question was complex, and the conceptual structure of Italian law unfamiliar. By contrast with *Bishopsgate*, there was 'less room here than there was in that case for the judge to apply his own legal training and experience... because Italian law deploys principles and concepts which are in some respects different from those of the common law'.[66] Importantly, however, the court recognized that even in such a case 'it seems to us to be appropriate for us to have at least some regard to our own experience and training'[67] and the court again articulated the view that questions of foreign law, where they can be resolved by reference to general principles of legal reasoning, are in effect questions of law.

It appears therefore that issues of foreign law cannot be classified simply as legal or factual. Law and fact merge when handling foreign law. As *Bishopsgate* confirms, the nature of the issue, and thus its juridical character, changes in so far as the construction of a foreign rule is within the skill and competence of the judge, when it becomes a matter of law. The nature of the mix may vary from case to case, as the Court of Appeal has noted. Sometimes, as in *Bishopsgate*, the legal aspect is to the fore. Sometimes, as in *SACE*, it is not, but, as the court in *SACE* recognized, it is unlikely to have no role at all.

This is not to imply, however, that the decisions in *Bishopsgate* and *SACE* are inconsistent with the decision in *Bumper*. *Bumper* correctly states the law governing information on foreign law. It confirms that issues of foreign law are issues of fact, and that a court cannot take judicial notice of foreign law. It explains why information

[61] Ibid., at [13]; see also *Neilson v Overseas Projects Corporation of Victoria Ltd* [2005] HCA 54, [199], per Kirby J.

[62] T Hodgkinson and M James, *Expert Evidence: Law and Practice* (2nd edn, London, 2007), 306.

[63] [1999] CLC 417 (CA), at [13]; see also [19].

[64] [1999] CLC 417 (CA).

[65] [2001] EWCA Civ 1932.

[66] At [51], [57].

[67] Ibid.

concerning foreign law is supplied in the form of evidence, but *Bishopsgate* and *SACE* are concerned with the evaluation of any evidence of foreign law. They do not permit a court to trespass beyond the evidence supplied, but they establish that the evaluation of that evidence may have a legal dimension. In such cases, a court does not take judicial notice of foreign law, but is applying English law.

This suggests that English law adopts a mixed approach to the foreign law problem. Issues of foreign law are for some purposes treated simply as issues of fact; for others they are approximated to questions of law. But this doctrinal conclusion implies a broader proposition. It is possible, indeed necessary, to treat different issues of foreign law differently. For some purposes, the enquiry is purely evidential, and no more can be expected than due process in the assessment of evidence. But in others it acquires the attributes of a legal enquiry, and may be judged accordingly.

But this prompts a final, important reflection. The resolution of questions of foreign law sometimes has the character of an enquiry into facts, and sometimes has the attributes of legal decision-making. But to say that the process may have a legal character does not mean that a court ever truly applies to foreign law. When a court draws on its inherent legal expertise it is drawing on methodologies derived from its own law, or from universal standards of reasoning and argumentation. To say that the process is not purely factual and evidential does not mean that a judge in one court has begun to mimic a judge elsewhere. As this confirms, the application of foreign law may have a legal character. But there is no meaningful sense in which courts apply foreign law.

b) Foreign law and the conflicts process

Again, the pragmatic approach undermines the choice-of-law process, as powerfully suggested by the approach of Kirby J in *Neilson*. By contrast with Gleeson CJ's approach, Kirby J was concerned that it would defeat the purpose of the choice of law process, which required the application of foreign law in certain cases, to allow the impairment of the accurate application of foreign law by treating the problem as one of evidence.

For Gleeson CJ, the proof of foreign law was not a search for truth about foreign law, but a question of evidence. Any finding on foreign law may be acceptable, provided that it has support (however slight) in the evidence, that it is plausible (or not 'inherently implausible'), and that the interests of the relevant foreign state are not implicated. A different perception informs the decision of Kirby J, who was concerned throughout that Chinese law should have been clearly and accurately determined, and who concluded not only that there was insufficient evidence of foreign law to allow it to be applied, but also that the presumption of identity between foreign and local law was inapplicable. For Kirby J, absent evidence as to how Chinese law would be applied, and given that the presumption was inapplicable, there was no sense in which the law of Australia applied instead. To accept that the evidence was sufficient to found any meaningful conclusion, and to resort to the presumption of identity, was in effect a betrayal of the objectives of the choice-of-law process. Those objectives were to 'ensure consistency of outcomes, to deny advantages of forum shopping and to fulfil ordinary human expectations'.[68] But they could be achieved only by arriving at a conclusion about the law of China based on proper evidence.[69]

This reveals two distinct reasons ways in which Kirby J treated the proof of foreign law as more than a matter of evidence. First, to see foreign law in strictly evidential terms, without resort to objectives of the conflicts process, undermines the objectives of the choice of law process—consistency, uniformity, and the satisfaction of expectations. Indeed, Kirby J apparently considered that respect for these objectives was compulsory, and he took the relevant Australian choice of law rule, whereby the *lex loci delicti* governs claims in tort, to be a mandatory rule.[70] Secondly, he assumed that applying foreign law meant applying it as the foreign court would. It is desirable in principle for a court to replicate the behaviour of foreign courts when applying foreign law. Unsatisfactory evidence of foreign law could not be excused by adverting to the factual nature of foreign law, and holding the evidence to be sufficient. Nor could it be circumvented by relying upon the evidential fiction that foreign law is the same as local law.

This difference of opinion in *Neilson* exposes clearly a tension which arises the moment one country's courts apply another country's laws, and which shapes and informs the courts' approach to foreign law. To what extent should a court aspire to apply foreign law as a foreign court would, or merely fashion norms for adjudication based on the evidence? Is justice served merely if a court approaches the evidence fairly and transparently, or only if foreign law is applied as a foreign court would apply it? Reflection suggests that these questions cannot be answered merely by declaring that the process of applying foreign law is factual and evidential. If the applicable law is foreign, the courts must take seriously the process of applying the applicable law.

Importantly, however, this does not mean falling into the trap of supposing that a court must act as a foreign court would. The kernel of truth in the pragmatic response is that the process is domesticated. There is no sense in which a court ceases to be a local court addressing an alien question. Kirby J in *Neilson* clearly recognized that this was the case. He regarded it as necessary to the proper implementation of the relevant choice-of-law rule that a court should apply 'the law that would be observed in China, were proceedings brought there'.[71] But he made it clear that this was a matter of evidence, and a matter for the court's inherent legal expertise. There was no sense in which a judge should assume the role of a judge in China. As Kirby J said in *Neilson:*[72]

> the duty of the primary judge in the forum was not (and could never properly be) to step into the shoes of a foreign judge, exercising that judge's powers as if sitting in the foreign court. Instead, it was to ascertain, according to the evidence or other available sources, how the foreign court itself would have resolved the substantive rights of the parties in a hypothetical trial conducted before it.

[68] At [199]. [69] At [199]. [70] At [215], [220].
[71] At [199]. [72] [2005] HCA 54, at [191].

As this suggests, there is no fallacy involved in saying that a court should aspire to apply foreign law as a foreign court would, provided it is recognized that this depends on evidence, and the inherent legal expertise of the court, and does involve masquerading as a foreign court.

IV. Conclusion

The problems associated with applying foreign law in national courts are partly technical, partly philosophical, and touch on the very nature of adjudication. They belong to the law of evidence, and to the conflict of laws. But the foreign law problem is important in two particular ways. It raises in acute form the epistemological puzzle at the heart of comparative law: what may we truly know of foreign laws? In the abstract this has an archly academic ring. But it has special resonance in the present context. Doubtless scholars of comparative law can master the laws of other countries. But how can counsel and the courts acquire the familiarity with foreign law necessary to apply it efficiently and fairly in the course of real proceedings?

Above all, perhaps, the problem of applying foreign law begs a question touching the very purpose and possibility of the choice of law process. The conflict of laws takes for granted that the applicable law may be foreign. Yet in some cases a proper understanding of foreign law seems impossible. This does not mean that the proof of foreign law will invariably fail. But it may sometimes fail, and whether it will succeed or not is often hard to discern. What future, then, for the conflict of laws if we cannot—or cannot with confidence—apply foreign law in national courts?

Arresting as it is, however, this rhetorical question is too grandiose. In reality, the foreign law problem is less extreme than might appear. Indeed, there may not be a substantial problem at all. What then is the true nature of the 'problem'? Differently expressed, by what measure may the application of foreign law be counted a success or failure?

Consider first the two extreme views of the process of applying foreign law. On the one hand, it is said that courts applying foreign law should replicate the decision-making of foreign courts. By that standard it is said that process is bound to fail. On the other, it is asserted that the process of establishing foreign law is purely evidential, reflecting the status of foreign laws as facts. By that measure, all that matters is that the relevant procedures are complied with.

Neither claim, taken literally, withstands inspection. It cannot realistically be expected that one court can mimic another court's processes, given that the material before it depends on evidence and the argument of local lawyers. But nor can it be right to conclude that coherence with foreign law is irrelevant given the factual, evidential nature of the enquiry. A more principled view is that the legal character of the foreign law enquiry must be respected, given that the integrity of the conflicts process, and the rights of the parties, depends on it. But this must be qualified by the realistic observation that a court can only act in accordance with the evidence and arguments placed before it. Even if the process is inherently domestic, a matter for the local judge, the enquiry can still aspire to determine foreign law as a foreign court does. Indeed, as we have seen, Kirby J in *Neilson* considered that respect for the choice-of-law process required the court to apply the laws of a foreign state as if proceedings were brought there.[73] But this was a matter of evidence. There is no sense in which a judge should assume the role of a foreign judge.

The message is that we cannot sensibly expect a local judge to impersonate a foreign judge in any meaningful sense. But nor is it adequate to shelter behind the proposition that foreign laws are merely facts, and insist that the process of establishing foreign law purely evidential. As this suggests, we cannot judge the process of establishing foreign law a failure on the ground that local courts can never truly act as foreign courts. That cannot be the measure. But nor we can say that the process is always satisfactory on the ground that it is just a matter of evidence. That is not the measure either.

Conformity with the foreign view of foreign law is thus an aspiration bounded by practicality, but an important one nonetheless. But consider how such conformity should be assessed. As we have seen, there is no jurisprudentially mature sense in which a court can achieve a 'right' answer to a question of foreign law, any more than it can achieve a 'right' answer to a question of local law. But it is plausible to expect that it will strive—or the evidential process should strive—to make the outcome authentic, in the sense that it coheres with the principles and methodology of the foreign system. As this suggests, one cannot meaningfully criticize a court for coming to a wrong conclusion about foreign law, unless this means a conclusion which a foreign court could not have reached.

In principle, there must remain a category of case in which even authenticity is impossible—in which, in a modified sense, there is no right answer. But the existence of such cases is no argument against the process of applying foreign law. To seek an authentic answer is an important aspiration. But, even if it fails in a given case, the process is not subverted. As we have seen, the process is inevitably domesticated. It can only be judged by standards appropriate to a *local* court applying a *foreign* law. Those standards comprise the principles governing the assessment of evidence, and, in so far as the court's legal expertise is deployed, the standards governing all legal reasoning—subject always to overriding principles of due process. These are domestic requirements, and do not concern conformity with foreign law. But the choice-of-law process, and the process of applying foreign law, are necessarily local institutions, and ultimately subject to such local standards. If a court has aspired to apply foreign law authentically but failed, there can be no complaint if those local principles of evidence, rationality, and due process are maintained.

As this suggests, the nature of the foreign law problem is beset by misunderstandings. It is misleading to expect too much of the application of foreign law. A judge in one country cannot impersonate a judge elsewhere. So we cannot judge the process a failure just because this does not happen. Nor can we expect of a judge in one country when applying foreign law more than we can of a foreign judge applying the same law. A decision on foreign law can be no more 'right' than a decision on domestic law. Nor, however, can we make the process of establishing foreign law too easy by declaring it

[73] At [199].

merely an evidential issue. In reality, the application of foreign law is always a domestic, not foreign matter, in the sense that the court can do no more than comply with the rules of evidence, reinforced by its inherent legal expertise. But this does not make it simply an evidential, not legal, matter. And it does not absolve a court from seeking to determine the parties' rights and duties under foreign law.

In the end, therefore, the pragmatists are answered. We can expect more of the application of foreign law than proficiency in the assessment of evidence. But so also the Cassandras are silenced. The enterprise of applying foreign law is not doomed to fail.

6

Foreign Law in International Legal Practice

*Guido Alpa**

I. 'Foreign law' in Italian legal culture: fashions and models from the 19th century to today

In Italian legal culture, the expression 'foreign law' has a quite restricted meaning, in as much as it refers to the law in force in other countries necessarily applied by the courts by virtue of the rules on the conflict of laws, or to the law chosen by agreement of the parties to govern the relationship established between them.[1] However, the expression may be used in a wider sense, which regards not only the statutory rules applied, but also the other 'legal formants', namely 'doctrine' (legal literature) and case law, according to the teachings of one of the most eminent Italian scholars of comparative law, Rodolfo Sacco.[2] From this perspective, we are to take into consideration the cultural models, the legal institutes, and the judgments coming from foreign experiences and which are used by individuals or by the courts in the solution of domestic legal problems.

In this wider meaning, the use of foreign law in Italy is the subject of a very rich history, still awaiting its narrator.[3] In summary, this history can be sub-divided into five periods: (i) the first period comprises the whole of the 19th century; (ii) the second the first half of the 20th; (iii) the third, the period which spans roughly two decades (from 1950 to 1970); (iv) the fourth regards the following two decades (from 1970 to 1990); and (v) the fifth, the last years of the 20th century. Each sub-division into periods is arbitrary and each period cannot be assumed as a monolith in which a sole and consistent approach took hold; however, taking a bird's eye view of the formation

* Professore ordinario di diritto civile, Università di Roma 'la Sapienza'; Presidente del Consiglio Nazionale Forense.

[1] The same perspective is adopted by U. Drobnig, 'The Use of Comparative Law by Courts: General Report', in U. Drobnig and S. van Erp (eds.), *The Use of Comparative Law by Courts*, XIVth International Congress of Comparative Law, Athens, 1997 (The Hague, London, Boston, 1999), at p. 6.

But what is striking is the use of foreign models to solve domestic cases: see B. Markesinis, 'Reading Through a Foreign Judgment', in P. Cane and J. Stapleton (eds.), *Essays in Celebration of John Fleming* (Oxford, 1998), p. 261 ff.

[2] R. Sacco and A. Gambaro, *Sistemi giuridici comparati* (Turin, 1996), at p. 6 ff.; G. Alpa (ed.), *Corso di sistemi giuridici comparati* (Turin, 1996) at p. 10.

[3] G. Gorla had studied the use of *lex alii loci* in the Middle Ages (*ius commune Europeum*): see ID., Il ricorso alla legge di un 'luogo vicino' nell'ambito del diritto comune europeo, in Foro italiano, 1973, V, 89 ff. For further details see P. Grossi, *L'ordine giuridico medievale* (Rome and Bari, 1998) *passim*.

Roman law is still mentioned in Italian decisions, but only *exornatione gratia* (G. Micali, 'Il diritto romano nella giurisprudenza della Corte suprema di cassazione', in *Giurisprudenza italiana*, 1993, IV, 489 ff.), while, according to the Spanish Civil Code, Roman law is the basis for interpreting the law through general principles.

of law in Italy, certain hues—which correspond to the periods previously mentioned—appear prevalent, thereby lending scientific credit to this temporal sub-division.[4]

1. The 19th century

The first period records a preponderant influence of French law, which reverberates over all the formants of our legal system, both the statutory formant, and legal literature and the decisions of the Courts.

As regards the statutory formant, the *Code Napoléon* constituted at first the law imposed by the General's armies in the provinces conquered from the Piedmontese, from the Austrians, the Lorraines, and the Bourbons; after the fall of Napoleon, his model of Civil Code is transplanted in several of the states into which Italy was divided (the Civil Code of the Kingdom of Two Sicilies; the Civil Code of the Duchy of Parma; the Civil Code of the Kingdom of Sardinia or 'Albertine Code') and is subsequently chosen as the model for the first Civil Code of unified Italy, which is born in 1865.

As for the legal literature formant, the *Ecole de l'Exégèse* becomes the method for analysis and application of universal law, so much so that the majority of the treatises and manuals of French law are first translated and then imitated by Italian legal writers. More than 600 of these works were translated over the whole century, which sees the coming into being of the Italian 'scuola dell'Esegesi' (School of Exegesis—Interpretation), which holds that law is only the statutory State-enacted law, and the legal writer's work is limited to an analytical commentary of the provisions of the same.

With reference to the case law formant, given the closeness of French law and Italian law, the judgments of the *Cour de Cassation* and of the French tribunals are quoted by legal writers and employed by judges with largesse, without regard for the fact that they have been rendered by foreign judges: French law is not considered by Italian jurists as a 'foreign' law, belonging to a *ius alienum*, that is to the system of a different State, and applied by judges belonging to the administration of a foreign State.

2. The early 20th century

The second period records a repudiation of the 'Scuola dell'Esegesi' (the school of interpretation), and the triumph of the Pandectist model, the historical School of Germanic origin, introduced in Italy by the scholars of Roman law. Even Roman law was not considered then, as it is not today, as a 'foreign' law in a proper sense: it is not only the primary source of the Italian legal language, but also of many of the institutes governing natural persons, property, contracts, torts, and the remedies thereto. Roman law is so widely diffused among the roots of our own legal culture that it constitutes, to this very day a fundamental subject matter of study for the formation of lawyers, is often quoted in decisions of the courts, and is studied in a 'current' dimension, almost

[4] Unfortunately the literature in English about this proceeding is very poor: see, among others, M. Bellomo, *The Common Legal Past of Europe (1000–1800)* (Washington, 1995); for new comments see P. Grossi, *La scienza giuridica in Italia nell'Ottocento* (Milan, 2000); G. Alpa, *La cultura delle regole. Storia del diritto civile italiano* (Rome and Bari, 2000).

as if it were not a body of rules and principles to be historically placed in the context of its bi-millennium evolution, but as a *corpus* of rules still in force.

The choice of moving from the French culture to the Pandectist culture was not only the product of a fashion, but rather born of a requirement that at the end of the 19th century and the beginning of the 20th was perceived as necessary: the intent was to dogmatically reconstruct Italian civil law, and consequently the method for studying the same. Savigny, Arndts, Dernburg, and Windscheid, among others, peep out from the bookshelves of lawyers, are top of the list in the courses of civil law, constitute the staple diet of jurists and therefore of judges, who, having received a Pandectist training, flaunt the same in their judgments. So much so, that a jurist of those times, Biagio Brugi, a famed author, a veritable scholar of Roman law and private law, and editor of one of the manuals of Institutions of Private Law most widely studied by generations of students,[5] could well state, in a lecture held in 1919, that 'no efficacy ever perhaps was had in Italy by foreign scientists, which can be comparable to that of the Germans in our day and age'. His was not a simple reckoning: it was a *cri de coeur*, aimed at fostering the awareness in Italian jurists of the bi-millennium history to which they were heirs, and which he now saw as being flattened in the books copied from the German jurists, and an attempt to recover these studies to the originality of the Italian model. It was also an invitation not to disregard the other aids of foreign legal science: the Italians—he suggested—'may indeed look as farther afield as to the English *common law* (in which often our own authors are still quoted) and to the decisions of North American Courts, in certain points inimitable'.[6]

Brugi's invitation was to remain unheeded: the influence of German culture was to remain unaltered up to the formulation of the new Civil Code in 1942, and further still for several more decades. However, due to the strange occurrences of legal history, at the end of the 1920s, an extraordinary event was recorded, thanks to the cosmopolitan climate which pervaded continental Europe during that period. In 1927 a bi-lateral commission officially installed by Italy and France drafted a uniform Code of Obligations. This initiative is due to another great jurist, a scholar of Roman law and private law, Vittorio Scialoja, and to the Frenchman, François Larnaude. Jurists from other countries, such as Belgium, Romania, Greece, and Canada, took part in the initiative at the beginning, but the same was finally restricted to the two founding nations.[7]

The purpose of the *Projet de Code des Obligations et des Contrats*, consisting of 739 articles, drafted in the two languages by the scholars of the 'sister Nations', was to 'create, with the consensus of all their strengths united, a body of laws which, within each of the two States, would represent that most perfect regime of law which legal science wished for and legal practice required.'

With the changing political balances, at the end of the 1930s, the German influence makes itself felt again; but the scholars of comparative law also continue to study the

[5] B. Brugi, *Istituzioni di diritto civile* (Milan, 1915).

[6] B. Brugi, *I danni dell'imitazione straniera nella nostra giurisprudenza, in Atti della R.Accademia Lucchese di Scienze,* Lettere ed Arti, vol. XXXVI (1919), at p. 7.

[7] Commissione reale per la riforma dei codici/Commission francaise d'etudes de l'union legislative entre les nations aliees et amies, Progetto di Codice delle Obbligazioni e dei Contratti, Testo definitivo approvato a Parigi nell'Ottobre 1927-Anno VI, Rome, 1928.

models of *common law*, taking into account not only institutes unheard of in Italy, such as *trusts*, but also company law.

3. 1950 to 1970

After the introduction of the new Civil Code, which incorporates also commercial law in a unified whole, from the 1950s onwards, we record a sort of closure, on the part of Italian jurists, towards foreign experiences: everyone is busy understanding, commenting, interpreting the new text, and references to comparison or to foreign laws are quite rare, both in legal literature and in court rulings.[8]

The most notable exception is that of Gino Gorla who, already in 1955, published a prodigious treatise on contracts in which, in addition to the historical perspective, a comparative approach is also adopted, by reliance on cases: reference to cases, then as today, becomes a way to seek in other experiences, in particular in common law, the similarities, the convergences, the more useful practical solutions.[9] We too can pride ourselves, as nowadays also the United Kingdom can pride itself, thanks to the works of Basil Markesinis, on scholars who are concerned in studying what unites us, more than what constitutes division, 'convergences' more than 'divergences', the formulas adaptable to the practical cases, rather than erudite musings which are an end unto themselves: scholars, in other words, animated by the longing for research, not to produce a sterile form of culture, but with the aim of seeking immediately functional, practical solutions.[10]

4. 1970 to 1990

The fourth period is the most lively, and to this we shall devote more time: it includes the influences recorded in decisions of the courts, from cases and from the other sources of foreign law, the influences of legal practice from other countries, in particular from the United States, and the deployment of remedies derived from those experiences.

5. The late 20th century

The current period records, in addition to the tendencies which developed during the fourth period, above all the incidence of the law of the European Union, and therefore the necessary circulation of the models of the Member States of the Union, which are merged in the regulations, in the directives, in the very language used by the European legislator and by the Court of Justice of the European Community.

[8] G. Alpa, *La cultura delle regole*, n. 4. [9] G. Gorla, *Il contratto* (Milan, 1955).

[10] This is the leitmotiv through the essays collected by B. Markesinis (ed.), *The Gradual Convergence. Foreign Ideas, Foreign Influences, and English Law on the Eve of the 21st Century* (Oxford, 1994).

II. Examples of foreign models used by Italian courts

The models of foreign judgments (or legal rules) used by Italian judges are still rare. Usually it is the lawyers who use these foreign elements in their defences and the judges, if they take them into account, make use of them in their motivations. But the recourse to foreign models is not only left to the culture of the lawyer or the judge, but also to the extent the quotation may be instrumental in bringing about the favourable decision of a dispute. However, it cannot be said that the use of comparative law is a usual and normal way of working for the Italian lawyer. Furthermore, many cases have been decided taking foreign models into account, but the judge does not reveal the sources of his reasoning, nor does he expressly quote them. Holding some of these cases against the light, however, we can surely note the influence of foreign experiences. Here are some examples.

1. Privacy

One of the first Italian cases in which the problem arose of the safeguarding in our system of the right to privacy[11] regards the tenor Caruso, whose family life during childhood had been depicted in the film 'Leggenda di una voce' (Legend of a voice). Certain sequences showed scenes of violence committed by his father, and Caruso himself had been portrayed as a short-tempered, heavy drinking man, of dubious morality. To uphold the right of Caruso to obtain compensation on the basis of *tort law*, the judges put the question whether there should be protection for a general right 'to confidentiality or privacy', qualified in Anglo-Saxon court rulings as a 'right of privacy'. The judges' reply—we are in the mid 1950s—is negative: the reasoning is formalistic, because in seeking a provision of the law aimed at protecting this specific right, and the judge having found only rules aimed at safeguarding the use of a person's name or image, or the person's decorum or reputation, but not privacy per se, the research is fruitless, and gives a negative result. Therefore, the judges conclude that 'in our legal system there is no right to privacy, but only individual subjective rights of the person are acknowledged and protected, in different ways; therefore, it is not forbidden to communicate, either privately or publicly, events, especially if imaginary, of another person's life, when knowledge of the same has not been obtained by means unlawful in themselves, or which impose an obligation of secrecy'.[12]

Gradually, however, the right of privacy charts its way through the Italian courts: this time, through the utilization of the European Convention on Human Rights and Fundamental Liberties, signed in Rome on 4 November 1950 and ratified in Italy with Statute n. 848 of 4 August 1955. The Convention—whose article 8 sets forth that '*toute personne a droit au respect de sa vie privée et familiare, de son domicile et de sa correspondance*' (every person has the right to the respect of his/her private and family

[11] G. Alpa, 'The Protection of Privacy in Italian Law', in B. Markesinis (ed.), *Protecting Privacy* (Oxford, 1999), at p. 105 ff.

[12] Tribunale di Roma, 14.9.1953, in Foro italiano, 1954, I, 115.

life, home and correspondence) is quoted as the basis for the decision which upheld, both on appeal, and in the Court of Cassation, the right of the family of Claretta Petacci, the unfortunate lover of Benito Mussolini, who had been executed alongside him, trying to shield him with her own body, to obtain damages. In this case, it was a book, in which Claretta Petacci's personality was described with scornful and discrediting phrases, which had prompted the family to claim their right of privacy, and the judges upheld the same, despite the fact that the injured party was deceased.[13]

2. Taking

Although no cases were expressly mentioned, nor was the legal theory of German origin relating to the subject matter, the Constitutional Court, in a landmark decision regarding the regulation of ownership, held that the legislator cannot, without compensation, compress the powers of the owner on a thing beyond the limits 'naturally attached to the right of ownership' such as they are acknowledged at the current time. The case regarded certain owners of land situated in the centre of the town of Palermo, land which was under a zoning ordinance which excluded the possibility of building on the same; the town plan was compliant with the zoning law, which envisaged no compensation for zoning ordinances or encumbrances which limited or compressed the rights of the owners. The court applied—as was immediately pointed out by the scholars of the subject matter—the German concept of 'Einzelakttheorie', according to which the individual right, the right of ownership in particular, must be considered as a sphere, on the surface of which the legislator can carve, that is can impose restrictions on the owner without compensation; but when restrictions carve onto the essential nucleus, and reach into the 'vital core' of the right, the sacrifice imposed on the owner must be compensated.[14]

3. Leasing

Leasing contracts made their appearance in an Italian court—according to the records—only in 1972. A small Tribunal in the province of Pavia, which is full of small businesses led by able and tireless entrepreneurs, had to solve the question of whether the machinery given by the lessor to the lessee for the manufacture of shoes should be considered the property of the lessor or of the lessee. The contract utilized was a leasing contract, unknown until then in the Italian experience, where, according to tradition, use of a thing can be the subject of a contract of rental or of a contract of sale, or of a contract creating property rights. The Tribunal instead referred to commercial practice—without, however, quoting the experience from which this type of contract had been imported—to acknowledge right of citizenship of the same in our own system, by virtue of the principle of freedom of contract.[15]

[13] Corte di Cassazione, 22.12.1956, n. 4487, ibi, 1957, I, 877.
[14] Corte costituzionale, 29.5.1968, n. 55, ibi, 1968, I, 1365.
[15] Tribunale di Vigevano, 14.12.1972, in Banca e borsa, 1973, II, 287.

4. Liability for prospectuses

Even for the presentation to the public of financial products, in the absence of statutes which would be enacted only in 1983, and then more widely in 1991, the judges—in this case the judges of the Tribunal and of the Appeals Court of the town of Milan, which is the main financial centre of the country—relied on foreign experience, in particular the English and US experience. They did not take care to mention any cases, but simply proceeded to follow the reasonings of the same. On that occasion there was a prospectus prepared by the issuer to favour the underwriting of debenture securities by investors; the issuer was the client of a bank, American Express Bank, subsequently American Service Bank s.p.a., which was in charge of placement of the securities on the Italian market; it had invited its clients to underwrite the debentures and assured them that the issuer was in an economically sound position; the investment, however, proved disastrous, because a few months later the issuer went bankrupt. In the first instance the bank was not held liable, because the judge ascertained that there was no contract of guarantee with clients;[16] in the appeal, instead, the bank was held liable in tort, because it had spread groundless information on the economic soundness of the issuer. In defining the limits of liability, the judges refer to liability for (misrepresentation in) prospectuses, well-known to common lawyers.

5. Nervous shock

In the Italian legal system, there has been great discussion as to the extent and qualification of personal injury. In addition to physical injury and so-called moral injury (which corresponds to the 'pain and suffering' of common law), a different type of injury, consisting of injury to health (so-called 'biological damage') has been ascertained. The purely psychological damage, due to the nervous shock produced by an accident, had never been taken into consideration as a legally relevant injury. However, the Constitutional Court, taking into account the English experience, specified as *obiter dictum,* in a case in which the issue was whether compensation was due to the relatives of the victim, that such psychological injury, if caused by fault (negligence) or wilful damage, gives rise to compensation. The writer of the judgment was one of the most noteworthy scholars of private law, Luigi Mengoni, a former Professor at the Catholic University in Milan, subsequently appointed to the Court. The judgment sets forth that liability for nervous shock must be tied to fault, it cannot be strict liability; on the other hand, the English courts which admit this principle, in order to avoid arbitrariness, and so as not to burden the risk of the insurance companies with an overly large number of claims, make the distinction of whether the claimant suffered shock as an occasional onlooker at the time of the accident, or if he was told of the event far away from the scene of the accident, upholding the claim in the first instance, but rejecting it in the second.[17]

[16] Tribunale di Milano, 11.1.1988, in Giurisprudenza commerciale, 1988, II, 585.
[17] Corte costituzionale, 27.10.1994, n. 372 in Foro italiano, 1994, I, 3297.

6. Italian trusts

The last example regards Trusts, a typical institute of *equity*, originally only available in the systems of English descent, and subsequently introduced, with different legal configurations, and on the basis of special statutes, also in countries of different legal traditions. Trusts were the subject of the Hague Convention of 1 July 1985, rendered executive in Italy by Statute n. 364 of 16 October 1989, which entered into force on 1 January 1992. The Convention deals with the applicable law, but contains certain provisions which give the definition of 'trust', for the purpose of extending the rules to all the types of this category, in the various forms in which the signing countries acknowledge the existence of the same. It is without doubt, in the Italian legal system, that a trust established abroad with a foreign trustee, relating to property located in Italy, is valid, even if the settlor is an Italian citizen. Italian citizens who intend to set up a trust mostly use foreign legal systems, mainly the rules applicable in Jersey, but also those applicable in Ireland. This choice is preferable for succession purposes, for fiscal reasons, for reasons of confidentiality, but also because the purposes achieved through the establishment of a trust are not equally available using the institutes of civil law, such as fiduciary contracts, fiduciary nomination, or registration, etc. Usually the following transaction takes place: the property is registered in the name of an Italian company, whose quotas or shares are in turn registered in the name of a foreign trustee.

After the approval, ratification, and entering into force even in Italy of the Hague Convention, the problem arose as to whether it was possible to set up a trust, obviously governed by a foreign law, with an Italian trustee. This is because the Convention, as it contained provisions on the definition of 'trusts', introduced in Italy rules of substantive law; trusts (in their structure at equity), governed by a foreign law, would now be fully compatible with Italian law, but only under condition that the trustee be a foreigner.

Decisions of the courts, extremely rare, are divided. The first case regarded compulsory purchases, promoted in Sardinia, in the 1950s, in order to enact the agrarian reform. The land subject to compulsory purchase had been set up in trust by an English national, by will and testament; the expropriating body had instituted proceedings against the surviving spouse, designated as the trustee, and not against their children designated in the will as 'beneficiaries'. The Tribunal of Oristano, a town on the island, had acknowledged the validity of a trust set up abroad on property located abroad, but had deemed incompatible with Italian law (in particular with the principles of so-called 'public policy') the institute of trust, when the same consisted of property located in Italy, as this would have been in contrast with the so-called 'numerus clausus' of property rights. The basic point of the ruling was the idea that in trust, ownership is split between *cestui que trust* and the trustee, and that this gives rise, therefore, to a form of property right which is not compatible with the wholeness of the right of ownership envisaged in the Italian Civil Code. For the judges, therefore, the alternative was between considering as owners either the surviving spouse or the children. By holding that the surviving spouse, as trustee, had only apparent title to the property, with powers to dispose of the same, but only in accordance with the aims of the trust, the Tribunal decided that the children had right of ownership, and therefore they should have been the recipients of the expropriation procedures, which, thus, had not been effected properly.[18]

The second case regarded a trust set up by an English national on property situated in Italy; the executor trustee had applied to the Italian judge (of the Tribunal of Casale Monferrato, a small town in the northern region of Piedmont) for authorization to sell the property; the judge, maintaining that the trust in question was similar to a fiduciary agreement 'cum amico' under civil law, refused authorization, and held that the same was not necessary, as the fiduciary agent was already the owner of the property, albeit on a fiduciary basis.[19]

The third case regarded a trust set up in Jersey by Italian nationals. The trustee was the settlor's wife, an Italian citizen, who held the property (that is the shares in two companies) in the interest of the beneficiaries, her children and her husband, the settlor himself. Having deposited the shares to take part in the Annual General Meetings of the two companies, the Directors of the companies then refused to return them to her. She had therefore acted to re-acquire possession of the shares; the Directors had objected, claiming that 'trusts' were not recognized in our own legal system, and that the trustee (who had been replaced in the meantime) could not claim any right to the shares. The judge instead ruled in favour of the plaintiff, without, however, discussing the nature of 'trusts' and their compatibility with the Italian legal system (which, according to the majority of authors, in the case at hand should have been ruled out, as the trustee was Italian); the judge based his ruling on the provisions relating to actions for recovery, which are regardless of the title to the property, but are based on the factual relationship with the property, such as possession.[20]

III. Use of *Anstalt* from Lichtenstein

For the purpose of tax savings, to invest capital abroad, for reasons of confidentiality, wide use has been made of the institute of *Anstalt*, a typical device of the law of Lichtenstein. It is similar to a foundation, set up by a sole subject; it has legal personality and is considered by Italian judges as a legal person existing under foreign law, recognized in Italy in the same way as our legal system recognizes other foreign legal entities. Under the laws of Lichtenstein, the necessary officers of the company are the founder and the administrator, while the Assembly and the Statutory Auditors are not strictly required. The administrator may dispose of the estate and may promote actions to safeguard the same. The general provisions of law (art. 16) and the Bruxelles Convention of 28 February 1968 (art. 1) are applied.

The first doubts that had been expressed by the Italian judges (in particular the Tribunal of Milan),[21] have been settled, and the Court of Cassation has upheld the legitimacy of *Anstalts* even if set up by founders who remain secret.[22]

18 Tribunale di Oristano, 15.3.1956, ibi, 1956, I, 1020.
19 Tribunale di Casale Monferrato, 13.4.1984 (decree), in Giurisprudenza italiana, 1984, I, 2, 754.
20 Pretura di Roma, 8.7.1999 (order), unpublished.
21 Tribunale di Milano, 11.1.1979, in Rivista di diritto internazionale, 1980, 523.
22 Corte di Cassazione, 21.1.1985, n. 198.

IV. The foreign models utilized in Italian contractual practice

In Italian contractual practice it is rare for the parties, if they are both Italian, to choose a foreign law to govern the contract. On the other hand, there are numerous institutes, types of contracts, negotiating practices, remedies which have been imported from foreign experiences, especially from English or US common law, to govern economic relations. Here are a few examples.

Many types of contract have been accepted in our legal system, by virtue of the principle of freedom of contract. These—as opposed to what occurred in other countries, such as France—have retained their original names: for instance, leasing contracts, factoring, franchising, merchandising, project financing, joint ventures, contracts regarding the use of information and data transmission technologies, and so forth. As with all contracts defined as 'atypical', because they are not comprised among the types regulated by the Civil Code or by statutes, they are governed by the contractual clauses negotiated between the parties. The judge's control is two-fold: on the one hand he verifies if they are worthy of protection under the Italian legal system, that is if the interests and the objectives they pursue are lawful and economically useful; on the other hand, in the event that a contract should fail to make adequate provisions for all the eventualities that may come about, the judge proceeds to qualify the same, taking into account the reference legal types. For instance, in the case of a leasing contract, reference is made either to the conditional sale agreements (with retention of title), or to rental contracts; for joint ventures, reference is made to association in participation, etc.

As for negotiating practices, the use of side-letters is frequent, and so is the use of letters of intent, letters of guarantee. Above all, for certain complex economic transactions, such as the sale of share holdings, the technique adopted in the United States is followed: a due diligence research is made, a first agreement is reached (closing) and then the parties proceed to the definitive contract.

Even as regards remedies, reference has been made to the experiences of common law, to better attain the interests of the parties: after some hesitation, the so-called 'autonomous contract of guarantee' has been accepted (configured at common law as bid bonds, etc.).

But it should be specified that often even among Italian parties, the use of US Standard Contract forms, drafted in English, is preferred.

Even if the contracts are complex, and therefore more articulate than the average contract utilized in Italy, we never arrive at the detailed regulation of US Contracts, consisting often of weighty files, in which every conceivable event is taken into account and provided for.

Usually professionals work on templates concerning the 'boiler-plate clauses'[23] and include in the content of contracts clauses providing 'no waiver', 'no oral amendments',

[23] M. Fontaine and F. De Ly, *Drafting International Contracts: An Analysis of Contract Clauses* (Leiden, 2nd edn, 2009); G. Cordero-Moss (ed.), *Boilerplate Clauses, International Commercial Contracts and the Applicable Law* (Cambridge, 2010); G. De Nova, *The Romanistic Tradition: Application of Boilerplate Clauses in Italian Law*, ivi, p. 227 ff.

'sole remedy', 'liquidated damages', 'representation and warranties', hardship, *force majeure*. Wording is similar to that used by lawyers in the US or UK, even if the parties are Italian and the applicable law is the Italian law. Some of these clauses are common also in Italian practice, others are new in content or in the way in which they are expressed. Interpretation and compliance with Italian law, mostly with the Italian Civil Code, is a difficult task for lawyers assisting their clients.

V. *Lex mercatoria* and principles of international commercial contracts processed by UNIDROIT

In international commercial contracts the Italian parties, when with a foreign counterparty they do not choose a foreign law, normally refer to the principles of *lex mercatoria*, or to the principles developed by the International Institute for the Unification of Private Law (UNIDROIT), with its Head Office in Rome.

1. *Lex mercatoria*

Even for the *lex mercatoria*—to which the Italian merchants of medieval times gave great impulse[24]—we can make the same observations as were made in relation to Roman law: it was not considered as a sort of foreign law, as in the history of our experience (not national but cultural); it is considered part of the history of Italian law. In any event, whilst the Italian judges have no difficulty in acknowledging it as a body of rules of conduct appraisable as widely used in the mercantile 'societas', the problems that may arise regard the possibility of making arbitration awards based on the same. The question is intertwined with the issue of international arbitration, which is not the subject of this paper.

It is worth recalling one of the few instances in which Italian judges have dealt with the matter.

The case regarded a contract entered into between an Italian company and a German one, containing an arbitration clause which referred the settlement of disputes to the Refined Sugar Association of London, which applies the principles of the *lex mercatoria*. The award was not motivated, in accordance with the practices of the Association. As the parties were citizens of two countries (Germany and Italy) which had signed the Geneva Convention of 21 April 1961 on International Commercial Arbitration, the Italian party (non-prevailing) claimed that the award was null and void, on the basis of the fact that the Convention envisages that where either party requests that the award be motivated, prior to the rendering of the decision, the award must be so motivated (art. 8). The German company had defended itself claiming that the Association belonged to a country (the United Kingdom), which had not signed the Convention, and therefore the award was valid.

The Court of Cassation issued a very elaborate ruling in which it upheld the claim of the Italian party. The motivation for this sets off from the notion of *lex mercatoria*

[24] P. Grossi, *L'ordine giuridico medievale*, n. 3.

previously mentioned; it went on to specify that *lex mercatoria* lacks sovereignty, because the mercantile 'societas' has no boundaries, but it does not have the enforceability of sovereign systems. Having therefore to refer to a legal system in order to render the arbitrators' decisions enforceable, the Court of Cassation deemed it appropriate to apply the Geneva Convention, claiming that the same has a more modern approach than that of New York. The choice is motivated in the sense that as the parties were citizens of countries which are signatories of this Convention, this Convention 'must be considered as recalled by implied reference in the contractual stipulations between entrepreneurs belonging to ratifying States of the same'.[25]

2. The principles of UNIDROIT

The principles of UNIDROIT represent a veritable melting-pot of the models from the most varied experiences, but above all represent a fortunate attempt to merge the principles of civil law, of common law, and of the *lex mercatoria*.[26] They move from the upholding of freedom of contract and they propose clear and simple rules which regard the binding force of contracts, the principle of good faith and reasonableness, the formation, interpretation and execution of the contract, in addition to rules on non-performance and damages. From the viewpoint of the Italian experience, of particular relevance is the envisaging of rules relating to situations of hardship.

In all systems, rules are established, expressly or construed from judicial or legal theory interpretation, regarding the eventuality that performance may become frustrated. In the Italian experience we can point out two occurrences: that in which frustration was extraordinary and unforeseeable, which bears with it the consequence of termination of the contract (art. 1467); and that in which the frustrating circumstances were foreseeable, but not actually envisaged by the parties. In this case, one has to ascertain the possibility of applying the theory of so-called 'pre-supposition' which, connected with the bona fide clause, with 'Causa' of the Contract, with the negotiating basis (that is with the assignment of advantages and risks) may entail the termination of the contract.

In international trade there is a trend, as underlined many times, toward keeping the contract alive. Therefore, the general rule according to which the parties are compelled to carry out their respective obligations, even if performance of the same has become more onerous (art. 6.2.1) is tempered by the institute of 'hardship'.

The features of this institute are outlined in article 6.2, where they are indicated as follows: frustration must be dependent on a risk not accepted in the contract, on external circumstances, which must not be ascribable to the party which invokes the same, and must have supervened or, if precedent, must not have been known or recognizable by the party who invokes them.

The effect of 'hardship' clauses is directed at maintaining the relationship alive. Therefore, the possibility is given to the party invoking the same to re-open

[25] Corte di Cassazione, 8.2.1982, n. 722, in Foro italiano, 1982, I, 2285.

[26] J. Bonell, *An International Restatement of Contract Law. The Unidroit Principles of International Commercial Contracts* (Irvington, NY, 1994).

negotiations without hindrance and without suspension of the performance due under the agreement.

Should negotiations fail, the interested party may apply to the judge (in our case to the arbitrator).

Here lies another scope for intervention, which in countries of codified law is totally ignored, indeed it is strenuously opposed: the judge, in fact, may—beyond the ruling of termination of the contract, which is the customary conclusion—'adapt the contract with the aim of re-establishing the balance between performances' (art. 6.2.3).

What is really extraordinary for civil lawyers is to admit the power of the judge to 're-write the contract' on behalf of the parties, in contrast with the principle of 'sanctity of contract'. But the aim of the principles is precisely to save the economic transaction and to render it feasible in accordance with the supervening risks.

VI. The rules of the common market of the European Union

Community law cannot be considered a 'foreign law', because it is one of the sources of the legal systems of the Member States. However, both Regulations and Directives tend to create uniform rules for the internal market; these rules are created originally by the organs of the Community, but can be traced back to the models coming from the individual countries of the Community; these rules are effective in the 'strong' models (the French, German, and English models) which are often adapted to the new exigencies; to those stronger models the weaker models (from a political, numerical, and economic viewpoint) adapt.[27] Thus it was, for instance, for the directive on 'unfair clauses in consumer contracts', for the directive on consumer credit, for the directives on banks and insurance companies, and, above all, for the rules on competition.

It is important to underline that from the complex of directives on the subject matter of contracts, special rules can be singled out which tend to become general: let us think of the use of the form of contract to protect the weaker party, to the ban on the abuse of bargaining (contracting) power; to the rules on prior and subsequent information in the stipulation of contracts; to the principle of good faith which is now at the basis of any type of contract.

Besides the proposal of many groups of an academic nature, devoted to the drafting of a 'European Civil Code', such as the Lando-Beale Commission, or the academics working on drafting the rules concerning the Acquis on Consumer Law, of a 'European Tort Law', the EC Commission and the EU Parliament are backing a proposal of Regulation on the Common European Sales Law (CESL) to facilitate cross-border transactions in the single market,[28] now enacted by the European Parliament, which embedded some general principles of contract law.[29]

[27] See B. Markesinis, 'Learning from Europe and Learning in Europe', in ID., *Foreign Law and Comparative Methodology: A Subject and a Thesis* (Oxford, 1997), p. 163 ff. and ID., 'Our Debt to Europe: Past, Present and Future', in *The Clifford Chance Millennium Lectures. The Coming Together of the Common Law and the Civil Law* (Oxford-Portland, 2000), p. 37 ff.

[28] European Commission, 11.10.2011 COM (2011) 635; G. Alpa, G. Conte, U. Perfetti, F. Graf von Westphalen (eds.), *The Proposed Common European Sales Law—The Lawyers View* (Munich, 2012).

[29] Resolution of the EU Parliament, 27 Feb. 2014.

VII. Some tentative conclusions

In rethinking the use of comparative law before the Italian civil courts, we may point out some caveats concerning the use of comparative law by not only national judges but also those belonging to the European *milieu*. Looking at this phenomenon from a very general perspective, we can dare to say that:

(i) comparative law is perceived in a narrow, typically 'Eurocentric' fashion: patterns of judgments are chosen from those legal systems which are more accessible for reasons of language, prestige, or tradition: in Italian eyes, these legal systems comprise a very limited range (the French and German systems, with that of England still perceived as a very distant planet);

(ii) 'Eurocentrism' is not a dangerous attitude, and is not a means by which to reduce the potential in comparative method: rather, this attitude is welcomed because it is more efficient in the process of harmonization of European private law, and it is developing almost 'naturally', thanks to the active role assumed by the European Institutions in drafting so many directives concerning contract law and consumer law. Enacting EC Directives, the national legislators are forced to accept notions, concepts, definitions, general principles, general 'standards', and general 'clauses' which are typical of other jurisdictions; the transplant of these legal elements plays an active role in the apparent or creeping convergence between systems;

(iii) in addition, the enormous effort made by the European Court of Justice in interpreting EC law leads to a common method of interpreting statutes and the underlying institutions of private law;

(iv) comparative law should be considered not from a static but a dynamic viewpoint: the comparison of written texts does not reflect the real situation of a foreign legal system, because the 'living law' (*diritto vivente* in Italian) is enriched by the case law. In codified systems some fields of law are almost wholly built on judicial rules which fill the gap between the needs of a complex society and the abstract texts conceived in previous times; this is an experience which is common to the German, French, and Italian systems, for example in tort law;

(v) reality is often different from the original ideas to which the lawyer is attached: many lawyers praise the divergences among legal systems, but reality leads to convergence: the most astonishing example is offered by the recent reform of the Book of Obligations of the German Civil Code, which has been shaped in accordance with the 'Principles of European Contract Law' drafted by the Lando-Beale Commission;

(vi) comparative law is sometimes grounded in ideological prejudices: for example, Roman law is not considered as it should be (i.e. the changing body of rules of an extinct empire) and is not described from a historical perspective, taking into account all the modifications, misinterpretations, adjustments made by Canon law, medieval law, the German 'reception', amalgamation with customary law, national adaptations and so on. Rather it is sometimes considered as a modern and living legal system, complete with all the abstractions and dogmas which were the by-product of the geometrical Roman law system created by Pandectists;

(vii) the citation of foreign judgments is done by extracting the case law from its original context, without any consideration of the legal principles which underlie the solution achieved; and

(viii) by way of a broad conclusion, the quotation of foreign judgments cannot be classified as a comparative law experiment; judges are not required to write a treatise of doctrinal thought, but only a means of justifying the solution envisaged in search of a better conclusion to their task. When a satisfying solution cannot be found (mainly in 'hard cases') in domestic case law, it is wise to look at other experiences, and possibly to find the door to the right exit abroad.

PART III

COMPARATIVE LAW WITHIN A EUROPEAN AND INTERNATIONAL LAW CONTEXT

7

Common Ground

A Starting Point or Destination for Comparative-Law Analysis by the European Court of Human Rights?

Paul Mahoney and Rachael Kondak***

I. The comparative-law method as inherent in Convention law

It is argued in this chapter that the comparative-law method (the search for consensus or, rather, a trend) is an interpretative tool which is an inherent part of the European Convention on Human Rights ('the Convention') system of protection. Comparative references to national law, as well as international law standards, in the European Court of Human Right's case law have steadily increased over the last decade. The conclusion that can be drawn from looking at the recent case law of the Court is that references to comparative law are not haphazard and underdeveloped, but rather a well-established part of the Court's judicial analysis and figure consistently in its Grand Chamber, as well as chamber, judgments. This is a direct result of the development and expansion of the Court's Research Division, as well as the professionalization of the comparative-law research process.[1]

As we know, 'Convention law' is made up of the vaguely worded text of the Convention fleshed out by the accumulated case law giving more specific and concrete meaning to that text in given contexts. The changing corpus of law known as 'Convention law' did not magically come into being from thin air and does not exist in a vacuum: there is an organic relationship between 'Convention law' and domestic law, as well as other international law. Comparative law is thus not merely a useful interpretative tool to which the Court can choose to have recourse now and again if it so wishes; rather the comparative-law method is inherent in the application and development of the Convention. It helps to preserve the delicate balance in the

* United Kingdom Judge, European Court of Human Rights.

** Lawyer, Research Division of the European Court of Human Rights. This chapter is an updated version of Paul Mahoney, 'The Comparative Method in Judgments of the European Court of Human Rights: Reference Back to National Law' in Andenas, Canivet, and Fairgrieve (eds.), *Comparative Law Before the Courts* (British Institute of International and Comparative Law, 2004) 135–50. The 2004 chapter was written by Paul Mahoney. The research and the greater part of the drafting for this updated version have been done by Rachael Kondak.

[1] As has been noted by other commentators—such as Luzius Wildhaber, Arnaldur Hjartarson, and Stephen Donnelly, 'No Consensus on Consensus? The Practice of the European Court of Human Rights' (2013) 31 *HRLJ* 257. See, in particular, the extensive case law cited in this very comprehensive article.

relations between the Strasbourg Court and national legal systems.[2] The Convention naturally establishes a two-way bridge between national law and international law. In one direction flows the international obligation for the Contracting States to make their national legal orders compatible with specified common standards, and in the other direction the inspiration and continuing source of those standards which derive from fundamental principles already recognized under the domestic law of all democratic countries.[3]

The place of comparative law in the interpretative process of the Convention is all the more natural because of certain characteristics of the Convention as a regional human rights treaty. One of these characteristics is that the enforcement machinery set up under the Convention is subsidiary to the national systems of protection of human rights. This creates a natural, on-going link between national-law standards and the interpretation of the Convention. The principle of subsidiarity and its consequence, the jurisprudentially developed interpretative doctrine of the margin of appreciation, have been recently reinforced by the addition of a new recital at the end of the preamble to the Convention by Protocol No 15, which was opened for signature in June 2013:

> Affirming that the High Contracting Parties, in accordance with the principle of subsidiarity, have the primary responsibility to secure the rights and freedoms defined in this Convention and the Protocols thereto, and that in doing so they enjoy a margin of appreciation, subject to the supervisory jurisdiction of the European Court of Human Rights established by this Convention.

Thus, one reason why the Court follows national patterns is because the Convention converts into an international obligation observance of those fundamental rights which pre-exist in domestic legal systems founded on political democracy and the rule of law. The Contracting States, in the Brighton Declaration 2012, also gave particular emphasis to the importance, in the international adjudicative process, of looking to the domestic legal systems in the interpretation and application of the guaranteed rights, encouraging the prominence of the principles of subsidiarity and the margin of appreciation. Convincing and reliable interpretative techniques, such as the search for common European ground, brings as much objectivity to the exercise as possible and serve to justify any law-making accomplished by the Court when filling interpretative gaps left in the Convention law. The comparative-law process thereby adds legitimacy to the judgments of the Court. It is precisely stressing this point of legitimacy that one commentator commends the Court of Justice of the European Union for relying more obviously on comparative law in its judgments.[4] While judgments that can be traced to common traits on the legislative face of the Convention community of States at national level are more likely to enjoy a higher degree of legitimacy and to be accepted

[2] Dean Spielmann, 'Consensus et marge d'appréciation nationale', Journal des tribunaux, 131e année, no. 6489 (22 Sept. 2012), pp. 592–3.

[3] Mahoney, 'The Comparative Method' (n **) 1.

[4] Gráinne de Búrca, 'After the EU Charter of Fundamental Rights: The Court of Justice as a Human Rights Adjudicator?' (2013) Public Law & Legal Theory Research Paper Series Working Paper No 13–51 (New York University School of Law).

more easily,[5] conversely failure to take account of national legal and constitutional traditions can lead to difficulties over execution of the Court's judgments.[6]

Yet, the fact that the comparative-law method is inherent in the adjudication system set up under the Convention does not mean that it will always be decisive for the outcome of cases. Establishing that there exists a national-law 'consensus' in the Council of Europe Member States is but one of the adjudicative tools that may be prayed in aid by the Strasbourg Court's judges, generally by way of confirmation or corroboration of a result arrived at by the classic means of interpretation. The comparative-law method in the Convention system is therefore perhaps best seen as serving as an evidentiary accompaniment or supporting factor for other interpretative considerations that point to a given outcome in a case. The existence of common ground helps the Court to interpret Convention notions and to decide whether a State's margin of appreciation should be wide or narrow.[7] The consensus-result is still neither binding nor dispositive of the outcome, but is nowadays more openly recognized as one of the indicative or persuasive factors capable of justifying interpretative leaps forward.

II. What the Court means by 'consensus'

It may be useful here to try to identify what the Court means by 'consensus'. 'Consensus' is sometimes defined as general agreement (whether tacit or overt) among members of a group.[8] In the Strasbourg Court's discourse, identifying 'consensus' appears to mean something less, namely looking for a possible trend in legislative development or practice. 'Consensus' is not the exclusive term used by the Court, however.[9] We also find 'common ground',[10] 'common European approach',[11] 'continuing international trend',[12] 'clear trend',[13] or even 'evolving convergence'.[14] Is this what has led one commentator to express the view that 'the [European Court of Human Rights'] experience of over 30 years in hundreds of cases demonstrates that it is simply unable to articulate and apply a clear, predictable, and workable consensus standard'?[15]

The question could be asked whether a uniform term employed by the Court would lead to less confusion.

[5] Wildhaber, Hjartarson, and Donnelly (n 2) 251.

[6] See for example the current stalemate in the United Kingdom over the Court's judgments in *Hirst v United Kingdom (no 2)* [GC] (App no 74025/01) ECHR, 6 October 2005, and *Greens and M.T. v United Kingdom* (App nos 60041/08 and 60054/08) ECHR, 20 November 2010 (extracts).

[7] Wildhaber, Hjartarson, and Donnelly (n 2), 248–51, who describe 'consensus' as an adjunct of the doctrine of the margin of appreciation.

[8] 'The Role of Consensus in the System of the European Convention on Human Rights', *Dialogue between Judges—2008* (European Court of Human Rights, Council of Europe, 2008) 7.

[9] For an example of where the Court uses the term 'consensus', see *A, B and C v Ireland* [GC] (App no 25579/05), ECHR, 16 December 2010, § 235.

[10] *Sitaropoulos and Giakoumopoulos v Greece* [GC] (App no 42202/07), ECHR, 15 March 2012, § 66.

[11] *Hirst* (n 7).

[12] *Christine Goodwin v United Kingdom* [GC] (App no 28957/95), ECHR 2002-VI, § 84.

[13] *S.H. and Others v Austria* [GC] (App no 57813/00), ECHR, 3 November 2011, § 96.

[14] *Herrmann v Germany* [GC] (App no 9300/07) ECHR, 26 June 2012, § 78.

[15] Jeffrey A. Brauch, 'The Dangerous Search for an Elusive Consensus: What the Supreme Court Should Learn from the European Court of Human Rights' (2009) 52 How L.J. 277.

Sometimes, rarely, it is possible to speak of a general agreement reflected in the internal laws of the Contracting States. For example, it was quite clear that a near full consensus could be said to exist in *Fabris v France*[16] (for 40 countries out of the surveyed 42, a child's status for inheritance purposes was independent of the marital status of their parents) and in *Bayatyan v Armenia*[17] (almost all the Member States of the Council of Europe which ever had or still had compulsory military service had introduced alternatives to such service in order to reconcile the possible conflict between individual conscience and military obligations). Yet, mostly the Court is asked to assess trends. Indeed, the joint partly dissenting opinion of seven judges in *X and Others v Austria* (which concerned second-parent adoption by same-sex couples)[18] underlines the point that consensus is rarely encountered in real life, and that it would be more appropriate and simpler to speak in terms of a 'trend'. The fact that there is not one exclusive term used by the Court would imply that the Court is looking to find a trend rather than an agreement as such or an outright majority, and it is therefore in this sense of trend that the word 'consensus' will hereafter be used in this chapter.

III. Evolutive interpretation

Consensus is, in fact, the basis of the evolution of Convention standards, the basis of interpretations going beyond what may have been in the minds of the drafters of the Convention when they adopted the text. It goes without saying nowadays that the Convention is, to quote the early judgment in *Tyrer v United Kingdom*[19] from 1978, 'a living instrument which . . . must be interpreted in the light of the present-day conditions'. In that case the Court 'could not but be influenced by the developments and commonly accepted standards in the penal policy of the Member States of the Council of Europe in this field'. This does not mean, however, that the Court has a blank cheque to rewrite the terms and reach of the Convention as it feels right on the back of the living-instrument doctrine and the identification of a given trend in national or international law. The minority in *Feldbrugge v Netherlands* made a similar point some 30 years ago:

> An evolutive interpretation allows variable and changing concepts already contained in the Convention to be construed in the light of modern-day conditions . . . but it does not allow entirely new concepts or spheres of application to be introduced into the Convention: that is the legislative function that belongs to the Member States of the Council of Europe.[20]

It is argued in this chapter that the evolutive approach should accompany change and even channel it where the text of the Convention itself implicitly incorporates the

[16] [GC] (App no 16574/08) ECHR, 7 February 2013 (extracts), § 34.
[17] [GC] (App no 23459/03) ECHR, 7 July 2011, § 123.
[18] [GC] (App no 19010/07) ECHR, 19 February 2013.
[19] *Tyrer v United Kingdom* (App no 5856/72) (1978) Series A no 26, § 31.
[20] (App no 9907/02) (1986) Series A no 99.

possibility of change in the level of protection granted as attitudes in a democratic society evolve,[21] but should not anticipate or impose it.

In *S.H. and Others v Austria* the Court concluded that, while there was a clear trend in the legislation of Contracting States towards allowing gamete donation for the purpose of *in vitro* fertilization, it was not based on settled and long-standing principles, but 'rather reflects a stage of development within a particularly dynamic field of law and does not decisively narrow the margin of appreciation of the State'.[22] Even in relation to such inherently evolving concepts, the Court's role is not to 'predict tomorrow's values' or to act as a radically progressive leader imposing on the 47 Contracting States and their democratic institutions social or moral policies which it, the Court, considers would be good for society. The Court's role is rather to protect, develop, and where necessary update the concepts provided for in the Convention. In the case of *Schalk and Kopf v Austria*[23] the Court based itself on the wording of Article 12, noting that Article 12 only granted the right to marry to 'men and women' and contrasted that Article to others which referred to 'everyone' and or 'no one' and cited the 'historical context' as being important:

> Moreover, regard must be had to the historical context in which the Convention was adopted. In the 1950s marriage was clearly understood in the traditional sense of being a union between partners of different sex.

The identification of consensus or a trend provides empirical justificatory support for evolutive leaps forward in interpretation and for the 'disabling of democracy'. By this latter phrase is meant that the Court has the competence under the Convention not only to sanction, through its rulings, bad-faith abuses of public power by national authorities, but also to find a violation of human rights in the product of the normal functioning of the democratic processes at national level if it is satisfied that the individual has had to bear an excessive burden in favour of the collective interest or the competing interest of some other group in society. The comparative-law method serves the purpose of consolidating the legitimacy of the Court's judgments that evolve the variable level of protection beyond its previously recognized boundaries, thereby 'disabling' democracy at national level in this sense, since the result finds its origins in some way in national legal systems.

One can also see the comparative-law exercise as an illustration of the Court seeking to be better informed; and the better informed the Court is, the more likely its judgments are to be convincing for the national authorities and legal commentators, as well as acceptable to the general public. The Convention is where law and politics, law and social policy, law and practice, and even law and morals meet. The rulings

[21] See the dictum regarding international law to more or less the same effect in the judgment of the International Court of Justice in the *San Juan River* case: 'there are situations in which the parties' intent upon conclusion of the treaty was, or may be presumed to have been, to give the terms used—or some of them—a meaning or content capable of evolving, not one fixed once and for all, so as to make allowance for, among other things, developments in international law' (*Dispute regarding Navigational and Related Rights (Costa Rica v Nicaragua)*, ICJ Reports 2009 242, § 64).

[22] See (n 14) § 96.

[23] (App no 30141/04) ECHR, 24 June 2010, § 55.

given by the Court are not simply derived from orthodox legal reasoning of the kind applicable to black-letter law, but necessarily involve a dose of value-judgment. Hence the desirability, in the adjudicative process under the Convention, of relying on empirical and objective considerations such as identifiable trends in national or international legislation.

Should the Court be following national patterns, or rather leading the way and providing an example? Some commentators stress the constitutionalist function and identity of the Court and contend that the Court has a duty to set universal standards.[24] So, for example, on the issue of homosexual marriage, it is argued that the Court's reliance on the margin of appreciation in *Schalk and Kopf v Austria*[25] was not the correct answer and has left homosexuals in a vulnerable position.[26] This is because 'relying on the margin of appreciation, States are free to introduce their own legislation and decide on judicial supervision of such legislation, without the reasons behind their decisions having to be examined by the Court'.[27] However, not only is this line of reasoning misconceived in the present authors' view, but it could also endanger the rule of law by reason of the Court's arrogating to itself a legislative function and a role of 'moral leadership' that are not invested in it under the Convention.

Another issue arising in the context of evolution in the variable content of some concepts found in the Convention is whether the quest for consensus could result in contracting rights rather than expanding them (think of draconian anti-terrorist legislation or surveillance laws brought in following major terror threats or other national-security threats perceived by governments). Is it possible that, in following national trends, the Court's jurisprudence is pulled down from previous levels to a new lowest common denominator?[28] Judge Casadevall in his partly dissenting opinion in *Gorou v Greece (no. 2)*[29] argued that the principle of non-regression must prevail, on the basis that acquired rights in the field of human rights are at least equal to acquired rights in other branches of the law:

> In this connection I am reminded of the 'standstill' technique. Also known as the 'ratchet mechanism', preventing a cogwheel from turning back once it has moved forward, the principle has been developed, particularly in legal opinion, in connection mainly with acquired social rights. It is the principle whereby the legislature is supposed not to pass laws that would have the effect of lowering a level of social protection already achieved.

[24] Fiona de Londras and Kanstantsin Dzehtsiarou, 'Case-Note on A, B & C v Ireland' (2013) 62 International and Comparative Law Quarterly, 250–62. See also George Letsas, 'The Truth in Autonomous Concepts: How to Interpret the ECHR' (2004) EJIL 15, 279–305, especially at p. 305.

[25] See n 24.

[26] Frances Hamilton, 'Why the Margin of Appreciation is Not the Answer to the Gay Marriage Debate' (2013) 1 EHRLR 47.

[27] Ibid., p. 50.

[28] The possibility, or not, of downward evolution has been discussed by one of the present authors in: Paul Mahoney, 'Judicial Activism and Judicial Self-Restraint in the European Court of Human Rights: Two Sides of the Same Coin' (1990) 11 HRLJ 57.

[29] [GC] (App no 12686/03), ECHR, 20 March 2009.

Should the ratchet mechanism or the notion of acquired rights apply equally to rights under the Convention? For the present authors, it should not be ruled out as a matter of principle that, while in the nature of things the level of human rights protection overall will be rising in line with progress in democratic society, exceptional circumstances may bring about a shift in the balance between a particular individual interest protected by the Convention and the general interest of the community or a competing Convention interest of other members of the community. What is at stake is not therefore to be correctly described as always being a regression of an 'acquired' Convention right, but could conceivably be a shift, prompted by changed circumstances in society as demonstrated by a European 'consensus', towards the necessity for greater protection of the Convention rights of other members of the community. In other words the legitimate need to strike a different balance between conflicting or competing human rights, not a regression in human rights protection as such. However, any such fundamental shift, although theoretically possible, will in practice need to be established by especially compelling evidence, and any case law change involving a lowering in the hitherto, jurisprudentially recognized level of protection of a specific right is something that, being prima facie undesirable, the Court can be expected to undertake with extreme caution.[30]

IV. The Court's comparative-law inquiry

Identifying consensus or a trend involves a comparative-law survey, undertaken by the Court's Research Division, which analyses the law and practice at the heart of the case, to see how other Member States address the same issue. The reports are requested by the judge rapporteur in a given case if he or she considers that a comparative-law analysis would contribute to the judicial decision-making. Grand Chamber cases involve a survey of roughly 40 Member States, sometimes more, and chamber cases involve comparative-law analysis of 30 to 35 Member States' law and practice. The national contributions are provided either by lawyers within the Court's own Research Division, or case-processing lawyers from the other legal divisions. Each national contribution is sent to the national judge for approval before inclusion in the final report. The reports prepared by the Research Division contain the analysis and conclusions of the survey (between 20 and 30 pages) as well as a lengthy annex with each individual State's contribution. The reports are distributed to the judges in advance of the deliberations, but remain confidential documents.

The Research Division now counts 12 lawyers and three assistants. It is a non-case-processing division falling under the ultimate supervision of the Court's Jurisconsult. The Division has considerably grown in size and standing since its first creation in 2001. In 2013 it produced 59 reports, 29 on Convention case law, 16 on comparative law, and 14 on international law (including European Union law). This is in addition to the Guides on the Court's case law which the Division is currently preparing for external publication. Apart from the reports prepared at the request of Council of

30 *Dialogue between Judges*—2008 (n 9).

Europe departments, all of the research reports are confidential. The justification for this practice is the secrecy of the deliberations. Internal material prepared for the purposes of the deliberations are considered to be part of the deliberative process and therefore not to be revealed to the outside world.

The Court's research efforts have in the past been criticized as rudimentary, under-developed, ad hoc, and inconsistent. Often these criticisms are based on case law from the 1990s or the early 2000s.[31] It may be that some of the criticism is based on a misconception as to the purpose served by the comparative method. These commentators are perhaps expecting too much of consensus and trends in the decision-making process of the Court. Nonetheless, it is a valid question to be posed whether the Court has refined its consensus inquiry during the last decade. Undoubtedly it has. In 2014 we can no longer speak of 'suboptimal methodology'[32] or flimsy or even incorrect evidence.

There are a number of reasons for this. Firstly, because of the growth and professionalization of the Research Division itself and the increased desire of the judges to have recourse to comparative-law research reports within the judicial decision-making process. Secondly, because often the empirical results of the Court's own internal surveys may be double-checked against independent information put forward either by the parties, who are increasingly relying on comparative-law analysis, or in third-party briefs. Some examples are instructive. In the case of *Anayo v Germany*[33] the comparative-law survey undertaken by the Court looked at whether, and under what circumstances, a biological father has a right to contact with his child where a different father exists in law. These results were extensively compared with an expert report drawn up by the German Institute for Youth, Human Services and Family Law which had been submitted by the German Government. In *Hirst v United Kingdom (no 2)*[34] comparative law was provided by the British Government by way of its diplomatic representations. In *Stübing v Germany*[35] the Court's own comparative data was double-checked against a report prepared by the Max Planck Institute for Comparative Law from 2007. In the recent case of *Oleksandr Volkov v Ukraine*[36] the comparative-law material was based on a research report entitled 'Judicial Independence in Transition' prepared by the Max Planck Institute for Comparative Public Law and International Law. Finally, in *X and Others v Austria*[37] the Court's comparative study was checked against comparative information which the Council of Europe's Commissioner for Human Rights had gathered in a study entitled 'Discrimination on grounds of sexual orientation and gender identity in Europe'.

Third-party briefs commenting on comparative law have also steadily increased over the last decade.[38] A few examples may be cited. In the case of *Nikula v Finland*[39]

[31] For example footnotes 41–43 in Kanstantin Dzehtsiarou, 'Does Consensus Matter? Legitimacy of European Consensus in the Case-Law of the European Court of Human Rights' (July 2011) *Public Law*, 534–53, where the judgments quoted date from 1992, 1993, and 2000.

[32] *De Londras and Dzehtsiarou* (n 25), 251.

[33] (App no. 20578/07), ECHR, 21 December 2010, §§ 32–40.

[34] See n 7.

[35] (App no 43547/08) ECHR, 12 April 2012, § 61.

[36] (App no 21722/11) ECHR 2013, § 81.

[37] See n 19, § 55.

[38] See by way of one example the large number of third-party interveners, including governments, in *Lautsi and Others v Italy* [GC] (App no 30814/06), ECHR, 9 January 2011 (extracts).

[39] (App no 31611/96), ECHR 2002-II, §§ 22–6.

comparative data was provided by Interights on privilege granted to lawyers for statements they make while representing clients in court. In *S. and Marper v United Kingdom*[40] the interveners, Liberty and Privacy International, were relied upon by the Court in the comparative-law section of the judgment referring in particular to the compulsory taking of fingerprints and cellular samples in the context of criminal proceedings and the storing on national databases or in other forms. In *Al-Khawaja and Tahery v United Kingdom*[41] Justice provided comparative information on the status of the hearsay rule in other common-law jurisdictions. Where independent empirical evidence is produced by the third party, the Court's own research findings can be compared and contrasted and ultimately double-checked. The third-party interventions are also said to render the exercise of power of the Strasbourg Court more legitimate through dialogue with civil society.[42] On a practical level, they enrich the case-file and put the judges in a better position to make the assessment as to compliance of the contested measure with the Convention standards.

The rising frequency of references to comparative-law material in the Court's judgments might be seen as signalling that the Court itself is increasing its reliance on comparative-law material in its decision-making process; perhaps even that the evolutive approach is steadily gaining in importance, in spite of the fact that comparative-law considerations constitute only one element in a complex law-making process. The increasing attention attached to 'consensus' led to the organization by the Court of a judicial seminar on the topic in 2008, entitled 'The Role of Consensus in the Convention System'.[43]

V. Comparative-law material in the judgments of the Strasbourg Court

A useful starting point is to analyse the specific relationship between the comparative-law material (the results of the consensus survey) and the outcome in a given case. This is not, however, with a view to establishing any thesis to the effect that the existence or absence of consensus should be decisive—although, when a large degree of consensus exists, this can generally be taken to be an indicator that the national margin of appreciation will be considerably narrowed; and, conversely, where there is an absence of consensus, the margin of appreciation enjoyed by the national authorities will generally be correspondingly wide.[44]

Let us begin by looking at some examples of a broad consensus in order to see how the Court uses the comparative-law findings in its analysis. Firstly, there are judgments where the establishment of a broad consensus provides support for finding a violation

[40] [GC] (App nos 30562/04 and 30566/04), ECHR 2008, § 45.

[41] [GC] (App nos 26766/05 and 22228/06), ECHR 2011.

[42] See Nicola Burli, '*Amicus Curiae* as a Means to Reinforce the Legitimacy of the European Court of Human Rights', in Tom Zwart et al. (eds.), *The European Court of Human Rights and its Discontents* (Edward Elgar, 2013) 135–46.

[43] *Dialogue between judges*—2008 (n 9).

[44] See Luzius Wildhaber, 'La place et l'avenir de la Convention europeene des droits de l'homme', speech delivered in Istanbul on 19 May 2004.

on the part of a respondent State that is out of line with its peers (this group of cases will be referred to as category 'A').

In *Stanev v Bulgaria*[45] the applicant complained about his placement in a social care home for people with mental disorders and his inability to obtain permission to leave the home. A comparative study of the domestic law of 20 Council of Europe Member States disclosed that in the vast majority of cases the law entitles individuals deprived of legal capacity to apply directly to the courts for discontinuation of the measure. These results were discussed under the Court's analysis of the applicant's Article 6 complaint:

> 18 of the 20 national legal systems studied in this context provide for direct access to the courts for any partially incapacitated persons wishing to have their status reviewed. In 17 States such access is open even to those declared fully incapable. This indicates that there is now a trend at European level towards granting legally incapacitated persons direct access to the courts to seek restoration of their capacity.
>
> . . .
>
> In the light of the foregoing, in particular the trends emerging in national legislation and the relevant international instruments, the Court considers that Article 6 § 1 of the Convention must be interpreted as guaranteeing in principle that anyone who has been declared partially incapable . . . has direct access to a court to seek restoration of his or her legal capacity.[46]

Here the comparative-law findings, coupled with the international-law instruments, can clearly be seen to have provided strong argument ('must be interpreted') for the Court's ruling on access to court.

In *Konstantin Markin v Russia* the applicant serviceman complained of the domestic authorities' refusal to grant him parental leave because he, unlike a servicewoman, had no statutory entitlement to three years' parental leave. The result of the Court's comparative-law research[47] was analysed under the Court's examination of the applicant's complaint under Article 14 taken in conjunction with Article 8:

> The relevant international- and comparative-law material demonstrates that the evolution of society—which began in the 1980s as acknowledged in the *Petrovic* case—has since significantly advanced. It shows that in a majority of European countries, including in Russia itself, the legislation now provides that parental leave may be taken by civilian men and women, while the countries limiting the parental leave entitlement to women are in a small minority. Even more important for the present case is the fact that in a significant number of the member States both servicemen and servicewomen are also entitled to parental leave. It follows from the above that contemporary European societies have moved towards a more equal sharing between men and women of responsibility for the upbringing of their children and that men's caring role has gained recognition. The Court cannot overlook the widespread and consistently developing views and associated legal changes to the domestic laws of Contracting States concerning this issue.[48]

[45] [GC] (App no 36760/06), ECHR 2012. [46] Ibid., §§ 243–5.
[47] Set out in some detail in §§ 71–75 of the judgment (see following footnote).
[48] [GC] App no 30078/06, § 140, ECHR 2012 (extracts).

Here, the Court used not merely the comparative-law findings in the instant case, but also those in a previous judgment considerably earlier[49] to show, as an empirical fact, a development towards a more equal sharing between men and women of responsibility for the upbringing of children. Unable to overlook these widespread and developing views in domestic law, the Court factored in these findings to its legal assessment of the contested measure, so as to hold that there had been discriminatory treatment in violation of Article 14 taken in conjunction with Article 8. It is interesting to mention the partly concurring, partly dissenting opinion of Judge Pinto de Albuquerque, who uses the comparative-law material to expand the State's obligation under Article 8. Concurring with the majority conclusion on Article 14 in conjunction with Article 8, Judge Pinto de Albuquerque derives a positive obligation for the Contracting Parties to the Convention to provide for a legal system of parental leave, drawing on *inter alia* the comparative-law findings:

> As a result of this wide international consensus in European and universal human rights law and international labour law, the approach taken by the Court in the case of *Petrovic v. Austria* is manifestly outdated. The basic argument presented at that time, according to which the majority of member States of the Council of Europe did not provide for parental leave for fathers, does not correspond to the reality any more today. But coherence demands that conclusions must be drawn from this new consensus. If it is correct to conclude that no reason remains for a distinction on the basis of sex with respect to parental leave, it is all the more to be concluded that the right to parental leave itself is now understood by almost all member States of the Council of Europe and the international community in general as an integral part and a constitutive element of the legal protection of the family and the parent-child relationship.[50]

The final example in this first category is the recent case of *Fabris v France*.[51] The applicant, a child born outside wedlock, alleged that he had suffered discrimination on grounds of birth in relation to the division of his mother's estate. The comparative-law material disclosed that in the great majority of the countries studied (40 States out of 42) a child's status for inheritance purposes was independent of the marital status of their parents.[52] Looking at the case law principles under Article 14 taken in conjunction with Article 1 of Protocol No 1, the Court leant on the comparative-law findings in order to narrow the national margin of appreciation as to making a possible distinction on the grounds of birth outside marriage:

> [C]ommon ground between the member States of the Council of Europe regarding the importance of equal treatment of children born within and children born outside marriage has been established for a long time, which has, moreover, led to a uniform approach today by the national legislatures on the subject—the principle of equality

[49] *Petrovic v Austria* (App no 20458/92) *Reports of Judgments and Decisions* 1998-II.

[50] While such resort to the comparative method might be taxed as straying into the realms of expanding the Convention rights into a wholly new area and, what is more, as involving a positive obligation on all the Contracting States to spend public money in a specific way, it should be stressed that this is an isolated minority view only.

[51] See n 17. [52] Ibid., § 34.

> eliminating the very concepts of legitimate children and children born outside marriage—and to social and legal developments definitively endorsing the objective of achieving equality between children...
>
> Accordingly, very weighty reasons have to be advanced before a distinction on grounds of birth outside marriage can be regarded as compatible with the Convention.[53]

In these category 'A' cases, consensus—in the sense of a trend—provides support for finding a violation by reason of there being a narrower range of choices available to the democratic decision-maker at the national level.

Moving from those judgments where the establishment of a broad trend provides support for finding a violation, we may turn to judgments where, although a broad trend exists, the final conclusion of the legal analysis is nonetheless one of no violation (we shall call these category 'B' cases). In these cases, consensus on its own, or in conjunction with other relevant factors, is not sufficient to find a violation: but why?

In *A, B and C v Ireland*[54] the first two applicants complained under Article 8 about, *inter alia*, the prohibition of abortion for health and well-being reasons in Ireland and the third applicant's main complaint concerned the alleged failure in practice to implement the constitutional right to an abortion in the case of a risk to the life of the woman. The findings of the comparative-law survey were clear and showed a broad trend permitting abortion on health grounds.[55] Nevertheless, and rather exceptionally, the Grand Chamber held that the broad trend did not decisively narrow the Irish Government's margin of appreciation:

> In the present case, and contrary to the Government's submission, the Court considers that there is indeed a consensus amongst a substantial majority of the Contracting States of the Council of Europe towards allowing abortion on broader grounds than accorded under Irish law. In particular, the Court notes that the first and second applicants could have obtained an abortion on request (according to certain criteria including gestational limits) in some 30 such States. The first applicant could have obtained an abortion justified on health and well-being grounds in approximately 40 Contracting States and the second applicant could have obtained an abortion justified on well-being grounds in some 35 Contracting States. Only three States have more restrictive access to abortion services than in Ireland namely, a prohibition on abortion regardless of the risk to the woman's life. Certain States have in recent years extended the grounds on which abortion can be obtained... Ireland is the only State which allows abortion solely where there is a risk to the life (including self-destruction) of the expectant mother. Given this consensus amongst a substantial majority of the Contracting States, it is not necessary to look further to international trends and views which the first two applicants and certain of the third parties argued also leant in favour of broader access to abortion.
>
> However, the Court does not consider that this consensus decisively narrows the broad margin of appreciation of the State.[56]

[53] See ibid., §§ 58–9. [54] See n 10. [55] Ibid., § 112. [56] Ibid., §§ 235–6.

Basing its reasoning on 'the profound moral views of the Irish people as to the nature of life' and the 'lengthy, complex and sensitive debate in Ireland', the Grand Chamber held that there had been no violation of Article 8 in relation to the first two applicants. Some commentators see the Court's reasoning as prioritizing an alleged internal consensus within one Member State over a European consensus.[57] According to the five partly dissenting judges:

> it is the first time that the Court has disregarded the existence of a European consensus on the basis of 'profound moral views'. Even assuming that these profound moral views are still well embedded in the conscience of the majority of Irish people, to consider that this can override the European consensus, which tends in a completely different direction, is a real and dangerous new departure in the Court's case-law. A case-law which to date has not distinguished between moral and other beliefs when determining the margin of appreciation which can be afforded to States in situations where a European consensus is at hand.

Does the Grand Chamber judgment in *A, B and C v Ireland* represent an abdication by the Court of its judicial responsibilities, as some critics maintain? In regard to intractable, philosophical issues of society such as abortion, which are by their very nature hardly susceptible of uniform legal regulation throughout a culturally diverse community of 47 States and in relation to which it cannot be maintained that the text of the Convention makes any clear provision, we should perhaps ask whether a country's cultural values, attitudes to morals, and constitutional traditions may not also have some relevance for situating the breadth or narrowness of the margin of appreciation? Democracy also implies diversity as well as commitment to protecting shared human rights; and as a corollary, the Strasbourg Court's mission of protecting shared human rights does not mean imposing centralized uniformity across the whole European 'legal space' in which a given human right deploys its effect. This view would appear to differ from the theory of the 'harmonizing' role of the Convention's case law as expounded by the partly dissenting judges. According to that theory, one of the paramount functions of the case law is to progressively create a harmonious application of human rights protection, cutting across national boundaries. Limits on this harmonizing role, say the minority, do exist; they come into play, notably, in contexts where European States differ considerably in the way that they protect individuals against the conduct by the State, and where no consensus exists. Hence, in non-consensus circumstances 'the Court refrains from playing its harmonising role, preferring not to become the first European body to "legislate" on a matter still undecided at European level'. The partly dissenting judges contest the judgment in *A, B and C v Ireland* precisely because the Court refrains from its harmonizing role in relation to very sensitive abortion issues even when a 'consensus' does exist.

However, the evident harmonizing function of the Court's jurisprudence should not, by sleight of interpretative hand, be metamorphosed into a steamroller which uniforms all before its path as soon as anything approaching a trend in a given direction can be identified. It is doubtless too simplistic to rely on a trend in national legislations so as to

[57] *De Londras and Dzehsiarou* (n 25), 250–62.

put an isolated country in violation of the Convention. It is well established in the Court's case law that democracy does not mean dictatorship of the majority as regards the enjoyment of human rights by individuals; neither should it mean dictatorship of the majority for the 47 culturally diverse States making up the Convention community of countries. Where the subject-matter is inherently one for each democratic society to decide according to proper democratic processes, a simple headcount of national legislations should surely not have the decisive consequence of removing democratic freedom of choice for those few States that prefer a different route. It is conceivable that in a given domain the margin of appreciation is per se extremely wide or wide enough to allow one or two States, acting in accordance with democratic processes and with the social and legal traditions of their society, to choose a different manner of implementing and regulating the exercise of the human right in question—different from that of the majority of the other States. The margin is also likely to be wider when it is a question of having to arbitrate between two human rights that are in conflict. European consensus will be one, perhaps influential, factor along with others, but not necessarily the sole or determining factor.

In this sense, the Grand Chamber's judgment in *A, B and C v Ireland* is not necessarily as worrying as some commentators may say.[58] This is so if one takes a 'democratic' approach to international human rights protection—that is to say, recognizing the liberty, as far as possible, for political democracies to choose their own lifestyle for their own people, and even to experiment, in relation to matters where no universal solution is imposed by the relevant human rights treaty, provided of course that the applicable human rights values embodied in the treaty are respected. The problem for the Strasbourg Court is to work out whether or not the contested measure falls within the democratic discretion of the Member State.

Where else does the Court find a consensus and yet conclude that the said consensus is not sufficient on its own to find a violation?

In *S.H. and Others v Austria* a consensus was found to exist but it was too 'fresh' to be relied upon; and, given that the particular area gave rise to sensitive moral and ethical issues, the margin of appreciation was held to remain wide:

> The Court would conclude that there is now a clear trend in the legislation of the Contracting States towards allowing gamete donation for the purpose of in vitro fertilisation, which reflects an emerging European consensus. That emerging consensus is not, however, based on settled and long-standing principles established in the law of the Member States but rather reflects a stage of development within a particularly dynamic field of law and does not decisively narrow the margin of appreciation of the State.[59]

[58] See *de Londras and Dzehtsiarou* (n 25); see also Bilyana Petkova, 'The Notion of Consensus as a Route to Democratic Adjudication' (2011–12) 14 Cambridge Yearbook of European Legal Studies, 663–95.

[59] See n 14, §§ 96–7. See also *Chapman v United Kingdom* [GC] (App no 27238/95) ECHR 2001-1, §§ 83–93: 'there may be said to be an emerging international consensus amongst the Contracting States of the Council of Europe recognising the special needs of minorities and an obligation to protect their security, identity and lifestyle (see…in particular the Framework Convention for the Protection of National Minorities), not only for the purpose of safeguarding the interest of the minorities themselves but to preserve a cultural diversity of value to the whole community. However, the Court is not persuaded that the

In *Sitaropoulos and Giakoumopoulos v Greece* the applicants, officials of the Council of Europe, alleged that their inability to vote from Strasbourg amounted to a disproportionate interference with the exercise of their right to vote in Greek parliamentary elections enshrined in Article 3 of Protocol No 1. The comparative material before the Grand Chamber revealed that out of 45 surveyed Member States, 37 allowed for voting from abroad (on the basis of a variety of arrangements) and eight did not. This data would appear to show a clear trend in favour of allowing voting from abroad, yet the Grand Chamber focused not so much on the numbers of Member States involved, but rather on the variety of different arrangements in place:

> In short, none of the legal instruments examined above forms a basis for concluding that, as the law currently stands, States are under an obligation to enable citizens living abroad to exercise the right to vote. As to the arrangements for exercising that right put in place by those Council of Europe Member States that allow voting from abroad, there is currently a wide variety of approaches.[60]

In our third category of cases (category 'C' cases), the comparative-law material shows a lack of consensus providing support for finding no violation. Many examples exist of these type of cases, and in a sense they are the corollary of category 'A' cases (where consensus may be taken as indicative of a narrowed margin of appreciation). Here the establishment of no European common ground is indicative of a broad margin of appreciation; the Member State has not stepped out of line because there is no clear line.

In the case of *Evans v United Kingdom*[61] the applicant complained that domestic law permitted her former partner effectively to withdraw his consent to the storage and use by her of embryos created jointly by them. The Grand Chamber considered that since the use of IVF treatment gave rise to sensitive moral and ethical issues against a background of fast-moving medical and scientific developments, and since the questions raised by the case touched on areas where there is no clear common ground amongst Member States, the margin of appreciation was accordingly to be a wide one. The relationship between no European common ground and a wide margin of appreciation was further underlined in the following cases: *Shavdarov v Bulgaria*,[62] a case concerning an applicant who believed he was the biological father of a child and wished to challenge the child's paternity; *Lautsi and Others v Italy*,[63] where the applicant mother complained about the presence of crucifixes in the State-school classroom of her children; *Scoppola v Italy (no 3)*,[64] a case which concerned voting rights of prisoners; *Van der Heijden v Netherlands*,[65] a case concerning the compellability of witnesses; and *Harroudj v France*,[66] where the applicant wished to adopt a child of Algerian nationality, who had been placed in her *kafala* care. In these cases the Court relied on

consensus is sufficiently concrete for it to derive any guidance as to the conduct or standards which Contracting States consider desirable in any particular situation.'

[60] See n 11, § 74. [61] [GC] (App no 6339/05) ECHR 2007-I, §§ 77–81, 92.
[62] (App no 3465/03) ECHR, 21 December 2010, §§ 46–48. [63] See n 39.
[64] [GC] (App no 126/05) ECHR, 22 May 2012, §§ 101–102.
[65] [GC] (App no 42857/05) ECHR, 3 April 2012, § 61.
[66] (App no 43631/09) ECHR, 4 October 2012, § 48.

the comparative data showing no conclusive European position on the subject at hand as one of the factors for holding that the margin of appreciation available to the Member State in the particular context was wide. In the majority of cases, an analysis of the specific facts of the case led to a conclusion of no violation.

However, this is not always so. Occasionally, despite no European consensus, and a wide margin of appreciation, the result may be a finding of a violation. This rather small category of cases—category 'D'—is well illustrated by *Hirst v United Kingdom (no 2)*:

> As regards the existence or not of any consensus among Contracting States, the Court notes that, although there is some disagreement about the legal position in certain States, it is undisputed that the United Kingdom is not alone among Convention countries in depriving all convicted prisoners of the right to vote. It may also be said that the law in the United Kingdom is less far-reaching than in certain other States. Not only are exceptions made for persons committed to prison for contempt of court or for default in paying fines, but unlike the position in some countries, the legal incapacity to vote is removed as soon as the person ceases to be detained. However, the fact remains that it is a minority of Contracting States in which a blanket restriction on the right of convicted prisoners to vote is imposed or in which there is no provision allowing prisoners to vote. Even according to the Government's own figures, the number of such States does not exceed 13. Moreover, and even if no common European approach to the problem can be discerned, this cannot in itself be determinative of the issue.[67]

Lack of consensus is indicative of a wide margin of appreciation, but only goes so far: there remains the further question whether, on the facts, the respondent State exceeded the admittedly wide margin of appreciation in adopting the contested measure. In the instant case, the Grand Chamber considered that the contested electoral legislation was a blunt instrument and stripped prisoners of their Convention right to vote in an indiscriminate way. As a result, a violation of Article 3 of Protocol No 1 was held to have occurred. Is it harder for the Member State, and the public at large, to accept the finding of a violation where no European consensus exists? The example of *Hirst (no 2)* shows that this is the case.

The use of the comparative data may, notably in relation to complaints of discrimination (under Article 14), be complicated by the precise manner in which the Court frames the Convention issue to be determined and by the sets of data that are compared. A few examples of cases where no conclusion could be drawn from the results of the comparative data demonstrate this phenomenon.

In *X and Others v Austria* the applicants alleged that they had been discriminated against in comparison with different-sex couples, as second-parent adoption was legally impossible for them. The comparative data, provided by a Court survey and double-checked by the results of an independent study prepared by the Council of Europe's Commissioner for Human Rights, was ultimately found inconclusive despite the research covering 39 Council of Europe Member States:

[67] See n 7, § 81.

> Furthermore, and solely in order to respond to the Government's assertion that no European consensus exists, it has to be borne in mind that the issue before the Court is not the general question of same-sex couples' access to second-parent adoption, but the difference in treatment between unmarried different-sex couples and same-sex couples in respect of this type of adoption . . . Consequently, only those ten Council of Europe Member States which allow second-parent adoption in unmarried couples may be regarded as a basis for comparison. Within that group, six States treat heterosexual couples and same-sex couples in the same manner, while four adopt the same position as Austria . . . The Court considers that the narrowness of this sample is such that no conclusions can be drawn as to the existence of a possible consensus among Council of Europe member States.[68]

The case of *Stübing v Germany* also shows that comparative data can be interpreted differently according to which precise group or sub-group is being compared:

> Applying the principles set out above to the instant case, the Court observes that there is no consensus between the Member States as to whether the consensual commitment of sexual acts between adult siblings should be criminally sanctioned . . . Still, a majority of altogether 24 out of the 44 States reviewed provide for criminal liability. The Court further notes that all the legal systems, including those which do not impose criminal liability, prohibit siblings from getting married. Thus, a broad consensus transpires that sexual relationships between siblings are neither accepted by the legal order nor by society as a whole. Conversely, there is no sufficient empirical support for the assumption of a general trend towards a decriminalisation of such acts. The Court further considers that the instant case concerns a question about the requirements of morals. It follows from the above principles that the domestic authorities enjoy a wide margin of appreciation in determining how to confront incestuous relationships between consenting adults, notwithstanding the fact that this decision concerns an intimate aspect of an individual's private life.[69]

In the case of *Van der Heijden v Netherlands*[70] there was a difference of approach between the judges as to the comparative-law findings. For the majority, the data evidenced 'the wide variety of practices among Council of Europe Member States relating to the compellability of witnesses'; whereas the dissenting minority took the results rather to favour finding a common ground. Again, the difference turns on the precise question being asked and the groups being compared. Thus, according to the joint dissenting opinion of five judges:

> In order to ascertain whether this interference was necessary in a democratic society, the majority begin by referring to the lack of common ground, which, although 'not in itself decisive . . . militates in favour of a wide margin of appreciation' . . . thus rendering any other argument superfluous. As Judges Casadevall and López Guerra have also observed, a more precise analysis of the comparative-law material presented by the Court concerning testimonial privilege in the Member States of the Council of Europe shows that, on the contrary, there is indeed common ground in this area, that is to say, that a majority of States would de facto have exempted the applicant from testifying in such a case . . . This

[68] See n 19. [69] See n 36, § 61. [70] See n 66.

observation confirms, once again, the relative nature of the Court's approach to the existence of a consensus and, more generally, raises the question whether it should not be 'disentangled' from the margin of appreciation in certain types of cases.

Sometimes it turns out not to be necessary for the Court to have recourse to the comparative-law data in its reasoning. In *Ahmet Yıldırım v Turkey*[71] the Court was asked to look into the blocking of the applicant's private internet site. Article 10 (freedom of expression) was held to have been breached on the basis that the domestic law did not provide for adequate safeguards to ensure that a blocking order in respect of a specific site was not used as a means of blocking access in general. This being so, the restrictive measure could not be regarded as having been 'prescribed by law', within the meaning of paragraph 2 of Article 10, with the consequence that the Court did not have to go on to examine whether the other requirement of 'necessity in a democratic society', as laid down in that paragraph, had been met. No cause for having recourse to the comparative-law material, which was nonetheless set out extensively in the judgment, therefore arose in the particular case.

VI. Comparative jurisprudence from non-Council of Europe Member States

The Court not only looks at domestic comparative law from Council of Europe Member States in its quest for finding the existence or not of elusive common ground. It also increasingly draws upon legal material from democratic non-Council of Europe States, such as the United States of America, Canada, and South Africa. It looks into this material to discover the possibility of evidence of an international trend relevant for the interpretation of the Convention standards.

In *Al-Khawaja and Tahery v United Kingdom*[72] the Grand Chamber set out in some detail the relevant case law of common-law courts from Australia, Canada, South Africa, Hong Kong, and the United States on the issue of hearsay rules. This was done partly in order to be able to deal with the arguments raised by the United Kingdom's Supreme Court in *R v Horncastle and Others*,[73] as well those raised by the third-party intervener, Justice, who questioned the Supreme Court's conclusions on the comparative material. In *Scoppola v Italy (no 3)*[74] the Grand Chamber examined the issue of prisoners' voting rights as seen by the South African Constitutional Court, the Australian High Court, and the Canadian Supreme Court. In *Vinter and Others v United Kingdom*[75] examples of prohibitions on grossly disproportionate sentences were given from the jurisprudence of Canada, Hong Kong, Mauritius, Namibia, New Zealand, South Africa, and the United States. Is there, it has been asked, an ever-increasing group of jurisdictions upon which the Court will rely?[76] In

[71] (App no 3111/10) ECHR, 18 December 2012. [72] See n 42.

[73] [2009] UKSC 14 (9 December 2009). [74] See n 65.

[75] [GC] App nos. 66069/09, 130/10 and 3896/10, ECHR 2013 (extracts).

[76] Christopher McCrudden, 'Using Comparative Reasoning in Human Rights Adjudication: The Court of Justice of the European Union and the European Court of Human Rights Compared' (2013) 15(1) Cambridge Yearbook of European Legal Studies, 383–415 (33).

the present authors' view, there must be limits on the extent to which case law and legislation from non-Member States can be of help to the Court in Strasbourg.

VII. International-law consensus

The comparative method as applied to sources of international law was not the focus of the previous chapter in 2004.[77] However, in much the same way as the last decade has seen a steady increase in references to comparative domestic law, examples of international-law standards are also an increasing reality in the Strasbourg case law. When it considers the object and purpose of the Convention provisions, the Court also takes into account the international-law background to the legal question before it. Being made up of a set of rules and principles that are accepted by the vast majority of States, the common international or domestic law standards of European States reflect a reality that the Court cannot disregard when it is called upon to clarify the scope of a Convention provision.[78] The Court's approach to international-law standards was set out at some length in the case of *Demir and Baykara v Turkey* where it concluded:

> The Court, in defining the meaning of terms and notions in the text of the Convention, can and must take into account elements of international law other than the Convention, the interpretation of such elements by competent organs, and the practice of European States reflecting their common values. The consensus emerging from specialised international instruments and from the practice of Contracting States may constitute a relevant consideration for the Court when it interprets the provisions of the Convention in specific cases.
>
> In this context, it is not necessary for the respondent State to have ratified the entire collection of instruments that are applicable in respect of the precise subject-matter of the case concerned. It will be sufficient for the Court that the relevant international instruments denote a continuous evolution in the norms and principles applied in international law or in the domestic law of the majority of Member States of the Council of Europe and show, in a precise area, that there is common ground in modern societies.[79]

International treaties may thus be taken as a sign of existing consensus—or lack of consensus, as in *Sitaropoulos and Giakoumopoulos v Greece*,[80] where the Grand Chamber found no international consensus on the issue of voting rights of nationals abroad.

Again, sometimes the intervening third parties may draw the Court's attention to international standards in a given area. One recent example is the case of *Bayatyan v Armenia*,[81] which dealt with conscientious objection of a Jehovah's Witness. The intervening non-governmental organizations provided a general overview of the gradual recognition of the right to conscientious objection at international and regional levels. On the international level, they focused in particular on the developments in the jurisprudence of the United Nations Human Rights Committee and its interpretation

[77] See n **. [78] *Demir and Baykara v Turkey* [GC] (App no 34503/97), ECHR 2008, § 76.
[79] Ibid., §§ 85–6. [80] See n 11. [81] See n 18, § 102.

of the counterpart provisions of the International Covenant on Civil and Political Rights, notably its General Comment no 22. They referred to the developments before other United Nations bodies, such as the United Nations Commission on Human Rights and the Working Group on Arbitrary Detention. At the regional level, the intervening organizations referred to the developments before the Council of Europe bodies, notably their recommendations urging recognition and greater protection of the right to conscientious objection. They also pointed out that the right to conscientious objection had been explicitly recognized by Article 10 of the Charter of Fundamental Rights of the European Union and by Article 12 of the Ibero-American Convention on Young People's Rights. They also relied on the Inter-American Commission on Human Rights. In its reasoning, the Grand Chamber drew upon these standards to justify its change in stance from the previous case law of the Commission and dealt with the complaint under Article 9 (religious freedom) alone and not in conjunction with Article 4 § 3(b) (prohibition of forced or compulsory labour). The Grand Chamber concluded that, given the overwhelming European and international consensus on the issue, the respondent State's margin of appreciation was limited, so that convincing and compelling reasons would have to be advanced to justify any interference with the guaranteed freedom. In the circumstances of the case, the respondent State was not able to do so and the Court, by a majority of 16 to 1, found a violation of Article 9.

Examples abound of references to international standards in the Court's jurisprudence. In *Rantsev v Cyprus and Russia*,[82] the Court referred to standards on slavery and trafficking of human beings as elaborated by the European Union, the United Nations, and case law from the International Criminal Tribunal for the Former Yugoslavia. Council of Europe Conventions have also been relied upon—for example, in the very recent judgment of the Grand Chamber in *Söderman v Sweden*,[83] where the Court cited the Convention on the Protection of Children against Sexual Exploitation and Sexual Abuse, drafted in October 2007. International instruments in specialized areas such as trade union freedom, data protection, and bioethics are relevant in so far as such texts may be regarded as sub-legislation regulating the specific aspects of the more general human rights set forth in the Convention.

In a number of judgments the Court has also used, for the purpose of interpreting the Convention, intrinsically non-binding instruments of Council of Europe bodies, in particular recommendations and resolutions of the Committee of Ministers and the Parliamentary Assembly.[84] In order to trace the exact scope of the rights and freedoms guaranteed by the Convention, the Court has also, for example, made use of the work of the European Committee of Social Rights,[85] the European Commission for Democracy through Law ('the Venice Commission'),[86] the European Commission against Racism and Intolerance,[87] the reports of the European Committee for the Prevention of

[82] (App no 25965/04), ECHR 2010 (extracts).
[83] [GC] (App no 5786/08) ECHR, 12 November 2013.
[84] *Demir and Baykara* (n 79).
[85] See *Stummer v Austria* [GC] (App no 37452/02) ECHR 2011, § 59.
[86] See *Sitaropoulos and Giakoumopoulos* (n 11).
[87] See *D.H. and Others v the Czech Republic* [GC] (App no 57325/00) ECHR 2007-IV, § 59.

Torture and Inhuman or Degrading Treatment or Punishment,[88] and the Council of Europe Commissioner for Human Rights.[89]

VIII. Conclusion

The conclusion of the first edition of this chapter in 2004 was that the comparative method was an interpretative tool that was inherent in the logic of the Convention. This has been confirmed by subsequent developments in judicial practice. However, what one might call the 'technical' aspect of the recourse to the comparative method by the Strasbourg Court in its reasoning has become more professionalized. Consequently, the use of objective, empirical comparative material (as one factor contributing to deciding the case one way or the other) has become more reliable; and the picture of what is going on in the judicial decision-making process is clearer. We now can speak of 'analysis' of comparative-law data in the case law of the Strasbourg Court. In practically every Grand Chamber case the Court will receive a lengthy research report, and sometimes three reports on comparative law, Convention law, and international law, covering most, but not all, of the 47 Contracting States. The theoretically influential role has come a long way since 2004 and is now an institutional reality.

Some commentators call for more transparency in the process, such as the Court's clearly acknowledging the sources of its comparative-law data, which, they say, would strengthen the legitimacy of its judgments.[90] In their view, a more transparent comparative-law process could counter criticisms that in choosing certain Member States and not others for its comparative analysis, the Court is 'cherry-picking'.[91] Or they argue that the adversarial nature of the proceedings would be enhanced by allowing the parties to see the comparative-law reports on which the Court itself relies.

Yet, is the result of the increasing use of comparative-law material that these considerations have taken on, or will take on, more weight in the complex judicial decision-making process? Has the Court's enquiry as to the existence or not of consensus acquired increasing importance in that process?[92] Does the Court, as the widely visible and indefatigable 'human rights locomotive',[93] continue to gain speed along its journey to universal European consensus or should the brakes be applied?

One should be wary about generalizing in answering such questions. Each case must still be analysed on its facts to determine the precise weight of influence of the comparative-law method in the actual decision-making. Patterns as to the incidence of the existence or absence of a 'consensus' can be found, as our analysis of the four categories of cases has shown, but it is still difficult to find watertight groups, and exceptions exist in every category. Thus, the President of the Court has written that

[88] See *Babar Ahmad and Others v United Kingdom* (App nos 24027/07, 11949/08, 36742/08, 66911/09 and 67354/09) ECHR, 10 April 2012, § 116.

[89] See *Rantsev v Cyprus and Russia* (n 83).

[90] See Kanstantin Dzehtsiarou and Vasily Lukashevich, 'Informed Decision-Making: The Comparative Endeavours of the Strasbourg Court' (2012) 3013 Netherlands Quarterly of Human Rights, 272–98.

[91] Ibid., quoting US Supreme Court Judge Scalia in *Roper v Simmons* (2005) 543 US 551, 125 S Ct 1183, 617, where he stated that 'all the Court has done today, to borrow from another context, is to look over the heads of the crowd and pick out its friends'.

[92] Brauch (n 16).

[93] Wildhaber, Hjartarson, and Donnelly (n 2).

while State practice (legislation, case law, administrative practice) may help to indicate consensus, absence of consensus (in the sense of absence of a common legal approach at national level) may have a variety of reasons, political as well as social, which do not necessarily prevent the Court from finding a relevant general trend as evidenced, for example, by international instruments.[94] Some topics and Convention Articles lend themselves more easily to the comparative-law approach, especially societal questions such as those raised under Article 8.[95] For other Articles of the Convention, such as Article 6, comparing domestic criminal or civil law systems proves difficult and sometimes futile.

Despite the advances over the last ten years or so, a good number of questions remain open to debate as concerns the role of the comparative method in the decision-making process of the Strasbourg Court, having regard to the way that the comparative method is employed in the Strasbourg case law to search for 'consensus' (or, more accurately, common ground or a trend)—notably as concerns the influence of comparative-law analysis on the 'living-instrument' doctrine, on the identification of positive obligations requiring public expenditure and, thus, on the Court's power to impose new, especially financial, obligations on the democratic organs of the Contracting States. It is our view that the European Convention on Human Rights and its international control mechanism are not about centralized uniformity and should not wholly take away the democratic discretion for political democracies to choose different routes. Rather the Convention allows diversity, even in relation to the enjoyment of Convention rights. The difficulty, of course, is where to draw the line between legitimate democratic discretion at national level and non-respect of a universal standard. The comparative method and the search for consensus, as an adjudicative tool, can help the Court in this task, without being able to provide the answer alone.

[94] Dean Spielmann, 'Allowing the Right Margin. The European Court of Human Rights and the National Margin of Appreciation Doctrine: Waiver or Subsidiarity of European Review?' (2011–2012) 14 Cambridge Yearbook of European Legal Studies, 381–418—citing, in particular, *Christine Goodwin v United Kingdom* (n 13), which concerned the legal status of post-operative transsexuals. See also Spielmann (n 3).

[95] According to recent research 45% of all cases which use the consensus argument are Article 8. See Wildhaber, Hjartarson, and Donnelly (n 2) 257.

8

The Comparative Law Method and the Court of Justice of the European Union

Interlocking Legal Orders Revisited

Koen Lenaerts and Kathleen Gutman***

I. Introduction

The comparative law method has a special meaning and place in the European Union (EU). As compared to other jurisdictions such as the United States of America (US), where the recourse to foreign and international law by the courts is more controversial,[1] the comparative law method is an established practice utilized by the Court of Justice of the European Union, which generally centres on the ways in which the Union courts look to the rules, principles, and traditions of the Member States from which EU law may be discerned for the purposes of adjudicating the particular case brought before them. In the previous edition of this work, the comparative law method of the Union courts was the subject of the contribution, 'Interlocking Legal Orders or the European Union Variant of *E Pluribus Unum*',[2] evidencing the considerable case law and literature on this subject going back to the early days of what was then the European Communities. Indeed, as depicted by the title of that contribution, unlike the American setting in which the debate about the relevance of a comparative law analysis largely emanated from the US Supreme Court's recourse to sources of foreign and international law that sit apart from, or are 'external' to, the domestic norms being interpreted, in the EU, the comparative law method of the Union courts is typically associated with the examination of the laws of the Member States, that is to say, national norms that are 'internal' to the Union legal order that inform and nourish the interpretation and formulation of EU law. As such, the stakes are somewhat different, and, in the EU judicial setting, the study of the

* Vice-President of the Court of Justice of the European Union and Professor of European Union Law, University of Leuven. All opinions expressed herein are strictly personal.

** Senior Affiliated Researcher at the Institute for European Law, University of Leuven.

[1] In the US, the reference to foreign and international law in connection with the interpretation of the US Constitution has generated a massive volume of literature, as well as initiatives at the federal and state levels to forbid the practice, and while its heyday may have passed, this debate sees no signs of abating in the literature or case law. See, eg, A Shinar and A Su, 'Religious Law as Foreign Law in Constitutional Interpretation' (2013) 11 International Journal of Constitutional Law 74; *McDonald v City of Chicago, Ill.*, 561 US 742 (2010); see also the contributions by M Minow, J Resnik, and J Waldron in the present volume.

[2] K Lenaerts, 'Interlocking Legal Orders or the European Union Variant of *E Pluribus Unum*' in G Canivet, M Andenas, and D Fairgrieve (eds.), *Comparative Law before the Courts* (British Institute of International and Comparative Law, 2004) 99. See also K Lenaerts, 'Interlocking Legal Orders in the European Union and Comparative Law' (2003) 52 ICLQ 873.

comparative law method more often rests on issues of how, as opposed to if, the Union's courts make use of the national laws and other legal sources in reaching a decision.

Over the past decade, this subject has come back to the forefront with a vengeance. The discussion of the use of comparative and international law by the Court of Justice[3] and the national (supreme or constitutional) courts in Europe[4] has now (or once again[5]) become a 'hot topic' in the scholarly literature. This has been spurred to a great extent by the entry into force of the Lisbon Treaty[6] and the changes brought about by that Treaty to the EU regime of fundamental rights, namely with respect to the EU's accession to the European Convention for the Protection of Human Rights and Fundamental Freedoms (ECHR) and the binding effects of the Charter of Fundamental Rights of the European Union (Charter).[7] This subject also intersects with several other related lines of scholarship, such as those placing renewed (and sometimes critical) attention on the formulation of general principles of EU law,[8] constitutional pluralism,[9] and the workings of the Court of Justice, with particular regard to its

[3] See, eg, G de Búrca, 'After the EU Charter of Fundamental Rights: The Court of Justice as a Human Rights Adjudicator?' (2013) 20 *MJ* 168; J Gerards, 'Judicial Argumentation in Fundamental Rights Cases—The EU Courts' Challenge' in U Neergard and R Nielsen (eds.), *European Legal Method—in a Multi-Level EU Legal Order* (UDJØF, 2012) 27; C McCrudden, 'Using Comparative Reasoning in Human Rights Adjudication: The Court of Justice of the European Union and the European Court of Human Rights Compared' (2012–2013) 15 *CYELS* 383; H Senden, *Interpretation of Fundamental Rights in a Multilevel System* (Intersentia, 2011) ch 13.

[4] Surely national courts outside of Europe are taken into account. See, eg, M Andenas and D Fairgrieve (eds.), *Tom Bingham and the Transformation of the Law—A Liber Amicorum* (Oxford University Press, 2009) pt V; S Muller and S Richards (eds.), *Highest Courts and Globalisation* (Hague Academic Press, 2010); 'Special Issue on Highest Courts and Transnational Interaction' (2012) 8 Utrecht Law Review No 2; M Bobek, *Comparative Reasoning in European Supreme Courts* (Oxford University Press, 2013); E Mak, *Judicial Decision Making in a Globalised World: A Comparative Analysis of the Changing Practices of Western Highest Courts* (Hart, 2013); B Markesinis and J Fedtke, *Engaging With Foreign Law* (Hart, 2009). As regards interaction between the Court of Justice and the national courts, see also, eg, M Claes, M de Visser, P Popelier, and C Van de Heyning (eds.), *Constitutional Conversations in Europe—Actors, Topics and Procedures* (Intersentia, 2012).

[5] In addition to the previous edition of this work cited in n 2, see already, eg, U Drobnig and S Van Erp (eds.), *The Use of Comparative Law by Courts* (Kluwer, 1999); M Kiikeri, *Comparative Legal Reasoning and European Law* (Kluwer, 2001).

[6] Treaty of Lisbon amending the Treaty on European Union and the Treaty establishing the European Community, [2007] OJ C306/1; consolidated versions of the Treaty on European Union (TEU), [2012] OJ C326/13, and the Treaty on the Functioning of the European Union (TFEU), [2012] OJ C326/47. For brevity's sake, quoted passages referring to the former Community or former provisions of the EU and EC Treaties may be replaced by the Union or the current provisions of the TEU or TFEU in brackets, and reference is made to the General Court (as opposed to the Court of First Instance) for cases decided before the entry into force of the Lisbon Treaty.

[7] See Art 6(1)–(2) TEU. The Charter of Fundamental Rights of the European Union, proclaimed at Nice on 7 Dec 2000, [2000] OJ C364/1, was re-enacted by the European Parliament, the Council, and the Commission on the day that the Lisbon Treaty was signed: Charter of Fundamental Rights of the European Union, proclaimed at Strasbourg on 12 Dec 2007, [2007] OJ C303/1, reprinted alongside the consolidated versions of the TEU and the TFEU, [2012] OJ C326/391 (Charter). With the entry into force of the Lisbon Treaty, the Charter has the same legal value as the Treaties, meaning that it has the status of binding primary Union law: Art 6(1), first para, TEU. See, in this regard, eg, Opinion of AG Sharpston in Case C-396/11 (Judgment of 29 Jan 2013) *Radu*, not reported in the ECR [ECLI:EU:C:2013:39], points 42–52.

[8] See, eg, K Lenaerts and JA Gutiérrez-Fons, 'The Constitutional Allocation of Powers and General Principles of EU Law' (2010) 47 *CMLR* 1629 and citations therein.

[9] See, eg, M Poiares Maduro, 'Interpreting European Law: Judicial Adjudication in a Context of Constitutional Pluralism' (2007) 1 *EJLS* 1; K Lachmayer, 'Constitutional Reasoning as Legitimacy of Constitutional Comparison' (2013) 14 *GLJ* 1463; C Saunders, 'Constitutional Reasoning as Legitimacy of

methods of interpretation,[10] its formulation of judge-made rules of Union law or so-called European 'federal common law',[11] and its supposed judicial activism,[12] not to mention the broader discourse on comparative constitutional law[13] and judicial globalization[14] beyond the confines of the EU.

In view of the changes taking place in the EU's legal and political system on numerous fronts, this presents an opportune time for revisiting this subject, and its implications should not be overlooked. The study of comparative law in the Court of Justice of the European Union is not a theoretical or academic exercise, but strikes at the heart of the relationship between the Union and the national legal orders and the dialogue between the Union courts and the national courts in particular, as well as the Union's relations with the international community in general, which are essential to the functioning and evolution of the European project, now more than ever.

The objective of this contribution is therefore to examine the comparative law method of the Court of Justice of the European Union in light of recent institutional and jurisprudential developments, building in relevant part on the previous contribution and other publications of the present authors in the field. It is divided into two main parts. The first part sets forth a general overview of the comparative law method in the EU judicial framework, thereby addressing the different expressions, sources, and actors involved, the legal bases in the Treaties governing the Union courts' potential recourse to this method, and the overarching aim or approach ('teleology') underpinning it, with illustrations from recent case law concerning the Union's non-contractual liability regime. The second part offers fresh reflection on

Constitutional Comparison: Comment on Konrad Lachmeyer' (2013) 14 *GLJ* 1493. See more generally, eg, M Avbelj and J Komárek (eds.), *Constitutional Pluralism in the European Union and Beyond* (Hart, 2012).

[10] See, eg, K Lenaerts and JA Gutiérrez-Fons, 'To Say What the Law of the EU Is: Methods of Interpretation and the European Court of Justice' (2014) 20 Columbia Journal of European Law 3 and citations therein. As regards renewed attention put on the Advocates General, see n 31.

[11] K Lenaerts and K Gutman, '"Federal Common Law" in the European Union: A Comparative Perspective from the United States' (2006) 54 *AJCL* 1.

[12] See, eg, M Adams, H de Waele, J Meeusen, and G Straetmans (eds.), *Judging Europe's Judges: The Legitimacy of the Case Law of the European Court of Justice* (Hart, 2013); M Dawson, B de Witte, and E Muir (eds.), *Judicial Activism at the European Court of Justice* (Edward Elgar, 2013); H-W Micklitz and B de Witte (eds.), *The European Court of Justice and the Autonomy of the Member States* (Intersentia, 2012); 'Special Issue: Perpetual momentum? Reconsidering the power of the European Court of Justice' (2012) 19 Journal of European Public Policy 1.

[13] For a brief selection, see, eg, T Ginsburg and R Dixon (eds.), *Comparative Constitutional Law* (Edward Elgar, 2011); M Rosenfeld and A Sajó (eds.), *The Oxford Handbook of Comparative Constitutional Law* (Oxford University Press, 2012); V Jackson and M Tushnet, *Comparative Constitutional Law*, 2nd edn (Foundation Press, 2003).

[14] For a brief selection, see, eg, A-M Slaughter, *A New World Order* (Princeton University Press, 2004) ch 2; 'Symposium: Judicialization and Globalization of the Judiciary' (2003) 38 Texas International Law Journal 397. In what has been called the 'battle of the metaphors' (V Perju, 'Constitutional Transplants, Borrowing, and Migrations' in *The Oxford Handbook of Comparative Constitutional Law*, n 13, 1304), there are, however, a growing number of terms that commentators have coined in describing the various kinds of interactions that implicate the recourse to foreign and international law by judges, such as 'conversation' (see, eg, M Claes, 'Introduction' in *Constitutional Conversations in Europe*, n 4, 1), 'dialogue' (see, eg, G Canivet, 'Trans-judicial Dialogue in a Global World' in *Highest Courts and Globalisation*, n 4, 21), 'engagement' (see, eg, V Jackson, *Constitutional Engagement in a Transnational Era* (Oxford University Press, 2010) 71), and 'migration' (see, eg, S Choudry, 'Migration as a New Metaphor in Comparative Constitutional Law' in S Choudry (ed), *The Migration of Constitutional Ideas* (Cambridge University Press, 2006) 1), which overlap with the discourse on comparative constitutional law and constitutionalism.

the conceptual framework or typology of the comparative law method in EU adjudication in terms of the three main situations in which the comparative law method arises in the case law of the Union courts—gap-filling, interpretation, and compatibility review—taking account of salient case law in several burgeoning areas, with particular regard to fundamental rights and other general principles of EU law, among others.

II. The comparative law method in the EU judicial framework

1. General overview

As already mentioned, the comparative law method generally signifies the ways in which the Court of Justice of the European Union looks to the rules, principles, and traditions of the Member States, as well as that of other jurisdictions to varying degrees, for the purposes of adjudicating the various types of cases provided for in the Treaties. While typically associated with the laws of the Member States, the comparative law method of the Union courts is not limited as such, and encompasses sources of foreign and international law in a broad sense. In other words, depending upon the particular case, it may comprise the law and case law of regional and international organizations and tribunals,[15] as well as that of third (non-EU) States, such as the US.[16] In particular, under settled case law, among the various international instruments from which the Court of Justice may draw inspiration (alongside the constitutional traditions common to the Member States) in respect of the EU fundamental rights regime, the ECHR is deemed to have 'special significance',[17] as indicated by the text of the Treaties.[18] Not surprisingly, given the changes brought about by the Lisbon Treaty in respect of this regime, there is growing emphasis put on the extent to which reference is made to decisions of the European Court of Human Rights (ECtHR) in the case law of the Court of Justice (and vice versa)[19] and other means of formal and informal dialogue between

[15] Eg, as regards the EFTA Court, see C Baudenbacher, 'The EFTA Court and Court of Justice of the European Union: Coming in Parts But Winning Together' in *The Court of Justice and the Construction of Europe: Analyses and Perspectives on Sixty Years of Case-Law* (TMC Asser Press, 2013) 183. See also, as regards the International Criminal Tribunal for Rwanda and the International Criminal Court, Opinion of AG Poiares Maduro in Joined Cases C-514/07 P, C-528/07 P, and C-532/07 P *Sweden and Others v API and Commission* [2010] ECR I-8533, point 26.

[16] See, eg, C Baudenbacher, 'Judicial Globalization: New Developments or Old Wine in New Bottles?' (2003) 38 Texas International Law Journal 505; FG Jacobs, 'Judicial Dialogue and the Cross-Fertilization of Legal Systems: The European Court of Justice' (2003) 38 Texas International Law Journal 547; A Rosas, 'With a Little Help from My Friends: International Case-Law as a Source of Reference for the EU Courts' in 1 *The Global Community—Yearbook of International Law and Jurisprudence 2005* (Oceana Publications, 2006) 203; A Rosas, 'The European Court of Justice in Context: Forms and Patterns of Judicial Dialogue' (2007) 1 EJLS 1. With particular regard to the US, see also n 37.

[17] See, eg, Joined Cases C-402/05 P and C-415/05 P *Kadi and Al Barakaat International Foundation v Council and Commission* [2008] ECR I-6351, para 283 and citations therein. For applications of other international instruments, see, eg, Case C-540/03 *European Parliament v Council* [2006] ECR I-5769, para 37; Case C-341/05 *Laval un Partneri* [2007] ECR I-11767, para 90; Case C-438/05 *The International Transport Workers' Federation and The Finnish Seamen's Union* ('*Viking Line*') [2007] ECR I-10779, para 43; Case C-244/06 *Dynamic Medien* [2008] ECR I-505, para 39.

[18] See Art 6(3) TEU: text accompanying n 64.

[19] See, eg, citations in n 3.

these two Courts, especially in view of the homogeneity between the interpretation of the Charter and that of the ECHR.[20]

Moreover, the comparative law method may be utilized by each of the three Union courts comprising the institution of the Court of Justice of the European Union—the Court of Justice (ECJ or Court),[21] the General Court (EGC), and the specialized courts, of which there is presently one, the EU Civil Service Tribunal (CST)[22]—pursuant to their respective bases of jurisdiction set forth in the Treaties.[23] For instance, as discussed below, one of the classic areas in which the comparative law method arises is in respect of the Union's non-contractual liability for which the General Court has been conferred first instance jurisdiction,[24] and the extent to which 'staff cases',[25] now under the jurisdiction of the EU Civil Service Tribunal, have constituted the basis for several notable examples of the comparative law method starting in early case law is striking.[26] The fact that focus is often put on the Court of Justice may be explained by virtue of its (so far exclusive[27]) jurisdiction to deliver preliminary rulings and its appellate jurisdiction in respect of the General Court's decisions, from which many landmark rulings involving the comparative law method have emanated. It may also be explained by the fact that, at present, Advocates General are attached only to the Court of Justice[28] and play a central role in this regard.

2. The role of the Advocate General

In the EU judicial framework, there is indeed the additional component of the Opinions of the Advocates General. At present, the Court of Justice is 'assisted' by nine Advocates General, though this number will increase to 11 in 2015.[29] Under

[20] See Charter, n 7, Art 52(3). See further, eg, K Lenaerts, 'The Court of Justice of the European Union and the Protection of Fundamental Rights' (2011) 31 Polish Yearbook of International Law 79, 98–103. See also Opinion of AG Ruiz-Jarabo Colomer in Case C-303/05 *Advocaten voor de Wereld* [2007] ECR I-3633, point 81 (emphasizing the emerging 'dialogue between the constitutional courts of the European Union', involving the national, Council of Europe, and EU spheres, in respect of fundamental rights).

[21] For clarity's sake, this contribution refers to the Court of Justice in the sense of the highest court of this institution.

[22] Art 19(1), first para, TEU.

[23] See K Lenaerts, I Maselis, and K Gutman (JT Nowak (ed)), *EU Procedural Law* (Oxford University Press, 2014) ch 2.

[24] See Art 256(1) TFEU; Art 268 TFEU. See further section II.3.

[25] That is to say, cases concerning disputes between the Union and its servants, which used to fall within the jurisdiction of the former Court of First Instance, now General Court. See Art 270 TFEU; Protocol (No 3), annexed to the TEU, TFEU, and the EAEC Treaty, on the Statute of the Court of Justice of the European Union, Annex I The European Union Civil Service Tribunal, [2012] OJ C326/10, as amended by Reg (EU, Euratom) No 741/2012 of the European Parliament and of the Council of 11 Aug 2012, [2012] OJ L228/1 (Statute). For detailed discussion, see, eg, Lenaerts, Maselis, and Gutman, n 23, ch 18.

[26] See, eg, JA Usher, 'The Influence of National Concepts on Decisions of the European Court' (1976) 1 *EL Rev* 359; Joined Cases 7/56 and 3/57 to 7/57 *Algera and Others v Common Assembly* [1957–1958] ECR 39, discussed at n 60 and accompanying text.

[27] While there is allowance under the Treaties for the General Court's jurisdiction over preliminary rulings, so far this has not yet occurred: see Lenaerts, Maselis, and Gutman, n 23, paras 2.47–2.48.

[28] There are no separate AGs attached to the EGC, but there is the possibility (used rarely) for a member of that Court to serve as an AG in a particular case. See Art 254, first para, TFEU; Statute, n 25, Art 49.

[29] See Art 19(2), first para, TEU; Art 252, first para, TFEU; Declaration (No 38), annexed to the Lisbon Treaty, on Art 252 TFEU regarding the number of Advocates-General in the Court of Justice, [2012] OJ

Article 252 TFEU, it is 'the duty of the Advocate-General, acting with complete impartiality and independence, to make, in open court, reasoned submissions' on cases that require his or her involvement.[30] In short, the primary duty of the Advocate General is to submit an Opinion as to how the particular case should be resolved. While there is ample literature on the Advocate General in the EU,[31] three points are relevant for this discussion. First, the Advocates General are members of the Court of Justice alongside the judges and fulfil a *sui generis* role in the EU by taking part in the process by which the Court reaches its decision.[32] Secondly, in line with the Advocate General's duty to 'assist' the Court, the Opinion brings to the Court's attention all possibly relevant matters that may help the Court to decide the case, which may include, inter alia, a fuller account of the background or context, detailed analysis of the parties' arguments as well as issues not raised by the parties, and a comparative analysis of the laws of the Member States and possibly other jurisdictions. This is all the more important, since the Court of Justice does not have any lower court record to work with, except for cases involving appeals from the General Court, and it has to decide all of the cases duly brought before it, without any sort of *certiorari* procedure.[33] Thirdly, the Opinion is not binding on the Court of Justice, but instead constitutes the Advocate General's 'opinion' as to how the Court should decide the case, which is taken into account as part of the Court's deliberations. Commentators have sought to analyse how often the Court has followed the Advocate General's Opinion,[34] but this presents difficulties because the Court's deliberations are secret[35] and hence it cannot be known for sure how much influence the Opinion had on the Court, even if it did not mention it or decide to follow it, in all or in part, in its decision. Nevertheless, the Advocate General's Opinion plays a significant role in EU jurisprudence, for instance, where the Court does not reach a certain issue or for prompting further development of the case law.[36]

Many of these functions, such as providing a fuller account of the case and paving the way for a future approach, help to explain why comparative analysis of the laws of

C326/352; Council Dec 2013/336/EU of 25 June 2013 increasing the number of Advocates-General of the Court of Justice of the European Union, [2013] OJ L179/92.

[30] Art 252, second para, TFEU. Not all cases require an AG Opinion: see Statute, n 25, Art 20, fifth para.

[31] For a brief selection, see, eg, C Barnard, M Gehring, and I Solanke (eds.), 'The Advocate General: Securing and Democracy in the EU Judicial Order' (2011–2012) 14 *CYELS* 507; N Burrows and R Greaves (eds.), *The Advocate General and EC Law* (Oxford University Press, 2007); E Sharpston, 'The Changing Role of the Advocate General' in A Arnull, P Eeckhout, and T Tridimas (eds.), *Continuity and Change in EU Law: Essays in Honour of Sir Francis Jacobs* (Oxford University Press, 2008) 20.

[32] Case C-13/94 (Order of 4 Feb 2000) *Emesa Sugar* [2000] ECR I-665, paras 10–15.

[33] Yet, in view of changes starting with the Nice Treaty, there have been means by which to streamline certain cases of importance to the Grand Chamber, while leaving others to be decided by three- and five-judge chambers. See K Lenaerts, 'The Unity of European Law and the Overload of the ECJ—The System of Preliminary Rulings Revisited' in *The Global Community*, n 16, 173.

[34] See, eg, C Ritter, 'A New Look at the Role and Impact of the Advocates-General—Collectively and Individually' (2006) 12 Columbia Journal of European Law 751.

[35] Statute, n 25, Art 35; Rules of Procedure of the Court of Justice of 25 Sept 2012, [2012] OJ L265/1, as amended on 18 June 2013, [2013] OJ L173/65 (ECJ Rules of Procedure), Art 32(1).

[36] Lenaerts, Maselis, and Gutman, n 23, para 2.16.

the Member States (as well as the laws of other jurisdictions as the case may be[37]) more often appears in the Opinions of the Advocates General than in the judgments of the Court of Justice. For instance, the Advocate General may utilize the comparative law method as part of setting out the general background or context of the case, as illustrated by Advocate General Jacobs' Opinion in *Garcia Avello*,[38] in which he elaborated on the approaches taken to names in the Member States as part of the backdrop to the case. This method may also be used by the Advocate General to highlight or advocate a particular approach,[39] which may or may not be taken up by the Court, or conversely, to highlight a difference in approach, in particular by explaining certain issues by contrasting what the EU is not. A notable example is Advocate

[37] As regards third (non-EU) States, it may be interesting to note that references to US law and case law appear in a wide variety of AG Opinions and serve several, and to some extent interrelated, functions, including those mentioned above as well as others, such as: (1) where a particular issue or doctrine has its origins in the US or US law has particular prominence in the area concerned; classic examples are found in antitrust, intellectual property, and anti-discrimination law; other applications range from the 'political question' doctrine (see, eg, Opinion of AG Poiares Maduro in Joined Cases C-402/05 P and C-415/05 P *Kadi and Al Barakaat International Foundation v Council and Commission* [2008] ECR I-6351, points 33–34 fns 39–40) to the discussion of notions or doctrines under the US Bill of Rights (see, eg, Opinion of AG Sharpston in Case C-467/04 *Gasparini and Others* [2006] ECR I-9199, point 72 fns 59–60 and point 111 fn 92; Opinion of AG Cruz Villalón in Joined Cases C-293/12 and C-594/12 (Judgment of 8 April 2014) *Digital Rights Ireland and Seitlinger and Others*, not reported in the ECR [ECLI: EU:C:2014:238], point 52 fn 46); (2) a sort of decorative quotation or flourish, often as a means of introducing the case, emphasizing the significance of a particular point, or borrowing a term from US law to help summarize or grasp the issue (see, eg, Opinion of AG Poiares Maduro in Case C-327/02 *Panayotova and Others* [2004] ECR I-11055, point 47 fn 33; Opinion of AG Poiares Maduro in Case C-422/05 *Commission v Belgium* [2007] ECR I-4749, point 1 fn 2; Opinion of AG Ruiz-Jarabo Colomer in Case C-553/07 *Rijkeboer* [2009] ECR I-3889, point 58 fn 46; Opinion of AG Wahl in Case C-321/12 (Judgment of 10 Oct 2013) *van der Helder and Farrington*, not reported in the ECR [ECLI:EU:C:2013:648], point 46 fn 21); (3) to highlight or advocate a similar approach (see, eg, n 39); (4) to highlight a difference in approach (see, eg, Opinion of AG Mengozzi in Case C-19/11 (Judgment of 28 June 2012) *Getl*, not reported in the ECR [ECLI:EU:C:2012:397], point 72 fn 15; see also n 42 and accompanying text); and (5) to be part of the comparative analysis conducted by the AG and thus placed side-by-side with the laws of the Member States (and other jurisdictions as the case may be) for the purposes of discerning EU rules on a particular issue (see, eg, ns 177, 234). For further discussion of the recourse to US law and case law in EU jurisprudence, see, eg, Baudenbacher, n 16, 517–20; L Faircloth Peoples, 'The Use of Foreign Law by the Advocates General of the Court of Justice of the European Communities' (2008) 35 Syracuse Journal of International and Comparative Law 219; L Faircloth Peoples, 'The Influence of Foreign Law Cited in the Opinions of the Advocates General on Community Law' (2009) 28 *YEL* 458; P Herzog, 'United States Supreme Court Cases in the Court of Justice of the European Communities' (1998) 21 Hastings International & Comparative Law Review 903; Jacobs, n 16, 554–6; K Lenaerts, 'Interpretation and the Court of Justice: A Basis for Comparative Reflection' (2007) 41 *International Lawyer* 1011. With respect to third States other than the US, see, eg, Opinion of AG Poiares Maduro in Case C-305/05 *Ordre des barreaux francophones and germanophone and Others* [2007] ECR I-5305, point 2 fn 3 (Canada); see also ns 39, 177.

[38] See Opinion of AG Jacobs in Case C-148/02 *Garcia Avello* [2003] ECR I-11613, points 5–22. See also, eg, Opinion of AG Sharpston in Case C-353/06 *Grunkin and Paul* [2008] ECR I-7639, points 6–8; Opinion of AG Sharpston in Case C-208/09 *Sayn-Wittgenstein* [2010] ECR I-13693, point 45 fn 34.

[39] See, eg, Opinion of AG Fennelly in Case C-376/98 *Germany v European Parliament and Council* ('*Tobacco Advertising*') [2000] ECR I-8419 and Case C-74/99 *Imperial Tobacco and Others* [2000] ECR I-8599, points 125–126 (citing Irish and US case law); Opinion of AG Poiares Maduro in Case C-305/05 *Ordre des barreaux francophones and germanophone and Others* [2007] ECR I-5305, point 71 fn 54 (citing US, UK, and Italian case law); Opinion of AG Mengozzi in Case C-48/09 P *Lego Juris v OHIM* [2010] ECR I-8403, point 62 fn 40 (basing his analysis on German and US law); Opinion of AG Cruz Villalón in Case C-509/09 *eDate Advertising and Others* [2011] ECR I-10269, point 60 fn 42 (citing German, UK, and Australian case law); Opinion of AG Cruz Villalón in Case C-523/10 (Judgment of 19 April 2012) *Wintersteiger*, not reported in the ECR [ECLI:EU:C:2012:220], points 27–29 fns 11–12 (citing French and US case law).

General Sharpston's Opinion in *Ruiz Zambrano*.[40] In her discussion of the scope of application of EU fundamental rights, she contemplated an approach that would make the availability of EU fundamental rights protection dependent on the existence and scope of a material EU competence,[41] but then pointed out that such an approach could not be taken unilaterally by the Court in the present case because it would involve introducing an overtly 'federal' element into the EU system, leading her to discuss the American incorporation doctrine with reference to US Supreme Court case law.[42] In this way, the comparative law method serves a number of key (and interrelated) functions in the Opinions of the Advocates General, which may or may not be determinative to the issue at hand and hence figure in the judgment of the Court of Justice.

Furthermore, the Advocate General's Opinion may be linked to other means by which the Court of Justice becomes, directly or indirectly, aware of a study on comparative law. For instance, parties involved in the proceedings before the Court of Justice[43] (or the other Union courts[44]), as well as the national courts in the order for reference in the case of preliminary rulings,[45] may utilize the comparative law method as part of their submissions, which may then prompt the Advocate General to examine that method in his or her Opinion and/or the respective Court to mention that method in its judgment. Likewise, comparative analysis conducted by the Commission or other Union institution or body as part of the groundwork for the adoption of a Union measure may filter into the interpretation of that measure before the Court.[46] In recent years, an interesting development has been the uses made of comparative materials formulated by various

[40] Opinion of AG Sharpston in Case C-34/09 *Ruiz Zambrano* [2011] ECR I-1177. For detailed discussion of this case, its broader implications, and related jurisprudence, see, eg, K Lenaerts, 'How the ECJ Thinks: A Study on Judicial Legitimacy' (2013) 36 Fordham International Law Journal 1302, 1351–69 and citations therein.

[41] Opinion of AG Sharpston in Case C-34/09 *Ruiz Zambrano*, points 163–170.

[42] Opinion of AG Sharpston in Case C-34/09 *Ruiz Zambrano*, points 171–173.

[43] See, eg, Case C-321/95 P *Greenpeace and Others v Commission* [1998] ECR I-1651, para 20.

[44] Of note, US antitrust and intellectual property law sometimes appear in parties' arguments before the General Court, but they rarely succeed, as that Court has consistently underscored the autonomy of EU law and evinces a subtle hostility to parties attempting to utilize US law to evade the application of EU rules in various circumstances. As regards the competition field, see, eg, Case T-203/01 *Michelin v Commission* [2003] ECR II-4071, para 112; Case T-329/01 *Archer Daniel Midlands v Commission* [2006] ECR II-3255, paras 35, 38–50 (appeal dismissed in Case C-510/06 P *Archer Daniel Midlands v Commission* [2009] ECR I-1843); as regards the intellectual property field involving trademark regulation, see, eg, Case T-109/11 (Judgment of 23 April 2013) *Apollo Tyres v OHIM*, not reported in the ECR [ECLI:EU:T:2013:211], paras 39, 41; Joined Cases T-102/11, T-369/12, T-370/12, and T-371/12 (Judgment of 12 March 2014) *American Express Marketing & Development Corp v OHIM*, not reported in the ECR [ECLI:EU:T:2014:118], para 35; see also, eg, as regards restrictive measures in the fight against terrorism, Case T-49/04 *Hassan v Council and Commission* [2006] ECR II-52*, Summ pub, paras 78, 94 (set aside on other grounds in Case C-399/06 P *Hassan v Council and Commission* [2009] ECR I-11393).

[45] See, eg, Case C-453/99 *Courage v Crehan* [2001] ECR I-6297, paras 13, 15 (the UK court cited US case law); Case C-168/00 *Leitner* [2002] ECR I-2631, para 12 (the Austrian court cited German law and case law).

[46] See, eg, Opinion of AG Léger in Case C-353/99 P *Council v Hautala* [2001] ECR I-9565, points 14, 54 fn 24, preceding his comparative analysis in points 55–59; see also Opinion of AG Tesauro in Case C-300/95 *Commission v United Kingdom* [1997] ECR I-2649, points 16–18 fns 6, 9 (citing US law and case law as part of the context for Council Dir 85/374/EEC on the approximation of the laws, regulations and administrative provisions of the Member States concerning liability for defective products, [1985] OJ L210/29).

academic projects as part of the ongoing debate about European private and contract law by parties as part of their arguments in the proceedings and by the Advocates General in their Opinions, but so far, these materials have not yet been employed by the Court of Justice or the General Court in the reasoning or operative parts of their judgments.[47]

Apart from this, there are many expressions of the comparative law method in the workings of the Court of Justice of the European Union that transcend the use of comparative analysis in the judgments of the Union courts and the Opinions of the Advocates General. Indeed, part of the 'standard mantra' in much of the literature over the past decades has been that the Union courts, and in particular the Court of Justice, embody a 'laboratory of comparative law'[48] or the 'perfect conditions for comparative work'[49] in view of their composition representing the various legal traditions of the Member States, their institutional set-up involving a translation service, and their resources by virtue of the comparative surveys drawn up by legal experts in the Court's Research and Documentation Service, with the result that the comparative law method 'permeates the daily activities' of the Union courts in many ways.[50]

While all of this is well and good in principle, there has been a rising crescendo of discord in the scholarly literature regarding the Court's comparative law method in practice. By and large, this relates, on the one hand, to the Court's lack of extensive (or much at all), comparative reasoning in its judgments, as compared to the Opinions of the Advocates General, which has been considered by some commentators to affect the legitimacy of the Court's rulings, especially with regard to its dialogue with the national courts, and, on the other hand, to the failure to make publicly available the comparative surveys utilized by the Court and the Advocates General.[51] This is certainly nothing new, and over the years, there have been good arguments put forward on both sides regarding these issues,[52] which to a great extent may be extrapolated to differing positions taken by jurists on the Court's reasoning in general. Suffice it to say, comparative analysis in the judgments of the Court of Justice may not be as extensive or as visible as that presented in the Opinions of the Advocates General. Nonetheless, this draws attention to the unique intermediary role played by the Opinions of the Advocates General by bringing to the Court's attention the law and case law of the Member States and other normative sources in relation to which they may have engaged in a comparative law analysis, even if the judges' consideration

[47] For further discussion, see, eg, K Gutman, *The Constitutional Foundations of European Contract Law: A Comparative Analysis* (Oxford University Press, 2014) ch 2 and citations therein; with respect to the Draft Common Frame of Reference, see also the contribution by T Kalouta in the present volume.

[48] M Hilf, 'The Role of Comparative Law in the Jurisprudence of the Court of Justice of the European Communities' in A de Mestral et al (eds.), *The Limitation of Human Rights in Comparative Constitutional Law* (Les Éditions Yvon Blais Inc., 1986) 549, 550 and citations therein.

[49] FC Mayer, 'Constitutional comparativism in action. The example of general principles of EU law and how they are made—a German perspective' (2013) 11 International Journal of Constitutional Law 1003, 1009.

[50] Lenaerts, *Comparative Law before the Courts*, n 2, 101–2.

[51] See, eg, Mayer, n 49, 1007–10; citations in n 3. For other concerns, see, eg, B Petkova, 'The Notion of Consensus as a Route to Democratic Adjudication?' (2011–2012) 14 *CYELS* 663, 685.

[52] Compare, eg, B Markesinis and J Fedtke, *Judicial Recourse to Foreign Law: A New Source of Inspiration* (Routledge-Cavendish, 2006) 121, with K Schiemann, 'The Judge as Comparatist', 358, 364–5.

of such sources, as the case may be, takes place behind the scenes and thus involves a more subtle undertaking.

3. Legal bases and overarching approach

The comparative law method may be relied upon by the Court of Justice of the European Union as an aid to interpretation, which is used alongside or in the service of the other such methods, such as consistent or teleological interpretation,[53] in order to carry out the tasks assigned to it under the Treaties.[54] In addition, the comparative law method is a tool for and informs judicial lawmaking, that is to say, the formulation of judge-made rules of Union law or so-called European 'federal common law', and thus is situated within the overarching system or allocation of jurisdiction conferred on the Union judicature in the Treaties.[55] In this context, there are both general and specific legal bases in the Treaties authorizing the Union courts to have recourse to the comparative law method for the purposes of their interpretative and lawmaking functions.

The first paragraph of Article 19(1) TEU, providing that the Court of Justice of the European Union 'shall ensure that in the interpretation and application of the Treaties the law is observed', constitutes a primary source of authority or general legal basis authorizing the Union courts to utilize the comparative law method. By reference to 'the law', this Treaty provision may be considered to task the Union judicature to take account of the laws of the Member States as part of carrying out its mission to uphold the rule of law in the Union legal order. As compared to its predecessor of Article 220 EC (ex Article 164 E(E)C) in the former EC Treaty,[56] this provision explicitly mentions the institution of the Court of Justice of the European Union, and not just the Court of Justice and (eventually) what is now the General Court.[57] Still, this mandate put on the Union judicature to ensure that 'the law' is observed has not changed since its original insertion into the Treaty framework.[58]

In the case law, the Court of Justice has recognized the link between its overarching duty under what is now Article 19(1) TEU and its recourse to the comparative law

[53] See, eg, Lenaerts and Gutiérrez-Fons, n 10. [54] See Art 19(3) TEU; Arts 251–281 TFEU.

[55] For detailed discussion of the framework governing the Union courts' competence to formulate European 'federal common law', see Lenaerts and Gutman, n 11, 12–19. For some illustrations, see section III.2.b).

[56] Initially, Art 220 EC (ex Art 164 E(E)C) stated: 'The Court of Justice shall ensure that in the interpretation and application of this Treaty the law is observed.' With the Nice Treaty, additional language was added to what became the first para of Art 220 EC to include what was then the Court of First Instance, now the General Court.

[57] See, eg, Case C-413/11 (Order of 18 April 2013) *Germanwings*, not reported in the ECR [ECLI:EU:C:2013:246], para 17; Opinion of AG Sharpston in Case C-40/12 P (Judgment of 26 Nov 2013) *Gascogne Sack Deutschland v Commission*, not reported in the ECR [ECLI:EU:C:2013:768], point 12.

[58] Incidentally, this used to be linked to the function played by the AG. Until the Nice Treaty, ex Art 222, second para, EC (ex Art 166, second para, E(E)C) stated that it was 'the duty of the Advocate-General . . . to make, in open court, reasoned submissions on cases brought before the Court of Justice, in order to assist the Court in the performance of the task assigned to it in Article 220'. This paragraph was changed by the Nice Treaty, so as to provide that it was 'the duty of the Advocate-General . . . to make, in open court, reasoned submissions on cases which, in accordance with the Statute of the Court of Justice, require his involvement'. This language has been retained with the entry into force of the Lisbon Treaty: see n 30 and accompanying text.

method. Early on, in *Algera*,[59] the Court considered that in a situation where the ECSC Treaty did not contain any rules, '[u]nless the Court is to deny justice it is therefore obliged to solve the problem by reference to the rules acknowledged by legislation, the learned writing and the case-law of the member countries'.[60] Thereafter, in *Brasserie du Pêcheur*,[61] the Court held that 'it is for the Court, in pursuance of the task conferred on it by Article [19(1) TEU] of ensuring that in the interpretation and application of the [Treaties] the law is observed, to rule on such a question in accordance with generally accepted methods of interpretation, in particular by reference to the fundamental principles of the [Union] legal system and, *where necessary, general principles common to the legal systems of the Member States*'.[62] This is also alluded to in certain Opinions of the Advocates General through to the present day.[63] It remains to be seen whether the Court may provide further support for this reading of Article 19(1) TEU in future case law. In any event, by virtue of the general mandate of Article 19(1) TEU, the Union courts' recourse to the comparative law method may arise on a case-by-case basis in many fields of EU law pursuant to the various bases of jurisdiction provided for in the Treaties.

As is well known, there are other Treaty provisions that explicitly counsel the Union courts to look to the laws of the Member States in certain areas and thus constitute specific legal bases for the comparative law method of the Union courts. In particular, Article 6(3) TEU, codifying the Court's early case law in the field of fundamental rights,

[59] Joined Cases 7/56 and 3/57 to 7/57 *Algera and Others v Common Assembly* [1957–1958] ECR 39.

[60] Joined Cases 7/56 and 3/57 to 7/57 *Algera*, 55.

[61] Joined Cases C-46/93 and C-48/93 *Brasserie du Pêcheur and Factortame and Others* [1996] ECR I-1029.

[62] Joined Cases C-46/93 and C-48/93 *Brasserie du Pêcheur,* para 27 (emphasis added). See also, eg, Opinion of AG Cosmas in Joined Cases C-94/95 and C-95/95 *Bonafaci and Others and Berto and Others* [1997] ECR I-3969, point 43 fn 19.

[63] See, eg, Opinion of AG Ruiz-Jarabo Colomer in Case C-228/96 *Aprile* [1998] ECR I-7141, point 54 ('In fact, the third question (as to whether national courts are bound by the principles laid down by the Court of Justice as "unwritten rules" of [Union] law) causes none of those parties to entertain any doubts: they take it for granted that those rules are binding, as a corollary of the duty to fulfil obligations deriving from the [Treaties] or from the acts of the [Union] institutions, it being the responsibility of the Court of Justice to ensure that in the interpretation and application of the Treat[ies] the law is observed (Article [19(1) TEU])'); Opinion of AG Mazák in Case C-411/05 *Palacios de la Villa* [2007] ECR I-8531, point 85 ('By formulating general principles of [Union] law—pursuant to its obligation under Article [19(1) TEU] to ensure observance of the law in the interpretation and application of the Treat[ies]—the Court has actually added flesh to the bones of [Union] law, which otherwise—being a legal order based on a framework treaty—would have remained a mere skeleton of rules, not quite constituting a proper legal "order"'); Opinion of AG Kokott in Case C-406/08 *Uniplex* [2010] ECR I-817, point 26 ('Certainly, when requirements of [Union] law are being interpreted, attention should always be paid to whether they can be fitted into national law with as little friction as possible. For all that, the Court's primary function is to ensure that in the interpretation and application of [EU] law the law is observed (first paragraph of Article [19 TEU]) and—working together with the national courts—to give effect to the rights which individuals derive from [Union] law'); Opinion of AG Kokott in Case C-550/07 P *Akzo Nobel Chemicals and Akcros Chemicals v Commission* [2010] ECR I-8301, point 92 ('it must be remembered first that the Court of Justice of the European Union—consisting of the Court of Justice, the General Court and specialised courts—is to ensure that in the interpretation and application of the Treaties the law is observed (Article 19(1) TEU). At an early stage, the Court of Justice inferred from the character of the Community (now: the European Union) as a community governed by the rule of law that, within its jurisdiction, certain principles based on the rule of law must apply and fundamental rights must be protected, even if they have not, or not yet, been laid down in writing').

states: 'Fundamental rights, as guaranteed by the European Convention for the Protection of Human Rights and Fundamental Freedoms and as they result from the *constitutional traditions common to the Member States*, shall constitute general principles of the Union's law.'[64] In addition, the second paragraph of Article 340 TFEU provides: 'In the case of non-contractual liability, the Union shall, in accordance with the *general principles common to the laws of the Member States*, make good any damage caused by its institutions or by its servants in the performance of their duties.'[65] These two provisions are essentially the 'gold standard' for examining the Union courts' recourse to the comparative law method in the formulation of various kinds of EU principles, rules, and concepts,[66] and have given way to an extensive and growing body of case law illustrating the Union courts' use of comparative law analysis and their overarching approach.

Whatever be the particular legal basis, it is also widely recognized in the case law and scholarly literature that the overarching aim or approach ('teleology') underpinning the comparative law method applied by the Union courts is to find, through the examination of the laws of the Member States (and other jurisdictions as the case may be), the solution which 'best suits' the objectives of the Union and which is 'acceptable' for the national legal orders responsible for implementing Union law.[67] Importantly, this overarching approach encompasses not one, but two related components: the former from the perspective of the Union in terms of finding a solution that is most appropriate for the needs and specific features of the Union legal order, and the latter from the perspective of the Member States in the sense of finding a solution that respects as much as possible the relevant national rules, principles, and traditions, since it is through the implementation of Union law in the national legal orders that EU law maintains its full effectiveness.[68] As could be expected, the more convergence there is among the national legal systems, the more the Union courts will tend to take up such an approach, adapting it as appropriate for the EU setting, whereas the greater the divergences among the national legal systems, the more the Union courts will be

[64] Art 6(3) TEU (emphasis added). See further section III.3.a).

[65] Art 340, second para, TFEU (emphasis added). See also Charter, n 7, Art 41(3). Similar language referring to the 'general principles common to the laws of the Member States' may be found in other provisions of the Treaties and secondary Union law dealing with non-contractual liability, eg, as regards the European Central Bank, see Art 340, third para, TFEU; as regards the non-contractual liability of the European Atomic Energy Community (EAEC), see Art 188, second para, EAEC. In tandem with the entry into force of the Lisbon Treaty, there is a new consolidated version of the EAEC Treaty ([2012] OJ C327/1) in which Art 188, second para, EAEC remains, but Art 151 EAEC was repealed and replaced by Art 268 TFEU. See Protocol No 2, annexed to the Lisbon Treaty, amending the EAEC Treaty, [2007] OJ C306/199. For detailed discussion, see, eg, Lenaerts, Maselis, and Gutman, n 23, ch 11 and citations therein.

[66] K Gutman, 'The Evolution of the Action for Damages Against the European Union and Its Place in the System of Judicial Protection' (2011) 48 *CMLR* 695, 738. To be clear, the recourse to 'general principles common to the laws of the Member States' under the second para of Art 340 TFEU is for the purposes of formulating EU rules on non-contractual liability, as opposed to using a specific national law as the governing rule: see, eg, Case C-221/10 P (Judgment of 19 April 2012) *Artegodan v Commission*, not reported in the ECR [ECLI:EU:C:2012:216], paras 45, 47, 80–82.

[67] Lenaerts, *Comparative Law before the Courts*, n 2, 105–10, 133. This may also be called, eg, an 'evaluative approach' (see Lenaerts and Gutiérrez-Fons, n 8), or 'evaluative comparison' (see Opinion of AG Kokott in Case C-550/07 P *Akzo Nobel Chemicals and Akcros Chemicals v Commission* [2010] ECR I-8301, point 94).

[68] See, eg, Lenaerts, *Comparative Law before the Courts*, n 2, 105–6; Lenaerts and Gutman, n 11, 17–19.

cautious in formulating a common 'EU' solution, but, as will be seen, the existence of such divergences does not automatically preclude the Union courts from adopting a solution recognized in only a small proportion of the Member States.[69] Basically, this approach is a functional one, which depends on the circumstances of the particular case and thus is not contingent on a certain 'magic' number of Member States, for example, that a particular rule must be found in all or a majority of Member States, or, conversely, must be reduced to the 'lowest common denominator'.[70] Indeed, as illustrated by recent case law concerning the Union's non-contractual liability regime, it involves a relative inquiry, and while the overarching approach is the same, these components may be assessed or weighed differently by the respective Union court and the Advocate General.

In *FIAMM and Others v Council and Commission*,[71] the Court of Justice was confronted with the question whether the Union could be held non-contractually liable in the absence of unlawful acts or conduct on the part of the Union institutions. In past years, the Court of Justice and the General Court had referred to the principle of Union liability in the absence of unlawful conduct, or no-fault liability, in hypothetical terms,[72] but it remained unclear whether such a principle was in fact recognized in EU law until 2005, when the General Court delivered five related rulings that affirmed this principle for the first time.[73] These rulings arose out of circumstances involving the EU's infringement of the World Trade Organization (WTO) rules, leading the US to take retaliatory measures against the EU that caused several undertakings to incur damage. They brought actions before the General Court seeking to hold the Union non-contractually liable on the basis of unlawful conduct, and, alternatively, in the absence of such conduct. As regards the latter ground, the General Court reasoned that what is now the second paragraph of Article 340 TFEU (ex Article 288 EC) did not restrict the ambit of 'general principles common to the laws of the Member States' solely to rules governing non-contractual liability for unlawful conduct and that '[n]ational laws on non-contractual liability allow individuals, albeit to varying degrees, in specific fields and in accordance with differing rules, to obtain compensation in legal proceedings for certain kinds of damage, even in the absence of unlawful action by the perpetrator of the damage'.[74] On that basis, it held that when damage is caused by conduct not shown to be unlawful, the Union is liable if the specific requirements as to sustaining actual damage, the causal link between that damage and the conduct of the

[69] Lenaerts and Gutiérrez-Fons, n 8, 1633–5. See further sections III.1.b)–2.a).

[70] See, eg, Opinion of AG Poiares Maduro in Joined Cases C-120/06 P and C-121/06 P *FIAMM and Others v Council and Commission* [2008] ECR I-6513, point 55 fn 59 and citations therein.

[71] Joined Cases C-120/06 P and C-121/06 P *FIAMM and Others v Council and Commission* [2008] ECR I-6513.

[72] See, eg, Case C-237/98 P *Dorsch Consult v Council and Commission* [2000] ECR I-4549, para 18 and citations therein.

[73] Case T-69/00 *FIAMM and FIAMM Technologies v Council and Commission* [2005] ECR II-5393; Case T-383/00 *Beamglow v European Parliament, Council and Commission* [2005] ECR II-5459; Case T-151/00 *Laboratoire du Bain v Council and Commission* [2005] ECR II-23*, Summ pub; Case T-320/00 *CD Cartondruck v Council and Commission* [2005] ECR II-27*, Summ pub; Case T-135/01 *Fedon & Figli and Others v Council and Commission* [2005] ECR II-29*, Summ pub. As these judgments are similar, only *FIAMM* is cited.

[74] Case T-69/00 *FIAMM*, paras 158–159.

institution concerned, and to the unusual and special nature of the damage in question were all met.[75] As these conditions were not fulfilled in the present proceedings, the cases were dismissed.[76]

Two of the General Court's rulings were appealed to the Court of Justice in *FIAMM and Others*.[77] In its judgment, the Court of Justice held that the General Court had erred in law by affirming the existence of a Union regime of non-contractual liability in the absence of unlawful conduct.[78] It explained that whereas the regime governing non-contractual liability for unlawful conduct was firmly established, this was not so with regard to that for lawful conduct. First, such a principle of no-fault liability could not be deduced from previous case law, in which the Court merely limited itself to specifying certain conditions under which such liability could be incurred if such a principle were to be recognized in Union law.[79] Secondly, as regards the liability regime recognized in Union law, the Court, on the basis of what is now the second paragraph of Article 340 TFEU, found that although the principles in the legal systems of the Member States governing the liability of public authorities for damage caused to individuals by legislative measures varied considerably, it was still possible to state that such authorities can only exceptionally and under special circumstances incur liability for such measures, which served as the basis for a strict approach taken to Union liability based on the fulfilment of certain requirements.[80] Finally, although comparative examination of the Member States' legal systems enabled the Court to make such a finding concerning convergence of those legal systems in the case of unlawful acts or omissions, including of a legislative nature, 'this is in no way the position' regarding the possible existence of a principle of liability in the case of lawful acts or omissions of public authorities, in particular where they are of a legislative nature.[81] In light of those considerations, the Court declared: 'as [Union] law currently stands, no liability regime exists under which the [Union] can incur liability for conduct falling within the sphere of its legislative competence in a situation where any failure of such conduct to comply with the WTO agreements cannot be relied upon before the [Union] courts.'[82]

In his Opinion, Advocate General Poiares Maduro took a different view.[83] In particular, he underlined that the Court's task is to draw on the legal traditions of the Member States in order to identify a solution that both respects those traditions and is appropriate to the needs and specific features of the Union legal system, and

[75] Case T-69/00 *FIAMM*, para 160.

[76] Case T-69/00 *FIAMM*, paras 202–214.

[77] Joined Cases C-120/06 P and C-121/06 P *FIAMM and Others v Council and Commission* [2008] ECR I-6513, para 1.

[78] Joined Cases C-120/06 P and C-121/06 P *FIAMM and Others*, para 179. Ultimately, however, the ECJ dismissed this ground of the appeal, since the EGC would have had to dismiss the applicants' claims in any event: paras 187–189.

[79] Joined Cases C-120/06 P and C-121/06 P *FIAMM and Others*, paras 168–169.

[80] Joined Cases C-120/06 P and C-121/06 P *FIAMM and Others*, paras 170–174.

[81] Joined Cases C-120/06 P and C-121/06 P *FIAMM and Others*, para 175.

[82] Joined Cases C-120/06 P and C-121/06 P *FIAMM and Others*, para 176; see also para 188.

[83] See Opinion of AG Poiares Maduro in Joined Cases C-120/06 P and C-121/06 P *FIAMM and Others*, which was divided into two subsections: the first dealing with the recognition of a principle of no-fault Union liability (points 54–63) and the second with its field of application (points 64–83).

therefore, even a solution adopted by a minority may be preferred if it best meets the requirements of the Union system, *in casu* the fact that only Spanish and French law provide for public authorities to incur liability by reason of a lawful legislative act cannot prevent such liability from being recognized in Union law.[84] In his view, the establishment of a principle of no-fault Union liability satisfied these requirements on several grounds, and could take its inspiration from certain elements of national law that accorded with the constitutional traditions common to the Member States.[85]

While the Advocate General's approach was not taken up by the Court, its judgment is not likely to be the end of the matter. To recall, the Court's holding in *FIAMM and Others* was prefaced by the wording 'as [Union] law currently stands', which leaves some room for manoeuvre as regards the reconsideration of this issue in the future.[86] Moreover, it was framed to a great extent within the particular circumstances of the proceedings, involving the Union institutions' compliance with the WTO agreements and linked to their legislative activity. Although not stated explicitly, the Court's emphasis on these aspects provides certain clues for reconciling the different positions.[87] The Court's reference to 'legislative' action may be viewed in the light of the defendant institutions' arguments relating to the lack of commonality among the national legal systems in relation to liability for lawful conduct in the legislative, as opposed to administrative, sphere,[88] since the Court had stronger grounds for rejecting the recognition of a principle of no-fault Union liability based on the 'general principles common to the laws of the Member States', as compared to the General Court's broader level of generality of the national legal systems. The specific linkage to the WTO agreements also suggests that the Court may have considered the recognition of such a principle as inappropriate in this context. In this way, the judgments of the Court of Justice and the General Court, as well as the Opinion of the Advocate General, may be considered to embody the same overarching approach in terms of identifying a solution that was appropriate to the Union legal order and respectful of the national legal traditions, even if they resulted in different outcomes.

A few months later, the Court of Justice delivered its judgment in *Masdar (UK) v Commission*,[89] which provides an apt comparison. This case confronted the Court of Justice on appeal with questions concerning the Union's potential non-contractual liability based on, inter alia, the principle of unjust enrichment.[90] In its ruling, the General Court accepted that the claim for unjust enrichment could in principle be brought within the context of what is now the second paragraph of Article 340 TFEU,

[84] Opinion of AG Poiares Maduro in Joined Cases C-120/06 P and C-121/06 P *FIAMM and Others*, points 55–56.

[85] Opinion of AG Poiares Maduro in Joined Cases C-120/06 P and C-121/06 P *FIAMM and Others*, points 57–63.

[86] Indeed, certain case law following this judgment continues to refer to the specific conditions of special and unusual damage and thus raises questions as to whether such liability may eventually be recognized in Union law under certain circumstances. See, eg, Case C-414/08 P *Sviluppo Italia Basilicata v Commission* [2010] ECR I-2559, paras 140–141; and Opinion of AG Trstenjak, points 236–237.

[87] Gutman, n 66, 743–4.

[88] See Joined Cases C-120/06 P and C-121/06 P *FIAMM and Others*, paras 141, 149–152, 156.

[89] Case C-47/07 P *Masdar (UK) v Commission* [2008] ECR I-9761, which was delivered on 16 Dec 2008; *FIAMM and Others* was delivered on 9 Sept 2008.

[90] For detailed discussion, see, eg, the case note by R Williams (2010) 47 *CMLR* 555.

since 'the rules on non-contractual liability, as provided for in the majority of national legal systems, do not necessarily contain a condition relating to the unlawfulness or fault with regard to the defendant's conduct'.[91] Yet, on the basis of the 'general principles common to the laws of the Member States', the General Court considered that such a claim could not succeed on account of the particular circumstances of the present case.[92]

In its judgment, the Court of Justice agreed, explaining that this type of action does not fall within the rules governing non-contractual liability in the strict sense, since it does not require proof of unlawful conduct on the part of the defendant.[93] Yet, if the second paragraph of Article 340 TFEU (and Article 268 TFEU) were construed as precluding the possibility of bringing such an action, the result would be contrary to the principle of effective judicial protection laid down in the case law and affirmed by Article 47 of the Charter.[94] Furthermore, unjust enrichment is a source of non-contractual obligation common to the legal systems of the Member States, such that the Union cannot be dispensed from the application to itself of the same principle where a natural and legal person alleges that the Union has been unjustly enriched to the detriment of that person.[95] The Court then upheld the General Court's finding as regards its application to the present proceedings.[96]

In his Opinion, Advocate General Mazák reiterated, following from Advocate General Poiares Maduro's Opinion in *FIAMM and Others*, that the solution applied by the Union courts in this context should be 'inspired by the basic characteristics of the relevant concepts in the national legal orders, adapted, where necessary, to meet the specific requirements of [Union] law'.[97] On the basis of a comparative analysis of the national legal systems, he found that the Member States took divergent approaches with respect to the principle of unjust enrichment, but still, where this principle existed as a basis for liability, it was generally possible to rely on it only under strict conditions as a subsidiary means of redress, and, therefore, the General Court's approach was consistent with the basic characteristics of this principle in the laws of the Member States.[98] Against this background, the Court's recognition and application of the principle of unjust enrichment in *Masdar* embodies its overarching approach to find a solution that is both appropriate for the Union legal order and respectful of the national legal orders, as evidenced by the Court's emphasis on the commonality of the national legal systems and the suitability of this principle to the Union's non-contractual liability regime, as compared to *FIAMM and Others*, in which those two components appeared to be more problematic.[99]

In contrast to the two foregoing judgments, it may be the case that, instead of a minority or majority on one side or other, there is in fact no common or dominant

[91] Case T-333/03 *Masdar (UK) v Commission* [2006] ECR II-4377, para 91.

[92] Case T-333/03 *Masdar*, paras 141–142.

[93] Case C-47/07 P *Masdar*, para 49.

[94] Case C-47/07 P *Masdar*, para 50.

[95] Case C-47/07 P *Masdar*, para 47.

[96] Case C-47/07 P *Masdar*, paras 52–61.

[97] Opinion of AG Mazák in Case C-47/07 P *Masdar*, point 45.

[98] Opinion of AG Mazák in Case C-47/07 P *Masdar*, points 47–51 (also discussing the principle of *negotiorum gestio* (the law of benevolent intervention in another's affairs) at issue in the case).

[99] Gutman, n 66, 746–7.

approach among the laws of the Member States that can be detected. As regards the Union's non-contractual liability, the Court's recent judgments in the three 'companion' cases of *Gascogne Sack Deutschland*,[100] *Kendrion*,[101] and *Groupe Gascogne*[102] are good examples. There, the applicants lodged appeals against the General Court's rulings dismissing their actions for annulment against the Commission decision finding that they had infringed the EU competition rules, alleging, among other things, that the General Court breached the second paragraph of Article 47 of the Charter on account of its failure to adjudicate within a reasonable time.[103] In her Opinion in *Groupe Gascogne*, Advocate General Sharpston dealt with this issue in depth,[104] underlining that there appeared to be no common approach in the legal traditions of the Member States, with one or more Member States taking a number of different routes for dealing with this issue, and thus, while neither of the two approaches taken by the Court in previous case law was perfect, she advocated the route of a separate action for damages brought before the General Court (under the *Der Grüne Punkt*[105] line of case law), as opposed to a reduction of the fine (under the *Baustahlgewebe*[106] line of case law).[107] In its judgment, the Court ruled, in line with the Advocate General's Opinion, that the sanction for a breach, by a Court of the European Union, of its obligation to adjudicate a case within a reasonable time under the second paragraph of Article 47 of the Charter must be an action for damages against the Union brought before the General Court. Indeed, such an action constitutes an effective remedy of general application for asserting and penalizing such a breach and can cover all the situations where a reasonable period of time has been exceeded in the proceedings, as opposed to the remedy of reducing the amount of the fine.[108] Accordingly, a claim for compensation for the damage caused by the General Court's failure to adjudicate in a reasonable time must be brought before that Court, sitting in a different composition from that which heard the dispute giving rise to the procedure whose duration is criticized, and assessed in accordance with certain criteria laid down by the Court of Justice.[109]

[100] Case C-40/12 P (Judgment of 26 Nov 2013) *Gascogne Sack Deutschland v Commission*, not reported in the ECR [ECLI:EU:C:2013:768].

[101] Case C-50/12 P (Judgment of 26 Nov 2013) *Kendrion v Commission*, not reported in the ECR [ECLI: EU:C:2013:771].

[102] Case C-58/12 P (Judgment of 26 Nov 2013) *Groupe Gascogne v Commission*, not reported in the ECR [ECLI:EU:C:2013:770].

[103] Art 47, second para, of the Charter, n 7, states in relevant part: 'Everyone is entitled to a fair and public hearing within a reasonable time by an independent and impartial tribunal previously established by law'. See further A McDonnell, 'Time is Money? Reasonable Duration of the Procedure by the European Courts as an Aspect of Effective and Timely Judicial Protection' in T Baumé, EO Elferink, P Phoa, and D Thiaville (eds.), *Today's Multi-layered Legal Order: Current Issues and Perspectives. Liber amicorum in honour of Arjen W.H. Meij* (Paris Legal Publishers, 2011) 183.

[104] See Opinion of AG Sharpston in Case C-58/12 P *Groupe Gascogne*, points 3, 70–150. She noted that the Court had invited the then 27 (now 28) Member States, the European Parliament, and the Council to indicate their views in writing: point 119.

[105] Case C-385/07 P *Der Grüne Punkt–Duales System Deutschland v Commission* [2009] ECR I-6155.

[106] Case C-185/95 P *Baustahlgewebe v Commission* [1998] ECR I-8417.

[107] Opinion of AG Sharpston in Case C-58/12 P *Groupe Gascogne*, points 118, 121–132, 148.

[108] Case C-40/12 P *Gascogne Sack Deutschland*, paras 86–89; Case C-50/12 P *Kendrion*, paras 91–94; Case C-58/12 P *Groupe Gascogne*, paras 80–83.

[109] Case C-40/12 P *Gascogne Sack Deutschland*, paras 90–96; Case C-50/12 P *Kendrion*, paras 95–101; Case C-58/12 P *Groupe Gascogne*, paras 84–90. In the present cases, the Court considered that the length of

III. The conceptual framework of the comparative law method in EU adjudication

As outlined in the previous contribution, there is a three-part conceptual framework or typology of the situations in which the Court of Justice of the European Union makes use of the comparative law method, which generally involve: first, filling a lacuna in the Union legal order (gap-filling); secondly, interpreting rules and concepts of EU law (interpretation); and thirdly, judging the compatibility of national law with EU law (compatibility review).[110] It may not be surprising that these situations largely correspond to the functions played by general principles of EU law,[111] including fundamental rights, in the Union legal order, since the establishment, application, and scope of such principles rest to a great extent on the comparative law method. Thus, while some overlap is unavoidable, each is taken in turn, and, as illustrated by salient case law, too, manifests the Union judicature's overarching approach to find a solution that best suits the needs of the Union legal system while respecting as far as possible the principles and traditions of the Member States.

1. Gap-filling

The case law of the Union courts is replete with numerous instances involving the Union courts' discovery and development of general principles of EU law based on the rules, principles, and traditions recognized in the Member States' legal orders.[112] In particular, this has come to the fore in the Court's jurisprudence concerning the prohibition of discrimination on grounds of sexual orientation since *Grant* and discrimination on grounds of age stemming from *Mangold*, which highlight occasions involving the convergence of and contradictions between national solutions, as well as

the proceedings (amounting to approximately five years and nine months) could not be justified under any of the particular circumstances and held that the procedure in the General Court breached the second para of Art 47 of the Charter according to the requisite conditions for incurring the Union's non-contractual liability: Case C-40/12 P *Gascogne Sack Deutschland*, paras 97–102; Case C-50/12 P *Kendrion*, paras 102–106; Case C-58/12 P *Groupe Gascogne*, paras 91–96.

110 See Lenaerts, *Comparative Law before the Courts*, n 2, 110.

111 See Lenaerts and Gutiérrez-Fons, n 8. See also, eg, Opinion of AG Bot in Case C-555/07 *Kücükdeveci* [2010] ECR I-365, point 80; Opinion of AG Trstenjak in Case C-282/10 (Judgment of 24 Jan 2012) *Dominguez*, not reported in the ECR [ECLI:EU:C:2012:33], point 93. As regards compatibility review, this also includes the Union courts' assessment of the compatibility of Union measures with higher ranking rules of EU law, including fundamental rights and other general principles of EU law. With the changes brought about by the Lisbon Treaty in respect of the binding force of the Charter, the Union courts have been faced with a growing number of cases concerning the compatibility of national measures as well as Union measures with provisions of the Charter. As regards Union measures, see, eg, Joined Cases C-92/09 and C-93/09 *Volker und Markus Schecke and Eifert* [2010] ECR I-11063; Case C-236/09 *Association Belge des Consommateurs Test-Achats and Others* [2011] ECR I-773; Joined Cases C-293/12 and C-594/12 (Judgment of 8 April 2014) *Digital Rights Ireland and Seitlinger and Others*, not reported in the ECR [ECLI:EU:C:2014:238]. As regards national measures, see section III.3.a).

112 For a general discussion and survey of general principles of EU law, including fundamental rights, in the Union legal order, see, eg, K Lenaerts and P Van Nuffel (R Bray and N Cambien (eds.)), *European Union Law*, 3rd edn (Sweet & Maxwell, 2011) paras 22-016–22-042.

legal and political developments taking place at the national and Union levels, which bear on the comparative law method.

a) *Prohibition of discrimination on grounds of sexual orientation: developments since* Grant

Under circumstances where comparative analysis of the laws of the Member States reveals contradictions between national solutions, the Court of Justice's 1998 judgment in *Grant*[113] was, and still is, a quintessential example.[114] There, the Court held that then Community (now Union) law, as it stood at the time, did not cover discrimination based on sexual orientation involving a person in a stable relationship with a person of the same sex.[115] It also ruled that, on the basis of comparative analysis of the laws of the Member States,[116] that in the present state of what was then Community law, stable relationships between two persons of the same sex were not to be regarded as equivalent to marriage or stable relationships between persons of the opposite sex, with the result that an employer was not required by Community law to treat the situation of a person who had a stable relationship with a partner of the same sex as equivalent to that of a person who is married to or has a stable relationship outside marriage with a partner of the opposite sex.[117] It added, however, that 'it is for the legislature alone to adopt, if appropriate, measures which may affect that position'.[118] As such, taking account of the positions of the Member States on the matter, the Court avoided establishing a solution that would not have had sufficient support in the Member States and left it to the political authorities to deal with the matter.

Indeed, as acknowledged by the Court in that judgment,[119] the Amsterdam Treaty entered into force the following year and introduced what is now Article 19 TFEU (ex Article 13 EC), which confers competence on the Union legislature to adopt measures to combat various forms of discrimination, including that based on sexual orientation.[120] One of the Union measures adopted pursuant to this Treaty provision is Directive 2000/78,[121] establishing a general framework for equal treatment in employment and occupation. The Court's interpretation of this Directive has produced a steady stream of cases affording protection against discrimination for same-sex couples.[122] For instance, in *Maruko*,[123] the Court ruled that Directive 2000/78 precludes national rules under which the surviving life partner does not receive a

[113] Case C-249/96 *Grant* [1998] ECR I-621.
[114] See Lenaerts, *Comparative Law before the Courts*, n 2, 120–1.
[115] Case C-249/96 *Grant*, para 47.
[116] Case C-249/96 *Grant*, para 32.
[117] Case C-249/96 *Grant*, para 35.
[118] Case C-249/96 *Grant*, para 36.
[119] Case C-249/96 *Grant*, para 48.
[120] See Art 19(1) TFEU (ex Art 13(1) EC). The Nice Treaty added a second paragraph, which is now Art 19(2) TEU (ex Art 13(2) EC).
[121] Council Dir 2000/78/EC of 27 Nov 2000 establishing a general framework for equal treatment in employment and occupation, [2000] OJ L303/16.
[122] See also Joined Cases C-124/11, C-125/11, and C-143/11 (Judgment of 6 Dec 2012) *Dittrich and Others*, not reported in the ECR [ECLI:EU:C:2012:771]. For detailed discussion, see, eg, G De Baere and K Gutman, 'The Impact of the EU and the ECJ on European Family Law' in JM Scherpe (ed), *Research Handbook on European Family Law* (Edward Elgar, forthcoming 2015) section 4.2 and citations therein.
[123] Case C-267/06 *Maruko* [2008] ECR I-1757.

survivor's benefit equivalent to that granted to a surviving spouse, even though, under national law, life partnership places persons of the same sex in a situation comparable to that of spouses as regards that survivor's benefit.[124] The Court left it to the national court to determine whether a surviving life partner is in a comparable position to that of a spouse who is entitled to a survivor's benefit, but it made clear that if the referring court made such a finding, the national rules at issue constituted direct discrimination within the meaning of the Directive.[125] In his Opinion, Advocate General Ruiz-Jarabo Colomer took stock of the Court's case law on the prohibition of discrimination on grounds of sexual orientation,[126] pointing out that *Grant* preceded Directive 2000/78 and that, by virtue of its reference to the Amsterdam Treaty, the Court 'hinted that the enactment of provisions prohibiting discrimination based on sexual orientation would have resulted in a different reply to the question analysed'.[127]

A few years later, in *Römer*,[128] the Court ruled that Directive 2000/78 precludes national rules in which a pensioner in a registered life partnership receives a lower supplementary retirement pension than that granted to a married pensioner, provided that in the Member State concerned, marriage is reserved to persons of different gender, whereas persons of the same gender only have access to a registered life partnership.[129] It found that there is indeed direct discrimination on grounds of sexual orientation where, under national law, that life partner is in a legal and factual situation comparable to that of a married person as regards such a pension, though again leaving it to the national court to determine the comparability in light of the benefit in question.[130] Notably, in his Opinion, Advocate General Jääskinen considered that the prohibition of discrimination on grounds of sexual orientation should be regarded as a general principle of EU law.[131] This was not dealt with by the Court in its judgment, since it found it unnecessary to give an answer to that question.[132] Thus, although it is not yet certain how the Court may rule on this issue in the future, the path of the case law since *Grant* attests to the dynamic nature of the comparative law method, taking account of and adjusting to legal and political developments at the national and Union levels.

b) Prohibition of discrimination on grounds of age: the Mangold *case law*

In the meantime, the Court's case law on other general principles of EU law provides fertile ground for recourse to the comparative law method, which may involve Directive 2000/78 (and even references to its judgment in *Grant* on occasion). One of the foremost examples is the *Mangold* line of case law. Famously, in *Mangold*,[133] the Court ruled that Directive 2000/78 did not itself lay down the principle of equal treatment in

124 Case C-267/06 *Maruko*, paras 65–73.

125 Case C-267/06 *Maruko*, para 72.

126 See Opinion of AG Ruiz-Jarabo Colomer in Case C-267/06 *Maruko*, points 87–95.

127 Opinion of AG Ruiz-Jarabo Colomer in Case C-267/06 *Maruko*, point 103. See also Opinion of AG Sharpston in Case C-427/06 *Bartsch* [2008] ECR I-7245, point 103 fn 94.

128 Case C-147/08 *Römer* [2011] ECR I-3591.

129 Case C-147/08 *Römer*, para 52.

130 Case C-147/08 *Römer*, para 52.

131 See Opinion of AG Jääskinen in Case C-147/08 *Römer*, points 125–131.

132 Case C-147/08 *Römer*, para 65.

133 Case C-144/04 *Mangold* [2005] ECR I-9981.

the field of employment and occupation, and that the source of the actual principle underlying the prohibition of discrimination on grounds of religion, disability, age, or sexual orientation was found, as was clear from the third and fourth recitals, in various international instruments *and in the constitutional traditions common to the Member States*.[134] On this basis, it proclaimed that the principle of non-discrimination on grounds of age must be regarded as a general principle of EU law, with the result that where national rules fall within the scope of EU law, as was the case in the present proceedings, the Court must, in line with its preliminary ruling jurisdiction, provide all of the criteria needed by the national court to determine whether those rules are compatible with this principle.[135]

Thereafter, the Court has been faced with further questions concerning its judgment in *Mangold*, as well as criticism from academics and certain Advocates General, in several cases, as neatly summarized by Advocate General Sharpston in her Opinion in *Bartsch*.[136] For instance, in his Opinion in *Palacios de la Villa*,[137] Advocate General Mazák took issue with the Court's elaboration of the general principle of non-discrimination on grounds of age,[138] pointing out that while various international instruments and constitutional traditions common to the Member States, to which the Court referred in *Mangold*, enshrined the general principle of equal treatment, this was not so, except in a few cases, with regard to the specific principle of non-discrimination on grounds of age.[139] In his view, neither what is now Article 19 TEU nor Directive 2000/78 necessarily reflected an already existing prohibition of all forms of discrimination to which they refer; rather, the intention was to leave it to the Union legislature and the Member States to take appropriate action to that effect, which is what the Court, too, seemed to suggest in *Grant*, concluding that then Community law, as it stood, did not cover discrimination based on sexual orientation.[140] Moreover, as noted in Advocate General Sharpston's Opinion in *Bartsch*,[141] certain parties challenged the existence of a general principle in EU law prohibiting age discrimination, arguing among other things that neither international instruments nor the constitutional traditions of the Member States provided an adequate basis for the recognition of such a principle.[142]

[134] Case C-144/04 *Mangold*, para 74 (emphasis added).

[135] Case C-144/04 *Mangold*, para 75. As is well known, much of the controversy underlying this case was because the main proceedings involved a dispute between private parties and when the contract at issue was concluded, the period for transposition of Dir 2000/78 had not yet expired. Nevertheless, the Court held that observance of the general principle of equal treatment, in particular in respect of age, cannot be conditional upon the expiry of the period allowed the Member States for the transposition of a directive intended to lay down a general framework for combating discrimination on the grounds of age and that it was the responsibility of the national court to guarantee the full effectiveness of the general principle of non-discrimination in respect of age, setting aside any provision of national law which may conflict with EU law, even where the transposition period for that directive has not yet expired: Case C-144/04 *Mangold*, paras 76–78. See further n 144 and accompanying text. For general discussion of these issues, see, eg, Lenaerts and Gutiérrez-Fons, n 8, 1639–49 and citations therein.

[136] Opinion of AG Sharpston in Case C-427/06 *Bartsch* [2008] ECR I-7245, points 28–65.

[137] Opinion of AG Mazák in Case C-411/05 *Palacios de la Villa* [2007] ECR I-8531.

[138] See Opinion of AG Mazák in Case C-411/05 *Palacios de la Villa*, points 79–99.

[139] Opinion of AG Mazák in Case C-411/05 *Palacios de la Villa*, point 88.

[140] Opinion of AG Mazák in Case C-411/05 *Palacios de la Villa*, point 95.

[141] Opinion of AG Sharpston in Case C-427/06 *Bartsch* [2008] ECR I-7245, point 29.

[142] In its judgment, the Court held that the national rules in question did not fall within the scope of EU law, distinguishing *Mangold* from the present proceedings: Case C-427/06 *Bartsch*, paras 14–25.

By comparison, in his Opinion in *Kücükdeveci*,[143] Advocate General Bot explained, amidst his discussion of *Mangold*,[144] that the existence of the prohibition of age discrimination as a general principle of EU law corresponded to the development of that right flowing from what is now Article 19(1) TFEU and Article 21(1) of the Charter.[145] He continued:

> The Court's reasoning would, of course, have been more convincing if it had been based on those factors, rather than merely on the international instruments and constitutional traditions common to the Member States, the majority of which do not recognise a specific principle prohibiting age discrimination. I think it is important, however, to emphasise that, by proclaiming that such a general principle of [EU] law exists, the Court is in accord with the wish expressed by the Member States and the [Union] institutions to counteract age discrimination effectively. From that point of view, it is not surprising that the prohibition of age discrimination, as a specific expression of the general principle of equal treatment and non-discrimination and as a fundamental right, should enjoy the eminent status of a general principle of [EU] law.[146]

As later explained by one Advocate General:

> [A]lthough the statement made in *Mangold* (and confirmed in *Kücükdeveci*) that the prohibition of discrimination on grounds of age is a general principle of EU law 'the source of [which is to be] found . . . in various international instruments and in the constitutional traditions common to the Member States', still holds absolutely true, the fact is that this principle has been enshrined in the 'Lisbon Charter' and it is therefore from this source that the possibilities and limitations of the principle's usefulness must flow.[147]

In effect, the *Mangold* case law evidences the Court's overarching approach of finding a solution that upholds the needs and fundamental objectives of the Union legal order and that accords with the general trend underpinning the constitutional values and traditions of the Member States taken as a whole, here embodied in the Charter, in the process of formulating general principles of EU law on the basis of the comparative law method,[148] even if at the time it was decided such a principle could be found in the laws

[143] Opinion of AG Bot in Case C-555/07 *Kücükdeveci* [2010] ECR I-365.

[144] See Opinion of AG Bot in Case C-555/07 *Kücükdeveci*, points 71–85.

[145] Opinion of AG Bot in Case C-555/07 *Kücükdeveci*, point 77.

[146] Opinion of AG Bot in Case C-555/07 *Kücükdeveci*, point 77. In its judgment, the Court acknowledged its recognition of the existence of the general principle of non-discrimination on grounds of age in *Mangold* and took note of Art 21(1) of the Charter, now having the same legal value as the Treaties under Art 6(1) TEU. See Case C-555/07 *Kücükdeveci* [2010] ECR I-365, paras 20–22, 50. See also, eg, Case C-476/11 (Judgment of 26 Sept 2013) *HK Danmark*, not reported in the ECR [ECLI:EU:C:2013:590], para 19.

[147] Opinion of AG Cruz Villalón in Case C-447/09 *Prigge and Others* [2011] ECR I-8003, point 26.

[148] *Mangold* may figure into the discussion of the potential recognition of other general principles of EU law in the Court's case law. Eg, as regards the question whether the right to annual paid leave should be regarded as a general principle of EU law, see Opinion of AG Trstenjak in Case C-282/10 (Judgment of 24 Jan 2012) *Dominguez*, not reported in the ECR [ECLI:EU:C:2012:33], points 89–114. The Court did not pronounce on the issue in its judgment, although it reiterated under settled case law that the entitlement of every worker to annual paid leave 'must be regarded as a particularly important principle of European Union social law': Case C-282/10 *Dominguez*, para 16.

of only a small number of Member States. This has become more apparent with the juxtaposition of *Mangold* and case law concerning the use of the comparative law method in the context of the interpretation of EU law, to which the discussion now turns.

2. Interpretation

As mentioned in the previous publication,[149] in the context of the interpretation of EU law, the Union courts may resort to the comparative law method where the EU norm at issue does not provide a solution to the problem. The comparative law method may reveal, on the one hand, a solution common to the laws of the Member States that is taken up for the interpretation of the EU rules concerned, as exemplified by *AM & S Europe v Commission* concerning the concept of 'legal professional privilege', or, on the other hand, divergences among the national laws, thereby justifying an autonomous EU interpretation or the formulation of judge-made rules of Union law, as illustrated by *Reed* and *D and Sweden v Council* concerning the concepts of 'spouse' and 'marriage', respectively. These two sets of judgments have been subject to subsequent developments in the national and Union legal orders, which shine further light on the dynamic nature of the comparative law method and the Court's overarching approach as detailed in the two sections that follow.

a) *Interpreting EU law:* AM & S Europe *and* Akzo Nobel

AM & S Europe v Commission,[150] decided in 1982, is one of the exceptional cases containing ample discussion of the comparative law method in the Court's judgment, as well as the Opinion(s) of the Advocate General.[151] It concerned an action for annulment brought by an undertaking against a decision taken by the Commission on the basis of what was then Regulation No 17[152] in the field of EU competition law, ordering the production of certain documents that the applicant claimed were protected by so-called 'legal professional privilege', namely, the protection of confidentiality of written communications between lawyers and their clients.[153] As there was no

[149] Lenaerts, *Comparative Law before the Courts*, n 2, 121–5.

[150] Case 155/79 *AM & S Europe v Commission* [1982] ECR 1575.

[151] As the oral procedure was reopened to allow for further briefing on the matter (see Case 155/79 *AM & S Europe*, 1603–1605), there were two AG Opinions in the case, both of which engaged in comparative analysis of the laws of the Member States: see, first, Opinion of AG Warner delivered on 20 Jan 1981 in Case 155/79 *AM & S Europe v Commission* [1982] ECR 1575, 1622–1623, 1630–1637; and secondly, Opinion of AG Sir Gordon Slynn delivered on 26 Jan 1982 in Case 155/79 *AM & S Europe v Commission* [1982] ECR 1575, 1648–1658, particularly 1649–1651 (regarding the overarching approach and difficulties of the comparative law method).

[152] Council Reg No 17 of 6 Feb 1962: First Reg implementing Arts 85 and 86 [later Arts 81 and 82] of the Treaty, [1959–1962] OJ Spec Edn 87, which has since been replaced by Council Reg (EC) No 1/2003 of 16 Dec 2002 on the implementation of the rules on competition laid down in Arts 81 and 82 [now Arts 101 and 102 TFEU] of the Treaty, [2003] OJ L1/1.

[153] As noted in that case, the label 'legal professional privilege' was a misnomer in English law, since it implied a privilege accorded to the legal profession: Opinion of AG Warner in Case 155/79 *AM & S Europe*, 1633. It garnered other labels, such as the protection or principle of confidentiality: see Case 155/79 *AM & S Europe*, headings above paras 18, 29. The case also figured into the determination of other aspects or

provision on point, it fell to the Court to decide on the applicability of this privilege in EU law. It declared that Community (now Union) law, 'which derives from not only the economic but also the legal interpenetration of the Member States, must take into account the principles and concepts common to the laws of those States concerning the observance of confidentiality, in particular as regards certain communications between lawyer and client'.[154] Despite some differences, 'there are to be found in the national laws of the Member States common criteria inasmuch as those laws protect, in similar circumstances, the confidentiality of written communications between lawyer and client', provided that, first, such communications are made for the purposes and in the interests of the client's rights of defence, and, secondly, they emanate from independent lawyers, that is to say, lawyers who are not bound to the client by a relationship of employment.[155] On that basis, Regulation No 17 must be interpreted as protecting the confidentiality of written lawyer–client communications subject to those two conditions, and thus incorporating such elements of that protection 'as are common to the laws of the Member States'.[156]

Nearly three decades later, *Akzo Nobel Chemicals and Akcros Chemicals v Commission*,[157] decided in 2010, presented the Court of Justice with the opportunity to reconsider its judgment in *AM & S Europe v Commission*. On appeal, the claimants sought to have the General Court's ruling set aside in so far as it rejected their claim of legal professional privilege for correspondence with the in-house lawyer of one of the claimants. In its ruling, the General Court held that following from *AM & S Europe*, communications with in-house lawyers, ie legal advisers bound to their clients by a relationship of employment, were excluded from protection under legal professional privilege.[158] It also rebuffed the claimants' argument, among others,[159] that it should extend the personal scope of such privilege beyond the limits established in *AM & S Europe*, since an examination of the laws of the Member States showed that even though specific recognition of the role of in-house lawyers and the protection of communications with such lawyers under such privilege was relatively more common today than when that case was decided, it was not possible 'to identify tendencies which are uniform or have clear majority support in that regard in the laws of the Member States'.[160] Specifically, a comparative examination of the laws of the Member States

principles related to lawyers' professional responsibility, eg, as regards lawyers' professional secrecy, see, eg, Opinion of AG Poiares Maduro in Case C-305/05 *Ordre des barreaux francophones and germanophone and Others* [2007] ECR I-5305, particularly point 39, though it was not mentioned in the Court's judgment. As regards rules governing lawyers before the Union courts, see also, eg, Case C-573/11 P (Order of 5 Sept 2013) *ClientEarth v Council*, not reported in the ECR [ECLI:EU:C:2013:564], para 11 and citations therein (highlighting that the conception of the lawyer's role in the EU legal order stems from the 'legal traditions common to the Member States' on which Art 19 of the Statute, n 25, is based).

154 Case 155/79 *AM & S Europe*, para 18.

155 Case 155/79 *AM & S Europe*, paras 20–21.

156 Case 155/79 *AM & S Europe*, para 22. The Court ultimately declared provisions of the Commission decision void in relation to certain documents considered to fall within legal professional privilege: see paras 34–36.

157 Case C-550/07 P *Akzo Nobel Chemicals and Akcros Chemicals v Commission* [2010] ECR I-8301.

158 Joined Cases T-125/03 and T-253/03 *Akzo Nobel Chemicals and Akcros Chemicals v Commission* [2007] ECR II-3523, paras 166–169.

159 See Joined Cases T-125/03 and T-253/03 *Akzo Nobel*, paras 172–176.

160 Joined Cases T-125/03 and T-253/03 *Akzo Nobel*, paras 170, 177.

showed that a large number of Member States still excluded in-house lawyers from protection under such privilege, and a considerable number did not allow in-house lawyers to be admitted to the Bar or Law Society and accordingly, did not recognize them as lawyers established in private practice; even in countries that did permit this possibility, the fact that in-house lawyers were admitted to a Bar or Law Society and subject to professional ethical rules did not always mean that communications were protected.[161]

In its judgment, the Court of Justice agreed, dismissing the appeal in full. It found that the General Court correctly applied the conditions set down in *AM & S Europe*, excluding communications with in-house lawyers from protection.[162] It also rejected the applicants' argument based on the evolution of the national legal systems. Following from the General Court's reasoning and comparative analysis, it found that 'no predominant trend towards protection under legal professional privilege of communications within a company or group with in-house lawyers may be discerned in the legal systems of the [then] 27 Member States of the European Union'.[163] Under those circumstances, the legal regime of one Member State[164] could not be regarded as signalling a developing trend in the Member States or as a relevant factor for determining the scope of this privilege.[165] It therefore considered that the legal situation in the Member States had not evolved since the judgment in *AM & S Europe* was delivered to an extent which would justify a change in the case law and recognition for in-house lawyers of the benefit of legal professional privilege.[166]

The Court's judgment should be read alongside Advocate General Kokott's Opinion, which delved further into the appellants' argument based on alleged changes 'in the legal landscape'.[167] In response to the claim that even changes in a small number of Member States were reason enough to reverse the Court's decision in *AM & S Europe*,[168] she pointed out that it was by no means inconceivable that a legal principle which is recognized or even firmly established in only a minority of Member States will be identified by the Union courts as forming part of EU law, particularly where, in view of the special characteristics of EU law, the aims and tasks of the Union, and the activities of its institutions, such a legal principle is of particular significance or where it constitutes a growing trend.[169] She found that this was the case with the Court's pronouncement of the general principle of non-discrimination on grounds of age in *Mangold*: even though at that time that principle did not appear to constitute a tendency which was uniform or had clear majority support in the national legal

[161] Joined Cases T-125/03 and T-253/03 *Akzo Nobel*, para 171. No specific Member States were mentioned.

[162] See Case C-550/07 P *Akzo Nobel*, paras 40–50.

[163] Case C-550/07 P *Akzo Nobel*, paras 71–74. Croatia acceded to the EU on 1 July 2013 after this case was decided.

[164] This was the Netherlands, where the in-house lawyer in the case was registered with the Bar: see Case C-550/07 P *Akzo Nobel*, para 3.

[165] Case C-550/07 P *Akzo Nobel*, para 75.

[166] Case C-550/07 P *Akzo Nobel*, para 76.

[167] Opinion of AG Kokott in Case C-550/07 P *Akzo Nobel*, points 87–113.

[168] See Opinion of AG Kokott in Case C-550/07 P *Akzo Nobel*, point 91.

[169] Opinion of AG Kokott in Case C-550/07 P *Akzo Nobel*, point 95.

systems or even in the constitutional law of the Member States,[170] it was consistent with a specific task incumbent on the EU in combating discrimination (Article 19 TFEU, ex Article 13 EC), had been given specific expression by the Union legislature in the form of a directive (Directive 2000/78), and mirrored a more recent trend in the protection of fundamental rights at Union level, to which the European Parliament, Council, and Commission had jointly given expression on the occasion of the proclamation of the Charter (Article 21).[171]

In contrast, with regard to the legal professional privilege at issue in the proceedings, the Advocate General considered that there were no comparable circumstances that would support the proposition that EU law should be brought into line with the legal position in a minority of Member States: the extension of the protection afforded by this privilege to in-house lawyers was not justified on grounds of any special characteristics exhibited by the tasks and activities of the Commission as competition authority, and it did not currently constitute a growing trend among the Member States, whether in competition law or other field.[172] As far as recent developments in the national legal systems were concerned, in her view, there was still no evidence of a clear—let alone growing—trend towards the protection of communications with in-house lawyers.[173] Of the then 27 Member States, a significant number (15)[174] continued to prohibit in-house lawyers from being members of a Bar or Law Society; in the vast majority of those States, this meant that in-house lawyers did not benefit from such privilege.[175] In a number of other Member States (6), the legal position could not be considered sufficiently established, either because there were no specific provisions, or because there was not yet any settled case law or administrative practice.[176] Only in a small minority of the Member States (6)[177] did the privilege apply to in-house lawyers, and the changes taking place in the laws of certain Member States (2 to 4)[178] appeared to be too isolated to be regarded as a clear trend.[179] Accordingly, she submitted that the

[170] She noted that such a prohibition is enshrined in Art 6 of the Finnish Constitution, and specifically in relation to employment, in Art 59(1) of the Portuguese Constitution: Opinion of AG Kokott in Case C-550/07 P *Akzo Nobel*, point 96 fn 78.

[171] Opinion of AG Kokott in Case C-550/07 P *Akzo Nobel*, point 96.

[172] Opinion of AG Kokott in Case C-550/07 P *Akzo Nobel*, point 98.

[173] Opinion of AG Kokott in Case C-550/07 P *Akzo Nobel*, point 100.

[174] She cited: 1) Austria, 2) Bulgaria, 3) Cyprus, 4) the Czech Republic, 5) Estonia, 6) Finland, 7) France, 8) Greece, 9) Hungary, 10) Italy, 11) Luxembourg, 12) Romania, 13) the Slovak Republic, 14) Slovenia, and 15) Sweden. Opinion of AG Kokott in Case C-550/07 P *Akzo Nobel*, point 101 fn 83.

[175] She cited certain exceptions regarding Germany and Greece: Opinion of AG Kokott in Case C-550/07 P *Akzo Nobel*, point 101 fn 84.

[176] She cited: 1) Denmark, 2) Latvia, 3) Lithuania, 4) Malta, 5) Romania, and 6) Spain. Opinion of AG Kokott in Case C-550/07 P *Akzo Nobel*, point 102 fn 85. She considered the legal position in Belgium was extremely unclear: point 102 fn 85. She further emphasized that as a result, national legislation, administrative practice, and case law seemed to draw on EU solutions, instead of the other way around, citing Belgium, Finland, and Slovenia: point 102 fn 86.

[177] She cited: 1) Greece, 2) Ireland, 3) the Netherlands, 4) Portugal, 5) Poland, and 6) the UK, considering that the legal position in Malta seemed unclear; she also compared the approaches taken by certain third States, the US and Australia. Opinion of AG Kokott in Case C-550/07 P *Akzo Nobel*, point 103 fns 87–88.

[178] She cited: 1) the Netherlands, 2) Poland, as well as 3) Belgium, though underlining that the position was unclear, and 4) France, though the matter was still under discussion. Opinion of AG Kokott in Case C-550/07 P *Akzo Nobel*, point 103 fn 89.

[179] Opinion of AG Kokott in Case C-550/07 P *Akzo Nobel*, point 103.

legal position of the Member States had not developed in such a way as to require a change in the Court's case law,[180] and hence that the appellants' claim based on a shift in the 'legal landscape' was to be rejected.[181]

This Opinion helps to flesh out the Court's approach taken in *Mangold* and offers some valuable insights into its overarching approach underlying the comparative law method generally. Certainly, the Court is more likely to establish general principles of EU law (or other rules of EU law as the case may be) on the basis of a common interpretation of the Member States. However, going back to the two components underlying its overarching approach, it may still do so where such principles may be found in only a minority of Member States, provided that there are certain other factors that 'tip the balance' in favour of recognition by virtue of the fact that such principle may be deemed to reflect specific objectives or tasks entrusted to the EU by the framers of the Treaties or to mirror a discernible trend in the laws of the Member States as a whole.

b) Judicial lawmaking: Reed *and* D and Sweden v Council

Alternatively, the comparative law method may reveal divergences in the laws of the Member States, which affords the basis for the Union courts to establish an autonomous EU interpretation of particular rules or concepts. This intersects with judicial lawmaking, since it may be the case that in the context of the interpretation of EU law, the Court of Justice (and the other Union courts) may be faced with formulating judge-made rules of Union law.[182] Among the most well known examples in the field of family law[183] is *Reed*,[184] concerning the concept of 'spouse', and *D and Sweden v Council*,[185] concerning the concept of 'marriage'.[186]

Decided in 1986, *Reed*[187] involved an action brought by Ms Reed against the Dutch authorities on account of their rejection of her application for a residence permit. She was an unmarried British citizen who had applied for such a permit on the grounds that she was cohabiting with another British citizen (of the opposite sex) for 'some five

[180] Opinion of AG Kokott in Case C-550/07 P *Akzo Nobel*, point 104. She also went on to find that activities of the Union legislature did not support the extension of the privilege to in-house lawyers: see points 105–112.

[181] Opinion of AG Kokott in Case C-550/07 P *Akzo Nobel*, point 113.

[182] See Lenaerts and Gutman, n 11, 9.

[183] See further De Baere and Gutman, n 122, section 4.3. Eg, compare Case C-34/10 *Brüstle* [2011] ECR I-9821, paras 24–38, in which the Court formulated the concept of 'human embryo' for the purposes of determining the scope of the exclusion of certain matters from patentability under the 'Biotechnology Directive' (Dir 98/44/EC of the European Parliament and of the Council of 6 July 1998 on the legal protection of biotechnological inventions, [1998] OJ L213/13). In doing so, it pointed out that 'although the definition of human embryo is a very sensitive social issue in many Member States, marked by their multiple traditions and value systems, the Court is not called upon, by the present order of reference, to broach questions of a medical or ethical nature, but must restrict itself to a legal interpretation of the relevant provisions of the Directive': Case C-34/10 *Brüstle*, para 30. This dovetailed with the AG's Opinion, noting the lack of a unanimous conception in the Member States: see Opinion of AG Bot in Case C-34/10 *Brüstle*, points 64–70.

[184] Case C-59/85 *Reed* [1986] ECR 1283.

[185] Joined Cases C-122/99 P and C-125/99 P *D and Sweden v Council* [2001] ECR I-4319.

[186] Lenaerts and Gutman, n 11, 50–5.

[187] Case C-59/85 *Reed* [1986] ECR 1283.

years standing'.[188] Article 10(1)(a) of Regulation No 1612/68[189] provided that certain members of the 'family' of a Union worker, including the 'spouse', have the right to install themselves with a worker who is a national of one Member State and employed in the territory of another Member State. Thus, the case turned on the issue whether Ms Reed could fall within the definition of 'spouse' under the Regulation so as to be granted the rights set forth in that provision. As the Regulation failed to define this concept, it fell to the Court, in a request for a preliminary ruling from the Dutch Supreme Court, to decide whether it included unmarried companions or cohabitees. In line with the argument put forth by the Netherlands Government, the Court ruled that 'any interpretation of a legal term on the basis of social developments must take into account the situation in the whole Community [now Union], not merely one Member State'.[190] On this basis and minding the Advocate General's Opinion indicating the variations among the Member States' cultural, social, and ethical traditions,[191] the Court fashioned an EU concept of 'spouse': 'In the absence of any indication of a general social development which would justify a broad construction, and in the absence of any indication to the contrary in the Regulation, it must be held that the term "spouse" in Article 10 of the Regulation refers to a marital relationship only.'[192]

Some years later, in 2001, the Court was confronted with elaborating the concept of 'marriage' in *D and Sweden v Council*.[193] This was a 'staff case',[194] involving the Council's rejection of an official's request to treat his same-sex relationship as equivalent to marriage in order to obtain certain benefits under the Staff Regulations, lodged before the Court of Justice on appeal. In his Opinion, Advocate General Mischo considered, in light of *Reed*, that if 'the situation in the whole of the Community [now Union]' is taken into account, 'it appears difficult to find otherwise than that in the context of the present case the definition of marriage includes only traditional marriage between two people of the opposite sex'.[195] He also stressed that the Union legislature had expressly decided not to adopt Sweden's request for modifying the Staff Regulations to assimilate same-sex registered partnerships with marriage, but to engage in further study of the matter.[196]

The Court's judgment heeded the Advocate General's Opinion on these points in upholding the General Court's interpretation of the Staff Regulations.[197] The Court held that 'according to the definition generally accepted by the Member States, the term "marriage" means a union between two persons of the opposite sex'.[198] Although an

[188] Case C-59/85 *Reed*, para 4.

[189] Council Reg (EEC) No 1612/68 of 15 Oct 1968 on freedom of movement for workers within the Community, [1968] OJ L257/2, now repealed by Reg (EU) No 492/2011 of the European Parliament and of the Council of 5 April 2011 on freedom of movement for workers within the Union, [2011] OJ L141/1.

[190] Case C-59/85 *Reed*, para 13.

[191] Opinion of AG Lenz in Case C-59/85 *Reed*, 1294.

[192] Case C-59/85 *Reed*, para 15.

[193] Joined Cases C-122/99 P and C-125/99 P *D and Sweden v Council* [2001] ECR I-4319.

[194] See n 25.

[195] Opinion of AG Mischo in Joined Cases C-122/99 P and C-125/99 P *D and Sweden v Council*, point 48.

[196] Opinion of AG Mischo in Joined Cases C-122/99 P and C-125/99 P *D and Sweden v Council*, points 51–53.

[197] Joined Cases C-122/99 P and C-125/99 P *D and Sweden v Council*, para 40.

[198] Joined Cases C-122/99 P and C-125/99 P *D and Sweden v Council*, para 34.

increasing number of Member States had 'introduced, alongside marriage, statutory arrangements granting legal recognition to various forms of union between partners of the same sex or of the opposite sex and conferring on such union certain effects which . . . are the same as or comparable to marriage', it considered that 'apart from their great diversity, such arrangements for registering partnerships between couples not previously recognised in law are regarded in the Member States as being distinct from marriage'.[199] Accordingly, the Court elaborated an EU concept of marriage in line with the national legal systems and the intent of Union legislature not to effect any changes to the Staff Regulations.[200]

Since those two judgments were delivered, the legal and social circumstances have evolved considerably at the national and Union levels. At Union level, after *D and Sweden v Council*, the Staff Regulations were amended,[201] and now provide a range of benefits to Union officials who are registered as a stable non-marital partner where certain conditions are satisfied.[202] At the national level, in light of the increasing recognition of same-sex marriage and other types of non-marital relationships in several Member States,[203] it remains to be seen whether the Court may be inclined to reconsider its position in future case law,[204] but the fact that the recognition of same-sex marriage remains highly controversial inside, as well as outside, the EU helps to give credence to the Court's cautious approach in the elaboration of these concepts taking account of the variation, and sometimes strongly opposing views, in the Member States at the time when those cases were decided.[205]

[199] Joined Cases C-122/99 P and C-125/99 P *D and Sweden v Council*, paras 35–36.

[200] See Joined Cases C-122/99 P and C-125/99 P *D and Sweden v Council*, paras 32, 37–38.

[201] See Council Reg (EC, Euratom) No 723/2004 of 22 March 2004 amending the Staff Regulations of officials of the European Communities and the Conditions of Employment of other servants of the European Communities, [2004] OJ L124/1, particularly seventh-eighth recitals. The Staff Regulations have been further amended, most recently by Reg (EU, Euratom) No 1023/2013 of the European Parliament and of the Council of 22 Oct 2013, [2013] OJ L287/15; see the consolidated version of the Staff Regulations, available at <http://ec.europa.eu/civil_service/index_en.htm>.

[202] But see, eg, Case F-86/09 (Judgment of 14 Oct 2010) *W v Commission*, not reported in the ECR [ECLI:EU:F:2010:125], in which the CST held that the condition of no prior access to marriage for same-sex non-marital partners should be interpreted flexibly in a situation where the applicant, on account of his dual Belgian-Moroccan nationality, did not marry his same-sex partner in Belgium, even though he had the right to do so, because he would have been subject to severe criminal prosecution if his same-sex marriage were to be notified to the Moroccan authorities. See also n 204.

[203] At the time of writing, the Member States with laws providing for same-sex marriage include: Belgium, Denmark, France, the Netherlands, Portugal, Spain, Sweden, and the UK (England, Scotland, and Wales); in Luxembourg, the law is expected to enter into force in 2015. See further <http://www.freedomtomarry.org/landscape/entry/c/international> (updated Oct 2014).

[204] These cases continue to be cited by the Union courts in more recent case law. See, eg, Case C-45/12 (Judgment of 13 June 2013) *Hadj Ahmed*, not reported in the ECR [ECLI:EU:C:2013:390], para 51 (holding, on the basis of *Reed*, that a mere cohabiting partner cannot be considered a 'spouse' for the purposes of Art 10(1)(a) of Reg 1612/68); Case T-58/08 P *Commission v Roodhuizen* [2009] ECR II-3797, paras 68–103 (upholding the CST's decision concerning its formulation of the concept of 'non-marital partnership' under the Staff Regulations, citing *Reed* and *D and Sweden v Council* though taking care to stress that unlike *D and Sweden v Council*, it was not being called upon to decide whether a 'registered partnership' can be deemed equivalent to marriage, but instead, was required to resolve the different matter of interpreting this concept expressly used in the Staff Regulations: see paras 75, 79–82).

[205] De Baere and Gutman, n 122, section 4.3.

3. Compatibility review

To a great extent, the discussion of the ways in which the comparative law method informs the Union courts' review of the compatibility of national law with EU law is intertwined with the previous sections. The Court's preliminary ruling jurisdiction on the interpretation of EU law indirectly determines whether a particular national rule complies with the provisions of EU law being interpreted. As explored in the sections below, the recourse to the comparative law method in this context has taken on renewed importance in the field of fundamental rights by virtue of the Charter and its interaction with the constitutional traditions common to the Member States,[206] and continues to arise in many other areas of EU law, as glimpsed by the Court's case law on the principles of national procedural autonomy, equivalence, and effectiveness.

a) The Charter and the constitutional traditions common to the Member States

In principle, the convergence of national solutions in relation to the EU regime of fundamental rights protection is embodied by the Charter, which, as indicated in its Preamble, reaffirms fundamental rights as they result from, inter alia, 'the constitutional traditions and international obligations common to the Member States'.[207] At present, one of the issues surrounding the Charter is its scope of application vis-à-vis the Member States.[208] As alluded to earlier,[209] the Charter is essentially the exact opposite of the American incorporation doctrine, since pursuant to Article 51, it applies to the Member States 'only when they are implementing Union law'.[210] If this is the case, then the 'last word' falls with the Union courts, whereas if not, the 'last word' falls with the national (supreme or constitutional) courts, that is to say, with the Member States. Consequently, this matter strikes at the heart of the comparative law method utilized by the Union courts for the purposes of discerning an 'EU' standard based on the constitutional traditions common to the Member States and the extent to which leeway is afforded to a particular national standard or constitutional tradition, as illustrated by *Åkerberg Fransson*,[211] as well

[206] It should not be overlooked, however, that the discussion of the constitutional traditions common to the Member States may figure into the assessment of the compatibility of national measures with EU law apart from the context of fundamental rights and other general principles of EU law: compare, eg, Case C-558/10 (Judgment of 5 July 2012) *Bourgès-Maunoury and Heitz*, not reported in the ECR [ECLI:EU:C:2012:418] (involving the indirect assessment of the compatibility of a national wealth tax capping mechanism with EU primary law), with Opinion of AG Cruz Villalón, points 58–62.

[207] Charter, n 7, Preamble, fifth para.

[208] For a brief selection, see, eg, S Peers, T Hervey, J Kenner, and A Ward (eds.), *The EU Charter of Fundamental Rights. A Commentary* (Nomos/CH Beck/Hart, 2014) pts I–II; V Kronenberger, MT D'Alessio, and V Placco (eds.), *De Rome à Lisbonne: les juridictions de l'Union européenne à la croisée des chemins. Mélanges en l'honneur de Paolo Mengozzi* (Bruylant, 2013) pt II; K Lenaerts, 'Exploring the Limits of the EU Charter of Fundamental Rights' (2012) 8 European Constitutional Law Review 375 and citations therein.

[209] See n 42 and accompanying text. [210] Charter, n 7, Art 51(1).

[211] Case C-617/10 (Judgment of 26 Feb 2013) *Åkerberg Fransson*, not reported in the ECR [ECLI:EU:C:2013:105].

as *Melloni*,[212] delivered by the Court of Justice on the same day,[213] and some prior case law.

Åkerberg Fransson[214] concerned a preliminary ruling from a Swedish court which turned on the issue of the application of the Charter (the *ne bis in idem* principle enshrined in Article 50) to national legislation allowing for two separate sets of proceedings, administrative and criminal, to punish the same wrongful conduct in the tax field.[215] In its judgment, the Court held that it had jurisdiction to answer the questions referred regarding the compatibility of the national legislation at issue with the Charter only in respect of the aspects of the case relating to the VAT, making clear that even though the national legislation was not adopted to transpose the relevant EU directive in the field, the application of that legislation was designed to penalize an infringement of that directive and further intended to implement the obligations imposed on the Member States under the Treaties to provide for effective penalties for conduct prejudicial to important financial interests of the EU, here in relation to the EU budget and the system of own resources.[216] On that basis, it held the Charter to be applicable and concluded that the *ne bis in idem* principle did not preclude a Member State from imposing successively, for the same acts of non-compliance with declaration obligations in the field of VAT, a tax penalty and a criminal penalty in so far as the first penalty was not criminal in nature, which was for the national court to determine.[217] In his Opinion, Advocate General Cruz Villalón, utilizing the comparative law method, took note of the varying positions of the Member States on the matter,[218] and emphasized that the lack of agreement among the Member States in respect of the incorporation of this principle into the ECHR system[219] coincided with the widespread existence and established nature in the Member States of systems in which both an administrative and criminal penalty may be imposed for the same offence, which 'could even be described as a common constitutional tradition of the Member States'.[220] This led him to advocate an independent interpretation of Article 50 of the Charter by the Court.[221] Accordingly, the Court's judgment may be viewed as establishing an 'EU' standard of Charter law in view of the divergent approaches in the Member States.

Yet, even where the Charter is deemed applicable, this does not exclude the viability of national constitutional traditions. As regards the scope and interpretation of the rights and principles enshrined in the Charter, Article 52 stipulates that: 'In so far as

[212] Case C-399/11 (Judgment of 26 Feb 2013) *Melloni*, not reported in the ECR [ECLI:EU:C:2013:107].

[213] For detailed discussion and broader implications of these judgments, see, eg, D Sarmiento, 'Who's Afraid of the Charter? The Court of Justice, National Courts and the New Framework of Fundamental Rights Protection in Europe' (2013) *CMLR* 1267; P Wattel, 'New wine into old wineskins: the scope of the Charter of Fundamental Rights of the EU after *Åkerberg Fransson*' (2013) 38 *EL Rev* 866; see also n 208.

[214] Case C-617/10 (Judgment of 26 Feb 2013) *Åkerberg Fransson*, not reported in the ECR [ECLI:EU:C:2013:105].

[215] See Case C-617/10 *Åkerberg Fransson*, paras 12–15.

[216] Case C-617/10 *Åkerberg Fransson*, paras 17–31. Compare Opinion of AG Cruz Villalón, points 47–64, which came to a different conclusion.

[217] Case C-617/10 *Åkerberg Fransson*, paras 32–37.

[218] See Opinion of AG Cruz Villalón in Case C-617/10 *Åkerberg Fransson*, point 83.

[219] See Opinion of AG Cruz Villalón in Case C-617/10 *Åkerberg Fransson*, points 71–74.

[220] Opinion of AG Cruz Villalón in Case C-617/10 *Åkerberg Fransson*, point 86.

[221] See Opinion of AG Cruz Villalón in Case C-617/10 *Åkerberg Fransson*, point 87.

this Charter recognises fundamental rights as they result from the constitutional traditions common to the Member States, those rights shall be interpreted in harmony with those traditions.'[222] By referring to the constitutional traditions common to the Member States, the Charter does not seek to define the fundamental rights recognized thereby in accordance with the 'smallest common denominator' of the Member States' constitutions, but instead, to interpret the fundamental rights enshrined therein in a way that offers a high level of protection that is adapted to the nature of EU law and that is, by its terms, in harmony with the national constitutional traditions.[223] As such, it harks back to the overarching approach underlying the comparative law method of the Union courts in terms of taking account of the national constitutional traditions in the process of interpreting the Charter, as evidenced by the case above.

Moreover, as regards the level of protection, Article 53 counsels that nothing in the Charter 'shall be interpreted as restricting or adversely affecting human rights and fundamental freedoms', as recognized by, inter alia, the Member States' constitutions.[224] Arguably, Article 53 may be read as a rule that strengthens the primacy of EU law by demanding that the Court state the reasons why it decided to follow, or depart from, the level of fundamental rights protection provided for in the Member States' constitutions, thereby representing an expression of 'constitutional pluralism' in the sense that so long as the essential interests of the EU are not adversely affected by national measures implementing EU law, the Court defers to the Member States the question of determining the level of protection of fundamental rights consistent with their national constitution.[225] As such, Article 53 is to be interpreted along the lines of *Omega*[226] and *Sayn-Wittgenstein*,[227] in which the Court ruled:

> [I]t is not indispensable for the restrictive measure issued by the authorities of a Member State to correspond to a conception shared by all Member States as regards the precise way in which the fundamental right or legitimate interest in question is to be protected and that, on the contrary, the need for, and proportionality of, the provisions adopted are not excluded merely because one Member State has chosen a system of protection different from that adopted by another State.[228]

This was recently confirmed in *Melloni*,[229] in which the Court held that as regards Article 53 of the Charter, 'Member States are free to apply national standards of protection of fundamental rights, provided that the level of protection provided for by the Charter, as interpreted by the Court, and the primacy, unity and effectiveness of EU law are not thereby compromised'.[230] In this way, going back to its overarching

[222] Charter, n 7, Art 52(4). [223] Lenaerts, n 208, 397. [224] Charter, n 7, Art 53.

[225] Lenaerts, n 208, 397–9 and citations therein. [226] Case C-36/02 *Omega* [2004] ECR I-9609.

[227] Case C-208/09 *Sayn-Wittgenstein* [2010] ECR I-13693.

[228] Case C-208/09 *Sayn-Wittgenstein*, para 91 (citing Case C-36/02 *Omega*, paras 37–38). For further discussion of these cases and their broader implications, see, eg, Lenaerts, n 40, 1327–32 and citations therein. See also, eg, Case C-244/06 *Dynamic Medien* [2008] ECR I-505, para 44.

[229] Case C-399/11 (Judgment of 26 February 2013) *Melloni*, not reported in the ECR [ECLI:EU:C:2013:107].

[230] Case C-399/11 *Melloni*, para 60. In the present proceedings, involving Union measures concerning the European arrest warrant, the Court found that this was not the case: see Case C-399/11 *Melloni*, paras 61–64. See also Opinion of AG Bot in Case C-399/11 *Melloni*, points 88–136, taking care to stress that such approach did not mean that account is not taken of the national identity of the Member States pursuant to

approach, the Court seeks to find a solution that ensures that the project of European integration is not put at risk, yet at the same time that its decision is sufficiently close to the national legal traditions so as to enjoy recognition and credibility in the Member States, including the national (constitutional and supreme) courts.[231]

With the status of the Charter as 'an authoritative catalogue of fundamental rights' based on the common constitutional traditions of the Member States,[232] it may be wondered whether this may detract from the Union courts' reliance on the comparative law method. For instance, in the context of *Laval un Partneri*[233]—the 'companion' case to *Viking Line*,[234] which together dealt with sensitive questions concerning the balancing of the fundamental right to take collective action with the free movement rules[235]—Advocate General Mengozzi considered, in the context of ascertaining the existence of such a fundamental right in the Union legal order,[236] that as regards the constitutional traditions of the Member States 'I am not of the view that they must be examined exhaustively, in view of the fact that . . . the Charter of Fundamental Rights . . . is principally intended to reaffirm the rights resulting in particular from those traditions.'[237]

Even so, to recall, under Article 6 TEU, the EU regime of fundamental rights protection rests on three complementary, as opposed to competing, normative sources—the Charter, the ECHR, and the constitutional traditions common to the Member States—the latter of which still operates as a source of inspiration in the interpretation and discovery of general principles of EU law, including but not limited to fundamental rights.[238] Furthermore, the comparative analysis of the constitutional

Art 4(2) TEU (points 137–142) and that the diversity of the national legal systems and traditions underpinned the EU's objectives to which the Union measures at issue pertained (points 143–145).

[231] Lenaerts and Gutiérrez-Fons, n 8, 1636.

[232] Opinion of AG Sharpston in Case C-396/11 (Judgment of 29 Jan 2013) *Radu*, not reported in the ECR [ECLI:EU:C:2013:39], point 48 (referring to its status pre-Lisbon); see also Opinion of AG Poiares Maduro in Case C-305/05 *Ordre des barreaux francophones and germanophone and Others* [2007] ECR I-5305, point 48; and Opinion of AG Poiares Maduro in Case C-465/07 *Elgafaji* [2009] ECR I-921, point 21 as regards the roles or dual function of the Charter (pre-Lisbon) as establishing a presumption of the existence of a fundamental right and for fleshing out the content, scope, and application of a fundamental right once identified.

[233] Case C-341/05 *Laval un Partneri* [2007] ECR I-11767.

[234] Case C-438/05 *International Transport Workers' Federation and Finnish Seamen's Union* ('*Viking Line*') [2007] ECR I-10778. In his Opinion, the AG referred to a comparative analysis of the case law of several Member State courts of which he cited 'only a random few' (the UK, Germany, the Netherlands, the Czech Republic, and Cyprus), as well as the US, as regards the horizontal effect of constitutional rights: see Opinion of AG Poiares Maduro in Case C-438/05 *Viking Line*, point 39 fn 38.

[235] For detailed discussion, see, eg, Lenaerts and Gutiérrez-Fons, n 8, 1664–7 and citations therein. See further, eg, Case C-271/08 *Commission v Germany* [2010] ECR I-7091, paras 38–50; see also Opinion of AG Trstenjak in Case C-271/08 *Commission v Germany*, points 179–199; Opinion of AG Trstenjak in Case C-81/09 *Idrima Tipou* [2010] ECR I-10161, points 81–88. Incidentally, in the latter case, the Court referred to the comparative analysis conducted by the AG as part of rejecting the existence of a general principle of company law: see Case C-81/09 *Idrima Tipou*, para 42.

[236] See Opinion of AG Mengozzi in Case C-341/05 *Laval un Partneri*, point 78.

[237] Opinion of AG Mengozzi in Case C-341/05 *Laval un Partneri*, point 77. He nevertheless pointed out that in this context 'the constitutional instruments of numerous Member States explicitly protect the right to establish trade unions and the defence of their interests by collective action, the right to strike being, in that connection, the method most regularly referred to'. Opinion of AG Mengozzi in Case C-341/05 *Laval un Partneri*, point 77.

[238] See n 64 and accompanying text.

traditions of the Member States plays an important role, in addition to other relevant instruments, especially where the fundamental right at issue in the case does not find its basis, or is not defined, in the Charter.[239] For instance, in *DEB*,[240] involving a request for a preliminary ruling from a German court as to whether the principle of effective judicial protection, as enshrined in Article 47 of the Charter, required legal aid to be granted to legal persons,[241] the Court of Justice pointed out that there was no indication in that provision of the Charter whether legal aid must be granted to legal persons (or of the nature of the costs covered by such aid), thereby necessitating analysis of the laws of the Member States, among other things.[242] On the basis of the Advocate General's Opinion, it found that 'examination of the law of the Member States brings to light the absence of a truly common principle which is shared by all those States as regards the award of legal aid to legal persons', although for those Member States that allow legal aid to be granted to legal persons 'there is a relatively widespread distinction between profit-making and non-profit-making legal persons'.[243] Ultimately, the Court concluded that the principle of effective judicial protection, as laid down in Article 47 of the Charter, must be interpreted as meaning that it is not impossible for legal persons to rely on that principle and that aid granted pursuant to that principle may cover, inter alia, dispensation from advance payment of the costs of proceedings and/or the assistance of a lawyer, laying down several criteria for the national court to take into account as part of its assessment drawn in relevant part from that comparative analysis.[244]

b) National procedural autonomy, equivalence, and effectiveness

Apart from fundamental rights, another area in which the comparative law method may be availed of in the context of the Union courts' review of the compatibility of national law with EU law concerns the Court's jurisprudence on the interplay between so-called 'national procedural autonomy' and the Union principles of equivalence and

[239] Eg, in *Schenker & Co. and Others*, the AG noted that the principle of *nulla poena sine culpa* (no punishment without fault) constituted a fundamental right common to the constitutional traditions of the Member States, even though it was not expressly mentioned in the Charter or the ECHR (though implicitly contained in certain provisions of those instruments): see Opinion of AG Kokott in Case C-681/11 (Judgment of 18 June 2013) *Schenker & Co. and Others*, not reported in the ECR [ECLI:EU:C:2013:404], point 41. The Court did not discuss this issue in its judgment.

[240] Case C-279/09 *DEB* [2010] ECR I-13849.

[241] The Court reframed the question posed by the national court, which had to do with the principle of effectiveness in connection with bringing a claim for State liability: see Case C-279/09 *DEB*, paras 27–33.

[242] Case C-279/09 *DEB*, paras 36–37 (also including its context, other provisions of EU law, and ECtHR case law).

[243] Case C-279/09 *DEB*, para 44. In his Opinion, AG Mengozzi referred to a 'small sample of national practices' (looking to those in France, Italy, Luxembourg, and Denmark: point 77 fns 38–41), from which he concluded, first, that there was the absence of a truly common principle which is shared by the Member States in awarding legal aid and which could, where appropriate, be reflected and established in EU law, and secondly, that the practice of distinguishing between commercial and non-commercial legal persons, with the effect that the latter were more readily given legal aid, was relatively commonplace across the Member States: Opinion of AG Mengozzi in Case C-279/09 *DEB*, points 76–80.

[244] Case C-279/09 *DEB*, paras 59–62.

effectiveness,[245] as demonstrated by classic cases such as *Factortame*,[246] *Eco-Swiss*,[247] and *Van Schijndel and Van Veen*.[248] Admittedly, there do not appear to be as many ready examples in more recent case law where the comparative law method is explicitly discussed in the Court's judgment. Yet, if one looks closely, this method may be detected beneath the surface of certain cases in this context.

For instance, in *Heemskerk and Schaap*,[249] by way of a reference for a preliminary ruling from a Dutch court, the Court was faced with the question whether a national court should invoke EU law of its own motion, in order to correct a violation of that law, where this would contravene the principle of Dutch law prohibiting *reformatio in pejus*, meaning that an individual bringing an action must not be placed in a less favourable position than if he had not brought that action.[250] In his Opinion, Advocate General Bot noted:

> An examination of the laws of the Member States reveals that, as in Netherlands administrative law, the principle of the prohibition on *reformatio in pejus* is closely associated with the principle that it is for the parties to delimit the subject-matter of the proceedings (the 'principe dispositif'). Accordingly, whether laid down by legislation or recognised by case-law, the prohibition on *reformatio in pejus* results from the idea that the party bringing an action does so in order to serve and protect his interests as set out and defined in the application submitted to the court. More general considerations are also put forward in different legal systems. Those considerations relate, inter alia, to legal certainty and, in particular, to litigants' expectations concerning the circumstances in which justice is done, expectations which do not allow the worsening of a situation that the use of a legal remedy was, on the contrary, intended to improve.[251]

In its judgment, the Court held that EU law did not require the Dutch courts to violate this principle, since '[s]uch an obligation would be contrary not only to the principles of respect for the rights of the defence, legal certainty and protection of legitimate expectations, which underlie the prohibition, but would expose an individual who brought an action against an act adversely affecting him to the risk that such an action would place him in a less favourable position than he would have been in, had he not brought the action'.[252] The Court's ruling, in affording deference to a principle of national procedural law, may also be read as respectful of the treatment of this matter in the national legal systems along the lines of its overarching approach underlying the comparative law method.

[245] See Lenaerts, *Comparative Law before the Courts*, n 2, 125–33. For detailed discussion, see, eg, Lenaerts, Maselis, and Gutman, n 23, ch 4 and citations therein.

[246] Case C-213/89 *Factortame and Others* [1990] ECR I-2433.

[247] Case C-126/97 *Eco Swiss* [1999] ECR I-3055.

[248] Joined Cases C-430/93 and C-431/93 *Van Schijndel and Van Veen* [1995] ECR I-4705.

[249] Case C-455/06 *Heemskerk and Schaap* [2008] ECR I-8763.

[250] See Case C-455/06 *Heemskerk and Schaap*, paras 44–45.

[251] Opinion of AG Bot in Case C-455/06 *Heemskerk and Schaap*, point 81 fn 21. However, he came to a different conclusion than the Court on this issue: see points 87–146.

[252] Case C-455/06 *Heemskerk and Schaap*, paras 46–48.

IV. Conclusion

In view of the foregoing discussion, the comparative law method constitutes an important, indeed crucial, tool for the Union courts as part of deciding all the various types of cases that are brought before them in all areas of EU law whether involving judicial interpretation or judicial lawmaking. The fact that more recent case law may not contain extensive comparative analysis of the national legal systems (or other relevant jurisdictions) should not be taken to mean that the comparative law method does not figure in EU adjudication, even if it may be more prevalent in the Opinions of the Advocates General or remain beneath the scenes of the Court's judgments in many cases. Likewise, the Union courts' overarching approach continues to involve a subtle, and increasingly delicate, balancing exercise between upholding the fundamental interests and objectives of the Union legal order and respecting as much as possible the rules, principles, and traditions of the Member States. As illustrated by several cases mentioned above, this approach is both a functional and fluid one, not only depending on the weighing of these two components, but also taking account of social and legal developments occurring at the national and Union levels. It remains as true today as in previous decades that the comparative law method in the workings of the Court of Justice of the European Union embodies the interlocking relationship between the Union and the national legal orders, and with the advancement of European integration, it is destined to play a central role in EU adjudication in the years to come.

9

National Judges and Strasbourg Case Law

Comparative Reflections about the Italian Experience

*Ermanno Calzolaio**

I. Introduction: the protection of human rights as case law

This contribution aims at giving some comparative reflections about the Strasbourg case law, moving from a simple but very important statement: the phenomenon of the protection of human rights in the European context has essentially a case law basis. Of course, no one could underestimate the importance of the European Convention for the Protection of Human Rights (ECHR) itself. But it is unquestionable that the protection of human rights lies on the concrete application of the ECHR by the European Court.

It is worth considering that until the end of the last century the system of protection of human rights in Europe was someway parallel and separate from the systems developed within the states. This was due essentially to the fact, on one side, that the ECHR was regarded as being a simple statute and, on the other side, that the Strasbourg Court had only a subsidiary role. The first 17 contracting parties wanted to set the way for a stable and pacific coexistence, in order to avoid the horrible attempts against human rights which were perpetrated during the Second World War, but they were in deep disagreement as to whether they should give rise to an autonomous supranational system of protection of human rights. That is why the jurisdiction of the ECtHR was limited to the voluntary initiative of the contracting states and subject to a previous leave by the European Commission of Human Rights, which was an institution created exactly in order to set a philtre of admissibility to the applications.[1]

In the 1990s, a deeper change took place. It is not the aim of this article to trace the steps of this development. It is sufficient to mention that the approval of Protocol no. 11, in force since 1 November 1998, had the effect of giving free access to individual applications and of giving to the Court the general binding competence on all the issues concerning the interpretation of the Convention and of its Protocols. As a result of this

* Professor of Private Comparative Law and Comparative Legal Systems and Dean of the Faculty of Law at the University of Macerata (Italy).

[1] D. Shelton, 'The Boundaries of Human Rights Jurisdiction in Europe', in Duke Journal of Comparative & International Law, n. 13, 2002, 95. The Commission ceased its activity in 1998. Its aim was to favour a friendly settlement of the controversy. In case of failure, it issued an opinion and submitted it to the Comity of Ministers. If the relevant State accepted the jurisdiction of the Court, the controversy could finally come to the Court. Only the States had recourse to the Court and not individuals.

reform, the activity of the Court now marks a huge increase of cases, moving from 45,000 applications in the whole period between 1955 and 1998 (i.e. about 1,000 per year), to over 56,000 per year today.[2]

As a consequence, national judges are now faced with an enormous block of judicial rules laid down by the Strasbourg Court. Moreover, as far as the European Union is concerned, the importance of the Strasbourg case law is more and more intense following the Treaty of Lisbon and the well-known acquisition of the same legal value of the Treaties by the Charter signed in Nice in 2000.

In short, it is possible to assert that almost every legal issue which arises in the domestic courts can have some implications in the light of the European Convention and so of the Strasbourg case law.[3]

If we are in front of a law which is essentially a 'case law', this has an immediate methodological consequence, from a comparative point of view, because it focuses the attention primarily on the characteristics of this case law. This methodological step about the *context* is essential and preliminary to any consideration about the *content* of the rules laid down by the Court.[4]

This contribution aims at raising some issues on this subject. It will be impossible to consider all the relevant aspects, such as the organization of the Court and the ways through which the judges are appointed. In this regard, it is only useful to mention that very recently, on 16 May 2013, Protocol no. 15 had been signed by the Committee of Ministers. It introduced significant changes concerning the appointment of judges, the relinquishment of a case by a Chamber in favour of the Grand Chamber, against which the parties do not have the right to object. Moreover, since 1 July 2013 the Court has adopted a new version of the Rules of the Court.

We will concentrate our attention on three aspects: i) the style of judgments; ii) the existence of a rule of precedent in the Convention system; iii) the position of Italian judges towards the European Convention. At the end, some remarks will be drawn about the role of comparative law in this subject.

II. The style of judgments

The expression 'style of judgments' indicates a series of characteristic and morphological aspects of judicial decisions, which are the manifestation of attitudes deeply rooted in the context of a legal system, such as the structure, the language used by the judges, the exposition of facts, the ways through which the issues are discussed and set, the referral to previous cases.[5]

It is well known that in civil law systems, the judgment is essentially a decision of the court itself, where usually a very short account of the facts is given by judges. In common law

[2] Since 2001, the statistics have been published on the website of the Court <http://www.echr.coe.int/Documents/Stats_annual_2014_ENG.pdf>. It is worth noting that the philtre of admissibility is very rigorous, as about 6% of petitions are declared admissible.

[3] Cf. M. O'Boyle, 'The Future of the European Court of Human Rights', in German Law Journal, 2011, 1862.

[4] About comparative law as 'science of context', see L. Moccia, *Comparazione giuridica e diritto europeo*, Milan, 2005, part 1.

[5] G. Gorla, 'Lo stile delle sentenze. Ricerca storico-comparativa' in *Quaderni de 'Il Foro italiano'*, 1967, 313.

systems, on the contrary, the judgment is formed by the opinions of the judges and there is always a deep consideration of the facts of the case. In the former, precedents are sometimes quoted and considered. In the latter, precedents are always considered.

The Strasbourg Court's judgments can be described as a kind of combination of these two models. Article 45 of the Convention only provides that all judgments should have reasons and that each judge can give separate opinions. Article 74 of the Rules of the Court gives more details and especially it provides that each judgment must indicate the official text (that is to say the language of the procedure) and the number of judges of the majority.

This last indication is very interesting because even if the judgments of the Strasbourg Court share with the continental model the characteristic of being collegial, they differ from it because they always indicate if the decision is adopted by the majority of judges or if it is a unanimous decision. Moreover, the judges can write separate opinions, which are reported at the end of the judgment. With a separate opinion, a judge can express a position of dissent, or an approval of the conclusions reached by the majority, but on different grounds.[6] This opportunity is very well known in the common law experience, but it is not familiar to the civil law systems.

Recent studies show that the recourse to separate opinions in the Strasbourg Court is very frequent. About 25 per cent of the judgments are adopted unanimously, 15 per cent have at least one dissenting opinion and 60 per cent at least a concurring opinion.[7]

This aspect is very often underestimated, especially in Italy and in general in the other civil law systems, but it is very important, because it indicates a methodological caution. The study of the Strasbourg Court case law should never be limited to the judgment itself, but it should take account of the separate opinions of judges, in order to consider the reasons given by them.[8] In this respect it is worth mentioning that studies on the case law of the Strasbourg Court show that the dissenting opinions are not given by judges coming from the state which is involved in the case, so that one could argue that they would be keen to develop arguments in defence of their respective system. It has been demonstrated that the dissenting opinions of national judges are very few, so that the reasons why a judge decides to add a separate opinion should be explored in different ways by considering the issues involved in the case.

An interesting example of this can be drawn from the case *S.H. and others v. Austria*, decided by the Grand Chamber in 2011, concerning the Austrian legislation on

[6] The possibility of writing separate opinions has some consequences on the structure of the judgment. At least five categories can be identified: i) a unanimous judgment; ii) a judgment and a dissenting opinion of one or more than one of the judges; iii) a judgment and a concurring opinion of one or more than one of the judges; iv) a judgment and concurring and dissenting opinions; v) a judgment and partially concurring or dissenting opinions. R.C.A. White, 'Judgments in the Strasbourg Court: Some Reflections', in M. Andenas-S. Vogenhauer (eds.), *A Matter of Style? The Form of Judgments in the United Kingdom and Abroad*, available at <http://ssrn.com/abstract=1435197>.

[7] F. Rivière, *Les opinions séparées des juges à la cour européenne des droit de l'homme*, Bruxelles, 2004; more recently, F.J. Bruinsma, *The Room at the Top: Separate Opinions in the Grand Chambers of the ECHR (1998–2006), Ancilla Juris*, 2008, 32, R.C.A. White-I Boussiakou, *Separate opinions in the European Court of Human Rights*, Human Rights Law Review, 2009, 37. About the role of the case law of the European Court see also J.G. Merrills, *The Development of International law by the European Court of Human Rights*, 2nd edn., Manchester, 1993.

[8] R.C.A. White-I Boussiakou, *Separate opinions etc.*, ibid., 55.

artificial insemination.[9] The Court concluded that the Austrian legislation which prohibits artificial insemination was in accordance with the Convention and great assistance for understanding the issues involved in this case comes from the two separate opinions, where the problems of the meaning of the 'margin of appreciation' of the states and of the relevance of new trends are debated.[10] In particular, one of the judges raises doubts about the assumption of the majority according to which a 'European consensus' on the subject matter under examination is an important consideration for determining whether or not there has been a violation of the Convention. His separate opinion asks core questions: Must a judge decide according to the majority principle in such matters? Does not history show that in Europe decisions against human rights have been adopted by a very large majority?[11]

Another example is the recent judgment of the Grand Chamber in the case of *X and others v. Austria*, concerning the issue of partner's same-sex adoption,[12] where the jointly partly dissenting opinion of seven judges raises very crucial issues about the comparative method of ascertaining a consensus between the states and of the meaning of evolutive method of interpretation.

These examples show that, despite the almost total absence of interest of civil law scholars and judges, separate opinions play a fundamental role in the case law of the Strasbourg Court, not only because they are personal voices which enrich the institutional discourse of the Court, but also because they correct the impersonal and sometimes bureaucratic style of its judgments, so that they are essential to an exact comprehension of the judgments themselves.

III. A rule of precedent?

Despite the central importance of Strasbourg case law, it is interesting to realize that there is general accordance between scholars that the Convention system does not provide a rule of binding precedent, as there is no statutory provision which compels the national courts to follow the Strasbourg precedents.[13]

If we look with more attention, the absence of statutory provisions in this respect is at least questionable. For instance, Protocol no. 14, which entered in force in 2011, provides that a panel of three judges can decide the case, without referring it to the Court, when it is possible to solve the issue through the application of previous judgments of the Court. This provision can easily be read as a recognition of the existence of a rule of precedent.

[9] *Case of S.H. and others v. Austria* (Application no. 57813/00), Grand Chamber, judgment 3 November 2011.

[10] For a deep comparative analysis, see M. Andenas-E. Bjorge, 'National Implementation of ECHR Rights', in A. Follesdal-B. Peters-G. Ulfstein (eds.), *Constituting Europe. The European Court of Human Rights in a National, European and Global Context*, Cambridge, 2013, 181, especially 194.

[11] Cf. dissenting opinion of Judge De Gaetano to the case quoted in n. 9.

[12] *Case of X and others v. Austria* (Application no. 19010/07), Grand Chamber, judgment 19 February 2013.

[13] Cf. M. Balcerzak, 'The Doctrine of Precedent in the International Court of Justice and the European Court of Human Rights', Polish Yearbook of International Studies, 2004, 131.

But, leaving aside the discussion whether or not an obligation to follow precedents exists, it is undeniable that the Strasbourg Court rarely departs from its precedents. In a very important case of 2002 the Grand Chamber said:

> 'While the Court is not formally bound to follow its previous judgments, it is in the interests of legal certainty, foreseeability and equality before the law that it should not depart, without good reason, from precedents laid down in previous cases (see, for example, Chapman v. the United Kingdom [GC], no. 27238/95, ECHR 2001-I, § 70). However, since the Convention is first and foremost a system for the protection of human rights, the Court must have regard to the changing conditions within the respondent State and within Contracting States generally and respond, for example, to any evolving convergence as to the standards to be achieved (see, amongst other authorities, the Cossey judgment, p. 14, § 35, and Stafford v. the United Kingdom [GC], no. 46295/99, judgment of 28 May 2002, to be published in ECHR 2002–, §§ 67–68). It is of crucial importance that the Convention is interpreted and applied in a manner which renders its rights practical and effective, not theoretical and illusory. A failure by the Court to maintain a dynamic and evolutive approach would indeed risk rendering it a bar to reform or improvement (see the above-cited Stafford v. the United Kingdom judgment, § 68).'[14]

This formulation has been repeated in many subsequent cases, so that we can conclude that the Court considers itself to be bound by its precedents, but at the same time the binding effect of precedents is not felt to be an absolute one, so that if there is a 'good reason' the Court feels free to depart from a precedent.[15]

From all that has been said so far, two statements can be made:

i) case law implies knowledge of the case, and so a study of it should not be limited to a principle of law which makes abstraction from the facts of the case;[16] one should take account of the entire judgment and of the separate opinions;
ii) the stability of precedents is of value for the Strasbourg Court, but this does not mean that the Court limits itself to mere uncritical adherence to the cases previously decided.

IV. The approach of Italian judges to the European Convention. Comparative remarks with the common law

Even before the enactment of the Treaty of Lisbon, Italian judges adopted a very open approach towards the ECHR, according to which the judge was entitled not to apply an Italian statute if it was in contrast with the rights guaranteed by the Convention. For instance, this happened in some cases concerning an Italian statute which permitted authorities to start building before expropriation. This statute provided that once a scheme has been declared to be in the public interest and the plans adopted, the

[14] *Christine Goodwin v. United Kingdom*, Grand Chamber, 11 July 2002.

[15] Cf. J. Mowbray, 'An Examination of the European Court of Human Rights' Approach to Overruling its Previous Case Law', in Human Rights Law Review, 2009, 179.

[16] In Italy, the 'massima' of a case is a short and synthetic exposition of the rule followed by the court, without reference to the facts involved in the case itself.

authorities could issue an expedited possession order, for a limited period not exceeding five years, in respect of the land to be expropriated. Once the order was issued, it would lapse if physical possession of the land was not taken within three months. This provision ensured that once the land had been possessed, a formal expropriation should take place, in order to provide adequate compensation to the owner. But the concrete application of this statute by Italian public authorities proved to be very different and it often happened that after taking possession of the land and the building finished, no formal expropriation occurred, and so no payment was directed to the owner. This phenomenon was at the origin of a huge litigation and in order to face the enormous financial difficulties, the Italian legislature adopted statutory measures, limiting the amount of compensation in favour of the owners. The ECtHR declared that this legislation was in open contrast with the European Convention.[17] As a consequence, Italian courts considered that they had the power not to apply the Italian legislation and recognized full compensation, according to the principles set by the case law of the ECtHR.[18]

Nevertheless, this approach was contradicted by the Italian Constitutional Court in two very important judgments issued in 2007.[19] The Court did not accept the view that a judge is entitled not to apply a national statute if he or she considers it contrary to the ECHR. The Court moved from art. 117 of the Italian Constitution, according to which the legislative power is exercised by the State and the Regions, consonant with Union law and international treaties. This means that no statute should contradict an international treaty, such as the ECHR. If this contradiction does occur, however, as international treaties do not have the same legal value as the Constitution itself, the judge is not entitled to refuse to apply the legislation, but should suspend the proceedings and ask the Constitutional Court to ascertain its constitutionality.

The Court estimates that the rules of the ECHR have not the same value as the rules of Union law, because they are binding for the State, but they do not have direct effect in the legal system. As a consequence of this, the Constitutional Court is the only judge to solve every problem of conflict between the ECHR and the internal law.

The approach of the Italian Constitutional Court was set before the enactment of the Treaty of Lisbon, which introduces very important changes in art. 6 of the Treaty on European Union (TEU). As is well known, the Charter of Nice now has the same legal value as the Treaties and the fundamental rights guaranteed by the ECHR, arising from the constitutional traditions common to the Member States, thereby they constitute general principles of the Union law.

After the enactment of the Treaty of Lisbon, some Italian judges claimed for the direct application of the ECHR in each legal system, so that Italian judges also should not apply the national law if it contradicts ECHR rights. According to this perspective, the principles laid down for Union law, such as direct effect and direct application, should also apply to the ECHR.

This position was notably expressed by the *Consiglio di Stato* (i.e. the Italian appellate jurisdiction for administrative law litigation), according to which the principles of the

[17] See especially *Belvedere Alberghiera srl v. Italy*, 30 May 2000, Hudoc.

[18] Corte app. Firenze, sez. I, 27 February 2005, n. 570, <www.dirittiuomo.it>.

[19] Corte Cost., 24 October 2007, n. 348, *Giur. cost.*, 2007, 5, 3475; Id., n. 349, *ivi*, 3535.

ECHR Convention are directly applicable to the internal law, after the Treaty of Lisbon and the new and more extensive formulation of art. 6 TEU.[20] From this perspective, the principles laid down by the European Court of Justice in the famous *Simmenthal* case should be applied, not only in Union law, but also in the field of the ECHR:

> A national court which is called upon, within the limits of its jurisdiction, to apply provisions of community law is under a duty to give full effect to those provisions, if necessary refusing of its own motion to apply any conflicting provision of national legislation, even if adopted subsequently, and it is not necessary for the court to request or await the prior setting aside of such provisions by legislative or other constitutional means.[21]

This approach has been rebutted once again by the Italian Constitutional Court, which continues to refuse the idea of a diffused judicial review. In 2011, the Court judged that the Treaty of Lisbon does not change the position of the ECHR in the hierarchy of the sources of law.[22] The adhesion of the EU to the Convention is still to be completed, and so the precise identification of its effects is not clear. Moreover, the Court rejects a second argument for the direct applicability of the Convention, grounded on art. 52.3 of the Charter of Nice (which has the same value as the Treaties according to art. 6.1 TEU): 'In so far as this Charter contains rights which correspond to rights guaranteed by the Convention for the Protection of Human Rights and Fundamental Freedoms, the meaning and scope of those rights shall be the same as those laid down by the said Convention'. As a consequence of this, it was claimed that when the rights guaranteed by the Convention correspond to the rights protected by the Charter, they should be considered to have the same strength of Union law. The Italian Constitutional Court rejected this argument, considering that the applicability of the Charter is limited to cases concerning the fields within the competences of Union law. In fact, art. 51.1 of the Charter provides that it 'does not extend the field of application of Union law beyond the powers of the Union or establish any new power or task for the Union, or modify powers and tasks as defined in the Treaties'.

The restrictive approach adopted by the Italian Constitutional Court seems to find now (perhaps unexpected) support by the European Court of Justice itself. In the case *Servet Kamberaj*, the Grand Chamber clearly states that art. 6.3 TEU 'does not govern the relationship between the ECHR and the legal systems of the Member States, nor does it lay down the consequences to be drawn by a national court in case of conflict between the rights guaranteed by that convention and a provision of national law'. So, it 'does not require the national court, in case of conflict between a provision of national law and the ECHR, to apply the provisions of that convention directly, disapplying the provision of national law incompatible with the convention.'[23]

[20] Cf. Cons. Stato, 2 March 2010, n. 1220, <www.giustizia-amministrativa.it> and Tar Lazio, sez. IIa bis, 18 May 2010, n. 11984, *ivi* and also Corte Conti reg., Friuli Venezia Giulia, sez. giurisd., Riv. Corte Conti, 2010, 119.

[21] EUCJ, 9 March 1978, *Amministrazione delle Finanze v. Simmenthal spa*, C-106/77.

[22] Corte Cost., 11 March 2011, n. 80.

[23] EUCJ (Gr. Ch.), *Servet Kamberaj v. Istituto per l'Edilizia sociale della Provincia autonoma di Bolzano*, 24 April 2012, C-571/10.

In this approach, one can easily see that the EUCJ is prudent in its progression towards a recognition of a 'Europeanization' of the ECHR, reserving for itself the power of determining if, when and how the Convention is effective within Union law.

So far, this approach substantially endorses the position of the Italian Constitutional Court and shows the extent to which the judicial dialogue between the European Courts and national judges still needs to be settled.

It is important not to overestimate the resistance of the Italian Constitutional Court with regards to direct application. Even if the judge is not entitled to directly apply the ECHR but is permitted to disapply an internal statute before the intervention of the Constitutional Court, it is worth noting that the so-called 'sub-constitutional' role accorded to the ECHR by the same Constitutional Court implies that all the legislation is to be interpreted in accordance with it, as applied by the European Court of Human Rights.

So, a deep value is afforded to the case law of the Strasbourg Court by the Italian Constitutional Court and this has a great impact, because every judge has to consider the text of the Convention in the light of its interpretation by the European Court.

At the same time, some critical considerations should be raised about the way in which this happens. In fact, in a judgment of 2009, the Court argued that when there is a decision from the Strasbourg Court, no power of interpretation is left to national judges. Consequently, the Constitutional Court cannot question the interpretation of the Convention given by the Strasbourg Court, to whom the contracting states gave this function.[24] This issue has been reinforced in another case, where one can read as follows: 'This Court cannot substitute its own interpretation of an article of the European Convention with that given by the Strasbourg Court, otherwise it will exceed its competence, in breach of a precise obligation of the Italian state deriving from the approval of the Convention.'[25]

On the one hand, the Italian Constitutional Court's recognition of the importance of a uniform interpretation of the ECHR is certainly welcome. On the other hand, however, this approach appears to be inconsistent with the mechanisms of case law. The European Court, like every judge, decides on the basis of concrete facts, to which the interpretation of the Convention is always linked. The former Italian judge, Vladimiro Zagrebelski, elucidates this method followed by the Strasbourg Court:

> the way of reasoning adopted by the Court, in the motivation of judgments and in the discussion between the judges, is essentially based on precedents. We move from the search of the relevant case and, when there is no one, the Court starts in an adventure within the interstices which are left open by the precedents. So it goes on distinguishing the case to decide from the one which has been decided, in order to come to find the relevant precedent or to the conclusion that the present case has not a precedent. In this case the Court considers all the precedents which have a useful ratio. In the absence of this, the Court tries to find out the meaning of the articles of the Convention.[26]

[24] Corte Cost., 26 November 2009, n. 311, *Riv. dir. int.*, 2010, p. 164.

[25] Corte Cost., 4 December 2009, n. 317, *ivi.*, 181.

[26] V. Zagrebelski, *La giurisprudenza casistica della Corte europea dei diritti dell'uomo; fatto e diritto alla luce dei precedenti*, in <www.giurisprudenza.unimib.it/V2/DATA/bacheca/File/convegni%20locandine/2009-2010/Zagrebelsky.pdf>.

If the Court works like this, the national judge should follow suit and adopt a similar method, without according Strasbourg decisions a value that they cannot have. For this reason, the position of the Italian Constitutional Court appears to be at least questionable, when it says that the judge cannot even interpret the ECHR because this task is not its task, as it has been delegated to the Strasbourg Court. This reveals a degree of cultural weakness: it is precisely the task of the national judge to analyse the case at hand, to compare it with the case decided by the Strasbourg Court, to find out the *ratio*, and to distinguish the case from the cases decided by the Court.

National judges are confronted by a real challenge, which is particularly serious for civil law judges, being less familiar with the dynamics of case law. From a comparative point of view, it is notable that English judges also experienced some discomfort soon after the enactment of the Human Rights Act 1998. As is well known, this Act requires English judges to 'take into account' Strasbourg case law (section 2(1)(a)) and, 'so far as it is possible to do so', to read and give effect to legislation in a way which is compatible with the Convention rights (section 3(1)). The (then) House of Lords adopted an approach which is not dissimilar from the one followed by the Italian Constitutional Court: 'courts should, in the absence of some special circumstances, follow any clear and constant jurisprudence of the Strasbourg court ... This reflects the fact that the Convention is an international instrument, *the correct interpretation of which can be authoritatively expounded only by the Strasbourg court*' (emphasis added). So, 'the duty of national courts is to keep pace with the Strasbourg jurisprudence as it evolves over time: no more, but certainly no less.'[27]

This passage gave rise to a number of very interesting questions and was substantially endorsed in later cases. For instance, in 2010 a judge of the Supreme Court said: 'Strasbourg has spoken, the case is closed.'[28] This wording gave rise to a reaction by the President of the Strasbourg Court himself, who observed that 'this is not the way in which I and my colleagues conceive the roles of the two Courts'.[29]

It is interesting to consider that a more cautious approach is now emerging, which seems to be more in accordance with the traditional common law perspective. Already in *Manchester City Council v. Pinnock* Lord Neuberger summarized his position as follows:

> This court is not bound to follow every decision of the European court. Not only would it be impractical to do so: it would sometimes be inappropriate, as it would destroy the ability of the court to engage in the constructive dialogue with the European court which is of value to the development of Convention law: see e g *R v Horncastle* [2010] 2 AC 373. Of course, we should usually follow a clear and constant line of decisions by the European court: *R (Ullah) v Special Adjudicator* [2004] 2 AC 323. But we are not actually bound to do so or (in theory, at least) to follow a decision of the Grand Chamber. As Lord Mance pointed out in *Doherty v Birmingham City Council* [2009] AC 367, para 126, section 2 of the 1998 Act requires our courts to 'take

[27] *R (Ullah) v. Special Adjudicator* [2004] UKHL 26 *per* Lord Bingham.

[28] *Secretary of State for the Home Department v. AF (No 3)* [2010] 2 AC 269, par. 98, *per* Lord Rodger.

[29] N. Bratza, 'The Relationship between the UK Courts and Strasbourg', in *European Human Rights Law Review*, 2011, 505. In this respect, see E. Bjorge, *The Courts and the ECHR: A Principled Approach to the Strasbourg Jurisprudence*, CLJ, 2013, 289, with an interesting analysis of the misunderstanding of the so called 'Ullah approach' (derived from the *dictum* of Lord Bingham, see n. 27).

> into account' European court decisions, not necessarily to follow them. Where, however, there is a clear and constant line of decisions whose effect is not inconsistent with some fundamental substantive or procedural aspect of our law, and whose reasoning does not appear to overlook or misunderstand some argument or point of principle, we consider that it would be wrong for this Court not to follow that line.[30]

In this respect, it is worth mentioning the position of a judge of the Supreme Court who, speaking extra-judicially, summarized his view by saying: 'Strasbourg has spoken, now it is our time to speak', and as he further explained 'there is no question of the one being the modest underworker of the other.'[31] This approach seems to find a significant endorsement in a recent case, where the Supreme Court acknowledges the need for a dialogue with the Strasbourg Court:

> In relation to authority consisting of one or more simple Chamber decisions, dialogue with Strasbourg by national courts, including the Supreme Court, has proved valuable in recent years. The process enables national courts to express their concerns and, in an appropriate case such as *R v Horncastle*, to refuse to follow Strasbourg case-law in the confidence that the reasoned expression of a diverging national viewpoint will lead to a serious review of the position in Strasbourg.[32]

Of course, this does not mean that national judges have to underestimate Strasbourg case law, but that they need to be the protagonists of a dialogue and not merely the executors of the European Court dicta.

V. Conclusion

The comparative remarks made in this chapter lead to the conclusion that national judges should take care of the nature and the dynamics of the Strasbourg case law: i) the Court gives judgments concerning cases and every judgment is linked to the facts considered, so that one should pay attention when drawing from it general principles overlooking the issues raised by the case itself; ii) one should also be aware that no one asks the national judges to consider the Strasbourg case law as a kind of legislative source which has to be strictly applied. On the contrary, a judgment is always a decision of a case and not a legislative act, so it calls for an effort of each judge to be the protagonist of a dialogue which does not admit any shortcut.

If our judges will not understand this challenge and their responsibility, it is easy to foresee that the growth of rights catalogues and the proliferation of judges dealing with them will lead to the paradox of the weakening of the protection of human rights.

[30] [2010] UKSC 45, [2011] 2 AC 104, para 48.

[31] Lord Kerr, 'The UK Supreme Court. The modest underworker of Strasbourg?', Clifford Chance Lecture 2012, <https://www.supremecourt.uk/docs/speech_120125.pdf>.

[32] *R (on the application of Chester) v. Secretary of State for Justice* [2014] 1 All ER 683.

10

Comparative Law and the European Union Civil Service Tribunal

*Haris Tagaras**

The role of comparative law in European integration and, in particular, in the case law of the Court of Justice of the European Union, has long been acknowledged, and extensively examined in legal literature.

This chapter builds on the above, but focuses specifically on the comparative-law aspects of the Civil Service Tribunal (CST), that is, on the requirement of the balanced composition of the Tribunal with respect 'to the national legal systems represented' and, more extensively, on the recourse by the Tribunal to comparative law (including comparative-law *methods*) when adjudicating cases.

However, the main bulk of the article will be preceded by a brief introductory section on the setting-up and main powers of the CST, since it is a relatively newly created judicial body, founded in 2004–2005, and not all readers are expected to be sufficiently familiar with the Tribunal.

I. Brief reminder of the institution and powers of the CST

Envisaged already at the end of the 1970s,[1] a specialized court for staff cases was eventually established by Council Decision 2004/752/EC[2] and began functioning in October 2005.

The primary objective behind its creation is generally said to have been to relieve the Court of First Instance of its very heavy workload.[3] Clearly, the CST is a specialized court and specialization is constantly mentioned as one of the major advantages following from the creation of the CST. However, it was evidently not the undoubted advantages of specialization themselves, but rather the concern about the very heavy workload of the Court of First Instance and about the resulting delays in adjudication of cases which prompted the creation of a specialized court for staff cases.

* Professor of Law at the Panteion University of Athens; Former Judge and Chamber President at the European Union Civil Service Tribunal. The author wishes to warmly thank his friend Paul Mahoney, former President of the Civil Service Tribunal and currently judge at the European Court of Human Rights, for the fruitful discussion they had on a number of questions addressed in this article, as well as for linguistic assistance on some points. This chapter takes into account developments up to September 2013.

[1] For the history of the creation of the CST, see R Grass, 'The Creation of the European Union Civil Service Tribunal: Some Recollections', (2011) 31 HRLJ 9.

[2] Council Decision of 2 November 2004 (2004/752/EC, Euratom, Official Journal of the European Union L 333, 9.11.2004).

[3] See P Mahoney, 'The Civil Service Tribunal: The Benefits and Drawbacks of a Specialized Judicial Body', (2011) 31 HRLJ 11, 13.

The jurisdiction of the CST encompasses all disputes between the Union institutions (including other bodies and agencies) and their servants; the CST is empowered to rule on the legality of acts adopted by the institutions, as well as on disputes of a financial character, for which it has unlimited jurisdiction. It is, however, a first-instance jurisdiction, with a right of appeal on points of law to the General Court and, thereafter, exceptionally, the possibility of a review by the Court of Justice.

The law to be applied by the CST is made up of the EU Staff Regulations and the Conditions of Employment of Other Servants (CEOS),[4] or the corresponding instruments of those institutions or bodies/agencies which have their own set of rules for employment relationships,[5] together with implementing texts adopted either individually by each institution and body/agency (e.g. for promotion of staff members) or at a more general level (e.g. for social security cases). It also includes secondary EU law to which the Staff Regulations (or other applicable instrument) refer.[6] Furthermore, the Tribunal, being a judicial body of the EU and part of the Court of Justice, is also bound by the general principles of law applicable in the EU, including notably principles for the protection of human rights.

The Decision establishing the CST[7] introduces three relatively important procedural reforms of the system of adjudication of staff cases: firstly, it does away with a second exchange of written pleadings; secondly, removes the previously existing exemption of staff members from the rule whereby the unsuccessful party pays the costs; thirdly, it expressly annunciates the objective of promoting attempts to reach a friendly settlement, calling on the CST to examine the possibilities of such settlement at all stages of the procedure, including when the application is filed.

However, the major novelty resides in the composition of the Tribunal. Firstly, it is composed of only seven members, which means that, at any given time, the large majority of Member States are *not* 'represented' in the Tribunal. Secondly, and more importantly, the selection of the candidates is no longer a privilege of the Member States, but the result of an open procedure, with individual applications and a recommendation by a selection committee (of 'wise men') to the Council, as to the candidates who possess the 'most suitable high-level experience';[8] the final decision on the appointment is taken by the Council, which, however, is required to ensure 'a balanced composition of the Tribunal on as broad a geographical basis as possible from among nationals of the Member States and with respect to the national legal systems represented.'[9]

The main question arising in this connection is whether the composition of the Tribunal is ultimately subject to a rotation requirement, in particular whether a more suitable candidate (that is, a candidate placed in a higher position on the

[4] Council Regulation (EEC, Euratom, ECSC) No 259/68 of 29 February 1968 (Official Journal of the European Communities L 56, 4.3.1968—Special Edition 1968, 1 December 1972), as amended.

[5] This is the case, e.g., for the European Central Bank and the European Investment Bank.

[6] Article 1e, para 2: 'Officials in active employment shall be accorded working conditions complying with appropriate health and safety standards at least equivalent to the minimum requirements applicable *under measures adopted in these areas pursuant to the Treaties*' (emphasis added).

[7] See n 2.

[8] Article 3, para 4, of the Annex to the Council Decision 2 November 2004, see n 2.

[9] Article 3, para 1, of the Annex to the Council Decision 2 November 2004, see n 2.

recommendation list drawn by the selection committee), but who comes from a Member State currently or recently 'represented' in the Tribunal, should yield before a 'less suitable' candidate coming from a Member State not so far represented. This is an interesting question, from both a political and a legal point of view, but for a number of reasons the present article limits itself to the observation that the Council practice up to now is tantamount to a clear adherence to the rotation system.

Nor, will there be any reference to or, *a fortiori*, comment on the substantive work of the Civil Service Tribunal or any general assessment as to what extent the Tribunal has accomplished effectively its tasks as expected. Not only would this be outside of the ambit of this article (save, of course, as regards what is written in sections III and IV below with regard to the comparative law), but in any case the present author's quality of former member clearly prevents him from doing so. There are many practitioners or academics, or EU officials, better placed for this task. It is not, however, without interest to close this section by recalling the British House of Lords' description of the Civil Service Tribunal as 'a success story'.[10]

II. The requirement of 'a balanced composition of the Civil Service Tribunal on as broad a geographical basis as possible ... with respect to the legal systems represented'

There can be various perceptions of a 'balanced' composition of a judicial body, e.g. with regard to the gender of its members or to their previous working experience as judges, lawyers, academics and so on. However, in the case of the CST, the requirement of balanced composition, as laid down in Article 3, paragraph 1, of the annex to Council Decision 2004/752, is expressly, and exclusively, linked to the 'geographical' dimension of the composition, which must be 'as broad as possible' with regard, firstly, to the nationality of the members and, secondly, to the legal systems 'represented'.

The first, and probably the main, question that comes to mind when reading the text of the above provision pertains to the added value of the second limb of the geographical dimension. Was it not enough to require the broadest possible representation of the EU Member States in the CST? Why was it considered necessary to extend this requirement, so as to encompass also the national legal systems represented? Is this not a tautology?

The obvious reply would be that not only did the authors of Decision 2004/752 wish to guarantee a 'right of representation' to each Member States (without prejudice to the frequency of the rotation), but they were also concerned to ensure that the CST reflect the variety of legal systems in Europe; and that they were in reality referring to the wider *law-families* of our continent and to the need for their representation in the Tribunal.

The present author does not find such an explanation convincing.

[10] House of Lords, European Union Committee, *The Workload of the Court of Justice of the European Union*, 14th Report of Session 2010–2011, paras 56 and 140.

It is true that, for historical reasons, some legal orders, notably those of countries with geographical proximity, have convergent or sometimes identical rules on specific questions (or other legal affinities). However, and notwithstanding whether a purely comparative-law study, building on such phenomena, could lead to a conclusion of the existence of specific law-families in the European Union, e.g. Scandinavian or East European (this being a question of undoubted interest, but as such outside the ambit of this article), in my perception, and with the exception to a certain extent of some common law concepts,[11] the recourse to national and/or comparative law by the EC/EU, including the Court of Justice, has *not* revealed, up to now at least, any distinguishable law-families *having their own specific impact* on the process of European integration.[12] Nor can the present author imagine that the drafters of Decision 2004/752 wished to put the selection committee and the Council before the herculean task of distinguishing and delimiting such law-families.

It is to be feared that the explanation is much simpler and less 'noble'. Member States, notoriously known for caring only for their own national interests when discussing EU issues (including institutional ones with regard to the Court of Justice, as the recent negotiations for the increase of the number of the judges at the General Court confirm), simply wanted to 'polish' the rule commanding a composition of the CST on the widest possible geographical basis *among their nationals*, which, as subsequent practice proved, is a rule perceived not only as excluding a second judge of the same Member State at any given moment, but also as excluding a second 'representation' by the same Member State before all other Member States have been represented (save of course in case of absolute absence of any suitable candidate from one or another so far unrepresented Member State).

However, the provision on 'national legal systems represented' is positive law and has to be interpreted and applied in a manner that does not render it redundant or obsolete. According to the present author, it may be construed in a two-fold way: as supplementing the rule requiring the balanced representation of Member States in the *composition* of the Tribunal (so as to encompass also a criterion of representativity of legal systems); and

[11] In EU law-making, the common law influence has been mainly felt in the field of civil jurisdiction (see the Schlosser Report on the accession of the United Kingdom, as well as Denmark and Ireland, to the Brussels Convention, Official Journal of the European Communities C 59, 5.3.1979, replaced by Regulations (EC) 44/2001 OJ L012 and, recently, (EC) 1215/2012 of 12 December 2012 L351/1; for an 'outsider's' view of the latter see P Hay, 'Notes on the European Union's Brussels-I "Recast" Regulation. An American Perspective', (2013) 12 The European Legal Forum 1); while, according to current ECJ President Skouris, 'Some Thoughts on the Comparative Dimension of Public Law in Europe', in Hilmar Fenge and Anastasia Grammaticaki-Alexiou (eds.), *ELPIS for Europe. The European and Comparative Dimension of Law Teaching in Europe* (Nomos, Baden-Baden 2006), pp. 123, 128, referring mainly to anti-trust law and quoting T Koopmans, 'The Birth of European Law at the Crossroads of Legal Traditions', (1991) 39 AJCL 493, the common law influence has 'penetrate[d]' the Court's decisions 'especially in matters of technique and procedure'.

[12] In order to avoid any misunderstanding that a quick reading of this paragraph might provoke, it should be made clear that no position as to the highly disputed issue of the existence or not (and their precise delimitation) of law-families in Europe is taken, a subject on which hundreds if not thousands of essays and articles have been written. What is addressed here is the much more specific question as to discernible traces of such law-families (admitting that they exist) on the EC/EU legal order and, in particular in the case law of the Court of Justice, this by opposition to discernible traces of influence by individual national legal systems (see the examples given by V. Skouris, ibid.).

as fulfilling at the same time a distinct function, related to the *adjudication* of cases. Both functions are clearly of interest from the comparative-law perspective.

With regard to the composition of the Tribunal, the provision on the 'national legal systems represented' can be interpreted as an invitation *to the selection committee and to the Council* not to take into account only the nationality of the candidates, but also the effective knowledge of their national legal system (or another legal system, preferably not 'represented' in the CST), so as to avoid, if possible, situations with two or three CST judges, irrespective of their nationalities, having the legal culture of one and the same Member State (or, due to their possible international career, having not maintained any sufficient contact with their, or any, national law). It is clear that the presence of judges possessing different legal cultures encourages and facilitates per se the recourse to comparative law.

In addition to that, the mere requirement of the widest possible representation of the existing national legal systems can only be seen as an invitation *to the CST* to make full use of comparative law when adjudicating cases. Indeed this requirement must be seen as serving a purpose; and what other purpose one could imagine than to ensure the optimal conditions for the recourse to comparative law?

III. The traditional comparative-law approach by the CST: recourse to national law

According to well-established EC/EU case law, of general application also by the CST, 'the need for uniform application of Union law and the principle of equality require that where a provision of Union law contains no express reference back to the law of the Member States for the purpose of determining its meaning and scope, it must normally be given an autonomous and uniform interpretation throughout the Union, which must be sought in the light of the context of the provision and the objective pursued by the rules in question'; on the other hand, 'even in the absence of an express reference back, the application of Union law may, where appropriate, involve making a reference to the laws of the Member States, in particular where the courts of the European Union cannot identify in Union law or in the general principles of Union law the elements which would allow it to define the content and scope of Union law by an autonomous interpretation.'[13]

A two-fold conclusion may be drawn from this case law. Firstly, that the autonomous interpretation constitutes the rule. Secondly, that the exception, that is reliance on national law, is not limited to the cases where EU law itself refers expressly back to such laws, but may also apply wherever appropriate, in particular in the absence of written EU law rules on the matter concerned (which is the case, for example, with regard to family-law concepts[14]).

[13] *Mandt v European Parliament*, F-45/07, para 62, referring to Case 327/82 *Ekro* [1984] ECR 107, para 11, Case T-43/90 *Díaz García v Parliament* [1992] ECR II-2619, para 36, and Case T-342/04 *Adam v Commission* [2006] ECR-SC I-A-2-23 and II-A-2-107, para 32.

[14] See para 63 of the *Mandt* case, ibid.: 'This is the case, in particular, in relation to personal status and family law (see, to that effect, Case 59/85 *Reed* [1986] ECR 1283, paragraph 15, and, in particular, Joined Cases C-122/99 P and C-125/99 P *D and Sweden v Council* [2001] ECR I-4319, paragraphs 34 to 38), as the

Comparative law thus operates mainly within the rule and not within the exception. The reason is that the exception does not involve a general and *in abstracto* recourse to national *laws* taken as a whole, but requires reliance on *one* specific national law. As a consequence, there is very limited, if any, room left for comparative-law approaches. Unless, of course, if we have in mind comparative *private international* law.[15] But in most cases brought before the CST the relevant connecting factors were located in the same country/legal order, and, therefore, the application of the national law of this country/legal order appeared as the evident and obvious solution, without the need to invoke private international law as a justificatory reasoning.[16] The best known exception in this respect was the *Mandt* case (discussed later), in which, as a result of the non-recognition of a divorce decision, the marital status of a person was clearly not the same in all Member States.

On the basis of the above premises, and in particular that comparative law operates mainly within the rule (that is, in cases of autonomous interpretation), the question to be answered is *how* this happens. Indeed, contrary to 'general' EU law, where comparative law has been recognized as having a core-role for many decades, as demonstrated not only by the reference in Article 215 EEC/288 TEC/340 TFEU, on non-contractual liability, to principles 'common in the laws of the Member States', but also by the comparative-law references in the Court of Justice's rulings and, much more frequently and extensively, in the Advocates General's opinions, leaving aside the comparative-law treatment to be found in legal literature, the CST appears, at first sight at least, quite discreet, when it comes to having recourse to comparative law in applying EU civil service law.

To begin with, there are many instances where the CST, while seeking the autonomous interpretation, appears to be 'constructing' such autonomous interpretation merely on the basis of the terms of the applicable provision and logic, although the case concerned raised difficult and subtle questions and more than one interpretative option was objectively conceivable and arguable. In this connection, particular mention can be made of the *Q* case (F-52/05), where what was at issue was the concept of harassment and, more specifically, the question whether the malicious intent of the

legal order of the Union has no written rules on such matters. In that regard, it has been held in particular that the formal validity of a maintenance agreement, as a condition of the grant of a survivor's pension to the divorced spouse under Article 27 of Annex VIII to the Staff Regulations, is governed by national law (Case T-172/01 *M v Court of Justice* [2004] ECR II-1075, paragraphs 72 and 73)'.

[15] The question arose in the field of maintenance law, in disputes related to the allowance for '*dependent* children'; see, in particular, the *Díaz García v Parlement* (T-43/90) and *Khouri v Commission* (T-85/91) cases.

[16] See, to this effect, *Klein v Commission*, Case F-32/08, concerning, inter alia, an invalidity pension and the definition of 'dependent child', as well as a death allowance, and in which the CST took for granted the applicability of French law, both for the question of the existence of legal maintenance obligations of an EU official towards his daughter and for the question of the latter's quality of unique heir of her father (paras 45 and 47), given that both were French nationals and were domiciled in France. See also *Tsirimiagos v Committee of the Regions*, Case F-100/07, on the mechanism of transfer of part of an EU official's emoluments outside the country of employment, holding that the legality of specific bank operations between accounts kept in a Member State is to be judged in the light of the legislation of that Member State. Moreover, in *Wilk v Commission*, Case F-32/10, full account was taken of a divorce decision rendered in a third country, without the validity of that decision (and its effects in the EU) being questioned in any way or contested by the parties.

alleged harasser is a necessary criterion for the classification of the impugned conduct as psychological harassment (paras 133 to 146). The CST replied in the negative. Its interpretation was upheld by the Tribunal of First Instance, and was even more generally welcomed by commentators,[17] but undoubtedly some comparative-law references would have enriched the judgment and strengthened the solution adopted. The same can be said of the *Bui Van* case (F-52/07) concerning the conditions governing withdrawal of a measure tainted with illegality, with particular regard to the requirement that such withdrawal should intervene within a reasonable time (paras 62 to 68).

Secondly, there have even been some cases where the CST, again in the context of 'autonomous' interpretation, has expressly dissociated the interpretation from the particular national law most closely connected to the case concerned (without 'compensating' this by reference to other national laws or to generally accepted principles/solutions in national legal orders). It did so (a) in *Roodhuijzen v Commission* (F-122/06) in relation to the question whether two persons having a cohabitation agreement under Dutch law could be regarded as 'non-marital' or 'unmarried' partners within the meaning of Article 72.1 of the EU Staff Regulations and Article 1.2 of their Annex VII (which would then have afforded them coverage by the EU Joint Sickness Insurance Scheme); (b) in *Efstathopoulos v Parliament*, F-144/07, on the issue of the inclusion or not of a 'productivity bonus' granted under Greek law in the calculation of the amount of 'gross income received by a former official in the context of his new duties' within the meaning of Regulation 2689/95 (with a view to determining whether an EU allowance paid to a former official should be cut); and (c) in *Bovagnet v Commission*, F-89/10, concerning the legal characterization to be given to a part of a school's fees called '*fonds d'investissment*' and '*fonds de roulement*', in accordance with Luxembourg law, for the purpose of calculating the 'education costs' which could be reimbursed to an official in accordance with Article 3.1 of Annex VII of the EU Staff Regulations.

While such an approach is clearly appropriate, in the sense that the concepts or terms of the kind in question should not be interpreted in the light of the relevant national law but 'autonomously', the question remains: how did the judge (in our case the CST) arrive at the autonomous interpretation and, in particular, was comparative law in any way taken into account in the interpretative process?

At first sight, the second limb of the question is to be answered in the negative. And this impression is confirmed by some other cases where the CST clearly appears to have disregarded not only the specific national law linked to the subject-matter at issue but national laws in general. Thus, in a number of cases concerning the applicant's 'habitual residence' (on which depend numerous pecuniary benefits), e.g. in *Petrilli v Commission* (F-100/08), this concept was defined as being the place where the former official 'has actually established his centre of interests, in other words the place in which the person concerned has established, with the intention that it should be of a lasting

[17] N Lhoëst, 'European Union Civil Service Tribunal Case-Law: How to Reconcile Judicial Review and the Human Dimension?', (2011) 31 HRLJ 36, 40; C Bernard-Glanz, L Levi, and S Rodriguez, 'Le contentieux de la fonction publique européenne–Une matière à (re)découvrir', (2010) JDE 97, 100; see also, by Judge, and since October 2011 CST President, S van Raepenbusch, 'Le juge face au harcèlement moral dans le cadre du contentieux de la fonction publique européenne', (2010) CDE 121.

character, the permanent or habitual centre of his interests and where he is deemed to incur his expenditure'; with this being added that 'irrespective of the purely quantitative element of the time spent by the person in a particular country, residence implies not only the actual fact of living in a given place, but also the intention of thereby achieving the continuity which stems from a stable way of life and from the course of normal social relations'. The judgments then go on to specify that this is a concept 'peculiar' to the EC/EU civil service and 'does not necessarily coincide with national meanings of the term'. Even more explicitly, in *Skareby v Commission* (F-95/09), when deciding whether an administrative request for assistance in a harassment case was time-barred or not, the CST took as comparator the legal action for damages available to EU officials, for which, according to settled case law, 'a point of reference may be derived from the limitation period of five years laid down in Article 46 of the Statute of the Court of Justice in actions for EU non-contractual liability'. After verifying that no 'relevant reason' ruled out taking this as a point of reference, the CST applied it to the different facts before it and declared the administrative request admissible, expressly rejecting the Commission's reliance on the circumstance that two Member States 'apply a limitation period of three years under criminal law for offences of psychological harassment'. Here again the impression is given that the CST is abstaining from any comparative-law recourse to national laws and that the sole comparative element in its reasoning is located in the application, by analogy, of 'other' EU rules, that is to say, rules of 'general' EU law and/or rules of different aspects of internal EU staff law.

This, however, can be seen to be a false impression on closer inspection. In reality, the CST is relying on comparative law—understood here in its traditional meaning, that is to say, linked to national legal orders—much more than the precedents above might suggest.

It has to be conceded that, compared with the '*scripta*' (the literal text of the CST judgments), such personal analysis has a lesser authority, even when its source is a former member of the Tribunal (and when it would appear to correspond to what leading commentators have said in the past[18]). However, it needs to be borne in mind that the CST is composed of only seven members and therefore, unless it has had the benefit of a research study prepared by the European Court of Justice research department, there is an evident risk for it in formally drawing comparative-law conclusions as to the state of the law, in general, in the Members States.[19] This circumstance does not prevent the Tribunal's members from seeking guidance and inspiration in their own legal systems (or in other legal systems of which they have knowledge). Indeed, the present author can confirm that they very often have done so,

[18] According to M Hilf, 'The Role of Comparative Law in the Jurisprudence of the Court of Justice of the European Communities', in A de Mestral, S Birks, M Bothe, I Cotler, D Klinck, A Morel (eds.), *The Limitation of Human Rights in Comparative Constitutional Law/La limitation des droits de l'homme en droit constitutionnel comparé* (Les Éditions Yvon Blais Inc., Québec 1986) 549, 561—'[s]ilence of the Court in its judgments is no evidence at all of the absence of comparative elements in the decision process within the Court'; while for current ECJ President Skouris, 'Some Thought in the Comparative Dimension of Public Law in Europe', n 11, at 124, 'everyone close to the course of European integration has to become more or less comparativist.'

[19] See, already for the Community of twelve, M Hilf, ibid., 561.

at least during his term of office,[20] although, admittedly, from that point to the inclusion of comparative-law positions in the judgments themselves is a long distance. In addition, given that time and resources for comparative-law research are necessarily limited, the Tribunal preferred, when seeking comparative law assistance/information, to give priority to 'horizontal' issues. There is, thus, for example, much comparative-law research underlying CST orders for costs and legal aid, as well as the CST practices in the field of friendly settlement of disputes.

Furthermore, there do exist a few judgments with explicit comparative-law reasoning.

Especially noteworthy in this context is *Mandt v Parliament* (F-45/07), concerning the pension payable to a surviving spouse. In *Mandt*, the status of surviving spouse in relation to the same, deceased, EC official was recognized to two different individuals. Initially the pension was claimed by (and granted to) the man whom the official had married in 2000 in the United States, and with whom she had been living up to her death in 2004. Two years later another man applied for receipt of the same pension. It emerged from the evidence submitted to the Parliament that this person had contracted marriage with the EC official concerned in 1993; and that the marriage had been dissolved soon thereafter by a Belgian divorce judgment, which had become final but which had been refused recognition in Germany. All three persons concerned were German nationals and had their residence in Germany, including the deceased EC official during the period after her retirement. Faced with this anomalous, not to say bizarre, situation, the Parliament decided to grant 'each surviving spouse' 50 per cent of the pension.

The *Mandt* case originated in the legal action brought by the husband who had been granted the pension in the first place (and at its full rate).[21] One of the grounds for annulment of the contested decision was that the other beneficiary of the pension (50 per cent of it) lacked the quality of 'surviving spouse'. Strictly legally speaking the issue raised was one of personal status. The CST accepted the Parliament's approach to determining the status of the other contested beneficiary '[through relying] mainly on considerations derived from the positive law and the legal order of one country, namely Germany, which clearly had very close links with both the situation of the [contested surviving spouse] and the dispute taken as a whole' (para 69—see also paras 70 and 71). The CST, however, extended its analysis by noting that 'in the great majority of the national legal orders, too, the marital status of the [contested surviving spouse] would be determined by application of German positive law and would be the status he was recognised to have in the legal order of that Member State' (para 72). Furthermore, while reiterating that the validity of the Belgian divorce judgment was not disputed in the Belgian legal order, the CST did not fail to qualify this finding by pointing out that it

[20] As it is admittedly the case for the other two EU jurisdictions (F Donnat, 'La CJUE et les droits nationaux: comparaisons, convergences', in O Cachard and L Nau (eds.), *Europäisches Privatrecht in Vielfalt geeint/Droit privé européen: l'unité dans la diversité* (Sellier, Munich 2012) 59, 62).

[21] The other husband had also challenged the Parliament's decision, but his action was rejected by the CST for failure to comply with admissibility conditions.

was 'without prejudice to [the Belgian judgment's] validity in other national legal orders' (para 83).

Strictly speaking, *Mandt* does not constitute an example of comparative law 'operating within the rule' (that is, within the autonomous interpretation), to repeat the terminology of this article used above, and of providing a tool for such interpretation. On the contrary, the questions raised, relating primarily to personal status and to family law, were in principle to be resolved on the basis of national law/laws; there was a settled case law on this, recalled in para 63 of *Mandt* (see footnote 13). One can, however, easily discern the CST's concern to introduce elements of autonomous interpretation in concepts that are primarily national-law concepts and to do so by means of a comparative-law approach. This is not exactly what one could call a traditional comparative-law approach, but who can claim that the EC/EU is a traditional scheme of international legal cooperation/integration?

Nor can the second noteworthy example of a more explicit comparative-law approach be characterized as traditional. The case *W v Commission* (F-86/09) concerned a same-sex couple and their right to family allowances. Under the terms of the EU Staff Regulations, 'stable non-marital partners' are entitled to family allowances, in particular of household allowance, subject to satisfying a number of conditions, including that the couple 'has no access to legal marriage in a Member State'. In *W*, the two partners had their residence in Belgium, a country that had introduced same-sex marriage. Consequently, being married appeared to be a requisite condition for obtaining the allowance sought. However, one of the partners possessed the nationality of a third country that not only prohibited same-sex marriage, but also criminalized homosexual acts, irrespective of where such acts were committed. Claiming that those circumstances excluded marriage in practice, the applicant argued for a kind of *de facto* autonomous interpretation of the condition of 'no access to legal marriage'. The CST followed this approach. It relied on jurisprudence of the European Court of Human Rights on the need for fundamental rights to be practical and effective, and not theoretical and illusory, and held that, in interpreting the relevant condition of the EU Staff Regulations, one 'cannot disregard the provisions of the law of another State with which the situation in question is closely connected because of the nationality of the persons concerned, where that law, although not applicable to matters relating to the formation of marriage, could render access to marriage and, therefore, the right to the household allowance theoretical and illusory' (para 45). While recalling to a certain extent Article 9 of the Rome I Regulation (539/08) on the *lois d'application immédiate* (overriding mandatory provisions), this passage can also be seen as another demonstration of an original recourse to comparative law.

The third case deserving mention, *Vienne v Parliament* (F-97/11), also relates, as did *Mandt*, to a divorce judgment, but from an entirely different perspective. What was at issue was not the recognition of the judgment (delivered by a Luxembourg court with Belgian law as *lex causae*), but simply the determination of the date from which the divorced official would cease receiving the household allowance. The CST established at the outset that this date should be that of the 'dissolution' of the marriage. Reliance was placed on the laws of Member States (in what can be seen as the first comparative-law reference of the judgment), providing that the mutual, including pecuniary, obligations arising out of the marriage (on the basis of which the household allowance was instituted) cease with the dissolution of the marriage (para 30). The CST went on to rule that, in the particular case, this should be taken to coincide with the date on which the divorce judgment became 'effective', since both national laws potentially applicable, namely Luxembourg law and Belgian law, adopted this solution.[22] As for the date of 'effectiveness', it 'recalled' that it is to be determined in accordance with the *lex fori*,[23] in the instant case Luxembourg law, which provided for a right of appeal within 40 days from service of the adversarial divorce judgment. Since no appeal had been lodged, the CST concluded that the marriage had been dissolved and the divorce judgment had become effective 40 days after service of the judgment. It goes on, however, to point out (para 42) that the application of Belgian law, which required the transcription of the divorce judgment in civil registries, could also have been rejected on the basis of substantive-law considerations, namely that in some national laws publicity procedures (such as the transcription foreseen in Belgian law) are not subject to any time-requirement, so that, by deliberately refraining from accomplishing such procedures, the divorced official could unduly conserve the allowance. This is a judicious, and welcome, comparative-law consideration (the second in the judgment), but queries may be expressed as to its consistency with the unreserved dictum that the date of effectiveness of the divorce judgment is to be determined by the *lex fori* (para 30); *quid* if, in another case, the *lex fori* is among those which do not impose any time-limit for the accomplishment of publicity requirement?

Finally, a more traditional, but at the same time more cautious, recourse to comparative law is to be found in *Landgren v European Training Foundation* (Case F-1/05), overturning a long-standing case law holding that no reasons need be given for dismissals from employment on contracts of indeterminate duration. Among legal developments justifying such a reversal of the pre-existing case law (which was upheld on appeal and also very favourably received by commentators[24]), the CST mentioned 'the development of the law concerning the protection of workers and the abusive recourse to successive fixed-term employment contracts' (para 65). It is true that, having regard to the following paragraph of the judgment, the 'development of the law' is most probably to be understood as being that represented by reference to the Framework Agreement on fixed-term work concluded by ETUC, UNICE, and CEEP[25]

[22] As drafted, paras 33–34 seem to imply that both under Luxembourg and Belgian law the date of dissolution of the marriage coincides with the date on which the divorce judgment becomes effective. However, only the Luxembourg provision cited has such a content. For Belgian law, the judgment cites Article 1278, first indent, of the Belgian Judicial Code (*Code judiciaire belge*), which, without any reference to the 'dissolution' of the marriage as such, addresses solely the question of the moment from when the divorce judgment produces its effects ('[l]e jugement ou l'arrêt qui prononce le divorce produit ses effets à l'égard de la personne des époux du jour où la décision acquiert force de chose jugée, et produit ses effets à l'égard des tiers du jour de la transcription').

[23] In spite of the use of the word 'recall', this position is not, however, evidenced by any reference to case law precedents.

[24] N Lhoëst, 'European Union Civil Service Tribunal Case-Law', n 17, at 37.

[25] These abbreviations stand for the European Trade Union Confederation (ETUC), the Union of Industrial and Employers' Confederations of Europe (UNICE) and the European Centre of Enterprises with Public Participation (CEEP).

and implemented by Council Directive 1999/70/EC. Nevertheless, even such an understanding does not preclude its being considered as a kind of comparative-law reference.

IV. Comparative law methods in the CST case law

In addition to the traditional comparative-law approach involving reference back to national laws as discussed in the foregoing section, the CST, in interpreting the applicable rules in each given case, often has recourse to rules and principles of other, non-national, legal orders or systems. This is not as such a comparative-law approach within the traditional meaning, but the methods have a lot in common. It was therefore considered appropriate to close this chapter with some brief references to such precedents.

In the field of *human rights*, the CST, like the Court of Justice and the General Court, has continued, even after the entry into force of the EU Charter of Fundamental Rights, to refer to the provisions of the ECHR, in common with the provisions of the Charter (unless the latter contains a provision with no equivalent in the ECHR). Moreover, the references to the ECHR are not limited to the mere quotation of its relevant provisions in addition to the provisions of the Charter. They go further. As already indicated, in *W v Commission* the CST applied to EU staff statutory rights the interpretative method of the ECHR Court as to 'practical and effective' (instead of 'theoretical or illusory') rights. Furthermore, In *Missir Mamachi di Lusignano v Commission* (F-50/09), the CST, faced with the question whether, for reasons of confidentiality, it was possible to derogate from the procedural rule whereby the Tribunal may take into consideration only documents made available to the parties' representatives and on which they have been given an opportunity to express their views, relied on a ruling of the ECHR Court, in the case of *A and Others v the United Kingdom*,[26] considering that, although not applicable as such (since it pertained to a criminal case), 'it does provide indications on which the Courts of the European Union may draw in the conduct of the cases before them' (para 154).

There are also a number of cases concerning statutory rights and obligations of EU staff members, in which the CST did not limit itself to the Staff Regulations, but felt obliged to refer to the *primary and secondary EU law*. In *O v Commission*, Joined Cases F-69/07 and F-60/08, the CST, called on to rule on the lawfulness of a decision by which the Commission had deferred medical cover for the applicant in accordance with the first paragraph of Article 100 of the CEOS, interpreted the staff provision in the light of the requirements flowing from freedom of movement for workers, as enshrined in Article 39 EC; while in *Strack v Commission*, F-120/07, the Tribunal relied on Directive 2003/88 in order to annul a Commission decision refusing the

[26] *A and Others v The United Kingdom* (App no 3455/05) ECHR 19 February 2009. The extract of the ECHR judgment cited reads as follows 'there may be restrictions on the right to a fully adversarial procedure where strictly necessary in the light of a strong countervailing public interest, such as national security, the need to keep secret certain police methods of investigation or the protection of the fundamental rights of another person. However, in order to ensure a fair trial, any difficulties caused to the defendant by a limitation on his rights must be sufficiently counterbalanced by the procedures followed by the judicial authorities' (paras 205–208).

applicant staff member the carry-over of more than 12 days of annual leave on the basis of an internal Commission rule authorizing such carry-over only for reasons related to the needs of service and not to illness, as claimed by the applicant.

Furthermore, in cases involving *institutions applying, not the EU Staff Regulations (or the CEOS), but their own set of staff rules*, which is the case mainly for the European Central Bank and the European Investment Bank (EIB), the Tribunal frequently needs to make comparative references to the equivalent provisions of the EU Staff Regulations (or the CEOS), since these other sets of staff rules often lack the clarity and completeness of the former. Such comparative references are no novelty; in proceeding so, the Tribunal follows well-established case law, going back many years, long before its own institution in 2004–2005. However, as a result of a review judgment delivered by the Court of Justice earlier this year (setting aside a judgment of the General Court which had upheld a CST judgment), a case called *Arango Jaramillo v European Investment Bank* (C-334/12 RX-II), fresh reflection on the matter is called for. In *Arango Jaramillo,* what was at issue was established case law according to which (a) in the absence of any provision setting time-limits for bringing proceedings in disputes between the EIB and its members of staff, such proceedings must be brought within a 'reasonable period' of time; and (b) the period of three months for bringing proceedings, laid down in Article 91.3 of the EU Staff Regulations, provided a 'relevant point of comparison' in assessing whether in each given case the applicant staff member had complied with that requirement (para 15 of the Court's judgment). This case law had in practice been understood as extending the three-month time-limit of the EU Staff Regulation to disputes between the EIB and its staff members. The *Arango Jaramillo* case settled that this was an erroneous interpretation. To the extent that the three-month period is not foreseen as such for legal actions brought against the EIB by staff members, but results by analogy from a EU Staff Regulation rule, it should not be applied as rigidly and strictly as the latter and, if it is exceeded, this should not entail automatically, and without consideration of the specific circumstances of the case, that the action is out of time. This review judgment shows clearly the limits and the inherent risks of the quasi comparative-law method used by the EU judge when interpreting, in the light of the EU Staff Regulations, other sets of staff rules.

11

Networks, Dialogue or One-Way Traffic?

An Empirical Analysis of Cross-Citations Between Ten of Europe's Highest Courts

Martin Gelter and Mathias Siems***

I. Introduction

Do highest courts from different countries interact with each other, for instance, by way of reading and citing each other's case law?[1] Previous research often found that courts rarely look abroad.[2] However, in a globalizing world, even in law, which has traditionally been a prerogative of the sovereign nation-state, some cross-border interaction seems likely.

For instance, Anne-Marie Slaughter contemplates that nowadays 'judges see each other not only as servants and representatives of a particular polity, but also as fellow professionals in an endeavour that transcends national borders'.[3] This statement was made in the context of transnational litigation, but it may also be a reflection of a more general trend. At the most basic level, the development of a 'one-way traffic' situation is conceivable when a court of a, perhaps, relatively small jurisdiction closely follows the jurisprudence of a larger one. With the development of a more intense interaction, this may become a dialogue if the latter jurisdiction begins to take some interest in the case law of the former country.[4] Going further, if countries belong to the same group of

* Associate Professor, Fordham Law School (US) and Research Associate, European Corporate Governance Institute.

** Professor of Commercial Law at Durham University (UK) and Research Associate at the Centre for Business Research of the University of Cambridge (UK). This chapter was initially published in (2012) 8 Utrecht Law Review 88 and is reprinted with permission (with references updated).

[1] A different question is whether cross-citations are desirable. For a summary of the main arguments see T Kadner Graziano, 'Is It Legitimate and Beneficial for Judges to Use Comparative Law?' (2013) 21 ERPL 687; M Bobek, *Comparative Reasoning in European Supreme Courts* (OUP Oxford 2013) 237–51. See now also M Gelter and M Siems, 'Citations to Foreign Courts – Illegitimate and Superfluous, or Unavoidable? Evidence from Europe' (2014) 62 AJCL 35.

[2] See, eg, B Markesinis and J Fedtke (eds.), *Judicial Recourse to Foreign Law* (Routledge-Cavendish Abingdon 2006); B Markesinis and J Fedtke, 'The Judge as Comparatist' (2005) 80 Tulane Law Review 11; G Canivet et al (eds.), *Comparative Law Before the Courts* (BIICL London 2004); G Canivet, 'The Practice of Comparative Law by the Supreme Courts: Brief Reflections on the Dialogue Between the Judges in French and European Experience' (2006) 80 Tulane Law Review 1377; U Drobnig and S Van Erp (eds.), *The Use of Comparative Law by Courts* (Kluwer London 1999).

[3] AM Slaughter, 'A Global Community of Courts' (2003) 44 Harvard International Law Journal 191 at 193. See also KG Young, 'The World, through the Judge's Eye' (2009) 28 Australian Yearbook of International Law 27 at 38 ('idea that a new, global, demos has challenged the territorial boundaries in which the basic unit of democracy can be understood').

[4] C L'Heureux-Dubé, 'The Importance of Dialogue: Globalization and the Impact of the Rehnquist Court' (1998) 34 Tulsa Law Journal 15 at 17 (change from reception to dialogue). See also Olga Frishman,

countries (for instance, the EU or the same legal family), it may be the case that the communication between highest courts forms part of a formal or informal network.[5]

Such interaction may take place in various forms. There is some direct transnational collaboration and communication between highest court judges,[6] but here we focus on cross-citations as a form of influence. Of course, the citation of a foreign court does not necessarily mean that foreign ideas were really a decisive consideration for the outcome of a case. Nonetheless, cross-citations can show to what extent courts use foreign law as a justification for a judicial decision, be it a positive or negative example. In the project from which this chapter derives,[7] we have collected data on how often and in which circumstances ten European highest courts cite each other. We managed to get access to the full text of almost all decisions of these highest courts for the period between 2000 and 2007. In total we have considered 636,172 decisions and we have found 1,430 cross-citations, as will be discussed in the following.

The remainder of this chapter is structured as follows. Section II summarizes the data considered and the search methodology used. Section III presents bar charts on cross-citations. Network presentations of the data follow in section IV. In section V we distinguish between outgoing and incoming citations. Section VI concludes.

II. Population and search methodology

Table 11.1 presents the list of countries and courts examined, the databases used, and the subject matter jurisdiction of the ten highest courts. It also indicates how many decisions the highest courts have published between 2000 and 2007 and how this translates into the number of decisions per 1,000 inhabitants.

In an associated article we describe the choice of countries and courts in detail.[8] In this article we also make it clear that our project does not aim to examine why, according to Table 1, not only the absolute number of cases but also the decisions per capita are very disparate. It would be the topic of a separate empirical study to explore this question. For instance, it possibly matters that there are differences in subject matter jurisdiction. Moreover, many further factors may influence the number of highest court decisions, such as appeal requirements and procedures, as well as ease of access to lower courts, availability of self-help and out-of-court settlement, differences in substantive law, legal culture etc.[9]

The actual data used in our project are the cross-citations between these ten courts. We managed to get access to the full text of (almost) all decisions of these highest

'Transnational Judicial Dialogue as an Organisational Field' (2013) 19 ELJ 739; GS Goodwin-Gill and H Lambert (eds.), *The Limits of Transnational Law: Refugee Law, Policy Harmonization and Judicial Dialogue in the European Union* (CUP Cambridge 2010).

[5] For details on the concept of networks in different disciplines see M Claes and M de Visser, 'Are You Networked Yet? On Dialogues in European Judicial Networks' (2012) 8 Utrecht Law Review 100.

[6] See eg, the Network of the Presidents of the Supreme Judicial Courts of the EU <http://www.network-presidents.eu>. See also Claes and de Visser, ibid.

[7] See also section II.

[8] M Gelter and M Siems, 'Language, Legal Origins, and Culture before the Courts: Cross-Citations between Supreme Courts in Europe' (2013) 21 Supreme Court Economic Review 215.

[9] Ibid.

Table 11.1 Countries and courts

Country	Population 2004[10]	Name of highest court	Database used	Subject matter jurisdiction of court	Total number of reported decisions 2000–2007	Decisions per 1,000 inhabitants
Austria	8,174,762	Oberster Gerichtshof	RIS[11]	Civil law (including employment and social law), criminal law	28,868	3.53
Belgium	10,348,276	Cour de cassation, Hof van Cassatie	Court website[12]	Civil law (including employment law), criminal law	24,053	2.42
England and Wales	53,057,000	Court of Appeal	Westlaw[13]	All areas of law	25,855	0.49
France	60,424,213	Cour de cassation	Legifrance[14] and court website[15]	Civil law (including employment law), criminal law	107,396	1.78
Germany	82,424,609	Bundes-gerichtshof	Beck Online[16]	Civil law (excluding employment and social security law), and criminal law	22,950	0.28
Ireland	3,969,558	High Court	Bailii[17] and Court website[18]	All areas of law (but not criminal appeals)	2,357	0.59
Italy	58,057,477	Corte di cassazione, Corte Suprema di Cassazione	De Jure[19]	All areas of law (with the exception of constitutional matters)	196,876	3.39
Netherlands	16,318,199	Hoge Raad	Court website[20]	Civil (including employment law), criminal and tax law	9,073 [36,020][21]	0.56 [2.20]
Spain	40,280,780	Tribunal Supremo	Court website[22]	All areas of law (with the exception of constitutional matters)	190,174	4.72
Switzerland	7,450,867	Bundesgericht	Court website[23]	All areas of law	27,570	3.70

[10] Sources: CIA Factbook, 2004 data available at <http://www.nationmaster.com/graph/peo_pop_cia_fac-people-population-cia-factbook&date=2004>. For England and Wales: National Statistics website, available at <http://www.ons.gov.uk/ons/taxonomy/index.html?nscl=Population>.

[11] <http://www.ris.bka.gv.at> (public law database of the Federal Chancellery).

[12] <http://jure.juridat.just.fgov.be/?lang=fr>. Source for the number of decisions: Rapport Annuel 2007, available at <http://justice.belgium.be/fr/ordre_judiciaire/cours_et_tribunaux/cour_de_cassation/documents/rapports_annuels/>, at 2201.

[13] <http://www.westlaw.co.uk> (Law Reports and Official Transcripts).

[14] <http://www.legifrance.gouv.fr>.

[15] <http://www.courdecassation.fr/> (for selected opinions of the *avocat general*).

[16] <http://www.beck-online.de>.

[17] <http://www.bailii.org/ie/cases/IEHC/>.

[18] <http://www.courts.ie/Judgments.nsf/advancedsearch?openform&l=en>.

[19] <http://dejure.giuffre.it/>.

[20] <http://uitspraken.rechtspraak.nl/>.

[21] Number of decisions according to the annual reports; see Jaarverslagen, available at <http://www.rechtspraak.nl/Organisatie/Publicaties-En-Brochures/Pages/Jaardocumenten.aspx>.

[22] <http://www.poderjudicial.es/search/>.

[23] <http://www.bger.ch/index/juridiction/jurisdiction-inherit-template/jurisdiction-recht/jurisdiction-recht-urteile2000.htm> and <http://www.polyreg.ch/d/informationen/bge.html>.

courts for the period between 2000 and 2007.[24] In order to locate citations to foreign courts covered by our study, we compiled an extensive list of search terms.[25] Then, in all countries, we first looked at the actual decisions. Where they were present (and available), we also included opinions by the reporting judge or the advocate general.[26] Inclusion of these documents was necessary because in some countries the legal justification of a decision that in other systems would be found in the decisions themselves, will appear only in the opinions of the reporting judge or advocate general.[27]

We checked all citations and classified them according to the reason why foreign courts had been cited: (a) case history and jurisdictional issues; (b) an underlying European or international legal basis; and (c) purely comparative reasons.[28] Citations of type (a) are the ones which a court usually cannot avoid. This type of citation is not exactly what we were looking for because such citations have no bearing on a possible transnational dialogue between the courts, or the influence of foreign legal arguments. Therefore, the following sections only report the total number of citations in categories (b) and (c), which have in common that judges have freedom of choice as to which foreign court (if any) to cite.[29]

III. Bar charts of cross-citations

There are different ways in which our data can be displayed. In this section we present bar charts that show how often the ten 'citing courts' have made reference to the ten 'cited courts'. Figure 11.1 is based on the absolute number of cross-citations. Figure 11.2 shows the cross-citations per all decisions of a particular court and Figure 11.3 the cross-citations per all of its cross-citations.[30]

It can be observed that the citations from Austria to Germany and from Ireland to England (and Wales)[31] dominate the picture: Austria has cited Germany 459 times, and Ireland has cited England 456 times. The other relationships trail behind these two by one order of magnitude: 58 and 45 citations from the Netherlands and

[24] Exception: the Netherlands (see Table 11.1).

[25] Usually, this was straightforward. However, for the citations of the High Court of Ireland to the Court of Appeal of England and Wales we had to rely on a random sample of decisions because citations to English courts do not always reveal whether the cited court is really the Court of Appeal (for details see Gelter and Siems, n 8, at 235).

[26] Opinions of the advocates general were included for Belgium and the Netherlands. For France we only got access to selected opinions of the advocate general and the reporting judge.

[27] For further details see Gelter and Siems, n 8, at 234.

[28] For similar classifications see JM Smits, 'Comparative Law and Its Influence on National Legal Systems' in M Reimann and R Zimmermann (eds.), *The Oxford Handbook of Comparative Law* (OUP Oxford 2006) 513; E Örücü, 'Comparative Law in Practice: The Courts and the Legislator' in E Örücü and D Nelken (eds.), *Comparative Law: A Handbook* (Hart Oxford 2007) 411; M Siems, 'Citation Patterns of the German Federal Supreme Court and of the Court of Appeal of England and Wales' (2010) 21 King's Law Journal 152.

[29] For this point see also Gelter and Siems, n 8, at 237–8.

[30] Abbreviations: AUT = Austria; BEL = Belgium; CH = Switzerland; ENG = England and Wales; FRA = France; GER = Germany; IRE = Republic of Ireland; ITA = Italy; NL = Netherlands; SPA = Spain. The full dataset of cross-citations is available at the project website: <http://www.cross-citations.blogspot.com>.

[31] In the following, the term 'England' is always to be read as referring to 'England and Wales'.

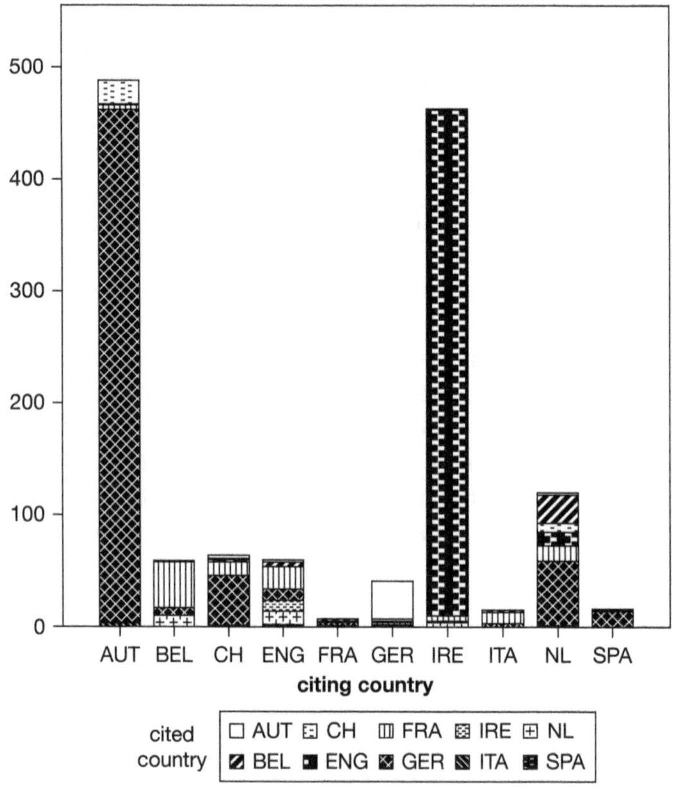

Figure 11.1 Absolute number of cross-citations

Switzerland to Germany, 41 citations from Belgium to France, and 34 citations from Germany to Austria.

A problem with Figure 11.1 is that it does not consider that the total number of highest court decisions varies widely between the ten countries (see Table 11.1). Figure 11.2 tries to rectify this problem but without much success since the distribution of the ten bars in Figure 11.2 is even more unequal than in Figure 11.1. The High Court of Ireland has cited the Court of Appeal of England and Wales in about 19 per cent of all of its decisions, well ahead of the next relationships—Austria and Netherlands to Germany in 1.6 per cent and 0.6 per cent respectively of all of the decisions of these courts.

It may be argued that this could make sense because of differences between common law and civil law countries: when common law countries cite each other, this is not seen as an 'import' of foreign law, but as a way to identify the common legal rules and principles (the 'common law is a whole'[32]). The fact that England does not cite Ireland very frequently may be regarded as a rare exception, since it can be shown empirically that the Court of Appeal of England and Wales frequently cites courts from

[32] Örücü, n 28, at 415. A possible caveat may be that this mainly concerns the relationships between Commonwealth countries since US law has diverged from many traditional common law rules. See Siems, n 28, at 164–5.

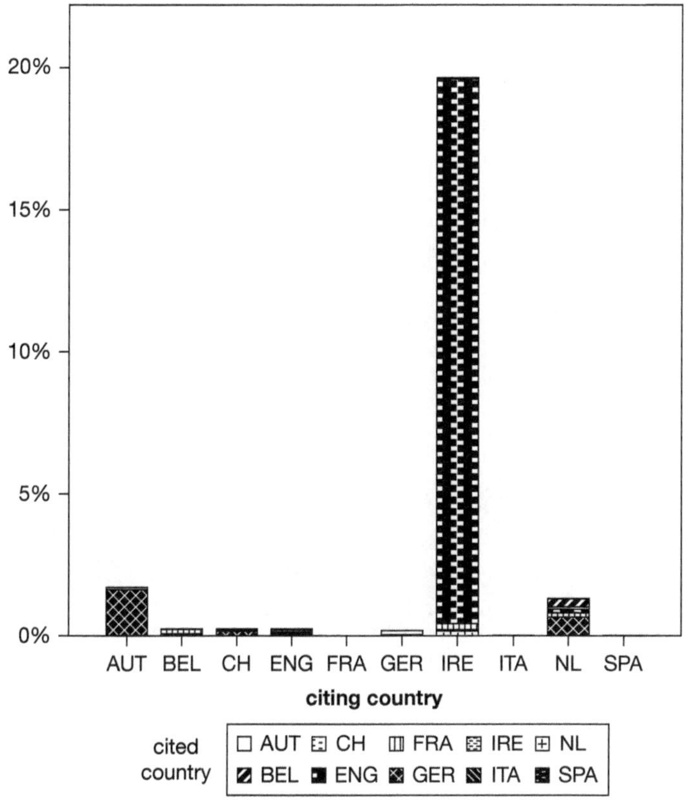

Figure 11.2 Cross-citations per all decisions of a particular court

Australia, Canada, and New Zealand.[33] However, a closer view has to lead to the conclusion that Figure 11.2 is not the most helpful presentation of our data. It is not clear to what extent the number of cross-citations is affected by the total number of decisions. One might suspect that cross-citations typically occur in the most important cases, in which there will be an appeal to the respective highest court in every country. Thus, theoretically, the total number of decisions need not affect the number of cross-citations.

Moreover, there are many factors other than the total number of decisions that may determine whether and how often foreign courts are cited. On a general level, it possibly matters who the highest court judges (and advocates general) are: for instance, how in each country judges are trained, appointed, and promoted,[34] and what 'judicial mentality' they have.[35] It also matters how (and for which audience)[36] judgments are

[33] Ibid. (Siems).

[34] See J Bell, *Judiciaries within Europe: A Comparative Review* (CUP Cambridge 2006) 13–24; C Guarnieri and P Pederzoli, *The Power of Judges: A Comparative Study of Courts and Democracy* (OUP Oxford 2001) 18–44.

[35] B Markesinis, 'Judicial Mentality: Mental Disposition or Outlook as a Factor. Impeding Recourse to Foreign Law' (2006) 80 Tulane Law Review 1325.

[36] N Garoupa and T Ginsburg, 'Judicial Audiences and Reputation: Perspectives from Comparative Law' (2009) 47 Columbia Journal of Transnational Law 451.

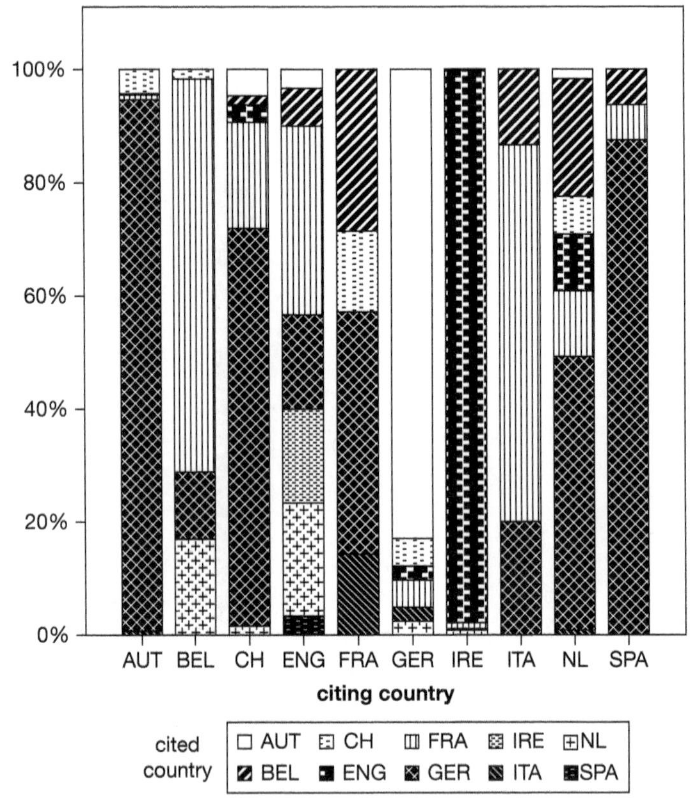

Figure 11.3 Cross-citations per all cross-citations of a particular court

drafted: while, for example, common law judges or the courts in German-speaking countries often write comparatively long opinions, French decisions tend to be short and written in an idiosyncratic formulaic style.[37] Furthermore, a low number of citations may simply reflect differences in citation style between the ten courts: in some countries it may be completely acceptable (or even expected) for judges or advocates general to look for inspiration from other countries and to indicate such findings in their opinions, whereas in other countries there may be social or legal restrictions on citing foreign law.[38]

Thus, in order to control for such unobserved differences between citing courts, Figure 11.3 is based on the citations per all cross-citations of the particular court. In contrast to Figures 11.1 and 11.2, this figure cannot be used in order to compare the differences in the total number of cross-citations (by definition, this is always 100 per cent).

[37] See also Bell, n 34, at 75.

[38] This seems to be the case particularly in France and Italy. See G Alpa, *Tradition and Europeanization in Italian Law* (BIICL London 2005) 102; Markesinis and Fedtke, above n 2, at 26–30. For the more general debate about the legitimacy of foreign citations see, eg, AM Hol, 'Internationalisation and Legitimacy of Decisions by the Highest Courts' in S Muller and M Loth (eds.), *Highest Courts and the Internationalisation of Law: Challenges and Changes* (Hague Academic Press The Hague 2009) 77.

Yet, Figure 11.3 is the most informative way of showing which of the cited courts each of the citing courts prefers to cite.

It can be seen that seven out of the ten courts have a favourite court accounting for more than 50 per cent of its foreign citations. These are the Irish citations to England (98 per cent), the Austrians to Germany (94 per cent), the Spanish to Germany (88 per cent), the Germans to Austria (83 per cent), the Belgians to France (70 per cent), the Swiss to Germany (70 per cent), and the Italians to France (67 per cent). In contrast to this, the citations of the English, French, and Dutch highest courts are more evenly split. In an associated article we have used regression analysis in order to determine which factors account for these differences in cross-citations. We found that language skills, membership of the same legal family, cultural, political, and economic indicators, and the population size of the cited country all matter for which countries are cited. The most important of these factors are language skills, with the possible policy implication that countries should provide English translations of their highest court decisions.[39]

IV. Network presentation of cross-citations

Network analysis has become increasingly popular in the last three decades.[40] It started in sociology but it has also been used in politics, economics, business, psychology, anthropology, and, more recently, law.[41] The main interest of social network analysis is to identify, visualize, compare, and analyse the relationships between individuals or entities. In the terminology of network analysis the individuals are called 'nodes' and the relationships are called 'ties' or 'edges'.

In the present case the 'nodes' are the ten countries and the 'ties' are the cross-citations between them. In Figure 11.4 all ties with more than five cross-citations (one way) are displayed. The strength of the ties, the size of the arrow heads, and the closeness of the countries in the chart[42] is determined by the logarithm of the absolute number of cross-citations. We have used the logarithm of the citations since a network presentation with the absolute numbers would not have been very revealing: Austria and Germany, and Ireland and England would have merged to one dot each, whereas the other pairs of countries would only have been connected by very thin lines. The logarithmic transformation has the advantage that it reduces the high numbers more than the lower ones, making the range of values more manageable.

[39] See Gelter and Siems, n 8, at 269.

[40] For general introduction see RA Hanneman and M Riddle, *Introduction to Social Network Methods* (2005), available at <http://faculty.ucr.edu/~hanneman/nettext/>; D Knoke and S Yang, *Social Network Analysis* 2nd edn (Sage Los Angeles 2008); J Scott and PJ Carrington (eds.), *The SAGE Handbook of Social Network Analysis* 2nd edn (Sage London 2011).

[41] For the last-mentioned see, eg, TA Smith, 'The Web of Law' (2007) 44 San Diego Law Review 309; R Dibadj, 'Networks of Heightened Scrutiny in Corporate Law' (2009) 46 San Diego Law Review 1; R Dibadj, 'Networks of Fairness Review in Corporate Law' (2008) 45 San Diego Law Review 1; MM Siems, 'The Web of Creditor and Shareholder Protection: A Comparative Legal Network Analysis' (2010) 27 Arizona Journal of International and Comparative Law 747.

[42] To be precise, this uses a technique called 'multi-dimensional scaling (adjust to the nearest Euclidean)', available in the network programme Ucinet.

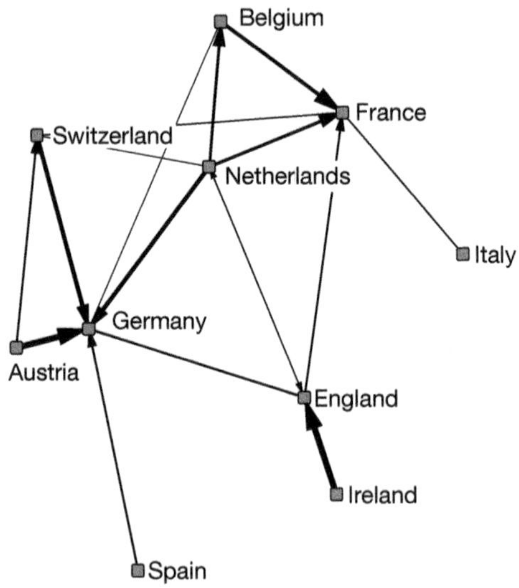

Figure 11.4 Network based on logarithm of absolute number of cross-citations

The first point to observe from Figure 11.4 is that we have no unconnected parts. In particular, it is worth noting that common and civil law countries, and Francophone, Germanophone, and Anglophone countries are not completely unconnected. Two countries, the Netherlands and Germany, are in the centre of the network since they are connected with five other countries. More isolated are Italy, Ireland, and Spain which are just connected with one of the other countries.

Almost all the arrow heads of Figure 11.4 show in one direction only (an exception is, for instance, the tie between the Netherlands and England). Thus, in terms of the direction of cross-citations, there seems to be mainly 'one-way traffic'. However, as noted already (see section III), the problem is that many unobserved factors influence the decision as to whether a particular highest court cites foreign courts at all. Here too, it is therefore preferable to consider the citations per the total number of cross-citations of this court.

Figure 11.5 displays all ties which denote more than 4 per cent of all cross-citations of this court. Ireland is again relatively isolated. Germany and France are in the centre since they are cited by many other countries, confirming that big countries are cited more often than smaller ones. It is also interesting to see that there are triangles between Italy, France and Belgium on the one hand, and Austria, Germany, and Switzerland on the other, indicating the relevance of common languages and legal cultures.[43] Finally, Austria and Germany are connected by a clear, dual-headed tie because both courts are the favourite cited courts of each other.[44] This seems to be different for the other relationships. Thus, again, we do not appear to find evidence of a judicial

[43] For a similar observation see D Barak-Erez, 'The Institutional Aspects of Comparative Law' (2009) 15 Columbia Journal of European Law 477 at 487 ('Courts find it easier to learn from precedents which have been formulated within their so-called "legal family"... or their legal culture understood in the broad sense.').

[44] This is different from the absolute numbers (see Figure 11.1) because there are 459 citations from the Austrian Supreme Court to the German one, but only 34 citations from the German to the Austrian one.

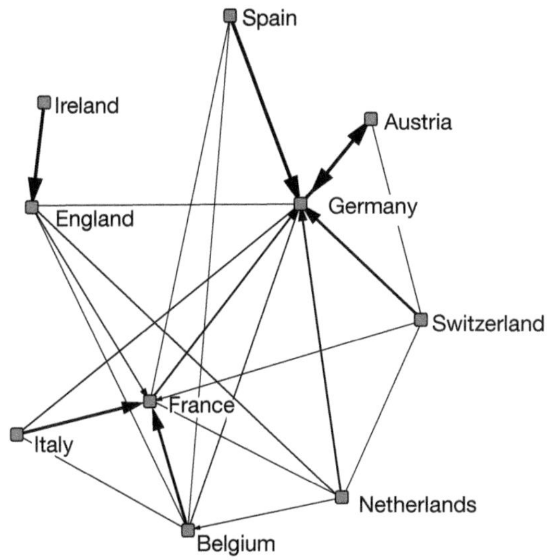

Figure 11.5 Network based on citations per all cross-citations of a particular court

dialogue. However, this should not be our final word on this issue because the following section will provide a more refined treatment of the association between outgoing and incoming citations.

V. Outgoing and incoming citations

Table 11.2 reports the correlation between the nine outgoing and incoming citations of each of the ten courts as well as the correlation between all ninety outgoing and incoming citations. The correlation coefficients of the absolute data (1) are problematic since unobserved factors influence the decision of the highest courts as to whether they cite any foreign court at all. Thus, the option which uses the cross-citations per all cross-citations of the court in question (2) is again preferable.

It follows from Table 11.2, model (2), that, overall, courts do 'return the favour' because there is a statistically significant positive relationship between incoming and outgoing citations. Austria, Ireland and Italy have very high correlation coefficients which can be explained by the fact that Austria almost only cites and is cited by Germany, Ireland almost only cites and is cited by England, and Italy almost only cites and is cited by France. With the exception of Spain, however, the other countries too have positive correlation coefficients.

Of course, the previous sections have also shown that some countries are more 'popular' (in terms of citations) than others, and that there are also differences in the frequency of citing foreign courts. So, despite positive correlation coefficients in Table 11.2, outgoing and incoming citations are not perfectly symmetrical with each other. Again, network analysis comes to our help, because it enables us to identify the core outgoing and incoming countries. This is done by way of a core-periphery

Table 11.2 Correlation between outgoing and incoming citations

	(1) Basis: absolute number of cross-citations	**(2) Basis: cross-citations per all cross-citations of a particular court**
Austria	*0.995***	0.999**
Belgium	*0.113*	0.790*
England	*0.191*	0.210
France	*0.231*	0.310
Germany	*0.992***	0.570
Ireland	*0.999***	0.999**
Italy	*−0.167*	0.970**
Netherlands	*0.130*	0.224
Spain	*−0.145*	−0.145
Switzerland	*−0.060*	0.328
All countries	*0.054*	0.367**

Note: **significant at the 0.01 level (two tailed)
*significant at the 0.1 level (two tailed)

Table 11.3 Blocked adjacency matrix of 2-mode categorical core-periphery model

		Cited courts									
		ENG	FRA	GER	BEL	AUT	IRE	ITA	NL	SPA	CH
Citing courts	NL	12	14	58	25	2		1			
	BEL		41	7					10		1
	CH	2	12	45	1	4					
	FRA			2	2			1			1
	AUT	1	4	464				3			21
	IRE	452	5	1	1				4		
	ITA		10	3	2						
	ENG		20	10	4	2	10		12	2	
	SPA		1	14	1						
	GER	1	2			34		1	1		2

model.[45] Such a model presupposes that, in terms of the present study, some countries are more popular outgoing countries and others are more popular incoming countries. Consequently, we cannot use the percentage form of our dataset (Figures 11.3 and 11.5) since, here, by definition, all outgoing citations of each court add up to 100 per cent. Thus, despite its previously mentioned problems, Table 11.3 is based on the absolute numbers of cross-citations (similar to Figure 11.1). The core cited and citing courts are in the shaded field.

It follows from Table 11.3 that England, France, and Germany are the core incoming countries, and that the Netherlands, Belgium, and Switzerland are the core outgoing ones. This is an interesting result. England, France, and Germany are often regarded as the three 'origin countries' whose legal systems have heavily influenced legal systems all

[45] For a technical definition see Hannemann and Riddle, n 40, at ch 17.

around the world.[46] Thus, it is not unexpected that these countries are most important in terms of incoming citations, with France and Germany being slightly ahead of England, possibly, because six out of seven of the remaining countries are civil law jurisdictions. The main explanation for the core outgoing countries seems to be linguistic diversity: Belgium and Switzerland are multilingual countries, and the Dutch Advocates General frequently cite English, French, German, and Dutch materials in their original languages. Thus, these judges and Advocates General may be more cosmopolitan than the ones of the other countries, as reflected in a high number of citations to different foreign courts.

VI. Caveats and conclusions

There is a general trend to use quantitative methods in order to compare court proceedings and judgments across countries.[47] For instance, the World Bank's Doing Business Report employs various indicators in order to measure 'the efficiency of the judicial system in resolving a commercial dispute'.[48] The European Commission for the Efficiency of Justice (CEPEJ) 'has undertaken a regular process for evaluating judicial systems of the Council of Europe's member states'.[49] The Netherlands Council for the Judiciary has assigned a study to 'design and implement a method to periodically compare the judiciary system of the Netherlands with that in other countries'.[50] And, at universities, a recent project of the University of Oxford has collected data on the costs and funding of civil litigation in various jurisdictions,[51] and a handbook of three Dutch universities has developed a methodology for measuring access to justice.[52]

It is clear that such quantitative research can always be challenged as being a rather simplistic way of comparing how courts actually work.[53] Thus, in the previous sections, we not only reported our results but also indicated where and to what extent the

[46] See, eg, E Glaeser and A Shleifer, 'Legal Origins' (2002) 117 The Quarterly Journal of Economics 1193; S Djankov et al, 'The New Comparative Economics' (2003) 31 Journal of Comparative Economics 595 at 605–6. For a critical summary see M Siems, 'Shareholder Protection Around the World (Leximetric II)' (2008) 33 Delaware Journal of Corporate Law 111 at 138–9.

[47] Starting with Blankenburg and Bruinsma in the 1980s. For a summary of their research see E Blankenburg, 'Civil Litigation Rates as Indicators for Legal Culture' in D Nelken (ed), *Comparing Legal Cultures* (Ashgate Dartmouth 1997) 41; M Siems, *Comparative Law* (CUP Cambridge 2014) 129–30.

[48] See <http://www.doingbusiness.org/MethodologySurveys/EnforcingContracts.aspx>. This derives from S Djankov et al, 'Courts' (2003) 118 Quarterly Journal of Economics 453.

[49] <http://www.coe.int/t/dghl/cooperation/cepej/evaluation/default_en.asp>.

[50] J Blank et al, *Benchmarking in an International Perspective: An International Comparison of the Mechanisms and Performance of the Judiciary System* (2004), available at <http://siteresources.worldbank.org/INTLAWJUSTINST/Resources/Benchmarking.pdf>, at 7.

[51] C Hodges et al (eds.), *The Costs and Funding of Civil Litigation: A Comparative Perspective* (Hart Oxford 2010).

[52] See <http://www.measuringaccesstojustice.com/>.

[53] See, eg, C Kern, *Justice between Simplification and Formalism* (Mohr Tübingen 2007). More generally see Siems, n 47, at 146–87 (on 'numerical comparative law'). See also the qualitative empirical work by E Mak, 'Why Do Dutch and UK Judges Cite Foreign Law?' (2011) 70 CLJ 420 and the survey research by B Flanagan and S Ahern, 'Judicial Decision-Making and Transnational Law: A Survey of Common-Law Supreme Court Judges' (2011) 60 ICLQ 1.

counting, in our case the counting of cross-citations between ten highest courts, has its limitations.

Overall, we observe some one-way traffic, some dialogue, and some networks. We were also able to identify why there is no mutual interaction between all of these highest courts: courts are more likely to cite each other when they are from the same legal tradition and the same language group. Furthermore, we found that larger jurisdictions are cited more frequently than smaller ones. Given these constraints, we would not expect legal systems to freely pick and choose 'the most efficient solution' (however defined), as had been suggested by Ugo Mattei.[54]

Cross-citations are important because they show to what extent courts use foreign law as a justification for a judicial decision. We do not argue that these citations have actually resulted in legal transplants. Indeed, a comparative analysis may also be used to explain the differences and reinforce national solutions rather than leading to uniformity.[55] Nevertheless, frequent cross-citations are evidence of some diffusion of ideas.[56] In this respect, our data may be seen as an empirical confirmation of Daphne Barak-Erez's observation that 'learning from other legal systems has always been a major technique in the development of law'.[57]

There can also be dialogue between highest courts that is not reflected in cross-citations. Highest court judges are increasingly involved in transnational networks with the aim of fostering collaboration and communication.[58] It may also be the case that in Europe ideas are often exchanged through intermediaries such as, say, the ECJ, its advocates general and the ECtHR,[59] or with references to European 'model laws' such as the instrument on European contract law.[60] A further caveat is that we do not know how much foreign case law may matter behind the scenes all the while that judges or advocates general do not mention it explicitly in their opinions.[61] But, as this chapter has shown, even limited to an analysis of visible cross-citations, there is some evidence of transnational legal thinking in some of the highest courts in Europe.

[54] U Mattei, 'Efficiency in Legal Transplants: An Essay in Comparative Law and Economics' (1994) 14 International Review of Law and Economics 3. Similarly, M Andenas and D Fairgrieve, 'There is A World Elsewhere - Lord Bingham and Comparative Law' in M Andenas and D Fairgrieve (eds.), *Tom Bingham and the Transformation of the Law: A Liber Amicorum* (OUP Oxford 2009) 831 ('international market place for judgements').

[55] G Canivet, 'Practice of Comparative Law', n 2, at 1395.

[56] See generally W Twining, 'Social Science and Diffusion of Law' (2005) 32 JLS 203.

[57] See Barak-Erez, n 43, at 478.

[58] See n 5.

[59] See also JM Smits, 'European Private Law and the Comparative Method' in C Twigg-Flesner (ed), *The Cambridge Companion to European Union Private Law* (CUP Cambridge 2010) 33 at 39–40.

[60] See MW Hesselink, 'A Toolbox for European Judges' (2011) 17 ELJ 441.

[61] For criticism see Canivet, 'Practice of Comparative Law', n 2, at 1398 ('Because the methods of courts ought in all circumstances to be transparent, it is obvious that the comparative analysis which the judge intends to include among the elements under examination ought to be . . . explicit').

12

The International Court of Justice's Methodology of Law Ascertainment and Comparative Law

*Eirik Bjorge**

I. Introduction

By relying upon the judgments and decisions of other international and regional courts and tribunals, the International Court of Justice reinforces the integrity of international law through use of comparative law. Moreover, it is not only the integrity of international law which is thereby strengthened; through its reliance upon comparative law, the International Court has also strengthened the integrity of international law's method of law-ascertainment.[1]

Differing views have been taken as to whether the International Court, designated by the UN Charter as the 'principal judicial organ of the United Nations',[2] should refer to the jurisprudence or practice of any other judicial organ or treaty body. Some commentators, such as Crawford and Andenas,[3] have argued that such references can reinforce the position of the UN's principal judicial organ at the apex of international law. The opposite view is sometimes cast in terms of the Registrar of the International Court who is said to have advised new Judges that no other courts and tribunals than the Court itself, and *a fortiori* no regional ones, were to be cited in the Court's jurisprudence.[4]

But differing views have also been taken with respect to the question of the exact extent to which the International Court, and its predecessor the Permanent Court of International Justice, has done so in fact. This could be thought to be a question which admitted only of a right and a wrong answer. Former President Guillaume of the International Court has pointed out that, to begin with, the International Court of Justice cited exclusively its own judgments and advisory opinions.[5]

* Shaw Foundation Junior Research Fellow, Jesus College, University of Oxford.

[1] On the terminology: H Thirlway, *The Sources of International Law* (Oxford University Press, 2014) 232 ('method of law-creation' and of 'law-ascertainment'); J d'Aspremont, *Formalism and the Sources of International Law: A Theory of the Ascertainment of Legal Rules* (Oxford University Press, 2011) 14 ('method of ascertainment of international legal rules'); 'Symposium on Method in International Law: Appraising the Methods of International Law' (1999) 93 AJIL 291–423 (simply 'method').

[2] Art 92, Charter of the United Nations, 26 June 1945, 892 UNTS 119.

[3] J Crawford, 'Chance, Order, Change: The Course of International Law' (2013) 365 Hague *Recueil* 9, 205–29; M Andenas, 'The Centre Reasserting Itself—From Fragmentation to Transformation of International Law' in M Derlén and J Lindholm (eds.), *Volume in Honor of Pär Hallström* (Iustus, 2012).

[4] See M Andenas, 'Case Concerning Ahmadou Sadio Diallo (Republic of Guinea v Democratic Republic of the Congo)' (2011) 60 ICLQ 810, 817. Compare: H Thirlway, *The Sources of International Law* (Oxford University Press, 2014) 120–4.

[5] G Guillaume, 'The Use of Precedent by International Judges and Arbitrators' (2011) 2 JIDS 5, 19.

This is not in actual fact true. Whilst it is the case that the predecessor of the International Court, the Permanent Court of International Justice, when in *Chorzów Factory* it drew on the arbitral award of Sole Arbitrator Huber in *British Claims in the Spanish Zone of Morocco*,[6] where Huber had characterized international responsibility as being the corollary of a right and as entailing when engaged the duty to make reparations, the Court did not cite *Spanish Zone of Morocco*.[7] This reticence on the part of the Permanent Court in *Chorzów Factory* could, however, be due more to modesty than anything else; the President of the Permanent Court at that time was the self-same Max Huber as had been the arbitrator in *Spanish Zone of Morocco*.

President McNair in 1954 pointed out that whilst the parties before the Permanent Court often cited decisions by other courts and tribunals than the Permanent and later International Court, those citations did not always find their way into the judgment of the Court. But he also observed that, already in the jurisprudence of the Permanent Court, there were occasions on which this had in fact happened.[8] In many cases, however, the Permanent Court did refer to the jurisprudence of other international courts and tribunals: in *Polish Postal Service in Danzig*[9] it referred to the arbitral award in *Pious Funds of the Californias*;[10] in *Lotus*[11] it referred to the arbitral award in *Costa Rica Packet*;[12] and in *Legal Status of Eastern Greenland*[13] it referred to the award handed down by Sole Arbitrator Huber in *Island of Palmas*.[14]

Succeeding the Permanent Court, the International Court then in the *Nottebohm Case* (Preliminary Objection) relied on and explicitly referred to the *Alabama* arbitration[15] of the Geneva Tribunal of 1871–2,[16] as having established the principle according to which tribunals have *competence-competence*:

> Since the *Alabama* case, it has been generally recognized, following the earlier precedents, that, in the absence of any agreement to the contrary, an international tribunal has the right to decide as to its own jurisdiction and has the power to interpret for this purpose the instruments which govern that jurisdiction.[17]

The International Court later, in *Continental Shelf (Tunisia/Libyan Arab Jamahiriya)*,[18] explicitly relied on and cited the arbitral award in the UK–France *Continental Shelf* case[19] by finding that 'so substantial a feature as the hurd Depp was not attributed such significance in the Franco-British Arbitration of 1977 concerning the Delimitation of

[6] *British Claims in the Spanish Zone of Morocco (Spain v United Kingdom)* (1925) 2 RIAA 615, 641.

[7] *Case Concerning the Factory at Chorzów (Claim for Indemnity)* PCIJ Rep Series A No 17, 47. Further: D Shelton, 'Righting Wrongs: Reparations in the Articles on State Responsibility' (2002) 96 AJIL 833, 835.

[8] AD McNair, *The Development of International Justice* (New York University Press, 1954) 12–13. Also: J Crawford, *Brownlie's Principles of Public International Law* (8th edn, Oxford University Press, 2012) 40–1.

[9] *Polish Postal Service in Danzig* (1925) PCIJ Ser B No 11, 30.

[10] *Pious Funds of the Californias* (1902) 9 RIAA 11.

[11] *Lotus* (1927) PCIJ Ser A 10, 26.

[12] *Costa Rica Packet* in Moore, 5 *Int Arb* 4948.

[13] *Legal Status of Eastern Greenland* (1933) PCIJ Ser A/B No 53, 45–6.

[14] *Island of Palmas* (1928) 2 RIAA 828.

[15] *Alabama Arbitration (Great Britain v US)* (1872) in Moore, 1 *Int Arb* 495.

[16] T Bingham, 'The *Alabama* Claims Arbitration' (2005) 50 ICLQ 1.

[17] *Nottebohm Case* (Preliminary Objection) (Judgment) 1953 ICJ Rep 11, 119.

[18] *Continental Shelf (Tunisia/Libyan Arab Jamahiriya)* (Judgment) 1982 ICJ Rep 18.

[19] *Delimitation of the Continental Shelf between the United Kingdom of Great Britain and Northern Ireland, and the French Republic (UK v France)* (1977–78) 18 RIAA 3.

the Continental Shelf'.[20] The International Court then in short order, in *Land, Island and Maritime Frontier Dispute*,[21] *Maritime Delimitation and Territorial Question between Qatar and Bahrain*,[22] *Sovereignty over Pulau Ligitan and Pulau Sipadan*,[23] and *Land and Maritime Boundary between Cameroon and Nigeria*,[24] cited a spate of arbitral awards in interstate disputes.[25] In *Kasikili/Sedudu*[26] the International Court referred to the judgment by the Tribunal in *Laguna del Desertio*.[27] There, however, the Court did so in order to show that it was not adopting the approach of the Tribunal in *Laguna del Desertio* to the question of whether in order to illuminate the meaning of words agreed upon in an old treaty the Court could take into account the present-day state of scientific knowledge.[28] Thus the reference to the Tribunal's judgment in *Laguna del Desertio* was prefaced with a 'compare'. The International Court has taken this approach further. In *Interim Accord of 13 September 1995*[29] on the issue of Greece's interpretation of Article 22 of the Interim Accord of 13 September 1995, the International Court noted that the breadth of the Greece's original contention that its rights and duties under a prior agreement take precedence over its obligation not to object to admission by the former Yugoslav Republic of Macedonia (FYROM) to an organization within the terms of Article 11(1). Such an interpretation of Article 22 would, if it were to be accepted, vitiate that obligation, as Greece could normally be expected to have a 'right' under prior agreements with third states to express a view on membership decisions. To this the Court observed that, considering that the parties did not intend Article 22 to render meaningless the first clause of Article 11(1), it was unable to accept the 'broad interpretation' originally advanced by Greece.[30] Here the Court found support in comparative law, as it pointed out that the Court of Justice of the European Communities too had rejected such an argument:

> In this regard, the Court notes that the Court of Justice of the European Communities has rejected a similar argument. In particular, that court has interpreted a provision of the Treaty establishing the European Economic Community which states that 'rights and obligations' under prior agreements 'shall not be affected by' the provisions of the treaty. The European Court has concluded that this language refers to the 'rights' of third countries and the 'obligations' of treaty parties, respectively.[31]

[20] *Continental Shelf (Tunisia/Libyan Arab Jamahiriya)* (Judgment) 1982 ICJ Rep 18, para 66.

[21] *Land, Island and Maritime Frontier Dispute (El Salvador/Honduras: Nicaragua Intervening)* (Judgment) 1992 ICJ Rep 351, paras 390–1.

[22] *Maritime Delimitation and Territorial Question between Qatar and Bahrain (Merits)* (Judgment) 2001 ICJ Rep 40, paras 100–17.

[23] *Sovereignty over Pulau Ligitan and Pulau Sipadan (Indonesia/Malaysia)* (Judgment) 2002 ICJ Rep 625, para 135.

[24] *Land and Maritime Boundary between Cameroon and Nigeria (Cameroon v Nigeria: Equatorial Guinea intervening)* (Judgment) 2002 ICJ Rep 303, para 222.

[25] G Guillaume, 'The Use of Precedent by International Judges and Arbitrators' (2011) 2 JIDS 5, 19.

[26] *Kasikili/Sedudu (Botswana/Namibia)* (Judgment) ICJ Rep 1045.

[27] *Dispute concerning the course of the frontier between BP 62 and Mount Fitzroy (Argentina/Chile)* ('*Laguna del Desertio*') (1994) 113 ILR 1, 76 at [115].

[28] *Kasikili/Sedudu (Botswana/Namibia)* (Judgment) ICJ Rep 1045, 1060 at [20].

[29] *Application of the Interim Accord of 13 September 1995 (FYROM v Greece)* ICJ Rep 2011 644.

[30] 678 at [109].

[31] 678–9 at [109] (referring to Case 10/61 *Commission v Italy* [1962] ECR, p 10 and Case C-249/06 *Commission v Sweden* [2009] ECR I-1348, para 34).

It was eloquent of the openness of the International Court to the jurisprudence of other courts and tribunals when Judge Greenwood, in *Diallo (Compensation)*, observed that:

> International law is not a series of fragmented specialist and self-contained bodies of law, each of which functions in isolation from the others; it is a single, unified system of law and each international court can, and should, draw on the jurisprudence of other international courts and tribunals, even though it is not bound necessarily to come to the same conclusions.[32]

The relationship between the reliance by the International Court upon comparative law and the method of law-ascertainment becomes apparent in relation to the issues often referred to under the etiquette 'fragmentation of international law'. Crawford has defined the terms of the debate as being: 'fragmentation' and 'proliferation'. The former refers to *substantive* fragmentation, that is, the product of conflicting but equally authoritative pronouncements on international law by courts and tribunals. The latter refers to *institutional* fragmentation, that is, the great expansion, in the last few decades, in the number of international courts and tribunals of competing jurisdiction.[33]

The International Law Commission, under the chairmanship of Martti Koskenniemi, observed in this connection that:

> Specialized law-making and institution-building tends to take place with relative ignorance of legislative and institutional activities in the adjoining field and of the general principles and practices of international law. The result is conflicts between rules or rule-systems, deviating institutional practices and, possibly the loss of an overall perspective on the law.[34]

President of the International Court Jennings feared that international law, on account of the parameters set out above, would develop 'without any overall plan'; there was, in his view, 'a danger that international law as a whole will become fragmented and unmanageable'.[35]

As will be seen, some commentators were led, against this background, to believe that the methods for law-ascertainment differed in the specialized sub-fields of international law from those in operation in general international law. As adumbrated above, this chapter makes the argument that that has been obviated through the International Court's opening up to comparative law.[36] The argument made in this chapter thus builds on what Andenas has argued in relation to the rule content of

[32] Declaration of Judge Greenwood in *Case Concerning Ahmadou Sadio Diallo (Republic of Guinea v Democratic Republic of the Congo)*, Compensation (Judgment) [2012] ICJ Rep 324, 394 at [8].

[33] J Crawford, *Chance, Order, Change: The Course of International Law* (2013) 365 Hague *Recueil* 9, 211–12.

[34] Report of the ILC Study Group, UN doc. a/Cn.4/L.682, 13 April 2006 p 11 at [8].

[35] RY Jennings, 'The Role of the International Court of Justice' (1997) 68 BYIL 1, 58–60.

[36] See generally PG Montaneri, *Methods of Comparative Law* (Edward Elgar, 2002). Also: K Zweigert and H Kötz, *An Introduction to Comparative Law* (T Weir tr, 3rd edn, Oxford University Press, 1998); H Muir Watt, 'Globalization and Comparative Law' in M Reimann and R Zimmermann (eds.), *The Oxford Handbook of Comparative Law* (paperback edn, Oxford University Press, 2008); M Reimann, 'Comparative Law and Neighbouring Disciplines' in M Bussani and U Mattei, *The Cambridge Companion to Comparative Law* (Cambridge University Press, 2012) 20–1.

various sub-fields of international law as compared to international law. He has argued that the International Court, by opening up its jurisprudence to the influences of other courts and tribunals, has been able to reassert itself as the centre of international law.[37] The argument made here is that this applied not only in connection with the rule content of international law but also in connection with the methods of law-ascertainment.

In connection with the issue of the fragmentation of international law, and whether special rules apply in special regimes of international law, Thirlway has posed the question, 'Do any of these special rules also purport to be based upon a source or sources other than, or independent of, the traditional triad of treaty, custom, and general principles?' This triad is expressed in Article 38(1)(a)–(c) of the Statute of the International Court of Justice:

> The Court, whose function is to decide in accordance with international law such disputes as are submitted to it, shall apply: a. international conventions, whether general or particular, establishing rules expressly recognized by the contesting states; b. international custom, as evidence of a general practice accepted as law; c. the general principles of law recognized by civilized nations.

Against that background, this chapter will focus on the use by the International Court of comparative law in connection with its ascertainment of legal rules following from international conventions and international custom, as evidence of a general practice accepted as law. This chapter sees the use by the International Court of Justice of comparative law, that is, the practice or jurisprudence of other courts and tribunals, in relation especially to the primary means by which international law is created: treaties and custom.

In relation to treaty law, this chapter will focus on the incidence of a particular situation: reference to the treaty bodies of human rights conventions. This is because, as will be seen, the field of human rights has been singled out as 'special' in relation to the methods of law-ascertainment both in connection with customary international law and in connection with treaties. In relation to custom, the chapter will, for the same reason, turn to references by the International Court to the same type of bodies, as with custom, too, the argument has been made that the normal rules of law-ascertainment need revision or at least cannot function in the way they ordinarily do.

II. Customary international law

Special Rapporteur Sir Michael Wood has, in the context of a study by the International Law Commission (ILC) on the formation of customary international law, stated that given the unity of international law and the fact that international law is a legal system, it is neither helpful nor in accordance with principle to break the law up into separate specialist fields. The same basic approach to the formation and identification of

[37] M Andenas, 'The Centre Reasserting Itself—From Fragmentation to Transformation of International Law' in M Derlén and J Lindholm (eds.), *Volume in Honor of Pär Hallström* (Iustus, 2012) 11–13.

customary international law, he said, applies regardless of the field of law under consideration:

> The formation and evidence of rules of customary international law in different fields may raise particular issues and it may therefore be for consideration whether, and if so to what degree, different weight may be given to different materials depending on the field in question, at the same time it should be recalled that, in the words of Judge Greenwood, '[i]nternational law is not a series of fragmented specialist and self-contained bodies of law, each of which functions in isolation from the others; it is a single, unified system of law'.[38]

The unified approach suggested by the Special Rapporteur must be the correct one. It is borne out especially by the way in which the International Court has relied, in cases where it has had to ascertain norms of customary international law, upon what could be called comparative law.

It has been argued, however, that ascertaining developments in customary international law presents particular difficulties in connection with human rights. Thus Thirlway avers that 'there is a problem with basing human rights law on custom'.[39] This, in his view, is because in the past the relationship of a State with its own subjects has been generally immune from the impact of developing customary law, the reason being, in his view, that custom derives from the *de facto* adjustment of conflicting claims and interests of the subjects of international law, and it has always been—and, he avers, probably still is—one of the most fundamental tenets of international law that individuals and private corporations are not subjects of international law.[40]

It bears mention, however, that it is now abundantly clear, as Greenwood has recently stated, that 'states can no longer be regarded as the only subjects of international law'.[41] Admitting that this is no longer the case, Thirlway nonetheless observes that 'teasing intellectual problems remain'.[42] In his view, the essence of custom, in the traditional view, is that its provisions have been hammered out in the resolution of conflicts of interests, or disputes, between States in their day-to-day relations. This leads to two problems, in his view. First, he cites Simma and Alston, who have observed that:

> An element of interaction—in a broad sense—is intrinsic to, and essential to, the kind of State practice leading to the formation of customary international law...The processes of customary international law can only be triggered, and continue working,

[38] International Law Commission, 'First Report on Formation and Evidence of Customary International Law, Report of the Special Rapporteur Sir Michael Wood' (2013) UN Doc A/CN.4/663 [19], citing *Ahmadou Sadio Diallo (Republic of Guinea v Democratic Republic of the Congo) (Compensation owed by the Democratic Republic of the Congo to the Republic of Guinea)* (Judgment) [2012] ICJ Rep 391 (Declaration by Greenwood J) [8].

[39] H Thirlway, *The Sources of International Law* (Oxford University Press, 2014) 176; H Thirlway, 'Working Paper on Human Rights in Customary International Law' presented at Oxford–FCO seminar 15 October 2014.

[40] See H Thirlway, *International Customary Law and Codification* (Brill, 1972) 7.

[41] C Greenwood, 'Sovereignty: A View from the International Bench' in R Rawlings, P Leyland, and A Young (eds.), *Sovereignty and the Law: Domestic, European and International Perspectives* (Oxford University Press, 2013) 255.

[42] H Thirlway, *The Sources of International Law* (Oxford University Press, 2014) 177.

> in situations in which States interact, where they apportion or delimit in some tangible way. But, at least in most cases, this is not what happens when a consensus about substantive human rights obligations, to be performed domestically, grows into international law.[43]

Secondly, Thirlway draws attention to 'the striking differences between the settings in which customary law traditionally arose and the issues on which it spoke, on the one hand, and the contemporary settings in which advocates of customary international law'—particularly, one might add, in the human rights field—'seek to employ customary norms, on the other'.[44]

Two points should be made in this regard. First the types of assertions on the part of states to which one must look for the ascertainment of customary international law in connection with human rights are more manifold than the ones which Thirlway is prepared to accept. It will by definition be a more complex matrix than only statements by Ministries of Foreign Affairs. Thus, in *Nicaragua*, the International Court, basing itself upon materials falling outside what Thirlway terms 'the interchange of State relations that normally constitutes the material element of custom',[45] observed that '[t]he existence in the *opinio juris* of States of the principle of non-intervention is backed by established and substantial practice', and relied in this connection on a single General Assembly resolution—General Assembly resolution 2625 (XXV).[46] This approach was acceptable, in the eyes of the International Court, in connection with the customary international law of non-intervention—why should it not be acceptable, too, in connection with what we have come to term human rights? In 1970 the International Court's first Registrar and President that year of the UN General Assembly, Edvard Hambro, had the following to say about the topic of customary international law and human rights:

> [The Universal Declaration of Human Rights] has been quoted in judicial decisions and incorporated in resolutions of the General Assembly... [Violations of the Universal Declaration] have been criticized, attacked and denounced by the General Assembly so consistently and so strongly that it is quite clear that in the eyes of the General Assembly there is an obligation to respect fundamental human rights... But it can be asked whether a repetition of a hortatory resolution makes it binding, however often it may be repeated. The answer probably is that repetition is the very essence of custom. That is the way customary law is created. *When the General Assembly again and again proceeds on the assumption and in the belief that it is illegal to violate human rights, it may be stated that a rule of customary international law is created.* Or perhaps

[43] B Simma and P Alston, 'The Sources of Human Rights Law: Custom, *Jus Cogens* and General Principles' (1988) 12 Australian Yearbook of International Law 82, 99.

[44] E Kadens and E Young, 'How Customary is Customary International Law?' (2013) 54 William & Mary Law Review 885, 914.

[45] H Thirlway, 'Working Paper on Human Rights in Customary International Law', n 39, para 5.

[46] *Military and Paramilitary Activities in and against Nicaragua (Nicaragua v United States of America)*, Merits, Judgment, ICJ Rep 1986 p 14, 106 at [202] ('It has moreover been presented as a corollary of the principle of the sovereign equality of States. A particular instance of this is General Assembly resolution 2625 (XXV), the Declaration on the Principles of International Law concerning Friendly Relations and Co-operation among States').

it is safer to say that such repetition may be an element in forming international custom, as evidence of a general practice accepted as law.[47]

In accordance with this approach, it is not the mere existence of the Universal Declaration that has contributed to rights contained therein having become part of customary international law (partly because custom cannot rise instantaneously); it is the repeated reliance by States upon them, in bodies such as the General Assembly.[48]

On the whole, it is not difficult to find examples of a State claiming, with respect to itself or a different State, that it (or the other State) is bound by what it perceives to be customary international law rules governing human rights. One example is Argentina's pleadings in *Suez v Argentina*, a case explicitly relied on by Thirlway,[49] where Argentina claimed that 'it adopted the measures [at issue] in order to safeguard the human right to water of the inhabitants of the country'.[50] Similarly Turkey, before the Grand Chamber of the European Court of Human Rights, in *Öcalan v Turkey*, defended its putative breach of Article 6 of the European Convention on Human Rights, by stating that 'the applicant had ... been brought before a Turkish judicial authority at the end of a lawful procedure, in conformity with customary international law'.[51] In *Loizidou v Turkey*, Cyprus argued before the Grand Chamber of the same court that Ms Loizidou had been the victim of a Turkish policy which was 'based upon racial discrimination in breach of ... customary international law'.[52] It is difficult to sustain the claim that human rights are so special in relation to customary international law.

Secondly, Thirlway observes that the concept of domestic jurisdiction and the recognized principle of sovereignty may stand in the way of human rights being capable of having the status of customary international law.[53] But the concept of 'domestic jurisdiction' is no ossuary. Challenges to this ossified concept of 'domestic jurisdiction' have a very respectable provenance in international law.[54] Addressing this same point, Hambro in 1970 pointed out that, although the principle expressed in Article 2(7) of the UN Charter of course remains intact, and 'the rule of domestic

[47] E Hambro, 'Human Rights and States' Rights' (1970) 56 American Bar Association Journal 360, 361 (emphasis added).

[48] The Universal Periodic Review (UPR) before the UN Human Rights Council may be another.

[49] H Thirlway, 'Working Paper on Human Rights in Customary International Law', n 39, para 17.

[50] *Suez, Sociedad General de Aguas de Barcelona SA v Argentina*, ICSID Case No. ARB/03/19, para 252; H Thirlway, 'Working Paper on Human Rights in Customary International Law', n 39, para 17.

[51] *Öcalan v Turkey*, App No 46221/99 (Merits and Just Satisfaction) 12 May 2005 at [82].

[52] *Loizidou v Turkey*, App No 15318/89 (Merits) 18 December 1996 at [36].

[53] H Thirlway, 'Working Paper on Human Rights in Customary International Law', n 39, para 7.

[54] See *Nationality Decrees Issued in Tunisia and Morocco (French Zone)* (Advisory Opinion) (1923) PCIJ Series B No 4; R Higgins, *Problems and Process* (Clarendon Press, 1994) 96–7 ('Once it is recognized that obligations are owed to individuals (because they have rights), then there is no reason of logic why the obligation should be owed only to foreign individuals, and not to nationals. It becomes unsustainable to regard the treatment of one's own nationals as matters falling essentially within domestic jurisdiction, and thus unreviewable by the international community.'); J Crawford, 'Chance, Order, Change: The Course of International Law' (2013) 365 Hague *Recueil* 9, 74–5 ('It is not only on the international plane that the limits of sovereignty are variable and flexible. The apparently clear boundary between the internal and the international also shifts as States enter into new treaties and as new areas of international activity evolve, for example with respect to human rights. The Permanent Court commented as early as 1923 that "whether a certain matter is or is not solely within the jurisdiction of a State is an essentially relative question" that "depends upon the development of international relations". This does not so much erode the notion of sovereignty as reconfigure it.').

jurisdiction exists', it should be realized that 'the content of what is within this domain has changed and does change continually'.[55] There is extremely good authority for this proposition in international law, the Permanent Court having observed in *Nationality Decrees issued in Tunis and Morocco* that '[t]he question whether a certain matter is or is not solely within the jurisdiction of a State is an essentially relative question; it depends upon the development of international relations.'[56] It is not impossible to imagine that a State should, in connection with how it treats individuals within its domestic jurisdiction, feel bound by rules of customary international law;[57] it is a question of framing the question in the right terms and taking on board that public international law, at the current stage of its development, admits of many other types of evidence of what is customary international law than the diplomatic note in bilateral state–state commerce.

Adding to this is the fact that the problems envisioned by Thirlway seem not to have arisen in the jurisprudence of the International Court, though that Court has had to deal with issues of customary international law dealing with human rights. It is suggested that it is partly through reliance upon comparative law that the International Court has avoided the problems discussed by Thirlway.

Whilst the norms of customary international law at issue in *Jurisdictional Immunities* were not in the strict sense human rights norms, but rather norms dealing with the duty of State authorities to respect recognized immunities, that judgment is a convenient point of departure. The International Court in *Jurisdictional Immunities* held that:

> It is of course axiomatic that the material of customary international law is to be looked for primarily in the actual practice and opinio juris of State, even though multilateral conventions may have an important role to play in recording and defining rules deriving from custom, or indeed in developing them.[58]

Although in that case State practice of particular significance was to be found in the judgments of national courts, the Court also pointed out that multilateral conventions, too, may have an important role to play in recording and defining rules deriving from custom, as well as in developing them. The International Court's approach here could be thought to be a far cry from the hammering out of custom in the resolutions of conflicts of interests, or disputes, between States in their day-to-day relations. Thirlway's approach seems to be based on a paradigm according to which international law is no more than a web of bilateral relationships whilst, for some time now, international law is a multilateral system consisting of several types of actors—of which a number of different courts are ones—and several types of instruments—of which multilateral treaties, too, are ones.

[55] E Hambro, 'Human Rights and States' Rights' (1970) 56 American Bar Association Journal 360, 363.

[56] *Nationality Decrees Issued in Tunisia and Morocco (French Zone)* (Advisory Opinion) (1923) PCIJ Series B No 4 p 24.

[57] See, here too, *Suez, Sociedad General de Aguas de Barcelona SA v Argentina* at [252] (within domestic territory); *Öcalan v Turkey* at [82] (outside of national territory); *Loizidou v Turkey* at [36] (in occupied territory).

[58] *Jurisdictional Immunities of the State (Germany v Italy; Greece intervening)* (Judgment) [2012] ICJ Rep 99, 122–3 [55].

The approach of the International Court in *Jurisdictional Immunities* might be thought to differ from the assertions of Thirlway in connection with whether, in principle, questions of human rights somehow are incapable of being expressed by way of customary international law, as in his words 'the "inter-State" element of custom creation remains a practical if not legal obstacle'.[59] The issues came to a head in the International Court's Advisory Opinion in *IFAD*.[60]

At issue in *IFAD* was 'the principle of equality of access to courts and tribunals', which could be thought to be either an expression of customary international law or, alternatively, a general principle of law recognized by civilized nations, in the sense of Article 38(1)(c) of the Statute of the International Court. The general principles referred to in Article 38(1)(c) are additional to, and therefore in principle independent of, the other sources of law in international law enumerated in Article 38. Customary law is not merely made up of rules; it contains also 'established principles', principles established in the same way as rules (by practice and *opinio juris*) or derived by extrapolation or analysis from such rules.[61] It seems that it was such a principle to which the International Court made reference in *IFAD*[62] when it referred to 'the principle of equality of access to courts and tribunals' in connection with the question whether the International Court should exercise its jurisdiction not to respond to the request in view of the anachronistic inequality of status between the employer and the employee. The issue arose in relation to the 'appeal' by the Director-General of the International Fund for Agricultural Development against a decision of the Administrative Tribunal of the International Labour Organization (ILOAT) upholding a staff member's claim against dismissal.[63] In order to establish the contents of this principle of customary law, and its development over time, the International Court adverted to the practice of the UN Human Rights Committee. In a paragraph that deserves to be quoted in full, the Court set out the principle of equality of arms thus:

> the development of the principle of equality of access to courts and tribunals since 1946, when the review procedure was established, may be seen in the significant differences between the two General Comments by the Human Rights Committee on Article 14, paragraph 1, of the International Covenant on Civil and Political Rights of 1966. That provision requires that '[a]ll persons shall be equal before the courts and tribunals'. The first Comment, adopted in 1984, just seven years after the Covenant came into force, did no more than repeat the terms of the provision and call on States to report more fully on steps taken to ensure equality before the courts, including equal access to the courts (HRC, General Comment No. 13: Article 14 (Administration of

[59] H Thirlway, *The Sources of International Law* (Oxford University Press, 2014) 177.

[60] *Judgment No 2867 of the Administrative Tribunal of the International Labour Organization upon a Complaint Filed against the International Fund for Agricultural Development* (Advisory Opinion) [2012] ICJ Rep 10.

[61] H Thirlway, *The Sources of International Law* (Oxford University Press, 2014) 94.

[62] *Judgment No 2867 of the Administrative Tribunal of the International Labour Organization upon a Complaint Filed against the International Fund for Agricultural Development* (Advisory Opinion) [2012] ICJ Rep 10, 27 at [39].

[63] Further, N Rodley, 'The International Court of Justice and Human Rights Treaty Bodies' in M Andenas and E Bjorge (eds.), *A Farewell to Fragmentation: Reassertion and Convergence in International Law* (Cambridge University Press, 2015).

> Justice), paras. 2–3). The later Comment, one adopted in 2007 on the basis of 30 years of experience in the application of the above-mentioned Article 14, gives detailed attention to equality before domestic courts and tribunals. According to the Committee, that right to equality guarantees equal access and equality of arms. While in non-criminal matters the right of equal access does not address the issue of the right of appeal, if procedural rights are accorded they must be provided to all the parties unless distinctions can be justified on objective and reasonable grounds (Human Rights Committee, General Comment No. 32: Right to Equality before Courts and Tribunals and to a Fair Trial, paras. 8–9, 12 and 13). In the case of the ILOAT, the Court is unable to see any such justification for the provision for review of the Tribunal's decisions which favours the employer to the disadvantage of the staff member.

As Rodley has observed, the International Court here stressed both equality of access and procedural equality, and the comparison it makes between the earlier and later General Comments is presumably intended to imply that if the scope of the principle was not clear in 1984, it was unmistakably so nearly a quarter of a century later. The reference to the fact that, he continues, under Article 14 of International Covenant on Civil and Political Rights of 1966[64] there is no automatic right of appeal in non-criminal matters, but that where there is appeal the parties should be equal is presumably made in order to offset any argument, in favour of IFAD, that the principles expressed in Article 14 would not apply to an appeal in a non-criminal case, as the only area of law in which the Covenant expressly requires provision for review of a judgment by a higher court is in the case of convictions for crimes, in Article 14(5).[65]

The Court further advised that, on the only other occasion in which a specialized agency had sought an opinion in terms of Article XII of the Annex to the Statute of the ILOLAT,[66] it had held that 'the principle of equality of the parties follows from the requirements of good administration of justice'.[67] The Court in *IFAD* went on to say that:

> that principle must now be understood as including access on an equal basis to available appellate or similar remedies unless en exception can be justified on objective and reasonable grounds.[68]

In order to set out the basic contours of the principle in issue, the International Court in *IFAD* relied on its own jurisprudence, ie the *UNESCO* Advisory Opinion.[69] But in

[64] International Covenant on Civil and Political Rights, 16 December 1966, 999 UNTS 171.

[65] N Rodley, 'The International Court of Justice and Human Rights Treaty Bodies' in M Andenas and E Bjorge (eds.), *A Farewell to Fragmentation: Reassertion and Convergence in International Law* (Cambridge University Press, 2015).

[66] Statute of the Administrative Tribunal of the International Labour Organization, 9 October 1946, C de Cooker (ed), *International Administration* (Martinus Nijhoff, 1990) doc.3.

[67] *Judgments of the Administrative Tribunal of the ILO upon complaints made against the UNESCO* (Advisory Opinion) ICJ Rep 1956 p 77, 86; *Judgment No 2867 of the Administrative Tribunal of the International Labour Organization upon a Complaint Filed against the International Fund for Agricultural Development* (Advisory Opinion) [2012] ICJ Rep 10, 29 at [44].

[68] *Judgment No 2867 of the Administrative Tribunal of the International Labour Organization upon a Complaint Filed against the International Fund for Agricultural Development* (Advisory Opinion) [2012] ICJ Rep 10, 29 at [44].

[69] *Judgments of the Administrative Tribunal of the ILO upon complaints made against the UNESCO* (Advisory Opinion) ICJ Rep 1956 p 77.

order to show how, since 1956, that principle of customary international law had developed, the Court relied, exclusively, upon the practice of the UN Human Rights Committee,[70] using the same techniques as it would have used in determining the content of a norm of customary international law of any other type.

Thus, in order to establish the customary rule in issue, the Court adverted to a multilateral convention which, through the practice of its treaty body, the UN Human Rights Committee, not only *defined* but also *developed* the content of the customary norm principle of equality of access to court. Through its reliance upon comparative law, that is, the practice of the UN Human Rights Committee, the International Court in *IFAD* showed how the rules for ascertainment of customary international law in respect of human rights in no way differ from the rules applying to other types of norm.

III. Treaty law

As was said in the introduction to this chapter, there is a connection between fragmentation with respect to the content of rules and fragmentation with respect to the law of treaties, that is to say fragmentation in the method of treaty interpretation. The techniques of treaty interpretation must not be seen only from the formal point of view; they also have material consequences, that is, consequences for the substance or contents of norms.[71]

The extent to which the International Court of Justice reinforces the integrity of international law, as well as of the integrity of international legal method or the methods relied on in the ascertainment of legal rules, is particularly clear in *Diallo*. There the International Court had to deal with questions relating to the protection of human rights and consular protection. Whilst the former is a relative newcomer in the jurisprudence of the International Court, the latter is a classic feature.[72]

In *Tehran Hostages* the International Court had said that that 'the rules of diplomatic law, in short, constitute a self-contained regime'.[73] The concept of 'self-contained regimes' has a long pedigree, deriving from the judgment of the Permanent Court of International Justice in *The SS 'Wimbledon'*,[74] where the Court was asked whether the provisions of the Treaty of Versailles applied to entitle non-neutral passage through the Kiel Canal in peacetime. Since the treaty contained a special section on the Kiel Canal which differed from the general provisions on watercourse contained in the treaty, said the Court, the provisions relating to the Kiel Canal must therefore be self-contained.

[70] UN Human Rights Committee (HRC), *CCPR General Comment No 13: Article 14 (Administration of Justice), Equality before the Courts and the Rights to a Fair Public Hearing by an Independent Court Established by Law*, 13 April 1984; UN Human Rights Committee (HRC), *General Comment No. 32, Article 14, Right to Equality before Courts and Tribunals and to a Fair Trial*, 23 August 2007, CCPR/C.GC.32.

[71] JM Dupuy and Y Kerbrat, *Droit international public* (10th edn, Dalloz, 2010), 352. Also, H Ruiz Fabri, 'La contribution de l'Organisation mondiale du commerce à la gestion de l'espace juridique mondial' in E Loquin and C Kessedjian (eds.), *La mondialisation du droit* (Litec, 2000) 369.

[72] See *Mavrommatis Palestine Concessions Case (Greece v United Kingdom)* (1924) PCIJ Series A No 2 p 12.

[73] *United States Diplomatic and Consular Staff in Tehran (United States of America v Iran)* (Judgment) [1980] ICJ Rep 3, 40 at [86].

[74] See J Crawford, *Chance, Order, Change: The Course of International Law* (2013) 365 Hague *Recueil* 9, 224.

If, the Court continued, they had to be supplemented by other provisions, they would lose their *raison d'être*.[75] By holding that the rules of diplomatic protection constituted a self-contained regime, the International Court in *Tehran Hostages* went further than it had done in *The SS 'Wimbledon'*.

As Crawford has observed with reliance upon the analysis of the 2006 Report of the Study Group of the International Law Commission (ILC):

> in a broad sense, a self-contained regime is little more than a strong form of *lex specialis*, by which a 'geographically or functionally limited treaty series' attempts to contract out of the secondary rules of international law that underpin the system as a whole.[76]

More broadly, the Report of the Study Group of the ILC made the point that conflict-resolution and interpretation cannot be distinguished from each other; whether there is a conflict and what can be done to it *prima facie* depends upon the way in which the relevant rules are interpreted. The ILC pointed to Article 31(3)(c) of the Vienna Convention on the Law of Treaties (VCLT)[77] as the 'master key' to the house of international law. But it also stressed that there is no need for formal reference to Article 31(3)(c) as 'other techniques provide sufficiently the need to take into account the normative environment' of a treaty.[78]

The principle of systemic integration, to which the ILC pointed with approval, has a long pedigree in international law. McNair pointed out how treaties must be 'applied and interpreted against the background of the general principles of international law'.[79] The arbitral tribunal in *Georges Pinson* even held that a treaty must be seen as referring 'tacitement au droit international commun, pour toutes les questions qu'elle ne résout pas elle-même en termes exprès et d'une façon différente'.[80] Not only has international law for many decades demanded that general international law has a role to play in treaty interpretation, it has also pointed to a need to take into account the normative environment more widely.[81] This point was made by the tribunal in *Tardieu-Jaspard*: 'il faut tenir compte du fait qu'il faut placer et interpréter l'accord Tardieu-Jaspar dans le cadre des accords de La Haye de janvier 1930, c'est-à-dire dans le cadre du Plan Young qui détermine soigneusement par quelle méthode les "paiements allemands" et les "transferts allemand" s'effectueront'.[82] The same point had been made even earlier, in the 1905 case *Muscat Dhows*,[83] where the tribunal set up by the Permanent Court of Arbitration had been asked to interpret the treaty term '*protégés*' in the Act of the

[75] *Case of the SS 'Wimbledon'* (1923) PCIJ Series A No 1, 15, 23–4.

[76] J Crawford, *Chance, Order, Change: The Course of International Law* (2013) 365 Hague *Recueil* 9, 226, citing Conclusions of the ILC Study Group, un doc. a/Cn.4/L.702, 18 July 2006, para 10.

[77] Vienna Convention on the Law of Treaties, 23 May 1969, 1155 UNTS 331; (1969) 8 ILM 679.

[78] M Koskenniemi, 'Fragmentation of International Law: Difficulties Arising from the Diversification and Expansion of International Law', Report of the Study Group of the International Law Commission, finalized by Martti Koskenniemi A/CN.4/L.682, at [420]–[421].

[79] AD McNair, *The Law of Treaties* (2nd edn, Oxford University Press, 1961), 466.

[80] *Georges Pinson (France/United Mexican States)* (1928) 5 RIAA 327, 422.

[81] M Koskenniemi, 'Fragmentation of International Law' (n 78), at [414].

[82] *Différend concernant l'accord Tardieu-Jaspard (Belgium/France)* (1930) 3 RIAA 1701, 1713.

[83] *Affaire des boutres de Mascate (France c Grande-Bretagne)* (1905) 11 RIAA 83.

Brussels Conference of 1890.[84] The Tribunal held that the interpretation must correspond to the intentions of the parties, as well as to 'principes du droit international tels qu'ils ont été exprimés dans les conventions en vigueur à cette époque, dans la législation nationale en tant qu'elle a obtenu une reconnaissance internationale et dans la pratique du droit des gens'.[85]

The International Court gave expression to much the same rule when it held in *Right of Passage* that 'it is a rule of interpretation that a text emanating from a Government must, in principle, be interpreted as producing and intended to produce effects in accordance with existing law and not in violation of it'.[86]

In principal there are, however, limits to such an approach. When it follows from the treaty to be interpreted, or from the jurisdictional title in issue, that the court is only to rely on the instrument before it, then it is in the normal course of events bound to do so. Here, as in other connections in the law of treaties, 'the intention of the parties should be controlling'.[87] This is exemplified especially in arbitral practice.

Relying as a matter of course on the Vienna rules, the Tribunal in *Kishenganga* (Final Award),[88] presided over by former President of the International Court Schwebel, in its interpretation of the Indian–Pakistani Indus Waters Treaty and Annexures,[89] underscored the importance of what the same Tribunal had said in *Kishenganga* (Partial Award), that is, that 'principles of international environmental law must be taken into account even when interpreting treaties concluded before the development of that body of law'.[90] Nonetheless, given the Indus Water Treaty and Annexures made clear that:

> the law to be applied by the Court shall be this Treaty and, whenever, necessary for its interpretation or application, but only to the extent necessary for that purpose, the following in the order in which they are listed: (a) International conventions establishing rules which are expressly recognized by the Parties; (b) Customary international law.

Thus the Tribunal noted 'that the place of customary international law in the interpretation and application of the Indus Waters Treaty remains subject to Paragraph 29'; 'this Treaty expressly limits the extent to which the Court may have recourse to, and apply, sources of law beyond the Treaty itself'.[91] The Tribunal concluded that: 'if customary international law were applied not to circumscribe, but to negate rights expressly granted in the Treaty, this would no longer be "*interpretation or application*" of the Treaty but the substitution of customary law *in place of* the Treaty.'[92]

Situations such as the one arising in *Kishenganga* are, however, relatively rare; they could even be said to be the exceptions that confirm the rule. Certainly none of the

[84] Declaration of the General Act of the Brussels Conference 2 July 1890, 173 CTS 188.
[85] *Affaire des boutres de Mascate* (n 83), 93–4.
[86] *Right of Passage over Indian Territory* (Preliminary Objections) [1957] ICJ Rep 125, 142.
[87] ILC Ybk 1964/I, 34.
[88] *Indus Waters Kishenganga (Pakistan v India)* (Final Award), 20 December 2013.
[89] Indus Waters Treaty, 19 September 1960, 419 UNTS 126.
[90] *Indus Waters Kishenganga (Pakistan v India)* (Partial Award) (2013) 154 ILR 1, 173 at [452].
[91] *Indus Waters Kishenganga (Pakistan v India)* (Final Award), 20 December 2013, at [111].
[92] *Indus Waters Kishenganga (Pakistan v India)* (Final Award), 20 December 2013, at [112] (emphases in original). Also: F Berman, 'Treaty "Interpretation" in a Judicial Context' (2004) 29 Yale JIL 315.

important multilateral treaties that govern international relations has clauses to this effect. It is possible, in principle, to argue that the effect of a self-contained regime would be the same, however, and in *Diallo*[93] the self-contained regime that had been in issue in *Tehran Hostages*[94]—the law of consular protection—was again at issue. The way in which the International Court distanced itself from the notion of self-contained regimes is eloquent of the open approach which the International Court now takes to international law. Gone is the insistence, in the case of consular protection, that the law of consular relations is a self-contained regime. Gone, too, is the notion that the Court refers only to its own jurisprudence. The extent to which these two developments were interlocked is clear from the way in which the Court dealt with the question of how consular protection interacted with human rights protection, and in establishing the level of protection to be afforded Mr Diallo, as well as how, in doing so, the Court relied on the practice of human rights treaty bodies.[95]

This was made explicit in the concurring opinion of Judge Cançado Trindade who stated that while the procedure for the claim for the vindication of the claim originally utilized was that of diplomatic protection, the substantive law applied by the Court was 'the International Law of Human Rights'.[96] The International Court made it clear that it was thus no longer the case that, to use the formula from *Tehran Hostages*, 'the rules of diplomatic law, in short, constitute a self-contained regime'.[97] This seemed to be in step with the criticism that had been levelled at *Tehran Hostages*, for example by Simma, who has argued that while the rules of diplomatic law, due to the dictum in *Tehran Hostages*, had become the rules of international law the most commonly associated with the notion of self-containment, but that in fact they were 'the least convincing example of a closed system of secondary rules.'[98]

In fact the International Court in *Diallo* went so far, in bringing human rights norms to bear upon the law of diplomatic protection, as to cite jurisprudence from the African Commission on Human and Peoples' Rights, the Inter-American Court of Human Rights, and the European Court of Human Rights.[99] As Rodley has shown, the reliance by the International Court upon the case law of such treaty bodies is interesting for two reasons: the first relates to the juridical status of the outputs of the treaty bodies;

[93] *Diallo (Republic of Guinea v Democratic Republic of the Congo)* (Preliminary Objections) [2007] ICJ Rep 582; *Ahmadou Sadio Diallo (Republic of Guinea v Democratic Republic of the Congo)* (Merits) (Judgment) [2010] ICJ Rep 639; *Ahmadou Sadio Diallo (Republic of Guinea v Democratic Republic of the Congo)*, Compensation (Judgment) [2012] ICJ Rep 324.

[94] *United States Diplomatic and Consular Staff in Tehran (United States of America v Iran)* (n 73), 40 at [86].

[95] *Ahmadou Sadio Diallo (Republic of Guinea v Democratic Republic of the Congo)* (Merits) (n 93), 662–73 at [63]–[98]; *Diallo (Republic of Guinea v Democratic Republic of the Congo)* (Preliminary Objections) (n 93) [2007] ICJ Rep 582, 599 at [39]. Also: Clapham, *Brierly's Law of Nations* (7th edn, Oxford University Press, 2012) 259–64.

[96] Concurring Opinion of Judge Cançado Trindade in *Ahmadou Sadio Diallo (Republic of Guinea v Democratic Republic of the Congo)* (Merits), 804 at [220].

[97] *United States Diplomatic and Consular Staff in Tehran (United States of America v Iran)* (n 73), 40 at [86].

[98] B Simma and D Pulkowski, 'Leges speciales and Self-Contained Regimes' in J Crawford and others (eds.), *The Law of International Responsibility* (Oxford: Oxford University Press 2010) 150.

[99] Andenas, 'Ahmadou Sadio Diallo' (n 4), 816–17.

the second, concerns the possible fragmentation of different fields of international law.[100]

In the earlier *Wall* case the International Court had referred with respect and approval to various outputs of the UN Human Rights Committee (HRC), of the UN Committee on Economic, Social and Cultural Rights. As Rodley explains, it did so, however, without indicating any general approach. In *Diallo* the International Court explained how, in the view of the Court, the General Comments of the Human Rights Committee and the decisions under the Optional Protocol were to be treated:

> Since it was created, the HRC has built up a considerable body of interpretative case law, in particular through its findings in response to the individual communications which may be submitted to it in respect of States parties to the first Optional Protocol, and in the form of its 'General Comments'.
>
> Although the Court is in no way obliged, in the exercise of its judicial functions, to model its own interpretation of the Covenant on that of the Committee, it believes that it should ascribe great weight to the interpretation adopted by this independent body that was established specifically to supervise the application of that treaty. The point here is to achieve the necessary clarity and the essential consistency of international law, as well as legal security, to which both the individuals with guaranteed rights and the State obliged to comply with treaty obligations are entitled.[101]

What has just been said about the interaction in *Diallo* between, on the one hand, consular protection and human rights protection and, on the other, the jurisprudence of the International Court and the practice of human rights treaty bodies has implications for the method of international law, especially treaty interpretation.

In the cases, such as *Diallo*, where the International Court has confirmed the coherence of international law as a system, the Court has also confirmed the coherence of the law of treaties with respect to interpretation. This shows the connection between the material substance of the rules in issue and of the methods used in order to establish that rule substance. There is a connection between fragmentation with respect to the content of rules and fragmentation with respect to the law of treaties, that is to say fragmentation in the method of treaty interpretation. The techniques of treaty interpretation must not be seen only from the formal point of view; they also have material consequences, that is, consequences for the substance or contents of norms.[102] In *Diallo* the International Court refused to see the area in issue as a self-contained regime—and specifically showed this by the styles of interpretation chosen.[103] What

[100] N Rodley, 'The International Court of Justice and Human Rights Bodies' in M Andenas and E Bjorge (eds.), *A Farewell to Fragmentation: Reassertion and Convergence in International Law* (Cambridge University Press, 2015).

[101] *Ahmadou Sadio Diallo (Republic of Guinea v Democratic Republic of the Congo)* (Merits) (Judgment) [2010] ICJ Rep 639, 663–4 at [66].

[102] Further: JM Dupuy and Y Kerbrat, *Droit international public* (10th edn, Dalloz, 2010) 352; H Ruiz Fabri, 'La contribution de l'Organisation mondiale du commerce à la gestion de l'espace juridique mondial' in E Loquin and C Kessedjian (eds.), *La mondialisation du droit* (Litec, 2000) 369; E Bjorge, *The Evolutionary Interpretation of Treaties* (Oxford University Press, 2014) Ch 2.

[103] Andenas, 'Ahmadou Sadio Diallo' (n 4), 813.

was in issue here was so-called effective interpretation: *ut res magis valeat quam pereat*.[104]

As was seen earlier, the approach of the International Court in *Tehran Hostages* had been criticized in the literature, and this criticism has not only centred on the idea of a '*self-contained* regime' but the idea of a '*regime*' itself. Crawford and Nevill have held that 'the institutions of diplomatic protection cannot be usefully described as a regime'. On their view it was both unfortunate and unnecessary that the International Court used the word 'regime':

> The Court was seeking to make the point that diplomatic relations is a self-contained system insofar as the arrangement for sanctions or taking measures against diplomats is set out in diplomatic law rather than any other part of general international law. But the specific rules sit within general international law, to which we resort alongside and in the absence of specific subject-matter rules.[105]

It would be better therefore if the word regime was used in a more discriminating way, and in particular was not used to describe branches of general international law. *Diallo* is an example of this type of argument prevailing. The International Court, in considering the provisions on the expulsion of an alien lawfully in the territory of a state, made clear that expulsion of Diallo could be effected only in accordance with the law, but that 'in accordance with the law' was not sufficient in itself. In addition, the applicable domestic law must be compatible with the other requirements of the relevant international law and the expulsion must not be arbitrary:

> it is clear that while 'accordance with law' as thus defined is a necessary condition for compliance with the above-mentioned provisions, it is not the sufficient condition. First, the applicable domestic law must itself be compatible with the other requirements of the Covenant and the African Charter; second, an expulsion must not be arbitrary in nature, since protection against arbitrary treatment lies at the heart of the rights guaranteed by the international norms protecting human rights.[106]

To focus in this way on the protection against arbitrary treatment, and to use that as a guiding principle in the interpretation of the provisions in issue, seems to be to take seriously the principle of effectiveness.[107] In fact, by concluding this way, the International Court in *Diallo* took more seriously than the European Court had done in similar cases the general exhortation, from *Airey v United Kingdom*, that human rights conventions such as the European Convention are 'intended to guarantee not rights

[104] 'That the thing may rather have effect than be destroyed.' Also: *Fisheries Jurisdiction (Spain v Canada) Jurisdiction of the Court* (Judgment) [1998] ICJ Rep 432, 455; *Dispute between Argentina and Chile concerning the Beagle Channel* (1977) 11 RIAA 53, 231; *Corfu Channel* [1949] ICJ Rep 4, 24; *Ambatielos case* (Jurisdiction) (Judgment) [1952] ICJ Rep 28, 45.

[105] J Crawford and P Nevill, 'Relations between International Courts and Tribunals: The "Regime Problem"' in MA Young (ed), *Regime Interaction in International Law: Facing Fragmentation* (Cambridge University Press, 2012) 259.

[106] *Ahmadou Sadio Diallo (Republic of Guinea v Democratic Republic of the Congo)* (Merits) (n 93), 663 at [65].

[107] Dispute between Argentina and Chile concerning the Beagle Channel (1977) 11 RIAA 53, 231; *Award in the Arbitration regarding the Iron Rhine ('Ijzeren Rijn') (Belgium v Netherlands)* (2005) 27 RIAA 35, 64.

that are theoretical or illusory but rights that are practical and effective'.[108] For it does seem to have been the case that the International Court went further than the human rights bodies have done in this regard, thus following that which has been seen to be the method of the human rights tribunals more scrupulously than those tribunals have done themselves. This will be explained in the following. Leading commentators have gone far in arguing that the sub-field of human rights has developed distinct methods of law-ascertainment and treaty interpretation, with a much greater focus upon effectiveness and teleology than what is the case in the general law of treaties.[109] It is this argument that the judgment of the International Court in *Diallo* refutes.

As has already been said, the International Court in *Diallo* relied directly on jurisprudence from other international and regional bodies, such as the United Nations Human Rights Committee[110] and the African Commission on Human and Peoples' Rights.[111] Moreover, it noted that the interpretation by the European Court of Human Rights and the Inter-American Court of Human Rights, respectively, of Article 1 of Protocol 7 to the European Convention and Article 22(6) of the American Convention—the said provisions being close in substance to those of the Covenant and the African Charter which the Court was applying in the present case—was consistent with what had been found in respect of the latter provisions.[112]

Judges Greenwood and Keith, however, pointed out that the cited jurisprudence on the expulsion provisions in issue did not, in point of fact, confer protection on substance, only on procedure.[113] This is borne out both by the jurisprudence of the European Court and of the Inter-American Commission.[114] The leading commentaries on the European Convention, too, seem to bear out this proposition. One commentary tersely states that the procedural guarantees of the pertinent provision provide no protection of substance, that is, relating to the grounds on which expulsion might be sought.[115] As a result, and as Judges Greenwood and Keith showed, the International

[108] *Airey v United Kingdom*, App No 6289/73, judgment 9 October 1979 at [24]; *Demir and Baykara v Turkey* App No 34503/97, judgment [GC] 12 November 2008 at [61].

[109] R Bernhardt, 'Evolutive Treaty Interpretation—Especially of the European Convention on Human Rights' (1999) 42 German Yearbook of International Law 11; G Letsas, 'Strasbourg's Interpretive Ethic: Lessons for the International Lawyer' (2010) 21 EJIL 509.

[110] *Maroufidou v Sweden* No 58/1979 at [9.3]; *Human Rights Committee, General Comment No 15: The position of aliens under the Covenant.*

[111] *Kenneth Good v Republic of Botswana*, No 313/05 at [204]; *World Organization against Torture and International Association of Democratic Lawyers, International Commission of Jurists, Interafrican Union for Human Rights v Rwanda*, Nos 27/89, 46/91, 49/91, 99/93.

[112] *Ahmadou Sadio Diallo (Republic of Guinea v Democratic Republic of the Congo)* (Merits) (n 93), 664 at [68].

[113] Separate Opinion Judges Greenwood and Keith in *Ahmadou Sadio Diallo (Republic of Guinea v Democratic Republic of the Congo)* (Merits) (n 93), 716–19 at [11]–[14].

[114] *Bolat v Russia*, App No 14139/03, judgment 5 October 2006 at [81]–[83]; *Lupsa v Romania* App No 10337/04, judgment 8 June 2006 at [54]–[61]; *Situations of Haitians in the Dominican Republic*, Inter-American Commission on Human Rights, Ann Rep 1991, 14 February 1992, ch V.

[115] RCA White and C Ovey, *Jacobs, White, and Ovey: The European Convention on Human Rights* (5th edn, Oxford University Press, 2010) 544–5. Also: D Harris, M O'Boyle, E Bates, and C Buckley, *Harris, O'Boyle and Warbrick: Law of the European Convention on Human Rights* (2nd edn, Oxford University Press, 2009) 747–8.

Court in effect went even further in its effective interpretation of the human rights provisions at issue than the human rights bodies had gone.[116]

IV. Conclusion

Galvanizing the approach of the Permanent Court, the International Court, already from *Nottebohm* (Preliminary Objection),[117] has relied on and referred to the decisions of other courts and tribunals than itself, in that case relying on the first modern arbitral award to be handed down, the *Alabama* arbitration.[118] From these auspicious beginnings the International Court developed its approach to one which, in order to avoid international law becoming a series of fragmented specialist and self-contained bodies of law functioning in isolation from another, it now refers to the practice and jurisprudence of other courts and tribunals when it deems that necessary, or, in Judge Greenwood's words, the Court, when faced with such situations, 'can, and should, draw on the jurisprudence of other international courts and tribunals, even though it is not bound necessarily to come to the same conclusions'.[119] The chapter has also suggested that, in addition to countervailing the fragmentation of international law in material terms, this practice on the part of the International Court contributes towards the de-fragmentation of the integrity of international law's method of law-ascertainment in connection both with treaty and custom. This too should be seen as a salutary contribution by the 'principal judicial organ of the United Nations',[120] as it reinforces the integrity of international law not only in material terms but also in terms of how international law is ascertained. That is of the highest importance, for 'if international law is to constrain to any degree, it must be ascertainable; one is not constrained by the unknown'.[121] In the same way that a fragmented international law is weak, a fragmented method of law-ascertainment will lead to a less effective international law. The more coherent and uniform the methods of law-ascertainment in international law are made to be by the International Court, the more effective international law will be. Opening up to comparative law, and by degrees refining its approach to doing so, the International Court has relied to a considerable degree on comparative law in this quest.

[116] E Bjorge, 'Ahmadou Sadio Diallo (Republic of Guinea v Democratic Republic of the Congo)' (2011) 105 AJIL 534, 539–40.

[117] *Nottebohm Case (Preliminary Objection)* (Judgment) 1953 ICJ Rep 11, 119.

[118] *Alabama Arbitration (Great Britain v US)* (1872) in Moore, 1 *Int Arb* 495.

[119] Declaration of Judge Greenwood in *Case Concerning Ahmadou Sadio Diallo (Republic of Guinea v Democratic Republic of the Congo)*, Compensation (Judgment) [2012] ICJ Rep 324, 394 at [8].

[120] Art 92, Charter of the United Nations, 26 June 1945, 892 UNTS 119.

[121] J Crawford, 'Chance, Order, Change: The Course of International Law' (2013) 365 Hague *Recueil* 9, 48.

PART IV

COMPARATIVE LAW BEFORE ADMINISTRATIVE COURTS

13

Comparative Law as an Essential Feature of French Public Law

The Influence of the European Union and of the European Convention on Human Rights

*Olivier Dutheillet de Lamothe**

Comparative law has long been a specific branch of legal scholarship in France. It was founded by Edouard René de Laboulaye who created in 1869 the 'Society of Comparative Legislation' ('*Société de Législation Comparée*') and introduced American legal culture in France with his book *Paris in America*, which he wrote in 1863. This scholarship has been significantly developed during the recent period, notably by the work of René David, who described the great systems of modern law: civil law, common law, once communist law, and today Islamic law. It is important to stress that David's purely theoretical approach is based on the analysis of the fundamental principles of each system, whereas Basil Markesinis, for example, takes a more pragmatic approach in which the comparatist begins by analysing specific cases and then demonstrates that similar solutions are offered by different legal systems.

Today, comparative law is much more than that. It is not only for scholars. It is also for judges and in particular for administrative judges. As Bernard Stirn, President of the Judicial Chamber of the Conseil d'Etat ('Council of State'), has declared: 'Comparative law has become a very common practice, in particular in big cases.'[1] Comparative law has become a way of thinking, a part of legal reasoning, 'business as usual'.

How did we get here? How did we go from the theoretical approach of Laboulaye and David to the daily practices of administrative judges today? I will try to demonstrate that the European Union (EU) and the European Convention on Human Rights (ECHR) have imposed on French public law a form of comparative legal pressure (I) that has led to the development of spontaneous comparative law (II).

* Président de la Section Sociale du Conseil d'Etat, France.

[1] B. Stirn, 'Le droit administratif français, européen et global: bilan et perspectives', ELN Interviews, n°1/2007, 5.

I. The EU and the ECHR have imposed on French public law a form of comparative legal pressure

1. Supremacy of EU law

All EU law is based on the primacy of EU Treaties on national law but also the primacy of European secondary legislation (Directives and Regulations) and of European Union Court of Justice (ECJ) case law.

This means that since 1958, French administrative courts have had to apply European Treaties, European secondary legislation, and the case law of the Court of Luxembourg. This has led to the importation into French civil law of many foreign concepts and in particular of Common Law concepts.

As regards legislation, I will give an example taken from my personal experience. When I was Director of Labour Relations at the Ministry of Labour, I negotiated many directives for France in the field of occupational health and safety. I remember hours and hours of discussion with the British delegation, which insisted that obligations imposed on employers should be imposed on them only insofar as they are 'reasonably practicable', a strange concept totally unknown in French civil law at the time. All directives are made of compromise, and so this concept was introduced in the directive. So now, in our French labour code we have expressions such as 'The employers must... 5° Take into account the evolution of technique 6° Replace what is dangerous with what is not dangerous or with what is less dangerous'.[2] EU legislation, which is extremely prolific, has led to the incorporation into French civil law of many British concepts, just as it has led to the introduction of many continental concepts in the United Kingdom.

As regards case law, I will also give an example related to the influence of preliminary rulings requested by other jurisdictions on the Council of State's decisions. One example is the Directive on money laundering, particularly its provisions applicable to barristers, which conflicted with attorney-client privilege, a key principle in allowing barristers to defend and advise their clients. Interestingly, the Council of State relied on the interpretation of the Directive given by a judgment of the ECJ on a preliminary ruling made at the request of the Constitutional Court of Belgium in order to rule on the conformity of the Regulation implementing the Directive to Article 6 (right to a fair trial) and 8 (right to respect for private life) of the ECHR. Though the judgment of the European Court did not rule explicitly on the point at stake in the case before the Council of State, the Council relied firstly on the opinion of the General Advocate before the European Court, Miguel Maduro, and secondly on the interpretation of the judgment by the Constitutional Court of Belgium.[3]

But most relevant is the Order for provisory settlement issued by the President of the Judicial Chamber of the Council of State on October 29, 2003, in the Société Techna case.[4]

[2] Article L. 4121-2 du Code du travail.

[3] Conseil d'Etat, Section, 10 avril 2008, Conseil National des Barreaux et autres, n° 296 845 et 296 907, conclusions Mattias Guyomar.

[4] Conseil d'Etat, Ordonnance de référé du 29 octobre 2003, Société TECHNA SA et autres, n° 260 768, 261 033, 261 034, AJDA 2004, p. 540 note Anne-Elisabeth Courrier.

This decision is very significant because it is the first time, since the creation of the Court in 1799, that the Council of State cites a foreign judgment in the decision itself—a judgment of the High Court of Justice.[5] The case was about a Directive which required animal food manufacturers to provide comprehensive ingredients lists on their product labels, which they claimed conflicted with their right to protect trade secrets. Since the Directive had to go into force for all Member States on a single date, all Member States were faced with the implementation of the Directive and the simultaneous petitions of the producers to suspend its implementation. The High Court of Justice decided on 6 October 2003, to suspend the implementation of the Directive and to request a preliminary ruling before the ECJ to assess the legal basis of the Directive and its conformity to the right of property and to the principle of proportionality. In order to make the same decision, the president of the Judicial Chamber of the Council of State himself explicitly cited the judgment of the High Court of Justice and decided that it was useless to ask for a preliminary ruling on the Directive by the ECJ since the High Court of Justice had already ruled on it. It is interesting to note that in the judgment of the High Court of Justice, Judge Davis stressed that the reason he had written such a long opinion was that he was aware that other judges were going to refer to it.

2. The contribution of ECHR to the introduction of foreign law into French Public Law

The ECHR has also contributed, since France ratified the protocol on individual applications in 1981, to introduce foreign law into French Public Law.

As in the United Kingdom with the Human Rights Act, the implementation of the ECHR has had a considerable impact on the French legal order. Since our Constitution expressly affirms the primacy of international law over national law,[6] and since the Constitutional Council decided that it was not for it, but for ordinary courts, to review the conformity of statutes with Treaties,[7] since 1989 the Council of State reviews the conformity of statutes to Treaties and in particular to the ECHR.[8] The implementation of the ECHR has introduced into French public law new concepts and new standards inspired by foreign law. I will give two examples.

First, as regards procedural law, the case law of the Strasbourg Court regarding article 6 of the Convention and the right to a fair trial has led French courts and administrative courts to adopt the concept of a 'fair and equitable trial ensuring the parties' rights' and of 'the necessary equality of arms between the parties' which derives from it, two concepts which are directly inspired by the due process standard of Common Law.

Second, as regards substantive law, the strict conception of the separation of powers by the Strasbourg Court and its condemnation of France in the *Zielinski* case[9] have led

[5] High Court of Justice, Queen's Bench Division, The Administrative Court, *Abna Ltd v Secretary of State for Health*, 6 October 2003, EWHC 2420 (Admin).

[6] Article 55 de la Constitution du 4 octobre 1958.

[7] Décision n° 75-54 DC du 15 Janvier 1975.

[8] Conseil d'Etat, Assemblée, 20 octobre 1989, Nicolo, R.F.D.A. 1989 p. 813 concl. Frydman, note Genevois.

[9] CEDH, 28 octobre 1999, Zielinski, Pradal, Gonzales et autres contre France.

French courts to restrict the ability of the legislator to validate acts which have been declared or are to be declared void by judges. In practice, financial considerations, however important they may be, cannot justify the validation of void acts by Parliament.

II. This form of imposed comparative law in the framework of the EU and ECHR has led to the development of spontaneous comparative law

Like Moliere's *Monsieur Jourdain* who discovered that he was speaking prose without knowing it, French judges have discovered that they were practising comparative law without knowing it. Confronted with foreign and international legal sources, they have begun to enjoy new concepts in comparative law. They have discovered the extraordinary intellectual stimulation and richness of comparative law. Every French judge, and in particular administrative judges, could say today like President Aharon Barak: 'For me, comparative law serves as a mirror. It makes me understand myself better.'[10]

Spontaneous comparative law is today present in the Council of State's adjudication and the expanding use of comparative law has become a policy of the Council.

1. Spontaneous comparative law is today present in the Council of State's adjudication

It is not easy to identify the place of foreign law in the Council of States case law for a structural reason: civil law judgments never quote a precedent, whether national or foreign.

Under the civil law tradition, French administrative courts and the Council of State apply the *stare decisis* principle in fact and not in law: when they apply a precedent, they reproduce it without changing a comma but never cite it.

Today, the use of foreign law takes two major forms in the Council of State's case law. First, it is very often used as an argument by the Advocates General that enriches their legal reasoning and supports their opinions. As president Stirn stressed, it is a very common practice, particularly in big cases. I will give just one example. To convince the Council of State to review the conformity of statutes to international treaties, Advocate General Patrick Frydman developed in his opinion the example of the American judicial review, which is based on exactly the same reasoning with regard to the Constitution.[11]

Secondly, foreign case law may be used as a precedent. This appears clearly when the foreign judgment is quoted in the decision itself, like the judgment of the High Court of Justice in the *Techna* case or the judgment of the ECJ in the *Conseil national des barreaux* case. But this is still rare. More often, the foreign precedent is quoted as a

[10] A. Barak, 'Comparative Law, Originalism and the Role of a Judge in a Democracy: A Reply to Justice Scalia' (Haifa, 2006).

[11] Nicolo, see n. 8.

reference in the official casebook of the Council of State, the 'Recueil Lebon', named after its 19th-century publisher. For example:

- the record of a decision of 16 December 2005 by the *Assemblée du contentieux*, which is the highest judicial panel of the Council of State, refers to a separate opinion of Judge Rubio Llorente in two cases of the Spanish constitutional tribunal;[12]
- the record of the Order for provisory settlement dated 6 March 2006, of a case related to the prohibition against wearing turbans in driver's licence photographs, considered to be discriminatory against Sikhs, refers both to a decision of the European Court of Human Rights (ECtHR) and to a decision of the Supreme Court of Canada dated 2 March 2006, *Multani c/Commission scolaire Marguerite-Bourgeoys*;[13]
- the record of another decision of the *Assemblée du Contentieux* concerning a very important case related to EU law refers both to the famous decision of the German Constitutional Court *Solange II*, dated 22 October 1986, and to the equally famous decision of the Italian Constitutional Court SpA *Fragd*, dated 13 April 1989.[14]

Foreign law and common law judgments have also triggered reforms in judgment writing style following a report by the Council of State that studied the writing style of foreign courts.[15] While retaining the deductive reasoning originating from the citation of the applicable text, then interpreting it and finally applying it to the specific case, the short, concise—some would say cryptic—traditional style of the Council of State is now more open to an argumentative style: in particular, the 'single sentence' and the 'whereas' is being phased out in favour of multiple sentences and the numbering of paragraphs. This reform, which has aroused great passion inside the Council of State and strong opposition from the young generation, is being implemented gradually and on a voluntary basis. It shows that a court's style reflects the very essence of this court: the way it reasons, the way it communicates, the way it is.

It is interesting to note the great diversity of foreign law used by the Council of State. Though one might have expected that the influence of civil law countries such as Germany or Italy would be dominant, in fact it is the contrary. The majority of the quotations, either in opinions of the Advocates General or in the judgments themselves, come from British and American courts and also from the Supreme Court of Canada. Following those are the civil law countries such as Italy, Belgium, Germany, and Spain and, less often, the Netherlands, Portugal, and Greece.[16]

It is also interesting to note that, unlike in the United States, there is no debate in French administrative courts about the use of foreign law. It is considered just as

[12] Conseil d'État, Assemblée, 16 décembre 2005, Ministre des Affaires sociales, du Travail et de la Solidarité et Syndicat national des huissiers de justice, Lebon p. 570.

[13] Conseil d'Etat, Ordonnance de référé, 6 mars 2006, Association United Sikhs et Mann Singh, Lebon p. 111.

[14] Conseil d'État, Assemblée, 8 février 2007, Société Arcelor Atlantique et Lorraine et autres, Lebon p. 56.

[15] The report is published on the website of the Council of State.

[16] See: F. Melleray, *L'utilisation du droit comparé par le Conseil d'Etat statuant au contentieux* (Mélanges Genevois, Dalloz 2009) 779.

normal to use foreign law as it is to use parliamentary debates to understand the scope of a statute. And I personally agree with Justice Breyer, who wrote in an opinion that there is no more risk of cherry-picking in foreign law than in the parliamentary debates of a statute.

2. Today, developing the use of comparative law has become a policy of the Council of State

It must be stressed that the Centre for Legal Research and Documentation (*Centre de Recherche et de Documentation Juridique*), which is an important service of the Judicial Chamber of the Council of State, has, since 2009, included a small team of comparative lawyers led by a scholar from Cornell University.

The Council of State has developed an active policy in international relations. The time of so-called French judicial isolationism is long bygone. The Council of State is more and more open to foreign influence. This does not mean that we have lapsed into legal expansionism. It is more a question of increasing interactions and cross-fertilizations between judges and scholars from various judicial backgrounds.

The European Courts—Luxembourg ECJ and Strasbourg ECtHR—are now day-to-day partners. Human and intellectual exchanges between Paris, Luxembourg, and Strasbourg are numerous. To date, no less than three members of the French Council are seconded to Luxembourg: the French judge of the Court of Justice, his principal clerk, and the French judge at the General Court. The former ECtHR Chief Justice was a French State Counsellor.

The most active network in that field is the Association of the Councils of State and the Supreme Administrative Jurisdictions of the Member States of the European Union (ACA-Europe) which was created in Stockholm in 1998 and includes the Councils of State or Supreme Administrative Courts of the 28 Member States of the EU, plus two observers (the Council of State of Turkey and the Supreme Court of Montenegro) and two permanent invited courts (the Supreme Court of Norway and the Supreme Court of Switzerland). The French Council of State has presided over ACA-Europe since June 2012 and continued to do so until June 2014.

The ACA-Europe organization has developed two databases. First, the DEC-NAT database: the research and documentation department of the ECJ holds files on around 21,000 national decisions. Pursuant to an agreement concluded between the Court of Justice and ACA-Europe, these data were transmitted to the association, which compiled them into a searchable database. DEC-NAT is regularly updated and translated into English. Second, the JURIFAST rapid information system for case law, which has been in operation since 1 February 2004. Using a login and password, the research and documentation departments of members courts of ACA-Europe can upload recent and unpublished decisions to the JURIFAST system. JURIFAST is accessible to the public in French and English via the ACA-Europe website. As of 1 July 2013 it contained 1,457 decisions.

At the international level, the International Association of Supreme Administrative Jurisdictions (*Association Internationale des Hautes Juridictions Administratives,*

AIHJA) was created in 1983 and includes 70 Supreme Administrative Courts. It held a triennial congress in Colombia in 2013.

These networks are completed by bilateral relations: for example, in 2013, the German Federal Administrative Court paid a visit to the Council of State, and the Council of State participated in a seminar organized by the Supreme Court of the United Kingdom.

An informal network was created on the two sides of the Channel. It was nicknamed FBI for Franco-British-Irish Judicial Committee. Every other year, judges from London, Paris, Edinburgh, Belfast, and Dublin convene for a two-day informal meeting. Last year the meeting took place in Scotland and addressed the issue of European citizenship. Our next meeting will take place in Paris in June 2015.

On 8 July 2013, the Bureau of the Council of State, which is its executive board, adopted a strategic approach to the development of international relations. Among the priorities defined was the development of exchanges with American universities: the conference on Comparative Administrative Law with the Yale Law School and the Supreme Court of the United Kingdom in March 2014 fell directly within the scope of this priority.

14

Comparative Legal Methodology of the *Conseil d'Etat*

Towards an Innovative Judicial Process?

Aurélie Bretonneau, Samuel Dahan,** and Duncan Fairgrieve****

Comparative law has often been treated as a purely theoretical subject, one used to classify major legal systems, to understand 'the other', or as a tool for transnational or harmonization projects, but this approach has changed radically in recent times, with the development of comparative law beyond Academe as a *practical* tool increasingly used in the forensic process, by lawyers and judges. This shift is well illustrated by the judicial processes of the *Conseil d'Etat*. As Bernard Stirn, President of the Judicial Committee of the Chambers, *Conseil d'Etat* has put it, 'comparative law has become a very common practice, particularly for big cases'.[1] In a similar vein, Olivier Dutheillet de Lamothe describes comparative law as a way of thinking, a part of legal reasoning, and 'business as usual'.[2] This supports Roland Drago's analysis regarding the use of comparative law: according to Drago, comparative law must not remain merely an academic subject, but must produce practical consequences—which is to say, legal systems must influence one another.[3]

While the use of foreign law in American courts is the subject of fierce debate in the United States,[4] quite the opposite is true within the practical arena in France:[5] comparative law is seen by leading administrative French judges as an important aspect of the judicial process. A comparative learning process has thus been developed at the *Conseil d'Etat* by several actors, notably Jean-Marc Sauvé, *Vice-Président du Conseil d'Etat*; Bernard Stirn, *Président de la Section du Contentieux*; and Olivier Dutheillet de Lamothe, *Président de la Section Sociale*. It is important, however, to stress that while the *Conseil d'Etat* has shown a significant interest in comparative law,

* Responsable du Centre de Recherche et de Documentation Juridique; Maître des Requêtes, *Conseil d'Etat.*

** Cornell Law Clerk, *Conseil d'Etat*, Cornell University Law School.

*** British Institute of International and Comparative Law, London; Université Paris Dauphine PSL.

[1] B. Stirn 'Le droit administratif français, européen et global: bilan et perspectives', ELN Interviews.

[2] O. Dutheillet de Lamothe 'Comparative Law as an Essential Feature of French Public Law: The Influence of the European Union and of the European Convention on Human Rights', Chapter 13 in this collection.

[3] R. Drago, 'Droit Comparé', in D. Alland and S. Rials (eds.), *Dictionnaire de la Culture Juridique* (Paris, Presse Universitaire de France, 2003), 455.

[4] See Chapter 23 in this collection, J. Resnik, 'Constructing the "Foreign": American Law's Relationship to Non-Domestic Sources'.

[5] For critical perspectives within French scholarship as regards the utility of comparative law: P. Legrand, *Le Droit Comparé* (Paris, PUF, 1999).

the judges recognize that there are limits as to the feasible use of comparative law—it cannot alas be ubiquitous as this would be a Herculean task, one that would be accompanied by significant drawbacks.[6]

In his comprehensive account of the increasing use of comparative law before administrative judges in France, François Lichère describes comparative law as being somewhere between optional and compulsory.[7] While Lichère's approach is more content-oriented, our approach in this chapter is more procedural as we examine the mechanisms governing the use of comparative law at the *Conseil d'Etat*, focusing more on the 'how' than the 'what'. Specifically, in this chapter we attempt to demonstrate that the growing use of comparative law is not dependent solely on subjective factors such as the willingness of judges to use it; rather, it relies on a method, not to say an organizational policy (section I) which, although it is still in development, may already be giving rise to a new form of judicial creative process (section II).

I. Method: comparative law as policy

While the decision to undertake comparative legal research at the *Conseil d'Etat* is, strictly speaking, personal and subjective—the *judges in charge of the case* have to request and initiate it—the use of comparative law has almost become a policy for important cases (*sous-section-réunies, plénière, section, assemblée*). This is probably why since 2008, the *Conseil d'Etat* has institutionalized and professionalized comparative legal research, notably through the creation of the Comparative Law Unit ('*Cellule de droit comparé*'), a team of foreign lawyers working under the supervision of *Centre de recherches et de diffusion juridiques* (CRDJ)(see section I.1). However, the *Conseil d'Etat* is conscious of the issues raised by the use of comparative law and is therefore cautious in its practice (see section 1.2).

1. Institutionalization of comparative legal practice: Comparative Law Unit

The *Conseil d'Etat* has, in the past few years, considerably strengthened its resources to develop its expertise in foreign law. First, it has developed an active policy in international relations that is aimed both at exporting French administrative law and importing foreign law. The most active network in that field is the Association of the Councils of State and Supreme Administrative Jurisdictions of the Member States of the European Union (ACA-Europe) which was created in Stockholm in 1998. The Vice-President of the French *Conseil d'Etat* has presided over the ACA since June 2012. This multilateral network is complemented by bilateral relations through which the *Conseil d'Etat* strengthens its relationship with its counterparts. For instance, the

[6] T. Groppi and M.-C. Ponthoreau, 'The Use of Foreign Precedents by Constitutional Judges: A Limited Practice, an Uncertain Future', in T. Groppi and M.-C. Ponthoreau (eds.), *The Use of Foreign Precedents by Constitutional Judges* (Oxford, Hart Publishing, 2013), 423.

[7] See Chapter 15 in this collection, F. Lichère, 'The Use of Comparative Law before the French Administrative Law Courts : Or the Triumph of Castles over Pyramids'.

German Federal Administrative Court and the Supreme Administrative Court of Finland have agreed to send representatives to the *Conseil d'Etat*. French administrative judges have, moreover, for many years undertaken short exchanges with UK judges under the aegis of a scheme organized by the *Comité franco-britannique de coopération judiciaire*,[8] and French judges have contributed to a series of seminars on the 'Rule of Law' organized by the Supreme Court of the United Kingdom, and have been part of a tripartite initiative, along with the Supreme Court of the United Kingdom and Yale Law School, that resulted in a common symposium in Yale dedicated to comparative administrative law. Finally, the executive board of the *Conseil d'Etat* agreed in its last meeting that developing exchanges with foreign universities was among its main priorities. For instance, the *Conseil d'Etat*, in collaboration with Cornell University, is hoping to organize an international conference in July 2015.

Beside bilateral and multilateral diplomacy, which is crucial to raising awareness of the importance of comparative law, the *Conseil d'Etat* has taken a step further and developed an integrated approach through the creation of the *Cellule de Droit Comparé* in 2008. The *Cellule* is affiliated with the *Centre de recherches et de diffusion juridiques* (CRDJ), which is a transversal unit working with both litigation and advisory departments of the *Conseil d'Etat*. The *Cellule* relies on several comparative lawyers with specialized training in different legal systems (for instance Italian, Spanish, German, and common law), supported by a few interns.[9]

The *Cellule* contributes to the research activity of the CRDJ in order to provide support for the Judicial and Advisory Chambers of the *Conseil d'Etat*. While the *Cellule* may have been somewhat improvised[10] at its inception—it only had two part-time lawyers—it has since been provided with significant resources (including extensive databases), thanks to the growing importance of comparative law at the *Conseil d'Etat*.

The importance of comparative law is obvious both from a qualitative and a quantitative standpoint. Whilst there were indeed examples of comparative law being drawn upon in an ad hoc way prior to the *Cellule*,[11] the institutional creation of a centre of expertise for comparative law means that resort to such information has now become commonplace in respect of important cases. It should thus be stressed that about 80 per cent of the cases decided by the *Conseil d'Etat* in plenary (*assemblée du*

[8] For more details, see <http://www.justice.gouv.fr/bulletin-officiel/saei87a.htm> (last accessed 4 July 2014).

[9] Since 2009, Cornell University has been funding the Cornell Clerkship programme by which a legal academic from the Cornell School of Law is seconded to the *Conseil d'Etat* to cover the common law area.

[10] The term 'bricolage' has been used: T. Groppi and M.-C. Ponthoreau, 'The Use of Foreign Precedents by Constitutional Judges: A Limited Practice, an Uncertain Future', in T. Groppi and M.-C. Ponthoreau (eds.), *The Use of Foreign Precedents by Constitutional Judges* (Oxford, Hart Publishing, 2013), 423; the term was used for the first time in 1999, M. Tushnet, 'The Possibilities of Comparative Constitutional Law', Yale Law Journal, 1999, 1225; V. Ferreres Comella, 'Comparative Modesty', European Constitutional Law Review, 2001, 517.

[11] An early example of this can be found in the case of *Kechichian*, concerning administrative liability for failure to supervise banks and was heard by the Plenary Chamber of the *Conseil d'Etat, Commissaire du Gouvernement* (as he then was) Alain Seban started his detailed *conclusions* with a survey of comparative law, covering Germany, America, and England, concluding with the remark that 'despite the different legal and administrative traditions, the same features may be found [in the three systems].' (CE 30 November 2001, *Kechichian*, conclusions Seban, *Les Petites Affiches*, N° 28, 7 February 2002, 7).

contentieux and *section*) were subject to comparative legal research. From a qualitative perspective, the *Cellule* has been designed as a very flexible instrument capable of responding quickly to the requests of the judges, but also producing substantial legal memoranda on a great diversity of foreign law.[12] Comparative research is usually requested by a *rapporteur*, although a request can also be made by other members of the *Conseil d'Etat* such as the *rapporteurs publics* or *Presidents de Section*. In this respect, the inquisitorial nature of the proceedings before French administrative courts has had an impact. It has often been argued that the information-gathering procedure of the French administrative courts, as well as the overall institutional structure with consultation amongst members of the *Conseil d'Etat*, and contributions from the *Rapporteur Publics* and reporting judges, facilitates the resolution of polycentric questions with multilateral implications.[13] It also facilitates the use of comparative law, with the judges being able to utilize comparative elements in their reflection even though the parties may not have requested it and without having to engage in a contradictory debate on these elements.

Over the past three years, the *Cellule* has produced more than 40 substantive studies each year.[14] These studies have focused mainly on tax law, bioethics, immigration law, civil service, labour law, and, to a lesser extent, administrative liability, administrative procedure, and implementation of EU Directives. In terms of coverage of the research, while the Unit may be requested, in certain cases to investigate a particular jurisdiction, substantive studies usually cover the following legal systems: civil law systems (Spanish, Italian, German, and Austrian law) and common law systems (English, American, and Canadian law when relevant). Depending on the complexity of the case, the comparative report can on occasion be quite detailed and can be further extended upon request. As for the research process itself, the research is mainly library-based, although it has proved useful to approach experts *in situ* (in academia, public sector, and law firms).

While it is difficult to measure the direct influence of these comparative law studies on the judicial reflexion, one can argue that *rapporteurs publics* have used these studies as a source of benchmarking. These studies are frequently cited by *rapporteurs publics* in the conclusions they deliver in open court during public hearings.[15] In this sense, the use of international or foreign materials is an extension of the *rapporteurs publics* general role of considering important questions in the round. In the case *Association la Cimade et M. O.*, the comparative law study was mentioned in the so-called '*feuille verte*'—a document elaborated by the *rapporteur public*, circulated among the judges

[12] Though one might have expected that the influence of civil law countries such as Germany or Italy would dominate, this is only partially true. Indeed, British and American courts generate great interest among the *rapporteurs publics*.

[13] See generally J.W.F. Allison, *A Continental Distinction in the Common Law* (Oxford, Oxford University Press, 1996); D. Fairgrieve, *State Liability in Tort: A Comparative Law Study* (Oxford, Oxford University Press, 2003).

[14] The Unit respectively produced 44, 43, and 41 studies in 2011, 2012, and 2013.

[15] See, for instance, CE, 11 avril 2012, assemblée, *Groupe d'Information et de Soutien des Immigrés (GISTI) et Fédération des Associations pour la Promotion et l'Insertion par le Logement (FAPIL)*, n° 322326; CE, assemblée, 21 décembre 2012, *Mlle Fofana*, n° 332491; CE, assemblée 14 février 2014, *Mme Lambert et autres*, n° 37508. For an earlier example of the use of comparative law in the conclusions of rapporteurs public, see CE 30 November 2001, *Kechichian*, conclusions Seban, *Les Petites Affiches*, N° 28, 7 February 2002, 7.

before the public hearing, listing the principal documents considered useful for the comprehension of the case. Furthermore, it is worth noting that although the rule of secrecy of deliberations prevents disclosure of discussions during the judicial deliberations, it would seem that the outcome of some deliberations has actually been reversed following the inclusion of comparative law research.

The role of the *Cellule* at the *Conseil d'Etat* is not confined to judicial review; it also plays an increasingly crucial part in the Conseil's advisory functions.[16] In the past three years, the *Cellule* has provided advisory departments with substantial studies, on various subjects such as electronic cigarettes, same-sex marriage, or the notion of confiscatory tax rates. Delivered at the request of the *rapporteur* of the legislative proposal examined by the department and appended to the documentation provided to its members, these studies are designed to present the legal framework of neighbouring countries and thereto inform discussion of the draft text submitted to the *Conseil d'Etat* by the French Government. Whilst the impact assessment study produced by the Government in respect of draft legislation contains a section devoted to comparative law, the *Conseil d'Etat* studies serve to complement and supplement this governmental study.

The *Cellule* also contributes to the production of two internal documents. The first is a case law review of important foreign supreme court decisions, a report that is also published in the *Revue Internationale de Droit Comparé*. The second document is a selection of relevant academic articles published in peer-reviewed public law journals. Finally, the members of the *Cellule* may contribute collectively to periodicals such as the *Recueil Dalloz*, or occasionally assist the justices in their private publications when they wish to consider important aspects of foreign law. For instance, the *Cellule* has recently published an article in the *Actualité Juridique Droit Administratif* at the request of the Vice-President of the *Conseil d'Etat*.[17]

2. Methodological challenges

Most comparatists know that every court is faced with serious challenges when using comparative law. The *Conseil d'Etat* and the *Cellule* are fully aware of these methodological difficulties.

A first challenge is that contextualization of laws should be regarded as an indispensable methodological characteristic of all comparative studies. As argued by Etienne Picard, 'the comparatist must become the interpreter of legal meaning.'[18] Indeed, it is 'the meaning of a law, its legal dynamic as well as its cultural dynamic, which he must understand if he wishes to spotlight its otherness.'[19] We believe that the *Conseil d'Etat*

[16] For further discussion of the *Conseil d'Etat*'s advisory function, see J. Bell, *French Legal Cultures* (Cambridge, Cambridge University Press, 2001), 172–5.

[17] The article concerns the Decision of the German Constitutional Court on the mandate violation of the European Central Bank; see S. Dahan, O. Fuchs, and M.-L. Layus, 'Whatever it Takes? A propos de la décision OMT de la Cour constitutionnelle fédérale d'Allemagne', AJDA July 2014.

[18] E. Picard, 'L'état du droit comparé en France, en 1999', RIDC 1999, n° 4, 896.

[19] J.M. Sauvé, 'Le Conseil d'Etat et la comparaison des droits', Hommage à Roland Drago, Colloque organisé par l'Institut français des sciences administratives et la Société de législation comparée, 14 Février 2014.

belongs to those Courts that try to contextualize their findings according to the French legal system and to distinguish the case before them from the equivalent foreign case.[20]

A second challenge is the temptation to engage in *cherry-picking*, citing only those foreign decisions that support the preferred result.[21] This misuse of comparative law could affect any supreme court, including the *Conseil d'Etat*. However, while the risk is real, its negative consequences might be overstated since cherry-picking, if applied correctly, has proven to be quite useful. As argued by Albie Sachs, 'yes, we cherry-pick all the time [but] it's got to be a cherry that fits.'[22]

It is important to stress that the members of the *Cellule*, when they receive a request, as well as the members of the *Conseil d'Etat*, are fully aware of these pitfalls. While this awareness cannot prevent all mistakes, it helps to avoid some of them. Two instances drawn from the *Conclusions* of the *rapporteurs publics* illustrate this dynamic. The first example can be found in the conclusions of Mattias Guyomar on the *Perreux* case, in which he asserts that what is fashionable among courts never constitutes a legal argument.[23] The *rapporteur public* reminds us that judges who rely on comparison should do so with caution, and that systematically importing foreign law is not a solution. A second example which can be found in several *Conclusions* further illustrates the restraint of the *Conseil d'Etat*. In the case *Torregrosa*, D. Botteghi stresses that the research effort made by the *Cellule* 'was not fruitful'.[24] Similarly, Xavier Domino in the *M. et Mme. Saidou Fall* case wrote in his *Conclusion* that sometimes 'One emerges unfulfilled [from one's travels in comparative lands], certain only that there is no unanimous or even dominant international standard leading one to interpret [a principle] in one direction or another.'[25]

These examples underscore once again the prudent approach taken by the *Conseil d'Etat* insofar as judges use comparative law only when strictly relevant and see the lack of result as a solution in itself. As argued by Lichère, comparative law may be irrelevant or sometimes counterproductive, particularly in fields that are too entrenched in the national legal culture to be subject to a thorough comparative investigation (for instance the law relating to public officials). The absence of a solution or the irrelevance of comparative legal research is a common challenge faced by the *Cellule* when the issues at stake diverge too far from what other systems have already encountered.[26]

[20] T. Groppi and M.-C. Ponthoreau, 'The Use of Foreign Precedents by Constitutional Judges: A Limited Practice, an Uncertain Future', in T. Groppi and M.-C. Ponthoreau (eds.), *The Use of Foreign Precedents by Constitutional Judges* (Oxford, Hart Publishing, 2013), 423.

[21] The concept was developed by Albie Sachs, Judge of the Constitutional Court of South Africa, cited by U. Bentele, 'Mining for Gold: The Constitutional Court of South Africa's Experience with Comparative Constitutional Law', 37 Georgia Journal of Comparative and International Law, 2009, 219.

[22] Ibid. 239.

[23] "Si un consensus jurisprudentiel sur l'application d'une règle commune n'est pas anodin, l'air du temps ne vaut pour autant jamais argument de droit"—see Conclusion M. Guyomar sur CE, 30 octobre 2009 *Perreux*, n°298348; cité par J.M. Sauvé, 'Le Conseil d'Etat et la comparaison des droits', Hommage à Roland Drago, Colloque organisé par l'Institut français des sciences administratives et la Société de législation comparée, 14 Février 2014.

[24] Conclusions D. Botteghi sur CE, 30 novembre 2011, Sect., *Torregrosa*, n° 348161.

[25] Conclusions X. Domino sur CE, 20 novembre 2013, *M. et Mme Saidou Fall*, n° 3686760.

[26] For instance, in the asbestos case regarding whether the State could be liable for negligence, after days of research, its members had to take the absence of a solution for an answer.

This methodological challenge is echoed by the judiciary in other systems: Lord Bingham in his famous judgment in *Fairchild v Glenhaven Funeral Services Ltd*, resorted to a sophisticated comparative law approach in that case, but nonetheless recognized the need for a nuanced approach to comparison.[27]

II. Roles of comparative law at the *Conseil d'Etat*: transforming the judicial process?

The legal world is today characterized by the opening-up and permeability of legal systems and a shift away from historically closed and hierarchical national legal systems, with a shift towards mutual influences and interdependencies.

This is the reason comparative legal practice, along with 'transjudicial' dialogue,[28] has been shaping a new form of judicial reasoning in most legal systems, even in the most reluctant ones.[29] As argued by Mattias Guyomar, there are cases when isolation would be 'pathetic' and 'destructive'[30] as it would result in an impoverishment of our own legal order.[31] Another factor is the increasingly complex issues with which modern courts are required to engage, whether they be fundamental rights, constitutional review, international law, or emerging areas such as biomedical issues, in which ethical and moral issues are increasingly prominent. It is noteworthy that judges look to each other for inspiration in 'hard cases', as the recent *Conseil d'Etat* judgment concerning the ending of medical treatment in the *Mme Lambert* case shows (discussed later in this section), or in earlier times in the context of wrongful birth cases in the *Epoux Quarez* decision.[32]

There seems to be a consensus on the transformative impact of comparative law on the judicial process of the *Conseil d'Etat.*

The first function is reflexive[33] in that comparative law helps to develop self-awareness, to better understand one's own legal system, to reconsider certain aspects of one's own legal system and to unveil its strengths and weaknesses in a new light.

[27] 'Development of the law in this country cannot of course depend on a head-count of decisions and codes adopted in other countries around the world, often against a background of different rules and traditions. The law must be developed coherently, in accordance with principle, so as to serve, even-handedly, the ends of justice. If, however, a decision is given in this country which offends one's basic sense of justice, and if consideration of international sources suggests that a different and more acceptable decision would be given in most other jurisdictions, whatever their legal tradition, this must prompt anxious review of the decision in question. In a shrinking world... there must be some virtue in uniformity of outcome whatever the diversity of approach in reaching that outcome.' [2002] UKHL 22, para 32.

[28] T. Groppi and M.-C. Ponthoreau, 'The Methodology of the Research: How to Assess the Reality of Transjudicial Communication?', in T. Groppi and M.-C. Ponthoreau (eds.), *The Use of Foreign Precedents by Constitutional Judges* (Oxford, Hart Publishing, 2013), 1.

[29] A. Sperti, 'United States of America: First Cautious Attempts of Judicial Use of Foreign Precedents in the Supreme Court's Jurisprudence', in T. Groppi and M.-C. Ponthoreau (eds.), *The Use of Foreign Precedents by Constitutional Judges* (Oxford, Hart Publishing, 2013), 393.

[30] Conclusion M. Guyomar sur CE, 30 octobre 2009 *Perreux*, n°298348.

[31] J.M. Sauvé, 'Le Conseil d'Etat et la comparaison des droits', Hommage à Roland Drago, Colloque organisé par l'Institut français des sciences administratives et la Société de législation comparée, 14 Février 2014.

[32] See the *conclusions* of CG Pécresse in CE 14 February 1997, *Epoux Quarez*, RFDA 1997.375, 379–80.

[33] This is what by E. Picard called 'reactive effect'; 'L'état du droit comparé en France, en 1999', *RIDC*, 1999, n° 4, p. 898.

Sometimes, comparative law is also useful in revising certain legal constructs, which are taken for granted, or, at least, in raising potential questions surrounding those constructs. Often it is through gaining an understanding of other systems that lawyers come to recognize the quality and strengths—as well as the flaws—of their own. As argued by Aharon Barak, Israel's Supreme Court President, 'for me, comparative law serves as a mirror. It makes me understand myself better.'[34]

Comparative law has a second function: to assert or challenge the legitimacy of the *Conseil d'Etat's* case law. Many courts use foreign precedents to support a preferred solution or to point out isolation. This form of 'probative argument'[35] has proven useful at the *Conseil d'Etat,* notably in the context of the EU integration process.[36] Indeed, the *Conseil* uses foreign precedents to see whether its position is consistent with other EU supreme courts.[37] In other words, foreign precedents are used as indicators of whether the *Conseil d'Etat* is 'pathetically isolated'[38] in its interpretation of EU law. In these cases, the *Cellule de Droit Comparé* makes a careful selection of the relevant foreign precedents that could result in transposable lessons. The recent decision on the retirement age of air traffic controllers[39] illustrates this dynamic insofar as the *Conseil d'Etat* has chosen to follow a solution that seems consistent with the trend followed by its neighbours.[40]

One may thus argue that comparative law can play a facilitating role in the convergence of national laws.[41] And this is probably true as far as EU law is concerned. In striving for an effective and uniform application of EU legislation and thus avoiding divergent interpretations amongst Member States, comparative law can prove decisive

[34] A. Barak, 'Comparative Law, Originalism and the Role of a Judge in a Democracy: A Reply to Justice Scalia', *The Fulbright Convention*, 29 January 2006.

[35] T. Groppi and M.-C. Ponthoreau, 'The Methodology of the Research: How to Assess the Reality of Transjudicial Communication?', in T. Groppi and M.-C. Ponthoreau (eds.), *The Use of Foreign Precedents by Constitutional Judges* (Oxford, Hart Publishing, 2013), 424.

[36] See further Chapter 15 in this collection, F. Lichère, 'The Use of Comparative Law before the French Administrative Law Courts: Or the Triumph of Castles over Pyramids'.

[37] For a parallel use of comparative law, see the English High Court judgment in *A v National Blood Authority* [2001] 3 All ER 289; [2001] Lloyd's Rep Med 187, which gave rise to a judgment in which Mr Justice Burton drew extensively upon comparative law as a core aspect of his decision-making. For a commentary on this, see generally M. Brooke and I. Forrester, 'The Use of Comparative Law in *A & Others v National Blood Authority*' (with postscript by Nicholas Underhill and afterword by Sir Michael Burton), in D. Fairgrieve (ed), *Product Liability in Comparative Perspective* (Cambridge, Cambridge University Press, 2005). See further Chapter 36 in this collection.

[38] The 'isolation' argument was developed by M. Guyomar in *Conclusion Perreux*; cited in Chapter 15 of this collection, F. Lichère, 'The Use of Comparative Law before the French Administrative Law Courts: Or the Triumph of Castles over Pyramids'.

[39] CE, 4 avril 2014, *Ministre de l'Ecologie, du développement durable et de l'énergie c/M. Z*, no 362785 et suivants.

[40] See paragraph 16 of the case.

[41] See examples in Chapter 13 in this collection, O. Dutheillet de Lamothe, 'Comparative Law as an Essential Feature of French Public Law: The Influence of the European Union and of the European Convention of Human Rights', p. 239 particularly, in decision of the *Conseil d'Etat* 16 décembre 2005, *Ministre des Affaires sociales, du Travail et de la Solidarité et Syndicat national des huissiers de justice*, Lebon p. 570; *Assemblée du Contentieux* referred to the opinion of Judge Rubio Llorente of the Spanish constitutional tribunal; also see *Conseil d'Etat*, 8 février 2007, *Société Arcelor Atlantique et Lorraine* et autres, Lebon p. 56, *Assemblée du Contentieux* referred to the famous decision of the German Constitutional Court *Solange II*, dated October 22, 1986, and to the equally famous decision of the Italian Constitutional Court SpA *Fragd,* dated April 13, 1989.

and become part of the legal rationale of the adopted solution. This explains why, whereas *Conseil d'Etat* decisions are seldom loquacious, there have been on occasion examples of foreign case law being cited in the judgments. In *Société TECHNA S.A. et autres*,[42] a decision of the High Court of Justice referring to the Court of Justice for a preliminary ruling is used as an argument to regard as illegal the deferred administrative act without need for referring to the Court of Justice a second time on a similar question; more originally, in *Conseil national des barreaux*,[43] the *Conseil d'Etat* uses a preliminary ruling issued by the *Cour d'arbitrage de Belgique* in order not to refer to the Court of Justice on a merely *resembling* question. In a quite different perspective, and even more unusual manner, a recent decision on the retirement age of air traffic controllers[44] refers to foreign legislation (and not only Member State) to assess the necessity and opportunity of the French legal framework and, therefore, its consistency with the relevant European Directive.[45]

However, comparative law can also be used as '*a contrario* argument' to assert the uniqueness or the 'glorious isolation' of a French solution. This is particularly true when foreign solutions are not compatible with French society and its legal system. This is consistent with the view that engagement with comparative law is an exercise which must be undertaken with sensitivity and in a nuanced way for it to be a successful endeavour.

Finally, comparative law can enhance the creative function of the administrative judges. When a new issue or an important societal question arises, and there are no domestic precedents, the *Conseil d'Etat* may look at how the issue has been addressed elsewhere before engaging in the interpretation of national statutes. For instance, in the recent *Mme Lambert* case[46] concerning the withdrawal of treatment for a patient in a vegetative state, the *Cellule de Droit Comparé* was asked to look at other foreign systems—particularly the United States and the United Kingdom—that had already dealt with the issue. While the complexity of something as sensitive as end-of-life issues does not allow a foreign precedent to be merely transposed from one system to another, several landmark cases, such as *Bland*[47] and *Schiavo*,[48] might have stimulated the imagination of the judges in order to provide a 'guiding horizon'.

While these effects are undeniable, an important question remains unanswered: is comparative law truly changing the judicial process? While it has played an increasingly significant role, is it only strengthening the 'official portrait'[49]—the official role—of the administrative judges?[50] The concept of the 'official portrait' has been developed

[42] Juge des référés, 29 octobre 2003, n° 260768 261033 261034.

[43] CE, Section, 10 avril 2008, n°s 296845 296907.

[44] CE, 4 avril 2014, *Ministre de l'Ecologie, du développement durable et de l'énergie c/M. Z*, n°s 362785 et suivants.

[45] Point 16.

[46] CE, Assemblée du Contentieux, 14 février 2014, *Mme P... U... et autres*, no 375081 et suivants.

[47] *Airedale NHS Trust v Bland* [1992] UKHL 5, 4 February 1993.

[48] *Bush v Schiavo*, 861 So. 2d 506 (2nd DCA 2003) (No. 2D03-5244).

[49] M. Lasser, 'Judicial (Self-) Portraits: Judicial Discourse in the French Legal System' [1995] Yale Law Journal 1325–410.

[50] See G. Ripert, *Les Forces Créatrices du Droit* (Paris, LGDJ, 1955), 'after a long period of distrust, the case law has been considered as a source of the law, as much as the statutes'.

by Mitch Lasser in order to challenge the archetype analysis of the French system of adjudication as a passive and mechanical system of a 'syllogism machine', by contrasting the official portrait of French adjudication with the hidden, unofficial portrait.[51] Lasser argued that while the judiciary has been incorrectly portrayed for a long time as a mere interpreter of the 'all-generating legal code',[52] it has in fact played a greater normative role. In other words, there has been a gap between the official portrait of the (mechanistic) civil judge and the unofficial (creative) portrait. The extensive use of comparative law in the judicial process is also consistent with this theory. Firstly, comparative law helps to confirm the 'official portrait' of the administrative judge, namely its normative power. Unlike the French ordinary judiciary,[53] the 'official portrait' of the French *Conseil d'Etat* has always been represented as a more creative and normative institution. Over and above that, it also confirms the significance of the unofficial portrait by emphasizing the importance of the invisible as well as the visible in the creative judicial process. Stereotypes as to common law and civil law approaches thus break down, in a way which has been explained by Président Bernard Stirn drawing parallels between the French administrative judge and the common lawyer in a piece eloquently entitled: '*Le Conseil d'Etat, so British?*'[54] One example of this is the way in which *Rapporteurs publics* therefore make use of external sources in a way which their common law brethren would do. Their *conclusions* are thus peppered with references to case law (sometimes referred to as 'precedent'),[55] as well as to policy discussion.[56] This is now complemented increasingly by comparative law references.[57] We believe that comparative law further strengthens this official standing by allowing French administrative judges to play an even more creative role when necessary, namely when a new issue is raised, or when the *Conseil d'Etat* is isolated.

[51] Lasser thus refers to two protagonists of this hidden, discursive sphere, the reporting judge and the advocate general, who via their respective *rapports* and *conclusions* 'demonstrate that the French judicial system possesses all of the attributes that traditional American comparative analyses have claimed that it lacks': See Mitchel De S.-O.-L'E Lasser, *Judicial Deliberations,: A Comparative Analysis of Judicial Transparency and Legitimacy* (Oxford, Oxford University Press, 2004).

[52] Ibid.; J.P. Dawson, 'The Oracles of the Law, University of Michigan Law School' [1968] Ann Arbor, MI (Reprinted in 1986 by William S. Hein & Co., Inc. Buffalo, New York).

[53] Ibid.; this skewed account has been corrected since. See M. Lasser, 'Judicial (Self-) Portraits: Judicial Discourse in the French Legal System' [1995] Yale Law Journal 1325–410.

[54] B. Stirn, 'Le Conseil d'Etat, so British?' in M. Andenas and D. Fairgrieve (eds.), *Tom Bingham and the Transformation of the Law: a Liber Amicorum* (Oxford, Oxford University Press, 2009).

[55] See ibid., 819. For a concrete example, see the conclusions of *Rapporteur Public* de Clausade in CE 23 September 1987, Monsieur et Madame *Ouaras*, Req 64.037.

[56] See, for instance, the reference to the 'defensive practices' policy concern in *conclusions*: D. Fairgrieve, *State Liability in Tort: A Comparative Law Study* (Oxford, Oxford University Press, 2003), 116.

[57] An early example of this can be found in the case of *Kechichian*, concerning administrative liability for failure to supervise banks and was heard by the Plenary Chamber of the *Conseil d'Etat, Commissaire du Gouvernement* (as he then was) Alain Seban started his detailed *conclusions* with a survey of comparative law, covering Germany, America, and England, concluding with the remark that 'despite the different legal and administrative traditions, the same features may be found [in the three systems].' (CE 30 November 2001, *Kechichian*, conclusions Seban, *Les Petites Affiches*, N° 28, 7 February 2002, 7.)

III. Conclusion: promising perspectives

This chapter has attempted to show 'how' and 'why' comparative law has developed at the *Conseil d'Etat*. While the method of comparison was a bit of a 'bricolage' in 2008, it has since become a significant component of the judicial process. As argued by Jean-Marc Sauvé, Vice President of the *Conseil d'Etat*, it is inconceivable to perform the function of a Supreme Court judge without inquiring about solutions brought by other supreme courts that have addressed questions that are posed in identical terms.[58] This is confirmed by the significant resources put at the disposal of the members of the *Conseil d'Etat*, as well as the institutionalization of comparative legal research, notably through the *Cellule de Droit Comparé*.

One may thus conclude that the comparing of different countries' laws is not merely cosmetic;[59] it seems to provide a genuine support for judges, support that takes many forms: reflexivity, legitimation, and new guiding horizons. President Dutheillet de Lamothe captures this transformation perfectly with the following comparison: like Molière's *Monsieur Jourdain,* who discovered that he was speaking prose without knowing it, French judges have discovered that they have been practising comparative law without knowing it.[60]

[58] J.M. Sauvé, 'Le Conseil d'Etat et la comparaison des droits', Hommage à Roland Drago, Colloque organisé par l'Institut français des sciences administratives et la Société de législation comparée, 14 Février 2014.

[59] Ibid.

[60] See Chapter 12 in this collection, O. Dutheillet de Lamothe, 'Comparative Law as an Essential Feature of French Public Law: The Influence of the European Union and of the European Convention of Human Rights'.

15

The Use of Comparative Law before the French Administrative Law Courts

Or the Triumph of Castles over Pyramids

*François Lichère**

*In memoriam Roger Errera***

I. Introduction

French administrative law is better known for its old origins than for its use of comparative law. Although its heritage does not go back as far as that of the civil law, it is difficult to contest the fact that France designed specific rules and established specific courts to deal with public authorities well before most other legal systems. Indeed it dates at least from 1799 when the Constitution of the 18 Frimaire an VIII created the Conseil d'Etat (Council of State) as both the advisor of the government which soon became also the supreme administrative court, but its origins can be traced back to the *ancient regime.*[1]

It is possible to argue that these ancient origins played a role in the non-use of comparative law to this regard. Even during most of the 19th century, the Conseil d'Etat would have met difficulties in finding something to compare—if one defines comparative law as encompassing foreign law but not French private law. For decades—if not centuries—administrative courts would not even think of looking abroad for the very reason that there was nothing to look at. Such a habit is likely to have lasted even after administrative law had developed in other countries. Although Edouard Laferrière, the famous Vice-President of the Conseil d'Etat, wrote in his still often quoted book *Traité des juridictions administratives* a substantial comparative chapter at the end of the 19th century, the use of comparative law before French administrative courts was almost non-existent until the end of the 20th century.

Another explanation of this insular approach might be found in a second characteristic of French administrative law: it has served as a model for many European countries—with the exception of the UK—and beyond. Countries such as Italy, Greece, Holland, Belgium, Spain, Germany[2]—to quote just a few among many—clearly based

* Professor of public law, University of Aix-Marseille.

** This article is largely based on the pioneer article written by Roger Errera in the first edition of this book who sadly passed away just before the publication of the second edition.

[1] Jean-Louis Mestre, *Introduction historique au Droit administratif* (PUF, 1985).

[2] Otto Maier, one of the founding fathers of German administrative law, wrote in 1896: 'We Germans play towards France the role of those who imitate and received' (quoted by Jean Rivero, 'Vers un droit commun européen: nouvelles perspectives en droit administratif', in Mauro Cappelletti, *Nouvelles perspectives d'un droit commun de l'Europe* (Bruylant, 1978), p. 395).

their administrative law on French law.[3] When everyone looks at you, it is quite tempting not to look at the others but instead to contemplate your own image in the mirror! However, it is now well established,[4] although not always recognized, that French administrative law has been less looked at since at least the mid-20th century. When you look at your own image, you may not spot that others are no longer looking at you. At some point, the French Conseil d'Etat was in danger of becoming narcissistic.

One may also argue that administrative law is more closely related to each country's public institutions than private law and for this reason is very national. The argument is debatable: if it were so, how come French administrative law has influenced so many other jurisdictions?

The real difference between administrative law and private law in this regard lies in the existence in private law—at least in the European continent—of a *jus commune* based on Roman law. Such a common substrate may help to create a sort of predisposition for private lawyers to look abroad—although it does not even secure it. However, it certainly does not prevent administrative lawyers from doing the same.

But French jurists—as well as other continental jurists—are nowadays often barred from making comparison by the absence of a common language. When King François I replaced Latin with French as the official language of France in 1539, he set the roots of a long decline of the common language for jurists. At the same time, the use of English spread throughout all common law countries.

The *stare decisis* is clearly another explanation for the more frequent use of comparative law in common law countries than in continental law countries: if no precedent can be found in one jurisdiction, why not look for other precedents in countries based on the same legal system?

Apart from the idea that until the 20th century, there was not too much to compare, all these potential explanations can be applicable to French civil law. Interestingly, the Conseil d'Etat now seems to be more inclined to use comparative law than the Cour de cassation.[5]

Indeed, in recent times there has been an evolution and one could now consider that the Conseil d'Etat has been cured of its narcissistic tendencies before they became lethal. The legislator started the medication: comparative law is often used by Parliament when drafting new legislation dealing with the Administration. This has clearly been the case for the reform of the status of civil servants,[6] the creation of the *Médiateur de la République* with an explicit reference to the Swedish Ombudsman,

[3] Bernard Schwartz, *French Administrative Law and the Common Law World* (New York University Press, 1954), for whom the former is the most 'sophisticated' administrative law; Les phénomènes d'imitation des modèles étrangers en droit administratif, in W.J. Ganshof Van Der Meersch, *Miscellanea* (Bruylant, 1972), vol. 3, p. 619; Yves Gaudemet, 'L'exportation du droit administratif français. Brèves remarques en forme de paradoxe', in Mélanges Philippe Ardant, LGDJ, 1999, p. 431; Michel Fromont, *Droit administratif des Etats européens* (PUF, 2006).

[4] See Fabrice Melleray, 'L'imitation de modèles étrangers en droit administratif français', AJDA 2004, p. 1224; Jean-Bernard Auby, 'Le droit administratif vu du droit comparé', AJDA 2013 p. 407.

[5] On this topic, see Alexis Albarian, Chapter 25 in this collection.

[6] Paul-Marie Gaudemet, *Le civil service britannique. Essai sur le régime de la fonction publique en Grande-Bretagne* (Armand Colin, 1952), p. 7.

of many independent regulatory agencies modelled on their American counterparts, or, more recently, for the *Contrats de partenariats* which the government itself claimed as the French 'Private Finance initiative'.[7] Of course, such examples are certainly closer to 'cross fertilization' than to 'legal transplants',[8] but nonetheless they show the recent importance of foreign laws. However, it only concerns the legislator and not the courts.

The situation of the latter has also dramatically evolved over the past 40 years or so. Comparative law is now quite often used by the administrative courts, although it rarely appears in the judgments[9]—certainly a vestige of the time when French administrative law was 'enlightening the world'[10] which made the Conseil d'Etat still reluctant to admit that it may now be enlightened by the world. But the opinion (conclusions) of the *rapporteur public* (formerly 'commissaire du gouvernement' and an equivalent of the advocate general before the European Court of Justice (ECJ)) illustrates the growing importance of comparative law. Such a comparative approach has been prepared by frequent references to comparative law in specific reports or in the annual report of the Conseil d'Etat which, apart from giving information on the activity of the administrative courts, also presents a study on a specific legal topic.[11]

Comparative law must be considered here in a relatively broad sense as including not only the search to compare French law with foreign law, but also as including the use of foreign law in a context where no comparison is made. It does not entail, however, situations ruled by private international law.

Bearing the latter in mind, in our view, comparative law before administrative courts is encapsulated in three ways: it is either compulsory or necessary or simply useful. The increasing use of comparative law before administrative courts can be explained by the fact that these three occurrences are nowadays likely to be met in an increasing number of circumstances.

II. Comparative law is compulsory

The situations where the administrative courts are obliged to study foreign law in the forensic process are scarce as we don't include in the study the situation where EU law takes examples from a national law. In the latter case, a foreign law is imposed upon national laws by way of EU law intermediation, i.e. in a vertical manner, but in such an indirect way and with such adaptation that it is difficult to see it as comparative law in a

[7] On these and other examples see F. Melleray, *L'argument de droit comparé en droit administratif français* (Bruylant, 2007).

[8] John Bell, 'Mechanisms for Cross-Fertilisation of Administrative Law in Europe', in Jack Beatson and Takis Tridimas (eds.), *New Directions in European Public Law* (Hart, 1998), ch. 11, 147.

[9] As does its own case law; see, for the first counter example, the Ordonnance (Order) of 9 January 2014, Ministre de l'intérieur c/Société Les Productions de la Plume et M. Dieudonné M'Bala M'Bala, available at <http://www.legifrance.gouv.fr/affichJuriAdmin.do?oldAction=rechJuriAdmin&idTexte=CETATEXT000028460200&fastReqId=419853244&fastPos=16>.

[10] 'Le rayonnement du Conseil d'Etat et le droit administratif à l'étranger', second part of the Livre jubilaire, Sirey, 1952, book review available in English at <http://journals.cambridge.org>.

[11] See, for example, the article of Prof. John Bell on independent administrative agencies in the 2001 report. This yearly report was created in 1947.

strict sense.[12] However, we have spotted at least three different situations in which foreign law has to be applied directly—i.e. in a horizontal way—and appears as such in the judgment. In most—but not all—cases this compulsory comparative law is related to—but not imposed by—European laws. EU law has created the basis for the use of comparative law by setting legal systems which involve cooperation between states, as is often the case, for example, in immigration law. The European Court of Human Rights has played a similar role but based on other grounds, the use of comparative law being required in order to assess if its standards are met. In other words, the increasing role of compulsory comparative law can be largely attributed to the increasing importance of European laws.

First, comparative law may take place when a court must establish if a decision to return an alien to a foreign country is likely to deprive him/her of his/her fundamental rights. In immigration law, it is quite often the case when it comes to extradition.

Regarding extradition to a country with the death penalty, the case law of the Conseil d'Etat applies the rule by which such an extradition is possible as long as the public authorities of the claimant country give sufficient guarantees that the extradited person won't be subject to death penalty. Contrary to its *Commissaire du Gouvernement*, the Conseil d'Etat held in the case of Joy Davis Aylor, who was convicted of the murder of her husband's mistress and of attempted murder of her husband, that the French government was right in extraditing her to the US.[13] Indeed, the Conseil d'Etat first analysed whether Texan law may lead to a death penalty for the alleged crime and then based its decision to uphold the extradition by quoting article 37-071 of the Texan Code of criminal procedure according to which capital punishment cannot be pronounced if not asked for by the prosecutor. The Conseil d'Etat then went on to say that the declaration of the prosecutor of the competent county not to require the death penalty was reliable enough. In the end, Mrs Aylor was indeed 'only' sentenced to life imprisonment.[14] The conclusions are remarkable, as they make reference not only to the Texan penal system but also to numerous foreign laws for other issues where it was not demanded to solve the case and remain, as of today, the most impressive conclusions with regard to comparative law.[15]

Extradition may also involve the use of comparative law in other circumstances. It is often necessary to assess whether criminal prosecution is time-barred.[16] Also, by application of Article 2§1 of the European convention of extradition which led the French government to reserve extradition to facts susceptible, in both countries, of sentences above a certain threshold, the Conseil d'Etat ruled that both German and

[12] On those examples, see Fabrice Melleray, 'L'imitation de modèles étrangers en droit administratif français', AJDA 2004, p. 1224.

[13] CE 15 October 1993, Mme Aylor, p. 283, concl. Vigouroux; RFDA 1993.1166. All the cases of the Conseil d'Etat posterior of 1979 and some of the cases anterior of 1980 can be freely found on <http://www.legifrance.gouv.fr>.

[14] <http://joyaylor.blogspot.fr>.

[15] Conclusions of Christian Vigouroux, RFDA 1993.1166: he quotes German, Dutch, Italian, Austrian, Danish, Swiss, and English law on the question of sufficient guarantees; and Canadian case law which admits extradition to the US because of the risks that many US murderers may otherwise immigrate to Canada.

[16] CE 3 December 2010, N° 334683.

French law met these conditions for 'attempted incitement to murder and repeated breaches of the court-ordered prohibition on visiting the victim's home or workplace or from maintaining any relationship with her.'[17]

One should also consider the situation where a non-EU citizen seeks asylum in a country after having arrived in another country. By application of the Dublin Convention,[18] he/she should therefore be sent back to the first EU country he had visited. But if he/she claims that he/she cannot return to the first country because of risk of a violation of his/her fundamental rights and requests judicial review of the decision to return him/her, this could lead a court to consider whether the foreign law is likely to do so. Such a circumstance has not been spotted in France, but it has been so in England with regard to the French law banning the concealment of the face in public (which eventually was not considered as violating article 3 of the ECHR[19]) and is potentially applicable the other way round.

Second, comparative law may need to be considered when the dispute resolution on the substance depends on the interpretation of a foreign law. Although quite rare, immigration is again likely to procure most of the examples of this category. For instance, the Conseil d'Etat held that the French Consul in Algiers was right to refuse a visa for an Algerian lady since her divorce had been regularly pronounced before she applied for a visa, as her ex-husband had given a power of attorney to sign the divorce on his behalf. According to the Conseil d'Etat, that power of attorney conformed to Algerian law.[20] In tax law, the Conseil d'Etat made reference to the Portuguese companies' Code in deciding that sums transferred to Portuguese subsidiaries were not characterized as a money advance but as part of the capital assets of the latter.[21] The need to look at foreign law for resolving litigation may increase if the Conseil d'Etat were to reconsider its position with regard to contracts subject to foreign law. For the moment, it refuses to accept jurisdiction in respect of those contracts, even if they are signed by a French authority,[22] but this solution has been highly criticized.[23]

Third, comparative law may also be obligatory in order to assess the urgency of a claim. We are here referring to a quite unusual situation which had led the *President of the Section du Contentieux* of the Conseil d'Etat to render in 2003 an injunction to suspend a decree by making reference to English, Dutch, and German law (and citing explicitly an English judgment).[24] The case regarded a decree transposing a European Directive—following mad cow disease—imposing on firms the requirement to inform the public about the precise content of animal food. The decree and indeed the

[17] 'tentative d'incitation au meurtre et violations répétées de l'interdiction judiciaire de se rendre chez la victime ou à son lieu de travail et d'entretenir tout relation avec elle' (CE 27 July 2005, N°269924).

[18] The Dublin Convention of 15 June 1990 (superseded in 2003 by Council Regulation (EC) No 343/2003, 'the Dublin II Regulation') established criteria and mechanisms for determining the single responsible state.

[19] High Court, 28 June 2013, Baradaran.

[20] CE 30 October 2002, N° 237441.

[21] CE 7 September 2009, SNC Immobilière GSE, n° 303560.

[22] CE Sect. 19 November 1999, Tegos, n° 183648; CE 30 March 2005, SCP de médecins de Reichheld et Sturtzer, n° 262964.

[23] Mattias Audit, Droit administratif, juin 2006, p. 2; Olivier Dubos, 'Le droit administratif et les situations transnationales: des droits étrangers au droit comparé?', in F. Melleray, *L'argument de droit comparé en droit administratif français* (Bruylant, 2007), p. 75.

[24] CE 29 October 2003, Société Techna S.A., N° 260768.

Directive raised concern about its compatibility with various EU treaty principles, such as the free exercise of professional activities, the protection of private property, and proportionality. In a claim brought by French firms, the judge considered that there was an urgency to suspend the decree since courts from other jurisdictions (such as the High Court which had asked for a preliminary ruling to the ECJ) or governments (like the Dutch, which had suspended the transposition of the Directive, or the German, which had not yet transposed the Directive) had issued decisions not to apply the Directive. As the French government had not done the same, the implementation of the decree would have distorted the competition between firms because the ones selling products in France would reveal their business secrets and industrial know-how while other sellers would not. As a matter of fact, said the judge, there was an urgency to suspend. Although not requiring an in-depth analysis, comparative law was necessary to assess the existence of a risk of distortion of competition to prove the urgency. Of course, the injunction is also based on the doubt that the judge had about the compatibility of the Directive with the above-mentioned EU principles. Interestingly, he for this purpose also quoted the ruling of the High Court asking for a preliminary ruling. But this quote was not necessary to solve the issue; it was only an argument to reinforce its doubts about the compatibility of this directive with EU principles.[25] This comparative law approach is, in broader terms, i.e. when comparative law is called to reinforce an internal argument but not compulsory, clearly the purpose of other uses of comparative law.

III. Comparative law is necessary

Comparative law may be drawn upon after an argument based on French law and it is quite often so when European law is at stake. Indeed, most of the cases where the *commissaires du gouvernements/rapporteurs publics* have made reference to comparative law are linked to the application of either EU law or ECHR law.

For an example of the former, when proposing to the Conseil d'Etat to overturn its 1978 case 'Cohn-Bendit' on the question of the direct effect of the Directive, the *Commissaire du Gouvernement* Mattias Guyomar made a thorough analysis of the solutions adopted throughout Europe. Although the former position of the Conseil d'Etat was explainable by a strict conception of the effect of Directives based on a literal interpretation of the texts, it was incompatible with the case law of the ECJ since 1978. But this incompatibility did not encourage the Conseil d'Etat to modify its position until 2009, at least in principle. Indeed, it had admitted so many exceptions to the principle of the absence of direct effect of Directives that several authors have talked about a '*petition de principe*',[26] i.e. a principle with so many exceptions that the principle almost only existed in theory. However, there remained situations where a claimant could face an impossibility to invoke a Directive which had not been fully

[25] Eventually, the ECJ ruled that the decree was not incompatible (ECJ 6 December 2005, C-453/03) and the Conseil d'Etat dismissed the judicial review but imposed a transitional period before the entry into force of the decree (CE 27 October 2006, Société Techna S.A., N° 260767).

[26] F. Raynaud and P. Fombeur, AJDA 1998, 403.

transposed into French law. That was the situation of Mrs Perreux, a judge from the civil courts, who argued that the decision of the Minister of Justice not to appoint her to a position she was seeking was based on her trade-union membership. She invoked article 10 of Council Directive 2000/78/EC of 27 November 2000 establishing a general framework for equal treatment in employment and occupation which reads that:

> the Member States shall take such measures as are necessary, in accordance with their national judicial systems, to ensure that, when persons who consider themselves wronged because the principle of equal treatment has not been applied to them establish, before a court or other competent authority, facts from which it may be presumed that there has been direct or indirect discrimination, it shall be for the respondent to prove that there has been no breach of the principle of equal treatment.

That article, which basically provides for a reversal of the burden of proof, had not been transposed into French law. Mattias Guyomar convinced the Conseil d'Etat to apply this provision directly to the case by making reference to a new constitutional provision which reinforced the duty of French authorities to apply EU law. This argument was reinforced by quotations of the position of many European courts on the topic which have recognized a direct effect of the Directives, namely the German, Belgian, Spanish, Portuguese, Greek, English, and Italian supreme courts.[27] And he considered, addressing the *Assemblée du Contentieux*, the most prestigious formation of the Conseil d'Etat, that 'some isolations are glorious, others are pathetic, yours on the question at stake today avoid both qualification. But it is quite worrying.'[28] The 'isolation' argument may have played an important role in this regard.

Comparative law is not only used as a way to denounce isolationism. Quite often, the reference is made to just a few foreign laws simply to reinforce a proposal. In that case, there is no need to quote many European countries. Generally, when doing so, the countries are carefully chosen among those representing different models. But it may also be that one foreign example is sufficient, especially when EU law is concerned. In a case related to mergers, the *Commissaire du Gouvernement* made references to US law and to EU law in order to convince the Conseil d'Etat to adopt the 'failing firm defence' theory.[29] In that case, one could avoid looking at other jurisdictions: in competition law, authors generally distinguish between a European approach and an American approach.[30] If both share a same concept, the common trend we were referring to above is established.

Finally, comparative law is sometimes used in order to show that there is not a clear trend at a European level. For instance, comparative law has been referred to in order to assess what should be the minimum thresholds above which public procurement

[27] RFDA 2009.1125.

[28] Ibid. 'Il est des isolements splendides; d'autres sont pathétiques. Le vôtre, sur la question qui nous intéresse aujourd'hui, échappe à ces deux qualificatifs. Mais il est pour le moins préoccupant.'

[29] CE Sect. 6 February 2004, Société Royal Philips Electronic, AJDA, 2004, p. 647, chron. Francis Donnat et Didier Casas; RFDA 2004, p. 286, concl. Emmanuel Glaser.

[30] See David Gerber, 'Les doctrines européenne et américaine du droit de la concurrence', in Guy Canivet (ed.), *La modernisation du droit de la concurrence* (LGDJ, 2006); *Comparative Antitrust Law, Oxford Handbook of Comparative Law* (OUP, 2006).

contracts should be subject to a minimum degree of transparency by application of the EU principle of transparency but with the result that no clear line could be drawn from the comparison.[31]

For an example of the use of comparative law when ECHR law is at stake, the ban on opinion polls two weeks prior to political elections was significant. The *Commissaire du Gouvernement* Jean-Claude Bonichot quoted Portugal, Germany, Italy, Greece, Ireland, Austria, Netherlands, Denmark, and the United Kingdom to convince the Conseil d'Etat that French law was consistent with Article 10 of the European Convention of Human Rights.[32] Interestingly, the law evolved in 2002 after the Cour de cassation issued an opposite view, overturning its own case law.[33] Also, when assessing whether a judge who took part in interlocutory proceedings could sit in the judgment on the substantive issues, the *Commissaire du gouvernement* Emmanuel Glaser quoted Austria, Belgium, Germany, Denmark, Finland, Greece, Ireland, Italy, Sweden, and the United Kingdom to illustrate the idea that such an approach is not incompatible in principle. However this comparative approach has been criticized as being somewhat secondary to arguments based on French law and not totally convincing, notably since Luxembourg and the Netherlands have ruled out this possibility as being incompatible with fair trial. The comparative argument was presented by critics as being a 'pretext'.[34]

In any case, these examples may lead to the consideration that in the case of application of European laws, comparative law is not only useful but is nowadays necessary. What we mean by this expression lies at the very heart of European law and at the growing consciousness of most of the European judges, at least at the supreme court level.

Such use of comparative law reveals the phenomenon of the *dialogue des juges* (or 'judges dialogue') that is taking place between national and European supreme courts.[35] This relatively new concept entails a circulation of legal reasoning and the idea of a network of courts rather than a hierarchical system as it was put by the current *Président de la Section du contentieux of the Conseil d'Etat*.[36] In this context, if a

[31] CE 10 February 2010, req. n° 329100, AJDA 2010.561: 'Les éléments quantitatifs émanant d'autres Etats de l'Union européenne sont quant à eux à considérer avec circonspection: les données que l'on vous soumet sont en effet en partie contradictoires et contre-productives: s'il semble par exemple que l'Allemagne n'organise pas de publicité en dessous d'un seuil, variable d'un Land à l'autre de 5 000 à 50,000 €, on y exige que des offres soient demandées et qu'une trace de ces demandes soit conservée. Il en va de même par exemple en Autriche', quoted by Camille Mialot, 'L'utilisation du droit comparé par le Conseil d'Etat, un changement dans la fabrique du droit', AJDA 2010, p. 1462.

[32] CE June 2, 1999, Meyet p. 161; LPA, June 8, 1999, No 113, p. 11, concl. Bonichot; AJDA 1999.560, note Raymand-Fombeur; LPA, October 11, no 202, p. 10, note Desfougères.

[33] Cass. Crim. 4 September 2001, N° 00-85.329.

[34] Antoine Claeys, 'L'évaluation de l'influence de l'argument de droit comparé sur l'appréhension du principe d'impartialité objective par le Conseil d'Etat français', in F. Melleray, *L'argument de droit comparé en droit administratif français* (Bruylant, 2007), p. 300.

[35] F. Lichère, L. Solis-Potvin, and A. Raynouard (eds.), *Le dialogue entre les juges nationaux et européens: incantation ou réalité?* (Bruylant, 2004).

[36] Bernard Stirn, 'Le droit administratif vu par le juge administratif', AJDA 2013, p. 387: 'Cette nouvelle architecture du droit administratif, qui relève davantage de la mise en réseau que du modèle pyramidal ou hiérarchique, conduit le juge administratif à prendre toute sa part à la construction du droit public européen, qui combine trois cercles, le droit de l'Union, le droit de la Convention et le droit des Etats européens. Aussi le droit comparé lui est-il de plus en plus nécessaire. La création en 2008 d'une cellule de droit comparé au sein du centre de recherches et de diffusion juridiques du Conseil d'Etat en témoigne.'

national court wishes to play a role in the construction of a European case law on a specific topic, it certainly will enhance the value of the argument and may well convince the European courts, which generally take steps after their national counterparts if comparative law is taken into careful consideration. A 2014 case illustrates the 'convincing' argument: in order to declare a French law, limiting the age of air traffic controllers to 57 years old, compatible with the European Directive 2000/78/CE, which admits discrimination based on age in limited circumstances,[37] the Conseil d'Etat made a thorough comparison to assess the necessity and the proportionality of the rule. It was also probably a way to establish a sort of common standard in the absence of a national one.[38]

On the other hand, the European courts may well take advantage of comparative law—as does notably the European Court of Human Rights but also the European Court of Justice[39]—in order to reach a satisfactory solution, i.e. a solution that may be better accepted by the largest number of national courts.

The image is not such of a Kelsenian pyramid than of a fort, each national supreme court being a corner tower and the European supreme courts being the two central towers. This means that not only do the central towers take part in the defence of the law but that each tower has a role to play. In the defence of a castle, not only the foundation of each tower is crucial but the communication with the different strategic parts of the castle is even more important. If the occupants of the two central towers may have the last word regarding the final strategy, they very much rely on how well the corner towers' occupants may inform them and communicate with them about it and also on how the corner towers communicate with each other.

[37] Art. 6.1: 'Notwithstanding Article 2(2), Member States may provide that differences of treatment on grounds of age shall not constitute discrimination, if, within the context of national law, they are objectively and reasonably justified by a legitimate aim, including legitimate employment policy, labour market and vocational training objectives, and if the means of achieving that aim are appropriate and necessary.'

Article 2.5: '5. This Directive shall be without prejudice to measures laid down by national law which, in a democratic society, are necessary for public security, for the maintenance of public order and the prevention of criminal offences, for the protection of health and for the protection of the rights and freedoms of others.'

Article 4.1: '1. Notwithstanding Article 2(1) and (2), Member States may provide that a difference of treatment which is based on a characteristic related to any of the grounds referred to in Article 1 shall not constitute discrimination where, by reason of the nature of the particular occupational activities concerned or of the context in which they are carried out, such a characteristic constitutes a genuine and determining occupational requirement, provided that the objective is legitimate and the requirement is proportionate.'

[38] Conseil d'État, Assemblée, 4 April 2014, n° 362785: 'En ce qui concerne la nécessité et la proportionnalité de la limite d'âge contestée: considérant qu'il ressort des pièces du dossier que si certains Etats, telle la Nouvelle-Zélande, ne fixent aucune limite d'âge particulière pour les agents chargés du contrôle de la circulation aérienne et si plusieurs Etats européens, dont l'Espagne et les pays scandinaves, ont fixé, pour ces derniers, une limite d'âge de 65 ans, les Etats membres du 'bloc d'espace aérien fonctionnel centre-européen', constitué sur le fondement de l'article 5 du règlement n° 551/2004 du 10 mars 2004 relatif à l'organisation et à l'utilisation de l'espace aérien dans le ciel unique européen et auquel appartient la France, ont tous adopté, pour les contrôleurs de la navigation aérienne, des limites d'âge dérogatoires au droit commun et inférieures à soixante ans; qu'elles varient ainsi entre 55 ans et 58 ans, en Belgique, en Allemagne et aux Pays-Bas; qu'une limite d'âge de 57 ans a été fixée au sein de l'organisation européenne pour la sécurité de la navigation aérienne ' Eurocontrol '; qu'enfin, la limite d'âge est fixée à 56 ans au Etats-Unis et à 60 ans en Italie, en Russie et en Chine.'

[39] Koen Lenaerts, 'Le droit comparé dans le travail du juge communautaire', RTD eur. 2001, p. 487.

IV. Comparative law is useful

Outside the scope of EU and ECHR law, comparative law may appear as simply useful and not necessary as it is not part of the construction of a common system. Interestingly, it mainly appears in situations that one may call societal issues but also with questions of the hierarchy of norms.

The usefulness is self-evident when the proposed solution is quite widespread abroad in continental Europe or in common law systems.

For instance, in 1997, the Conseil d'Etat had to decide if the behaviour of the hospital which had led the mother not to ask for an amniocentesis was likely to have caused loss to the parents of a disabled child that was subsequently born, as the mother had thus been deprived of the possibility of seeking an abortion. The Conseil d'Etat held the hospital liable and ordered it to pay damages to the parents during the lifetime of the child but did not award damages to the handicapped child. In her conclusions the Commissaire du Gouvernement quoted the concept of 'wrongful life' from English and American case law (including the case law of state supreme courts) in support of her argument not to indemnify the child for being born disabled.[40]

Regarding the question of the relationships between internal and international norms, comparative law is often used when European law is at stake, as shown earlier with the Perreux case, but also when it is not. For instance, regarding international customs, the Conseil d'Etat held that they do not take precedence over statutes, although they may have a legal effect if not contrary to a statute. The *Commissaire du Gouvernement* quoted the US but also Sweden, India, Germany, Italy, and Greece either for the question of the value of international customs and for the interpretation of the relevant custom.[41]

In case of matters outside the scope of European law, the examples discussed showed that societal issues and questions of the hierarchy of norms represent a favourable field for comparison. But there is, in our view, no more reason to undertake comparative law in these fields than in, lets say, urban planning law—which is still a very national law—or State liability. Indeed, comparative law has, for instance, been referred to in the conclusions of the *Commissaire du Gouvernement* of a case dealing with the liability of the State for the lack of supervision of the banking sector.[42] And before deciding to adopt the possibility of giving *ex nunc* effect to judgments of administrative courts, the Conseil d'Etat asked two of its members to prepare a report which quoted largely comparative law, noting that even if systems of law admit different principles (*ex tunc* effects or *ex nunc* effects), they all allow for *ex nunc* effects under certain circumstances.[43]

However, comparative law is not always useful; indeed it may be counterproductive for an inferior court or a *rapporteur public* or a claimant to make reference to it in some circumstances. The reason for this reluctance may be found, in our view, in the idea

[40] CE 14 February 1997, Centre Hospitalier de Nice, concl. Pécresse; RFDA 1997.374, concl. Pécresse and note Mathieu.

[41] CE 6 June 1997, Aquarone, p 206, concl. Bachelier; RFDA 1997.1068.

[42] CE 30 November 2001, Ministre de l'Economie, des Finances et de l'Industrie v Kechichian et al., Les Petits Affiches, No. 28, February 7, 2002, concl. Seban; AJDA 2002.136.

[43] Jacques-Henri Stahl, Anne Courèges, RFDA 2004, N° 3, p. 438.

that sometimes foreign law is too specific to a country or to a legal system which appears too far from the French one. Two examples come to mind.

The first one is related to the estoppel principle. The Conseil d'Etat was asked by a plaintiff to adopt this common law principle in tax law. The Conseil d'Etat, in response to this argument which was explicitly based on the estoppel principle, held that the principle was not applicable—despite the French origin of the term[44]—since the statutes already gave certain, though not equivalent, guarantees.[45]

The second example is linked to legitimate expectations. Within the scope of EU law, the Conseil d'Etat admits this principle as applicable, although it has rarely actually sanctioned the administration for violating it. Outside the scope of EU law, the Conseil d'Etat still refuses to admit its applicability. It has reiterated its position after the administrative court of first instance of Strasbourg took an opposite view, based on the importance of this principle in German and EU law. The case related to an unjustifiably sudden change of regulations and more precisely to a sudden ban on import of waste. The Strasbourg court of first instance had then imposed a transitional period before the ban could enter into force.[46] The Conseil d'Etat refused to apply such a principle to the same case in 2001.[47] However, in 2006, it applied the same solution as the one applied by the Strasbourg administrative court of first instance, i.e. the need in certain circumstances to respect a transitional period in case of change in the regulation. But it refused to call it legitimate expectations and based its reasoning on the legal certainty principle.[48]

The topicality of this case is twofold. First, it shows again that comparative law may be counterproductive when the concept at stake is not widely applicable abroad and/or too much related to one specific legal system. Second, it may also show that judges sometimes have a loose view of foreign concepts. Indeed, the concept of legitimate expectations in German law ('Vertrauensschutz') looks very much like the rule applied in the case law of the Conseil d'Etat. Legitimate expectations in German law covers numerous hypotheses, most of which are already enshrined in the case law of the Conseil d'Etat based on the idea of legal certainty.[49] It is clear that EU law as well as German law on legitimate expectation are not that demanding for public authorities and probably not incompatible with the French doctrine of *Puissance publique.*[50] In other words, comparative law may have been counterproductive here, not really because the concept was too much attached to a foreign law, but because foreign law was not known enough. One might (legitimately) expect that the Conseil d'Etat will one day merge the two principles of legitimate expectations and legal certainty.

[44] Derived from the old French 'Estoupail' meaning cork, itself deriving from the Latin word 'Stuppa'; see Eric Agostini commenting on the Cour de cassation case law integrating the Estoppel principle in French civil law, <http://actu.dalloz-etudiant.fr/fileadmin/actualites/pdfs/D2006-1424.pdf>.

[45] CE 1 April 2010, N° 334465.

[46] Tribunal administratif de Strasbourg, 8 December 1994, Enterprise Freymuth c. Ministre de l'Environnement, AJDA 1995.555. Concl. Pommier; commented by Errera, [1995] PL.

[47] CE 9 May 2001, Entreprise Freymuth, N° 210944.

[48] CE Ass. 24 mars 2006, KPMG, n°288460.

[49] See Paraskevi Mouzouraki, *Le principe de confiance légitime en droit allemand, français et anglais: un exemple de convergences des droits administratifs des pays européens?* (Bruylant, 2011).

[50] For an opposite view, Sylvia Calmes, *Du principe de protection de la confiance légitime en droits allemands, communautaires et français* (Dalloz, 2001).

The frequency of comparative law when it is non-compulsory or not recommended mainly relies on technical and subjective factors. Techniques have evolved recently so that they facilitate access to foreign law, in particular thanks to electronic resources. When one looks at the 1993 conclusions of Christian Vigouroux, the *commissaire du gouvernement* in the Joy Davis Aylor extradition case quoted earlier, they mainly referred to books or articles published in French or in English. With many databases of case law available online now, most of them freely accessible, one can hardly argue that access is too difficult anymore. In addition, the Conseil d'Etat created in 2008 a comparative law cell ('cellule de droit comparé') with lawyers with foreign experience who can help the judges to find the relevant references.[51] On the other hand, the Conseil d'Etat now offers on its website a selection of its judgments translated into English, Arabic, German, Chinese, and Spanish. It seems that comparative law becomes a new strategy to enlighten the legal world as much as being enlightened by the legal world.

Subjectivity comes with the judges themselves. Non-compulsory comparative law still relies on the will of the judges to look abroad, in other words on their openness. In this respect, the current *Président de la section du contentieux* of the Conseil d'Etat (like his predecessor) could be representative of a modern approach which is based on the idea that the law is more valuable if arguments include comparative approaches. The simple fact that the school in which almost all the members of the Conseil d'Etat study ('Sciences Po Paris') now imposes on its students the requirement to spend one year abroad will certainly reinforce the importance of comparative law once the young judges become in charge. The existence of formal (such as in the *Association des Conseils d'États et juridictions suprêmes de l'Union européenne*)[52] or informal relationships and meetings between judges of supreme courts shall play the same role. Finally, the consciousness that economies are interdependent and that globalization makes it inevitable that the firms will compare jurisdictions may also favour such a comparison.[53] It may be that the judgments of the Conseil d'Etat may soon be quoting foreign law even if this is not compulsory. Indeed, a first step has been taken when the Conseil d'Etat issued an 'Avis contentieux'—i.e. a preliminary ruling after a question of law posed by an inferior administrative court—about the civil liability of the French State for its action towards Jewish people during the second world war, which led the Conseil d'Etat to state that past laws have sufficiently indemnified the victims by quoting foreign examples.[54]

[51] On this topic, see A. Bretonneau, S. Dahan, and D. Fairgrieve, 'Comparative Legal Methodology of the *Conseil d'Etat*: Towards an Innovative Judicial Process?' Chapter 13 in this collection.

[52] Bernard Stirn, 'De l'intérêt de faire vivre le droit comparé', La Semaine Juridique Edition Générale n° 39, 24 September 2012, doctr. 1025.

[53] Jean-Bernard Auby, *La globalisation, le droit et l'Etat* (Montchrestien, 2003); see also the World Bank reports 'doing business' existing since 2004 which do not concern administrative law directly but which have made administrative judges react.

[54] CE (Avis) 16 February 2009, Madame H., n° 315499, AJDA 2009.589, chron. S.-J. Liéber et D. Botteghi; RFDA 2009.316, concl. F. Lenica, 525, note B. Delaunay et 536, note P. Roche: 'Prises dans leur ensemble et bien qu'elles aient procédé d'une démarche très graduelle et reposé sur des bases largement forfaitaires, ces mesures, comparables, tant par leur nature que dans leur montant, à celles adoptées par les autres Etats européens dont les autorités ont commis de semblables agissements.'

When it is compulsory to do so, the Conseil d'Etat may also take advantage of the *amicus curia* procedure—which has been recently introduced—in order to call on the expertise of a foreign professor of law.

The image that comes to mind here, i.e. in a non-European context, is very much of watch towers. If their occupants can defend themselves, they reinforce their defence by being informed by other watch towers which first implies that they must look at them.

V. Conclusion

Comparative law is more often compulsory, recommended, and useful than it used to be. In particular, European law renders it necessary as the systems look very much like a fort rather than a pyramid.

The result of this 'European castle' may well be that their occupants, speaking different languages and having different cultures, might develop a little bit of their own strategy in wartime. In peacetime, each tower occupants may be gardening around their tower in their own way and so gardens around the European castle may resemble an English garden (with many sorts of trees and plants in a lightly organized manner) rather than a French garden (with very symmetric and clear cut alleys of trees and plants carefully selected). But it does not deprive each national court from building its own watch tower and garden around in its own way when European laws are not at stake. As for the European garden, we as French people would have certainly preferred the French way at first sight. But why not concede to the English if the garden is much wider and offers a better view?

16

The Use of Comparative Law before the Italian Public Law Courts

*Aldo Sandulli**

I. The relevance of comparative law during a decision's preparation and the difficulties of evaluating its role concretely

What part does comparative law play in the Italian public law courts? This is a question that is not easy to answer. How important for Licurgus were the journeys to Crete, Asia, and Egypt documented by Plutarch? Or the study of the laws in the other Greek cities for Solon, *kállista nomothetêsai* ('author of the finest laws')? It is difficult to establish the boundaries between exogenous contributions and an endogenous capacity for creation.

What is certain is that foreign models have always had a part in the construction of national legal systems. Such systems thrive on comparisons between analogies and differences. They evolve through a process of cross-fertilization, forming conceptual models on a comparative basis by drawing analogies but also by noting contrasts.

The evolution of the English and French models provides the most significant example of this process. It has been demonstrated that these two European legal archetypes (considered irreconcilable on account of the idealization and radicalization effected by Dicey and Hauriou) have developed through a process of reciprocal contamination and transplantation. This has brought them so close to one another and has made the borderline between common law and civil law so difficult to identify that one wonders whether it is more a case of convergence in different contexts or one of differences in similar contexts.

Returning to the original question, comparative law appears to have had a significant influence on the Italian public law courts in the past and to be even more relevant today.

The problem that anyone studying this subject faces is the difficulty of documenting this role concretely. This is because recourse to comparative law for the purposes of reaching a decision has a conditioning effect both on the judge's preliminary investigation and hearing, but it does not always have an express impact on the decision. Indeed, it is not rendered explicit in the text of the judgment and frequently remains hovering just out of sight. Sometimes, therefore, it has a decisive influence because it

* Full Professor of Administrative Law and Dean of the Faculty of Law of the University Suor Orsola Benincasa of Naples.

constitutes the element inspiring the decision, but it is one that nevertheless remains shadowy—in the realm of the unsaid—and must be traced by inductive reasoning.

Then there is the fact that, very frequently, the influence comparative law exerts is a derived one, having passed through the filter of the legislator or legal theory. The present analysis is obviously only concerned with the second category.

Moreover, over the last decade, the cases in which Italian courts (and, in particular, the Italian Constitutional Court) directly uses foreign law have significantly increased.

This chapter is divided into three sections. The first takes a brief look at the links with organizations through which the Italian public law courts build relations with corresponding European bodies for the purpose of discovering new solutions to common problems. The second section proposes to highlight comparative law's historical relevance to the administrative judge's goal of developing both principles of administration and forms of judicial protection for the citizen vis à vis the administration. The third section examines the considerable opening to comparative law brought about recently by the increasing relevance of European law and by the growing process of judicial globalization. Such analysis will include examples of the influence comparative law has exercised on the national constitutional and administrative judge's work and certain conclusions will be drawn.

II. The links with organizations through which comparative law may surface in the Italian public law courts

The increasing relevance the Italian public law courts attach to comparative law may also be deduced from their close links with other organizations and the frequent cultural exchanges that they arrange with the corresponding courts in other European countries.

The Italian Constitutional Court runs a Research Unit which has an office specially dedicated to in-depth studies in the field of comparative constitutional law. This Comparative Law Department is composed of young lawyers from many different countries. This office prepares a number of comparative law reports, at the request of the judges, on a subject which is going to be discussed by the Court: yet, only seldom can an echo of this research be read in the judgment. Through this office, the Court studies other models of constitutional justice and the solutions adopted in other countries in relation to the main common problems. An example of the careful monitoring of other systems can be found in the five volumes developed between September and October 1992 on the principle of reasonableness, following which the Constitutional Court carried out an even more penetrating examination of the reasonableness of legislation. In many cases foreign law is quoted by the parties, as an argument to persuade the Court: the Comparative Law Department established within the Court prepared comparative law dossiers, but the Court very rarely explicitly (i.e. in the text of the judgment) takes into account such arguments. Furthermore, the Court hosts judges from superior appellate jurisdictions in other countries and foreign university lecturers in public law for periods of research and cultural exchange.

The Council of State, the supreme organ of administrative justice, is equally active at the level of international relations. The need for a knowledge of the other systems of administrative justice is evidenced by the fact that it was precisely the Italian Council of State that promoted the foundation of the Association of the Councils of State and Supreme Administrative Jurisdictions of the European Union, approximately 15 years ago. The organizations belonging to the association meet every two years to discuss methods they have discovered for solving common problems and those concerning the application of European law in the Member States, in particular. For example, at the end of a meeting taking place at the beginning of the 1990s, a decalogue of the principles common to the various systems of administrative justice was developed. Moreover, Italian administrative judges maintain relations of a scientific nature with their French, Spanish, and German counterparts through special associations which periodically organize bilateral conferences.

This intense activity aimed at learning about other experiences and comparing them with their own reality, demonstrates how, at least recently, the Italian public law courts have opened up to models from other countries. It does not demonstrate, however, that the migration of ideas has resulted in comparative law operating a concrete influence, since that can only be demonstrated by analysing decisions of the courts. It is thus on such an analysis that we must dwell.

To such an end, I will focus, in the second section, on the administrative judge's activity, since it seems most interesting to reconstruct the historical developments that have accompanied the evolution of administrative justice. There are two reasons for this.

On the one hand, contrary to Jean Rivero's assertions (that administrative laws are more open than other laws to syncretisms and a certain type of ecumenism that transcends nations and closed systems), Italian administrative law has always been considered the branch of the law least lending itself to comparison on account of its typically national stamp. Administrative judges' receptiveness to comparative law thus assumes a particular significance.

The other reason is that even if the Constitutional Court's function (as the constitutional check on the legality of laws) has made it more constantly open to the influence of comparative law, its history is very short (the first decision of the Italian Constitutional Court dates back to 1957); on the contrary, focus on administrative Courts allows the rebuilding of the entire evolution of Italian history (the Council of State was established in 1831, by the King of Sardinia, three decades before the unification of Italy, in 1861).

III. Developments in Italian public law since judges have started drawing legal comparisons

Legal theory and the Orlandian school,[1] in particular, have played a fundamental part in the construction of Italian administrative law. It must, however, be recognized that the general principles of administration and judicial protection of the citizen vis à vis the administration have been established in Italy precisely by virtue of the influence comparative law has had on administrative courts' decisions.

[1] Vittorio Emanuele Orlando (1860–1952) and his students, Santi Romano (1875–1946), Federico Cammeo (1872–1940), and Oreste Ranelletti (1868–1956), above all.

Amongst the fields to choose from, the judicial protection of citizens' rights and liberties must doubtless be pinpointed. In contrast to the developments in substantive law (in relation to which reasoning followed domestic lines for long periods), a greater interest in comparative law has marked the methods employed in the field of judicial safeguards against oppressive state practices. Activity dedicated to developing suitable procedural safeguards is characterized by a widespread communality of problems constituting a fertile ground of enquiry for comparative law. Thus, at least under this profile, comparative law seems to have had a not indifferent role as regards the activities of the national public law courts and the administrative judge in particular.

At the end of the 19th century (the Council of State's Fourth Division, covering litigation, was founded in 1889) administrative court decisions were heavily conditioned by two influences. On the one hand, they were affected by German legal theory (particularly by Otto Mayer's theses which had made their appearance in Italy primarily through Vittorio Emanuele Orlando's studies) and, consequently, by a Hegelian metaphysical concept of the State. On the other, the French model of judicial protection and, in particular, its typical and original character inherited from the French *Conseil d'Etat* (the creative force of praetorian decisions developing rules and principles by integrating and completing a positive datum) also left its mark.

In this context, the interpretation of the ground of review of abuse of power constitutes a decisive step forward for constructing principles of administration. Following the guidance of the French experience, Italian administrative judges have understood abuse of power as a *détournement de pouvoir*, i.e. as a misuse of power rather than an overflow or excess (from the French *empiément de pouvoir*), which is how the legislator appears to have understood it. The consequences for the limits of administrative judicial review have been extremely important, since judges have found themselves able to carry out judicial review of the exercise of discretionary power. It is from this initial orientation, inspired by the experience of the *Conseil d'Etat*, that the more than century-old evolution of judicial review descends. Even if the Italian Council of State distanced itself right from the beginning of the 20th century from the route taken by its French counterpart, it preserved and still preserves the French model's original inspiration as part of its own genetic heritage.

During the central decades of the 20th century, the decisions of the courts saw comparative references lessen as they evolved along autonomous lines of development. At the height of the Fascist period and during the 1930s in particular, the courts' decisions became the administrative system's centre of gravity for two main reasons. On the one hand, they carried out the task of counterbalancing the administration by protecting the sphere of safeguarding citizens' rights and, on the other, they substituted legal theory in the role of constructing administrative law. During the second post-war period, as the law reacquired its supremacy in the wake of Kelsen's theories, the return to normativism and to an Enlightenment faith in legislation (conceived as the pre-eminent source of law) reduced the judge's role to that of executing legislation. Thus, from 1920 to 1980, a distancing or, rather, a gradual isolation of Italian administrative courts' decisions may be recorded in relation to the lines of development in corresponding European courts. During this period, Italian judges followed autarchic courses that were not influenced externally if not through isolated studies of legal theory in foreign models which gradually found their way into the orientation of the courts' decisions. In this respect, we must remember the contribution made by one of the greatest 20th-century Italian administrative lawyers, Massimo Severo Giannini. His work has allowed an understanding of how fundamental it was to see national administrative law in a comparative light.

During the 1980s, Italian administrative courts' decisions maintained a closed attitude despite the fact that European law was acquiring increasing importance. If first instance judges (the Regional Administrative Court in Lombardy, in particular) demonstrated a greater sensitivity towards the *acquis communautaire*, the Council of State was extremely wary of opening the national system's doors to Community law. Suffice it to say that the Council of State made its first Preliminary Reference to the European Court of Justice in 1991. A sudden change of trend occurred at the beginning of the 1990s when the Council of State first recognized, with the *Fratelli Costanzo* case,[2] the direct effect of Community legislation at a national level and subsequently gradually took the Court of Justice's guidelines into account.

The close tie established between the Court of Justice and national administrative judges in recent years has fuelled a renewed interest in comparative law on the part of Italian judges. As is known, the Court of Justice has developed a series of legal principles, drawing its inspiration from the 'better law' criterion, i.e. by choosing from amongst the solutions accepted in each Member State the one considered most appropriate and compatible with the European system.

European law has, moreover, revealed itself to be an exceptional point of convergence for common law and civil law models. If, in fact, the comparative perspective for Continental European legal systems was, if anything, oriented towards the Franco-German dimension during the middle period of the 20th century, it has also turned in the direction of common law models in recent years. The mutual exchange has led the civil law systems to attach less importance to the authority of unilateral legal regimes and the common law systems to attribute increasing importance to the fact that administrative action is carried out in pursuit of the public interest.

Increasing reciprocal contamination between models of administration has led to the assertion that 'the domestic approach to administrative law that went unopposed during the last century appears inadequate today, in the face of trends differing in origin and nature but converging univocally upon meeting points between the major systems that allow significant merits for comparison.'[3]

Cases in which principles and institutions deriving from other European countries have been introduced into the national system through judges' pronouncements have clearly multiplied over the last decades. This is primarily by virtue of the process of European integration and the greater attention legal theory has paid to foreign systems; secondly by virtue of the increasing process of judicial globalization.

[2] Council of State, Vth Section, 6 April 1991, no. 452, in *Le grandi decisioni del Consiglio di Stato*, a cura di G. Pasquini e A. Sandulli, Milano, Giuffrè, 2001, 571.

[3] M.P. Chiti, *Diritto amministrativo comparato*, in *Digesto. Discipline pubblicistiche*, vol. V, Torino, Utet, 1990, p. 206.

Thus, through the vehicular function of European and global law and the filter of legal theory, national constitutional and administrative judges have re-opened the doors to comparative law. They have done this, however, in a manner that is one stage removed, only using comparative law directly in very rare circumstances.

With the aim of demonstrating this statement, it appears appropriate to look at some of the examples of constitutional and administrative decisions considered to be most significant for the purposes of the present investigation.

IV. Some examples of how the Italian public law courts have used comparative law

It is useful to start from decisions of the Italian Constitutional Court, because, in recent years, this judge made the most significant steps in the direction of 'strong' use of foreign law. This is not so much in terms of quantity (the cases where the Italian Constitutional Court directly uses foreign law are still few) as in terms of quality: there was an undoubted growth in the judicial use of foreign law.

As Maurizia De Bellis demonstrated,[4] while in the past the Italian Constitutional Court used generic expressions to refer to foreign law ('experience of other countries', 'the majority of the countries', 'mature democracies' (No. 341/1994), 'countries of ancient and consolidated liberal tradition' (No. 313/1995)), in recent years it has begun to refer to specific legal orders. The Italian Constitutional Court takes into account mostly the experience of four countries: two of civil law (France and Germany, 11 cases each), and two of common law (United Kingdom, 8 cases, and United States, 6). Traditionally, these countries have been regarded as examples and exporters of legal models by the Italian legal scholarship.

During the past century, the direct use of foreign law by the Italian Constitutional Court was very rare. A remarkable exception is judgment no. 329/1992, the most ancient case referring both to foreign law and foreign precedents, as well as to a high number of foreign countries: not only France, Germany, UK, and US, but also Switzerland, Australia, Canada, Pakistan, Singapore, and South Africa. The case originated from the confiscation of a cargo owned by the Government of Nigeria, authorized by the Tribunal of Pisa and upon request of Nigerian companies to whom the Nigerian Government owned some money (the Nigerian companies were, on the other side, debtors of some Italian firms). The confiscation had been repealed by the Ministry of Justice, as a national law dating back to 1926 did not authorize acts of confiscation on the goods of a sovereign State, without the authorization of the Ministry itself. The reasoning of the Italian Constitutional Court takes into account a general trend, in all the aforementioned countries, marking the progressive abandonment of the concept of 'absolute' State immunity from enforcement measures to a more

[4] M. De Bellis, *Foreign Precedents in Constitutional Litigation. The Italian Constitutional Court and Comparative Law: A Tale of Two Courts*, in Società italiana per la Ricerca nel Diritto Comparato (SIRD), *Rapports Nationaux Italiens /Italian National Report Au XIX Congrès International de droit comparé – Vienne 2014 / To the XIX International Congress of Comparative Law – Vienna 2014*, Giuffrè, 2014, pp. 673–700.

limited and 'restrictive' approach. Applying this type of approach, the Italian Court declared the national law to be unlawful in the part in which it made State immunity broader than what international law recognized.

This judgment (in many respects, exceptional) 'is probably the one in which the comparative method is used in the most extensive and deepest way by the Italian Constitutional Court, not only because of the number of foreign examples which are taken into account, but especially for the way in which such comparative reasoning constitutes the grounds of the decision itself (a "strong" use of foreign law).'[5]

During the year 2000, an elaborated use of foreign law was more common than in the past. Instead of selecting one or two examples, the Court took into account a variety of cases.

In judgment no. 250/2010, the Court was assessing the legitimacy of a national law about immigration, requiring the application of a monetary sanction when a foreign individual enters into the national borders without the permissions asked for by the Italian law. The Court considered this solution to be legitimate. Its reasoning is grounded on principles set forth in the Italian Constitution. Yet, the Court used the comparative argument in a 'weak way' or as a 'probative comparison': it supported its reasoning by citing other legislations applying monetary sanctions to illegitimate immigration (France, Germany, Spain, and UK are mentioned). Also, in judgment no. 32/2011, concerning exactly the same provision about immigration, the Court used a comparative reasoning to strengthen its arguments (the foreign laws quoted in this judgment are exactly the same as in judgment no. 250/2010).

In judgment no. 270/2010, an Italian law providing for a specific exception to the usual procedure about merger control was challenged. According to the Court, it was legitimate to provide for such exception when specific and relevant general public interests were involved. In so ruling—hence, again, using comparative law as a 'probative comparison'—the Italian Constitutional Court engaged in an in-depth discussion of the French, German, and British laws about mergers, all admitting some exceptions to the general rules when reasons of general interests were involved (even though the definition of such interests can vary across countries).

Another judgment making an extensive use of a comparative methodology is judgment no. 13/2012. This judgment is different from those examined above in that it is not about a constitutional matter. It was adopted by the Court within its competence on judging whether a *referendum* through which the electorate would be asked to decide whether to abrogate a law could be admitted or not. The law which it was asked to abrogate was the electoral one, which had abrogated the previous one. The legal problem the Court had to deal with was the one of whether, if the *referendum* repealed the existing law, such repeal would revive the law that had been previously repealed, in the absence of a specific provision reviving it. The negative answer of the Court came after the examination of a number of foreign solutions, both coming from legal texts and case laws (UK, France, Spain, US, and Germany are referred to), and all excluding that a legal act previously repealed could revive unless a normative act would

[5] Ibid.

explicitly revive it. Also in this judgment, though, the legal grounds of the decision are found in national legal principles, while the comparative argument has a supportive role.

> The analysis above shows that even though, from a quantitative point of view, the frequency in the use of foreign law and precedents is still very rare, from a qualitative point of view there was a tremendous evolution in the activity of the Court.[6]

Now we can focus on the decisions of the Italian administrative courts.

The process of cross-breeding administrative law between legal systems can occur through court decisions in one of three ways: through the direct or indirect influence of European law; through the spread of knowledge via legal theory; or following a transplant deriving from an autonomous urge on the part of the courts. The first two possibilities occur more frequently.

There are cases in which a principle or institution developed in other European systems has made its appearance in Italy through the 'better law' filter applied by European judges. An all but analogous analysis goes for the vehicular function of the European Court of Human Rights and the influence of its decisions on national decisions, in both the constitutional and the administrative courts.

The principle of proportionality constitutes the most significant example for the Italian system. As is known, such principle had its birth in Germany (*Verhältnismäßigkeitsprinzip*), spreading first to the other German-speaking systems and then to France (*contrôle de la proportionnalité de l'acte*), before being acknowledged finally by the European Court of Justice. The process of European integration has acted in such a way that, through European judges' decisions, the principle has been applied by national judges in countries where it still had not been recognized as a general legal principle. England and Italy are two such countries.

The Italian and English stories are very similar, despite the differences between their judicial review systems. In both orders, the introduction of the principle of proportionality has led to a far more extensive judicial review of the exercise of discretionary power than in the past.

The evolutionary process leading to the principle's recognition has been long and tortuous for both legal systems. The argument by which the courts and a branch of legal theory excluded the application of the principle of proportionality from domestic law for more than a decade is also common to both: judges meddling with the executive's exercise of discretionary power would lead to the judiciary taking the place of public authorities in choosing the solutions to be adopted.

Both in Italy and England, before the supervisory jurisdiction introduced by proportionality, judicial review of administrative action was limited to verifying the reasonableness of the action. The latter implies a qualitative assessment inherent in balancing the interests involved. Proportionality, as is known, requires the administration to adopt the solution that is appropriate and commensurate and causes the least possible sacrifice of interests simultaneously present. In such a way, judicial review has

[6] Ibid.

been extended to a quantitative examination of the right measure of administrative power exercised by public authorities.

Italian administrative judges' definitive recognition of the principle of proportionality is very recent. It dates to just three years ago. There had already been previous pronouncements that had applied the principle either expressly or, more frequently, implicitly. But it was in the *SEA Aeroporti di Milano* case[7] that the Council of State, adopting an orientation expressed by the Regional Administrative Court in Lombardy, weighed up respect for the principle of proportionality as far as suitability, necessity, and proportionality in the strict sense were concerned. This it did under the guidance of methods developed by the German public law courts and assimilated by the European Court of Justice. The principle was then applied to so many decisions of the Courts (one meriting mention is that made in the *Enel Trade* case)[8] that it may now be considered a fully acknowledged general principle of administrative law.

There are numerous cases where comparative law has made an impact through the filter of European law. Some of the most important ones are to be noted for the way they have introduced the notion of bodies governed by public law into the Italian order when applying European legislation.

As is known, the requirements outlined by European law for identifying a body governed by public law have been formulated by mingling elements of European law with components typical of the French legal system.[9] In particular, the requirement of 'needs of a general interest of a non-industrial and non-commercial nature' is derived from the combination of the concept of 'needs of a general interest' (which has a European circulation) and that of 'an industrial and commercial nature', which is typical of the French system. Only if one interprets the second part of the phrase as bearing the typical meaning applied in France after the second world war is it possible to understand that only the legal persons operating in the direct interests of the collective whole, without seeking profit, can be deemed a body governed by public law.

From amongst the pronouncements made by Italian administrative judges regarding bodies governed by public law, the case of the *Casa Religiosa della Compagnia di Gesù*[10] merits a mention. Here, a private ecclesiastical body that had received public funding to restore a work of art was held to be subject to the public law rules governing public tenders.

In other cases, it is the filtering action of legal theory, rather than European influence, that has been decisive.

The *Enel Trade* case just quoted and the earlier *Spirito* case[11] represent valid examples both of the Council of State's different sensitivity towards comparative law and of the fact that very often the latter's influence is of a derived rather than a direct nature.

[7] Council of State, VIth Section, 1 April 2000, no. 1885, in *Rivista italiana di diritto pubblico comunitario*, 2000, 439.

[8] Council of State, VIth Section, 1 October 2002, no. 5156, in *Giustamm.it*, 2002, n. 10.

[9] See, in particular, the *arrêt Monpeurt*, Conseil d'Etat, 31 juillet 1942, in *Recueil*, 1942, J, 138. See also C. Eisenmann, *L'arrêt Monpeurt. Légende et réalité*, in *Etudes en l'honneur d'Achille Mestre*, Paris, 221 ss.

[10] Council of State, Vth Section, 7 June 1999, no. 295, in *Giornale di diritto amministrativo*, 1999, 1057.

[11] Council of State, IVth Section, 9 April 1999, no. 601, in *Giornale di diritto amministrativo*, 1999, 1179.

The two judgments are significant for our purposes because they make use of indeterminate legal concepts (*umbestimmte Rechtsbegriffe*) likewise developed from German law in order to solve an issue regarding the degree to which the actions of the Italian Antitrust authority are challengeable. More precisely, the Council of State has established (in the *Enel Trade* case) that complex technical assessments (i.e. those where the moment of technical assessment and a careful consideration of the public interest appear fused and blurred) involve the evaluation of a series of factual elements that are the fruit of inexact and debatable sciences (of a prevalently economic nature). These, it has held, may be used to define indeterminate legal concepts (such as, in the case in point, those of the relevant market, a dominant position, and anti-competitive agreements). This leads to the impossibility of effecting a 'strong' judicial review of complex technical assessments processed by the Antitrust Authority: only a 'weak' judicial review is possible, with the judge ending up substituting the Authority's debatable assessment with his own, equally debatable one. On the other hand, the fact that the possibility of carrying out a judicial review (albeit a weak one) of complex assessments has been recognized as important because it allows a distinction to be drawn between technical discretionary power (reviewable within certain parameters) and the administrative merits which, entailing an examination of opportuneness, are never reviewable.

The arrival of these ideas from the German legal system is not attributable to trends in court decisions, however, but rather to studies carried out by academics over the last 20 years and to a book written in 1995 by Daria De Pretis, in particular.[12] This work faced the issue and solved it precisely through an analysis of the German experience.

As I said earlier, it is only very rarely that an administrative judge has direct recourse to comparative law. The *Borrelli* case[13] offers us a significant example. Here, the Council of State was analysing the provisions that introduced exclusive jurisdiction for administrative judges in relation to public utilities (article 33 of Legislative Decree no. 80/1998, reproduced with slight amendments as article 7 of Law no. 205/2000, reforming administrative trial procedure). It interpreted such law as introducing into the national legal system the criterion of jurisdictional allocation adopted in the French order and based on the concept of '*service public*'. As a consequence, the legislator would have employed a broader notion of 'public utility service' than hitherto recognized in the Italian order: therefore, the provision would refer directly to the use the French order makes of the concept rather than those other uses already applied within the Italian system. Recourse to the French concept of *service public* is instrumentally useful to the administrative judge for asserting his own exclusive jurisdiction over all activity carried out in pursuit of the collective interest and exercised through channels that do not constitute public authorities, i.e. without making use of *puissance publique*. Therefore, rather than the legal nature of the person/entity initiating the act, it is the activity (of whatever type) linked to the protection of collective interests that assumes significance, whether it is carried out by public or private persons. In this sense, one

[12] D. De Pretis, *Valutazioni amministrative e discrezionalità tecnica*, Padova, Cedam, 1995.

[13] Council of State, adunanza plenaria, 30 March 2000, no. 1, in *Giornale di diritto amministrativo*, 2000, 576.

could also state that the choice was dictated by a desire to draw inspiration from the German model by attributing to the administrative judge all cases involving administration (understood in the community—and therefore broad—sense of the term). Thus, the administrative judge's plenary jurisdiction has seen its boundaries greatly expand at the expense of the ordinary judge who, not without reason, has demonstrated perplexity at the administrative judge's interpretation of the legislation.[14] The concept of *service public* has therefore brought about a genuine regulation of the jurisdictional boundary lines between ordinary judges and administrative ones. The point of particular interest in the case in question is that reference was made to a concept of *service public* that, by now, differs from that currently in force in France, finding its theoretical reference in the works of Léon Duguit and Gaston Jèze as well as Charles Eisenmann's subsequent studies.[15] In this way, whereas in France the general allocation of jurisdiction has been substituted by an allocation based on *blocs de compétence* precisely by virtue of a crisis regarding the concept of *service public*, in Italy a genuine general jurisdictional allocation has been introduced in the guise of a *bloc de compétence.*

V. Conclusions

A somewhat contradictory overall picture results from what I have been saying.

On the one hand, one can still perceive a sort of cultural gap that is revealed in judges' and barristers' lack of familiarity in handling concrete issues in the light of general principles, seeking possible solutions by referring to institutions existing in other legal systems. The leaning is still towards a hand-made, domestic product. The Italian barrister well knows that a judge remains more impressed by the citation of one of his own precedents than by a reference to a case decided in another legal system.

On the other hand, there is no doubt that the number of enlightened judges looking with great interest over the domestic hedge is increasing. This is due, in great part, to the process of cross-breeding determined by the direct and indirect influence of European law and by the growing process of judicial globalization.

The acknowledgement of foreign experiences through the mediation of both the said law and the decisions of the Court of Justice and the European Court of Human Rights has allowed a *corpus* of fundamental principles that are common to the various European orders to be identified. This is a phenomenon that is in expansion and now irreversible.

However, it is the influence of European law rather than the use of comparative law that one perceives in such cases. When comparative law penetrates the national system through the filter of European law, the former ends up remaining in the background whilst the latter takes the limelight. Essentially, a sort of novation takes place by which

[14] Corte di Cassazione, sezioni unite, 30 March 2000, no. 72, in *Corriere giuridico*, 2000, 592. See also Corte di Cassazione, sezioni unite, 12 novembre 2001, n. 14032, in *Giustizia civile*, 2002, I, 374.

[15] L. Duguit, *Transformations du Droit public*, Paris, Colin, 1913; G. Jèze, *Principes généraux du droit administratif*, 3 ed., Paris, 1925; C. Eisenmann, *Cours de droit administratif*, vol. I, *Cours de 1951–1952*, Paris, LGDJ, 1982, 21 ss.

the principle or institution becomes part of the national system not so much as an expression of foreign law as a source of European law.

There is no doubt, in any case, that the Italian public law courts' use of comparative law is becoming increasingly important even if the latter's role often remains hidden.

The Constitutional Court has been using comparative law steadily for some time now; more and more often it uses foreign law in a direct way rather than in hidden mode.

Administrative court decisions, traditionally anchored to a domestic approach, are increasingly expressly applying principles and institutions from other legal systems.

On the other hand, the cases examined earlier constitute examples of inter-family comparison, concerning the French system in the majority of cases or, at most, the German one. It could therefore seem that, in accordance with Pierre Legrand's famous comments on *la mentalité*, the Italian courts look at civil law regimes only in rare cases and never at all at common law ones.

In reality, there are evolutionary tendencies of a more general nature that are moving towards a point of convergence for systems. These are the expression not only of judges' orientations but also those of the legislator and academic opinion and they constitute the foundations of the slow but steady changes in course made by legal systems.

The most significant of these tendencies concerns the gradual spread of a hybrid (public/private) law following, on the one hand, the privatization of public corporations and, on the other, private law's penetration of public law in the civil law countries and an awareness of the split between public law and private law in the common law countries. With regard to the affirmation of such general trends, the national courts are called to make their contribution, often by applying European and national sources of law. Thus, in this case too, there is a mediated comparative influence, with the trend in courts' decisions acting not as a driving force but as the application of a positive datum.

Nevertheless, the transformations currently under way thanks to the spread of hybrid law represent a favourable opportunity for the Italian public law courts to further open up the system of judicial protection to the stimulus of comparative law.

And yet the administrative reforms occurring in Italy over the last 25 years seem to be proceeding precisely in this direction: from Law no. 241/1990 on administrative procedure (which has apparently narrowed the gap between the administration and the citizen and has favoured the spread of contracts in pursuit of the public interest) to Law decree no. 104/2010, on administrative court proceedings, giving the administrative judge the power to protect citizens by awarding compensation for damage.[16]

Here, too, one can perceive how the civil law and common law models are drawing closer together as they rediscover the basis of a common feeling. In the era of Dicey and Hauriou the questions asked related to what constituted the most effective form of judicial protection: an *annullamento* (an order similar to that of *certiorari*), typical of

[16] Administrative judges' powers were limited (until 1999) to making orders quashing administrative actions. It was therefore formerly necessary to bring a second, separate action for damages which would be heard by an ordinary judge.

administrative law, or damages, typical of private law. The fact that the Italian administrative judge has been vested with the authority to make both types of order is symptomatic of the unstoppable process of convergence the two legal models are undergoing.

Common principles are, therefore, gradually adopted in the context of a progressive universalization of the principles of law or, as it has been pointed out, of a 'universality that has been regained and can be further developed'.[17]

In this process of gradual globalization of law, courts are called upon to play a primary role, sometimes aimed at enhancing the convergence, sometimes intended to emphasize the differences between systems, but always in the direction of 'removing barriers to granting the greater respect possible for values set by foreign legal systems'.[18]

[17] S. Cassese, *L'universalità del diritto*, Napoli, Editoriale Scientifica, 2005.

[18] M. Cappelletti, *Il valore delle sentenze straniere in Italia*, in *Riv. dir. proc.*, 1965, 220.

PART V

CONSTITUTIONAL COURTS AS USERS OF COMPARATIVE LAW

17

Cooperation of Constitutional Courts in Europe

The Openness of the German Constitution to International, European, and Comparative Constitutional Law

*Peter M. Huber and Andreas L. Paulus**

The following sections are each written by a justice from one of the two Senates of the 'twin court' that is the German Bundesverfassungsgericht, the First Senate dealing mainly with fundamental rights, the Second serving as 'State Courts' that deals also with Germany's international relations. The first section (I) is written by Peter Huber, the second and third (II and III) by Andreas Paulus.

The sections are based on the responses we have given on behalf of the Court, but in our personal capacity, to a questionnaire of the XVIth Congress of the Conference of European Constitutional Courts meeting in Vienna in May 2014.[1] It reflects the openness of the German Grundgesetz to international and European law, but also of the Federal Constitutional Court towards the jurisprudence of other constitutional courts in Europe and in the world, and to the inclusion of their insights into its own case law. In accordance with the will of the German constituent legislator to make Germany an equal member of a united Europe, the Federal Constitutional Court has always endeavoured to carry into effect the Basic Law's openness to European law, and to international law, without losing sight of the foundations of national constitutional law. It has, for instance, generally acknowledged the precedence of application of European Union (EU) law, and has incorporated the values of the European Convention on Human Rights (ECHR) into its interpretation of the Basic Law. The Federal Constitutional Court has accorded decisions of European and international courts, within their competences, a 'function of orientation and guidance' for its own interpretation. Apart from this, the Federal Constitutional Court makes extensive reference to decisions of other national and European Courts which are not binding on it. This, however, finds its limits in the German fundamental rights ('Solange'), the competences conferred to the EU ('*ultra vires*'), and Germany's constitutional identity. The inter-woven nature of the case law of European constitutional courts, including the Court of Justice of the European Union and the European Court of Human Rights, has resulted in what Federal Constitutional Court President Andreas Vosskuhle has

* Prof Dr Peter M. Huber is a Justice of the Second Senate; Prof Dr Andreas L. Paulus is a Justice of the First Senate of the Federal Constitutional Court. We thank Duncan Fairgrieve and Maik Knaust for their outstanding editorial support.

[1] Peter M. Huber, Andreas L. Paulus, 'The Federal Constitutional Court of Germany', in: *The Cooperation of Constitutional Courts in Europe. Current Situation and Perspectives* (Wien, Verlag Österreich, 2014), vol. 1, pp. 217–234.

labelled a 'Verfassungsgerichtsverbund', a Multilevel Cooperation of the European Constitutional Courts[2] in which Courts respect each other's judgments in the framework of their respective jurisdiction, but in which they do this in their proper constitutional frameworks. Thus conflict is not entirely excluded, but remains exceptional and rare. Thus, as yet, the Federal Constitutional Court has not had to establish a genuine divergence that would have made it impossible to implement decisions of supranational courts. With regard to the case law before different constitutional courts, the relationship is one of mutual learning and persuasive, but not of binding authority.

I. Constitutional courts between constitutional law and European law

The sole standard for judgments of the Federal Constitutional Court is the Basic Law.[3] Since, however, the Court is bound by the principle of open statehood ('*offene Staatlichkeit*'), an indirect legal obligation also exists under the so-called 'hinge provisions' ('*Scharniernormen*')—Art. 1 sec. 2, Art. 23 sec. 1, and Art. 24 sec. 1 GG—to take into account European (and international) law to the extent that this supersedes, re-shapes or influences the provisions of the Basic Law. The Federal Constitutional Court therefore derives from the Basic Law the principles of openness to European law[4] and to international law,[5] which oblige it to give wide-ranging regard to EU law and international law and the decisions of European and international courts, to avoid as far as possible conflicts between the obligations of the Federal Republic of Germany under EU law and international law, and national law.[6]

1. The influence of European law

Even though EU law is not the standard by which the Federal Constitutional Court undertakes its decision-making, it does, nevertheless, play an indirect role today in many proceedings. For example, the extent to which the standards set by the Basic Law may be applied to a certain case depends on the provisions of EU law. The opening up of statehood under Art. 23 sec. 1 GG generally allows the legislator to give priority to EU law, over even the standards and value judgments set out in the Constitution, which

[2] A. Voßkuhle, 'Multilevel Cooperation of the European Constitutional Courts: Der europäische Verfassungsgerichtsverbund', 6 Const L Rev (2010) 175.

[3] Hereinafter *Grundgesetz*, GG.

[4] BVerfGE [Decisions of the Federal Constitutional Court] 123, 267 <354>—*Lisbon*; 126, 286 <303>—*Honeywell*; 129, 124 <172>—*Assistance for Greece and EFSF.*

[5] BVerfGE 128, 326 <368 and 369>—*Preventive detention II.* The principle has been developed there only in relation to treaties on fundamental rights and human rights. Earlier decisions draw a distinction between openness to international law and an obligation, under constitutional law, of the legislator to comply with international law in BVerfGE 6, 309 <362 and 363>, 41, 88 <120 and 121>. In another decision, the Federal Constitutional Court derived from openness to international law differentiated obligations to respect international law, BVerfGE 112, 1 <26 and 27>—*Soviet expropriations.*

[6] BVerfGE 109, 13 <23 and 24>; 109, 38 <50>; 111, 307 <318, 328>—*Görgülü*; 112, 1 <25>—*Land reform III*; 123, 267 <344 et seq., 347>—*Lisbon*; 128, 326 <368 and 369>—*Preventive detention II.*

is what has implicitly taken place with the ratification of the European treaties—these being at present the Treaty on European Union (TEU) and the Treaty on the Functioning of the European Union (TFEU) of 2012.[7] Within the reach of EU law, German laws, administrative measures, and court decisions may, therefore, normally be measured against the Basic Law, only to the extent that EU law allows corresponding room to manoeuvre.[8] Against this background, the Federal Constitutional Court must consider EU law if for no other reason than to be able to determine the remaining area of application for the standards set in the Basic Law.

The only exception to this would be if the measure in question under EU law were to represent a clear or structurally significant *ultra vires* act[9] or if it were detrimental to Germany's constitutional identity as protected under Art. 79 sec. 3 GG, including the minimum standard of protection of fundamental rights[10] demanded by the Basic Law. Such exceptions have not, however, so far been necessary in practice; in the event that they should become relevant, the principle of openness to European law obliges the Federal Constitutional Court to find a solution that is as little detrimental as possible to the integrity of EU law.

The ECHR enjoys the rank of a federal law in the German legal system (Art. 59 sec. 2 GG).[11] It is therefore lower in rank than the Basic Law and thus, generally, does not set a standard for decisions by the Federal Constitutional Court. Therefore, one cannot take direct action against a violation of the Convention by means of a constitutional complaint.

Nevertheless, the guarantees under the Convention do possess significance in constitutional law, as they influence the interpretation of the fundamental rights and rule of law principles of the Basic Law. The dogmatic basis for this is provided by Art. 1 sec. 2 GG, which contains an acknowledgement of inviolable and inalienable human rights by the German people and makes it clear that the fundamental rights under the Basic Law are to be understood as a manifestation of human rights, which they have incorporated as a minimum standard.[12] According to the consistent jurisprudence of the Federal Constitutional Court, the Convention and the jurisprudence of the European Court of Human Rights, which gives it concrete definition, are to be considered, therefore, as aids to interpretation for defining the content and range of the fundamental rights and rule of law principles of the Basic Law. On the one hand, this serves to give the guarantees under the Convention the widest possible area of application and can, on the other hand, help to avoid the Federal Republic of Germany being convicted

[7] In favour of an 'expansion of the application' of the Basic Law's fundamental rights if this is required by European law, see BVerfGE 129, 78 <99 and 100>—*Le Corbusier furniture*.

[8] BVerfGE 118, 79 <95 et seq.>—*Emission allowances*.

[9] BVerfGE 89, 155 <187 and 188>—*Maastricht*; 123, 267 <353, 400>—*Lisbon*; 126, 286 <304>—*Honeywell*.

[10] BVerfGE 37, 271 <278 et seq.>—*Solange I*; 73, 339 <375 et seq.>—*Solange II*; 89, 155—*Maastricht*; 102, 147—*Banana market*.

[11] BVerfGE 74, 358 <370>—*Private suits*; 82, 106, <120>—*Presumption of innocence*; 111, 307 <316 and 317>—*Görgülü*; 128, 326 <367>—*Preventive detention II*.

[12] BVerfGE 74, 358 <370>—*Private suits*; 111, 307 <329>—*Görgülü*; 128, 326 <368 and 369>—*Preventive detention II*.

of violations. The ECHR is included in the interpretation of the Basic Law not schematically but in a way that is results-oriented.[13]

2. Influence of international law

The jurisprudence of the Federal Constitutional Court was already including references to the ECHR in the 1950s.[14] These references have considerably increased since the late 1980s and are found today in most Senate decisions involving the protection of fundamental rights.[15]

References to the Charter of Fundamental Rights (CFREU) can be found in many decisions of the Federal Constitutional Court since 2000 which concern the protection of fundamental rights at European Union level.[16] The CFREU, not unlike the ECHR, is also referred to in order to determine the level of common European protection of fundamental rights.[17]

Other European instruments of law impact the jurisprudence of the Federal Constitutional Court as well; these include, since 2008, the European Convention for the Protection of Animals Kept for Farming Purposes,[18] the European Convention on Nationality,[19] and the European Convention on the Adoption of Children.[20]

In the last five years alone, Senate decisions of the Federal Constitutional Court have made reference—in some cases frequently so—, *inter alia*, to the Charter of the United Nations,[21] the International Covenant for Social, Economic and Cultural Rights[21a] the North Atlantic Treaty,[22] the Vienna Convention on the Law of Treaties,[23] and the United Nations Convention on the Rights of Persons with Disabilities.[24]

If the jurisprudence of the Chambers is included, the picture becomes even more diverse.[25] Since comparative law, which is sometimes designated as the fifth method of interpretation,[26] has gained significantly in importance in the practice of the Federal

[13] BVerfGE 111, 307 <316 with further references, 322>—*Görgülü*; 128, 326 <370, 374 et seq., 391 et seq.>—*Preventive detention II.*

[14] BVerfGE 4, 110 <111>; 6, 389 <440 and 441>.

[15] Most recently BVerfGE 124, 199 <220>—VBL [federal and state pension institution], n. 88; 128, 326 <367 et seq.; 375 et seq.>—*Preventive detention II*; 131, 268 <296 ff.>—*Reservation of the right to order preventive detention*, n. 92 et seq.; BVerfG [Federal Constitutional Court], Order of 11 July 2013—2 BvR 2302/11, 2 BvR 1279/12, EuropäischeGrundrechte-Zeitschrift (EuGRZ) 2013, 536 <544 et seq.>—ThUG (Therapeutic Confinement Act), n. 69 et seq., 84 et seq., 88 et seq.

[16] Cf. BVerfGE 126, 286 <290>—*Honeywell*, n. 78; BVerfG, Judgment of 24 April 2013—1 BvR 1215/07, EuGRZ 2013, 174 <184>—Counter-terrorism database, n. 88 et seq.

[17] BVerfGE 124, 199 <220>—*VBL* (Discrimination on grounds of sexual orientation) n. 88.

[18] BVerfGE 127, 293 <334>—*Keeping of laying hens.*

[19] BVerfGE 116, 24 <48>—*Naturalization obtained by deception.*

[20] BVerfGE 79, 51 <67>—*Foster parents, care process.*

[21] BVerfGE 121, 30 <55>—*Hessian Private Broadcasting Act*; 123, 267 <423>—*Lisbon.*

[21a] BVerfGE 134, 1 <16 para. 43>—*Student Fees*, 134, 204 <229, para. 88>—Authors' Remuneration.

[22] BVerfGE 121, 135 <170>—*AWACS deployment* (Turkey); 122, 120 <148>—*Data retention* (preliminary injunction); 123, 263 <423 and 424>—*Lisbon.*

[23] BVerfGE 123, 267 <396>—*Lisbon*; 132, 195 <286>—*ESM* (preliminary injunction).

[24] BVerfGE 128, 138 <156> *Pension reduction, invalidity pension*; 128, 282 <306 and 307, 311, 315>—*Compulsory treatment.*

[25] See the references in BVerfGK (Chamber Decisions of the Federal Constitutional Court) 18, 539 and 540; 19, 492.

[26] P. Häberle, *Europäische Verfassungslehre* (7th edn., Baden-Baden, Nomos, 2011), p. 250 et seq. with further references.

Constitutional Court (cf. section II of this chapter), the grounds for decisions also include many informational references to international sources of law of the kind in question here.[27]

a) *The impact of decisions of the European courts of justice and the European Court of Human Rights*

i. Constitutional provisions

Under Art. 20 sec. 3 GG, the Federal Constitutional Court is bound by law and justice, as are all courts. Furthermore, it has derived the principle of openness to European law from the first sentence of Art. 23 sec. 1, by which it is itself bound. On this basis, the Federal Constitutional Court is not only obliged to consider and respect (even defective) decisions of the Court of Justice of the European Union (ECJ) up to the threshold of the *ultra vires* act or the limit of constitutional identity, it must also give the ECJ the opportunity, by means of a preliminary ruling procedure under Art. 267 TFEU, to remove any transgression of boundaries itself, before the Federal Constitutional Court can establish such boundaries for Germany.[28]

From Art. 1 sec. 2 GG, the Federal Constitutional Court has derived not only the obligation to invoke the ECHR as an aid to interpreting the Basic Law, but also, beyond the individual case being decided, to respect the jurisprudence of the European Court of Human Rights.[29] This is an expression of the openness of the Basic Law to international law and is based on what is, at any rate, the *de facto* function of orientation and guidance accorded to the jurisprudence of the Strasbourg Court of Justice for the interpretation of the ECHR, which goes beyond the specific individual case being decided.[30]

ii. Approach of the Federal Constitutional Court

In view of the fact that the Federal Constitutional Court is indirectly *legally* obliged to consider the jurisprudence of the European courts, there is little room left for any more wide-ranging influence *in practice*. Admittedly, however, the jurisprudence in the *Solange* cases[31] and *obiter dicta* in the *Maastricht* judgment[32] or in the judgment concerning the counter-terrorism database[33] may also be regarded as deliberate signals to the European Court of Justice and reactions to the influence of its jurisprudence in practice.

Moreover, the jurisprudence of the Federal Constitutional Court shows that an effort is made to keep divergences from the jurisprudence of the European Court of Human

[27] BVerfGE 124, 199 <220>—*VBL* (Discrimination on grounds of sexual orientation) n. 88.

[28] BVerfGE 123, 267 <354>—*Lisbon*; 126, 286 <303>—*Honeywell*; 129, 124 <172>—*Assistance for Greece and EFSF*.

[29] BVerfGE 128, 326 <367 and 368>—*Preventive detention II*.

[30] BVerfGE 111, 307 <320>—*Görgülü*; 128, 326 <368>—*Preventive detention II*; BVerfGK 10, 66 <77 and 78>; 10, 234 <239>.

[31] See n. 10.

[32] BVerfGE 89, 155 <210>—*Maastricht*.

[33] BVerfG, Judgment of 24 April 2013—1 BvR 1215/07, EuGRZ 2013, 174 <184>—*Counter-terrorism database*, n. 88 et seq.

Rights to a minimum and to avoid judgments being rendered against the Federal Republic of Germany. Both with regard to the rights of personality of prominent individuals and in the area of preventive detention, this has resulted in the attempt to build 'bridges' to the jurisprudence of the Strasbourg court.

We have already seen that EU law and the European Convention are cross-sectional in nature and, apart from a few matters of law purely concerning the organization of the state, are relevant for nearly all cases upon which the Federal Constitutional Court is called upon to decide. To this extent, the Federal Constitutional Court has always referred to the jurisprudence of the Court of Justice of the European Union and the European Court of Human Rights.

There are many examples.[34] The most important decisions from an historical point of view are, however, probably the *Solange II*,[35] the *Maastricht*,[36] and the *Banana Market* decisions,[37] in which it has been established that the Court of Justice of the European Union guarantees in its jurisprudence a standard of fundamental rights that fulfils the minimum required by the Basic Law.

Again, just to name a few examples, reference has been made to the jurisprudence of the European Court of Human Rights in the definition of the area of protection of Art. 13 GG,[38] in the definition of the effective area of protection of the right of personality of prominent individuals,[39] in family law, in the definition of inadmissible evidence in criminal trials,[40] and, most recently, in particular in connection with the law concerning preventive detention,[41] the reservation of the right to order preventive detention,[42] and therapeutic confinement.[43]

3. Divergences between the Federal Constitutional Court and European courts

In theory, there are two substantial divergences between the Federal Constitutional Court and the Court of Justice of the European Union. Firstly, the Federal Constitutional Court, contrary to the jurisprudence of the court in Luxembourg,[44] accepts no

34 See *pars pro toto* e.g. BVerfGE 115, 276 <305, 309, 314, 317>—ODDSET-betting with reference to the Gambelli decision of the ECJ.

35 BVerfGE 73, 339 <368>—*Solange II*.

36 BVerfGE 89, 155 <202>—*Maastricht*.

37 BVerfGE 102, 147 <153 and 154>—*Banana market*.

38 BVerfGE 130, 1 <31>—*Inadmissibility of evidence in criminal trials*.

39 BVerfGE 120, 180 <201 et seq.>—*Caroline v Hannover III*; without reference to the ECHR BVerfGE 101, 361 et seq.—*Caroline I*; BVerfG, NJW (Neue Juristische Wochenschrift) 2005, 1857 et seq.—*Caroline II* (Decision of the 1st Chamber of the 1st Senate).

40 BVerfGE 130, 1 <30 and 31>—*Inadmissibility of evidence in criminal trials*.

41 BVerfGE 128, 326 <370, 375 and 376>—*Preventive detention II*.

42 BVerfGE 131, 268 <296 and 297>—*Reservation of the right to order preventive detention*.

43 BVerfG, Judgment of the Second Senate of 11 July 2013—2 BvR 2302/11, 2 BvR 1279/12, EuGRZ 2013, p. 536 <543 and 544>, n. 61 et seq.—*Therapeutic Confinement Act*.

44 ECJ Case 6/64 (*Costa v ENEL*), ECR 1964, 1251; Case 11/70 (*InternationaleHandelsgesellschaftmbH*), ECR 1970, 1125; Case 106/77 (*Simmenthal*) ECR 1978, 629, n. 24; Case C-13/91 and Case C-113/91 (*Debus*), ECR 1992, I-3617, n. 32; Case C-119/05 (*Lucchini*), ECR. 2007, I-6199, n. 61; Case C-115/08 (*CEZ*) ECR 2009, I-0000, n. 138; Case C-314/08 (*Filipiak*), ECR 2009-I-11049, n. 81 et seq.; Case C-147/08 (*Römer*), ECR 2011 I-3591, n. 54.

blanket precedence of EU law over national constitutional law.[45] Since the precedence of EU law, as far as Germany is concerned, is based on the national act ratifying the European treaties and since this act must satisfy the primacy of the Constitution, the precedence of application is necessarily limited, in the opinion of the Federal Constitutional Court, by the core of identity of the Basic Law, which, under the third sentence of Art 23 sec. 1 in conjunction with Art. 79 sec. 3 GG, is not open to integration. The task of guarding the integrity of the Basic Law belongs to the Federal Constitutional Court and is not the same as the obligation of the Court of Justice of the European Union under the first sentence of Art. 4 sec. 2 of the TEU to give regard to the national identity, which is understood more broadly by the Member States.

Secondly, the Federal Constitutional Court finds that it is obliged to declare as non-applicable *ultra vires* acts by organs and offices of the European Union in Germany. EU law has its democratic legitimacy in Germany within the meaning of Art. 20 sec. 1 and sec. 2 GG primarily by virtue of the German act consenting to the programme of integration laid down in the European treaties. This means that in the final analysis, according to the principle of sovereignty of the people, every action by public authorities in Germany must have its legitimacy in the people of the state; therefore, the Federal Constitutional Court sees itself as being obliged to monitor at least those actions that arbitrarily exceed the limits of the programme of integration, that is, the competences accorded to the European Union, and if necessary to find such legal acts to be inapplicable in Germany.[46]

However, so far, that is, up to the middle of December 2013, the Federal Constitutional Court has not identified any violation of the constitutional identity of the Basic Law or any *ultra vires* act.[47] Even with regard to the assumption, which is somewhat questionable from a dogmatic point of view, by the Court of Justice of the European Union that prohibition of age discrimination can be seen as a general principle of law under EU law,[48] the Second Senate, apart from the dissenting opinion of Justice Landau,[49] did not find any clear and structurally significant transgression of boundaries.[50]

In relation to the European Court of Human Rights, there have so far been three main areas in which divergences in jurisprudence have existed at least temporarily. These are the balancing of the protection of the privacy of prominent individuals with the freedom of the press, the position of the biological father in family law, and the law concerning preventive detention.

In the complex relationship between the protection of the privacy of prominent individuals and the freedom of the press, the Federal Constitutional Court has, from the very beginning,[51] tended towards following a line privileging press freedom

[45] BVerfGE 73, 339 <375>—*Solange II*; 123, 267 <398>—*Lisbon*; 126, 286 <302>—*Honeywell*.

[46] BVerfGE 58, 1 <30 and 31>—*Eurocontrol*; 75, 223 <235, 242>—*6th VAT Directive*; 89, 155 <188>—*Maastricht*; 123, 267 <354>—*Lisbon*; 126, 286 <308>—*Honeywell*.

[47] Differently however Czech Constitutional Court, Decision of 31 January 2012—Pl.ÚS 5/12 (*Holoubec*); see also the reference to the ECJ in BVerfGE 135, 155—OMT.

[48] ECJ Case C 144/04 (*Mangold*), ECR 2005, I-9981.

[49] BVerfGE 126, 286 <318>—*Honeywell*.

[50] BVerfGE 126, 286 <307 et seq.>—*Honeywell*.

[51] To some extent already BVerfGE 7, 198 <221 and 222>—*Lüth*.

because, among other reasons, this fundamental right is constitutive of the very basis of the free and democratic basic order. Thus, in its decision in *Caroline v Hannover I*, the First Senate fundamentally approved the idea developed in the jurisprudence of the civil courts of the 'absolute person of contemporary history' and also suggested that people in the public eye who do not hold public office should accept reporting about themselves to a greater degree than is otherwise the case.[52] The Senate found that the public has a 'legitimate interest in learning whether such persons, who are often regarded as a role-model or as an example, convincingly bring into agreement the behaviour that they show in their public function and their personal behaviour.'[53] Conversely, the European Court of Human Rights, in its *von Hannover v Germany* judgment of 24 June 2004, found that the freedom of the press, protected under Art. 10 of the ECHR, did not have predominant interests, except when reporting about political matters or other matters of importance, at least to a certain degree.[54] The regular German courts thereupon to a large extent based their balancing of conflicting fundamental rights in the individual case on the (narrower) criteria set by the European Court of Human Rights. In its *Caroline v Hannover III* decision, the Federal Constitutional Court gave this solution to the conflict of fundamental rights its blessing, since it, too, was in conformity with the Constitution.[55]

In its *Görgülü* decision, the Second Senate of the Federal Constitutional Court overturned decisions by the ordinary courts concerning the rights of custody and access of the father of an illegitimate child because they had not given sufficient consideration[56] to a previous successful fundamental rights complaint by the father.[57] The Senate ruled that the ECHR participates in the primacy of the law (Art. 20 sec. 3 GG) and must insofar also be accorded due consideration by the ordinary courts. 'Taking into account' does not, however, mean strict compliance, but 'taking notice of the Convention provision as interpreted by the ECHR and applying it to the case, provided the application does not violate prior-ranking law, in particular constitutional law.'[58] It is also important 'how taking account of the decision takes place in the system of the field of law in question', so that the Convention does not automatically take precedence over other (ordinary) federal law. Finally, it should be noted that proceedings before the court in Strasbourg do not adequately depict the legal positions and interests involved in a multi-polar, especially civil law, legal situation.[59]

In the case of preventive detention, on the other hand, the Second Senate of the Federal Constitutional Court in 2004 initially approved the retrospective removal of time-limits for preventive detention.[60] However, when in 2009 the European Court of

[52] BVerfGE 101, 361 <390 et seq.>—*Caroline I*; previously already BVerfGE 34, 269 <283>.

[53] BVerfGE 101, 361 <393>—*Caroline I*.

[54] ECtHR (3rd Section) Judgment of 24 June 2004, *von Hannover v Germany*, Application no. 59320/00, n. 64; see further ECtHR (4th Section) Judgment of 16 November 2004, *Karhuvaara and Iltalehti v Finland*, Application no. 53678/00, n. 45.

[55] BVerfGE 120, 180 <220 and 221>—*Caroline III*.

[56] BVerfGE 111, 307 <330 et seq.>—*Görgülü*.

[57] ECtHR, Judgment of 26 February 2004, *Görgülü v Germany*, Application no. 74969/01.

[58] BVerfGE 111, 307 <329>—*Görgülü*.

[59] BVerfGE 111, 307 <328 and 329>—*Görgülü*.

[60] BVerfGE 109, 133 <159>—*Preventive detention I*.

Human Rights saw in this just as much of a violation of Art. 5 and Art. 7 sec. 1 ECHR as the institution of retrospective preventive detention,[61] the Federal Constitutional Court then ultimately[62] took this largely into account in its judgment of 4 May 2011 and its later decisions concerning the reservation of the right to order preventive detention and therapeutic confinement. It is true that the Federal Constitutional Court stressed that the ECHR and the jurisprudence of the European Court of Human Rights should (only) be considered in a results-oriented way,[63] and thus, unlike the Strasbourg Court, regarded the ordering of retrospective preventive detention or the retrospective extension of its maximum duration not as a problem of retrospective effect under Art. 104 sec. 2 GG, but as a fundamentally disproportionate impairment of the freedom of the person (Art. 2 sec. 2 GG).[64] Ultimately, however, the Federal Constitutional Court did end up objecting to retrospective preventive detention in the way in which it was implemented, that is, to the retrospective extension of its maximum duration, and in doing so gave particular consideration to the principles of the ECHR.[65] It did, however, acknowledge an exception to the general ban on retrospective preventive detention 'if a high risk of the detainee's committing most serious crimes of violence or sexual offences can be inferred from specific circumstances of the detainee's person or conduct and . . . the detainee suffers from a mental disorder'; without this being based on relevant indications by the Strasbourg Court, but grounded in Art. 5 sec. 1(e) of the ECHR.[66] In its most recent decision concerning the Therapeutic Confinement Act, the Senate has further reinforced this approach and dealt, in detail, with the concept of mental illness ('unsound mind' or 'true mental disorder').[67] It is still open as to whether the European Court of Human Rights will step on to this 'bridge'.[68] In view of these

[61] Fundamentally ECtHR, Judgment of 17 December 2009, *Mücke v Germany*, Application no. 19359/04.

[62] Regarding the various constructions C. Grabenwarter, 'Die deutsche Sicherungsverwahrung als Treffpunkt grundrechtlicher Parallelwelten', EuGRZ 2012, 507 et seq.

[63] BVerfGE 128, 326 <370>—*Preventive detention II.*

[64] BVerfGE 128, 326 <372 et seq., 392 and 393>—*Preventive detention II.*

[65] BVerfGE 128, 326 <388 et seq., 391 et seq.>—*Preventive detention II.*

[66] BVerfGE 128, 326 <332, 396 et seq.>—*Preventive detention II.*

[67] BVerfG, Judgment of the Second Senate of 11 July 2013—2 BvR 2302/11, 2 BvR 1279/12, EuGRZ 2013, p. 536 <543 and 544>, n. 88 et seq.—*Therapeutic Confinement Act.*

[68] The Court has partially rejected the criterion of mental disorder (cf. ECtHR, Judgment of 17 December 2009, Application no. 19359/04, *Mücke v Germany*, n. 103), or at least cast doubt on it (cf. ECtHR, Judgment of 13 January 2011, Application no. 17792/07, *Kallweit v Germany*, n. 55; Judgment of 24 November 2011, Application no. 4646/08, *O.H. v Germany*, n. 86; Judgment of 19 January 2012, Application no. 21906/09, *Kronfeldner v Germany*, n. 79). In this it was guided by the differentiation, at the time to be drawn under national law, between the confinement of dangerous offenders in preventive detention on the one hand and the confinement of persons of unsound mind who have committed crimes in a state of absence of criminal responsibility or significantly diminished criminal responsibility in a psychiatric hospital on the other hand (cf. ECtHR, Judgment of 13 January 2011, Application no. 17792/07, *Kallweit v Germany*, n. 55) and based its decision on the finding of the domestic courts, which had rejected confinement of the affected person under § 63 of the German Criminal Code (StGB) (cf. ECtHR, Judgment of 17 December 2009, Application no. 19359/04, *Mücke v Germany*, n. 22, 103; Judgment of 13 January 2011, Complaint No. 17792/07, *Kallweit v Germany*, n. 55; Judgment of 13 January 2011, Application no. 6587/04, *Haidn v Germany*, n. 92, there regarding provisions of federal state law). Further, the ECtHR found, without rendering a final decision in all cases on the question of mental disorder, that the domestic courts were not, in any case, the competent body to examine whether a mental disorder existed and that the confinement decision was not based on mental disorder (cf. ECtHR, Judgment of 17 December 2009, Application no. 19359/04, *Mücke v Germany*, n. 103; Judgment of 13 January 2011, Application no. 17792/07, *Kallweit v*

decisions, it is to be expected that the decisions of the two courts will be compatible even with regard to this difficult question. This is particularly significant not least because it is possible that the duty incumbent upon the state to protect life and physical integrity under Art. 2 sec. 2 GG prohibits the German legislator from allowing highly dangerous and mentally disturbed criminals, who cannot necessarily claim diminished criminal responsibility, to go free when there is a specific risk that they will be a danger to the life and limb of others.

4. The approach of other national courts

It is correct to say that other national courts do consider the jurisprudence of European courts of justice as a result of the constitutional court taking it into consideration in its decisions. A few examples can be given.

The Federal Constitutional Court proceeds in its consistent jurisprudence from the assumption that an arbitrary violation of the duty incumbent upon the courts of last instance under Art. 267 sec. 3 TFEU to refer matters where no legal remedy is available under national law for a preliminary ruling (*Vorlagepflicht*) is at the same time a violation of the guarantee of the lawful judge, and has found in favour of numerous constitutional complaints on these grounds.[69] This has lastingly and across the board reinforced the willingness of the ordinary courts to refer matters concerning the validity and interpretation of EU law to the European Court of Justice, and not just in the specific cases in question.

As far as the European Court of Human Rights is concerned, it is only the treatment of the areas of reference dealt with earlier—protection of rights of personality, the role of the fathers of illegitimate children, and preventive detention—by the Federal Constitutional Court that has created the legal certainty that has enabled the regular courts to incorporate the jurisprudence from Strasbourg.

5. Reciprocal influences: how the European Courts are influenced by the case law of the Federal Constitutional Court

It may be taken as certain that in EU law, the decisions of the European Court of Justice concerning fundamental rights have been crucially influenced, at least since the *Nold*

Germany, n. 56; Judgment of 13 January 2011, Application no. 6587/04, *Haidn v Germany*, n. 93; Judgment of 24 November 2011, Application no. 4646/08, *O.H. v Germany*, n. 86; Judgment of 19 January 2012, Application no. 21906/09, *Kronfeldner v Germany*, n. 79). Beyond this, in the Court's opinion, there is no justification, again irrespective of mental disorder, under the second sentence letter e of Art. 5 sec. 1 ECHR, because the confinement was not carried out in an establishment that was appropriate for persons of unsound mind (cf. ECtHR, Judgment of 13 January 2011, Application no. 17792/07, *Kallweit v Germany*, n. 57 Judgment of 13 January 2011, Application no. 6587/04, *Haidn v Germany*, n. 94; Judgment of 24 November 2011, Application no. 4646/08, *O.H. v Germany*, n. 87 et seq.; Judgment of 19 January 2012, Application no. 21906/09, *Kronfeldner v Germany*, n. 80 et seq.). Most recently see ECtHR, Judgment of 28 June 2012, 3300/10, juris n. 92 et seq.; Judgment of 16 May 2013, Application no. 20084/07, *Radu v Germany*, EuGRZ 40 (2013), 584 <592>, n. 91 et seq.

[69] BVerfGE 75, 223 <234>; 82, 159 <192 and 193>; 128, 157 <187>; 129, 78 <105>; consistent jurisprudence.

judgment, by the *Solange* decision of the Federal Constitutional Court (and the *Frontini* decision of the Italian *Corte Costituzionale*). The same can be demonstrated for the adoption of the principle of proportionality, a feature of Prussian police law which entered German constitutional law via the jurisprudence of the Federal Constitutional Court in the 1950s. A similar process may be seen at work in the attention paid by the European Court of Justice to the subject of constitutional identity, which has been a *cantus firmus* in the jurisprudence of the Federal Constitutional Court as a limit of integration since the *Solange* decision and has now been codified in the first sentence of Art. 4 sec. 2 TEU,[70] even if, as has already been mentioned, the way in which this guarantee functions is understood differently in Karlsruhe and Luxembourg.

To mention another example, in its 1996 opinion concerning the accession of the European Union to the ECHR,[71] the European Court of Justice adopted the restrictive conditions established in the *Maastricht* judgment regarding Art. 308 of the EC Treaty (now Art. 352 TFEU) almost word-for-word. Similarly, the ECJ reproduced the Federal Constitutional Court's 2010 judgment on preventive data retention almost verbatim in its own judgment on the matter.[71a]

The autonomous interpretation of the Convention, and the restriction to English and French as the authentic languages of the Convention, emphasized by the European Court of Human Rights, make it difficult to provide evidence of the influence of the jurisprudence of the Federal Constitutional Court on the jurisprudence of the European Court of Human Rights. On the other hand, the similarities between the jurisprudence of the two courts regarding the concept, function, and structure of the protection of fundamental rights is so great[72] that a considerable indirect influence may be assumed.

More specifically, the conflict areas mentioned earlier, namely protection of the rights of personality of prominent individuals[73] and preventive detention,[74] demonstrate that the European Court of Human Rights reacts constructively to the adaptability shown in the jurisprudence of the Federal Constitutional Court. So the discursive basis of the cooperation between European constitutional courts (*europäischer Verfassungsgerichtsverbund*) does indeed entail a certain degree of influence.

II. Interactions between constitutional courts

The Basic Law does not restrict the ways in which the Federal Constitutional Court may take the decisions of other constitutional courts into account in its jurisprudence.

[70] See ECJ, Case C-285/98, *Tanja Kreil*, ECR 2000, I—69, closing statement by the Attorney General *La Pergola*; Case C-36/02, *Omega Spielhallen*, ECR 2004, I-9609, n. 39.

[71] ECJ, Opinion 2/94, *ECHR*, ECR 1996, I-1759 n. 29 et seq.

[71a] BVerfG 125, 260 <212>—*Preventive Data Retention*; cf ECJ, Case C-293/12 and C-594/12 <para. 37 *et passim*>.

[72] Cf. the summary in C. Grabenwarter, *Europäische Menschenrechtskonvention* (5th edn., Munich, Beck, 2012), § 18.

[73] ECtHR, Judgment of 7 February 2012, Application nos. 40660/08, 60641/08, *von Hannover v Germany*, juris; Judgment of 19 September 2013, Application no. 8772/10, *von Hannover v Germany*, juris.

[74] ECtHR, Judgment of 24 November 2011, Application no. 4646/08, *O.H. v Germany*; Judgment of 19 April 2012, Application no. 61272/09, *B v Germany*; Judgment of 16 May 2013, Application no. 20084/07, *Radu v Germany*, EuGRZ 40 (2013), 584 <592>, n. 91 et seq.

Reference to, indeed even respect for, international judgments is part and parcel of judicial independence. Comparative law is even regarded by some as a method of interpretation of equal standing with the others.[75] Article 1 sec. 2 GG states that '[t]he German people... acknowledge inviolable and inalienable human rights as the basis of every community, of peace and of justice in the world'. While there is some argument as to the meaning of this provision,[76] the Federal Constitutional Court and commentators on the Basic Law do, however, agree for the most part that international guarantees of human rights may and should be referred to in order to support the interpretation of human rights under the Basic Law.[77]

1. Reference to the jurisprudence of other constitutional courts

The Federal Constitutional Court refers to the decisions of other European or non-European constitutional courts and supreme courts in many of its decisions,[78] without any noticeable bias towards German-speaking or European courts.

The Federal Constitutional Court has always paid particular attention to the rulings of the US Supreme Court.[79] Recent judgments have concerned such various subjects as respect for the rulings of the International Court of Justice[80] or the right to demonstrate at airports—with the theory of 'public space' being supported additionally with reference to the jurisprudence practice of the Supreme Court of Canada.[81]

These citations do not mean, however, that the Federal Constitutional Court would feel itself bound by the decisions of other constitutional courts if its opinion were to deviate from them. Rather, the Court sees it as a matter of professionalism in a highly interwoven international (legal) world not only to be aware of legal concepts and ideas

[75] S.P. Häberle, *Europäische Verfassungslehre* (7th edn., Baden-Baden, Nomos, 2011), p. 250 et seq. with further references.

[76] Cf. e.g. M. Herdegen, in Maunz/Dürig, GG (Munich, Beck, March 2006), Art. 1 sec. 2 n. 39 (Incorporation of the 'core' standards of human rights under international law); representing the opposing view H. Dreier, GG, Vol. I (3rd edn., Tübingen, Mohr Siebeck, 2013), Art. 1 sec. 2 n. 20 with further references.

[77] See just for the ECHR BVerfGE [Decisions of the Federal Constitutional Court] 111, 307 <329>—*Görgülü*; BVerfGE 128, 326 <367 et seq.>—*Preventive detention*; for other guarantees of human rights cf. BVerfGE 128, 282 <306>—*Psychiatric confinement*; 132, 134 <161 and 162, n. 68>—*Asylum Seekers' Benefits Act* (*Asylbewerberleistungsgesetz*); BVerfG; from the literature see e.g. Herdegen, in: Maunz-Dürig, GG (Munich, Beck, March 2006), Art. 1 sec.2 n. 47; opposing view Höfling, in: Sachs, GG (6th edn., Munich: Beck, 2011), nn. 76 and 77.

[78] Cf. for European Decisions: BVerfG, Decision of 14 January 2014—2 BvR 2728/13, <www.bverfg.de>, para. 30—*OMT*; Decision of 18 March 2014—2 BvR 1390/12, <www.bverfg.de>, paras. 211–20; Decision of 12 September 2012—2 BvR 1824/12, <www.bverfg.de>, para. 12—*ESM* (Provisional measures); Non-European Decisions: BVerfG, Decision of 22 February 2011—1 BvR 699/06, <www.bverfg.de>, paras. 70, 105—*Fraport*; Decision of 19 September 2006—2 BvR 2115/01, <www.bverfg.de>, paras. 16–20—*LaGrand*; Decision of 30 April 1963—2 BvM 1/62, <www.bverfg.de>, paras. 44 f, 73 ff.—*Iranian Embassy*.

[79] E.g. BVerfG, Decision of 30 April 1963—2 BvM 1/62, <www.bverfg.de>, paras. 79 ff.—*Iranian Embassy*; Decision of 24 February 1971—1 BvR 435/68, <www.bverfg.de>, para. 116—*Mephisto*; Decision of 15 April 1980—2 BvR 842/77, <www.bverfg.de>, para. 75—*Expatriation*; Decision of 14 July 1986—2 BvE 2/84, 2 BvR 442/84, <www.bverfg.de>, para. 187.

[80] See in this regard BVerfGK [Chamber decisions of the Federal Constitutional Court] 9, 174 <186 et seq., 191> (duty to take into consideration); BVerfGK 17, 390 <399 et seq.>; recently BVerfG, Decision of 5 November 2013—2 BvR 1579/11, <www.bverfg.de>; BGH Federal Court of Justice, *Der Strafverteidiger*—StV 2011, 603; cf. opposing US Supreme Court, *Sanchez-Llamas v Oregon*, 548 US 338 (2006); *Medellín v Texas*, 552 US 491 (2008).

[81] BVerfGE 128, 226 <253>—*Fraport*.

from other countries, but also to confront those concepts and ideas and interrogate them. As an example, a Chamber of the Second Senate, in the process of implementing the decisions of the International Court of Justice in the *LaGrand*[82] and *Avena*[83] cases, reached the conclusion that the opinion of the minority of their American colleagues should be followed in the German legal system, and not that of the majority.[84]

Moreover, the published decisions alone do not provide the full picture of the full range covered by consideration of international decisions. Many, if not most, of the drafts leading to decisions involve a careful analysis of the legal situation in other countries, even if the findings from such analyses are not incorporated into the reasons given for the decisions.

Notwithstanding the above, the Federal Constitutional Court does have a particular affinity with its sister courts in the German-speaking countries, especially in Austria and Switzerland.[85] However, this is not merely for linguistic and cultural reasons, but is also based in part on some similarity of federal structures and common legal traditions. Wherever there are parallel problems in Austria and Switzerland, there is a good chance that they are reflected in German constitutional jurisprudence[86]—which does not mean that the solutions found there are seen as binding. Unlike perhaps in common law, there is no theory of 'binding prejudice' in Germany which could have an effect on the citation of foreign court decisions. It is a matter of exchanging arguments and practical experience with certain regulatory and interpretative approaches, but also of the ability of German solutions to be part of the German and European linguistic and legal zone.[87]

It is not possible to determine clearly the fields of law in which the Constitutional Court refers particularly to the jurisprudence of other constitutional courts, as there are no rules exempting any particular field. It is most likely to occur in matters of international and European law[88] and in the area of the ECHR,[89] as foreign legal practice has an impact here on the interpretation and application of norms in other countries.[90] In contrast, matters of 'simple' ordinary law—civil, criminal, and public law—are (still) of a mostly national character and are also not subject to full review by

[82] *LaGrand (Germany v United States)* ICJ Rep 2001, 466.

[83] *Avena (Mexico v United States)* ICJ Rep 2004, 12.

[84] BVerfG, BVerfGK 9, 174 <189 et seq.>; BVerfGK 17, 390 <398>; cf. BVerfGE 111, 307 <319>—*Görgülü*; BVerfGE 128, 326 <367 et seq.>—*Preventive detention II* (both concerning the duty to take into account decisions by the European Court of Human Rights).

[85] E.g. BVerfGE 1, 97 <102>—*Survivor Pension*; 1, 322 <324 f.>; 59, 280 <283>; 4, 31 <37>; 39, 1 <70, 93 ff.>—*Abortion I*; 32, 54 <66>; 46, 342 <369 f.>—*Philippine Embassy*.

[86] E.g. BVerfGE 1, 97 <102>—*Survivor Pension*; 39, 1 <70, 93 ff.>—*Abortion I*; 32, 54 <66>; 46, 342 <369 f.>—*Philippine Embassy*, or, recently, BVerfG, Decision of 15 January 2014—1 BvR 1656/09 -, <www.bverfg.de>, EuGRZ 2014, 373, para. 56—*Second Home Tax*, referring to Schweizerisches Bundesgericht, Judgment of the second public law section of 1 June 2007—2P.43/2006 -, BGE 133 I, 206 <220>.

[87] Conclusion of the so-called 'Solange-Rechtsprechung': BVerfGE 37, 271—*Solange I*; 73, 339—*Solange II*; 89, 155—*Maastricht*; 102, 147—*Banana market regulation*; 123, 267—*Lisbon*.

[88] E.g. BVerfGE 123, 267 <401>—*Lisbon*; 89, 155—*Maastricht*; 112, 1 <27>—*Land reform III*; 118, 124 <137, 155>—*National Emergency*.

[89] E.g. BVerfGE 133, 59 <81 ff.>—*Successive adoption*; 130, 240 <252, 255>—*Landeserziehungsgeldgesetz*; 123, 267 <373>—*Lisbon*.

[90] E.g. BVerfGE 95, 335 <364 ff.>—*Surplus mandates*; 65, 1 <34>—*National Census*; 128, 226 <253>—*Fraport*.

the Federal Constitutional Court. Thus, less reference is made to foreign decisions by domestic Courts.

2. Reciprocal influences on other constitutional courts?

The reciprocal influence of the Federal Constitutional Court on other foreign constitutional courts has mostly occurred in the area of European law, as noted earlier, in which the influence on other national courts is also relatively high, not necessarily in the sense of word-for-word adoption, but rather as inspiration[91] (or even incentive). As an example, the decision by the Czech Constitutional Court to apply the *ultra vires* doctrine[92] to a decision by the Court of Justice of the European Union can be traced back *inter alia* to the *Honeywell* decision of the Second Senate,[93] without following it in every detail.

As far as we can see, no comprehensive study exists of the influence of the Federal Constitutional Court on other constitutional courts.[94] However, for example, German jurisprudence and practice regarding the principle of proportionality has had a marked influence on international jurisprudence on human rights and fundamental rights.[95]

[91] Cf. J. Isensee, 'Positivität und Überpositivität der Grundrechte' in: Merten/Papier (eds.), *Handbuch der Grundrechte II* (Munich, Beck, 2006) § 26 n. 104 (for the ECHR and the development of international human rights).

[92] Czech Constitutional Court, Decision of 31 January 2012—Pl.ÚS 5/12 - Slovak Pensions (*Holoubec*); also M. Faix, Genesis eines mehrpoligen Justizkonflikts: Das Verfassungsgericht der Tschechischen Republik wertet ein EuGH-Urteil als Ultra-vires-Akt, EuGRZ 2012, 597 et seq.; A. Vincze, Das tschechische Verfassungsgericht stoppt den EuGH, EuR 2013, 194 et seq.; J. Komárek, 'Czech constitutional court playing with matches: the Czech constitutional court declares a judgment of the court of justice of the EU ultra vires', European Constitutional Law Review 8 (2012) 323 et seq.

[93] BVerfGE 126, 286 <302 et seq.>—*Honeywell.*

[94] See generally C. Tomuschat, 'Das Bundesverfassungsgericht im Kreise anderer nationaler Verfassungsgerichte' in: P. Badura and H. Dreier (eds.), *Festschrift 50 Jahre Bundesverfassungsgericht* (Tübingen, Mohr Siebeck, 2001) 245 et seq. (with critical notes on the lack of citation practice ibid., p. 285 et seq. and note on citing other constitutional courts in deviating opinions, e.g. BVerfGE 39, 68 (71, 74)—*Termination of pregnancy I*, Dissenting opinions *Rupp v Brünneck, Simon*—and in BVerfGE 73, 339 (376)—*Solange II*). For individual impressions see László Sólyom 'Worte des Hörers', in: M. Stolleis (ed.), *Herzkammern der Republik* (Munich, Beck, 2011), p. 224 et seq.; A. Zoll, 'Verfassungsrichter in Polen und in der BRD. Rechtliche Regelungen im Vergleich', ibid., p. 247 et seq. Differences from the French Conseil constitutionnel are emphasized by E. François, 'Das Bundesverfassungsgericht und die deutsche Rechtskultur: Ein Blick aus Frankreich', ibid., p. 52 et seq.; O. Jouanjan, 'Conseil constitutionnel und Bundesverfassungsgericht: zwei verschiedene Modelle der europäischen Verfassungsgerichtsbarkeit', ibid., p. 137 et seq.

[95] On the development of the principle of proportionality and the influence of the Federal Constitutional Court see A. Barak, *Proportionality* (Cambridge, Cambridge University Press, 2012), p. 178 et seq. (with a detailed description of the history of that influence in Europe and beyond); D. Merten, 'Verhältnismäßigkeitsgrundsatz' in Merten/Papier (eds.), *Handbuch der Grundrechte III* (Munich, Beck, 2009) Sec. 68 n. 6 et seq. For the origins of the principle see the Kreuzberg Decision by the Prussian Higher Administrative Court of 14 June 1882, E (Decisions) 9, 353 (370 et seq.). See now the second sentence of Art. 52 (1) of the Charter of Fundamental Rights of the European Union and Art. 18 of the European Convention on Human Rights (hereinafter ECHR). On the influence of the Federal Constitutional Court generally see also recent collections and handbooks such as Merten/Papier (eds.), *Handbuch der Grundrechte* (Munich, Beck, 2004 ff.); v. Bogdandy/Huber (eds.), *Ius Publicum Europaeum* (Munich, Beck, 2007 ff.); on the ECHR see O. Dörr, R. Grote, and T. Marauhn, *EMRK/GG Konkordanzkommentar ECHR and Basic Law* (GG) (2nd edn., Tübingen, Mohr Siebeck, 2013).

3. Other forms of cooperation

Innumerable mutual visits are undertaken among European constitutional courts and supreme courts as well as meetings with the Court of Justice of the European Union in Luxembourg and the nearby European Court of Human Rights in Strasbourg. There are also many encounters on a personal level. There is, for example, an informal discussion group comprising members of the Federal Constitutional Court, the British Supreme Court, and the French Conseil d'État that deals with the fundamental principles of European constitutional and administrative law in the jurisprudence of the respective national courts and the cross-referencing, but also the differences between their respective jurisprudence. Supra national handbook projects by legal scholars, some of whom are also justices, complement this cooperation, which is close, but for the most part, as we have said, informal.

III. Interactions between European courts in the jurisprudence of constitutional courts

Interactions between European courts and the Federal Constitutional Court are much more formal. This is mainly because the decisions of European courts, namely the Court of Justice of the European Union and the European Court of Human Rights, formally have a function of orientation and guidance for the interpretation and application of the relevant Treaties.[96] The European courts can, in particular, exert considerable pressure for the implementation of their decisions, including sanctions which the Court of Justice of the European Union is able to impose for non-implementation of its decisions (Art. 260 sec. 2 subsection 2 TFEU). The Committee of Ministers of the Council of Europe monitors the enforcement of decisions of the European Court of Human Rights, and, as is well known, the Court now uses the binding nature of its decisions under Art. 46 of the ECHR to issue so-called 'pilot judgments',[97] which can, if necessary, demand that signatory countries take rather drastic measures to prevent future violations of the Convention.[98]

But a distinction must be drawn here: while the decisions of the Court of Justice of the European Union are part of the precedence of application of EU law, as is acknowledged in the consistent jurisprudence of the Federal Constitutional Court,[99] the Federal Constitutional Court has accorded the decisions of the European Court of Human Rights (only) a 'function of orientation and guidance' in the application of the ECHR within German jurisdiction,[100] but no final and binding effect within the

[96] See BVerfGE 111, 307 <319>—*Görgülü*; BVerfGE 128, 326 <367 et seq.>—*Preventive detention II.*

[97] *Broniowski v Poland* (Grand Chamber), Application no. 31443/96, 2004-V, EuGRZ 2004, 472; in this regard see e.g. S. Schmahl, EuGRZ 2008, 369 et seq.; *Rumpf v Germany*, Application No. 46344/06, EuGRZ 2010, 700, p. 59 et seq.

[98] See as a reaction to the Rumpf Decision the Law concerning legal protection in over-long court proceedings and criminal investigation proceedings of 24 November 2011, Bundesgesetzblatt (BGBl). [Federal Law Gazette] I 2302, with many changes to the entire German trial and court constitution law with the introduction of the remedy of a formal objection to delay (*Verzögerungsrüge*).

[99] See BVerfGE 126, 286 <301>—*Honeywell*; BVerfGE 129, 78 <97>—*Le Corbusier furniture.*

[100] See e.g. BVerfGE 111, 307 <320>—*Görgülü*; BVerfGE 128, 326 <368>—*Preventive detention.*

domestic legal system. Any deviation, however, requires a great deal of time and effort to be put into its substantiation, which means that it occurs extremely rarely, if at all.

Thus, as far as can be seen, the Federal Constitutional Court has not so far denied the effectiveness within German jurisdiction of any decisions of either of the two European courts. In the *Lisbon* judgment,[101] the *Honeywell* decision,[102] and in the judgment concerning the counter-terrorism database,[103] it has, however, imposed limits—which have so far remained theoretical—regarding the acknowledgement of judgments of the Court of Justice of the European Union. Similarly, in its second judgment concerning preventive detention, it has imposed limits in relation to decisions by the European Court of Human Rights.[104]

1. References to European Union law in the jurisprudence of the European Court of Human Rights and its impact on the jurisprudence of the constitutional court

The Federal Constitutional Court incorporates the jurisprudence of the Court of Justice of the European Union into its own jurisprudence; there is no need in Germany for a separate incorporation by the European Court of Human Rights. The Federal Constitutional Court has consistently established that it fundamentally acknowledges the precedence of European law in its jurisprudence.[105] This includes the binding nature of decisions by the Court of Justice of the European Union in matters of EU law. For instance, the First Senate has used the precedence of application of European law and the jurisprudence of the Court of Justice concerning the prohibition of discrimination on the grounds of nationality (Art. 18 TFEU) to substantiate its finding—over and above the wording of Art. 19 sec. 3 GG[106]—that the fundamental rights under the Basic Law are also applicable to legal entities domiciled in other Member States of the European Union.[107]

This does not, however, apply in the same way for areas that EU law reserves either expressly or, for lack of conferred powers, tacitly, for national law. The Court of Justice of the European Union has extended the application of European fundamental rights to cover the entire area of application of EU law, including exceptions from the fundamental freedoms provided for in the Treaties[108] and the scope for decision-making left to the discretion of the Member States, and has upheld this despite the restriction under Art. 51 sec. 1 CFREU, which provides for their application 'only

[101] BVerfGE 123, 267 <398>—*Lisbon Treaty*; see already BVerfGE 73, 339 <375>—*Solange II*.

[102] BVerfGE 126, 286 <302 et seq.>—*Honeywell*.

[103] BVerfG, Judgment of 24 April 2013, *Neue Juristische Wochenschrift (NJW)* [2013], 1499; BVerfG, Judgment of 24 April 2013—1 BvR 1215/07—*Counter-terrorism database*, <www.bverfg.de>, n. 91.

[104] BVerfGE 128, 326 <371 and 372>—*Preventive detention II*; 111, 307 <327>—*Görgülü*.

[105] BVerfGE 126, 286 <301>; BVerfGE 129, 78 <97>.

[106] Art. 19 (3) GG reads: 'The basic rights shall also apply to *domestic* artificial persons to the extent that the nature of such rights permits' (emphasis added).

[107] BVerfGE 129, 78 <94 et seq.>—*Le Corbusier furniture*.

[108] Regarding the area of application of EU law see now ECJ, *Åklagaren v ÅkerbergFransson*, Judgment of 26 February 2013, Case C-617/10, n. 19 with further references; cf. D.-E. Khan, in: Geiger/Khan/Kotzur, *EUV/AEUV* (3rd edn., Munich, Beck, 2010), Art. 18 AEUV n. 12 with further references; cf. in this regard, BVerfGE 123, 267 <349 et seq.>; 126, 286 <302>; 129, 78 <98>.

when... implementing Union law'.[109] However, in its decision concerning emission allowances, the Federal Constitutional Court has clarified that the fundamental rights under the Basic Law apply to the full extent in this area and will be subject to its oversight.[110] Only in cases where EU law imposes mandatory requirements leaving no scope for discretion in implementation are solely the fundamental rights of the EU applicable; in this instance, the Federal Constitutional Court has merely a residual competence for ascertaining that essentially the same effective protection of fundamental rights vis-à-vis EU jurisdiction is generally guaranteed in the EU as is required under the Basic Law, while moreover generally guaranteeing the essential content of the respective fundamental rights.[111] In reaction to the expansive jurisprudence of the Court of Justice of the European Union, the Federal Constitutional Court has once again, in its judgment on the German Counter-Terrorism Database Act,[112] confirmed its jurisprudence to the effect that German fundamental rights are fully applicable, not in the area of mandatory EU law, but, in contrast, outside the area of application of EU law and within the scope for discretion left to the Member States by EU law even within its area of application.

In terms of content, the Federal Constitutional Court addresses decisions by the Court of Justice of the European Union above all where the German law implements EU law. In these cases, it ensures that the national courts' duty under Art. 267 sec. 3 TFEU to refer matters for a preliminary ruling (*Vorlagepflicht*) is complied with. It assesses this duty to refer matters for a preliminary ruling according to the provisos of the relevant—expansive—jurisprudence of the Court of Justice of the European Union.[113]

Just as with regard to respecting the competences of national courts, it does not, however, exercise full control here, but leaves the regular courts room for discretion in their judgments. The Federal Constitutional Court overturns judgments by the regular courts as violations of the right to one's lawful judge (second sentence of Art. 101 sec. 1 GG), which is equivalent to a fundamental right, only in cases in which the manner in which the regular courts deal with the European duty of referral for a preliminary ruling is untenable; particularly when regular Courts have ignored the duty of referral as such, have deliberately deviated from the ECJ case-law or have arbitrarily failed to refer an uncertain question of European Law to the ECJ in spite of the incompleteness of European jurisprudence in the matter.[114] This has happened multiple times in practice.[115]

[109] Åkerberg Fransson, Judgment of 26 February 2013, C-617/10, n. 19 et seq. Critical of this e.g. P.M. Huber, 'Auslegung und Anwendung der Charta der Grundrechte', NJW 2011, 2385.

[110] BVerfGE 118, 79 <95 et seq.>—*Emission trading*; confirmed in BVerfG, Judgment of 24 April 2013—1 BvR 1215/07—*Counter-terrorism database*, juris, n. 88.

[111] BVerfGE 73, 339 <387>—*Solange II*; 102, 147 <162 et seq.>—*Regulation of the banana market*; 118, 79 <95>—*Emission trading*.

[112] Judgment of 24 April 2013 (n. 27)—*Counter-terrorism database*, n. 88–91.

[113] Cf. BVerfGE 129, 78 <105 and 106>; BVerfG, Judgment of the Second Senate of 28 January 2014—2 BvR 1561/12—n. 177 et seq.

[114] See BVerfGE 128, 157 <187 et seq.>; 129, 78 <106 and 107>; BVerfG, Judgment of the Second Senate of 28 January 2014—2 BvR 1561/12—n. 179 et seq.; regarding restriction to examination of untenability BVerfGE 126, 286 <317 and 318>—*Honeywell*.

[115] See e.g. BVerfGK 17, 533 <543 et seq.>—*Printers and plotters*.

The Federal Constitutional Court frequently gives regard to the content of EU jurisprudence, even outside the area of application of EU law, where EU law has no binding effect in the case in question. Nonetheless, German law also goes over and above the standard set by EU law (cf. Art. 53 CFREU); for example, workplaces and places of business fall under the protection of the inviolability of the home under Art. 13 sec. 1 GG,[116] whereas this was at least for a time not clear in the jurisprudence of the Court of Justice of the European Union.[117]

2. The influence of the jurisprudence of constitutional courts on the relationship between the European Court of Human Rights and the Court of Justice of the European Union?

Until the accession of the European Union to the ECHR (cf. Art. 6 sec. 1 TEU) is completed—not only in the accession treaties but also in practice—it is difficult to predict the influence of the jurisprudence of the constitutional courts on the relationship between the European courts. After the rejection of the draft accession agreement, the future relationship between the two European Courts is more uncertain than ever.[118]

However, the so-called 'co-respondent mechanism', that is, the mechanism providing for the opinion of the Court of Justice of the European Union before an ECtHR judgment,[119] raises many questions as to its domestic effectiveness if this opinion deviates from the previous jurisprudence of the Court of Justice of the European Union, for example in order to avert a possible conviction of the EU by the European Court of Human Rights. The prior assessment of compatibility with the Convention rights (*Vorabbefassung*) under Art. 3 sec. 6 of the draft accession treaty, on the other hand, is intended to lead to a judgment by the Court of Justice of the European Union which, under Art. 19 sec. 1 TEU, is part of the precedence of application of Union law. However, the means by which such a prior assessment can be brought about under EU law do not yet seem quite clear.

National constitutional courts will have a say in this, just as they have already influenced the interpretation and application of the ECHR in their jurisprudence. Moreover, they have, from the outset, influenced the constitutional traditions common to the Member States of the European Union which, under Art. 6 sec. 3 TEU, will

[116] See BVerfGE 76, 83 <88>; 97, 228 <265>—*short reporting*; 120, 274 <309>—*Acoustic surveillance of residential space*.

[117] Opposing this ECJ, Case 46/87—*Hoechst*, ECR 1989, 2859 n. 18 and 19; but affirming subject to restrictions ECtHR, *Deés v Hungary*, Application No. 2345/06 of 9 November 2010, n. 21; while open ECJ, Case 94/00, *Roquette Frère SA*, Judgment of 22 October 2002, ECR 2002, I-9032, n. 29.

[118] See the 'Draft revised agreement on the accession of the European Union to the Convention for the Protection of Human Rights and Fundamental Freedoms', in: Final report to the CDDH (Steering Committee for Human Rights) of 10 June 2013, Doc. 47+1(2013)008rev2, Appendix 1; see in this regard J. Polakiewicz, 'Der Abkommensentwurf über den Beitritt der Europäischen Union zur Europäischen Menschenrechtskonvention', EuGRZ 2013, 472. But see, recently, Opinion 2/13 of the Court of Justice of the European Union of 18 December 2014, rejecting the accession in the current form of the accession agreement.

[119] Draft revised agreement, ibid., Art. 3, in this regard Polakiewicz, EuGRZ 2013, 472 <476 et seq.>.

continue to be part of EU law as general principles. However, the Charter of Fundamental Rights contains so many and such expansive fundamental rights that these constitutional traditions are likely to decline in relevance.[120] Nevertheless, their significance for the interpretation and application of fundamental European rights—and especially for the Charter—should not be underestimated.

3. The impact of the differences between the jurisprudence of the European Court of Human Rights and the Court of Justice of the European Union on the jurisprudence of the Federal Constitutional Court

The jurisprudence of the European Court of Human Rights has a function of orientation and guidance for the interpretation of the Convention and for its application in the domestic jurisdiction. It may on occasion have to be 'integrated' and reconceived to fit the overall structure of the national legal system.[121] The national context may even require other—national—constitutional institutions or constitutional rights to be used rather than the Convention. Not everything with the same name has the same meaning. But the Convention is an expression of a common European standard, a common foundation of human rights for the whole of Europe. As far as can be seen, the possibility of asserting the primacy of the Constitution and disregarding the Convention in extreme cases has so far stayed within the realms of the theoretical. Ultimately, at any rate, the signatories are obliged to respect the Convention and the decisions of the European Court of Human Rights (see Art. 46 ECHR).[122]

This is also true of the Court of Justice of the European Union as the guardian of the EU treaties (second sentence of Art. 19 sec. 1 TEU). However, this court adjudicates only within the area of application of EU law, and in the area of fundamental rights when implementing the law of the EU (Art. 51 sec. 1 CFREU). The Federal Constitutional Court generally does not exercise its competence for protecting fundamental rights in Germany[123] within the area of mandatory EU law.[124] From a formal point of view, the ECJ's decisions are not binding in national law when it does not implement mandatory European law.

Of course, this is to understate the informal influence exercised by European law. In the event of a divergence from the European Court of Human Rights, the following applies: when implementing EU law, EU law, including European fundamental rights, prevails. In all other respects, the jurisprudence of the European Court of Human Rights has a function of orientation and guidance for the jurisprudence of the Federal Constitutional Court in the application of human rights.

[120] T. Kingreen, in: C. Calliess and M. Ruffert (eds.), *EUV/AEUV* (4th edn., Munich, Beck, 2011), Art. 6 TEU n. 17 and 18, questions entirely the justification for regarding constitutional tradition as a source of law alongside the Charta; R. Streinz, in: C. Calliess and M. Ruffert (eds.), *EUV/AEUV* (2nd edn., Munich, Beck, 2012), Art. 6 TEU n. 35 is more positive.

[121] See BVerfGE 111, 307 <327>; 128, 326 <370 and 371>—*Preventive detention II.*

[122] See in this regard BVerfGE 128, 326 <370 and 371>—*Preventive detention II.*

[123] Cf. BVerfGE 89, 155 (156, 175)—*Treaty of Maastricht.*

[124] BVerfGE 118, 79 <95 et seq.>—*Emission trading*; confirmed in BVerfG, Judgment of 24 April 2013—1 BvR 1215/07—*Counter-terrorism database*, <www.bverfg.de>, n. 88.

18

Judicial Dialogue in a Multilevel Constitutional Network

The Role of the Portuguese Constitutional Court

Ana Maria Guerra Martins and Miguel Prata Roque***

I. Introductory remarks

The purpose of this article is to research whether the Portuguese Constitutional Court establishes a judicial dialogue with other courts, namely international, European, or even foreign constitutional courts. As multilevel constitutionalism implies the existence of a considerable number of common values, principles, and rules that emerge precisely from the interaction between national, international, and European law, the courts—as appliers of the law—surely play a significant role in the disclosure of those values, principles, and rules. Therefore, 'judicial dialogue' should be seen as a powerful tool in a multilevel constitutional system.

First of all, we will focus on the meaning of the expressions 'multilevel constitutionalism', 'transnational constitutionalism', and 'constitutional pluralism', since they are not synonymous. Secondly, we will clarify what 'judicial dialogue' means in a multilevel constitutional system and we will draw attention to the difficulties that it usually faces. Thirdly, we will briefly mention the openness of the Portuguese Constitution to the multilevel constitutional system; and, fourthly, we will concentrate on the Portuguese Constitutional Court and its case law. After explaining the reasons why and how this Court uses European, international and even foreign law, we will analyse some decisions in four particular matters that illustrate rather well the position of the Court.

II. A brief overview on multilevel constitutionalism, transnational constitutionalism, and constitutional pluralism

Although we cannot discuss and develop the concept of multilevel constitutionalism[1] in this study, nor distinguish it from some other closed concepts, such as transnational

* Professor at the Faculty of Law of the University of Lisbon. Judge of the Portuguese Constitutional Court.

** Professor at the Faculty of Law of the University of Lisbon. Ex-Advisor at the Cabinet of Judges of the Portuguese Constitutional Court.

[1] On the concept of multilevel constitutionalism see, among many others, Ingolf Pernice, 'Multilevel Constitutionalism in the European Union' (2002), 27 European Law Review 511–29; Ingolf Pernice and Franz C. Mayer, 'De la Constitution composée de l'Europe' (2000), 6 Revue Trimestrielle de Droit Européen 623–48; Ana Maria Guerra Martins, *A natureza jurídica da revisão do Tratado da União Europeia* (Lex, Lisbon, 2000); Ana Maria Guerra Martins, *Curso de Direito Constitucional da União Europeia* (Almedina,

constitutionalism[2] and constitutional pluralism,[3] we will briefly mention that nowadays there are a significant number of centres of political decision that legislate beyond the State, since some competences, *per definitionem*, overcome the territorial scope of it. Therefore, they can only be effectively implemented at a supranational or a transnational level.[4]

By adopting legal rules that are not only applied to the States but also potentially to the citizens of each State,[5] those political centres dispute the political power of the State. Consequently, one has to accept that the concepts of constitution and constitutionalism are no longer exclusively linked and limited to the State.[6] For those who accept either the multilevel constitutionalism or the constitutional pluralism,[7] the substantive concept of constitution—we are not talking about the formal one—applies not only to the national level but also to the supranational or the transnational levels of political power. Moreover, each level has its legal order, each one establishing a horizontal and non-hierarchical relationship with the others.

As a matter of fact, after World War II, one can clearly distinguish a global legal order, some regional legal orders, and many national legal orders, where, according to some scholars,[8] one can identify public powers—the normative, the executive, and the judicial one—as well as some forms of participation of the citizens. Therefore, the birth of a constitutional global order and a European constitutional order cannot be denied.[9]

The awareness of the difficulties faced by every single State in overcoming the challenges of globalization on its own[10] leads to a 'Global Law' that tends to disclose

Coimbra, 2004); Ana Maria Guerra Martins, *Manual de Direito da União Europeia* (Almedina, Lisbon, 2012); Franz C. Mayer and Mattias Wendel, 'Multilevel Constitutionalism and Constitutional Pluralism—Querelle Allemande or Querelle d'Allemand?', in Matej Avbelj and Jan Komárek, *Constitutional Pluralism in the European Union and Beyond* (Hart, Oxford, 2012) 127–51.

2 For a critical view of the transnational constitutionalism see Marcelo Neves, *Transconstitucionalismo* (WMF Martins Fontes, São Paulo, 2009) 83 *ff.*

3 On the birth, spread, and diffusion of the idea of constitutional pluralism see Matej Avbelj and Jan Komárek (n 1) 2–9.

4 Ana Maria Guerra Martins, *Manual de Direito da União Europeia* (Almedina, Lisbon, 2012) 35.

5 Nisha Mukherjee and Jonathan Krieckhaus, 'Globalization and Human Well-Being' (2012), 33 International Political Science Review, 150–70.

6 Ana Maria Guerra Martins, *Manual de Direito da União Europeia* (Almedina, Lisbon, 2012) 37 *ff.*

7 Ibid., 35 *ff.*

8 Fausto de Quadros, 'Global Law, Plural Constitutionalism and Global Administrative Law', in Javier Robalino-Orellana and Jaime Rodríguez-Arana Muñoz, *Global Administrative Law Towards Lex Administrativa* (CMP Publishing, London, 2010) 329–40; Sabino Cassese, 'La globalisation du Droit', in *Mélanges en honneur de Jean-Paul Costa* (Dalloz, Paris, 2011) 124–5; Carlo Focarelli, 'Costituzionalismo internazionale e costituzionalizzazione della Global Governance: Alla richercha del diritto global' (2011), 42 Politica del Diritto, 201–37.

9 Ana Maria Guerra Martins (n 6) 41 *ff.*

10 Matthias Herdegen, 'Constitutional Rights and the Diminishing State', in *Constitutionalism, Universalism and Democracy—a comparative analysis* (Baden-Baden, Nomos Verlagsgesellschaft, 1999) 183–90; Gonzalo Maestro Buelga, 'Globalización y Constitución débil' (2001), Teoría y Realidad Constitucional n 7, 139; Joseph Stiglitz, *Globalization and its Discontents* (Norton & Company, Inc., New York, 2003) 3–52; Anne-Marie Slaughter, 'Sovereignty and Power in a Networked World Order' (2004), 40 Stanford Journal of International Law 283, 284; Christoph Ohler, *Die Kollisionsordnung des Allgemeinen Verwaltungsrechts—Strukturen des deutschen Internationalen Verwaltungsrechts* (Mohr Siebeck, Tübingen, 2005) 11–12; Daniel Esty, 'Good Governance at the Supranational Scale: Globalizing Administrative Law' (2006), 115 YLJ 1493; Ulrich Beck, *Was ist Globalisierung?: Irrtümer des Globalismus—Antworten auf Globalisierung* (Suhrkamp Taschenbuch Verlag, Frankfurt am Main, 2007); Wolfgang Hoffmann-Riem,

a real 'boomerang effect' (or 'cross-fertilization'[11]) through which the national legal systems start to influence the formation of a worldwide common parameter and end by suffering its subsequent binding effect.[12] This process of normativity consolidation takes advantage of some national consolidated rules and principles, in order to fabricate a truly renewed complex of binding global parameters. In the pursuit of the building of new legal mechanisms able to face the consequences of the freedom of movement, which characterizes contemporary global society, the national constitutional courts have been developing a 'judicial dialogue'.

In fact, the development of international organizations and international rules led to a global legal order, where the normative power is composed, at a first level, by international treaties and international customary law and, at a second level, by rules adopted by international organizations, which apply not only to the States, but also to the civil society inside the States: human beings, undertakings, and non-governmental organizations. At the global legal order, a centralized heart of executive power does not exist, but one can identify numerous international organs that have executive functions. Furthermore, after 1990 a considerable number of international courts had been created with the aim to guarantee and protect international rights and duties. The global legal order has significantly limited the sovereignty of the State.[13]

This 'Global Law' is not only built by formal or classical international forms of negotiation between State authorities, but rather forged by a spider web of private institutions and individuals that cooperate, in a voluntary or in an informal way, to produce binding norms and principles through the adoption of 'codes of conduct' and

'Constitutional court judge's roundtable: comparative constitutionalism in practice' (2005), (Sixth World Congress of the International Association of Constitutional Law, Santiago, Chile, 14–16 January 2004, 4 International Journal of Constitutional Law), 5578; Sabino Cassese, *Il Diritto Globale—Giustizia e Democracia Oltre lo Stato* (Einaudi, Torino, 2009) 5; Jaime Rodrígues-Araña Muñoz, 'El Derecho Administrativo Global: un Derecho principial' (2010), 1 Revista de Derecho Publico de la Universidad de El Salvador, 40; Colaço Antunes, *A Ciência Jurídico-Administrativa* (Almedina, Coimbra, 2012) 29.

[11] Norman Dorsen, Michel Rosenfeld, Amdrás Sajó, and Susanne Baer, *Comparative Constitutionalism—Cases and Materials* (Thomson, Toronto, 2003) *iii*; Romano Orrú, 'Uno sguardo esterno sulla giurisprudenza costituzionale portoghese: "Ius est ars boni et aequi": il Tribunal Constitucional, la comparazione e le sfide della preservazione dello "Stato Costituzionale"', *XXV Anos de Jurisprudência Constitucional Portuguesa* (Coimbra Editora, Coimbra, 2009) 442; Luiz Magno Pinto Bastos (jr) and Cecilia Caballero Lois, 'Beyond the Borders of the National Constitution: Cross-Fertilization and Global Constitutionalism' (2009), in <http://paperroom.ipsa.org/papers/paper_2833.pdf>; Vlad Perju, 'Constitutional Transplants, Borrowing, and Migrations', in M. Rosenfeld and A. Sajo (eds.), *Oxford Handbook of Comparative Law* (Oxford University Press, Oxford, 2012) 1305–9; Christa Rautenbach, 'South Africa: Teaching an "Old Dog" New Tricks? An Empirical Study of the Use of Foreign Precedents by the South African Constitutional Court', Tania Groppi and Marie-Claire Ponthoreau (eds.), *The Use of Foreign Precedents by Constitutional Judges* (Hart Publishing, Oxford, 2013) 185.

[12] Juliane Kokott, 'From Reception and Transplantation to Convergence of Constitutional Models', *Constitutionalism, Universalism and Democracy—a comparative analysis* (Nomos Verlagsgesellschaft, Baden-Baden, 1999) 74; Hannah Buxbaum, 'From Empire to Globalization . . . and Back? A Post-Colonial View of Transjudicialism' (2004), 11 International Journal of Global Legal Studies, 184; Gábor Halmai, 'The Use of Foreign Law in Constitutional Interpretation', in Sujit Choudry (ed), *The Migration of Constitutional Ideas* (Cambridge University Press, Cambridge, 2007) 1328; Romano Orrú (n 11); Christa Rautenbach and Lourens du Plessis, 'In the name of comparative constitutional jurisprudence: The consideration of German precedents by South African Constitutional Court judges' (2013), 8 German Law Review, 1539. Accordingly, Decision n. 104/2006 of the Portuguese Constitutional Court even noticed the existence of a 'common constitutional heritage of the European countries'.

[13] Ana M. Guerra Martins (n 6) 41 *ff.*

'technical patterns'. These norms and principles benefit from national experiences in order to form a real 'global set of normativity'.

Nevertheless, one has to point out that the global legal order has not yet achieved the same degree of perfection and effectiveness as the constitutional national orders and the European Union legal order. As a matter of fact, the sectorial character of its legal rules, as well as the lack of a global government, cannot be underestimated. Even the global judicial power reveals itself as less coherent and effective than the national and the European Union one. To sum up, the national State still plays a determinant role in the global legal order.[14]

Besides the global legal order, some regional legal experiences, such as the European Convention on Human Rights, adopted by the Council of Europe, and, obviously, the European Union, have been playing a significant role in the theorization of multilevel constitutionalism. Honestly speaking, the birth of the idea first emerged in the context of European integration. The European Union does not only possess the public powers already mentioned, but also shares the principles and values that are the foundations of the State, such as the rule of law, democracy, and the protection of fundamental rights. That means the European Union stays a step ahead of other international entities.[15]

However, it is important to underline that multilevel constitutionalism relies upon an intricate web of values, principles, and rules, without necessarily demanding a complete worldwide unification of the applicable binding commands. Accordingly, it is acceptable to maintain specific national regulations, as long as they are able to secure the high standards claimed by a truly global society. In order to achieve this goal, there are two main strategies: *i)* to forecast national 'conflict rules' that allow the courts and the administrative authorities to apply global/European/foreign law;[16] *ii)* to assure that the national 'substantive rules' are duly interpreted in a way that benefits from the experiences of other global/European/foreign legal systems and (specially) from the jurisprudence.[17]

14 Ana Maria Guerra Martins (n 6) 42. 15 Ana Maria Guerra Martins (n 6) 43.

16 Generally, about this possibility, see Gerhard Thallinger, *Grundrechte und extraterritoriale Hoheitsakte—Ausländseinsätze des Bundesheeres und Europäisches Menschenrechtskonvention* (Springer, Wien/New York, 2008); Martin Kment, *Grenzüberschreitendes Verwaltungshandeln—Transnationale Elemente deutschen Verwaltungsrechts* (Mohr Siebeck, Tübingen, 2010); Jörg Menzel, *Internationales Öffentliches Recht: Verfassungs- und Verwaltungsgrenzenrecht in Zeiten offener Staatlichkeit* (Mohr Siebeck, Tübingen, 2011).

17 Vicki C. Jackson and Mark Tushnet, *Comparative Constitutional Law* (Foundation Press, New York, 1999) *v* and 144; David Fontana, 'Refined Comparativism in Constitutional Law' (2001), 49 UCLA Law Review, 557–62; David Fontana, 'The Next Generation of Transnational/Domestic Constitutional Law Scholarship: A Reply to Professor Tushnet' (2004), 38 Loyola L.A. Law Review 449–50; Anna-Verena Bauer and Christoph Mikulaschek, 'Looking Beyond the National Constitution—The Growing Role of Contemporary International Constitutional Law. Reflections on the First Vienna Workshop on International Constitutional Law' (2005), 7 German Law Journal, 1110; Jan Smits, 'Comparative Law and its Influence on National Legal Systems', in Mathias Reimann and Reinhard Zimmermann (eds.), *Oxford Handbook of Comparative Law* (Oxford University Press, Oxford, 2006) 486; Gábor Halmai (n 12) 1329–30; Hélène Lambert, 'Transnational judicial dialogue, harmonization and the Common European Asylum System' (2009), 3 International and Comparative Law Quarterly, 520; Luiz Magno Pinto Bastos (jr) and Cecilia Caballero Lois (n 11), 2; Christopher Whytock, 'Foreign Law in Domestic Courts: Different Uses, Different Implications', in Donald W. Jackson, Michael C. Tolley, and Mary L. Volcansek (eds.), *Globalizing Justice: Critical Perspectives on Transnational Law and Cross-Border Migration of Legal Norms* (State University of New York Press, New York, 2010) 48–9; Daniel Rauch, 'Same Difference: Inter-State Legal Citation and the Supreme Court's Use of Foreign Law' (2011), 1 Journal of Politics & Society, 40.

From a strictly constitutional perspective, one has to acknowledge that if the direct application of European law can be easily conceived, by contrast, the possibility of a direct application of global public law by national courts is hardly acceptable.[18] The prejudice against the full extraterritoriality of public law still grows strong among the major democratic legal systems.[19] That is why 'judicial dialogue' presents itself as a privileged instrument for achieving a worldwide consensus about the fundamental sketches of public law and, especially, of human rights protection.[20]

In the next section, we will clarify the meaning of 'judicial dialogue' and how important it is in a multilevel constitutional system. We will concentrate on the 'judicial dialogue' that benefits constitutional courts, including the Supreme Courts charged with the competence to control the respect of constitutional law by legislative acts.

III. Judicial dialogue in a multilevel constitutional system

When referring to 'judicial dialogue', we must distinguish it according to:

- Its subjects:
  (a) Direct dialogue between courts—not so uncommonly, national constitutional courts maintain formal cooperative proceedings, namely by the establishment of several judicial networks that are charged with activities like the exchange of information, organization of summits and conferences, editing of papers and books about Constitutional Law;[21]

[18] Showing that Constitutional Courts are more willing to enforce international law rather than foreign law, see Andrea Lollini, 'Legal argumentation based on foreign law: an example from case law of South African Constitutional Court' (2007), 3 Utrecht Law Review, 64; Christa Rautenbach (n 11) 187.

[19] Léon Duguit, *Traité de droit constitutionnel*, Tome II (2nd edn, E. de Boccard, Paris, 1923) 47; Michel Fromont (tr) and Ernst Forsthoff, *Traité de Droit Administratif Allemand* (Bruylant, Brussels, 1969) 36–7 and 252; Juan Alfonso Santamaría Pastor, *Fundamentos de Derecho Administrativo* (1st edn, Editorial Centro de Estudios Ramón Areces, Madrid, 1991) 367–8; Martens Bos, 'Droit international public et droit international privé: deux identités bien distinctes', in *Theory of International Law at Threshold of the 21st Century—Essays in honour of Krzyztof Skubiszewski* (Kluwer Law International, The Hague/London/Boston, 1996) 94; Eduardo García de Enterría and Tomás-Ramón Fernández, *Curso de Derecho Administrativo*, I (8th edn, Editorial Civitas, Madrid, 1997) 81; Eberhard Schmidt-Aβmann, 'Strukturen des Europäischen Verwaltungsrechts: Einleitende Problemskizze', in Eberhard Schmidt-Aßmann and Wolfgang Hoffmann-Riem, *Strukturen des Europäischen Verwaltungsrechts* (Nomos Verlagsgesellschaft, Baden-Baden, 1999) 18–19; Luciano Parejo Alfonso, Tomás de la Quadra-Salcedo, and António Estella de Noriega, *Manual de Derecho Administrativo Comunitario* (Editorial Centro de Estudios Ramón Areces, S.A., 2002) 2; Paulo Otero, 'Normas administrativas de conflitos: as situações jurídico-administrativas transnacionais', in *Estudos em Memória do Professor António Marques dos Santos* (Coimbra Editora, Coimbra, 2005) 781–2.

[20] Vicki C. Jackson, Mark Tushnet (n 17) 144.

[21] For instance, the Portuguese Constitutional Court is a regular member of the Ibero-American Conference of Constitutional Justice (see <http://www.cijc.org/Paginas/Default.aspx>), of the European Constitutional Courts Conference (see <http://www.vfgh.gv.at/cms/vfgh-kongress/en/index.html>), of the Constitutional Jurisdictions of Portuguese Official Language Conference and of the Trilateral Conference (that also includes Italy and Spain). On these cooperative proceedings, see Juliane Kokott (n 12) 74; Olivier Dutheillet de Lamothe, 'Constitutional court judge's roundtable: comparative constitutionalism in practice' (2005), (Sixth World Congress of the International Association of Constitutional Law, Santiago, Chile, 14–16 January 2004), 4 International Journal of Constitutional Law, 555–6; Austen Parrish, 'Storm in a teacup: The U.S. Supreme Court's use of foreign law' (2007), 2 University of Illinois L. Rev., 675; Romano Orrú (n 11) 467–9; When-Chen Chang and David Law, 'The limits of global judicial dialogue' (2011), 68 Washington Law Review, 535–8; Anne Meutwese and Marnix Snel, 'Constitutional Dialgogue: An Overview' (2013), 9 Utrecht Law Review, 131.

(b) Mediated dialogue between courts—this kind of '*judicial dialogue*' expresses itself through the analysis and reception of other foreign courts' jurisprudence. This is not a direct dialogue because it does not demand a formal '*judiciary assistance*', namely by the request and delivery of authenticated copies of the foreign constitutional decisions. On the contrary, the mere enquiry of public databases of other Constitutional Courts enables its taking into account;[22]
(c) Voluntary dialogue through the reception of legal scholarship—it is rather common to find plenteous quotations of foreign authors along the decisions of the Constitutional Courts.[23]

- Its object:
  (a) Written legal texts;[24]
  (b) Jurisprudence;[25]
  (c) Legal scholarship.[26]
- Its source:
  (a) European;
  (b) International;[27]

[22] Thereby, see Alec Stone, *The Birth of Judicial Politics in France—The Constitutional Council in Comparative Perspective* (Oxford University Press, Oxford, 1992) 7–8; Juliane Kokott (n 12) 74; Neil Walker, 'The migrations of constitutional ideas and the migration of the constitutional idea: the EU case' (2005), EUI Working Paper Law nº 04, 3; Juan Colombo Campell, 'Constitutional court judge's roundtable: comparative constitutionalism in practice' (2005), (Sixth World Congress of the International Association of Constitutional Law, Santiago, Chile, 14–16 January 2004), 4 International Journal of Constitutional Law, 544; Dutheillet de Lamothe (n 21) 553–5; Hélène Lambert (n 17) 520; Romano Orrú (n 11) 457–8 and 464–5; Pinto Bastos (Jr)/Cecília Lois (n 11) 5; Teresa Violante, 'A adjudicação constitucional e o Direito Comparado', *Teoria da Argumentação e Neo-Constitucionalismo—Um Conjunto de Perspectivas* (Almedina, Coimbra, 2011) 338; David Law and Wen-Chen Chang (n 21) 526; Anne Meutwese and Marnix Snel (n 21) 130–1.

[23] Thus, see Iddo Porat, 'The use of foreign law in Israeli constitutional adjudication' (2011), in <http://www.clb.ac.il/uploads/Porat%20-%20Foreign%20Law%20-%20May%204.pdf>, Tel Aviv University, 2011, 3; Mila Verseeg and David Law, 'The Evolution and Ideology of Global Constitutionalism' (2011), 99 California Law Review, 1166–7; Anne Meutwese and Marnix Snel (n 21), 123–4. As regards Portuguese Constitutional Court, see Romano Orrú (n 12) 462.

[24] Nevertheless, this is crucial to bear in mind that all foreign written texts must be understood as a part of a historic legislative (or even customary) process of consolidation of a set of binding rules and principles. Accordingly, it is also necessary to analyse the reasoning that was involved in the adoption of the foreign constitutional rules. Therefore, see José de Sousa e Brito, 'The ways of public reason—Comparative Constitutional Law and pragmatics' (1996), International Journal for the Semiotics of Law, 26, 175; Bruce Ackerman, 'The Rise of World Constitutionalism' (1977), 83 Virginia Law Review, 794; Sujit Choudry, 'The Lochner era and comparative constitutionalism' (2004), 1 International Journal of Constitutional Law, 4; Vicki C. Jackson, 'Comparative constitutional federalism and transnational judicial discourse' (2004), 1 International Journal of Constitutional Law, 93; Wolfgang Hoffmann-Riem (n 10) 559; Daniel Rauch (n 17) 56–8; Vlad Perju (n 11) 1309–10.

[25] Dutheillet de Lamothe (n 21) 553–5.

[26] Some authors show that there is a constant dialogue between the academics and the jurisprudence of the Portuguese Constitutional Court that mutually influence each other. Thereby, see Romano Orrú (n 11) 449; Teresa Violante (n 22) 353. In general, speaking about the influence of an interchange of legal scholarship, see Alec Stone (n 22) 7–8; Juliane Kokott (n 12) 74–5 and 77; Ulrich Karpen, 'Teaching Constitutional Law', *Constitutionalism, Universalism and Democracy—a comparative analysis* (Nomos Verlagsgesellschaft, Baden-Baden, 1999) 341 and 343; David Fontana (2004) (n 17) 445–83; Luiz Magno Pinto Bastos (jr) and Cecilia Caballero Lois (n 11) 9–10.

[27] For a severe criticism of the use of these international sources as a national constitutional parameter, see Roger Alford, 'Misusing International Sources to Interpret the Constitution' (2004), American Journal

(c) Transnational/Global;[28]
(d) Foreign.[29]

The continuous growth of an effective 'Global Community of Public Law' reinforces the urge for a permanent 'judicial dialogue' among the judiciary authorities of each country.[30] This dialogue is not doomed to any institutional or formal proceedings. By contrast, it is founded on an inorganic and voluntary quest for knowledge of global, international, European and foreign laws, jurisprudence, and legal scholarship. The increment of technological means of distance communication[31] and the use of English language[32] as a worldwide common language have strengthened the ability for national courts, lawyers, and academic communities to accede to external sources of constitutional normativity.

The main goal of 'judicial dialogue' is to achieve an effective and transparent 'benchmarking' of several potential legal solutions that apply on international/European/foreign ground.[33]

In comparative terms, constitutional academics tend to distinguish among the international/European/foreign-friendly jurisdictions and the sceptical ones. It is usual to identify as friendly jurisdictions the ones pertaining to common law and,

of International Law, 57, 57–8 and 67–9; Robert Delahunty and John Yoo, 'Against Foreign Law' (2005), 1 Harvard Journal of Law & Public Policy, 313–16.

[28] Sujit Choudry (n 24) 4; Vicki C. Jackson (n 24) 91–2; Gábor Halmai (n 12) 1328–9; Austen Parrish (n 21) 662–3.

[29] Against the use of foreign law, see, among many others, Richard Posner, 'No thanks, we already have our own laws: The Court should never view a foreign legal decision as a precedent in any way' (2004), Legal Affairs, July/August, 40–2; Robert Delahunty and John Yoo (n 27) 291–330.

[30] Thereby, see François Venter, *Constitutional Comparision—Japan, Germany, Canada & South Africa as Constitutional States* (Kluwer Law International, Lansdowne, 2000) 256; Norman Dorsen/Michel Rosenfeld/Amdrás Sajó/Susanne Baer (n 11) *iii*; Teresa Violante (n 22) 340–1.

[31] Juliane Kokott (n 12) 74; Gábor Halmai (n 12) 1328–9; Ran Hirschl, 'The Rise of Comparative Constitutional Law: Thoughts on substance and method' (2008), Indian Journal of Constitutional Law, 11; Raza Husain and Hélène Lambert, 'The British judiciary and the search for reciprocal relations with its continental partners', in Guy Goodwin-Gill and Hélène Lambert (eds.), *The Limits of Transnational Law* (Cambridge University Press, Cambridge, 2010) 142; When-Chen Chang and David Law (n 21) 526; David Law and Mila Versteeg (n 23) 1183; Vlad Perju (n 11) 1305.

[32] Hélène Lambert (n 17) 531; Paul Tiedemann, 'The use of foreign asylum jurisprudence in the German administrative courts', in Guy Goodwin-Gill and Hélène Lambert (eds.), *The Limits of Transnational Law* (Cambridge University Press, Cambridge, 2010) 67; Raza Husain and Hélène Lambert (n 31) 141; David Law and Mila Versteeg (n 23) 1183.

[33] Not far from this guidance, Konrad Zweigert, 'Der Einfluß des Europäischen Gemeinschaftsrecht auf die Rechtsordnung der Mitgliedstaaten' (1964), 28 Rabels Z, 611 expressed a real idyllic thought according to which this comparative method should allow to identify the better solution to give to a specific case: 'The general principle of law is generally the one that emerges as the best solution after a critical analysis of the solutions obtain after a journey along some comparative horizons'. About the comparative method as a modern trace of a global and networked public system, see also Albrecht Weber, 'Sviluppi nel Diritto Amministrativo Europeo' (1998), 3–4 Revue Iinternational de Droit Public, 592; Vicki C. Jackson and Mark Tushnet (n 17) 144; Rudolph Streinz, 'Der Einfluß des Europäische Verwaltungsrechts auf das Verwaltungrecht der Mitgliedstaaten', in Michael Schweitzer (ed), *Europäisches Verwaltungsrecht* (Österreichischen Akademie der Wissenschaften, Wien, 1991) 244; Júrgen Schwarze, 'Enlargement, the European Constitution and Administrative Law' (2004), 53 International Comparative Law Quarterly, 970; Claus-Dieter Classen, 'Die entwicklung eines Internationalen Verwaltungsrecht als aufgabe der rechtswissenschaft' (2008), 67 Veröffentlichungen der Vereinigung der Deutschen Staatsrechtslehrer, 370–3; Sam Halabi, 'Constitutional Borrowing as Jurisprudential and Political Doctrine in Shri DK Basu v. State of West Bengal' (2013), 3 Notre Dame Journal of International & Comparative Law, 8–12.

specially, countries that take (or took) part in the Commonwealth: Australia, Canada, India, Israel, New Zealand, South Africa, and the United Kingdom. Well known for their nationalist positions are the US, French, and German constitutional courts. They are very restrictive in their acceptance of foreign law (and jurisprudence) as a direct source of their judicial reasoning. That does not mean that they don't consider it.[34] By contrast, they only give notice of its existence, with the goal of reassuring the full applicability of national binding rules and principles. There is a well-known statement of Chief Justice Marshall, of the US Supreme Court, according to which:

> [t]he jurisdiction of the nation within its own territory is necessarily exclusive and absolute. It is susceptible of no limitation not imposed by it. Any restriction upon it deriving validity from an external source would imply a diminution of its sovereignty to the extent of the restriction and an investment of that sovereignty to the same extent in that power which could impose such restriction.[35]

In spite of a progressive awareness about the need to ponder foreign law (its jurisprudence and legal scholarship),[36] the US courts persist in disregarding the possibility of applying it instead of their national laws.

This bias against the enforcement of international/European/foreign law is perfectly compatible with an undisputed 'homeward trend' that runs all major contemporary legal systems.[37, 38] All across the world, each national court is tempted to put its own laws ahead.

[34] Actually, the 'principle of legal certainty' claims a certain foreseeability of the judicial decision to be taken. Even if a national legal system does not rely upon a precedent method, that urge for security may demand that a Constitutional Court considers foreign laws (including jurisprudence and doctrine) in order to assure a compatibility between its decisions and previous other decisions taken by foreign courts on the same matter. Thereby, see Paul Tiedemann (n 32) 64.

[35] *The Schooner Exchange v McFaddon*, of 2 March, 1812 (see 11 U.S. 136, available at <http://supreme.justia.com/cases/federal/us/11/116/case.html>). For an approach to this decision, see E. N. Kleffens, 'Sovereignty in International Law' (1953), Recueil des Cours de l'Academie de Droit International, 82, (I), 86; Lee M. Caplan, 'State immunity, human rights, and "jus cogens": A critique of the normative hierarchy theory' (2003), 87 American Journal of International Law, 745–7; Lewis S. Yelin, 'Head of State immunity as sole executive lawmaking' (2011), 44 Vanderbilt Journal of International Law, 931–4.

[36] In that sense, Chief Justice William Rehnquist, of the US Supreme Court even came to predict this evolution: 'The United States courts, and legal scholarship in our country generally, have been somewhat laggard in relying on comparative law and decisions of other countries. But I predict that with so many thriving constitutional courts in the world today...that approach will be changed in the near future' *in* 'Constitutional Courts—Comparative Remarks' (1989), *Germany and Its Basic Law: Past, Present and Future—A German-American Symposium* (Nomos Verlagsgesellschaft, Baden-Baden, 1993) 413.

[37] As a matter of fact, the administrative international law legal scholarship has underlined a notorious homeward trend from the national courts that is strengthened by the difficulty of access to foreign law and by the lack of formation in International Law and Comparative Law. Thus, see Rudolph Heiz, *Das fremde öffentliche Recht im internationalen Kollisionsrecht—der Einfluß der Public Policy auf ausländisches Straf-, Steuer, Devisen-, Konfiskations- und Enteignungsrecht* (Polygraphischer Verlag, Zürich, 1960) 115 and 131; Christine Breining-Kaufmann, 'Internationales Verwaltungsrecht' (2006), 125 Zeitschrift für Schweizerisches Recht, 7–73, 30; Martin Kment (n 16) 139–40. Similarly, reporting to Private International Law, see Marques dos Santos, *As normas de aplicação imediata no Direito Internacional Privado—Esboço de uma teoria geral*, I Vol. (Almedina, Coimbra, 1991) 44 and 62–4; Luís de Lima Pinheiro, 'The "Denationalization of Transnational Relationships"—Regulation of transnational relationships by Public International Law, European Community Law and Transnational Law', *Estudos de Direito Internacional Privado—Direito de Conflitos, Competência Internacional e Reconhecimento de Decisões Estrangeiras* (Almedina, Coimbra, 2006) 190.

[38] Some time ago, now overtaken, when globalization was still in an embryonic state, even a territorialist such as Vogel forecast that the principle of territoriality is also bound to a specific historical circumstance

Nevertheless, the acceptance of truly complex global binding rules and principles—'Global Law'—has currently increased. This comprehends the core of the common constitutional parameters that bind every State and political community, independently of their national cultural and anthropological specificities.[39]

The role of the constitutional courts in this work-in-progress is rather crucial because they tend to be much more eager to learn from foreign experiences and to interpret national binding rules in a more flexible way.

The 'judicial dialogue' also raises some problematic issues. It may lead the national legal systems to a dangerous 'race-to-the-bottom' (or 'Delaware effect'). After a 'benchmarking' of several national legal solutions, each country may be tempted to reduce its level of public protection of human rights, in order to render into a competition with countries that adopt much more flexible regimes. Currently, we may identify a visible trend to reduce the scope of protection of the binding rules of the countries that are most committed to human rights and to democratic proceedings of public decision.

The 'Global Law', which started as a privileged tool to export human rights and legal protection all over the world, now risks becoming an instrument that will reduce living conditions among the major world democratic regimes. In order to assure an adequate 'medium level of human rights protection', one must stress that 'judicial dialogue' does not allow national courts to degrade—more than allowed by the proportionality and other constitutional principles—the scope of protection of their own national constitutions, unless there are democratic proceedings that legitimate that external influence. While those external sources of normativity do not assure democratic approval proceedings,[40] they cannot truly attempt a removal of the national constitutional binding rules. Otherwise, the democratic force of Constitutional Law would be completely shattered.

and its acknowledgment, as a core principle of the contemporary law—specially of the modern Administrative and Tax Law—should lastly rely upon the ascertainment if those founding conditions still persist today' (see Klaus Vogel, *Der räumliche Anwendungbereich der Verwaltungsrechtsnorm—Eine Untersuchung über die Grundfragen des sog. Internationalen Verwaltungs- und Steuerrechts* (Alfred Metzner Verlag, Frankfurt Am Main/Berlin, 1965) 59).

[39] Thus, reporting the formation of a concept of 'universal commonly recognized values', see Ronaldo Quadri, 'La tutela penale degli interessi stranieri e internazionali', in *Scritti Giuridici*, III (Diritto delle comunità europee—Diritto Pubblico—Teoria Generale del Diritto) (Giuffrè Editore, Milano, 1988); Juan Jose Diez Sanchez, *El Derecho Penal Internacional (Ambito espacial de la Ley Penal)* (Editorial Colex, Madrid, 1990) 174; Vicki C. Jackson (n 24) 91–2; Gábor Halmai (n 12) 1329; Austen Parrish (n 21) 642–4; Paulo Otero, *Instituições Políticas e Constitucionais*, Volume I (Almedina, Coimbra, 2007) 488; Ran Hirschl (n 31) 12; Georg Nolte, 'Das Verfassungsrecht vor den Herausforderungen der Globalisierung' (2008), 67 Veröffentlichungen der Vereinigung der Deutschen Staatsrechtslehrer, 137–9; Pedro Caeiro, *Fundamento, Conteúdo e Limites da Jurisdição Penal do Estado* (Coimbra Editora, Coimbra, 2010) 242–6; David Law and When-Chen Chang (n 21) 525–6; John Bell, 'The Relevance of Foreign Examples to Legal Development' (2011), 21 Duke Journal of Comparative & International Law, 458–9; Maria José Rangel de Mesquita, *Os Direitos Fundamentais dos Estrangeiros na Ordem Jurídica Portuguesa* (Almedina, Coimbra, 2013) 182–91; Sam Halabi (n 33) 13–15. Reporting that even the American founding fathers have included in the Declaration of Independence the need for 'a decent respect to the opinions of Mankind', see Ruth Bader Ginsburg, 'A Decent Respect to the Opinions of [Human]kind: The Value of Comparative Perspective in Constitutional Adjudication' (2005), 3 Cambridge Law Journal, 578–9.

[40] For a critical overview about the democracy of the procedures within international and transnational structures, see A. Frowein, 'Constitutionalism in the Face of the Changing Nation State', *Constitutionalism, Universalism and Democracy—a comparative analysis* (Nomos Verlagsgesellschaft, Baden-Baden, 1999) 60–2 and 69–70.

In fact, it is rather uncommon to ascertain national courts' decisions—concerning constitutional matters—that assume a direct enforcement of global, international, European, or foreign laws. International parameters mostly coincide with national law, and constitutional regimes tend to be followed by the written legal texts. That means international conventions do not usually add any significant normative protection to the one that comes from the national legal system. The Portuguese Constitutional Court provides an example of a court that usually refuses to evaluate an alleged breach of international law, stating that it would be unnecessary or even superfluous (see Decisions n. 352/1998, n. 12/2005, n. 682/2006, and n. 185/2010).[41]

As a matter of fact, the Portuguese Constitutional Court has not yet enforced any binding parameter stemming from those sources of Global Law. On the contrary, the Court has adopted a traditional and cautious approach.

IV. The openness of the Portuguese constitutional order to the multilevel constitutionalism

Before concentrating our attention on the dialogue between the Portuguese Constitutional Court and other international/European/foreign courts, it is important to underline that the Constitution of the Portuguese Republic (CPR) of 1976,[42] last revised in 2005,[43] deals with multilevel constitutionalism, since it is deeply committed to a 'friendship' towards international law in general and, particularly, to European Union law.

Above all, the Portuguese constitutional 'friendship' with multilevel constitutionalism in general arises from Article 7 CPR, concerning international relations. This provision implicitly contains a principle of respect for international law,[44] with a special reference to the human rights and the rights of the peoples, incorporating into the Constitution[45] some principles that are also contained in the Charter of the United Nations, such as respect for human rights.

Article 7(2) CPR contains the guidelines of Portuguese external policy, some of which hold notably less relevance nowadays.[46] Article 7(4) CPR stresses, in accordance with our history, that 'Portugal shall maintain privileged ties of friendship and cooperation with Portuguese-speaking countries'.

[41] All decisions of the Portuguese Constitutional Court that are mentioned during this paper may be found, in Portuguese, at <http://www.tribunalconstitucional.pt/tc/acordaos/>. Summaries of some of them in English are also available at the same website.

[42] An English version of the Constitution is available at <http://www.tribunalconstitucional.pt/tc/conteudo/files/constituicaoingles.pdf>.

[43] Constitutional Law No 1/2005 is available at <http://debates.parlamento.pt/catalog.aspx?cid=r3.dar_s2rc>.

[44] See J. J. Gomes Canotilho and Vital Moreira, *Constituição da República Portuguesa, Anotada*, vol. I (4th edn., Coimbra Editora, Coimbra, 2007) 240.

[45] Jorge Miranda, 'Commentary to Article 7', in J. Miranda and R. Medeiros, *Constituição Portuguesa Anotada*, vol. I (2nd edn., Coimbra Editora, Coimbra, 2010) 152.

[46] Jorge Miranda (n 45) 154.

Moreover, Article 7(5) and (6) CPR comprises a constitutional clause of engagement with the construction and deepening of European integration.[47] These two paragraphs shall be read together with Article 8(4) CPR, which will be mentioned below.

Paragraph (5) of Article 7 CPR reads:

> Portugal shall make every effort to reinforce the European identity and to strengthen the European states' actions in favour of democracy, peace, economic progress and justice in the relations between peoples.

Article 7(6) explicitly admits:

> Subject to reciprocity and to respect for the fundamental principles of a democratic state based on the rule of law and for the principle of subsidiarity, and with a view to the achievement of the economic, social and territorial cohesion of an area of freedom, security and justice and the definition and implementation of a common external, security and defence policy, Portugal may enter into agreements for the exercise jointly, in cooperation or by the Union's institutions, of the powers needed to construct and deepen the European Union.

Finally, Article 7(7) CPR constitutes a general clause of acceptance of the Rome Statute into the Portuguese constitutional order,[48] including the jurisdiction of the International Criminal Court. This provision must be interpreted in the context of the protection of human rights and the rights of the peoples. It was added by the constitutional revision of 2001, in order to overcome the constitutional difficulties of ratification of the Rome Statute.[49]

Furthermore, Article 16(1) CPR on the scope and the interpretation of fundamental rights states that 'the fundamental rights enshrined in the Constitution shall not exclude any others set out in applicable international laws and legal rules'. This clause expresses the openness of the Constitution to the international and European human rights law. To put it in other words, Article 16(1) CPR foresees an 'open clause' in matters of fundamental rights, meaning that our Constitution receives all human rights contained in other sources of law (including in international law), as if they were part of the written Portuguese Constitution. However, one should draw attention to the fact that since the constitutional catalogue of fundamental rights is rather broad, in practical terms; this provision does not apply very often.

Additionally, the Portuguese Constitution rules the reception and position of international law into the Portuguese legal order and the reception and supremacy of European Union law over the Portuguese legal order.

As regards international customary law, in accordance with Article 8(1) CPR, 'the rules and principles of general or common international law shall form an integral part of Portuguese law'. This includes human rights resulting from universal international customary law, such as the equal dignity of every person, the right to life, the right to the integrity of the person, the prohibition of torture and inhuman or degrading

[47] J. J. Gomes Canotilho and Vital Moreira (n 44) 243; Paulo Otero, *Direito Constitucional Português*, vol. I (Almedina, Coimbra, 2010) 132.

[48] J. J. Gomes Canotilho and Vital Moreira (n 44) 248.

[49] Jorge Miranda (n 45) 157.

treatment or punishment, the prohibition of slavery and forced labour, the right to self-determination of the peoples, freedom of speech, freedom of thought, conscience and religion, etc.

A significant number of Portuguese scholars[50] argue that these rules and principles are directly binding on the Portuguese state and, consequently, they do not need any internal specific procedure of reception.

Furthermore, Article 16(2) CPR confers a supra-constitutional value to the Universal Declaration of Human Rights (UDHR), given that 'the provisions of this Constitution and of laws concerning fundamental rights shall be interpreted and construed in accordance with the Universal Declaration of Human Rights'. In other words, Article 16(2) CPR expressly guarantees that all constitutional principles and norms shall be interpreted and applied in the light of the UDHR.

As for the position of the human rights that derive from the rules and principles of general or common international law within the hierarchy of the Portuguese sources of law, Article 8(1) of the Constitution just states that they are considered 'an integral part of Portuguese law', without responding to the question of whether they prevail or not over national law, including the Constitution. Therefore, scholars are divided concerning the solution to this problem. On the one hand, there are some scholars who distinguish between the human rights integrated in the peremptory norms of international law (*jus cogens*)[51] and the human rights that merely belong to international customary law, considering that only the first prevail over national law, including constitutional law.[52] The rules and principles of general or common international law, which cannot be assessed as *jus cogens*, only prevail over national legislative acts, but they shall respect the constitutional law.[53] On the other hand, there are also some supporters of the complete supremacy of these rules and principles over national law, including constitutional law.[54]

As regards international covenants, Article 8(2) CPR states that all international conventions are binding on the Portuguese Republic, when duly ratified[55] or signed[56] by the Head of State, as long as they remain in force at the international level. The ratification or the signature of the Head of State depends on the documents being

[50] Paulo Otero, 'A Declaração Universal dos Direitos do Homem e Constituição: a inconstitucionalidade de normas constitucionais?' (1990), O Direito 122/3, 613; André Gonçalves Pereira and Fausto de Quadros, *Manual de Direito Internacional Público* (Almedina, Coimbra, 2005) 283–4; Ana Maria Guerra Martins, *Direito Internacional dos Direitos Humanos* (Almedina, Coimbra, 2006) 110 *ff*; J. J. Gomes Canotilho and Vital Moreira (n 44) 256; Jorge Miranda, *Curso de Direito Internacional Público* (4th edn, Principia, Cascais, 2009) 152–3.

[51] According to Articles 53 and 64 of the Vienna Convention on the Law of Treaties, some provisions of the universal international human rights law are qualified as peremptory norms of international law ('*jus cogens*'), for instance, the prohibition of torture, the prohibition of genocide, the right to self-determination. They prevail over every single rule and they do not allow their removal through any kind of corrective interpretation. On the problem of the relationship between *jus cogens* and human rights in general, see Olivier De Schutter, *International Human Rights Law* (Cambridge University Press, Cambridge, 2010) 64–89; Javaid Rehman, *International Human Rights Law*, 2nd edn. (Harlow, Pearson Education, 2010) 25–6; D. Moeckli, S. Shah, and S. Sivakumaran, *International Human Rights Law* (Oxford University Press, Oxford, 2010) 113–14.

[52] Jorge Miranda (n 50) 152. [53] Jorge Miranda (n 50) 153.

[54] Gomes Canotilho and Vital Moreira (n 44) 261.

[55] Article 135(b) CPR. [56] Article 134(b) CPR.

deemed as 'treaties' or 'agreements'. In order to prevent eventual conflicts with constitutional law, Article 278(1) CPR provides an abstract a priori control:

> [t]he President of the Republic may ask the Constitutional Court to conduct a prior review of the constitutionality of any rule laid down by an international treaty that is submitted to him for ratification . . . or by any international agreement, the decree passing which is sent to him for signature.

However, the fact is that conflicts can emerge and Article 8(2) CPR does not give any clear solution to this problem. As a consequence, Portuguese academics and judicial authorities have been expressing different points of view. The mainstream opinion supports the position that international sources of law—including European conventions on human rights—prevail over ordinary law but they do not prevail over the Constitution.[57] By contrast, they must respect it, mainly basing this opinion on the following arguments:

- Article 204 CPR concerning compliance with the Constitution reads: '[i]n matters that are brought to trial, the courts shall not apply rules that contravene the provisions of this Constitution or the principles enshrined therein'. As the provision does not distinguish between internal sources of law and international ones, this school considers that the courts shall not apply any source, including international sources, that contravene the Constitution;
- Article 277 CPR allows the Portuguese Constitutional Court to control the compatibility of any rule—including international rules—with the principles and rules guaranteed by Fundamental Law;
- Article 278 CPR permits an abstract preventive control of constitutionality.

In spite of the strength of these arguments, there are also some scholars that maintain the primacy of the international conventions over the Constitution in matters concerning human rights, due to the friendship of the Portuguese Constitution towards international law, mainly expressed in Article 7,[58] mentioned earlier.

The reception of EU law and its supremacy over Portuguese legal order are ruled by Article 8(3) and (4) CPR.

Regarding Article 8(3) CPR 'rules issued by the competent bodies of international organizations to which Portugal belongs shall come directly into force in Portuguese internal law, on condition that this is laid down in the respective constituent treaties'. This provision was introduced by the constitutional revision of 1982, due to the Portuguese accession to the European Communities.[59] Its purpose was to automatically receive EU secondary law and to integrate it into the national legal order without any procedure of reception.[60] However, due to the wording of the provision—'rules issued by the competent bodies of international organizations'—it can also be applied outside the European Union law context.[61] In fact, the evolution of international law in

[57] Gomes Canotilho and Vital Moreira (n 44) 261.

[58] Fausto de Quadros, *A protecção da propriedade privada pelo Direito Internacional* (Almedina, Coimbra, 1998) 531.

[59] The Portuguese Republic has been a member of the EU since 1 January 1986.

[60] Gomes Canotilho and Vital Moreira (n 44) 263.

[61] Gomes Canotilho and Vital Moreira (n 44) 263.

the last two decades has led to the emergence of a normative power before the states within some international organizations. According to Article 8(3) CPR, provided they have this power, their mandatory rules come directly into force in the Portuguese legal order.

Article 8(4) of the CPR stipulates, 'the provisions of the treaties that govern the European Union and the rules issued by its institutions in the exercise of their respective responsibilities shall apply in Portuguese internal law in accordance with Union law and with respect for the fundamental principles of a democratic state based on the rule of law'. Historically, this paragraph was introduced in the Constitution by the revision of 2004, with the aim of ensuring the compatibility of Portuguese constitutional law with the new Treaty establishing a Constitution for Europe, which provided in Article I 6 the principle that EU law prevails over the law of Member States. In spite of the failure of this Treaty, due to the negative *referenda* in France and in the Netherlands, the Portuguese Constitutional provision remains in force and shall be interpreted and applied according to the Treaty of Lisbon. That means 'the Treaties and the law adopted by the Union on the basis of the Treaties have primacy over the law of Member States, under the conditions [well settled by the case law of the Court of Justice of the European Union (CJEU)]', as the Declaration concerning primacy recalls.

On the one hand, the solution of the conflicts between EU law and national law results from a constituent decision indirectly taken by the Portuguese citizens, through their representatives, and, on the other hand, the Constitution recognizes that the solution of the conflicts between primary and secondary EU law adopted by European institutions within their competencies belongs to EU law. Therefore, it prevails over every single internal rule, including constitutional norms.[62] However, the supremacy of EU law over domestic law does not lead to the invalidity of the national rule, but only to its inapplicability.[63] Actually, there is no replacement mechanism of the national rule by the EU law rule.

The introduction of this paragraph into Article 8 CPR has been strongly criticized by the most nationalist school of academics,[64] given that it represents a loss of sovereignty. In our opinion,[65] EU law prevails over the national legal order, including the Constitution, except when it violates the fundamental principles of a democratic state based on the rule of law. The question of which jurisdiction is competent to declare whether such a violation exists or not is disputable. On the one hand, the Constitutional Court (and the national courts in general) is the guardian of the principles of a democratic state based on the rule of law according to Portuguese law. On the other hand, the CJEU is the guardian of EU law. Taking into account the fact that no judicial hierarchy exists between the national courts and the European courts, but that their relationship is governed by a system of cooperation, the solution for this issue must be based on the

62 Paulo Otero (n 47) 133; J. J. Gomes Canotilho and Vital Moreira (n 44) 265.

63 Paulo Otero (n 47) 133–4; J. J. Gomes Canotilho and Vital Moreira (n 44) 266.

64 Jorge Miranda, 'Commentary to Article 8', in J. Miranda and R. Medeiros, *Constituição Portuguesa Anotada*, vol. I (2nd edn, Coimbra Editora, Coimbra, 2010b) 172 *ff.*

65 Ana Maria Guerra Martins (n 6) 511; Ana Maria Guerra Martins and Miguel Prata Roque, 'Chapter 18—Universality and Binding Effect of Human Rights from a Portuguese Perspective', in Rainer Arnold, *The Universalism of Human Rights* (Springer, Dordrecht, 2013) 313.

principle of primacy of EU law over domestic law.[66] According to this principle, EU law cannot be declared unconstitutional and the national courts shall not apply domestic law that contravenes EU law. In cases where doubt remains, it may or shall make a preliminary reference to the CJEU, under the terms of Article 267 of the Treaty on the Functioning of the European Union (TFEU) (including the Constitutional Court).

V. The Portuguese Constitutional Court and the 'judicial dialogue'

Taking into consideration how the Portuguese Constitution deals with multilevel constitutionalism, the Portuguese legal system (and scholars, as well as judges) could be strongly committed to a sincere and natural openness to external sources of normativity. Other reasons could also lead to this conclusion: Portuguese history is highly influenced by multiple connections with other people,[67] and the Portuguese constitutional review system encloses its own originality, rarely seen in other national legal regimes. Since 1989, the law that regulates the proceedings before the Constitutional Court allows the judicial review of decisions rejecting the application of a rule appearing in a legislative act on the grounds that it contradicts an international convention, or that applies it contrary to what has been previously decided on the matter by the Constitutional Court (see article 70(1)(*i*), of the Constitutional Court Law). That means a Portuguese legislative rule may be invalidated by the Court when it disrespects an international convention that has already entered into force in Portugal.[68] Accordingly, international law operates as a real 'parametric tool'.

Notwithstanding, the Portuguese Constitutional Court has never afforded to neglect a direct enforcement of foreign law as an autonomous constitutional parameter. By contrast, international law has been often used, for constitutional review purposes, as a rhetoric 'reinforcement tool' or as an 'interpretative tool' through which the constitutional judges strengthen their final decisions by showing that they have rendered extensive research work about the matter that they have in hand.[69] The usage of international law

[66] J. J. Gomes Canotilho and Vital Moreira (n 44) 270.

[67] Numerous foreign civilizations and tribes that have settled themselves in the southern European territory from Ancient Times to the Middle Ages, the Portuguese Maritime Discoveries, the French Invasion, during the first decades of the 19th century, and the military help of the British Empire, the adhesion to the European Union, in 1986, and the adoption of the Euro currency in 2000 are some examples of Portuguese cosmopolitanism.

[68] On the contrary, the French Constitutional Court (*'Conseil Constitutionnel'*) has been seriously reluctant to accept its jurisdiction over the breaches of international conventions by national legal acts. For criticism, see Mauro Cappelletti and William Cohen, *Comparative Constitutional Law—Cases and Materials* (Bobbs-Merrill, Indianapolis, 1979) 152–5.

[69] Thereby, Alec Stone (n 22) 10–11; Vicki C. Jackson and Mark Tushnet (n 17) 168–9; Christian Starck, 'The Legitimacy of Constitutional Adjudication and Democracy', in *Constitutionalism, Universalism and Democracy—a comparative analysis* (Nomos Verlagsgesellschaft, Baden-Baden, 1999) 21; Francois Venter (n 30) 17–19; Vicki C. Jackson (n 24) 92–3; Anna-Verena Bauer and Christoph Mikulaschek (n 17) 1118–19; Gábor Halmai (n 12) 1333; Stephen Sedley, 'Constitutional court judge's roundtable: comparative constitutionalism in practice' (2005) (Sixth World Congress of the International Association of Constitutional Law, Santiago, Chile, 14–16 January 2004), in 4 International Journal of Constitutional Law, 570; Austen Parrish (n 21) 674; Christopher Whytock (n 17) 49; Daniel Rauch (n 17) 40; Teresa Violante (n 22) 348; David Law and When-Chen Chang (n 31) 525; John Bell (n 39) 449; Anne Meutwese and Marnix Snel (n 21), 126). Referring himself to the German judicial system, see Paul Tiedemann (n 32) 62–3.

shows the consistency of the Court's decisions with Global Law and the legal solutions adopted abroad.[70]

Actually, it is rather common to observe several quotations of international/European/foreign jurisprudence and academic literature among some of the Portuguese Constitutional Court's decisions.[71] Excluding the decisions that we will develop in the next item, we may detach:

- Decision n. 12/2005 takes the European Court of Human Rights (ECtHR) jurisprudence on pecuniary indemnity for preventive arrest in case of major error into account;[72]
- Decision n. 589/2006 takes the ECtHR jurisprudence on justice confidentiality and the access to documents attached to criminal proceedings into consideration;[73]
- Decision n. 416/2007 states that the Constitutional Court is bound to the international sources of law, namely the European Convention on Human Rights (ECHR) and the Charter of Fundamental Rights of the European Union;
- Decisions n. 216/2010, n. 548/2011, and n. 41/2012 quote the UDHR and the ECtHR jurisprudence relating to legal support to companies and other institutional subjects;
- Decision n. 281/2011 ponders the ECtHR jurisprudence about impartiality warranties and the participation of judges that had intervened in the appealed decisions of the court of appeal;[74]
- Decision n. 527/2011 takes the ECtHR jurisprudence on defence rights and the right to be notified of the counter-allegations of the Public Attorney into consideration;[75]
- Decision n. 340/2013 considers the ECtHR case law on the right against self-incrimination in criminal procedures ('*nemo tenetur se ipsum accusare*').[76]

To sum up, one has to emphasize that for the Portuguese Constitutional Court, international law figures as a privileged instrument for discovering the real scope of every single fundamental right, but it is hardly an autonomous ground for dismissal of

[70] As noticed by Martin Shapiro, *Courts: A Comparative and Political Analysis* (Chicago University Press, Chicago, 1980) 1, it comes from common sociological knowledge that whenever two persons cannot reach a compromise about a dispute the only solution to solve the conflict is to refer to a third person to settle the dispute. Comparative Constitutional Law acts as that third person, giving a different insight about the question to settle. In a similar way, see John Bell (n 39) 460.

[71] Unlike several other foreign courts—for instance, the American Supreme Court and the English courts (see Hélène Lambert (n 17) 531)—the Portuguese Constitutional Court does not restrict itself to English written doctrine. On the contrary, it is rather usual to find different quotations in French, German, Italian, and Spanish.

[72] For instance, see Decisions *Brogan v United Kingdom, Ciulla v United Kingdom, N.C. v Italy*, and *Sekanina v Austria* of the ECtHR.

[73] For instance, see Decisions *Lamy v Belgium, Lietzow v Germany, Garcia Alva v Germany*, and *Schöps v Germany* of the ECtHR.

[74] For instance, see Decisions *Saraiva de Carvalho v Portugal, Procola v Luxembourg, Hauschildt v Denmark, Morel v France*, and *Warsicka v Polónia* of the ECtHR.

[75] Namely, Decision *Feliciano Bichão v Portugal* of the ECtHR.

[76] Namely, Decision *Funke v France, J.B. v Suisse, Shannon v United Kingdom*, and *Saunders v United Kingdom* of the ECtHR.

a national binding rule, for constitutional purposes.[77] Otherwise, foreign law is frequently used as a productive point for comparison. It helps the constitutional judges to ponder similar legislative solutions, particularly, in order to speculate about potential alternative measures that could induce a breach of the proportionality principle.[78]

This reasoning of the Court can be mainly explained by three factors: *a)* the incorporation in the Portuguese Constitution of some solutions of international law and the advances of foreign constitutional law all over the world; *b)* the wideness of the catalogue of fundamental rights, including civil and political rights and social, economic and cultural rights;[79] and *c)* the system of jurisdictional review of the constitutionality of normative rules.[80] As we have already mentioned, almost all internationally consecrated fundamental rights are also foreseen by the Portuguese Constitution. The jurisprudence of the Portuguese Constitutional Court has usually stressed that international binding rules and principles are commonly used as an additional interpretative tool rather than directly applied (see, for instance, Decisions n. 352/1998, n. 12/2005, n. 682/2006, and n. 185/2010).

The Portuguese Constitutional Court has even stated (*vide* Decision n. 101/2009) that any reference to foreign law, pursuing comparative purposes, cannot be deemed as an acceptance of those foreign rules and principles as an autonomous parameter for the control of constitutionality. They can help the Court to clarify the best solution for each case,[81] but

[77] Even on one of the few occasions when the Court expressly accepted international law has a pattern of validity (see Decision n. 416/2007), it also self-restrained, using those international parameters as an auxiliary tool for the fixation of the scope of the 'right to proprietorship'. In a claim concerning the definition of the amount of an indemnity for expropriation, the Court stated: 'Moreover, it should be stressed that this pluridimensionality of the right to proprietorship directly stems from International Law (see article 17 of the Universal Declaration on Human Rights, article 1(1) of the Additional Protocol to the European Convention on Human Rights, of the 20th March 1952) that, according to (2) of article 8 and (1) of article 16 of the Portuguese Constitution, immediately binds the Portuguese legislator and—particularly—this Constitutional Court. Furthermore, it shall even be mentioned (1) of article 17 of the European Union Charter of Fundamental Rights, that protects the right to proprietorship, in its different shapes, expressly disentangling 'the right to enjoy the property of his legally acquired assets, the right to use them, the right to dispose of them and the right to transmit them during life or by death. In short the international concept of the right to proprietorship shall also be considered, for purposes of interpretation of the normative scope of (1) of article 62 of the Portuguese Constitution' (Decision n.º 416/2007, available, in Portuguese, at <http://www.tribunalconstitucional.pt/tc/acordaos/>).

[78] Thus, see Neil Walker (n 22) 3; Anna-Verena Bauer and Christoph Mikulaschek (n 17) 1119–20; Gábor Halmai (n 12) 1330–1; Ran Hirschl (n 31) 12; Michael Rosenfeld, 'Principle or Ideology? A Comparativist Perspective on the U.S. Controversy Over Supreme Court Citations to Foreign Authorities' (2006), Benjamin N. Cardozo School of Law/Jacob Burns Institute for Advanced Legal Studies 2008 Working Paper No. 213, in <http://papers.ssrn.com/sol3/papers.cfm?abstract_id=1081854>, 8; John Bell (n 39) 449.

[79] Further reading on the protection of fundamental rights by Portuguese Constitutional Law, see Ana Maria Guerra Martins and Miguel Prata Roque (n 65) 312–14.

[80] Ana Maria Guerra Martins and Miguel Prata Roque, 'Jurisprudence—Constitutional/Constitutionnelle 2007' (2008), 20 Revue Européenne de Droit Public, 1245 *ff.*

[81] As a matter of fact, this refusal of enforcing foreign law as a constitutional parameter of decision has been frequently discussed among all Constitutional Courts. That position was well evidenced by a discussion promoted by the US Association of Constitutional Law, on 13 January 2005, between Justice Antonin Scalia and Justice Stephen Breyer, both judges of the US Supreme Court. Thus, Vicki C. Jackson and Mark Tushnet (n 17) 144; David Fontana (2004) (n 17) 462–7; Gábor Halmai (n 12) 1332, n. 30; Austen Parrish (n 21) 644; David Law and When-Chen Chang (n 31) 530, n. 20; Carla Zoethout, 'The Dilemma of Constitutional Comparativism' (2011), 71 Zeitschrift für ausländisches öffentliches Recht und Völkerrecht, 794–5.

they cannot substitute the national grounds for a non-constitutionality judgment. However, a correct and wise approach of foreign law may shed some light on a global consensus about some specific matters, particularly when they contend with world-wide recognized civil rights.

In the following section we will study some specific Court decisions, where one can confirm what has just been said.

VI. Analysis of some Portuguese constitutional decisions

The Portuguese Constitutional Court takes international/European/foreign law into account, mainly in the abstract *preventive* and 'successive procedures'.[82] That does not mean that we cannot find any 'appeal procedures', where international, European, and foreign law have been weighted, but due to the general binding character of the preventive and successive decisions, we will mostly draw attention to Decisions based on these two kinds of procedures.

1. Decisions on voluntary termination of pregnancy

The first group of decisions that deeply considers international/European/foreign law, in order to reinforce or interpret national law, concerns the matter of the criminalization (or decriminalization) of the voluntary termination of pregnancy when justified by the will of the pregnant woman until the 12th week.[83] Since 1984, several requests of judicial review have been submitted to the Portuguese Constitutional Court (Decisions n. 25/1984, n. 288/1998, n. 617/2006, and n. 75/2010). Two of them were integrated in 'referendum procedures' (the ones of 1998 and 2006).

a) Decision n. 25/1984

After the entry into force of the Penal Code of 1982, the parliament adopted a new law that decriminalized the voluntary termination of pregnancy in three exceptional situations (e.g. risk of death or irreversible injury/lesion for the pregnant woman; eugenic abortion until the 16th week; pregnancy due to a rape until the 12th week), as long as the final decision was submitted to medical certification and to a second doctor's opinion. In a Catholic society, as Portuguese society used to be, this parliamentary decision brought forth a huge public discussion. In order to strengthen its arguments, the Court analysed several legislative solutions adopted abroad (see, particularly, § V of the decision)—the French Loi n. 75-17, of 17 January 1975; the German Penal Code or

[82] On the Portuguese system of constitutional review, see Ana Guerra Martins and Miguel Prata Roque (n 80) 1245–56.

[83] Actually, judicial review of ordinary criminal laws concerning the decriminalization of the voluntary termination of pregnancy (in certain circumstances) has been one of the most polemic topics in the course of all constitutional courts jurisprudence. In these terms, see Mauro Cappelletti and William Cohen (n 68) 563–622; Vicki C. Jackson and Mark Tushnet (n 17) 1–143.

'*Strafrechtsgesetz*' of 1871 with the reviews of 1974 and 1976;[84] and the Italian Legge n. 194, of 22 May 1978. Afterwards, it also developed an extensive study of the constitutional jurisprudence of those countries.[85]

Noteworthy is the criticism of the decision taken by the Federal Constitutional Court of West Germany (*Bundesverfassungsgerichthof*), on 25 February 1975.[86] After stressing that constitutional courts should restrict themselves to reviewing the most polemic political decisions adopted by the parliaments, the Portuguese Constitutional Court stated that the above-mentioned German decision must be faced as one of the few exceptions where the German Court had surpassed this method of restraint.[87] Accordingly, Decision n. 25/1984 did not accept the German Court perspective. In spite of recognizing that the fundamental right to life comprises the right to life of the unborn, it concluded that there are other constitutional values that must be protected and may justify an exceptional lack of punishment of voluntary termination of pregnancy.

To sum up, in this case the Portuguese Constitutional Court invoked foreign law as a 'reinforcement tool'.

b) *Decision n. 288/98*

In 1998, throughout a preventive review of a question to be submitted to a referendum, the Portuguese Constitutional Court had analysed the constitutional conformity of a legislative act that would decriminalize the voluntary termination of pregnancy when justified by the will of the pregnant woman up to the 12th week. In this decision, the Court established a comparative analysis of other legal regimes,[88] giving special attention to the German new 'system of delays' that was adopted as a consequence of the modification of the German Criminal Code in 1992. Bearing in mind the Decision of 28 May 1993 of the German Constitutional Court (*Bundesverfassungsgerichtshof*),[89]

[84] For an extensive overview of the German constitutional jurisprudence concerning this topic, see Vicki C. Jackson and Mark Tushnet (n 17) 113–40.

[85] On the case law of the German, French, and Italian courts, see, among many others, Mauro Cappelletti and William Cohen (n 68) 563–622.

[86] Drawing attention to the importance of this German decision in the dynamics of the Portuguese Constitutional Court jurisprudence, see José de Sousa e Brito (n 24) 178–80.

[87] See § V, 1. of Decision n. 25/1984: 'If we can say that German constitutional court (federate and federal) has known, in general, to adequately trace the boundaries between law and politics, such a statement is not worthy, however, without exception. Deserving much more criticism than agreement, it appears, for instance, the decision of the Federal Constitutional Court of 25th February 1975 that declared null and void a 1974 law that largely attenuated and partially eliminated the punishment of abortion… However, the question about deciding if the protection is better secured by other means (for example, by consultancy and assistance services, etc.), the question about deciding if protection starts immediately after the conception or only after 12 weeks, the question about knowing if there are reasons, and which, that may lead to deem as exceptionally admissible an abortion (medical, eugenic, criminological or social indication, etc.) – all these questions do not find any immediate answer in the Constitution and the legislator must dispose from a large margin of freedom. In this case, the (German) Court has invaded this margin of freedom that makes any criticism seem to be justified'.

[88] In the Decision n. 288/1998 the Court had expressly quoted Ronald Dworkin, *Life's Dominion—An Argument about Abortion and Euthanasia* (Knopf, New York, 1993).

[89] On this decision, see Vicki C. Jackson and Mark Tushnet (n 17) 134–40.

as well as the famous Decision *Roe v Wade*[90] of the US Supreme Court, taken in 1983, and the subsequent *Planned Parenthood of Southeastern Pennsylvania v Casey* of 1992, the Court underlined that although the Constitution is committed to protect the right to life—including the foetus to be born—this goal can be reached either by a 'repressive method' (i.e. the criminalization of voluntary termination of pregnancy) or by a 'preventive method' (e.g. sexual education and reproductive planning). Accordingly, the Court concluded that the possibility of decriminalization of the voluntary termination of pregnancy—in some exceptional circumstances, such as the ones in discussion in that lawsuit—would not be a disproportionate restriction of the right to life, taking other constitutional protected values into account, such as the self-determination and the life of the pregnant woman.

In order to achieve this result, the Court developed an exhaustive research on the criminal law of the Member States of the European Union (back-to-date), taking their laws and their constitutional jurisprudence into consideration. The Decision clarified that some countries did not punish the voluntary termination of pregnancy until a certain delay, which in the case of Austria (since 1975) was during the first three weeks; Belgium (since 1990), Denmark (since 1973), Greece, Luxembourg (since 1978), Sweden (since 1974) until the 12th week of pregnancy; Finland (since 1970) until the 16th week of pregnancy; and France (since 1975) until the 10th week of pregnancy, which was accentuated by the Decision of 15 January 1976, of the French *Conseil Constitutionnel*. The Netherlands did not punish in case of medical assistance without a legal delay, but usually deemed as only allowed until the 20th week of pregnancy (1981).

Other countries were more restrictive. This was the case of the United Kingdom, that did not punish until the 24th week of pregnancy, in case of threat to life or personal integrity to the pregnant woman, in case of rape, and in case of malformation of the foetus (since 1967 and 1990); Italy did not punish in case of threat to life or personal integrity to the pregnant woman, in case of rape, and in case of malformation of the foetus (since 1978), pursuing a Decision of the Italian Constitutional Court (*Corte Costituzionale*) of 1975, and later confirmed by another Decision of 1981. However, this Court has not accepted a referendum on the decriminalization of the voluntary termination of pregnancy by the will of the mother until the 12th week, on the basis of a Decision taken in 1997, stating that it could be a disproportionate restriction to the right to life of the unborn. In Spain, the Criminal Code did not allow the voluntary termination of pregnancy by the will of the mother, but it was widely accepted that a doctor may authorize it, taking the psychological health of the pregnant woman into consideration, since the Decision of the Spanish Constitutional Court of 11 April 1985.

The sole country that criminalized the voluntary termination of pregnancy in any circumstances was Ireland.

One has to point out that Decision n. 288/1998 shows rather well how far the Portuguese Constitutional Court goes into its quest for foreign law. Actually, the

[90] On the importance of the *Roe v Wade* case, for purposes of Comparative Constitutional Law, see José de Sousa e Brito (n 24) 173–8; Vicki C. Jackson and Mark Tushnet (n 17) 5–25; Michael Rosenfeld (n 78) 7–8.

Comparative Constitutional Law has been called upon as a 'reinforcement tool'. Building this parallelism, the Court even underlined that:

> the majority of the foreign jurisdictions where there is a Constitutional Court or a similar institution—and that has been called to take a decision on matters of decriminalization of abortion by the will of the pregnant—has acknowledged the constitutional protection of intra-uterine life, Austria being the only exception. Nevertheless, that starting point did not prevent those constitutional jurisdictions of, sooner or later, albeit following different tracks, coming to accept the constitutional conformity of the decriminalization of the abortion, not only when concurring certain circumstances, but also during the first third of the pregnancy, by a free decision of the pregnant mother, when faced with that situation.

c) Decision n. 617/2006

The above approach was later retaken by the Decision n. 617/2006. First of all, the Court noticed that since it had been faced with the decriminalization of the voluntary termination of pregnancy, no country has receded in this issue. In order to justify this statement, the Portuguese Constitutional Court put through an overview of all European legal regimes, namely with the help of contemporary legal scholarship. For instance, it referred to Article L 2212-1 of the French Public Health Code (*Code de la Santé Publique*), approved by Law n. 2000-548, of 15 June 2000, that enhanced the voluntary termination of pregnancy by will from 10 to 12 weeks, and the correspondent decision of the French Constitutional Court (*Conseil Constitutionnel*)[91] of 27 June 2001 that did not declare any breach of the Constitution. Furthermore, the Court considered the Irish referendum of March 2002, by which the Irish people voted against a change of the Constitution in order to prevent some jurisprudence that allowed the acquittal of any pregnant woman put in danger of suicide due to her pregnancy.[92] The Decision also mentioned the case law of the ECtHR in *Vo v France*, of July 2004, on a voluntary termination of pregnancy caused by medical negligence, according to which it is disputable to say whether the foetus may be deemed as a person, even though it benefits from a certain level of legal protection. Lastly, the Portuguese Constitutional Court quoted the resolution of the European Parliament in favour of the 'preventive method'. It recommends that EU Member States adopt a public policy on sexual and reproductive health that may assure and potentiate a decreasing number of voluntary terminations of pregnancy and prevent the death of pregnant women due to

[91] On the *'Conseil Constitutionnel'*, in a comparative perspective, see Alec Stone (n 22); Dominique Rosseau, 'The Conseil Constitutionnel confronted with comparative law and the theory of constitutional justice: or Louis Favoreu's untenable paradoxes' (2007), 1 International Journal of Constitutional Law, 28–43.

[92] In fact, there was a consolidated criminal jurisprudence, among the Irish courts, according to which a young 14-year-old girl who was pregnant after having been raped should not be punished if she did not carry on her pregnancy, in case of risk of committing suicide. The referendum aimed to clarify that the risk of death did not include self-inflicted death, but the majority of voters disapproved such a restrictive solution. See Lisa Smith, *Abortion and Nation—The Politics of Reproduction in Contemporary Ireland* (Ashgate Publishing, London, 2005) 17–20.

complications arising from illegal abortions.[93] This resolution was followed by Regulation (CE) n. 1567/2003 of the European Parliament and the Council of 15 July 2003, which adopted several legislative measures concerning the EU's assistance to the public policy on reproductive and sexual health of its Member States.[94]

At the end of the day, Decision n. 617/2006 considered admissible a referendum on the decriminalization of voluntary termination of pregnancy performed until the 12th week of pregnancy only grounded on the will of the pregnant woman.

Contrary to the first referendum on this subject, in this one—in spite of not achieving the minimum percentage of electing participation—the *yes* vote won.

d) *Decision n. 75/2010*

Following the above-mentioned referendum, the parliament adopted Law n. 16/2007 of 17 April, which enabled public hospitals to welcome pregnant women that, for several reasons (e.g. extreme poverty, unemployment, extensive families, etc.) have decided not to carry the pregnancy to term.

A group of conservative members of the Portuguese Parliament[95] required the control of the constitutionality of some provisions of that Law before the Constitutional Court. Decision n. 75/2010 stated the compatibility of the decriminalization of the voluntary termination of pregnancy with the UDHR and the ECHR. On the one hand, it stressed the specific nature of the UDHR as a repository of customary international law, despite the denial of its conventional binding nature. On the other hand, this Decision clarified that there was no need to apply those international texts because the Portuguese written Constitution also foresaw the same patterns harboured by the latter ones. Accordingly, when applying the national written rules, the Court would be also applying the same criteria adopted by those international texts.

Revisiting the topic of the conflict of rights held by the pregnant woman and the foetus, Decision n. 75/2010 considered that the legislative solution of granting an exceptional criminal exemption in case of voluntary termination of pregnancy until the 12th week does not constitute a disproportionate restriction of the right to life. Following the German Constitutional Court (Decision of 28 May 1993[96]), the Portuguese Court made a different approach as either the pregnancy is still in its beginning or as it is in its final weeks of gestation.

Otherwise, the Court updated the research on the decriminalization of the voluntary termination of pregnancy that it had made in its former decisions. It quotes the criminal laws of several European countries, such as Austria, Belgium, Bosnia-Herzegovina, Denmark, Estonia, France, Greece, Macedonia, Netherlands, Romania, Spain,

[93] See Resolution of the European Parliament on Rights in Matters of Reproductive and Sexual Health, *in* [2003] OJ C, 271-E.

[94] [2003] OJ L, 224.

[95] According to Article 281(2)(*f*), of the Portuguese Constitution, 10% of the 230 members of the Parliament have the capacity to request a review of any legislative act by the Portuguese Constitutional Court, in order to declare its unconstitutionality.

[96] On this German constitutional decision, see José de Sousa e Brito (n 24) 181–2. The full text of the decision can be found, in German, at BVerfGE (88, 203 *ff*, 253).

Sweden, Switzerland, Turkey, and the United Kingdom. In this decision the commitment of the Portuguese Constitutional Court to Comparative Constitutional Law is obvious.

To conclude, Decision n. 75/2010 considers that there are several possible solutions for the conflict of the rights of the pregnant woman and of the foetus that could be in conformity with the Constitution. The solution chosen by the Portuguese legislator is aligned with several other foreign experiences. As a result, it reckons that there is no evidence of a disproportionate breach of the right to life as foreseen by the Portuguese Constitution and by international law.

2. Decisions on wiretapping

Another group of decisions that takes international/European/foreign law into consideration relates to wiretapping.

Before 2007, Article 188(3) of the Portuguese Criminal Procedure Code foresaw that any conversation held by a suspect and a third person that had been recorded through a subsequently authorized wiretapping deemed as irrelevant by a preliminary judge should be fully destroyed. Decisions n. 660/2006, n. 450/2007, and n. 451/2007 acknowledged the unconstitutionality of this provision, considering that the full and definitive destruction of the records would prevent the defendants from using them in order to contextualize the conversations held. By contrast, after the submission of the appeal to the Plenary of the Constitutional Court, by its President, Decision n. 70/2008 decided that, in case of a conflict between the rights of defence of an indicted person and the rights of privacy of third persons, the privacy should prevail and, consequently, it prescribed the destruction of the recorded conversations. In this Decision the Court invoked the jurisprudence of the ECtHR, namely Decisions *Huvig*, of 24 April 1990 (see § 34), *Kruslin*, of 24 April 1990 (see § 35), *Valenzuela Contreras*, of 30 July 1998 (see §§ 46, IV and 59), and *Prado Bugallo*, of 18 February 2003 (see § 30).[97]

Actually, the former Decision n. 660/2006 had already called upon the referred jurisprudence (and also upon some comparative analysis) to sustain a diametric point of view because the ECtHR only admitted the possibility of destroying the records when the criminal proceeding would be definitely dismissed or in case of a *res judicata* effect over the criminal conviction. Through a laborious reasoning, Decision n. 70/2008 provoked a shift of the constitutional jurisprudence. This decision was adopted by the majority of the Portuguese Constitutional Court.[98]

[97] Among many others, see Lee Bygrave, 'Data Protection Pursuant to the Right to Privacy in Human Rights Treaties' (1998), 6 International Journal of Law and Information Technology, 247–84; Aileen McHarg, 'Reconciling Human Rights and the Public Interest: Conceptual Problems and Doctrinal Uncertainty in the Jurisprudence of the European Court of Human Rights' (1999), 5 Modern Law Review, 671–96; Yaman Akdeniz, Nick Taylor, and Clive Walker, 'Regulation of Investigatory Powers Act 2000 (1): Bigbrother.gov.uk: State surveillance in the age of information and rights' (February 2001), Criminal Law Review, 73–90; Evelin Browe, 'Legality and Data Protection Law: The Forgotten Purpose of Purpose Limitation', *The Eclipse of the Legality Principle in the European Union* (Wolters Kluwer, Alphen aan den Rijn, 2011) 284–6.

[98] The referred judgment was taken by 8 to 5 votes of the Court's members. All the defeated judges enclosed a written dissenting opinion stating their particular points of view.

Although it is fairly debatable whether this reasoning is compatible with the ECtHR case law, one must highlight that Decision n. 70/2008 has never risked to neglect or to contradict European jurisprudence. On the contrary, the Portuguese Court was extremely cautious to disclaim any contradiction between its new decision and the former decisions of the ECtHR. Accordingly, even when disagreeing with that jurisprudence, the Portuguese Constitutional Court is very aware of the need to comply with it.

After the amendment of the Criminal Procedure Code in 2007, the law came to admit that those records (obtained by wiretapping) could be kept until the end of the criminal proceedings, although in secrecy, in order to allow the interested parties to use them for contextualization purposes.

3. Decision on medically assisted procreation

After the entry into force of Law n. 32/2006 (that regulated, for the first time, the use of medically assisted procreation therapeutics), a group of conservative members of the Portuguese Parliament requested the review of its constitutionality by the Constitutional Court. According to that plea, several of its provisions were against the Convention on Human Rights and Biomedicine (Oviedo Convention) and the UDHR that, under the terms of Article 8(2) of the Constitution, are part of the substantive constitution.

In order to judge this request, the Portuguese Constitutional Court started by admitting the lack of specific constitutional written rules on medically assisted procreation. As a consequence, the need for comparative and international analysis of relevant rules and principles increased. Decision n. 101/2009 took into consideration not only the UDHR, but also the Universal Declaration on the Human Genome and Human Rights, the Oviedo Convention, and its Additional Protocol on the Prohibition of Human Cloning. As we have already mentioned, Article 16(1) of the Portuguese Constitution does not exclude any other fundamental rights set out in the applicable international conventions.

Furthermore, the Court underlined that the use of Comparative Constitutional Law would help find a reasonable solution because the problems conjured up by medically assisted procreation had both global range and meaning. This universal range[99] led the Court to a comparative analysis with other legislative solutions—even if it also clarified that those foreign law patterns would not be assembled as an autonomous constitutional parameter for national purposes. In its wise wording:

> The importance of all these elements must be understood in view of the openness of the Portuguese constitutional parameters applicable on matters of medically assisted procreation but this last will be the ones to offer the conclusive criteria for the decision to be taken.[100]

[99] Referring to the fact that Comparative Constitutional Law is often used whenever there is a universal standard to be pondered, see Vicki C. Jackson (n 24) 91–2; Francois Venter (n 30) 34.

[100] See Decision n. 101/2009, § 5, *a), in fine*.

This judgment is one of the most important Court statements about the reception of international normative parameters by the Portuguese Constitution. Not only does the Court recognize their universal binding force (as *ius cogens*), but it also stresses that any human rights foreseen by an international source takes part of the substantive national set of constitutional normativity, following Article 16(1) of the Constitution.[101] Afterwards, Decision n. 101/2009 embraces a division between the typology of international sources that may be deemed as a national constitutional parameter. On the one hand, the Court affirmed the binding effect of the Oviedo Convention and its Additional Protocol on the Prohibition of Human Cloning—due to its nature of a binding treaty—but, on the other hand, it also stated that the Universal Declaration on the Human Genome and Human Rights would not benefit from this binding force because this is a political resolution adopted by the General Conference of the UN Educational, Scientific and Cultural Organization (UNESCO), during its 29th session, in 1997.

Regarding the Oviedo Convention, the Court also clarified that, even the binding Article 67(2)(*e*) of the Portuguese Constitution expressly set out that parliament should legislate over medically assisted procreation, in a way compatible with human dignity. Accordingly, the ordinary laws should address the relevant international binding rules, but the latter should also be in accordance with national constitutional parameters. In the negative case, they would relinquish to the Portuguese Constitution. That meant the national legislator would benefit from a wide margin of discretion. Following this approach, Decision n. 101/2009 concluded that those international rules and principles could not be used as an autonomous standard of constitutionality, but only because national written constitutional rules already assured the same effect.

4. Decision on same-sex marriages

Another impressive example of the cosmopolitan trend that crosses the Portuguese Constitutional Court's jurisprudence is the case of same-sex marriage. Confronted by a President of the Republic's request, the Court discussed whether the concept of marriage included in Article 16(1) of the UDHR[102] forced the national legislator to confine civil marriage to opposite-sex spouses. Based on a strict interpretation of the wording of that clause, the President of the Republic maintained that it should be forbidden to extend civil marriage to same-sex couples.

In order to address the request, Decision n. 121/2010 discussed the meaning and the influence of the UDHR in the Portuguese legal order, since, as we have already mentioned, Article 16(2) of the Portuguese Constitution expressly foresees that the latter must be used as an interpretative tool for constitutional review purposes. Although the Court reinforced the constitutional significance of the UDHR, it also clarified that it could only be used with the aim of enlarging the protection of human

[101] See Decision n. 101/2009, § 5, *b)*.

[102] According to this article: '(1) Men and women of full age, without any limitation due to race, nationality or religion, have the right to marry and to found a family. They are entitled to equal rights as to marriage, during marriage and at its dissolution.'

rights and not to diminish it.[103] According to the Court, any restriction of a human right should be directly and expressly foreseen by the written Constitution and not by means of an indirect interpretation of an international text, even when it is binding. Hence, the Court stated that the UDHR could not be used as a tool to restrain the full range of the constitutional protection to the right to marry.[104]

Furthermore, Decision n. 121/2010 also proceeds to an extensive analysis of comparative law on the matter of same-sex marriage, concluding that some countries had already allowed it (Belgium, Netherlands, Norway, Spain, State of California, Sweden) and others had adopted different civil union regimes for same-sex couples (Canada, Denmark, Finland, France,[105] Germany, Iceland, Switzerland, United Kingdom). However, Decision n. 101/2009 explicitly clarifies that:

> comparative law still deserves a special reference. It is clear that the Law of other countries is not a parameter of constitutionality. But there is no doubt that some matters that are linked with human problems as universal as the ones related to medically assisted procreation may assume relevance to know what happens in other juridical experiences and (without losing the sense of autonomy of each juridical system) to take conclusion, especially when it is possible to deduce common principles from those experiences.

Moreover, the Court did not spare itself from an accurate overview of several judicial foreign[106] decisions concerning the subject:

- Decision of the German Constitutional Court (*Bundesverfassungsgerichtshof*) of 17 July 2002 that judged in favour of the constitutional compatibility of the law of

[103] Thus, referring to a 'race to the top', during which each country tries to strengthen the scope of protection of their human rights, see David S. Law, 'Globalization and the Future of Constitutional Rights' (2008), in Northwestern University Law Review 102, 1277; Iddo Porat (n 23) 23; David Law and Mila Versteeg (n 23) 1175–7. Now and then, American courts tend to refuse to directly enforce foreign law because they state that American legal regimes are more protective than the aforementioned. Accordingly, see Daniel Rauch (n 17) 48.

[104] For a different view, Decision n. 121/2010 even quotes a judgment taken by the South African Constitutional Court, in the case *Minister of Home Affairs v Fourie*, whereby it considered that the wording of Article 16(1), of the UDHR should be interpreted as only allowing an opposite-sex marriage (although it also stated that this conception was cultural and historically dated).

[105] Since the approval of Decision n. 121/2010, France has also approved a bill that opened civil marriage for same-sex couples. The bill was voted on 12 February 2013, by the National Assembly, and on 12 and 23 April 2013 by the Senate. After a request from a conservative group of members of the parliament, the French Constitutional Court (*'Conseil Constitutionnel'*) also ruled that the law was not unconstitutional, on 17 May 2012, and the French President immediately promulgated the bill. Decision n. 2013-669 DC of the French Constitutional Court is available at <http://www.conseil-constitutionnel.fr/conseil-constitutionnel/root/bank/pdf/conseil-constitutionnel-137046.pdf>.

[106] Referring itself to a former judgment (see Decision n. 359/2009), the Court also mentioned several judicial decisions taken in Canada and South Africa. Likewise, the German Constitutional Court also analysed the legal regimes of several other countries concerning same-sex marriages, in order to rule over their constitutionality (see BVerfGE 105, 315). Accordingly, see Gábor Halmai (n 12) 1338. Similarly, referring to the US Supreme Court jurisprudence about LGBT rights—for instance *Lawrence v Texas*, 539 US 548 (2003), see David Fontana (2004) (n 17) 450–7; Anna-Verena Bauer and Christoph Mikulaschek (n 17) 1111; Ruth Ginsburg (n 39) 589; Noga Morag-Levine, 'Judges, Legislators, and Europe's Law: Common-Law Constitutionalism and Foreign Precedents' (2006), 65 Maryland Law Review, 109; Michael Rosenfeld (n 78) 2 and 16–27; Robert Leckey, 'Thick Instrumentalism and Comparative Constitutionalism: The Case of Gay Rights' (2009), 40 Columbia Human Rights Law Review, 427 and 442; Carla Zoethout (n 81) 791.

same-sex civil unions (*Lebenspartnerschaftgesetz*) that forbid the marriage of same-sex couples;

- Decision n. 159/2004 of the Belgium Constitutional Court (*Cour d'Arbitrage*) of 20 October 2004 that considered same-sex marriage to be in accordance with the Constitution;
- Decision of the Supreme Court of Hawaii (USA) of 1993 (case *Baher v Levin*) that clarified that the federative Constitution could only limit civil marriage to opposite-sex couples if a 'compelling interest' could be shown;
- Decision of the Supreme Court of Vermont (USA) of 20 December 1999 (case *Baker v State*) ruled that the principle of equality forbids the exclusion of same-sex partners from social benefits and warranties similar to the ones given by the force of marriage;
- Decision of the Supreme Court of Massachusetts (USA) of 2003 (case *Goodridge*), which decided in favour of the unconstitutionality of an exclusive opposite-sex marriage clause for breach of the principle of equality;
- Decision of the Supreme Court of Massachusetts (USA) of 15 May 2008 (case *In Re Marriage*) ruled in favour of the unconstitutionality of an exclusive opposite-sex marriage clause for breach of the principle of equality;
- Decision of the Canadian Supreme Court of 1866 (case *Hyde v Hyde*) stated that a Christian concept of marriage forbids its extension to same-sex couples;
- Decision of the Canadian Supreme Court of 9 December 2004 (case *Reference Re Same-Sex Marriage*) judged that the principle of equality demanded the extension of civil marriage to same sex-couples.

The Portuguese Constitutional Court also took the international background of same-sex marriages into consideration.[107] Decision n. 121/2010 quoted several resolutions from European institutions, such as the European Parliament of the European Union and the Parliamentary Assembly of the Council of Europe.

In order to strengthen the idea that it is widely accepted in democratic States that they shall remove any legislative measures which provokes a discriminatory treatment grounded on sexual orientation, the Portuguese Constitutional Court also summoned the abundant jurisprudence of the ECtHR.[108] Cases, such as *Dudgeon v United Kingdom*, of 22 October 1981, *Norris v Ireland*, of 26 October 1988, *Modinos v Cyprus*, of 22 April 1993, and *A.D.T. v United Kingdom*, of 31 July 2000 ruled that the criminalization of consensual intercourse between free and willing same-sex adults would be a serious violation of the right to respect for private life and also a violation of the principle of non-discrimination. Furthermore, the Portuguese Court also referred to the Decisions *L. and V. v Austria* and *S. and L. v Austria*, both of 9 January 2003, in which the ECtHR declared that there was no objective and reasonable reasoning for the conservation of a different legal age for authorized sexual intercourse, as well as to

[107] For a comparative overview of the principle of discrimination, see Harry Groves, *Comparative Constitutional Law* (Oceana Publications, Dobbs Ferry, NY, 1963) 49–187; Juliane Kokott (n 12) 88–91.

[108] All decisions of the ECtHR are available at <http://cmiskp.echr.coe.int>.

Decision *Baczkowski and others v Poland*, of 3 May 2007, in which the Court ruled that the denial of authorization for purposes of public demonstration of lesbian, gay, bisexual, and transgender (LGBT) supporters by the authorities of Warsaw was contrary to the freedom of assembly, as well as against the prohibition of discrimination. In another case (*E.B. v France*, of 22 January 2008), the European Court also deemed as a breach of the non-discrimination principle, the denial of a candidature of a lesbian woman for purposes of single adoption of a child.

Lastly, the Portuguese Constitutional Court also noticed that there had been an evolution of the ECtHR's jurisprudence about the meaning of marriage. At an early stage, this court tended to assume marriage as a specific legal institution only available for a relation between a man and a woman.[109] However, when it evaluated a case of transsexuality (case *Christine Goodwin v United Kingdom*, of 11 July 2002), the ECtHR not only recognized that the right to have a family could not be a mandatory condition of the right to marry[110]—namely, in case of infertility or impossibility to conceive by natural means—but it also clarified that the meaning of civil marriage had been suffering a strong influence of new social and cultural approaches that implied a new viewpoint on its contemporary scope of protection.[111] Taking the lack of uniformity of the modern concept of marriage into account, the ECtHR declared that the Member States of the Convention benefit from a wide margin of discretion in order to regulate same-sex couples (see cases *Mata Estevez v Spain*, of 10 May 2001, and *Karner v Austria*, 24 July 2003).

Following that lead, the Portuguese Constitutional Court concluded that international (and national) constitutional law authorizes the ordinary legislator to choose between the existing options, as long as it assures the non-discrimination of same-sex couples. The granting of the right to marry to same-sex couples—which concerns one of the options—does not represent either a breach of any international, or of any national, constitutional parameter. Accordingly, the decision must stay in the hands of the legislative branch and, at the end of the day, in the hands of the people of each country by means of regular and democratic elections.

The same-sex marriages constitutional controversy highlights the importance of international and foreign law in a globalized world.

VII. Conclusions

The current study permits us to extract the following conclusions:

1. The issue of 'judicial dialogue' in a multilevel constitutional network is currently one of the most interesting topics of public law. As a matter of fact, after World War II, one can clearly distinguish a global legal order, some regional legal orders, and an increasing number of national legal orders, where one can identify public

[109] Thereby, see *Rees v United Kingdom*, of 10 October 1986 (see § 49), *Cossey v United Kingdom*, of 27 September 1990 (see § 43), and *Sheffield and Horsham v United Kingdom*, of 30 July 1998 (see § 60).

[110] See Decision *Christine Goodwin v United Kingdom*, § 98. About this ECtHR decision, see Carla Zoethout (n 81) 797–9.

[111] See Decision *Christine Goodwin v United Kingdom*, § 100.

powers—the normative, the executive, and the judicial—as well as some forms of participation of the citizens.

2. As the State cannot overcome on its own the multiple challenges of a globalized world, the emergence of worldwide common constitutional parameters has become a reality. This 'global set of normativity' suffers the influence of national legal experiences and simultaneously provokes rather significant changes in national law, contributing to the appearance of a multilevel constitutional network.
3. In spite of the above-mentioned, the national courts still maintain a strong reluctance with regard to the direct application of global constitutional parameters, due to the prejudice against the extraterritoriality of public law. Therefore, the dialogue between the courts or, in other words, the 'judicial dialogue' presents itself as a privileged means for achieving and applying a worldwide consensus about the main issues of public law, such as the protection of human rights.
4. The Portuguese Constitutional Order and the Portuguese Constitutional Court could not exclude themselves from this evolution. In fact, the Portuguese Constitution deals with multilevel constitutionalism, since it is deeply committed to a 'friendship' towards international law, in general, and European Union law, in particular, as well as to international and European human rights law.
5. Consequently, the Portuguese Constitutional Court has been rather open to mentioning external sources of normativity in its decisions, such as international, European, and even foreign law, but strictly as a rhetorical 'reinforcement tool' or as an 'interpretative tool'. Like many other constitutional courts, the Portuguese Constitutional Court has never afforded to consider any external source as an autonomous 'parametric tool' of constitutionality.

19

Judges and Professors

The Influence of Foreign Scholarship on Constitutional Courts' Decisions

*Lucio Pegoraro**

I. The use of comparison in deciding cases

This chapter aims at examining the use of legal literature by constitutional or supreme courts in a selected number of countries. As scholars have already noticed, courts have been participating in the circulation of legal solutions—as well as of principles and ideas—at a steady rate. In particular, this is due to the role that constitutional, international, and transnational courts play in the dissemination of ideas and principles.[1] We will not focus on international and EU law—indeed, they cause what can be termed as the problem of 'vertical' circulation in interpretative activities. On the contrary, we will consider how comparative law displays an important auxiliary function in deciding cases in a 'horizontal', judicial dialogue.[2]

Like scholars with a background in private law, scholars of constitutional law have started studying the use of comparative law by constitutional courts.[3] We have already

* Full Professor of Comparative Public Law, University of Bologna. This research has benefited from the contribution of the project PRIN 2010–2011. Translation by Antonio Alderuccio and Eleonora Lena. Revised by Matteo Nicolini.

[1] On the topic see, among others, Vv.Aa., 'The International Judicial Dialogue: When Domestic Constitutional Courts Join the Conversation' (2001), 114 Harv L.Rev 1943; A-M Slaughter, '40th Anniversary Perspective: Judicial Globalization' (2000), 40 Va Int'l L.J. 403; C.L. L'Heureux-Dubé, 'The Importance of Dialogue: Globalization and the International Impact of the Rehnquist Court' (1998), 34 Tulsa L.J. 15; M. Claes et al. (eds.), *Constitutional Conversation in Europe. Actors, Topics and Procedures* (Intersentia, Cambridge-Antwerp-Portland 2012); H. Nogueira Alcalá (ed.), *Diálogo judicial multinivel y principios interpretativos favor persona y de proporcionalidad* (Librotecnia, Santiago de Chile 2013).

[2] On horizontal circulation see: U. Drobnig, S. Van Erp (eds.), *The Use of Comparative Law by Courts. XIV Congrès international de droit compare* (Kluwer Law Int., The Hague-London-Boston 1999); A. Somma, *L'uso giurisprudenziale della comparazione nel diritto interno e comunitario* (Giuffrè, Milano 2001); G. Canivet, M. Andenas, D. Fairgrieve (eds.), *Comparative Law Before the Courts* (British Institute of International and Comparative Law, London 2004); G. Alpa (ed.), *Il giudice e l'uso delle sentenze straniere. Modalità e tecniche dell'interpretazione giuridica* (Giuffrè, Milano 2006); B. Markesinis, J. Fedtke, *Judicial Recourse to Foreign Law: a New Source of Inspiration?* (U.C.L. Press, London 2006); T. Groppi, M.-Cl. Ponthoreau (eds.), *The Use of Foreign Precedents by Constitutional Judges* (Hart Pub, Oxford 2013); E. Ferrer Mac-Gregor, A. Herrera García (eds.), *Diálogo jurisprudencial en Derechos Humanos entre Tribunales Constitucionales y Cortes Internacionales* (Tirant Lo Blanch México, México 2013). See also the essays collected in 14 (8) German L.J. (2013).

[3] G.F. Ferrari, A. Gambaro (eds.), *Corti nazionali e comparazione giuridica* (Esi, Napoli 2006); G. de Vergottini, *Oltre il dialogo tra le Corti. Giudici, diritto straniero, comparazione* (il Mulino, Bologna 2010); D. Maus, 'Le recours aux précedents étrangers et le dialogue des cours constitutionnelles' (2009), 2 *Rev. fr. dr. const.*; M.C. Ponthoreau, *La reconnaissance des droits non écrits par les cours constitutionnelles italienne et français. Essai sur le pouvoir créateur du juge constitutionnel* (Èconomica, Paris 1994); Id., *Le recours à*

delivered the results of such research, which we will here summarize.[4] First, there is a strict connection between the use of comparison by the ordinary courts and the use of comparison by the constitutional courts. If a supreme court carries out the judicial review of legislation, the use of comparison in common and constitutional proceedings unavoidably overlaps. Hence, legal education and the background of judges—either 'ordinary' or 'constitutional'—plays a crucial role in the use of comparison.

Second, common law courts use foreign law more than civil law ones.[5] There are, however, relevant exceptions: in the Latin American area, quotations of foreign law are very numerous.

Third, judges who usually cite foreign judicial precedents do also have recourse to other formants (legislation and literature) as well. Thus, constitutional courts do not use only a single formant; references to foreign law comprise judicial precedents, legislation, and (with exceptions) doctrine.

Finally, there is extensive quotation of international or transnational courts' judgments in deciding domestic cases. However, a distinction must be drawn: on the one hand, judges 'have to' apply precedents—because judicial precedents are binding; on the other, they quote foreign rulings in order to complement their reasoning with additional arguments. If it is the case, references to international or regional courts' judgments—such as the European or the Inter-American ones—count as the court referring to the constitutional court's rulings.

II. The references to legal literature

As for quotations of legal literature, foreign law does not only display its influence through the comparative arguments directly used by judges. On the contrary, they also refer to legal works, and analyse domestic law through the lenses of comparison.[6] In this respect, reference to legal literature necessarily entails an unconscious reference to foreign law. This 'indirect' influence of comparative law may be more intense than that

'l'argument de droit comparé' par le juge constitutionnel. Quelques problems théoriques et tecniques, in F. Melin-Soucramanien (ed.), *L'interprétation constitutionnelle* (Dalloz, Paris 2005).

[4] L. Pegoraro, 'L'argomento comparatistico nella giurisprudenza della Corte costituzionale italiana', in G.F. Ferrari, A. Gambaro (eds.), *Corti nazionali e comparazione giuridica* (n 3); Id., *La Corte costituzionale italiana e il diritto comparato: un'analisi comparatistica* (Clueb, Bologna 2006); Id., *La Corte costituzionale e il diritto comparato nelle sentenze degli anni '80* (3 *Quad. cost.* 1987); L. Pegoraro, P. Damiani, 'Comparative law in the judgments of Constitutional Courts', in A.M. Rabello, A. Zanotti (eds.), *Developments in European, Italian and Israeli Law* (Giuffrè, Milano 2001), Spanish translation 'El Derecho comparado en la jurisprudencia de los Tribunales constitucionales' (1999), 26 *Rev. Jur. Castilla-La Mancha*, and in L. Pegoraro, *Ensayos sobre justicia constitucional, la descentralización y las libertades* (Porrúa, Ciudad de Mexico 2006).

[5] According to M. Andenas, D. Fairgrieve, 'Intent on making mischief: seven ways of using comparative law', in P.G. Monateri (ed.), *Methods of Comparative Law* (Edward Elgar, Cheltenham (UK), Northampton (MA) 2012): 'Across the national borders dividing the Commonwealth, the seamless nature of the common law, from its origins in English law, through its permutations across to former colonies and beyond, provided a reason and justification for courts to look to each other's jurisprudence, exchange solutions and thereby create a network of persuasive authority.'

[6] A. Gerber, 'Der Einfluss des ausländischen Rechts in der Rechtsprechung des Bundesgericht', in Vv. Aa., *Perméabilité des orders juridiques* (20 Publications de l'Isdc, Zürich 1992); F. Werro, *La jurisprudence et le droit comparé* (20 Publications de l'Isdc, Zürich 1992).

determined by the explicit and conscious reference to foreign legislation and judgments. It is quite evident that legal literature must set appropriate patterns for the reception of foreign legal solutions in domestic judgments.

We have already mentioned the peculiarities of common law: judges are used to moving beyond domestic law, and naturally use foreign precedents drawn from the same legal tradition. This has fostered their open-minded legal culture. Alongside judicial precedents, they often quote foreign law, as well as legal literature—although in a more selective and differentiated way—in order to support judicial reasoning.

Unlike references to foreign precedent, the *ratio* governing quotations of foreign literature and legislation usually consists in validating a ruling or an interpretative choice.

References to legal literature achieve an additional and differentiated purpose if compared to that resting on either binding or persuasive precedents: it confers authority to the decision. In judge-made law systems, however, comparative reference doesn't necessarily supplement the *ratio decidendi*. This, however, can occur: for example, courts decide cases without referring to a precedent in point delivered by other common law courts, which hardly happens now.[7] (In civil law systems, on the contrary, the weave of jurisprudence provides the argumentative basis to compose the system with rationality.)[8]

There are also legal systems where judges normally strengthen arguments with specific references to monographs, articles, essays, encyclopedia articles, and even doctoral theses (as in Canada and Switzerland). In other systems, these references are considered, if not sacrilegious, at least useless—and legislation prohibits references to legal literature.[9] In some circumstances, praxis suggests not to quote legal doctrine in rulings. Once having entered the profession, such prohibition separates the judge from legal studies, which are more attentive to literature. This also persuades judges to look for useful precedents in case law, even in countries based on codified legislation. Hence, courts do not benefit from the development of comparative legal studies.[10]

As already noticed, a *continuum* links ordinary to constitutional courts. As a consequence, if ordinary courts do not refer to literature, constitutional ones will do the same. Reference to domestic and foreign literature is caused by several factors: how rulings are delivered, objective occurrences (like globalization of law), as well as subjective factors.

[7] For M. Andenas, D. Fairgrieve, (n 5), 'Comparative law has been seen to provide courts with persuasive and non-binding arguments. At the current stage, there is an argument about the consequences of a call for more consistency. One question is whether courts are ever bound to make use of comparative law sources, for instance in certain situations when an authority is based on comparative law sources'. M.R. Legeais, 'L'utilisation du droit comparé par les tribunaux' (1994), 2 Rev. int. dr. comp., makes a distinction between 'recours obligatoire au droit comparé' and 'l'utilisation libre du droit comparé'.

[8] I refer to my textbooks *Giustizia costituzionale comparata* (Giappichelli, Torino 2015), and *La justicia constitucional. Una perspectiva comparada* (Dykinson, Madrid 1998).

[9] For Italy, see art. 118 of the provisions enhancing the code of civil procedure.

[10] The influence of university studies is emphasized by U. Drobnig, 'The Use of Comparative Law by Courts', in U. Drobnig, S. Van Erp (eds.), *The Use of Comparative Law by Courts* (n 2), in relation to the legal systems of Luxembourg, Brazil, and Quebec, and explained by the influence of codifications and the subsequent contents of the teachings.

The first factor regards the appointment of judges. Ordinary judges, professors, lawyers, officials (sometimes politicians), now interact and spend more time studying abroad. When they come back to their own country, they bring new legal/cultural trends and attitudes. The legal culture of the judge may vary depending on the place of education, and on the place where the judge spent time in fruitful studies and specializations.[11] A second variable is represented by the need to ensure coherence and rational basis to judgments. The 'younger' courts cannot draw authorities from their precedents in order to guarantee legal certainty. Therefore, they seek it in authoritative law books.

III. Purpose and method of research

In this chapter, I will anticipate some topics that will be fully developed in a scientific research project that involves 14 Italian universities and dozens of scholars from all continents. The project analyses how constitutional courts (European and international) of around 30 countries handle internal and foreign literature.

The main purposes are:

- Exploring circulation of formants (both the propositions about law made by jurists and judges), and checking their alignment or fracture.[12] In fact, it might happen that courts prefer to refer to the opinions of jurists rather than to normative formants (the Constitution and the law) or to judicial ones (the precedents). In this way, they distance themselves from the law in force. Vice versa, they can find that arguments reaffirm alignment in legal literature (either native or foreign).
- Studying the reasoning of the various constitutional courts from this peculiar perspective, which has never been investigated so far. Hence, the project analyses how the mindset of judges is formed and justified, by focusing both on the opinion of the majority and on concurring or dissenting opinions, where permitted.
- Verifying whether and how the opinion of the courts and of individual judges takes into account non-legal studies (such as psychology, medicine,

[11] Let me make references to some articles of mine: 'Estudio introductorio. Trasplantes, injertos, diálogos. Jurisprudencia y doctrina frente a los retos del derecho comparado', in E. Ferrer Mac-Gregor, A. Herrera García (eds.), *Diálogo jurisprudencial en Derechos Humanos entre Tribunales Constitucionales y Cortes Internacionales* (n 2), and 'Derecho nacional, derecho internacional, derecho europeo: la circulación orizontal y vertical entre formantes', 17 *Anuario Iberoam. Justicia Const.* (2013), and 19 *Rev. Iberoamer. Der. Procesal Const.* (2013).

[12] The expression 'formants' of the legal system was coined by R. Sacco, 'Legal Formants: a Dynamic Approach to Comparative Law' (1991), 39 Am. J. of Comp. Law 1; Id., *Introduzione al diritto comparato*, (5th edn., Utet, Torino 1992). It refers to different sets of rules and propositions that, in the context of a legal system, concur in creating the legal order of a group, in a certain place and at a certain time. In other words, 'a "formant" of the Law is a group, a type of personnel, or a community, institutionally involved in the activity of creating Law': see P.G. Monateri, *Introduction*, in Id. (ed.), *Methods in comparative law: an intellectual overview*, (n 5). About the rift between formants, see A. Somma, *Introducción crítica al Derecho Comparado* (Ara, Lima 2006).

anthropology). Hence, deciding a case often needs the contribution of non-legal sciences or 'cultural mediations'. Moreover, the aim is to ascertain which the different lines are behind: philosophy, political doctrine, and general theory of law, that explicitly function as a support to an argument.

- Reflecting on the legal education of constitutional judges—at least, where it is possible to detect the quote to be attributed to a specific judge, which is not always easy for the majority decisions. In particular, the project aims at verifying whether there is any link between academic, forensic, bureaucratic, or political origin and opening to foreign law.
- Understanding the flows of ideas among the various legal systems—who absorbs ideas, who exports them, who are the authors that stand out more and where they come from, in relation to what matter (either civil or constitutional or administrative or criminal etc.); whether there is continuity or not with the legal history of the country (e.g., how much the doctrine of a colonizing country in an already colonized state, now independent, counts today); to what extent the language barrier represents a brake to the circulation of ideas.
- Updating, from a practical point of view, the ranking of universities and schools. Many universities are ranked because they have an ancient and glorious history rather than because they exert a real influence over the mindset of the globalized world. How many universities are there? For which of them is the assumption valid? Which are the emerging universities? On an individual level, do judges quote the great masters of the past, the jurists that had studied in the last decades, or the contemporary ones? Who are the professors that influence constitutional courts' decisions in different fields of law (and philosophy)? And where do they teach? To what extent do some schools replace others as time goes by? Do scholars assert themselves while others are forgotten?

We will give a partial explanation to the results of some 'coring', which are functional to a more comprehensive, systematic, and exhaustive study. Indeed, a full worldwide research should be based on temporally homogeneous, statistically reliable, geo-culturally differentiated data sufficient to detect the reasons supporting the interest in this research.

First, we will examine only explicit quotations, although behind them are readings and a whole culture. Second, the pioneering character of the study suggests a focus on some mixed jurisdictions (Philippines, South Africa, Israel). Hence, the mix of several legal cultures seems forthcoming and interesting. For the same reason, we will then examine the quotes of the Supreme Court of Argentina in the years 2008–2011, in order to verify the dissemination of foreign legal cultures in a jurisdiction that can be traced back, as for private law, to the civil law legal tradition, whereas domestic constitutional and public law is very much indebted to the US model, as occurs in Latin America.

As the work is in progress, we will not always offer full information about every single jurisdiction in a homogeneous way (in some cases, we will omit information about judges' education, even though we have gathered it. In others, we will set aside single quotation analysis in order to examine the aggregation of the data).

IV. Philippines

1. Introductory remarks

The Philippines are a melting pot of legal cultures. Civil law legacies comprise legislation that had been implanted by the Spanish colonization in the 19th century. From an institutional point of view, there is a clear influence of US law, and such influence continues even after full independence was gained in 1946. This obviously arouses curiosity (and has inspired expansive literature) about the mixture of conflicting legal traditions, the way they impact on constitutional judicial review—in particular, the use of legislative sources and the appeal to the *stare decisis*.

The structure of the Constitutional Court is construed as a clone of the US one, (appointment and composition, functions and rituals, dissent). There are also interesting, domestic peculiarities, like those related to the *recurso de amparo*. Quotations normally imply a reference to a specific work, and not a generic reference to the opinion of a single scholar.

Given the dual roots of the mixed jurisdiction, it should be argued that judges draw more from the civil law tradition in civil matters, and refer more to US authors in relation to public law, freedom, and trial matters. That is what we will verify.

2. Source of quotations

Given the impressive size of pronunciations and quotations, the spectrum of sentences is limited to those delivered between January 2008 and December 2011. The majority of authors quoted by the Supreme Court are from the Philippines, irrespective of the legal field of law involved (civil, criminal, constitutional, etc.).

As for quotations of foreign scholars, referred to by the Court, more than a half are from the US, and they are equally distributed among judgments on constitutional, criminal, and civil matters. This points out how the common law mentality has eventually superseded the civilian one. This assumption is held if we consider the quotations of various British, Canadian, Australian, and Indian authors. References appear both in the majority opinions and in the dissenting and concurrent ones. Among the mentioned authors there are judges and lawyers. They are quoted, however, because of their publications.[13]

Apart from the famous *Black's Law Dictionary*—which is quoted for plagiarism, performance of obligations, and standing[14]—the Court refers to public law authorities

[13] For example Donald Verilli—former partner in a well-known law firm and then appointed Vice Attorney General by Obama—is quoted about procedural proofs (G.R. n. 189122, 03/17/2010); the Court also quoted: 'The rights of others: protection and advocacy organizations associational standing to sue' by the historian and political activist Kelsey McCowan Heilman (G.R. 122846, 01/10/2009); M.M. Whiteman (internationalist and official of the State Department till the Seventies) on the subject of maritime boundaries (G.R. 187167, 08/16/2011); the criminal lawyer Paul Cramm (on the importance of DNA proof: G.R. 176389, G.R. 176864, 12/14/2010); Armand Arabian (G.R. 176389, G.R. 176864, 12/14/2010), former Judge of the Supreme Court of California, about the definition of 'informed consent' on the theme of medical responsibility.

[14] AM 10717-SC, 02/8/2011, G.R. 171702, 02/12/2009, and G.R. 191342, 03/17/2010 respectively.

as well. Among constitutionalists, Judges Brandeis and Warren are quoted about *privacy*;[15] the book *Electoral law* by Daniel P. Tokaji (professor of Constitutional Law at the Ohio State University) is also mentioned;[16] M. Gerhardt (professor at Columbia Law School) is quoted for *impeachment*;[17] Paul Freund (known Harvard professor) for the legislation on morality matters;[18] Lawrence Tribe (professor at Harvard University) about gay rights.[19] Among the internationalists, the Court referred to Edwin Borchard (the distinction between treaties and executive agreements, as well as on diplomatic protection), and to C. Ku, on the geopolitical problems of the archipelago.[20]

On procedure and criminal law, the Court quoted M. Schoenfeld as for specific cases of the absolute certainty that the evidence of a crime must have; Roger Park, about the necessary reliability of evidence; Ronald J. Allen is referred to in a judgment dealing with evidence in a case of drug detention.[21] Among the versatile scholars—of Constitutional Law, Jurisprudence, Comparative law, Legal theory—there are Steven G. Calabresi (Yale, Northwestern University)—morals cannot be disciplined by the law; and R. Posner (judge and professor at the University of Chicago[22]); Maurice Rosenberg, on the discretion of the judge.[23]

In the broader field of civil law, the Court quotes H.W. Ballantine (on the possibility for other shareholders to buy shares); Earl Crawford (on an apparent inconsistency between §. 4 and §. 8 of art. VIII of the Constitution); Harry G. Henn (about sole proprietorships, which is not soused in the Filipino commercial range); William Meade Fletcher (the decision regards the interests of the heirs and appointment of an administrator); Roger E. Schechter and John R. Thomas (both on right of publicity, trademark, and intellectual property law); the same Schechter on intellectual property; William Prosser (in a case about harmful conduct for the right to *privacy*); Richard E. Shugrue, about the consent given by the patient and the need that the information provided are always appropriate; M.J. Stephey, on the evolution of credit card systems; Laurie Sterns, about the possibility of distinguishing between plagiarism and *copyright* infringement; Joyce C. George (quoted both by the majority and in a *dissent*) as to whether the reasons for the judgment are protected or not by copyright; finally, Angela

[15] The first was member of the Supreme Court of the United States from 1916 to 1939, the second graduated from Harvard in 1875, then became Chief Justice: judgment 10/18/2011, G.R.181881.

[16] G.R. 188456, 09/10/2009. [17] AM 10-7-17-SC, 02/08/2011.

[18] G.R. 171947–48, 02/15/2011. [19] G.R. 190582, 04/08/2010.

[20] Bochard was law professor at Yale University until the 1950s; Ku was Executive Director of the American Society of International Law (ASIL) and former professor at Johns Hopkins University and at the University of Virginia. See the judgments G.R. 175888; G.R. 176051; G.R. 176222, 02/11/2009; G.R. 162230, 04/28/2010; G.R. 187167, 08/16/2011.

[21] Schoenfeld has been criminal scholar at Harvard, then at the Cleveland-Marshall College of Law, and finally at the Villanova University. Park was trained at Harvard, and then became professor at the UC Hastings College of Law in San Francisco. Allen is a lawyer and a professor of Procedural Law at the Northwestern University, the University of Nebraska, and the State University in New York. The cases are: G.R. 182010, 08/25/2010 and G.R.178757, 03/13/2009; G.R.178757, 03/13/2009; G.R.178757, 03/13/2009.

[22] 01/10/2009, G.R. 122846, which also refers to O.W. Holmes on the same theme. As for R. Posner, see the judgment AM n. 10-7-17-SC of 02/08/2011: 'Plagiarism is a species of intellectual fraud'.

[23] Law professor at the Syracuse University and the Columbia University; see G.R. 189122, 03/17/2010.

Schneeman, author of *Law Corporations, The Law of Corporations and Other Business Organizations*.[24]

Among the US non-jurists, the Supreme Court quoted both social and natural science scientists. A concurring opinion of Judge Corona[25] refers to a sentence from the essay *The third wave* by Alvin Toffler—well-known US mass-mediologist—on the unavoidability of IT choices. In the case G.R. 165424 9.6.2009, the Court uses contributions of some psychologists.[26] In G.R. 189546 of 21.9.2010 the Court identifies the definition of source-code by referring to David Wagner, professor of Computer Science at Berkeley University.

In the Philippines, the dominance of the common law reasoning is also attested by the numerous references to the legal literature of England and other Commonwealth countries, and by numerous quotations of legal professionals (rarely academic): in the field of international law, the Court quoted Andreas O'Shea,[27] Susan McCrory,[28] and Ian Brownlie.[29] In corporate matters, the Court refers to Stuart Sime, quoting his work *A Practical Approach To Civil Procedure*.[30] Among Canadians, there are Don Stuart, professor of criminology at Queen's University in Ontario, on the concept of fair process; the University of Edmonton's specialists in administrative law, D.P. Jones and A.S. De Villars[31] about the peremptoriness of appeal terms. As for Australia, there is Eugenia Levine.[32] Finally, the Court quotes a work of the Chief Justice of India, A.S. Anand, whose education was at University College, London, where it asserts the need that the judicial power does not interfere with the executive one.[33]

The peculiar characteristics of the Philippines legal system also explain quotations—albeit infrequent—of civilian professors. They are mainly German or Austrian, both philosophers and positive jurists. Among philosophers, there is Max Hamburger, a scholar of Aristotle educated at the Universities of Heidelberg and Würzburg, whose

[24] G.R. 157479, 11/24/2010; G.R. 191342, 03/17/2010; G.R. 175048, 02/10/2009; G.R. 177066, 09/11/2009; G.R. 175048, 02/10/2009; G.R. 185917, 06/01/2011; AM 10-7-17-SC, 02/08/2011; G.R.181881, 10/18/2011; G.R. 165279, 06/07/2011; G.R. 174269, 08/25/2010; AM 10717-SC, 02/08/2011; AM 10-7-17-SC, 02/08/2011; G.R. 175048, 02/10/2009.

[25] G.R. 188456, 09/10/2009.

[26] The quoted authors were professors at many US universities. Among non-lawyers, in G.R. 176389/G. R. 176864 of 12/14/2010, the Court used, as an argument in favour of one of the accused, the lack of DNA of the latter on the body of any of the victims by referring to a book by Ron C. Michaelis, biologist, geneticist, researcher of DNA, a graduate of Vanderbilt University.

[27] Barrister and international law expert and author of *Amnesty for crime in international law and practice*: see G.R. 162230, 04/28/2010, on topics related to the book recalled.

[28] Director of the Research Centre of the International Council on Human Rights: see G.R. 182498, 12/03/2009, on the notion of 'forced disappearance'.

[29] Lawyer and professor at the Universities of Leeds, Oxford, and the London School of Economics: G.R. 183871, 02/18/2010, on the substantial equivalence of customary law to other sources of international law.

[30] Of the Oxford University Faculty of Law, where he teaches Civil and Commercial Litigation and Corporate Law: G.R. 153142, 03/29/2010.

[31] Authors of *Principles of Administrative Law* (Carswell 1985).

[32] Who trained at the Columbia Law School and is now an internationalist lawyer, on the theme of command responsibility (title of one of her books).

[33] See G.R. 176389 and G.R. 176864, 12/14/2010; G.R. 190582, 04/08/2010; G.R. 183871, 02/18/2010; G.R. 171947–48, 02/15/2011, respectively.

excerpts on the relationship between morality and law are mentioned. Among jurists, Dieter Fleck, whose studies are evoked when referring to the principles of international law in matters of the jurisdiction of the State hosting foreign armed forces.[34] In addition, the Austrian professor Alfred von Verdross is quoted on the existence of valid *erga omnes* rules towards the countries.[35] Among Eastern Europe professors, the Supreme Court quotes, about the responsibility for war crimes, Serbs Iavor Rangelov and Jovan Ninic, as well as Polish internationalist Jerzy Sztucky's *Jus Cogens and the Vienna Convention on the Law of Treaties*.[36] Only an Argentine professor, Juan E. Mendez, whose book *Disappearances and the Inter-American Court: Reflections on a Litigation Experience* is quoted to explain the juridical characteristics of forced disappearance, represents the rest of the world.[37]

3. Analysis of quotations

The judgments during 2008–2011 seem to contend that the Philippines can continue to be considered as a 'culturally' mixed system. From a linguistic point of view, the only language used in quotes is English; most of the references are to US authors, and among the others the majority belongs to Commonwealth countries. The ancient links with Spain have been completely cut off. German authors only maintain a significant presence, whereas representatives of other countries are quoted mainly in the field of international law (and sometimes they do not come from the academic world). Even non-legal citations (either medical or psychological or political science ones) are traced back to American university scholars.

Universities, from which come quoted authors, are very different. This demonstrates the international dimension, not only of the distinguished Harvard and Yale, but also of other US institutions, while for the United Kingdom, Oxford is present alongside other universities (such as Leeds or the London School of Economics).

The contribution of foreign scholars is recorded in all areas of law, both public and private. It confirms once again the capitulation of the civilian legacies and the affirmation of common law dominance. It should be noted that the Philippine Supreme Court is indifferent even to continental European constitutional law—and, as a consequence, to its categories, which are not related to legal families, but transcend them. There are sporadic references connected to civil rights (but the authors are internationalists).

[34] Former director of the German Federal Ministry of Defense, an expert in international agreements and policy: see G.R. 122846, 01/10/2009, G.R. 175888, G.R. 176051, and G.R. 176222, 02/11/2009.

[35] Professor of International Law at the Universities of Wien (1924) and Wroclaw (1932), in G.R. 162230, 04/28/2010.

[36] Expert in international law at the Centre for the Study of Global Governance in London; operator of the Humanitarian Law Center; professor and operator in Lodz, Rome, Uppsala, respectively. The cases are: G.R. 183871, 02/18/2010, and G.R. 162230, 04/28/2010.

[37] Professor at the Georgetown Law Center, the Johns Hopkins School of Advanced International Studies, and the University of Oxford: G.R. 162230 dated 04/28/2010.

V. South Africa

1. Introductory remarks

The South African legal system is known for its ambivalent character, which is due to the establishment of the Cape Colony by the Dutch in 1652, to the British conquest and annexation of Natal, Transvaal, and Orange, up to the *Union* of the four colonies sanctioned in 1909. The current Constitution consecrates an evolution marked by various stages, such as after independence, where the 1961 Constitution and that of 1983 make a cautious first opening in the breach of apartheid, at least in favour of those of mixed race and Asians.

The system of constitutional judicial review represents a hybrid; the judicial review is in fact conferred on the High Courts. The Constitutional Court only intervenes when there's an appeal from the parties or when there has been a declaration of unconstitutionality by such courts. However, it has exclusive jurisdiction in matters of conflicts between institutions and constitutional bodies, as well as on the conduct of the President. The appointment of the judges emanates from the President of the Republic, after consultation with the leaders of the parties represented in the National Assembly and the Judicial Service Commission.

2. Source of quotations

As for South Africa, the analysed period consists of the first five years after the entry into force of the 1996 Constitution (1996–2000). As already noticed, it is in fact plausible that a new constitutional court gives rationality and continuity to its reasoning by relying more on literature than on its smattering of precedents. There are 24 references to legal literature; quotations are numerous, and are equally distributed between domestic and foreign authors. The Court almost always quotes the legal works. For reasons of space, the information about around 30 South African authors will be omitted.

Among foreigner scholars, 25 authors are from the US—however, quotations are even more numerous, since some of them are multiple. There is Lucius J. Barker, a constitutionalist, emeritus professor at Stanford University, in the judgment n. 2/1996 on privacy;[38] Lawrence G. Baxter, a professor of Judicial Practice at Duke Law School;[39] William Joseph Brennan, Jr, theorist and constitutionalist educated at Harvard, judge of the Supreme Court;[40] Benjamin Nathan Cardozo (1870–1938), judge of the Supreme Court, from Columbia Law School. In the judgment n. 9/1999, the Court quotes *The*

[38] The Court quotes his *Civil Liberties and the Constitution* (Prentice-Hall 1970).

[39] Also an expert on administrative law, comparative law, criminal law, constitutional law. He is well reputed, because he had started his career at the University of Natal in South Africa. His book *Administrative Law* (Juta 1984) is quoted in the judgment n. 6/1998 on certain profiles of due process; and in the judgment n. 8/2000, on the discretionary use of power. (The judgment regarded the right of spouses to live together and the principle of dignity.)

[40] *Reason, Passion, and the Progress of the Law, The Forty-Second Annual Benjamin N. Cardozo Lecture*, judgment n. 15/1999.

Nature of the Judicial Process, where the great jurist rejects the opinion that a judge can always be 'absolutely' neutral. As for privacy, the Court also refers to Angela C. Carmella, a Harvard graduate and professor at Seton Hall;[41] to P. Allan Dionisopoulos and Craig R. Ducat, respectively professors of Political Science and Constitutional Law Policies at Northern Illinois University.[42]

The Court then refers to William E. Burghardt Du Bois (1868–1963), historian, essayist, publisher, PhD at Harvard, founder of the department of Sociology at the University of Atlanta;[43] to Ronald Dworkin, famous constitutionalist who trained at Harvard but was a professor at Yale[44] (a dissent in the judgment n. 2/1996 refers to its rather obvious phrase[45]); to Thomas Irwin Emerson (1907–1991), theorist of law, especially of civil liberties, and professor at Yale Law School for 30 years (on freedom of expression);[46] to Kathleen Ferraro, professor of Sociology at Northern Arizona University, whose *Irreconcilable Differences—Battered Women, Police and the Law*, is referred to in the judgment n. 19/2000 on the subject of domestic violence and family relationships; to Thomas C. Grey, which is quoted in the judgment n. 15/1999 in its critical passage about anti-sodomy laws;[47] to A. Leon Higginbotham (1928–1998) lawyer and judge of the Federal Court of Appeal, who trained at Yale Law School, and Michael F. Higginbotham, a professor at the University of Baltimore School of Law;[48] to Christine Littleton, professor of Women's Rights at UCLA, whose article 'Reconstructing Sexual Equality' is quoted in the judgment n. 15/1999 (sodomy).

Furthermore, the Court quotes other American authors: Martha Minow, Dean of Harvard Law School and professor of Civil Procedure, Constitutional Law, Family Law, International Criminal Justice;[49] John E. Nowak and Ronald D. Rotunda, co-authors of the famous manual of constitutional law;[50] Dorothy Q. Thomas, activist for human rights whose preparation is non-academic (on domestic violence);[51] Laurence H. Tribe, professor of Constitutional Law at Harvard University—the Court uses his famous

[41] See judgment n. 11/2000 (on the relationship between corporal punishment and religious freedom). The book mentioned is Mary Ann Glendon, *Religious Liberty: The Social Nature of the Person and the Public Nature of Religion.*

[42] Judgment n. 2/1996, with a quote from their book *The Right to Privacy.*

[43] Currently Clark, Atlanta University. In the judgment n. 15/1999 (on sodomy), the Court cites his work *The Souls of Black Folk: Essays and Sketches.*

[44] And member of the New York University School of Law.

[45] 'Freedom should not mean license', in the judgment n. 7/1996; another dissent remembers a passage on the relationship between freedom of expression and pornography.

[46] Judgment n. 7/1996, which quotes his *The System of Freedom and Expression.*

[47] Legal theorist and historian of the development of American legal thought, former judge in the Court of Appeals for the District of Columbia Circuit and professor at Stanford Law School.

[48] They are co-authors with a South African judge of the article 'De Jure Housing Segregation in the United States and South Africa: The Difficult Pursuit for Racial Justice' (judgment n. 2/2000).

[49] Judgment n. 19/2000 on domestic violence. The cited work is *Between Vengeance and Forgiveness: Feminist Responses to Violent Injustice.*

[50] Professor of Constitutional Law at the Loyola University, and constitutionalist as well, a graduate of Harvard Law School and a professor at the Chapman University Dale E. Fowler School of Law, respectively. See judgment n. 5/1997, about the review of the economic and social laws. Nowak and Rotunda are also mentioned in the judgment n. 15/1999 on sodomy. In the same judgment, the Court quotes *Naked Preferences and the Constitution* by Cass R. Sunstein, former professor of Constitutional Law and Administrative Law at the University of Chicago Law School and currently a professor at Harvard Law School.

[51] Judgment n. 19/2000.

American Constitutional Law several times;[52] Michael Walzer, in the judgment n. 15/1999 on sodomy.[53] In the same judgment, P. Williams, PhD at Harvard and professor of law at Columbia University, advocate of critical race theory, is also mentioned. Finally, there are references to Adrien Katherine Wing and, in the same case, to Robert Maxwell Young.[54]

From the British homeland, the Court quotes many jurists (and non-jurists). Apart from Lord Acton,[55] the reasoning of the majority or the minority opinions often refer to classical authors, such as A.V. Dicey (quoted five times[56]); R. Jennings, mentioned in judgment n. 17/2000 (on the rights of homosexual couples), and in n. 29/2000 (on the definition of international agreement[57]); W. Wade (1918–2004), father of British administrative law, and professor at Harvard and at Trinity College in Cambridge, cited in judgment n. 6/1998 on corporate law.

The Constitutional Court quotes several jurists. Among others: Stephen Bailey (School of Law, University of Nottingham), mentioned in judgment n. 6/1998; Jean Brownlie (Leeds, Oxford, London School of Economics, and lawyer), also quoted by the Court of the Philippines (on the Vienna Convention reflecting common international law);[58] Stanley A. de Smith, who trained at Cambridge and is a professor at the London School of Economics, at the University of London and at Cambridge;[59] Paul P. Craig (Oxford), specialist of administrative and European law (on the suspension of school scholarships without reasonable notice);[60] Christopher F. Forsyth, professor of Public Law and Private International Law at Cambridge, on preventive detention;[61] Denis Galligan, professor of Administrative Law at Oxford;[62] Jeffrey Jowell, professor of Constitutional Law, Administrative Law and Human Rights at UCL in London;[63] Carol Harlow, emeritus professor of Public/Administrative law at the London School of Economics, and Richard Rawlings, a professor at University College in London.[64]

[52] Judgments n. 15/1999 on sodomy, n. 11/2000 on the subject of religion, and n. 15/2000 on the relation between the President and the Congress on the constitutionality of a bill.

[53] Professor of Political, Social and Moral Philosophy at the Institute for Advanced Study at Princeton. The book recalled is *Spheres of Justice: A Defence of Pluralism and Equality*.

[54] Judgment n. 15/1999 on sodomy: the quoted work is *Critical race Feminism: a reader*. Wing graduated from Princeton, UCLA, and Stanford, and is now a professor of Human and International Rights at the University of Iowa College of Law. Young is a science historian specializing in Darwinian thought, a biological and human sciences philosopher, and a psychotherapist.

[55] Judgment n. 6/1998, on corporate matters, quotes his sentence: 'there is no worse heresy than that the office sanctifies the holder of it'.

[56] N. 6/1998, 17/1999, 8/2000 on rule of law, on balance among powers (judgment n. 15/2000), on due process (n. 16/2000).

[57] Professor of International Law at Cambridge (who specialized at Harvard), judge and President of the International Court of Justice since 1982.

[58] Judgment n. 29/2000 (extradition).

[59] Judgment n. 1/2000 (on the role of courts in the control of public discretional power).

[60] The quoted work is *Legitimate Expectations: A Conceptual Analysis. Substantive Legitimate Expectations in Domestic and Community Law*, in the judgment n. 20/1999.

[61] Judgment n. 17/1999 and n. 20/1999.

[62] Judgment n. 8/2000 (cohabitation of spouses), and judgment n. 16/2000 (on due process).

[63] Judgment n. 1/2000 (on the role of the courts).

[64] Judgment n. 8/2000 (on the right of spouses to live together), which quotes their book *Law and Administration*.

Stephen Sedley, Geraldine Van Bueren, Arthur Watts, Robert Wintemute, Harry Kenneth Woolf are also quoted.[65]

It is well known that South Africa regarded Canada as a model in the construction of its new institutional framework—it is an example of a balanced, multicultural society. Hence, Canadian scholars are repeatedly quoted in the judgments of the Constitutional Court: for example, Peter W. Hogg, the leading Canadian constitutional law scholar, who is mentioned five times.[66] Among others, the Court refers to James A. Fontana, an Ontario judge, who trained at the Universities of Toronto, Ottawa, and at Osgoode Hall Law School; David A. Wright, a lawyer who specialized in human rights at the Court of Ontario and professor of Administrative Law at Osgoode Hall Law School; Jennifer Nedelsky, professor of law at the University of Toronto and formerly professor of Politics at Princeton University; Betsy Gibbons (researcher at Manitoba), co-author of the essay *Domestic Violence Protection Orders: A Comparative Review.*[67] Among the non-lawyers, there is Otto Klineberg (1899–1992) psychologist at Columbia University and at the University of Paris.[68]

As for other common law systems, there are references to the Irish constitutionalist at Trinity College in Oxford, John M. Kelly, who is quoted in the judgment n. 15/2000 concerning the powers of the President in legislative proceedings. Among the Australians, the Court refers to the volume *Constitutional and Administrative Law: Basic Principles* by Laurence Boulle, judge and professor of law at Bond University; John F. Mitchell, jurist and philosopher of law at University College, Oxford and the University of Notre Dame; Moira Paterson, professor of IT law at Monash University in Australia.[69] Despite the massive presence of an Asian community, Indian scholars are not specifically mentioned—albeit some quotations of the Supreme Court of India are not infrequent.[70] As for Israel, the quotation regards Natan Lerner, who graduated from the University of Buenos Aires, specialized in international law and is a professor at IDC in Herzliya.[71] From Zimbabwe there is a quotation from Bede

[65] Sedley was a Judge of the Court of Appeal of England and Wales from 1999 to 2011, educated at Queens' College, Cambridge; Van Bueren is a lawyer and professor of International Law of Human Rights at Queen Mary, University of London; Watts is an internationalist lawyer and diplomat, who trained at a military boarding school and then at Cambridge, mentioned twice; Wintemute is professor of Human Rights at King's College, London; Woolf, non-academic (who studied law at University College London). See in the order: judgment n. 1/2000 on the role of the courts; judgment n. 11/2000, on religious education; judgments n. 17/2000 (same-sex couples) and 29/2000 (extradition); judgment n. 15/1999 on sodomy; judgment n. 1/2000 on the control of the courts.

[66] Educated at the University of New Zealand, at Harvard, and at the Monash University in Melbourne, then professor of law at Osgoode Hall Law School—York University in Toronto. He is quoted in judgments n. 3/1996 on the central and provincial jurisdictions on school matters; n. 5/1997, on criminal liability; 15/1999, on sodomy; 15/2000 on the presidential veto; 17/2000, on homosexual couples.

[67] Judgment n. 2/1996, on monition; judgment n. 20/1999, on scholarships and child custody; judgment n. 19/2000 (domestic violence).

[68] Judgment n. 4/1996, on the use of languages in education.

[69] Judgment n. 1/2000, on the role of the courts; judgment n. 15/1999 on sodomy (the Court quoted the essay *Law, Morality and Sexual Orientation*); judgment n. 20/1999, on child custody.

[70] The only quoted authors are a judge—Asaf Ali Asghar Fyzee—educated in Bombay and at St. John's College in Cambridge (the judgment n. 1/1996, on adoption, quotes the volume *Outlines of Muhammadan Law in India*); and the constitutionalist Hormasji Maneckji Seervai (*Constitutional Law of India*, mentioned in the judgment n. 4/1996 on discrimination in school).

[71] Judgment n. 4/1996, on educational rights.

Harris.[72] Finally, the Court refers to the famous Egyptian Mahmoud C. Bassiouni: trained in the US, he is an internationalist and a criminal scholar, emeritus professor at DePaul University College of Law in Chicago.

The mixed nature of the South African law should lead us to imagine a balanced presence of European authors, especially the Dutch ones. On the contrary, there are only two quotations between 1996 and 2001: Pieter Van Dijk and Godefridus J.H. Van Hoof.[73] The only German scholar, to which the Court refers, is Rainer Forst, a professor of Political Theory and Philosophy at the Goethe University in Frankfurt (who is mentioned in the same judgment n. 2/1996).The Austrian Erwin Bernat, professor at the Institute of Public Law, University of Graz, is quoted as for corporal punishment in schools in the judgment n. 11/2000. Only a quotation of the French sociologist, philosopher, psychologist, and historian Paul M. Foucault—evoked in the judgment n. 15/1999 on sodomy—represents France. As for Italy, only Francesco Capotorti is quoted.[74]

3. Analysis of quotations

The South African experience points out a considerable receding of the civil law legal tradition. Like in the Philippines, the majority of bibliographic references are in English; apart from local authors, the majority of the quotations regard US or Commonwealth authors. Even whilst referring to administrative law (whose *raison d'être* correspond to the civil law), British or American authors are quoted. The cultural Boer stock (Roman-Dutch Law) disappeared. There are sporadic quotations of Austrian and German scholars, whereas French and Italian ones are absent or almost absent.

Hence, the prestige of universities where the quoted authors teach still counts. Some famous academic institutions still exert their charm, irrespective of the branch of law involved. In particular, Harvard, Yale, Oxford, and Cambridge continue to provide vital nourishment to the formation of the legal thought that is most highly regarded in South Africa, although there are numerous less ancient universities (or, in theory, less prestigious). It should be recalled that there is a close connection between the Court of South Africa and Canadian universities. The common problems faced by the two countries, with reference to the concept of multi-ethnic, multilingual, and multicultural cohabitation, justify various quotes of social scientists (however not only Canadians) in the judgments of the Constitutional Court.

VI. Israel

1. Introductory remarks

Since the British conquest of Palestine between 1917 and 1918, the Ottoman law had been gradually supplanted by the doctrine of the English courts—which were

[72] Professor at the Universities of Natal, Pietermaritzburg, Waikato, James Cook, and Canberra, about judicial review and the role of the courts (judgment n. 1/2000).

[73] Of whom in judgment 2/1996 the book *Theory and Practice of the European Convention on Human Rights* is remembered, in relation to the right to privacy.

[74] N. 4/1996, on the importance of educational rights.

established in the conquered territories—by the legislation passed at Westminster, by the codification of unwritten principles in the legal provisions adopted by the agent administration.

The judicial system partly reflects the British imprinting. In Israel, the Supreme Court—not an ad hoc tribunal—exercises the judicial review of legislation. The parameter does not consist in a written constitution, but in the Fundamental Laws subsequently approved by a qualified majority in the Knesset.

The analysis of the scholars quoted by the Supreme Court certifies this trend. Moreover, Israel has many other reasons of interest in relation to the topic of study. First, it is true that there is a British cultural lineage; however, the creation of a homeland for the Jewish people entailed the arrival in ancient Palestine (now the State of Israel) of people and jurists educated in cultures different from the Anglo-Saxon one. This could have provoked a changing in legal mentality after World War II. Second, it will be interesting to verify the endurance of the English influence, which has to face the competition from other areas of common law, such as the United States and Canada. Finally, as for the several waves of migration, it will be necessary to prove whether there has been inputs or recoveries of the European continental doctrine.

To test the working hypothesis, we will carry out a dynamic study. We will first analyse the judgments of the early years after independence. Then, we will choose 'random' sample judgments delivered in the past decades.

2. Source of quotations

The essay examines 35 judgments delivered in the period 1948–1958—14 judgments contain doctrinal references. We will omit those related only to the Israeli doctrine. A case of 4/12/1950 deals with the question of whether Israel should take over Palestine, including in the payment of debts. The Court quoted a passage by Kelsen on the topic of the responsibility of States. Four days later, in the field of private international law (divorce between spouses who were French citizens living in France, and of custody of the children), it quotes *Conflict of Laws* by A. Dicey. A ruling of 3/29/1951, on the delicate issue of polygamy, defines the term 'discrimination' according to the *Encyclopaedia of the Social Sciences*. The Court also referred to such work in the judgment of 10/16/1953, on freedom of expression—during which it remembers the American constitutionalist Zechariah Chafee (1885–1957), and the British jurist and scholar William Blackstone (1723–1780)—and in the judgment of 4/4/1955, where it quoted the definitions of 'interest' and 'usury' given in the same work by the Swiss scholar Edgar Salin. The Court also referred to Chafee in the case *Kol Ha'Am v Minister of Interior*, on information, in numerous passages of his work *Free Speech in the United States*, written in 1948.[75]

Dicey and the German jurist and philosopher Christian Wolff (1679–1754)—the Court quoted his *Private International Law*—are evoked in the judgment 6/4/1953, on the conflict of law rules (insurances). On usufruct and Ottoman law, there is a reference

[75] Respectively: C.A. 41/49; 16.4.1950, HJC 125/49; CRIM. A.112/50; HCJ.101/54; C.A. 248/53; 7 P.D. 871, 1953.

to a volume by George Young, *Corps de droit Ottoman* in the judgment 7/28/1954. As for family law, the Court quoted W.E. Beckett's *The Recognition of Polygamous Marriages under English Law*, and P.B. Maxwell, *Interpretation of Statutes*, in the decision 1/15/1954 (divorce and religious marriage), in a passage related to the *jus superveniens*; P.H. Winfield, *Chief Sources of Legal History* (and the Welsh criminal specialist Glanville Williams) are referred to on the use of a precedent in a case concerning retirement. The same Glanville Williams, along with some criminologists and psychiatrists and Jerome Hall, a law professor at Indiana University, were quoted in the judgment 2/24/1956.[76] Finally, judgment 10/24/1956, on causality connections in a case of manslaughter, mentioned Arnold D. McNair;[77] and a judgment of 02/13/1958 (the jurisdiction of the Courts in the occupied Palestine areas) quoted the internationalists Georg Schwarzenberger (University of London), Lassa Oppenheim, of German descent, professor in Basel but emigrated to the United Kingdom and naturalized British in 1900, and Eric Barendt, from Oxford and professor of Media Law at University College London.[78]

In the second period we have analysed, there is a progressive detachment from the English legal literature, and a greater reliance on the US, as well as a kind of 'allowance' of the German one. Because of the memory of the Holocaust, the latter had been relegated to a cryptic role, without expressed quotations. The migration to Israel and the different educations of the judges tend to internationalize even more, whenever possible, the doctrine of the Supreme Court.

The British cultural background, however, still continues, as in the case of quotations of classical works, such as in *The Academic Center of Law and Business v Minister of Finance*, which deals with the unconstitutionality of a law, which entrusted the management of individual prisons to private corporations. The Court quotes Hobbes, Locke, Adam Smith, and Isaiah Berlin.[79]

Among American ones, authors, scholars, teachers and lawyers from Stanford, Yale, and Harvard are mentioned at a steady rate, as in the case of *Ressler v Minister of Defence*,[80] on standing. Quotations encompass Peter Cane, lecturer, reader, and professor at Yale Law School; Kenneth E. Scott and Wayne McCormick, both professors at Stanford (the latter also at the Universities of Utah and Texas); Kenneth C. Davis. In previous judgments, the Court had quoted T.I. Emerson, a professor at Yale Law School, J.A. Barron, a professor at George Washington University Law School, and Melville Nimmer (trained at Berkeley and Harvard, and professor at UCLA School of Law).[81]

[76] The authors are: a famous Scottish psychiatrist, Angus MacNiven; the Polish-American criminologist Sheldon Glueck, educated at Harvard and professor at the same university; the American criminologists E.R. Keedy and the same Sheldon Glueck from Harvard, both passed away. The quoted cases are: C.A.118/51; 02/19/1954, C.A.191/51; C.A.238/53; 04/06/1953, H.C.J.176/54; CRIM.A.118/53. In judgment n. 02/24/1956 the Court recalls also a passage from *Hamlet* by Shakespeare and the XVII century jurist Matthew Hale, about murders and mental illnesses.

[77] 1885–1975, British jurist, professor at the Universities of Cambridge and Liverpool, judge, and first President of the European Court of Human Rights.

[78] See CRIM.A. 47/56, and H.C.J. 103/57; HC 399/85, 41 PD 255, 1987.

[79] HCJ 2605/05, 11/19/2009.

[80] 42 PD 441, 1988.

[81] *Kahane v Broadcasting Authority*, HC 399/85, 41 PD 255, 1987.

German and Austrian authors are also mentioned in *Miller v Minister of Transport*. Texts and opinions of the former Presidents of the Constitutional Court of Austria Ludwig Adamovich and Walter Antoniolli are quoted.[82] There are also manifold references to philosophical or general theory works that analyse the relationship between law and society, such as those of Schmitt, Habermas, Ehrlich, Forsthoff—professor of constitutional law at the Universities of Vienna, Hamburg and Heidelberg—and Max Weber, who is mentioned in the case *Academic Center Law and Business v Minister of Finance*.[83]

Other classics mentioned several times are Cesare Beccaria, whose work *On Crimes and Punishments* is the subject of study and analysis in the case *Barzilai v Government of Israel*,[84] along with authors belonging to the French tradition such as Montesquieu or Rousseau.[85]

Among the continental authors, *Local Building and Construction Committee v Holzman* refers to the studies of the Italian specialist in administrative law Domenico Sorace (University of Florence) to explain the circumstances in which it is possible to get expropriation and commensurate compensation. In *The Public Committee v The Government of Israel*, the Court refers to the works of the internationalist Antonio Cassese (University 'La Sapienza' in Rome).[86] The American political analyst Philip Pettit, from Princeton, is quoted for an article published in a book edited by three philosophers of law from the University of Bologna (Bongiovanni, Sartor, and Valentini) in *Academic Center for Law and Business v Minister of Finance*.

3. Analysis of quotations

The impressive number of doctrinal quotes in the decisions of the Supreme Court of Israel precludes analysing them in an analytical way. Some majority opinions—and individual ones—can be considered as essays, equipped with notes, in which the references to common law precedents (initially mainly British, then also from US and other jurisdictions) are accompanied by references to the legislation and—the most relevant feature—to legal and non-legal literature.

Thus, the Supreme Court clearly expresses the idea that the law not only rests on statutes, but also on their interpretations—precedents—and on works of scholars. The Court also confirms that there can be mismatches between the three levels of formants. Indeed, the levels are used jointly, when aligned, or separately, if conflicting. The Court not only rests on local legal heritage (which it could not do at the beginning), but also on comparative law. Such 'openness' is particularly facilitated in Israel by the peculiar history of the country, from the differentiated roots and the patchy formation of the

[82] The quoted texts are *Verwaltungsrecht* and *AllgemeinesVerwaltungsrecht*.

[83] HCJ 311/60, 15 PD 1989, and HCJ 2605/05, PD 2009.

[84] HCJ 428/86, 08/06/1986.

[85] Montesquieu is quoted in the judgments *Supreme Monitoring Committee v Prime Minister; Leon v Acting District Commissioner of Tel-Aviv* (HCJ 5/48); *Academic Center Law and Business v Minister of Finance* (HCJ 2605/05, PD 2009); and Rousseau in the judgments *Bassil Abu Aita v The Regional Commander of Judea and Samaria* (HCJ 69/81).

[86] See CA 5546/97, CA 6417/97, HCJ 769/02, 12/11/2005 and HGC 2605/05 1, 11/19/2009.

judges, coming from different stories and universities. It is not easy to ascribe the cultural origins of a doctrinal reference: judges often have different training, partly in Europe, partly in the United States, and only those of the last generation were all (or nearly all) born in Israel and often trained in the prestigious Universities of Jerusalem and Tel-Aviv. Nevertheless, cosmopolitanism is still marked, as evidenced by the use of comparison (and citations of foreign authors) also in the last decade, although the mentioned authors, even though not Israelis, are often Jews.

It is true that the legal sources with major influence in Israel—as in other analysed countries—are those from US universities, especially the most known ones. From the Anglo-Saxon world there are also influences from Canada, as well as from the UK. Albeit Israel has civilian foundations that make it a mixed jurisdiction, the European continental legal literatures were absent in the first period. They then became recessive—when compared to the Anglo-Saxon one—during the course of the whole life of the country.

This is due to the fact that the Supreme Court has been gradually transformed into a court of constitutionality and 'jurisdiction of freedom'. This is a general trend in comparative legal studies; in Israel, however, it corresponds to the growing importance assumed by Fundamental Laws on the subject of freedom as benchmarks. The private and civil issues the Court deals with (which would justify a more extensive use of European continental doctrine) are numerically less frequent. Furthermore, this can be considered as a consequence of the already mentioned reluctance to explicitly evoke German influences, which characterized the early years of jurisprudence.

Finally, there is a scarcity of quotation of French, Italian, and Spanish scholars.

VII. Argentina

1. Introductory remarks

The legal and institutional history of Argentina is characterized by some significant landmarks: the first Spanish settlements in the early 16th century; independence in 1810, the Constitutions of 1853, 1949, and 1994; the period of the dictatorship (since 1976); the restoration of democracy. These landmarks shall not detain us here; suffice to say that, as in other Latin American jurisdictions, civil law (imported from Spain) has been affected by the influence of the US model, as in the case of the constitutional design.

The assumption is also valid for constitutional litigation of both levels of governments—provincial and federal—which is basically organized in order to ensure the appointment of judges with a background in law. Judges are appointed by the President with the consent of the Senate by a majority of two-thirds.

2. Source of quotations

Between 2008 and 2011, there were 39 judgments with references. Setting aside the numerous citations of domestic legal doctrine (the Court is not used to citing living

Argentine authors), out of a total of 104 citations, there are only 49 Argentines. This demonstrates a huge recourse of the Court to comparative law.

Some references have regard to Latin American jurists, such as the constitutionalist Uruguayans Agustín de Vedia (on impeachment) and Héctor Gros Espiell (human rights); the renowned civil law expert Héctor Lafaille; the tax lawyers Juan Eduardo Azzini and Ramón Valdés Costa;[87] the Colombian constitutionalist Florentino González (1843–1910), who was also quoted in judgment 10/6/2009 regarding indictments against the President of the Republic.

The number of quotations of US authors is considerable, and the Supreme Court sometimes refers to them in labour law and administrative law, as well as for institutional issues. The only US author quoted in two judgments is Corwin:[88] his work, *The Constitution and what it means today,* provides the Court with a contribution on the method of legal interpretation. Among others, there are some classics: Alexander Hamilton, Thomas M. Cooley (1824–1898, judge and professor at the University of Michigan), and J.W. Paschal (1812–1878, professor at Georgetown University);[89] Nathaniel C. Towle—the Court remembers the 1861 volume *A History and Analysis of the Constitution of the United States* (on impeachment).[90]

The remaining authors are contemporary: Dinah Shelton, professor of International Law at the Faculty of Law in Washington (the judgment 12/7/2010 quotes a passage related to the inalienability of rights in labour law); Philip Alston, about safety in the workplace; Wayne Morrison (judgment 8/11/2009, on people illegally abducted and disappeared during the military dictatorship).[91] On sources of law we find Lawrence Tribe, Professor of Constitutional Law at Harvard Law School;[92] Jeremy T. Gunn, about the concreteness of the constitutionality judgment (the case concerned a deputy who claimed standing).[93] Among the non-jurists, J. Mann, a doctor author of writings on health and rights, is quoted in judgment 12/7/2010[94] on these topics.

As for civil law legal literature, there are a relevant number of Spanish authors, quoted by dissenting judges. This indicates the continuing influence of ancient homeland, facilitated by the use of a common language.

[87] Respectively 10/06/2009 (M1514.XLIII), 08/10/2010 (A.374.XLIII), 08/04/2009 (L.314.XL), 04/22/2008 (O.259.XLI), 06/15/2010 (A.910.XXXVII).

[88] E.S. Corwin, a famous scholar of political doctrines and a political expert, educated at the Universities of Michigan and Pennsylvania, judgments 08/12/2008 (G.1326.XXXIX), and 12/14/2010 (A.246.XXXIX).

[89] 06/15/2010 (A.910.XXXVII), on taxation; 02/10/2009 (M.565.XL), on interstate commerce; 10/6/2009 (M.1514.XLIII), on impeachment.

[90] 10/06/2009, M.1514.XLIII.

[91] Alston is an internationalist of Australian origin, trained at the Universities of Melbourne and Berkeley, professor at New York University School of Law; Morrison, from the University of Wisconsin, Stanford Law School, San Francisco State University, a professor of Criminal Law and Family Law at the St. Louis School of Law, Washington University.

[92] The references are: A. 1023. XLIII, cit.; 03/31/2009, T.205.XLIV; G. 291.XLIII; G. 291.XLIII.

[93] Case 06/15/2010, T.117.XLVI. J.T. Gunn is professor at the Faculty of Arts and Sciences at the University of Al Akhawayn in Ifrane, Morocco, Senior Fellow in Religion and Human Rights at the Center for the Study of Law and Religion at Emory University School of Law and former director of the ACLU programme on freedom of religion and belief. PhD at Harvard, educated at Boston and Chicago. He has filled various positions in the US government, also in the US State Department.

[94] A.1023.XLIII.

For example, the Court quotes the constitutionalists Camino Vidal Fueyo (judgment 6/15/2010 on the principles of rationality and proportionality as requirements for the activity of the State),[95] and Eduardo García de Enterría, emeritus professor at the University Complutense of Madrid (case 4/22/2008, on the equivalence between service charge and tax); the experts in procedure Ferrandiz, Castro-Prieto, and Francisco Ramos Méndez,[96] on preventive seizure as a measure of temporary restriction of the right to property; and González Navarro, professor of Administrative Procedural Law at the Escuela Nacional de Administración Pública, in judgment 11/4/2008, on matters of entry to the Bar of the State.

In addition, Elisa Perez-Vera is quoted in relation to the 1980 Hague Convention related to the civil aspects of international child abduction—the Court refers to her as framer of the Convention;[97] José María Rodríguez de Santiago is referred to on the principles of rationality and proportionality;[98] the labourist Pérez Botija is mentioned on compensation for damages to workers;[99] Salvador Alvarez del Castillo-Cedrón, Professor of Tax Law at the University of Salamanca, is quoted for his *Consideraciones sobre las presunciones jurídicas en materia impositiva* (the title of his article is also the theme of the judgment).[100] Finally, there is the legal philosopher Luis Recasens Siches.[101]

The European continental doctrine is represented by French authors, such as Eduardo Laboulaye, lawyer and politician of the 19th century, and author of *Curso de Legislación comparada*, mentioned in case 10/6/2009 on impeachment; G. Burdeau, professor of Constitutional Law at the Sorbonne; Pierre Lambert, whose book *Les partis liberticides et la Convention européenne des droits de l'homme* is quoted;[102] Henri Donnedieu de Vabres, criminal expert at the Sorbonne and judge in the Nuremberg trials; Maurice Travers, author of an international criminal law manual, in judgment 5/19/2010, on extradition and prescription; Karel Vasak;[103] and Philippe Cahier, author of a *Derecho Diplomático Contemporáneo*.[104]

The Court also quotes Italian scholars. Hence, there are quotations from the two major experts in adjective law, Francesco Carnelutti and Piero Calamandrei, on standing;[105] the expert in labour law, Louis Barassi (Perugia, Genoa, Bari, and the

[95] Professor of Constitutional Law at the University of Burgos, of whom the Court remembers the article 'El principio de proporcionalidad como parámetro de constitucionalidad de la actividad del juez'.

[96] The latter, professor of Procedural Law at the University Pompeu Fabra in Barcelona, of whom the textbook *Derecho Procesal Civil* is recalled in the case 06/15/2010 (n 93).

[97] Judge of the Tribunal Constitucional, professor in Granada, at the Universidad Autónoma de Madrid, in Santiago de Compostela: judgment 10/21/2010, R.390.XLVI.

[98] Professor of Administrative Law at the Universidad Autónoma de Madrid, in case 6/15/2010, cit.

[99] 8/12/2008, cit. The Court remembers his 'Curso de Derecho del Trabajo' (Madrid, 1948).

[100] Judgment 06/15/2010, H.442.XXXVIII.

[101] Professor at the Universities of Santiago de Compostela, Salamanca, Valladolid, Madrid, and then at the UNAM in Mexico, quoted on the nature of the interpretation in the case 02/24/2009 (A.1792.XLII), on social security.

[102] In judgment 03/17/2009, P.1469.XLI, on political anti-system parties, and 05/29/2010, cit.

[103] Born in Czechoslovakia and then moved to France to study law, international official and university professor: case 12/07/2010, cit., on labour law.

[104] Case 04/08/2008, S.2102XL, on extradition and double incrimination matters.

[105] Carnelutti taught at the Universities of Milano-Bocconi, Catania, Padua, Milano-Statale, Rome; Calamandrei belonged to a Pisa and Florentine school. Both are quoted in judgment n. 06/15/2010.

Catholic University of Milan), is referred to in judgment 8/12/2008, concerning the right of workers to participate in the profits of the enterprise. The Court quotes the already mentioned internationalist Antonio Cassese,[106] and Luigi Ferrajoli, philosopher of law and professor in Rome, well known in Latin America (case 5/27/2009 on the role of judges and individual rights).[107]

There are also quotations from German scholars. Most of them are classical authors: the theorist and philosopher Gustav Radbruch (Munich, Leipzig, and Berlin); the great expert in criminal law, educated at Jena and working in Munich in the early 19th century, Paul Johann Anselm Ritter von Feuerbach;[108] Hermann Heller, jurist and politician between the two World Wars, on the definition of 'people' contained in the *Teoría del Estado* (case of 2/24/2009 concerning confidentiality).[109] Ernst Rudolf Huber is also recalled in case 11/4/2008, on the Bar Association;[110] the internationalist and diplomat Jan Woischnik,[111] about the impartiality of judges, guarantees for the accused, and the constraints of international conventions; the expert in public law Martín (judgment n. 6/24/2008, on the balance between the right to information and protection of honour, and judgment n. 11/9/2010, on the legal recognition of a neo-Nazi party).[112]

Hans Kelsen represents German and Austrian legal scholars. His famous essay *La garantía jurisdiccional de la Constitución* is quoted in relation to the judicial review of legislation.[113] Manfred Nowak is referred to for freedom of association in the field of labour and in relation to international agreements on the subject.[114]

Quotations from British scholars only comprise Matthew Craven (professor of International Law at the Faculty of Law, University of London, both in terms of labour and the rights of the person protected by international agreements[115]), and the 19th-century jurist O.M. Wilson, of whom the Court cites a *Digesto de la Ley Parlamentaria* (case 10/6/2009, on impeachment).

3. Analysis of quotations

The Argentine Supreme Court makes a significant use of quotations. To put it another way, borders do not impede a legal dialogue. The Court's legal culture is enriched by a valuable comparative propensity.

The circulation of foreign legal literature does not follow a merely geographical line, marked by territorial proximity (as for Uruguayans or Colombian authors.) The basin

[106] Internationalist and professor in Florence, case 12/07/2010, cit., remembered for his statement on the supremacy of international jurisdictions compared to state ones on rights matters.

[107] T.639.XLII. [108] Judgment 08/11/2009, cit. (extradition and rights).

[109] H.270.XLII.

[110] Scholar of constitutional law between the two wars, compromised with Nazism, a professor at the Universities of Bonn, Leipzig, and Strasbourg, and, in the postwar period, in the Universities of Freiburg and Göttingen.

[111] Educated in Heidelberg, Freiburg, and Mainz, judgment 05/27/2009 (T.639.XLII).

[112] Respectively P.2297.XL and D.828. X. Kriele, educated at Yale and Muenster, is professor in Koeln.

[113] Case 5/19/2010, C.205.XLV.

[114] In judgment 11/11/2008, A.201.XL. Nowak was director of the Institut für Menschenrechte Ludwig Boltzmann, and then of a similar institute at the University of Utrecht.

[115] Judgment 8/20/2010 (A. 374. XLIII), and judgment 12/07/2010, cit.

is mostly represented by contiguity in legal culture, as attested by the numerous references to Spanish scientific legal literature. Moreover, Spanish scholars are not only quoted for their commentaries; there are also contributions of theorists, philosophers, constitutionalists, experts in labour law, tax experts, etc. This similarly occurs with Italian and French scholars. As for the former, there are quotations of the great masters of adjective law of the first postwar period,[116] along with authors who had delved into civil rights. As for French scholars, the Court refers to works on constitutional law and liberties, as well as on the relationship between State powers—in the constitutional structure of Argentina, the frame of government was influenced by the US model. Quotations of German legal literature leave room for different interpretations. Some of them evoke the 'ghosts of the past' (as for the political parties), whereas others draw from the immense theoretical and philosophical heritage of Germany and Austria, or from the production in distinct areas of constitutional law. Moreover, there are no quotes about private law.

As for common law authors, the discourse is identical: in addition to the classics, the Argentine Supreme Court quotes writings concerning labour law and administrative law of US authors, although the majority refer to cases affecting rights and freedoms. There has been no penetration of Canadian doctrine, and the British one is unsatisfactory.

The universities that trained and taught the mentioned authors are both the classic and the 'new' ones: Harvard is represented alongside Stanford, Wisconsin, New York, Michigan, Pennsylvania, St. Louis, Washington, etc.; the Sorbonne appears only for an author now deceased; Complutense and Salamanca are quoted together with Granada, Santiago de Compostela, Valladolid; Bologna is absent, and Italy is represented by Rome and Florence, with authors both contemporary and deceased. Among living German scholars, the Court only quotes a constitutionalist from Cologne.

As for legal culture, the impression is that Argentina looks like a 'mixed' jurisdiction more than the other systems analysed. It is an example of cross globalization, where the constitutional doctrine draws heavily from domestic, European, and Anglo-Saxon doctrine with no apparent connections with the foundations of the normative formants (civil law) or with the institutional models adopted (United States). There is, therefore, a considerable cleavage between the formants: the literature-based formant follows its own roads, and shapes the others. In addition, it does not follow the wave of dissemination stemming from ancient (the codification) and new transplants (the political-institutional order). A justification could lie in the choice of inserting a system of judicial review of legislation (borrowed from the US model) into a civilian *corpus*. This led to a mutual influence: judicial review of legislation makes an undifferentiated use of common law and civil law legal literature. Furthermore, some topics (especially as for rights and freedoms) are irrespective to the civil law–common law dichotomy. This occurs, however, in all the legal systems we have examined.

[116] On the role of the first one during the foundation of the 'Derecho procesal constitucional' see E. Ferrer Mac-Gregor, *Derecho Procesal Constitucional. Origen científico (1928–1956)* (Marcial Pons, Madrid-Barcelona-Buenos Aires 2008).

VIII. Concluding remarks

The survey has examined a selected number of legal systems. As for the method, the data has been deliberately exposed with uneven, different criteria. The main purposes of the chapter were the following: to ascertain whether it is possible to promote a subsequent, extensive, and scientifically reliable research, and to establish whether the research may have recourse to a broad, uniform statistical basis of the judicial doctrine in order to achieve the scientific goals. Furthermore, subsequent research should expose the results through compact 'grids' based on distinct elements: the quantification of the use of legal literature by the courts; the identification of cultures, countries, and universities of provenance; the distinction between macro and micro areas of the quotations (e.g., civil law, family law, criminal law, rights and liberties, powers of the state, decentralization, constitutional process, etc.); the identification of the setting of quotations (majority or dissent opinions, type of judgment, etc.); the analysis of the argumentation, training of the judges, etc.

The examination suggests some hypotheses for future research.

First, the survey challenges the presiding traditional criteria classification of legal systems. In this respect, such criteria do not correspond to the results of the research conducted through the dichotomy between legal literature and doctrine. In some jurisdictions—traditionally termed as 'mixed'—there is a striking affirmation of the common law legal culture, which undermines the civil law one. The circulation of legal literature also seems to infiltrate in legal systems numbered within the civil law legal tradition. Hence, the penetration of the Anglo-Saxon doctrine (especially the US one) is massive.

This seems to attest to the correctness of the argument (proposed by Sacco and his pupils), which highlights the breakdown of the equation among formants. Indeed, it is impossible to read comparative law in a compact and homogeneous way—this is, however, the ways scholars still examine domestic legal systems.

Moreover, the chapter upholds the assumption that some ideas, principles, values, and concepts circulate—regardless of the origins of the importing and exporting countries. For example, the survey seems to confirm that circulation of civil rights and freedoms does not take into account both the classification of legal systems and the frame of government—and, probably, the form of the State (this is the outcome of other 'probing', of which I could not give account). US, Spanish, Latin, and Italian jurists, regardless of families and schools of origin, share some ideas, and they are often quoted together (as for the so-called neo-constitutionalism).

More specifically, the German legal culture continues to disseminate ideas, despite the barrier of a language, which is no more (or even less) a vehicular one. Thus, this legal culture opposes (though with difficulty) the prevalence of English-speaking jurists. French and Italian scholars are mostly represented by masters of the past decades. Spanish scholars are still gripping in Latin America, but they are not so overwhelming. (The analyses of several hundreds of Mexican and Peruvian judgments, whose data I have not shown here, still do not give clear results. In this regard, the data on language barriers appears in countertrend.)

There are also provisional results, which offer some hypotheses for additional future research. They are more sociological than legal. Some prestigious universities such as the Sorbonne and Bologna, as well as Cambridge, are gradually losing ground in this particular ranking, whereas other universities maintain a strong dominance (especially Harvard, encouraged by the penetration of US legal thought, as well as some ancient German universities). Several authors come from universities from all over the world, and hundreds of research centres are represented through quotations. Normally, jurists were trained and/or have taught in various universities. This seems to confirm that, in order to be internationally renowned, it is useful to get a multi-faceted culture. On the contrary, the fact of being a student, and then a professor in the same university does not contribute to internationalization.

20

South Africa: Teaching an 'Old Dog' New Tricks?

An Empirical Study of the Use of Foreign Precedents by the South African Constitutional Court (1995–2010)

*Christa Rautenbach**

I. Introduction

For many years the maxim *iudicis est ius dicere sed non dare* (it is the province of a judge to interpret the law and not to make it) relegated the function of judges in South Africa to mere interpreters of the law.[1] In earlier decisions of the South African courts the task of the judiciary was seen as being 'to establish what the law is and then to judge in accordance with the law so found'.[2] Within this framework the South African judiciary has used foreign precedents as extra-textual aids to assist in the process of constitutional interpretation.[3] In doing so, the judges focused mainly on foreign precedents which had historical links with the South African legal system.[4] The justification offered for this type of historical comparative interpretation was that there was a relationship of subordination between the country borrowing and the country borrowed from, especially in the case of former colonial countries looking to the colonizers for judicial guidance by comparing foreign situations with domestic ones.[5] This process of 'cross-fertilization' took the form of a monologue more often

* B Iuris LLB LLM LLD Professor of Law, Faculty of Law, North-West University (Potchefstroom Campus), South Africa. I am grateful to the National Research Foundation (South Africa) and the Alexander von Humboldt Foundation (Germany) for their financial assistance whilst conducting this research. Nevertheless, I am solely responsible for my viewpoints and mistakes. An earlier version of this paper was published in T Groppi and M-C Ponthoreau, *The Use of Foreign Precedents by Constitutional Judges* (Hart, 2013).

[1] See, eg, *Union Government (Minister of Mines) v Thompson* [1919] AD 404 at 425; *Estate Reid v Goodwin* [1920] AD 367 at 373; *R v Tebetha* [1959] 2 SA 337 (A) 346G; *S v Khanyapa* [1979] 1 SA 824 (A) 835; *S v Blaauw* [1980] 1 SA 536 (C) 537H.

[2] *Bloem v State President of the RSA* [1986] 4 SA 1064 OPD 1075I-J.

[3] The mixed nature of South Africa's legal system necessitated a comparative legal approach to find, develop, and make the law, and the South African courts were discreetly doing this behind the scenes. See the discussion of LWH Ackermann, 'Constitutional Comparativism in South Africa' (2006) 123 South African Law Journal 497, 500.

[4] South Africa was formerly a colony first of the Netherlands and then of the United Kingdom. See overview in section II of this chapter.

[5] See the explanation of A Lollini, 'Legal Argumentation Based on Foreign Law: An Example from Case Law of the South African Constitutional Court' (2007) 3 Utrecht Law Review 60, 61–2.

than a dialogue.[6] The colonies borrowed from the colonial powers, and not the other way round.

All indications are, however, that the influence of the colonial powers is fading and that a distinct form of judicial globalization is gaining momentum, partly as a result of South Africa's new constitutional dispensation and its re-entry into the global community, and partly as a result of the South African judiciary's willingness to engage in global judicial debates. It is trite that South Africa's two Constitutions since 1994[7] have introduced a new constitutional dispensation based on the supremacy of the Constitution and the rule of law. The implication of this transformation is particularly evident when assessing the contemporary role of the judiciary in general, and the techniques of judicial reasoning in particular, especially in the context of foreign case law. Justice Chaskalson's statement in *S v Makwanyane*,[8] which dealt with the constitutionality of the death sentence in South Africa, seems to suggest that the judiciary keeps itself busy with judicial comparativism because it is the right thing to do. He states:[9]

> The international and foreign authorities are of value because they analyse arguments for and against the death sentence and show how courts of other jurisdictions have dealt with this vexed issue. *For that reason alone they require our attention.* (emphasis added)

It is believed, seemingly without foundation,[10] that the most important catalyst for judicial comparativism in South Africa today is the unique interpretation clause in the Constitution, viz section 39(1) of the Constitution which reads:

> When interpreting the Bill of Rights, a court, tribunal or forum–
> (a) must promote the values that underlie an open and democratic society based on human dignity, equality and freedom;
> (b) *must consider international law*; and
> (c) *may consider foreign law*. (emphasis added)

Subsections (b) and (c) provide a totally new dimension to comparative interpretation by authorizing courts to consider international and foreign law when interpreting the Bill of Rights.[11] There are important differences between these two cues to forms of interpretation in a South African context. The first difference is evident in the dissimilarity of the wording of subsections (b) and (c). In the case of international law the court *must* consider it, and in the case of foreign law the courts *may* consider it. Though there is a clear difference between the two auxiliary verbs 'may' and 'must', both of them are linked with the verb 'consider', which implies nothing more than

[6] HL Buxbaum, 'From Empire to Globalization . . . and Back? A Post-Colonial View of Transjudicialism' (2004) 11 Indiana Journal of Global Legal Studies 183, 185, 187.

[7] Constitution of the Republic of South Africa 200 of 1993 (the interim Constitution) in operation from 27 April 1994 to 3 February 1997; and the Constitution of the Republic of South Africa 1996 (the Constitution) in operation since 4 February 1997.

[8] *S v Makwanyane* [1995] 3 SA 391 (CC).

[9] See (n 8) at 34.

[10] Ackermann, 'Constitutional Comparativism' (n 3) 500 points out: 'I have not the slightest doubt that, because of the comparative law ethos in South Africa, the Court would have placed the same reliance on foreign law even had there been no such provision in the Constitutions.'

[11] S 11(2) of the Constitution of the Republic of Malawi of 1997 contains a similar provision.

carefully thinking about or reflecting on something. In the case of international law, the courts are obliged to go through (ie 'must consider') this thinking process, whilst in the case of foreign law there is merely a suggestion that they may think (ie 'may consider') about it.[12] In other words, the courts have the discretion to consider foreign law but an obligation to consider international law.

The second difference between subsections (b) and (c) has to do with the less obvious distinction based on the relationship between South Africa's domestic law and international law. South Africa follows a dualistic approach to the incorporation of international law, which in essence requires the formal transformation of international law into domestic law.[13] South African courts must also prefer an interpretation of legislation consistent with international law.[14] Thus, in addition to section 39(1)(c), international law is connected to South Africa's domestic legal system through ratification procedures[15] and a directive to prefer legislative interpretation in line with international law. In *S v Makwanyane*[16] Justice Chaskalson explained the use of comparative international law by pointing out that international law may include binding and non-binding law.[17] Both forms of international law may be used in the interpretation process.[18] On the other hand, there is no similar distinction in respect of foreign law and the statutory permission to consider foreign law during the interpretation process authorizes courts only to '"have regard to" such law', and there is 'no injunction to do more than this'.[19]

Other scholars have also recognized the important differences between considering foreign law and considering international law in the South African Constitution. As Lollini[20] explains:

> [M]aking effective international public law norms binding in South Africa has nothing to do with the interpretive procedure based on *extra*-systemic parameters. On the one hand, norms are applied that have been produced by a system outside of the national sphere, but to which South Africa formally belongs. On the other, interpretive solutions created or decreed by foreign constitutional courts may be freely used for interpreting the South African Constitution.

The strategies of considering foreign law and international law are thus poles apart, and one should not lose sight of this fact when assessing the Court's use of foreign precedent.

[12] See also *S v Makwanyane* (n 8) 37.

[13] J Dugard, *International Law: A South African Perspective* (Juta, Landsdowne 2005) 47–8.

[14] See s 233 of the Constitution.

[15] The most important procedures are contained in the Constitution in s 231 (international agreements) and s 232 (customary international law).

[16] *S v Makwanyane* (n 8) 35. The Court considered the implication of s 35(1) of the interim Constitution, which is almost identical to s 39(1) of the Constitution.

[17] Binding international law will be international law ratified and acceded to in terms of s 231 of the interim Constitution, which is similar to s 231 of the new Constitution. See also s 232 regarding the position of customary international law and s 233, which obliges courts to give preference to international law when alternative interpretation outcomes exist.

[18] For a general discussion of the Constitutional Court's use of international law, see E De Wet, 'The "Friendly but Cautious" Reception of International Law in the Jurisprudence of the South African Constitutional Court: Some Critical Remarks' (2005) 28 Fordham International Law Review 1529.

[19] In *S v Makwanyane* (n 8) 37.

[20] Lollini, 'Legal Argumentation' (n 5) 64.

Contrary to the status of international law in the South African legal system, the status of foreign law is fairly unclear. The use of the words 'comparable foreign law' in the interim Constitution, which might have given us a clue in this regard, were changed in the final Constitution to refer only to 'foreign law'. Does this omission imply that foreign law no longer has to be comparable before it may be considered? There is no clear answer to this question but, in its dealings with foreign law, the Constitutional Court has given some direction as to the factors relevant for the comparison process. For example, in *S v Makwanyane*[21] Justice Chaskalson pointed out that foreign law is important in the early stages of transition where there is 'no developed indigenous [rights] jurisprudence on which to draw' but one should 'appreciate that this will not necessarily offer a safe guide to the interpretation' of the Bill of Rights. In addition, the nature of the South African legal system, its history and circumstances, and the structure and language of the Constitution are important factors to bear in mind when dealing with foreign law.[22]

Another important aspect which must be taken into consideration in a discussion such as this is the difference between constitutional and ordinary statutory interpretation, which is not always readily apparent. Justice Froneman in *Matiso v Commanding Officer, Port Elizabeth Prison*[23] explained the difference as follows:

> The interpretation of the Constitution will be directed at ascertaining the foundational values inherent to the Constitution, whilst the interpretation of the particular legislation will be directed at ascertaining whether that legislation is capable of an interpretation which conforms with the fundamental values or principles of the Constitution. *Constitutional interpretation in this sense is thus primarily concerned with the recognition and application of constitutional values and not with a search to find the literal meaning of statutes.* The values and principles contained in the Constitution are, and could only be, formulated and expressed in wide and general terms, because they are to be of general application. In terms of the Constitution the courts bear the responsibility of giving specific content to those values and principles in any given situation. *In doing so judges will invariably 'create' law.* (emphasis added)

Justice Froneman's viewpoint is a clear breakaway from the traditional viewpoint that judges should interpret and not make the law. In the new dispensation of constitutional supremacy, judges are not merely an extended arm of the executive, but reviewers and law-makers in their own sphere (thus a separate segment of government).[24] This notion of judicial law-making is also explained by Justice Froneman as an important function of judicial review which should be based on constitutional supremacy and not take place under the 'guise of simply seeking and giving expression to the will of the majority in Parliament'. He makes it clear that judicial law-making in the form of judicial review differs fundamentally from making law by means of legislation, and says:[25]

[21] *S v Makwanyane* (n 8) 37. [22] *S v Makwanyane* (n 8) 39.

[23] *Matiso v Commanding Officer, Port Elizabeth Prison* [1994] 3 BCLR 80 (SE) 87. *S v Makwanyane* (n 8) 87.

[24] The concept of separation of powers was fully investigated by the Constitutional Court in *Doctors for Life International v Speaker of the National Assembly* [2006] 6 SA 416 (CC).

[25] *Matiso v Commanding Officer* (n 23). This viewpoint also accords with the notion that the courts have a developmental function, as expressed in ss 8(3) and 39(2) of the Constitution.

> In contrast to legislative law-making the process of judicial review is not partisan in the sense that it is initiated by the law-makers themselves. Judges do not initiate litigation; individual litigants do. And the adjudication process 'creating' law is done by an impartial and independent Judge; not by the majority party who initiates legislation in the legislature.[26]

Since its establishment in 1994 the Constitutional Court, which is regarded as the most authoritative interpreter of the Constitution[27] of South Africa, has considered foreign precedents on numerous occasions.[28] The very first judgment the Constitutional Court handed down on 5 April 1995, *S v Zuma*,[29] cited no less than 25[30] foreign precedents of countries such as the United States, the United Kingdom, Canada, Hong Kong, Namibia, China, and Botswana. Justice Kentridge, who delivered a unanimous decision, gave no content to the comparable enabling provision in the interim Constitution,[31] but he did caution (by implication) against ignoring 'all the principles of law which have hitherto governed our courts' and neglecting 'the language of the Constitution' in favour of a misguided use of the underlying constitutional values determined, amongst others, by foreign law.[32] Without giving any guidelines as to when and which foreign precedents would be relevant in the comparison process, Justice Kentridge referred to the different solutions of foreign precedents to the problem of reconciling presumptions of reverse onus simply as 'illuminating',[33] without shedding light on the (un)compelling value of the foreign precedents that he considered.

The Constitutional Court's next judgment, *S v Makwanyane*,[34] which found the death penalty to be unconstitutional, may be considered as the Court's inaugural decision. Every one of the 11 judges on the bench delivered a separate judgment and each one of them considered foreign precedent. Justice Chaskalson earns first place on the podium with 124 foreign case citations and the second place is taken by Justice Ackermann with 33 foreign case citations. In total there were 220 foreign case citations from 11 countries and three supranational courts.[35] To date this record has not been

[26] Other authors, such as LM Du Plessis, 'Interpretation of Statutes and the Constitution' in loose-leaf *Bill of Rights Compendium* (LexisNexis, Durban 2002) 2C50 point out that the maxim *iudices est ius dicere sed non dare* has not disappeared from the scenery in its totality, since it still has a role to play in the realm of statutory interpretation, and it could also act as a restraining mechanism to an interpreter's preferences and prejudices. For that reason Du Plessis proposes the rephrasing of the maxim to read: 'it is the province of the interpreter of an enacted law-text primarily to give the best possible effect to the text as it stands and not to (try and) re-enact (or rewrite) it'.

[27] See s 167 of the Constitution.

[28] The Constitutional Court was formally opened on 14 February 1995. The Court consists of the Chief Justice, the Deputy Chief Justice and nine other judges and is the highest court in all constitutional matters. See ss 167 and 173 of the Constitution.

[29] *S v Zuma* [1995] 2 SA 642 (CC). This case dealt with the constitutionality of the presumption relating to the admissibility of confessions in terms of the former s 217 of the Criminal Procedure Act 51 of 1977.

[30] Some of the foreign cases were referred to more than once, bringing the total citations of foreign cases up to 32.

[31] The provision enabling the use of foreign law in that Constitution was similar to s 39(1)(c) of the new Constitution but referred to 'comparable foreign case law'. The word 'comparable' was discarded from the latter which refers only to 'foreign case law'.

[32] *S v Zuma* (n 29) 17. [33] *S v Zuma* (n 29) 19. [34] *S v Makwanyane* (n 8).

[35] Some of the foreign cases were referred to more than once, bringing the total citations of foreign cases up to 220.

broken and *S v Makwanyane* remains one of the most remarkable judgments delivered by the Constitutional Court in many respects.

Statistics confirm that since its inception in 1994 the Constitutional Court has been considering foreign precedents on an ongoing basis. This may be explained partly by the fact that the newly established Court under a newly adopted Constitution was called upon to develop, through its jurisprudence, a sound foundation for the interpretation and application of that Constitution in the almost complete absence of domestic precedent.[36] This comparative process of referring to foreign case law has many names and several layered meanings and nuances. It has been called 'transjudicialism',[37] 'transjudicial communication',[38] 'constitutionalist dialogue',[39] 'judicial globalism',[40] 'constitutional cross-fertilisation',[41] 'transnational contextualisation',[42] 'globalisation of judgment',[43] 'globalisation of national courts',[44] and 'judicial comparativism'.[45] But there is also another explanation for this phenomenon which has nothing to do with the Court's desire to develop jurisprudence in constitutional issues, and this has to do with the global trend of constitutional judges to communicate with one another. The statistics discussed in Figure 20.1 point in this direction.[46]

Against this background I have conducted an empirical survey from 1995 to 2010 to establish the use of foreign precedents by the South African Constitutional Court. I commence with a brief overview of South Africa's historical and constitutional context[47] before I set out the methodology that I employed to do this research.[48] Then I focus on the empirical results and the inferences one can draw therefrom.[49] Finally, I conclude this contribution with a few remarks on the propensity of the Constitutional Court to consider foreign law from both a qualitative and a quantitative point of view.[50] The ultimate question is whether the Constitutional Court's use of foreign precedents as a method of constitutional interpretation, especially in the development of human rights jurisprudence, rather than a method of statutory

[36] See *S v Makwanyane* (n 8) 37.

[37] DS Wood, 'In Defence of Transjudicialism' (2005) 44 Duquesne Law Review 93.

[38] RC Black and L Epstein, '(Re-)Setting the Scholarly Agenda on Transjudicial Communication' (2007) 32 Law and Social Inquiry 789. A valuable contribution to the debate is the scholarly article of A-M Slaughter, 'A Typology of Transjudicial Communication' (1994) 29 University of Richmond Law Review 99. According to her the overarching term for the process of 'cross-fertilisation' between courts in various jurisdictions is 'transjudicial communication'. This phenomenon takes place within the formal treaty context (references to international law and supra-national courts) and within an informal context (references to foreign law).

[39] B Bryde, 'The Constitutional Judge and the International Constitutionalist Dialogue' (2005) 80 Tulane Law Review 203, 213–14. He points out that although the use of foreign law is mostly 'inspirational', it is also used as a genuine legal argument.

[40] Buxbaum, 'From Empire to Globalization' (n 6) 183.

[41] Buxbaum, 'From Empire to Globalization' (n 6) 184.

[42] LM Du Plessis, 'Interpretation' in S Woolman, M Bishop, and J Brickhill (eds.), *Constitutional Law of South Africa* (Juta, Kenwyn 2010) 32.171.

[43] R Bahdi, 'Globalization of Judgment: Transjudicialism and the Five Faces of International Law in Domestic Courts' (2002) 34 The George Washington International Law Review 555.

[44] MJ Tawfik, 'No Longer in Splendid Isolation: The Globalization of National Courts and the Internationalization of Intellectual Property Law' (2007) 32 Queen's Law Journal 573.

[45] DC Gray, 'Why Justice Scalia should be a Constitutional Comparativist... Sometimes' (2007) 59 Stanford Law Review 1249. See also Ackermann, 'Constitutional Comparativism' (n 3) 497.

[46] See section III.2.a.i. [47] See section II. [48] See section III.1.

[49] See section III.2. [50] See section IV.

interpretation, boils down to a 'new' form of interpretation, or whether it is merely a matter of teaching an old dog new tricks.

II. Historical and constitutional context

The South African Court's tendency to refer to foreign precedents must be understood in its historical and constitutional context.[51] European involvement in South Africa became prominent in 1652 when the Dutch East India Company established a refreshment station in the Cape of Good Hope with permanent settlers. The British seized the Cape in 1795, and then briefly relinquished it back to the Dutch in 1803 before definitively conquering it in 1806, annexing it as a Crown colony. This colony was gradually extended eastwards and northwards by conquest, barter, and cession. Furthermore, the interior of Southern Africa was systematically occupied from 1836 onwards by migrating non-British pioneer farmers whose purpose was to break away from British colonial rule. For more than 60 years the country which was later to become South Africa consisted of two British colonies and two sovereign 'Boer' republics.

The Anglo-Boer War of 1899–1902 ended in the annexation of the two 'Boer' republics as new British colonies. On 31 May 1910 the Union of South Africa came into being but it continued to be under British rule. The constitutional dispensation of the Union was typically that of a British *dominion* with a Westminster-type parliament entrusted with legislative sovereignty, which precluded the adoption of a Bill of Rights and substantive judicial review. When the Union was transformed into the Republic of South Africa in 1961, these constitutional characteristics remained in place, making the unfolding of the apartheid system possible.

In 1990 a turning point was reached when the government officially accepted the unavoidability of the introduction of comprehensive democracy and launched a process of negotiating a thoroughly new constitutional dispensation. The main role players in the multi-party constitutional negotiations that produced the interim Constitution were representatives of socialistically-inclined liberation movements on the one hand, and on the other of an order that was established and was functioning under a constitutional dispensation founded in English legal thinking. Nevertheless, as common ground was found in contemporary constitutionalist thinking, the negotiations produced what the first paragraph of the preamble to the interim Constitution referred to as a 'sovereign and democratic constitutional state' and the provisions of the Constitution provided for the realization of the different elements of the constitutional state. The introduction of a justiciable, supreme Constitution including a Bill of Rights as a key component changed the essence of the system significantly.

The interim Constitution required a 'final constitution' to be drafted, which led to the adoption of the 1996 and final Constitution. This (current) Constitution was largely based on the interim Constitution and preserved the most salient features of the former

[51] For a detailed discussion of the constitutional history of South Africa, see S Woolman and J Swanepoel, 'Constitutional History' in S Woolman, M Bishop, and J Brickhill (eds.), *Constitutional Law of South Africa* (Juta, Kenwyn 2010) 2.1–2.49.

document, including its human-rights-based dispensation[52] founded upon a supreme basic law[53] of which the Constitutional Court is the authoritative interpreter.[54]

Many comparative insights were incorporated in the Bill of Rights, including other modern Constitutions and international human rights instruments.[55] The two national Constitutions that most strongly influenced the drafting of the final Constitution both in its structural provisions and its Bill of Rights were the German *Grundgesetz* of 1949 and the Canadian Constitution Act of 1982.

III. Empirical analysis: making sense of statistics

1. Methodology

The Constitutional Court,[56] the Supreme Court of Appeal,[57] and the High Courts of South Africa all have constitutional jurisdiction and may thus use foreign law in their judicial reasoning, but since it would be a mammoth task to survey all of the decisions dealing with constitutional issues within these courts this empirical study focuses only on the judgments of the Constitutional Court for the last 16 years.[58]

The empirical survey follows both a quantitative and qualitative approach by counting and evaluating explicit citations of foreign precedents. The qualitative approach entails the collection of empirical information such as the number of foreign precedents cited per year, per judge, per foreign case, and per country, as well as by categorizing the type of issue dealt with under the headings 'human rights issues', 'institutional issues', or 'other issues'. The quantitative approach makes use of formal and substantive factors to determine the actual or potential influence of the foreign precedents on South African Constitutional Court judges. Formal indicators include the following: whether the judge considering a foreign case delivered a majority, dissenting, or separate judgment; whether a reference to the foreign case was merely a reference or a quote; whether the reference was made in the majority or dissenting decision of the foreign case; and whether the foreign case was referred to in the text or footnote of the South African case. The substantive indicators require an analysis of the legal reasoning applied by the judges, and in doing this three categories were used, viz: the reasoning (or argumentative) phase; the 'even there'-approach; and the '*a contrario*'-approach.[59]

[52] S 8(1) of the Constitution applies the 'Bill of Rights to all law, and binds the legislature, the executive, the judiciary and all organs of state'.

[53] S 2 of the Constitution confirms the supremacy of the Constitution.

[54] S 165(2) of the Constitution vests judicial authority in the courts and reads: 'The courts are independent and subject only to the Constitution and the law, which they must apply impartially and without fear, favour or prejudice'. S 167 confirms that the Constitutional Court is the highest court in all constitutional matters.

[55] Du Plessis, 'Interpretation' (n 42) 32.183.

[56] See ss 166 and 167 of the Constitution.

[57] The Supreme Court of Appeal is the highest court of appeal except in constitutional matters. See ss 166 and 168 of the Constitution.

[58] The empirical results have been captured in a searchable database accessible at <http://www4-win2.p.nwu.ac.za/dbtw-wpd/textbases/ccj.htm>. The database is still in a developmental phase and additional data is being uploaded on a regular basis. Preliminary results are available and are discussed in this contribution. Searches can be conducted by means of keywords or empirical results. For more information, see the database.

[59] See section III.2.b. for an explanation of the three categories.

It is important to point out that the term 'citations' in this contribution does not necessarily refer to the number of foreign precedents considered but the number of times a judge referred to a foreign precedent. In other words, the word 'citations' refers to the number of foreign case citations and not to the number of foreign cases in each constitutional court case.

2. Explicit citations of foreign precedents

a) Quantitative approach

i. Citations of foreign precedents: the cases

Since the establishment of the South African Constitutional Court, the Court has been handing down judgments that have had a profound impact on the law in South Africa.[60] In *Mistry v Interim National Medical and Dental Council of South Africa*[61] Justice Chaskalson recognized the value of foreign case law and emphasized that the Constitutional Court will continue to consult foreign law in areas where constitutional principles have not been established. In other words, foreign precedents will be used to 'create' law where there is none. Similar views were expressed by Justice Sachs, giving a dissenting opinion, in *Coetzee v The Government of RSA; Matiso v Commanding Officer, Port Elizabeth Prison.*[62] He agreed that the interpretation clause in the interim Constitution[63] invites judges to have regard to international experience where applicable when seeking to interpret provisions relating to fundamental rights: 'As I understand it, this section requires us to give due attention to such experience *with a view to finding principles rather than to extracting rigid formulae, and to look for rationales rather than rules* (emphasis added).'[64]

From 1995 to 2010 the Constitutional Court delivered a total number of 403 judgments with at least 2,742 foreign citations.[65] At least 194 of these judgments do

[60] Since the rule of precedent or *stare decisis* applies in South Africa, courts will be bound by decisions of certain other high courts, especially the Supreme Court of Appeal and the Constitutional Court, thus obviating the need to re-interpret the law (especially constitutional law) every time by taking foreign precedent into account.

[61] *Mistry v Interim National Medical and Dental Council of South Africa* [1998] 4 SA 1127 (CC). At para 3 the Court said: 'Cases fall to be decided on a principled basis. Each case that is decided adds to the body of South African constitutional law, and establishes principles relevant to the decision of cases which may arise in the future. Particularly where principles have not yet been established, courts may draw on the burgeoning international jurisprudence on constitutional rights.'

[62] *Coetzee v The Government of RSA; Matiso v Commanding Officer, Port Elizabeth Prison* [1995] 4 SA 631 (CC).

[63] S 35, which is similar in wording to s 39 of the new Constitution.

[64] *Coetzee v The Government of RSA; Matiso v Commanding Officer, Port Elizabeth Prison* (n 62) 57.

[65] Not included in this number is the Constitutional Court's citation of other international or supranational institutions. For example, from 1995 to 2010, the judgments from the following institutions have been cited: African Commission on Human and Peoples' Rights (two citations); Benelux Court of Justice (one citation); European Commission of Human Rights (four citations); European Court of Human Rights (138 citations); European Court of Justice (eight citations); Inter-American Commission on Human Rights (two citations); International Court of Justice (14 citations); International Criminal Tribunal for Rwanda (six citations); International Criminal Tribunal for the former Yugoslavia (three citations); International Tribunal for Arbitration (three citations); Iran-United States Claims Tribunal (one citation); UN Human Rights Committee (12 citations); and UK Privy Council (81 citations).

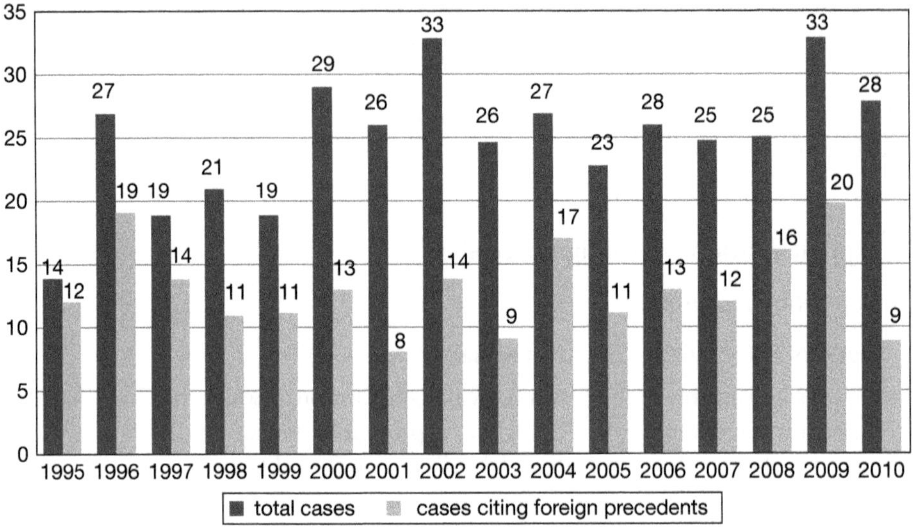

Figure 20.1 Cases per year divided according to those citing and total

not refer to foreign precedents and at least 52 per cent of the total number of judgments considered foreign precedents in comparison with the 48 per cent which did not consider foreign precedents over the period of 16 years. In other words, the number of judgments citing foreign precedents at the end of 2010 was 4 per cent more than the number of those which did not cite any foreign precedents. This illustrates the Court's favourable disposition towards foreign precedents, as reflected in Figure 20.1.

So far the Court has cited foreign precedents quite extensively in its adjudication of constitutional issues, but legal scholars predicted a decline in the Constitutional Court's reliance on foreign law in interpreting the Bill of Rights as it begins to develop a jurisprudence of its own.[66] An assessment of the statistics reveals that although there has been a steady decline in the Constitutional Court's citation of foreign precedents since 1995, the rate increased again in 2004 and has since remained more or less consistent, except for 2010, when it declined again. For instance, in 1995, 12 constitutional judgments of a total of 14 (ie 86 per cent) cited foreign precedents, whilst only 11 judgments of a total of 25 (ie 39 per cent) cited foreign judgments in 2003.[67] The citation rate increased again in 2004 to 63 per cent and, except for a slight drop during the next three years (2005–07), the rate hovered around 60 per cent again during 2008 and 2009. In 2010 it dropped again to 32 per cent. The latest drop is perhaps due to the appointment of a number of new judges at the Constitutional Court.

The tendency of the Constitutional Court to keep on citing foreign precedents despite the lack of an obvious motivation for doing so is in line with the argument that South African courts, in particular the South African Constitutional Court, want to

[66] DM Davis, 'Constitutional Borrowing: The Influence of Legal Culture and Local History in the Reconstruction of Comparative Influence: The South African Experience' (2003) 1 International Journal of Constitutional Law 181, 194.

[67] The percentage of cases referring to foreign law increased to 59% in 2004.

keep in step with the global community and thus participate in the global exchange of judicial knowledge on an ongoing basis.[68] Justice Moseneke's receptiveness towards foreign precedents came to the fore in an interview he had with an American legal scholar, Bentele,[69] where he said:

> most legal issues are not of exclusive or immediate origin . . . Even in this country . . . there's been judicial reasoning and adjudication for at least two and a half centuries— and I think as it is helpful to look at domestic jurisprudence, it must surely be helpful to look at what other jurisdictions say.

Though the Constitutional Court judges show a great openness to foreign jurisprudence, as is evident in the statistics in Figure 20.1, the persuasive value of the precedents so cited is less obvious than the number of citations. Or, as another author puts it: '[t]he South African court's engagement with foreign law does not, however, treat such sources [foreign precedents] as "authority", even in the broadest sense of the term'.[70]

ii. Citation of foreign precedents: the judges

At this moment,[71] the Constitutional Court has 11 current judges, 11 former judges, and has had 12 acting judges. The judges most active in considering foreign precedents are those with permanent appointments and thus include the current and former judges, except for Justice Kentridge, who had an appointment as an acting judge.

The statistics reveal that Justice Ackermann has included the most citations during his term of office, viz an average of 55 foreign case citations per year from 1994 to 2004. He is followed by Justice Chaskalson with an average of 46.5 foreign case citations per year during the same period; and in third place is Justice Kentridge with an average of 41.5 foreign case citations during the period from 1995 to 1996.

The high rate of foreign citation by some of the judges reveals that they generally do not shy away from considering foreign law. Nevertheless, an early warning was issued by Justice Chaskalson in *S v Makwanyane*,[72] viz:

> In dealing with comparative law, we must bear in mind that we are required to construe the South African Constitution, and not an international instrument or the constitution of some foreign country, and that this has to be done with due regard to our legal system, our history and circumstances, and the structure and language of our own Constitution. We can derive assistance from public international law and foreign case law, but we are in no way bound to follow it.

The willingness of the judiciary to consider foreign law is illustrated by members' personal views as documented by Bentele in her scholarly work.[73] She refers, amongst others, to the viewpoint of Justice Van der Westhuizen that people (including judges)

[68] Janet McLean, 'From Empire to Globalization: The New Zealand Experience' (2004) 11 Indiana Journal of Global Legal Studies 161, 166–9.

[69] Ursula Bentele, 'Mining for Gold: The Constitutional Court of South Africa's Experience with Comparative Constitutional Law' (2009) 37 Georgia Journal of International and Comparative Law 219, 222–3.

[70] Bentele, 'Mining for Gold' (n 69) 226.

[71] As at March 2011.

[72] *S v Makwanyane* (n 8) 39.

[73] Bentele, 'Mining for Gold' (n 69) 229–32.

were eager to become part and parcel of the international community again, and that considering foreign precedents has been a logical consequence of such a desire.[74] Justice Kriegler echoed these sentiments, expressing the people's wish to participate in important international developments.[75] Justices Chaskalson and Goldstone also expressed the opinion that one should be open to learning valuable lessons from jurisdictions other than one's own.[76] In *Du Plessis v De Klerk*[77] Justice Kentridge remarked as follows: '[t]he purpose of this perhaps overlong account of constitutional adjudication elsewhere is to see what guidance it might provide in the interpretation of the South African Constitution'.

Nevertheless, the approach to foreign precedent, albeit friendly, has been cautious in many respects. Justice O'Regan, for instance, in *Fose v Minister of Safety and Security*,[78] pointed out that '[a]s in all exercises in legal comparativism, it is important to be astute not to equate legal institutions which are not, in truth, comparable'. She calls this form of comparativism (where the legal institutions are not comparable) 'shallow comparison' which should be avoided, but indicates that:

> It would seem unduly parochial to consider that no guidance, whether positive or negative, could be drawn from other legal systems' grappling with issues similar to those with which we are confronted. Consideration of the responses of other legal systems may enlighten us in analysing our own law, and assist us in developing it further. It is for this very reason that our Constitution contains an express provision authorising courts to consider the law of other countries when interpreting the Bill of Rights. It is clear that in looking to the jurisprudence of other countries, *all the dangers of shallow comparativism must be avoided. To forbid any comparative review because of those risks, however, would be to deprive our legal system of the benefits of the learning and wisdom to be found in other jurisdictions.* Our courts will look at other jurisdictions for enlightenment and assistance in developing our own law. The question of whether we will find assistance will depend on whether the jurisprudence considered is of itself valuable and persuasive. If it is, the courts and our law will benefit. If it is not, the courts will say so, and no harm will be done. (emphasis added)[79]

There is thus, according to her, not much of a danger that 'shallow comparison' would lead to harmful results, because in considering foreign precedents the Court will assess the persuasive value of the foreign precedents and deal with it accordingly.

iii. Number of foreign precedents: per year, judge, and country

The total number of constitutional cases citing foreign precedents sorted by countries discloses some interesting tendencies. Most evident is the fact that the Court no longer prefers the countries with which South Africa had historical links but also cites, almost haphazardly, other jurisdictions such as Canada, the United States of America (USA), and Germany, as reflected in Figure 20.2.

[74] Ibid., 229. [75] Ibid., 230. [76] Ibid., 230–1.
[77] *Du Plessis v De Klerk* [1996] 3 SA 850 (CC) 41.
[78] *Fose v Minister of Safety and Security* [1997] 3 SA 786 (CC) 34.
[79] Bentele, 'Mining for Gold' (n 69) 35.

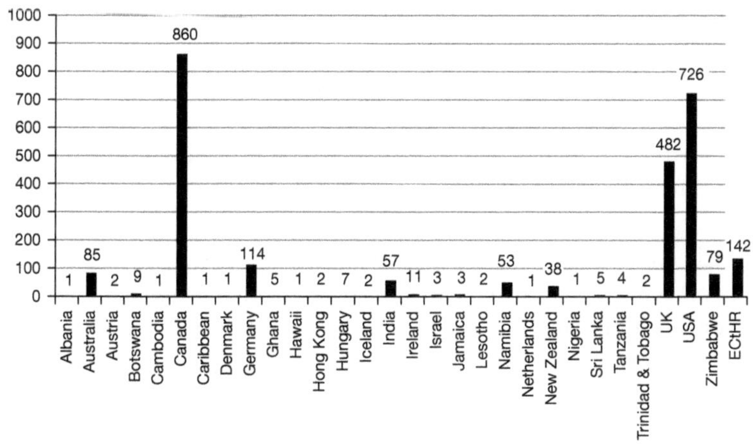

Figure 20.2 Total foreign countries cited: 1995–2010[80]

Although the use of international law has been excluded from my research findings, it is important to point out that there have been circumstances where the Constitutional Court considered the judgments of international or supranational institutions in a comparative way. One such example is the judgments of the European Court of Human Rights (ECtHR). South Africa is not a member of the Council of Europe and thus not a party to the European Convention on Human Rights (ECHR). Nevertheless, it has cited the judgments of the ECtHR at least 142 times during the period under investigation. It is, however, difficult to determine if these comparisons have been done in the context of 'international law' or 'foreign law' as prescribed by section 39(1)(b) or (c) of the Constitution respectively.

The four foreign jurisdictions most cited by the top five judges[81] are, in descending numerical order, Canada and the USA, followed by the United Kingdom (UK) and, finally, Germany.

The overall statistics for foreign countries cited also show that Canadian precedents are the most popular with the South African judges. The popularity of Canadian precedents comes as no surprise and can be attributed mainly to the huge influence that the Canadian Charter of Rights and Freedoms had upon the drafters of the South African Bill of Rights.[82] The top three Canadian precedents cited by the Constitutional Court include *Thomson Newspapers Ltd v Canada (Director of Investigation and Research, Restrictive Trade Practices Commission)*[83] with 50 citations, *R v Big M Drug Mart Ltd*[84] with 31

[80] Fig 20.2 includes the citation of the ECtHR.

[81] By the 'top five judges' I mean those who have referred the most to foreign precedents during the 15-year period, viz Ackermann, Chaskalson, Kriegler, Langa, and O'Regan.

[82] The Charter was enacted as Schedule B to the Canada Act 1982, which came into force on 17 April 1982. See also the discussion of D Davis, 'Democracy—Its Influence upon the Process of Constitutional Interpretation' (1994) 10 South African Journal on Human Rights 103, 115.

[83] *Thomson Newspapers Ltd v Canada (Director of Investigation and Research, Restrictive Trade Practices Commission)* [1990] 1 SCR 425. At least seven different Constitutional Court judgments cited this case.

[84] *R v Big M Drug Mart Ltd* [1985] 1 SCR 295. At least 12 different Constitutional Court judgments cited this case.

citations, and *Egan v Canada*[85] with 18 citations. All three Canadian cases generally deal with the interpretation of human rights issues and are cited by both the majority and dissenting South African judges, sometimes even in the same case. For instance, the Canadian case *Thomson Newspapers Ltd v Canada (Director of Investigation and Research, Restrictive Trade Practices Commission)*[86] was cited not only by the majority in *Harksen v Lane*[87] but also by the dissenting judge, Kriegler J, in *President of the RSA v Hugo.*[88]

Interestingly enough, there has been some exchange of ideas between the Canadian Supreme Court and the South African Constitutional Court, which accords with the idea that conversations among courts today take the form of a dialogue.[89] A few examples exist where the Canadian Supreme Court has cited South African cases but not nearly as many as the Constitutional Court's citations of Canadian precedents.[90] For example, in *Arsenault-Cameron v Prince Edward Island,*[91] Judge Bastarache applied the Constitutional Court case, *President of the RSA v South African Rugby and Football Union,*[92] in deciding whether or not a motion for recusal should be allowed. Similarly, in *Sauvé v Canada (Chief Electoral Officer),*[93] McLachlin CJ referred to the Constitutional Court case *August v Independent Electoral Commission*[94] to draw a parallel between a citizen's right to vote and his or her dignity. Two other examples where the Canadian Supreme Court cited South African precedents without much authority include *R v Hall*[95] and *Grant v Torstar Corp.*[96]

USA precedents are statistically the most cited by the top Constitutional Court judges, but generally without attaching much actual authority to them. The reasons for this high citation rate are less obvious than are those of the Canadian precedents, and they are mostly based on the contention that the USA is an 'open and democratic society based on freedom and equality'.[97] Furthermore, citing USA precedents in spite of the absence of a clear connection between South African and USA jurisprudence illustrates a move towards the universality of legal norms in a global community of

[85] *Egan v Canada* (1995) 29 CRR (2nd) 79. At least nine different Constitutional Court judgments cited this case.

[86] *Thomson Newspapers Ltd v Canada (Director of Investigation and Research, Restrictive Trade Practices Commission)* (n 83).

[87] *Harksen v Lane* [1998] 1 SA 300 (CC) 50 and 93.

[88] *President of the RSA v Hugo* [1997] 4 SA (CC) 80. Incidentally, the same Canadian case was also cited by Goldstone and Justice Mokgoro, who delivered the majority judgment (see 41 and 92).

[89] Buxbaum, 'From Empire to Globalization' (n 6) 185, 187.

[90] I have not not performed in-depth research in this regard, and an empirical survey might reveal that there has been more cross-pollination.

[91] *Arsenault-Cameron v Prince Edward Island* [1999] 3 SCR 851 4.

[92] *RSA v South African Rugby and Football Union* [2002] 2 SA 64 (CC).

[93] *Sauvé v Canada (Chief Electoral Officer)* [2002] SCC 68, [2002] 3 SCR 519 35.

[94] *August v Independent Electoral Commission* [1999] 3 SA 1 (CC).

[95] *R v Hall* [2002] 3 SCR 309, 2002 SCC 64. See para 115, where the Court distinguished the social conditions in *S v Dlamini; S v Dladla; S v Joubert; S v Schietekat* [1999] 4 SA 623 (CC) with the social conditions *in casu.*

[96] *Grant v Torstar Corp* [2009] SCC 61 68. The Court compared the jurisprudence of other common law democracies including South Africa but did nothing more than merely refer to *Du Plessis v De Klerk* (n 77) and *National Media Ltd v Bogoshi* [1998] 4 SA 1196 (SCA).

[97] See the words of Ackermann in *Ferreira v Levin; Vryenhoek v Powell* [1996] 1 SA 984 (CC) 72.

judges, at least in the case of constitutional adjudication in South Africa. This fact is demonstrated by the words of Justice Ackermann in *Ferreira v Levin; Vryenhoek v Powell*,[98] where he declared as follows:

> [S]ection 35(1)[99] obliges us to promote the values underlying such a society when we interpret Chapter 3 [the Bill of Rights] and encourages us to have regard to comparable case law. In construing and applying our Constitution, *we are dealing with fundamental legal norms which are steadily becoming more universal in character.* When, for example, the United States Supreme Court finds that a statutory provision is or is not in accordance with the 'due process of law' or when the Canadian Supreme Court decides that a deprivation of liberty is not 'in accordance with the principles of fundamental justice'... we have regard to these findings, not in order to draw direct analogies, but *to identify the underlying reasoning with a view to establishing the norms that apply in other open and democratic societies based on freedom and equality.*
> (emphasis added)

In other words, regarding foreign precedents is more than just comparing for the sake of interpretation; it also means making law by establishing or using norms that apply or exist in other democracies. This paradigm shift from mere interpretation of the law to the making of the law explains why transjudicialism is not limited to comparable foreign jurisdictions but to all foreign jurisdictions which can make a valuable contribution to the law-making process.

Contrary to the Canadian precedents citing South African cases, the relationship between the South African and USA judiciaries is pretty much one-sided. The USA judiciary generally treats foreign precedents with suspicion and very few judgments refer to foreign law.[100] In this context communication between the South African and USA courts is 'more readily conceptualised as monologue than dialogue'.[101] In spite of huge differences between the USA Constitution and the South African Constitution,[102] USA precedents remain popular with South African judges, although their influence on South African law remains doubtful. Statistics reveal that 700 of the total of 726 citations were referred to by South African judges during the first stage of the interpretative process when they were orientating their judgments.[103] The fact that American interns also work on legal opinions in the Constitutional Court from time to

[98] Ibid. [99] Interim Constitution.

[100] USA judges generally fear that transjudicialism might endanger the principles of sovereignty and separation of powers, including the concern that judges might find justification for their subjective viewpoints in foreign precedent. See, eg, where these fears are discussed by Wood, 'In Defence of Transjudicialism' (n 37) 93; B Markesinis, 'Understanding American Law by Looking at it through Foreign Eyes: Towards a Wider Theory for the Study and Use of Foreign Law' (2006) 81 Tulane Law Review 123; and Gray, 'Justice Scalia' (n 45) 1249. There are, however, a few examples where the USA courts have cited South African cases. A recent example (decided on 17 May 2010) is *Abbott v Abbott* [2008] FLR 1451 (Case 08-645, accessible at <http://www.supremecourt.gov/opinions/09pdf/08-645.pdf>), which cited the South African Constitutional Court case, *Sonderup v Tondelli* [2001] 1 SA 1171 (CC), that deals with the custody of minor children.

[101] See Slaughter, 'A Typology of Transjudicial Communication' (n 38) 113.

[102] The difference was pointed out by Chaskalson P in *Ferreira v Levin; Vryenhoek v Powell* (n 97), 175–6.

[103] See the discussion at section III.2.b.ii.

time definitely has an influence on the citation of USA precedents.[104] These judgments are mostly referred to in passing and seem to have no influence on the final conclusion reached by the Court.

The third highest total of foreign cases cited is those of the UK. This phenomenon can probably be attributed to South Africa's historical links with Britain. The latter was a colonial power in South Africa on two occasions, finishing in the 1960s.[105] Although the rationale for the citation of UK precedents was initially based on historical grounds and the subordinate relationship between the UK and South Africa, this is no longer so. Nevertheless, empirical research into the propensity of the UK court to cite South African courts would be needed in order to determine whether the recent equal relationship between these two countries has led to cross-pollination or not.

The Constitutional Court's citing of German precedents is explicable in the light of the fact that the South African Constitution contains some elements of the German Constitution.[106] Although German precedents are inaccessible to most South African judges as a result of the fact that they are expressed in the German language,[107] other factors have helped to develop a sound base for comparison. For example, the practice of appointing German lawyers from time to time as judges' clerks at the Constitutional Court, the availability of English translations, research visits of South African Constitution writers to Germany, and other scholarly contributions from German scholars[108] have all contributed to the seepage of German precedent into the Constitutional Court's jurisprudence.[109] For example, the textbook of Kommers[110] on the constitutional jurisprudence of Germany is referred to in quite a number of Constitutional Court cases.[111] Another classic example is the case of *Du Plessis v de*

[104] In this regard one can refer to the interview with Justice van der Westhuizen documented by Bentele, 'Mining for Gold' (n 69) 244. He acknowledges the fact that the Harvard Law School intern contributed to the approximately 25 USA citations in *Magajane v Chairperson North West Gambling Board* [2006] 5 SA 250 (CC).

[105] The first British occupation was from 1795 to 1803, and the second from 1806 to 1910. After this date, the Union of South Africa became an independent dominion within the British Commonwealth and in 1961 South Africa became an independent Republic.

[106] Referred to as the 'German presence' by Du Plessis. He also points out some similarities between the German and South African Constitutions. See L Du Plessis, 'Learned Staatsrecht from the Heartland of the Reichtsstaat: Observations on the Significance of South African-German Interaction in Constitutional Scholarship' (2005) 8 Potchefstroom Electronic Law Journal 76, 81, 89–91, accessible at <http://www.puk.ac.za/opencms/export/PUK/html/fakulteite/regte/per/issue05v1.html>.

[107] See the remark made by Kriegler J in *Du Plessis v De Klerk* (n 77) 39: 'The German jurisprudence on this subject is not by any means easy to summarise, especially for one who does not read German.'

[108] eg, Prof Jochen Frowein (Max Planck Institute for Comparative Public and International Law). Justice Kriegler, because he had difficulties in reading German jurisprudence, referred to the scholarly works of German authors to gain access to the German cases. His conclusions are thus based on secondary information and the inherent danger in such an approach is quite well known.

[109] Ackermann, 'Constitutional Comparativism' (n 3) 505 refers to two professors, viz Francois Venter (North-West University) and Gerhard Erasmus (Stellenbosch University). See also the discussion of Du Plessis, 'Learned Staatsrecht' (n 106).

[110] DP Kommers, *The Constitutional Jurisprudence of the Federal Republic of Germany* (Duke University Press, Durham 1997).

[111] See *Matatiele Municipality v President of the RSA* (No 2) [2007] 6 SA 477 (CC) at n 11; *Doctors for Life International v Speaker of the National Assembly* [2006] 6 SA 416 (CC) at n 70; *Affordable Medicines Trust v Minister of Health* [2006] 3 SA 247 (CC) at n 53; *First National Bank of SA Ltd t/a Wesbank v Commissioner, SARS; First National Bank of SA Ltd t/a Wesbank v Minister of Finance* [2002] 4 SA 768 (CC) at nn 136 and 139; *Khumalo v Holomisa* [2002] 5 SA 401 (CC) at n 40; *Beyers v Elf Regters van die*

Klerk,[112] where the German principle of 'drittwirkung' in the field of private law was compared with the application of the South African Bill of Rights in private law.[113]

Not all of the judges are comfortable with the consideration of German precedents in the Constitutional Court, especially because of their difficulties with the German language. In this regard, Kriegler states:[114]

> It [German] is not an easy language, and it's certainly not technically an easy language. And there are writing styles, techniques, [and] mannerisms in legal writing in German, quite apart from always putting the verb in the wrong place. And people blindly concurred with Laurie [Ackermann]'s judgments. I couldn't do that; if I can't get to the guts of what it's about, if I don't understand what they are really saying, what is built on that, I can't go along with it.

However, Justice Kriegler, who indicated his uneasiness with German precedents, made ample use of German law in the *Du Plessis v de Klerk*[115] case, though he made use mainly of secondary sources to find the law. He seems to be comfortable using translations or interpretations of German case law but does not trust the judgments of his own colleagues.

The high citation rate of foreign cases by the South African Constitutional Court also confirms what Lollini[116] calls the 'circulation' of foreign law between constitutional judges or a 'dialogue between judges'. He argues convincingly that the question is no longer whether this phenomenon exists or not. The task rather is to determine and discuss the theories and methods of this form of legal reasoning.[117] Lollini[118] refers to the whole process as one of 'interpretation based on *extra*-systemic parameters' and argues that this process has the potential to transform the interpretative practices of judges into a process where they look to substantiate their normative arguments or viewpoints pertaining to constitutional issues in foreign law. He finally applies his extra-systemic parameters' framework to the South African setting and convincingly comes to the conclusion that there are various reasons why the application of extra-systemic parameters in post-apartheid South Africa is working, namely:[119]

Grondwetlike Hof [2002] 6 SA 630 (CC) at para 7; *Ex Parte President of the RSA: In re Constitutionality of the Liquor Bill* [2000] 1 SA 732 (CC) at n 11; *Christian Education SA v Minister of Education* [2000] 4 SA 757 (CC) at n 24; *Maphahlele v First National Bank of SA Ltd* [1999] 1 SACR 373 (CC) at n 10; *Du Plessis v De Klerk* (n 77) in the notes at 104; *S v Makwanyane* (n 8) at nn 89 and 164.

[112] *Du Plessis v De Klerk* (n 77) 41.

[113] The judgment was delivered when the interim Constitution was still in operation and it is generally accepted that the new Constitution applies directly to private law. See in general the discussion of Stu Woolman, 'Application' in S Woolman, M Bishop, and J Brickhill (eds.), *Constitutional Law of South Africa* (Juta, Kenwyn 2008) 31.3–31.161.

[114] His views were expressed during an interview; see Bentele, 'Mining for Gold' (n 69) 242–3.

[115] *Du Plessis v De Klerk* (n 77) 41. He declared: 'In my opinion there is at least one positive lesson to be learnt from the Canadian and German approaches to the problem before us. Both Canada and Germany have developed a strong culture of individual human rights, which finds expression in the decisions of their courts.'

[116] Lollini, 'Legal Argumentation' (n 5) 60.

[117] Lollini, 'Legal Argumentation' (n 5) 61–2.

[118] Lollini, 'Legal Argumentation' (n 5) 62.

[119] Lollini, 'Legal Argumentation' (n 5) 63–4.

- The express provision in the South African Constitution which allows judges to use extra-systemic parameters (viz foreign precedents).
- South Africa needs to obtain international legitimacy after years of human rights infringements.
- The judiciary needs to search for international principles to aid the interpretation of the South African Constitution, especially the Bill of Rights.
- The judiciary is aware that judicial review in a post-apartheid South Africa would require a period of legal learning which could be provided by the global legal (especially constitutional) arena.

iv. Number of foreign precedents: human rights, institutional or other issues

Each foreign citation was categorized according to the issue it dealt with. Three issues are distinguished, viz 'human rights issues',[120] 'institutional issues',[121] and 'other issues' (see Figure 20.3).[122] A clear division among these three issues is not always possible. For example, a decision by an institution can sometimes also be classified as a human rights issue under the heading 'just administrative action'[123] and thus could fall under both the heading 'institutional issues' and the heading 'human rights issues'. From 1995 to 2010 the Constitutional Court had a total of about 2,152 foreign case citations in the context of human rights issues, approximately 472 foreign case citations dealing with institutional issues, and approximately 2,206 citations which can be classified as other issues.

Furthermore, in order to limit the number of human rights issues involved, the human rights issues have been categorized according to the main provisions in the Bill of Rights. For instance, the right to a fair trial is strictly speaking a right on its own but it is placed in the category 'arrested, detained and accused persons'.[124] In some instances, more information on the particular right falling under the main category is given under the heading 'other issues'. In other words, the right to a fair trial will be categorized as a human rights issue under the heading 'arrested, detained and accused persons' but then simultaneously as a right to a fair trial under the heading 'other issues'. The numbers of citations under 'human rights issues' (as set out in Figure 20.4 below) and 'institutional issues' are thus fairly accurate at this stage but the number of citations under 'other issues' remains problematic.

[120] In order to limit the number of entries the human rights issues are categorized according to the human rights listed in the Bill of Rights. See ch 2 of the Constitution.

[121] Institutional issues may overlap with human rights issues, eg, a decision of a school board may infringe human rights such as equality, freedom of expression, and cultural rights but may also be classified as an institutional issue. An example is *MEC for Education Kwazulu-Natal v Pillay* [2008] 1 SA 474 (CC), where the decision of the school board to prohibit a learner from wearing a nose stud can be categorized under both issues.

[122] Other issues include interpretation, constitutional values, the limitation of rights, the rule of law, etc. The other-issues option was also used to refine a particular human right included in the broad categories of human rights listed in Fig 20.3; eg, the right to a fair trial will be included under other issues but also forms part of the statistics in the category of 'arrested, detained and accused persons' in Fig 20.3.

[123] See s 33 of the Constitution.

[124] See s 35 of the Constitution.

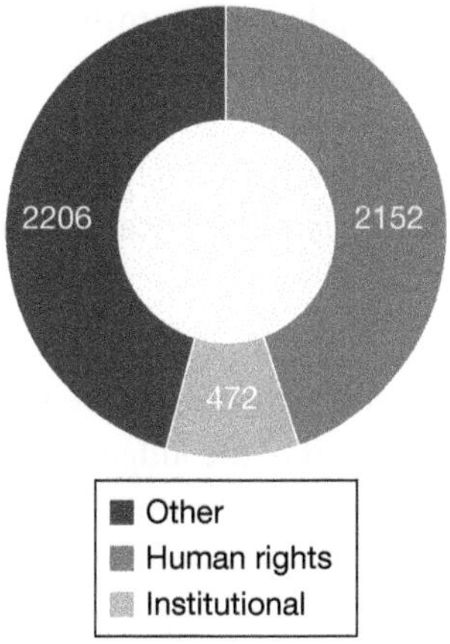

Figure 20.3 Number of citations vis-à-vis issues

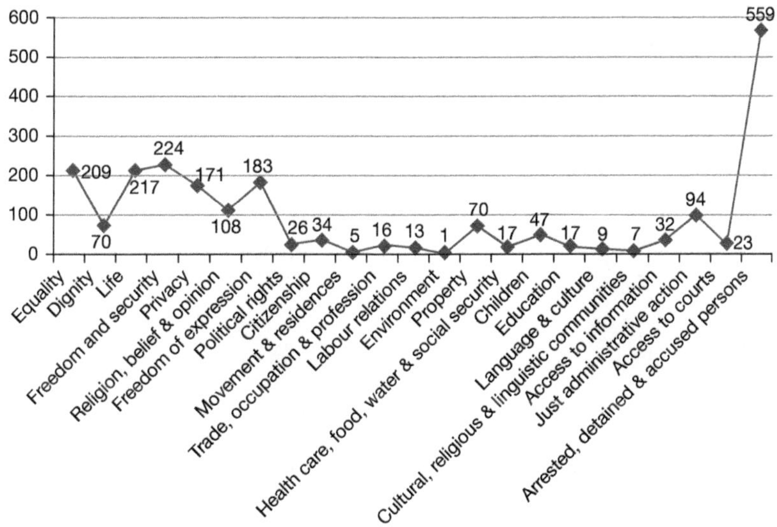

Figure 20.4 The number of foreign citations pertaining to human rights issues[125]

b) Qualitative approach

i. Formal indicators

By using formal indicators one can determine to an extent just how influential foreign cases have been on the South African judiciary. The formal indicators used in the survey are, first and foremost, the mode of citation used by the Court. A citation could be made either in a footnote or in the text, and it could also be a mere reference to or a

[125] Fig 20.4 illustrates the number and classes of human rights issues most likely to elicit the consideration of foreign precedents by the judges. It is extremely difficult to give exact numbers since a particular foreign precedent might have been cited more than once and also in connection with more than one human right.

quote from a foreign case. The second group of formal indicators looks at the question of who is citing whose foreign judgments. The mode of citation does not really tell us what the value of the particular citation for South African law was; a foreign case could be followed by the South African judge but merely referred to in a footnote, or a foreign case could be discussed at length only to be discarded (*a contrario*) at the end.

Mode of citation

No clear indications as to the authoritative value of a foreign case can be derived from looking at where it was cited in the text of the judgment. It can be cited either in the text or in a footnote and the citation could either be a mere reference to or a quote from the foreign case. According to the statistics, however, it appears that mere references to foreign cases are most common, as are citations in footnotes rather than in the text (see Figure 20.5).

Who is citing whom?

As to the question 'who cites foreign precedents', the statistics reveal what we have suspected, which is that judges delivering majority, dissenting, and separate judgments all consider foreign precedents. However, as reflected in Figure 20.6, the vast majority

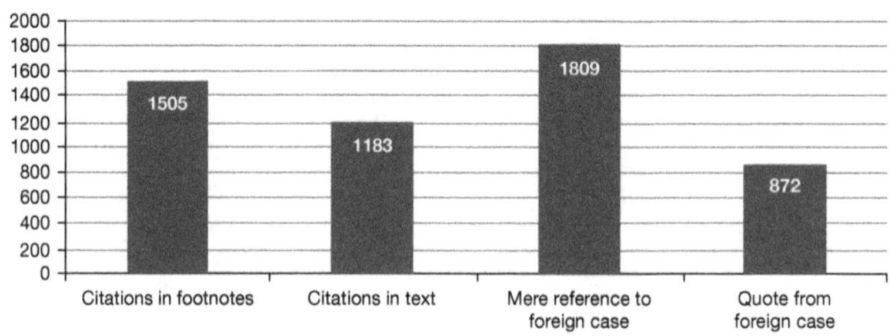

Figure 20.5 The number of citations according to the mode of citation

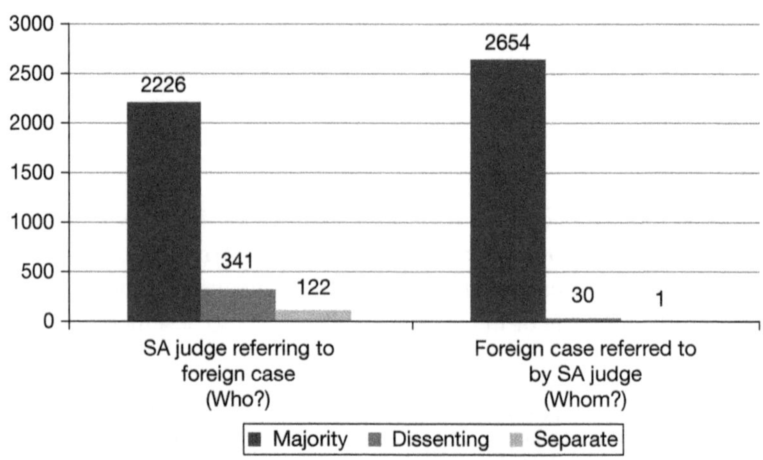

Figure 20.6 The number of citations according to majority, dissenting, or separate judgments

of the Constitutional Court judges citing foreign cases delivered the majority decision and also referred to the majority judgment of the foreign case.

The fact that judges refer to minority judgments in foreign precedents might not be surprising. Interestingly, though, a foreign case is sometimes considered by the judges delivering the majority, dissenting, and/or separate judgments, all in one case. For instance, in the well-known case dealing with the constitutionality of legislation prohibiting the selling of liquor on certain days and at certain times, viz *S v Lawrence; S v Negal; S v Solberg*,[126] Justice Chaskalson, delivering the majority judgment, considered the Canadian case, *R v Big M Drug Mart Ltd*,[127] and came to the conclusion that it was unnecessary for him to decide whether or not he should follow the Canadian approach to legislation dealing with the selling of liquor on Sundays because of the final decision that he reached.[128] In the same case Justice O'Regan, who delivered a minority judgment, also referred to *R v Big M Drug Mart Ltd*[129] in passing.[130] In a separate but concurring judgment, Justice Sachs too referred to *R v Big M Drug Mart Ltd*[131] but, whilst Justice Chaskalson implicitly stated that he need not follow the Canadian case, Justice Sachs indicated that he endorsed the viewpoint of the latter.[132]

As to the question 'who is cited by the South African judges', the statistics reveal a very interesting phenomenon. Although the majority of foreign case citations (ie 2,654) refer to the majority decisions of foreign precedents, there are also many foreign case citations (ie 30) where the dissenting decisions of the foreign precedents were considered by the South African judges. For example, in *Prince v President, Cape Law Society*,[133] a case dealing with the illegal use of cannabis by Rastafarians, the Constitutional Court judges referred 13 times to the USA case *Employment Division, Department of Human Resources of Oregon v Smith*.[134] A break-up of the statistics reveals the following interesting facts:

- Justices Chaskalson, Ackermann, and Kriegler delivered the majority judgment and cited the USA case at least nine times. Six times they referred to the majority judgment[135] and the other three times they referred to the dissenting judgment in the USA case.[136] The three justices found the dissenting judgment to be more consistent with the South African Constitution.[137]

[126] *S v Lawrence; S v Negal; S v Solberg* [1997] 4 SA 1176 (CC) 87, 88, 92, 98, and 104.

[127] *R v Big M Drug Mart Ltd* (n 84).

[128] *S v Lawrence; S v Negal; S v Solberg* (n 126), 98. He came to the conclusion that Sundays are normally the day that most South Africans do not work and '[a] restriction on the sale of liquor on Sundays is, therefore, likely to be more effective in curtailing the consumption of liquor than a restriction on the sale of liquor on any other day of the week' (see 106).

[129] *R v Big M Drug Mart Ltd* (n 84).

[130] Without indicating the weight afforded to the Canadian case, she merely refers to it in a footnote. See *S v Lawrence; S v Negal; S v Solberg* (n 126), 126.

[131] *R v Big M Drug Mart Ltd* (n 84).

[132] See *S v Lawrence; S v Negal; S v Solberg* (n 126), 126.

[133] *Prince v President, Cape Law Society* [2002] 2 SA 794 (CC).

[134] *Employment Division, Department of Human Resources of Oregon v Smith* [1990] 494 US 872.

[135] *Prince v President, Cape Law Society* (n 133) 119–21, 123, and 128–9. The majority judgment was delivered by Judge Scalia.

[136] *Prince v President, Cape Law Society* (n 133) 122 and 128–9. Judge Blackmun delivered a dissenting opinion and was joined by Judges Brennan and Marchall.

[137] See *Prince v President, Cape Law Society* (n 133) 122, 128.

- Justice Ngcobo, delivering a dissenting judgment, cited the USA case only once by referring to the dissenting opinion of Judge Blackmun.[138] He did not indicate, however, if the opinion of Judge Blackmun had any influence on his final decision.
- Justice Sachs, who delivered a separate dissenting judgment, referred to the dissenting opinion of Blackmun (which he too favoured) in the USA case at least three times.[139] He recognized the differences between the situation in South Africa (ie a Rastafarian's use of marijuana/dagga) and that of the USA (ie native Americans using peyote) and came to the conclusion that to 'read as a whole his judgment [the dissenting decision of Judge Blackmun] is inconsistent with the granting of a narrowly tailored religious exemption in South Africa for the sacramental use by Rastafari of dagga'.[140]

In all likelihood South African Constitutional Court judges refrain from citing foreign precedents which are not directly to the point or comparable with the facts before the Court. This fact was made clear by Justice Langa in *SABC v National Director of Public Prosecutions*[141] with regard to the foreign precedents referred to by the council for the SABC.

ii. Substantial indicators: judicial reasoning

By using substantial indicators it is possible broadly to classify the legal reasoning of the judge citing foreign law into the following three categories:[142]

- Citations used at the very first stage of the process when reasoning must be oriented.[143] In this context, citations of foreign precedents may be useful to illustrate the range of potential choices or consequences. During this stage the influence of a particular foreign precedent is not always clear. In most instances the judges merely refer to the foreign precedents in passing. Using foreign precedents during this stage, without giving consideration to the (potential) value of a particular foreign case so cited, is also the method disapproved of by some critics. According to the statistics, approximately 2,534 foreign citations fall into this category.
- Citations used with the purpose of proving that 'even there' a certain measure was adopted, which the court intends to adopt 'even here'.[144] An example of where this line of reasoning was applied is *Coetzee v The Government of RSA; Matiso v Commanding Officer, Port Elizabeth Prison*.[145] In this case Justice Sachs, delivering

[138] *Prince v President, Cape Law Society* (n 133) 47.

[139] *Prince v President, Cape Law Society* (n 133) 152, 155, 163.

[140] *Prince v President, Cape Law Society* (n 133) 152.

[141] *SABC v National Director of Public Prosecutions* [2007] 1 SA 523 (CC) 56 and 59.

[142] Placing a foreign citation in one of the three categories is not an easy task and this process is still ongoing.

[143] This phase can also be described as the 'inspirational' phase as discussed by Bryde, 'The Constitutional Judge' (n 39) 213–14.

[144] This phase can also be described as the 'legal argument' phase as described by Bryde, 'The Constitutional Judge' (n 39) 214–19.

[145] *Coetzee v The Government of RSA; Matiso v Commanding Officer, Port Elizabeth Prison* (n 62). This judgment has at least 149 foreign case citations.

a separate opinion, interpreted the word 'necessary' in the limitation clause[146] and, in doing so, considered foreign case law.[147] He then explained the value of the foreign precedents by saying that the term 'necessary', as indicated by the foreign case citations:[148]

> is not made the subject of rigid definition, but rather is regarded as implying a series of inter-related elements in which central place is given to the proportionality of the means used to achieve a pressing and legitimate public purpose. Turning to the South African Constitution, I will not attempt a full definition of the word 'necessary', but, *bearing international experience in mind*, make the following observations.
> (emphasis added).

According to the statistics there are only 147 foreign citations in this category.

- Citations used as an example not to be followed (*a contrario*) in order to set aside some of the potential interpretative readings. Only about 22 foreign case citations fall in this category.

The high rate of foreign case citations during the reasoning phase without any indication of what the explicit influences of the foreign cases are might leave one with some discomfort. If 'considering' foreign law, as authorized by section 39(1)(c) of the Constitution, means nothing more than paying lip service to foreign law, what then is the point of the whole exercise? As explained by Justice Moseneke,[149] judges 'cherry pick all the time' when they refer to domestic or foreign cases. According to him the process of judicial adjudication:

> implies a selection, and a reasoned and rational process to search for the truth by weeding out what's irrelevant and finding what is cohesive and that best answers... the problem before us.[150]

The dealings of the Constitutional Court judges in citing foreign law during the reasoning phase have been all-encompassing rather than restrictive. The advantage of such a method is, of course, that nobody can blame the Court afterwards for not considering all of the available foreign case law on a particular issue.

IV. Concluding remarks

Whilst the international community is hotly debating the pros and cons of judicial comparativism, the South African Constitutional Court has been developing, without much ado, an impressive reference list of foreign precedents. Never considering foreign precedents to be binding or persuasive, the Court has been protecting its independence. Justice Ackermann, in a scholarly article, declared as follows:[151]

[146] As contained in s 33 of the interim Constitution and similar to s 36 in the Constitution.

[147] See *Coetzee v The Government of RSA; Matiso v Commanding Officer, Port Elizabeth Prison* (n 62). Justice Sachs has about 30 foreign case citations in his judgment.

[148] *Coetzee v The Government of RSA; Matiso v Commanding Officer, Port Elizabeth Prison* (n 62), 60.

[149] See Bentele, 'Mining for Gold' (n 69) 239.

[150] Quoted in Bentele, 'Mining for Gold' (n 69) 239.

[151] Ackermann, 'Constitutional Comparativism' (n 3) 510–13. He also supplies a long list of examples where foreign precedents have proved to be instructive and helpful in the judgments of the Constitutional Court.

> [F]oreign law is not in any sense binding on the court that refers to it. There seems to be the fear that in referring to foreign law one is bowing to foreign authority and thereby endangering the national sovereignty of one's own legal system. This is manifestly not so. One may be seeking information, guidance, stimulation, clarification or even enlightenment, but never authority binding on one's own decision. One is doing no more than keeping the judicial mind open to new ideas, problems, arguments, and solutions.

Furthermore, the justices consider primarily open and democratic societies and they are not afraid to recognize the differences and commonalities between the South African legal system and other jurisdictions, or those of the issues before them and the analogous foreign issues. These features, in a nutshell, have been described by Justice Ackermann in *National Coalition for Gay and Lesbian Equality v Minister of Justice*[152] as follows:

> In referring to these [foreign] judgments from the highest courts of other jurisdictions I do not overlook the different nature of their histories, legal systems and constitutional contexts nor that, in the last two cases, the issue was one essentially of statutory construction and not constitutional invalidity. Nevertheless, these judgments give expression to norms and values in other open and democratic societies based on human dignity, equality and freedom which, in my view, give clear expression to the growing concern for, understanding of, and sensitivity towards human diversity in general and to gays and lesbians and their relationships in particular. This is an important source from which to illuminate our understanding of the Constitution and the promotion of its informing norms.

The results of the empirical survey reveal an unprecedented willingness on the part of the Constitutional Court to participate in the constitutional dialogue happening in the global world. It is, nevertheless, dangerous to conclude that the South African Constitution is the main catalyst for the Court's engagement in constitutional comparativism. South African judges have always used foreign precedents in their judicial reasoning and it is quite natural that a newly established court such as the Constitutional Court would continue to do so. In this regard, it might be more truthful to conclude that it is a 'new' dog with 'old' tricks. That being said, it is also true that South Africa did not have a Bill of Rights before, and neither did the foreign jurisdictions that the South African courts used to refer to. For that reason, at least, the section 39 mandate could be seen as a new development enabling the South African courts to refer to foreign case law when interpreting the human rights provisions in the South African Constitution.

Also, although tempting, it is difficult to reach a crystal-clear conclusion that the Constitutional Court's jurisprudence reveals a consistent line of authority that indicates an approach towards foreign precedents which is universally accepted. Such a conclusion could lead to the utopian world of transjudicialism as imagined by Slaughter:[153]

> Imagine a world of regular and interactive transjudicial communication—among... courts... It would be a world in which courts perceived themselves independent of,

[152] *National Coalition for Gay and Lesbian Equality v Minister of Justice* [2000] 2 SA 1 (CC) 48.
[153] Slaughter, 'A Typology of Transjudicial Communication' (n 38) 132.

> although linked to, their fellow political institutions, open to persuasive authority, and engaged in a common enterprise of interpreting and applying national and international law, protecting individual rights, and ensuring that power is corralled by law. National differences would not obscure common problems nor block the adoption of foreign solutions. Courts would relate to each other in ways that could circumvent and constrain other branches of national governments and that could forge an independent link between national and international institutions. In this conception, the phenomenon of transjudicial communication is a pillar of a compelling vision of global legal relations.

We can all dream about this wonderful world she describes but we all know that the real world does not work this way. At least the statistics of the South African Constitutional Court reveal that the Court does not shy away from judicial globalism but on the contrary is open to dialogue with other jurisdictions—an attitude that is commendable.

21

Enhancing Constitutional Self-Understanding through Comparative Law

An Empirical Study of the Use of Foreign Case Law by the Supreme Court of Canada (1982–2013)

*Gianluca Gentili**

I. Introduction

The 'migration of constitutional ideas'[1] represents a distinctive feature of contemporary constitutionalism. This expression[2] captures the increased exchange of legal ideas that has occurred between constitutional systems since the end of the 20th century, when a new wave of constitution-making endeavours prompted the adoption of a new generation of national charters of rights.[3] One declination of this exchange is the practice of judges citing foreign case law when interpreting national constitutions, a trend variously referred to as 'judicial dialogue',[4] 'judicial internationalization', 'trans-judicialism', 'judicial cosmopolitanism', 'judicial globalisation',[5] or 'judicial engagement with foreign law'.[6] While a handful of fundamental charters worldwide expressly allow this engagement,[7] the majority remains silent on a practice that has grown controversial.

* Research Associate in Transnational Constitutional Law, School of Law, University of Manchester (Manchester, UK). I wish to thank Tania Groppi, Marie-Claire Ponthoreau, Cheryl Saunders, Jean-François Gaudreault-DesBiens, and Richard Kay for helpful discussions and comments on previous drafts of this article. All remaining inaccuracies are mine. An earlier version of this chapter was published in T Groppi and M-C Ponthoreau, *The Use of Foreign Precedents by Constitutional Judges* (Hart, Oxford 2013).

[1] S Choudhry (ed), *The Migration of Constitutional Ideas* (Cambridge University Press, Cambridge 2006).

[2] This concept has also been described as 'importation of constitutional law': C Dupré, 'The Importation of Law: A New Comparative Perspective and the Hungarian Constitutional Court' in A Harding and E Orocu (eds.), *Comparative Law in the 21st Century* (Kluwer, The Hague 2002); 'constitutional borrowing': B Friedman and C Saunders, 'Editor's Introduction' (2003), 1 International Journal of Constitutional Law 177; 'cross-constitutional influence': KL Scheppele, 'Aspirational and Aversive Constitutionalism: The Case for Studying Cross-Constitutional Influence through Negative Models' (2003), 1 International Journal of Constitutional Law 296.

[3] J Elster, 'Forces and Mechanisms in the Constitution-Making Process' (1995), 45 Duke Law Journal 364, 368. Cheryl Saunders notes that, worldwide, '91 new constitutions or constitutional-type instruments for states and other distinct polities have come into force since 1990': C Saunders, 'Judicial Engagement with Comparative Law' in T Ginsburg and R Dixon (eds.), *Comparative Constitutional Law* (Edward Elgar, Cheltenham 2011) 574, fn 22.

[4] S Harding, 'Comparative Reasoning and Judicial Review' (2003), 28 Yale Journal of International Law 409.

[5] S Muller and S Richards (eds.), *Highest Courts and Globalisation* (Asser Press, The Hague 2010) 4.

[6] V Jackson, *Constitutional Engagement in a Transnational Era* (Oxford University Press, New York 2010).

[7] s 11(2)(c) of the Constitution of the Republic of Malawi, 1994; s 39(1) of the Constitution of South Africa, 1996; s 32(2) of the *Charter of Human Rights and Responsibilities Act 2006* (Victoria). Interestingly,

A view indeed holds that constitutions—which, since the rise of the nation-state, have been understood as the product of a given ethos—should be interpreted exclusively on the basis of domestic, rather than foreign, legal materials. The topic has received uneven scholarly attention: studies have focused extensively on the theoretical aspects of this practice (legitimacy and methodology), while empirical analyses on the frequency and meaning of citations remain generally still rare.

Since the adoption of the 1982 *Charter of Rights and Freedoms*[8] (*Charter*), the Supreme Court of Canada (SCC or Court) has established itself as one of the most progressive constitutional judges worldwide. Expressly endowing the Court with powers of judicial review for the protection of constitutionally entrenched rights, this constitutional Bill of Rights changed the Court's role and hermeneutic approach, in a system rooted in the British tradition of parliamentary supremacy.[9] The *Charter*—inspired by the United States *Bill of Rights* and several other international human rights documents—fostered an openness to foreign legal sources typical of a common law high court, and prompted the Court to refer to an even broader range of foreign jurisdictions.

This contribution will present an empirical analysis of the Court's decisions issued during the first 32 years of application of the *Charter*, between 1982 and 2013. Its main purpose is to achieve a better understanding of the decision-making process informing the Court's activity in today's globalized legal context and of the role played by the *Charter* in this process. Specifically, this work will provide empirical evidence supporting the view that the SCC, in deciding constitutional cases and interpreting the newly enacted *Charter*, has consistently considered other jurisdictions. Referring to cases decided by American, Australian, British, and European courts, the Court has, over the years, established its *Charter* jurisprudence by drawing critical inspiration from foreign judicial decisions and adapting their legal principles to the unique features of Canada's legal system and society.

Section II will provide an overview of Canada's constitutional and institutional history since the country's foundation as a member of the British Commonwealth. Section III will focus on the empirical study, its methodology, qualitative and quantitative results, detailing the Court's use of foreign case law in constitutional cases, both in general and with specific regard to United States precedents.

II. The context

1. Canada's constitutional origins: the British North America Act, 1867

Canada as a political entity came into being in 1867, when several North American political systems north of the United States (US) united into a Federation. The *British*

art 84 of the 1990 *Basic Law* of the Hong Kong Special Administrative Region indicates that, in the adjudication of cases, courts of that Region 'may refer to precedents of other common law jurisdictions'.

[8] *Charter of Rights and Freedoms*, Part I of the *Constitution Act, 1982* being Schedule B to the *Canada Act 1982* (UK), 1982, c 11.

[9] In a legal system based on this principle, no constraints are imposed upon what Parliament can do, because it is thought that Parliament represents the best place to draw the appropriate balance between individual freedoms and a broader public interest.

North America Act of 1867 (BNAA or *Act*)—the main document that served as Canada's constitution until 1982—created the Dominion of Canada out of three separate entities and established the framework for admission of other colonies and territories in the future.[10] Since none of the then existing Canadian entities was independent, this process was overseen by the British Foreign Office, with the BNAA enacted as ordinary legislation by the United Kingdom (UK) Parliament. The *Act* did not terminate the relationship with the UK—independence was not sought at that time—and the new Dominion remained a British colony. For the same reason, the BNAA contained no provision for a domestic amendment procedure: Canada, therefore, was required to resort to the UK Parliament for constitutional change.

While representing one of the key components of Canada's constitution, care should be taken to distinguish the BNAA and 'the constitution' of Canada.[11] The 19th-century Canadian constitution, in fact, was traditionally understood as an instrument of government wider in scope than the BNAA,[12] and could not be found in one single, written document. Following the British political tradition, it was formed by a heterogeneous set of materials including a compendium of Acts and statutes along with common law decisions and customary practices ('constitutional conventions'[13]) that together organized the political life of the nation and prescribed how the government was to operate.[14]

Despite just being a part of the Canadian constitution, the BNAA was a significant one nonetheless. The *Act* defined the basic institutional framework of the new Federal government and provided for the distribution of legislative powers between the Federal Parliament and the legislatures of the Provinces.[15] Furthermore, its Preamble contained an important interpretative statement to determine Canada's form of government, prescribing for Canada 'a Constitution similar in Principle to that of the United Kingdom'.[16]

[10] The original three Provinces were New Brunswick, Nova Scotia, and the United Province of Canada, comprising present-day Ontario and Quebec. Between 1867 and 1949, six more Provinces joined (British Columbia, Prince Edward Island, and Newfoundland) or were created from federal territories (Manitoba, Saskatchewan, and Alberta). Now Canada has ten Provinces and three federal territories (Yukon, Northwestern Territories, and Nunavut).

[11] Throughout this work, the Canadian 'constitution' will not be capitalized, while the US 'Constitution' will be. Indeed, in the case of the US, usage refers to a distinctive document, whereas with regard to Canada the term refers to a collection of documents (including, but not limited to, the *Constitution Act, 1867* and the *Constitution Act, 1982*) along with a substantial unwritten constitution.

[12] Drafters of the BNAA had a limited purpose: creating a governmental structure ('the Dominion of Canada') for the three English colonies in North America. Accordingly, it did not include a Bill of Rights. Under that system, the Provinces retained considerable autonomy, and the Dominion as a whole was under the authority of the English Crown. MC McKenna, 'Introduction: A Legacy of Questions' in MC McKenna (ed), *The Canadian and American Constitutions in Comparative Perspective* (Calgary University Press, Calgary 1993) XV.

[13] Albert Venn Dicey maintained that political actors and institutions were bound by two sets of rules, the first being 'laws' in the strict sense, and the second defined as 'conventions, understandings, habits, or practices which, though they may regulate the conduct of the several members of the sovereign power, of the Ministry, or of other officials', are not 'laws' and hence not enforceable by courts: AV Dicey, *An Introduction to the Study of the Law of the Constitution* (10th edn, Macmillan, London 1960) 23.

[14] For the sources of Canadian constitutional law, see PW Hogg, *Constitutional Law of Canada* (4th edn, Carswell, Toronto 1997) ch 1.

[15] Arts 91–95 BNAA. [16] Preamble, BNAA.

2. Enhancing protection of fundamental rights

Before the adoption of the *Charter* in 1982, the legislative powers of the Federal and Provincial parliaments were subject to very few limits. Cases raising civil liberties issues were addressed under the BNAA provisions outlining the division of power between the Federal and Provincial governments.[17]

One of the first attempts to develop limits to the governments' powers, with a view to protecting fundamental rights, saw Canadian courts resorting to the idea of an 'implied bill of rights'. In the *Alberta Press* case,[18] Chief Justice Duff found that limitations to governmental actions could be found in the idea that citizens' rights and freedoms were necessary to the proper functioning of a 'responsible government'. Although the theory received some support, it was never endorsed by a majority of the SCC, and was eventually rejected.[19]

After the Second World War, more articulate attempts were made—both at the Federal and Provincial levels—to ensure fundamental rights protection.

Beginning in 1947, several Provinces adopted human rights statutes, effective within their territories: Saskatchewan, Ontario, Nova Scotia, Alberta, New Brunswick, Prince Edward Island, Newfoundland, British Columbia, Manitoba, and Quebec.[20] In 1960 a *Canadian Bill of Rights*[21] (*Bill* or CBoR) was enacted as an ordinary statute by the Canadian Parliament. The *Bill*, still in effect today, is an interpretative Bill of Rights listing a series of fundamental freedoms and providing that all other laws be 'so construed and applied so as not to abrogate, abridge or infringe' any of the rights or freedoms declared in the *Bill* itself.[22] Almost completely superseded by the 1982 *Charter*, it nonetheless contains some guarantees not included in this latter document.[23] The CBoR, however, suffered three main shortcomings: a) it only applied to

[17] In *Saumur v City of Quebec* (1953) 2 SCR 299, the SCC upheld a Jehovah's Witness' challenge to a Quebec law against street distribution of literature without prior police permission. Although the case addressed religious freedom issues, the SCC based its judgment on the federal division of power, ruling that the power to regulate religious practices fell under the purview of national government rather than of the Provinces.

[18] *Reference re Alberta Statutes* [1938] 2 SCR 100 ('*Alberta Press* case'). The implied Bill of Rights theory was invoked mostly before the *Charter*'s enactment (eg *Reference re Persons of Japanese Race* [1946] SCR 248) and received its most explicit articulation in *Switzman v Elbling* [1957] SCR 285.

[19] In 1978, a Court's majority rejected this theory declaring that no civil liberty, including those inherited from the UK, 'is so enshrined in the Constitution as to be beyond the reach of competent legislation': *AG Canada and Dupond v Montreal* [1978] 2 SCR 770, 796. The idea, however, has been revisited in a recent opinion: *Reference re Remuneration of Judges of the Provincial Court of Prince Edward Island* [1997] 3 SCR 3.

[20] *Saskatchewan Bill of Rights Act*, SS 1947, c 35; *Ontario Human Rights Code*, SO 1961–62, c 93; *Nova Scotia Human Rights Act*, SNS 1963, c 5; *Alberta Human Rights Act*, SA 1966, c 39; *New Brunswick Human Rights Act*, SNB 1967, c 13; *PEI Human Rights Act*, S PEI 1968, c 24; *Nfld Human Rights Act*, S Nfld 1969, no 75; *BC Human Rights Act*, SBC 1969, c 10; *Manitoba Human Rights Act*, SM 1970, c 104; *Charter of Human Rights and Freedoms*, SQ 1975, c 6.

[21] *Canadian Bill of Rights*, 'An Act for the Recognition and Protection of Human Rights and Fundamental Freedoms' SC 1960, c 44. For the *Bill*'s legislative history: WS Tarnopolsky, *The Canadian Bill of Rights*, 2nd rev edn (Carleton University Press, Toronto 1978) 11–14.

[22] Pt I, s 2 *Bill*.

[23] eg s 1(a) *Bill* protects the right of property, while s 2(e) *Bill* guarantees everyone 'the right to a fair hearing in accordance with the principles of fundamental justice for the determination of his rights and obligations'. The *Charter* does not protect property rights, and the guarantee to a fair hearing is deemed narrower.

Federal laws, therefore not affecting Provincial enactments;[24] b) it could be derogated from by a subsequent Act of the Canadian Parliament (with an express declaration that the Act could operate notwithstanding the *Bill*);[25] c) as an ordinary Act of Parliament it was not part of the Canadian constitution, and could be repealed at any time by the Federal Parliament, without recourse to the amending procedure.[26] This latter feature, together with an attitude of deference to the legislator imbued in the judiciary, represents the main reason why, with just one exception,[27] courts have been reluctant to consider the *Bill* as conferring upon the judiciary the authority to invalidate other duly enacted laws; this concept, without an express constitutional grant of power, seemed to Canadian courts to run against the basic rule of parliamentary supremacy.[28] The CBoR has therefore mostly been used by courts as a guide to the interpretation of other statutes, receiving narrow judicial application.

In 1977, the Federal government enacted the *Canadian Human Rights Act* (CHRA), a statute whose aim is to counter discriminatory practices based on a list of prohibited grounds set out in the document.[29] While the CHRA finds application throughout Canada, it only affects federally regulated activities.

Finally, in 1978, the Supreme Court rejected the idea that fundamental freedoms could be derived from the Preamble to the BNAA.[30]

This being the constitutional landscape at the beginning of the 1980s, in 1982 a major change occurred within the Canadian legal system, due to the enactment of two statutes of the UK Parliament. The first, the *Canada Act, 1982*, terminated the legislative authority of the UK over Canada.[31] The second, the *Constitution Act, 1982*, an annex to the *Canada Act, 1982*, along with declaring a list of 30 Acts and statutes—including the *Constitution Act* itself and the BNAA (renamed the *Constitution Act, 1867*)—to be the supreme law of Canada, contained two Parts relevant for this study. Part V of the *Constitution Act, 1982*, 'patriated' the constitution introducing amending procedures that could be promoted entirely by Canadian institutions. Part I introduced a *Charter of Rights and Freedoms*, a constitutional Bill of Rights entrenching fundamental personal freedoms against legislative and executive action. The

[24] s 5, c 2 *Bill*. This is unlike the *Charter*, which has application to both Federal and Provincial governments. It should be noted that much of the SCC's activity after 1982 has involved challenges to provincial legislation.

[25] s 2 *Bill*.

[26] The *Charter*, conversely, is a constitutionally entrenched document which expressly overrides inconsistent statutes.

[27] *R v Drybones* [1970] SCR 282.

[28] Other common law courts, however, concluded otherwise. In *Simpson v AG*, 3 NZLR 667, 706 (1994), the New Zealand Court of Appeals, interpreting that country's 1990 (statutory) *Bill of Rights Act*, noted that lack of constitutional status 'makes no difference to the strength of the Bill of Rights where it is to be applied'. In some authors' view 'this and other recent decisions of the Court of Appeals indicate that the [New Zealand] *Bill of Rights*, though unentrenched, may gradually gather sufficient legal authority to allow courts to exercise most of the powers of scrutiny and control they would have had under a system of full-scale judicial review', gaining de facto entrenched status: R Hirschl, 'The Struggle for Hegemony: Understanding Judicial Empowerment Through Constitutionalization in Culturally Divided Polities' (2000), 36 Stanford Journal of International Law 73, 110 fn 173.

[29] The CHRA established the Canadian Human Rights Commission, a body investigating claims of discrimination, along with the Canadian Human Rights Tribunal that judges these cases.

[30] *Canada (AG) v City of Montreal*, 2 SCR 770 (1978).

[31] *Canada Act, 1982*, 1982 c 11.

Charter's enactment caused the Canadian system to move away from a pure British tradition of parliamentary supremacy, closer to the American concept of judicial supremacy.[32]

3. The *Canadian Charter of Rights and Freedoms*

The *Charter* is a constitutional declaration of fundamental rights drawing inspiration from various international human rights covenants and from the 1791 *Bill of Rights* to the US Constitution. The connection between these two declarations of rights is so intense that it could be defined—in the words of a famous scholar—as 'genetic'.[33] Despite being significantly influenced by a document almost two centuries older (the US *Bill of Rights*), the Canadian *Charter* fully participates in the expansive conception of rights characteristic of contemporary constitutionalism, due to the concurrent influence on the *Charter*'s drafters of international human rights treaties and conventions.[34]

The *Charter* represented the fulfilment of a project furthered by Pierre Trudeau's Liberal government against the initial objections of most Provinces, concerned that the declaration would increase the judicial power to interfere with the policies of elected governments. To counter these concerns, Conservative and Socialist Provincial governments supported inclusion in the *Charter* of a provision—section 33—allowing Provincial and Federal legislatures to enact laws for a renewable five-year period, notwithstanding the fundamental freedoms and legal rights protected therein.[35] Although seldom resorted to, section 33 represents a defining feature of Canadian constitutionalism.

As an entrenched document, the *Charter* has supremacy over all Federal and Provincial enactments. The power to strike down legislation inconsistent with the *Charter* is expressly codified in section 52(1) of the *Constitution Act, 1982*, which entrenches the Canadian version of the US Supremacy Clause, providing that the constitution, including the *Charter*, is the supreme law of Canada, and mandating that laws that are inconsistent

[32] L Weinrib, 'Canada's Constitutional Revolution: From Legislative to Constitutional State' (1999), 33 Israeli Law Review 13.

[33] The two documents being 'genetically related'. In Louis Henkin's view, constitutional documents are genetically related if one influenced the framing of the other, or if both were framed under the influence of a third: L Henkin, 'A New Birth of Constitutionalism: Genetic Influences and Genetic Defects' (1993), 14 Cardozo Law Review 533, 536–8. On the influence exerted by the US *Bill of Rights* and the US Supreme Court's jurisprudence on the *Charter*'s drafters, see L Weinrib, 'Of Diligence and Dice, Reconstituting Canada's Constitution' (1990), 42 University of Toronto Law Journal 207, 220, where the author details the unsuccessful effort, amidst the drafting process, to disengage from consideration of US jurisprudence.

[34] See J Claydon, 'International Human Rights Law and the Interpretation of the Canadian Charter of Rights and Freedoms' (1982), 4 Supreme Court Law Review 287, 295–302, noting the influence of the European Convention on Human Rights (ECHR), the UN Universal Declaration of Human Rights (UDHR), and other international human rights instruments upon the *Charter*.

[35] *Charter of Rights and Freedoms*, s 33: (1) Parliament or the legislature of a Province may expressly declare in an Act of Parliament or of the legislature, as the case may be, that the act or a provision thereof shall operate notwithstanding a provision included in section 2 or sections 7 to 15 of this Charter... (3) A declaration made under subsection (1) shall cease to have effect five years after it comes into force or on such earlier date as may be specified in the declaration.

with it are of no force or effect 'to the extent of the inconsistency'.[36] This makes this document a stronger Bill of Rights than the interpretative one enacted in 1960 in Canada and of those in force in New Zealand and the UK.[37] At the same time, the *Charter* differs from the US *Bill of Rights* in that it hosts in its section 1 a general 'salvage' or 'limitations' clause allowing the government to justify reasonable limits on rights,[38] an innovation subsequently adopted in New Zealand and South Africa. Unlike India or Ireland, or under the European Convention on Human Rights (ECHR), the Canadian limitations clause is open-ended and does not prescribe the reasons that legitimately justify limitations of rights.[39] The *Charter* therefore protects fundamental freedoms and rights, subject to the limitation set out in section 1, implicitly acknowledging that no legal system can treat any right as an absolute. This way, courts are permitted to uphold statutes found to infringe *Charter* rights, provided that legislation meets the procedural ('prescribed by law') and substantive ('demonstrably justified in a free and democratic society') requirements of section 1.[40] Section 24(1) gives the Court the power to devise remedies for those whose *Charter* rights have been violated.[41] A joint reading of sections 52(1) and 24(1) of the *Charter* vests the power of judicial review in the Canadian courts. Finally, section 32(2) of the *Charter* originally provided that the right to equality protected by section 15 would become effective three years after enactment of the document.

[36] *Constitution Act, 1982* being Schedule B to the *Canada Act, 1982* (UK), 1982, c 11, s 52(1).

[37] For a comparison of the Bills of Rights adopted in Canada, the UK, and New Zealand, which, in different forms, accommodate judicial protection of fundamental rights with claims of parliamentary sovereignty, see S Gardbaum, *The New Commonwealth Model of Constitutionalism. Theory and Practice* (Cambridge University Press, New York 2013).

[38] s 1 *Charter* famously states: 'The *Canadian Charter of Rights and Freedoms* guarantees the rights and freedoms set out in it subject only to such reasonable limits prescribed by law as can be demonstrably justified in a free and democratic society.'

[39] This clause derives from some earlier 20th-century human rights instruments: art 29(2) of the UDHR includes a limitations clause which, in turn, inspired analogous provisions in the ECHR and the International Covenant on Civil and Political Rights (ICCPR). Other constitutions also included similar clauses: Bahamas (1973), Barbados (1966), Botswana (1966), Grenada (1973), India (1949), Jamaica (1962), Kenya (2010), Malta (1964), Mauritius (1968), Nigeria (1960), Pakistan (1973), Samoa (1960), Trinidad and Tobago (1976). See V Jackson, *Constitutional Engagement in a Transnational Era* (Oxford University Press, Oxford 2009) 86, fns 89–90.

[40] In *R v Oakes*, 1 SCR 103 (1986), a case dealing with the constitutionality of a reverse onus provision of the *Narcotic Control Act*, RSC 1970, the SCC developed the test for the application of the balancing mechanism set out in section 1. According to the two-stage '*Oakes* test' courts first need to establish whether there has been an infringement of a *Charter* right. If an infringement is found, and the government action has been authorized by law, the Court then moves to the second step to decide whether the right was legitimately denied under section 1 and the violation—and corresponding law—can be 'demonstrably justified in a free and democratic society', and therefore 'salvaged' from a declaration of unconstitutionality. This second step has three important components, requiring a court to assess whether: 1) 'the measures adopted... [are] reasonably connected to the objective' (rationality); 2) 'the means... impair "as little as possible" the right or freedom in question' (minimal impairment); 3) there is 'proportionality between the effects of the measure responsible for limiting the Charter right and the objective which has been identified as of "sufficient importance"' (proportionality as such): *R v Oakes*, 139.

[41] s 24(1) *Charter* provides: 'Anyone whose rights or freedoms, as guaranteed by this Charter, have been infringed or denied may apply to a court of competent jurisdiction to obtain such remedy as the court considers appropriate and just in the circumstances.'

4. The Supreme Court of Canada

The BNAA only made a brief reference to the establishment of a national High Court,[42] without detailing the Court's composition, authority, functions, and jurisdiction. This silence is explained by the fact that, at the time, appeals from the courts of the British North American colonies could be lodged with the Judicial Committee of the Privy Council (PC or Privy Council), a London-based final court of appeal which, after the creation of the Dominion of Canada in 1867, entertained cases directly from the Provincial courts of appeal.[43]

Pressure for the development of a national High Court led to the adoption, in 1875, of the *Supreme and Exchequer Courts Act* (SECA), an ordinary Act of Parliament, and to the creation of the SCC.[44] The SECA established the Court's jurisdiction over all Provincial and Federal legal issues, common and statutory law. The SCC, however, did not immediately become the Court of last resort for Canada, its decisions remaining subject to appeal to the Privy Council until 1949, when that right was completely terminated. This occurred gradually: criminal appeals to the Privy Council were terminated in 1933 (with a few exceptions) while civil appeals ended in 1949.[45] Until then, the PC had a significant influence upon the evolution of the Canadian constitution, establishing the principles to be adopted in the interpretation of the BNAA, favouring strict literal interpretation and Provincial powers over those of the Federal government.

Originally composed of six members, the Court's composition grew over the years to reach the current total of nine. According to the *Supreme Court Act*, the Court is composed of one Chief Justice and eight Puisne (Associate) Justices exercising jurisdiction over appeals from Provincial courts in civil and criminal matters.[46] The Court's composition takes into account regional representation, selecting its members among different regions.[47]

In 1975, an amendment to the *Supreme Court Act* abolished most appeals as of right, introducing a leave to appeal mechanism that gave the Court control over its own docket.[48] Since the Court could now select the cases it would review, its docket

[42] s 101 *Constitution Act, 1867*, granted power to the Federal Parliament to create a new 'General Court of Appeal for Canada... and any additional Courts for the better administration of the Law of Canada'.

[43] The Council consisted of English judges, members of the House of Lords. LP Beth, 'The Judicial Committee: Its Development, Organisation and Procedure' (1975) 3, Public Law 219, 222–23, 232; ibid., 'The Judicial Committee of the Privy Council and the Development of Judicial Review' (1976), 24 American Journal of Comparative Law 22, 22–23.

[44] *Supreme and Exchequer Courts Act*, RS, 1900, c 154, later known as the *Supreme Court Act*.

[45] The last Canadian case was heard by the PC in 1959, as the case had been grandfathered: *Ponoka-Calmar Oils Ltd and anor v Earl F Wakefield Co, and ors* [1959] UKPC 20.

[46] *Supreme Court Act*, RSC, 1985, c S-26, s 4(1). In 1875 the Supreme Court was composed of six members. The number was raised to seven in 1927 and finally reached the current number of nine in 1949.

[47] Regional representation results from a combination of legislation and conventions. The *Supreme Court Act* requires three judges to come from Quebec: *Supreme Court Act*, RS 1985, c S-26, s 6. Of the Court's remaining seats, conventionally, three are allocated to Ontario, two to the Western Provinces and one to Atlantic Canada.

[48] Two years earlier, Bora Laskin had been appointed the 14th Chief Justice of Canada, a moment usually considered 'the beginning of the modern era of the Court': P McCormick, 'Blocs, Swarms, and Outliers: Conceptualizing Disagreement on the Modern Supreme Court of Canada' (2004), 42 Osgoode Hall Law Journal 99, 105.

decreased rapidly, enabling the Court to focus on cases with national relevance. Furthermore, unlike its US counterpart, the Court has the possibility of delivering advisory opinions, so-called 'reference cases', on constitutional or other issues referred by Federal or Provincial governments.[49]

The enactment of the *Constitution Act, 1982*, prompted another momentous change in the Court's status, functions, and role. Originally lacking formal recognition in the BNAA, some aspects of the Court came to enjoy entrenched status in the amending formula of sections 41–42.[50] Furthermore, since the beginning of its activity, the Court had reviewed legislation and executive actions to ensure consistency with the BNAA (now *Constitution Act, 1867*). This had consisted, primarily, in enforcing the allocation of legislative competences between Provincial and Federal governments pursuant to sections 91–92 of the *Constitution Act, 1867*.[51] The *Charter*'s enactment endowed the Court with explicit powers of judicial review over now constitutionally entrenched rights, radically transforming the Court's powers. The SCC's docket changed significantly[52] as the Court started to address new issues concerning the balance between governmental actions and individual or group freedoms, and developing a rights' jurisprudence.[53] The express judicial obligation to set aside legal provisions conflicting with the *Charter* caused the Court's authority to extend beyond the area of rights protection into areas previously addressed by the legislator, changing the balance of power in favour of the judiciary and eventually moving the system's focus away from the principle of Parliamentary supremacy.[54] Since then, in the effort to protect

[49] *Supreme Court Act*, RSC, 1985, c S-26, s 53.

[50] *Constitution Act, 1982*, ss 41 and 42.

[51] The BNAA provides specific lists of 'exclusive' powers for both levels of government. Unless otherwise stated (see ss 92(3) and 95 BNAA), these powers are mutually exclusive, rather than concurrent as in the US. s 91 grants the Federal government exclusive authority over issues of national importance, like 'trade and commerce' and criminal and family law; the BNAA's drafters' purpose was indeed to create a stronger Federal government than the one in the US. s 92, in turn, grants the provincial governments 'exclusive' authority in a number of broadly defined legislative areas, such as natural resources and land management, education, family institutions, property and civil rights, and other matters of a 'merely local or private nature'. It should be noted, however, that despite ss 91–92's textual emphasis on exclusiveness, the current dominant interpretative trend embraces more an overlapping conception of federalism than a 'watertight compartments' approach. Until the *Charter*'s enactment, the SCC was almost exclusively concerned with cases involving the Federal structure. This circumstance was summarized in the statement that 'historically, federalism cases have been the heart and soul of Canadian Constitutional law': D Beatty, *Constitutional Law in theory and Practice* (Toronto University Press, Toronto 1995) 2.

[52] Since the *Charter*'s enactment, 'cases in the areas of criminal law and civil liberties have increased dramatically while cases dealing with private law and economic interests have fallen significantly': D Songer, *The Transformation of the Supreme Court of Canada: An Empirical Examination* (Toronto University Press, Toronto 2008) 58–67.

[53] Unlike the US *Bill of Rights* and the 1960 statutory CBoR, the *Charter* explicitly recognizes group rights. It also expressly protects the special status of the French-speaking minority.

[54] A phenomenon termed as 'judicialisation of politics': R Hirschl, 'The New Constitutionalization and the Judicialization of Pure Politics Worldwide' (2006), 75 Fordham Law Review 721, 741–2. Frequently cited examples of this trend are the 'Patriation Reference' (*Reference re: Resolution to Amend the Constitution*, 1 SCR 754 (1981)) and the 'Quebec Secession Reference' (*Reference Re: Secession of Quebec*, 2 SCR 217 (1998)), where the Court dealt with fundamental issues like the nature of the Canadian polity, sovereignty, self-determination, and the extent of the Court's powers. See S Harding, 'The Supreme Court of Canada' in AAVV, *Annuario di Diritto Comparato e Studi Legislativi* (Napoli, ESI 2011) 281; R Hirschl, 'The New Constitutionalization and the Judicialization of Pure Politics Worldwide' (2006), 75 Fordham Law Review 721, 741–2. See also PH Russell, 'The Effect of the Charter of Rights on the Policy-Making Role of Canadian

fundamental rights, reliance has been placed more on adjudication (and strategic litigation) than on the enactment of legislation.

This reliance is also related to the Court's choice of interpretative theories. The Court's most frequently employed hermeneutical approach to the *Charter* is one of 'purposive interpretation', that considers rights likely to change with the passing of time and the varying of circumstances.[55] This hermeneutical approach is consistent with the Court's commitment to the idea of a 'living constitution' and the view of the constitution as a 'living tree', a notion that has deep roots in Canadian constitutional interpretation[56] and whose application to the *Charter* also came as a reaction against the much-criticized judicial self-restraint applied to the 1960 statutory *Canadian Bill of Rights*.[57]

Despite allegations of judicial activism, especially during the first years of the *Charter*'s application,[58] the Court has eventually embraced a more shared approach to decision-making, engaging the legislator in a dialogic process of constitutional interpretation.[59] The 'dialogue' metaphor, in the Canadian context, has a twofold meaning: not only does it describe the shared interpretative responsibilities of the Court and the other democratic institutions within the system;[60] in a second, more structural meaning, it also

Courts' (1982), 25 Canadian Public Administration 1; Id, 'The Political Purposes of the Canadian Charter of Rights and Freedoms' (1983), 61 Canadian Bar Review 30, 51.

[55] Harding, 'The Supreme Court of Canada' (n 54) 288. In Peter Hogg's view this approach allows the Court to go beyond a traditional understanding of rights to embrace an interpretation that fits with the broader goals of the *Charter* and the constitution as a whole: P Hogg, *Constitutional Law of Canada* (Carswell Legal 2003) 724–5.

[56] The 'living tree' metaphor and subsequent doctrine of constitutional interpretation trace back to Lord Sankey's opinion for the Privy Council in the '*Persons Case*' recognizing the right of women to sit in the Canadian Senate: 'The British North America Act planted in Canada a living tree capable of growth and expansion within its natural limits ... Their Lordships do not conceive it to be the duty of this Board ... to cut down the provisions of the Act by a narrow and technical construction, but rather to give it a large and liberal interpretation': *Edward v Canada (AG)*, AC 124 (1930) 136. According to Vicki Jackson, 'the constitution as a "living tree" ... exists in interaction with changing social understanding; ... the metaphor implicitly acknowledges limitations on interpretive evolutions that may arise from the text and (possibly) the need to distinguish between those areas in which meaning can change through interpretation and those in which a formal amendment through constitutionally specified processes is required': V Jackson, 'Constitutional Interpretation in Comparative Perspective', in T Ginsburg and R Dixon (eds.), *Comparative Constitutional Law* (Edward Elgar, Cheltenham 2011) 601; ibid., 'Constitutions as Living Trees? Comparative Constitutional Law and Interpretive Metaphors' (2006), 75 Fordham Law Review 921.

[57] Justice Wilson characterized the *Charter* as sending 'a clear message to the courts that the restrictive attitude which at times characterised their approach to the Canadian Bill of Rights ought to be reexamined': *Singh v Minister of Employment & Immigration* [1985] 1 SCR 177.

[58] Scholars noted a rise in activism in the first cases under the *Charter*, followed by a drop in the following years: FL Morton, P Russell, and M Withey, 'The Supreme Court's First One Hundred Charter of Rights Decisions: A Statistical Analysis' (1992), 30 Osgoode Hall Law Journal 1, 14; C Manfredi, *Judicial Power and the Charter: Canada and the Paradox of Liberal Constitutionalism* (Oxford University Press, Oxford 2001).

[59] The 'dialogue' approach is traced back to PW Hogg and A Bushell, 'The Charter Dialogue Between Courts and Legislatures (Or Perhaps the Charter of Rights Isn't Such a Bad Thing after All)' (1997), 35 Osgoode Hall Law Journal 75. See also S Choudhry, 'Globalization in Search of Justification: Toward a Theory of Comparative Constitutional Interpretation' (1999), 74 Indiana Law Journal 819, exploring the dialogue approach in the Court's attitude to foreign law. A critique of this phenomenon is given in LB Tremblay, 'The Legitimacy of Judicial Review: The Limits of Dialogue between Courts and Legislatures' (2005), 4 International Journal of Constitutional Law 617.

[60] K Roach, *The Supreme Court on Trial: Judicial Activism or Democratic Dialogue* (Irwin Law, Toronto 2001); C Manfredi, 'Life of a Metaphor: Dialogue in the Supreme Court, 1998–2003' (2004), 23 Supreme Court Law Review (2nd) 105; R Dixon, 'The Supreme Court of Canada, Charter Dialogue, and Deference' (2009), 47 Oosgode Hall Law Journal 235, 240.

refers to the possibility, for the National or Provincial legislators—each within their respective areas of competence—to re-enact legislation pursuant to section 33 of the *Charter* most likely in response to a declaration of unconstitutionality.[61] In fact, the Court does not enjoy the final say in constitutional interpretation, and pursuant to the so-called 'notwithstanding clause', legislatures have been granted the power to re-enact a statute notwithstanding the *Charter*'s individual rights provisions, for a renewable five-year period.[62] This mechanism has shaped what has been defined as a 'weak-form' of constitutional review,[63] one that stresses legislative—rather than exclusively judicial—responsibility for adherence to constitutional norms.

III. The empirical research

1. Methodology

In light of the complexity of Canada's legal history and constitutional system, my research relied on a few methodological choices. Citations of judgments of some international adjudicatory bodies, like the International Court of Justice or the International Criminal Court, were excluded from consideration, with the exception of decisions of the European Court of Human Rights (ECtHR) and the Court of Justice of the European Union (CJEU), since Canada is a signatory to neither of these Treaties and decisions of these two Courts exercise only persuasive, rather than binding, authority in Canada.[64] More importantly, since 1986[65] and increasingly in the past 20 years, judgments of the ECtHR have represented a fundamental point of reference for the SCC in the effort to protect fundamental rights domestically. With only this—rather significant—exception, my analysis focused on what has been defined 'horizontal communication' between national courts, to the exclusion of vertical and mixed vertical–horizontal interactions.[66] Citations of sources of law other than case law (ie international

[61] *Constitution Act, 1982*, s 33(1).

[62] The clause does not apply to voting and language rights.

[63] As opposed to 'strong' forms of constitutional review, typically represented by the US system of judicial review. According to Mark Tushnet, '[w]eak-form review combines some sort of power in courts to find legislation inconsistent with constitutional norms with some mechanism whereby the enacting legislature can respond to a court decision to that effect': M Tushnet, 'The Rise of Weak-form Judicial Review' in T Ginsburg and R Dixon (eds.), *Comparative Constitutional Law* (Edward Elgar, Cheltenham 2011) 322; M Tushnet, 'Judicial Activism and Restraint in a Section 33 World' (2003), 53 University of Toronto Law Journal 89; M Tushnet, *Weak Courts, Strong Rights: Judicial Review and Social Welfare Rights in Comparative Constitutional Law* (Princeton University Press, Princeton 2007).

[64] On the difference between persuasive and binding authority, see HP Glenn, 'Persuasive Authority' (1987), 32 McGill Law Journal 261, 263, emphasizing that persuasive authority is an 'authority which attracts adherence as opposed to obliging it'; M-C Ponthoreau, 'L'argument fondé sur la comparaison dans le raisonnement juridique' in P Legrand (ed), *Comparer les droits, résolument* (Presses Universitaires de France, Paris 2009) 548.

[65] When in *R v Oakes* [1986] 1 SCR 103, the SCC cited for the first time a decision of the European Commission of Human Rights, a body operating until 1998 as a filter to the ECtHR. See Table 21.2.

[66] See A-M Slaughter, 'A Typology of Transjudicial Communication' (1994), 29 University of Richmond Law Review 99. According to the author, horizontal communication occurs between courts of similar status across international borders; vertical communication occurs when there exists a hierarchical relationship between national and international or supranational institutions; mixed vertical–horizontal communication takes place when supranational tribunals serve as a conduit for horizontal communication.

treaties, foreign statutes, or codes, etc) were likewise excluded, in order to focus the investigation on an assessment of the reality and extent of trans-judicial communication.

With regard to its functions, the SCC has been frequently called to exercise its advisory jurisdiction and has indeed rendered some of its most important determinations in the form of 'reference' opinions.[67] For this reason, and despite their precedential value being controversial, I decided to include these determinations among the Court's acts surveyed for citations to foreign case law.[68]

Canada's former membership of the British Commonwealth of Nations and its subjection to the jurisdiction of the Privy Council mandated a few additional methodological choices. While in 1933 the right of appeal to the PC was abolished for criminal cases, only in 1949 did a complete abolition of that right (ie, also including civil cases) come into effect. This development carries momentous importance for this study, since, in my opinion, it requires to regard criminal cases decided and lodged with the PC and other English courts before 1933 and civil cases adjudicated and filed before 1949—whenever cited by the SCC—as 'domestic', rather than foreign, authority for Canada, and therefore ones that should be excluded from consideration in the quantitative assessment of citations to foreign case law.[69] Indeed, before the colonies acquired independence, the Privy Council could hardly be considered a foreign court.[70] At some point, however, the colonies became independent but continued to accept the jurisdiction of the Privy Council. From this time, and for as long as the colonies still accepted its jurisdiction, the Privy Council operated as a supranational Court (whose decisions, as seen, are excluded from this research, due to their binding authority on Member States). On this basis, it is my view that only decisions issued by the Privy Council and other English courts in criminal and civil cases lodged, respectively, after 1933 and 1949, can genuinely be considered as foreign precedents for Canada, and legitimately included in the research when cited by the SCC.

Finally, since one of the main purposes of the study is to assess the *Charter*'s impact on the SCC's citation attitude, the study will cover the years from 1982 to 2013.[71] In

[67] See, eg *Reference re Secession of Quebec*, 2 SCR 217 (1998); *Reference re Same-Sex Marriage*, 3 SCR 698 (2004). All of SCC's determinations (both judgments and reference opinions) are available at <scc.lexum.org>.

[68] An argument for the exclusion of advisory opinions from this study could also have been made considering that the presumption of constitutionality normally applied by a court when reviewing 'ex post' the constitutionality of statutes, does not find application when that same review is conducted 'a priori', that is, when the statute has not yet been enacted. However, as indicated, advisory opinions were eventually included in the research in light of their relevance in the general system of rights protection developed by the SCC.

[69] See also R Lefler, 'A Comparison of Comparison: Use of Foreign Case Law as Persuasive Authority by the United States Supreme Court, the Supreme Court of Canada and the High Court of Australia' (2001–02), 11 Southern California Interdisciplinary Law Journal 165, 166.

[70] This principle applies not just to PC decisions on cases originating from Canada, representing the overwhelming majority of citations, but to all PC judgments; under the then-prevailing doctrine of precedent, 'decisions of the Judicial Committee of the Privy Council bind all colonial courts of whatever status or jurisdiction': TO Elias, 'Colonial Courts and the Doctrine of Judicial Precedent' (1955), 18 Modern Law Review 356, 361.

[71] Covering therefore the work of four Chief Justices: Bora Laskin (CJ from 1973–84), Brian Dickson (1984–90), Antonio Lamer (1990–2000), and Beverley McLachlin (2000–13).

choosing this time period, I was aware of the view, expressed by some authors,[72] that a study on the frequency of foreign citations should avoid the uncommonly high number of references to foreign jurisprudence expected during the so-called 'formative period' of domestic jurisprudence, seen as a potentially anomalous phase. Nonetheless, I eventually decided to start my investigation from the year of the *Charter*'s enactment for two reasons: first, because I claim that a comprehensive study on citations of foreign case law should also include 'formative periods' to better determine the effects of the new document on the constitutional system as a whole and on the Court's functions and role; and second, due to practical difficulties in defining the temporal limits of the so-called 'formative periods' supposedly to be excluded from the analysis, and in determining a specific moment when the interpretation of the *Charter* would became 'mature'.

2. Quantitative and qualitative results

Scholars have identified some general, systemic reasons to help explain the practice of citation of foreign precedents, some of which may also find application to the SCC and the Canadian legal system.

Common law jurisdictions, like Canada, for a variety of reasons[73] appear to be more prone to citing foreign case law than civil law countries. However, some of these jurisdictions have shown signs of 'discomfort' with this practice, as is the case with the US, Singapore, and Malaysia.[74]

Canada's former membership of the British Commonwealth may prove, therefore, a more persuasive argument. The use of foreign case law received stimulus from the Commonwealth practice of considering the common law as a single, unified legal system with a high degree of permeability between jurisprudences.[75] When addressing judicial review issues, under the Constitution of one Commonwealth Member, the Privy Council would refer to cases involving other Members' Constitutions, making comparison a familiar exercise in constitutional adjudication and practice.[76] Canadian legal actors therefore became accustomed to reading cases from the UK, Australia, and

[72] eg B Roy, 'An Empirical Survey of Foreign Jurisprudence and International Instruments in Charter Litigation' (2004), 62 University of Toronto Faculty Law Review 99, 103.

[73] Among these, Vicki Jackson includes i) a less deeply positivistic culture than civil law countries; ii) 'familiarity and comfort with the idea that constitutionalism involves principles that exist outside of written legal commitments': Jackson, *Constitutional Engagement in a Transnational Era* (2009) (n 6) 243. Cheryl Saunders identifies further reasons in: a) the fact that cases in the common law tradition are established by reference to earlier cases (whether domestic or foreign, binding or merely persuasive) considered analogous; b) the form of judicial decisions, requiring written reasons for the judgment and an analysis of how legal authorities are used; c) the fact that constitutional cases are determined by the courts that also administer the rest of the law, promoting interdependence of the constitution with the rest of the legal system; d) reliance on adversarial procedure and the fact that foreign experiences enter judicial deliberations through parties and amici briefs, and are in turn expected to be reflected in its reasons: Saunders, 'Judicial Engagement with Comparative Law' (n 3) 575.

[74] Saunders, 'Judicial Engagement with Comparative Law' (n 3) 574.

[75] The theory was that there was a single, monolithic body of common law: see WR Lederman, *Continuing Canadian Constitutional Dilemmas* (Butterworths, Toronto 1981) 68; 'a comprehensive body of doctrine… uniform throughout the British Empire': Hogg, *Constitutional Law of Canada* (2007) (n 14) 32.

[76] Jackson, *Constitutional Engagement in a Transnational Era* (2009) (n 6) 96.

New Zealand, all English-speaking countries sharing the same Commonwealth history and similar social and economic conditions. While Canada is no longer a member of this system, extra-systemic materials are today resorted to due to perceived membership of a single cultural space which justifies jurisprudential cross-references.

Several other reasons, more specifically related to Canada, have been put forth to explain the SCC's use of foreign case law.[77] From an institutional standpoint, Canada is a bilingual and bijural country.[78] It is thought that familiarity with more than one language and legal tradition—originating from Quebec's French linguistic heritage and civilian legal tradition—would make Canadian lawyers and judges more accustomed to understanding multiple legal systems, more likely to access and understand foreign legal materials, and more prone to include them in their briefs and amici curiae (lawyers) and decisions (judges).[79]

The aforementioned progressive hermeneutical approach of the SCC (the 'living tree' metaphor) also arguably plays a central role in explaining the Court's use of foreign case law. As pointed out by Vicki Jackson, 'while living constitutionalism need not necessarily embrace consideration of foreign case law, it is more open to them than intentionalists or originalists modes of interpretation'.[80] Furthermore, international covenants and human rights treaties played an important role in the *Charter*'s drafting. It should not come as a surprise, therefore, that in interpreting the *Charter*, the SCC is open to citation of foreign materials coming from the ECtHR or from other worldwide jurisdictions.[81] Finally, considering the experiences of Hungary and South Africa, extensive revision or enactment of a new constitutional document and corresponding lack of a line of domestic precedents interpreting the new provisions, may promote recourse to foreign case law.[82]

A comparison of columns B and D and columns E and F of Table 21.1 illustrates that the SSC's tendency to refer to foreign case law is present not only in constitutional

[77] Roy, 'An Empirical Survey of Foreign Jurisprudence' (n 72).

[78] J-F Gaudreault-DesBiens, *Les solitudes du bijuridisme canadien. Essai sur les rapports de pouvoir entre les traditions juridiques et la résilience des atavismes identitaires* (Thémis, Montréal 2007).

[79] However, as Table 21.2 and Figure 21.4 show further, the citation process is overwhelmingly dominated by decisions from common law countries, that is, from only one of Canada's languages and legal cultures. On this point, see also P McCormick, 'Waiting for Globalization: An Empirical Study of the McLachlin Court's Foreign Judicial Citations' (2009–2010), 41 Ottawa Law Review 209.

[80] Jackson, *Constitutional Engagement in a Transnational Era* (2009) (n 6) 97.

[81] On the *Charter*'s relationship to other international and human rights documents, see AF Bayefsky, 'International Human Rights Law in Canadian Courts' in I Cotler and FP Eliadis (eds.), *International Human Rights Law: Theory and Practice* (1992) 115, 125–9. The timing of the adoption of the *Charter* may have reinforced Canadian openness to foreign influences, particularly since the *Charter* was drafted, negotiated and adopted shortly after Canada's 1976 ratifications of the International Covenant on Civil and Political Rights (ICCPR) and the International Covenant on Economic, Social and Cultural Rights (ICESCR): Jackson, *Constitutional Engagement in a Transnational Era* (2009) (n 6) 239.

[82] *Charter* claims were qualitatively different from earlier arguments relying on the BNAA in that they were based on direct constitutional protection of civil liberties. This made pre-*Charter* precedent of little help to judges seeking guidance on civil liberties issues. On this, then-Justice McLachlin noted: 'the difficulty is that the Canadian Charter ... is a new experience. We have not had anything like it before. Our judges cannot rely on their own experience to breathe life into the *Charter*; instead they must find that life elsewhere': B McLachlin, 'The Charter of Rights and Freedoms: A Judicial Perspective' (1988–1989), 23 University of British Columbia Law Review, 579, 580. The tendency to resort to foreign case law is likely to decline when a significant line of domestic jurisprudence becomes available.

Table 21.1 Number of decisions and citations to foreign precedents (CFPs) (1982–2013)

	A	B	C	D	E	F
Year	Total decisions per year	Cases with CFPs (constitutional & others)	Constitutional cases	Constitutional cases with CFPs (% of total decisions)	Total CFPs per year	Total CFPs in constitutional cases per year
1982	119	39 (32.8%)	15	4 (3.4%)	113	10
1983	90	17 (18.9%)	12	2 (2.2%)	36	4
1984	64	15 (23.4%)	13	3 (4.7%)	112	13
1985	84	31 (36.9%)	28	9 (10.7%)	182	48
1986	76	32 (42.1%)	19	9 (11.8%)	200	97
1987	94	28 (29.8%)	34	12 (12.8%)	178	89
1988	106	31 (29.2%)	32	12 (11.3%)	155	66
1989	133	49 (36.8%)	61	26 (19.5%)	209	122
1990	144	60 (41.7%)	80	33 (22.9%)	327	196
1991	108	29 (26.8%)	38	15 (13.9%)	180	103
1992	109	39 (35.7%)	49	20 (18.3%)	235	57
1993	138	40 (28.9%)	53	21 (15.2%)	204	88
1994	111	33 (29.7%)	41	17 (15.3%)	169	81
1995	108	37 (34.2%)	39	21 (22.7%)	201	122
1996	121	39 (32.2%)	54	23 (19.0%)	136	78
1997	110	43 (39.1%)	33	18 (16.4%)	195	83
1998	90	27 (30.0%)	33	15 (16.7%)	80	37
1999	80	26 (32.5%)	36	13 (16.3%)	163	82
2000	69	21 (30.4%)	20	7 (10.1%)	111	26
2001	94	32 (34.0%)	34	15 (16.0%)	161	90
2002	86	38 (44.2%)	38	21 (24.4%)	184	55
2003	74	21 (28.4%)	27	8 (10.8%)	67	21
2004	83	18 (21.7%)	28	7 (8.4%)	53	26
2005	87	19 (21.8%)	30	8 (9.2%)	59	19
2006	59	20 (33.8%)	18	3 (5.1%)	64	3
2007	55	28 (50.9%)	20	12 (21.8%)	157	77
2008	72	25 (34.7%)	19	7 (9.7%)	110	52
2009	62	19 (30.6%)	18	7 (11.3%)	114	86
2010	67	17 (25.4%)	27	9 (13.4%)	84	66
2011	67	16 (23.9%)	20	5 (7.5%)	100	37
2012	75	24 (32.0%)	19	10 (13.3%)	55	18
2013	74	30 (40.5%)	16	8 (10.8%)	106	20

cases,[83] but also in other areas of law, a fact highlighting the SCC's general, favourable attitude towards cross-section citation of foreign case law (see also Figure 21.1). Furthermore, the results of my research show that references to foreign precedents follow a distinctive pattern across the various areas of law: the incidence of US and ECtHR decisions is higher in constitutional cases, given the US Supreme Court's extensive experience in constitutional interpretation and the ECtHR's focus on human rights cases; on the other hand, the areas of tort, contract, and property law still appear to be very much reserved to British common law rulings.

[83] The expression 'constitutional cases' is used here broadly, to include not only cases involving necessarily the interpretation and application of constitutional provisions, but also those dealing with institutional and/or human rights issues.

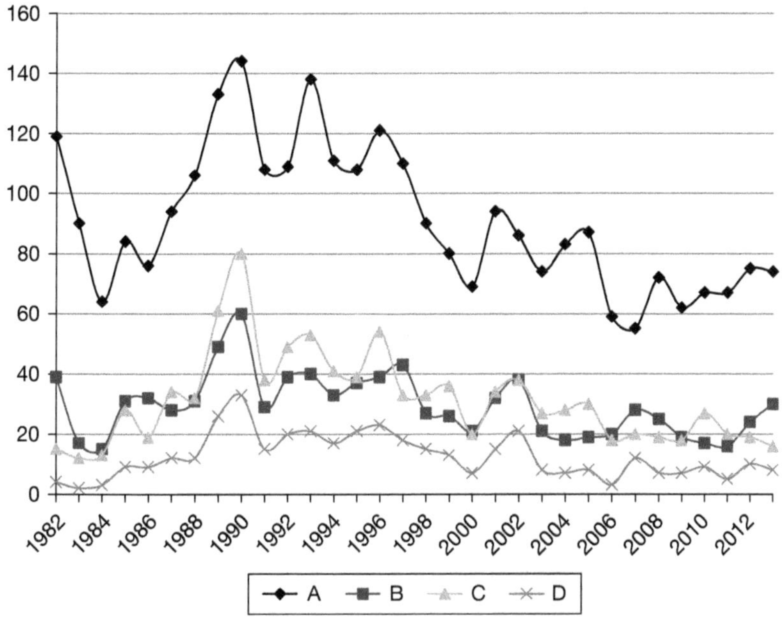

Figure 21.1 Constitutional cases citing foreign precedents out of all constitutional cases (1982–2013)

A: Total number of decisions issued per year by the Court
B: Decisions citing foreign precedents
C: Constitutional cases
D: Constitutional cases citing foreign precedents

From a quantitative standpoint, Table 21.1 shows that the number of cases granted leave to the SCC increased at its maximum between the end of the 1980s and the first half of the 1990s,[84] reaching its peak in 1990 and remaining high at least until 1997: arguably the period when most of the new *Charter* cases reached the Court.

While the openness to foreign case law remained unchanged, citations rates of foreign jurisprudence declined between the end of the 1990s and the end of the 2000s (see Table 21.1, column D and Figure 21.1).[85] Indeed, the research shows that once the SCC had developed a sufficient domestic jurisprudence, it relied less on foreign sources and more upon its own domestic body of established law, citing extensively to domestic precedents.[86]

[84] This is roughly the time when s 15, which took effect in 1985, received its first serious judicial interpretation by the SCC, in *Andrews v Law Society of British Columbia* [1989] 1 SCR 143. Other early equality cases are described, along with US comparison, in JM Pellicciotti, 'The Constitutional Guarantee of Equal Protection in Canada and the United States: Comparative Analysis of the Standards for Determining the Validity of Governmental Action' (1997), 5 Tulsa Journal of Comparative and International Law 1.

[85] With the total number of foreign precedents per year in constitutional cases dropping (see Table 21.1, column F). This is also due to the highly diminished number of cases granted leave to the SCC, which, in the 2000s amounted to 741, that is, 33.8% fewer than the cases reaching the Court in the 1990s (1119).

[86] 'When courts are relatively new and fragile, reliance on the views of other, better established courts, may contribute to enhance the reputation and independent adjudicatory capacity of the court within its own country', Jackson, *Constitutional Engagement in a Transnational Era* (2009) (n 6) 197.

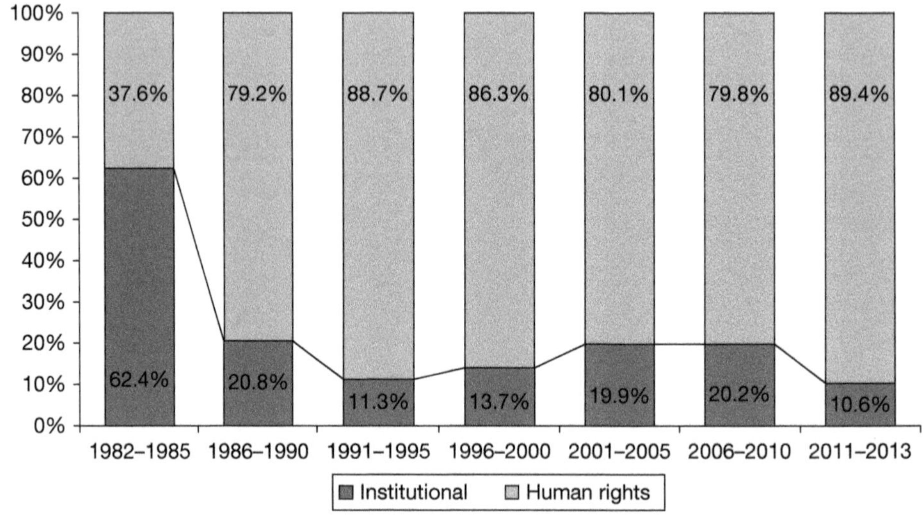

Figure 21.2 Human rights or institutional cases out of constitutional cases (1982–2013)
1982–1985: 37.6% Human rights—62.4% Institutional
1986–1990: 79.2% Human rights—20.8% Institutional
1991–1995: 88.7% Human rights—11.3% Institutional
1996–2000: 86.3% Human rights—13.7% Institutional
2001–2005: 80.1% Human rights—19.9% Institutional
2006–2010: 79.8% Human rights—20.2% Institutional
2011–2013: 89.4% Human rights—10.6% Institutional

The impact of the *Charter*'s enactment on the SCC's docket can also be analysed considering the type of cases—whether dealing with institutional or human rights issues—that the Court addressed in the period under consideration (see Figure 21.2).

With the new functions that the *Constitution Act, 1982* vested with the Court, the vast majority of judicial review cases fell under the *Charter*'s purview, and civil liberties cases rapidly increased in number, bringing Canada closer to the US in the level of rights-based litigation.[87] The majority of these citations are in cases involving questions of individual rights, rather than questions of allocation of powers among the levels of government. However, use of foreign precedents is certainly not reserved only to fundamental rights cases. A small number of significant institutional cases—addressing the boundaries between Federal and Provincial powers—is dealt with each year by the Court.[88]

In analysing these two different typologies of cases, a clear pattern emerged: English or domestic cases are cited predominantly for federalism issues while US, Australian,

[87] Table 21.1 shows that the total SCC's caseload increased significantly in the first 10 years under the *Charter*, with constitutional cases accounting for around 50% of the Court's total judgments. However, the caseload rapidly decreased in the second half of the 2000s bringing the SCC even closer to the US Supreme Court in terms of cases adjudicated per year.

[88] See, eg, *General Motors of Canada Ltd v City National Leasing* [1989] 1 SCR 641; *Ontario Hydro v Ontario (Labour Relations Board)* [1993] 3 SCR 327; *Reference re Secession of Quebec* [1998] 2 SCR 217; *BC v Imperial Tobacco Canada Ltd* [2005] 2 SCR 473; *Canadian Western Bank v Alberta* [2007] 2 SCR 3; *British Columbia (AG) v Lafarge Canada Inc* [2007] 2 SCR 86; *Consolidated Fastfrate Inc v Western Canada Council of Teamsters* [2009] 3 SCR 407; *Marine Services International Ltd v Ryan Estate* [2013] 3 SCR 53.

Table 21.2 Citations of foreign precedents in constitutional cases per country (1982–2013)

Year	UK	US	AU	ECtHR	NZ	Other jurisdictions
1982	5	5	–	–	–	–
1983	4	–	–	–	–	–
1984	6	6	1	–	–	–
1985	12	31	–	–	–	Bahamas: 2; Cyprus: 1; Pakistan: 2
1986	12	70	–	4	2	–
1987	18	69	–	1	1	–
1988	22	33	4	7	2	Germany: 1
1989	32	74	5	9	–	Belgium: 1; EU: 1
1990	23	157	2	9	1	India: 2
1991	5	92	2	2	1	Ireland: 1
1992	20	25	1	2	–	–
1993	31	50	2	2	2	–
1994	32	40	11	1	1	Germany: 2; Hong Kong: 1; Israel: 1; South Africa: 1
1995	39	77	3	2	–	–
1996	24	50	1	–	3	–
1997	12	63	6	–	2	–
1998	18	14	2	2		France: 1
1999	34	33	5	–	5	EU: 1; India: 1; South Africa: 1
2000	11	15	–	–	–	–
2001	23	51	10	6		–
2002	22	24	4	4	–	Israel: 1; South Africa: 1
2003	10	11	–	–	–	–
2004	2	23	–	1	–	–
2005	5	8	–	–	–	EU: 2; France: 4
2006	–	3	–	–	–	–
2007	14	40	5	4	2	France: 4; Israel: 4; South Africa: 1
2008	19	24	6	–	2	Hong Kong: 1
2009	26	30	7	3	4	South Africa: 3
2010	19	28	4	8	4	Netherlands: 1; South Africa: 1
2011	4	13	6	2	1	France: 7; Germany: 4
2012	7	9	–	–	2	–
2013	3	17	–	–	–	–
Total	**516**	**1183**	**87**	**69**	**35**	France: **16**; South Africa: **8**; Germany: **7**; Israel: **6**; EU: **4**; India: **3**; Bahamas: **2**; Hong Kong: **2**; Pakistan: **2**; Belgium: **1**; Cyprus: **1**; Ireland: **1**; The Netherlands: **1.**

New Zealand, and ECtHR precedents are cited for human rights cases. This very limited recourse to US precedents in federalism cases originates in the fact that litigation over the allocation of legislative powers among levels of government represented the main area of constitutional decision-making even before the *Charter*'s enactment and a long line of precedents was already available; also, differences in the constitutional provisions—and corresponding design—of Canadian and US federalism[89] and a peculiar hermeneutical approach of the PC[90] made US precedents unlikely to be considered in recent federalism issues.

This rather interesting dichotomy (UK precedents cited predominantly in institutional cases; US precedents in human rights decisions) helps to explain the data presented in

[89] See n 51. [90] See n 97 and corresponding text.

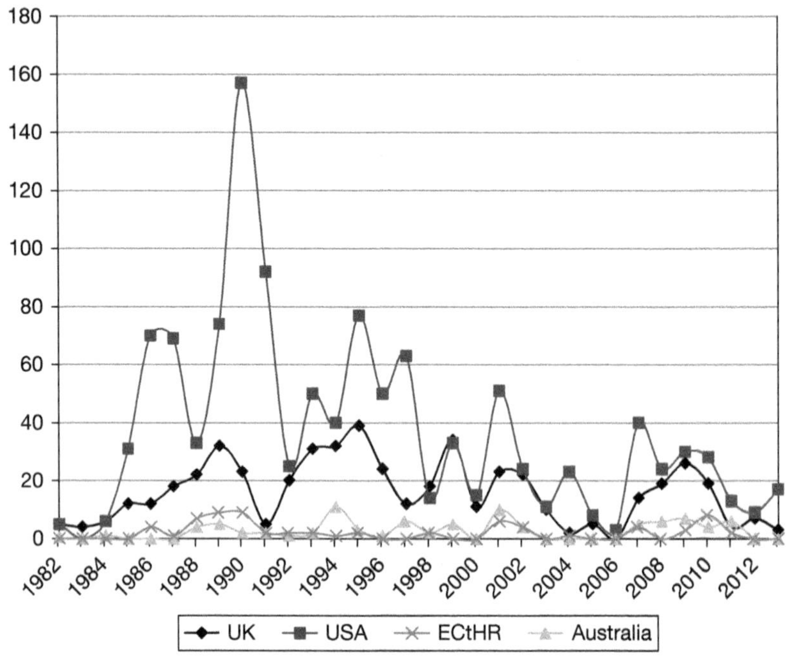

Figure 21.3 Citations of foreign precedents per country in constitutional cases (four most-often cited jurisdictions) (1982–2013)

Table 21.2 and Figures 21.3 and 21.4. Indeed, the steady increase in human rights cases reaching the SCC, combined with the lack of domestic jurisprudence interpreting the *Charter* account for the extensive use of US precedents displayed.

Citations of British precedents are not surprising, given the historical ties that existed between the Canadian court system and the UK and Commonwealth systems. The *Charter*'s enactment, however, at least with regard to constitutional cases, soon brought to an end the 'English captivity',[91] determining a rapid decline in institutional cases and a corresponding decrease in the number of UK precedents cited by the SCC. Conversely, the increase in human rights cases reaching the SCC made US precedents valuable resources, extensively resorted to, reaching a peak in the early 1990s. This rise was determined mainly by two reasons: claims of civil rights' violations previously filed under the BNAA's provisions concerning the allocation of legislative competences between the Federation and the Provinces started to be filed under *Charter* provisions; furthermore, the *Charter*'s enactment changed citizens' attitudes towards the protection of fundamental rights. The Parliament was no longer the only appropriate place to protect and advance fundamental rights protection, with courts becoming a privileged locus for this type of claim.

Arguably, language also plays an important role in the choice of the foreign jurisdictions considered. As shown by Figure 21.4, in the 32 years of SCC's activity surveyed by

[91] B Laskin, 'The Supreme Court of Canada: A Final Court of and for Canadians' (1951), 29 Canadian Bar Review 1038, 1045–6.

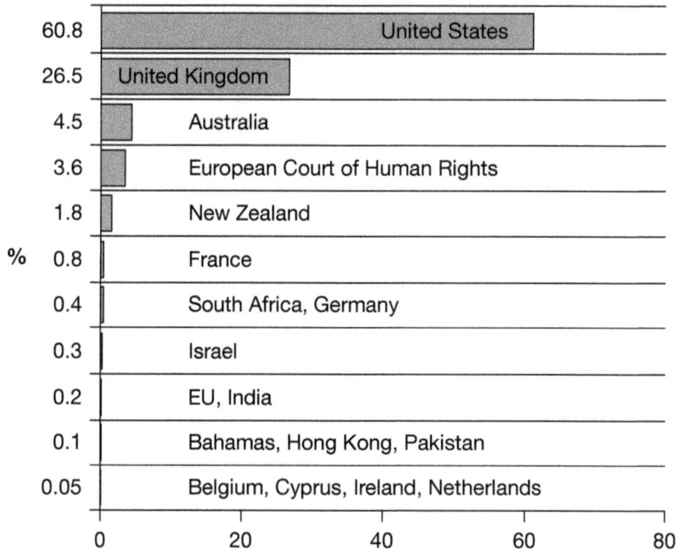

Figure 21.4 Percentage of constitutional cases using foreign precedents, sorted by country (1982–2013)

the research, more than 98 per cent of the SCC's decisions in constitutional cases made reference to six main jurisdictions and one supranational court, either being former Members of the British Commonwealth or speaking familiar languages (English and French, both official languages in Canada): the US, the UK, Australia, the ECtHR (whose decisions are published in both English and French), New Zealand, France, and South Africa, listed in order of frequency of citations. Citations to US and UK precedents alone account for 87 per cent of the total foreign citations in constitutional cases.

The numerous references to UK, Australian and New Zealand precedents illustrated by Table 21.2 and Figure 21.3 can be explained through the so-called 'genealogic interpretation'[92] theory: as mentioned, a common law court may find it useful to resort to precedents of a foreign court of a country belonging (presently or in the past) to the same (cultural or legal) space to address controversial cases, whenever suitable legislative or jurisprudential aids are missing within its own legal system.[93]

Regarding the types of opinion hosting references to foreign precedents, citations are not limited to only one typology—whether majority, concurring, or dissenting—but, conversely, are equally present in all different types. While SCC decisions are notable for their high rate of unanimity (around 65 per cent of the total),[94] as Figure 21.5 shows, the highest numbers of citations of foreign precedents are found in majority and dissenting opinions. This is a sign that the number of foreign precedents cited increases along with the level of disagreement on a specific issue and the number of opinions

[92] Choudhry, 'Globalization in Search of Justification' (n 59) 838ff.

[93] G de Vergottini, *Oltre il dialogo tra le Corti. Giudici, diritto straniero, comparazione* (Il Mulino, Bologna 2010) 108.

[94] An attitude that has not changed after the *Charter*'s enactment, despite the increase in more controversial cases. D Songer, *The Transformation of the Supreme Court of Canada* (2008) (n 52).

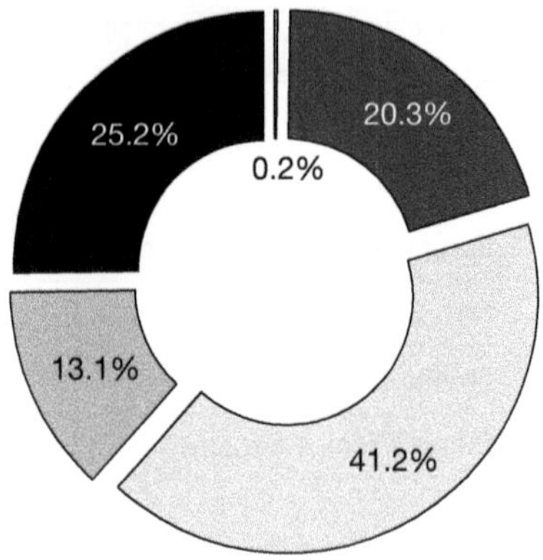

Figure 21.5 Location of citations to foreign precedents in constitutional cases

filed. Judges seem to feel compelled to cite a higher number of precedents not only to overcome opposition from colleagues but also to make their decisions more acceptable to the public and to other institutional actors with enforcement powers. Also, on average, judges appear to resort more to foreign precedents when overturning government action than when upholding it.[95]

3. Use of United States precedents

Together with the aforementioned general features favouring the use of foreign citations, two elements, specific to Canada, deserve more careful consideration: the special value accorded to US precedents and the role of section 1 of the *Charter*.

The use of US precedents has featured in Canadian judicial decision-making since Confederation. Indeed, the first years after 1867 were characterized by references of Canadian courts to US constitutional cases, and by discussions about the similarities and differences between the two constitutional systems.[96] The Privy Council, however,

[95] See, eg, *R v Morgentaler* [1988] 1 SCR 30 (19 foreign precedents); *Committee for the Commonwealth of Canada v Canada* [1991] 1 SCR 139 (20 foreign precedents); *R v Seaboyer* [1991] 2 SCR 577 (18 foreign precedents); *Miron v Trudel* [1995] 2 SCR 418 (14 foreign precedents); *R v Ruzic* [2001] 1 SCR 687 (23 foreign precedents); *R v Kang-Brown* [2008] 1 SCR 456 (13 foreign precedents).

[96] The study of the use of US case law by Canadian courts has long-standing roots: O Mowat, 'Observation on the Use and Value of American Reports in Reference to Canadian Jurisprudence' (1857), 3 Upper Canada Law Journal; Lex, 'The Authority of American Decisions in Canadian and English Courts' (1899), 35 Canada Law Journal 518; JM MacIntyre, 'The Use of American Cases in Canadian Courts' (1964–66), 2 University of British Columbia Law Review 478: the articles suggest that, after an initial period of acceptance, a bias emerged against American authorities; SI Bushnell, 'The Use of American Cases' (1986), 35 University of New Brunswick Law Journal 157: Bushnell found that the use of American cases declined in the 1920s to re-emerge only in the 1970s. CP Manfredi, 'The Use of United States Decisions by

soon established a formalist approach to statutory interpretation and indicated that US decisions bore no relevance in the adjudication of cases arising from Canada.[97] The interpretation of the *Constitution Act, 1867* developed, therefore, along domestic lines, making foreign precedents of no utility in resolving hermeneutical issues. This situation did not change even in 1949 when the SCC became Canada's highest appellate court.

The *Charter*'s enactment radically changed this landscape: at the outset, the US experience with civil rights jurisprudence was explicitly considered during the *Charter*'s drafting process, when the phrasing of some sections was changed as a result of concerns arising from the US experience.[98]

Then, language similarities with the US *Bill of Rights* made US jurisprudence immediately relevant.[99] Indeed, while, on one hand, the sections dealing with group rights[100] addressed distinctive aspects of Canadian society and the override provision of section 33 reflected concerns of judicial activism and the willingness to safeguard—at least to some extent—the British tradition of parliamentary sovereignty,[101] on the other hand, both the US and Canadian declarations entrench a series of negative rights (substantive and procedural) protecting the individual from State unconstitutional actions, leaving outside of their purview positive or social rights.[102] These rights are included in section 2 and sections 7 to 15 of the *Charter* and are expressed in broad

the Supreme Court of Canada under the Charter of Rights and Freedoms' (1990), 23 Canadian Journal of Political Science 499: Manfredi notes that between 1949–68 American cases constituted less than 2% of all citations; conversely, between 1969–78 a significant increase in US citations occurred. American jurisprudence therefore influenced Canadian legal doctrine even before 1982, showing that in Canada enhancement of fundamental rights and reference to US cases were connected even before the *Charter*'s enactment. See also: PW Hogg, 'Canada: From Privy Council to Supreme Court' in J Goldsworthy (ed), *Interpreting Constitutions. A Comparative Study* (Oxford University Press, Oxford 2007) 55.

[97] Early PC case law rejected the view that US authority would be controlling in the interpretation of the Canadian constitution: *Bank of Toronto v Lambe*, 1887 12 AC 575, 587 (PC) (appeal taken from Canada).

[98] The October 1980 draft of s 1 referred to 'reasonable limits... in a free and democratic society with a parliamentary system of government'. The *Charter*'s drafters eventually removed reference to 'a parliamentary system of government' from s 1 in order not to imply the irrelevance of US jurisprudence in *Charter* adjudication: PW Hogg, *Constitutional Law of Canada* (2nd edn, Carswell, Toronto 1985) 679, n 149. On the other hand, provincial concerns about the interpretation given to the expression 'due process' by US courts led to its replacement with 'principles of fundamental justice' in s 7 of the *Charter*: R Romanow, J White, and H Leeson, *Canada Notwithstanding: The Making of the Constitution, 1976–1982* (Carswell, Toronto 1984) 245–6.

[99] For early comparisons between the *Charter* and the US Constitution, see D Stone and FK Walpole, 'The Canadian Constitution Act and the Constitution of the United States: A Comparative Analysis' (1983), 2 Canadian-American Law Journal 1; WS Tarnopolsky, 'The New Canadian Charter of Rights and Freedoms as Compared and Contrasted with the American Bill of Rights' (1983), 5 Human Rights Quarterly 227; P Bender, 'The Canadian Charter of Rights and Freedoms and the United States Bill of Rights: A Comparison' (1983), 28 McGill Law Journal 811; FL Morton, 'The Politics of Rights: What Canadians Should Know About the American Bill of Rights' (1989), 1 Windsor Review of Legal & Social Issues 61.

[100] That is, s 23 (minority language education rights), s 25 (aboriginal rights), and s 28 (affirmative actions), entrenching a distinctive Canadian perspective on multiculturalism, one embracing linguistic and cultural diversity ('ethnic mosaic'). US pluralism tends, conversely, to pursue assimilation to a common national identity ('melting pot').

[101] Other specific Canadian issues were the 'patriation' of the Canadian constitution and the different process of legal consent the *Charter* underwent compared to the US Constitution.

[102] M McKenna (ed), *The Canadian and American Constitutions* (1993) (n 12).

terms analogous to the First, Fourth, Fifth, Sixth, Eighth, and Fourteenth Amendments to the US Constitution, subject only to the limitation of section 1. The *Charter*, therefore, brought US and Canadian cultures closer, the latter acquiring a rights-based foundation the former had already experienced for decades, and making US precedents relevant to the interpretation of Canadian laws.[103] It came naturally to the SCC to resort to US case law interpreting cognate constitutional provisions to those entrenched in the *Charter*.[104] Furthermore, even when the language of the *Charter* differed from the one of the US *Bill of Rights*, US cases represented a useful source of ideas and comparisons, in order to foresee possible, long-term outcomes of certain interpretations.

From a qualitative standpoint, my research shows that while the SCC's use of American precedents in constitutional cases is focused on US cases decided in the latter half of the 20th century, these are not necessarily recent decisions.[105] Furthermore, the fact that the SCC has cited US rulings coming not only from the US Supreme Court but from across all levels of US courts (including lower US federal and state court judgments), suggests a rather sophisticated understanding of US jurisprudence by Canadian judges. Despite the significant (positive or negative) influence exerted on the Canadian legal system, US precedents have never enjoyed more than mere persuasive authority.[106]

In addition to textual similarities between the two Constitutions, several other elements concurred in making US precedents a suitable resource for Canadian courts and arguably explain the SCC's high rate of citation of US precedents.

Focusing exclusively on legal and institutional features, both countries share a background as former British colonies, although the relationship with the UK was terminated in two rather different ways.[107] They both established their constitutional systems—and federal systems of government—more than a century ago[108] and belong to the same common law legal tradition of British origin that in both cases needed to be

[103] CP Manfredi, 'Adjudication, Policy-Making and the Supreme Court of Canada: Lessons from the Experience of the United States' (1989), 22 Canadian Journal of Political Science 313.

[104] CJ Dickson expressed willingness to examine US case law: 'the American courts have the benefit of two hundred years of experience in constitutional interpretation. This wealth of experience may offer guidance to the judiciary in this country', *R v Simmons* [1988] 2 SCR 495, 516. The same spirit is evident in Justice L'Heureux-Dubé's concurring opinion in *R v Elshaw* [1991] 3 SCR 24, 57: 'to reject the American experience out of hand and to refuse to engage in its examination, at least as a comparative exercise, would surely be... a [great] mistake'. See also C L'Heureux-Dubé, 'Two Supreme Courts: A Study in Contrast', in M McKenna (ed), *The Canadian and American Constitutions in Comparative Perspectives* (Calgary University Press, Calgary 1993) 163.

[105] The majority of Canadian citations concerns US Supreme Court decisions taken during the Warren and Burger Courts (1953 to 1986). See C L'Heureux-Dubé, 'The Importance of Dialogue: Globalization and the International Impact of the Rehnquist Court' (1998), 34 Tulsa Law Journal 15, 29: 'An informal analysis of Canadian Supreme Court decisions since 1986 revealed that the Rehnquist court was cited in fewer than one-half as many cases as the Warren Court, and in just under one-third the number of Burger Court cases.'

[106] Unlike in Argentina, where, due to the influence of the US Constitution on the 1853 Argentine Constitution, for a certain number of years, decisions of the US Supreme Court enjoyed binding authority: see JM Miller, 'The Authority of a Foreign Talisman: A Study of US Constitutional Practice as Authority in Nineteenth Century Argentina and the Argentine Elite's Leap of Faith' (1997), 46 American University Law Review 1483.

[107] Canada experienced an incrementalist—rather than revolutionary, as in the US—development from colony to independent sovereign State.

[108] However, as seen, the division of legislative powers is designed differently in the US and Canada: see (n 50).

adapted to social and geographical circumstances markedly different from those in the UK. Furthermore, Canada followed the US—rather than the British—model of legal education when, in the 20th century, it established legal education within its universities. Finally, both countries have a 'generalist' Supreme Court with jurisdiction over ordinary and constitutional legal issues.[109]

Another significant reason for frequent use of US precedents lies in the fact that, following the *Charter*'s enactment, Canada developed a system of strategic litigation. In other words, the *Charter* created new ways to further protection and advancement of fundamental rights in which judicial bodies—rather than the legislator, as in the British constitutional tradition—played an influential role, attracting interest groups looking for ways to influence public policy and employing court litigation to promote their objectives, analogous to well-established US dynamics.

Looking beyond one's own borders does not necessarily imply, however, automatic acceptance and adoption of foreign solutions. This represents probably the most striking feature of the Canadian attitude towards citation of US precedents. While there are, certainly, a few instances of endorsement of US interpretations of the *Bill of Right*'s provisions,[110] my research shows that, in the majority of cases, results achieved by US courts have not been followed.[111] The different structure of the *Charter*, especially with regard to its general limitation clause (s 1), represented a starting point for the development of a distinctively Canadian jurisprudence.[112]

The Court is extremely conscious of the risks involved in citing foreign case law. In *Lavigne v Ontario Public Service Employees Union*,[113] Justice Wilson wrote:

> This Court has consistently stated that even although it may undoubtedly benefit from the experience of American and other courts in adjudicating constitutional issues, it is by no means bound by that experience or the jurisprudence it has generated. The uniqueness of the Canadian Charter flows not only from its distinctive structure if

[109] For these and additional elements, see Jackson, *Constitutional Engagement in a Transnational Era* (2009) (n 6) 240ff.

[110] eg, in *Hunter v Southam* [1984] 2 SCR 145, the SCC, in addressing the s 8 *Charter* guarantee of freedom from unreasonable search or seizure, adopted the warrant requirement set forth in *Katz v United States*, 389 US 347, 88 S Ct 507 (1967), despite the *Charter* making no reference to such requirement. In obscenity cases, the SCC has relied extensively on US case law to develop a similar test for assessing the constitutionality of obscenity statutes: see *The Queen v Butler* [1992] 1 SCR 452. In *United Food & Commercial Workers Local 1518 v Kmart Can Ltd* [1999] 2 SCR 1083, in determining whether different standards apply in reviewing the constitutionality of leafleting and picketing bans, the SCC adopted the distinction between these two activities established in US First Amendment jurisprudence. In *Vriend v Alberta* [1998] 1 SCR 493, the SCC, in dealing with employment discrimination based on sexual orientation, cited with approval the US Supreme Court's decision in *Romer v Evans*, 517 US 620, 116 S Ct 1620 (1996).

[111] With regard to the outcome of the cases, between 1982 and 2013, out of 281 constitutional cases with citations to US case law, US solutions have been followed in only 14% of these cases, while being distinguished in 29% of them. The remainder of cases (57%) presents merely informative references to US precedents (neither followed, nor distinguished).

[112] In *R v Keegstra* [1990] 3 SCR 697, 740, Chief Justice Dickson, for the majority, stated: 'applying the *Charter* to the legislation challenged in this appeal reveals important differences between Canadian and American constitutional perspectives... Section 1 has no equivalent in the United States, a fact previously alluded to by this Court in selectively utilizing American constitutional jurisprudence.'

[113] *Lavigne v Ontario Public Service Employees Union* [1991] 2 SCR 211.

compared to the American Bill of Rights but also from the special features of the Canadian cultural, historical, social and political traditions.

This is consistent with the view that engagement with foreign law is first and foremost an exercise in (constitutional) self-understanding, which leads to identification of the distinguishing elements of Canadian society.[114] In other words, 'engagement' is a stance 'primarily concerned with the self-reflective elements of constitutional adjudication',[115] rather than a finalistic exercise in comparative reasoning within judicial decision-making. As a result, consideration of US precedents by the SCC is mainly 'aversive' or 'negative'.[116] The results of my study indicate that the Court is willing to be receptive to foreign solutions only when they are compatible with the principles informing Canadian society and its legal system.

The Canadian '*manifesto*' of this aversive attitude was expressed in the early days of *Charter* adjudication by Justice La Forest, who maintained that judges 'should be wary of drawing too ready a parallel between constitutions born to different countries in different ages and in very different circumstances ... American jurisprudence, like the British, *must be viewed as a tool, not as a master*' (emphasis added).[117] A recent example of this stance is found in *R v Sinclair*, a 2010 case dealing with a detainee's right to counsel, where the SCC refused to adopt the guarantee established by the US Supreme Court in *Miranda v Arizona*,[118] indicating: 'We are not persuaded that the (American) Miranda rule should be transplanted in Canadian soil ... Adopting procedural protections from other jurisdictions in a piecemeal fashion risks upsetting the balance that has been struck by Canadian courts and legislatures.'[119]

For those who studied the Court's use of US jurisprudence *before* the enactment of the *Charter*, this is not surprising, and is consistent with 'a fluctuating attitude

[114] Saunders, 'Judicial Engagement with Comparative Law' (n 3) 582, where the author indicates that 'comparative constitutional law can assist constitutional self-understanding by ... identifying dimensions of local experience that are distinctive by contrast with others'.

[115] Jackson, *Constitutional Engagement in a Transnational Era* (2009) (n 6) 71.

[116] CL Ostberg, ME Wetstein, and CR Ducat, 'Attitudes, Precedents, and Cultural Change: Explaining the Citation of Foreign Precedents by the Supreme Court of Canada' (2001), 34 Canadian Journal of Political Science 377.

[117] *R v Rahey* [1987] 1 SCR 588.

[118] *Miranda v Arizona*, 384 US 436. 86 S Ct 1602 (1966).

[119] *R v Sinclair* [2010] 2 SCR 310. Other examples of this 'aversive' attitude are: *Reference re Section 94(2) of the British Columbia Motor Vehicles Act* [1985] 2 SCR 486: at issue was the meaning of s 7's 'principles of fundamental justice'; Justice Lamer (as he then was), on the basis of ss 52, 33, and 1 rejected the US distinction between substantive and procedural due process in light of 'fundamental structural differences between the two constitutions': see GV La Forest, 'The Use of International and Foreign Material in the Supreme Court of Canada' (1988), 17 Canadian Council of International Law 238; J Cameron, 'The Motor Vehicle Reference and the Relevance of American Doctrine in Charter Adjudication' in R Sharpe (ed), *Charter Litigation* (Butterworths, Toronto 1987) 69. In *R v Keegstra* [1990] 3 SCR 697, the SCC upheld a statute prohibiting public hate speech directed at vulnerable groups, rejecting the rationale developed in the US First Amendment case *Beauharnais v Illinois*, 343 US 250, 72 S Ct 725 (1952); in *Reference re Provincial Electoral Boundaries (Sask)* [1991] 2 SCR 158 the SCC rejected the US principle of 'one man, one vote' from *Baker v Carr* (1962), to embrace a principle of 'effective representation' for the right to vote entrenched in s 3 *Charter*; in *Hill v Church of Scientology of Toronto* [1995] 2 SCR 1130, the SCC considered the consequences of the adoption of the US 'actual malice' standard, concluding that it was undesirable in Canada, due to the consequences it would have determined.

toward American jurisprudence'.[120] Probably a striking Canadian feature, the awareness of a national and constitutional uniqueness, even more present after the *Charter*'s enactment, suggests a considerate approach to foreign sources. Nowadays, on most *Charter* issues, Canadian law diverges significantly from US law, substantive rights having usually been interpreted in a broader fashion, before being tested in relation to section 1.

4. The role played by section 1 of the *Charter*

A most important role in furthering the SCC's recourse to foreign case law has been played by the presence of the general 'salvage' or 'limitations' clause in section 1 of the *Charter*. As an explicit balancing and limiting provision, section 1 acknowledges that even fundamental rights cannot be absolute, and mandates consideration of the people's will in a 'free and democratic society' in the process of reviewing governmental activity allegedly infringing such rights.

Determining what limitations are justified in a 'free and democratic society', however, requires some degree of comparison, since the words 'free and democratic' imply a contrast with societies that are not, and, conversely, commonality with others sharing the same features. It is clear, therefore, that such provision de facto represents 'a directive to engage in comparative exercise and research the position in other jurisdictions' and not to 'blindly [accept] the Canadian experience as the last word on how a free and democratic society ought to conduct itself.'[121] Indeed, in some scholars' view, section 1 represents something analogous to the express authorization to cite foreign case law codified in the Constitutions of South Africa and Malawi,[122] and determines in Canada a framework where 'comparative analysis is regarded as internal to the activity of constitutional adjudication'.[123] This view was reaffirmed in Justice Wilson's statement that 'our courts have found the experience in other "free and democratic" societies useful in determining whether means adopted in this country are the best alternative'.[124]

My investigation confirms the view that the SCC has been receptive to this invitation, making use of the experience of other free and democratic countries and citing

[120] Roy, 'An Empirical Survey of Foreign Jurisprudence' 135, citing Bushnell, *The Use of American Cases* 167.

[121] C L'Heureux-Dubé, 'Two Supreme Courts: A Study in Contrast' in MC McKenna (ed), *The Canadian and American Constitutions* (1993) (n 104) 164; see also La Forest, 'Use of International and Foreign Material' (n 119) 236.

[122] See B-O Bryde, 'The Constitutional Judge and the International Constitutionalism Dialogue' in B Markesinis and J Fedtke (eds.), *Judicial Recourse to Foreign Law* (Routledge, New York 2006) 306, where the author suggests that in the case of limitation clauses analogous to s 1 the 'text of the national constitution cannot be understood without comparative analysis'. See also C Saunders, who, comparing s 1 *Charter* to s 39 of the 1996 Constitution of South Africa, emphasizes that 'a requirement of the kind in section 1 of the Charter... anticipates reference to foreign experience': Saunders, 'Judicial Engagement with Comparative Law' (2012) (n 3) 574. Vicki Jackson looks at this clause as probably requiring comparison: Jackson, *Constitutional Engagement in a Transnational Era* (2009) (n 6) 73.

[123] L Weinrib, 'Constitutional Conceptions and Constitutional Comparativism' in V Jackson and M Tushnet (eds.), *Defining the Field of Comparative Constitutional Law* (Praeger Publishers Inc, Westport, Connecticut 2002) 3–4.

[124] *Lavigne v Ontario Public Service Employees Union* [1991] 2 SCR 211, 298 (Can).

foreign case law not only in defining the substance of the rights at issue, but also in assessing the constitutionality of limitations.[125]

Furthermore, section 1 probably entrenches the most relevant difference between the *Charter* and the US *Bill of Rights*, one that determines much of the aversive attitude of the SCC toward US precedents. In fact, this provision mandates to the SCC a rather different hermeneutical approach to the one required by the US *Bill of Rights*, where rights are expressed in absolute terms and limitations are developed by judicial interpretation in the very process of defining the substance of rights. Section 1, conversely, allows the SCC to balance the rights and freedoms protected by the *Charter* against other values without limiting the substance of the provisions. It appears clear, therefore, that in most cases the substantive definition of rights determined in the US may appear too narrow to Canadian courts.[126]

IV. Conclusions

The attitude of the SCC towards citation of foreign case law is still in flux. Confronted with the major demands that the *Charter*'s enactment brought on the Court, the SCC resorted to the example provided by foreign case law to develop domestic jurisprudence.

External sources, however, have never been dispositive of the outcome of a case before the Court. The SCC, through a principled approach towards citation of foreign precedents, seems to provide evidence that concerns about 'cherry picking'[127] should be, at least to some extent, reconsidered, in light of the numerous aversive citations. More precisely, the SCC shows that comparative reasoning—usually associated with a finalistic approach, aiming to emphasize analogies more than differences—can also be used aversively, in order to reassert differences with other jurisdictions and define the identity of a domestic constitutional system.[128] In the words of Chief Justice Beverly McLachlin, 'a willingness to look at foreign law is no impediment to developing and maintaining distinctive legal approaches that respond to the particular history, values and needs of a nation'.[129]

[125] eg *Charkaoui v Canada (Citizenship and Immigration)* [2007] 1 SCR 350.

[126] See eg, *Ford v Attorney General of Quebec* [1988] 2 SCR 712, where the Court indicated that s 1 'permitted the Court to give a large and liberal interpretation to s. 2(b) . . . leading to the inclusion of commercial expression within its ambit', something notoriously in contrast with the US Supreme Court's jurisprudence on the issue.

[127] Critics of the use of foreign precedents in constitutional adjudication argue that when judges quote foreign decisions, they would be unable to use these resources in a principled manner and would not resist 'cherry picking', ie citing only foreign decisions supporting their preferred result.

[128] A concept defined by Pierre Legrand as 'prioritization of difference': P Legrand, 'The Same and the Different' in P Legrand and R Munday (eds.), *Comparative Legal Studies: Traditions and Transitions* (Cambridge University Press, Cambridge 2003) 240ff, 292ff; de Vergottini, *Oltre il dialogo tra le Corti* (2010) 35.

[129] Keynote Address of Chief Justice Beverly McLachlin on 'The Use of Foreign Law—A Comparative View of Canada and the United States', delivered on 26 April 2010 at the 104th ASIL's Annual Meeting in Washington, DC, USA. A video recording of the entire Address is available at: <www.fora.tv>. The phrase quoted can be found at minute 41:00 of the recording. A written, edited version of the Address is available as B McLachlin, 'The Use of Foreign Law—A Comparative View of Canada and the United States' (2010), 104 American Society of International Law Proceedings 491.

If the use of comparative law and recourse to foreign case law is not done with finalistic intents, the utilitarian component of the practice is, conversely, undeniable. When domestic jurisprudence on the interpretation of a newly enacted document is insufficiently developed, judges resort to foreign solutions in order to foresee possible consequences for the various interpretations of the constitutional provisions theoretically available.[130] This 'dialogical interpretation' helps the Court to become more self-aware and aware of the direction that its own jurisprudence is taking.[131] Foreign precedents can also 'alert [the Court] to some of the theories about which we might want to think'.[132]

Along with reasons connected to processes of legal adjudication, citation of foreign case law may also involve some policy elements. Indeed, in recent times, the political reasons behind citation of foreign precedents have become the subject of relevant consideration. The SCC seems to be aware of the relevant role that its jurisprudence plays on the international arena and the importance to be regarded as a progressive and outward-looking judicial body in the area of fundamental rights protection. By citing civil liberties cases from other countries extensively, Canadian judges have become part of a global debate on the extent of human rights in democratic societies. Openness towards citation of foreign judgments has also been perceived as an invitation to other courts to interact and has encouraged other jurisdictions to cite Canadian precedents in the exercise of their own adjudicatory functions.[133] This has also had an effect on constitution-drafting efforts worldwide, leading some scholars to observe that 'the Canadian Charter of Rights and Freedoms has, in recent years, become a leading alternative' to the US *Bill of Rights* as a model for constitution-making.[134]

In light of this policy component, one may wonder whether the SCC's citations of foreign decisions, in recent years, are still inspirational or have rather taken on a more cosmetic use. After all, 'judges from Canada may experience satisfaction from being regarded as committed to a cooperative transnational project of judging and human rights'.[135]

Regarding this aspect, my investigation seems to reveal a recent trend in citation of foreign judgments. Citation of foreign cases may be declining due to the development

[130] SI Smithey, 'A Tool, Not A Master. The Use of Foreign Case Law in Canada and South Africa' (2001), 34 Comparative Political Studies 1188.

[131] Choudhry, *Globalization in Search of Justification* (n 59) 836; C Saunders, 'Judicial Dialogue in Common Law Countries' in AAVV, *Renouveau du droit constitutionnel. Mélanges en l'honneur de L Favoreau* (Dalloz, Paris 2007) 423.

[132] M Tushnet, 'The Possibilities of Comparative Constitutional Law' (1999), 108 Yale Law Journal 1225.

[133] 'Canadian law serves as a source of inspiration for many countries around the world': A Barak, 'Foreword: A Judge on Judging: The Role of a Supreme Court in a Democracy' (2002), 116 Harvard Law Review 19, 114. Recent studies detailed the influence of the SCC's decisions on other jurisdictions' high courts: T Groppi, 'A User-friendly Court. The Influence of Supreme Court of Canada Decisions Since 1982 on Court Decisions in Other Liberal Democracies' (2007), 36 Supreme Court Law Review 337.

[134] S Choudhry, 'Globalization in Search of Justification' (n 59) 822; Anne-Marie Slaughter suggests that Canada and South Africa are 'looking around the world and canvassing the opinions of their fellow constitutional courts, and each is disproportionally influential as a result', A-M Slaughter, 'A Brave New Judicial World' in M Ignatieff (ed), *American Exceptionalism and Human Rights* (Princeton University Press, Princeton 2005) 289. See also DS Law, M Versteeg, 'The Declining Influence of the United States Constitution' (2012), 87 New York University Law Review 762.

[135] Jackson, *Constitutional Engagement in a Transnational Era* (2009) (n 6) 240.

of significant lines of domestic precedents, but the SCC's openness to foreign case law has not changed, now focusing mostly on cases dealing with previously unaddressed issues. While consideration of political reasons may be unavoidable, to a certain degree, the SCC appears genuinely to perceive itself as operating within a new 'worldwide rights culture'[136] implying a genuine, optimistic view of legal cosmopolitanism and a 'sincere outward-looking interest in the views of other societies'.[137]

136 Keynote Address of Chief Justice Beverly McLachlin on 'The Use of Foreign Law—A Comparative View of Canada and the United States', (n 129) available at: <www.fora.tv>.

137 G La Forest, 'The Use of American Precedents in Canadian Courts' (1994), 46 Maine Law Review 211.

22

Comparative Law before the Supreme Courts of the UK and the Netherlands

An Empirical and Comparative Analysis

*Elaine Mak**

I. Introduction

In recent years, legal scholars, political scientists, and social scientists have explored the use of non-binding foreign law, in particular the case law of foreign national courts, in judicial decision-making of the courts in Western legal systems. However, their studies have focused mostly on common law jurisdictions, in particular the United States,[1] or on large jurisdictions, such as the United Kingdom (UK), France, and Germany.[2] To obtain a better insight into the use of foreign law as a source for judicial decision-making, it seems interesting to contrast the practices of courts in common law and civil law systems and to see whether and, if so, which similarities and differences exist between judicial practices in large and small jurisdictions. A more detailed study of this kind seems valuable in light of identified factors which influence cross-citations between national jurisdictions in Europe: legal tradition, language group, and the size of the jurisdiction.[3] For this reason, this chapter analyses the use of foreign law in the Supreme Court of the UK and the highest courts of the Netherlands.

The focus on the courts in these two legal systems is pertinent for several reasons. Firstly, few scholars have as yet addressed the specific case of the use of foreign law in judicial decision-making in the Dutch legal system.[4] Moreover, the particularities of the Dutch constitutional framework, in particular its openness towards international and European law, might have an influence on the approaches of judges to the use of

* Endowed Professor of Empirical Study of Public Law, in particular of Rule-of-Law Institutions, at Erasmus School of Law (Erasmus University Rotterdam, the Netherlands). This contribution is based on research supported by a post-doctoral VENI grant from the Netherlands Organisation for Scientific Research (NWO). The chapter uses parts of two previous publications: E Mak, 'Why Do Dutch and UK Judges Cite Foreign Law?' (2011) 70 Cambridge Law Journal 420; E Mak, 'Globalisation of the National Judiciary and the Dutch Constitution' (2013) 9 Utrecht Law Review 36.

[1] See inter alia VC Jackson, *Constitutional Engagement in a Transnational Era* (OUP, Oxford 2009); B Flanagan and S Ahern, 'Judicial Decision-Making and Transnational Law: A Survey of Common Law Supreme Court Judges' (2011) 60 International and Comparative Law Quarterly 1.

[2] See inter alia B Markesinis and J Fedtke, *Judicial Recourse to Foreign Law* (Routledge-Cavendish, Abingdon 2006).

[3] M Gelter and M Siems, 'Networks, Dialogue or One-Way Traffic? An Empirical Analysis of Cross-Citations Between Ten of Europe's Highest Courts' (2012) 8 Utrecht Law Review 88.

[4] M Adams and E Mak, 'Buitenlands recht in nationale rechtspleging: onder welke voorwaarden is dat feitelijk nuttig en mogelijk?' (2011) 86 Nederlands Juristenblad 2912; M Adams, 'Globaliserende rechtspraak: democratisch omstreden?' (2012) 61 Ars Aequi 531.

foreign law. Because of this openness, Dutch judges are familiar with the interpretation and application of legal sources originating outside of the national legal system, and with the precedence which such sources can take over national laws.[5] Concerning the UK, the changes of the constitutional system in the last decades provide reasons for a closer analysis of the judicial practices in this system. In particular, the implementation of the Human Rights Act 1998 and the establishment of the Supreme Court in 2009, replacing the Appellate Committee of the House of Lords (the 'Law Lords'), might have influenced the judicial reference to comparative legal sources.

The need to reconsider judicial approaches under the influence of globalization is arguably most pressing at the level of the highest national courts, which hold responsibility with regard to the interpretation and development of the law.[6] For this reason, this chapter analyses the practices of the UK Supreme Court and the two most significant highest national courts in the Dutch legal system: the Hoge Raad der Nederlanden (Supreme Court of the Netherlands, hereafter: Hoge Raad) and the Afdeling bestuursrechtspraak van de Raad van State (Administrative Jurisdiction Division of the Council of State, hereafter: Afdeling bestuursrechtspraak).[7] The central research question, which forms the starting-point for the analysis, is: what role does comparative law play in the deliberations and reasoning of the British and Dutch highest courts, taking into account the similarities and differences between the two legal systems in terms of legal tradition as well as organization and working methods of the highest courts? The analysis will address the characteristics of the courts, their practices with regard to the use of foreign law, and the legitimacy of these practices in light of the constitutional normative frameworks for judicial decision-making in the British and Dutch legal systems.

The chapter combines a socio-legal analysis of the judicial decision-making of the examined courts with a legal-theoretical analysis of the constitutional implications of the identified practices. The socio-legal research took the form of semi-structured interviews and aimed to present an inside story concerning the changing practices of the highest courts examined. Since judicial deliberations are not public and not all considerations made by individual judges are revealed in the judgments, talking to the judges themselves seemed an adequate approach to establish how the use of foreign law in the highest courts has developed and how influential the personal approaches of judges are in this regard.[8] In the UK, interviews were held with seven Supreme Court

[5] See further LFM Besselink, 'The Proliferation of Constitutional Law and Constitutional Adjudication, or How American Judicial Review Came to Europe After All' (2013) 9 Utrecht Law Review 19.

[6] S Muller and S Richards (eds.), *Highest Courts and Globalisation* (Hague Academic Press, The Hague 2010) 2.

[7] Two specialized tribunals with final jurisdiction in administrative cases will not be included in the analysis in this article. The Centrale Raad van Beroep (Central Appeals Tribunal), based in Utrecht, rules on appeals in social security and civil service cases. The College van Beroep voor het bedrijfsleven (Trade and Industry Appeals Tribunal), based in The Hague, decides cases in the field of social-economic law and is the court of appeal for cases arising under specific laws, including the Competition Act and the Telecommunications Act. These two tribunals, because of their small size, occupy a relatively less prominent place in the Dutch judicial system when compared to the other highest courts.

[8] For a further explanation of the research design, see E Mak, 'Why Do Dutch and UK Judges Cite Foreign Law?' (2011) 70 Cambridge Law Journal 420, 421–3; E Mak, 'Globalisation of the National Judiciary and the Dutch Constitution' (2013) 9 Utrecht Law Review 36, 40–1.

judges and one recently retired Law Lord. The interviews took place in November 2009.[9] In the Netherlands, interviews were held with 13 judges of the Hoge Raad, as well as with five Advocates General. These interviews took place in September and October 2009. Both in the UK and in the Netherlands, additional information was obtained through meetings with judicial assistants at the courts. Interviews with two members of the Afdeling bestuursrechtspraak and with a liaison officer took place in March 2011.

The outline of the chapter is as follows. In section II, the competences and organization of the courts are presented and compared. Section III examines to what extent the use of foreign law has been integrated into the practices of the UK Supreme Court, the Hoge Raad, and the Afdeling bestuursrechtspraak. Section IV sets out the normative implications of the judicial recourse to foreign law at the constitutional level. Section V presents some concluding remarks.

II. The courts

The UK Supreme Court fits the Anglo-Saxon model, which is characterized by a single highest court at the apex of the judicial system. The Anglo-Saxon legal systems, which include the UK as well as inter alia Canada and the United States, are closely tied by historical connections relating to the former British Empire. The further development of the common law is still an important responsibility of judges in the Commonwealth, and also engages to a lesser extent judges in the United States. The highest courts in the Anglo-Saxon legal systems play an important role as the final interpreter of the law at the national level, and as participants in the development of the law across national borders. The Dutch court system, by contrast, has been inspired by the French model, in which multiple highest courts exist next to each other. The court system features a judicial branch charged with the judgment of civil and criminal cases, and an administrative branch charged with the judgment of administrative cases. This system was introduced in the Netherlands during the French occupation of 1795 to 1813.[10] Significant reforms of the court system have taken place since, in particular concerning the integration of administrative adjudication into the general courts of first instance and the clearer organizational separation between the legislative and judicial functions in the Raad van State (Council of State).[11] However, the highest courts still reflect the general characteristics of the original model. The three courts examined are introduced in more detail in the next paragraphs.

[9] In May 2009, three exploratory interviews were held with judges of the Court of Appeal of England and Wales. The information obtained through these interviews was used for the set-up of the interviews at the British and Dutch Supreme Courts. Although the results are not included in this book, it should be noted that the experiences of the interviewed Court of Appeal judges correspond in many respects with those of the judges of the UK Supreme Court.

[10] KJ Kraan, 'Het Koninkrijk der Nederlanden' in L Prakke and CAJM Kortmann (eds.), *Het staatsrecht van de landen van de Europese Unie* (Kluwer, Deventer 2004) 559.

[11] See section II.3.

1. UK Supreme Court

The Supreme Court for the United Kingdom was established in 2009 to replace the Appellate Committee of the House of Lords, which dated from 1876 and had origins as far back as the 14th century.[12] This reform, set in motion by the Constitutional Reform Act 2005, can be seen as 'the last step in the separation of powers' in the British legal system.[13] The Supreme Court is based in the Middlesex Guildhall in London, opposite the Houses of Parliament.

The UK Supreme Court's jurisdiction regards the final appeal of civil cases in the United Kingdom and criminal cases in England, Wales, and Northern Ireland.[14] No constitutional review of legislative acts exists, but the Human Rights Act 1998 goes a long way in this direction. This Act introduced the judicial competence to declare Acts of Parliament incompatible with fundamental rights provisions transposed from the European Convention on Human Rights (ECHR).[15]

At the time of the interviews, the UK Supreme Court was composed of 11 judges. Most of these judges were former Law Lords, who took up office in the new Supreme Court in October 2009. The 12th position in the Court was filled by the appointment of Sir John (now Lord) Dyson as Justice of the Supreme Court in 2010. Following the untimely death of Lord Rodger and the retirement of Lord Collins and Lord Saville, three new judges were appointed in 2011. Lord Wilson was sworn in in May 2011 and Lord Sumption in January 2012. The new Scottish judge, Lord Reed, was appointed in December 2011 to take the place of Lord Rodger. Lord Brown, who retired in April 2012, was succeeded by Lord Carnwath, a former judge of the Court of Appeal.[16] Lord Phillips retired in September 2012 and Lord Neuberger was appointed as the new President of the Supreme Court.[17]

Cases in the UK Supreme Court are judged by a panel of five judges, and occasionally, at the discretion of the President, by a panel of seven or nine judges.[18] Criteria used when considering a larger panel are: the possibility of a reversal of the case law; the constitutional importance of the case; the public importance of the case; the need to

[12] See <http://www.supremecourt.uk/about/appellate-committee.html>. Concerning this historical background, see, inter alia, R Stevens, *Law and Politics: The House of Lords as a Judicial Body, 1800–1976* (Weidenfeld and Nicolson, London 1979); R Stevens, *The English Judges: Their Role in the Changing Constitution* (Hart, Oxford 2002); L Blom-Cooper, B Dickson, and G Drewry (eds.), *The Judicial House of Lords 1876–2009* (OUP, Oxford 2009).

[13] 'UK Supreme Court judges sworn in', *BBC News* (London), 1 October 2009, available at <http://news.bbc.co.uk/2/hi/uk_news/8283939.stm>.

[14] The judges of the Supreme Court also sit on the Judicial Committee of the Privy Council (JCPC), which is the final court for cases from Commonwealth jurisdictions; see <http://www.jcpc.uk>. Some of the former and current judges of the Supreme Court are Non-Permanent Judges of the Court of Final Appeal of Hong Kong; see <http://www.judiciary.gov.hk/en/organization/judges.htm>.

[15] Human Rights Act 1998, s 4.

[16] See <http://www.supremecourt.uk/about/biographies-of-the-justices.html>.

[17] UK Supreme Court, 'Press Notice: Lord Phillips, President of the Supreme Court, to retire next summer' (London, 11 October 2011), available at <http://www.supremecourt.uk/docs/pr_1110.pdf>; UK Supreme Court, 'News Release: New President of the Supreme Court' (London, 12 July 2012), available at <http://www.supremecourt.uk/news/new-president-of-the-supreme-court.html>.

[18] For an overview, see UK Supreme Court, *The Supreme Court Annual Report and Accounts 2009–2010*, 24–5, available at <http://www.supremecourt.uk/docs/ar_2009_10.pdf>.

reconcile a conflict of the case laws of the House of Lords, the Privy Council, and the Supreme Court; and the need to consider an important question in light of the ECHR.[19] The use of a larger panel was considered desirable by some of the interviewed judges in order to avoid inconsistencies between panels. However, this is difficult to realize because of the time constraints the Court has to deal with. The judges have support from seven judicial assistants, who work cooperatively. Judicial assistants are appointed for one judicial year, which runs from the beginning of September until the end of July. Their task is to carry out research regarding pending cases, and to summarize applications for permission to appeal.[20] Importantly, the judges of the UK Supreme Court feel that counsel should bring forward all legal materials which are relevant for deciding the case, including foreign judgments and academic resources concerning foreign law. This view fits the British adversarial system for court proceedings, in which the parties present their case and all relevant arguments to the court.[21]

Concerning the UK Supreme Court, appeal is possible in cases where leave to appeal has been granted by the lower court—in most cases this is the Court of Appeal of England and Wales—or where a case has been admitted by the Supreme Court itself. The criterion for case selection is the 'general public importance' of arguable points of law.[22] In 2009, the Appellate Committee of the House of Lords disposed of 104 applications for permission to appeal and had a caseload of 40 cases.[23] Its successor the Supreme Court received 135 applications for permission to appeal between its start on 1 October 2009 and the end of the Court's financial year on 31 March 2010.[24] The Court heard 43 appeals and gave judgments in 42 cases. In 19 cases, the appeal was allowed.[25] Between 1 April 2010 and 31 March 2011, 228 applications for permission to appeal were received by the Supreme Court, 76 appeals were heard, and judgments were given in 56 cases. In 28 of the decided cases, the appeal was allowed.[26]

2. Hoge Raad der Nederlanden

The Hoge Raad is the court of final appeal in civil, criminal, and tax law cases in the Netherlands. It is a court of cassation, meaning that its jurisdiction is limited to the judgment of questions of law, and does not include the judgment of facts.[27] The Hoge

[19] See <http://www.supremecourt.uk/procedures/panel-numbers-criteria.html>.

[20] Applications for seven temporary posts of judicial assistants for the term of 10 September 2012 until 31 July 2013 were solicited through the Supreme Court's website in March 2012.

[21] Lord Woolf, *Access to Justice: Interim Report to the Lord Chancellor on the Civil Justice System in England and Wales* (Lord Chancellor's Department, London 1995).

[22] See <http://www.supremecourt.uk/about/role-of-the-supreme-court.html>.

[23] Ministry of Justice (UK), *Judicial and Court Statistics 2009*, available at <http://www.justice.gov.uk/downloads/statistics/mojstats/jcs-stats-2009-211010.pdf>.

[24] The financial year is defined by s 54(3) of the Constitutional Reform Act 2005. Section 54(1) of this Act provides that '[a]s soon as practicable after each financial year, the chief executive of the Supreme Court must prepare a report about the business of the Supreme Court during that year'.

[25] UK Supreme Court, *The Supreme Court Annual Report and Accounts 2009–2010*, 22–3.

[26] UK Supreme Court, *The Supreme Court Annual Report and Accounts 2010–2011*, 21–2, available at <http://www.supremecourt.uk/docs/ar_2010_11.pdf>.

[27] Judiciary Organisation Act 1827 (Wet op de rechterlijke organisatie), s 79.

Raad cannot review parliamentary acts in light of the Constitution.[28] However, the court is allowed to decide on the conformity of acts of Parliament with provisions of international treaties binding the state.[29]

The Hoge Raad has a number of additional competences. These competences include advice to the Government concerning legislative bills or reform plans for the judiciary,[30] the judgment of applications for cassation in the interests of the uniform application of the law ('*cassatie in het belang der wet*'),[31] the judgment of applications by the Procurator General concerning the suspension or discharge of judges,[32] and the judgment of public-office offences committed by members of the States General, ministers, and state secretaries.[33] On 1 July 2012, a law entered into force which allows the lower courts in the Netherlands to ask the Hoge Raad for a preliminary ruling on legal questions which have arisen in a large number of similar cases. This procedure is limited to civil cases.[34]

The Hoge Raad at the time of the interviews consisted of the President, six Vice-Presidents, 31 Supreme Court judges, and three extraordinary judges. The judges are distributed over three chambers: the Civil Law Chamber; the Criminal Law Chamber; and the Tax Law Chamber. Cases are judged by a panel of three or five judges. There is a Procurator-General's Office at the Hoge Raad, which consists of the Procurator-General, the Deputy Procurator-General, and 21 Advocates General. The Procurator General's Office provides a '*conclusie*' (opinion) to the Court in most cases, rather like that of the Advocate-General before the Court of Justice of the European Union (CJEU), and thus acts as an advisor to the Court on how to decide the questions of law raised in the case at hand. The Advocates General work in one of the three fields of competence of the Hoge Raad. The Court has a support staff, which is organized in the Court's Research Service (Wetenschappelijk Bureau). Judges in the Criminal and Tax Law Chambers have personal judicial assistants. In the Civil Law Chamber, two assistants are available for all judges together.

During the research period, the Hoge Raad did not have the competence to select cases. In 2009, judgments were given in 527 cases by the Civil Law Chamber, in 3,464 cases by the Criminal Law Chamber, and in 999 cases by the Tax Law Chamber.[35] An exception to the general rules of the Court concerned the possibility for the Advocates General in tax cases (but not in criminal or civil cases) to select the cases for which they will write an opinion addressed to the court.[36] Furthermore, the Court had the competence to dismiss appeals with a shortened reasoning if it considered that there were no grounds for cassation and the case did not raise any legal questions which should be answered in the interest of legal uniformity or the development of the law.[37] However, these cases would still have to go through the entire cassation trajectory, and

[28] Constitution 1983 (Grondwet), art 120.
[29] Constitution 1983, arts 93 and 94.
[30] Judiciary Organisation Act 1827, s 74.
[31] Judiciary Organisation Act 1827, s 78(1).
[32] Judiciary Organisation Act 1827, s 111.
[33] Constitution 1983, s 119.
[34] Supreme Court Preliminary Questions Act 2012 (Wet prejudiciële vragen aan de Hoge Raad), Staatsblad 2012, 65.
[35] Hoge Raad, *Verslag over 2009–2010*, 53, 63 and 76, available at <http://www.rechtspraak.nl>.
[36] One of the interviewed Advocates General suggested that this exception relates to the absence of mandatory legal representation in tax cases.
[37] Judiciary Organisation Act 1827, s 81.

in this way took up a considerable amount of time and resources. In order to improve the quality and efficiency of the cassation procedure, a reform was initiated in 2008 with the aim of establishing a general mechanism of case selection.[38] Since 1 July 2012, the Hoge Raad has been allowed to dismiss an appeal directly at the beginning of the cassation procedure if this appeal apparently cannot lead to cassation or if the applicant apparently does not have a sufficient interest.[39]

3. Afdeling bestuursrechtspraak van de Raad van State

The highest administrative court in Netherlands, the Afdeling bestuursrechtspraak, is part of the historically developed institution of the Council of State, which combines the tasks of legislative consultation and the judgment of administrative cases.[40] The competence of the supreme administrative court mirrors that of the court of cassation. However, the Afdeling bestuursrechtspraak has the additional competence to judge some cases as a first instance court.[41] Like the Hoge Raad, the supreme administrative court has the competence to review the conformity of parliamentary acts in light of international treaty provisions but not in light of the Constitution.[42] Criticism of the combination of political and judicial tasks in the Council of State has in recent years led to a reform of the internal organization of the Council, in particular consisting of a stricter division of legislative and judicial functions.[43]

The Council of State is formally headed by the King of the Netherlands, who holds the position of President. In practice, the Council is headed by the Vice-President. This position is currently held by Piet Hein Donner, who succeeded Herman Tjeenk Willink in February 2012.[44] The Council of State is further composed of a maximum of 10 members, approximately 40 State Councillors, and a small number of Extraordinary Councillors.[45] Amongst the Extraordinary Councillors are one or two members of the Hoge Raad, whose role is to contribute to the consistency of the case law of the highest courts.[46] To guarantee the independence of the judicial decision-making, no more than 10 members and State Councillors may combine functions in the advisory and judicial divisions of the Council of State.[47] Members and State Councillors who take part in the judicial division are appointed for life by Royal Decree.[48] The selection of candidates is

[38] Hammerstein Committee, *Improving Cassation Procedure* (The Hague, February 2008), available at <http://www.rechtspraak.nl/Organisatie/Hoge-Raad/OverDeHogeRaad/publicaties/Pages/default.aspx>.

[39] Judiciary Organisation Act 1827, s 80a.

[40] Constitution 1983, art 73. See further the Council of State Act 1962 (Wet op de Raad van State).

[41] See General Administrative Law Act 1994 (Algemene wet bestuursrecht), s 8:105 and Annex on Administrative Jurisdiction Competence (Bevoegdheidsregeling bestuursrechtspraak), s 2.

[42] Constitution 1983, art 120.

[43] Council of State Restructuring Act 2010 (Wet herstructurering Raad van State), Staatsblad 2010, 175.

[44] 'Donner benoemd tot vicepresident Raad van State' (The Hague, 16 December 2011), available at <http://www.rijksoverheid.nl/nieuws/2011/12/16/donner-benoemd-tot-vicepresident-raad-van-state.html>.

[45] See <http://www.raadvanstate.nl/the_council_of_state>.

[46] Concerning this practice, see S Kingma, 'Raadsheer Snijders verbindingsofficier met de Raad van State' (Cassatieblog, 15 November 2011), available at <http://cassatieblog.nl/category/hoge-raad-algemeen>.

[47] Council of State Act 1962 (Wet op de Raad van State), s 2(3).

[48] ibid., ss 2(1) and 8(3).

made by the Council of State itself, and candidates are considered on the basis of their expertise and experience in the fields of legislation, government, or the judiciary. If a member or State Councillor is solely appointed to the judicial division, prior legal training is a requirement for appointment.[49]

The Afdeling bestuursrechtspraak consists of three chambers, each dealing with cases concerning a specific field of administrative law. The Spatial Planning Chamber decides cases in first and final instance under specific legislative acts, including the Spatial Planning Act, the Nature Conservancy Act, and the Transport Infrastructure (Planning Procedures) Act. The Aliens Chamber judges appeals in the field of immigration and asylum law under the Aliens Act 2000. The General Chamber, finally, decides cases under a variety of legislative acts, including the Environmental Permitting (General Provisions) Act, the Government Information (Public Access) Act, as well as cases under general municipal byelaws and cases concerning planning permissions and the like.[50] Until 1 June 2011, environment cases were dealt with by a separate chamber in the division. This chamber was integrated in the General Chamber on the occasion of the entry into force of the Environmental Permitting (General Provisions) Act.[51] Each chamber of the judicial division is composed of a Chamber President, one or more Vice-Presidents, and a number of members, which in 2010 ranged between 11 and 24.[52] These members can be part of more than one chamber. The Afdeling bestuursrechtspraak is assisted by lawyers and support staff, who work in the Administrative Jurisdiction Department. The entire support staff of the Council of State comprises around 600 persons, including 250 lawyers.[53]

The Afdeling bestuursrechtspraak cannot select its cases. On average, the judicial division decides approximately 13,000 cases per year, as well as around 1,050 applications for provisional relief ('*voorlopige voorziening*').[54] In 2009, the Afdeling bestuursrechtspraak decided 1,951 cases in first and final instance and gave judgment on 690 applications for provisional relief. Also, judgments were handed down concerning 2,692 general appeals and 347 applications for provisional relief on appeal. As concerns the appeal in immigration and asylum cases, 4,432 cases were decided as well as 408 applications for provisional relief.[55] In 2010, the Afdeling bestuursrechtspraak dealt with 2,132 cases in first and final instance, and decided on 810 applications for provisional relief. The general appeals decided reached the number of 2,396 and 310 decisions on applications for provisional relief. In immigration and asylum cases, finally, 6,077 judgments were handed down, as well as 1,649 decisions on applications for provisional relief.[56] The caseload per chamber of the judicial division was as follows in 2010: the Spatial Planning Chamber handed down 1,150 judgments, the Environment Chamber 982, the General Chamber 2,396, and the Aliens Chamber 6,077.[57]

[49] ibid., s 2(4). [50] See <http://www.raadvanstate.nl/the_council_of_state>.
[51] Raad van State, *Jaarverslag 2010*, 207, available at <http://www.raadvanstate.nl/publicaties/jaarverslagen>.
[52] ibid., 223–7. [53] See <http://www.raadvanstate.nl/the_council_of_state>.
[54] See <http://www.raadvanstate.nl/the_council_of_state>.
[55] Raad van State, *Jaarverslag 2010*, 228–33. [56] ibid. [57] ibid., 234.

4. Comparability

On the basis of the particularities of their jurisdiction and organization, some differences can be expected regarding the use of foreign legal sources in the British and Dutch highest courts. These differences relate mostly to the number of judges and the caseload that the courts have to deal with. Concerning the composition of the courts, the small number of judges in the UK Supreme Court entails that the judges are not formally specialized and will regularly sit on cases with each of their colleagues. The judges in the Hoge Raad and Afdeling bestuursrechtspraak, by contrast, act within the context of a specific chamber, and their exchange of ideas will thus be restricted to a specific field of law and a less varied group of colleagues. Because of this internal specialization, judicial ideas about the use of foreign legal sources might differ between the specific chambers. In private law cases, criminal cases, or administrative law cases, different types of foreign law can be discussed and the frequency of such discussions can vary depending on the specific area of the law. In particular, the occurrence of international law aspects or human rights aspects is likely to stimulate the judicial debate about foreign legal sources. However, we will also consider whether the use of foreign law has developed in cases concerning the interpretation of purely national law. In any case, the organizational surroundings of individual judges, concerning both the types of cases in which they are involved and the possibilities for exchange with their colleagues, can be thought to have an influence on these judges' familiarity with and personal approach to the use of foreign law.

As concerns caseload, in contrast to the UK Supreme Court, the Dutch Courts at the time of the interviews had no formal possibility of case selection. Therefore, the judges had less time to spend on individual cases and on the insights which foreign law might offer in these cases. This is different for the British judges, who decide only a small number of cases each year and can devote more time to the study of relevant legal sources in these cases. Moreover, in the Anglo-Saxon model, the counsel for the parties is supposed to put forward all arguments and relevant materials, while the judges in the Dutch courts conduct research into relevant materials themselves. Yet, the Dutch Courts seem to benefit from a larger research staff and the input of internal advisors, such as Advocates General. We will examine in section III how these organizational differences concerning caseload and research tasks and facilities play out in the context of the use of foreign legal sources.

III. Practice

In the interviews, the judges of the UK Supreme Court, the Hoge Raad, and the Afdeling bestuursrechtspraak outlined their experiences with the use of foreign legal sources and they shared their views concerning the usefulness of references to these sources in judicial decision-making. We will first examine the judicial considerations and next analyse the judicial practices developed regarding the use of foreign law.

1. Judicial considerations: the usefulness of foreign law in judicial decision-making

What motives do the highest court judges in the UK and in the Netherlands have for using non-binding foreign law in their deliberations and judgments? Based on the interviews, a number of observations can be made.

a) *UK perspective*

The interviewed judges in the United Kingdom pointed out that in their judgments they cite all arguments which they consider to be persuasive. Indeed, in the common law conception, the judge feels that he owes a duty to counsel to explain why their arguments are not accepted. The judge is very courteous to the parties and their counsel, and his or her judgment can even be considered as an excuse to the losing party and its counsel.[58] The wish for completeness of judicial reasoning is apparent in the treatment of non-binding foreign legal sources by the British judges.

It was indicated in the interviews that comparative legal sources feature regularly in the decisions of the UK Supreme Court, and previously in the judgments of the Appellate Committee of the House of Lords. Such sources include the judgments of foreign courts. The idea of the judges is that arguments for their reasoning may be found in decisions of foreign judges just as well as in other legal sources. If an argument is found in a foreign judgment and used in the reasoning of the case at hand, it is only courteous to mention the author, as one Supreme Court judge stated. However, foreign judgments are considered to have no binding value of precedent.[59] Several judges pointed out that the citation of foreign judgments is often used merely to buttress the decision which was taken on the basis of binding legal sources. Examples mentioned by the interviewed judges will be discussed hereunder.

Other non-binding sources can also play a role in the legal reasoning of the British judges. An example is formed by unimplemented treaties. As already explained, international treaty law needs to be integrated into the legal system of the UK through domestic legislation. This requirement entails that no cases can be brought to the domestic courts concerning the violation of obligations under treaties which have not been transposed into national law.[60] Still, unimplemented treaties are sometimes considered legally relevant in the judicial decision-making of the British common law courts. In the judgment of the English Court of Appeal in *Ahmad v ILEA*, for example, it was considered that:

> [I]t is no longer possible to argue that because the international treaty obligations of the United Kingdom do not become law unless enacted by Parliament our courts pay no regard to our international obligations. They pay very serious regard to them: in

[58] A Touffait and A Tunc, 'Pour une motivation plus explicite des décisions de justice notamment celles de la Cour de cassation' (1974) 72 Revue trimestrielle de droit civil 491.

[59] Concerning the concept of 'precedent', see F Schauer, 'Precedent' in A Marmor (ed), *The Routledge Companion to Philosophy of Law* (Routledge, London 2012) 123–36.

[60] G van Ert, 'Using Treaties in Canadian Courts' (2000) 38 Canadian Yearbook of International Law 3, 19.

> particular, they will interpret statutory language and apply common law principles, wherever possible, so as to reach a conclusion consistent with our international obligations.[61]

b) Dutch perspective

References to foreign case law and legal doctrines in principle do not occur in the published judgments of the Hoge Raad and are relatively scarce in the opinions of the Advocates General. Most of the interviewed judges expressed the fear that the discussion of foreign judgments in their decisions would give rise to criticism concerning the legal systems to which reference is made: why look at one system, but not at another? References to foreign judgments would thus risk weakening the authority of the judgments of the Hoge Raad. Indeed, the discussion of foreign judgments would not fit the Dutch tradition of judgments, which might no longer be apodictic but are still reasoned more 'economically' than is the style in the common law tradition. Moreover, citations of case law are already rare in the case law of the highest courts, as no formal system of precedent exists in the Netherlands.[62] In this context, the judges consider that the citation of foreign judgments in the decisions of the Hoge Raad would be a bridge too far. They feel that the opinions of the Advocates General, which are published alongside the Court's judgments and which sometimes contain a discussion of arguments from foreign law, are sufficient to give more insight into the background of the Court's reasoning. These opinions clarify to some extent whether, and if so which, foreign sources have played a role in the decision-making of the Supreme Court.

Judges in the Hoge Raad further mentioned that sometimes a specific approach to the use of foreign legal sources is dictated by the subject-matter of the case at hand. In extradition cases, for example, the starting-point is mutual trust between states. The Court, because of this mutual trust, will try to grant requests for extradition to the largest possible extent. This involves the comparison of the national law and the law of the foreign legal system which sent the request for extradition. The study of the law of a foreign legal system here is an essential element to the judgment of the case at hand and the consistency of the interpretation of legal provisions is an important aim of judicial decision-making.

At the Council of State, the influence of comparative law is considered to be more significant in the Council's function as an advisory body on legislation than in its function as the highest general administrative court in the Netherlands. An interviewed judge observed that in judging one has to limit one's focus to what matters for the case at hand. In that specific context, comparative law generally only has limited usefulness. Why would one choose to be guided by the German Bundesverfassungsgericht, which functions under a different system regarding the implementation of international law? Or by French law which is much less direct than the equivalent Dutch law? The judge indicated that, if a choice has to be made, the judges in the Afdeling bestuursrechtspraak prefer to engage in a vertical comparison, for example with the CJEU or the European Court of Human Rights (ECtHR), rather than in a horizontal comparison

[61] *Ahmad v ILEA* [1978] 1 QB 36 (CA) para 48D–E (Scarman LJ); Van Ert, 'Using Treaties', ibid., 28.
[62] See Gelter and Siems, 'Networks, Dialogue or One-Way Traffic?', n 3.

with courts in other national jurisdictions. The European courts are considered to be the 'cassation judges' for the law of the European Union (EU) and the ECHR, which makes it interesting and legitimate for the *Raad van State* to pay attention to the case law of these courts. Concerning the horizontal comparison with other national courts, the particularities of national legal systems and procedural laws are thought to form an obstacle for a fruitful study of the judgments of these foreign courts. The judge made an exception for the Grondwettelijk Hof van België (Constitutional Court of Belgium), previously the Arbitragehof (Court of Arbitration).[63] This Court is considered to function in a similar system of the implementation of international law as the Afdeling bestuursrechtspraak. This provides a basis for legal comparison, for example concerning the concept of the 'reading together' of fundamental rights provisions. In the case *Jezus redt*, for example, Articles 6 and 7 of the Dutch Constitution, concerning the freedom of religion and the freedom of expression, were read together with Articles 9 and 10 of the ECHR, concerning the same fundamental freedoms.[64]

This judge further considered that comparative law is interesting for judges only in an abstract sense. The judge felt that comparative law should only be used at the level of concepts and that it should only serve as an inspiration. Concerning the deciding of individual cases, from a practical point of view, time constraints limit the possible engagement of judges with foreign law.[65] From a principled point of view, this judge's reservations concerned the usefulness of comparative law in light of the argument that foreign legal systems are very different from the domestic legal system of the Netherlands, and that these foreign legal systems do not provide specific solutions. The judge considered that the point of departure for the use of comparative law should be the usefulness for pending cases, combined with the requirement of the celerity of proceedings.

In sum, particularities of the views in the British and in the Dutch highest courts relate to the legal tradition and developed style of reasoning in the examined courts. Citations of non-binding foreign law are less problematic in the common law tradition, in which judges attach much value to the persuasiveness of legal arguments, than in the civil law tradition, in which the formal validity of legal sources is a predominant concern in judicial reasoning. Still, judges in both legal systems are developing their approaches in light of the increased 'global' influence on judicial decision-making and its implications for judicial deliberations. Some judges, in the UK as well as the Netherlands, consider it a necessity to take account of the position of states and highest national courts in a context of increased intertwinement of legal orders. Other judges, in both examined legal systems, are more sceptical with regard to the need and usefulness of engagement with foreign law.

2. Judicial practices: the use of foreign law in judicial decision-making

Information from the interviews and other published sources, in combination with an analysis of case law, provide the following picture regarding the use of foreign law in the decision-making of the three examined courts.

63 See <http://www.const-court.be>.

64 ABRvS, 14 July 2010, LJN BN1135. See further section III.2.

65 See section III.2.

a) UK perspective

Some examples given by the British judges shed more light on the way in which they use non-binding foreign case law in their decision-making. The *Reynolds* case, first, concerned the liability for libel in the light of qualified privilege for political events. The question to be answered by the House of Lords was if a libellous statement of fact made in the course of political discussion is free from liability if published in good faith or if liability may also arise if, having regard to the source of the information and all the circumstances, it was not in the public interest for the newspaper to have published the information as it did.[66] In this judgment, explicit mention was made of solutions adopted in other countries. In particular, attention was paid to the United States, where the *Sullivan* case[67] is the leading authority on the topic at hand. The overview of foreign case law in the judgment of the UK Supreme Court further included an analysis of Canadian, Indian, Australian, South African, and New Zealand case law.[68] The study of comparative sources in this specific case seemed to be connected to the wish to show that no uniform or non-controversial case law existed in the area in question. Lord Nicholls stated that:

> Before turning to the issues raised by this appeal mention must be made, necessarily briefly, of the solutions adopted in certain other countries. As is to be expected, the solutions are not uniform. As also to be expected, the chosen solutions have not lacked critics in their own countries.[69]

Another example is the *Jewish Free School* case, which concerned the admission policy of a religious school.[70] The school's policy was to give preference to those whose status as Jews is recognized by the Office of the Chief Rabbi of the United Hebrew Congregation of the Commonwealth (OCR), meaning 'those children whose mothers satisfy the matrilineal test or who are Jews by conversion by Orthodox standards'.[71] The question to be answered by the Supreme Court was whether this policy constituted a violation of section 1 of the Race Relations Act 1976. In deciding this case, the nine judges on the special panel of the UK Supreme Court paid attention, inter alia, to the case law of the Supreme Court of Israel.[72] Several members of the panel indicated that extra comparative legal research was done at the request of the judges themselves.

Extra research was also demanded by the judges in a number of cases concerning the freezing of assets of suspected terrorists. In the Supreme Court's judgment of 27 January 2010, reference is made to the measures adopted in Australia and New Zealand regarding the implementation of the applicable UN Resolutions.[73] The relevant

[66] *Reynolds v Times Newspapers Ltd and others* [2001] 2 AC 127.

[67] *New York Times Co v Sullivan*, 376 US 254, 84 S Ct 710 (1964).

[68] [2001] 2 AC 127, 199 (Lord Nicholls) and 209 (Lord Steyn).

[69] [2001] 2 AC 127, 198.

[70] *R (E) v Governing Body of JFS* [2009] UKSC 15, [2010] 2 AC 728.

[71] ibid., para 5 (Lord Phillips).

[72] ibid., para 159 (Lord Hope), where reference is made to *No'ar K'halacha v Ministry of Education*, HCJ 1067/08, 6 August 2009.

[73] *Her Majesty's Treasury v Mohammed Jabar Ahmed and others (FC)* [2010] UKSC 2, [2010] 2 AC 534, para 50 (Lord Hope, with whom Lord Walker and Lady Hale agree). See also this judgment at paras 120–22 (Lord Phillips), in which two New Zealand cases put forward by counsel for the defendant are analysed.

European judgment in *Kadi v Council of the European Union*[74] is analysed in the light of Canadian and US case law. An interviewed judge indicated to have suggested looking at Canadian case law, as this might give guidance on how to judge the case. However, the cited foreign case law was considered not to be decisive for the case at hand.[75]

In a more general sense, the British judges considered that citations of foreign law mostly occur in human rights cases and in private law cases. In human rights cases, the judges hope to find guidance in case law concerning the interpretation of the ECHR or concerning comparable instruments for human rights protection. In contract and tort cases, the shared background with other common law legal systems is thought to make legal comparison often useful. One of the judges indicated that in particular tort law is still relatively untouched by statute law and thus leaves room for comparison with other common law jurisdictions. Appreciation was voiced for Australian case law in particular, which was mentioned by several judges for its high quality. Australian case law was further mentioned as a source of inspiration for the judgment of asylum and refugee cases. When looking at the published judgments of the British judges in recent years, citations to Australian judgments can indeed be found in a number of cases. An inventory of the Law Reports of 2008 reveals that in 37 published cases of the Law Lords in which foreign law was cited, reference to Australian judgments was made in nine cases, yielding a total of 11 Australian judgments cited in the judicial opinions.[76]

The use of foreign law is less frequent in criminal cases. However, several judges indicated a personal interest in French or German case law. A judge remembered having looked at French case law in a case concerning the balancing of the anonymity of parties and the interest of media coverage in the light of the right to a fair trial and the principle of open justice. Another judge, speaking about the same legal question, mentioned having searched German law and having made inquiries with personal contacts in Germany in order to find useful information, which then might give rise to a question to counsel to base arguments on this information. In the decision given on 27 January 2010, Lord Rodger, who delivered the unanimous judgment, remarked that:

> Unfortunately, no real additional help with the question of anonymity orders can be obtained from examining the practices of courts in Europe when issuing judgments. In all the principal systems, at least, steps can apparently now be taken, where appropriate, to anonymise reports of matrimonial disputes and disputes relating to children. Apart from that, however, what is striking is the variety of approaches.[77]

This observation was followed by an overview of French, Italian, and German case law.[78] The responses of the interviewed judges and the reasoning in the judgment

[74] Case C-402/05 P *Kadi and Al Barakaat International Foundation v Council and Commission* [2008] ECR I-06351.

[75] [2010] UKSC 2, para 71 (Lord Hope).

[76] Most noteworthy among these judgments were *OBG Ltd v Allan* [2007] UKHL 21, [2008] AC 1 concerning actions for economic loss in English law (four Australian judgments cited), and *Sempra Metals Ltd v IRC* [2007] UKHL 34, [2008] 1 AC 561 concerning the calculation of interest in a case regarding restitution for unjust enrichment (five Australian judgments cited).

[77] [2010] UKSC 1, [2010] 2 WLR 325, para 53.

[78] ibid., paras 54–7. The judgment also contains a careful analysis of relevant ECtHR case law concerning arts 8 and 10 of the ECHR; see ibid paras 22–52.

suggest that the comparative analysis in this case was carried out with the aim of getting a clearer insight into the state of the domestic law. The observed variety of approaches can be considered a justifying argument for the decision taken, which stays very close to the facts of this specific case. Furthermore, the foreign case law gives an indication of factors to be taken into account when balancing the right of privacy against the rights of the press. In this way, the knowledge of the practices in other legal systems seems to have helped the judges to mark out the relevant questions during the process of discovery.

Finally, the British judges sometimes take account of 'soft law' instruments which are considered to have a certain prestige. References to the Principles of European Contract Law (PECL), developed by the Lando Commission, can be found in a small number of judgments of the Law Lords and the UK Supreme Court. A search of BAILII yielded five judgments given between 2001 and 2009.[79] However, these references appear to have no impact on the interpretation of domestic law. They are used as guidance for the interpretation of European law, such as the Unfair Contract Terms Directive,[80] or to highlight the differences between the English and the continental legal traditions. This latter argument transpires, for example, from the opinion of Lord Hoffmann in *Chartbrook Ltd v Persimmon Homes Ltd*, in which the judge observed that the PECL and related instruments 'reflect the French philosophy of contractual interpretation, which is altogether different from that of English law'.[81] An interviewed judge further considered that taking into account the PECL or the Draft Common Frame of Reference (DCFR) developed at the initiative of the European Commission would not make sense, because this source is too vague and academic in comparison with the domestic law. This judge considered that the DCFR might develop into an optional system in Europe 'as an ever closer union'.[82] However, it is this judge's belief that practical hindrances to commerce will remain as a result of efficiency considerations and costliness. The judge therefore considered that the DCFR can be no more than an inspiration for the UK Supreme Court.

b) Dutch perspective

Because of the absence of citations of non-binding foreign law in published judgments, it is difficult to assess the impact of comparative law on the decisions taken by the Dutch highest courts. Indeed, a research of the case law of the Afdeling bestuursrechtspraak yielded only a few citations of judgments of national courts in other jurisdictions. An interviewed judge recalled the judgment of the Afdeling bestuursrechtspraak in the case of the *Mothers of Srebrenica Citizens' Association*, which had requested the disclosure of documents concerning the UN Protection Force in the

[79] See <http://www.bailii.org> (search term 'Principles of European Contract Law').

[80] Directive 93/13/EEC, which was interpreted in *Director General of Fair Trading v First National Bank* [2001] UKHL 52, [2001] 2 All ER (Comm) 1000, paras 36–37 and 45.

[81] *Chartbrook Ltd v Persimmon Homes Ltd and others* [2009] UKHL 38, [2009] 4 All ER 677, para 39.

[82] Preambles to the EC Treaty and the EU Treaty.

former Yugoslavia.[83] In this case, assistance for the interpretation of the UN Convention on Privileges and Immunities was found in Belgian case law. The Afdeling bestuursrechtspraak considered:

> According to [appellants], the judgment delivered by the Tribunal de Première Instance de Bruxelles on 11 May 1966 in Manderlier v The United Nations (Journal des Tribunaux 1966, p 721ff; 'Manderlier') confirms that the privileges and immunities of the UN may not be accepted unreservedly but must be subject to review.[84]

The Afdeling bestuursrechtspraak cited its own earlier case law, in which it had held that the UN Convention prohibited the Minister of Defence from granting the application for disclosure of requested UN documents.[85] After discussing the United Nations' view concerning the confidentiality of the documents requested in the case at hand, the Afdeling bestuursrechtspraak discussed the argument advanced by the appellants on the basis of the *Manderlier* judgment. The supreme administrative court considered:

> The Manderlier judgment at first instance gives no reason to conclude otherwise. In its judgment the court of first instance in Brussels dismissed the plaintiff's civil claim against the UN because the UN invoked its immunity from every form of legal process pursuant to article II, section 2 of the UN Convention on Privileges and Immunities. In its judgment of 15 September 1969 (Revue critique de jurisprudence belge 1971, p 449 ff) the Cour d'Appel de Bruxelles upheld the court of first instance's judgment. In its judgment, the appeal court held that by acceding to the UN Convention on Privileges and Immunities, the parties to the UN Charter have established the necessary privileges and immunities and that the courts would be exceeding their authority were they to assume the right to evaluate the necessity of the immunities vested in the UN by that convention.[86]

The Afdeling bestuursrechtspraak held that the argument of the appellants was untenable and that the appeal therefore was unfounded. It upheld the contested judgment of the District Court of Amsterdam.[87] It seems that the Belgian judgments in this case were discussed primarily to give a reply to the arguments put forward by counsel for the appellants. An interviewed judge pointed out that in principle the Afdeling bestuursrechtspraak does not refer to the case law of foreign courts for the interpretation of international treaties, if sufficient information is available through international courts, in particular the European courts. This approach is taken with regard to all foreign courts, including constitutional courts. Therefore, the described case should indeed be considered to constitute an exception.

Concerning the Hoge Raad, its Annual Report 2007–2008 addressed 'international dimensions' in the Civil Law Chamber's case law.[88] However, comparative legal research was merely mentioned as a tool used to identify the meaning of rules of

[83] ABRvS 3 March 2010, LJN BL6245. The judgment also contains a discussion of EU law and CJEU judgments mentioned in the arguments of the appellants.
[84] ibid., para 2. [85] ABRvS 25 March 2009, LJN BH7691.
[86] ABRvS 3 March 2010, LJN BL6245, para 2. [87] ibid.
[88] Hoge Raad, *Verslag 2007 en 2008*, 50–9, available at <http://www.rechtspraak.nl>.

uniform private law, and only two specific examples were given of cases in this category in which the Supreme Court's decision was based on the use of international and comparative law.[89] This was slightly different in the Annual Report 2009–2010, which was entirely dedicated to the internationalization of the Hoge Raad's decision-making. The chapter of the report concerning the Civil Law Chamber contained a detailed explanation of the Court's use of the comparative method of interpretation, which has become the standard in cases in which no supranational court exists to which a request for a preliminary ruling can be sent.[90] The information obtained from judges and Advocates General confirmed that, in this type of case, comparative law at least plays a role in the phase of discovery before the judgment is written.

For the judges of the Dutch Hoge Raad, foreign judgments which are taken into account in the judicial deliberations mostly originate in France and Germany, and sometimes in England or the United States. Several judges mentioned consulting the German Bundesgerichtshof's case law in cases regarding commercial law, for example, the law on bills of exchange, and in intellectual property cases. The Hoge Raad, for example, considered the case law of the Bundesgerichtshof in deciding whether LEGO, after the expiry of its patent, could halt the copying of its toy building blocks through an action based on precise imitation ('*slaafse nabootsing*').[91] Another example concerned the comparison of Dutch and German judgments in cases where the interpretation of the Convention on the Contract for the International Carriage of Goods by Road (CMR), which forms part of transnational uniform commercial law, is required. A famous example in which the Court was informed about relevant non-binding foreign law by the Advocate General concerned the *Baby Kelly* case regarding a 'wrongful life' claim, meaning a claim for damages in the name of a severely handicapped child born as a result of an incorrect diagnosis during the mother's pregnancy. In his opinion for this case, Advocate General Hartkamp included an extensive discussion of, inter alia, French and German case law.[92]

In criminal cases, most of the interviewed judges of the Hoge Raad considered that references to foreign judgments occur more often with regard to questions of substantive law than with regard to questions of procedural law. These references seem to aim to better identify the current state of the domestic law. Examples which were mentioned concern the comparison with German law regarding the absoluteness of the right of non-disclosure;[93] the explanation on rights of appeal ('*Rechtsmittelbelehrung*'); and the interpretation of the concept of self-defence ('*noodweer*').[94] In a case concerning the insulting of a group ('*groepsbelediging*'), extra literature and case law were added to the judges' file by the reporting judge, and, on the suggestion of another judge,

[89] ibid., 55–6. [90] Hoge Raad, *Verslag over 2009–2010*, 17–21.

[91] *LEGO v Mega Brands* HR 20 November 2009, LJN BJ6999. Advocate General Verkade, para 4.6, discusses BGH 2 December 2004, I ZR 30/02, GRUR 2005/4, 349.

[92] *Baby Kelly* HR 18 March 2005, NJ 2006, 606 (opinion of Advocate General Hartkamp). On the transnational judicial dialogue in wrongful life cases, see further I Giesen, 'The Use and Influence of Comparative Law in "Wrongful Life" Cases' (2012) 8 Utrecht Law Review 35.

[93] See, eg HR 12 October 2010, LJN BN0526 (opinion of Advocate General Jörg), para 90, citing German, French, Swiss and US legal sources which define the scope of the right of non-disclosure.

[94] See, eg HR 4 January 2011, LJN BO4475 (opinion of Advocate General Silvis), para 10, citing German doctrine and the case law of the Bundesgerichtshof as sources which confirm the case law of the Hoge Raad.

a judgment of the British Law Lords was used in the deliberations in chambers. Concerning the right to a fair trial, US law is considered instructive in addition to the ECHR.

Concerning tax law, in some cases the case law of courts in other member states of the Organisation for Economic Co-operation and Development (OECD) is analysed to find guidelines for the application of the OECD Model Tax Convention (MTC).[95] Furthermore, the example was mentioned of a case in which the Court of Appeal for England and Wales was contacted because it seemed that pending preliminary questions of this Court to the CJEU might be of use for the decision of the Dutch case as well. In yet another case, the judgment of a Greek court was deemed relevant for a decision regarding unjustified VAT reclaims. However, here the problem of understanding the context and language of the decision came up.[96]

Finally, judges in the Hoge Raad indicated that they sometimes take account of prestigious 'soft law' instruments when judging cases. A Dutch judge in tax cases mentioned that regulations of the International Accounting Standards Board[97] have been used by the Hoge Raad as a guideline for its decision-making. Likewise, the OECD Commentary to the MTC is considered an aid to the interpretation of this treaty. In the Civil Law Chamber, the PECL are sometimes used as a source of reference. A search of the published judgments of the Hoge Raad yielded 23 judgments of the Civil Law Chamber, given between 2002 and 2012, in which reference was made to the PECL or commentaries of these Principles. All references are to be found in the opinions of the Advocates General.[98] The interviewed judges and Advocates General asserted that the PECL are used for guidance only. An Advocate General mentioned the example of assessing the termination of a breach of contract, taking account of fundamental interests of the parties. The analysed case law of the Hoge Raad corroborates this view. In a case concerning the interpretation of the termination clause included in a contract of employment, Advocate General Huydecoper observed that two kinds of interpretation identified in the Dutch academic literature in some foreign legal doctrines are considered to be identical.[99] In a footnote to this observation, he remarked that:

> Notwithstanding many differences, the sources of law for our neighbouring countries indicate a remarkable unanimity as regards the idea a) that contracts are to be interpreted in the first place on the basis of the intentions of the parties, which unless proved otherwise have to be interpreted in light of the standard of the 'reasonable man'; and b) that an addition to what was agreed upon in the absence of proved or reasonably assumed intentions of the parties has to take place with reference to what reasonably judging parties in the given case would have assumed.[100]

[95] See <http://www.oecd.org>.

[96] Concerning these practical obstacles to the use of comparative law, see further section IV.3.

[97] See <http://www.ifrs.org>.

[98] See <http://www.rechtspraak.nl> (search term 'Principles of European Contract Law').

[99] HR 13 November 2009, LJN BJ8724 (opinion of Advocate General Huydecoper), para 20.

[100] HR 13 November 2009, LJN BJ8724 (opinion of Advocate General Huydecoper), note 18 (my translation).

The influence of these observations on the deliberations and on the decision of the Hoge Raad is not evident from the judgment, since the judgment was given with the shortened reasoning allowed by section 81 of the Judicial Organisation Act 1827.[101]

3. Comparison

Although the use of non-binding foreign legal materials is not always easily apparent in the published judgments of the highest courts, the interviews clarify that foreign law is studied and discussed and, if not persuasive, at least has a guiding role in the deciding of some domestic cases in the highest courts of the UK and the Netherlands. With regard to the use of non-binding foreign law, an important observation concerns the distinction between the use of materials in judicial deliberations and in the published reasoning of judgments. In the Netherlands, the tradition of the courts is that no citations of foreign case law are included in judgments. However, this does not mean that no foreign sources are considered during the process of discovery of relevant arguments for the decision. Indeed, the experiences of the Dutch judges, described earlier, provide evidence that the highest national courts consult the case law of courts in other jurisdictions more frequently than might be expected on the basis of an analysis of their published judgments. The described examples from the case law of the UK Supreme Court and the two Dutch Courts confirm the outcomes of other research regarding the influence of legal tradition and language in the selection of comparative legal sources.[102] The British judges mention Canadian, US, and Australian case law as important sources of reference. The Dutch judges mention French and German case law. Besides the genealogical relations between legal systems, it seems that the prestige of foreign courts, such as the German Bundesverfassungsgericht and Bundesgerichtshof and the Supreme Courts of Canada and the US, have an influence on judicial approaches. In this regard, the analysis confirms the relation between the size and influence of jurisdictions.[103] The analysis further clarifies that the use of foreign law in the highest courts currently does not seem to follow a specific logic. Examples found in the case law of the courts are few,[104] and the presentation of the practice by the interviewed judges is mostly of an anecdotal nature.

In order to better understand the practices that have developed, we will next focus our attention on the constitutional normative framework for the judicial decision-making of the highest courts. Under what conditions is the use of non-binding foreign law by domestic highest courts legitimate? This part of the analysis will clarify whether the changed judicial practices of the British and Dutch highest courts fit within the existing constitutional frameworks of the two legal systems or whether an adaptation of these frameworks should be considered in light of the evolved legal context for judicial decision-making.

[101] See section II.2. [102] See Gelter and Siems, 'Networks, Dialogue or One-Way Traffic?', n 3.
[103] ibid. [104] ibid.

IV. Constitutional implications

What consequences does the trend of judicial internationalization just described have for the constitutional normative framework concerning the judicial decision-making of the highest courts in the UK and the Netherlands? This section will consider relevant aspects which emerge from our empirical and comparative research and which should be taken into account in efforts to adapt the British and Dutch constitutional frameworks to the needs of the current globalized legal context. Three aspects seem to be involved. Firstly, the research reveals a shifting emphasis in judicial approaches from the formal status of legal sources, based on their democratic legitimation, to the substantive value of legal sources for the deciding of cases. Secondly, legal tradition and the nature of cases are significant factors taken into account by judges when making choices concerning the use of foreign law in judicial decision-making. Finally, the use of foreign law is affected by considerations concerning the effectiveness and efficiency of judicial decision-making. The analysis of these three aspects will enable us to identify the impact of legal and judicial internationalization on the constitutional normative framework regarding the functioning of the highest courts.

1. Democratic justification of judicial decisions

The functioning of the highest national courts in Western legal systems contains a problematic aspect, in the sense that judges in these courts are appointed, not elected. For this reason, the highest courts do not enjoy the direct democratic legitimation of their decisions that national Parliaments have with regard to enacted laws. When considering the judicial use of foreign law, this democratic legitimacy could pose a problem. In particular, the justification of judicial decisions could be endangered by the contestation of the authority of sources consulted by the courts.

The question of the authority of sources for judicial decision-making is more complicated than the positivist distinction between sources which *have* and sources which *have not* been approved as binding sources of domestic law by the competent national authorities. Analyses of judicial approaches in case law, for example concerning the use of foreign law by the US Supreme Court, demonstrate that the authority of legal sources is connected to the development of the use of these sources. In an informal and incremental process, a source will often become less or more binding in proportion to the frequency with which use is made of this source in the judgment of cases.[105]

The underlying issue, in this respect, is whether or not the recourse to foreign legal sources is considered desirable. Arguments in favour of and against the use of foreign law have been formulated by judges, academics, and political actors on the basis of diverse normative points of view. It has been argued that disagreement on this topic can be traced back to attitudes concerning the role of judges, such as pragmatist and legalist views or liberal and conservative views.[106] In the context of the globalized legal

[105] Adams, 'Globaliserende rechtspraak', n 4, 534. See also F Schauer, 'Authority and Authorities' (2008) 94 Virginia Law Review 1931.

[106] Adams, 'Globaliserende rechtspraak', n 4, 535.

context, judicial attitudes concerning the appropriate practices of the highest national courts can be considered to translate into globalist and localist views.[107] Globalist judges focus on the possibilities of finding inspiration in other jurisdictions for the solution of shared legal questions. These judges feel that in hard cases it is their duty to search for the best interpretation of relevant concepts and principles, using all sources which could be relevant for this interpretation.[108] From this perspective, foreign law can provide useful insights and guidance in the search for a solution of domestic cases. By contrast, localist judges take two different views on the use of foreign law. First, they might contest the competence of the national courts to use materials which are not formally binding as a source for judicial decision-making at the domestic level.[109] Secondly, they might point out the limitations of the comparative approach in light of the cultural differences between legal systems.[110] Vicki Jackson has made a further classification by relating the approaches of courts in different jurisdictions concerning the internationalization of judicial decision-making to three different postures: the resistance to global influences; the aspiration of the cross-border convergence of legal rules; and the engagement with foreign legal sources as 'interlocutors' in judicial decision-making.[111] Localist judges can be expected to take a posture of resistance to the use of foreign law, while globalist judges can be expected to represent postures of convergence or engagement.

The empirical research presented in this chapter reveals that none of the interviewed judges in the British and Dutch highest courts are absolutely against the study of foreign law. Indeed, the arguments of judges with a localist view differ. Judges who take an absolutely resistant posture oppose the use of non-binding foreign legal sources on the basis of the absence of formal authority of these sources within the highest court's jurisdiction. US Supreme Court Justice Antonin Scalia, who has expressed his views in dissenting opinions, speeches, and publications, is perhaps the most well-known proponent of this view. He has argued that the citation of foreign law in judicial reasoning cannot be considered to be merely of a supportive nature besides the reasoning based on the national law. In his view, if the Supreme Court acknowledges foreign support for a specific interpretation of the law, it grants to the foreign law the value of an authoritative source for its decision-making.[112] Other localist judges, including several of the interviewed British and Dutch judges, do not contest the use of foreign law in judicial deliberations as such. However, they are doubtful about the guidance which might be derived from the study of foreign law. These judges emphasize that judgments handed down in foreign jurisdictions cannot provide specific solutions for domestic cases, because of the differences between national legal systems

[107] ibid. [108] cf R Dworkin, *Law's Empire* (Hart, Oxford 1998, original edn 1986).

[109] cf HLA Hart, *The Concept of Law* (2nd edn OUP, Oxford 1997).

[110] See, eg M Reimann and R Zimmermann (eds.), *The Oxford Handbook of Comparative Law* (OUP, Oxford 2008); M Adams and J Bomhoff (eds.), *The Theory and Practice of Comparative Law* (CUP, Cambridge 2012). In the field of constitutional law, see R Hirschl, 'The Question of Case Selection in Comparative Constitutional Law' (2005) 53 American Journal of Comparative Law 125.

[111] Jackson, *Constitutional Engagement*, n 1.

[112] See inter alia N Dorsen, 'The Relevance of Foreign Legal Materials in US Constitutional Cases: A Conversation between Justice Antonin Scalia and Justice Stephen Breyer' (2005) International Journal of Constitutional Law 519.

based on the national legal culture. In this respect, the time-consuming nature of comparative legal research might be an additional reason for abstaining from an inquiry into foreign legal sources.

Globalist judges appear in two types. Most of the judges included in this study are not absolutely in favour of striving for convergence with the laws of other countries or with international law. Indeed, and befitting the balanced nature of the judicial function, the majority of the judges seem to have a nuanced approach regarding the use of foreign law in judicial decision-making. These judges fit the posture of engagement with foreign law. The judges expressed different degrees of willingness to engage with global influences. This willingness seems to be related to the perceived usefulness of foreign legal sources in the decision-making in concrete cases. The mentioned limitations of comparative legal research for the judgment of concrete cases echo the criticism expressed by localist judges. However, globalist judges underline the inspiration which foreign concepts and solutions can bring for decision-making in difficult cases and cases of public importance. The yardstick or example provided by foreign case law can help judges to find a solution or support for their decision. The globalist judges feel that this can strengthen the judicial reasoning and enhance the public trust in the court's judgment. Moreover, they are of the opinion that the study of foreign law can assist them in making sure that their standards for decision-making are of the same quality as those of their foreign peers. Finally, the study of foreign law is considered useful for assessing whether a domestic judgment would be following general trends in the development of the law in other Western legal systems. These considerations fit the idea, voiced by John Bell, that the use of foreign law can add force to arguments based on domestic law on the basis of 'a sense of fairness that similar situations should receive similar solutions across legal systems'.[113] While acknowledging that the justification of judgments should still be connected to the domestic law, Bell considers that foreign case law can provide a 'reflecting mirror' which enables a better judicial analysis of the domestic law.[114]

2. Legal tradition and the nature of cases

Concerning legal tradition, it seems that the doctrine of precedent, which is typical for the common law tradition but not for the civil law tradition, has only a limited influence on judicial practices regarding the reference to non-binding foreign case law. Indeed, it appears that most of the interviewed judges, when judging difficult cases, are more concerned with the persuasive force of legal arguments than with the formal source from which these arguments derive. In this sense, the authority of legal sources in the decision-making of the highest courts does not depend so much on the formally binding or non-binding nature of these sources. Rather, judges consider the persuasiveness of legal arguments which were developed in non-binding foreign legal materials, for example, the arguments discussed in the case law of other Western courts regarding a similar legal matter as the domestic case which needs to be decided.

[113] J Bell, 'The Argumentative Status of Foreign Legal Arguments' (2012) 8 Utrecht Law Review 8, 18.
[114] ibid.

Interestingly, a relevant difference between the UK Supreme Court and the Dutch highest courts relates to the style of judicial reasoning. The interviewed Dutch judges pointed out that the citation of case law as such is rare in the judgments of their highest courts. For reasons of tradition and the requirement of a unanimous decision, judgments in this civil law system tend to be relatively short. In this light, the citation of foreign law would be exceptional. Indeed, some interviewed judges felt that the reasoning of a judgment might be weakened because of possible criticism of the highest court's use of foreign law, for example, with regard to the scope and relevance of the legal comparison with other jurisdictions. The citation of foreign legal materials is more easily accepted in the UK Supreme Court, which stands in the tradition of law development through case law and which permits individual judges to issue their own opinion on cases. A question of concern amongst judges in this Court is the question of whether a presentation of foreign law in the court's reasoning should consist of a 'full' discussion of all materials found or whether the court is allowed to mention only those foreign references which support its own decision. British judges have indicated that they do not find the latter approach problematic. They differ, in this respect, from some of their American colleagues who have criticized the use of foreign law if it consists of 'cherry picking'.[115] Still, the British judges seem to agree with their transatlantic peers on the point that the discussion of foreign law in judicial deliberations should be as comprehensive as possible.

Finally, legal tradition plays a role in the selection of non-binding foreign legal materials for comparison by a specific highest national court. The genealogical relation between the legal system of the UK and other common law systems, such as Canada and the United States, makes it more natural for the UK Supreme Court to look to these systems for inspiration than to legal systems which do not share this British origin. The exchange between courts in these jurisdictions, furthermore, is made easier by their shared language. The Dutch highest courts, by contrast, most often study foreign sources which originated in other civil law jurisdictions. The Dutch courts consider that the French and German influences in the Dutch legal system provide reasons for looking to these systems first when engaging in a comparative legal study. Besides language, all interviewed judges also take into account the prestige of specific foreign courts when selecting case law for a legal comparison.

The interviews clarified that the nature of cases plays a role in the judicial use of foreign law, too. The study of foreign law can be a requirement in cases in a specific field of law, such as international private law cases or extradition cases. However, the use of foreign law is certainly not restricted to cases which by their nature require of judges to engage in such an exercise. Many of the interviewed judges pointed out the usefulness of a comparative analysis of non-binding foreign legal materials for the judgment of difficult cases, in which no precedent existed in the national legal system. The examples from case law, presented in section III, give further insight into the rich palette of cases in which judges in the highest courts examined in this chapter have

[115] Consider for example the views of the Chief Justice of the US Supreme Court: 'Confirmation Hearing on the Nomination of John G. Roberts, Jr. to be Chief Justice of the United States', available at <http://www.gpo.gov>.

made use of both binding and non-binding foreign law. At the same time, the interviews clarify that so far no systematic approach has been developed with regard to the use of comparative legal sources in the judicial decision-making of the highest courts.

3. The effectiveness and efficiency of judicial decision-making

It can be argued that the use of non-binding foreign law by the highest national courts might have a negative effect on the effectiveness and efficiency of the decision-making of these courts.[116] After all, the research of foreign legal sources and the discussion of these sources in judicial deliberations might not yield arguments which are essential to the deciding of the case. Furthermore, this research might be time-consuming. Still, the effectiveness of the judicial decision-making could increase if the research of foreign law yields substantial input for the deciding of a case. Besides these considerations of principle, it is likely that the possibilities for the highest courts to engage in the study of foreign law will be limited by practical constraints. Such constraints may concern the knowledge of foreign languages, the access to foreign legal sources, and the availability of assistance with the conduct of comparative legal research.

Indeed, the interviews confirmed that judges take into account the costs, in terms of time spent on the research and study of foreign legal materials, and the benefits of this exercise, in terms of useful concepts and arguments for their decision in a domestic case. The research provides helpful information to add further nuance to this conclusion.

The costs of the comparative exercise, first, vary for judges depending on: (1) the assistance which they can make use of for this research; (2) their personal affinity with and ability to conduct comparative legal research; and (3) the accessibility of foreign legal sources, for example, through databases, judicial networks, and personal contacts. The availability of judicial assistance differs between the highest courts examined, as do the possibilities of commissioning universities to carry out comparative legal research. An important distinction exists between the proceedings before the UK Supreme Court, in which the legal counsel of a party has an important responsibility in bringing the relevant legal sources to the attention of the court, and the proceedings before the highest courts of the Netherlands, in which the judges themselves and Advocates General have a role in the research of relevant legal materials for the deciding of the case. The ability of judges to conduct comparative research, and the accessibility of sources, are related to the legal training and experience of the judges as well as to their involvement in transnational judicial exchanges. In sum, both organizational and personal factors in the highest courts have an influence on the costs of using comparative law in judicial decision-making.

[116] On the notions of 'effectiveness' and 'efficiency' in relation to the functioning of judicial systems, see E Mak, *De rechtspraak in balans* (Wolf Legal Publishing, Nijmegen 2007). See also GY Ng, *Quality of Judicial Organisation and Checks and Balances* (Intersentia, Antwerp 2007); D Piana, *Judicial Accountabilities in New Europe: From Rule of Law to Quality of Justice* (Ashgate, Farnham 2010).

Concerning the benefits of the study of non-binding foreign law, a clear relation exists with the postures of judges concerning the role of their highest court in the globalized legal context.[117] Globalist judges consider the study of foreign law to be more useful for their court's decision-making than localist judges. For this reason, depending on personal affinity and ability, globalist judges will engage in the study of foreign law more readily than their localist counterparts. Interestingly, the approaches of judges of a similar mind but working in different highest courts might be closer to each other than the approaches of two judges at the same highest court but holding opposite views on the usefulness of the study of foreign law.

4. An evolving constitutional normative framework

The justification of judicial decisions, legal tradition and the nature of cases, and the effectiveness and efficiency of judicial decision-making are all significant factors in the developing practices of the British and Dutch highest courts concerning the use of foreign law. The analysis of these changing judicial practices provides insight into a process of incremental constitutional change related to the internationalization of the law.

The most significant change at the normative level, in particular for courts functioning in the civil law tradition, concerns the slow but steady shift from a formal-positivist approach to the use of legal sources to an approach based on the substance of legal sources. This shift can be understood in light of the more general trend of legal globalization and the dissolution of national legal borders which is caused by this trend. US Supreme Court Justice Stephen Breyer, discussing the impact of international and foreign law on his professional life, has observed about this development:

> For one thing, my description blurs the differences between what my law professors used to call comparative law and public international law. That refusal to distinguish (at least for present purposes) may simply reflect reality. The commercial law of various States, for example, has become close to a single, unified body of law, in part through the work of uniform state law commissioners, in part through a pattern of similar judicial responses to similar problems, in part because of the work of intermediate judicial institutions such as federal bankruptcy courts, in part because the interstate nature of commercial contracts means that judges in different states apply each other's law. Formally speaking, state law is state law. But practically speaking, much of that law is national, if not international in scope. Analogous developments internationally, including the development of regional or specialised international legal bodies, also tend to produce cross-country results that resemble each other more and more, exhibiting common, if not universal, principles in various legal areas.[118]

This observation reveals the inadequacy of traditional state-oriented constitutions to capture the current relations between national, binding international and non-binding

[117] See section IV.1.

[118] S Breyer, 'The Supreme Court and the New International Law' (American Society of International Law, Washington, DC, 4 April 2003).

foreign legal rules. The substance of legal rules is increasingly converging, both vertically between national and international legal orders and horizontally between national legal orders. In this respect, the distinction between dualist and monist mechanisms for the implementation of international law in national legal systems is becoming less important. Still, the traditional openness of the Dutch monist system might have paved the way for the current willingness of many judges of the Hoge Raad and the Afdeling bestuursrechtspraak to consider foreign legal sources. These judges have been educated and they have built up judicial experience in a system which places a high responsibility on judges concerning the establishment of the relationship between international and national legal rules. Whereas Justice Breyer's statement might give rise to debate in the dualist US legal system,[119] many of the interviewed Dutch judges would not seem to have any problem in accepting his description of the globalized legal context. In the UK, the connections between legal systems in the framework of the Commonwealth make it natural for judges to consider themselves as part of a transnational legal community. Moreover, the strict separation made by the UK's dualist system between the international and domestic legal orders has been nuanced in a very significant manner by the incorporation of the ECHR[120] into the domestic law and the interaction of the UK Supreme Court with the ECtHR concerning the interpretation of Convention rights.[121]

This openness of the British and Dutch judges to engage with legal rules developed outside of the national legal system further seems to be connected with the involvement of the UK and the Netherlands in the process of legal integration within the EU. While this process aims at the harmonization of national laws within the European legal context, it respects the fundamental differences between the national constitutions of the EU Member States. This recognition of constitutional pluralism enables national courts to engage in a dialogue with the CJEU, steering clear from the traditional emphasis on the vertical relation between the Member States and the supranational legal order.[122] In a similar way, the 'global community of courts', as described by Anne-Marie Slaughter,[123] finds its legitimacy in the recognition of shared fundamental values from which judges can derive inspiration for the judgment of domestic cases, and the simultaneous recognition of national cultural differences which delimit the scope of useful comparative exercises. Concerning this relative usefulness, the research clarifies

[119] Concerning the debate amongst US Supreme Court Justices regarding the use of foreign law in judicial decision-making, see N Dorsen, 'The Relevance of Foreign Legal Materials in US Constitutional Cases: A Conversation between Justice Antonin Scalia and Justice Stephen Breyer' (2005) 3 International Journal of Constitutional Law 519; MA Waters, 'Creeping Monism: The Judicial Trend toward Interpretive Incorporation of Human Rights Treaties' (2007) 107 Columbia Law Review 628.

[120] Concerning this reform, see eg A Kavanagh, *Constitutional Review under the UK Human Rights Act* (CUP, Cambridge 2009); T Hickman, *Public Law after the Human Rights Act* (Hart, Oxford 2010).

[121] Concerning this interaction, and the British and Dutch public debates about the legitimacy of the ECtHR's judgments, see JH Gerards and JWA Fleuren (eds.), *Implementation of the European Convention on Human Rights and of the Judgments of the ECtHR in National Case Law: A Comparative Analysis* (Intersentia, Antwerp 2014).

[122] See in this respect A Torres Pérez, *Conflicts of Rights in the European Union: A Theory of Supranational Adjudication* (OUP, Oxford 2009); M Avbelj and J Komarek (eds.), *Constitutional Pluralism in the European Union and Beyond* (Hart, Oxford 2011).

[123] A-M Slaughter, 'A Global Community of Courts' (2003) 44 Harvard International Law Journal 191.

that the recourse to foreign law is considered by judges more readily if a shared legal framework exists because of historical ties with another legal system, or if the nature of the case to be decided invites a legal comparison.

V. Concluding remarks

The interviews with judges in the Supreme Courts of the UK and the Netherlands reveal that foreign law plays an increasingly important role in the judicial decision-making of these highest national courts. Ever more often, judges use non-binding foreign legal materials as a source of inspiration, and sometimes also to find additional supporting arguments for the decision in a specific case. In this chapter, it has been shown which views and approaches to the use of foreign law can be identified in the British and Dutch highest courts. By relating the interviews to the relevant case law and other available public information, a picture emerged of evolving judicial views and practices in the highest national courts of a large common law jurisdiction and a small civil law jurisdiction. In addition to the established literature on the judicial use of foreign law, the chapter in particular makes visible the variety of views within specific highest courts and the lack of a systematic approach to the use of foreign legal materials.

The analysis further clarifies that the constitutional normative framework for judicial decision-making in the British and Dutch highest courts is evolving. The judicial practices of the UK Supreme Court, the Hoge Raad, and the Afdeling bestuursrechtspraak reflect acknowledgment of the increasing intertwinement of legal orders and the search for a judicial approach which fits with this globalized legal context. This approach seems to have been found in an increased emphasis on the persuasiveness of legal arguments rather than on the source from which these arguments originate. Concerning the use of non-binding foreign law, which is considered to have supporting rather than controlling value in judicial decision-making, no formal constitutional arrangements seem to be required. The developed judicial approaches and the views expressed by the interviewed judges in the British and Dutch courts reveal a careful and nuanced reflection. Domestic law still remains the basis for all judicial decisions. Further judicial exchanges and academic debates can facilitate the development of a methodology of comparative legal research for the benefit of judicial decision-making, and clarify the argumentative possibilities for the use of foreign legal sources in the legal reasoning of judgments.

PART VI

COMPARATIVE LAW BEFORE GENERAL COURTS

23

Constructing the 'Foreign'

American Law's Relationship to Non-Domestic Sources

*Judith Resnik**

> No decisions in law or equity in Great Britain after July 4, 1776 'shall be received or read in any court of law or equity' as 'law or evidence of the law, or elucidation or explanation thereof.'[1]
>
> New Jersey, Act of June 13, 1799, § 5

> No treaty or executive agreement shall be made respecting the rights of citizens of the United States protected by this Constitution.[2]
>
> The Bricker Amendment, 1952

> Neither the Supreme Court of the United States nor any lower Federal court shall, in the purported exercise of judicial power to interpret and apply the Constitution of the United States, employ the constitution, laws, administrative rules, executive orders, directives, policies, or judicial decisions of any international organization or foreign state, except for the English constitutional and common law or other sources of law relied upon by the Framers of the Constitution of the United States.[3]
>
> The Proposed American Justice for American Citizens Act of 2004

> It is beyond comprehension why we should look . . . to a country . . . with . . . a legal, political, and social culture quite different from our own.[4]
>
> Justice Antonin Scalia, *Roper v. Simmons* (2005)(dissenting)

> Any court, arbitration, tribunal or administrative agency ruling or decision shall violate the public policy of this state and be void and unenforceable if the court, arbitration, tribunal or administrative agency bases its ruling or decisions in the

* Arthur Liman Professor of Law, Yale Law School. Thanks to Susan Rose-Ackerman for prompting this essay, to Duncan Fairgrieve for his invitation to turn the essay into a chapter and his thoughtful review of its claims, to Bruce Ackerman, Joseph Blocher, Martha Davis, Vicki Jackson, Johanna Kalb, Marty Lederman, David Nachman, Kim Scheppele, Reva Siegel, and Denny Curtis for discussions on these topics, to the indefatigable Yale law librarian Michael Van der Heijden, and for insightful and able research help to Mathew Andrews, Caitlin Bellis, Jason Bertoldi, James Dawson, Daniel Hessel, Mark Kelley, Bilyana Petkova, Devon Porter, Bonnie Posick, Megan Wachspress, Jonas Wang, Benjamin Woodring, and Mary Yanik.

[1] Act of June 13, 1799, § 5, 1799 N.J. Laws 435–6, *superseded by* Act Relative to Foreign Reports, 1811 N. J. Laws 81–82 (re-enacting the prohibition on reference to British law and additionally penalizing violators with a one-year suspension), *repealed* May 25, 1820, Acts of the 44th General Assembly of the State of New Jersey, at 126–27 (1820).

[2] S.J. Res. 130, 82d Cong. (1952), *reprinted in* Duane Tananbaum, *The Bricker Amendment Controversy: A Test of Eisenhower's Political Leadership* 222 (1988).

[3] H.R. 4118, 108th Cong. (2004). The bill was introduced by Representatives Ron Paul, Republican representing Texas, and Marilyn Musgrave, Republican representing Colorado.

[4] *Roper v Simmons*, 543 U.S. 551, 626–7 (2005) (Scalia, J., dissenting).

> matter at issue in whole or in part on any foreign law, legal code or system that would not grant the parties affected by the ruling or decision the same fundamental liberties, rights and privileges granted under the United States and Kansas Constitutions.
>
> Kansas, House Substitute for Senate, Bill No. 79, enacted May 2012

The opening quotations track a vivid narrative in the United States about the use of non-United States law. Justices on the Supreme Court have written opinions objecting to non-domestic sources, and legislators have proposed statutes and constitutional amendments enjoining government officials from relying on foreign sources.

But a counter-narrative exists, which is central to this chapter. America is a country of migrants, as is our law.[5] The construction of law as 'domestic' or 'foreign' and the attachment of positive or negative valences take place in many venues, national and subnational, shaping 'American' understandings of its own production of and nexus to law. Borders are porous, and various routes serve to domesticate as well as exile 'foreign' law. Indeed, the reason I have placed 'foreign' in quotes is to underscore the work entailed in that branding and to invite interrogation of the choices made when labelling law domestic or foreign.

This chapter explores various routes through which Americanization and 'foreignization' (to offer an awkward but parallel locution) take place. I analyse how foreign sources have been acknowledged, embraced, ignored, and ostracized[6] to show both the impossibility of avoiding foreign sources in a legal system built on liberal federalism principles and the irresistibility, in a networked age, of learning from and being influenced by foreign law.

Yet debate continues, as new bans are proposed on using non-domestic sources. Therefore, more examination is needed of when and why courts, the executive branch, and legislatures at national, state, and local levels look abroad—either to welcome foreign sources or to preclude them. To probe the role played by directives to judges on what legal sources to use, I address not only the contemporary prohibitions but also whether mandates to *require* judges to consider foreign law would be constitutional. My questions include whether the U.S. Constitution itself invites or prohibits foreign law and whether theories about constitutional structure and the allocation of powers among branches in the federated government make judges subject to, or immune from, directions on the sources to consult when rendering judgments.

As I detail, a thicket of case law exists, which puts judges to the task of parsing competing lines of doctrine—on separation of powers, judicial independence, due process, the First Amendment, and federalism—so as to decide the scope of authority of common law judges in state and federal systems. As the many opinions reflect, conceptions of the judicial role are embedded in transnational histories, practices, and

[5] In a related essay, I examine the permeability of the physical borders of the country, of federal and state law, and of the law of the citizen and the alien. See Judith Resnik, 'Bordering by Law: The Migration of Law, Crimes, Sovereignty, and the Mail' *in NOMOS LVI: Immigration and Emigration* (Jack Knight ed., forthcoming 2015).

[6] The competing themes in American discourse are examined in Rogers M. Smith, *Civic Ideals: Conflicting Visions of Citizenship in U.S. History* (1997).

doctrine. By exploring the legality of legislative directives on judging, I illustrate that judicial agency is unavoidable, as judges have a host of choices when interpreting the parameters of the Constitution. In short, the turn to foreign sources is neither exotic nor intrinsically less disciplined than looking at other resources.

This chapter has another purpose, which is to reflect on the relationship of using foreign sources to the grounding of the United States's identity in legal commitments. 'Sovereignty' is one term capturing the political effort to make a community into a unified legal force. Directing judges to use certain legal sources is a means of locating sovereign identity in law. But one can delineate identity through law without insisting on the exclusivity of a national legal regime. My hope is to undo an equation of a sovereigntist stance with isolationism. To do so, I sketch how, in the name of its legal system, the United States could—as some legal systems currently do—insist on its own individuated legal identity even when requiring consideration of external sources. In short, to appreciate a role for the 'foreign' does not necessarily result in diminution of the United States as a liberal constitutional order, reliant on its law as a source of identity and of affiliation.

I. Incorporating 'foreign' law

> ... nor shall any state deprive any person of life, liberty, or property, without due process of law.
>
> U.S. Const. amend. XIV, § 1 (1868)

> The dignity of the human being is inviolable. No person shall be denied equal protection of the laws.
>
> Constitution, State of Montana, art. II, § 4 (1972)

> The Board of Supervisors of the City and County of San Francisco hereby finds and declares as follows:
>
> 'The Convention on the Elimination of All Forms of Discrimination Against Women [CEDAW], an international human rights treaty, provides a universal definition of discrimination against women and brings attention to a whole range of issues concerning women's human rights...
>
> The City shall work towards integrating gender equity and human rights principles into all of its operations, including policy, program and budgetary decision-making. The Commission shall train selected departments in human rights with a gender perspective.'
>
> Section 12.K.4. Implementation of the Principles of CEDAW, adopted 1998

> The department shall consider chemicals listed as a suspected carcinogen, reproductive or developmental toxicant, or as being persistent, bioaccumulative, and toxic...by a state, federal, or international agency. These agencies may include, but are not limited to, the California Environmental Protection Agency, the Washington Department of Ecology, the United States Department of Health, the United States Environmental Protection Agency, the United Nation's World Health Organization, and European Parliament Annex XIV concerning the Registration, Evaluation, Authorization, and Restriction of Chemicals.
>
> Minn. Stat. 2009 § 116.9402

These quotations illustrate different routes through which foreign law makes its way into the United States. Because debates in the United States about the propriety of using foreign law often gloss over distinctions among forms of law, I use the term foreign law to include international treaties to which the United States is a party (some of which Congress has implemented domestically), treaties that the United States has not ratified, international customary law, and law from other countries.[7] My focus is less on the various methods of putting foreign law to work inside judicial opinions and more on the legality and sociology of using foreign sources.[8]

The relevant actors and the modes of exchange are diverse. Those serving as conduits for law's migration range across the branches of government, the tiers in the federation, and the public and private sectors. Some of their efforts to bring international and comparative law 'home' are express and others unacknowledged, and, at times, the non-domestic roots of the legal principles advanced may not be known. Because the arenas of law in which foreign materials play a part involve both civil and criminal law, affect constitutional and statutory provisions, and a host of topics, a brief tour of various venues for and methods of importing foreign law is in order.

1. Framing constitutional commitments

Federal constitutional law is, today, a visible site of conflict about the role to be played by non-domestic law.[9] Yet, unself-conscious examples of incorporation of non-U.S. law are plentiful. One place to begin is with the text, 'due process of law', often positioned (proudly) as a particularly 'American' statement of our law's best aspirations. But wrapping oneself in these words should not obscure that they (like the colours on the American flag) came from transnational exchanges about people's relationship to government.

The phrase 'due process of law', found in the Fifth Amendment of 1791 and in the Fourteenth Amendment of 1868, was borrowed from England and France and made its way through early state constitutions into the national discourse. As the historian Charles Miller documented, the words 'the law of the land' ('per legem terrae') can be traced to Chapter 39 of the English Magna Carta of 1215.[10] The term 'process of law' ('process de ley') stems from a French phrase in an English legal document of the 14th century, which helped to produce the words 'by due process of law' in the reissued 1354 Magna Carta.

[7] In contrast to my approach, a recent study of the use of foreign law focused only on explicit citations by constitutional courts. See *The Use of Foreign Precedents by Constitutional Judges* 6–7 (Tania Groppi and Marie-Claire Ponthoreau eds., 2013).

[8] See, e.g., Damiano Canale, 'Comparative Reasoning in Legal Adjudication', Bocconi University Legal Studies Research Paper Series, 2014, SSRN 2466552.

[9] My focus is on citations in federal courts; examples abound of state court use of non-U.S. law. See, e.g., *Commonwealth v Gautreaux*, 458 Mass. 741 (2011); *In re Marriage Cases*, 183 P.3d 384 (Cal. 2008). See *generally* Martha Davis, 'The Spirit of Our Times: State Constitutions and International Human Rights', 30 N.Y.U. Rev. L. & Soc. Change 359 (2006); Margaret H. Marshall, '"Wise Parents Do Not Hesitate to Learn From Their Children": Interpreting State Constitutions in an Age of Global Jurisprudence', 79 N.Y.U. L. Rev. 1633 (2004).

[10] Charles A. Miller, 'The Forest of Due Process Law', *in NOMOS XVIII: Due Process* 3–12 (J. Roland Pennock and John W. Chapman eds., 1977).

The 1776 Constitution of Virginia picked up Blackstone's elaborations when it required that 'no man be deprived of his liberty, except by the law of the land or the judgment of his peers',[11] a locution that was then common. Miller argued that the selection of the phrase 'due process of law' for the federal Constitution aimed to protect individuals from arbitrary government decision-making.[12] Major renovations of the meaning of 'due process' came during the 20th century when justices read the words (over dissents) not only to require conformity with legally prescribed procedures but also to license independent assessments of the quality of legislative and executive procedural directives.[13]

More generally, historians describe the U.S. Constitution as an 'international document', drafted with foreign sovereigns as a source of pressure for restructuring the confederated government and as an important audience for the result.[14] The founding generation was imbued in the ideologies of the European Enlightenment; even when seeking to generate a government with sufficient girth to compete with Europe, the drafters shared many political and legal precepts with their counterparts across the Atlantic.[15] A parallel in the 21st century is the South African Constitution, which describes its aim to use law to join the 'family of nations'.[16] Similarly, the U.S. Constitution of 1789 aspired to help the young country gain recognition as a 'civilized state', worthy of equal respect in the international community.[17] Using the Constitution to affiliate with the 'law of nations', the drafters shaped institutional structures, such as the jurisdiction given to life-tenured federal judges, to help insulate those responsible for enforcing treaties from anti-foreign sentiments held by some sectors of the population.[18]

2. Dignity domesticated

A more recent example of the effects of non-U.S. law on constitutional interpretation comes from the incorporation of dignity into Supreme Court interpretation of the U.S. Bill of Rights.[19] Even as concepts linked to dignity were implicit in the founding

[11] Va. Const. of 1776, art 1, § 8. [12] Miller, n 10, at 3, 4–5.

[13] I explore the development and debates about due process in Judith Resnik, 'Fairness in Numbers: A Comment on *AT&T v Concepcion, Wal-Mart v Dukes*, and *Turner v Rogers*', 125 Harv. L. Rev. 78 (2011); and in Judith Resnik, 'Constitutional Entitlements to and in Courts: Remedial Rights in an Age of Egalitarianism: The Childress Lecture', 56 St. Louis U. L.J. 916 (2012).

[14] David M. Golove and Daniel J. Hulsebosch, 'A Civilized Nation: The Early American Constitution, the Law of Nations, and the Pursuit of International Recognition', 85 N.Y.U. L. Rev. 923, 924–46 (2010). See Vicki C. Jackson, *Constitutional Engagement in a Transnational Era* 6–8, 257–79 (2010).

[15] References to foreign law are sprinkled throughout the Federalist Papers. See David J. Seipp, 'Our Law, Their Law, History, and the Citation of Foreign Law', 86 Boston U. L. Rev. 1417, 1429 (2006). Seipp counted 504 references to foreign places; 154 were to the British Isles. Ibid. at n. 68.

[16] The Constitution of the Republic of South Africa, 1996 pmbl., provides:
'We, the people of South Africa ... adopt this Constitution ... so as to ... establish a society based on democratic values, social justice and fundamental human rights ... and build a united and democratic South Africa able to take its rightful place as a sovereign state in the family of nations.'

[17] Golove and Hulsebosch, n 14, at 935.

[18] Golove and Hulsebosch, n 14, at 981–8; 993–5; 1001–10.

[19] This discussion builds on Judith Resnik and Julie Chi-hye Suk, 'Adding Insult to Injury: Questioning the Role of Dignity in Conceptions of Sovereignty', 55 Stan. L. Rev. 1921 (2003).

commitments to liberty and equality, the 1789 Constitution did not use that term.[20] That absence is not surprising; dignity was not an attribute ascribed in the 18th century to all persons but was, in Western legal traditions, largely reserved for nobility and for government and religious authorities.[21]

That understanding of dignity is reflected in the volumes of the U.S. Supreme Court's reporters.[22] The word can be found hundreds of times—used during the 18th, 19th, and early 20th centuries, as opinions refer to dignity in discussions of nations,[23] states,[24] and of legal institutions such as courts[25] and their judges.[26]

That usage persists. Justices continue to discuss the 'peace and dignity' of the state.[27] Indeed, it was the invocation in the 1990s of dignity as a rationale for expanding state sovereign immunity that sparked my interest in the term's deployment.[28] In rulings limiting the capacity of individuals to enforce federal rights against states, justices regularly concluded that permitting such damage actions would undermine states' dignity.[29]

In contrast to the centuries of constitutional concern for the dignity of institutions, the attention paid to individual dignity is of more recent vintage. Not until the 1940s did justices on the U.S. Supreme Court turn to the vocabulary of dignity to explain the constitutional protections accorded to individuals. The link between humans and dignity appeared first in 1942 and 1943 in relation to criminal defendants' rights to counsel[30] and detained individuals' rights to be brought before a neutral third party.[31] As Justice Felix Frankfurter explained in 1943, an arrested person had to be taken promptly before a

[20] Gerald L. Neuman, 'Human Dignity in United States Constitutional Law', *in Zur Autonomie Des Individuums: Liber Amicorum for Spiros Simitis* 249 (Dieter Simon and Manfred Weiss eds., 2000).

[21] See, e.g., James Q. Whitman, 'Enforcing Civility and Respect: Three Societies', 109 Yale L.J. 1279 (2000) (arguing that the protection of dignity in Germany and France derives not only from post-World War II concerns for human rights but also from aristocratic cultures grounded in hierarchy).

[22] Resnik and Suk, n 19, at 1933–34; about two-thirds of the 900 references to dignity as of 2003 were written in the Court's decisions of the 20th century.

[23] See, e.g., *Bas v Tingy*, 4 U.S. (4 Dall.) 37, 39 (1800) (commenting that references to nations as '*enemies*' serves the 'honour and dignity of both nations').

[24] See, e.g., *Chisholm v Georgia*, 2 U.S. (2 Dall.) 419, 451 (1793) (discussing the immunity of a state from suit).

[25] See, e.g., *Green v Lessee of Neal*, 31 U.S. (6 Pet.) 291, 298 (1832) (finding that local statutes revising Supreme Court rulings would be inconsistent with the 'dignity of this tribunal').

[26] See, e.g., *Ex parte Milligan*, 71 U.S. (4 Wall.) 2, 39 (1866) (referring to the 'dignity and independence of the judges').

[27] See, e.g., *Tenn. Student Assistance Corp. v Hood*, 541 U.S. 440, 460 (2004) (Thomas, J., dissenting, joined by Scalia, J.) (arguing that a limited in rem exception to state sovereignty in bankruptcy could permit a proceeding to be 'resolved by motion without offending the dignity of the State'); *United States v Lara*, 541 U.S. 193, 197 (2004) (stating that, when an individual commits an act that 'violates the "peace and dignity" of two sovereigns', prosecutions are permissible by each).

[28] See, e.g., *Alden v Maine*, 527 U.S. 706 (1999); see also Daniel J. Meltzer, 'State Sovereign Immunity: Five Authors in Search of a Theory', 75 Notre Dame L. Rev. 1011, 1037–41 (2000).

[29] See, e.g., *Shelby County, Alabama v Holder*, 133 S. Ct. 2612, 2623 (2013); *Sossamon v Texas*, 131 S. Ct. 1651, 1657–8 (2011).

[30] *Glasser v United States*, 315 U.S. 60, 89 (1942) (Frankfurter, J., dissenting).

[31] *McNabb v United States*, 318 U.S. 332 (1943). The phrase 'human dignity' first appears in the text of a Supreme Court opinion in 1946. See *In re Yamashita*, 327 U.S. 1, 29 (1946) (Murphy, J., dissenting) ('[i]f we are ever to develop an orderly international community based upon a recognition of human dignity it is of the utmost importance that the necessary punishment of those guilty of atrocities be as free as possible from the ugly stigma of revenge and vindictiveness').

committing authority because a 'democratic society, in which respect for the dignity of all men is central, naturally guards against the misuse of the law enforcement process.'[32]

The context for such concerns was fascism and World War II. In the aftermath, the 1948 Universal Declaration of Human Rights (UDHR) begins with the recognition of the 'inherent dignity' of all people.[33] Many other transnational agreements followed with express commitments to human dignity, including the International Covenant on Economic, Social and Cultural Rights (ICESCR),[34] the International Covenant on Civil and Political Rights (ICCPR),[35] the International Convention on the Elimination of All Forms of Racial Discrimination (CERD),[36] and the Convention on the Elimination of All Forms of Discrimination Against Women (CEDAW).[37] Most national constitutions or Basic Laws drafted during the second half of the 20th century also invoke dignity.[38]

In addition to the case law, dignity entered U.S. constitutional discourse through the constitutions of its subparts that were enacted or amended after World War II. For example, the 1952 Constitution of Puerto Rico states that the 'dignity of the human being is inviolable'; the 1967 Constitution of American Samoa provides that the 'dignity of the individual shall be respected'.[39] Further, as quoted at the opening of this section, in 1972 Montana amended its constitution to provide that the 'dignity of the human being is inviolable', when it also specified that rights of 'equal protection of the laws' protected individuals from discrimination by either the state or 'any person, firm, corporation, or institution' on the basis of 'race, color, sex, culture, social origin or condition, or political or religious ideas'.[40]

Louisiana followed in 1974 by labelling a section of its constitution the 'Right to Individual Dignity', even as the word does not appear in the text that follows, guaranteeing equal protection and prohibiting 'slavery and involuntary servitude'.[41] Dignity gained more widespread currency in state constitutions with a wave of amendments in the 1970s and 1980s providing rights for crime victims. More than a

[32] *McNabb v United States*, 318 U.S. 332, 343 (1943).

[33] The 'recognition of the inherent dignity and of the equal and inalienable rights of all members of the human family is the foundation of freedom, justice and peace in the world.' Universal Declaration of Human Rights, G.A. Res. 217 (III) A, U.N. Doc. A/RES/217(III), at 71 (Dec. 10, 1948, Preamble). The first article states: 'All human beings are born free and equal in dignity and rights.' Ibid. at 72.

[34] International Covenant on Economic, Social and Cultural Rights, 16 Dec. 1966, S. Treaty Doc. No. 95-19, 6 I.L.M. 360 (adopted 1966; effective 1976), 993 U.N.T.S. 3.

[35] International Covenant on Civil and Political Rights, S. Treaty Doc. No. 95-20, 6 I.L.M. 368 (adopted 1966; effective 1976), 999 U.N.T.S. 171.

[36] International Convention on the Elimination of All Forms of Racial Discrimination, S. Treaty Doc. No. 95-2 (adopted 1965; effective 1969), 660 U.N.T.S. 195.

[37] Convention on the Elimination of All Forms of Discrimination Against Women, S. Treaty Doc. No. 95-2 (adopted 1979; effective 1981), 1249 U.N.T.S. 13.

[38] For example, in 1949, Germany adopted the Basic Rights of Persons in the Basic Law of Germany; '(1) The dignity of man is inviolable. To respect and protect it is the duty of all state authority.' Grundgesetz für die Bundesrepublik Deutschland [Grundgesetz] [GG] [Basic Law], May 23, 1949, BGBl. I (Ger.), art. 1. In 1992, Israel adopted a Basic Law on Human Dignity and Liberty; Section 2 declares: 'There shall be no violation of the life, body or dignity of any person as such'; Section 4 entitles all persons to the protection of 'their life, body, and dignity'. Basic Law on Human Dignity and Liberty, SH No. 1391 (3/25/1992), HC p. 60 (Isr.).

[39] See P.R. Const. art. 2, § 1; Am. Samoa Const. art. 1, § 4.

[40] See Mont. Const. art. 2, § 4 (1972).

[41] La. Const. art. 1, § 3 (1974).

dozen states added formulations for victims to be 'treated with dignity' and to participate in criminal proceedings.[42]

Returning to the jurisprudence of the U.S. Supreme Court, since the second half of the 20th century, justices have regularly relied on dignity to explicate the import of the Bill of Rights. Personal dignity has played a role in discussions of the First Amendment protection of religious freedom,[43] the Fourth Amendment right to be free from unreasonable searches and seizures,[44] and the Fifth Amendment shelter against coercive interrogations.[45]

Dignity is at the centre of Eighth Amendment jurisprudence explicating the prohibition on cruel and unusual punishment as it relates to treatment in prisons[46] and to the death penalty.[47] Indeed, when deciding that a conviction for desertion could not serve as the basis for a loss of citizenship, the Supreme Court explained that the core premise of the Eighth Amendment prohibition on cruel and unusual punishment was 'the dignity of man'.[48] Chief Justice Earl Warren reasoned that, to render a person stateless would be to strip 'the citizen of his status in the national and international community', and thereby was 'offensive to the cardinal principles for which the Constitution stands'.[49]

Personal dignity is also regularly linked to equal protection, liberty, and due process under the Fourteenth Amendment.[50] As Justice Anthony Kennedy explained for the majority in *Lawrence v Texas*, states cannot make criminal the act of same-sex sodomy because 'adults may choose to enter upon this relationship in the confines of their homes and their own private lives and still retain their dignity as free persons'.[51] In his decision in *United States v Windsor*, finding the congressional refusal to recognize same-sex

[42] States adopting victims' rights amendments include Alaska, Arizona, Idaho, Illinois, Louisiana, Maryland, Michigan, Mississippi, New Mexico, Ohio, Oklahamo, Oregon, Rhode Island, South Carolina, Texas, Virgina, Washington, and Wisconsin. See generally Alice Koskela, 'Victims' Rights Amendments: An Irresistible Political Force Transforms the Criminal Justice System', 34 Idaho L. Rev. 157 (1997).

[43] *Elk Grove Unified Sch. Dist. v Newdow*, 542 U.S. 1, 41 (2004) (O'Connor, J., concurring) (discussing how to 'acknowledge the religious origins of our Nation's belief in the "individuality and the dignity of the human being"' (citation omitted)).

[44] *E.g., United States v Flores-Montano*, 541 U.S. 149, 152 (2004) (concluding that the 'dignity and privacy interests of the person being searched' was not undermined in a vehicle search).

[45] *E.g., Chavez v Martinez*, 538 U.S. 760, 774 (2003) (discussing whether questioning was 'so offensive to human dignity' as to violate due process (quoting *Rochin v California*, 342 U.S. 165, 172 (1952))).

[46] *E.g., Hope v Pelzer*, 536 U.S. 730, 745 (2002) (identifying an Eighth Amendment violation when prison guards tied an inmate to a hitching post for hours, an action called 'antithetical to human dignity'); *Brown v Plata*, 131 S. Ct. 1910, 1928 (2011) ('The basic concept underlying the Eighth Amendment is nothing less than the dignity of man.') (quoting *Atkins v Virginia*, 536 U.S. 304, 311 (2002)).

[47] *E.g., Roper v Simmons*, 543 U.S. 551, 560 (2005) (commenting that by 'protecting even those convicted of heinous crimes, the Eighth Amendment reaffirms the duty of the government to respect the dignity of all persons').

[48] *Trop v Dulles*, 356 U.S. 86, 100 (1958). See generally Patrick Weil, *The Sovereign Citizen: Denaturalization and the Origins of the American Republic* (2012).

[49] *Trop*, at 101–2.

[50] See *Tennessee v Lane*, 541 U.S. 509, 537 (2004) (Ginsburg, J., concurring, joined by Souter and Breyer, J.J.) (discussing how legislation 'calling upon all government actors to respect the dignity of individuals with disabilities is entirely compatible' with commitments to federalism).

[51] *Lawrence v Texas*, 539 U.S. 558, 567; see also *Planned Parenthood of Se. Pa. v Casey*, 505 U.S. 833, 851 (1992) ('These matters, involving the most intimate and personal choices a person may make in a lifetime, choices central to personal dignity and autonomy, are central to the liberty protected by the Fourteenth Amendment.').

marriages to be unconstitutional, Justice Kennedy again wrote of relational rights in dignity terms.[52]

Harms to dignity do not, however, necessarily result in conclusions of unconstitutionality, as they might in some legal systems.[53] For example, when describing strip searches of individuals detained by the police as a 'serious affront to human dignity', Justice Samuel Alito nonetheless concurred in upholding their use as he also raised the potential for limiting the decision's reach.[54]

In these many references to dignity, justices generally do not offer citation to the U.N. Charter, the UDHR or other conventions and constitutions.[55] However, as documents from the United Nations, from other countries, and from state constitutions came to embrace dignity, that word seeped into U.S. constitutional jurisprudence and thereafter came to be understood as central to its commitments.[56]

Dignity is a complex concept, with widely varying legal import both in U.S. case law and in different legal systems. Analyses abound about the relevance of its Catholic and aristocratic origins, the nuances and distinctions in legal systems, and about what distinguishes dignity from autonomy, liberty, equality, and privacy.[57] Further, while some theorists insist dignity relates solely to human beings, I have argued that dignity can usefully be deployed instrumentally to protect institutional roles, for example, of indigenous communities or of state interests.[58] The purpose of discussing dignity here, however, is not to explore these facets but to underscore the degree to which core

[52] *United States v Windsor*, 133 S. Ct. 2675, 2693 (2013).

[53] For example, Germany describes dignity as an absolute legal obligation. In contrast, the Basic Laws of Israel expressly provide that dignity harms are to be balanced through a proportionality analysis. See Susanne Baer, 'Dignity, Liberty, Equality: A Fundamental Rights Triangle of Constitutionalism', 59 U. Toronto L.J. 417 (2009); Aharon Barak, 'Foreword: A Judge on Judging: The Role of a Supreme Court in a Democracy', 116 Harv. L. Rev. 16, 44–6 (2002).

[54] *Florence v Bd. of Chosen Freeholders*, 132 S. Ct. 1510, 1527 (2012) (Alito, J., concurring).

[55] A few opinions reference practices abroad. For example, in *Trop*, 356 U.S. at 102–3, Chief Justice Warren referred to a U.N. survey finding that only two countries permitted denationalization for deserting, as he concluded that 'civilized nations of the world are in virtual unanimity that statelessness is not to be imposed as punishment for crime'.

[56] See also Karl N. Llewellyn, 'The Law, Human Dignity, and Human Civilization', *in Science, Philosophy and Religion: Third Symposium* 297, 297–9 (Lyman Bryson and Louis Finkelstein eds., 1943), *reprinted in* Karl N. Llewellyn, *Jurisprudence: Realism in Theory and Practice* 476, 476–77 (1962) (discussing the 'negative' side of 'Human Dignity' as a source of prohibitions on slavery and the 'positive' side that legal systems ought to aspire to as an ideal); Richard A. Primus, *The American Language of Rights* 182 (1999) (focusing on the influence of Hannah Arendt on the turn in American political and legal theory to 'human dignity'); Richard Primus, Note, 'A Brooding Omnipresence: Totalitarianism in Postwar Constitutional Thought', 106 Yale L.J. 423, 429 (1996) (finding that during the 1930s, The Yale Law Journal published no articles on natural law and universal rights; after World War II, such articles appeared regularly).

[57] See, e.g., Reva Siegel, 'Dignity and the Politics of Protection: Abortion Restrictions Under *Casey/Carhart*', 117 Yale L.J. 1694 (2008); Christopher McCrudden, 'Human Dignity and Judicial Interpretation of Human Rights', 19 EJIL 655 (2008); Christopher McCrudden, 'Dignity and Religion', *in Islam and English Law: Rights, Responsibilities and the Place of Shari'a* 94–106 (Robin Griffith-Jones ed., 2013). Moreover, sometimes dignity is argued to provide an independent basis for a decision and potentially more protection than U.S. Constitutional rights, while in other instances, dignity appears as a 'secondary and at best complementary role.' See Vicki C. Jackson, 'Constitutional Dialogue and Human Dignity: States and Transnational Constitutional Discourse', 65 Mont. L. Rev. 15, 28 (2004).

[58] See Resnik and Suk, n 19, at 1929–33. We argued that recognizing a state's dignity interests does not compel a conclusion that states be immune from suits. Indeed, the ability to sue and be sued acknowledges the authority and dignity of both persons and entities.

'American' constitutional obligations are forged in the context of worldwide constitutional discourse, whether expressly or *sub silentio*.[59]

3. Shaping criminal defendants' rights via transnational exchanges

Another example of non-U.S. law's impact on constitutional analyses takes a more familiar form—express comparative analyses that offer other systems as positive or negative examplars. The development of criminal defendants' rights during the middle of the 20th century is laced with references to other countries. Illustrative is the 1950s decision of a federal appellate court, deriding the New York City police for holding a man 'incommunicado' for 27 hours, for 'refusing to allow his lawyer, his family, and his friends to consult him', and for questioning him continuously in a cell that made 'sleep virtually impossible'.[60] Because that isolation and psychological pressure was so abusive, the court threw out the confession, explaining that '[a]ll decent Americans soundly condemn [such] satanic practices, [used only by] totalitarian regimes [not abiding by] . . . the barest minimums of civilized principles of justice.'[61]

The contrast between totalitarian treatment of defendants and U.S. values was repeated in various judgments addressing criminal defendants' rights.[62] A famous example is *Miranda v Arizona*[63] where foreign law appeared in both the briefing and the decision. John Frank's argument on behalf of the petitioner, Ernesto Miranda, picked up the motif of the foreign as the negative exemplar. 'We are not talking with some learned historicity about the *lettre de cachet* of pre-Revolutionary France or the secret prisons of a distant Russia. We are talking about conditions in the United States, in the Twentieth Century, and now.'[64]

Chief Justice Warren in turn, writing for the five-person majority decision holding that the Fifth Amendment imposed a constitutional prohibition against compelled self-incrimination, referenced foreign practices negatively.[65] In contrast, when explaining the remedy, the *Miranda* majority reported on legal safeguards on interrogation provided in Scotland, India, and Ceylon, as well as by the U.S. Federal Bureau of Investigation and the Uniform Code of Military Justice.[66] The Chief Justice was not chastised by his colleagues for referencing foreign practices. Rather, Justice Tom Clark, dissenting in part, disagreed with the majority's evaluation of the rules cited: 'none of these jurisdictions

[59] See Jackson, *Constitutional Engagement*, n 14; William Twining, *General Jurisprudence: Understanding Law from a Global Perspective* (2009); Judith Resnik, 'Law's Migration: American Exceptionalism, Silent Dialogues, and Federalism's Multiple Ports of Entry', 115 Yale L. J. 1564 (2006). The view that words common across legal cultures lack shared meanings—making the costs of understanding and using foreign law too high—is explained in Thomas O. Main, 'The Word Commons and Foreign Laws', 46 Cornell Int'l L.J. 219 (2013).

[60] *United States ex rel. Caminito v Murphy*, 222 F.2d 698, 701 (2d Cir. 1955).

[61] *Caminito*, 222 F.2d at 701. See generally Kim Lane Scheppele, 'Aspirational and Aversive Constitutionalism: The Case for Studying Cross-Constitutional Influence Through Negative Models', 1 Int'l. J. Comp. L. 296 (2003).

[62] See Hope Metcalf and Judith Resnik, 'Gideon at Guantánamo: Democratic and Despotic Detention', 122 Yale L. J. 2504 (2013).

[63] 384 U.S. 436 (1966).

[64] Brief for Petitioner at 46–7, *Miranda v Arizona*, 384 U.S. 436 (1966) (No. 759).

[65] *Miranda*, 384 U.S. at 442. [66] Ibid. at 488 (majority opinion).

has struck so one-sided a balance as the Court does today'.[67] *Miranda* also offers an example of the import/export trade; some jurisdictions outside the U.S. reference *Miranda*—as a guide, or as an example of too much protection for defendants, or too little.[68]

4. Naming and bringing human rights 'home'

The use of non-U.S. sources in constitutional law has drawn a good deal of attention. Yet courts are but one port of entry. The ordinariness of using non-U.S. sources can be seen from a few examples of executive and legislative action. Kevin Cope has recently surveyed some federal statutes to identify when, to borrow his term, Congress 'elects' to consider international law when enacting domestic legislation.[69] Here, I bring into focus the activities of state and local actors affiliating with international conventions and incorporating non-U.S. materials when drafting regulatory standards.

One example comes from the debate about CEDAW, signed in 1980 by President Jimmy Carter. Although the United States Senate has not exercised its constitutional authority to ratify, the City and County of San Francisco have taken up CEDAW's precepts by making it local law.

In 1998, the San Francisco Board of Supervisors endorsed CEDAW's 'universal definition of discrimination against women' across a 'whole range of issues' and committed to 'work towards integrating gender equity and human rights principles into all of its operations, including policy, program and budgetary decision-making'.[70] San Francisco's approach to CEDAW relies on what the United Nations, the Council of Europe, and the Commonwealth Secretariat call 'gender mainstreaming', considering how gender is implicated across a wide range of policies.[71] San Francisco uses CEDAW precepts when assessing the impact of street lighting and parking lots

[67] *Miranda*, 384 U.S. at 521 (Clark, J., dissenting in part and concurring in part).

[68] For example, in 1972, the Supreme Court of Canada discussed *Miranda* when holding that compelling citizens to submit to breathalyser tests did not violate what was then Canada's Bill of Rights. *Curr v The Queen*, 1972 S.C.R. 889. The Court explained decades later: 'We are not persuaded that the *Miranda* rule should be transplanted in Canadian soil.' *Jude (Raymond) v HM Advocate*, 2011 S.C.L. 569. In contrast, when deciding what warnings were due a suspected drunk driver, the German Constitutional Court concluded that *Miranda* and its progeny were too restrictive; whether in custody or not, warnings about self-incrimination had to be given prior to interrogation. BGHSt 38, 215 (218); see also Stephen C. Thaman, '*Miranda* in Comparative Law', 45 St. Louis U. L.J. 581, 598 (2001). *Miranda* has also played a role in transnational European law. In *Ambrose v Harris*, the Supreme Court of the United Kingdom explored *Miranda*'s 'custodial approach' when reflecting on whether the European Court of Human Rights would ultimately adopt a similar framework, [2011] UKSC 54, para. 37. The 2012 Directive of the European Parliament, creating a floor of procedural uniformity for criminal defendants, established 'information about procedural rights' for suspects and accused individuals—provided through a written 'Letter of Rights' detailing rights of access to lawyers, to remain silent, and to other safeguards. See Council Directive 2012/13, On the Right to Information in Criminal Proceedings, 2012 O.J. (L 141) 1 (EU).

[69] Kevin L. Cope, 'Elective International Law in Congress', 113 Mich. L. Rev. (forthcoming 2015). Cope analysed the legislative history of statutes and identified legislators referencing non-U.S. law in discussing the wisdom, practicality, and impact of various enactments, such as the Marijuana on the High Seas Act.

[70] S.F., Cal., Admin. Code § 12K.1 (as amended in 2000).

[71] See generally Council of Europe, Group of Specialists on Mainstreaming, Gender Mainstreaming: Conceptual Framework, Methodology and Presentation of Good Practice 4–5 (1998). See also Christopher McCrudden, 'Mainstreaming Human Rights', *in Human Rights in the Community* 9–28 (Colin Harvey ed., 2005).

on work opportunities of women and men, when considering options for leave and telecommuting, and when analysing job assignments in the Department of the Environment.[72]

Some localities, such as California's Los Angeles in 2003 and Berkeley in 2012, have also adopted ordinances to implement CEDAW,[73] and the Mayor of Salt Lake City, Utah has relied on a CEDAW framework to assess women's rights there.[74] Many more cities and some states have issued what I have termed 'expressive' resolutions, calling on the Senate to ratify CEDAW.[75]

The efforts to incorporate human rights conventions in localities are part of a translocal, transnational social movement. São Paolo, Brazil has also adopted CEDAW; the City Councils of Chicago and Los Angeles have endorsed the Convention on the Rights of the Child.[76] Portland, Oregon has incorporated the UDHR,[77] as has Carrboro, North Carolina; Pittsburgh, Pennsylvania; Eugene, Oregon, and many other localities, identify themselves as 'human rights cities'.[78] Some also use the drafting of self-analyses, common in some human rights treaties, to assess compliance with such norms.[79]

Advocacy for such efforts comes in part from non-governmental organizations, the now-familiar NGOs. Other important supporters are translocal organizations of government actors that, I have suggested, merit their own acronym—TOGAs—to capture their distinctive attributes.[80] These private organizations gain their political capital through their members, because they hold public offices. Illustrative is the U.S. Conference of Mayors (USCM), created in 1933 during the Depression to help mayors work effectively in Washington.[81] The agenda of the USCM has expanded beyond lobbying to policy networking and law reform. The USCM has resolutions on many issues, including climate change, immigration policies, and endorsements of a related, transnational group—Mayors for Peace.[82]

72 See, e.g., Martha F. Davis, Johanna Kalb, and Risa E. Kaufman, *Human Rights Advocacy in the United States* (2014); *Bringing Human Rights Home: How State and Local Governments Can Use Human Rights to Advance Local Policy* 22 (Columbia Law School, Human Rights Institute, Dec. 2012).

73 Ordinance No. 7,224-N.S., Adopting the Operative Principles of the United Nations Convention on the Elimination of All Forms of Discrimination Against Women, codified at Ch. 13.20, enacted 2012.

74 *Bringing Human Rights Home*, n 72, at 20.

75 See Resnik, 'Law's Migration', n 59, at 1633–42.

76 *Bringing Human Rights Home*, n 72, at 10.

77 São Paolo, unlike San Francisco, is in a country also a party to CEDAW. See Karen Knop, 'International Law and the Disaggregated Democratic State: Two Case Studies on Women's Human Rights and the United States', Rapoport Center Human Rights Working Paper Series, 16 (2012); See generally Risa E. Kaufman, '"By Some Other Means": Considering the Executive's Role in Fostering Subnational Human Rights Compliance', 33 Cardozo L. Rev. 1971 (2012).

78 See *Bringing Human Rights Home*, n 72, at 11–12.

79 Ibid. at 21.

80 See Judith Resnik, Joshua Civin, and Joseph Frueh, 'Ratifying Kyoto at the Local Level: Sovereigntism, Federalism, and Translocal Organizations of Government Actors (TOGAs)', 50 Ariz. L. Rev. 709, 769–86 (2008). See also Judith Resnik, 'The Internationalism of American Federalism: *Missouri* and *Holland*' (the 2008 Earl F. Nelson Lecture), 73 Miss. L. Rev. 1105 (2008).

81 See Richard M. Flanagan, 'Roosevelt, Mayors, and the New Deal Regime: The Origins of Intergovernmental Lobbying and Administration', 3 Polity 415 (Mar. 1999).

82 U.S. Conference of Mayors, Calling for U.S. Leadership in Global Elimination of Nuclear Weapons and Redirection of Nuclear Weapons Spending to Meet the Urgent Needs of Cities (2012), <http://www.usmayors.org/resolutions/80th_conference/international08.asp>.

Appreciation of the scope of the transnational import/export of rights requires moving beyond activities in the United States. In 2004, United Cities and Local Governments (UCLG) was founded by merging various local government organizations, including the International Union of Local Authorities (IULA), the United Towns Organisation (UTO), and Metropolis.[83] Headquartered in Barcelona, Spain, UCLG counts more than 1,000 cities and 112 national associations as its members, and therefore has associations with 140 of the 192 United Nations (UN) members. UCLG's goals include reinforcing roles for local and regional authorities in international decision-making. The topics include development, sustainability, migration, human rights, gender equality, and transnational cooperation. In 2011, UCLG adopted a 'Global Charter-Agenda for Human Rights in the City', and set forth as the first of its 'values and principles' that 'the dignity of every human being' was 'a supreme value'.[84] In short, transnational as well as translocal organizations of government actors criss-cross boundaries to reshape laws and policies.

5. Toxic toys and precautionary principles

Even when shifting from courts to legislators and from the national to local levels, discussion about the propriety of importing law often centres on issues related to personal liberties and equality. But the borrowing of legal precepts sourced abroad occurs in diverse arenas. Illustrative are regulations of chemicals and other risks to the environment and health.

A 2009 Minnesota law, the Toxic Free Kids Act (quoted at the beginning of section I) requires its agencies, when evaluating toxicity of chemicals, to consider 'chemicals listed . . . by a state, federal, or international agency'. The Act also authorizes consideration of chemicals listed by 'the California Environmental Protection Agency, the Washington Department of Ecology, the United States Department of Health, the United States Environmental Protection Agency, the . . . World Health Organization, and European Parliament Annex XIV concerning the Registration, Evaluation, Authorisation, and Restriction of Chemicals'.[85]

Minnesota is one of many states looking to Europe for standard-setting[86] as part of a transnational 'drive for safer chemical policy'.[87] California is another, albeit less explicitly. In 2007, Governor Arnold Schwarzenegger signed into law an amendment

[83] See <http://www.uclg.org/en/organisation/about>.

[84] Committee on Social Inclusion, Participatory Democracy and Human Rights, United Cities and Local Governments (UCLG), Circular 52, <http://www.uclg-cisdp.org/sites/default/files/cisdp_circular52_en.pdf> (announcing the UCLG World Council adopted the Global Charter-Agenda for Human Rights in the City on 11 December 2011).

[85] See Minn. Stat. § 116.9402 (2009).

[86] In Connecticut, for example, the Act Concerning Banning Bisphenol-A in Children's Products and Food Products did not reference European law but the legislative hearings cited to Europe dozens of time. See Environmental Committee Hearing Transcript 0/3/02/2009 and H.B. 6572, 2009 Gen. Assembly, Jan. Sess. (Conn. 2009). See also Washington Dep't of Ecology of Children's Safety Product Act Report, July 2009.

[87] See generally Michael E. Belliveau, 'The Drive for a Safer Chemicals Policy in the United States', 21 New Solutions 359 (2011).

to that state's Health and Safety Code. Aimed at 'toxic toys',[88] the statute provided that, as of 2009, 'no person or entity shall manufacture, sell, or distribute in commerce any toy or child care article that contains' certain chemicals.[89] Proponents, initially seeking to address cosmetics as well as toys, credited a 2003 European law as an influence. In 2004, the California draft proposed to define a 'prohibited substance' to include those prohibited, as of 2003, by the 'European Parliament and the Council of the European Union'.[90] As enacted, the legislation focused on toys, specified which chemicals are banned, and did not directly link the prohibitions to those in Europe.[91]

6. The diversity of cross-border topics, methods, and legal actors

I have offered glimpses of a small fraction of the diverse ways in which governments at different levels cross borders. One focus is the environment, with joint ventures, conferences, and protocols. For example, states and Canadian provinces have projects to address the Great Lakes; Mexico and U.S. border-states have sought to share ways to protect endangered species. Other initiatives are commercial, aspiring to improve localities or regions' economic bases through developing 'sister city' relations or other ties abroad. On other occasions, the efforts target transnational human rights, such as by imposing bans on products made with forced labour or on using funds from investors who provide services for oppressive regimes.

The legal actors are likewise varied, including appointed or elected judges, legislators and local officials, corporations, NGOs, and TOGAs. Their reliance on non-U.S.

[88] See Mark Schapiro, 'Toxic Toys: Why Europe's Children Are Safer than Ours', The Nation, Nov. 5, 2007, vol. 285 at 11–17, *available at* <http://www.thenation.com/article/toxic-toys>.

[89] See A.B. 1108, 2006–2007 Reg. Sess. (Cal. 2007).

[90] The California proposal provided:

'(c) "Prohibited substance" means either of the following:

(1) A substance identified in Annex I of Directive 67/648/EEC of the European Union as a category 1, 2, or 3 carcinogen, mutagen, or reproductive toxicant and prohibited from use in cosmetic products pursuant to Article 4b of Directive 2003/15/EC, adopted by the European Parliament and the Council of the European Union on February 27, 2003.

(2) A substance prohibited from forming part of the composition of cosmetic products pursuant to Annex II of Directive 76/768/EEC, as adopted by the European Parliament and the Council of the European Union.'

A.B. 2025, 2003–2004 Reg. Sess. (Cal. 2004). In the late 1990s, the European Union imposed a ban on the use of six phthalates in children's toys. See European Parliament and Council Directive 2005/84, 2005 O.J. (L 344) 40 (EC). Additional regulations were put into place in 2011. See Commission Directive 2011/8/EU, 28 Jan. 2011 (amending Direction 2002/72/EC as regards the restriction of use of Bisphenol-A in plastic infant feeding bottles).

[91] Such efforts to regulate at the subnational level had provoked opposition, including lawsuits filed by business associations arguing that state and local action is preempted by federal law. But in the Consumer Product Safety Improvement Act of 2008, §§ 101–107, Pub. L. No. 110–314, 122 Stat. 3016, which banned the sale of children's toys and child care articles containing a certain concentration of specific forms of phthalates, Congress specified that nothing in that act 'shall be construed to preempt or otherwise affect any State requirement with respect to any phthalate alternative not specifically regulated in a consumer product safety standard under the Consumer Product Safety Act.' Ibid. § 108(d). Additional regulations in states followed. The interaction between Europe's 'Regulation, Evaluation, Authorization, and Restriction of Chemicals (REACH)' and the United States is analysed in 'Across the Pond: Assessing REACH's First Big Impact on U.S. Companies and Chemicals' (Environmental Defense Fund, Jan. 2009). See generally *Environmental Protection: European Law and Governance* (Joanne Scott ed., 2009).

sources range from constitutional comparisons, transnational incorporation, and using scientific data to borrowing standards and mandating methods of enforcement, such as CEDAW analyses. Some of these interactions name the sources of law, and others have absorbed legal precepts without expressly acknowledging the roots in other legal systems.

Given the different mandates of the officials (elected/appointed, legislative, executive, and judicial), the legal and normative implications of these various border-crossings vary. The criticisms levelled against using foreign sources are mostly focused on the judiciary, to which I turn after bringing into view another posture—that of overt hostility to sources from abroad.

II. Othering 'foreign' law

In light of the many methods of incorporation of non-U.S. law and the diverse actors doing so, coupled with the background of centuries of transnational religious, imperial, and mercantile law production, a puzzle emerges about why and how foreign law has come to be negatively freighted. My purpose here is not to rehearse the literature on 'American exceptionalism' but rather to show how much work and energy is required to make foreign law suspect.

1. 'Domestic jurisdiction' and the Universal Declaration of Human Rights

This chapter's opening quoted a 1799 New Jersey law prohibiting the use of English law. In the 18th century, the rebellion against England prompted New Jersey and other states to seek to become distinctive legal communities; one technique some states employed was to decree that the law of Great Britain was not to be used in their courts.[92] The New Jersey statute was, as one commentator recently explained, 'Anglophobia, not xenophobia'.[93] By 1820, New Jersey had repealed the provision.[94] More generally, English law has been an important resource for American courts across a variety of domains.[95]

Skipping to the 20th century, the creation of the League of Nations and the United Nations raised a host of anxieties that shaped new anti-foreign campaigns. A major exemplar was the mid-20th century proposal to amend the United States Constitution. Senator John Bricker, a Republican from Ohio, sought to prevent a treaty that 'conflicts with the Constitution' from having any 'force or effect', because, in his view, 'human rights' were for the 'domestic jurisdiction' of each nation-state. His fear of the foreign

[92] Act of June 13, 1799, § 5, 1799 N.J. Laws 435–36, n 1. Pennsylvania had a more complex approach—that it was not 'lawful to read or quote in any court in this Commonwealth, any British precedent or adjudication' originating before 4 July 1776 but that the provision should not be 'construed to prohibit the reading of any precedent of maritime law, or of the law of nations.' See Act of Mar. 19, 1810, ch. 98, in Acts of the General Assembly of the Commonwealth of Pennsylvania 136 (Phila., John Bioren 1810).

[93] Seipp, n 15, at 1427. [94] See n 1.

[95] See generally William A. Fletcher, 'The General Common Law and Section 34 of the Judiciary Act of 1789: The Example of Marine Insurance', 97 Harv. L. Rev. 1513 (1984).

was very specific. Bricker worried that, were the UDHR to be part of American law, it would undermine the racial and gender hierarchies then entrenched.

Bricker was right to understand that transnational egalitarian movements put systems of discrimination at risk. In 1946, 1947, and 1951, three appeals—filed respectively by the National Association for the Advancement of Colored People (NAACP), the National Negro Congress (NNC), and the Civil Rights Congress (CRC)—petitioned the UN to protect black Americans.[96] But the agreement that forged the UN had embedded recognition of the 'domestic' as a place immune from oversight. The UN Charter states: 'Nothing contained in the present Charter shall authorize the United Nations to intervene in matters which are essentially within the domestic jurisdiction of any state or shall require the members to submit such matters to settlement under the present Charter.'[97] The history of the drafting suggests the purpose was to leave the United States free to join the Charter while unencumbered by a mandate to change its race relations.[98]

The question is, of course, what matters are deemed 'essentially within the domestic jurisdiction' of a state. As I have already detailed, 'domestic' matters—from constitutional rules on criminal defendants' rights to local laws on health, safety, and equality—may draw on and could be seen as implicating 'foreign affairs'; further, the 'foreign' routinely influences the domestic.[99] Bricker was not the first to make an essentialist effort to delineate the two as discrete and unrelated. Proponents of slavery once relied on the idea that localities—rather than the federal government—had exclusive authority of 'master/servant' relationships, just as efforts to obtain national redress for women's subordination were met with claims that family life was for state governance. World-wide movements against slavery and for women's rights reframed these claims as forms of discrimination to be addressed by international, national, and local 'domestic' law.[100]

[96] See Nat'l Negro Council, *A Petition to the United Nations on Behalf of 13 Million Oppressed Negro Citizens of the United States of America* (1946); NAACP, *An Appeal to the World!: A Statement on the Denial of Human Rights to Minorities in the Case of Citizens of Negro Descent in the United States of America and an Appeal to the United Nations for Redress* (1947). The State Department responded that the Charter did not apply because, as they had no distinct culture or language, Negroes were not 'national minorities'. See Carol Anderson, *Eyes Off the Prize: The United Nations and the African American Struggle for Human Rights, 1944–1955* 72–82 (2003).

The NAACP's efforts prompted Eleanor Roosevelt to threaten to leave its board, and soon thereafter, the NAACP retreated from its international human rights agenda. Ibid. at 102–11, 130–61; see also Mary L. Dudziak, 'Desegregation as a Cold War Imperative', 41 Stan. L. Rev. 61 (1988). In 1951, the third petition was filed, with some 90 individuals joining the Civil Rights Congress in a 200-page document listing individuals who had died as well as estimates that U.S. economic and social policies caused 30,000 unnecessary deaths annually. See *We Charge Genocide: The Historic Petition to the United Nations for Relief from a Crime of the United States Government Against the Negro People* 57–125 (Int'l. Publishers Co. ed. 1970) (1951). The UN did not respond.

[97] UN Charter art. 2, para. 7. [98] See Anderson, n 96, at 40–9.

[99] Judith Resnik, 'Foreign as Domestic Affairs: Rethinking Horizontal Federalism and Foreign Affairs Preemption in Light of Translocal Internationalism', 57 Emory L.J. 31 (2007).

[100] See, e.g., Council of Europe Convention on Preventing and Combating Violence Against Women and Domestic Violence, Art.1 (a), May 11, 2011, Council of Europe Treaty Series No. 210 (2011); *Valiulienė v Lithuania*, Appl. No. 33234/07, Eur. Ct. H.R. 26 March 2013, ¶¶ 74, 75, 86. See generally Judith Resnik, 'Federalisms' Forms and Norms' *in NOMOS LV: Federalism and Subsidiary* (James Fleming ed., 2014).

The Bricker amendment failed in the Senate by one vote. Its legacy ('the ghost of Senator Bricker') continues to constrain action on some conventions.[101] Yet his efforts could not stop the international currents of dignity and equality, joining domestic social movements, which undid many of the hierarchies that Bricker and others had hoped to leave in place.[102]

Bricker's anxieties continue to resonate—replayed in contemporary debates about the citation of foreign law, immigration, climate change policies, and conventions addressed to the law of the sea and to children. In the wake of 9/11, hostility to and anxiety about the impact of transnational movements gained new ground as activists interested in freighting the foreign seek to do so in various venues. In the following sections, I draw examples from three sites—Supreme Court decisions, Congress, and state legislation.

2. The platform provided by the Supreme Court

Disagreements among justices on the Supreme Court have been central to the narrative of the foreign as a suspect resource for domestic constitutional law production. Justice Antonin Scalia has been a vocal actor, arguing in 1989 against the use of foreign sources in a case involving interpretation of the Eighth Amendment prohibition against 'cruel and unusual punishment'.[103] He insisted that '[w]e must never forget that it is a Constitution for the United States of America that we are expounding…[W]here there is not first a settled consensus among our own people, the views of other nations, however enlightened the Justices of this Court may think them to be, cannot be imposed upon Americans through the Constitution.'

The focus on the Eighth Amendment raises specific questions. Given the textual concern about whether a punishment was 'unusual', one could have read the Eighth Amendment to require consideration of law beyond that of the United States so as to make that determination. Indeed, 19th century Supreme Court decisions did so.[104] But undeterred by commentators arguing that he was wrong as a matter of text and the Court's prior interpretive practices,[105] Justice Scalia has persisted in pursuing his anti-foreign law arguments. In a case involving execution of a mentally disabled person, the majority acknowledged the role of non-U.S. law in a footnote commenting that the 'national consensus' against execution of cognitively limited individuals comported with views of the 'world community'.[106] Justice Scalia called his colleagues to task:

[101] Louis Henkin, 'U.S. Ratification of Human Rights Conventions: The Ghost of Senator Bricker', 89 Am. J. Int'l L. 341 (1995).

[102] Resnik, 'Law's Migration', n 59, at 1606–10 (2006).

[103] *Thompson v Oklahoma*, 487 U.S. 815, 868 n.4 (1989) (Scalia, J., dissenting).

[104] See *Wilkerson v Utah*, 99 U.S. 130, 134–5 (1879).

[105] See, e.g., Sarah Cleveland, 'Our International Constitution', 31 Yale J. Int'l L. 1 (2006); Steven G. Calabresi and Stephanie Dotson Simdahl, 'The Supreme Court and Foreign Sources of Law: Two Hundred Years of Practice and the Juvenile Death Penalty Decision', 47 Wm. & Mary L. Rev. 743 (2005); Vicki C. Jackson, 'Constitutional Comparisons: Convergence, Resistance, Engagement', 119 Harv. L. Rev. 109 (2005); see also Jeremy Waldron, 'Foreign Law and the Modern Ius Gentium', 119 Harv. L. Rev. 129 (2005).

[106] *Atkins*, 536 U.S. 304, 316 & n. 21 (2002). The European Union and several United States diplomats had filed briefs arguing that executing those of limited mental capacities violated transnational

'thankfully', the views of other nations were 'not always those of our people', and the views of other nations, 'however enlightened the Justices of this Court may think them to be, cannot be imposed upon Americans through the Constitution'.[107]

The disagreement returned in 2005, when a majority held in *Roper v Simmons* that the Eighth Amendment prohibited the execution of minors. Foreign law played a role, albeit an unclear one. Justice Kennedy, writing for that majority, read the Eighth Amendment as requiring the Court to ascertain whether a national 'consensus' had developed that the death penalty for juveniles was cruel and unusual and, further, to exercise its own 'independent judgment' about whether that punishment was 'disproportionate'.[108] In the final segment of the opinion,[109] Justice Kennedy discussed the English Parliament's 1948 prohibition against the death penalty for juveniles as well as several international conventions that ban the practice.[110] He explained its decision to refer to 'the overwhelming weight of international opinion' as 'confirmation for' but not as 'controlling' the correctness of its interpretation of the Eighth Amendment.[111] The majority could therefore be read as trying to give legitimacy to such references—and forcing the conflict about them into the open—without actually having foreign law do real legal work on the merits.

Justice Scalia's dissent, joined by Chief Justice William Rehnquist and Justice Clarence Thomas, objected on the merits and to the mention of such sources. In characteristically aggressive prose, Justice Scalia asserted that:

> It is beyond comprehension why we should look, for that purpose, to a country that has developed, in the centuries since the Revolutionary War—and with increasing speed since the United Kingdom's recent submission to the jurisprudence of

understandings of human rights and interfered with American diplomatic efforts to reduce human rights abuses. See Brief of Amicus Curiae the European Union in Support of the Petitioner, *McCarver v North Carolina*, 533 U.S. 975 (2001) (No. 00-8727) (reintroduced in *Atkins*, see Joint Motion of All Amici in *McCarver v North Carolina*, No. 00-8727, To Have Their *McCarver* Amicus Briefs Considered in this Case in Support of Petitioner, *Atkins*, 536 U.S. 304 (No. 00-8452), 2001 WL 1682012); Brief of Amici Curiae Diplomats Morton Abromowitz et al. in support of Petitioner, *McCarver v North Carolina*, 533 U.S. 975 (2001) (No. 00-8727) (also reintroduced in *Atkins*).

[107] Both the dissent by the Chief Justice (joined by Justices Scalia and Thomas) and the dissent by Justice Scalia (joined by the Chief Justice and Justice Thomas) objected to the mention of views of other countries. *Atkins*, 536 U.S. at 324–5, 328 (Rehnquist, C.J., dissenting); ibid. at 347–8 (Scalia, J., dissenting) (quoting *Thompson v Oklahoma*, 487 U.S. 815, 868 n.4 (1988) (Scalia, J., dissenting)).

[108] *Roper*, 543 U.S. 551, 564 (2005).

[109] Ibid. at 575–9. The majority opinion did note that when the United States ratified the ICCPR, it did so subject to a reservation on Article 6(5), which 'prohibits capital punishment for juveniles'. Ibid. at 567. The Court found that, because five states had subsequently outlawed capital punishment for juveniles and because Congress had not extended that punishment to juveniles when enacting the Federal Death Penalty Act in 1994, that reservation was 'only faint support for' the argument that no national consensus against the practice existed. Ibid.

[110] Justice Kennedy cited the Convention on the Rights of the Child; the International Covenant on Civil and Political Rights; the American Convention on Human Rights: Pact of San José, Costa Rica; and the African Charter on the Rights and Welfare of the Child. Ibid. at 576.

[111] *Roper*, 543 U.S. at 578. In *Graham v Florida*, holding that sentencing juveniles to life without parole violates the Eighth Amendment, Justice Kennedy commented that 'judgments of other nations and the international community are not dispositive as to the meaning of the Eighth Amendment', but their views 'support' the Court's 'independent conclusion' that sentencing juveniles to life without parole is cruel and unusual. 560 U.S. 48, 80, 130 (2010). See generally Ernest A. Young, Comment, 'Foreign Law and the Denominator Problem', 119 Harv. L. Rev. 148, 153 (2005).

> European courts dominated by continental jurists—a legal, political, and social culture quite different from our own.[112]

His ire prompted Justice Sandra Day O'Connor (even as she too dissented on the merits) to distance herself from what she described as a claim that 'foreign and international law have no place in our Eighth Amendment jurisprudence'.[113] Rather, the 'special character' of the Eighth Amendment appropriately 'draws its meaning directly from the maturing values of civilized society'.[114]

These debates continued, on and off the bench. For example, in *McDonald v City of Chicago*, decided in 2010, the Supreme Court held, 5–4, that the Second Amendment applied to the City of Chicago and restrained it from imposing a form of gun regulation. Justice John Paul Stevens dissented, invoking 'the experience of other advanced democracies, including those that share our British heritage', to undermine 'the notion that an expansive right to keep and bear arms is intrinsic to ordered liberty. Many of these countries place restrictions on the possession, use, and carriage of firearms far more onerous than the restrictions found in this Nation'.[115] As Justice Stevens explained, locating the United States as 'an international outlier in the permissiveness of its approach to guns' was not to 'suggest that our laws are bad laws. It does suggest that this Court may not need to assume responsibility for making our laws still more permissive.'[116] Thus, it was 'silly—indeed, arrogant—to think we have nothing to learn about liberty from the billions of people beyond our borders'.[117]

Justice Scalia, concurring, had provoked that accusation of arrogance by objecting to what he called the 'follow-the-foreign-crowd requirement' that would 'foreclose rights that we have held... are incorporated, but that other "advanced" nations do not recognize—from the exclusionary rule to the Establishment Clause.'[118] Justice Scalia used the example that U.S. law is more permissive on abortion, a contention that is empirically disputed, yet was asserted as fact.[119]

Although Justice Scalia has been at the forefront of arguing the legal boundaries of domestic law, on occasion he too has relied on legal precepts shaped across borders. An example comes from his dissent in *Arizona v United States*, a 2012 decision by a five-person majority holding that federal law preempted Arizona's criminalization of migration.[120] The majority based its ruling in part on the need for a unified federal

[112] *Roper*, 543 U.S. at 626 (Scalia, J., dissenting).

[113] Ibid. at 604 (O'Connor, J., dissenting).

[114] *Roper*, 543 U.S. at 604 (O'Connor, J., dissenting). Justice O'Connor agreed with the majority about the need to understand domestic opinion but disagreed that a 'genuine *national* consensus' against the practice existed. Ibid.

[115] *McDonald v City of Chicago*, 130 S. Ct. 3020, 3110 (2010) (citing to the City's brief, which discussed laws from England, Canada, Australia, Japan, Denmark, Finland, Luxembourg, and New Zealand).

[116] Ibid. [117] Ibid. [118] Ibid. at 3056.

[119] In rejecting Justice Stevens' approach, Justice Scalia noted that it would require the court to 'either throw all of those rights overboard or... simply ignore foreign law when it undermines the desired conclusion, see, e.g., Casey, 505 U.S. 833... (making no mention of foreign law).' *McDonald*, 130 S. Ct. at 3056. Reva Siegel's comparative work on abortion makes plain that the United States and Germany have some convergences and further, that several jurisdictions have liberal abortion rights. See Reva Siegel, 'The Constitutionalization of Abortion', *in The Oxford Handbook of Comparative Constitutional Law* 1057 (Michel Rosenfeld and András Sajó eds., 2012).

[120] *Arizona v United States*, 132 S.Ct. 2492 (2011).

position (speaking with 'one voice') on immigration, as implicating foreign affairs. Disagreeing with the preclusion of state-level law-making, Justice Scalia turned repeatedly to international law as a resource for ideas about states' sovereign authority.[121]

As these interactions illustrate, several justices embrace cross-border exchanges on questions of U.S. constitutional law. Justice Ruth Bader Ginsburg has been one such steady voice; in a speech, 'A Decent Respect for the Opinions of [Human]kind', she explained that, as a 'matter of comity and in a spirit of humility',[122] consideration of responses by other courts is an important facet of judicial decision-making that, she has elsewhere described as an 'international human rights dialogue'.[123] She joins Justices O'Connor, Stevens, Kennedy, and Stephen Breyer in arguing the utility of learning from, without being bound by, judgments from abroad.[124]

To be clear, the intensity of *Roper, McDonald, Arizona*—and several other cases in which foreign law is referenced—is fuelled by layers of disagreement, first about the particular issue at hand (the legality of capital punishment, gun control, immigration); second about which legal actors (judges, legislatures, municipalities, state or federal) have the power to condemn or condone a practice; third about what normative sources (national, local, or transnational texts, case law, legislative history, structural interpretations reflecting moral and political theory) should be the basis for whatever rules are made; and fourth about what weight to accord non-domestic sources. The effort to delegitimize the use of foreign law is, in short, interrelated with battles about the role of judges in the American polity, the allocation of power in the federation, the authority of federal courts to shape legal rules, the meaning of American constitutional obligations, and the preferred methods of constitutional interpretation.

3. 'American justice' in Congress

Legislative efforts—akin to Senator Bricker's proposed constitutional amendment—continue to reflect conflicts about the permissibility of interacting with legal developments abroad. A recent example (quoted at the outset) from Congress, the proposed federal 'American Justice for American Citizens Act of 2004', instructs that '[n]either the Supreme Court of the United States nor any lower Federal court shall . . . employ the

[121] 132 S. Ct. at 2511 (Scalia, J., dissenting) (citing both a source that pre-dated the founding of the United States—Emer de Vattel's 'seminal 1758 treatise'—and another from the following century—I.R. Phillimore, *Commentaries upon International Law* (1854)).

[122] Justice Ruth Bader Ginsburg, Remarks to the International Academy of Comparative Law: 'A Decent Respect to the Opinions of [Human]kind: The Value of a Comparative Perspective in Constitutional Analysis' (July 30, 2010); Justice Ruth Bader Ginsburg, Remarks to the Constitutional Court of South Africa: 'A Decent Respect to the Opinions of [Human]kind: The Value of a Comparative Perspective in Constitutional Adjudication', (Feb. 7, 2006), transcripts available at <http://www.supremecourt.gov/publicinfo/speeches/speeches.aspx>.

[123] Ruth Bader Ginsburg and Deborah Merritt, 'Affirmative Action: An International Human Rights Dialogue', 21 Cardozo L. Rev. 253 (1999).

[124] See, e.g., 'A Conversation Between U.S. Supreme Court Justices: The relevance of foreign legal materials in U.S. constitutional cases: Justice Antonin Scalia and Justice Stephen Breyer', 3 Int'l J. Const. L. 519, 530 (2005); Sandra Day O'Connor, 'Remarks at the 79th Annual Meeting of the American Law Institute', 15 May 2002, in 79 A.L.I. PROC. 245, 247–9 (2002).

constitution, laws, administrative rules, executive orders, directives, policies, or judicial decisions of any international organization or foreign state, except for the English constitutional and common law or other sources of law relied upon by the Framers of the Constitution of the United States.'[125] The political expressive quality of this legislation gave it a high profile, even as its likelihood of passage was remote.[126]

Another means by which Senators can register concerns about the use of foreign law—without needing to get any of their colleagues to vote with them—is through questioning individuals nominated to the federal bench and subject for confirmation to the advice and consent of the Senate. All of the last four nominees to the Supreme Court were interrogated about whether they would turn to sources outside the United States when interpreting domestic constitutional obligations. All four abjured a plan to be importers, albeit with different explanations and qualifications.

In the exchanges over his nomination, then Judge John Roberts (now the Chief Justice) cited 'democratic theory' as a basis for his view that using non-U.S. law for constitutional interpretation was unwise, albeit not violative of a judge's oath of office—and implicitly—not appropriately prohibited by Congress.[127] The Chief Justice explained that the American system of judicial selection through the political branches (the federal constitution gives the power of nomination to the President and confirmation to the Senate) legitimated judicial authority, anchored judges' power in 'democratic theory', and thereby licensed their judgments. To use law developed from outside (he referenced several countries, including Germany and Indonesia) on 'what our Constitution means' would, he inferred, undercut accountability. Further, foreign law was too open-ended:

> [R]elying on foreign precedent doesn't confine judges. It doesn't limit their discretion the way relying on domestic precedent does... In foreign law you can find anything you want... [L]ooking at foreign law for support is like looking out over a crowd and picking out your friends... It allows the judge to incorporate his or her own personal preferences, cloak them with the authority of precedent because they are finding precedent in foreign law, and use that to determine the meaning of the Constitution.[128]

[125] H.R. 4118, 108th Cong. (2004).

[126] In 2005, Congress enacted new legislation related to the enforcement of the Geneva Conventions; a subsection stated that '[n]o foreign or international source of law shall supply a basis for a rule of decision in the courts of the United States.' 18 U.S.C. § 2441 (6)(a)(2). This provision was part of the Military Commission Act of 2006 (later amended in 2009), which was responsive to criticisms about and sought to insulate the government from claims brought by detainees held at Guantánamo Bay. The Supreme Court ruled aspects of the 2006 MCA that limited access to court for those detainees to be unconstitutional. See *Boumedienne v Bush*, 553 U.S. 723 (2008). The provision on foreign law was not in issue in the case but, in addition to the issues discussed later about the legality of such provisions in general, could raise due process problems, if defendants, charged with offences against the laws of war, wanted to argue that international standards aided their defense.

[127] *Confirmation Hearing on the Nomination of John G. Roberts, Jr to be Chief Justice of the United States: Hearing Before the Comm. on the Judiciary*, 109th Cong. at 201 (2005).

[128] Ibid. These critiques echo the debates in the literature. Overviews can be found in Vicki C. Jackson, 'Constitutional Comparisons: Convergence, Resistance, Engagement', 119 Harv. L. Rev. 109 (2005), in Christopher McCrudden, 'Judicial Comparativism and Human Rights', 371–98, in *Comparative Law: A Handbook* at 371–98 (Esin Orucu and David Nelkin eds., 2007), and in Neil Duxbury, 'The Law of the Land', 78 Modern L. Rev. 26 (2015).

Thus, aside from the interpretation of contracts (which may stipulate using another jurisdiction's law) and of treaties, the Chief Justice explained that he thought foreign law ought not to be used as a 'precedent on the meaning of American law'.

Justice Samuel Alito also bracketed treaties and private law questions during his confirmation hearings, when he too rejected foreign law for constitutional interpretation ('We have our own law. We have our own traditions. We have our own precedents. And we should look to that in interpreting our Constitution.').[129] In 2009, Justice Sonia Sotomayor was asked several times about the issue. Commenting that she shared Justice Ginsburg's view of foreign law's educational use, Justice Sotomayor stated, 'American law does not permit the use of foreign law or international law to interpret the Constitution'.[130] Justice Elena Kagan likewise registered an insistence on the use of American sources: 'Our Constitution is our own. It's . . . the text that we have been handed down from generation to generation . . . And except with respect to a very limited number of issues . . . the fundamental sources of legal support and legal argument for that Constitution ought to be American.'[131]

Some dismiss confirmation hearings as political theatre, but my view is that such performances provide windows into salient concerns, as Senators aim to please constituencies and shape agendas. By reading transcripts of hearings, one can see the changes in the questions asked. For example, during the 1970s and 1980s, a nominee's views of whether the Fourteenth Amendment should be read to apply to women became relevant.[132] Similarly, by reading confirmation hearings, one can track when foreign law became a topic with a political resonance that prompted four individuals—with very different backgrounds—all to be wary of embracing the legitimacy of its use in constitutional interpretation.

4. 'American law for American courts'

Federalism offers additional venues for debates about the judicial role and the place of foreign law. While some states and localities are importers of foreign law, other state-level action aims to buffer against it. For example, after 9/11, a new translocal, transnational movement emerged to provide a spate of anti-foreign law efforts, often coupled with anti-immigrant legislation.[133] The 'American Laws for American States' movement is itself border-crossing, propelled by translocal organizations such as the

[129] *Confirmation Hearing on the Nomination of Samuel A. Alito, Jr. To Be an Associate Justice of the Supreme Court of the United States: Hearing Before the S. Comm. on the Judiciary*, 109th Cong. at 370 (2006).

[130] *Confirmation Hearing on the Nomination of Sonia Sotomayor To Be an Associate Justice of the Supreme Court of the United States: Hearing Before the S. Comm. on the Judiciary*, 111th Cong. at 442 (2009).

[131] *Confirmation Hearing on the Nomination of Elena Kagan To Be an Associate Justice of the Supreme Court of the United States: Hearing Before the S. Comm. on the Judiciary*, 111th Cong. at 127 (June 29, 2010). She also noted that in 'a number of circumstances' (such as when deciding 'who counts as an ambassador'), international law would be relevant. Ibid.

[132] See Judith Resnik, 'Judicial Selection and Democratic Theory: Demand, Supply, and Life Tenure', 26 Cardozo L. Rev. 579, 631–5 (2005).

[133] See, e.g., Monica W. Varsanyi, 'Neoliberalism and Nativism: Local Anti-Immigration Policy Activism and the Emerging Politics of Scale', 35 Int'l J. Urban & Reg'l Res. 295, 296 (2011).

American Public Policy Alliance, the Center for Security Policy, ACT! For America, Society of Americans for National Existence (SANE), and Stop the Islamization of America, an entity related to Stop the Islamization of Europe.[134] These efforts have had significant political success, even after litigation challenging the legality of some of the mandates. Directives limiting the use of non-domestic law have become codified in both constitutions and statues.

In 2010, 70 percent of those who voted supported an Oklahoma constitutional amendment ('Save our State'), instructing that state's judges not to 'look to the legal precepts of other nations or cultures' and, specifically, not to consider either 'international or Sharia law'.[135] Thereafter, Muneer Awad, a practising Muslim and the Executive Director of a local chapter of the Council on American-Islamic Relations, asked a federal judge to enjoin the provision. Awad's lawsuit argued that the 'official condemnation' of his religion was an unconstitutional stigmatization that interfered with his religious freedom to execute his will in a manner he wished.[136] Both the trial and appellate federal courts agreed that Oklahoma had violated Awad's First Amendment rights and the provision could not survive strict scrutiny.[137] After that ruling, Oklahoma enacted a statute that no longer mentioned Sharia but which banned reliance on foreign law if not providing 'the same fundamental liberties, rights, and privileges granted under the United States and Oklahoma Constitutions.'[138]

As Oklahoma's new statute reflects, the 2012 federal court's invalidation of the constitutional provision had an impact on the wording of proposed bans but not on their popularity.[139] By 2013, anti-foreign law prohibitions had been introduced in 31

[134] David Yerushalmi, a founder of SANE and General Counsel for the Center for Security Policy and Stop Islamization of America, drafted a model statute. See 'About Us', Law Offices of David Yerushalmi, P.C., *available at* <http://www.davidyerushalmilaw.com/aboutus.php> (last visited Apr. 17, 2011). Some funding came from the William H. Donner and Sarah Scaife Foundations. See IRS Form 990-PF, William H. Donner Foundation (2009); Sarah Scaife Foundation, Annual Report 2 (2009), *available at* <http://www.scaife.com/sarah09.pdf>. See also Wajahat Ali, Eli Clifton, Matthew Duss, Lee Fang, Scott Keyes, and Faiz Shakir, *Fear, Inc.: The Roots of the Islamaphobia Network in America* (Center for American Progress, 2011). That report estimated that several organizations had contributed more than 40 million dollars between 2001 and 2009 to this work. Ibid. at 3.

[135] State Question Number 755/Legislative Referendum Number 355, Enr. H. J. R. No. 1056, Amending Oklahoma Constitution Art. 7, § 1 (May 25, 2010). The provision also required judges to 'uphold and adhere to the law as provided' by federal and state law 'and if necessary the law of another state of the United States provided the law of the other state does not include Sharia Law, in making judicial decisions.' Ibid. See generally Martha F. Davis and Johanna Kalb, 'Oklahoma State Question 755 and an Analysis of Anti-International Law Initiatives', ACS Issue Brief, Jan. 2011; 'Oklahoma and Beyond: Understanding the Wave of State Anti-Transnational Law Initiatives', 87 Ind. L.J. Supp. 1 (2011).

[136] Complaint at 7–8, 754 F. Supp. 2d 1298 (W.D. Okla. 2010) (No. Civ. 10-1186).

[137] *Awak v Ziriak*, 670 F.3d 1111 (10th Cir. 2012).

[138] See Okla. Stat. Ann. tit. 12, § 20 B (West 2014) ('Any court, arbitration, tribunal, or administrative agency ruling or decision shall violate the public policy of this state and be void and unenforceable if the court, arbitration, tribunal, or administrative agency bases its rulings or decisions in the matter at issue in whole or in part on foreign law that would not grant the parties affected by the ruling or decision the same fundamental liberties, rights, and privileges granted under the United States and Oklahoma Constitutions, including but not limited to due process, freedom of religion, speech, or press, and any right of privacy or marriage as specifically defined by the Constitution of this state.').

[139] See generally Amara S. Chaudry-Kravitz, 'The New Facially Neutral Anti-Sharia Bills: A Constitutional Analysis', 20 Wash & Lee J. Civil Rights & Soc. Justice 25 (2013).

other states,[140] with more than 100 different proposed bills. Some referenced 'Sharia' directly,[141] while others proposed to ban 'religious laws', 'foreign religious codes', the 'legal precepts of other nations or cultures', and/or 'international law'.[142] To avoid the many business agreements choosing another jurisdiction's law to govern conflicts if they arise, some proposals specified their application only to 'natural persons' and not to corporations.[143] Further, some proposals permitted foreign law more generally, if private contracts include choice of law clauses or if the U.S. has made treaties domestically applicable.

The texts of the proposals regularly posit 'foreign law' to be in tension with American rights. For example, the proposed 'American and Alabama Laws for Alabama Courts Amendment' (approved by a wide margin of voters in the autumn of 2014[144]) defined foreign law as 'any law, rule, or legal code, or system established, used, or applied in a jurisdiction outside of the states or territories of the United States, or which exist as a separate body of law, legal code, or system adopted or used anywhere by any people, group, or culture different from the Constitution and laws of the United States or the State of Alabama.' Alabama then mandated that a 'court, arbitrator, administrative agency, or other adjudicative, arbitrative, or enforcement authority shall not apply or enforce a foreign law if doing so would violate any state law or a right guaranteed by the Constitution of this state or of the United States.'[145]

The injunction in Kansas, which became law in May of 2012,[146] instructs against the use of 'any foreign law, legal code or system that would not grant the parties affected by

[140] See Faiza Patel, Matthew Duss, and Amos Toh, *Foreign Law Bans: Legal Uncertainties and Practical Problems* 1 (Center for American Progress, May 2013) [hereinafter *Foreign Legal Bans*]. See, e.g., S.B. 62, 2011 S., Reg. Sess. (Ala. 2011); H.B. 88, 27th Leg., 1st Sess. (Alaska 2011); S. Con. Res. 1010, 50th Leg., 1st Reg. Sess. (Ariz. 2011); S.B. 97, 88th Gen. Assemb., Reg. Sess. (Ark. 2011); S.B. 1360, 2012 S., 114th Reg. Sess. (Fla. 2012); H.B. 45, 151st Gen. Assemb., Reg. Sess. (Ga. 2011); S.J. Res. 16, 117 Gen. Assemb., 1st Reg. Sess. (Ind. 2011); H. Conc. Res. 44, 60th Leg., 2nd Reg. Sess. (Idaho 2010); H.B. 575, 84th Gen. Assemb., Reg. Sess. (Iowa 2011); S.B. 79, 84th Leg., Reg. Sess. (Kan. 2012); H.B. 386, Reg. Sess. (Ky. 2012); H.B. 785, Reg. Sess. (La. 2010); H.B. 811, 125th Leg., 1st Reg. Sess. (Me. 2011); H.B. 4769, 96th Leg., Reg. Sess. (Mich. 2011); S.B. 2281, 87th Leg., 2nd Reg. Sess. (Minn. 2011); H.B. 301, 126th Leg., Reg. Sess. (Miss. 2011); H.J. Res. 31, 96th Gen. Assemb., 1st Reg. Sess. (Mo. 2011); Leg. B. 647, 102nd Leg., 1st Reg. Sess. (Neb. 2011); H.B. 1422, 162nd Gen. Ct., Reg. Sess. (N.H. 2011); Assemb. B. 919, 215th Leg., 1st Ann. Sess. (N.J. 2012); S.J. Res. 18, 50th Leg., 1st Sess. (N.M. 2011); H.B. 640, 2011 Gen. Assemb., Reg. Sess (N.C. 2011); H.B. 2029, 195th Gen. Assemb., Reg. Sess. (Pa. 2011); S.B. 444, 119th Gen. Assemb., 1st Reg. Sess. (S.C. 2011); H.J. Res. 1004, 86th Leg. Assemb., Reg. Sess. (S.D. 2011); H.B. 3768, 169th Gen. Assemb., Reg. Sess. (Tenn. 2010); H.J. Res. 57, 82nd Leg., Reg. Sess. (Tex. 2011); H.B. 296, 58th Leg., Gen. Sess. (Utah 2010); H.B. 631, Reg. Sess. (Va. 2012); H.B. 3220, 80th Leg., Reg. Sess. (West. Va. 2011); H.J. Res. 8, 61st Leg., Gen. Sess. (Wyo. 2011). Similar legislation has also been introduced on the federal level. The 'Constitution Restoration Act' would have demanded the impeachment of federal judges for any citation to foreign law when interpreting the Constitution. See H.R. 3799, 108th Cong., tit. II § 201, tit. III §§ 301–302 (2004); S. 520, 109th Cong., tit. I § 101, tit. II §§ 301–302 (2005).

[141] See, e.g., S.J. Res. 18, 50th Leg., 1st Sess. (N.M. 2011). Some statutes used the term 'Sharia law', while the correct description would be 'Shari'a'—as it is law.

[142] See, e.g., S.B. 79, 84th Leg., Reg. Sess. (Kan. 2012).

[143] See, e.g., H.B. 3768, 169th Gen. Assemb., Reg. Sess. (Tenn. 2010).

[144] S. 4, 2013 Leg. Sess. (Ala. 2013).

[145] S. 4, 2013-269, Leg. Sess. (Ala. 2013); Ala. Const. Amend. DCCCLXXXIV (proclaimed ratified, Dec. 1, 2014).

[146] See Ariz. Rev. Stat. §§ 12-3101 to 3103 (2012); Kan. Stat. Ann. § 60-5103 (West 2012); La. Rev. Stat. Ann. § 9:6001 (2011); S.D. Codified Laws § 19-8-7 (2012); Tenn. Code Ann. §§ 20-15-101 to 20-15-106 (West 2012).

the ruling or decision the same fundamental liberties, rights and privileges granted under the United States and Kansas Constitutions.'[147] In addition to Oklahoma's constitutional and statutory enactments, Alabama's constitutional provision, and Kansas's law, the states of Arizona, Louisiana, South Dakota, and Tennessee have put into their laws variously worded prohibitions against 'foreign' law.

5. The legality of illegalization

The anti-foreign laws have prompted congressional hearings[148] and a good deal of commentary, much of it criticizing these provisions on various grounds.[149] In addition to focusing on their xenophobic quality, critics claim that such laws unwisely insert uncertainty into an array of legal exchanges.[150] Others dismiss the provisions as publicity stunts. How could judges, in a given case, scan a foreign law 'system' and compare it to all of American law? And given that state judges cannot otherwise violate the federal constitution, prohibitions on using foreign law to do so are superfluous. In addition, judges can avoid the threatened sanctions (such as their judgments being voided or, in a few formulations, their own impeachment) by not citing foreign sources even if using them.

I want to hold aside the potential for ready evasion through silence or through findings that U.S. law permits a result. Further, I will not rehearse the arguments about why foreign law bans can intrude on individual rights, as exemplified by the ruling that Oklahoma's constitutional amendment violated an individual's freedom of religion.[151] Nor will I explore here claims that such bans constitute targeted discrimination against minorities, unconstitutional interferences with contractual relationships, and that they undermine states' obligations under the Full Faith and Credit Clause to enforce judgments rendered in other states.

Instead I focus on the question of whether directions to judges not to cite foreign law violate structural aspects of U.S. law, in terms of federalism and separation of powers. To sharpen an understanding of what problems could exist, I probe not only the bans

[147] Kansas, House Substitute for Senate Bill No. 79, enacted May 2012. The variations are analysed in *Foreign Legal Bans*, n 140, at 15–20. A Louisiana statute, enacted in 2010, declares that no 'court, administrative agency, or other adjudicative, mediation, or enforcement authority shall enforce a foreign law if doing so would violate a right guaranteed by the constitution of this state or of the United States.' 2010 La. Sess. Law Serv. Act 714 (H.B. 785). See also 2010 Tenn. Laws Pub. Ch. 983 (H.B. 3768) (a similar provision).

[148] See, e.g., *Appropriate Role of Foreign Judgments in the Interpretation of American Law,* Hearing before the Subcom. On the Constitution of the Comm. On the Judiciary, U.S. House of Rep., 108th Cong. 2d Sess. H. Res. 568 (March 25, 2004) 14–18.

[149] See generally Cynthia Brougher, 'Application of Religious Law in U.S. Courts: Selected Legal Issues', Congressional Research Service, 705700, R41824, May 18, 2011.

[150] See Patel, Duss, and Toh, *Foreign Law Bans*, n 140, at 16–22.

[151] State Question Number 755/Legislative Referendum Number 355, Enr. H. J. R. No. 1056, Amending Oklahoma Constitution Art. 7, § 1 (May 25, 2010). The provision also required judges to 'uphold and adhere to the law as provided' by federal and state law 'and if necessary the law of another state of the United States provided the law of the other state does not include Sharia Law, in making judicial decisions.' Id. See generally Martha F. Davis and Johanna Kalb, 'Oklahoma State Question 755 and an Analysis of Anti-International Law Initiatives', ACS Issue Brief, Jan. 2011; 'Oklahoma and Beyond: Understanding the Wave of State Anti-Transnational Law Initiatives', 87 Ind. L. J. Supp. 1 (2011).

that have been enacted or proposed but their opposite—directives to judges requiring them to consider foreign sources. While largely hypothetical in the U.S. context, the idea is familiar—if one looks abroad. In contrast to the American directives to judges *against* referencing foreign law, many countries have provisions calling for judges *to* look outside their legal systems when making decisions about their own law.

The sources of and the terms vary: some constitutions call for 'respect for international law', or that a state must ensure 'that its laws comply with international law';[152] others recognize that international law 'shall have supremacy over the national legislation',[153] or require that a country 'observe obligations' under international law.[154] Some constitutions also specify that certain international agreements are superior to domestic constitutional law.[155] Others call for consideration of law from abroad. The Constitution of South Africa is the familiar exemplar, providing that '[w]hen interpreting the Bill of Rights, a court, tribunal or forum (a) must promote the values that underlie an open and democratic society based on human dignity, equality and freedom; (b) must consider international law; and (c) may consider foreign law.'[156]

[152] Const. of Belarus, art. 8. [153] Const. of Montenegro, art. 9.

[154] Const. of the Czech Republic, ch. 1, art. 1. See also Art. 44 of the French Constitution of Oct. 4, 1958.

[155] See, e.g., Article 51 (c), Constitution of India (1950) ('The State shall endeavour to... foster respect for international and treaty obligations in the dealings of organized people with each other'); Article 5(4), Federation of Constitution of the Swiss Confederation (1999) ('The Confederation and the Cantons shall respect international law'); Constitution of Spain, art. 10(2) (that fundamental rights guaranteed by the Constitution 'shall be construed in conformity with the Universal Declaration of Human Rights and international treaties and agreements thereon ratified by Spain').

Examples of statements of the higher authority of international law come from Art. 7 (1) of the Costa Rica Constitution (1949) ('Public treaties, international agreements and concordats duly approved by the Legislative Assembly have a higher authority than the laws upon their enactment or from the day that they designate.') Ch. IV Argentina, § 75, No. 22 (1994) ('Treaties and concordats have a higher hierarchy than laws. The American Declaration of the Rights and Duties of Man; the Universal Declaration of Human Rights; the American Convention on Human Rights; the International Pact on Economic, Social and Cultural Rights; the International Pact on Civil and Political Rights and its empowering Protocol; the Convention on the Prevention and Punishment of Genocide; the International Convention on the Elimination of all Forms of Racial Discrimination; the Convention on the Elimination of all Forms of Discrimination against Women; the Convention against Torture and other Cruel, Inhuman or Degrading Treatments or Punishments; the Convention on the Rights of the Child; in the full force of their provisions, they have constitutional hierarchy, do no repeal any section of the First Part of this Constitution and are to be understood as complementing the rights and guarantees recognized herein. They shall only be denounced, in such event, by the National Executive Power after the approval of two-thirds of all the members of each House. In order to attain constitutional hierarchy, the other treaties and conventions on human rights shall require the vote of two-thirds of all the members of each House, after their approval by Congress'); 2009 Const. of Bolivia art. 13(IV) ('The international treaties and conventions ratified by the Plurinational Legislative Assembly [Bolivia's unicameral Congress], that recognize human rights, and that prohibit their limitation during Emergency Situations prevail in the domestic order. The rights and duties established in this Constitution shall be interpreted in accordance with the international human rights treaties ratified by Bolivia.').

[156] Constitution of South Africa, Chapter Two: Bill of Rights, Art. 39 (adopted May 8, 1996) *available at* <http://www.gov.za/documents/constitution-republic-south-africa-1996>. The Constitution of Malawi, Article 11(2) has a similar statement, that when 'interpreting the provisions of this Constitution a court of law... (c) where applicable, have regard to current norms of public international and comparative foreign law.' Constitution of the Republic of Malawi (adopted May 16, 1994) *available at* <http://www.wipo.int/wipolex/en/text.jsp?file_id=218796>. South Africa also requires that, when 'interpreting any legislation, every court must prefer any reasonable interpretation of the legislation that is consistent with international law over any alternative interpretation that is inconsistent with international law.' Const. of South Africa, at Art. 233. In the United States, the 'Charming Betsy' canon, articulated in *Murray v Schooner Charming Betsy*, 6 U.S. 64 (1804), stands for a similar proposition—that acts of Congress

My question is not about how such obligations function in practice,[157] but rather about the structural legality of either bans or injunctions to use foreign law. Would it be lawful in the United States for federal or state constitutions or legislatures to require that in 'any case involving human rights and civil liberties, judges *must consider* international human rights law and may consider comparative law'? Do such directives—emanating from different legal actors by way of constitutions or statutes—trench on courts' inherent powers, federalism, judicial independence, or judges' freedom of thought?

Given the enactments at the state level (exemplified here with details of the bans in Oklahoma, Kansas, and Alabama, and the mandates in San Francisco to use CEDAW), a first issue is about the power of states and localities to address non-U.S. sources through constitutions, statutes, or executive action.[158] A doctrine in the United States takes the view that the federal government has exclusive authority over foreign affairs. If one categorized directives—banning or requiring foreign law—as intruding on that power, federal law would block state law-making under a doctrine known as 'foreign affairs preemption', which is sometimes described as 'implied' or 'dormant'. Those modifiers reflect that, while the U.S. Constitution mentions the word 'foreign' in six contexts (from commerce to the coinage of money, titles of nobility, jurisdiction, and entering into compacts or treaties[159]), none requires a reading of total federal exclusivity in relationship to all forms of foreign interactions.

Nonetheless, several Supreme Court rulings have held certain kinds of state decisions to infringe on federal authority. For example, the Court has relied on implied foreign affairs doctrine to prohibit the State of Massachusetts from banning the use of its own funds to buy products made through forced labour in a country then called Burma.[160] Likewise, the foreign affairs preemption doctrine served to invalidate a California statute requiring companies offering insurance to disclose their dealings

'ought never to be construed to violate the law of nations, if any other possible construction remains.' Ibid. at 118.

[157] See, e.g., Christa Rautenbach, 'South Africa: Teaching an "Old Dog" New Tricks? An Empirical Study of the Use of Foreign Precedents by the South African Constitutional Court' (1995–2010) in *The Use of Foreign Precedents*, n 7, at 186–209. See also Aparna Chandra, *Fostering Respect? The Supreme Court of India's Approach to International Law: A Call for Caution* (JSD dissertation, 2013).

[158] I do not address questions internal to a state, about whether a particular state's doctrine of separation of powers, inherent powers, or other provisions would apply—other than to note the argument that state court common lawmaking authority could be greater than that of the federal courts—making state courts more immune from directives from their legislatures than the federal courts.

[159] See Art. I § 8 Cl. 2 ('Congress shall have Power' 'To regulate Commerce with foreign Nations and among the several States, and with the Indian Tribes.'); Art. I § 8 Cl. 5 (giving Congress the power to 'coin Money, regulate the Value thereof, and of foreign Coin, and fix the Standard of Weights and Measures'); Art. I § 9 Cl. 8 ('no Person holding any Office of Profit or Trust under them, shall, without the Consent of the Congress, accept of any present, Emolument, Office, or Title, of any kind whatever, from any King, Prince, or foreign State'); Art. I § 10 Cl. 3 ('No State shall, without the Consent of Congress... enter into any Agreement or Compact with another State, or with a foreign Power...'); Art. III § 2 ('The judicial Power shall extend to all Cases, in Law and Equity, arising under this Constitution, the Laws of the United States, and Treaties made, or which shall be made, under their Authority... to Controversies... between a State, or the Citizens thereof, and foreign States, Citizens or Subjects'); Eleventh amend. ('The Judicial power of the United States shall not be construed to extend to any suit in law or equity, commenced or prosecuted against... Citizens or Subjects of any Foreign State').

[160] *Crosby v National Foreign Trade Council*, 530 U.S. 363 (2000).

during the Holocaust.[161] Similarly, when ruling that Arizona's criminalization of migration was preempted by federal statutes, locating authority for prosecution in the Attorney General, the majority in *Arizona v United States* asserted the importance of speaking on issues affecting international affairs with 'one voice'.[162]

These decisions rely on extrapolations of the treaty power, the mention of the word 'foreign nations' in the Commerce Clause, and ideas about what inheres in sovereignty. Indeed, the various contexts in which the doctrine has been deployed render the nomenclature of 'foreign affairs preemption' insufficient, as judges at times rely on 'war powers preemption' or 'foreign commerce preemption'.[163] Further, in some cases, the claim of exclusive national authority is predicated on a federal statute, while in other instances, preemption rests on the potential for conflict with national policies of the Executive branch.

Elsewhere, I have disagreed with this expansive form of preemption and, more generally, with the Court's over-use of preemption.[164] The thousands of exchanges among states and localities that cross borders (ranging, as noted, from 'sister city' programmes aiming to expand commercial activities to regulation of chemicals and human rights initiatives) make federal control implausible, undesirable, and harmful to federalist virtues. Absent clear directions from Congress that U.S. policy requires a single point and form of interaction, the Court ought not craft its own foreign affairs policies by precluding state interactions—be they for or against using foreign law.

Yet, even if states were precluded from enacting foreign law edicts, federal supremacy arguments do not prevent the federal government from giving instructions to its judges.[165] This chapter opened with a 2004 proposed congressional formulation—instructing federal judges not to 'employ the constitution, laws, administrative rules, executive orders, directives, policies, or judicial decisions of any international organization or foreign state', aside from sources extant at the founding and relied on by 'the Founders'.[166] Given the unlikelihood of a constitutional amendment, would such directives from Congress—as well as mandates to consider foreign sources—be lawful? Does the Constitution itself have a position on the use of foreign sources in interpretation? Do separation of powers doctrine or ideas about inherent judicial power, the independence of the judiciary, or speech rights of judges render such directives unconstitutional?

Recall that some historians of the U.S. Constitution read it as speaking to both a domestic and an external audience and as drawing its legitimacy from functioning on both dimensions.[167] One could interpret that history, coupled with textual references to the 'Law of Nations', the decision to make treaties the supreme law of the land, and the

[161] *American Insurance Ass'n v Garamendi*, 539 U.S. 396 (2003).

[162] *Arizona v United States*, 132 S. Ct. at 2507 (Kennedy, J. for the majority).

[163] See, e.g., *Deutsch v Turner Corp.*, 324 F.3d 692 (9th Cir. 2003); *National Foreign Trade Council v Giannoulias*, 523 F. Supp. 731 (N.D. Ill. 2007).

[164] See, e.g., Resnik, 'Foreign as Domestic Affairs', n 99.

[165] The Supreme Court has also recognized congressional authority to require state courts to enforce federal law, and hence I focus here on interactions between Congress and the federal courts.

[166] H.R. 4118, 108th Cong. (2004). The bill was introduced by Representatives Ron Paul, Republican representing Texas, and Marilyn Musgrave, Republican representing Colorado.

[167] See Golove and Hulsebosch, n 14.

jurisdictional provisions for foreigners in federal courts,[168] as a thin version of the South African directive to look abroad for resources, or at least as permitting such inquiries. And, as noted, specific constitutional provisions—'cruel and unusual punishment' or 'unreasonable' searches and seizures, or the liberty related to gun control—may be understood as calling for a border-crossing analysis to interpret the meaning of their terms. Yet an alternative approach is to read the constitutional text as banning such exchanges. For example, the Supremacy Clause's statement that the 'Constitution and the laws of the United States which are made pursuant thereof shall be the supreme law of the land' could be the basis for an argument precluding foreign law's relevance.[169]

Return then to the hypothetical congressional statute addressing the issues. Under current doctrine, if the Constitution provides an answer, Congress may implement it but cannot alter its underlying meaning. In 1997, in *City of Boerne v Flores*, the Court held that Congress had infringed its prerogative to determine the contours of the constitutional guarantee of freedom of religion. 'While the line between measures that remedy or prevent unconstitutional actions and measures that make a substantive change in the governing law is not easy to discern, and Congress must have wide latitude in determining where it lies, the distinction exists and must be observed.'[170]

One could therefore read the Constitution as itself directive on the issue of foreign sources, affirming or negating their reference. With or without that construction, other facets of the Constitution also come into play. Article III both states that the 'judicial power' shall extend to a series of kinds of cases and provides that federal judges have life tenure and salaries that cannot be diminished.[171] Further, freedom of thought and expression are enshrined in the First Amendment. Linking Article III commitments to judicial independence with the First Amendment could require that judges be unfettered in deciding what materials are relevant to their work.

Judges' authority over their own evaluative choices has a good deal of appeal;[172] traditions of judicial independence date from the English Act of Settlement of 1701 and moved through state constitutions into Article III's protections. Commitments to those protections may be the reason why some members of Congress have proposed a 'resolution' providing the 'sense' of Congress on the impropriety of the use of foreign law, rather than—as other members have—a statute banning its use.[173] Indeed, some of the justices identified as hostile to the use of foreign law are among those most committed to certain prerogatives of life-tenured judges—striking, for example, specific grants of power to bankruptcy judges (who lack life tenure), as well as congressional efforts to reinstate cases wrongly dismissed under the Court's interpretation of a federal

[168] See U.S. Const, Art. I. sec. 8, cl. 10; Art. VI; Art. III sec. 2 cls. 1 and 2.

[169] See *Appropriate Role of Foreign Judgments in the Interpretation of American Law: Hearing Before the H. Comm. on the Judiciary*, 108th Cong. at 1 (2004) (Statement of Representative Chabot) [hereinafter *2004 Appropriate Role of Foreign Judgments House Hearing*].

[170] 521 U.S. 507, 508 (1997).

[171] See Judith Resnik, 'Judicial Independence and Article III: Too Much and Too Little', 72 U.S.C. L. Rev. 657 (1999).

[172] *2004 Appropriate Role of Foreign Judgments Hearing*, n 169, at 14–18 (statement of Vicki Jackson, Professor of Law, Georgetown University Law Center).

[173] See H. Res. 568, discussed in *2004 Appropriate Role of Foreign Judgments Hearing*, n 169.

statute.[174] Justice Scalia has invoked the idea of the judicial 'department', which is not a term the Constitution uses, to underscore the judiciary's institutional authority to render final judgments without congressional superintendence.[175] Thus, even as Justice Scalia inveighed against the use of foreign law, he also cautioned against congressional directives preventing judges from using it.[176]

Yet Justice Scalia has also declined to ascribe general common law powers to the federal judiciary and has read the remedial authority of judges to be deeply dependent on Congress.[177] Further, Article III offers little textual direction on the contours of 'the judicial power', and judicial freedom is routinely curtailed by Congress—detailing the scope of federal court jurisdiction, creating or abolishing causes of action, requiring courts to apply certain law, and at times structuring decision-making and remedial authority. Sometimes Congress's focus is on standards, procedures, and remedies for statutory rights, and at other times statutes address constitutional claims.

The First Amendment is likewise not necessarily a safe haven, even as it has been the source of limiting state regulation of judicial elections. While candidates for judicial office have robust speech rights,[178] and judicial decisions may also have First Amendment protections,[179] codes of ethics constrain judicial speech, and more generally government employees' speech can be subject to significant control by their employers, albeit not in all circumstances.[180] Compelling speech (such as doctors or lawyers being required to give specific information) if interfering with professional judgments[181] may raise special concerns.[182] But if congressional directives to judges—either to consider or abjure from considering foreign law—were to be understood as justified by a compelling government interest, speech rights would give way.

In short, the parameters of congressional authority over the courts have produced dozens of decisions and decades of commentary struggling to delineate permissible directives from unconstitutional 'intrusions'. Those in search of criticism of, or of support for, directions on foreign law can find authority for their positions by drawing on competing lines of cases. For example, statutes dating from the 1930s governing

[174] See, e.g., *Plaut v Spendthrift Farm, Inc.*, 514 U.S. 211 (1995) (Scalia, J., writing for the Court); *Stern v Marshall*, 131 S. Ct. 2594 (2011) (Roberts, C.J., writing for the Court).

[175] Plaut, 514 U.S. at 218, 221.

[176] See Charles Lane, 'Scalia Tells Congress to Mind Its Own Business', Washington Post, May 19, 2006, available at <http://www.washingtonpost.com/wp-dyn/content/article/2006/05/18/AR2006051801961.html>.

[177] See, e.g., *Grupo Mexicano de Desarrollo, S.A. v Alliance Bond Fund*, 527 U.S. 308 (1999), discussed in Judith Resnik, 'Constricting Remedies: The Rehnquist Judiciary, Congress, and Federal Power', 78 Ind. L.J. 223, 234 (2003).

[178] *Republican Party v White*, 536 U.S. 765 (2002). In 2015, the Supreme Court considered whether the First Amendment prohibited a state from banning the direct solicitation of funds by candidates for judicial office. The Supreme Court of Florida had concluded that such an ethical limitation promoted the state's compelling interests in the integrity of the judicial and public confidence in the judiciary. The U.S. Supreme Court affirmed in a 5–4 decision. See *Williams-Yulee v Florida Bar*, 135 S. Ct. 1656 (2015).

[179] See, e.g., *In re Kendall*, 712 F.3d 814 (3d Cir. 2013); *Harrison v Coffman*, 35 F. Supp. 3d 722 (E.D. Ark. 1999).

[180] *Garcetti v Ceballos*, 547 U.S. 410 (2006); *Lane v Franks*, 134 S. Ct. 2369 (2014).

[181] See, e.g., *Legal Services Corp. v Velazquez*, 531 U.S. 533 (2001).

[182] *Rust v Sullivan*, 500 U.S. 173 (1991); *Agency for International Development v Alliance for Open Society International*, 133 S. Ct. 2321 (2013).

disputes about labour, utilities, and taxes limit judicial authority by specifying what findings judges must make as predicates to the issuance of injunctions.[183]

One might posit these examples as about only statutory rights, over which the power of Congress would be at its height. But some enactments address constitutional rights enforcement. For example, in 1996, Congress enacted the Prison Litigation Reform Act (PLRA) specifically to limit the powers of judges to respond to lawsuits charging that conditions in state prisons violated constitutional prohibitions on cruel and unusual punishment. When the statute was proposed, its acronym was 'STOP', and its point—explained in hearings—was to halt decades of federal adjudication on behalf of prisoners in Texas, Philadelphia, and elsewhere.

In the PLRA, Congress required judges to make specific findings before issuing injunctions;[184] precluded certain remedies such as releasing inmates to relieve over-crowding absent additional findings;[185] authorized parties or interveners to move to terminate injunctions two years after their issuance unless judges made new findings that relief was still necessary;[186] and deemed such motions as imposing an automatic stay of previously entered remedial orders injunctions, albeit with some potential for postponement.[187] A few lower courts held that some of these provisions were unconstitutional intrusions on judicial power (in part because final injunctions put into place were undone[188]). But the Supreme Court approved congressional imposition of an automatic stay, and concluded that the statute did not unconstitutionally reopen a judgment; rather the Court construed the statute to structure the 'prospective effect of previously entered injunctions'.[189] Further, the Court held that the time limitations were not so constraining as to create a due process problem. Thereafter, other PLRA constraints have generally been assumed to be constitutional.

The PLRA is legislation aiming to curb 'liberal' judges. Others want to slow down 'conservative' judges through superintending court decision-making. For example, scholars who viewed the Court as too ready to strike congressional statutes have argued that Congress could impose a super-majority voting rule as a predicate to the Court's finding a statute unconstitutional.[190] These analyses draw on lines of constitutional precedents and scholarly commentary positing that the Congress has virtually plenary control over the lower federal courts and a great deal of authority over the Supreme Court, aside from its original jurisdiction.

[183] See, e.g., *Lauf v Shinner*, 303 U.S. 323 (1938), and the Norris-LaGuardia Act of 1932, 29 U.S.C. §§ 1010–115.

[184] 18 U.S.C. § 3626(a) (2012).

[185] Ibid. See *Brown v Plata*, 131 S. Ct. 1910 (2011) (upholding a cap on the number of prisoners in the California prison system).

[186] See 18 U.S.C. § 3626(b). [187] See 18 U.S.C. § 3626(e).

[188] See, e.g., *Ruiz v Johnson*, 37 F. Supp. 2d 855 (S.D. Tex., 1999), rev'd in *Ruiz v United States*, 243 F. 3d 941 (5th Cir. 2001); *French v Duckworth*, 178 F.3d 437 (7th Cir. 1999), rev'd sub nom. *Miller v French*, 530 U.S. 327 (2000).

[189] *Miller v French*, 530 U.S. 327, 344 (2000).

[190] See Evan H. Caminker, 'Thayerian Deference to Congress and Supreme Court Supermajority Rule: Lessons from the Past', 78 Indiana L.J. 72 (2002); Jed Handelsman Shugarman, 'A Six-Three Rule: Reviving Consensus and Deference on the Supreme Court', 37 Ga. L. Rev. 893 (2003).

Yet the Court has also imposed limits on congressional powers by relying on Article III, structural commitment to separation of powers, guarantees of habeas corpus and due process and (as *City of Boerne* illustrates) the Court's sense of itself as the final arbiter of constitutionality. A famous example is the post-Civil War case, *United States v Klein*, which held unconstitutional a congressional statute requiring courts to find that a presidential pardon was proof of disloyalty to the Union.[191] Depending on how broadly one reads *Klein* (which could be understood as preventing Congress from directing a rule of decision in a particular case or from permitting judges to interfere with the presidential pardon power),[192] directives on foreign law could be impermissible. Similarly, a case dealing with the Military Commissions Act of 2006 struck limits on federal judges' decision-making under guarantees that the right of habeas corpus not be suspended;[193] the Court ruled that Congress had unduly restricted the role of federal judges as fact finders when individuals challenged their detention. But once again, other statutes, which could be seen to be as intrusive as that invalidated in *Klein*—such as a provision enacted to address two pending cases and directing that the Bureau of Land Management had met the statutory criteria—have not been found to be *Klein* problems; the Court read the statute as altering the substantive standards of adjudication rather than directing an outcome, even as, by doing so, the statute did resolve pending cases.[194]

Thus, the relevant lines of cases provide a good deal of interpretative licence in deciding if and when Congress has impermissibly trenched upon the judicial power. Indeed, the doctrine governing Court–Congress relationships is full of the kinds of judicial judgments that critics of citations to foreign law see as its vices—unaccountable judges reasoning through concepts about judicial role and legislative authority by choosing among competing lines of cases ('picking friends') and by making interpretative choices to resolve pressing legal questions.

What then is the relationship between democratic theory and consideration of foreign sources and between the constitutional creation of a federal judiciary and congressional directives? Chief Justice Roberts, joining several commentators, argued that democratic practices made the turn to foreign law inappropriate because law had to be made by judges selected through domestic democratic practices. In contrast, I see democratic theory as a resource for judicial use of foreign materials as well as other bodies of information. Democratic theory posits judges to be independent actors. That understanding of the judicial role developed over several centuries as sovereignty shifted from monarchies to the people. Transnational precepts altered the conception of judges, who were once positioned as loyal servants of the state. Instead, judges became a distinct kind of government employee—licensed by governments, yet authorized to sit in judgment of the very governments that deploy them. Further, transnational

[191] *Klein v United States*, 80 U.S. 128 (1871).

[192] See William Young, 'A Critical Reassessment of the Case Law Bearing on Congress's Power to Restrict the Jurisdiction of the Lower Federal Courts', 54 Maryland L. Rev. 132 (1995).

[193] *Boumediene v Bush*, 553 U.S. 723 (2008). See n 126.

[194] *Robertson v Seattle Audubon Soc'y*, 503 U.S. 429 (1992).

understandings reshaped courts as venues obliged to treat all persons—regardless of race, ethnicity, and gender—as equal and dignified participants, entitled to be heard.[195]

It is this conception of the judiciary that limits the authority of legislatures to constrain the intellectual resources available to judges. Congress may be able to structure the processes and predicates for decision-making and establish the standards by which actions are judged. Congress may also request that judges consider a host of factors and entertain a variety of materials, domestic or foreign. But legislatures cannot, in a democracy, attempt to constrain judicial thought-processes by banning consideration of a category of materials, labelled 'foreign'.

Yet, as I have also shown, that conclusion rests on choices among the doctrines about the contours of congressional control over the judiciary. In short, given the competing understanding of judges and the myriad of congressional directives to which they are subject, the legality of statutes prohibiting citations to foreign law—like that of many other statutes—illuminates the choices that judges have as they shape the meaning of the 'judicial power' as well as of the 'foreign'.

III. Affiliation by law

A review is in order. First, in constitutional doctrine, statutes, and administrative regulation, the use of non-domestic law in United States law is ordinary and often goes unremarked upon. Further, a lively import and export trade is facilitated by a myriad of cross-border crossings, enthusiastically supported by a host of government officials. Moreover, avoiding law without 'foreign' sources is functionally impossible. Thus, and second, significant work is required to try to chill such use, as the recent wave of political mobilization to 'save' America for 'American law' illustrates.

Third, the proposed 'American law for American Courts' formulations are either unconstitutional limits on religious practices (the Oklahoma example) or readily avoidable. State-based efforts may also be illegal under current foreign affairs preemption doctrine, although that approach rests on judicial expansiveness aiming to limit state and local initiatives beyond what Congress has expressly directed.

Deciding the legality of congressional directives on foreign sources requires either a view that the Constitution decides the question or extrapolation from constitutional theories about judicial role, separation of powers, and First Amendment theories. Admonitions to consider foreign law comport with the idea of a common law judge reasoning from a mix of text, precedents, and ideas. In contrast, proposals to ban consideration of resources from abroad are in tension with the conception of a democratic government welcoming the intellectual freedom of judges. Yet case law has tolerated other constraints on judging—leaving the decision about whether such directives impermissibly encroached the judicial power in the hands of judges, choosing among lines of doctrine and theory that have been shaped through transnational construction of judges as independent.

[195] See Judith Resnik and Dennis Curtis, *Representing Justice: Invention, Controversy and Rights in City-States and Democratic Courtrooms* (2011).

Fourth, the contemporary political successes of anti-foreign law initiatives prompt another kind of inquiry—about the desirability of playing the 'law card' when inscribing political identity. In a well-known book about the formation of nation-states, Benedict Anderson saw maps and museums, the construction of a shared history, census-taking, and wars as the building blocks of the 'imagined community' that constitutes the state.[196] Proponents of 'American law for American Courts' add another source, by looking to law as central to the construction of identity.

For professional jurists, the idea of law-as-affiliation ought to be heartening.[197] In lieu of ethnic, religious, or other divides, law serves to create identity and ties. That stance has echoes of Robert Cover's insistence on attending to the interaction between the jurisgenerativity of paideic communities and the law of the state. Cover described some operations of the state as jurispathic, able—through power and force—to displace law generated from other sites.[198] (His examples included the challenges that insular communities, such as the Mennonites, posed for American efforts to create universal educational requirements, and the conflicts between some religious orders, committed to racial segregation, and equality principles.[199])

Sovereigntists such as the supporters of 'American law for American Courts', as well as Senator Bricker and Justice Scalia, could be understood as appreciating Cover's insights, for they too put the processes of law-generation on the table as a social and political practice. The acts of pronouncing, adhering to, reiterating, and implementing legal obligations are ways in which to make certain stances constituent of community membership,[200] and legislators in Oklahoma, Alabama, Kansas, and elsewhere are demonstrating that they can generate popular interest in law as central to identity.

What is disquieting about objections to foreign law is not the effort to build community through law but the commitment that distinctive legal polities are forged through unilateral law-production walled off from and inhospitable to different precepts.[201] That position ignores that the origins of laws blur. Certain precepts now seen to be foundational to the United States ought to be labelled 'made in the USA' only if one knows that—like other 'American' products—some of the parts and designs are produced abroad. Yet the sovereigntist efforts also serve as reminders that branding a precept as 'American' is an act of ownership with consequences that cosmopolitans and internationalists may too easily discount.

196 Benedict Anderson, *Imagined Communities: Reflections on the Origin and Spread of Nationalism* (2006, revised edition; first published in 1983).

197 Bruce Ackerman's series of books on *We the People* provides a powerful example. See *We the People 3, The Civil Rights Revolution* (2014).

198 Robert M. Cover, 'The Supreme Court, 1982 Term—Forward: Nomos and Narrative', 97 Harv. L. Rev. 4, 12–14 (1983).

199 Ibid. at 60–6.

200 Judith Resnik, 'Living One's Legal Commitments: Paideic Communities, Courts and Robert Cover', 17 Yale J. L. and Humanities 17 (2006). See also Jean L. Cohen, 'Changing Paradigms of Citizenship and the Exclusiveness of the Demos', 14 Int'l Sociology 245 (1999); Seyla Benhabib, 'On Michel Rosenfeld's *The Identity of the Constitutional Subject*', 33 Cardozo L. Rev. 1889 (2012); Jean L. Cohen, *Globalization and Sovereignty: Rethinking Legality, Legitimacy, and Constitutionalism* (2012); James Bohman, *Democracy Across Borders: From Dêmos to Dêmoi* (2007).

201 See Seyla Benhabib, *Dignity in Adversity: Human Rights in Troubled Times* 6–19; 66–76 (2011).

One can, however, embrace 'American law' without becoming an exclusive sovereigntist. The alternative obligations from constitutions around the world—calling for legal orders to 'respect' or to 'consider' or to be bound by law from abroad—are no less sovereigntist. They too insist that identity requires interactions with law, albeit inclusively so, by recognizing jurists and communities elsewhere as important interpreters.[202] To acknowledge those links is not to underestimate the importance of identifying with and using law in demos-making.

[202] See, e.g., Johanna Kalb, 'The Judicial Role in New Democracies: A Strategic Account of Comparative Citation', 38 Yale J. Int'l L. 423 (2013); Gary Jeffrey Jacobsohn, 'The Permeability of Constitutional Borders', 82 Tex. L. Rev. 1763 (2004). See generally Jackson, *Constitutional Engagement*, n 14.

24

The Use of Comparative Law before the French Private Law Courts

*Guy Canivet**

I. Introduction

As globalization increasingly exposes us to problems that transcend national boundaries and legal systems, it seems that the importance of the judiciary is clearly increasing. In our advanced democracies, there is a general demand for judicial intervention to solve serious social problems. In whichever legal system he or she belongs, be it common law or civil law, one of the judge's main roles is to adapt the law to the evolution of society. The great changes of our times take the form, as we all know, of a vertiginous scientific and technological progress and of the speeding-up of trade globalization. All these phenomena deeply call into question the economic, social, and cultural equilibrium of a country and challenge its system of values.[1]

The specific role of the judge is to accompany these changes by laying down the framework inside which they will produce their effects. There clearly is a bipolarity in the exercise of the judicial function. A first pole of fluidity is represented by scientific and technological progress. This pole is matched by a second pole of stability, represented by society's foundational values. The judge is always guided by the protection of social values. The task is to constantly create a bridge between the law and the values of the society in which he or she lives, both with the means of his own legal culture and with the aid of comparative law.

In this chapter, I would like to argue that the use of comparative law is essential to the fulfilment of a supreme court's role in a modern democracy. I will use the example of the French Cour de cassation, which is the supreme court on civil and criminal affairs in my country. In section II of this chapter, I will try to lay down a theoretical framework that can help us account for and assess a supreme court's role in the preservation of social values in an ever-changing world. In section III, I will then try to analyse the importance of comparative law in this enterprise by giving some examples from the Cour de cassation's practice. My working hypothesis is that comparative law is not ornamental, a favourite pastime for Olympian judges isolated in their ivory tower; on the contrary, it is becoming more and more important, both for the resolution of conflicts and for the protection of democratic values by the judiciary.

* Conseil Constitutionnel, France.

[1] See generally William Twining, *Globalisation and Legal Theory* (London, Butterworths, 2000).

II. The protection of social values by a supreme court

As we all know, the opening of the courtroom to scientific progress and innovation is one of the main factors of development of new case law. New trends in scientific evidence, like genetic expertise, inevitably widen the horizon of the judge by inducing creative legal reasoning.[2] But this reasoning cannot do without legal protection and adjustment of social values. For it is obvious that globalization increasingly exposes the judge to systems of thought and to cultures that transcend national borders. And since judges assume an ever-widening role in the resolution of social conflicts, they are destined to tackle head-on the legal problems spurred by the process of globalization. Even though the task is novel, they have all the requisites of success.

The French private law judges are no longer—if they ever really were—considered as the 'mouth that produces the words of the law' (according to the famous expressions by Montesquieu).[3] They are commissioned to adjust the law to the values of their society. In this task, they might find of use their own legal culture, of course, but also comparative law. Anyway, local and foreign legal cultures constantly interact. The judges must, by necessity, maintain the coherence and integrity of a full-blown legal system by relentlessly referring to the abiding features of their own law and legal culture. But no legal culture is exclusively inward-looking; it can favour, at least in the long run, the emergence of a common law for a specified legal region, without denying, for that reason, national identities and traditions.

The law does not just regulate social relations. It also reflects widely shared social values. The judges understand their society's law as a coherent ensemble that evolves together with a social reality in perpetual motion. This is clearly the case in common law countries. Their legal systems encapsulate several centuries of flexible responsiveness of the law to social changes. But this is also the case in civil law countries like mine, where the courts complete and give meaning to legislative changes through their work of interpretation.

How does the judge preserve widely shared values by assimilating social changes? The judge's work cannot be conceived under the model of revolution or of discontinuity. Every judgment must maintain the normative coherence of the legal system by implementing its fundamental values. The courts of a country, especially the high courts, must integrate every judicial decision in a narrative that gives voice to its legal traditions. Every judge must, in a sense, contribute to the 'chain novel' of law that is constantly being written, according to the celebrated analogy of legal philosopher Ronald Dworkin.[4]

The judge cannot but strive after a certain consistency and constancy of the law, hostile to any disruption or jolt. The basis of justification for action is not political will,

[2] This point was first made by a great American judge, Benjamin Cardozo. See his famous lecture *The Nature of the Judicial Process* (New Haven, Conn., Yale University Press, 1921) and also Benjamin N. Cardozo, *The Paradoxes of Legal Science* 10–11 (Westport, Conn., Greenwood Press, 1970) (1928).

[3] Charles de Secondat, baron de Montesquieu, *The Spirit of Laws* 209 (David Wallace Carrithers intro., notes and appendices, Berkeley, Cal., University of California Press, 1977) (1750).

[4] Ronald Dworkin, *Law's Empire* 229 (Cambridge, Mass., Belknap Press, 1986).

which is an essentially capricious thing, but argumentative transparency and honesty. The judges are not permitted to propel transformations by themselves. In common law countries, this idea takes the form of the rule of *stare decisis*, that requires that all distinctions of a judicial precedent be expressly founded on a convincing argument.[5] In civil law countries like France, this idea is mostly expressed as the requirement that every reversal in case law should follow a change in the spirit of legislation. Even in the areas where transformations are speedy (like bioethics), the structure of the fundamental principles and values the judge has to protect always gives a certain stability to legal change.[6]

Other factors play also a role in this tendency toward a more evolutionary than revolutionary change in case law. The judge never has the initiative of change; he or she inevitably depends on the petition submitting a case to the court. Thus, the judges do not have the means of promoting a political agenda, since the changes in law they can induce are, after all, limited and interstitial. Only the political branches can master the mass of data that is necessary to global decision-making and can mobilize institutions in order to obtain desired results.[7] Lastly, even judicial interpretations that are creative and dynamic are always dependent on the perception and the legitimate expectations of the legal community and of the public at large. The settled expectations and the reliance of jurists and of citizens who read judicial opinions do not permit the judge to overstep boundaries in the name of experimentation or of innovative interpretation. Judges dispose of a legitimacy capital they should not manage in the short run.[8]

One can resume the preceding developments by saying that a main task of a supreme court is to stabilize legal norms by seeking consistency and by implementing incremental changes in the law. Two concepts are instrumental in the judge's effort to maintain this pole of stability: 'fundamental principles' and 'human rights'. These concepts provide the ground for judicial innovation—including the use of comparative law—because they express the principles of political morality that underlie the law and tie it down to societal values.[9]

[5] See generally Rupert Cross and J.W. Harris, *Precedent in English Law* (Oxford, Clarendon Press and New York, Oxford University Press, 4th edn., 1991), and Neil MacCormick and Robert S. Summers (eds.), *Interpreting Precedents: A Comparative Study* (Brookfield, Vt., Aldershot, Ashgate, 1997).

[6] On the judge's role as collaborator with the legislator in statutory interpretation, see generally William D. Popkin, *Statutes in Court: The History and Theory of Statutory Interpretation* (Durham, N.C., 1999). Professor William N. Eskridge, Jr exposes powerfully the idea of a hermeneutic back-and-forth process between social values and statutory law in his book *Dynamic Statutory Interpretation* (Cambridge, Mass., Harvard University Press, 1994).

[7] These data are so-called 'legislative facts', that are gathered and processed on a wide scale by the legislative branch in order to invent a new policy or to reshape an institution; they are to be distinguished from 'adjudicative facts', that are the facts necessary for the resolution of a concrete case or controversy before a court. On this distinction, see, e.g., Kenneth L. Karst, 'Legislative Facts in Constitutional Litigation', Supreme Court Review 75 (1960), and Henry P. Monaghan, 'Constitutional Fact Review', 85 Columbia Law Review 229 (1985).

[8] American sociology of law has been insistent on this point; see Gerald Rosenberg, *The Hollow Hope: Can Courts Bring About Social Change?* (Chicago, Ill., University of Chicago Press, 1991). Cf. M.D.A. Freeman, 'Standards of Adjudication, Judicial Law-Making and Prospective Overruling', 26 Current Legal Problems 166, 181 (1973): 'To understand the judicial role and apprise the legitimacy of judicial creativity one must explore the shared expectations which define the role of the judge.'

[9] For the notion of 'public values' expounded by the law, see Cass R. Sunstein, *The Partial Constitution* (Cambridge, Mass., Harvard University Press, 1993). The legal philosopher Ronald Dworkin used the term

Fundamental principles—or foundational values—of law underlie and justify the legal rules of a given society. Without their 'gravitational force' (according to Dworkin's expression),[10] legal rules would be atomized and would coagulate in a heap of precepts lacking any internal coherence. Fundamental principles are the reason why the texture of the law is open, but by no means discontinuous.[11] They are the normative background against which legal texts will be interpreted and enforced. In other words, fundamental principles give meaning and restrain at the same time any legal change, because they attach positive law to a certain number of values that shape the public morality of a country. Thus, any influence or inroad of comparative law on national practice is necessarily mediated by the domestic legal system's fundamental principles.

For our purposes, it is important to acknowledge at this point the double nature of fundamental legal principles. Indeed, fundamental principles are at the same time aspirational[12] and instrumental; they express the objectives of a legal system and the means that system uses to achieve them. A fundamental principle such as due process of law (or adjudicative fairness), for example, simultaneously expresses an ideal of society and a body of technical legal rules apt to approximate this ideal. Thus, any comparison of a domestic legal system or institution with a foreign one necessarily passes through the filter of the fundamental principles of the former.[13] Moreover, fundamental principles run the whole spectrum from grand principles (such as substantive justice or fair treatment) to social standards of behaviour (such as the 'reasonable man' or the 'good faith' standards in tort and contract law, respectively). They help us place the legal concepts or institutions we want to compare at the proper level of generality, which is not always the same between differing legal systems.[14]

Human rights made a staggering appearance on the scene in the wake of World War II. They were integrated in the postwar Constitutions and undoubtedly became the horizon of western democracies.[15] Respect for human rights nowadays condition every economic or social policy. The dynamic character of human rights is the result of the fact that they sometimes put a break on, and sometimes accelerate, changes. If we

'political morality' to express the same idea; see Ronald Dworkin, *Taking Rights Seriously* (London, Duckworth, 1977) and *A Matter of Principle* (Cambridge, Mass., Harvard University Press, 1985).

[10] Ronald Dworkin, *Taking Rights Seriously*, ibid, 26–7. William Eskridge builds on that notion by writing that 'public values have a gravitational force that varies according to their source... and the degree of our historical and contemporary commitment to these values' (William N. Eskridge, Jr, 'Public Values in Statutory Interpretation', 137 *University of Pennsylvania Law Review* 1007, 1018 (1989)).

[11] On the 'open texture of the law', see H.L.A. Hart, *The Concept of Law* 121–32 (Oxford, Clarendon Press, 1961).

[12] The expression is Lon Fuller's; see Lon L. Fuller, *The Morality of Law* 5–19, 41–4 (New Haven, Conn., Yale University Press, 1964).

[13] As I will try to show in section III.

[14] It is only by understanding the functionality of a principle in a given legal system that we can assess the similarity between two principles of a different pedigree. Thus, a comparative law research permits us to understand that the principles of 'good faith' in civil law systems and of 'reasonableness' in common law systems share the same function; cf. Roger Brownsword, Norma J. Hird, and Geraint Howells (eds.), *Good Faith in Contract: Concept and Context* (Brookfield, Vt., Aldershot, 1999) with American Law Institute, *Restatement (Second) of Contracts*, § 204 (Washington, D.C., May 17, 1979) (St. Paul, Minn., American Law Institute Publishers, 1981).

[15] See Louis Henkin, *The Age of Rights* (New York, Columbia University Press, 1990) and Charles R. Epp, *The Rights Revolution: Lawyers, Activists, and Supreme Courts in Comparative Perspective* (Chicago, Ill., University of Chicago Press, 1998).

take the example of human dignity, which is the matrix of all human rights, one cannot but acknowledge its role as a double-edged knife: sometimes, for example as regards human cloning, human dignity is used as the last moral bastion against possible transgressions of the human species' intrinsic qualities; sometimes, for example as regards the rights of the disabled, human dignity is used as a catalyst for consciousness-raising and for acceptance of the problem by the society.[16]

Accordingly, fundamental principles of law and human rights partake in the reception and assimilation of worldwide legal changes by judges, by stepping sometimes on the accelerator, sometimes on the breaks. In any case, they give judges a normative structure without which there can be no opening up of legal systems to foreign influences. In front of an increasingly large tendency to harmonize or unify individual legal systems, French private law judges remain sensitive to those cultural differences which are characteristic of their legal traditions. But these traditions, entrenched as they may be, are surely not impermeable to other perspectives or other methods of reasoning.[17]

That is the reason why a reflection on the accommodation of foreign concepts and institutions by a legal system—in short, a reflection on comparative law—is in order. If we look at the development of comparative law, we will see that some of the most important advances have resulted from 'cross-fertilization' between different legal systems, and that comparison enables the existence of 'a strong measure of objective neutrality and critical self-assessment'.[18] The increasing consciousness by national legislators of the value of comparative law has materialized, for instance, in the creation of the English and Scottish Law Commissions. These bodies inquire into the function of legal principles and the framework within which they operate.[19] To do this, they try to ascertain whether a specific legal rule or institution has been successful in achieving what it has set out to do. The point I want to make in section III of this article is based on that idea. In brief, I will try to show that the utility of comparative law research by a domestic supreme court lies not so much in the empirical comparison between rules as

16 The literature on the principle of human dignity and bioethics has, as is well known, acquired very big dimensions, even though this principle became central to the common law legal cultures only quite recently. To the contrary, the recent history of tyranny in a country like Germany permanently shaped its legal culture; suffice it to observe that the German Constitution starts by recognizing the inalienable character of human dignity. See notably Michael J. Meyer and William A. Parent (eds.), *The Constitution of Rights: Human Dignity and American Values* (Ithaca, N.Y., Cornell University Press, 1992) and Edward J. Eberle, *Dignity and Liberty: Constitutional Visions in Germany and the United States* (Westport, Conn., Praeger, 2002). In French, see notably Béatrice Maurer, *Le principe de respect de la dignité humaine et la Convention européenne des droits de l'homme*, pref. Frédéric Sudre (Paris, La documentation française, 1999).

17 One should be mindful that there is a doctrinal controversy on whether legal systems actually converge or not. Professor Basil Markesinis, for instance, thinks that there is no doubt that a convergence is taking place (see Basil Markesinis (ed.), *The Gradual Convergence* (Oxford, Clarendon Press and New York, Oxford University Press, 1994)), whereas Professor Pierre Legrand is of the opinion that legal cultures do not really converge, even though contingent legal rules do tend to become uniform in some areas of law (see Pierre Legrand, 'European legal systems are not converging', 45 *International and Comparative Law Quarterly* 59 (1996)).

18 Peter de Cruz, *Comparative Law in a Changing World* 17 (London and Sydney, Cavendish Publishing, 1999 (1st edn. 1995)).

19 The two Law Commissions are the children of the British Law Commissions Act, § 3(1)(f), enacted in 1965.

in the inspiration from the *interpretative methodology* foreign supreme courts use in order to ascertain whether a rule has successfully fulfilled its function.

III. The importance of comparative law in the practice of the Cour de cassation

The status of comparative law varies according to the specific traditions of each legal culture. There are cultures that are more hospitable to foreign law and others that are more provincial. The Supreme Court of Canada, for instance, is particularly open to legal experiences stemming from other countries, especially anglophone common law countries. On the contrary, the Supreme Court of the United States is more reticent about this type of arguments, even though some recent decisions[20] show a certain opening because of their discussion of the international parameters of certain controversial issues.[21]

In France, the Cour de cassation is structurally inhibited, because of its traditional style of writing that makes no mention of precedents in the body of the decision, from referring to foreign law.[22] A hasty reader of the Court's case law would draw the conclusion that comparative law is of no significance whatsoever and that the Court lacks judicial techniques to incorporate foreign legal sources. This is certainly not true, as I will try to show in this section. But first, let me elaborate on the importance of comparative law for a supreme court judge's task to preserve social values in a changing world.[23]

What are the uses a national judge can make of comparative law? We can start by stating the obvious, that is that comparison with other legal cultures unquestionably enlarges the judge's horizon. Comparative law multiplies the available viewpoints and interpretative options. With globalization, different national institutions are increasingly called to treat the same kinds of legal problems. Therefore, to the extent similarities exist between legal values, the judges can better fulfil their role because of the enhancement of his stock of possibilities. But at a deeper level, we can see that many fundamental principles underpinning a legal system are common between democratic

[20] Notably *Atkins v Virginia*, 536 U.S. 304 (2002) on the death penalty, and *Lawrence v Texas* (June 26, 2003) on sodomy laws, where Justice Kennedy's opinion for the Court explicitly mentioned the 1981 European Court of Human Rights case *Dudgeon v United Kingdom.*

[21] A retired judge of the Supreme Court of Canada, Claire L'Heureux-Dubé, criticizes the United States Supreme Court's provincialism in her article 'The Importance of Dialogue: Globalization, the Rehnquist Court and Human Rights', *in* Martin H. Belsky (ed.), *The Rehnquist Court: A Retrospective* 234 (New York, Oxford University Press, 2002). Paradoxically, the U.S. Supreme Court's relative closure to international and comparative law does not deter foreign courts from being inspired from that court's interpretation of the U.S. Constitution; see, e.g., Anthony Lester, 'The Overseas Trade in the American Bill of Rights', 88 Columbia Law Review 537 (1988).

[22] On the French Cour de cassation's style of judicial writing, see Mitchel de S.-O.-l'E. Lasser, 'Judicial (Self-) Portraits: Judicial Discourse in the French Legal System', 104 Yale Law Journal 1325 (1995).

[23] The use of comparative law by the courts is discussed in Ulrich Drobnig and Sjef van Erp (eds.), *The Use of Comparative Law by Courts*, 14th International Congress of Comparative Law, Athens, 1997 (The Hague and Boston, Kluwer Law International, 1999), and by Professor H. Patrick Glenn in two important recent works: *Legal Traditions of the World: Sustainable Diversity in Law* (Oxford and New York, Oxford University Press, 2000), and 'Comparative Law and Legal Practice: On Removing the Borders', 75 Tulane Law Review 977 (2001).

societies. It is only natural that legal comparison can reveal those options by bringing them out into the open.[24]

The structure of comparison is always more complicated than a simple lining up of rules or institutions coming from different countries. We should not simply compare sporadic legal solutions on this or that problem; we should also examine the failures and successes of these solutions vis-à-vis the fundamental principles of the legal system in question. In other words, comparative law is always useful for the local judges because it makes them understand the coherence between a judicial precedent and a body of fundamental principles that underlie a legal system. Thus, judges will be better equipped to perform by themselves this work of harmonization in their own legal system.

If two legal systems share basic cultural features, it should be possible to use comparative law as a source of inspiration for the judge's task of interpreting written law. The judge can learn a lot from foreign Constitutions or statutes about the aims pursued by another legal system and about the arrangement of legal means with a view to obtaining these aims.[25] Once more, the utility of the comparison does not consist so much in the alignment of concrete legal solutions as in the interpretative methodology, that is in the way a legal culture approaches a problem and arranges the means it has at its disposal in order to resolve it. The judges will not be that much influenced by concrete legal solutions found in another legal system; they will be mostly influenced by this hermeneutic come-and-go between the specific or general goals of a legal rule or institution and the practical solutions that foreign judges have conceived in order to pursue those goals. The judges will, in the end, be more inspired by the mechanisms of interpretative decoding they will find in a legal culture that is not their own than by ready-made solutions they can easily discover by simply consulting legal textbooks.[26]

The interpretative inspiration from comparative law can easily be ascertained from the Cour de cassation's application of international law, prominently of the European Convention for the Protection of Human Rights and Fundamental Freedoms (ECHR) of 4 November 1950. Like any other court in Europe, the Cour de cassation is bound to apply this supranational law, that has a binding force superior to French domestic law.[27] The Court achieves this by referring to the respective case law and methods of this supranational legal order.[28] It thus continuously incorporates in the French legal

[24] This distinction is inspired by the fundamental distinction between 'microcomparison' (comparison between topics or institutions of two or more legal systems) and 'macrocomparison' (comparison between two or more entire legal systems) made by Konrad Zweigert and Hein Kotz, 1 *Introduction to Comparative Law* 4–5 (Tony Weir trans. Oxford, Clarendon Press, 2nd edn., 1987), who draw on Max Rheinstein, 'Comparative Law—Its Functions, Methods, and Usages', 22 Arkansas Law Review and Bar Association Journal 415 (1968).

[25] For a discussion of the range of comparative law methodologies in the constitutional law context, see Mark Tushnet, 'The Possibilities of Comparative Constitutional Law', 108 Yale Law Journal 1225 (1999), and more recently, Vicki C. Jackson and Mark Tushnet (eds.), *Defining the Field of Comparative Constitutional Law*, William H. Rehnquist foreword (Westport, Conn., Praeger, 2002).

[26] In an important article, Professor George P. Fletcher explores the implications of this interpretative function of comparative law; see George P. Fletcher, 'Comparative Law as a Subversive Discipline', 46 American Journal of Comparative Law 683 (1998).

[27] According to art. 55 of the French Constitution of 1958.

[28] There are many examples of the Cour de cassation's referring openly to the case law of the European Court of Human Rights; see, e.g., the decisions Cour de cassation, Chambre commerciale, *Rey c. directeur général des Impôts, Bulletin civil*, 2002, IV, N° 124, p. 113, and *Barbet, Ruth et Société Auchan c. Conseil*

order legal principles rooted in a different legal system. Since the ECHR enshrines basic democratic and liberal values that the French legal order shares, it is only natural that the country's supreme civil and criminal court will be heavily influenced in its own case law by the interpretative methodology of the Strasbourg judges. In short, the normative overlap between two integrated legal orders (like the French legal order and the ECHR or the European Community Law) obviously stimulates a comparative law reasoning on the part of the domestic judge.

Hence, the Cour de cassation has by now become familiar with the comparative law methodology via its normative commitment to the European legal order. We must not be oblivious to the fact that European legal integration, together with the first signs of an emergent European legal culture, do not result only from authoritarian black-letter unification, but also involve the gradual internalization of common values by each of the national legal systems. At least as far as European Community law and the law of the European Convention for Human Rights are concerned, harmonization is not necessarily the result of imposed uniformity.[29] It is not always the impact of European law on the content of given national rules that is important. Harmonization may also—albeit more exceptionally—be the effect of a spontaneous, incremental growth towards common perspectives and standpoints. It is important for French judges to discover signs evidencing the progressive development of a specifically European way of looking at things. This certainly is the point where comparative law is most useful.

However, even if European human rights law does not open a space of legal uniformity, the dynamics of the ECHR is such that citizens and judges of states which share more or less similar cultures and enjoy a similar level of economic development are less and less likely to accept that situations raising the same issues of fact yield different results because of the difference in the legal rules to be applied. There is a trend, one might even say a strong demand, that compatible solutions be reached, regardless of the differences in the underlying applicable rules of law. This is true, for example, in the field of privacy law. The case *Fretté v France*,[30] in which the European Court of Human Rights declared that the denial by the French legislation of the right of homosexuals to adopt children does not contravene the Convention, brought lawyers and public opinion into disarray. One can legitimately ask what justifies here the existence of different legal rules between countries having common cultural values and recognizing the concept of human dignity as pre-eminent.

This example shows that in European countries at least, the judiciary needs to follow a step-by-step approach in order to develop a specifically European legal culture in at

National de l'Ordre des Pharmaciens, Chambre criminelle, 10 January 2001 (unpublished). These references are quite impressive, if we keep in mind the French courts' traditional refusal to cite judicial precedents in their decisions.

[29] This is obvious enough from the European Court of Human Rights (Grand Chamber) case *Open Door and Dublin Well Woman v Ireland* of 29 October 1992. In that case, the Strasbourg court declared contrary to the ECHR a ban on advertisement and counselling for Irish women who wished to travel abroad so as to have an abortion (which remains illegal in their country). There was no effort by the Court to enact a unified substantive law on abortion rights throughout the member states of the ECHR; rather, the effort of the Court was to balance the individuals' right to information with the national states' value system, and it did this by applying the 'proportionality' standard, that proved fatal to the Irish legislation.

[30] Case *Fretté v France* of the European Court of Human Rights (3rd section), 26 May 2002.

least some highly important moral issues that are treated by law. The first thing a domestic supreme court like the Cour de cassation will need to do is to find the solutions given by other supreme courts to hard cases. In the French judicial system, which conceives justice as a 'public service', no court can address itself to a legal expert or 'special master' for the ascertainment of a legal solution, since the determination of questions of a legal nature cannot be delegated to a third party.[31] Interestingly, this procedural impossibility opened up the way to a new technique akin to the *amicus curiae* in common law legal systems.[32]

The Cour de cassation has twice resorted to this technique. It asked the French Comparative Law Institute to issue a research report, firstly regarding a case of wrongful birth,[33] and secondly regarding the possible conviction for manslaughter of a person who had caused a miscarriage in a car accident he was responsible for.[34] These reports were then notified to the parties and to the *ministère public* (the public prosecutor's office at the Cour de cassation) for use in their briefs before the Court. In those two cases, the research undertaken was not limited to the technical aspects of foreign positive law, but also included an analysis of the legal, economic, and cultural context inside which similar cases were decided by judges in the foreign countries in question. The admittance of comprehensive and relevant studies enabled the Cour de cassation to open up its deliberations to comparative legal methodology.

Even though this trend is gaining importance in the Cour de cassation's practice, it is by no means a novel one. We must not forget that like their common law colleagues, civil law judges and lawyers have always worked inside a transnational judicial culture.[35] Supreme courts in common law jurisdictions enjoy a long tradition of working with reference to the English legal system and to the case law of its senior courts. It is, therefore, for them quite natural to base their decisions on common law precedents and to be attentive to the evolution of the common law in each of the systems which partake of the same working methods, judicial precedents, legal sources, and legal practices. Consequently, it is not infrequent that supreme courts of English-speaking countries make explicit references in their opinions to the case law of one another.[36] This link is

[31] The possibility of appointing special masters is, on the contrary, specifically provided for in the United States; see Federal Rule of Civil Procedure 53(b).

[32] On the *amicus curiæ* in common law countries, see the report by Alexander B. Aikman, Mary E. Elsner, and Frederick G. Miller, *Friends of the Court: Lawyers as Supplemental Judicial Resources* (Williamsburg, Va., National Center for State Courts, 1987), as well as the recent monograph by Ian R. Brodie, *Friends of the Court: The Privileging of Interest Group Litigants in Canada* (Albany, N.Y., State University of New York Press, 2002).

[33] The famous case *Perruche* of the Cour de cassation, Assemblée plénière, 17 November 2000, *Dalloz* 332 (2001), note Denis Mazeaud and Patrice Jourdain.

[34] Case *Procureur général près la cour d'appel de Metz* of the Cour de cassation, Assemblée plénière, 29 June 2001, in *Dalloz* 2916 (2001), note Yves Mayaud.

[35] Professor Slaughter has argued forcefully for the existence of a 'transjudicial communication'; see, *inter alia*, Anne-Marie Slaughter, 'Judicial Globalization', 40 Virginia Journal of International Law 1103 (2000), and 'A Typology of Transjudicial Communication', 20 University of Richmond Law Review 99 (1994).

[36] Of course, this does not mean that there is an uncritical acceptance of each and any precedent coming from a foreign Anglo-American supreme court. The best example, in that regard, is the attitude Canadian courts have towards U.S. case law: 'While it is natural and even desirable for Canadian courts to refer to American constitutional jurisprudence in seeking to elucidate the meaning of Charter guarantees that have counterparts in the United States Constitution, they should be wary of drawing too ready a parallel between

easier to make, of course, because of the fact that judicial opinions stem from the same origin in the common law and are written in the same language. There is also easy access to the case reports of the anglophone countries' supreme courts, so that judicial opinions are readily accessed, read, and adapted to the domestic stream of precedents.

Civil law countries, even though they do not share this common historical and linguistic background that cements their belonging to a common legal culture, did face a similar movement at the beginning of the 19th century. But the particularity of this movement is that it revolved around the historical phenomenon of codification. With the enactment of the Napoleon Civil Code in 1804 and its adoption by many states during the 19th century, a host of countries engaged in a common interpretation of this Code, as expounded by their courts. Of course, this trend has long terminated since the abandonment of these first French-inspired Civil Codes, which have been revised, or overhauled, or have undergone such changes that common references have by now become irrelevant.

If we take the example of two neighbouring countries which share many historical and cultural traditions, namely France and Belgium, we can still observe—albeit rarely—cross-references to judicial decisions of their respective Cours de cassation. Of course, since (as we saw) these courts never cite precedents in their decisions, it is difficult to ascertain the real influence which they no doubt still exert on one another. By now, the main instrument of exchange of information on landmark decisions between French-speaking jurisdictions is the Cour de cassation's Annual Report.[37] As for the French-speaking African countries, which still have legal systems inherited from the French one, reference to the case law of the French Cour de cassation is not surprising.[38]

These remnants of a common legal space revolving around the splendour of the French Civil Code undoubtedly formed the background against which legal transplants were performed and comparative law methodology made its way through the French courts and legal academy. But, since this common space was fuelled more by the French Empire's political power or prestige and less by the efficiency of the French 'legal product', the radiance of French civil law culture slowly began to wane in the 20th century, accustoming our national courts to a rather provincial state of mind. Even today, after the European Community and European human rights legal revolutions fundamentally altered the balance of power between national and supranational legal institutions, French law is quite reticent about opening up the judicial forum to foreign law. We can see this in the conflict of laws area, whose rules command the French courts to apply foreign law. Taking into account—or maybe under the pretext of—the difficulty of knowing the applicable foreign law with reasonable certainty, recent Cour de cassation case law has limited the cases in

constitutions born to different countries in different ages and in very different circumstances' (*Rahey v The Queen* [1987] 1 SCR 588, 639).

[37] The latest French Cour de cassation Annual Report is on civil liability (Cour de cassation, Rapport 2002, *La responsabilité*, Paris, La documentation française, 2003).

[38] Reports of African supreme court decisions are gathered since 1891 in a review called *Penant. Revue de droit des pays d'Afrique.*

which there is an obligation for the lower courts to apply foreign law when no party has raised the conflict of law issue.[39]

This deference of French courts, and first of all of the Cour de cassation, to the self-sufficiency of national law is by now obsolete, due to the fantastic strike force of European law. Even though there is no mention of foreign or international law, or of comparative methodology of law, in the body of the Cour de cassation's decisions, there is theoretical work to be done on the importance comparative law has in the conclusions and reports that frame and clarify the decisions of the Cour de cassation. These conclusions and reports are not, technically speaking, a part of the judicial decision having a *res judicata* effect; but they *are* a part of the pertinent legal materials lawyers can consult, especially on the Internet,[40] in order to understand the case law.

[39] See, e.g., Cour de cassation, Chambre sociale, *Application moderne des plastiques A.M.P. c. Cremades*, Bulletin civil, 1992, V, N° 593, p. 374.

[40] The Cour de cassation's website has put online several 'internal documents', such as conclusions or reports accompanying important cases that have been decided by the Court; see <http://www.courdecassation.fr>.

25

The Use of Comparative Law before the French *Cour de Cassation*

The View from Academia

*Alexis Albarian**

I. Introduction: The less and less 'hidden use' of comparative law before the *Cour de cassation*

Section 39 of the South African constitution provides that '(1) when interpreting the Bill of Rights, a court, tribunal or forum... (c) *may consider foreign law*.'[1] Of course, the French constitution does not contain such a provision. Moreover, since the *Cour de cassation*'s decisions are—by nature—very short,[2] one can *prima facie* easily think that the use of comparative law is totally absent from the French judicial world. This brevity of the French court's decisions also explains the fact that foreign courts do not—often—refer to French precedents in their own rulings.[3] In other words, this *imperatoria brevitas*[4] would *ipso facto* exclude the use of comparative law before the French 'supreme' court.[5] As a result—traditionally—a clear and direct reference to foreign solutions is rather rare in French case law.[6] That is typically the reason why some authors described the use of comparative law by French judges as a 'hidden'[7] one or—in the best case scenario—as an 'unconscious'[8] one. However, today's factual reality is

* Associate Professor of Private Law, Aix-Marseille University, France, Economic Law Center (EA 4224).

[1] <http://www.servat.unibe.ch/icl/sf00000_.html>.

[2] P. Deumier, 'Création du droit et rédaction des arrêts par la Cour de cassation', in *La création du droit par le juge*, Archives de philosophie du droit, tome 50, 2007, p. 50, n° 1.

[3] T. Rambaud, *Introduction au droit comparé. Les grandes traditions juridiques dans le monde*, PUF, 2014, p. 250: '*Les arrêts français sont rédigés avec une concision, remarquable à plus d'un titre, mais qui n'invite pas volontiers à l'imitation en droit comparé*'.

[4] A. Touffait and A. Tunc, 'Pour une motivation plus explicite des décisions de justice notamment de celles de la Cour de cassation', RTDC, 1974, p. 487. Most of this article is reproduced in the following book: B. Rudden, *A source-book on French Law. Public Law: Constitutional and administrative law. Private law: Structure, contract*, 3rd edn., Clarendon Press, Oxford, 1991, p. 281.

[5] G. Canivet, 'The use of comparative law before the French private law courts', in *Comparative Law Before the Courts*, ed. G. Canivet, M. Andenas, and D. Fairgrieve, British Institute of International & Comparative Law, 2004, p. 187. *Adde*, P. Bellet, 'France. La Cour de cassation', RIDC, 1978, p. 213.

[6] R. David and C. Jauffret-Spinosi, *Les grands systèmes de droit contemporains*, 11th edn., Dalloz, 2002, p. 6, n° 5: '*La doctrine française s'intéresse de plus en plus de nos jours au droit comparé, mais il est vrai qu'un usage restreint même aujourd'hui en est fait par la jurisprudence.*'

[7] S. Van Erp, 'The use of comparative law method by the judiciary—Dutch report', in *The use of comparative law method by courts. XIVth International Law Congress*, ed. U. Drobnig and S. Van Erp, Kluwer, 1999, p. 243.

[8] Y.-M. Laithier, *Droit comparé*, Dalloz, 2009, p. 18, n° 10.

much more nuanced. Indeed, it is possible to discern different degrees of the use of comparative law, especially in the preparatory works of the *Cour de cassation*'s rulings.

II. The different degrees of the use of comparative law in the preparatory works ('*travaux préparatoires*') of the *Cour de cassation*'s decisions

The 'comparative argument'[9] can either be mentioned as a mere 'ornamental' reference, or as a rather solid and tangible justification of the court's decision. As a result, the use of comparative law appears less and less hidden and less and less unconscious before the *Cour de cassation.* A cultural or psychological revolution—or at least an evolution of this kind—seems to be underway in the French 'supreme' court.

1. The notion of preparatory works ('*travaux préparatoires*')

The expression '*travaux préparatoires*'[10] translates literally as 'preparatory works'. The general definition of this phrase is the following: 'materials used in preparation of the ultimate form of an agreement or statute'[11] or—in our case—a court's decision. Those works tend to massively inspire the judges in the writing of their final opinion. Those 'preparatory works', as far as the *Cour de cassation* is concerned, are mainly composed of two kinds of important materials: the *Rapport* of the *Conseiller rapporteur* (a) and the *Avis* of the *Avocat général* (b).

a) The rapport *of the* conseiller rapporteur

> The function of the *conseiller rapporteur* is (a) to review the lower court record, (b) to identify the issues and, finally, (c) to recommend a solution. After explaining the facts and the history of the case, the *conseiller* presents to the court a personal opinion, based mainly on a detailed analysis of relevant past decisions and taking into account policy considerations.[12]

This opinion is called a *rapport* (a report).

b) The Avis *of the* Avocat général

The function of the *Avocat général* in the *Cour de cassation* is:

> to submit an opinion from an independent standpoint representative of the public interest and further ensuring that the law is construed and applied correctly. In the exercise of this function, the *Avocat général* does not act as a member of the panel

[9] *L'argument de droit comparé en droit administratif*, ed. F. Melleray and J.-B. Auby, Bruylant, 2007. See also M. Bobek, *Comparative reasoning in European supreme courts*, Oxford University Press, 2013.

[10] See on this notion, *Le raisonnement juridique. Recherche sur les travaux préparatoires des arrêts*, ed. P. Deumier, Dalloz, coll. Méthodes du droit, 2013.

[11] B. A. Garner, *Black's Law Dictionary*, 9th edn., West, 2009, V[is] '*Travaux préparatoires*', p. 1638.

[12] E. Steiner, *French Law. A comparative approach*, Oxford University Press, 2010, p. 186.

hearing the appeal; his role is instead to "guide" the court on the most appropriate outcome for each individual case. Like the *conseiller rapporteur*, the *Avocat général* examines and analyses relevant judicial precedents, and, in the light of them, makes recommendations on how the case should be decided in a document called [*avis*]. In his [*avis*] the *Avocat général* frequently presents a line of reasoning based on social, economic, or institutional considerations; in this respect going further than the *conseiller rapporteur* by not hesitating, when appropriate, to call for a change in established precedent, thus preparing the ground for legislative reform. Unlike the *conseiller rapporteur*, the *Avocat général*, not being a member of the panel hearing the appeal, feels freer to suggest such modifications to the court.[13]

Those two documents—the *rapport* of the *conseiller rapporteur* and the *avis* of the *Avocat général*[14]—are systematically published by the *Cour de cassation* itself in the most crucial and technical cases. The latter are held before the most 'solemn' divisions of the French 'supreme' court, *i.e.* a *Chambre mixte* or the *Assemblée plénière.*[15] Those pieces of 'preparatory works' can be easily consulted on the *Cour de cassation*'s website.[16] As President Canivet mentions: *'l'exigence de transparence implique également que l'intégration des éléments de droit comparé au raisonnement du juge soit explicite... dans les documents préparatoires: rapport du juge [conseiller rapporteur] et avis du ministère public [avocat général], comme cela est désormais pratiqué en France'*.[17] The promotion and the diffusion of those preparatory works are an essential

[13] Ibid.

[14] For further details regarding those 'preparatory works', see M. Lasser, 'Judicial (self-) portraits: judicial discourse in the French legal system', Yale Law Journal, 1995, Vol. 104, pp. 1325–410; M. Lasser, '*La Macdonald-isation du discours judiciaire français*', in *L'américanisation du droit*, Archives de philosophie du droit, tome 45, 2001, pp. 137–48. *Adde*, M. Lasser, *Judicial deliberations: a comparative analysis of transparency and legitimacy*, Oxford University Press, 2009.

[15] 'The Court of Cassation is also comprised of temporary benches which either include judges from each of the divisions (Full Court/plenary sessions: *Assemblée plénière*) or judges from at least three divisions (Mixed Divisions: *Chambre mixte*). These benches are presided over by the President or by the most senior divisional presiding judge of the Court. A total of 19 judges sit in plenary sessions. These include all the divisional presiding judges and senior trial judges (doyens) together with a trial judge from each of the divisions. The decision to hear a case in Full Court is made by the President or by the division to which the appeal is referred. *This is indeed the case when a matter of principle is involved.* However it is mandatory if after an initial decision or judgment has been quashed by the Court of Cassation the decision of the second court to which the matter was referred is challenged again on the same grounds or if the request for a plenary session is made by the General Prosecutor (procureur général) before the appeal is heard. It is important to note that the points of law laid down in a ruling by the Full Court which quashes a lower court's decision are binding on the court to which the case is then referred. In addition to the President or Deputy President, mixed divisions include four judges from each of the divisions (the presiding judge, the senior trial judge, and two trial judges). This would represent a total of 13 judges if a mixed division were comprised of judges from the three divisions. If a given case normally falls within the scope of several divisions or if diverging rulings have been issued or are likely to be issued by the divisions, it must be heard by a mixed division. This is also the case if the division which heard the appeal initially reached a shared vote. Prior to the hearing, the General Prosecutor may also request for a given case to be heard by a mixed division. The foremost purpose of this type of bench is to settle inconsistencies in case law between the divisions', <http://www.courdecassation.fr/about_the_court_9256.html>.

[16] As for the rulings of a *Chambre mixte*, see <http://www.courdecassation.fr/jurisprudence_2/chambres_mixtes_2740/>. As for the rulings of the *Assemblée plénière*, see <http://www.courdecassation.fr/jurisprudence_2/assemblee_pleniere_22/>.

[17] G. Canivet, 'Préface', in S. B. Markesinis, *Juges et universitaires face au droit comparé. Histoire des trente-cinq dernières années*, Dalloz, 2006, p. VIII.

part of the current 'case law policy' of the *Cour de cassation*[18] and also part of a 'quiet revolution'[19] of its own.

2. The comparative argument as a mere 'ornamental' reference

Sometimes references to foreign legal solutions are used (for example, in preparatory works) for 'documentary reasons' only. In this case, the author of the *avis* or *rapport* could be compared to a PhD student mentioning comparative arguments in the introduction of his or her thesis only as it is a traditionally mandatory stage in France, like in many other countries. In this specific situation, the foreign precedent is to be considered as a 'documentary authority' (*autorité documentaire*[20]).

This 'comparative quotation' ('*citation comparative*'[21]) can take on various forms but never longer than a sentence or a short paragraph. Here, amongst others,[22] is an illustration of this process: '*Les auteurs s'accordent en définitive pour retenir qu'en réalité, le mode de libération de la caution institué par l'article 2037 du Code civil, mode qui existe depuis le droit romain et* est commun aux systèmes juridiques qui en sont issus ainsi qu'à ceux de common law, *n'entre dans le moule d'aucun concept éprouvé et qui n'a d'autre justification que "l'idée de juste rétribution des conduites de chacun tel que la tradition des juristes et l'expérience des précédents l'ont établi"*'.[23] This is what an author calls a 'blink of an eye comparison' ('*comparaison en clin d'oeil*').[24]

3. The comparative argument as a justification of the court's decision

In recent times, one of the most significant and emblematic uses of comparative law before the *Cour de cassation* is the famous case held by the *Assemblée Plénière* on 29 March 1991: *Association des centres éducatifs du Limousin v Blieck*.[25] This landmark has admitted that article 1384 paragraph 1[26] of the French civil code contained not only a principle of liability for objects in one's custody, but also a general principle of vicarious liability. More specifically, even since this leading case, 'there is now, in

[18] G. Canivet and N. Molfessis, 'La politique jurisprudentielle', in *La création du droit jurisprudentiel. Mélanges en l'honneur de Jacques Boré*, Dalloz, 2007, p. 95: 'La publication des rapports, avis et mémoires constitue ici un apport évident, qui présente le double intérêt de fournir une explicitation du message comme de ses ressorts et, dans le même temps, d'inciter les magistrats à formaliser les choix et raisonnements choisis.'

[19] P. Jestaz, J.-P. Marguénaud, C. Jamin, 'Révolution tranquille à la Cour de cassation', D. 2014, p. 2061.

[20] D. Maus, 'Le recours aux précédents étrangers et le dialogue des cours constitutionnelles', RFDC, octobre 2009, n° 80, pp. 675–95.

[21] S. Bouabdallah, '*La comparaison des droits*', in *Le raisonnement juridique. Recherche sur les travaux préparatoires des arrêts*, ed. P. Deumier, Dalloz, coll. Méthodes du droit, 2013, p. 205, n° 235.

[22] See for many other illustrations, P. Deumier, 'Les "motifs des motifs" des arrêts de la Cour de cassation. Études des travaux préparatoires', in *Principes de justice. Mélanges en l'honneur de Jean-François Burgelin*, 2009, p. 125; S. Bouabdallah, ibid., p. 205–7, n°s 235–236.

[23] *Rapport Conseiller* Cachelot, Ch. Mixte, 10 juin 2005, n° 02-21.296: <http://www.courdecassation.fr/jurisprudence_2/chambres_mixtes_2740/cachelot_conseiller_519.html>.

[24] X. Thunis, 'Comparer: de la réaction spontanée à l'outil méthodologique', ADI, vol. 66, 2006, n°s 1–2, p. 38.

[25] D. 1991, note C. Larroumet.

[26] 'A person is liable not only for the damages he causes by his own act, but also for that which is caused by the acts of persons for whom he is responsible, or by things which are in his custody.'

French law, a general principle of liability for acts carried out by persons who are in the area of institutions or organisations where patients or residents are supervised on a long-term basis and in a structured environment'.[27] Yet this solution is massively inspired by article 1054 of the civil of code of Quebec as it had been interpreted by the Privy Council in 1920.[28] Here is the way the *Avocat général* Dontenwille wrote his *conclusions*:[29]

> And yet our world is moving outside France. Even the countries most permeated by our civil code have distanced themselves. This is not an exhaustive list of course, but some touches... that broaden the horizon.
>
> Germany: 'One who, by virtue of the law, is obliged to supervise a person, who, because of his minority or because of his mental or physical condition, needs to be monitored, is required to repair the damage caused by that person to others...'
>
> Quebec: striking parallel between our article 1384 and article 1054 of the civil code of Quebec.
>
> '– However, the list of principles of liability at the hands of someone else is substantially larger: father and mother, tutors, trustees or others with legal custody of the mentally incapacitated, teachers, master craftsmen and principals...
> – Moreover, the general formula preceding these particular principles uses an expression with a more targeted impact than ours: (the person) "is responsible for the damages caused by the fault of those of whom were in their custody..."
>
> This allowed an eminent lawyer of the Privy Council to assert the existence in paragraph 1 of Article 1054 of the Quebec civil code, of two general principles of liability: of objects in one's custody, and of vicarious liability.
>
> Finally, it is interesting to note that the German civil code just cited has been imitated in its general principle, applicable to all persons charged with the supervision of

[27] E. Steiner, *French Law. A comparative approach*, Oxford University Press, 2010, p. 371.

[28] *Quebec Railway, Light, Heat and Power Co. v Vandry*, Privy Council, A.C. 662 [1920].

[29] (Our translation) '*Et pourtant notre monde bouge en dehors de notre hexagone. Même les pays les plus imprégnés de notre code civil ont pris leurs distances. Pas de liste exhaustive bien sûr, mais quelques touches... qui apportent un peu d'oxygène.*

Allemagne: "Celui qui, en vertu de la loi est obligé d'exercer la surveillance sur une personne qui, à raison de sa minorité ou de son état mental ou physique a besoin d'être surveillée, est tenu de réparer le préjudice causé par cette personne à autrui..." (C. civ. allemand, art. 832).
Québec: Parallélisme très prononcé entre notre article 1384 et l'article 1054 du Code civil du Québec.

'– Cependant la liste des présomptions de responsabilité du fait d'autrui est sensiblement plus large: père et mère, tuteurs, curateurs ou autres ayant légalement la garde des insensés, instituteurs et artisans maîtres et commettants...
– En outre la formule générale précédant les présomptions particulières utilise une expression à la portée plus ciblée que la nôtre: (la personne) "est responsable du dommage causé par la faute de ceux dont elle a le contrôle..." Ce qui a permis à un éminent juriste du conseil privé de Londres d'affirmer l'existence, dans l'alinéa 1 de l'article 1054 du Québec, de deux présomptions générales de responsabilité, du fait des choses mais aussi d'autrui.

Enfin, il n'est pas sans intérêt de noter que le Code civil allemand que nous venons d'évoquer a été imité en son principe général applicable à toute personne chargée de la surveillance d'autrui, quelle que soit la cause de cet état de dépendance, par des pays tels que l'Algérie, l'Egypte, la Grèce et le Japon.

Ce survol des positions adoptées par les pays étrangers n'est bien sûr ici qu'une esquisse.'

another, regardless of the cause of this state of dependency, by countries such as Algeria, Egypt, Greece, and Japan.

This overview of positions adopted by foreign countries is, of course, only an outline.'[30]

This example illustrates very clearly the importance of those preparatory works—such as the *avis* of the *avocat général*—in the comprehension process of the *Court de cassation*'s rulings.[31]

Another 'classical' illustration of this phenomenon is the introduction into French case law—by the *Cour de cassation*—of the important distinction between 'obligations to achieve a particular result' ('*obligations de résultat*') and 'obligations to use reasonable care'—or 'best-efforts obligations'—('*obligations de moyens*'). 'The fundamental idea that lies behind this distinction is that one must scrutinize both what has been promised and what can reasonably be expected. If a precise result is promised (for instance, delivery of goods at a certain date), it is an *obligation de résultat*; if, on the contrary, one promises to use all appropriate means in order to achieve a result (for instance, in order to cure a patient), it is an *obligation de moyens*'.[32] This distinction, conceptualized by René Demogue[33] in 1925 and taken up by the *Cour de cassation* later on, was directly inspired from Italian law, itself influenced by German law.[34]

Much more recently, another very emblematic example can illustrate this trend in favour of comparative arguments. That is what in France is called the '*Baby loup*' case.[35] The applicant had been fired from her job at *Baby Loup*, a private crèche and nursery, for violating the organization's rules of procedure. By wearing the *hijab*, the applicant purportedly breached the rule that the principle of freedom of conscience and of religion of each staff member may not impede respect for the principles of *laïcité* [secularism] and neutrality that apply in the exercise of developmental activities, either on the premises of the crèche, or during outside activities in which staff accompany children enrolled in the crèche. This is the latest case to be held before the *Assemblée plénière* and, in order to measure its importance, it should be mentioned that a whole book was written after it.[36] The preparatory works of this (controversial) ruling contains a great deal of comparative material, especially the *rapport* of the *Conseiller rapporteur* Laurent Truchot. Indeed, four full pages are dedicated to 'comparative elements' ('*éléments de droit comparé*'). German, Austrian, Belgium, Danish, Spanish, Dutch, English, Algerian, Moroccan, and Canadian solutions are exposed and contextualized in this report.[37]

In the above illustrations, the foreign legal solutions are used as a 'persuasive authority' ('*autorité de persuasion*'[38]). Therefore, comparative arguments contribute

[30] La Semaine Juridique Edition Générale n° 21, 22 Mai 1991, II 21673, conclu. Premier Avocat Général Dontenwille.

[31] R. Legeais, 'L'utilisation du droit comparé par les tribunaux', RIDC, 1994, p. 358.

[32] *Ius commune casebooks for the common law of Europe, Cases, Materials and Text on Contract Law*, ed. H. Beale, B. Fauvarque-Cosson, J. Rutgers, D. Tallon, and S. Vogenauer, Hart Publishing, 2010, pp. 722–3.

[33] R. Demogue, *Traité des obligations*, Vol. V., A. Rousseau, 1925, § 1237.

[34] Y.-M. Laithier, *Droit comparé*, Dalloz, 2009, p. 18, n° 10.

[35] Ass. Plén., 25 juin 2014, n° 13-28.369, *Madame Fatima X. v Association Baby loup.*

[36] S. Hennette-Vauchez and V. Valentin, *L'affaire Baby loup ou la nouvelle laïcité*, LGDJ, 2014.

[37] Rapport Truchot: <http://www.courdecassation.fr/IMG///Rapport_Truchot_pleniere_140625ano.pdf>.

[38] D. Maus, 'Le recours aux précédents étrangers et le dialogue des cours constitutionnelles', RFDC, octobre 2009, n° 80, pp. 675–95.

massively to the elaboration of the final opinion. In other words, these arguments could be considered as a part of the *ratio decidendi.*

This comparative methodology is even more relevant and useful (and logical) when the case to be ruled deals with a notion that belongs to another legal tradition. Recent case law before the *Cour de cassation* gives interesting illustrations of the phenomenon. The most significant example is—of course—the case that decided to introduce the common law notion of 'estoppel' into French law[39] in the field of arbitration. Indeed, a ruling of the *Assemblée plénière* of 27 February 2009 held that '*la seule circonstance qu'une partie se contredise au détriment d'autrui n'emporte pas nécessairement fin de non-recevoir*'.[40] Moreover, the same decision added that '*ce comportement doit être sanctionné, en vertu du principe suivant lequel une partie ne peut se contredire au détriment d'autrui (théorie de l'*estoppel)'. One can then remark that the term 'estoppel' is directly used in this ruling which is very rare in French case law. In the light of this, this case provides one of the clearest illustrations of a 'legal transplant'.[41] Thus, both the *avis*[42] and the *rapport*,[43] related to this famous case, contain very long developments about the notion of estoppel under English law. One can, nonetheless, regret that the works mentioned and analysed in these two 'preparatory works' are (almost) exclusively written by French scholars or practitioners. Therefore, the standards of the usual comparative methodology do not seem to be respected as—in this field—it is always highly recommended to work on 'genuine' materials, *i.e.* on internal sources of the legal system being analysed, instead of on 'second-hand', or, even, sometimes—'third-hand' materials. Here certainly lies a major form of improvement for the *Cour de cassation.* Lastly, this case is the source of a real doctrine of estoppel '*à la française*', indicated by the fact that no fewer than four main precedents[44] were subsequently issued by the *Cour de cassation* regarding this specific question. Similar research and investigations were undertaken by the *Cour de cassation*[45] concerning the critical issue of whether to introduce the well-known common law notion of mitigation of damages.[46] In the field of tort law, the *Cour de cassation*'s position is clear (mitigation of damages is banned): '*l'auteur d'un accident doit en réparer toutes les conséquences dommageables... La*

[39] See on this specific point, O. Moréteau, 'Estoppel' in *Les 100 mots du droit anglais. 100 notions fondamentales du droit anglais à l'épreuve du droit français*, ed. A. Albarian, Wolters Kluwer, coll. Axe droit, 2013, p. 267.

[40] Ass. Plén. 27 février 2009, n° 07-19.841; D. 2009, p. 1245, note D. Houtcieff.

[41] A. Watson, *Legal transplants. An approach to comparative law*, 2nd edn., The University of Georgia Press, 1993. *Adde*, C. VALCKE, '*La greffe juridique en droit comparé*', in Internationalisation du droit, Internationalisation de la justice, 3e Congrès de l'AHJUCAF, 21–23 juin 2010: see <http://www.ahjucaf.org/La-greffe-juridique-en-droit.html>.

[42] See <http://www.courdecassation.fr/jurisprudence_2/assemblee_pleniere_22/gouttes_premier_12303.html>.

[43] See <http://www.courdecassation.fr/jurisprudence_2/assemblee_pleniere_22/boval_conseiller_12302.html>.

[44] Cass. 1ère civ., 3 février 2010, n° 08-21.288; Cass. 1ère civ., 8 juillet 2010, n° 09-14.280; Cass. com., 20 septembre 2011, n° 10-22. 888; Cass. 1ère civ., 24 septembre 2014, n° 13-14.534.

[45] G. Canivet, 'Préface', in S. B. Markesinis, *Juges et universitaires face au droit comparé. Histoire des trente-cinq dernières années*, Dalloz, 2006, p. VIII, n° 10, note 1: 'La Cour de cassation s'est intéressée à la pratique anglo-saxonne de "*mitigation of damages*"'.

[46] See *Les 100 mots du droit anglais. 100 notions fondamentales du droit anglais à l'épreuve du droit français*, ed. A. Albarian, Wolters Kluwer, coll. Axe droit, 2013, pp. 222–3, n° 297.

victime n'est pas tenue de limiter son prejudice dans l'intérêt du responsable'.[47] Nevertheless, in the field of contract law, the door is ajar.[48]

However, how does the *Cour de cassation* access comparative law material?

III. How does the *Cour de cassation* access comparative law material?

The *Cour de cassation* possesses both internal and external means of accessing comparative law material.

1. Internal means

The '*service de documentation et d'études*'[49] ('The documentation, research and reporting department') of the *Cour de cassation,* since 2008, 'has its own European law monitoring unit (*Observatoire du droit européen*) allowing the issues raised by domestic courts with regard to the application of European law to be answered'.[50] This department publishes two sets of documents related to comparative law on the *Cour de cassation*'s website:

- The '*veilles bimestrielles de droit européen*'[51] ('bimonthly oversights of European law') which contain a specific section dedicated to comparative law. Unfortunately, this piece of work only mentions bibliographical references written by French scholars (*sic*!);
- The '*Études thématiques*'[52] ('thematic studies') which present the foreign legal solutions related to the specific issue of each study. However, to date, only six studies have been published and the latest one is from the year 2009 (*sic bis*!).

The *Cour de cassation* can also rely on 'twinning covenants' ('*conventions de jumelages*') with other supreme courts in order to gather information related to foreign judicial systems. The French 'supreme' court has—indeed—signed such agreements with more than 20 foreign supreme courts.[53] In the same vein, the *Cour de cassation* belongs to many both non-European and European networks of supreme courts,[54]

47 Cass. 2e civ., 25 octobre 2012; D. 2013, p. 415, note A. Guégan-Lécuyer. *Adde*, Cass. 2e civ., 19 juin 2003, n° 00-22.302.

48 Cass. 2e civ., 24 novembre 2011, n° 10-25.635; D. 2012, p. 141, note H. Adida-Canac. *Adde*, F. Terré, P. Simler, and Y. Lequette, *Droit civil. Les obligations*, 11th ed., Dalloz, 2013, p. 962, n° 899, *in fine*.

49 J. Léonnet, 'Le service de documentation et d'études. Mémoire de la Cour de cassation', in *L'image doctrinale de la Cour de cassation*, La documentation française, 1994, p. 63.

50 <http://www.courdecassation.fr/about_the_court_9256.html>.

51 <http://www.courdecassation.fr/publications_26/publications_observatoire_droit_europeen_2185/veilles_bimestrielles_droit_europeen_3556/>.

52 <http://www.courdecassation.fr/publications_26/publications_observatoire_droit_europeen_2185/etudes_thematiques_3166/>.

53 <http://www.courdecassation.fr/venements_23/activite_internationale_5/conventions_jumelage_628/>. *Adde*, M. Douchy-Oudot, 'Droit judiciaire privé et recours au droit comparé', in *Le recours au droit comparé par le juge*, ed. T. Di Manno, Bruylant, 2014, p. 151, n° 29.

54 <http://www.courdecassation.fr/venements_23/activite_internationale_5/reseaux_cours_supremes_9195.html>. *Adde*, M. Douchy-Oudot, ibid., p. 150–1, n° 28.

such as the 'Network of The Presidents of the Supreme Judicial Courts of the European Union'.[55] These kinds of associations and organizations unquestionably facilitate 'dialogue between judges'[56] from different horizons. Lastly, the judges from the *Cour de cassation* could also possibly call on means belonging to the judiciary, namely the 'liaison judges' ('*magistrats de liaison*'), who are:

> French judge[s] or public prosecutor[s], seconded to the Foreign Ministry by the Justice Ministry. He/she works in [three] areas:
> - mutual assistance in international criminal matters;
> - mutual assistance in civilian and commercial legal matters;
> - comparative law.[57]

One of the main missions of this special sort of judge is to carry out comparative studies related to specific issues.[58] Therefore, it could be very useful to consult him or her but, in practice, it is quite rare that the *Cour de cassation* takes advantage of this option.

As a result, those internal means may appear insufficient; that is the reason why the *Cour de cassation* mobilizes external means as well, in order to get more relevant, accurate, technical, and documented material regarding foreign laws.

2. External means

As President Canivet and Professor Molfessis wrote: '*le droit comparé est devenu une priorité, que manifestent les accords entre la Cour de cassation et celles des universités sollicitées qui ont bien voulu lui apporter leurs concours*'.[59] Therefore, sometimes, for the issues of considerable importance, the *Cour de cassation* could commission a comparative study by the '*Unité mixte de recherche de droit comparé de Paris (Université Paris I)*' or by another university research centre specializing in comparative law.

Thus:

> The *Cour de cassation*...asked the French Comparative Law Institute to issue a research report, the first time regarding a case of wrongful birth,[60] and the second time regarding the possible conviction for manslaughter of a person who had caused a miscarriage in a car accident he was responsible for.[61] These reports were then notified to the parties and to the *Ministère public* (the public prosecutor's office at the *Cour de*

[55] <http://www.network-presidents.eu/>.

[56] S. Caron, *La Cour de cassation et le dialogue des juges*, Phd thesis, Grenoble, 2011. *Adde*, G. Canivet, 'La pratique du droit comparé par les cours suprêmes. Brèves réflexions sur le dialogue des juges dans les expériences française et européenne: en commentaire de l'article de Sir Basil Markesinis et Jörg Fedtke *Le juge en tant que comparatiste*, [2005] 80 Tul. L. Rev. 221'.

[57] <http://www.ambafrance-uk.org/Liaison-Judge-s-Office>.

[58] <http://www.justice.gouv.fr/art_pix/1_fp_magistrat_liaison.pdf>.

[59] G. Canivet and N. Molfessis, 'La politique jurisprudentielle', in *La création du droit jurisprudentiel. Mélanges en l'honneur de Jacques Boré*, Dalloz, 2007, p. 94, n° 28, note 17.

[60] Ass. Plén., 17 novembre 2000, n° 99-13.701, '*Perruche case*'.

[61] Ass. Plén., 29 juin 2001, n° 99-85.973. See <http://www.courdecassation.fr/publications_26/bulletin_information_cour_cassation_27/bulletins_information_2001_1367/n_540_1444/#1>.

> *cassation*) for use in their briefs before the Court. In those two cases, the research undertaken was not limited to technical aspects of foreign positive law, but included an analysis of the legal, economic, and cultural context inside which similar cases were decided by judges in the foreign countries in question. The admittance of comprehensive and relevant studies enabled the *Cour de cassation* to open up its deliberations to comparative legal methodology.[62]

The 'comparative concern' reaches its climax when complementary studies based on comparative law are annexed to the preparatory work. Such was the case for the ruling held before the *Assemblée plénière* on 7 July 2006 regarding the issue of *Res judicata* and the retroactive effect of overrulings.[63] In such a situation—paradoxically—the elements of foreign laws are rather short in the preparatory works, as the latter mainly consist of referrals to the annexed study.

In almost the same vein, the latest initiative of the *Cour de cassation* is to have foreign scholars and French scholars presenting comparative studies about very important and crucial issues. A case held before a *Chambre mixte* in May 2013,[64] regarding the important and controversial issue of 'linked transactions', illustrates this 'new approach' to comparative law. One has to remark that, in this process, the final comparative report was not annexed to the preparatory works but was published elsewhere—namely in a law review.[65] As for this initiative, however, the picture is a mixed one, given that none of the preparatory works of this case—*avis* or *rapport*—significantly referred to the comparative elements presented before the Court by the parties' respective counsels.

In order to (temporarily) conclude this point, let us leave the last word—once again—to President Canivet:[66]

> French case law has been propelled in recent months by particularly beneficial lessons arising from foreign experiences with regards to retroactivity of reversals in jurisprudence. The experiment was repeated on the issue of the limitation of liability clauses in contracts for land transport and those concerning 'la force majeure' in different branches of law. These studies have not only been conducted in countries with civil law: some common law solutions are ideal for transposition into French law, provided that they are surrounded by a sufficient number of relevant similarities.

[62] G. Canivet, 'The use of comparative law before the French private law courts', in *Comparative Law Before the Courts*, ed. G. Canivet, M. Andenas, and D. Fairgrieve, British Institute of International & Comparative Law, 2004, p. 191.

[63] <http://www.courdecassation.fr/IMG/File/Plen-06-07-07-0410672-rapport-definitif-anonymise-annexe-2.pdf>.

[64] Ch. Mixte, 17 mai 2013, n°s 11-22.768 & 11-22.927; RDC, 2013, p. 849.

[65] RDC, 2013, p. 1079–120.

[66] (Our translation) '*La jurisprudence française a ainsi pu tirer, ces derniers mois, des leçons particulièrement bénéfiques des expériences étrangères en matière de rétroactivité des revirements de jurisprudence. L'expérience a été renouvelée sur le thème des clauses limitatives de responsabilité dans les contrats de transport terrestre et sur celle de la force majeure dans les différentes branches du droit. Ces recherches n'ont pas été menées uniquement dans les pays de Code civil: certaines solutions de* common law *se prêtent parfaitement à une transposition en droit français, pourvu qu'elles soient entourées d'un nombre suffisant de concordances pertinentes*'.

Lastly, it would be reasonable and legitimate to assume that the '*Fondation pour le droit continental*'[67] ('Foundation for civil law initiative') could be asked by the *Cour de cassation* to coordinate and finance comparative studies. That could be a valuable initiative since the Foundation's network consists of legal experts (scholars and practitioners) present throughout the world.

IV. Conclusion: Is the *Cour de cassation* an 'ideal supreme court' with respect to comparative law?

As a result, the *Cour de cassation* is still far from an 'ideal supreme court'[68] with respect to the use of comparative law, even though a large number of improvements have already been made and should be accomplished in the forthcoming years. For the time being, the use of comparative law before the *Cour de cassation* could be summed up as follows:[69]

> Resort to comparative law is also common in the perfection, completion or adaptation of national laws. This occurs mainly in cases where national law contains a loophole, or even an anachronism, or when it is much in need of modernization. Judges also use an evaluation of solutions provided by foreign law to decide new, complex cases that give rise to lively discussions. The example of foreign law is already considered with interest by the courts when a problem is common to several countries, and when it seems preferable to adopt an identical response in all systems of law, particularly when the solution has an economic impact that exceeds the limits of the legal area to which it pertains. Before choosing a position, the judge may still be tempted to test its efficiency in the foreign systems. Finally, reference to external laws and precedents always proves useful and rarely discussed in highly technical matters, sometimes unfamiliar to all ethical, political or social considerations.[70]

Therefore, the use of comparative law before the *Cour de cassation* is certainly no longer hidden and unconscious. Indeed, it is now visible and even, sometimes, claimed. However, its methodology, as well as its whole underlying philosophy, could be improved in the following ways:

67 <http://www.fondation-droitcontinental.org/en/>.

68 A. Tunc, 'Conclusions: la Cour suprême idéale', RIDC, 1978, p. 433.

69 (Our translation) '*[. . .] le recours au droit comparé est également habituel aux fins de parfaire, completer ou adapter les droits nationaux. Cette situation se rencontre principalement dans les hypothèses où le droit national contient une lacune, un anachronisme ou bien encore lorsqu'il doit être modernisé. Les juges ont aussi recours à une évaluation des solutions données par les droits étrangers pour trancher des cas nouveaux, complexes et qui donnent lieu à des vives discussions. L'exemple des droits étrangers est encore considéré avec intérêt par les juridictions lorsqu'un problème est commun à plusieurs pays et qu'il semble préférable d'adopter une réponse identique dans tous les systèmes de droit, en particulier, lorsque la solution a une portée économique qui dépasse les limites de l'espace juridique auquel elle s'applique. Avant d'adopter une position, le juge peut être encore tenté d'en vérifier l'efficacité dans les systèmes étrangers qui ont précédé. Enfin, la référence aux lois et précédents externes s'avère toujours utile et peu discuté dans les matières hautement techniques, parfois étrangères à toutes considérations éthiques, politiques ou sociales.*'

70 G. Canivet, 'Préface', in S. B. Markesinis, *Juges et universitaires face au droit comparé. Histoire des trente-cinq dernières années*, Dalloz, 2006, p. VII–VIII, n° 10.

- It is mandatory that:
    - 'The research which [is] undertaken [is] not limited to aspects of foreign law but [includes] an analysis of the foreign solutions in the legal, cultural and economic context of the countries involved. This [would enable] the *Cour de cassation* to refer in the course of its decision making process to comprehensive and relevant studies on those issues at stake. Thus, it is not only comparative law which [should be] introduced in the working method of the Court, but comparative science as a whole. This is the way [the Court] should proceed, by taking a judicial action which gives to comparative law all its significance in bridging the divide between different systems of law and in the approximation of the rules of law';[71]
    - French judges work much more on 'genuine' materials (original statute and case laws) and not on studies written by French scholars only;
    - The internal means and resources of the *Cour de cassation* are updated and highly increased.
- Moreover, the equivalent of the Comparative Law Unit ('*Cellule de droit comparé*') of the *Conseil d'État could be created* at the *Cour de cassation*.[72]
- The 'liaison judges' should be consulted on a more regular and substantial basis by the *Cour de cassation*. A partnership agreement could be set up between the 'Foundation for civil law initiative' and the Court.
- Exchanges of judges *via* professional internships abroad could be encouraged.

Hence, the use of comparative law before the *Cour de cassation*: work in progress!

[71] G. Canivet's speech pronounced on 18 November 2002 at the BIICL during the 'Grotius Dinner'.

[72] Particularly knowing the fact that a member of this Unit has contributed to the study related to this issue of 'linked transactions' mentioned earlier in this chapter.

26

Italian Courts and Comparative Law

*Annalisa Aschieri**

I. Introduction

The purpose of this chapter is to highlight whether, and to what extent, Italian courts tend to refer to foreign judgments in their decisions. This chapter will first focus on Italian decisions that mention non-domestic case law when applying foreign statutory laws in compliance with internal rules of international private law.[1] It will be stressed that these decisions long arose out of Italian case law attached to the idea that the analysis of foreign legal systems' decisions could be left behind, with its interpretation and application accepted on the basis of the mere wording of a foreign law. In this respect, it will be underlined how this kind of approach does not allow a full understanding of the actual content of a given foreign law.

Secondly, an outline will be provided of significant cases in which Italian courts were asked to consider foreign case law in the application of international legal instruments of uniform law. In particular, with regard to the latter, it will be stressed that if every legal system adopts its own domestic interpretation criteria, the consistency of such texts of law is undermined. Therefore, it will be shown the vital importance of relying on an interpretation of international conventions, autonomous and different from the ones given by the various domestic legal systems. In order to develop courts' awareness of the need to consider foreign case law, so as to guarantee an international and uniform interpretation of international conventions, it is important to foster true coordination amongst the decisions that apply these conventions, particularly when they are such important sources of law. However, such awareness does not necessarily imply acceptance of a supranational *stare decisis* doctrine.[2]

In this regard, it is specifically Italian case law concerning issues related to international sales of movable assets mentioning foreign decisions, which will be considered. Moreover, there is a notable tendency amongst certain Italian courts to refer to non-domestic decisions in order to identify the prevailing interpretation that persists at an international level.

Finally, the analysis will examine cases in which Italian courts have spontaneously mentioned foreign case law exclusively in order to enhance their decisions as already

* Ph.D. Candidate, Department of Law, University of Turin and University of Maastricht. I want to thank Professor Silvia Ferreri and Professor Joerg Luther who gave me precious help supporting me in the research and drafting of this chapter. All mistakes are mine.

[1] In Italy, an important private international law reform was enacted in 1995 with Law n. 218.

[2] See, Marco Torsello, 'Foreign Judge-made Law e sua ricezione nel diritto interno', in Gianmaria Ajani, Antonio Gambaro, Michele Graziadei, Rodolfo Sacco, Vincenzo Vigoriti and Michel Waelbroek (eds.), *Scritti in onore di Aldo Frignani* (Giappichelli, 2011), pp. 479–99.

elaborated after autonomous evaluations of the situation *de facto*, or in order to provide a decision of the case at stake more in line with the broader context affected by the decision. The most significant trait of these Italian decisions is related to the fact that, once in the Italian system, a rule expressed by a court that referred to foreign case law—as not arising out of foreign statutory or conventional laws—tends to become part of the domestic legal system more easily, and eventually, in a more permanent way.

Lastly, this chapter seeks to highlight that Italian courts are overall willing and open to foreign judge-made law references. This is particularly remarkable if considering today's projects of European and transnational harmonization of the law, as courts' support in the pursuit of such goal is not always easy to achieve.[3] Therefore, even if Italian decisions mentioning foreign case law are still few, they are nonetheless noteworthy. Indeed, it should be noted that Italian courts could foster an effective circulation of foreign judge-made law, promoting a faster and deeper level of harmonization of rules—to which the mere unification of statutory laws would never lead.

The so-called judge-made law plays a key role in the development of a uniform and harmonized supranational law. In this direction, Italian courts—even if only occasionally—have been shown to be open-minded. They understood that they need to look beyond their own legal and geographical boundaries when searching for the applicable *regulae iuris* for the decision of the case at stake.

The Italian case law considered in this chapter can be seen as an 'enlightened minority'.[4] Not taking into account foreign decisions is the prevailing attitude among Italian courts. In fact, non-domestic decisions are unfortunately still normally regarded as *tamquam non esset* for the solution of both domestic disputes and cases, in which the applicable foreign law would require an analysis of the relevant precedents.[5]

The above is true of both the Supreme Court and Italian first instance courts. In the case of the latter, it can be specified that in Italy there are ordinary and administrative courts of first and second instance which normally—except for administrative courts—bear the name of the Italian city in which they are located. They decide on the *quaestio facti* and *iuris*, as presented by the parties, and are usually composed of a body of judges. Once a first instance decision is appealed, there is not a third level of judgment. In fact, it is possible to file a claim before the Italian Supreme Court in order to exclusively obtain a decision on a *questio iuris*. Moreover, with the Italian legal system governed by civil law, precedents do not have a binding effect, but are instead recognized as having a persuasive value, especially if they are Supreme Court decisions. Furthermore, administrative courts are able to provide a short decision if it contains specific references to one or more relevant previous judgments.

[3] At the European level, the Green Paper from the Commission of 1 July 2010 on policy options for progress towards a European Contract Law for consumers and businesses [COM(2010) 348 final].

[4] See, for instance, Marco Torsello, 'Italy', in Franco Ferrari (ed.), *The CISG and Its Impact on National Legal Systems* (Sellier, European Law Publishers, 2008); see, Marco Torsello, 'Foreign Judge-made Law e sua ricezione nel diritto interno', in Gianmaria Ajani, Antonio Gambaro, Michele Graziadei, Rodolfo Sacco, Vincenzo Vigoriti and Michel Waelbroek (eds.), *Scritti in onore di Aldo Frignani* (Giappichelli, 2011), pp. 479–99.

[5] Accordingly see, for instance, Francesco Galgano, *La globalizzazione nello specchio del diritto* (Il Mulino, 2005) 117.

II. Private international law and reference to foreign case law

In Italy an important private international law reform[6] was enacted in 1995 with Law n. 218. Article 15 of Law n. 218/1995 provides that a foreign law must be applied according to its own interpretation and application criteria over time.

The Italian Court of Pesaro,[7] in one of its decisions of 2001, had to apply Articles 17 and 18 of the English Sale of Goods Act in order to identify the moment of actual transfer of ownership in a shipbuilding contract. The court, while outlining its arguments, referred to foreign judgments that were considered relevant and further mentioned a leading case[8] in this field, decided by the English House of Lords. Specifically, the Italian court ended up stating that the assumption founded on contractual provisions of anticipated partial payments—as also stressed by following English judgments[9]—was now to be considered as 'strong'. What's more, the Italian court's decision explicitly indicated the use and application of criteria developed by English judges.[10]

In another Italian case[11] concerning a licence and distribution agreement, English law had to be applied because of an *electio iuris* made from the parties themselves. The court had to decide on a penalty clause and, even if large support came from the work of an expert specifically appointed according to Article 14 of Italian Law n. 218/95,[12] a famous English case, *Dunlop v New Garage Ltd*,[13] was explicitly mentioned, as well as other previous and subsequent English decisions. The aim was to provide a unique answer to the question of the courts' power to reduce an evidently excessive penalty clause according to English law.[14] The court finally stated that, given the extensive English case law on the issue, it could now be stated that English judges tend to consider a clause as a penalty only if there is an evident case of clause stipulated *in terrorem*.[15] Therefore, a contractual provision can be qualified as a penalty clause if its amount is clearly excessive and disproportionate to the prejudice foreseen by the parties at the time of signing the contract for events of contractual breaches.

It is clear from the aforementioned decisions that Italian courts refer more commonly to foreign judgments when they are essential and connected to the application of a foreign statutory provision. Thus, the external reference becomes a natural consequence of the existence of a domestic rule of private international law. Following the

[6] Italian Law 31 May 1995, n. 218.

[7] Trib. Pesaro, [24 April 2001], in Riv. dir. proc., [2002], 457.

[8] *Dunlop Pneumatic Tyre Co. v New Garage & Motor Co. Ltd* [1915] AC 79.

[9] For instance, *Sir James Laing & Sons, Limited v Barclay, Curle & Co. Limited* [1908] AC 35 and *Blyth Shipbuilding and Dry Docks Company, Limited* [1926] CH 494.

[10] The Court in fact literally stated that 'in tale operazione di esegesi il Collegio ha fatto applicazione dei suesposti criteri elaborati dalla giurisprudenza inglese' ('For this interpretation the court applied criteria developed by the English case law').

[11] Trib. Rovereto, [15 March 2007], in Riv. dir. int. priv. proc., [2008], 179.

[12] Article 14 of the Italian Law n. 218/95.

[13] [1915] AC 79.

[14] See Marco Torsello, 'I rimedi all'inadempimento', in Francesco Galgano (ed), *Atlante di diritto privato comparato*, 145.

[15] Trib. Rovereto, [15 March 2007], in Riv. dir. int. priv. proc., [2008], 179.

Italian reform of private international law,[16] the actual chance for Italian courts to mention foreign decisions appears to rest on a specific provision of law,[17] given that a foreign law must now be applied according to its own interpretation and implementation criteria. Indeed, there have been scholars that have argued that the use of non-domestic criteria to interpret and implement a foreign law—at least in civil law systems—means essentially the employment of principles provided by statutory laws, without necessarily recalling case law.[18]

However, the picture changes if a foreign law is conceived as a 'legal system'[19] as a whole. This acknowledgement, along with the duty of Italian judges to interpret and implement a foreign law in the same way as a judge of that legal order would, forces domestic judges to unavoidably consider the foreign relevant case law, the latter being a vital part of that legal system. Such an investigation hence becomes inevitable and goes beyond the wording of a provision of law. Thus, Italian courts are somehow forced to broaden their analysis and take into account the relevant non-domestic decisions in order to define the actual content of a specific external statutory provision within the considered foreign legal system.

Moreover, since every Italian court[20] is directly burdened with the investigation of a foreign law, they are provided with specific tools that help them to verify its content. These tools seem to be shaped in order to offer courts a comprehensive understanding of the content of every important component of the studied legal system. In fact, for such an accomplishment, Italian courts can rely on the relevant international conventions, on the information acquired from the Italian Minister of Justice, or on the support given by experts or specialized institutions.[21] As a matter of fact, whenever a court is assisted—in the verification of the content of a foreign law—by the work of an expert, the latter will identify the content of a foreign law by considering all the elements that constitute the considered legal system, and, therefore, also its case law.

Furthermore, the above-mentioned Italian decisions show that there is a slowly growing awareness. In these cases, Italian courts have understood the importance of not limiting their analysis exclusively to the text of law that they need to apply. They realized that it is vital to broaden the investigation to the relevant foreign case law in order to verify the exact content of the law that they need to use and implement for the solution of the concrete case.

[16] Italian Law 31 May 1995, n. 218.

[17] Article 15, Italian Law 31 May 1995, n. 218 according to which a foreign law is applied according to its own interpretation and application criteria.

[18] Nerina Boschiero, 'Art. 15', in Stefania Bariatti (eds.), *Commentario: Riforma del sistema italiano di diritto internazionale privato (l. 31 maggio 1995, n. 218),* 1043; Sergio Maria Carbone, 'Articolo 15 (Interpretazione e applicazione della legge straniera)', in Pocar, Treves, Giardina, Luzzatto, Mosconi, Clerici, (eds.), *Commentario del nuovo diritto internazionale privato* (Padova, 1996, 72).

[19] Specifically according to the government's report to the Italian Law 31 May 1995, n. 218.

[20] Article 14, Italian Law of 31 May 1995, n. 218. The principle provided by the latter article has been recently qualified by the Italian Supreme Court as a general principle of the Italian legal system relevant also within criminal proceedings. Cass. Pen., [5 November 2009], n. 49532, in Cass. pen., [2010], 6, 2177; Gentiloni Silveri, *Il reato di corruzione internazionale: tra globalizzazione del diritto penale e (difficile) adattamento all'ordinamento interno*, (in Cass. pen., 2010, 6), 2177.

[21] Italian Law of 31 May 1995, n. 218. See, for instance, Ilaria Pittaluga, *La prova del diritto straniero: evoluzioni giurisprudenziali in Francia e Italia* (in Riv. dir. int. priv. proc., 2002), 675.

However, it could be argued that in the aforesaid Italian decisions, courts applied provisions of a common law system where statutory laws are known to be rare or at least marginally important. Moreover, if we look for Italian courts applying foreign civil law system's provisions, it is quite exceptional to find references to non-domestic case law.[22]

As per the Italian Supreme Court's judgments, a significant reference to foreign case law cannot be found. Such a tendency is, in fact, not yet common among its decisions. Nonetheless, in 2002[23] the Italian highest court had the chance to deal more closely with the issue of interpreting a foreign law, as provided by Italian Law n. 218/1995.[24] Similarly, in 2009[25] the Supreme Court confirmed the existence in the Italian legal system of a general rule according to which, when deemed necessary for the decision at stake, Italian courts are obliged to consider foreign laws.[26] In the same decision, our highest judges pointed out that following Law n. 218/1995, the knowledge of a foreign law by Italian courts, as well as its interpretation according to the criteria provided by the Article 15 of Law n. 218/1995, is no longer regulated as a *quaestio facti*, but has become a *quaestio iuris*. Nevertheless, it was underlined that the conditions for the applicability of a particular foreign law still depend on the existence of connecting criteria based on facts, which must be ritually acquired during the proceeding.[27]

In fact, according to Article 14 of Italian Law n. 218/1995 and in compliance with the principle *iura novit curia*, every Italian court must identify the foreign applicable law. The Italian legislator expressly qualified foreign statutory provisions as legal rules. Therefore, in case of mistakes in the application of a foreign law a claim can be filed[28] before the Italian Supreme Court. If the investigation of a foreign law was regarded as a *quaestio facti*, it would have not been possible to have a Supreme Court's judgment. However, a claim can be filed before the highest court in case of violation or erroneous application of a foreign law. This is the case because in Italy the inquiry of a foreign law is not regarded as a *quaestio facti*, but as a *questio iuris*.[29] On practical grounds, this means that during a proceeding, parties are not required to provide evidence of the content and applicability of a foreign law, as they are in this respect free from an actual burden of proof.

However, it must be highlighted that the principle *iura aliena novit curia* does not imply that Italian courts must have a full knowledge of every foreign law. It just means that they must study and investigate them in order to obtain such knowledge, in this

[22] See, for example, Trib. Chieti, 4 February 2005, n. 114, in PQM, [2005], 76; Michele Pezone, *Sulla condizione di reciprocità ex. art. 16 delle Preleggi* (in PQM, 2005), 76.

[23] Italian Supreme Court, [26 February 2002], n. 2791, (in Nuova giur. civ. comm., 2003, I), 22.

[24] Article 15, Italian Law 31 May 1995, n. 218.

[25] Italian Supreme Court, [5 June 2009], n. 13087 (in Riv. dir. int. priv. proc., 2010).

[26] The so-called 'regola generale della rilevabilità e accertamento d'ufficio del diritto straniero'.

[27] Italian Supreme Court, [5 June 2009], n. 13087, ibid.

[28] Article 360 of the Italian Civil Procedure Code. See Italian Supreme Court, [21 April 2005], n. 8360, (in Dir. com. int., 3/4, 2006).

[29] See, among others, Antonio Coaccioli, *Manuale di Diritto Internazionale Privato e Processuale* (Giuffrè Editore, 2011), 123. Filippo Preite, Pugliese Gazzanti, Antonio di Crotone, *Atti notarili nel diritto comunitario e internazionale—Vol. 1: Diritto Internazionale Privato* (Utet Giuridica, 2011).

way also complying with Article 113[30] of the Italian Civil Procedure Code.[31] Today, Italian courts can expressly rely on experts or specialized institutions in order to understand the content of a foreign law,[32] while parties are burdened with the duty of supporting the court—for instance by providing experts' reports or documental evidence—in the identification of the foreign applicable law.[33]

As per the understanding of a foreign law[34] and the role played by non-domestic case law, it is worth considering the aforesaid case decided by the Supreme Court in 2002.[35] The Court had to deal with an issue of natural paternity of a child. The mother, a citizen of the Republic of Cameroon, claimed that the father of her daughter was an Italian citizen. However, the latter exclusively admitted of having provided food and clothing to the child without recognizing her as his natural daughter. The court of first instance admitted the woman to pursue her claim and pointed out that, on the issue at stake, the law of the Republic of Cameroon provides that such an action can be filed within two years from the birth of the child or whenever the father ceases to provide food and clothing. In this case, the claim was filed more than two years after the birth of the young girl. However, it could have been brought forward because the Italian man himself stated that he once provided clothing and food to the child.

The appeal filed by the Italian citizen was further dismissed. Particularly, it was rejected in the part where he asked the court to take into consideration the interpretation criteria used in the Cameroonian legal system. In this respect, the Court of Appeal held that the reference made by Article 15 of Law n. 218/1995 to the interpretation and application criteria of a foreign law does not imply that an Italian court must investigate how a foreign provision of law that has to be applied is specifically interpreted in the considered legal system. A court should simply return to the general interpretation rules governing that legal order. Specifically, as per the Cameroonian law regulating the issue at stake, the court observed that it had to be interpreted in the sense that a claim can also be filed if the supposed father ceases to provide food and clothing. In the case hereby considered, the man expressly declared that he once provided economic aid, food, and clothing to the child.

Furthermore, the Italian citizen brought the case before the Supreme Court, but the claim was again rejected. With regard to the objection that the Cameroonian text of law should have been legalized by an appropriate Italian institute, the Supreme Court held that an Italian judge must be able to cope with a foreign statutory provision in the same way as with an Italian one: by specifically having the duty to verify its content and

[30] This Article provides that every Italian judge must decide its cases according to the relevant and applicable legal rules.

[31] Lastly, among others, Italian Supreme Court, [9 May 2007], n. 10549, (in Dir. Rel. Ind., 1, 2008).

[32] Italian Supreme Court, [7 December 1976], n. 458, (in Riv. Dir. Intern., 1976), 577.

[33] See Italian Supreme Court, Sez. Un. (Plenary Chamber) [18 May 1978], n. 2392, (in Dir. mar., 1979); Italian Supreme Court, [27 January 1995], n. 995, (in Giust. civ. mass., 1995).

[34] See also Michele Zamboni, *Sugli strumenti di conoscenza della legge straniera da parte del giudice italiano*, (in Nuova giur. civ. comm., 2003, I), 26; Antonello Di Muro, *La ricerca e l'interpretazione del diritto straniero. La Cassazione di fronte agli artt. 14 e 15 della legge n. 218/1995*, (in Giur. it., 2003) 479; Italian Supreme Court, [5 June 2009], n. 13087, (in Riv. dir. int. priv. proc., 2010), 140; Chiara Tuo, *Obbligazioni contrattuali ed applicazione della legge straniera. Un preoccupante segnale di regresso da parte della Corte di Cassazione* (in Riv. dir. int. priv. proc., 2010,) 55.

[35] Italian Supreme Court, [26 February 2002], n. 2791, (in Nuova giur. civ. comm., 2003, I), 22.

assure its application. In this regard, an Italian court can also refer to information acquired by experts, specialized institutions, its personal knowledge, or evidence provided by the parties. In the case at hand, the court underlined that the translated text of law came from the Cameroonian Embassy that attested its authenticity. Therefore, the Court of Appeal correctly used and studied it, and also provided that the claimant did not file any specific objection on the trustworthiness of the said translation. Moreover, the Italian man claimed a violation of Article 15[36] of Italian Law n. 218/1995. In this respect, the Italian Supreme Court[37] remarkably held that a foreign provision should indeed be interpreted and implemented considering the whole legal system to which it belongs, in its entireness and global dimension. Nonetheless, it further specified that such requirement does not imply that an Italian court must retrieve foreign case law or scholarly works supporting one or another interpretation given to the considered statutory provision. In its investigation, an Italian court should simply apply the general interpretation criteria existing in that legal system.

On the one hand, it can be argued that it would be inconceivable to indiscriminately ask Italian courts to generally comply with previous foreign case law, applying the relevant statutory provisions for the decision of the case at stake. In fact, while in common law systems, courts must adhere to precedents of earlier cases as sources of law, according to the so-called *stare decisis* principle,[38] in civil law systems courts must not comply with previous case law, the latter holding merely persuasive value. On the other hand, it would also be incorrect—and probably excessive—to state that there is no duty at all for Italian courts to consider a foreign legal system in its global dimension—hence including its case law—when defining its actual content for the decision of the case.

Along with the latter consideration, the Italian Supreme Court[39] carried on pointing out that, on practical grounds, a specific foreign case law orientation on the implementation of a certain statutory provision could not have yet been developed. Therefore, an investigation of the Italian judge in this direction, which could also turn out to be excessively complex and, at times, impossible, may risk being insufficient, incomplete, or outdated. It could hence lead to a deceptive result and recognition of a binding effect to former decisions of the considered foreign legal system.

Overall, the statements of the Supreme Court's judgment of 2002 can be perceived as somehow puzzling. In fact, generally speaking, the court proved to be remarkably open when stating that a foreign law must be interpreted and applied as a legal system as a whole, considered in its global and actual dimension. However, from a practical point

[36] According to which a foreign law must be applied pursuant to its own interpretation and application criteria over time.

[37] Italian Supreme Court, [26 February 2002], n. 2791, (in Nuova giur. civ. comm., 2003, I), 22.

[38] On the *stare decisis* principle within the Italian legal system see, *inter alia*, Marino Bin, *Il precedente giudiziario in Italia* (in Contratto e Impresa, 1988), 192; Angelo Bonsignori, *L'art. 65 dell'ordinamento giudiziario* (in Contratto e Impresa, 1988), 526; Gino Gorla, reference: 'Precedente giudiziale', in *Enc. giur. Treccani*, XXIII, Roma, 1990; Michele Taruffo, *Precedente ed esempio nella decisione giudiziaria* (in Riv. tri. dir. proc. civ., 1994), 19; Francesco Galgano, *L'efficacia vincolante del precedente di Cassazione* (in Contratto e Impresa, 1999), 889; Letizia Vacca (ed), *Lo stile delle sentenze e l'utilizzazione dei precedenti* (Torino, 2000).

[39] Italian Supreme Court, [26 February 2002], n. 2791 (in Nuova giur. civ. comm., 2003, I), 22.

of view, the court stepped back and held that, the above notwithstanding, there is no actual duty for Italian courts to refer to foreign case law supporting a certain interpretation rather than another, the use of foreign interpretation criteria when applying a non-domestic provision of law being sufficient. Therefore, even if in principle it is the global dimension of each legal system that is important, practically speaking, such openness is eclipsed by the concrete difficulties of retrieving the foreign case law interpreting the non-domestic provision that has to be applied.

However, if an Italian court has to apply a foreign common law provision, it should refer and comply with the relevant previous case law, as being bound to an interpretation and application in compliance with the criteria of that legal system. Likewise, when dealing with the interpretation of an external civil law provision, former decisions would not be binding, but should anyway be taken into account by Italian courts as key elements of that legal system globally considered.

It should be further noticed that by complying with Italian private international rules and related civil procedure provisions, foreign case law may be specifically referred to by Italian judges when they are asked to recognize non-domestic decisions. Nevertheless, this possibility is of little interest for this analysis, as in these cases Italian courts simply verify whether a foreign decision can be qualified and accepted—according to the general principles of the Italian legal system—as an ultimate judgment for the case at stake. Therefore, an Italian court checks the consistency of a foreign decision with the principles that shape the Italian legal system in order to recognize its binding effect on a specific case. Whilst the non-domestic judgment gets clearly mentioned, it is expressly regarded as having limited effects—hence having few possibilities to actually circulate and, eventually, affect the Italian legal system as a whole.

III. International conventions and reference to foreign decisions

In 1996 a remarkable decision of the Court of Cuneo[40] referred to foreign case law while applying an International Convention. The Court of Cuneo had to apply Articles 38 and 39 of the Vienna Convention[41] with regard to certain alleged defects of sold assets. The court held that the foreign case law retrieved on the issue—even if few—appeared to be quite rigorous. The Italian court mentioned, for instance, a Swiss decision[42]—identical as per the nationality of the parties—in order to state that in the event of evident defects of sold assets, this must be immediately disclosed to the seller. Specifically, the Swiss case concerned the supply of movable assets between an Italian seller and a Swiss purchaser. Moreover, the Court of Cuneo highlighted that in another identical case with regard to the type of sold assets—clothing—a German court[43] considered as late a notice given to the seller 16 days after the delivery of the goods.

40 Trib. Cuneo, 31st January 1996, n. 45, in Dir. Comm. Int., [1996].

41 United Nations Convention on Contracts for the International Sale of Goods (Vienna, 1980) (CISG).

42 See District Court Locarno Campagna, 27 April 1992, n. 6252, in UNILEX [1995].

43 See Landgericht Stuttgart (District Court of Stuttgart), 31 August 1989, available at <http://cisgw3.law.pace.edu/cases/890831g1.html> (last accessed 24 January 2014).

In another case, the Court of Pavia[44] had to decide on an issue concerning interest due for unpaid sums according to the Vienna Convention.[45] The Italian court referred to foreign case law[46] in order to confirm its solution already developed after a study of the text of the Convention. The Court of Pavia observed that such an issue was not regulated by the Vienna Convention. Therefore, it had to be solved by referring to internal rules of international private law, hence to domestic rules. Thus, in this way the Court of Pavia followed the solution adopted by the mentioned[47] foreign case law.

Notably, in this case, an Italian court not only referred to foreign case law, but also specified that even if foreign decisions are not binding, they should be taken into account. This is in compliance, for instance, with Article 7, paragraph 1, of the United Nations Convention.[48] An Italian court therefore specifically outlined the principle that will be further confirmed by following case law, according to which references to other States' decisions—practice that the Court of Pavia wanted to be fostered among Italian Courts—has merely a persuasive—but not binding—effect.[49]

Moreover, in the 2000s we assisted in an evolution of referencing foreign case law by Italian courts. The first decision worth mentioning is that of the Court of Vigevano[50] of 12 July 2000. In this decision, the court referred to around 40 foreign decisions and arbitration awards concerning different aspects of the issue investigated by the Italian court. These foreign judgments were of different legal systems such as the German, Dutch, Austrian, Swiss, French, and US.[51] Given the important role played by the foreign case law cited, the Court of Vigevano stated that even if not binding, those non-domestic decisions had to be taken into account in order to assure and foster the uniform application of the United Nations Conventions, as required by Article 7, paragraph 1,[52] of the Convention.

Additionally, the decision of the Court of Vigevano for the first time largely referred to foreign case law by specifying the law reviews or electronic databases[53] in which they

[44] Trib. Pavia, 29 December 1999, in Corr. giur., [2000]; See Franco Ferrari, 'Rapporto tra diritto materiale uniforme di origine convenzionale e diritto internazionale privato' [2000] Corr. giur. 933.

[45] See on the issue, among others, Burghard Piltz, *Internationales Kaufrecht Das UN-Kaufrecht in praxisorientierter Darstellung* (Verlag C.H. Beck, München, 2008, 2. Auflage, XX) 492; Franco Ferrari, 'CISG Case Law: A New Challenge for Interpreters?' [2005] 17 Journal of Law and Commerce 245–61.

[46] As, for instance, District Court Locarno Campagna, 16 December 1991, available at <http://cisgw3.law.pace.edu/cases/911216s1.html> (last accessed 30 January 2014).

[47] See the decision of the District Court Locarno Campagna of 1991.

[48] Trib. Pavia, 29 December 1999, in Corr. giur., [2000]. The recognition of foreign case law as having a binding effect, as there was a sort of supranational *stare decisis* principle, would be very likely fostered by the existence of a supranational Court. On the issue see, for instance, M. Torsello, *Common Features of Uniform Commercial Law Conventions. A Comparative Study Beyond the 1980 Vienna Sales Law* (Sellier, European Law Publishers, 2004).

[49] Trib. Rimini, 26 Novembre 2002, n. 3095, in Giur. it., [2003]; See Franco Ferrari, 'Problematiche tipiche della Convenzione di Vienna sui contratti di vendita internazionale di beni mobili risolte in una prospettiva uniforme' [2001] Giur. it. 281.

[50] Trib. Vigevano, 12 July 2000, in Giur. it., [2001].

[51] It is also undoubtedly significant that this decision got translated in various languages, almost to confirm its capability of being a reference model for future Courts' decisions.

[52] In this sense, see also Trib. Pavia, 29 December 1999, n. 468, in Corr. giur., [2000].

[53] See, among others, Anna Veneziano, 'Uniform Interpretation: What is being done? Unofficial Efforts and Their Impact' and Filip De Ly, 'Uniform Interpretation: What is being done? Official Efforts', in Franco Ferrari (ed), *The 1980 Uniform Sales Law. Old Issues Revisited in the Light of Recent Experiences* (Giuffrè & Sellier, European Law Publishers, 2003).

were found. The importance of referring to foreign decisions was also recognized by a posterior Italian decision, innovative and noteworthy in virtue of the several and different foreign judgments that it mentioned.[54] The Court of Rimini[55] stated that if every State interpreted International Conventions, in a different way, there would have been opposite and conflicting results on practical grounds. Nonetheless, the Court of Rimini observed that this risk was not too high when considering the United Nations Convention on international purchase agreements of movable assets. In fact, there are luckily quite a few tools that undermine the development of different interpretation approaches as, for instance, databases publishing international case law on the issue,[56] or law reviews such as the *Internationales Handelsrecht*.[57]

Following the Court of Vigevano's decision, a few other cases decided by the Court of Padova[58] widely referred to foreign case law in relation, *inter alia*, to remedies in the event of breach of contract,[59] form of contracts, terms of payment, interest rates in case of late payment,[60] and definition of 'fundamental breach' and relevant consequences.[61]

Given the above, it can be said that the overall number of Italian decisions referring to foreign case law is still a minority. Nonetheless, it is possible to find some enlightened Italian courts[62] that have been amenable to the needs of a harmonized law at an international level.[63] There are, in fact, Italian courts that referred to foreign case law when applying Conventions other than the Vienna Convention.[64] For instance, in 2006 the Court of Venice[65] had to apply the Rome Convention[66] criterion, according to which it is the law of the country with which the contract is most closely connected to that must be chosen.[67] The Court of Venice stated that because of the specific

[54] Trib. Rimini, 26 Novembre 2002, n. 3095, in Giur. it., [2003].

[55] Trib. Rimini, 26 Novembre 2002, n. 3095, in Giur. it., [2003]. Available at <http://cisgw3.law.pace.edu/cases/021126i3.html> (last accessed 30 January 2014).

[56] As the decisions available at <www.unilex.info> (last accessed 30 January 2014).

[57] Trib. Rimini, 26 Novembre 2002, n. 3095, in Giur. it., [2003].

[58] For instance, see Trib. Padova, 10 January 2006, in Giur. mer., [2006].

[59] Trib. Padova, 25 February 2004, in Giur. it., [2004]. On remedies in case of breach of contract under the Vienna Convention see, *inter alia*, Marco Torsello, 'Remedies for Breach of Contract under the 1980 Convention on Contracts for the International Sale of Goods' [2005] 9 Vindobona Journal of International Commercial Law and Arbitration 253.

[60] Trib. Padova, 31 March 2004, in Giur. mer., [2004] 1065, available at <http://cisgw3.law.pace.edu/cases/040225i3.html> (last accessed 30 January 2014); see also Franco Ferrari, 'La disciplina sostanziale della vendita internazionale ed il saggio di interessi' [2004] Giur. mer. 1069.

[61] Trib. Padova, 10 January 2006, in Giur. mer., [2006] 1408.

[62] See, Marco Torsello, 'Foreign Judge-made Law e sua ricezione nel diritto interno', in Gianmaria Ajani, Antonio Gambaro, Michele Graziadei, Rodolfo Sacco, Vincenzo Vigoriti and Michel Waelbroek (eds.), *Scritti in onore di Aldo Frignani* (Giappichelli, 2011), pp. 479–99.

[63] Accordingly, see, for instance, Marco Torsello, 'Italy', in Franco Ferrari (ed), The CISG and Its Impact on National Legal Systems (Sellier, European Law Publishers, 2008) 215. As per the procedure laid down in Article 267 TFEU, its function is to ensure uniform interpretation and validity specifically of EU law, across all Member States. In fact, according to the preliminary reference procedure a national court or tribunal can refer a question of EU law to the European Court of Justice (CJEU) for a preliminary ruling so as to decide the case before it.

[64] For instance, the Geneva Convention of 1956 on international transport of goods by road. Trib. Biella, 15 May 1998, in Dir. marittimo [1999] 833.

[65] Trib. Venezia, 20 February 2006, in Riv. dir. int. priv. e proc., 2007;

[66] Convention 80/934/ECC on the law applicable to contractual obligations opened for signature in Rome on 19 June 1980.

[67] According to Article 4, paragraph 2, of the Convention of Rome 1980.

circumstances of the case at stake, the criterion provided by Article 4, paragraph 2, of the Rome Convention could not be applied and specifically referred to by an English Court of Appeal's decision of 2001.[68] The Italian court also pointed out that the above-mentioned criterion can be applied only if the one provided in paragraph 1 of the same Article[69] is not applicable.

In another case, the Court of Rovereto[70] had to decide whether general terms and conditions placed on the back of a written contract proposal—in the event that these are mentioned in the contract document which contains the body of the proposal—can be considered as an integral part of the proposal itself. The Italian court stated that (as the case law interpreting the Vienna Convention also highlighted),[71] for the purposes of the completeness of a contract proposal, it is not necessary that the general conditions are outlined in the contract, considering instead a reference in the text of the proposal of the document containing them to be sufficient. What is noteworthy is that this decision of the Court of Rovereto largely referred to case law of States that are part of the Vienna Convention that applied Articles 8 and 14 of the said Convention.[72]

Moreover, there are two other decisions of the Court of Forlì which are particularly significant for the number of different foreign decisions mentioned. At first, in 2008[73] the Court of Forlì decided on a dispute arising from defective purchased goods. The court verified its jurisdiction according to EU Regulation n. 44/2001 and then largely referred to European and domestic case law applying this Regulation.[74] The court confirmed its jurisdiction and unfolded its decision on the specific facts of the case at stake by expressly mentioning about 53 foreign decisions.

Furthermore, in 2009 the Court of Forlì[75] continued in its reference of non-domestic decisions. In fact, in this latter decision, the Court of Forlì ended up mentioning up to 31 foreign judgments with specific indication of their location. Hence, the court showed that foreign decisions can be usefully implemented by Italian courts when applying a uniform text of law. In the case at hand, the existence of defects on certain purchased goods was communicated 13 months after their delivery. The Court of Forlì stated that the general approach followed by both Italian and foreign decisions, even if not binding, unequivocally indicated that the aforesaid period of notice was excessively long. The court highlighted that there were previous decisions stating that such a notice made a few months after the delivery of the goods could not in any case be considered

[68] *Samcrete Egypt Engineers and Contractors s.a.e. v Land Rover Exports Limited* [2001] EWCA Civ 2019.

[69] Article 4, paragraph 1, of the Convention of Rome 1980.

[70] Trib. Rovereto, 21 November 2007, available at <http://cisgw3.law.pace.edu/cases/071121i3.html> (last accessed 30 January 2014).

[71] Specifically, reference was made to the *Bundesgerichtshof*, 31 October 2001, available at <http://cisgw3.law.pace.edu/cases/011031g1.html> (last accessed 30 January 2014).

[72] For instance, the *Bundesgerichtshof* of 31 October 2001, ibid.

[73] Trib. Forlì, 11 December 2008, available at <http://cisgw3.law.pace.edu/cases/081211i3.html> (last accessed 30 January 2014).

[74] The Court, in fact, directly refers to the decision of the *Voorzieningenrechter Rechtbank's Gravenhage*, in Ned. Int. Priv., 2005, 232.

[75] Trib. Forlì, 16 February 2009, available at <http://cisgw3.law.pace.edu/cases/090216i3.html> (last accessed 30 January 2014).

as promptly given.[76] In addition, the Court of Forlì remarked that when applying international rules of uniform law, an Italian court should take both foreign and Italian case law into consideration. This, not because such judgments are binding, but because they are an adequate tool that can support the judge in the interpretation of the law.

Overall, from the Italian cases discussed it can be noticed that Italian courts have sometimes taken into consideration foreign decisions when applying uniform and conventional rules.[77] It is specifically the Vienna Convention of 1980[78]—because of the several decisions on the issues regulated by the Convention—that represents the most significant and emblematic case in which Italian courts applied provisions of international conventions and referred to non-domestic judgments. It is, in fact, straightforward that a mere harmonization of the law does not guarantee an even implementation of the said law in every legal system that adopts it.[79] Therefore, the latter needs to be applied in the same way by national courts in order to be able to rely on similar decisions on disputes arising from international contracts of the sale of goods regulated by the Convention.[80]

Thus, rules on interpretation of International Conventions become crucial. In this respect, it is noteworthy that almost every contractual Convention of uniform law recurs to interpretation clauses that are fundamentally alike.[81] Within the Vienna Convention, such a clause can be found in Article 7, paragraph 1. The latter requires that the interpretation of the Convention must be carried out bearing in mind the international trait of the Convention and the goal of achieving a harmonized application of the Convention, while assuring at the same time the respect of the principle of good faith in international trade.[82]

Article 7 of the United Nations Convention provides for interpretation guidelines aiming to support courts in the solution of difficulties arising from the application of this international uniform law. Scholars have long remarked on the observance of good faith in international trade.[83] However, for the present analysis, according to paragraph

[76] For instance in LG Berlin, 16 September 1992, available at <http://cisgw3.law.pace.edu/cases/920916g1.html> accessed 30 January 2014, the months were three and a half, while in OLG Düsseldorf, 10 February 1994, in *Recht der Internationalen Wirtschaft*, 1995, 53, were two.

[77] See, for instance, Marco Torsello, *Common Features of Uniform Commercial Law Conventions. A Comparative Study Beyond the 1980 Vienna Sales Law* (Sellier, European Law Publishers, 2004).

[78] See, *inter alia*, Peter Winship, 'The Scope of the Vienna Convention on International Sales Contracts', in Galston and Smit (eds.), *International Sales: The United Nations Convention on Contracts for the International Sale of Goods* (Matthew Bender, 1984), available at <http://www.cisg.law.pace.edu/cisg/biblio/winship5.html> (last accessed 30 January 2014); Bianca–Bonell, *Commentary on the International Sales Law* (Giuffrè, 1987, Milan).

[79] L.M. Ryan, 'The Convention on Contracts for the International Sale of Goods: Divergent Interpretations' [1995] 4 Tulane J. Int'l & Comp. 101.

[80] Franco Ferrari, 'Nuove e vecchie questioni in materia di vendita internazionale tra interpretazione autonoma e ricorso alla giurisprudenza straniera', Nota a Trib. Padova, sez. distaccata di Este, 25 febbraio 2004, in Giur. It., 2004; Roderick Munday, 'The Uniform Interpretation of International Conventions' [1978] 27 ICLQ 404.

[81] Marco Torsello, *Common Features of Uniform Commercial Law Conventions. A Comparative Study Beyond the 1980 Vienna Sales Law* (Sellier, European Law Publishers, 2004) 157.

[82] On Article 7 of the Vienna Convention see, *inter alia*, Peter M. Gerhart, 'The Sales Convention in Courts: Uniformity, Adaptability, and Adoptability', in Peter Sarcevic and Paul Volken (ed), *International Sale of Goods Revisited* (Kluwer Law International, 2001).

[83] See, among others, Michael Joachim Bonell, 'Article 7', in Bianca–Bonell (eds.), *Commentary on the International Sales Law* (Giuffrè, Milan, 1987) 65–94; Troy Keily, 'Good Faith and the Vienna Convention

1 of the aforementioned Article 7, the interpretation of the Convention has to be carried out with regard both to its international character and to the need to promote uniformity in its application. This clearly evinces the importance of an autonomous interpretation of the Convention.[84] In fact, with such an expression, Article 7 goes beyond the idea according to which Conventions, once introduced within national legal systems, can be interpreted pursuant to domestic interpretation criteria.[85]

Thus, the interpretation clause of the Vienna Convention expressly provides that courts must be aware of the need of promoting a harmonized application of the Convention. Hence, in order to achieve such a goal, the Convention should be considered as an autonomous *corpus* of law and should be accordingly implemented.[86] In this respect, the essential role[87] played by drafting works,[88] scholarly,[89] and comparative studies on the different solutions adopted by domestic legal systems must be recognized. However, the key role is still played by the understanding of domestic and foreign decisions[90] as, not binding,[91] but certainly persuasive[92] precedents.

Likewise, the Italian highest court is well aware of the fact that an international convention should be considered as an autonomous *corpus* of law, interpreted accordingly. In fact, in one of its decisions in 1968,[93] the court stated that an international provision of law regulating international trade could not be interpreted by means of an internal rule. A meaning should not be given to such a provision that differs from the one resulting from the common intentions of the contracting States. Moreover, the Supreme Court highlighted that international provisions of law are fully part of the Italian legal system. Yet, they cannot be interpreted as if they were domestic rules, hence by referring to national criteria. The arguments unfolded by the Supreme Court expressly showed the need of relying on an autonomous interpretation of

on Contracts for the International Sale of Goods (CISG)' [1999] 3 Vindobona Journal of International Commercial Law and Arbitration, Issue 1, 15–40.

[84] Michael Joachim Bonell, ibid., 74.

[85] See also, Franco Ferrari, 'CISG Case Law: A New Challenge for Interpreters?' [1999] 17 Journal of Law and Commerce, 245–61.

[86] Paul Volken, 'The Vienna Convention: Scope, Interpretation, and Gap-filling', in Petar Sarcevic and Paul Volken (eds.), *International Sale of Goods: Dubrovnik Lectures* (Oceana, 1986, Ch. 2), 19–53.

[87] Stefania Bariatti, 'L'interpretazione delle convenzioni internazionali di diritto uniforme' [1986] Riv. dir. int. priv. e proc. 163.

[88] See, *inter alia*, John O. Honnold, *Uniform Law for International Sales under the 1980 United Nations Convention* (Kluwer Law International, The Hague, 3rd edn., 1999) 141; Stefania Bariatti, 'L'interpretazione delle convenzioni internazionali di diritto uniforme', ibid., 204.

[89] See E. Bodenheimer, 'Doctrine as a Source of the International Unification of Law' [1986] 34 American Journal of Comparative Law, Supplement, 67–79.

[90] See Franco Ferrari, 'Interprétation uniforme de la Convention de Vienne de 1980 sur la vente internationale' [1996] Rev. Int. dr. comp. 813.

[91] See, for instance, Larry A. DiMatteo, 'An International Contract Law Formula: The Informality of International Business Transactions Plus the Internationalization of Contract Law Equals Unexpected Contract Liability' [1997] 23 Syracuse Journal of International Law and Commerce 79.

[92] See, *inter alia*, M. Torsello, *Common Features of Uniform Commercial Law Conventions. A Comparative Study Beyond the 1980 Uniform Sales Law* (European Law Publishers, 2004) 164.

[93] Italian Supreme Court 24 June 1968, n. 2106, in Riv. dir. int. priv. proc., 1969, 914; Michael J. Bonell, 'L'interpretazione del diritto uniforme alla luce dell'art. 7 della convenzione di Vienna sulla vendita internazionale' [1986] 2 Rivista di diritto civile 225.

supranational provisions of law. However, it has to be pointed out that this awareness did not receive the extensive attention that was expected and somehow desired.

In recent years such consciousness slowly started to grow again, gaining consent among Italian courts. The latter understood that even if there is an autonomous interpretation, for instance, of the Vienna Convention, this still does not guarantee its uniform application. Italian courts became conscious of their decisive role. In fact, a mere autonomous interpretation of an international convention, hence an interpretation that does not make reference to the meaning given by national legal systems, is not *per se* sufficient for the fostering of the harmonization of the law as intended by international conventions.[94] It is vital that courts refer and take into account the relevant domestic and foreign decisions that apply a uniform text of law, in order to—by paying attention to what occurs beyond each national boundary[95]—achieve the aforesaid goal of uniform application and harmonization of the law.

IV. Italian courts' brainstorming and foreign case law

The Court of Napoli in 2002[96] decided on a case of alleged unauthorized use of the trademark 'Playboy'. At first, the court referred to one of its previous decisions in order to reaffirm that, given the extreme popularity gained by that brand, the latter now played a preeminent and characteristic role in every potential customer's choice. Moreover, the Court of Napoli referred to external decisions in order to further enrich its own. Specifically, the court held that it was particularly remarkable that the US District Court of the State of New York in 1996 declared—with the aim of protecting the 'Playboy' trademark—not accessible from the United States website playmen.it.

In the aforementioned Italian decision, the reference to a foreign precedent was clearly made in order to support and enhance the decision of the Court of Napoli by means of an *id quod plerumque accidit,* hence by a merely enriching use of foreign case law.[97] Furthermore, there is another noteworthy case decided by the Court of Monza[98] on an alleged responsibility of an internet server provider. In this decision, the Italian court referred to foreign case law in order to provide an appropriate analysis of the case at stake, carried out under the correct light and within the right framework. It has to be noticed that the dispute did not *per se* have any transnational element. However, the Court of Monza drew inspiration from non-domestic decisions and mentioned them even if going against the approach followed by previous internal decisions.

The Italian Court of Monza firstly stated that a provider should be considered—as it actually usually is—a mere internet manager. Secondly, it referred to both foreign and domestic previous decisions which recognized the provider's responsibility for the

[94] Trib. Padova, 25 February 2004, in Giur. it., 2004, 1403.

[95] On these decisions see, among others, Franco Ferrari, 'Do Courts Interpret the CISG Uniformly?', in Franco Ferrari (ed), *Quo Vadis CISG? Celebrating the 25th Anniversary of the United Nations Convention on contracts for the International Sale of Goods* (Brulyant/Sellier European Law Publishers/FEC, 2005) 3.

[96] As the Court of Napoli stated on 24 March 1999.

[97] See, for instance, A. Loiodice, 'Il Giudice e l'uso delle sentenze straniere', in Guido Alpa (ed), *Modalità e tecniche della comparazione giuridica* (Milan, 2006) 79.

[98] *Soc. Doctor Glass Group v Soc. Nexia* Trib. Monza, 14 May 2001, in Corriere giuridico, 2001.

unlawful acts committed through the managed websites. For instance, the Court of Monza mentioned the *Cour d'Appel* of Paris of 10 February 1999[99] that decided for the provider's responsibility in a case of disclosure of photographs which were considered harmful with regard to the right to protection of one's image.

Notwithstanding the above-mentioned domestic and foreign case law approach, the Court of Monza—after a careful study of external decisions—decided differently. The Italian court built its arguments specifically upon a large number of US decisions on the same topic that affirmed the principle according to which the provider is not responsible for the unlawful acts committed on the internet. Specifically, the Court of Monza referred to a case, *Cubby v Compuserve*,[100] where the US court qualified the provider as a magazine or review seller and not as an editor, thus excluding the provider's responsibility for an online release—in newsgroups or forums—of defamatory materials.

Moreover, the Court of Monza mentioned the US case *Stratton Oakmont v Prodigy*,[101] which recognized the provider's responsibility. The court, however, specified that this happened just because in that case the provider had spontaneously activated an automatic filtering system. Therefore, the court stated that the provider could no longer be considered as a technical operator, but almost as a newspaper headline director, with all the relevant duties and responsibilities. Furthermore, the Court of Monza stressed that European case law excluded a *per se* provider's responsibility, hence only because of its position.[102] In this regard, the Italian court remarked that a provider is considered responsible for the unlawful acts committed on the internet only if he could have directly known or somehow recognized them, according to the ordinary duty of care. Moreover, the Court of Monza mentioned a 1996[103] decision of the District Court of the Hague that excluded the provider's responsibility in case of copyright violations carried out by a newsgroup.

Furthermore, other Italian decisions referred to foreign case law in order to better identify the rule governing the case at stake, or the applicability limits of certain domestic legal institutes originated by external influences.

Consider, for instance, a recent case of legal separation of spouses. A claim pursuant to Article 709-*ter* of the Italian Civil Procedure Code[104] was filed before the Court of Varese.[105] The Italian court was asked—by the filing party—to provide a judgment that followed a certain Italian case law approach according to which the said provision is considered in terms of punitive damages.[106] The Court of Varese rejected the claim in the part not supported by a precise cause-effect relation between the behaviour and the

99 Cour d'Appel de Paris of [10 février 1999], in La semaine juridique, édition générale, [1999], II.

100 *Cubby v Compuserve* [1990] 90 Civ. 6571 [1991], United States District for the Southern District of New York.

101 *Stratton Oakmont v Prodigy* [1994] 31063 Supreme Court of New York [1995].

102 The so-called '*responsabilità oggettiva*'.

103 District Court of Aja, 12 March 1996, n. 96/160.

104 Article 709-*ter* of the Italian Civil Procedure Code concerns disputes between parents arising out the exercise of parental authority and/or children's custody.

105 Trib. Varese, 7 May 2010, in Redazione Giuffrè, 2010.

106 See Trib. Messina, 5 April 2007, in Dir. famiglia, 2007, 1795; Trib. Messina, 25 September 2007, in Giur. locale-Messina,2008. Trib. Palermo, 2 November 2007, in Redazione Giuffrè 2008.

actual prejudice suffered. This, *inter alia,* was on account of the fact that the legal concept of punitive damages, as developed in legal systems such as that of the US, is normally linked to the person that, with one single action, damages several people, going along with specific compensation limits. Reference was made to a decision of the Federal Court for the District of New Jersey of 1989[107] and to one of the US Supreme Court of 1991.[108]

Also the Italian Supreme Court showed awareness of the fact that looking at foreign judgments helps to provide the right perspective on the case that has to be decided. For instance, the highest Italian court in one of its decisions[109] referred to foreign case law[110] in order to interpret and evaluate the parties' contractual intent with regard to a certain clause. Precisely, the Supreme Court pointed out that the interpretation of the clause under discussion was straightforward, and that an English court[111] had conclusively stated so in a different case.[112] In this respect, it can be noticed that, through this judgment, a certain principle became part of the domestic legal system under circumstances that required to focus also on transnational elements. However, the Supreme Court's case law, by referring to foreign judgments in other circumstances, could more easily welcome foreign principles within the Italian legal system, that could later lose their external relation and eventually become part of our legal system.

Overall, the Italian decisions referring to foreign case law can be comprehensively considered as cases in which courts looked at non-domestic judgments in the application of typical national provisions of law. In fact, there was no duty, nor specific need, to mention foreign case law. References to foreign decisions were made spontaneously and used as sources of free inspiration.

Unarguably, it is a practice that still occurs in a limited number of Italian decisions.[113] However, if we pay attention to the ongoing progress made by Italian case law in this regard, it can no longer be considered a question of numbers.[114] What's important is that there actually are cases in which Italian courts naturally referred to foreign decisions directly drawing inspiration from them, fostering, in this way, the circulation of the law between different States by means of a simple case law flow.

Moreover, it should not be forgotten that there are cases in which foreign judgments are covertly referred to.[115] Hence the arguments of a certain decision do not expressly disclose the external source of inspiration. Thus, it is the reader that has to recognize the reference made to non-domestic decisions and bring it to the fore,[116] undoubtedly

[107] Federal Court for the District of New Jersey, 9 March 1989, in Foro it., 1990, IV, 78.

[108] Supreme Court of the US, 4 March 1991, in Foro it., 1991, IV, 235.

[109] Italian Supreme Court, *Jp Morgan Chase Bank National Association v Poste it.* [2007] Giust. civ. 2007, 2, I.

[110] *Bankers Trust International plc v RCS Editori s.p.a.* [1996] CLC.

[111] Specifically, the Queen's Bench Division (Commercial Court).

[112] *Bankers Trust International plc v RCS Editori s.p.a.*, n 108.

[113] See Roberto Sacco, *Introduzione al diritto comparato* (UTET, 1992) 136.

[114] See, for instance, Antonio Gambaro, 'Il diritto comparato nelle aule di giustizia ed immediati dintorni', in AA.VV., *L'uso giurisprudenziale della comparazione giuridica* (Quad. riv. trim. dir. e proc. civ., n. 7, Giuffrè, Milano, 2004) 3.

[115] See, *inter alia*, Alessandro Somma, *L'uso giurisprudenziale della comparazione nel diritto interno e comunitario* (Milan, 2006).

[116] See Alessandro Somma, 'Metodi e scopi della comparazione giuridica nelle decisioni delle corti', in Guido Alpa (ed), *Il giudice e l'uso delle sentenze straniere* (Giuffrè, 2008) 6–7.

remaining with a degree of uncertainty in regards to the exact source of inspiration used. In this respect, given that references to foreign decisions could also be indirect or implicit, it could be argued that a court did not draw inspiration from foreign decisions, but simply from domestic scholars that looked to foreign scholars' case law studies.

Considering all that has been discussed, it can hence be pointed out that there are Italian courts that explicitly and spontaneously referred to non-domestic decisions, considering them as reference models or as means of enhancement of their conclusions achieved after autonomous studies of the case at stake.

V. Conclusion

The study of so-called judge-made law is indeed extremely interesting: how it evolves according to different times and geographical areas; that it represents one of the key components of every legal system.[117] It is certainly challenging, but at the same time worthwhile, to investigate whether and how foreign decisions circulate and are adopted by legal systems that are different from the system of origin.

Comparative scholars found that the structure of a legal system[118] that reverts to 'the law of a neighbor' and imitates a foreign legal model, shapes itself accordingly, such an attitude being one of the most significant mechanisms contributing to the development[119] of the law. In particular, every legal system's case law, being an important source of the law itself, can evolve when driven by external influences.[120] Domestic judges, for instance, may recall foreign courts' decisions because national scholars have studied non-domestic decisions.[121] In some other cases, national judges may—even if not always explicitly[122]—directly draw inspiration from foreign decisions.[123]

Before the modern codifications and the following nationalization of the European legal systems, the case law of a neighbour legal order was commonly referred to as a frequent practice both in civil[124] and common law[125] areas. Nowadays, with the ongoing debate on how to identify the concrete ways through which to achieve

[117] See, Marco Torsello, 'Foreign Judge-made Law e sua ricezione nel diritto interno', in Gianmaria Ajani, Antonio Gambaro, Michele Graziadei, Rodolfo Sacco, Vincenzo Vigoriti and Michel Waelbroek (eds.), *Scritti in onore di Aldo Frignani* (Giappichelli, 2011), pp. 479–99.

[118] See, among others Gino Gorla, *Il ricorso alla legge di un 'luogo vicino' nell'ambito del diritto comune europeo* (in Foro it. 1977, V) 91; Basil Markesinis and Jörg Fedtke, *Giudici e diritto straniero. La pratica del diritto comparato* (Bologna, 2009).

[119] See Alan Watson, *Legal Transplants. An Approach to Comparative Law* (Edinburgh, 1974); Michele Graziadei, 'Comparative Law as the Study of Transplants and Receptions', in Reiman and Zimmermann (eds.), *The Oxford Handbook of Comparative Law* (Oxford, 2006) 441.

[120] See, for instance, Marino Bin, *Il precedente giudiziario* (Padova, 1995).

[121] See, for example, Vincenzo Zeno Zencovich, *Come fumo negli occhi: sempre più limiti alla pubblicità del tabacco* (in Foro it., 1995) 3458; the decision Corte App. Roma [7/3/05] n. 1015; Rodolfo Sacco, *Introduzione al diritto comparato* (Torino, 2005) 137; Antonio Gambaro and Rodolfo Sacco, *Sistemi giuridici comparati* (3rd edn., Torino, 2008) 33.

[122] See, among others, Alessandro Somma, *L'uso giurisprudenziale della comparazione nel diritto interno e comunitario*, ibid.

[123] See Erik Jayne, *Precedente e Rechtsfortbildung nel sistema tedesco dell'illecito civile. L'influenza del diritto comparato* (in Foro it., 1988, V) 366.

[124] See Chapter 6, Guido Alpa, 'Foreign Law in International Legal Practice'.

[125] See especially the studies carried out by Gino Gorla, *Diritto comparato e diritto comune europeo* (Milano, 1981).

harmonization of European[126] and transnational[127] private law, the capability of judge-made law to circulate between the different Member States merits a renewed and careful study.[128]

It is within this picture, and for the above-mentioned reasons, that this chapter aimed to highlight how and to what extent Italian courts referred to foreign case law,[129] with particular emphasis on the function recognized by Italian courts to non-domestic decisions and consequently on their capability to affect the national legal system, always bearing in mind the greater goal of fostering the Europeanization and globalization of the law.[130]

[126] See, *inter alia*, from a comparative perspective, Mauro Bussani, *Diritto privato Europeo* (in Enc. dir., Annali, II, 2, Milan, 2008) 417; Luigi Moccia, *Comparazione giuridica e diritto europeo* (Milan, 2005).

[127] For instance, Aldo Frignani and Marco Torsello, *Il contratto internazionale. Diritto comparato e prassi commerciale* (2nd edn., Padova, 2010), 53.

[128] See, for example, the *XXX Tavola rotonda di diritto comunitario* held at the University of Genova on 25–26 September 2009 on '*L'applicazione della legge straniera da parte delle autorità giudiziarie e non giudiziarie in Europa*'.

[129] See, for instance, Antonio Gambaro, *Il diritto comparato nelle aule di giustizia ed immediate dintorni* (in AA. VV., L'uso giurisprudenziale della comparazione giuridica) 3.

[130] See Francesco Galgano, *La globalizzazione nello specchio del diritto* (Bologna, 2005).

27

The Controversial Status of International and Comparative Law in the United States

*Martha Minow**

I. Introduction

In recent years, I have watched the swirling debate over whether the United States courts should consult international or comparative law. As a law professor, the debate has puzzled me: international and comparative legal materials have always appeared in the sources consulted by American lawyers and judges. So this article is really a search for the roots of the contemporary controversy. Why is there a controversy? And what can we learn from it?

I will suggest three conjectures to explain the fact of the contemporary debate over the proper role of international law within the United States:

(1) a basic concern emphasizes that we risk being taken over, or losing what we are by engaging with others;

(2) a second worry stresses that the United States is exceptional and thus faces politically motivated attacks as the last superpower;

(3) a third, very specific, trepidation arises from the unusual nature of 'customary international law'.

My hope is that, by locating the sources of the controversy over the place of international law within the United States, we can dismiss artificial issues and focus on genuine and significant developments—broader changes that offer a window onto the prospects for more effective human governance. The debate diverts attention from developments that might be instructive to us, not just in what US courts do, but, more importantly, in how we design legislation and legal institutions and how we understand our place in the world.

First, we need to see the puzzle: what is the contemporary debate and how does it relate to judicial practice in the United States?

II. The contemporary debate and the puzzle

Here is the puzzle: no one disagrees that United States judges have long consulted and referred to materials from other countries as well as international sources; yet for the

* Martha Minow is the Morgan and Helen Chu Dean and Professor of Law at Harvard Law School.

past nine or so years, citing foreign and international sources has provoked intense controversy.

The evidence of the longstanding practice is undisputed and well-forecast by one of the Federalist Papers, which asserted, 'attention to the judgment of other nations is important to every government' as a matter of foreign policy and also as a check on 'strong passion or momentary interest' within the nation.[1] The US Constitution itself accords to Congress the authority to 'define and punish Piracies and Felonies committed on the high Seas, and Offences against the Law of Nations'.[2] Citations to foreign law appear in Supreme Court opinions from 1823 (dealing with Native Americans),[3] 1832 (defining the status of Indian tribes),[4] 1877 (concerning personal jurisdiction),[5] and 1879 (rejecting polygamy).[6] In 1900, the Supreme Court ruled that 'international law is part of our law'.[7] Justices on the Supreme Court have consulted and referred to the laws of other nations in addressing slavery,[8] mandatory vaccinations,[9] regulation of wheat markets,[10] emergency governmental powers,[11] the meaning of cruel and unusual punishment,[12] rights upon arrest,[13] abortion,[14] sodomy,[15] and end-of-life treatment.[16] Judge Frank Easterbrook reviewed the use of foreign sources by US courts and concluded that the practice 'has been stable for a long time; any suggestion that the practice has skyrocketed recently is unfounded'.[17]

Others have noted that consideration by US judges of decisions or practices from other countries and international bodies is fundamentally no different than references to law review articles, materials from state courts, or Shakespeare, in that each is 'filtered through the analytical machinery of a US court' and treated not as binding but merely as potentially instructive.[18]

[1] The Federalist No. 63 (James Madison). See also 4 William Blackstone, Commentaries *67 (stating that the common law adopts the law of nations).

[2] US Const art I, § 8.

[3] *Johnson v M'Intosh*, 21 US (8 Wheat.) 543, 574–85, 592–6 (1823).

[4] *Worcester v Georgia*, 31 US 515, 551–2 (1832).

[5] *Pennoyer v Neff*, 95 US 714, 729–30 (1877).

[6] *Reynolds v United States*, 98 US 145, 164–5 (1879).

[7] *The Paquete Habana*, 175 US 677, 700 (1900). See also *Murray v Schooner Charming Betsy*, 6 US 64, 80 (1804) (Chief Justice Marshall agreed with the complainant that 'an act of Congress ought never to be construed to violate the law of nations if any other possible construction remains').

[8] *Dred Scott v Sanford*, 60 US 393, 407–8, 451 (1857).

[9] *Jacobson v Massachusetts*, 197 US 11, 31–2 (1905).

[10] *Wickard v Filburn*, 317 US 111, 125–6 (1942).

[11] *Youngstown Sheet & Tube Co. v Sawyer*, 343 US 579, 651–2 (1952) (Jackson, J., concurring).

[12] *Trop v Dulles*, 356 US 86, 103 (1958).

[13] *Miranda v Arizona*, 384 US 436, 486–7 (1966).

[14] *Roe v Wade*, 410 US 113, 136–8 (1973).

[15] *Lawrence v Texas*, 539 US 558, 573 (2003).

[16] *Washington v Glucksberg*, 521 US 702, 718 n.16 (1997). See generally Steven G. Calabresi and Stephanie Dotson Zimdahl, 'The Supreme Court and Foreign Sources of Law: Two Hundred Years of Practice and the Juvenile Death Penalty Decision' (2005), 47 WM. & MARY L. REV. 743.

[17] Frank H. Easterbrook, 'Foreign Sources and the American Constitution' (2006), 30 Harv. J.L & Pub. Pol'y 223, 223.

[18] Chimène I. Keitner, 'International and Foreign Law Sources: Siren Song for US Judges?' (2009), 3 Advance: J ACS Issue Groups 215; See also Easterbrook, 'Foreign Sources' (n 17) (cautioning against citation of any sources to support judicially-announced changes in the Constitution or national law).

Whether identified as foreign law, international law, or comparative law, what if any role should legal materials originating from outside domestic US practice play inside the legal system of this country? It is worth noting at the outset that the discussion tends to merge these categories—international and comparative law—although all that they share is 'not US in origin'. Let me flag for later emphasis: where international law does have endorsement by the United States, then it too is US law. Although this point gets obscured, let us acknowledge that the debate sweeps in consultation of constitutions, statutes, and judicial decisions from other countries, as well as international treaties we have not signed, international treaties we have signed, and other sources of international law.

Current members of the US Supreme Court advance the most visible edge of the contemporary debate over this issue. When Justices of the United States Supreme Court give public speeches, they seldom replay fights internal to the Court on the results of particular cases, but more commonly explore disagreements about methods of interpretation and the roles of judges and the judiciary.

During his Senate confirmation hearing, Chief Justice John Roberts objected to reference to international law by US courts because international law 'doesn't limit [judges'] discretion the way relying on domestic precedent does', and consulting how other countries treat particular legal questions pending in the United States is like 'looking out over a crowd and picking out your friends'.[19] During his own confirmation hearing, Justice Samuel Alito emphasized that 'The Framers [of the United States Constitution] did not want Americans to have the rights of people in France or the rights of people in Russia, or any of the other countries on the continent of Europe at the time. They wanted them to have the rights of Americans, and . . . I don't think it's appropriate to look to foreign law.'[20]

Justice Thomas wrote concurring in a denial of certiorari: 'While Congress, as a legislature, may wish to consider the actions of other nations on any issue it likes, this Court's Eighth Amendment jurisprudence should not impose foreign moods, fads, or fashions on Americans.'[21] In a 2004 opinion, Justice Antonin Scalia chided fellow Justices for implying that the 'law of nations', which he described as 'redefined to mean the consensus of states on any subject', could ever bind citizens in our territory because, he wrote, this idea is 'a 20th-century invention of internationalist law professors and human rights advocates'[22] and is inconsistent with both the understanding of our Constitution's framers and democracy. Scalia viewed international human rights law to be 'a fantasy'.[23] In another recent opinion, Justice Scalia objected to the citation of the laws of other

[19] 'Confirmation Hearing on the Nomination of John G. Roberts, Jr. to be Chief Justice of the United States: Hearing Before the S Comm on the Judiciary', 109th Cong. 201 (2005) (statement of Judge John G. Roberts, Jr.).

[20] 'Confirmation Hearing on the Nomination of Samuel A. Alito to be an Associate Justice of the Supreme Court of the United States: Hearing Before the S Comm on the Judiciary', 109th Cong. 471 (2006) (statement of Judge Samuel A. Alito).

[21] *Foster v Florida*, 537 US 990, 123 S Ct 470, (2002) 990 n. 1 (Thomas, J., concurring in the denial of certiorari).

[22] *Sosa v Alvarez-Machain*, 542 US 692, 749–50 (2004) (Scalia, J., concurring in part and concurring in the judgment).

[23] Harlan Grant Cohen, 'Supremacy and Diplomacy: The International Law of the US Supreme Court' (2006), 24 Berkeley J Int'l L 273, 310.

nations as irrelevant and inconsistent, and also noted that '"[a]cknowledgment" of foreign approval has no place in the legal opinion of this Court unless it is part of the basis for the Court's judgment—which is surely what it parades as today.'[24]

Some members of Congress decided to join the fray and even suggested censure or impeachment of a judge who cites non-US sources.[25] Members of Congress have repeatedly introduced resolutions such as this one: 'judicial interpretations regarding the meaning of the Constitution of the United States should not be based in whole or in part on judgments, laws, or pronouncements of foreign institutions unless such foreign judgments, laws, or pronouncements inform an understanding of the original meaning of the Constitution of the United States.'[26] Senator John Cornyn introduced this resolution into the Senate by warning that a trend of citing foreign decisions, if real, would mean that 'the American people may be losing control over the meaning of our laws and of our Constitution. If this trend continues, foreign governments may even begin to dictate what our laws and our Constitution mean, and what our policies in America should be.'[27] During the Senate confirmation hearings for Justice Elena Kagan, Senator Jon Kyl said he was troubled by the suggestion 'you can turn to foreign law to get good ideas.'[28] Former Attorney General Alberto Gonzales objected that foreign legal sources should not be used in US courts because their authors 'are not accountable to the American people.'[29] In sum, critics charge that references to non-US sources by American judges can be selective, faddish, and cover for the judges' own unaccountable views, or a departure from American democracy and authority.

When it comes to keeping Congress out of their business, perhaps all the Justices could agree. Hence, Justice Scalia in a speech in 2006 declared: 'As much as I think that it is improper to use foreign law to determine the meaning of the Constitution, I don't think it's any of [Congress's] business.'[30]

But on the place of foreign and international law within US law, Justices Breyer, Ginsburg, and Kennedy have diverged from the views already described. Justice Breyer does not only refer to foreign and international legal sources,[31] he also emphatically defends this practice, noting:

> [W]hen I do read things, I can read what I want. If I see something written by a man or a woman who has a job like mine in another country, and who is interpreting a document somewhat like mine and who in fact has a problem in front of the court

[24] *Roper v Simmons*, 543 US 551, 628 (2005) (Scalia, J., dissenting).

[25] See Judicial Conduct Act of 2007, H.R. 2898, 110th Cong. (2007); Dana Milbank, 'And the Verdict on Justice Kennedy Is: Guilty', *Washington Post* (9 April 2005) A3.

[26] H.R. Res. 372, 110th Cong. (2007); S. Res. 92, 109th Cong. (2005).

[27] 151 Cong. Rec. S3109 (daily ed. 20 March 2005) (statement of Sen. John Cornyn).

[28] *Confirmation Hearing on the Nomination of Elena Kagan to be an Associate Justice of the Supreme Court of the United States: Hearing Before the S. Comm. on the Judiciary*, 111th Cong. (30 June 2010).

[29] Alberto Gonzales, US Att'y Gen., Remarks at George Mason University (18 Oct. 2005) (transcript *available at* <http://www.justice.gov/archive/ag/speeches/2005/ag_speech_051018.html>).

[30] 'Scalia Criticizes Use of Foreign Law in Interpreting US Constitution', *Fox News* (18 May 2006) *available at* <http://www.foxnews.com/story/2006/05/18/scalia-criticizes-use-foreign-law-in-interpreting-us-constitution/>.

[31] See, e.g., *Knight v Florida*, 528 US 990, 120 S Ct 459, 462–463 (1999) (Breyer, J., dissenting) (mem.) (citing decisions from Jamaica, India, Zimbabwe, and the European Court of Human Rights).

> somewhat like mine, why can't I read it, see what they've done? I might learn something.[32]

Justice Breyer has asserted that international law importantly reflects a globalization of human rights and 'near-universal desire for judicial institutions that, through guarantees of fair treatment, help to provide the security necessary for investment and, in turn, economic prosperity.'[33] Foreign governmental responses, in this view, may 'cast an empirical light on the consequences of different solutions to a common legal problem.'[34] Justice Breyer has also commented: 'I know it's not binding', when the authority comes from outside the United States, and, in his words, 'so what's the problem?'[35]

Justice Ruth Bader Ginsburg similarly has commented that:

> Judges in the United States are free to consult all manner of commentary—Restatements, Treatises, what law professors or even law students write copiously in law reviews . . . why not the analysis of a question similar to one we confront contained in an opinion of the Supreme Court of Canada, the Constitutional Court of South Africa, the German Constitutional Court, or the European Court of Human Rights?[36]

More controversially, she has stated: 'We are losers if we neglect what others can tell us about endeavors to eradicate bias against women, minorities, and other disadvantaged groups.'[37] Indeed, she stresses that lack of engagement with foreign decisions has reduced the influence of the Supreme Court.[38] Following the Senate confirmation hearings for Justice Kagan, Justice Ginsburg speech stressed: 'The US judicial system will be the poorer, I have urged, if we do not both share our experience with, and learn from, legal systems with values and a commitment to democracy similar to our own.'[39] Citing reference to foreign opinion or law by the authors of the Declaration of Independence, the authors of the Federalist Papers, and by Supreme Court opinions, Justice Ginburg predicted that the US Supreme Court will continue to accord 'a "decent Respect to the Opinions of [Human]kind" as a matter of comity and in a spirit of humility.'[40]

[32] Jesse J. Holland, 'Justice Breyer Says Debate Over Foreign Law is Irrelevant', *Associated Press* (2 April 2010), *available at* <http://www.law.com/jsp/scm/PrintFriendly.jsp?id=1202447364424>.

[33] Associate Justice Stephen Breyer, 'Keynote Address: The Supreme Court And The New International Law' (2003), 97 Am. Soc'y Int'l L. Proc. 265, 267.

[34] Ibid.

[35] Holland, 'Justice Breyer says debate over foreign law is irrelevant' (n 32).

[36] Ruth Bader Ginsburg, Associate Justice, Supreme Court of the United States, Speech at the Constitutional Court of South Africa, '"A Decent Respect to the Opinions of [Human]kind": The Value of a Comparative Perspective in Constitutional Adjudication' (7 February 2006) <http://www.supremecourt.gov/publicinfo/speeches/viewspeeches.aspx?Filename=sp_02-07b-06.html>.

[37] Breyer, 'The Supreme Court And The New International Law' (n 33) (quoting Ginsburg, J.).

[38] Adam Liptak, 'Ginsburg Shares Views on Influence of Foreign Law on Her Court, and Vice Versa' *N.Y. Times* (12 April 2009) A14.

[39] Ruth Bader Ginsburg, Associate Justice, Supreme Court of the United States, Speech at the International Academy of Comparative Law, American University: '"A Decent Respect to the Opinions of [Human]kind": The Value of a Comparative Perspective in Constitutional Adjudication' (30 July 2010) <http://www.supremecourt.gov/publicinfo/speeches/viewspeeches.aspx?Filename=sp_08-02-10.html>. Noting how the framers set the 'high importance' of observing the 'laws of nations,' Justice Ginsburg reiterated Elena Kagan's position that foreign opinions 'set no binding precedent for the US judge. But they can add to the store of knowledge relevant to the solution of trying questions'.

[40] Bader Ginsburg, 'A Decent Respect to the Opinions of Human kind' (n 39).

Justice Anthony Kennedy previously objected to the idea that judgments from foreign constitutional courts could contribute to the development of American constitutional law, but in recent years he has cited foreign sources in key opinions. In *Lawrence v Texas*, invalidating Texas' sodomy statute, Justice Kennedy pointed to the decriminalization of sodomy by the British Parliament in 1967, the European Convention on Human Rights, and a 1981 European Court of Human Rights decision.[41] In *Roper v Simmons*, explaining the Court's rejection of the death penalty applied to a crime committed by a minor, Justice Kennedy's analysis of the Eighth Amendment Cruel and Unusual Punishment Clause included consideration of 'the world community' as providing 'respected and significant confirmation for our own conclusions.'[42] Justice Kennedy added: 'It does not lessen fidelity to the Constitution . . . to acknowledge that the express affirmation of certain fundamental rights by other nations and peoples underscores the centrality of those same rights within our own heritage of freedom.'[43]

Justice Sonia Sotomayor has also supported 'broader consideration of foreign and international law in US judicial opinions',[44] and in 2009 in a speech stated, 'to the extent that we have freedom of ideas, international law and foreign law will be very important in the discussion of how to think about the unsettled issues in our legal system',[45] though she has also maintained that such sources have 'very limited formal force' and she joins Justices Scalia and Thomas in warning of selection bias in the use of international legal sources.[46] While on the Court, Chief Justice Rehnquist and Justice Sandra Day O'Connor at times supported judicial consultation of decisions of other constitutional courts outside the United States.[47]

Yet since 2003, a serious political—as well as theoretical—fight over judicial reference by US judges to non-US sources has broken out in the opinions of Supreme Court Justices, on the lecture circuit, in law reviews, and in Congress. Intensity of feeling

[41] *Lawrence v Texas*, 539 US 558 123 S ct 2472 (2003) 572–3.

[42] *Roper v Simmons*, 543 US 551 125 S Ct 1183 (2005) 578.

[43] *Roper v Simmons* (n 42).

[44] Collin Levy, Op-Ed, 'Sotomayor and International Law', Wall St. Journal (14 July 2009) A13.

[45] Steven Groves, 'Questions for Justice Sotomayor on the Use of Foreign and International Law', *The Heritage Foundation* (6 July 2009) <http://www.heritage.org/Research/Reports/2009/07/Questions-for-Judge-Sotomayor-on-the-Use-of-Foreign-and-International-Law> at note 12 and accompanying text (quoting speech by Sotomayor, J. to the ACLU in Puerto Rico).

[46] Ibid.

[47] See William Rehnquist, 'Constitutional Courts—Comparative Remarks' in Paul Kirchhof and Donald P. Kommers (eds.), *14 Germany And Its Basic Law: Past, Present And Future—Turererman—American Symposium* (Nomos 1993) 411, 412 ('now that constitutional law is solidly grounded in so many countries, it is time that the United States courts begin looking to the decisions of other constitutional courts to aid in their own deliberative processes'); Sandra Day O'Connor, *The Majesty Of The Law: Reflections Of A Supreme Court Justice* (Random House 2003) 234. ('As the American model of judicial review of legislation spreads further around the globe, I think that we Supreme Court Justices will find ourselves looking more frequently to the decisions of other constitutional courts, especially other common-law courts that have struggled with the same basic constitutional questions that we have: equal protection, due process, the Rule of Law in constitutional democracies . . . All of these courts have something to teach us about the civilizing function of constitutional law'). On the bench, however, in interpreting the Eighth Amendment, Chief Justice Rehnquist wrote, 'if it is evidence of a *national* consensus for which we are looking, then the viewpoints of other countries simply are not relevant.' *Atkins v Virginia*, 536 US 304, 325 (Rehnquist, C.J., dissenting).

around these debates should not be underestimated. Justice Ginsburg reported a death threat that was posted on a website in 2005 against both her and Justice O'Connor in reference to their discussions of international law in the context of judicial decision-making.[48] Justice Ginsburg cautioned that the congressional debates seemed to 'fuel the irrational fringe.'[49]

III. Why the big fight?

1. Fear of being taken over and losing control

Senator Cornyn offered a cogent explanation of the first source of the fight over turning to foreign law: a basic concern about identity and autonomy—that we risk being taken over and losing what we are by engaging with others. This concern squarely hits the use of comparative law, the law of Germany, Canada, South Africa, Israel, or other countries, rather than consultation of international law, though that, too, could raise similar worries. There is an obvious intersection between this set of concerns and debates over judicial interpretation and constitutional construction. Justice Scalia, for example, is explicit in his advocacy of 'originalism', directing judges to construe the United States Constitution to discern the meaning of its drafters. Justice Scalia connects this method to his resistance to foreign sources in noting, 'the men who founded our republic did not aspire to emulate Europeans, much less the rest of the world... and nothing has changed.'[50] Justice Breyer emphasizes, in contrast, that the Declaration of Independence itself points to a 'decent respect to the opinions of mankind',[51] and Justice Breyer has articulated a philosophy of judicial interpretation that pursues the underlying values of fostering democracy and the well-being of citizens.[52]

For Senator Cornyn and others, US judges risk losing tight adherence to strictly US text and values if they consult the laws or decisions of other nations to construe terms within the US Constitution. Attacks against consideration of foreign sources can reflect not only concerns about confining judges to the views held by the Constitution's framers but also disagreements over the results in cases like *Lawrence v Texas*—striking down a statute criminalizing sodomy—and *Roper v Simmons*—rejecting the death penalty applied to a crime committed by a minor. An author posting on the National Review website comments that this consultation of foreign and international law to assist interpretation of the US Constitution could allow a judge to 'reach the result he wants to reach' with no restrictions, and with the effect of 'depriving American citizens of their powers of representative government by selectively imposing on them favored

[48] See Bill Mears, 'Justice Ginsburg Details Death Threat', *CNN* (15 March 2006) <http://www.cnn.com/2006/LAW/03/15/scotus.threat>.

[49] Ibid.

[50] Antonin Scalia, Associate Justice, Supreme Court of the United States, Remarks at the American Enterprise Institute on the Role that International and Foreign Law Should Play in American Judicial Decision-Making (21 February 2006) (transcript available from CQ Transcriptions).

[51] Tom Curry, 'A Flap over Foreign Matter at the Supreme Court', *MSNBC* (11 March 2004) <http://www.msnbc.msn.com/id/4506232>.

[52] Stephen Breyer, *Active Liberty* (Alfred A. Knopf 2005).

policies of Europe's leftist elites.'[53] As no one argues that foreign sources are in any way binding on the United States, the objection merely to consulting them is thus often simply part of the critique of the outcomes.

Yet there is another worry about the consultation of foreign sources that seems to operate at a psychological or sociological level of concern. The sheer act of looking at decisions or opinions from non-US sources is the apparent problem—so why? There seems to be a fear of temptation or loss of control. If merely looking at what others are doing causes the worry, the concern seems to be about caving to peer pressure or being an outlier—some kind of contagion effect. Justice Breyer must sense this objection for he responds, 'comparative use of foreign constitutional decisions will not lead us blindly to follow the foreign court', and 'of course, we are interpreting our own Constitution . . . and there may be relevant political and structural differences between their systems and our own.'[54]

This recognition of differences offers a response to the fear that our judges will be contaminated, unable to resist, or taken over if they consult constitutional materials from other countries. The assumption that looking at what others do leads to following them neglects the genuine possibility that looking at others will lead to greater conviction about remaining different or to increased clarity about the reasons for going a different way. As Professor Vicki Jackson emphasizes, the process of engagement with comparative materials is as likely to help American judges clarify what is not consistent with the text and traditions of the United States as it is to be instructive in interpreting American commitments.[55] For example, in viewing the treatment of hate speech in Canada and Germany, where courts have upheld and applied restrictions, analysis of the American constitutional tradition rejects the path pursued elsewhere as disconnected from our text and commitments, as well as reflective of different contexts and concerns.[56] Looking at what others do may sharpen our sense of our differences rather than produce a sense of pressure to conform.

This reminds me of the critical lesson my mother taught my sisters and me. As my sister Nell explained recently:

> One of the greatest gifts my mother ever gave me was when I was in kindergarten and I told her that everyone else was allowed to go to a friend's house after school without getting permission first except me. She said, 'Now is a good time for you to learn that

[53] Ed Whelan, 'Obama Supreme Court Candidate Harold Koh—Part 1' (24 Sept. 2008), *Bench Memos, National Review Online*, <http://www.nationalreview.com/bench-memos/50710/obama-supreme-court-candidate-harold-koh-mdash-part-1/ed-whelan> (criticizing judicial transnationalism as interpreted in Harold H. Koh, 'Why Transnational Law Matters' (2006), 24 PENN. ST. INT'L L. REV. 745, 749–50).

[54] Breyer, n 33.

[55] Vicki C. Jackson, *Constitutional Engagement In A Transnational Era* (Oxford University Press 2009) 115; see also Vicki C. Jackson, 'Constitutional Comparisons: Convergence, Resistance, Engagement' (2005), 119 Harv. L. Rev. 109.

[56] Ronald J. Krotoszynski, Jr, *The First Amendment In Cross-Cultural Perspective* (New York University Press 2006) 51–2, 137–8; Frederick Schauer, 'The Exceptional First Amendment', in Michael Ignatieff (ed), *American Exceptionalism And Human Rights* (Princeton University Press 2005) 29, 32–8. See also *Doe v Michigan*, 721 F. Supp. 852, 860–67 (E.D. Mich 1989) (discussing the various restrictions on free speech allowed by US Courts under the First Amendment).

> that reason will never work in our family. If there's a reason that something is right for us, I want to hear about it. But what everyone else is doing is never a reason for us to do it.'[57]

My sister reflected:

> What an utterly liberating idea. I never thought about trying to be like everyone else again. Now that backfired a little on my mother when she tried to tell me that everyone else wears shoes at their wedding, but other than that, we've both been very happy with it.[58]

I do not mean to minimize concerns about peer pressure or influence but, instead, to emphasize that confidence in who we are, what our values and traditions are, and how we interpret them over time stems from a source deeper than a refusal to look at what others do.

2. Defense of American exceptionalism

Announcement of American difference, however, is a further reason for the resistance to judicial consideration of foreign or international sources. The view of American uniqueness has roots in ideas from the Puritans, ideals of the Revolution, comments by observers like Alexis de Tocqueville,[59] and visions of leaders like Abraham Lincoln, whose Gettysburg Address locates America as a nation 'conceived in liberty, and dedicated to the proposition that all men are created equal.'[60] After the fall of the Soviet Union, American exceptionalism also became associated with recognition of the nation as the last superpower, and some have argued that as the United States has been expected to play—and is often playing—the leading role in many international affairs, this country should be understood as an 'exception' to the law of nations. Some make this claim affirmatively and others do so critically.[61] In this context, reference to international law in decisions by American judges can be fraught with political charge, especially if it seems to signal adherence to international documents outside the official process of treaty agreement involving the Congress and the President.

[57] Nell Minow, Sermon delivered at Beth El Hebrew Congregation, Alexandra, Virginia 4 (30 April 2010) (transcript on file with the Harvard International Law Journal).

[58] See n 57.

[59] Phillips Bradley (ed), Henry Reeve (tr), Alexis De Tocqueville, *Democracy In America* (Alfred A. Knopf 1987, first published in 1831).

[60] Abraham Lincoln, President of the United States, 'Gettysburg Address' (19 November 1863) in Ray P. Basler (ed), *The Collected Works Of Abraham Lincoln* (Rutger University Press 1953). See also Seymour Martin Lipset, *American Exceptionalism: A Double-Edged Sword* (Norton and Company 1997) 31. ('G. K. Chesterton put it: "America is the only nation in the world that is founded on a creed. That creed is set forth with dogmatic and even theological lucidity in the Declaration of Independence"') (citations omitted).

[61] See, e.g., Discussion among Neal K. Katyal, Michael S. Paulsen, David B. Rivkin, Jr, Nadine Strossen, and Steven G. Calabresi, 'American Exceptionalism, the War on Terror and the Rule of Law in the Islamic World' The Federalist Society (17 November 2007) <http://www.fed-soc.org/multimedia/detail/american-exceptionalism-the-war-on-terror-and-the-rule-of-law-in-the-islamic-world-event-audiovideo>; Michael Ignatieff (ed), *American Exceptionalism And Human Rights* (Princeton University Press 2005).

For some, reference to foreign sources in Justice Kennedy's opinion for the five-Justice majority striking down the death penalty for crimes committed by juveniles in *Roper v Simmons* is especially controversial, because even the majority acknowledged that 'when the Senate ratified the International Covenant on Civil and Political Rights . . . it did so subject to the President's proposed reservation regarding Article 6(5) of that treaty, which prohibits capital punishment for juveniles.'[62] Justice Kennedy's consideration of practices by other nations thus, to some, looked like an end run around that treaty process. It is worth noting, however, that Justice Kennedy's opinion expressly interprets United States law, namely, the 'cruel and unusual punishment' language in the Eighth Amendment of our Constitution, and considers foreign practice only alongside practices within our states and expert opinions within the United States as data to assess, as our Eighth Amendment directs, whether punishment is 'cruel and unusual'.[63] The relevance of the law of other nations is only as provided by United States law that itself directs judges to consider what is or has become 'cruel and unusual'.

The issue of American exceptionalism arises additionally with regard to international legal sources, and the clear rule is that the United States is bound by international law when that law has been duly incorporated into US law, pursuant to our own procedures for doing so. One of the treaties we have not signed establishes the International Criminal Court (ICC) (technically: President Bill Clinton signed the governing Rome Statute, President George Bush 'unsigned' it, and Congress has never ratified it).[64] US critics assail this court—empowered to investigate and prosecute crimes against humanity, war crimes, and genocide—as an infringement of national sovereignty, as operating with vague and unaccountable power, and as subject to politically motivated prosecutions.[65] It does pose the unusual feature that even nations that have not signed onto the court could face prosecutions if the situation involving an alleged international crime within the court's jurisdiction is referred to the ICC prosecutor by the United Nations Security Council under Chapter VII of the Charter of the United Nations.[66] The United States has itself embraced the Charter of the United Nations, so this provision is itself consistent with the law of the United States. That the United States holds a veto at the United Nations Security Council should be some reassurance that checks exist to protect the United States.[67] But with calls for war crimes prosecutions against various officials in the United States for incidents ranging

[62] *Roper v Simmons*, 543 US 551, 567. [63] *Roper v Simmons*, 543 US 551, 276–8.

[64] See 'Braced for the Aftershock' *The Economist* (5 March 2009) 66.

[65] John Bolton, 'Speech Two: Reject and Oppose the International Criminal Court', *in* Alton Frye (ed), *Toward An International Criminal Court?* (Council on Foreign Relations Press 1999) 37, 43–5, 47.

[66] Rome Statute of the International Criminal Court art. 13(b), 12 July 1998, 2187 UNTS. 900 [hereinafter Rome Statute]. A non-state party may also consent to ICC jurisdiction over crimes committed within its territory or over its nationals. Rome Statute, art 12.

[67] In addition, under the 'complementarity' provision, should any case arise from the conduct of a United States national, the case is inadmissible before the ICC if the case 'is being investigated or prosecuted' within the United States or if it 'has been investigated' here and the State 'has decided not to prosecute the person concerned, unless the decision resulted from the unwillingness or inability of the State genuinely to prosecute.' Rome Statute, arts 17(1)(a), 17(1)(b) (n 66).

from the conflicts in Vietnam to the conflict in Iraq, these concerns could contribute to the heat over reference to international sources by the United States judiciary.

The proper resolution of this matter, once more, is to be found in the directives of US law itself. In a series of recent decisions, the US Supreme Court addressed the place of international law as a limit to the conduct of the executive branch and clearly reinforced this ground rule: where the United States has made international law part of our domestic legal system, it is binding and enforceable law inside the country, even against the executive during a time of armed conflict. Hence, in *Hamdan v Rumsfeld*, the Court found fatal defects in the military commissions established during the administration of George W. Bush to hold trials for detainees at Guantanamo Bay because their structures and procedures violated two sources of US law: the Uniform Code of Military Justice and Common Article 3 of the Geneva Conventions, signed in 1949 and codified in US law and ensuring detainees a 'regularly constituted court affording all the judicial guarantees which are recognized as indispensable by civilized peoples.'[68] In his concurring opinion, producing the fifth vote for this view, Justice Kennedy reasoned:

> The terms of this general standard are yet to be elaborated and further defined, but Congress has required compliance with it by referring to the 'law of war' in §821. The Court correctly concludes that the military commission here does not comply with this provision.
>
> Common Article 3's standard of a 'regularly constituted court affording all the judicial guarantees which are recognized as indispensable by civilized peoples,' ... supports, at the least, a uniformity principle....

Absent more concrete statutory guidance, this historical and statutory background—which suggests that some practical need must justify deviations from the court-martial model—informs the understanding of which military courts are 'regularly constituted' under United States law.[69]

Explicit Congressional authority would be necessary before the executive could bypass these otherwise existing US norms. No claim of American exceptionalism can give the President of the United States unilateral authority to suspend the Geneva Conventions;[70] for those who care about the capacity of the United States to operate apart from developments in international law, the internal domestic structures of the

[68] *Hamdan v Rumsfeld*, 548 US 557, 126 S Ct 2749, (2006) 642 (Kennedy, J. concurring) (quoting Geneva Convention (III) Relative to the Treatment of Prisoners of War, Aug. 12, 1949, 6 UST at 3318).

[69] Ibid., at 644.

[70] President Bush had so claimed. See Memorandum from George W. Bush, President of the United States to The Vice President, the Sec'y of State, the Sec'y of Def., the Attorney Gen., Chief of Staff to the President, Dir. Of Cent. Intelligence, Assistant to the President for Nat'l Sec. Affairs & Chairman of the Joint Chiefs of Staff (7 February 2002), reprinted in Mark Danner, *Torture And Truth: America, Abu Ghraib, And The War On Terror* (The New York Review of Books 2004) 105. See also Memorandum from Alberto R. Gonzales, Attorney Gen., to George W. Bush, President of the United States (25 January 2002), reprinted in Mark Danner, n 70, at 83. By their terms, common art. III of the Geneva Conventions cannot be repudiated by a signatory during an ongoing conflict. Geneva Convention [No III] Relative To The Treatment Of Prisoners Of War, (adopted 12 August 1949, entered into force 21 October 1950) 75 UNTS 135. 6 UST 3316.

United States Constitution—notably, congressional action, subject to presidential veto and judicial review—provide the proper avenues.

3. Customary international law

Heated concerns over bypassing domestic legal structures lie behind the specific objection to judicial application of what is known as 'customary international law'. Understanding those concerns can help explain some of the anxieties about judicial application of international law. 'Customary international law' can be defined as 'rules of law derived from the consistent conduct of States acting out of the belief that the law required them to act in that way.'[71] Analogous in some ways to the common law in the Anglo-American tradition, customary international law—which has, according to observers such as the authors of the 1987 Restatement (Third) of Foreign Relations Law of the United States, long included the international crimes of slavery, genocide, and war crimes, as well as the principles of immunity for visiting heads of state and the right to humanitarian intervention—thought by some to be binding, not merely advisory.[72] The Restatement itself, written by American law professors Louis Henkin, Andreas Lowenfeld, Louis Sohn, and Detlev Vagts, was the first effort to assert inclusion of customary international law within the US federal law; the prior edition has indicated that its status was an open question.[73] In a powerful law review article published in 1997, law professors Curtis Bradley and Jack Goldsmith argued against treating customary international law as part of US law, in part by showing the absence of any actual judicial opinion or federal statute clearly making customary international law part of US law.[74]

Two sources of US law make customary international law pertinent. The first is the United Nations Charter—over which the United States played a key role and to which our nation subscribes. The United Nations Charter includes a provision directing the International Court of Justice to apply 'international custom, as evidence of a general practice accepted as law.'[75] Discerned in assessments of general, consistent, and widespread practice, this source of norms has governed relations among diplomats and rules of war. The second instance is the Alien Tort Statute, enacted as a clause of the Judiciary Act of 1789, directing that federal district courts 'shall also have cognizance, concurrent with the courts of the several States, or the circuit courts, as the case may be, of all causes where an alien sues for a tort only in violation of the law of nations

[71] Shabtai Rosenne, *Practice and Methods of International Law* (Oceana Pubns 1984) 55. Shabtai Rosenne is the former Ambassador of Israel to the United Nations and a leading expert on international courts. See also Jean-Marie Henckaerts and Louise Doswald-Beck, *1 Customary International Humanitarian Law* (Cambridge University Press 2005) xxxi–xlii (exploring customary international law which is not written and which is reflected in state practice and conviction in the international community that such practice is required as a matter of law).

[72] Restatement (Third) Of The Foreign Relations Law Of The United States § 404 (1987).

[73] Curtis A. Bradley and Jack L. Goldsmith, 'Customary International Law as Federal Common Law: A Critique of the Modern Position' (1997), 110 Harv. L. Rev. 815, 834–6.

[74] Bradley and Goldsmith, 'Customary International Law as Federal Common Law' pp 849–70 (n 73). Ibid. at 849–70.

[75] The Statute of the International Court of Justice, annex to the UN Charter, art. 38(1)(b).

or a treaty of the United States.'[76] Ignored or neglected for centuries, this provision has recently been deployed as a vehicle for international human rights litigation in US federal courts. In 1980, the Federal Court of Appeals for the Second Circuit found jurisdiction and held that deliberate torture perpetrated under colour of official authority 'violates universally accepted norms of the international law of human rights, regardless of the nationality of the parties'—and under that holding, the court ruled that US federal courts could hear cases alleging violations of public international law or treaties brought by non-US citizens even for conduct occurring outside the United States.[77] Ultimately, in this case, a federal court announced civil damages liability against the former police inspector general of Paraguay following the kidnapping and torturing of a 17-year-old son of the plaintiff in reaction to his father's political activities.[78]

With this case and its progeny, as well as assertions by some human rights advocates that customary international law constrains the executive branch of the United States, customary international law has generated controversy. Why should the federal courts address extra-territorial matters? They impose burdens of work; they strain the courts' expertise; and they may unmoor the courts from US law, some may object. These objections may grow in the face of assertions that customary international law is evolving to include economic and social rights, to prohibit the death penalty, and to regulate discrimination on the basis of sexual orientation.[79] Professors Bradley and Goldsmith note that customary international law is now articulated, not only by actual practices of states, but by treaties, resolutions, and views of academics.[80] They also note how customary international law is growing rapidly and addressing topics—such as labour organizing, primary education, and hate speech—historically treated only by domestic law.[81] Other examples, claimed to be customary international law, include the protection of refugees from being sent back to places where their lives or liberties are in jeopardy, immunities for visiting foreign heads of state, a right of humanitarian intervention, and prohibitions of slavery, genocide, and crimes against humanity, although no one claims that these were consistent practices among civilized nations at the time of the founding of the United States. Very fair questions arise, thus, over what counts as consistent practice, who decides, and why practices never explicitly endorsed or embraced within the United States come to trump rules adopted pursuant to the legislative, judicial, and executive practices of US states and the nation.[82]

Among the powerful critiques developed by Professors Bradley and Goldsmith is one telling argument that portrays dramatic shifts in prevailing understandings of law itself within the United States. They note how, for a time, customary international law was viewed by judges, scholars, and lawyers in this country as part of 'general common law', inherited from England or simply the 'law of the land' with no attention to its

[76] Judiciary Act of 1789, ch. 20, § 9, 1 Stat. 73, 77 (current version at 28 USC § 1350) ('The district courts shall have original jurisdiction of any civil action by an alien for a tort only, committed in violation of the law of nations or a treaty of the United States.').

[77] *Filartiga v Pena-Irala*, 630 F.2d 876, 878 (2d Cir. 1980).

[78] Ibid.

[79] See Bradley and Goldsmith, 'Customary International Law as Federal Common Law' (n 73) 818.

[80] Ibid., at 839.

[81] Ibid., at 840–2.

[82] Ibid., at 838, 857–9, 870–6.

source in particular judicial or legislative authority.[83] This fits a dominant pattern before 1938, when even federal courts could claim to be simply finding the general common law of torts or contracts even if that meant contradicting what a state law said. Oliver Wendell Holmes, Jr, with disparagement, called this conception of general common law that of 'a transcendental body of law outside of any particular State'[84] and he instead argued that the common law evolves and reflects the interests and times of those articulating it.[85] So rather than one universal body of law, the common law reflected rules and decisions created by particular decision-makers. In its 1938 decision in *Erie Railroad Co. v Tompkins*, the Supreme Court embraced this view and rejected assertions by federal courts of a power to announce general common law; 'law in the sense in which courts speak of it today does not exist without some definite authority behind it' and hence '[e]xcept in matters governed by the Federal Constitution or by Acts of Congress, the law to be applied in any case is the law of the State.'[86] Scholars gradually recognized that this knocked the legs out from under federal court articulations of customary international law as well, and that is the argument that Bradley and Goldsmith emphasized.[87] Hence, a federal court cannot apply customary international law 'in the absence of some domestic authorization to do so.'[88]

The US Supreme Court actually had a chance to weigh in on this question—and the status of customary international law in federal courts—in a case in which a Mexican citizen brought a claim under the Alien Tort Statute asserting false arrest by US Drug Enforcement Agency and a Mexican national hired to help the US government. A district court and the Court of Appeals for the Ninth Circuit ruled that the Alien Tort Statute created a private cause of action for the Mexican citizen to claim a violation of international law due to the arbitrary arrest and detention against Jose Francisco Sosa, the Mexican citizen hired to help the US agency. Defendant Sosa argued that US courts have no authority to announce or apply customary international law; the plaintiff argued that not only do the federal courts have that power, but that it extended to the instance of false arrest he claimed. The Supreme Court struck a middle course. Using a close study of evidence about how the framers of the Constitution approached international law, the Supreme Court unanimously ruled that the international common law claims authorized for enforcement in the federal courts do not include the claim in this case, and federal courts should not recognize as claims violations of international law norms 'with less definite content and acceptance among civilized nations than the 18th-century paradigms familiar' when the Alien Tort Statute was enacted in 1789—such as those against piracy, prohibiting offences

[83] Ibid., at 822–3.

[84] *Black & White Taxicab Transfer Co. v Brown & Yellow Taxicab & Transfer Co.*, 276 US 518, 533 (1928) (Holmes, Jr, J. dissenting).

[85] Oliver Wendell Holmes, Jr, *The Common Law* (1881), *available at* <http://pds.lib.harvard.edu/pds/view/10253629>.

[86] *Erie R.R. Co. v Tompkins*, 304 US 64, 78–9 (1938).

[87] Bradley and Goldsmith, 'Customary International Law as Federal Common Law' (n 73) 827–8, 846–7, 852.

[88] Ibid., at 853.

against ambassadors, and ensuring safe conduct into or out of a country, whether during war, truce, or peacetime.[89]

Justice Scalia concurred in the result in the case and concurred in the assessment of the historical understanding. But, in a separate opinion, Justice Scalia asserted that recent developments—including the post-*Erie* treatment of common law—preclude the federal courts from recognizing any further developments in international common law. He objected that 'the law of nations, redefined to mean the consensus of states on any subject' is merely 'a 20th-century invention of internationalist law professors and human rights advocates' inconsistent with the intent of the Constitution's framers and the democratic project.'[90] Nonetheless, even Justice Scalia did not dispute that Congress in 1789 authorized federal courts to enforce a small number of international norms even without further specific authorization by Congress.[91] A six-Justice majority kept the door open to new statements of federal common law by federal courts, given two centuries of acknowledgment of international law by the United States and the supplemental authority given by Congress to permit judicial consideration of torture victim cases.[92] But even this group of Justices emphasized, as I already mentioned, that 'federal courts should not recognize private claims under federal common law for violations of any international law norm with less definite content and acceptance among civilized nations than the historical paradigms familiar' when the Judiciary Act of 1789 was enacted.[93] And in addition, cautioned the Court, practical consequences of making a claim available to litigants should be considered.[94]

Because the subject of customary international law remains one where federal courts might exercise some limited and restrained discretion, the topic could generate anxieties about federal court consideration of international law. The historical shifts in prevailing understandings of the nature of law's development and authority—and the increasing recognition that judges do not merely discover preexisting law, they help create it—may increase concerns over the sources judges can consult. The Supreme Court has tethered consultation of customary international law to traditions and understandings in this country in 1789. This seems a sound precaution given growing evidence that first actors in announcing developments in customary international law may themselves retreat or alter their positions over time.[95] Where there are disagreements across nations about the content of customary

[89] *Sosa v Alvarez-Machain*, 542 US 692, 124 S Ct 2739 (2004) 732. The Court noted that the United States announced their reception of the 'law of nations' at the time of the Declaration of Independence, and that included, as summarized ultimately by Blackstone, violation of safe conducts, infringement of the rights of ambassadors, and piracy. Ibid., at 713–14. One historical inquiry suggests that the framers had in mind only safe conducts, not piracy or ambassadorial infringements. Thomas H. Lee, 'The Safe-Conduct Theory of the Alien Tort Statute' (2006), 106 COLUM L REV 830.

[90] *Sosa v Alvarez-Machain* (n 89) 749–50 (Scalia, J., concurring in part and concurring in the judgment).

[91] *Sosa v Alvarez-Machain* (n 89) 728–30 (discussing Scalia, J. concurring opinion and referring back to sections I and II, endorsed by Justice Scalia).

[92] Ibid., at 724–5. [93] Ibid., at 732. [94] Ibid., at 732–3.

[95] See, e.g., Máximo Langer, 'The Diplomacy of Universal Jurisdiction: The Regulating Role of the Political Branches in the Transnational Prosecution of International Crimes' (2010), Harvard Law School Faculty Workshop, Working Paper, 47–52 (discussing developments in universal jurisdiction) (on file with Harvard International Law Journal).

international law, it seems almost definitional that the topic in question does not yield a norm of such general practice and acceptance as to rise to the level of customary international law.

In exploring the sources of concern over judicial consultation of foreign and international law, I have suggested worries about customary international law, risks to America given politically motivated uses of law, and fears of being taken over or losing control. To be frank, those who raise these concerns are likely to be more worried about what others will do than about themselves. But I hope that the recent history I have recounted gives assurance that the Supreme Court has affirmed rigorous adherence to American law and traditions when the Justices turn to foreign or international law and has emphasized restraint even then.

IV. Reclaiming the chance to learn

Those who object to references to foreign or international law even when US law directs attention to these sources run risks of inciting anxieties and fears, as the death threats to Justices Ginsburg and O'Connor indicate. There are other costs that spread beyond judges and courts.

Neglecting developments in international and comparative law could vitiate the vitality, nimbleness, and effectiveness of American law or simply leave us without the best tools and insights as we design and run institutions, pass legislation, and work to govern ourselves.

Consider two examples of extra-domestic—and extra-judicial—learning that would be helpful; the absence of which would be a loss. First, regulators, citizens, and indeed anyone interested in governance could learn about emerging forms of what is called 'soft law' in the context of the European Union. Unlike government-issued rules that carry sanctions, enforceable by courts or agencies, soft law includes voluntary standards that depend on consensual action, and which are embraced by private actors and also informal institutions.[96] Soft law can proceed through private and voluntary codes, certification and labelling systems, or transparency obligations placed on government where the disclosure of information deters misconduct and empowers observers to monitor government action.[97] And, as summarized by John Kirton and Michael Trebilcock, soft law offers the advantages of 'timely action when governments are stalemated; bottom-up initiatives that bring additional legitimacy, expertise, and other resources for making and enforcing new norms and standards; and an effective means for direct civil society participation in global governance.'[98] In trade, labour relations, environmental protection, and other fields, these techniques can elicit changes in behaviour, attract cooperation, and also at times work as a precursor to, or substitute

[96] See John J. Kirton and Michael J. Trebilcock, 'Introduction: Hard Choices and Soft Law in Sustainable Global Governance' (2004), in John J. Kirton and Michael J. Trebilcock (eds.), *Hard Choices, Soft Law: Voluntary Standards in Global Trade, Environment and Social Governance* (Ashgate 2004) 3, 9; Mary Ellen O'Connell, *The Power And Purpose Of International Law: Insights from the Theory and Practice of Enforcement* (Oxford University Press 2008) 12.

[97] Ibid., at 10. [98] Ibid., at 5.

for, 'hard law' with sanctions. These kinds of devices pervade international law and also identify tools that are often useful within a country, state, or town.[99]

Of course, we use some of these devices already, both domestically and in our international ties. But learning about developments elsewhere could offer new tools and refinements even while helping us clarify how law works. It is easy to emphasize that foreign and international legal materials—analogous to soft law—represent no binding force within the United States, except where American law itself endorses, incorporates, or calls for consultation of international or foreign law. Non-binding authorities, including law reviews, scholarly treatises, and judgments of sister circuit courts are often and widely consulted. Especially in issues of first impression or evolving legal norms, consultation of non-binding sources can be instructive and clarifying, though never binding.

A second topic offering potentially useful learning to lawyers, judges, and citizens in the United States is the International Criminal Court. It is the institutional design that offers instruction here. Any worries about prosecutions of United States citizens are not only unwarranted, but they also risk obscuring fascinating features of that experiment that might offer intriguing ideas for domestic work here. Chief among them is the idea of complementarity, built into the Court: the Court defers to actions within nations and in fact loses the ability to proceed with a case if the case 'is being investigated or prosecuted' within a country having jurisdiction over it or even if it 'has been investigated' here and the State 'has decided not to prosecute the person concerned, unless the decision resulted from the unwillingness or inability of the State genuinely to prosecute.'[100] This device has several consequences. It puts power in the hands of individual nations to avoid ICC action—if only the individual nation takes up the investigation of the matter otherwise headed to the ICC. It thereby creates a device for limiting the ICC's business and power. It also creates an incentive for increasing capacity and political will in individual nations for enforcing the norms against genocide and crimes against humanity. It preserves decentralization and national sovereignty in ways that might offer models on some matters for the relationships between the national and state governments within the United States, between Indian Tribes and the United States, between government and non-governmental entities, or in other instances where multiple agents may have an interest in a given matter. A dean might try this with students, or a parent might even try this with a child—I'll check into your conduct unless you do so and do so credibly.

The complementarity device of the ICC is simply one example of international legal materials offering potential instruction to people in the United States—not because it is our law but because it offers an approach to issues of institutional design that we often face. Moreover, we as Americans, who contributed so much to modern international

[99] See Gerda Falkner, et al., *Complying with Europe: EU Harmonisation and Soft Law in the Member States* (Cambridge University Press 2005) 179–80; Dinah Shelton, 'Soft Law', in David Armstrong (ed.), *Routledge Handbook of International Law* (Routledge 2009) 68; David M. Trubek, Patrick Cottrell, and Mark Nance, '"Soft Law", "Hard Law" and "EU Integration"', in Gráinne De Búrca and Joanne Scott (eds.), *Law and New Governance in the EU and US* (Hart Publishing 2006) 65, 69.

[100] Rome Statute, art 17(1)(a), 17(1)(b).

law, remain involved in it. Even Americans who report scepticism about the efficiency of the UN respond very positively to the recommendations of the UN.[101]

One last thought: we might actually learn something from an instance about which I think there is considerable pride in this country. Our Supreme Court's landmark decision, *Brown v Board of Education*, is a legal moment about which our nation is justifiably proud. However partial and limited is the fulfilment of its ultimate vision of racial integration, *Brown*'s rejection of 'separate but equal' schools spurred the end of segregation in retail stores, theatres, swimming pools, and employment, though often only after a struggle and legislative or litigated reforms.[102] The steps from Jim Crow segregation to the election of President Barack Obama were many and non-linear, but *Brown* played a role in mobilizing changes in ideas as well as in practices and opportunities. *Brown*'s influence inside schools but outside of the context of race has profoundly altered the discussions and treatment of gender, disability, language, ethnicity, and national origin, with further changes in the way educational and life opportunities of students are affected by their sexual orientation, religion, economic class, or status as Native Hawai'ians or Native Americans.[103] Well beyond schooling, *Brown* and the efforts surrounding it have created the model for social and legal reforms in the United States on behalf of girls and women, persons with disabilities, members of religious minorities, and advocates for economic justice, environmental protection, and other issues.[104]

As I researched my book on *Brown*'s influence,[105] I was struck by how much our landmark case and the struggle behind it have served as an evocative reference point for advocates pursuing equal opportunity and social change around the world. Advocates in Northern Ireland, South Africa, India, and Eastern Europe have pointed to *Brown* in their own efforts to use law to overcome social division within educational systems and even in initiatives addressing social hierarchy and exclusion without connection to race or education. Although this international perspective echoes *Brown*'s mixed legacy in actually realizing equal opportunity in practice, looking across the world, it is undeniable that Chief Justice Warren's opinion for a unanimous Supreme Court has become a powerful resource for change agents everywhere.

Brown v Board of Education has played a prominent role in efforts both to combat this segregated education system and to transition away from the apartheid regime

[101] Katerina Linos, 'How International Norms Shape Voter Choices' (2010), 103 Am. Soc'y Int'l L Proc. 10, 11.

[102] See, e.g., Jeff Wiltse, *Contested Waters: A Social History Of Swimming Pools In America* (The University of North Carolina Press 2007); Richard C. Cortner, *Civil Rights And Public Accommodations: The Heart Of Atlanta Motel And Mcclung Cases* (University Press of Kansas 2001). See generally Gary Gerstle, *American Crucible: Race And Nation In The Twentieth Century* (Princeton University Press 2001); Michael J. Klarman, *Unfinished Business: Racial Equality In American History* (Oxford University Press 2007) 160–203; Richard Wormser, *The Rise and Fall of Jim Crow* (St. Martin's Press 2003).

[103] See Martha Minow, *In Brown's Wake: Legacies Of America's Constitutional Landmark* (Oxford University Press 2010) 33–83, 96–108.

[104] See, e.g., Beverly Wright, 'The Deep South Center for Environmental Justice: Education and Empowerment for an Engaged Citizenry' (2004), 8 Diversity Digest 11, <http://www.diversityweb.org/Digest/vol8no2/wright.cfm>; David S. Meyer and Steven A. Boutcher, 'Signals and Spillover: Brown v. Board of Education and other Social Movements' (2007), 5 Persp on Pol 81.

[105] Minow, *In Brown's Wake* (n 103).

more generally. In 1958, Britain's Prime Minister Harold Macmillian cited *Brown* while critiquing apartheid in an address to South Africa's Parliament.[106] During the 1980s, two lawyers who worked closely with Thurgood Marshall on *Brown v Board of Education* assisted lawyers in South Africa to develop judicial strategies to terminate apartheid.[107] After the fall of apartheid and the creation of a new constitutional regime, the South African Constitutional Court has repeatedly cited *Brown v Board of Education* in cases. For the case of *In re The School Education Bill of 1995*, the Court relied on *Brown* in discussing the important role of education in developing and maintaining a democratic society, but reflected the history of South Africa and the global human rights movement in rejecting the claim that the government had a constitutional duty to establish or fund Afrikaans schools while recognizing the right of private groups to maintain such schools.[108] One author argues that the tensions over school desegregation and affirmative action in the United States influenced drafters of the South African Constitution in their decision to shield remedial uses of racial categories from constitutional challenge.[109]

And last October, the South African Constitutional Court worked to accommodate language rights while tackling ongoing exclusion of black South Africans from educational opportunities. An Afrikaans-language school had extra spaces and black South Africans wanted access, but the school asserted a right to instruct only in Afrikaans. The Constitutional Court acknowledged the constitutional right to be taught in an official language of one's choice but directed the school's own governing body to reassess its language policy and provide sufficient spaces for English learners for the coming school year.[110] Affirming equality as respect for the language of one's own choice, in this case, involved protecting a minority language of the historically privileged group;[111] the Court then expressly pointed to the Constitutional design to

[106] See Anthony Lester, 'Brown v. Board of Education Overseas' (2004), 148 Proc. Am. Phil. Soc'y 455, 459.

[107] See Richard J. Goldstone and Brian Ray, 'The International Legacy of Brown v. Board of Education' (2004), 35 MCGEORGE L REV 105, 114 (discussing efforts by Constance Baker Motley and Jack Greenberg).

[108] *In re Dispute Concerning the Constitutionality of Certain Provisions of the School Education Bill of 1995*, 1996 (3) SA 165 (CC) at ¶¶ 47–52 (S. Afr.); see also Penelope Andrews, 'Perspectives on Brown: The South African Experience' (2005), 49 NYL Sch. L Rev. 1155, 1165–7; Rassie Malherbe, 'A Fresh Start I: Education Rights in South Africa' (2000), 4 Eur J for Educ. & Pol'y 49, 50–1. Courts in other countries have also referenced *Brown* for the general proposition that education is pivotal in a democratic society. See, e.g., *R v Jones* [1986] 2 SCR 284, ¶ 22 (Can.); see also Goldstone and Ray, 'The International Legacy of Brown v. Board of Education' (n 107) 117–18 (discussing case in Trinidad and Tobago).

[109] Andrews, 'Perspectives on Brown' (n 108) 1158–65; See generally Mark S. Kende, *Constitutional Rights In Two Worlds: South Africa And The United States* (Cambridge University Press 2009).

[110] *Head of Dep't: Mpumalanga Dep't of Educ v Ermelo*, (CCT 40/09) (2009) ZACC 32 (14 October 2009) (Saflii), *available at* <http://www.saflii.org/za/cases/ZACC/2009/32.pdf> (unpublished).

[111] The case thus offers a striking contrast to *Lau v Nichols*, 414 US 563, 94 S Ct 786 (1974), in which a minority immigrant group of Chinese-speaking students successfully argued that instruction solely in English failed to provide equal educational opportunity. See Minow, *In Brown's Wake* (n 103) 37–40. The historic power and resources held in the Afrikaaner community complicate protection for its autonomy; but for that, the case has some similarities with issues confronted by indigenous groups at risk of forced assimilation unless they can maintain their own culture. See Minow, *In Brown's Wake* (n 103) 96–108.

transform public education and South African society by addressing unequal access to educational resources.[112]

In Eastern Europe, the European Roma Rights Centre in Budapest joined with others, including Czech attorney David Strupek, in 2000 to challenge student placement practices in the Czech Republic, where a disproportionately large number of Roma children were being placed in schools for students with mental or learning disabilities rather than mainstream schools.[113] Lawyers and others working on behalf of the Roma students explicitly discussed *Brown* and the movement surrounding it.[114] They initiated a case known as *D.H.* as the centrepiece of the Roma rights movement's litigation strategy,[115] which was designed to pursue cases that could change existing practices 'through liberal and far-reaching judicial interpretation, as well as to trigger comprehensive reform of legislation.'[116] *D.H.*—like the cases combined into *Brown*—focused on systematic discrimination and mindsets perpetuating second-class status for an entire group of people. Lawyers from the United States, Great Britain, and many European nations contributed to the advocacy strategy and commentary about it.[117]

And the European Court of Human Rights ruled in favour of the Roma applicants by a vote of 13 to 4.[118] Finding that the special schools offered an often inferior curriculum, as well as diminished educational and employment prospects,[119] and finding that the placement in special schools likely increased stigma for Roma children, the Grand Chamber quoted, with approval, the European Commissioner for Human Rights, who said that 'segregated education denies both the Roma and non-Roma children the chance to know each other and to learn to live as equal citizens.'[120] The Grand Chamber cited research from the United States about racial inequity in special education,[121] noting the

[112] *Head of Dep't: Mpumalanga Dep't of Educ. v Ermelo*, (CCT 40/09) (2009) ZACC 32 at 45–7.

[113] European Roma Rights Centre, Strasbourg Application by Roma Challenges Racial Segregation in Czech Schools (29 April 2000), *available at* <http://www.errc.org/cikk.php?cikk=219>.

[114] William New, '*D.H. & Others v C.Z.*: A Narrative Analysis of Romani Education Policymaking', Remarks at the Annual Meeting of The Law and Society Association (6 July 2006) (transcript on file with the Harvard International Law Journal).

[115] Morag Goodwin, 'Developments, *D.H. and Others v. Czech Republic*: A Major Set-back for the Development of Non-discrimination Norms in Europe' (2006), 7 German LJ 421.

[116] European Roma Rights Centre Legal Activities, <http://www.errc.org/> (last visited 17 March 2015), cited in Jennifer Devroye, 'The Case of D.H. and Others v. the Czech Republic' (2009), 7 N.W. U. J. Int'l Hum. Rts. 81.

[117] See Bob Hepple, 'The European Legacy of Brown v. Board of Education' (2006), U. Ill. L. Rev. 605. Sir Bob Hepple, a distinguished English law professor, was born in South Africa and is a frequent lecturer there.

[118] Grand Chamber Judgment, Case of *D.H. & Others v Czech Republic*, App. No. 57325/00, 47 Eur. H.R. Rep. 3 (2008), *available at* <http://www.echr.coe.int/echr/en/hudoc/> [hereinafter D.H. Grand Chamber Judgment]. The decision is notable in clarifying that, at least in the context of education, the European Convention on Human Rights applies not only to cases of individual discrimination but also to systemic discrimination; that a prima facie case of discrimination can be shown through evidence of disproportionately negative effects on one racial group in the application of an apparently neutral rule; that statistical evidence can show such a prima facie case, and upon the showing of a prima facie case, the burden of proof shifts to the responding party to try to demonstrate that the rule or practice was objectively and reasonably justified. Ibid.

[119] Hepple, 'The European Legacy of Brown' (n 117) 207.

[120] Ibid., at 50 (quoting the commissioner for human rights).

[121] Ibid., at 44 (citing Daniel J. Losen and Gary Orfield, 'Introduction', in Daniel J. Losen and Gary Orfield (eds.), *Racial Inequity In Special Education* (Harvard Educational Pub Group 2002) xv).

negative effects of early tracking.[122] It located its judgment in the context of sources from the Council of Europe,[123] including European Community law and practice concerning indirect discrimination and disparate impact of tests on minority populations;[124] United Nations materials;[125] and a set of 'other sources', including the US Supreme Court's interpretation of the 1964 Civil Rights Act, allowing evidence of the disparate racial impact of a test as evidence of racial discrimination.[126] The European Court ultimately ruled that demonstration of invidious intention was not necessary to show a pattern of separation and disadvantage for children from one background and, in this dimension, struck out on a path quite different from the constitutional interpretation of the US Supreme Court, which demands proof of intentional discrimination to establish a violation of the US Constitution.

One more echo of *Brown* can be heard in Northern Ireland which has long been divided between 'controlled' schools—which are government run, have Protestant roots, and serve about 50 per cent of the students—and 'managed' schools, which are maintained by Catholic organizations and educate about 45 per cent of the children. Historically, these separate school systems have taught contrasting versions of regional history and as a result have not reduced but have contributed to the tensions and violence of 'the Troubles', which began in the 1960s and have continued even after the Belfast agreement of 1998. In the 1980s, a group of parents started the Northern Ireland Council for Integrated Education as a voluntary organization to develop schools that would bring together students from the two communities. With government aid, the Council allows parents to launch new, integrated schools; the Council also developed a procedure by which parents could vote to convert an existing school into an integrated school.[127] These schools give general instruction in Christianity rather than strict instruction in Protestantism or Catholicism.[128] The Department of Education incorporates such schools only after they show sufficient enrolment and a waiting list for pre-school.[129]

By 2009, the Council had produced, with aid from English charitable trusts, 19 integrated nursery schools, 41 integrated primary schools, and 20 integrated second-level colleges—showing impressive growth, but reaching barely 5 per cent of the population.[130] Across the country, integrated schools have generated considerable parental demand, with long waiting lists. Perhaps by having a strategy of integrating schools only with supportive parents and starting such schools on a small scale, the

[122] Ibid., at 52–3.

[123] Ibid., at 54–80 (citing recommendations adopted by the Committee of Ministers of Council of Europe, the Parliamentary Assembly of the Council of Europe, the Framework Convention for the Protection of National Minorities, and the Commissioner for Human Rights).

[124] Ibid., at 81–91. [125] Ibid., at 92–102.

[126] Ibid., at 107 (citing *Griggs v Duke Power Co.*, 401 US 424 (1971)).

[127] Roy Gardner, Jo Cairns and Dennis Lawton (eds.), *Faith Schools: Consensus Or Conflict?* (2005) 159.

[128] See Northern Ireland Council for Integrated Education, 'What Is Integrated Education?' <http://www.nicie.org/about-us/integrated-education/what-is-integrated-education/> (last visited 6 Aug. 2010).

[129] Colin Knox and Pádraic Quirk, *Peace Building In Northern Ireland, Israel And South Africa: Transition, Transformation And Reconciliation* (Palgrave Macmillan 2000) 63–4.

[130] Northern Ireland Council for Integrated Education (n 128).

project ensured, from the start, a base of support rather than conflict—even before the larger community conflict quieted down.

After a decade of relative peace following a process producing political power-sharing, Northern Ireland experienced a spike in intergroup violence in March 2009. The murder of a Northern Irish police officer in Ulster occurred two days after the murders of two British soldiers, and a resurgence of acts of terror committed by dissident groups wracked the region.[131] Johann Hari, a British journalist, suggested 'Northern Ireland needs its own version of *Brown v. Board of Education*.'[132] Citing a six-year study by researchers at Queen's University, Hari noted that individuals who attended the integrated schools were 'significantly more likely' to oppose sectarianism, had more friends across the divide, and identified as 'Northern Irish' rather than as 'British' or 'Irish'.[133] Stressing that '[i]t's difficult to caricature people you've known since you were a child: great sweeping hatreds are dissolved by the grey complexity of individual human beings', Hari marvelled that '82 percent reported that they personally support the idea of integrated schooling, and 55 percent of parents say the only reason their kids don't go to an integrated school is because' they cannot get into one.[134] Taking one more page from US history, this British journalist concluded: 'Who knows—a hefty push for school integration could yield, in a few decades, a Northern Irish Obama, carrying both sides in his veins.'[135]

There might even be lessons to take back to the United States about the potential influence of a parent-based movement for integration. But *Brown* itself, as it turns out, even before the US Supreme Court, reflected important influence from comparative and international concerns. The Swedish scholar Gunnar Myrdal's *American Dilemma*, with its searing indictment of America's treatment of the 'Negro', became a key citation in the Court's famous footnote 11.[136] Initially, President Eisenhower showed no sympathy for the school integration project and expressed suspicion that the United Nations and international economic and social rights activists were betraying socialist or even communist leanings in supporting the brief.[137] But as the United States tried to position itself as a leader in human rights and supporter of the United Nations, the

[131] 'New Wave of Violence Grips Northern Ireland' *Voanews* (10 March 2009), <http://www1.voanews.com/english/news/a-13-2009-03-10-voa30-68813047.html>; Henry McDonald and Owen Bowcott, 'Ulster Violence Escalates as Policeman Is Shot Dead' *Guardian* (10 March 2009) 1.

[132] Johann Hari, 'Northern Ireland Needs Its Own Version of "Brown vs. The Board of Education"—and Fast' *Huffington Post* (14 March 2009), <http://www.huffingtonpost.com/johann-hari/northern-ireland-needs-it_b_174939.html>. Hari is a Scottish-born journalist, based in London, with the *Independent*; in 2008 he became the youngest person ever to be awarded the George Orwell Prize for political journalism.

[133] 'New Wave of Violence Grips Northern Ireland' *Voanews* (n 131). The piece explains that among those who attended integrated schools, 'politics were far more amenable to peace: Some 80 percent of Protestants favour the union with Britain, but only 65 percent of those at integrated schools do. Some 51 percent of Catholics who went to a segregated school want unification with Ireland, but only 35 percent of those from integrated schools do. The middle ground—for a devolved Northern Ireland with links to both countries, within the EU—was fatter and happier.' Ibid.

[134] Ibid. [135] Ibid.

[136] *Brown v Board of Education*, 347 US 483, 74 S Ct 686 (1954) 494 n.11; see Gunnar Myrdal, *An American Dilemma* (Harper & Bros 1944); Walter A. Jackson, *Gunnar Myrdal And America's Conscience: Social Engineering And Racial Liberalism* (The University of North Carolina Press 1994) 1938–87.

[137] See Carol Anderson, *Eyes Off The Prize: United Nations and the African American Struggle for Human Rights* (Cambridge University Press 2003) 1944–55. Anderson argues that anticommunism contributed to the narrowing of the civil rights agenda.

Cold War orientation of Eisenhower's Republican administration gave rise to interest in ending official segregation, lynchings, and cross burnings in order to elevate the American image internationally. The Department of Justice collaborated with the State Department on an amicus brief that argued that ending racially segregated schools could terminate the Soviet critique of the tolerance of racial abuses by the US system of government and thereby help combat global communism.[138] Ending segregation emerged as part of a strategy to secure more influence than the Soviet Union over the 'Third World'. African-American civil rights leader and journalist Roger Wilkins later recalled that ending official segregation became urgent as black ambassadors started to visit Washington, DC and the United Nations in New York City.[139]

At our best, we have learned from a global perspective; my small (and I hope not too controversial) thought is that judges and lawyers, citizens and residents of this country can and should continue to learn from global perspectives in order to advance the best version of ourselves.

[138] See Mary L. Dudziak, *Cold War Civil Rights: Race and the Image of American Democracy* (Princeton University Press 2000) 99–102. See also Lester, n 106, at 457–9 (noting Department of Justice brief in pre-*Brown* civil rights cases indicating how the nation's foreign relations were embarrassed by its domestic acts of discrimination).

[139] 'Black/White and Brown: Brown versus the Board of Education of Topeka' *KTWU/Channel 11 broadcast* (3 May 2004) (transcript *available at* <http://brownvboard.org/> (statement of Roger Wilkins).

28

Foreign Law and the Modern *Ius Gentium*

*Jeremy Waldron**

I. Introduction

Is it ever appropriate for American courts to cite or defer to foreign law? The question arose in a bitter dispute among the Justices of the US Supreme Court in *Roper v Simmons*,[1] the juvenile death penalty case.[2] One of the frustrating things about *Roper*, however, is that no one on the Court bothered to articulate a general theory of the citation and authority of foreign law.[3] Writing for the Court, Justice Kennedy said that it was 'proper' to take foreign law into account and that referring to the laws of other countries could be 'instructive' for the Court's interpretation of the Eighth Amendment.[4] But he did not explain the jurisprudence behind this view.[5] Nor did the *Roper* dissenters articulate a theory of citation to foreign law that they could squarely refute; they simply denounced the practice.

The theory that is called for is not necessarily a complete jurisprudence. But it has to be complicated enough to answer a host of questions raised by the practice: about the authority accorded foreign law (persuasive versus conclusive); about the areas in which foreign law should and should not be cited (private law, for example, compared to constitutional law); and about which foreign legal systems should be cited (only democracies, for example, or tyrannies as well). The theory has to be broad enough to explain the use of foreign law in all appropriate cases: too many scholars call for a theory that will explain the citation of foreign law only in constitutional cases.[6] The theory has to be persuasive enough to dispel the serious misgivings that many Americans have about this practice: why should American courts cite anything other than American law? Above all, it has to be a theory of law. The argument cannot just be that good diplomacy requires us to ingratiate ourselves with the Europeans.[7] It must explain

* University Professor at New York University School of Law.

[1] *Roper v Simmons,* 543 US 551, 125 S Ct 1183 (2005).

[2] The relevant controversy in *Roper* concerned the invocation of international as well as foreign law. This Comment will consider only the latter, though much of my argument is applicable to the former as well.

[3] Cf. Roger P. Alford, 'In Search of a Theory for Constitutional Comparativism' (2005) 52 UCLA L. Rev. 639, 639 ('[T]he notion that international and foreign material should be used to interpret the US Constitution... is gaining currency. Yet proponents of this practice rarely offer a firm theoretical justification for the practice.').

[4] *Roper v Simmons,* 543 US 551, 125 S Ct 1198–1200 (2005).

[5] Justice O'Connor was more forthcoming in her dissent, but her analysis focused specifically on the dignitarian aspects of the Eighth Amendment and is of limited use for other cases in which foreign law is introduced. See ibid. at 1215–16 (O'Connor, J., dissenting).

[6] See, e.g., Alford, 'In Search of a Theory for Constitutional Comparativism' (n 3) (focusing exclusively on constitutional law).

[7] See Joan L. Larsen, 'Importing Constitutional Norms from a "Wider Civilization". *Lawrence* and the Rehnquist Court's Use of Foreign and International Law in Domestic Constitutional Interpretation' (2004)

why American courts are legally permitted (or obliged) to cite non-American sources and how that practice connects with the status of courts as legal institutions.

An example may help get at the sort of theory I have in mind. When courts cite their own precedents, they do so on the basis of the theory of *stare decisis*, which provides a platform on which judges can articulate and defend their deference to precedent. It explains why deference is appropriate even for cases in which justice or policy seems to require a different result. It explains why precedent is more important in some cases than in others. And it explains its relation to various sources of law (the difference between *stare decisis* in common law and in constitutional interpretation, for instance). No doubt the details of *stare decisis* are controversial.[8] But even if one disagrees with a judge's conception, it is surely better that he should articulate such a theory than that he simply give the impression that he thinks deferring to precedent is a good idea. We should require nothing less for the citation of foreign law.

In his dissent in *Roper*, Justice Scalia said that the Court's citation of foreign law was unprincipled and opportunistic.[9] Even this observation, however, does not mean that there cannot be a good theory to support the practice. Using my analogy again, Justice Scalia has sometimes argued that the Court's following and departing from precedent in cases involving individual rights is unprincipled and opportunistic.[10] But it does not follow that he rejects *stare decisis* or that he thinks it is not worth developing a theory of precedent. Similarly, we should not reject the idea of a theory of the citation of foreign law simply because we see foreign law being cited opportunistically; we should reject it only if we think inconsistent and unprincipled citation is inevitable under the auspices of such a theory.

Though it appears from his dissent in *Roper* that Justice Scalia's denunciation of the citation of foreign law proceeds without any appreciation that such citation should be based on a theory, dicta from his recent concurrence in *Sosa v Alvarez-Machain*[11] indicate that he does have in mind a theory of the authority of foreign law (albeit one he wishes to refute). Though the *Roper* Court did not engage with this theory, it merits closer consideration.

Sosa concerned a claim under the Alien Tort Statute[12] (ATS). A physician, kidnapped from Mexico by persons working for the US Drug Enforcement Agency, sued

65 Ohio. St. L.J. 1283, 1316–18 (mentioning the foreign policy argument that is sometimes used to justify US courts' reliance on foreign law: citing foreign law will reduce American diplomatic isolation on human rights issues).

[8] There are several rival conceptions of *stare decisis*—the Dworkinian theory of law as integrity, see generally Ronald Dworkin, *Law's Empire* (Belknap Press 1986); the pragmatic theory of predictability and secure expectations, see generally Richard A. Posner, *The Problematics Of Moral And Legal Theory* (igg); and the old idea of the common law 'work[ing] itself pure', *Omychund v Barker* (1744) 1 Atk 21, 33, 26 ER 15, 23 (argument by the future Lord Mansfield) (emphasis omitted); see also Lon L. Fuller, *The Law In Quest Of Itself* (The Foundation Press 1940) 140.

[9] See *Roper* case, 543 US 551, 125 S Ct 1228 & n.9 (2005) (Scalia, J., dissenting) ('To invoke alien law when it agrees with one's own thinking, and ignore it otherwise, is not reasoned decisionmaking, but sophistry... Either America's principles are its own, or they follow the world; one cannot have it both ways.').

[10] See *Lawrence v Texas*, 539 US 558, 123 S Ct 2472, 2488–91 (2003) (Scalia, J., dissenting); *Planned Parenthood of Southeastern Pennsylvania v Casey*, 505 US 833, 982, 992–3 (1992) (Scalia, J., dissenting).

[11] *Sosa v Alvarez*, 542 US 692, 124 S Ct, 2739 (2004).

[12] 28 USC § 1350 (2000).

under the ATS for damages arising from his unlawful arrest.[13] The ATS, first enacted as part of the Judiciary Act of 1789,[14] provides that federal district courts 'shall have original jurisdiction of any civil action by an alien for a tort only, committed in violation of the law of nations',[15] Alvarez-Machain argued that his kidnapping was just such a violation. The Supreme Court rejected his claim for damages, holding that the Court's 1938 decision in *Erie Railroad Co. v Tompkins*[16] seriously curtailed the ability of litigants in American courts to generate new causes of action under 'the law of nations'.[17] The Court in *Sosa* said that the federal courts now have only very limited discretion to recognize new causes of action in this regard, discretion that the Court declined to exercise in the plaintiff's favour.

Justice Scalia, concurring, took a somewhat different approach. He argued that the ATS must be read in the narrow sense that its framers understood it—to refer exclusively to 'the accepted practices of nations in their dealings with one another (treatment of ambassadors, immunity of foreign sovereigns from suit, etc.) and with actors on the high seas hostile to all nations and beyond all their territorial jurisdictions (pirates).'[18] Justice Scalia denied that the federal courts had even limited discretion to recognize new grounds of action under the rubric of the law of nations. Then he added this:

> The notion that a law of nations, redefined to mean the consensus of states on any subject, can be used by a private citizen to control a sovereign's treatment of its own citizens within its own territory is a 20th-century invention of internationalist law professors and human-rights advocates. The Framers would, I am confident, be appalled by the proposition that, for example, the American peoples' democratic adoption of the death penalty could be judicially nullified because of the disapproving views of foreigners.[19]

That last comment looks forward to cases, like *Roper*, that do not involve the ATS, but do involve reference to the sort of global legal consensus underlying the idea of the law of nations. I think Justice Scalia is right in thinking that this is the implicit theory behind the Court's citation of foreign law in cases like *Roper*.

Developing an argument that the citation of foreign law can rest on the idea of the law of nations requires a number of steps. In section II, I define the law of nations and distinguish it from natural law. Section III contrasts the approaches these two theories take toward the solution of modern legal problems. Section IV examines how the law of nations approach might bear on the juvenile death penalty. In section V, I show that American jurisprudence is still capable of recognizing the law of nations for the purposes of a case like *Roper*, despite the inhibiting positivism of *Erie*. In this regard, we need to go beyond the stodgy Latin apparatus of *ius gentium* and start thinking directly about legal problems in a way that makes this account of the citation of foreign law appealing. I set out an account of this kind in section VI. I will end, in section VII,

[13] *Sosa v Alvarez*, 542 US 692, 124 S Ct 2746–47 (2004). [14] Ch. 20, I Stat. 73.
[15] 28 USC § 1350. [16] 304 US 64 (1938).
[17] See *Sosa v Alvarez*, 542 US 692, 124 S Ct 2739–62 (2004).
[18] *Sosa v Alvarez*, 542 US 692, 2775 (2004) (Scalia, J., concurring).
[19] *Sosa v Alvarez*, 542 US 692, 2776 (2004) (emphases omitted) (citations omitted).

with some brief comments on the relation between this theory and the rather casual invocation of foreign law in cases like *Roper*.

II. The law of nations (*ius gentium*)

The law of nations is often used as a synonym for international law. But it once had a broader meaning, comprising something like the common law of mankind, not just on issues between sovereigns but on legal issues generally—on contract, property, crime, and tort. It was a set of principles that had established itself as a sort of consensus among judges, jurists, and lawmakers around the world. This chapter seeks to return the phrase to this broader meaning.

An analogy that I use throughout this chapter is between the law of nations and the established body of scientific findings. Existing science claims neither unanimity among scientists nor infallibility; nevertheless, it stands as a repository of enormous value to individual researchers as they go about their work, and it is unthinkable that any of them would try to proceed without drawing on that repository to supplement their own individual research and to provide a basis for its critique and evaluation. Similarly, the law of nations is available to lawmakers and judges as an established body of legal insight, reminding them that their particular problem has been confronted before and that they, like scientists, should try to think it through in the company of those who have already dealt with it.

Terminology is a particular problem in this area. The law of nations is often referred to using terms like 'general common law', 'federal common law', and 'customary international law'. There is nothing wrong with these labels. But I shall use the Latin phrase '*ius gentium*' to refer to the law of nations in the more comprehensive sense—a body of law purporting to represent what various domestic legal systems share in the way of common answers to common problems. Terms like 'federal common law' I regard as functional terms that are used to indicate particular roles that the law of nations may play in the complex structure of American federalism. One of my arguments is that the fact that an appeal to the law of nations is precluded in some contexts does not necessarily make it unavailable in others. Rejecting the idea of general common law, for example, does not show that *ius gentium* may not figure in a case like *Roper* as a legitimate source of legal inspiration.

In the history of jurisprudence, *ius gentium* represented the coming together of two ancient ideas. One was the idea of natural law, understood (in the words of Cicero) as 'right reason in agreement with nature [,] ... of universal application, unchanging and everlasting.'[20] The other was a more technical jurisprudence that developed in Rome to address the legal interests of foreigners who did not have the benefit of Roman law itself (*ius civile*). As Sir Henry Maine observed, the Romans resorted to the expedient of applying certain rules held to be common to Roman law and the laws of the surrounding non-Roman Italian communities. They called this body of rules 'ius gentium',

[20] Clinton Walker Keyes (tr), Cicero, *The Republic*, bk. III, 33 (Harvard University Press 1928) 211.

which they understood as law common to all nations (or at least all the nations with substantial numbers of immigrants in Rome).[21]

At its inception, the Romans had no particular respect for *ius gentium*. They did not think of it as capturing the essence of law, but merely as an expedient. Only after it became associated with the Greek idea of natural law did it begin to be regarded as 'a great though as yet imperfectly developed model to which all law ought as far as possible to conform.'[22]

Now, natural law also involved the idea of commonality: just as fire burns in Persia as well as in Greece, so murder is wrong in Carthage and in Rome. The difference was that the law of nature posed itself explicitly as an ideal: what did human reason as such say about the basics of human action and relationship, justice and injustice, right and wrong? *Ius gentium*, on the other hand, afforded a more grounded focus of aspiration, looking not just to philosophic reason but to what law had actually achieved in the world.[23] Natural law might have provided the very basic premises of a normative account, but *ius gentium* embodied a set of enduring intermediate principles that one might use as touchstones for real-world legal systems.[24] This difference of emphasis between natural law and *ius gentium* led sometimes to differences in content: slavery, which was always thought to be an affront to the law of nature, was plainly an incident of *ius gentium* in ancient times. And the two bodies of law might differ also in their character: *ius gentium* could change and evolve while the law of nature by definition was immutable. These differences were inevitable once natural law was brought down to earth from the lofty heights of purely philosophical speculation and became, so to speak, a brooding omnipresence on the ground.

In its early association with natural law, *ius gentium* took on a role similar to that of equity in later jurisprudence—a method of cutting through layers of local technicalities and idiosyncrasies to get at the essence of justice. As such, it came to be seen as an additional body of law that could correct and supplement the *ius civile* on its home ground. So the author of the *Institutes of Justinian* was able to say:

> Every community governed by laws and customs uses partly its own law, partly laws common to all mankind. The law which a people makes for its own government belongs exclusively to that state, and is called the civil law [*ius civile*], as being the law of the particular state. But the law which natural reason appoints for all mankind obtains equally among all nations, and is called the law of nations [*ius gentium*], because all nations make use of it.[25]

[21] See Henry Sumner Maine, *Ancient Law* (3d ed, J. Murray, London 1866) 49.

[22] Henry Sumner Maine, *Ancient Law* (3d ed, J. Murray, London 1866) 52.

[23] Many natural law-oriented jurists preferred to focus their normative study on *ius gentium*. See Richard Tuck, *Natural Rights Theories* (Cambridge University Press 1979) 34.

[24] See R.J. Henle (tr), St. Thomas Aquinas, *Summa Theologica* Pt. I–II, Q. 95, Art. 4 (University of Notre Dame Press 1993) 298. ('The Law of Nations is indeed in some way natural to man inasmuch as it is rational, since it is derived from the Natural Law by way of a conclusion, which is not very far from the principles').

[25] Thomas Collett Sanders (tr), *The Institutes of Justinian* 1.2.1 (2d ed, John W. Parker & Son, London 1859) 80. For a more detailed investigation of the historical development of *ius gentium*, see Genc Trnavci, 'The Meaning and Scope of the Law of Nations in the Context of the Alien Tort Claims Act and International Law' (2005) 26 U. Pa. J. Int'l Econ. L. 193, 199–222.

If *ius gentium* concerns relations and transactions in what we would regard as domestic law—in torts, crimes, contracts, and property—how did it become so tightly associated with international law? In its early usage, *ius gentium* often dealt with issues, like the status of ambassadors, that we would regard as international law issues, along with issues concerning merchants, sojourners, and immigrants.[26] But as international law began to develop into an independent body of law, legal positivists began to wonder if *ius gentium* was really a separate body of law or if it had all been subsumed under international law. Jeremy Bentham's scrutiny was the most devastating: he said 'the law of nations' meant nothing more than international law, defined as 'the mutual transactions between sovereigns as such',[27] or it meant the law of private mercantile and maritime transactions, or it meant natural law.[28] Of these possible meanings, Bentham did not consider natural law to be law, and he thought mercantile transactions were already covered by municipal law. That left only international law to give meaning to the phrase.[29]

But the overlap between *ius gentium* and *ius inter gentes*—international law—was never complete. The residual connotations of *ius gentium* allowed it also to capture issues that were not just matters between sovereigns. The distinction between international law and domestic law was much less crisp at the time Bentham was writing (around the time of the founding of the United States) than it was in the middle of the 20th century,[30] and it has become less crisp again with the emergence of human rights law.

Ius gentium is still both an inspiration for domestic law and a guiding ideal for a uniform body of transnational law. A quick survey of modern scholarship reveals that experts believe that *ius gentium* affords a useful framework for thinking about such topics as data protection,[31] antitrust,[32] and copyright.[33] And even in strictly domestic cases something like *ius gentium* serves as a basis for solving otherwise intractable problems. Consider the well-known case of *Riggs v Palmer*,[34] in which a man murdered his grandfather and then claimed an inheritance under his grandfather's validly executed will. The court in *Riggs* declared:

> [All] laws, as well as all contracts, may be controlled in their operation and effect by general, fundamental maxims of the common law. No one shall be permitted to profit by his own fraud, . . . or to acquire property by his own crime. These maxims are

[26] David J. Bederman, 'World Law Transcendent' (2005) 54 Emory L.J. 53, 62–4.

[27] J.H. Burns and H.L.A. Hart (eds.), Jeremy Bentham, *An Introduction To The Principles Of Morals And Legislation* 296 & n.x. (Univ. of London 1970) 789.

[28] See Harold J. Berman, 'World Law' (1995) 18 Fordham Int'l L.J. 1617, 1617.

[29] Ibid.

[30] See Harold Hongju Koh, 'International Law as Part of Our Law' (2004) 98 Am. J. Int'l L. 43, 45. ('[A]t the beginning of the Republic, U.S. courts drew no sharp line between international and foreign law, precisely because of the extensive overlap of these two bodies of law.')

[31] See, e.g., Marsha Cope Huie et al., 'The Right to Privacy in Personal Data: The EU Prods the U.S. and Controversy Continues' (2002) 9 Tulsa J. Comp. & Int'l L. 391, 402–3.

[32] See, e.g., Friedrich K. Juenger, 'The "Extraterritorial" Application of American Antitrust Law and the New Foreign Relations Law Restatement' (1990) 40 Wirtschaft und Wettbewerb 602, 612–3.

[33] See, e.g., Graeme B. Dinwoodie, 'A New Copyright Order: Why National Courts Should Create Global Norms' (1990) 149 U. Pa. L. Rev. 469, 475–6; William Patry, 'Choice of Law and International Copyright' (2000) 48 Am. J. Comp. L. 383, 417–18.

[34] *Riggs v Palmer*, 22 NE 188 (N.Y. 1889).

dictated by public policy, have their foundation in universal law administered in all civilized countries, and have nowhere been superseded by statutes.[35]

In recent years, Ronald Dworkin has made *Riggs* the leitmotif of an entire jurisprudence, arguing that law comprises deep legal principles as well as rules embodied in texts and precedents.[36] But it is worth noting also that the court in *Riggs* referred to these principles in exactly the terms that jurists have used down the ages to refer to the law of nations.

Historians of jurisprudence have spent gallons of ink on the question of whether *ius gentium* was conceived as natural law or positive law.[37] The fact is that at various times and for various purposes it has been both, as well as the product of a sort of reflective equilibrium between the two. It was not enough for *ius gentium* to serve only as a basis for philosophical discussion of natural law or only as a barometer of legal consensus. If consensus was to function normatively, it had to be less than complete (so that it guided someone's choices). But incomplete consensus required choices to be made, and those choices would necessarily be guided by a sense of justice.[38] That sense of justice would not be idiosyncratic but would itself be informed by the extent, depth, and character of the consensus on the question at hand.

This process of back-and-forth, which is well understood in moral philosophy,[39] accounts for the dual nature of *ius gentium*.

How courts have invoked *ius gentium* has depended in part on the purposes, traditions, and categories of the particular court using it. In cases involving law between nations, the law of nations is referred to as 'customary international law'.[40] In private law cases, on the other hand, *ius gentium* is associated with the heritage of the common law,[41] though judges still used the words of Cicero to refer to it as 'not the law of a single country only, but of the commercial world. Non erit alia lex Rome, alia Athenis, alia nunc, alia posthac, sed et apud omnes gentes, et omni tempore, una eademque lex obtenebit.'[42] *Riggs* referred to *ius gentium* both as 'fundamental maxims of the common law' and as 'universal law administered in all civilized countries'.[43] As I have already indicated, these labels and the differences between them should not preoccupy us. 'General common law' and 'customary international law' are not so much separate

[35] *Riggs v Palmer,* 22 NE 188, 190 (N.Y. 1889).

[36] See Ronald Dworkin, *Taking Rights Seriously* (Harvard University Press 1977) 40.

[37] See Trnavci (n 25), at 200–2, for a characterization of the debate on this issue. See also H.F. Jolowicz and Barry Nicholas, *Historical Introduction To The Study Of Roman Law* (3d ed. Cambridge University Press 1972) 104–6; John R. Kroger, 'The Philosophical Foundations of Roman Law: Aristotle, the Stoics, and Roman Theories of Natural Law' (2004) WIS. L. REV. 905, 909–10.

[38] Dworkin would consider this process 'interpretive'. Cf Dworkin Dworkin, *Law's Empire* (Belknap Press 1986) 76–8 (explaining the relation between fit and moral appeal in interpretation).

[39] See generally John Rawls, *A Theory Of Justice* (Oxford University Press 1971) 48–51 (establishing and explaining the concept of reflective equilibrium); Norman Daniels, 'Wide Reflective Equilibrium and Theory Acceptance in Ethics' (1979) 76 J. PHIL. 256 (expanding and elaborating on Rawls's conception).

[40] See, e.g., *The Paquete Habana*, 175 US 677, 707, 20 S Ct 290 (1900); *Filartiga v Pena-Irala*, 630 F 2d 876, 882 ((2d Cir), 1980).

[41] See, e.g., *Swift v Tyson*, 41 US (16 Pet.) 1, 10 L. Ed. 865 (1842); *Luke v Lyde (1759)*, 2 Burr. 882, 887, 97 ER 614, 617.

[42] *Swift v Tyson*, 41 US (16 Pet.) 1, 19.

[43] *Riggs v Palmer*, 22 N.E. 188, 190 (N.Y. 1889).

bodies of law as different ways of referencing one and the same jurisprudential enterprise.

III. Contrast with modern natural law argumentation

Some scholars have argued that the citation of foreign law in modern American cases is best understood as an application of natural law.[44] But the connection between natural law and foreign law is unclear. Modern natural law theory validates the posing of direct moral questions about justice and rights. According to modern natural law theory, judges are often required to make moral judgments as part and parcel of identifying the law applicable to their cases.[45] These judgments are not mere personal preferences. Judges ask questions about justice and rights in a spirit of objectivity; they may get the answers wrong, but they aspire to be right, and they accept that their judgments are answerable to the moral facts. But if this is what natural law adjudication involves, then the citation of foreign law seems mysterious: if the true law is independently discoverable, why would one defer to other people's answers to these moral questions (let alone the answers of Frenchmen or Zimbabweans)? Why not just ask and answer the questions oneself?

There is a cynical response to this point. Perhaps judges are embarrassed to make moral pronouncements in their own voice, even under the cover of the objectivity of natural law. Justice Scalia once remarked:

> It's pretty hard to put together a respectable number of pages setting forth (as a legal opinion is supposed to do) analytical reasons for newly imposed constitutional prescriptions or prohibitions that do not at all rest... upon logic or analysis, but rest instead upon one's moral sentiments, one's view of natural law, one's philosophy, or one's religion.[46]

Reference to official judgments, whether local or foreign, helps rescue judges from a feeling of intellectual nakedness. Just asserting that it is objectively wrong to execute individuals for crimes committed when they were children might be viewed as an expression of subjective sentiment rather than an insight into moral fact. But judges sound more substantial when they talk about 'the overwhelming weight of international opinion against the juvenile death penalty'.[47]

[44] See, e.g., Roger P. Alford, 'In Search of a Theory for Constitutional Comparativism' (2005) 52 UCLA L. Rev. 639, 659–73.

[45] See, e.g. Michael Moore, 'Moral Reality' (1982) Wis. L. Rev. 1061, for a natural law approach of this kind.

[46] Justice Antonin Scalia, Keynote Address Before the Ninety-Eighth Annual Meeting of the American Society of International Law: 'Foreign Legal Authority in the Federal Courts' (2004) 98 Am. Soc'y Int'l L. Proc. 305, 308.

[47] *Roper v Simmons*, 543 US 551, 125 S Ct 1200. One can see how the difficulty arises. Analytic philosophers have rightly insisted that if moral realism is true, then ordinary first-level moral propositions like 'The juvenile death penalty is wrong' are the appropriate vehicle for conveying beliefs about moral reality. One does not need to add any qualifier such as 'objectively' to the word 'wrong'. See, e.g., Ronald Dworkin, 'Objectivity and Truth: You'd Better Believe It' (1996) 25 Phil. & Pub. Aff. 87 (arguing that moral values do exist and cannot be quantified as 'objective'). The trouble is, however, that these are also the formulations one would use to express purely personal attitudes if emotivism were true, i.e., if there were no

However, this may be more of a problem for *modern* natural law theory than for the natural law tradition. Natural law jurisprudence never used to be a matter of individuals just inserting their own moral judgments into legal reasoning, any more than natural science was ever just a matter of idiosyncratic observations about energy or gravity. In both instances, the goal was the accumulation of knowledge, not just the validation of individual intuitions. No one in the modern world would take seriously novel claims about energy or gravity that did not refer to the work of the scientific community at large. It is hard for us, however, to imagine something similar for rights or justice, accustomed as we are to the privileges of the individual conscience. Yet this is exactly what *ius gentium* provided—the accumulated wisdom of the world on rights and justice. The knowledge is accumulated not from the musings of philosophers in their attics but from the decisions of judges and lawmakers grappling with real problems. And it was 'accumulated' not just in the crude sense of one thing adding to another, but in the sense of overlap, duplication, mutual elaboration, and the checking and rechecking of results that is characteristic of true science. *Ius gentium*, conceived in this way, is no guarantor of truth: a consensus in either the law or the natural sciences can be wrong. In neither field, however, is there a sensible alternative to paying attention to the established body of findings to which others have contributed over the years.

IV. *Ius gentium* and the juvenile death penalty

If the law of nations comprised nothing but customary international law, then it would not be easy to invoke it in an essentially domestic case like *Roper*. But it would not be impossible. Modern international law, preoccupied as it is with human rights, has expanded outward from being purely *ius inter gentes* to looking at the way states treat their subjects in their internal dealings. It is not inconceivable that penal practices might come under international law scrutiny in the same sort of way. But this argument does not need to be made. *Ius gentium* has never been entirely displaced by the law of nations in the narrower sense of international law. The aspirational elements of *ius gentium* may serve as a source of guidance as much in areas of crime and punishment as in transnational contexts.

Does this mean that *ius gentium* is omnipresent? Is there no area of law where people are entitled to rely on their own customs, traditions, and democratic instincts? The question, I think, misunderstands the authority of *ius gentium*. In subject areas where municipal legal systems already have their own applicable law, the function of *ius gentium* is not to preempt that law but to guide its elaboration and development. The

such thing as moral facts or natural law. cf. Jeremy Waldron, 'The Irrelevance of Moral Objectivity', in Robert P. George (ed), *Natural Law Theory: Contemporary Essays* (Oxford University Press 1992) 164–71. So speaking this way is an uncomfortable thing to do in a world where your audience is divided—or even mystified—as to whether there is an objective natural law. Half the audience will think that there are no moral facts and that you are just imposing your own values; the other half (who do believe in moral facts) will be divided between those who agree with you and those who think you have the moral facts wrong!

real question is whether seeking guidance from *ius gentium* would be inappropriate for any particular areas of law.

Some have speculated that law is essentially relative to local conditions, varying according to climate, geography, or the temper and virtue of a people.[48] But that does not preclude the application of *ius gentium*. We should still seek guidance from the accumulated legal experience of mankind as to which norms should be sensitive to circumstances, and as to the nature and extent of that variability. Others have suggested that law is essentially relative to the peculiarities of local customs.[49] No doubt there are some areas where the lawmakers of a society will stick to their own customs or preferences no matter what the international community thinks. The United States has taken this sort of stand with regard to the death penalty itself.[50] Even so, there are many contested legal questions about the administration of the death penalty for which *ius gentium*'s guidance is appropriate. The question of whether the Eighth Amendment forbids the juvenile death penalty is a question of this kind. Other societies do not face exactly this question, but they have faced questions about rights, dignity, and death penalty administration that are so close to it that it would be churlish and irrational to ignore the guidance of whatever consensus has been reached among the nations on this point.

Another way of putting the matter is this: we may have simply decided, as a matter of national will, not to rule out the death penalty altogether. But a case can still be made that we should not just *decide* whether it is cruel or unjust to execute adults for crimes committed when they were children. Since it is an open question in our system whether this practice is constitutional, we should look not just for a decision but for a way of figuring out the complex rights and wrongs of the matter, as well as the vexing issues of culpability and responsibility. In addressing this problem, we need all the help we can get. If these issues have been wrestled with in a number of other jurisdictions, then our commitment to the pursuit of justice should lead us to examine the end product of their labours for guidance. So even if the modern death penalty is quintessentially and peculiarly American, the accumulated legal wisdom of mankind, embodied in *ius gentium*, may still have something to offer us.

[48] The locus classicus is Montesquieu, *The Spirit of the Laws*, Anne M. Cohler et al. (eds. & trs.), Montesquieu, *The Spirit of the Laws* (Cambridge University Press 1989) 0748. See ibid., book 14, 231–45 ('On the laws in their relation to the nature of the climate'); ibid., book 18, 285–307 ('On the laws in their relation with the nature of the terrain'); ibid., book 19, at 308–33 ('On the laws in their relation with the principles forming the general spirit, the mores, and the manners of a nation').

[49] See Abraham Hayward (tr), Frederick Charles Von Savigny, *Of the Vocation of our Age for Legislation and Jurisprudence* 27 (Legal Classics Library 1986) 1828 (noting the 'organic connection of law with the being and character of the people', and analogizing a people's law to their language); Sarah K. Harding, 'Comparative Reasoning and Judicial Review' (2003) 28 Yale J. Int'l L. 409, 411 ('Legal systems reflect the cultures within which they are situated and thus have unique and highly contingent identities... Given this close connection between law and local culture, foreign law seems to have very little place in judicial reasoning').

[50] See, e.g., US S. Exec. Doc. No. 102–23, (1992) 11–12 (indicating that despite its ratification of the International Covenant on Civil and Political Rights, '[t]he United States reserves the right, subject to its Constitutional constraints, to impose capital punishment on any person (other than a pregnant woman) duly convicted under existing or future laws permitting the imposition of capital punishment').

V. The challenge of *Erie*

I now want to turn to a different sort of challenge to the theory that I have been considering. In his concurrence in *Sosa*, Justice Scalia referred to the 'avulsive change' in our thinking about the law of nations wrought by the decision of the Supreme Court in *Erie*.[51] So here is the challenge. If we accept what *Erie* said about general common law, can we still treat *ius gentium* as a resource for courts to use in the general way that I have indicated? And, if we accept what the *Sosa* Court said about the radically attenuated meaning to be given now to 'the law of nations', is there any way in which the law of nations can be invoked outside the ATS context to address the issues that arise in a case like *Roper*?

I think the answer in both cases is 'Yes'. It is true that both precedents place severe limits on people's ability to ground particular claims in the law of nations and on their ability to cite it as conclusive authority in particular contexts. But what gets invoked in a diversity case or what gets considered as the substantive ground of a claim under the ATS does not necessarily determine the status of the law of nations or *ius gentium* in other contexts. As we have seen, *ius gentium* makes its appearance in the legal systems of the world at different places and under different labels, and most of the doctrines licensing or restricting its appearance are context-sensitive. Some recent discussions ignore this important point. Professors Curtis Bradley and Jack Goldsmith, for example, say that '[d]omestic law [has] absorbed the private-law elements of the law of nations',[52] implying that everything useful that *ius gentium* did in regard to private law is now done by domestic private law. Even if that is true, it neglects the process by which that absorption has taken place and it begs the question of whether it is still taking place. Anyway, Professors Bradley and Goldsmith entirely ignore the critical and suggestive role that *ius gentium* may still play in the domain of domestic law. If we are evaluating domestic doctrine or wrestling with unresolved doctrinal issues, we may look to *ius gentium* as a source of insight. But if we can do that, then its absorption into domestic law so far as its positive law uses are concerned says nothing about its status as a critical resource.

I think the real difficulty with the position I am outlining is that some of the scepticism about *ius gentium*—particularly the scepticism expressed in *Erie*—is not just functional, but ontological. In this regard, the Court in *Erie* seemed to draw on and endorse[53] the dogmatic theory of Justice Holmes in his dissent in *Black & White Taxicab & Transfer Co. v Brown & Yellow Taxicab & Transfer Co.*[54]

In *Taxicab*, Justice Holmes spoke of the 'subtle fallacy' involved in referring to a body of law as though it could exist apart from the institutional provenance that furnished its authority.[55] There is no such thing as general common law, Justice

[51] *Sosa v Alvarez-Machain*, 542 US 692, 124 S Ct 2739, 2773, 2775 (2004) (Scalia, J., concurring).

[52] Curtis A. Bradley and Jack L. Goldsmith, 'Customary International Law as Federal Common Law: A Critique of the Modern Position' (1997) 110 Harv. L. Rev. 815, 822.

[53] See *Erie R.R. Co. v Tompkins*, 304 US 64, 79, 58 S Ct 817 (1928); *Erie R.R. Co. v Tompkins*, 304 US 64, 79 (938).

[54] *Black & White Cab v Yellow Cab*, 276 US 518 (1928).

[55] *Black & White Cab v Yellow Cab*, 276 US 518, 532–3 (1928) (Holmes, J., dissenting).

Holmes argued; there is just the common law of a particular jurisdiction. Law does not float free in a way that transcends the political sources of its authority:

> If there were such a transcendental body of law outside of any particular State but obligatory within it unless and until changed by statute, the Courts of the United States might be right in using their independent judgment as to what it was. But there is no such body of law. The fallacy and illusion that I think exist consist in supposing that there is this outside thing to be found.[56]

Justice Holmes applied this reasoning to the idea of general common law, which was cited by the 19th-century Court as '[n]on . . . alia lex Romae, alia Athenis, . . . sed . . . apud omnes gentes'.[57] A body of law, said Justice Holmes, cannot just be. Law 'in the sense in which courts speak of it today does not exist without some definite authority behind it', and the definite authority must be that of a particular state.[58] In this sense the endorsement of Justice Holmes's view in *Erie* is said to have lent to legal positivism the authority of the Supreme Court.[59] And if that position is now authoritative, then it seems there is simply nothing for courts to look to under the heading '*ius gentium*'. Like 'the law of Middle Earth', the phrase denotes something imaginary, something that does not exist.

There are, however, a number of reasons for rejecting this line of argument. First, *Erie*'s endorsement of Justice Holmes's theoretical observations is dicta; it was not necessary for the decision in *Erie*, which is better understood as a case about the role of federal courts than as a case about the concept of law.[60] Second, the particular version of positivism embodied in Justice Holmes's dicta—the crude sovereignty-centred positivism of John Austin[61]—is now almost universally rejected among positivists, and the forms of positivism that have replaced it by no means support Justice Holmes's dogmatic rejection of general common law.[62] In any case, positivism's general credentials are suspect today,[63] and among the theories that look to supplant positivism are some that place front and centre principles of the sort that *Riggs* associated with 'universal law administered in all civilized countries'.[64]

Even if by some chance a dictum in *Erie* quoting a dissent in *Taxicab*, drawing on a discredited jurisprudence, were to be regarded as authoritative on what law is, it would still not preclude an appeal to *ius gentium* as something that judges might appropriately consider in solving legal problems. For in this critical natural law role, it is not

[56] *Black & White Cab v Yellow Cab*, 276 US 518, 533 (1928).

[57] *Swift v Tyson*, 41 US (16 Pet.) 1, 19 (1842); see (n 41) 137.

[58] *Black & White Cab v Yellow Cab*, 276 US 518, 533 (1928).

[59] See Louise Weinberg, 'Back to the Future: The New General Common Law' (2004) 35 J. Mar. L. & Com. 523, 539.

[60] See Ernest A. Young, 'Sorting Out the Debate over Customary International Law' (2002) 42 Va. J. Int'l L. 365, 492.

[61] See generally John Austin, *The Province Of Jurisprudence Determined* (John Murray, London 1832).

[62] See H.L.A. Hart, *The Concept of Law* (2d ed. Oxford University Press 1994) 50–78; Jack Goldsmith and Steven Walt, 'Erie and the Irrelevance of Legal Positivism' (1998) 84 VA. L. REV. 673, 694–700.

[63] See, e.g., Ronald Dworkin, 'Thirty Years On' (2002) 115 HARV. L. REV. 1655, 1677–8 (reviewing Jules L. Coleman, *The Practice of Principle: In Defence of a Pragmatist Approach to Legal Theory* (Oxford University Press 2001)).

[64] See Ronald Dworkin, *Taking Rights Seriously* (Harvard University Press 1977) 23–39.

necessary that *ius gentium* be understood positivistically; it need only be seen as a source of normative insight grounded in the positive law of various countries and relevant to the solution of legal problems in this country. In this sense the whole *Erie/Taxicab* apparatus is irrelevant to the sort of role that—on my account—*ius gentium* plays in *Roper*.

VI. Legal problems and legal science

We do not live in an age in which uttering magic words like '*ius gentium*' is sufficient to license the practice of basing American legal conclusions on non-American legal premises. Invoking the law of nations may confer some jurisprudential respectability. But we also need to consider directly what reasons there are for taking this line of thought seriously at the beginning of the 21st century.

I have invoked the image of science and of scientific problem-solving several times to illustrate how a foreign law consensus may be relevant to US legal decision-making. Let me now set out this analogy in full. Consider how we would expect our public health authorities to deal with a new disease or epidemic appearing within our borders. It would be ridiculous to say that because this problem had arisen in the United States, we should look only to American science to solve it. On the contrary, we would want to look abroad to see what scientific conclusions and strategies had emerged, had been tested, and had been mutually validated in the public health practices of other countries. We can think of citation to foreign law in *Roper* in the same way. The relation between the juvenile death penalty and the values embodied in the Eighth Amendment is a difficult problem for us. The dignitarian issues and the tangled issues of culpability and responsibility are hard to think through. By paying attention to what other jurists have done with this relation or similar relations, we treat it as a problem to be solved in part by attending to the established deliverances of legal science—the enterprise, which many legal systems share, of grappling with, untangling, and resolving the rival rights and claims that come together in issues of this kind.

Of course it is ultimately our decision: '[I]t is a Constitution for the United States of America that we are expounding.'[65] But that does not preclude turning to the legal consensus of civilized nations for assistance any more than the American origin of an epidemic precludes Americans' turning to foreign scientists for guidance. It is possible that geographic or cultural peculiarities may distinguish the American experience with the epidemic from experience elsewhere. Still, we would not want to respond arbitrarily to local peculiarities; we should respond on a scientific basis to ascertain which peculiarities should be taken into account and how.

I have emphasized the point that referring to *ius gentium* treats the problems that arise in our courts as though they were questions for legal science. It does not simply look to 'foreign moods, fads, or fashions'.[66] It relies instead on the idea that solutions to

[65] *Thompson v Oklahoma*, 487 US 815, 868, 108 S Ct 2687 (1988) (Scalia, J., dissenting).

[66] *Foster v Florida*, 537 US 990, 990, 123 S Ct 470 (2002) (Thomas, J., concurring in denial of certiorari) ('[T]his Court's Eighth Amendment jurisprudence should not impose foreign moods, fads, or fashions on Americans').

certain kinds of problems in the law might get established in the way that scientific theories are established. They do not get established as infallible, they change over the years, and there are always outliers who refuse to accept them—some cranky, some whose reluctance leads eventually to progress. But to ignore foreign solutions, or to refrain from attending to them because they are foreign, betokens not just an objectionable parochialism, but an obtuseness as to the nature of the problems we face.

Under the theory of foreign law citation that I have been outlining, the appeal to foreign law is not a piecemeal practice—as though our courts were taking some inspiration from Britain, some other inspiration from France, and so on. Some defences of the citation of foreign law take this approach, as though it were a casual matter of getting a little bit of help here and a little bit of help there.[67] A lot of criticisms of the practice presuppose this approach too. Critics react as though the Supreme Court had cited British law forgetting that the United States declared its independence from Britain 230 years ago,[68] or as though we had deferred to Zimbabwean law forgetting about President Mugabe's human rights record.[69] Such piecemeal citation would be easy to discredit. Now it might be thought that if it is not alright to cite any particular foreign law or precedent, then it is not alright to cite any consensus or accumulation of foreign authorities. But that way of thinking commits the fallacy of composition. On the analogy I have been using, what characterizes a consensus in biology or epidemiology is not just that it is an accumulation of authorities, but that it represents a dense network of checking and rechecking results, experimental duplication, credentialing, mutual elaboration, and building on one another's work. Likewise, *ius gentium* is more than the sum of its parts, and, as a dense and mutually reinforced consensus, it may have a pertinence to our law that its individual constituents do not have. This fact means that *ius gentium* may not be 'foreign' in the objectionable sense in which the constituent elements of it are foreign.[70]

In the public health analogy, we would certainly expect our scientists to look only to findings we had reason to trust; they would not look to the work of suspect or disreputable laboratories. Similarly, an *ius gentium* inquiry may restrict itself to consensus among 'civilized' or 'freedom-loving' countries.[71] As I said earlier, discerning the

[67] See Mary Ann Glendon, *Rights Talk* (Free Press 1998) 146–59 (1ggi); Justice Stephen Breyer, Key-note Address Before the Ninety-Seventh Annual Meeting of the American Society of International Law (2003), in 97 Am. Soc'y Int'l L. Proc. 265, 266 (mentioning 'the enormous value in any discipline of trying to learn from the similar experience of others').

[68] Thus Congressman Ted Poe of Texas reminded us of all the patriots who 'spilled their blood . . . to sever ties with England forever . . . Now, justices in this land of America . . . use British court decisions . . . in interpreting our Constitution. What the British could not accomplish by force, our Supreme Court has surrendered to them voluntarily.' 151 US Cong. Rec. H3105 (daily ed. May, 2005) (statement of Rep. Poe).

[69] See *Knight v Florida,* 528 US 990, 996, 120 S Ct 459 (1999) (Breyer, J., dissenting from denial of certiorari) (citing the Supreme Court of Zimbabwe).

[70] Cf. Daniel R. Coquillette, 'Ideology and Incorporation III: Reason Regulated—The Post-Restoration English Civilians', 1653–1735, 67 B.U. L. Rev. 289, 294 (1987) ('By Roman law definition, ius gentium was not "foreign" law because it was an inherent part of the law of all, or most, countries').

[71] *Reynolds v United States,* 98 US 145 (1879), presents a remarkable instance of an appeal to a very restricted consensus. See ibid. at 164 ('Polygamy has always been odious among the northern and western nations of Europe, and, until the establishment of the Mormon Church, was almost exclusively a feature of the life of Asiatic and of African people').

normatively relevant consensus is a matter of reflective equilibrium between the positive law experience and our sense of the right premises with which to approach this problem. Since *ius gentium* is not a purely descriptive consensus, an appeal to it need not be indiscriminate as to the quality of the laws on which it draws. Maybe we should not give weight to courts in Zimbabwe or the Sudan. By analogy we might not expect our public health officials to look to North Korea for guidance in their response to a possible avian flu epidemic.

I do not expect any of this to convince those who see law as purely a matter of will.[72] If you think that legal problems are ultimately solved in a simple Alexandrian fashion—just cutting through the Gordian knot with a determination to privilege *this* value or to promote *that* policy—then you will be uninterested in the logic of a jurisprudence that talks about patient analysis, the untangling of issues, the ascertaining of just resolutions, and the learning and cooperation that is characteristic of a scientific approach. For you it is just a matter of will, and the question is 'Whose will should prevail?'. And you will see in the citation of foreign law nothing much more than 'the subjective views of five Members of this Court and like-minded foreigners.'[73] I have presented law in a different light, as essentially a problem-solving enterprise. And I am sure that if the invocation of foreign law is to be defended, then it has to be on grounds like this.

VII. Conclusion

My aim in this chapter has been to present a theory of the citation of foreign law, not a justification of the actual use that American courts have made of foreign law. What troubled me at the outset of this chapter was that the Supreme Court in *Roper* failed to articulate any general ideas or standards by which its use of foreign law might be evaluated. For reasons I have indicated, a pure theory of natural law does not fit the bill, but a theory articulated in terms of *ius gentium* does.

I am under no illusion, however, that the practice of the Supreme Court in *Roper* and in other cases[74] actually answers to the characterization I have given. Practice often falls short of theory—particularly when the practitioners have not shown much awareness of the theory in question! And there are all sorts of pitfalls and temptations associated with a theory as loose as this. No crisp or precise litmus test defines the sort of international consensus that makes up *ius gentium* on any particular subject. It is, as we have seen, a matter of interpretation, and so there is always the prospect that a judge will invoke this theory opportunistically, picking and choosing the consensus he relies on, to reinforce conclusions that he wanted to reach anyway. For those who see law as a matter of will, this sort of theory is at best just an opportunity for haphazard legitimation. But for those who do see legal decision as a matter of reasoning one's way through problems, my account may help to explain why courts turn naturally to

[72] See Herbert Wechsler, 'Toward Neutral Principles of Constitutional Law' (1959) 73 Harv. L. Rev. 1, ii (cautioning that '[t]hose who perceive in law only the element of fiat . . . will not join gladly in the search for standards of the kind I have in mind').

[73] Roper, 125 S. Ct. at 1217 (Scalia, J., dissenting).

[74] See *Lawrence v Texas*, 123 S. Ct. 2472, 2483 (2003); *Atkins v Virginia*, 536 US 304, 317 n 21 (2002); *Thompson v Oklahoma*, 487 US 815, 830–1 (1988) (plurality opinion).

foreign law. The real contrast between those who oppose and those who defend the use of foreign law in American legal reasoning is not that jurists in the first group are parochial and the second cosmopolitan. It is rather this contrast between law as will and law as reason. Those who approach the law as a matter of will do not see any reason why expressions of will elsewhere in the world should affect our expressions of will in America. But those who see law as a matter of reason may well be willing to approach it in a scientific spirit that relies not just on our own reasoning but on some rational relation between what we are wrestling with and what others have figured out.

29

Comparative Law before the Spanish Private Law Courts in the 21st Century

Marta Requejo Isidro and Marta Otero Crespo***

I. Introduction

In the third edition of their renowned *An Introduction to Comparative Law* (1998), K. Zweigert and H. Kötz stated that:

> comparative law, as it is practised today, has two quite distinct roots: 'legislative comparative law', when foreign laws are invoked in the process of drafting new national laws, and 'scientific or theoretical comparative law', when the comparison of different legal systems is undertaken simply in order to improve our legal knowledge.[1]

Nowadays, it can be said that comparative law is not only invoked during legislative processes and in purely academic scenarios as previously mentioned, but also as a *jurisprudential element* across European jurisdictions.

In this regard, the Spanish courts are no exception. With this in mind, our contribution aims to explore the role of comparative law before the Spanish private law tribunals,[2] to which a general description of the Spanish background on the resort to comparative law is indispensable: not only for imbuing academic studies, but also as a source of inspiration for drafting the private law rules, and, finally (as of recently), as a tool confidently (even if, quantitatively speaking, not too frequently) handled by the Spanish private law courts. Section II will address these aspects. Moreover, an explanation of the relevant data which have conditioned—and which still do condition—the role of comparative law in the working of the Spanish courts will be provided to render a more coherent understanding of the overall situation.

Empirical data will be examined in section III, where a further classification has been made between *non-mandatory* and *mandatory* uses of comparative law.[3]

* Dr Marta Requejo Isidro is a Senior Research Fellow at Max Planck Institute Luxembourg.

** Dr Marta Otero Crespo is a Senior Lecturer in Civil Law at Universidad de Santiago de Compostela. This publication has been produced with the financial support of the *Programa de consolidación y estructuración de unidades de investigación competitivas del Sistema universitario de Galicia [exp. GPC2014/024]: financiado por la Xunta de Galicia y el FEDER.*

[1] Zweigert and Kötz, *An Introduction to Comparative Law* (3rd ed, Oxford University Press 1998) 51.

[2] For this study we have used the two most relevant Spanish databases: a privately run one, Aranzadi Westlaw (RTC, RJ, AC or JUR references), and the publicly owned CENDOJ (CENDOJ references). The latter database is accessible for free via <http://www.poderjudicial.es/search/index.jsp>

[3] This division between mandatory and non-mandatory resort to comparative law is inspired by Bobek's tripartition between mandatory, advisable, and voluntary uses: Bobek, *Comparative Reasoning in European Supreme Courts* (Oxford University Press 2013) 19 ff.

Non-mandatory resource is identifiable whenever there is no distinct basis in the domestic legal system for resorting to an alien law. Conversely, in the case of mandatory use, the national legal system expressly imposes the application of foreign law—and with it, the need to resort to comparative law tools; a typical example is the designation of a foreign legal system by a conflict-of-laws rule.

II. A few words on the background

Both Spanish academia and law-makers have dealt with comparative law issues in the past. From the academic perspective, in 1851 the University of Madrid created the first Chair in Comparative Law (*Cátedra de legislación comparada*), which is considered to be the first academic Chair in the world.[4] Thanks to this Chair, comparative law studies formally took root in Spain, with a fair number of law schools offering comparative law as an autonomous subject in the curriculum. Nonetheless, this fact did not automatically imply the success of comparative law studies in our country, nor the acceptance of the discipline as the answer to a real need within our frontiers. In the mid 20th century, Professor De Castro—a leading private law academic—still declared that the study of foreign laws and doctrines, whilst useful, can also be a source of perverse deviation.[5] In the 21st century this viewpoint is clearly untenable: comparative law studies have spread across law schools as an independent, educational subject, as well as an element regularly present in the teaching of civil law and of private international law (PIL). Further, it is extremely difficult to find a civil law or a PIL PhD dissertation without a comparative law ingredient. In addition, the comparative method is nearly always present in academic works: publications with references to foreign laws or case law—mainly from Anglo-Saxon, German, French, and Italian sources—and a matching comparative analysis are commonplace.

As for the law-maker, the influence of foreign laws and the resort to comparative law on private law legislative processes is perfectly traceable since the time of codification in the 19th century. Following the Napoleonic French Code of 1804, Art. 258 of the Spanish Constitution of 1812[6] proclaimed the need to adopt a 'single' Civil Code—together with a commercial and criminal codes—in place of the mere dispersion of numerous rules characteristic of that era. While the commercial and criminal codification processes succeeded relatively quickly,[7] the civil codification path can only be described as long and full of stones: several drafts were dismissed before the final

[4] Prof. Montalbán was the first to hold the Chair. See Hoffman Elizande, *Introducción al estudio del Derecho comparado* (2nd ed, Universidad Iberoamericana, México D. F. 1998) 151. Prior to the 19th century some Spanish authors had dealt with a sort of 'comparative law': Villalobos, *Antinomia Regni Hispaniarum et civilis* (Salamanca, 1569); Martín de Olano, *Concordia et nova reduction antinomiarum iuris communis et regni hispaniarum* (1575); or Ximénez, *Concordia sea concordantiae utriusquae iuris civilis et canonici* (1569). These and further references are included in García Cantero, 'Nacimiento, desarrollo e importancia actual del Derecho comparado' (2000), *Actualidad Civil*, N°1, 2000, 72 ff.

[5] Literally, 'el estudio del Derecho comparado de legislaciones extranjeras y forasteras doctrinas puede ser útil, es ajena experiencia aprovechable, pero puede ser causa de desviaciones perturbadoras y de servil seguir ajenas modas', in De Castro, *Derecho civil de España* (Civitas, Madrid, reprinted 1984) 138.

[6] This is the first Spanish Constitution, drawn up in Cádiz on 19 March 1812.

[7] The Commercial Code was approved in 1829; the Criminal Code in 1822.

approval of the Civil Code in 1889. One of these drafts was the Civil Code project of 1851, also called '*Proyecto de García Goyena*'.[8] In his acclaimed work '*Concordancias, motivos y comentarios del Código civil español*',[9] Florencio García Goyena analyses every single article of Project 1851, including comparative notes related to foreign Civil Codes—French, Dutch, Austrian, Prussian, and Bavarian Codes, amongst others—which had inspired the text submitted by the Spanish Law Commission of the Ministry of Justice.

What about case law? It has been said that the 20th century witnessed the rise, the decay, and, subsequently, the revitalization of comparative law.[10] This assertion cannot be blindly endorsed when discussing the Spanish context. While the stimulus of foreign laws in scholarly writings—as well as in the legislative processes of drafting private law rules—is clear, their impact on Spanish case law is almost undetectable until the mid 20th century. Only then did the Spanish Supreme Court in its First Chamber (the civil chamber, *Sala de lo Civil*) start to feel confident enough to gently venture into foreign and comparative law; comparative law only became more of a common feature of our case law in the 1990s. Several circumstances concur to explain the situation. First, it must be recalled that under the former political regime prior to the Spanish Constitution of 1978—a dictatorship, abolished in 1975 after Franco's death—Spain was a country closed to influences from other legal systems. Second, according to the traditional—and still in force—method of access to the judiciary, candidates have to pass a series of exams for which national law is the unique subject of study. Furthermore, almost no private international law rules are included as topics of examination. A third element to consider is the linguistic barrier: knowledge of foreign languages is a pre-requisite to accessing comparative law—one unfortunately neglected in the Spanish curricula. Indeed, command of foreign languages is, if at all, acquired by judges by their own means.[11]

There remains one additional factor. The rule on 'Evidence' of the Spanish Code of Civil Procedure (*Ley de enjuiciamiento civil* 2000—LEC) states that 'foreign law must be proved as regards its content and its validity; the court may use any means of verification it considers to be necessary for its implementation' (Art. 281.2 *in fine* LEC). The provision exempts foreign law from the *iura novit curia* principle, and therefore releases the judge from having to investigate it.[12] Besides, it does not explain the consequences of any of the parties to the proceedings effectively proving the applicable foreign law—i.e., according to the wording of the provision, the burden of proof does not fall upon the judge, even under such circumstances. The Spanish Constitutional Court has provided for some guidance, pointing towards a different interpretation and therefore imposing a more active role on the judge in order to determine the foreign

[8] This project was about to be finally passed. See Repáraz Padrós, 'La crítica contemporánea al Proyecto de Código Civil de 1851' (1997), *Anuario de Derecho civil*, Vol. 50, nº 3, 1015 ff.

[9] García Goyena, *Concordancias, motivos y comentarios del Código civil español* (Cometa, Zaragoza 1974 (original published in Madrid, 1852)).

[10] B. Fauvarque-Cosson, 'The Rise of Comparative Law: a Challenge for Legal Education in Europe', Walter van Gerven Lectures (7), Leuven Centre for a Common Law of Europe, Belgium, 2007, 3.

[11] See n 53.

[12] And this in spite of the fact that in Spain the conflict-of-law rules are conceived as compulsory for the judge, and applicable *ex officio* by him: see Art. 12.6 Civil Code.

law designated by the conflict-of-laws rule. The actual reach of the mandate, however, is far from clear.[13]

In spite of the foregoing, resource to comparative law in Spain today is more than a purely academic exercise deprived of practical effects. As in many other jurisdictions, legal research has become more European (rather, transnational and global) and less inward looking, a fact that accounts for an increasing presence of comparative law in the daily practice of the tribunals. Furthermore, foreign materials are much more accessible in the digital era: judges have an easier access to them if they wish to. As previously stated, Spanish private law courts have resorted to comparative law in their decisions over the last 20 years, and for a number of different functions, as we will immediately see.

III. Empirical data on the use of comparative law before the private law courts

1. Non-mandatory uses of comparative law: purely domestic cases

a) General remarks

In purely domestic, non-cross-border settings, the ordinary point of departure leading to a comparative law analysis is a situation where the judge does not need to refer 'compulsorily' to any legal system but the Spanish one, to which he/she is legally bound. The judge is not compelled to resort to foreign law, but is not told not to either. This actually means that the judge is given a choice of two attitudes: a positive and a negative. The positive attitude represents the active choice of the judge, who, even though not obliged to do so, still opts to look to external references provided for by foreign law. On the contrary, if the negative attitude dominates, the judge will ignore any foreign legal system and remain focused on his/her national law.

For obvious reasons, in this study attention is only paid to those cases where the judge supports the positive choice. The ground for such a preference may indeed vary. Often the judge has to fulfil lacunae, or to interpret national existing rules of unclear meaning. When none of those situations are at the source of the positive choice, the possibility that the judge voluntarily turns to foreign law due to his/her expertise or knowledge, especially because of his/her academic background, cannot be excluded.[14]

Once the judge has made a positive choice, the need for comparative law as a tool comes to the forefront. In the light of the case law we have reviewed (to which we return later), an explanation of what Spanish courts understand by 'comparative law' is advisable: in particular, in order to exclude a common prejudice—i.e., that comparative

[13] See *Sentencia del Tribunal Constitucional*, 10/2000 of 17 January (RTC 2000/10), on the proof of Armenian law applicable to a divorce case of a couple living in Spain.

[14] Professor E. Roca Trías is a good example of this attitude: during her appointment as judge of the Spanish Supreme Court (Civil Chamber) she issued a great number of judgments including comparative law elements in her capacity as reporting judge.

law is limited to foreign legislative or/and jurisprudential texts. Over the last decades, several academic movements aiming at studying and promoting the harmonization of European law have spread across Europe. These heterogeneous initiatives, originating from different legal backgrounds, have carried through an outstanding comparative work, resulting in a series of written pieces to publicize the results of the research. Amongst the texts that have emerged, some deserve particular attention: the Principles of European Contract Law (PECL), the Principles of European Tort Law (PETL), the Principles of European Family Law,[15] and the Draft Common Frame of Reference (DCFR). Leaving aside the wide variety of topics covered and their diverse impact on national systems, all of them intend to serve as a model for the European legislators. Besides, they have actually been functioning as soft law before the courts; if we have a look at the way in which the Spanish courts deal with them, particularly in purely domestic constellations,[16] it can be said that they are already a source for inspiration. In other words, foreign law, foreign case law, and scholars' work are not the only materials on which comparison is built; soft law instruments are also considered. That's why we will split the presentation of Spanish case law into two headings: *comparative law in a strict sense*, meaning quotation of foreign law, doctrine, or jurisprudence; and *comparative law: wider approach*, for the soft law realm. We will briefly outline some examples falling within those two areas. Decisions where the judiciary just mentions the 'Derecho comparado', without further ado, have not been taken into account.[17]

A final point worth mentioning here is that of the effects of the use of comparative law devices by the courts in a non-mandatory setting. The answer is largely conditioned by the role of jurisprudence itself as a source of law within our legal system. Article 1 of the Civil Code states the relevant sources of law in the private law context.[18] According to paragraph 5, the case law (*jurisprudencia*) shall *complement* the legal system by means of the doctrine repeatedly upheld by the Supreme Court in its interpretation and application of statutes, customs, and general legal principles. To put it another way, case law is *not* a source of law. Consequently, comparative law used by Spanish courts in the framework baptized 'non-mandatory' will never be a means of implementing foreign law into our jurisdiction.[19]

[15] This comprises the Principles on Divorce and Maintenance between former spouses, the Principles on Parental Responsibilities, and the Principles on Property Relations between Spouses.

[16] As opposed to cross-border cases.

[17] A mere reference to 'Derecho comparado' without including concrete foreign laws, authors, or case law is made by the *Sentencia del Tribunal Supremo (Sala de lo Civil, Sección 1ª)*, 10 January 2011, on a child custody case. See also *Sentencia del Tribunal Supremo (Sala de lo Civil, Sección 1ª)*, 20 June 1959, where 'Derecho extranjero' is mentioned to recall the foreign influences on the modification of the Code of civil procedure. The same kind of non-specific citing is also found in the *Sentencia del Tribunal Supremo (Sala de lo Civil, Sección 1ª)*, 25 February 1960, in a buy-and-sell business, or the *Sentencia del Tribunal Supremo (Sala de lo Civil, Sección 1ª)*, 23 June 1960, in an urban renting case.

[18] The Spanish Civil Code was passed in 1889; the regulation therein contained on legal rules, their application and effectiveness was of general application. However, the situation changed in 1978, after the coming into force of the Spanish Constitution: first, the Constitution is now the main source of law; secondly, it establishes itself a rank of the different types of normative rules. The classification of the sources of law established in the Civil Code has never been abolished, but since 1978 its interpretation has to be consistent with the Constitution.

[19] See García Rubio, *Introducción al Derecho civil* (Cálamo, Barcelona 2002) 109 ff.

b) Comparative law—strict sense

As we have already seen in section II, comparative law references—doctrine, legislation, and case law—are not alien to the Spanish judiciary. Allusions to comparative law can be traced from the mid 20th century. One of the leading examples is the *Sentencia del Tribunal Supremo (Sala de lo civil, sección 1ª)*, 15 October 1957,[20] in which the reporting Judge, Mr Francisco Eyre Varela, alludes to comparative doctrine (Enneccerus and his commentators) together with comparative law (Swiss and German Codes) in a case where the mental capacity to make a will was at stake due to the alcoholism of the testator. The magistrate specifically mentions that the decision cannot be grounded on the solutions adopted by foreign laws (and authors), but those external answers may be taken into consideration to interpret the lacuna identified in our Civil Code—alcoholism per se was not included as a cause for declaring null and void the will of the testator who suffers that disease. The judge was fully aware of the virtues of comparative law and endorsed it as a means of interpretation.

Another illustrative case is the *Sentencia del Tribunal Supremo (Sala de lo Civil)*, 29 April 2008,[21] where the judge rapporteur—Dr E. Roca Trías—refers to the United Nations Convention on the rights of persons with disabilities 2006, and to how this Convention has been transposed into national laws. The Civil Code of Quebec (Art. 285), the Italian Civil Code (Art. 404), the French Civil Code (Arts. 491–492) and the German BGB (paragraphs 1869 and 1902) are cited in Recital number six, under the heading 'Comparative law' (*Derecho comparado*). The magistrate turns to those foreign sources to reach the conclusion that, albeit under different names, neighbouring legal systems effectively establish legal mechanisms in order to protect disabled people.

The Supreme Court has expressly quoted foreign regulation on family law as well. Child custody criteria are a good illustration. In 2005 the Spanish Civil Code was amended to explicitly include joint custody as a child custody option available after a divorce or separation.[22] However, the legislator did not include the guiding rules to be taken into consideration when the judge has to decide about the child custody regime. The Supreme Court has fulfilled this lack of guidance with references to foreign legal systems which provide, not only for the joint custody as a preferred option, but also for hints on how to implement it. For instance, the decision of the *Tribunal Supremo (Sala de lo Civil, Sección 1ª)*, 8 October 2009,[23] cites many European jurisdictions which provide for joint custody only if both parents agree on this solution (Germany or Norway), together with countries where the judge has the power to select joint custody when this is the option which favours the best interest of the child, even if the parents reject the model (Belgium, France, England, Wales, Scotland—and the Catalonian Family Law Code). Further, about the criteria to be considered, the Court confronts

[20] *Sentencia del Tribunal Supremo*, 1502/1957, 15 October 1957, CENDOJ: 28079110011957100680.

[21] RJ 2009/2901.

[22] Besides its regulation within the sphere of matrimonial crisis, those provisions are applicable to children born outside marriage as well.

[23] RJ 2009/4606.

the silence of the Spanish Civil Code with the French (Code civil) or English (Children Act) regulations.[24]

c) Comparative law—wider approach

In recent years, the number of occasions in which the civil chamber of the Supreme Court has referred to soft law instruments is (proportionally) high. Soft law texts have become popular amongst the Spanish judiciary, especially when the reporting judges hold an academic background. If we look for references to PECL, PETL, DCFR, or UNIDROIT Principles, the amount of judgments is remarkable. One of the main causes for this may be the structural deficiency of the Spanish regulation on patrimonial law (contract and tort law). The Spanish rules on obligations and contracts contained in the Civil Code 1889 have been said to be obsolete—as they have not been modified according to the real needs of the 20th and 21st centuries—and vague—as they do not define key general concepts. To overcome these flaws, the Supreme Court has resorted to those 'alternative sources' of law. For instance, the decision of the *Tribunal Supremo (Sala de lo Civil),* 11 February 2013, mentions Art. 9:501 (2) PECL as a mechanism to define the features of *lucrum cessans* as a head of damage, when assessing damages in a contractual scenario. Following this criterion, this type of damage shall be awarded when it can be equated to a future loss which is reasonably likely to occur. Another example is the decision of the *Tribunal Supremo (Sala de lo Civil),* 27 June 2013,[25] in an agency contract case: when assessing the damages to be awarded in that context, the court mentions both the Spanish Agency Act and Art. IV.D—3: 312 (4) DCFR. Another is the judgment of the *Tribunal Supremo (Sala de lo Civil),* 25 October 2013,[26] that turns to Art 7.3.1. [2b] UNIDROIT Principles when interpreting the right to terminate the contract following Art. 1124 of the Spanish Civil Code.

Within the tort law context, the PETL have proven to be really helpful when interpreting Art. 1902 ff of the Spanish Civil Code. The *Sentencia del Tribunal Supremo (Sala de lo Civil),* 17 July 2007,[27] expressly recognizes that criteria established in PETL might be of help when interpreting and integrating the notion of fault and standard of care (*culpa/estándar de conducta exigible*) derived from Art. 1902 CC in parallel to Art. 4:102 PETL. In the same vein, the *Sentencia del Tribunal Supremo (Sala de lo Civil),* 10 September 2012,[28] must be mentioned: the judge rapporteur, Mr Xiol Ríos, uses Art. 3:102 PETL to shed light onto the conflicting debate on potentially multiple causation applicable to a car crash case (to conclude that in the face of multiple activities, where each of them alone could have caused the damage at the same time, each activity is regarded as a cause of the victim's damage).

In addition to this interpretative function, on many occasions the Supreme Court has referred to soft law instruments in a purely 'ornamental' manner, that is, to

[24] The *Sentencia del Tribunal Supremo,* 6 February 2013 (RJ 2014/736) also deals with a 'foreign' family law institution—surrogacy motherhood.

[25] *Sentencia del Tribunal Supremo,* 7 of June 2013, CENDOJ: 28079110012013100403.

[26] RJ 2013/7257. [27] RJ 2007/4895. [28] RJ 2012/11046.

underpin the content or the interpretation given to national provisions. For instance, the *Sentencia del Tribunal Supremo (Sala de lo Civil, Sección 1ª)*, 25 May 2009:[29] when deciding on a life annuity contract (*contrato de vitalicio*), the Magistrate alludes to Art. 5:106 PECL and Art. II-8: 106 DCFR to support the rule established in Art. 1284 CC (if a clause of a contract shall admit several meanings it must be interpreted according to the most suitable meaning to be effective). More recently, the *Sentencia del Tribunal Supremo (Sala de lo Civil)*, 20 January 2013,[30] cites Art. 1:201 PECL 'Good faith and fair dealing' in parallel to Art. 7 Civil Code (general duty to act according to good faith—general principle of law), when analysing the bank's duties to inform and provide advice to its clients about a banking product.

To sum up, comparative law in a broad sense is not only familiar to the Spanish Supreme Court, but seems to be in the process of becoming a more common tool when drafting judgments.[31]

2. Comparative law and private international law: the mandatory(?) use of comparative law

a) General remarks

Because they both deal with foreign legal systems, PIL and comparative law have been said to entertain an intimate relationship.[32] A separate heading addressing the rapport between the two disciplines thus seems appropriate.[33]

To be truthful, the assertion we have just reproduced does not reveal much about the working together of PIL and comparative law, or about comparative reasoning as a tool for the application of PIL by the judiciary. As a matter of fact, at the first stage of exploring the issue, it may even be tempting to disagree with the statement. Foreign law enters the forum via a conflict of laws rule of the forum itself: in other words, the use of foreign law is mandatory, judges do not have the choice to apply it or not, nor do they experience the need to be open to it; they simply follow the national rules that

[29] *Sentencia del Tribunal Supremo (Sala de lo Civil)*, 25 of May 2009. Judge rapporteur: E. Roca Trías. RJ 2009/2417.

[30] RJ 2014/781.

[31] To the point that scholars have felt the need to remind us that the Principles are not positive law: Díez-Picazo Giménez/Arana de la Fuente, *El desbordamiento del Derecho de daños. Jurisprudencia reciente* (Civitas 2009) 29.

[32] Reinmann, 'Comparative Law and Private International Law', in Reimann, Zimmermann, *The Oxford Handbook of Comparative Law* (Oxford University Press 2008) 1364; Fauverque-Cosson, 'Droit comparé et droit international privé: la confrontation de deux logiques à travers l'exemple des droits fondamentaux' (2002), 54 Revue International de Droit Comparé, 798–9; Ciuro Caldani, 'El Derecho comparado y su relación con el Derecho Internacional Privado', lecture at the Universidad Notarial Argentina, on file with the author.

[33] The question mark in the heading indicates doubts over whether under the Spanish system the application of foreign law—carrying with it comparative law as a tool—is really mandatory, in spite of the clear mandate of Art. 12.6 Civil Code as regards the conflict-of-laws rule ('Los Tribunales y autoridades aplicarán de oficio las normas de conflicto del derecho español'). See also section II, on the proof of foreign law in Spain.

command the application of foreign law. Comparative reasoning seems to have little relevance here.[34]

However, the foregoing assumption is manifestly much too simplistic. It ignores the multiple evidence pointing to the contrary, starting with the many cases of institutions (such as universities, institutes and the like) that couple both disciplines and offer masters programs or specialized courses,[35] or which are devoted to a combined research of the two subject matters.[36] Legal and juridical comparison, sometimes explicitly and on many occasions just implicitly, is part of the constitution, the development, and the application of PIL rules by the national authorities. The idea of a *Droit international privé comparé* has become a topic in legal literature.[37] The following list provides for concrete examples of the uses of comparative law for PIL:

- The identification of the foreign element of a situation and the assessment of its relevance/irrelevance (i.e., whether it weighs enough to require a differentiated legal treatment), already implies the use of a comparative reasoning.[38]
- Legal comparison may intervene to fill gaps of the national PIL system, or gaps emerging in its functioning.[39]
- Interpretation of PIL rules as a part of the qualification mechanism may be done in several ways, one of them being the construction by the judge of autonomous concepts built upon a comparative analysis of the legal systems at stake.[40]
- Proper application of the foreign legal system appointed by the national conflict-of-laws rule commands its correct understanding and apprehension; the same happens with foreign decisions. For such purposes, comparative reasoning with other systems, starting with that of the forum, is needed.[41]
- Comparison between systems is required when a choice among the substantive rules of several legal systems is required from the judge: for instance, in case he/she has to apply a conflict-of-laws rule that points towards a particular outcome, such as the formal validity of a will or a marriage.[42]

[34] That's the approach, for instance, of Bobek, *Comparative Reasoning in European Supreme Courts* (Oxford University Press 2013).

[35] Among many others, the Masters in *Droit international privé comparé* (M2) of the Law Faculty, Paris-Assas University, in which one of the authors (Marta Requejo) has taught.

[36] The most renowned being the *Max Planck Institute für ausländisches und internationales Privatrecht*, Hamburg.

[37] As explained by Prof. B. Ancel in his course entitled 'Droit international privé comparé', addressed to second-year masters students, 'Il n'existe pas plus de droit international privé comparé qu'il n'existe de droit comparé si le sens propre des termes qui composent ces désignations ne doit recouvrir que le droit positif édicté et sanctionné par l'Etat. En revanche, d'une part, le droit international privé, comme le droit civil ou le droit commercial ou le droit judiciaire privé, existe assurément; et, d'autre part, dès lors que ces objets juridiques, ces manifestations du phénomène juridique se présentent dans les réalisations diverses qu'en offrent les ordres juridiques nationaux, il est permis, il est même recommandé de pratiquer la comparaison entre eux.'

[38] Ciuro Caldani, 'El Derecho comparado y su relación con el Derecho Internacional Privado' (n 33), 3.

[39] See under section b.i.

[40] This was the proposal of Rabel, 'Das Problem der Qualification' (1931), 5 RabelsZ 241.

[41] Below, under subheadings 'The understanding of foreign institutions' and 'Understanding the foreign decision'.

[42] Below, under subheading 'Result-oriented conflict of laws rules'.

- Legal comparison is compulsory for the operation of devices such as the public policy clause, be it within the framework of the conflict-of-laws rule or to decide on a request of recognition or enforcement.[43]
- Uniform or harmonized PIL texts also need comparison to ensure interpretation in a uniform way.

But, do these assertions also hold true for Spain?

b) Comparative law, PIL, and the Spanish courts

The resort of the judiciary to comparative reasoning in the field of PIL varies widely depending on the country under consideration. For several motives—some of them already mentioned in section II—Spain could have developed a good tradition in this regard from 1975 on, yet it has not.

The end of General Franco's dictatorship in 1975 and the gradual building of democracy led to the renewal of many laws in force, comporting the will to break with the immediate past, on the one hand; and the need to look elsewhere, beyond the borders, to find legal inspiration, on the other. PIL was one of the fields where both the will and necessity were (presumptively) more acute. The broad opening of the borders of the country, which began before the passing away of the dictator, meant the expansion and increase of private law cases with a foreign element. The main instrument at hand was the provisions contained in the *Título Preliminar* of the Civil Code, which had certainly been reviewed in 1974, but which still remained underdeveloped: it only contained conflict-of-laws rules, drafted still under the particular policy and social perceptions of General Franco's period. No rules on jurisdiction were provided for—another ten years elapsed before the lawgiver produced them;[44] the rules on recognition and exequatur were limited to some provisions dating back to the end of the 19th century, which invoked reciprocity in the first place.[45] Against this backdrop, comparative law being accorded a relevant role wouldn't have come as a surprise.

Another good reason for comparative reasoning becoming part of the everyday work of the Spanish judiciary should have been the incorporation of Spain in the European Community in 1985: uniform PIL instruments such as the Convention of 27 September 1968, on jurisdiction and the enforcement of judgments in civil and commercial matters, or the Convention of 19 June on the Law Applicable to Contractual Obligations, and later, the European regulations substituting the conventions or adding to them, entered into force. Spanish judges had to learn about how to deal with them; a regard to what other Member States were doing would have been advisable. The same could be said about the numerous international conventions in the field of PIL, from The Hague Conference and other institutions, signed and ratified by Spain in the 1980s.[46]

[43] Below, under subheadings 'Compatibility with public policy' and 'Public policy'.

[44] *Ley Orgánica 6/1985*, 1 July, *del Poder Judicial (LOPJ)*, Arts. 21, 22.

[45] *Ley de Enjuiciamiento Civil*, 3 February 1881, Arts. 951–958.

[46] To mention just some: the Convention on the Service Abroad of Judicial and Extrajudicial Documents in Civil or Commercial Matters (adopted 15 November 1965, in force in Spain since 1987) 658 UNTS 9432;

In spite of these circumstances, comparative law reasoning in the Spanish practice of PIL has occupied, and still occupies, a modest place, in clear contrast with the one it has in academia.[47] Comparative analysis is rare, or at best rarely identifiable in Spanish PIL decisions; it is also limited, in the sense that to a large extent the case law which resorts to comparative expedients concentrates on a few topical situations, mostly linked to Islamic law; in addition, the argumentation therein developed is poor.[48] The grounds on which international jurisdiction is founded are usually not stated, consequently no comparative explanation appears either. In the area of recognition and enforcement of foreign judgments, the concise style which has become inherent to the decisions—especially to those granting the requested recognition/exequatur—may account for the brevity of the comparative reasoning. The fact, already mentioned,[49] that the foreign law designated by the conflict-of-laws rule has to be proved by the party interested in its application—i.e., there is no *ex officio* application—and that if he/she fails to do so Spanish law will apply instead,[50] has led to many cases of abandonment of foreign law, and with it, of any reference to comparative law. The meagre equipment of the Spanish judiciary as regards the basics of comparative law analysis, starting with the formation at university level and followed by the subject-matter programme of the exams that give access to the judicial corps, must also be recalled. Confusion between the notions of comparative law and foreign law is sometimes evidenced, as exemplified by the *Sentencia del Tribunal Central de Trabajo*, 6 May 1982: 'As to comparative law, it is known that beyond the cases in which the rules of private international law, mainly those contained in arts. 8, 9, 10, 11 and 12 C. Civ, are applicable . . . the laws and regulations of other countries do not have any binding force in Spain'[51] (this notwithstanding—rather, in open contradiction—the Court was engaged in a thorough analysis of English and French law). Reference to comparative law is sometimes made only to highlight its limits, as illustrated by the *Sentencia de la Audiencia Provincial de Zaragoza (Sección 5ª)*, 21 July 2006, in a case where French law is invoked by the claimant to underpin his position. The Court answers in the following way: 'This rule of foreign law is not applicable in any way, nor can the study of comparative law force the interpretation of Spanish law in force in the intended manner'.[52]

Convention on the Taking of Evidence Abroad in Civil or Commercial Matters (adopted 18 March 1970, signed by Spain in 1976, entered into force in 1987) 847 UNTS 231; the Convention on the Law Applicable To Traffic Accidents, (adopted 4 May 1971, in force in Spain since 1987) 965 UNTS 411; Convention on the Law Applicable to Products Liability, (adopted 2 October 1973, in force in Spain since 1989) 1056 UNTS 187.

[47] The support given by comparative law to academia is acknowledged by the judiciary: see e.g. the *Auto del Tribunal Supremo (Sala de lo Civil)*, 5 October 1982, RJ/1982/5539.

[48] Compare with some decisions in purely domestic cases, such as the *Sentencia del Tribunal Supremo (Sala de lo Civil)*, 17 September 2007, RJ/2007/4968, on gender dysphoria and the changing of the individual name. Also, those quoted in sections 1.b and 1.c.

[49] See section II.

[50] There is no legal provision addressing the problem of a deficit in the proof of the applicable foreign law; the solution indicated in the text is the one preferred by scholars and courts.

[51] RTC 1982/3236. [52] JUR 2006/224732.

Finally, as already said, a proverbial deficit in the command of foreign languages contributes as well to the under-use of the tools provided by the comparative law method.[53]

Still, in spite of the foregoing, and even if it does not amount to deny the caveats above expressed on both the scarcity of the case law and the poorness of the reasoning, some case law has been identified of either direct or indirect evidence of comparative analysis in Spanish PIL court decisions. The examples will be presented under the next headings, following the traditional tripartite classification of PIL: jurisdiction; applicable law; recognition and enforcement of foreign judgments.

i. Jurisdiction

References to comparative law are scarce in Spanish case law in this area of PIL. As stated before, the interpretation of the European procedural law for cross-border litigation in civil and commercial cases appears as one of the most suitable areas for comparative reasoning. Suffice to remember that most of the provisions should be interpreted in an autonomous way, 'autonomous' meaning a combination of two ingredients: first, the objectives and scheme of the document to which they belong; secondly, to the general principles which stem from the corpus of the national legal systems. The latter element clearly calls for a comparative analysis:[54] however, the tendency of the Spanish tribunals has been to rely solely on the interpretive guidance given by the European Court of Justice (ECJ), neglecting (or so it seems, in the light of the lack of quotations) the information that the practice of other Member States could provide in this respect.[55]

As for Spanish common law, the rules establishing the grounds of international jurisdiction for the first time in this country entered into force in 1985 (*Ley Orgánica del Poder Judicial*).[56] The Act followed the Brussels Convention of 1968 as closely as possible. No forum of necessity existed in the Convention, and none was included in the Spanish *Ley Orgánica del Poder Judicial*. That is why the resource to this notion in order to assert the jurisdiction of a Spanish tribunal, and to the conditions that should be complied with for it to be applied, may be regarded as the outcome of (among other factors)[57] a comparative reasoning, even if no explicit reference to it is made in the judicial text. The decision of the *Audiencia Provincial de Murcia (Sección 1ª)*, 12 May 2003,[58] is one of the few cases where the idea of a forum of necessity is explicitly alluded

[53] Private knowledge is shown in separate opinions, such as that of I. Sancho Gargallo to the *Sentencia del Tribunal Supremo (Sala de lo Civil, Sección 1ª)*, 21 May 2012, RJ 2012/6537, where he interprets a Spanish insolvency rule in the light of its French predecessor and source of inspiration.

[54] In practice the relevance of the second element is clearly inferior; the ECJ has a distinct preference for the first one.

[55] The *Sentencia del Tribunal Supremo (Sala de lo Civil)*, 20 January 1978, CENDOJ: 28079110011978100286, could be considered as an example of a comparative analysis related to the comprehension of a conventional uniform rule to which reference is made—probably, the Convention providing for a Uniform Law for Bills of Exchange, although it is not absolutely clear—together with German Law, as supporting the understanding of some provisions of the Spanish Commercial Code.

[56] See n 44.

[57] The principal argument is always provided by Art. 24 Spanish Constitution, i.e., the right to a due process.

[58] AC 2003/1676.

to—without any mention of comparative law. The Spanish tribunal is considered competent to rule on parental responsibility over a common child in a situation where otherwise the Moroccan courts would have jurisdiction, but the claimant (the mother) could not litigate there for fear of the presumed consequences that such a move could have on her.

ii. Applicable law

Comparative reasoning plays a main role as regards the understanding of foreign institutions; also, for the assessment of the compatibility of the application of the foreign law with the public policy of the forum (see the first two sections that follow). Comparison is also needed to choose between several potentially applicable legal systems in the framework of a conflict of laws rule imposing a particular outcome, i.e., when the rule is not neutral but policy- or result-oriented (see the third section that follows).

The understanding of foreign institutions

The landscape of Spain has changed a lot in the last 40 years in as far as flux of population is concerned. Traditionally a country of emigration, Spain has become a country of reception of immigrants. A good number of them come from Islamic countries. Once in Spain, family litigation raised before the courts triggers the application of the foreign law appointed by the Spanish conflict of law rule. Study of foreign institutions is inextricably intertwined with their comparison with those known by the judges—first and foremost, with domestic law—to get a proper understanding of their meaning and function, which is essential to implement foreign law in the way required by the Spanish law: the national judge is duty bound to apply foreign law as a foreign judge would do.[59]

An example of the use of comparative reasoning to the purposes pointed out earlier is provided by the decision of the *Audencia Provincial de Barcelona (sección 12ª)*, 17 October 2009:[60] the applicable law being the Moroccan Family Code, the Spanish court examined the institution called 'Mut'a' and equated it with the Spanish 'pensión compensatoria'; it also calculated the amount to be paid monthly to the claimant and the duration of such payments, comparing the Moroccan system with the Spanish one (Código civil, but also the Catalonian *Codi de Familia*).

Compatibility with forum public policy

The foreign law designated by the conflict of laws rule must be discarded in case of incompatibility between its application (rather, the outcome of such application) and the public policy of the forum. The assessment of the compatibility/incompatibility is a

[59] Reference to this command is traditional in case law: see e.g. *Sentencia del Tribunal Supremo (Sala de lo Civil)*, 5 November 1971, CENDOJ: 28079110011971100272. That is also the reason why an isolated quotation of a foreign code or act is not considered to provide enough proof of it: evidence is also required as to the contents, the validity, and the understanding of the applicable provisions in their system of origin. See among many others the *Sentencia del Tribunal Supremo (Sala de lo Civil)*, 3 February 1975, CENDOJ: 28079110011975100082.

[60] JUR 2010/44285.

case for comparative reasoning, as shown, for instance, by the *Sentencia de la Audiencia Provincial de Madrid (Sección 22ª)*, 22 June 2001:[61] the contrast between the Moroccan and the Spanish legal systems would have permitted a decision on the basis of the former in a case of a matrimonial crisis; the claimant's *petitio* was for separation, which does not exist under Moroccan law; nonetheless the factual situation (consolidation of the matrimonial failure) would have allowed for another possibility (divorce) in application of that legal system. The comparative analysis led the Spanish court to conclude that the absence of legal separation does not make Moroccan law contrary to Spanish public policy, as the foreign system offers other options to face matrimonial crisis, which are similar to ours.

A third example of comparative analysis is provided by joint wills: in spite of their ban in the Spanish Civil Code, Art. 669, compatibility with the Spanish public policy of a German joint will granted on the basis of the BGB is affirmed in the *Sentencia del Tribunal Supremo (Sala de lo Civil, Sección primera)*, 8 October 2010,[62] after comparison with the systems of Aragón, Catalonia, and Navarra (i.e., other in-force Spanish legal orders), which admit it.

Result-oriented conflict of laws rules

Spanish PIL is familiar with the technique known as 'materially oriented conflict-of-laws'. Maintenance obligations and the formal validity of contracts and wills have been traditional cases, both in the conventional and in the common frame.[63] Case law demonstrates courts' awareness of the fact that such a method implicates, at least potentially, a comparison of the contents of the different legal systems at stake; however, we have been unable to find any specimen of such a comparison. With some effort, the *Sentencia de la Audiencia Territorial de Granada*, 22 April 1966, relating to a holographic will, may count as an exception.[64]

iii. Recognition and enforcement

Phenomena similar to those already described with regard to the application of foreign law occur in the context of the recognition of foreign judgments: what the foreign judge has decided must be understood by the requested Spanish authority, and therefore a comparative exercise is required (see following section). The public policy exception, which may intervene as an obstacle to the recognition or exequatur, also asks for comparison (below, subheading *Public policy*).

[61] AC 2001/1539. The same court had reached the same conclusion previously, under similar circumstances: *Sentencia de la Audiencia Provincial de Madrid (Sección 22ª)*, 21 February 2000, AC 2000/111.

[62] RJ 2010/8009.

[63] Solutions of the kind were already present in the Hague Convention of 2 October 1973 on the Law Applicable to Maintenance Obligations, as well as in Art. 9.7 Civil Code, for maintenance obligations. For the formal validity of contracts, see Art. 9 of the Convention of 19 June on the Law Applicable to Contractual Obligations provided for alternative connecting factors, as did Art. 11.1 Civil Code; for the formal validity of wills see Convention on the Conflicts of Laws Relating to the Form of Testamentary Dispositions (adopted on 5 October 1961) 510 UNTS 177.

[64] *Revista Profesional del Ilustre Colegio de Abogados de Granada*, 1966, 43–7.

Understanding the foreign decision

Spanish courts facing applications for the recognition of Moroccan 'kafala' decisions[65] usually get involved in reasoning comporting comparison, in a two-step process: first, the features of the foreign institution as it is in the original system are presented; secondly, a functionally analogous figure is sought within Spanish law.[66] The common conclusion being the absence of equivalence with our adoption, a 'kafala' is equated with the so-called 'acogimiento familiar': as stated by the *Auto de la Audiencia Provincial de Barcelona (Sección 18ª)*, 8 July 2008, 'Through the PIL legal technique of *functional characterization* it may be understood that such institution, unknown to Spanish law, develops abroad the function that in Spain is displayed by foster care'.[67] Many other *Autos* corroborate this pattern;[68] in some cases, however, after examining it and comparing it with domestic law, guardianship has been preferred as the domestic equivalent of 'kafala'.[69]

Public policy

The recognition of a foreign decision will be refused if such recognition is manifestly contrary to public policy in the Member State in which it is sought. To determine whether this is the case, a comparative analysis of the judgment is needed: not with a hypothetical domestic counterpart,[70] but with the principles and values integrating the public policy clause. Actually, comparison has become usual in this context, although case law reflects a variable degree of detail. For instance, regarding an American award of punitive damages, the Spanish *Tribunal Supremo*[71] accorded its recognition after asserting that the institution is oriented to the defence of interests 'which, within the framework of a market economy are not only of local relevance, but of general and universal appreciation in the States involved similar legal, social and economic conceptions'.[72] Recognition has been granted to foreign divorce decrees issued by Notaries after a deeper inquiry, related to the functions of the public authority according to the State of origin, and to its similarities to the role of the Spanish judges, vested with *imperium*. Cuba is the country of origin of most cases; decisions from Morocco and Egypt have provoked an analogous comparative reasoning.[73]

[65] The claim is usually for the recognition as an adoption, or as constituting an intermediary step in this direction. A comparative analysis has also been performed for other purposes, such as for determining who holds parental authority over the child: *Auto de la Audiencia Provincial de Cádiz (Sección 5ª)*, of 23 March 2012.

[66] The high number of similar cases has led to a comparative study by the *Dirección General de los Registros y el Notariado*, published as Resolución 2/2006, 21 March 2006, and Resolución Circular of 30 August 2006.

[67] JUR 2008/315373.

[68] *Audiencia Provincial de Tarragona (Sección 1ª)*, 23 June 2008, AC 2008/1710; *Auto de la Audiencia Provincial de Barcelona (Sección 18ª)*, 3 November 2011, JUR 2012/33503; *Auto de la Audiencia Provincial de Madrid (Sección 22ª)*, 2 December 2011, JUR 2012/22180.

[69] *Auto de la Audiencia Provincial de Barcelona (Sección 18ª)*, 28 March 2006, JUR 2008/149354; *Auto de la Audiencia Provincial de Cádiz (Sección 5ª)*, 11 December 2008, JUR 2009/59788.

[70] Reinmann, 'Comparative Law and Private International Law' (n 33), 1383.

[71] Which at the time was the only competent court for recognition requests according to the common PIL system.

[72] *Auto del Tribunal Supremo (ATS)*, 13 November 2001 (Exequatur No. 2039/1999).

[73] Among other Cuban decisions, see *Auto del Tribunal Supremo (Sala de lo Civil)*, 20 January 1998, RJ 1998/2667 (Cuba); *Auto del Tribunal Supremo (Sala de lo Civil)*, 7 July 1998, RJ 1998/6087; *Auto del*

Still in the domain of family law, recognition has been denied to divorce decrees which—according to the foreign (Moroccan) legal system—did not carry the final dissolution of the marriage, but just a provisional and revocable one;[74] to reach the outcome comparative arguments have been used by the Court. Conversely, recognition has been awarded to a so-called 'kohle' decision, also from Morocco, once the court established its similarity to Spanish divorce: both the wife and the husband are allowed to apply for it (therefore foreign law is not discriminatory); it is non-revocable.[75]

Comparative arguments have given support to dissenting opinions in particularly sensitive family matters, as is the case of surrogate motherhood. Invoking incompatibility with the public policy of the forum, the Spanish Supreme Court ruled against the appellants seeking to have their parenthood established as regards two children, born in California to a surrogate mother. In a separate dissenting opinion, one of the magistrates defended the contrary view, backed, among other arguments, on 'the trends shown in comparative law, which point to the regularization and relaxation of such situations'.[76]

Applications for recognition of arbitral awards have also led to references to comparative law in the framework of compatibility with the forum's *ordre public*. However, the way it's done is somehow different from what we have seen so far: comparative law is alluded to in order to explain in the abstract the diverse positions adopted in neighbouring legal systems regarding public policy in the framework of arbitration. The explanation is usually followed by a presentation of the two main Spanish doctrinal trends in the same field. To the extent that the predominant one coincides with the prevailing foreign tendency, the comparative arguments may be considered to come to reinforce the court's final decision: this is the case of the *Auto de la Audiencia Provincial de Barcelona (Sección 15ª)*, 24 May 2004.[77] It should be noted, however, that the converse situation—i.e., the comparison with foreign conceptions of public policy as applied to the recognition of arbitral awards in order to highlight the Spanish divergences—is more common: in this regard, see decisions such as the *Auto de la Audiencia Provincial (Sección 15ª)*, 28 May 2008; *Auto de la Audiencia Provincial de Barcelona (Sección 15ª)*, 4 May 2009; *Auto de la Audiencia Provincial de Barcelona (Sección 15ª)*, 15 January 2010.[78]

Tribunal Supremo (Sala de lo Civil), 23 February 1999, RJ 1999/1892; *Auto del Tribunal Supremo (Sala de lo Civil, Sección 1ª)*, 27 July 2004, JUR 2004/272915. On the recognition of a decision from Morocco, see *Auto del Tribunal Supremo (Sala de lo Civil)*, 8 June 1999, RJ 1999/4346; on the basis of an Egyptian decision: *Auto del Tribunal Supremo (Sala de lo Civil)*, 21 April 1998, RJ 1998/3563.

[74] *Auto del Tribunal Supremo (Sala de lo Civil)*, 23 July 1996, RJ 1998/2907. *The Auto del Tribunal Supremo (Sala de lo Civil)*, 21 April 1998, RJ 1998/3563, awarded recognition to a non-final Egyptian divorce because under the particular circumstances the outcome of doing so did not collide with the Spanish public policy. The same solution is to be found in the *Auto de Tribunal Supremo (Sala de lo Civil, Sección 1ª)*, 27 July 2004, JUR 2004/290634, regarding a divorce decision in application of Mauritanian law.

[75] *Auto del Tribunal Supremo (Sala de lo Civil)*, 27 January 1998, RJ 1998/2924.

[76] *Sentencia del Tribunal Supremo (Sala de lo Civil, Sección Pleno)*, 6 February 2013, RJ 2014/736; dissenting opinion of R. Sarazá Jimena.

[77] JUR 2005/36597.

[78] JUR 2008/266910; JUR 2009/412368; JUR 2010/149846, respectively.

IV. Conclusion

What can be concluded about the role of comparative law before the Spanish courts? The case law analysed allows us to assert that in the 20th century, after a long time of closure and inward-looking due to political reasons, our tribunals became perfectly aware of the possibilities opened by comparative law as bases for legal reasoning, both in purely domestic and in international settings. However, at the beginning of the 21st century resort to foreign elements and comparative tools is still not as common as it could, or even should, be. This seems particularly clear within the PIL domain: here, the tie to foreign legal systems is the unavoidable consequence of both the factual settings and of the legal mandate (the conflict-of-laws rules as well as the rules on jurisdiction and on recognition and exequatur); a priori, a place for comparative reasoning could be taken for granted. Yet the examples found via a thorough research in both private and public jurisprudence databases point towards a different outcome: little comparative work is done in order to apply the grounds of international jurisdiction—even those contained in European or conventional instruments, for which a uniform interpretation by the Member States/States parties to the convention is most desirable, if not compulsory. Application of the foreign law designated by the conflict-of-laws rules has certainly triggered comparison so as to get a better understanding of unknown institutions, to search for their equivalents within its own system, and/or (as the case may be) assess their compatibility with public policy. However, it has mainly focused on one field (family law), and mostly in relation to specific (Islamic) legal systems. In the area of recognition and exequatur, the comparative law ingredient appears more often, helping in a similar way: it comes into play to provide a better comprehension of the foreign legal product, and also to determine its contrariety or its consistency with the *ordre public* clause.

Outside the PIL domain, there are two remarkable features of the use of comparative law methodology: first, a clear preference of the courts for non-compulsory instruments born out of comparative legal research, such as the PETL, PECL, or the DCFR; second, a link between resorting to comparison and the reporting judge of the decision holding an academic background. Keeping in mind that the Spanish Civil Code limits the role of the jurisprudence, these *soft law* instruments and other references to foreign laws are used in a purely ornamental way, in the sense that by no means do they amount to the application of foreign law in Spain; but they are also a means of interpreting Spanish private law rules (mainly 19th century Civil Code provisions, still in force).

All in all, we can conclude that in Spain comparative law is no longer rooted in academic research and in legislative drafting, but that it has still a way to go to develop all its potential. It is here submitted that further education of judges, aiming to open up their minds to see beyond territorial and juridical borders, as well as to strengthen (sometimes, to create *ab initio*) their command of foreign languages, is a must in this regard.

30

Comparative Legal Reasoning and the Courts

A View from the Americas

*H. Patrick Glenn**

I. Introduction

It has been axiomatic in western legal theory in the last two centuries that comparative law has little or no place before the courts and is not a source of law. This view is now being challenged as judges and courts engage in an increasingly vigorous conversation across borders and as state-centric views of the sources of law gradually decline. The view that excludes comparative reasoning from the functioning of courts was closely associated with legal positivism and the concept of a self-sufficient national legal system. Comparative law did, however, play a fundamental role in the construction of national legal systems from, say, the 16th century. There was in Europe, from that point, a massive process of mining of Roman, customary, canonical, and other sources of law, in both civil and common law traditions, for purposes of construction of national law.[1] Codification and the emergence of the notion of stare decisis marked the end of this process, since they both signalled a turning away from residual or supplementary sources of law and an exclusivist concentration on current sources of state law. There was variation in this process from jurisdiction to jurisdiction. In some continental jurisdictions, however, such as Prussia, Spain, Switzerland, and Italy, citation of non-state sources of law was even prohibited by formal enactment.[2]

Comparative law thus achieved some initial prominence as a resource for the construction of state law. This process of construction being seen as largely completed in Europe in the 19th century, comparative law then assumed a further or auxiliary role, once again in support of state law. It could thus provide advice in the ongoing process of improvement of local sources, acting as a kind of scientific filter for foreign experience, absorbing and translating it for whatever purpose judged acceptable by

* The editors sadly record the author's passing away in 2014 before the publication of the second edition. Peter M. Laing Professor of Law, McGill University.

[1] See generally H. P. Glenn, 'The Nationalist Heritage' in P. Legrand and R. Munday, *Comparative Legal Studies [:] Traditions and Transitions* (Cambridge: Cambridge University Press, 2003) 76; W. Wijffels, 'Arthur Duck et le *ius commune* européen', Rev. d'histoire des Facultés de droit 1990.193 (notably for the influence of English civilians on English law); and for French law, J.-L. Thireau, 'Le comparatisme et la naissance du droit français', Rev. d'histoire des Facultés de droit 1990.153.

[2] See H. P. Glenn, *On Commons Laws* (Oxford: Oxford University Press, 2007) 46, note 8, with references. Professor Zimmermann has concluded that Prussian prohibitions were 'doomed to failure,' as were 'all… attempts to enact statutes prohibiting to comment upon, interpret and develop the law.' R. Zimmermann, '*Statuta sunt stricte interpretanda?* Statutes and the Common Law: A Continental Perspective' (1997) 56 Camb. L.J. 315 at 326. On the long tradition, however, of the *Zitiergesetz*, now re-emerging in some U.S. states through laws or popular referenda, G. Teipel, 'Zitiergesetze in der romanistischen Tradition' (1955) 72 ZRG RA 245. On U. S. developments see n 33.

local law-making institutions. As well, state legal systems having developed in multiple form, comparative law could undertake the scientific function of taxonomic ordering of these state forms of law, conferring further legitimacy by categorizing them in accordance with various mega-criteria for legal identification.[3] State sources of law being presumed complete, however, there could be no use in principle of comparative law before the courts, since this would directly challenge the presumption of exclusivity of state sources. Comparative law used in this way can be seen as filling a subversive function.[4] Further, there could be no resort to transnational or general principles of law, demonstrated though comparative reasoning, for trans-border cases, and the assignation of such cases to one or another national legal system became the basic premise of private international law.[5] This general theory was remarkably successful in Europe and comparative legal reasoning in large measure disappeared from the courts, retaining some minor visibility only in the common law tradition where English courts would, on occasion, refer to extra-territorial common law authority. In both the civil and common law worlds of Europe, however, comparative legal reasoning was not a direct source of law. It could be only a source of law-making, channelled through local institutions.

Twentieth-century legal positivism very much reinforced this marginal role for comparative legal reasoning, in teaching that legal systems existed as matters of fact. Hart described his work both as analytical and as 'descriptive' of existing municipal legal systems.[6] For him, a legal system would exist once two minimal conditions were met, those of general public obedience and, as well, acceptance by the officials of the system of its rules of recognition and change.[7] Since legal systems simply existed, occupying a given space, it followed that they were incompatible with other legal systems, in that same space. Hart spoke of each of them having 'a certain kind of *supremacy* within its territory and *independence* of other systems'.[8] Joseph Raz explained that '[a]ll legal systems . . . are potentially incompatible at least to a certain extent. Since all legal systems claim to be supreme with respect to their subject-community, none can acknowledge any claims to supremacy over the same community which may be made by another legal system.'[9] There would thus be an inherent presumption that a system should not be in the business of giving effect to laws other than its own. It would be, in principle, 'undesirable and an unstable situation' for a community to practise two legal systems.[10] Moreover, since legal systems simply exist, with no necessary normative justifications, they in principle can tell us nothing as

[3] On this taxonomic function of comparative law the fullest justification is the three-volume treatise of L. Constantinesco, *Traité de droit comparé* (Paris: L.G.D.J., 1972–83).

[4] H. Muir Watt, 'La fonction subversive du droit comparé', Rev. int. dr. comp. 2000. 503; G. Fletcher, 'Comparative Law as a Subversive Discipline' (1988) 46 Am. J. Comp. L. 683.

[5] For the presumption of completeness of state law as the philosophical foundation of private international law, see H. Batiffol, *Aspects philosophiques du droit international privé* (Paris: Dalloz, 1956) at 16, 24.

[6] H. L. A. Hart, *The Concept of Law*, 3rd ed. (Oxford: Oxford University Press, 2012) at vi.

[7] Hart, n 6, at 116.

[8] Hart, n 6, at 24.

[9] J. Raz, *The Authority of Law [:] Essays on Law and Morality*, 2nd ed. (Oxford: Oxford University Press, 2009) at 119.

[10] Raz, n 9, at 118.

to when they should yield to, or adopt as a result of comparative reasoning, rules drawn from another legal order or tradition. Legal systems are large, and silent, seen from without.

Today there are major doubts, however, both as to the existence and as to the completeness of legal systems. In some areas of the world, states and their legal systems are said to have 'failed', and there is doubt as to what might replace them.[11] Even where states appear well established, the range of contemporary problems is such that existing legal systems appear inevitably inadequate. The contemporary inadequacy of national legal systems has led Professor Bucher, of Switzerland, to conclude that tradition must be recognized as a source of law, and that external sources of law are an inherent element of tradition.[12] In France the Court of Cassation is increasingly relying on 'general principles of law' as justification for its decisions, and less on posited, national texts.[13] A number of books, including this one and its predecessor, as well as a small mountain of periodical literature, have developed on the topic.[14] These legal developments are complemented by those in contemporary philosophy, where it is said that the distinction between fact and value, upon which legal systems are based, has now collapsed.[15]

There is therefore renewed interest in legal theory in the use of comparative law before the courts. To be more precise, there is renewed interest in comparative legal reasoning before the courts, since comparative law, in its static, taxonomic dimension, is not that which is now being urged. It is rather a more dynamic process of comparative legal reasoning which has become relevant, in which local law and foreign models are assessed against one another, for purposes of application in a given case. From the perspective of European legal theory, this may be seen as a recent development, the return of pre-19th-century judicial practice, but it is also the case, as the experience of the Americas shows in general, that it represents a process which has never disappeared from legal practice before the courts. The practice has not been well represented by Western legal theory, which has devoted its attention almost exclusively to the construction of state law over the last four centuries, but its theoretical interest is now becoming evident, once again. New forms of transnational law and 'transgovernmentalism'

[11] See N. Lante Wallace-Bruce, 'Of Collapsed, Dysfunctional and Disoriented States: Challenges to International Law' (2000) 47 Neth. Int. L. Rev. 3; also for 'quasi'-states, R. Jackson, *Quasi-States: Sovereignty, International Relations and the Third World* (Cambridge: Cambridge University Press, 1990), notably at 20–1 (as 'juridical statehood', lacking institutional strength or effective hierarchy); C. Morris, *An Essay on the Modern State* (Cambridge: Cambridge University Press, 1998) at 52 (states in name only though recognized by international order of states); S. Kaplan, *Fixing Fragile States[:] A New Paradigm for Development* (Westport: Praeger, 2008) at 6 (for LICUS, low-income countries under stress). For tables of 'state fragility', M. Marshall and B. Cole, *Global Report 2009: Conflict, Governance and State Fragility* (Severn: Center for Systemic Peace), accessible at <http://www.humansecuritygateway.com>, at 25ff. (Sudan, Somalia of highest fragility, quantified at 25, 23 respectively; only some 21 states, some 10% of those in the world, have 0 fragility).

[12] E. Bucher, 'Rechtsüberlieferung und heutiges Recht', ZeuP 2000.394.

[13] J.-P. Gridel, 'La Cour de cassation française et les principes généraux du droit privé', D. 2002.I.228.

[14] See also U. Drobnig and S. van Erp (eds.), *The Use of Comparative Law by Courts* (The Hague: Kluwer Law International, 1999). Professor Alford has counted some 3000 law review articles on the subject in the U.S.; R. Alford, 'Lower Courts and Constitutional Comparativism' (2008) 77 Fordham Law Review 647.

[15] *Voir* H. Putnam, *The Collapse of the Fact/Value Dichotomy* (Cambridge, MA: Harvard University Press, 2002).

are now emerging and comparative legal reasoning is an essential element in these processes.[16]

The Americas are, however, a large and legally diverse geographic area. They have never been the object of a single ius commune or common law, and they are not now, and are unlikely ever to be, the object of overarching political or judicial authorities such as those which exist in the European Union. Neither NAFTA nor MERCOSUR presently entail such institutions, and any Free Trade Agreement of the Americas, should one ever come into existence, is unlikely to bring about their creation. Nor do the free trade areas of the Americas imply any formal programme of harmonization of law, such that there remains ample occasion for genuinely comparative reflection on the basis of ongoing national diversity. The Americas are different, moreover, from Europe, in that they represent a much larger number of private law jurisdictions, but much less linguistic diversity. In NAFTA alone there are some 99 private law jurisdictions and this number would increase to approximately 130 in any free trade area of the Americas. Cross-border communication is facilitated, however, by the existence of only four major official legal languages (English, French, Spanish, and Portuguese) of trans-border or transnational dimensions.

It is possible to identify a variety of attitudes to comparative legal reasoning in the Americas, notably those which prevail with respect to aboriginal or chthonic peoples, and also those which prevail amongst the European legal traditions received in the Americas. Further attention should be given, moreover, to the methods of comparative legal reasoning in the context of American free trade areas.

II. Comparative legal reasoning and aboriginal or chthonic law

A number of European legal traditions have been received in the Americas, but it is constant throughout all American territories that adjustment to those traditions has been necessary in light of the existence of pre-existing aboriginal or chthonic law. The existence of the law of the first peoples of America is widely recognized in national constitutions and national legislation, and has become the object of major litigation in many jurisdictions. In Latin America there has been a major, and recent, movement towards entrenchment of indigenous law and legal institutions in the most recent constitutions.[17] There have also been major recent Latin American efforts of theoretical conceptualization of indigenous law.[18] This formal anchoring of non-written indigenous law in basic texts of state law effectively removes objection to its proof and application before state tribunals, and there must be corresponding adjustment to second order state rules of sources and proof of law. In the United States of America

[16] H. P. Glenn, 'A Transnational Concept of Law' in P. Cane and M. Tushnet, *Oxford Handbook of Legal Studies* (Oxford: Oxford University Press, 2003) 839; A.-M. Slaughter, 'Judicial Globalization' (2000) 40 Virginia J. Int'l. L. 1103.

[17] See generally W. Assies, G. Van der Haar, and A. Hoekema, *The Challenge of Diversity [:] Indigenous peoples and reform of the State in Latin America* (Amsterdam: Thela Thesis, 2000).

[18] For example, C. Durand Alcántara, M. Sámano Rentería, and G. Gómez González, *Hacia una fundamentación teórica de la costumbre jurídica india* (Chapingo: Plaza y Valdés, 2000); and for historical dimensions of Maya, Aztec law, O. Cruz Barney, *Historia del derecho en México* (Mexico: Oxford University Press, 1999) 3 ff.

the fundamental concept is that of 'tribal sovereignty', indicating a fundamental, irreducible core of application of tribal law, though there is ongoing and vigorous debate over the interpretation given to this concept, notably by the United States Supreme Court.[19] In Canada, article 25 of the *Canadian Charter of Rights and Liberties* provides that the guarantees of the *Charter* do not abrogate or derogate from 'aboriginal, treaty or other rights and freedoms' pertaining to aboriginal populations. From the 19th century, in both the U.S.A. and Canada, there has been ongoing litigation on the extent of aboriginal land claims, rooted in aboriginal law, and major decisions of the Supreme Courts of both countries have addressed the issue.

In dealing with all types of claim rooted in aboriginal law, state courts must be open to effective means of its proof, usually in oral form, by community members or by anthropological experts, and must come to terms with law radically different from state law. This is most evident in land claims, where a notion of a communal usufructary interest is said to underlie aboriginal title, but it is also the case in other areas of law. Adoption, for example, is highly informal in Inuit communities in the Canadian Arctic, but has been accepted by state courts as appropriate for the needs of children in a severe climate. The reasoning in all of these types of cases is comparative, since the institutions of a *lex non scripta* must first be understood, by lawyers and judges not initially familiar with them, and then it must be decided whether the institutions are recognizable by state courts. The extent of divergence from state law is relevant to this enquiry, as is the suitability of the particular institution for the circumstances in which it is invoked. It is also comparative *legal* reasoning, since the view that such unwritten law is not law, or that it is too imprecise for cognizance to be taken of it by a state court, or that it is incommensurable with state law, has now been effectively repudiated throughout the Americas.

III. Comparative legal reasoning and European legal traditions

It is possible to identify a number of zones of law in the Americas, according to the European legal traditions which have been received. Latin America has thus been characterized by a large process of reception of Spanish law, adjusted to local circumstance (*il derecho indiano*). The common law of England has been received into a number of Caribbean Commonwealth jurisdictions as well as into the Canadian common law provinces. French civil law has been received in diverse measure in Quebec and Louisiana. The U.S.A. has undergone a complex process of reception first of English common law and then a later, 19th-century process of adoption of major institutions of continental civil law.[20] There are different forms and levels of comparative legal reasoning in each of these zones of law, according to the traditions received. More generally, however, it is the case that all manifestations of European-

[19] See, for example, *Nevada v Hicks*, 533 U.S. 3553 (2001) (tribal jurisdiction over non-members); *Arizona Department of Revenue v Blaze Construction Co.*, 526 U.S. 32 (1999) (state jurisdiction over tribes); D. Getches, 'Conquering the Cultural Frontier: The New Subjectivism of the Supreme Court in Indian Law' (1996) 84 Cal. L. Rev. 1573.

[20] See A. von Mehren, *The U.S. Legal System: Between the Common Law and Civil Law Legal Traditions* (Rome: Centro di studi e ricerche di diritto comparato straniero, 2000).

derived law in the Americas result from a process of trans-border transferral of law, originally in the circumstances of colonialism. Thus, while today almost all American jurisdictions are politically independent, and have been so in some cases for hundreds of years, law has not been thought of in exclusively national terms for much of the history of the countries or jurisdictions concerned. American judicial practice has had as its primary historical concern the adjustment of European legal models, or common laws, to American circumstances. The process is one of comparative legal reasoning. Exclusivist concepts of state law have thus had less influence in the Americas than in Europe and Western, state-centric legal theory is only partially relevant to legal and judicial practice. There are particular and different manifestations of this general phenomenon.

In Latin America it is the Spanish variant of the civilian, continental tradition which has been received, largely in the form of the *Siete Partidas* but also subsequently in the form of the *derecho indiano*. Since much of this law was in the form of classic texts, in the case of the *Siete Partidas* going back to the 13th century, doctrinal exposition of it was fundamental to its ongoing adaptation and application. Comparative legal reasoning thus took place and takes place today within the cadre of this particular, ongoing, hispanic ius commune, and according to its traditional sources. The style of judgment in Latin America is generally discursive, and Latin American judges thus cite non-legislative sources of law, including Roman law and European legal authors. This may not be a frequent practice but it certainly does occur and there has historically been little objection to it, as a form of comparative legal reasoning.[21] It is also the case that opinions of local legal authors may be presented to the court, as expert opinions, and these may involve extensive citing of foreign material, usually in doctrinal form.[22] In matters of public or constitutional law, U.S. law may also be cited, given the importance of the U.S. model in the development of Latin American constitutional law. There appears to have been no instance in Latin America of formal prohibition of citing of foreign authors, as occurred in Spain, and the ongoing use of extra-territorial sources of comparative legal reasoning prevailed even over strongly territorialist legal and political attitudes which largely precluded application of foreign law in private international cases (the Calvo clause and doctrine). Some form of closure certainly did occur and in Mexico, for example, between 1995 and 2010, citation to foreign cases was apparently reduced to between 0.5 and 3 per cent of total judicial review public law cases, the latter figure being those of minority judgments.[23] Often, however, the Mexican Supreme Court was obviously following foreign models without expressly acknowledging it and

[21] See, for Mexican examples, W. L. Butte, 'Stare decisis, Doctrine, and Jurisprudence in Mexico and Elsewhere' in J. Dainow (ed.), *The Role of Judicial Decisions and Doctrine in Civil Law and in Mixed Jurisdictions* (Baton Rouge: Louisiana State University Press, 1974) 311.

[22] See, for example, the opinion of Professor da Silva Pereira, citing Roman law, Troplong, Savatier, Josserand (France), Ruggiero and Marci (Italy), Rossel and Mentra (Switzerland), in K. Karst and K. S. Rosenn, *Law and Development in Latin America* (Berkeley: University of California Press, 1975) at 7.

[23] E. F. MacGregor and R. S. Gil, 'Mexico: Struggling for an Open View in Constitutional Adjudication' in T. Groppi and M.-C. Ponthoreau, *The Use of Foreign Precedents by Constitutional Judges* (Oxford: Hart, 2013) 301, at 308–9.

today it is said that there is 'an increasing comparative influence in our legal theory and adjudication'.[24]

In the Commonwealth jurisdictions of the Americas the common law has never been seen as a purely national product. Reception statutes typically set a date of reception for English law during colonial times, but the entire process of reception depended on local judicial appreciation of whether metropolitan legislation and case law were 'suitable' for circumstances overseas.[25] The process was widespread and involved a constant comparative evaluation of potentially receivable law. Results varied widely through the Commonwealth. Moreover, case law subsequent to the stipulated date of reception was considered capable of ongoing reception, as persuasive authority, since the common law was not seen as a positive, systemic construction, but rather as a form of ongoing judicial dialogue on what the law should be. The judges acted, and continue to act, according to what has recently been described as the 'philosophy of the common law'.[26] The judicial dialogue could obviously take place across the borders of political authority, in whatever form it took. In this environment notions of national stare decisis, when they emerged in the 19th century, could obtain only a tenuous place. Given the contemporary decline of stare decisis, under the avalanche of decisions, the search for legal principle across borders is now once again well under way, in fields as diverse as human rights, intellectual property, and commercial law. Studies of citation patterns in Canada show widespread use of extra-jurisdictional case law, drawn largely from the Commonwealth and the U.S., but extending also on occasion to civil law jurisdictions.[27] Judges also participate in transnational judicial meetings and now exchange legal information through electronic means of communication. They are coming to be recognized as a transnational 'epistemic community'.[28]

In the North American civil law outposts of Quebec and Louisiana there is further diversity in the method and extent of comparative legal reasoning. In both jurisdictions the methods of the common law have been adopted in matters of court structures and jurisdiction (notably in matters of administrative law), procedure, and styles of judgment. Judgments are therefore discursive, as everywhere in the Americas, and judges are able to record the comparative legal reasoning which they engage in. There is perhaps more of this in public law than in private law, since the surrounding jurisdictions share the same public law tradition. In private law matters, where the law is civilian in origin, there are two recognizable directions to the comparison. The first is towards the original metropolitan jurisdictions, France in the case of Quebec, and

[24] MacGregor and Gil, n 23, at 311 ('Copying a well-known Spanish precedent but without saying it was doing so', introducing balancing test), 312 ('clearly inspired' by American constitutional doctrine), and 320 (for 'increasing comparative influence').

[25] See generally H. P. Glenn, 'Persuasive Authority' (1987) 32 McGill L.J. 261 at 271–3.

[26] G. Posterma, 'Philosophy of the Common Law' in J. Coleman and S. Shapiro (eds.), *The Oxford Handbook of Jurisprudence and Philosophy of Law* (Oxford: Oxford University Press, 2002) 588.

[27] See H. P. Glenn, 'The Common Law in Canada' (1995) 74 Can. Bar Rev. 261, at 286–8, with references; and, more recently, C. Gentili, 'Canada: Protecting Rights in a "Worldwide Rights Culture". An Empirical Study of the Use of Foreign Precedents by the Supreme Court of Canada (1982–2010)' in T. Groppi and M.-C. Ponthoreau, *The Use of Foreign Precedents by Constitutional Judges* (Oxford: Hart, 2013) 39, reporting at 40 Supreme Court Canada 'has consistently considered other jurisdictions', and at 53 with rates of 19% to 51% of all cases containing foreign references.

[28] A.-M. Slaughter, 'A Typology of Transjudicial Communication' (1994) 29 U. Richmond L. Rev. 99.

France and Spain in the case of Louisiana. It is the legal writing of the European countries which is now looked to as a source of possible inspiration and the ongoing linguistic commonality between France and Quebec has greatly facilitated this process.[29] It is sometimes said to be less vigorous in Louisiana.[30] The other direction of comparison is towards the common law jurisdictions of North America and this has occurred with varying degrees of tension. There have been varying forms of reification of the civil and common laws, and calls for their ongoing integrity and resistance to influence, but the judicial practice of comparison has been issue-specific and resistant to large-scale generalization.

The U.S.A. went through a period of intense comparative legal reasoning in the 19th century, the process very much paralleling the mining of Roman and other sources which preceded national legal closures in Europe.[31] The process was one of constructive borrowing or comparison, for purposes of national law making. Much civil law thinking was thereby incorporated into U.S. law, notably through the great treatises of Story and Kent. As in Europe, the process of comparative legal reasoning declined thereafter, though it has never disappeared entirely. Studies of case citation patterns show a steady decline of citation of out-of-state and foreign cases from the later decades of the 19th century through the 20th century.[32] By 1970 the California Supreme Court was citing to other state courts and foreign courts in only 10 per cent of its citations.[33] The notion of Anglo-American law was still alive, though not in the best of health. More recently, however, a U.S. commentator has concluded that there is 'increasing use of foreign law' in U.S. courts, at least in connection with trans-border cases, that there is ongoing use of Spanish law in matrimonial property and water rights cases in a number of southern states, and that 'episodic' comparison occurs in judicial practice elsewhere.[34] Perhaps more significantly, there is now a major debate within the U.S. judiciary and law reviews as to the need and appropriateness of acknowledging and using foreign sources of law.[35] The debate has also attracted popular and political attention.[36] The United States Supreme Court has been divided on the issue, though a

[29] P.-G. Jobin, 'Les réactions de la doctrine à la création du droit civil québécois par les juges: le début d'une affaire de famille' (1980) 21 C. de D. 257; H. P. Glenn, 'La Cour suprême du Canada et la tradition du droit civil' (2001) 80 Can. Bar Rev. 151.

[30] T. Yiannopoulos, 'Louisiana Civil Law: A Lost Cause?' (1980) Tul. L. Rev. 830, but see at 845, 846 ('solutions reached in civil law jurisdictions, especially France, are always pertinent and frequently persuasive').

[31] See text accompanying n 1.

[32] L. M. Friedmann, et al, 'State Supreme Courts: A Century of Style and Citation' (1981) 33 Stan. L. Rev. 773.

[33] J. H. Merryman, 'Toward a Theory of Citations: An Empirical Study of the Citation Pattern of the California Supreme Court in 1950, 1960, and 1970' (1977) 50 Cal. L. Rev. 381, notably at 394–400.

[34] D. Clark, 'The Use of Comparative Law by American Courts I' (1994) 42 Am. J. Comp. L. (Supp.) 23, at 23, 24, 40; see also A. Levasseur, 'The Use of Comparative Law by American Courts II' (1994) 42 Am. J. Comp. L. (Supp.) 41 (on what would be a decline in influence in the U.S. of continental law).

[35] For the law review literature, see Alford, n 14.

[36] For recent U.S. appreciations of legislative resolutions and laws, popular referenda on the subject, see R. Ginsburg, '"A Decent Respect to the Opinions of [Human]kind": The Value of a Comparative Perspective in Constitutional Adjudication' (2005) 64 Camb. L. J. 575, at 582 (concern that legislative resolutions on foreign citations 'fuel the irrational fringe'); S. Symeonides, 'Choice of Law in the American Courts in 2010' (2011) 59 Am. J. Comp. L. 303, at 320 ('xenophobic hysteria'). Popular referenda

majority judgment has recently cited European authority.[37] There have also been calls by state judges for increased use of enlightening foreign material.[38] As elsewhere, this process appears driven by the intractable nature of many problems now appearing before the courts and increasing communication, at a transnational level, amongst judges.

Comparative legal reasoning has also appeared in judicial practice in the Americas with respect to immigrant and minority populations, since personal laws are often invoked by members of such populations as justification for conduct before the courts. Here the question is whether implanted European legal traditions will cede in some measure before non-European ones. The answer is that they will, in some measure, though the practice falls short of recognition of personal laws. The comparative legal reasoning which takes place in such cases is designated as the process of 'reasonable accommodation' of personal law or so-called cultural practices,[39] or the recognition, in criminal matters, of a so-called 'cultural defence', usually limited to questions of sanction rather than guilt.[40]

IV. Comparative legal reasoning in the context of free trade

Free trade areas are now multiplying throughout the Americas and there remains a (slim) possibility of a single, large, free trade area. Comparative legal reasoning plays an important role in free trade areas, for a number of reasons. First, it is unlikely that the free trade area would have come into being without a great deal of comparative legal reasoning already having been undertaken, in the intensifying legal relations which precede the formal conclusion of the free trade agreement. In this sense, the emergence of a free trade area can be seen as the culmination of a process as much as the beginning of a process.[41] Second, the coming into force of a free trade agreement has a major effect on the volume of trans-border transactions and trans-border litigation. This inevitably intensifies cross-border legal relations and it is possible to identify a major process of unilateral adjustment of national law to accommodate the new circumstances of the free trade area. Free trade has a kind of informal slip-stream effect on

prohibiting application of particular laws, such as the shari'a, will, however, be contrary to the equal treatment guaranteed by the First Amendment; *Award v Ziriax*, 670 F. 3d 1111 (10th Cir. 2012).

37 *Laurence v Texas*, 539 U.S. 558 (2003), the dissenting judgment of Scalia J. referring to the citations as 'meaningless' and 'dangerous' dicta. Compare the earlier remarks of Breyer J. in *Printz v United States*, 521 U.S. 898 (1997) at 970–1, with those of Scalia J. at 935.

38 See S. S. Abrahamson and M. J. Fischer, 'All the World's a Courtroom: Judging in the New Millenium' (1997) 26 Hofstra L. Rev. 273.

39 J. Woehrling, 'L'obligation d'accommodement raisonnable et l'adaptation de la société à la diversité religieuse' (1998) 43 McGill L. J. 325, with references.

40 See A. Dundes Renteln, *The Cultural Defense* (New York: Oxford University Press, 2004).

41 On pre-NAFTA processes of convergence in North America, see V. Loungnarath, 'L'intégration juridique dans la zone ALENA: Un chantier axé sur les processus' (2001) 61 R. du Barreau 1 at 15; and on the phenomenon generally, D. Trubek, Y. Dezalay, R. Buchanan, and J. Davis, 'Global Restructuring and the Law: Studies of the Internationalization of Legal Fields and the Creation of Transnational Arenas' (1994) 44 Case W. Res. L. Rev. 407 at 466. To say that convergence facilitates the creation of free trade areas is not to say, however, that it is irreversible, or that it eliminates major elements of diversity. See the following discussion in the text.

national law and national legal institutions. Adjustment to national law takes place as a result of comparative evaluation of national law against other laws in the free trade area and the needs of participants in the free trade.[42] The comparative law which is here identifiable may be seen in some measure, however, as comparative law of the constructive type, a means of informing and facilitating the reform of national law by national institutions. In the practice of free trade, however, there is a much more active process of comparative legal reasoning, which occurs in legal practice generally, as well as before the courts.

In the North American free trade context there are two features of the process of comparative legal reasoning which are worthy of mention. The first is the development of trans-border law firms, which now exist in trans-state or trans-provincial form in all of the NAFTA countries and which have now developed across national borders. The trans-border law firm generates a more intense and sophisticated form of comparative legal reasoning than has been previously known. It straddles political boundaries, may survey and choose amongst jurisdictional laws according to criteria and expertise from within its own structures, and may function in any number of jurisdictions with its own, locally qualified resources. The situation is very different from the historical one in which single practitioners would have contact with foreign law only through the medium of rules of private international law and formal opinions from foreign colleagues or academic institutions. Trans-border law firms thrive in large measure on their ability to engage in comparative legal reasoning, and it has been said that in matters of contemporary transnational commercial law it is 'practising lawyers who are making the running.'[43] Where a case is litigated is thus much more the result of comparative legal reasoning than has historically been the case.

The second feature of relevant practice before the courts in the Americas is the absence of any rule, or the absence of any enforced rule, to the effect that rules of private international law are applicable in a mandatory way (*d'office, von Amts wegen*) by the judge. The contrary rule, that judges are obliged to apply conflicts rules to any trans-border case and eventually to apply the designated law, exists in a number of European countries. It is the result of an apparently laudable attempt to offset the local bias of exclusivist national legal theory by ensuring that foreign states are treated on an equal footing with the state of the litigation. It is a highly unsuitable rule for a free trade area, however, since it creates a presumption that differences in national laws must be treated as conflicts of laws (in spite of results which may frequently be similar) and subjects all trans-border litigation to an expensive and time-consuming second-order process of court-directed choice of law. It may now happily be avoided in some

[42] See, for this process in the context of NAFTA, H. P. Glenn, 'Conflicting Laws in a Common Market? The NAFTA Experiment' (2001) 76 Chicago-Kent Law Review 1789–1819; H. P. Glenn, 'North America as a Medieval Legal Construction' (2002) Global Jurist, vol. 2, Issue 1, Article 1 <http://www.bepress.com> and in M. Bussani and U. Mattei (eds.), *The Common Core of European Private Law* (The Hague: Kluwer Law International, 2003) 49.

[43] R. Goode, 'International Restatements and National Law' in W. Swadling and G. Jones (eds.), *The Search for Principle [:] Essays in Honour of Lord Goff of Chieveley* (Oxford: Oxford University Press) 45 at 57.

jurisdictions by the notion of the 'equivalence' of laws.[44] The absence of such a rule in the Americas means that parties are able to bury formal differences of laws and litigate according to the *lex fori* if they agree that it is appropriate to do so. The presumption is one of harmony rather than of conflict, though the presumption may be reversed by either party pleading foreign law if they feel it is necessary to their case. The result is productive of comparative legal reasoning, since appreciation of foreign law cannot be left to the court and an eventual opinion by an institute specializing in foreign law, but must rather be the object of immediate appreciation and evaluation by litigants and their counsel. This active process of comparative legal reasoning, combined with a presumption of harmony of laws, means that there is no movement towards formal harmonization of laws in the Americas.[45] Given generalized knowledge of different laws, legal and judicial practice is perfectly capable of facilitating the functioning of a free trade area through a process of conciliation of laws. Comparative legal reasoning is fundamental to this process.

V. Conclusion

A great deal has been written recently to favour or to oppose the citation of foreign legal sources. There are many reasons which support either position, particularly since high courts are often engaged in many countries in deciding on the compatibility of particular laws with guarantees of fundamental rights. Citation of foreign sources may therefore be seen as fundamentally important to democratic forces and questions of national identity. There is a fundamental question, however, of whether citation of foreign sources can be examined as a particular topic or whether it must be situated within the larger context of judicial opinion writing and the constraints on that process in a particular, national setting. The French Court of Cassation, for example, never cites anything other than national legislation in its decisions, though it engages in intense comparative research before arriving at its conclusions.[46] It is therefore a court which is very open to foreign authority, though such authority is never cited in its actual decisions.

In some measure, therefore, concern with the citation of foreign decisions is a concern of those jurisdictions with a tradition of discursive, judicial opinion writing, and these are in the main common law jurisdictions. Civilian judges and jurisdictions may be cosmopolitan in other ways than citation practice. This conclusion is supported in part by a recent study of citation practices in public law across a wide range or jurisdictions, which concluded that '[t]here is an almost perfect correlation' between

[44] For the decisional law in France, for example, S. Godechot-Patris, 'Retour sur la notion d'équivalence au service de la coordination des systèmes' Rev. crit. d.i.p. 2010.271.

[45] See H. P. Glenn, 'Harmony of Laws in the Americas' (2003) 34 Inter-American Law Rev. 223.

[46] G. Canivet,'Use of Comparative Law Before French Private Law Courts' in G. Canivet, M. Andenas, and D. Fairgrieve (eds.), *Comparative Law Before the Courts* (London: British Institute of International and Comparative Law, 2004), notably at 193 ('deference... to the self-sufficiency of national law is now obsolete').

courts citing foreign materials and the legal traditions that the courts belong to.[47] Common law jurisdictions will cite foreign materials; civil law jurisdiction will generally not, and the force of the tradition 'seems to prevail over the special structural features of constitutional adjudication'.[48] Jurisdictions of the Americas would not deviate from this pattern, though the opposition to citation in the U.S.A. is an indication that it is not remaining entirely true to its origins as a common law jurisdiction but is being influenced by the wave of civilian method and substance which it experienced in the 19th century, which taught above all that law should be conceived as a national phenomenon. Legal traditions therefore matter, but citation practices are not necessarily an accurate guide to the cosmopolitan character of a court.

[47] T. Groppi and M.-C. Ponthoreau, 'Conclusion. The Use of Foreign Precedents by Constitutional Judges: A Limited Practice, An Uncertain Future' in T. Groppi and M.-C. Ponthoreau, *The Use of Foreign Precedents by Constitutional Judges* (Oxford: Hart, 2013) 411, at 412.

[48] Groppi and Ponthoreau, n 47, at 413.

31

Comparative Law in the German Courts

*Hannes Unberath and Astrid Stadler**

I. Introduction

Comparative law in the German courts is a topic that has occupied German academics with some measure of regularity.[1] The conclusions drawn are usually pessimistic in tone and, on the basis of detailed statistical evaluations, state the limited role foreign law has played so far before their courts. Yet, the significance of the topic is rapidly growing with the infiltration into German law of European law, especially in the field of private and private international law, and the increased importance of international conventions. In short: private law in Europe is in the process of reacquiring a transnational character.[2]

The purpose of the present chapter is modest. Rather than giving a comprehensive overview[3] it highlights only aspects of this broad theme, and we are hoping thus to reveal the specific problems of comparative law before national courts and offer some insights into its usefulness as a tool for the national judge. The enquiry is further limited to the areas in which comparative law has played a role in German private law. Comparative law may provide assistance to national courts in some quite different respects. In the first section comparative law will be discussed as a necessary tool and in the second section comparative law as a voluntary enterprise. The concluding section explores the future role of comparative law.

* University of Konstanz; Erasmus School of Law, Rotterdam. In the first edition of this volume Hannes Unberath was responsible for the chapter on 'Comparative Law in the German Courts'. On 28 January 2013 Hannes Unberath sadly passed away at the age of 39. It is a great honour for me to become responsible for this chapter in the second edition. I have kept the main structure of the text and the line of arguments of the text written by Hannes Unberath and made only a few supplements in order to update the chapter.

[1] Selection: H. Koch, 'Prozessrechtsvergleichung zur Kennzeichnung von Rechtskreisen' ZEuP (*Zeitschrift für Europäisches Privatrecht*) 2007, 735; R. Schulz and G. Ajani (eds.), *Gemeinsame Prinzipien des Europäischen Privatrechts* (2003); H. Kötz, 'Der Bundesgerichtshof und die Rechtsvergleichung' in A. Heldrich and K. Hopt (eds.), *50 Jahre Bundesgerichtshof* (2000) vol. 2, p. 824; U. Drobnig, 'The Use of Foreign Law by German Courts' in U. Drobnig and S. van Erp (eds.), *The Use of Comparative Law by Courts* (1999), p. 127; B. Großfeld, 'Vom Beitrag der Rechtsvergleichung zum deutschen Recht' AcP 184 (1984) 289; J.M. Mössner, 'Rechtsvergleichung und Verfassungsrechtsprechung' AöR 99 (1974) 193; B. Aubin, 'Die rechtsvergleichende Interpretation autonom-internen Rechts in der deutschen Rechtsprechung' RabelsZ 34 (1970) 458; H. Dölle, 'Der Beitrag der Rechtsvergleichung zum deutschen Recht' in *Festschrift zum 100jährigen Bestehen des deutschen Juristentages* (1960), p. 19.

[2] As Professor R. Zimmermann remarked in his Clarendon Lecture; *Roman Law, Contemporary Law, European Law* (2001), p. 108. Cf. H. Kötz, n. 1, p. 842.

[3] See for a survey in English: B.S. Markesinis, *Comparative Law in the Courtroom and Classroom* (2003), p. 107.

II. Comparative law as a necessary tool

1. Legal transplants—reception of foreign rules

As a matter of course national courts normally apply domestic law, and only in cross-border cases does the situation occur when foreign law has to be applied based on the forum's conflict of laws rules. From a more general perspective, however, courts will also look into foreign law if their own law is a legal transplant—for whatever reasons[4]—from another legal system. There are numerous examples throughout legal history of legal institutions or whole sets of rules moving across political and cultural borders. It is common knowledge that the French Code Civil has been adopted—sometimes without much change—in Louisiana, Quebec, and a large number of states in Latin America;[5] in 1926 the Swiss Civil Code and Code of Obligations were adopted by Turkey;[6] and, during the 19th century, German civil law had a strong influence on new codifications in Greece, Japan, South Korea, and even in China at the end of the Qing Dynasty. Again, in the 1990s, when at the end of the Cold War the Central and Eastern European countries gained independence and implemented new laws, German civil law was often taken into account. Where legal transplants were successful and depending on how far-reaching and detailed the adoption of foreign law was, it is obvious that courts in applying the 'transplants' often look into the case law and developments in the law's country of origin for the interpretation of their law. Although—vice versa—it is also very interesting for the original legal system to learn how legal transplants develop in another socio-legal and cultural environment, this seems to be a domain of academic research rather than court practice. As far as can be seen, at least in Germany, there is not much evidence of courts taking into consideration how foreign courts apply rules or legal institutions that have been adopted from German law. Legal interpretation based on the history of a rule methodologically seems to be a one-way road and the comparative method is still not part of the broadly accepted canon of legal methodology in Germany.[7]

2. Conflict of laws—'most favourable law'—approach

On very rare occasions courts could also be legally obliged to look into foreign law, particularly how it is applied by foreign courts, and to compare the results of their

[4] For a discussion of the various reasons for law moving from one state to another see R. Zajac Sannerholm, '"Cut-and-paste?" Rule of law promotion and legal transplants in war to peace transitions' in A Bakardjieva Engelbrekt and J. Nergelius (eds.), *New Directions in Comparative Law* (2009), p. 56 et seq.

[5] M. Rainer, *Europäisches Privatrecht—Die Rechtsvergleichung* (2nd edn. 2007), § 4.

[6] K. Zweigert and H. Kötz *Einführung in die Rechtsvergleichung* (3rd edn. 1996), pp. 175–6; E. Hirsch, *Das schweizerische Zivilgesetzbuch in der Türkei* Schweizer Juristenzeitung 50 (1954) 337; G. Jonas, 'Ein zeitgenössischer Rezeptionsprozess am Beispiel des türkischen Zivilrechts' JuS (*Juristische Schulung*) 1987, p. 266; the change that the Swiss regulations underwent in Turkey is described by D. Damar and H. Rösler, 'Türkisches Zivil-, Handels- und Kollisionsrecht im Zeichen der Modernisierung—Reform- und Systemfragen' ZEuP 2011, 616.

[7] For the role of comparative law in a European methodology T. Henninger, *Europäisches Privatrecht* (2009).

research with the *lex fori*. German law provided a rare example of such a necessary comparison in its conflict of laws rules which were applied for many years based on case law. Before Article 40 of the German Introductory Act to the Civil Code came into force in 1999 (which for its part was replaced in 2009 by Article 4 of the Rome II Regulation), conflict of laws rules with respect to tort cases were based on the so-called 'most favourable law' approach.[8] In case of cross-border torts according to this prevailing doctrine, courts had to apply either the tort law of the state where the injury or damage occurred or the law of the state where the tortious act had been admitted. The tort victim had the right to opt for the law which was the most favourable for his or her damages claim. If the plaintiff did not make an explicit choice with respect to the applicable law during the litigation, German courts were held to do a comparative research *ex officio* and had to apply the law which was the most favourable for the tort victim. This required a comparison of the tort laws which came into consideration, and given the fact that German courts had jurisdiction to try the case in the first place, German law was very likely to be one option.[9] In practice, courts were, however, very reluctant to make a detailed comparison and sometimes very quickly took recourse to the domestic rules, particularly if German law granted full compensation of the tort victim's damage anyway.[10] When a codification of the conflict rules was under debate in the late 1990s, it was clearly pointed out, particularly by the German legislature, that an *ex officio* comparative research by the courts was no longer deemed to be efficient and that this should be left to the plaintiff and his or her lawyer to be done in preparation of the lawsuit.[11]

3. International conventions

Nevertheless, German courts still sometimes (and even increasingly) have to take into consideration how foreign courts handle some cases and apply certain rules, namely when it comes to the application of international conventions or European regulations. The aim of any international convention is to harmonize the law. For uniformity to be preserved it is essential to take into account its international character and the interpretation given to the convention in other contracting states. A perfect illustration

[8] B. von Hoffmann in *Staudinger's Kommentar zum BGB*, 2001, Article 40 para. 6.

[9] Within the European Union, Article 5 no. 3 of the Brussels I Regulation provides international jurisdiction for the courts in the Member State where either the tortious act was committed or where the injury or damage occurred.

[10] In this case, foreign law could only be more favourable for the plaintiff if he or she would have been entitled to punitive damages under the foreign tort rules. German courts, however, would have rejected the application of foreign law with respect to punitive damages as a matter of public policy anyhow. This was later reflected by Article 40 para. 3 which did not permit the application of foreign tort law to the extent that punitive damages would be available. Today Article 26 of the Rome II Regulation has a similar effect (see Recital 32 of the Regulation).

[11] Therefore Article 40 of the Introductory Act to the German Civil Code finally left the selection of the applicable tort law to the tort victim. If he or she did not make a choice during the litigation, the law of the state where the tortious act was committed applied automatically. Courts were only held to inform the plaintiff whether he or she could make such a choice, but they were no longer held to find out *ex officio* what the most favourable set of rules was, see B. von Hoffmann in the Commentary of Staudinger, *German Civil Code*, 2001, Article 40 para. 9.

can be found in Article 7(1) of the Convention on Contracts for the International Sale of Goods (CISG): 'In the interpretation of this Convention, regard is to be had to its international character and to the need to promote uniformity in its application and the observance of good faith in international trade.'[12] Maritime law is an area of the law dominated by international conventions such as The Hague Rules where international practice is of paramount importance.[13] Here, German courts have frequently referred to English law. This is not surprising, for in this field English law has much to offer. Not only is the case law a gold mine for any civil lawyer; often the contracts of carriage themselves incorporate English terms or concepts.[14] This area is thus a perfect example of how English law has benefited the development of international practice. Recent developments lead one to believe that this is not a one-way road. Even the more 'advanced' English system may benefit from looking at the position of German law.[15] It is interesting to note that German courts tend to cite English textbooks (e.g. *Scrutton on Charterparties*), the Carriage of Goods by Sea Act, or accounts of English law in German[16] rather than the case itself.[17] This hesitation to base a (German) decision on an (English) case is understandable, since the German judge may not be in the best position to distinguish cases and weigh the authoritative value in the foreign system. At the same time this in itself emphasizes the need for the comparative lawyer to act as a bridge between different systems. In recent years, the German Federal Court also referred to foreign case law when it had to apply other international conventions in order to guarantee a uniform application of the respective convention.[18] References

[12] For the interpretation of the CISG see A. Janssen and O. Meyer, *CISG Methodology* (2009). The degree of autonomy of the supra-national source of law is increased and the importance of comparative law lessened to some degree if a supra-national court is empowered with the final interpretation of the source. Such is the case with the European legislation but as Judge Lenaerts has powerfully explained the comparative method remains essential in preparing the decisions of the European Court of Justice and the Court of First Instance (see his paper). For the role of comparative law in interpreting European regulations, see section I.5.

[13] BGH, decision of the German Supreme Court (*Bundesgerichtshof*, BGH) of 28 June 1971, BGHZ 56, 300 illustrates this point well. 'International practice' was the court's guiding principle in deciding whether a shipper is answerable for the master of the ship in relation to the seaworthiness of the ship and in limiting the liability of a time-charterer to that of a shipowner. The latter aspect is particularly noteworthy because at the time the Brussels convention on limitation of liability of shipowners of 1957 was only about to be ratified in Germany (in England this had happened in the Merchant Shipping (Liability of Shipowners and others) Act 1958). Thus the court followed international practice even before the legislator had fully adapted German law (now: Sec. 486 HGB). See for further examples: Drobnig, n. 1, p. 135.

[14] E.g. BGH, decision of 20 May 1952, 'on deck at shipper's risk', BGHZ 6, 127; BGH, decision of 26 September 1957, 'Quality, contents and weight unknown', BGHZ 25, 250; BGH, decision of 18 December 1958, arbitration clause, BGHZ 29, 120; Hanseatisches Oberlandesgericht Hamburg, decision of 7 November 1974, MDR 1975, 406, Himalaya clause; BGH, decision of 22 January 1990, VersR 1990, 503 (identity of carrier clause); BGH, decision of 21 September 2000 (carriage of goods by air), BGHZ 145, 170. English law is also referred to when bill of ladings are to be construed; e.g. BGHZ 44, 303, decision of 15 November 1965; BGHZ 60, 102, decision of 25 January 1973.

[15] See *The Starsin* [2003] UKHL 12, where Lord Millett and Lord Hobhouse of Woodborough referred to German law in support of their view.

[16] The leading but now outdated commentary on maritime law by G. Schaps and H.J. Abraham, *Seerecht* (4th edn. 1978) contains detailed and elegant glosses on English case law.

[17] As for instance in BGHZ 60, 102 (n. 14).

[18] BGH, decision of 14 February 2008 (I ZR 183/05), IPRax (*Praxis des Internationalen Privat- und Verfahrensrechts*) 2008, 541 para. 25 (application of the Convention on the contract for carriage of goods by road (CMR), reference to case law in England, Belgium, France, The Netherlands); BGH, decision of 14 June 2007 (I ZR 50/05) NJW 2008, 289 para. 28 (CMR: Italy, Austria); BGH, decision of 12 March 2002

are, however, typically very short and the German Federal Court rarely considers in detail the arguments on which a foreign decision is based.

4. Conflict of laws—qualification, recognition, and enforcement of foreign judgments

Another area of the law where national courts are bound to consider foreign law is private international law which has been mentioned already. Under conflict of laws rules German courts may be called upon to apply foreign law. According to the present reading given to section 293 of the Code of Civil Procedure, the court is also entrusted with the task to determine the foreign law. This explains why according to German practice *the court* commissions a report on the position of the foreign legal system in question.[19] However, although foreign law is here routinely applied by national courts which in itself sometimes provides beautiful examples of cross-fertilization between the different systems,[20] the comparative method is only needed in hard cases. Apart from the 'most favourable law' approach already mentioned, another example can be given: according to the traditional approach of the so-called *lege fori* qualification it is necessary to compare the foreign rule with German substantive law in order to determine which specific German conflict of laws rule covers the foreign rule of substantive law.[21] Often this will not involve any difficulties. However, a more elaborate comparative approach is crucial where foreign law provides for remedies unknown to the national system. It is then essential to take into account the function of the unknown concept and compare it to the purpose of remedies in one's own system in singling out the applicable conflicts rule.[22]

(X ZR 43/01) para. 33 (European Patent Convention); BGH, decision of 17 February 2000 (I ZR 194, 97), NJW-RR 2001, 38 (application of the Revised Berne Convention for the Protection of Literary and Artistic Works, reference to Austrian and French courts); BGH, decision of 16 August 2000 (XII ZB 210/99) NJW 2000, 3349 para. 13 (Convention on Civil Aspects of International Child Abduction; reference to US and Dutch courts); BGH, decision of 13 November 1997 (I ZR 157/95) NJW-RR 1998, 896 para. 13 (CMR, reference to Austrian and French courts), BGH, decision of 23 March 1976 (VI ZR 150/74) NJW 1976, 1587 (Warsaw Convention, reference to French and Dutch courts).

[19] Usually reports are provided by a comparative law institute such as the *Max-Planck-Institut für ausländisches und internationals Privatrecht* in Hamburg. Even further back goes the tradition of the Institute of Comparative Law in Munich which under the directorship of Ernst Rabel was declared to be available for such requests as early as 1924. See 'Bekanntmachung des Bayerischen Staatsministeriums der Justiz' in *Justizministerialblatt für den Freistaat Bayern vom 21. Juli 1924*, N. 13326.

[20] This applies especially where the national judge assumes the role of his foreign counterpart in developing the law because the enquiry into foreign law does not yield an unequivocal answer. From the English jurisprudence *City of Gotha and Federal Republic of Germany v Sotheby's and Cobert Finance SA* Queen's Bench Case No. 1993 C 3428 and 1997 G 185. Reproduced and translated in M.H. Carl, H. Güttler, and K. Siehr, *Kunstdiebstahl vor Gericht* (2001), offers an excellent illustration. Mr Justice Moses, in deciding whether the German city of Gotha was entitled to a claim in restitution against Sotheby's in relation to a Dutch painting confiscated by Soviet authorities after the war, applied German law. The elegant High Court judgment was to become the first judicial authority on the relevant provision Sec. 221 (now Sec. 198) of the German Civil Code.

[21] See Drobnig, n. 1, p. 130.

[22] E.g. the concept of *Mahr* (*Morgengabe*), existing in most Islamic systems, according to which the husband undertakes to pay the wife a certain sum upon dissolution of the marriage; cf. A. Heldrich, 'Das juristische Kuckucksei aus dem Morgenland' IPRax 1983, 64. From the rich case law: BGH NJW 1987, 2161, decision of 28 January 1987.

The same applies when foreign decisions are to be enforced in Germany. Both the Brussels Ia Regulation[23] (applicable for decisions from other Member States) and Sec. 328 of the German Civil Procedure Code (applicable for third state judgments) permit a public policy objection which requires comparing whether the foreign judgment's effects may violate fundamental principles of German law. There is rich case law in this respect, but worth being mentioned is a seminal decision, in which the German Federal Court in 1992 rejected a full recognition of US punitive damages awards by comparing the objectives of this US instrument to similar instruments of German procedural and substantive law.[24] Similar aspects become important once a foreign decision is to be recognized in Germany when it comes to the question what practical consequences follow from such recognition. German domestic law (Sec. 328 Civil Procedure Code) and the Brussels Ia Regulation apply the so-called 'effects doctrine' which means that all procedural and substantive law effects that the judgment has in its country of origin are to be extended to Germany as the country of recognition and enforcement. Therefore, again, German courts must scrutinize foreign law in order to determine the effects of recognition of a particular judgment.

5. European law

In general, European regulations today provide a very important and vast field for comparison. This is particularly true for the Brussels Ia Regulation[25] which—together with its predecessor, the Brussels I Convention and the Brussels I Regulation —has been a long-established instrument of judicial cooperation with ample case law all over Europe. Although these regulations do not exactly require the comparison of domestic and foreign law, there is at least the need for national courts to take into consideration how courts in other Member States interpret European regulations in order to preserve uniformity. By contrast to international conventions, the European Court of Justice (ECJ) plays a prominent role in this respect[26] and with respect to many articles the court favours a so-called 'autonomous interpretation'. As a consequence most of the expressions used in the Brussels I Regulation must not be interpreted according to national law but by taking into account the Regulation's context and goals and—if available—a common standard in the Member States. Thus it is very helpful for national courts to consider how the regulation is interpreted in other Member States. The German Federal Court (*Bundesgerichthof*) has done so on several occasions.[27]

[23] See section II.5.

[24] BGH, decision of 4 June 1992 (IX ZR 149/91), BGHZ 118, 311 (= NJW 1992, 3096).

[25] On 10 January 2015 a recast of the Brussels I Regulation (Regulation 44/2001) came into force: Regulation 1215/2012 ('Brussels Ia').

[26] See n. 12.

[27] BGH, decision of 31 May 2011 (VI ZR 154/10) NJW 2011, 2809, para. 39 (Lugano Convention); BGH, decision of 14 March 2007 (XII ZB 174/04), NJW (*Neue Juristische Wochenschrift*) 2007, 3433 paras. 32–35 (scope of admissible objections in exequatur proceedings: England, France, Switzerland); BGH, decision of 19 February 2013 (VI ZR 45/12) BGHZ 196, 180 para. 18 (lis pendens: Italy); BGH, decision of 15 July 1999 (I ZR 130/96), EuZW (*Europäische Zeitschrift für Wirtschaftsrecht*) 1999, 697 (competition law: Austria, Switzerland).

Particularly when a court considers referring a case to the ECJ for a binding interpretation of a particular Article of the Brussels I Regulation, it must demonstrate the need for a reference which is not permitted in case of an 'acte claire'. Therefore, courts considering a reference must not only take into account the ECJ case law, but also relevant decisions given by courts in the Member States. Experience proves that this is something which can primarily be expected from higher courts, although reference can be made by any court of last instance in a particular case.[28] The German Federal Court thus referred to case law in other Member States in a number of cases.[29]

6. Comparative law as a voluntary enterprise

a) *Foreign law as a source of inspiration*

In the examples discussed until now comparative law is a necessary element of the judicial process. The true challenge for comparative law lies elsewhere. This is whether a comparative lawyer can succeed in persuading practitioners to consider what Lord Bingham called the wider jurisprudence[30] even in cases where national law, alone, is concerned. There are prominent examples in German law where courts had recourse to comparative law either to support their view or to distance themselves from a foreign position.

One should note at the outset that German courts are less free to develop the law than their English counterparts. In civil law systems adjudication is to a great extent determined by the codal and relevant statutory regime. Law reform is a task mainly performed by the legislator.[31] On the other hand it is a misconception to conclude that the courts are a passive part of the legal machinery, devoid of creative powers when applying the meagre, scarce, and dead letter of the law![32] As the 'case-law revolution'[33] following the coming into force of the German Civil Code (*Bürgerliches Gesetzbuch*—BGB) in 1900 demonstrates, there is room for creative thinking and thus also for comparative law.

[28] In this respect it has to be emphasized how important it is to have easy access to foreign decisions (and translations thereof). Whereas there are really good data bases for the CISG, for example, this cannot be said to be true for EU law.

[29] BGH, decision of 18 September 2013 (V ZB 163/12) BeckRS (online data base available at: <https://beck-online.beck.de/>) 2013, 19171 para. 18 (suspension of litigation based on Article 27 Brussels I Regulation); BGH, decision of 13 December 2012 (I ZR 217/10) NJW-RR (*Neue Juristische Wochenschrift—Rechtsprechungsreport*) 2013, 555 paras. 31–33 (reference to Austrian and French High Courts); BGH, decision of 1 February 2011 (KZR 8/10) GRUR 2011, 554 para. 12 (various Member States); BGH, decision of 10 November 2009 (VI ZR 217/08) EuZW 2010, 313 paras. 9, 16 (reference to French courts); BGH, decision of 26 March 1992 (VII ZR 158/91) EuZW 1992, 514 (Brussels Convention). For a reference to the ECJ made in European trademark law see BGH, decision of 23 November 2000 (I ZB 18/98), MarkenR (*Markenrecht*) 2001, 71 para. 33 (US courts).

[30] *Fairchild v. Glenhaven Funeral Services Ltd* [2002] UKHL 22, no. 23–32.

[31] See for a detailed analysis of the generous use of foreign material by the German legislator Markesinis, n. 3, p. 114 ff.

[32] Rudolph von Jhering warned strongly against this type of 'positivistic' judge. See his inaugural lecture held in Vienna, 16 October 1868, reproduced in O. Behrends (ed.), *Ist die Jurisprudenz eine Wissenschaft?* (1998), at p. 50.

[33] Zimmermann, n. 2, p. 55.

An example where the courts 'corrected' the initial approach of the legislator and, interestingly for our purpose, did so under the impression of comparative material is the development of the right to damages for privacy invasions. The fathers of the Civil Code had ruled out the possibility of damages for interference with privacy. The report of the Committee of the BGB states in uncompromising terms that it would be 'repugnant to the dominant opinion among the population to place non-material values on the same level as property interests and to make good with money interferences with non-material interests.'[34] By the time the German Federal Court reconsidered the issue in the *Herrenreiter* case in 1958[35] the climate had dramatically changed. Two factors seem to have been decisive: the 'constitutionalization' of private law; and the (comparative) academic studies available to the court. Ironically, the same two factors may initiate the introduction of a general privacy right into English law.

The Basic Law of 1949 attributed human dignity the highest value. Only weeks before the decision in the *Herrenreiter* case the Constitutional Court had developed the theory of indirect horizontal effect of the Constitution,[36] thus bringing human dignity, as well, to the forefront in the area of private law. According to the *Drittwirkung* doctrine[37] the rules of private law must be interpreted in conformity with the fundamental values of the Constitution. The *Bundesgerichtshof* in the *Herrenreiter* case did not yet expressly refer to this new doctrine but applied its rationale when it said:

> Now that the Constitution guarantees a comprehensive protection to the personality and recognises human dignity and the right to free development of the personality as a fundamental value, it has done away with the dogma held by the original draftsmen of the BGB that there can be no civil law protection of general personality right.[38]

Foreign law was not referred to at this stage when the court granted compensation for immaterial damage, but academic writings were taken into account. There was at the time a strong current of opinion in German academic literature in favour of recognizing a general right of privacy.[39] Noteworthy in particular is the systematic treatise on the subject by Heinrich Hubmann,[40] who strongly suggested that the time was ripe for the recognition of a right of privacy and that its violation should give rise to a right to claim damages. Interestingly enough, one of his arguments was that the right of privacy

[34] For details see B.S. Markesinis and H. Unberath, *German Law of Torts* (4th edn. 2002), pp. 74, 406, 472. There was some protection of privacy, though random, often incidental and overall very limited, before the ground-breaking *Herrenreiter* case.

[35] BGHZ 26, 349, decision of 14 February 1958; translated in Markesinis/Unberath, n. 34, p. 415. The plaintiff acted as a gentleman show-jumper. The defendant disseminated a poster with a picture of the show-jumper advertising a pharmaceutical preparation which purportedly increased sexual potency.

[36] In the famous *Lüth* case: BVerfGE 7, 198, decision of 15 January 1958, translated in Markesinis/Unberath, n. 34, p. 392.

[37] See for a comparative examination: B.S. Markesinis (1999) 115 LQR 47.

[38] BGHZ 26, 349, decision of 14 February 1958 (= NJW [*Neue Juristische Wochenschrift*] 827 at 830).

[39] See H. Coing in *Staudinger's Kommentar zum BGB* (11th edn. 1957) Vorbem. § 1 Rn. 20 with references.

[40] Heinrich Hubmann, *Das Persönlichkeitsrecht* (1953, 2nd edn. 1967). Cited by the BGH in an earlier seminal judgment, in which the right to freely develop one's personality was recognized as one of the interests protected by the general tort provision Sec. 823 I BGB: BGHZ 24, 72, decision of 2 April 1957.

was recognized in other legal systems.[41] There can be no doubt that this was at the back of the mind of the judges when *Herrenreiter* was decided and that the judges took confidence in the fact that recognizing a right of privacy had been successfully tested in other legal systems. Thus it cannot come as a surprise that when a few years later the court was criticized for interfering with the freedom of the press, the *Bundesgerichtshof* was quick to emphasize that:

> in almost all legal systems in which the value of a person plays a central role damages is recognised as an adequate remedy for invasions of privacy. Also in these systems freedom of the press is of fundamental importance and continues to be so despite the recoverability of damages. Therefore, the objection is unfounded that recognising the right to damages for violations of the right of privacy would unreasonably interfere with the freedom of the press.[42]

While in these decisions the references to comparative material are fairly general and can only be understood against the background of academic studies available to the court, the fine-tuning of this right of privacy prompted the German courts to examine foreign material in more detail. Thus, this time expressly following the Swiss model, the court limited the right to damages to cases in which the violation of privacy was of considerable weight.[43] In the *Caroline* litigation the *Bundesgerichtshof* looked once again at other jurisdictions[44] and held that the princess even though a public figure was entitled to privacy in places accessible to the public provided that it was obvious that the person wished to be let alone and crucially the location offered some seclusion from the public. Thus the publication of photographs taken in a restaurant was said to interfere with the right of privacy. The reference here was to a decision of the Supreme Court of the United States.[45] By contrast, photographs taken of the princess walking on the street did not constitute an infringement of privacy. The court explicitly rejected the more radical French approach[46] according to which the unsolicited publication of a photograph is prohibited unless it shows the person performing a public duty.

The privacy cases are in a number of ways a useful illustration of how comparative law can benefit the development of the law before national courts. First, they show how a new concept came more easily to be recognized because other legal systems had successfully incorporated it. Secondly, the comparative method was used also on a more specific level to justify refinements and the application to the individual case. Thirdly, the development reminds one of the present situation in English law.[47] What has taken place in Germany over many years seems—some would argue—about to

[41] 1st edn. p. 38, 251; § 17 of the 2nd edn. gives a detailed account of the situation in Switzerland (which he regarded as a suitable model), France, Austria, and Italy. English law was also examined, though he correctly stated that English courts did not recognize a right of privacy and concluded that the situation was 'somewhat unsatisfactory'.

[42] BGHZ 39, 124, 132, decision of 5 March 1963. In a similar vein the Constitutional Court stressed that this line of cases of the BGH brought German law into line with international developments, BVerfGE 34, 269, 291, decision of 14 February 1973.

[43] BGHZ 35, 363, decision of 19 September 1961.

[44] BGHZ 131, 332, decision of 19 December 1995; reproduced in Markesinis and Unberath n. 34, p. 444.

[45] *Katz v. United States* 389 Supreme Court (1967) 347.

[46] Cour de Cassation, Bulletin des arrêts Chambres civiles, No. 98, p. 67.

[47] See Markesinis and Unberath n. 34, p. 411 with references.

begin in England. Finally, the privacy cases may be typical in so far as they suggest that the comparative method is particularly attractive when a radical departure from previous practice is at stake or a novel issue arises and the local solution is not strongly dictated by a local statute or long-established practice.

b) Foreign law as a supportive argument

This last aspect is confirmed by two other decisions. In the first the *Bundesgerichtshof* rejected a wrongful life claim.[48] This time the German Supreme Court preferred the approach adopted by the English Court of Appeal in the *McKay* case[49] to the more liberal view expressed in some American decisions. In the second the Court had to decide whether a doctor who negligently removed the only kidney of a child was liable in damages to the child's mother who donated one of her own kidneys to rescue the child.[50] However, the *Bundesgerichtshof* used comparative material also in other contexts in which the issues were not genuinely new but potentially controversial.[51]

Overall, however, the German record still does not compare well with the willingness of English courts[52] to embrace foreign ideas. However, the situation has changed rapidly. Professor Kötz concluded in his study published in 2000 that the number of cases where the *Bundesgerichtshof* referred to foreign law without the need to do so was only around a dozen.[53] Today an increasing number of those decisions exist. The main

[48] BGHZ 35, 363, decision of 19 September 1961.

[49] *McKay v. Essex Health Authority* [1982] 2 WLR 890.

[50] BGHZ 101, 215, decision of 30 June 1987, reproduced in Markesinis and Unberath, n. 34, p. 660. Liability was established and the court referred to the rescue doctrine as applied in US decisions.

[51] See e.g. BGH, decision of 16 September 1987 (sale of goods, reference to Swiss and US law) BGHZ 101, 337; BGH, decision of 5 November 1974 (liability for sport injuries, reference to French law) BGHZ 63, 140; BGH, decision of 22 June 1956, BGHZ 21, 112, and BGH, decision of 13 May 1957 (commercial agents, references to Swiss, French, Italian, and Austrian law), BGHZ 24, 214.

[52] *White v. Jones* [1995] 2 AC 207 (cf. W. Lorenz JZ 1995, 317); *Henderson v. Merrett Syndicates Ltd* [1995] 2 AC 145 (cf. Markesinis and Unberath, n. 34, p. 337); *Hunter v. Canary Wharf Ltd* [1997] AC 655; *Barry v. Midland Bank plc* [1998] 1 All ER 805; *Kleinwort Benson Ltd v. Lincoln CC* [1999] 2 AC 349; *McFarlane v. Tayside Health Board* [2000] 2 AC 59 (cf. Markesinis and Unberath, n. 34, p.197); *Arthur JS Hall & Co v. Simons* [2000] 3 WLR 543 (cf. Markesinis and Unberath, n. 34, p. 330); *Michael Douglas, Catherine Zeta-Jones, Northerm and Shell plc. v. Hello! Ltd* [2000] EWCA Civ 353; *Alfred McAlpine Construction Ltd v. Panatown Ltd* [2001] 1 AC 518 (cf. H. Unberath *Transferred Loss* (2003) p. 205); *Greatorex v. Greatorex* [2000] 1 WLR 1970 (cf. Markesinis, n. 3, p. 157); *A v. National Blood Authority* [2001] EWHC QB 446; *Campbell v. Mirror Group Newspapers Ltd* [2002] EWCA Civ 1373; *Fairchild v. Glenhaven Funeral Services Ltd* [2002] UKHL 22; *The Starsin* [2003] UKHL 12. An overview gives K. Schiemann L.J., 'Aktuelle Einflüsse des deutschen Rechts auf die richterliche Fortbildung des englischen Rechts' EuR 2003, 17. This is in fact a renaissance of comparative law in England if one remembers for instance that comparative law formed part of major treatises of the 19th century, e.g. J. Chitty, *A Treatise on the Law of Contracts and upon the Defences to Actions Thereon* (6th edn. 1857 by J.A. Russel); C. Blackburn, *A Treatise on the Effect of the Contract of Sale* (1845). See as to these developments and the reasons for the change in attitude: B.S. Markesinis, 'Our Debt to Europe' in B.S. Markesinis (ed.), *Clifford Chance Millenium Lectures* (2000), p. 37.

[53] Including criminal law; Kötz, n. 1, p. 832, for example BGH, decision of 5 November 1974 (VI ZR 100/73), BGHZ 63, 140 para. 11 (liability for injury suffered during football match: reference to Austrian and French case law); BGH, decision of 13 November 1970 (1 StR 412/70) NJW 1971, 1093 (legal duty to maintain safety on ski slopes: reference to Austrian, French, and Swiss courts); BGH, decision of 10 December 1998 (I ZR 20/96) NJW 1999, 1186 para. 19 (trade mark law, reference to US Supreme Court); BGH, decision of 27 April 1999 (KZR 35/97), NJW-RR 2000, 773 para. 8 (competition law, reference to US Supreme Court).

reason for the initial absence of wide-ranging comparative jurisprudence in Germany can be easily identified. With the emergence of the Civil Code in the year 1900, a major achievement of the Pandectist school but also comparative evaluation,[54] German scholarship and the courts focussed all their energy on interpreting the Code and filling it with life. Roman law was marginalized as a study in the history of law and the comparative approach had become superfluous.[55]

Fortunately this self-chosen isolation has come to end. There is hardly any major monograph nowadays that does not include at least a comparative chapter. The German legislator was increasingly anxious to bring German law into line with international practice. The modernization of the German law of obligations in 2002 was a perfect example.[56] Courts have also followed suit and there are, meanwhile, more examples for decisions of the German Federal Court in which the judges refer to foreign law in order to obtain additional arguments to legitimate the results they have found for the interpretation of national law.[57]

III. Comparative law: outlook

If a European Civil Code were ever to be adopted,[58] this would mean within the Code's scope the end of comparative law in its traditional form. But new challenges would of course appear immediately, because a uniform application would not be easy to be achieved. However, this course of events does not seem likely. The Commission itself has abandoned the idea of a more modest Contract Code in favour of creating an optional body of EU contract law and consolidating the existing law.[59] When the Draft Common Frame of Reference (DCFR) was published in 2009[60] it met considerable criticism[61] for both political reasons and with respect to how particular rules were designed. As a consequence the project was boiled down to a proposal for a Common

[54] See Dölle, n. 1, p. 25 ff. with references.

[55] Cf. Zimmermann, n. 2, p. 40 ff.

[56] *Gesetz zur Modernisierung des Schuldrechts vom 26.11.2001*, BGBl. I S. 3138 implementing Directive 1999/44/EC on consumer sales. The directive in turn is in part modelled after Art. 35 CISG. Unlike the English Sale and Supply of Goods to Consumers Regulations 2002 (cf. M. Bridge (2003) 119 LQR 173) the German legislator extended the approach of the directive beyond consumer sales to sale of goods generally. Moreover the whole system of remedies for irregularities of performance was changed. See for an account in English: R. Zimmermann, *Breach of Contract and Remedies under the New German Law of Obligations*, Saggi, conferenze e seminari, vol. 48, Centro di studi e ricerche di diritto comparato e straniero (2002); for the use of comparative material for this reform: Markesinis, n. 3, p. 114.

[57] BGH, decision of 28 May 2008 (I ZR 61/06) BGHZ 176, 365 (= NJW-RR 2008, 1169), para. 32 (recognition of divorce decision issued by private institution); BGH, decision of 11 September 2007 (X ZR 27/04) GRUR (*Gewerblicher Rechtsschutz und Urheberrecht*) 2008, 145 (patent law).

[58] Opinions vary from strongly in favour: O. Lando, 'Does the European Union need a Civil Code?' RIW 2003, 1; to strongly against: Y. Lequette, 'Quelques remarques à propos du projet der code civil européen de M. von Bar' D. 2002, Chron. p. 2202.

[59] COM (2003) 68 final, 12 February 2003.

[60] Chr. v. Bar, E. Clive, and H. Schulte-Nölke et al. (eds.), *Draft Common Frame of Reference* (outline edition, 2009); P. Legrand, 'Antivonbar' (2006) Journal of Comp. L. 13.

[61] There is a vast number of publications discussing the DCFR in European literature, see for example the contributions in ZEuP, vol. 4, 2008.

European Sales Law (CESL) in 2011 with a much more limited scope of application.[62] Even for this opt-in instrument, the scope of application has finally been narrowed further to contracts made on the internet.[63] The Commission has now abandoned the project which is nothing to bewail as it would have provided only a quite narrow experimental ground for harmonized contract law. 'Harmonisation' on a large scale would not only make the comparative method superfluous eventually (if it is successful), but it would also sweep away the heritage of centuries. Traditions may be worth preserving but it is equally important that legal scholarship as well as adjudication transcends the boundaries of one's own legal system. Great assistance and fresh ideas were expected from the different study groups on European private law.[64] A lesson learned from the process which led to the DCFR, however, was that Europe needed an institution corresponding to the American Law Institute.[65] As a consequence, in June 2011 the European Law Institute (ELI) was established and already started a couple of comparative studies.[66] It is still a long way to go before something like 'European Principles'[67] can acquire the same persuasive force *in the courtroom* as the Restatements prepared by the American Law Institute. Perhaps one has to be sceptical whether this will be the case. One reason is that legal systems like the common law system which are primarily based on case law generate a stronger demand for 'principles' than the continental systems. Furthermore, in Europe, the systemic differences between the legal orders are still too great to be dissolved by compromise decisions. Thus Sir Roy Goode, who was a member of the Lando Commission, has once remarked that he had accepted specific performance as a primary remedy under the Principles of European Contract Law,[68] but it would be quite another thing to have this as a rule of English law.[69] For the future a very promising approach is comparative research done with the English practising lawyer in mind. Professor Basil Markesinis has called this the right packaging of foreign law.[70] If it is accompanied by making the material

[62] EU Commission, Draft for a Regulation on a Common European Sales Law, COM(2011)0635. In Germany, the German Association of Civil Lawyers held a special meeting in April 2012 in Bonn to discuss the CESL, contributions are published in AcP (*Archiv für die civilistische Praxis*) 2012 vol. 212, pp. 467–852.

[63] Position of the European Parliament, published 26 February 2014: Oral P7_TA-PROV(2014)0159.

[64] O. Lando, E. Clive, A. Prüm, and R. Zimmermann (eds.), *The Principles of European Contract Law* (2003) had a considerable influence on the Draft Common Frame of Reference, mainly edited by *The Study Group on a European Civil Code* (Chairman: C. von Bar) and the Acquis Group. With respect to tort law there are several efforts, such as the *European Group on Tort Law* (the former Tilburg Group; <http://www.egtl.org/>) which published its Principles of European Tort Law (PETL) in 2005, the Institute for European Tort Law (ETL) and the European Centre of Tort and Insurance Law (ECTIL), both based in Vienna.

[65] R. Zimmermann, 'Reflections on a European Law Institute' ZEuP 2010, 719.

[66] For the activities of ELI, see: <https://www.europeanlawinstitute.eu/>.

[67] The Draft Common Frame of Reference turned out to be not a very promising attempt in this respect. Although the initial idea of the European Commission when implementing the Study Group was to receive a frame of common principles, definitions and general rules. In the end, the Study Group drafted a rather detailed 'code' and went far beyond just gathering existing rules. The result was a number of new regulations—based on comparative research and both political and academic compromise. Thus, different from the 'principles' published by the American Law Institute, the DCFR includes a number of innovative ideas and rules which nowhere in Europe currently exist in the way they are laid down in the DCFR.

[68] Article 9:102. Both, the DCFR and the CESL are based on the concept of specific performance and rejected the common law approach.

[69] In his reply to the Commission's Communication on European Contract Law, COM(2001)398 final.

[70] See n. 3, p. 215.

available in the English language,[71] this method seems most successful and worth copying in Germany.[72]

Comparative law should be presented in such a way that it appeals to a national lawyer. Its appeal will be strong if the research is directed at specific topics while at the same time the comparative lawyer undertaking the research is familiar with and ideally trained in both legal systems and understands the philosophical and historical foundations of both.[73] This service, which comparative law can provide, should not be belittled as a minor task. Comparative law is not only a service to the national legal system. It is a cause—an end in itself. The great jurist *Rudolph von Jhering* remarked more than 100 years ago in a well-known but little adhered to passage from his *Geist des römischen Rechts*:[74]

> The times have forever passed when Roman law united most of European jurisprudence. Legal scholarship is now national scholarship; the limits of legal science coincide with political borders. What a humiliating, unworthy state of affairs! Yet it is for legal scholarship to free itself from these limitations and to regain what it possessed for so long, to regain its universal character for all times to come, albeit under the different guise of comparative law. Its method will be different, its perspective wider, its judgment more mature, and thus the apparent loss will turn out to be its saviour, elevating legal science to a higher level.

With an increasing number of European regulations which require an autonomous and uniform interpretation, courts need different tools to assist them in deciding cases. Databases which make court decisions from other Member States available are being developed, but are not yet widely used by local courts. However, another instrument with which particularly German courts are familiar to work with is undergoing a slow, but significant change: the so-called 'commentaries' in which academics and practitioners explain legal provisions and provide the relevant case law to courts become more and more international. This applies to the traditional Commentaries of the German Civil Code only to some extent, but commentaries of the increasing number of European regulations are now often written by a team of international scholars and practitioners, and as a matter of course refer to the leading cases in different Member States.[75] With respect to the CESL, the European Parliament recently suggested that the blessings of 'commentary' on the text should be explicitly emphasized in a new recital of a CESL Regulation (recital 34 a).[76] The process takes time, but it has started. Comparative law is able to ensure that convergence between the different legal systems

[71] As done for instance on the website of the Institute of Global Law, University College London: <http://www.ucl.ac.uk/laws/global_law/cases/index.html>.

[72] Professor Kötz emphasizes that it is the task of the comparative lawyer to make the practitioner aware of the foreign material, n. 1, p. 841.

[73] Even study books for students are increasingly based on a comparative approach, see F. Ranieri, *Europäsiches Obligationenrecht* (3rd ed. 2009); R. Schulze and H. Schulte-Nölke (eds.), *Casebook Europäisches Verbraucherrecht* (1999).

[74] Vol. 1 (5th edn. 1891) p. 14 f.

[75] A good example is provided by the Commentary on the Brussels I Regulation edited by Rainer Hausmann and Thomas Simons (unalex *Kommentar Internationales Zivilprozessrecht - Brüssel I Verordnung*, IPR Verlag Munich 2012).

[76] See n. 62.

will emerge gradually and organically. By pursuing this path, rather than imposing extensive harmonization from above, the traditional approaches of national legal systems are preserved, and from these competing ideas the national judge will be able to choose the most compelling solution while preserving coherence within his own dear law.

32

Comparative Law in the Syariah Courts

A Case Study of Singapore, Malaysia, and Brunei

*Kerstin Steiner**

This chapter will explore how comparative law is used in the Syariah[1] courts of Singapore, Malaysia, and Brunei. These countries have been chosen because they all (1) belong to the common law legal tradition as a result of their colonial experiences; (2) adhere to the same *maddhab* (classic Islamic school of legal thought), namely the Shafi'i school of legal thought; and (3) have developed a similar approach towards administering law for Muslims.

During the colonial period, the law applicable to all Muslims in what are now Malaysia, Singapore, and Brunei was seen by the British colonial administration as a separate body of law. A hybrid mixture of legal doctrine developed through a long and complex process of regulatory intervention and judicial interpretation that Hooker, with a nod to British Indian 'Anglo-Mohammedan Law', has called the 'Anglo-Malay maddhab'.[2]

As a result, the Syariah courts in Singapore, Malaysia, and Brunei are all to some degree navigating the difficult question of whether they are principally located in a British common law tradition or an Islamic legal tradition; and whether they are common law courts or something else altogether.[3]

This observation suggests several lines of inquiry from a comparative law perspective, including investigation into the legal origin and path dependency of Islamic law in these countries, or to phrase it differently, how influential is this legal history in shaping the Syariah courts today? Is the historic influence of common law traditions or Islamic law more decisive? The observation also enables a reflection of the sources of law and the techniques employed by judges when making a decision, asking whether they are grounded in the common law tradition, Islamic legal tradition, or both.

It is the latter question that is the focus of this chapter. Following an introduction that provides the context for Islamic law in Singapore, Malaysia, and Brunei, this

* Dr Kerstin Steiner, Senior Lecturer at the Department of Business Law and Taxation, Monash Business School, Monash University and Associate of the Asian Law Centre, The University of Melbourne. The author would like to thank Professor Tim Lindsey for his kind permission to use some of the material from our project and publications, T. Lindsey and K. Steiner, *Islam, Law and the State in Malaysia and Brunei* (London: I.B.Tauris, 2012) and T. Lindsey and K. Steiner, *Islam, Law and the State in Singapore* (London: I.B.Tauris, 2012), and his comments on an earlier draft of the chapter.

[1] *Syariah* means 'Islamic law'. There are a variety of different spellings used for Arabic terms in Southeast Asia. I have chosen one of the most common spellings of these terms in the region and provide a short definition in order to assist the reader the first time such a term is used.

[2] Lindsey and Steiner, *Islam, Law and the State in Singapore*, 15.

[3] Lindsey and Steiner, *Islam, Law and the State in Singapore*, 207.

chapter discusses how comparative law is being used in the Syariah courts of Singapore, Malaysia, and Brunei today. The focus is on the different sources of law used in the Syariah courts and the style of reasoning relied upon to answer legal questions. It examines selected cases from each jurisdiction, referring to various arguably 'foreign' legal sources, such as the primary sources of Islamic law, the classical Islamic school of legal thoughts, and the Anglo-Malay maddhab. It also comments on how this material is used by judges in dealing with these sources. By taking this approach, the chapter will answer the question of how much of the colonial legacy is still evident in the decisions of the Syariah courts of Singapore, Malaysia, and Brunei.

I. Introductory context: history of Islam, law, and the state in Singapore, Malaysia, and Brunei

Singapore, Malaysia, and Brunei share a plural legal system in which Islamic law and secular law coexist. This existence of different norms next to each other is a result of the histories of these countries.

Islam reached the Malay Peninsula by the 14th century and spread with the territorial expansion of the Malacca Sultanate during the 15th century.[4] In pre-colonial Malaysia, the sultans or rajahs were the political leaders and the head of religion in their respective states. In this sense, there was no formal, institutionalized separation between politics, Islam, and law.[5]

This situation changed during the British colonial period as the status of Islam in the British colonial territories varied. The Straits Settlement,[6] to which Singapore belonged, was a crown colony and sovereignty rested with the British. Under British rule, Islam was not the official religion,[7] and the authority of Islam depended on the Charter of Justice, statute and precedent, and the accommodation there made for Islam. Unlike the situation in the neighbouring Malay states, that were also effectively controlled by the British, Islamic law was never the law of the land in the Straits Settlements. In the Federated Malay States, Unfederated Malay States, and Brunei, the status of Islam was recognized by the colonial treaties as within the sovereignty of the sultan.[8] Under the colonial administration, these sultans lost—to various degrees depending on the exact colonial status of their respective territories—their political power but still retained their religious authority.

[4] K. G. Tregonning, *A History of Modern Malaysia and Singapore* (Singapore: Eastern University Press, 1972), 16–21.

[5] For an account of this relationship, see, for instance, A. C. Milner, 'Islam and Malay Kingship' in A. Ibrahim, S. Siddique, and Y. Hussain (eds.), *Readings on Islam in Southeast Asia* (Singapore: ISEAS, 1985), 25–35.

[6] The Straits Settlement consisted of Malacca, Penang, and Singapore as well as Labuan (from 1907). It was established in 1826 by the British East India Company and became a crown colony in 1867. The territories are now part of the modern nations of Singapore and Malaysia.

[7] G. P. Means, 'The Role of Islam in the Political Development of Malaysia', *Comparative Politics,* 1(2) (1969) 264 at 275.

[8] Means, 'The Role of Islam', at 274, quoting the first agreement, the Pangkor Engagement, which stated that the Ruler 'receive and provide a suitable residence for a British Officer . . . whose advice must be asked and acted upon on all questions other than those touching Malay Religion and Custom.'

In all of these colonial territories, the basic tenor of how Islamic law was to be administered was the same. British colonial administration saw Mohammedan law as a separate body of law. Yet, through regulatory intervention and judicial interpretation, British common law and its legal traditions, procedures, and principles created the hybrid mix that Hooker labelled the Anglo-Malay maddhab. Occasionally, Islamic law was even supplanted by case law. For instance, in the case of *In the Goods of Abdulah,*[9] it was held that a Muslim could dispose of his property by will. The issue at hand was whether or not a letter of administration granted to the deceased's wife should be revoked on the grounds that the deceased had, in fact, executed a will. The judge, Malkin R., held that a Muslim could, by will, dispose of his complete property, even if this was not permissible under Islamic law. This adjudication on Islamic law by non-Muslims, in particular British officials, was sometimes the source of 'considerable embarrassment to British officers' who were 'disturbed' by their dual judicial responsibility.[10]

In postcolonial times, partial relicts of this dual judicial responsibility can still be found in the negotiation of the hierarchy and jurisdictional division between the Syariah courts and the civil courts. During colonial times and the early years of independence in Singapore and Malaysia, the jurisdictional division between the civil courts and the Syariah courts was not settled. It was quite common that Syariah court decisions could be appealed in the civil courts, a problem that continued to challenge the new states well after independence.[11]

Singapore, Malaysia, and Brunei all inherited British judicial precedent and legislation following independence. Based on their colonial heritage, the newly independent states started to negotiate their own approach towards accommodating Islam in their respective legal and political frameworks.

Singapore's road to independence was arguably influenced, in part at least, by the ruling elite's attitude towards Islam. In 1959, the island became self-governing with official elections being held. The People's Action Party (PAP), dominated by non-Muslims, won these elections—and every subsequent election until the time of writing. In 1963, Singapore merged with the Federation of Malaya, only to leave 23 months later to become an independent nation on its own. Singapore's expulsion from the Federation of Malaya was a result of persistent disagreement between the Chinese-dominated PAP and Malaya's ruling Malay-dominated Alliance. This disagreement was partially caused by religious concerns, one being the role that Islam should play within the state. Islam was supposed to be the official religion of the Federation of Malaya, as it still is in Malaysia today. This approach did not sit well with the

[9] *In the Goods of Abdullah* (1835) 2 Ky Ecc 8.

[10] Emily Sadka as cited in R. H. Hickling, 'The Influence of Islam on Singapore Law' in *Essays in Singapore Law* (Petaling Jaya: Pelanduk Publications, 1992), 111–61, 125.

[11] In what is now Malaysia, for example, sections 4 and 45(6) of the Administration of Muslim Law Enactment, No. 3 of 1952 (Selangor), allowed for cases to be appealed to civil courts. This was addressed in 1988 by the newly enacted article 121 (1A) of the Federal Constitution (Malaysia) which arguably abolished appeals to civil courts. In the case of Singapore, section 56(A) of the Administration of Muslim Law Act, cap. 3, No. 27 of 1966, rev. ed., 2009 (Singapore), hereafter called the AMLA of 2009 (Singapore), defined the exclusivity of the jurisdiction of the Syariah courts.

non-Muslim majority in Singapore. In addition, communal tensions between the majority non-Muslim population and the Muslim minority in Singapore were rising in the 1950s and 1960s.[12] It is therefore no surprise that the Republic of Singapore maintained a model for the administration of law for Muslims built upon the colonial experience. This meant that Islam was to be accommodated within a secular system,[13] restricting religion to the personal sphere and consequently limiting Islamic law to private legal matters. It also meant subjugating Islam to the interests of the ruling party.

This is in contrast to Malaysia and Brunei, where Islam is part of the political, ideological, and constitutional framework.[14] Pursuant to article 3 of the Federal Constitution (Malaysia), Islam is the official religion of the Federation and thus has a privileged position compared to any other religion. The result of this is a politically and socially hotly contested debate over whether or not Malaysia is an Islamic state.[15] Moreover, two of the main political parties—UMNO and PAS—regularly try to out-Islamize each other.[16] This meant that the institutionalization and bureaucratization of Islam continued in post-independence Malaysia, a phenomenon unprecedented before British arrival.

Brunei is at the other end of the spectrum compared to Singapore in the sense that Islam is part of the Brunei Malay Muslim Monarchy (Melayu Islam Beraja or MIB). As Lindsey and Steiner have commented, 'MIB conflates sovereignty and political legitimacy with the Sultanate, Islam and Malay identity', and, to a certain degree, the underpinning ideas of MIB are a continuum from the colonial period, 'when pre-colonial notions of authority of the Crown were relied upon as a tool of British colonial rule'.[17]

Despite the differences in approach towards Islam in Singapore, Malaysia, and Brunei—ranging from a careful management and supervision, to co-option, and integration into the political landscape—the cornerstones, legally speaking, had been set by the British colonial powers. None of those states sought to change the parallel

[12] Lindsey and Steiner, *Islam, Law and the State in Singapore*, 239.

[13] For details on the Singaporean approach to secularism and the Muslim minority, see K. Steiner, 'Religion and Politics in Singapore—Matters of National Identity and Security? A Case Study of the Muslim Minority in a Secular State', *Osaka University Law Review*, 58 (2011), 107–34, 107.

[14] Lindsey and Steiner, *Islam, Law and the State in Malaysia and Brunei*.

[15] Globally, there is no theoretical consensus as to what constitutes an Islamic state. For an overview of the different possibilities of defining Islamic state in the context of Malaysia, see A. Harding, 'The Keris, the Crescent and the Blind Goddess: The State, Islam and the Constitution in Malaysia', Singapore Journal of International and Comparative Law, 6 (2002), 154–80.

Tunku Abdul Rahman, who later became the first prime minister, commented that 'this country is not an Islamic state as it is generally understood . . . Islam shall be the official religion of the state' and that 'unless we are prepared to drown every non-Malay, we can never think of an Islamic Administration'. See Ahmad Ibrahim, 'The Position of Islam in the Constitution of Malaysia' in Ibrahim, Siddique, and Hussain (eds.), *Readings on Islam*, 213–20, 213, and F. R. Von Der Mehden, 'Religion and Politics in Malaysia', *Asian Survey*, 3(12) (1963), 609–15, 611.

In 2001, the prime minister at the time, Dr Mahathir Mohamad declared that Malaysia should be regarded as an Islamic state. In 2007, this sentiment was partially re-asserted by Deputy Prime Minister Najib Razak, who declared that Malaysia was never a secular state: see 'Malaysia Not Secular State, Says Najib', *Betnama*, 17 July 2007.

[16] Lindsey and Steiner, *Islam, Law and the State in Malaysia and Brunei*, 13–16.

[17] Lindsey and Steiner, *Islam, Law and the State in Malaysia and Brunei*, 345.

nature of the legal system, and changes to broaden the jurisdiction of Syariah courts were, arguably, negligible at least in Islamic family law, which is the focus of this chapter.

II. The Syariah court systems in Singapore, Malaysia, and Brunei

Singapore, Malaysia, and Brunei share a similar framework in regards to their court systems. As a result of colonial British heritage, all three countries have adopted a parallel legal system with a secular jurisdiction and Syariah jurisdiction. The jurisdiction of the Syariah courts in Singapore, Malaysia, and Brunei is mostly confined to personal law for Muslims,[18] with Malaysia and Brunei[19] also providing for certain limited Islamic criminal law matters to be heard in the Syariah courts. The selected case studies in this section[20] will only refer to matters of personal law.

As previously mentioned, British colonization in Singapore, Malaysia, and Brunei resulted in the introduction of common law traditions and institutions. In the case of the Syariah courts, the common law tradition is evident in the style of judgment. First, the existence of a written judgment as such is in itself testament to the influence of common law tradition, as cases were not formally reported in the Islamic legal tradition.[21]

The structure of reported cases follows the traditional common law formula of decisions starting with the judge setting out the application, including the reason for applying, the relief sought, and grounds relied upon. The next part of the decision then discusses whether or not the court has jurisdiction to hear the case, and if so, on what

[18] See, for example, in the case of Singapore, section 35 of the AMLA of 2009 (Singapore).

As Malaysia is a federal system, the powers—legislative and partially judicial—are divided between the states and the federal level. While the Federal Constitution in Schedule 9, List I (Federal List), Item 4 provides for the administration of general law to be a federal responsibility, Schedule 9, List II (State List), Item 1 provides that Islam is a matter for the individual states. Therefore, the jurisdiction of the Syariah courts is laid down in the various state enactments. For the purpose of this chapter, I refer only to the enactments of the Federal Territories as this is the model that has been adopted by most of the other states. The civil jurisdiction of the Syariah High Court is defined in section 46(2)(b) of the Administration of Islamic Law Act, No. 505 of 1993 (Federal Territories), and for the Syariah Subordinate Court, in section 47(2)(b) of the same act.

In the case of Brunei's Syariah courts, the Syariah Court Act, cap. 184, 2000 (Brunei), provides for the different jurisdictions. The civil jurisdiction of Brunei's Syariah High Court is laid down in section 15(b) and for the Subordinate Syariah High Court in section 16(b) of the same act.

[19] Compare in the case of Malaysia where the Syariah courts also have criminal jurisdiction: see, for instance, section 46(2)(a) of the Administration of Islamic Law Act, No. 505 of 1993 (Federal Territories) for the Syariah High Court and section 47(2)(a) of the same act for the Syariah Subordinate Court. For Brunei's Syariah High Court, the criminal jurisdiction is laid down in section 15(a), and for the Syariah Subordinate Court in section 16(a) of the Syariah Court Act, cap. 184, 2000 (Brunei).

[20] The selection is partially based on a study conducted by Lindsey and Steiner, who collected and analysed 50 cases from the Syariah courts in Singapore; 17 cases from various Syariah courts in Malaysia; and 17 cases from the Syariah courts in Brunei. See Lindsey and Steiner, *Islam, Law and the State in Malaysia and Brunei*; Lindsey and Steiner, *Islam, Law and the State in Singapore*.

[21] Lindsey and Steiner, *Islam, Law and the State in Malaysia and Brunei*, 463.

legal basis. This is followed by a brief case history and a summary of the submissions of the parties, including their legal arguments. The reasoning underpinning the decision, or *ulasan*, is usually the focus of the judgment. Here, the judge weighs the evidence given by the parties and decides whether or not the legal requirements have been satisfied. The last part of the judgment is the actual decision and the making of orders.[22] It is, however, noteworthy that the surveyed Malaysian and Singaporean Syariah courts' decisions do break with the common law tradition of including majority and dissenting opinions in a judgment. In these Syariah courts, the reasons are written by one judge, either in his own name or on behalf of the court, with no dissenting opinions recorded or mentioned.[23]

Furthermore, common law decisions follow a specific formula that consists of a detailed judgment, in which judges spend time identifying principles of law in previous decisions and drawing analogies with cases before them or distinguishing their facts from previous decisions.[24] This doctrine of *stare decisis* or binding precedent is one of the main characteristics of the common law legal tradition. Conversely, in classical Islamic judicial process, the judge is not bound by previous decisions but decides the case on its merits, usually applying one of the classical maddhab.[25]

This adherence to common law technique is especially evident in cases where the Syariah courts refer to cases decided by Syariah courts outside their jurisdiction, specifically within the 'new' Anglo-Malay maddhab. While decisions of this maddhab are, of course, not binding on the other Syariah courts, as they are from a different national jurisdiction, judges take particular care when using these cases and even more so when distinguishing their cases from them.

The legislative frameworks for Islamic law in Singapore, Malaysia, and Brunei basically invite judges to use comparative law in their decisions. The legislative frameworks of these countries are very similar in the sense that, in none of the countries, the Islamic legal framework is concerned with codifying the substance of Islamic law but is rather occupied with providing a framework for administering Islamic law. The lack of substantive rules makes it necessary for judges to locate the substance in arguably 'foreign' law, which is inherently an exercise in comparative law. In regards to these external sources, they can be categorized into three types: (1) classical primary Islamic legal sources; (2) a particular maddhab; or (3) Islamic law as it was developed within a certain cultural environment, that is, Muslim law as varied by Malay custom or the so-called Anglo-Malay maddhab.

The rest of this chapter will show how these sources are used in selected cases from all three jurisdictions.

[22] See Lindsey and Steiner, *Islam, Law and the State in Malaysia and Brunei*, 234, 463–4.

[23] Lindsey and Steiner, *Islam, Law and the State in Malaysia and Brunei*, 234; Lindsey and Steiner, *Islam, Law and the State in Singapore*, 214.

[24] For details on the type of legal arguments and methodology used in both the common law and Islamic legal traditions, see W. B. Hallaq, 'The Logic of Legal Reasoning in Religious and Non-Religious Cultures: The Case of Islamic Law and the Common Law', Cleveland State Law Review, 34(1) (1985–1986), 79–96, 79.

[25] N. Coulson, *A History of Islamic Law* (Edinburgh: University Press, 1964), 30.

1. References to primary Islamic sources: the Qur'an, Sunnah, and Hadith

The various legislation enforced in particular in Malaysia[26] and Brunei[27] refer to Islamic law per se, that is, stating 'hukum syariah' should be applied. Implicit in this phrasing is the reference to Islamic legal primary sources, that is, the Qur'an, *sunnah*,[28] and *hadith*.[29] As argued elsewhere, classical Islamic primary sources can be perceived as a form of global norm, albeit a contested one and therefore need interpretation and contextualization when applied.[30] Judges have to use human reasoning and engage with the primary sources of Islamic law. This means that it is left to the judge, at least to a certain degree, to locate and argue for the substance of these legal rules based on the classical Islamic legal sources. Hallaq describes this as the two-level approach upon which Muslim jurists operate; on the first level, they are 'bound by the explicit textual statements and commands', while on the second level the jurists are 'allowed a certain, although limited, freedom of interpretation in deciding the new case, due to the ambiguous nature of the textual precedents'.[31] The question is therefore how the judges in the Syariah court approach this material and what methods they employ in doing so.

In the early 2000s, Brunei's Syariah court system underwent significant change, most notably that any provision of the newly enacted Syariah Courts Act, cap. 184, 2000 (Brunei) has to be read in light of Islamic law (*hukum syariah*) with any inconsistencies resolved in favour of Islamic law.[32] This means that the Qur'an, *sunnah*, and *hadith* should take precedence when interpreting statutes. In reality, however, common legal methodology prevails, and classical sources are thus generally only used as an addendum to support legislative provisions and to legitimize the decision. Traditional Islamic legal sources are also used in assisting statutory interpretation by, for example, filling gaps in the legislation[33] or explaining technical Arabic terms.[34]

A similar observation—that Islamic law and state legislation are used in tandem—can be made in Malaysia. In the case of *Intan Shahira Mohd Shairun v Md Aszerul*

[26] See, for instance, the Syariah Court Civil Procedure (Amendment) Act, No. A1251 of 2005 (Federal Territories) which amended the English translation of the Syariah Court Civil Procedure Act, No. 585 of 1998 (Federal Territories) by substituting for the words 'Islamic law' and 'Islamic Law' wherever they appear, except in the definition of 'Administration Act' in subsection 3(1), with the words 'hukum syarak'—syarak being an alternative spelling of syariah.

[27] See, for instance, section 39 of Religious Council and Kadis Court Act, cap. 77, 1984 (Brunei) or section 144 of the Islamic Family Law, cap. 217, 2012 (Brunei) which makes 'hukum syariah' the default law if no provision is made for any other law to be applicable.

[28] *Sunnah* means the way, derived from *hadith*, sayings and deeds of the Prophet Muhammad.

[29] *Hadith* are the traditions, the recorded words, and deeds of the Prophet Muhammed.

[30] K. Steiner, 'Variations of "Unpacking" a Global Norm in a Local Context: An Historical Overview of the Epistemic Communities that are shaping Zakat Practice in Malaysia' in J. Gillespie and P. Nicholson (eds.), *Law and Development and the Global Discourses of Legal Transfers* (Cambridge: Cambridge University Press, 2011), 356–78.

[31] Hallaq, 'The Logic of Legal Reasoning', 88.

[32] Section 2(2) and (3) of the Syariah Courts Act, cap. 184, 2000 (Brunei).

[33] *Hjh Siti Tiewa binti Awg Hj Iring v Hj Reduan bin Lalal*, Unreported Case No. MRHS/MAL/BM/567/2006, 14 February 2007.

[34] *Pg Hj Mohd Yussof bin Pg Hj Jaludin v Dayang Haryati @ Erni Haryati Nurulhidayah binti Hj Awang Ismail*, Unreported Case No. MRHS/MAL/BM/360/2003, 29 April 2009.

Nizam Abdullah,[35] a wife sought an interim injunction against her husband to prevent him from giving interviews about their marital litigation. The husband had previously sought to have his wife declared *nusyuz* (disobedient), as she refused to see him on the advice of her family.

In his decision, the judge condemned the husband for going to the media and disclosing this information, stating that it 'may lead to slanders and back biting between the parties'. Then he quoted from the Qur'an, surah *Al-Hujarat*, verse 12, stating that '[a]nd do not let some of you slander others. Does one of you like to eat the flesh of his dead brother? Surely you abhor it; and keep your duty to Allah, for Allah is Oft-returning and Most Merciful.'

The judge also engaged in a discussion about whether the husband's interview was protected under Article 10 of the Federal Constitution (Malaysia), which grants freedom of speech. Correctly, he clarified that freedom of speech is not without limitations, in particular as regards 'acts of derision which [would] also fray the administration of justice'. He then supported this by reference to the Qur'an, surah *Al-Maidah*, verse 8, quoting, 'O you who believe! Be those who always uphold justice in the name of Allah, and never allow your hatred of others to make you act unjustly; act fairly (to everyone), for being fair is closer to that of piety. And keep your duty to Allah; surely Allah is Aware of all that you do.' Reference to this supposed harmonious synergy between the Constitution, human rights, and Islamic law is quite common in Malaysian court decisions.[36] In this case, it was quite appropriate.

This raises the question which source of law, state or divine, is given more weight in the Syariah court decisions. Unlike their counterparts in Brunei and Singapore, discussed later, Syariah courts in Malaysia rely far more on classical Islamic legal sources. From an Islamic perspective, this is arguably correct, as both a constitution and the Qur'an are binding positivist law. However, the Qur'an is divine in its origin, arguably a higher legal source against which national law can be checked. This approach of devaluing national positive regulation has been criticized by some Syariah appeal boards. This was particularly true of decisions in the 1990s cases handed down by Ahmad Ibrahim, a member of the Syariah Appeal Board of Kuala Lumpur.[37] This practice of emphasizing Islamic law over state positive law is still common in Malaysia, and is still criticized, but today mostly from outside the Islamic judiciary.[38]

[35] *Intan Shahira Mohd Shairun v Md Aszerul Nizam Abdullah* [2011] 1 CLJ (SYA) 477.

[36] In 1988, amendments to article 121 (1A) of the Federal Constitution (Malaysia) changed the delineation of jurisdictions between the civil and the Syariah courts. Since then, the 'harmonious' relationship between Islamic law and the Constitution has been questioned in particular with regard to cases of freedom of religion, apostasy, and unilateral conversion of children to Islam by one parent. Shaq Saleem Faruqi commented on this by saying 'with the slightest whiff of Islamic jurisprudence, our superior court abdicates in favour of the syariah courts even though momentous issues of constitutionality may be at stake or even if one of the parties is a non-Muslim.' Shaq Saleem Faruqi, 'Operating at the Periphery', *The Star Online*, 14 November 2007 available at <http://mstar.com.my/berita/cerita.asp?file=/2007/11/14/TERKINI/Mutakhir/Operating_at_the_periphery&sec=mstar_berita> last accessed 5 September 2013.

[37] See, for example, *Re: Mohd Hussin bin Abdul Ghani & Anor* [1990] 2 MLJ llxxv; *Rojmah binti Abdul Kadir v Mohsin bin Ahmad* [1991] 3 MLJ xxx; *Mejar Mohammed Sultan bin Ismail Dan Saodah binti Hj Abdul Kadir* [1991] 8(1) JH 266; *Jasni bin Abdul Rahim v Rahmah binti Mohd Jono* [1992] 1 MLJ cxliii.

[38] A coalition of numerous NGOs including the All Women's Action Society; Bar Council Malaysia; Catholic Lawyers' Society; Malaysian Civil Liberties Society; Protem Committee; Malaysian Consultative

Conversely, it is rather unsurprising that, in Singapore, the Syariah courts give primacy to state legislation, the AMLA of 2009 (Singapore). This approach is logical and pragmatic given that their formal authority is entirely based on the state and therefore 'to do otherwise would be to subvert the very instrument to which they owe their existence'.[39] In only one of 50 cases did Lindsey and Steiner find that a different approach was used.[40] In the case of *Katijah Bee binte Ahmad v Abdullah bin Mira Sahib*,[41] the judge prioritized his understanding of Islamic principles over state law. This was overall a very poorly argued decision; the judge clearly favoured the husband and found the wife at fault for seeking a divorce despite the fact that her husband, after some negotiations, had divorced her by *talak*.[42] Paradoxically, the judge even used a secular analogy to employment law, stating that 'if a wife requests a divorce she is like a worker who asks to resign from her job . . . the person who [resigns] does not deserve to claim any compensation or redundancy payment/pension or any right to something for which she no longer wants to bear any responsibility.'

There appears to be a divide between the two courts—the lower Syariah Court and the Syariah Appeal Board. The Appeal Board, writing mostly in English, refers more often to AMLA of 2009 (Singapore) and uses Islamic principles to support legislative interpretation, and as already mentioned, this method can also be observed in the Bruneian Syariah courts. In the case of *Aminah binte Abdullah v Mohahd Rais bin Rai*,[43] the Appeal Board even used both statute and Islamic law in order to criticize the subordinate Syariah Court for not adhering to the principles of fair hearing and the right to be heard. The decision started by acknowledging that this issue was 'quite familiar to common law practitioners but uncharacteristically still new turf to Syariah lawyers'.

In *Aminah binte Abdullah v Mohahd Rais bin Rai*, a divorce was being negotiated between a husband and wife. When the supposedly agreed terms were read out by the Syariah Court judge, the wife refused to sign off on the previously agreed upon terms. Notwithstanding her refusal to consent, the terms were recorded and formed the basis of the order by the court. The wife complained that she did not get the agreed compensation and was not provided with an opportunity to dispute her husband's comments. The Appeal Board referred to section 35(2) of the AMLA of 2009

Council of Buddhism, Christianity, Hinduism, Sikhism and Taoism; HAKAM; Sisters in Islam; Suara Rakyat Malaysia; Vivekananda Youth Movement, Seremban; Women's Aid Organisation; and Women's Development Collective formed Article 11 named after the constitutional provision for providing freedom of religion. The original website at <http://www.article11.org> appears to be dysfunctional now but the petition affirming the secular supremacy of the Federal Constitution over Islamic law can be accessed and signatories are listed at <http://www.petitiononline.com/petitions/constsup/signatures> last accessed 4 September 2013.

39 Lindsey and Steiner, *Islam, Law and the State in Singapore*, 209.

40 Lindsey and Steiner, *Islam, Law and the State in Singapore*, 212.

41 *Katijah Bee binte Ahmad v Abdullah bin Mira Sahib*, Syariah Summons, No. 18726.

42 The judge commented, for example, that the 'actions of the wife in applying for a divorce destroyed the sweet dream of the husband' and that 'the wife wanted profit, that is profit from the destruction of her family and the death of her marriage'.

43 *Aminah binte Abdullah v Mohahd Rais bin Rai*, Appeal Case No. 15/1987.

(Singapore), stating that the 'Syariah court shall *hear and determine* [emphasis added]'. The Appeal Board criticized the Syariah Court for failing to realize that 'the moment the Appellant declined to endorse the minutes the Court should have abstained from handing down any decision—in any event not before evidence from the parties and their witnesses had been heard'. The Appeal Board then referred to a *hadith* narrated by Ahmad, Abu Daud, and Termizi collected in *Nailil Awtar* (volume 8, page 24), which read that 'Ali (peace be upon him) narrated that the Messenger of Allah (peace be upon him) said: Ya! Ali, if two persons in dispute appear before you, you should not judge between them until you have heard the latter as you have heard the former. Then only the judgement will be (clear to you).'

In conclusion, in the case of *Aminah binte Abdullah v Mohahd Rais bin Rai*, the Syariah Appeal Board upheld the appeal by the wife on the grounds that her right to be heard during the proceedings had been violated, a right that the Syariah Appeal Board grounded in both the secular legislative provisions and divine law.

Interestingly, some of the secondary sources arguably detailing *fiqh*, Islamic jurisprudence, are catalogued in section 114 of the AMLA of 2009 (Singapore). This provision lists authoritative texts for Muslim law on succession and inheritance, some of which are texts from British India dating from the 19th to the 20th centuries.[44] The relevance and suitability of these sources for contemporary Singapore are highly questionable, but this has not been brought up yet in discussions of reforming AMLA. In the survey conducted by Lindsey and Steiner,[45] only two cases referred to these archaic texts; both cases were from the 1980s. It appears that this section is a leftover colonial legacy that, while still part of the legislative provisions, is no longer utilized. Watson described something similar when he referred to dysfunctional law as 'little bits and pieces, left over from other periods. Very often, these fragments survive precisely because they are so minor that it is hardly worth the trouble to wipe them off the face of the earth.'[46]

Unlike Malaysia, where the sunnah and hadith but moreover the Qur'an appear to take precedence over state law, the Syariah courts in Brunei and Singapore use them as a supplement in order to support state law. This leads to the question of how another source of classical Islamic law, that is, the different schools of thought, are being used.

[44] In two cases, namely *Zaleha binti Yusoff v Zakaria Bin Ahmat*, Appeal Case No. 01/1989 and *Mohd Rashid bin Mohd Hussein*, Appeal Case No. 01/1988, the Syariah Court expressly quoted from some of the sources first prescribed under British colonial rule and then incorporated under Section 114 AMLA of 2009 (Singapore) namely: (a) *The English translation of the Quran*, by Yusuf Ali or Marmaduke Pickthall; (b) *Anglo-Muhammadan Law*, by Sir Roland Knyvet Wilson, 6th edition revised by A. Yusuf Ali; and (c) *Muhammadan Law*, by F.B. Tyabji.

The other sources listed in Section 114 AMLA of 2009 (Singapore) that were omitted in these decisions were: (a) *Mohammedan Law*, by Syed Ameer Ali; (b) *Minhaj et Talibin* by Nawawi, translated by E. C. Howard from the French translation of Van den Berg; (c) *Digest of Moohummudan Law*, by Neil B. E. Baililie; and (d) *Outlines of Muhammadan Law*, by A.A. Fyzee. No reason is offered in the decisions for their omission.

[45] Lindsey and Steiner, *Islam, Law and the State in Singapore*, 210.

[46] A. Watson, 'Legal Change: Sources of Law and Legal Culture', University of Pennsylvania Law Review, 131 (1983), 1121–57 at 1139.

2. Reference to a particular classical Islamic maddhab: the Shafi'i school of legal thought

Adherence to the Shafi'i school of legal thought was a pre-colonial practice[47] and continued under colonial administration. In Malaysia, colonial legislation explicitly referred to the Shafi'i maddhab. For example, sections 30 to 42 of the Administration of Muslim Law Enactment, No. 3 of 1952 (Selangor), fixed the Shafi'i school as the main reference for the *mufti* (Muslim jurist capable of giving an authoritative legal opinion) and the Fatwa Committee in deciding issues among Muslims. Reference to the Shafi'i madhhab as the applicable school of legal thought has partially continued after Independence; however, the legislative framework is more flexible nowadays, a flexibility that is somewhat exploited by some Syariah courts.

In post-independence Malaysia, section 39(1) of the Administration of Islamic Law Act, No. 505 of 1993 (Federal Territories) also refers to the Shafi'i school of legal thought as the main maddhab to be used when giving a *fatwa*;[48] although, subsection 2 allows the Mufti to use any of the other Sunni maddhab[49] where 'public interest' so requires.[50] The Shafi'i maddhab is not exclusively mentioned as a source for the Syariah courts; instead *hukum syariak* is defined as 'Islamic law according to any recognized maddhab'.[51] It is noteworthy in this context, that if legislation lists the applicable maddhab for Syariah courts, it usually refers to the Shafi'i school of legal thought first, mentioning the others more or less as an afterthought; for example, section 3 of the Syariah Court Evidence Act, No. 561 of 1997 (Federal Territories) mentions 'Mazhab Shafie, or according to any one of the Mazhab Maliki, Hanafi or Hanbali', the same expression also being used in section 2, of the Islamic Family Law Act, No. 303 of 1984 (Federal Territories).[52]

The Syariah courts have therefore some flexibility in choosing a maddhab. In the case of *Datin Fauziah Haron v Dato Kadar Shah Tun Sulaiman*,[53] for example, the court took a noteworthy approach in making a decision as to which maddhab was

[47] A. Ibrahim, *Islamic Law in Malaya* (Singapore: Malaysian Sociological Research Institute, 1965), 152.

[48] *Fatwa* is a legal opinion of a qualified religious scholar in a particular situation. Traditionally, a *fatwa* is not binding, but legislative provisions in Southeast Asia have made them binding in particular circumstances.

[49] The four Sunni schools of Islamic legal thought are Hanbali, Hanafi, Maliki, and Shafi'i.

[50] Not all states followed the same approach. Other early independence legislation, Administration of Muslim Law Enactment, No. 3 of 1964 (Perlis), in section 7(4), simply stated, for example, that the Islamic Religious Council and the Syariah Committee shall follow the Qur'an and the sunnah of the Prophet.

[51] Section 2 of the Administration of Islamic Law Act, No. 505 of 1993 (Federal Territories).

[52] The Federal Territories in general have been more flexible with regard to adherence to a particular school of legal thought than some of the other states. This has been particularly obvious in reforms to Islamic family law. The Islamic Family Law Act, No. 303 of 1984 (Federal Territories), for instance, provides in section 52 several grounds under which a wife can seek a *fasakh* divorce, which is a divorce initiated by the wife on the grounds that the husband has not fulfilled certain obligations. These reasons are taken from a combination of schools of thought, including the Maliki. Conversely, the states of Kelantan, Terengganu, and Perak decided to adhere only to the Shafi'i school of legal thought and provide fewer circumstances under which a wife can divorce her husband. See A. Ibrahim and A. Joned, *Sistem Undang-Undang Di Malaysia* (Kuala Lumpur: Dewan Bahasa & Pustaka, 1986), 67, as cited by N. M. Hashim, *Towards a Fairer System in Awarding Maintenance for Children after Divorce: A Study of the Assessment Process in the Syariah Courts in Malaysia* (PhD Thesis, Melbourne: The University of Melbourne, 2013), 30.

[53] *Datin Fauziah Haron v Dato Kadar Shah Tun Sulaiman* [2010] 1 CLJ (SYA) 47.

applicable. The maddhab in question was not identified by the judge as the maddhab to which the parties adhered but rather the maddhab that would provide the remedies sought. The parties were married in Jakarta, Indonesia, in 1980. In 2003, the plaintiff, the wife, sought to obtain a divorce in the Syariah Subordinate Court, Shah Alam, Selangor, and applied for orders with regard to her maintenance for *iddah*,[54] *muta'ah*,[55] and matrimonial property. The Syariah Subordinate Court held that the marriage was irregular because it was not entered into correctly according to Islamic law, and consequently declined to make any orders. The wife then went to the Syariah High Court in Kuala Lumpur, claiming the same relief. The defendant objected to the jurisdiction of the court and stated that, since the Syariah Subordinate Court had ruled that the marriage was irregular, the plaintiff was not his lawful wife and therefore had no right to seek these remedies. Discussing whether the Syariah High Court was allowed to hear the case, the judge considered what the consequences of an irregular marriage would be for the claims. The judge stated that the Shafi'i school of legal thought 'did not prescribe any provisions pertaining the status of claims from irregular marriages'. The judge therefore felt free to consult the Hanafi and Maliki maddhab. The Hanafi school of legal thought was basically discarded, as the Maliki remedies were considered more relevant and applicable, or in common law terms, more likely to achieve a fair and equitable outcome, given that the couple had been married for 27 years and had three children together. Quoting from several Maliki textbooks, the judge held that, notwithstanding that parties of disputed irregular marriages should be separated, their respective marital and proprietary rights remained enforceable in law. Overall, the judge took a very utilitarian approach to choosing the applicable maddhab.

In Brunei, as in Malaysia, the Shafi'i maddhab is slightly more favoured, at least in the legislative provisions, as compared to the other Islamic schools of thought. Article 2(1) of the Constitution of 1959 (Brunei) states that the '"Muslim Religion" means the Muslim Religion according to the Shafeite sect of that religion'. This preference for the Shafi'i maddhab is also seen in section 43(1) of the Religious Council and Kadis Courts Act, cap. 77, 1984 (Brunei). This section provides that the Shafi'i maddhab is to be followed by the Majlis (Religious Council) and its Legal Committee when giving a *fatwa*. No similar provision is made for the authority of the Shafii maddhab in the Syariah courts. Therefore it is no surprise that the Syariah courts use classical sources of a particular school of legal thought only very rarely. If reference to an Islamic school of thought is made, the Brunei Syariah courts use this opportunity only to support existing legislative provisions and to legitimize their decision. This was done, for instance, in the case of *PG Hjh N... binti Pg Hj Z... v Pg Hj I... bin Pg Hj H...*[56] where the judge referred to Syeikh Muhammad's *Al-Khatib As-Syarbini's Mughni Al-Mutaj*—a classical textbook of the Shafii maddhab—in order to confirm a statutory provision, that is, section 87(1) of the Religious Council and Kadis Courts Act, cap. 77,

[54] *Iddah* is the prescribed waiting period for a woman following divorce or the death of her husband before she can marry again.

[55] *Muta'ah* is a consolatory gift on divorce if a specific dowry had not been specified.

[56] *PG Hjh N... binti Pg Hj Z... v Pg Hj I... bin Pg Hj H...*, Unreported Case No. TC/BM 54/2002, 12 October 2002. I have anonymised unreported cases that contain allegations of violence or sexual misconduct. Copies of all cases are on file with the author.

1984 (Brunei), which provided that the judge had the power to hear a case in the absence of the defendant.

Singapore has opted for a similar approach to Malaysia and Brunei. The requirement to 'ordinarily follow the tenets of the Shafi'i school of law' is only explicitly made for the Majlis Ugama Islam Singapura (Islamic Religious Council of Singapore or MUIS) and its legal committee.[57] Such an explicit reference is missing for the Syariah courts. In Singapore, the Syariah courts in general appear to avoid discussion of different schools of legal thought. In a study by Lindsey and Steiner, only one out of 50 cases made explicit mention of a particular maddhab.[58] This is in the case of *Mohd Rashid bin Mohd Hussin*,[59] discussed in more detail in section II.3. Even there, the Appeal Board avoided making a decision as to what the substantive rule of a particular maddhab was. The Singaporean Syariah courts, however, have to apply 'Muslim law, as varied where applicable by Malay custom', according to section 35(3) AMLA of 2009 (Singapore), which was one of the key issues of this case.

The next section looks at how this particular reference to 'Muslim law as varied by Malay custom' is dealt with in Singapore and in Malaysia and Brunei as it basically refers to the Anglo-Malay maddhab.

3. Reference to 'foreign' judgments: the Anglo-Malay maddhab

The Anglo-Malay maddhab is, in principle, a variation of the Anglo-Mohammedan maddhab in India that has been described by numerous scholars.[60] The creation of Anglo-Mohammedan law arose out of the principle that native law and customs be recognized 'subject to justice, equity, and good conscience'.[61] This principle affected both common law and Islamic law in its development. Common law and equity were adapted to Indian circumstances and society;[62] and 'the *syari'at*, as modified by English law, both common and statutory, and equity, in the varying social and cultural conditions of the sub-continent.'[63] This legal historical link between the states has been reinforced and continued into the post-independence era through legislative initiatives. As Hooker describes it, the 'codes in Southeast Asia have more in common than not.

[57] Section 33(1) of the AMLA of 2009 (Singapore).

[58] Lindsey and Steiner, *Islam, Law and the State in Singapore*. The study covered 50 cases on matters of divorce spanning 30 years from 1976 to 2006, selected from the Syariah Court, the Appeal Board, and a few High Court decisions.

[59] *Mohd Rashid bin Mohd Hussein*, Appeal Case No. 01/1988.

[60] For a description of the Anglo-Mohammedan law, see, for example, A. A. Fyzee, *Outlines of Mohammedan Law* (London: Oxford University Press, 1974). The Anglo-Malay maddhab has been described by M. B. Hooker, 'Muhammadan Law and Islamic Law' in M. B. Hooker (ed.), *Islam in South-East Asia* (Leiden: E. J. Brill, 1983), 160–82, and M. B. Hooker, *Islamic Law in Southeast Asia* (Singapore: Oxford University Press, 1984).

[61] This principle was included in Hastings's Mufassil Regulation of 1772, repeated in the Regulation of 1780.

[62] See, for example, R. K. Wilson, *Anglo-Muhammadan Law* (6th edn., London: Oxford University Press, 1930) for a complete account.

[63] A. A. Fyzee, *Cases in the Muhammadan Law of India and Pakistan* (Oxford: Clarendon Press, 1965), xxi.

Judges from one state would find themselves pretty well at home with the Codes of one or more of the others.'[64]

In Singapore, section 35(3) of the AMLA of 2009 (Singapore) refers to 'Muslim law, as varied where applicable by Malay custom' as the law to be applied in matters falling within the jurisdiction of the Syariah Court. This notion of Muslim law as varied by a particular custom is another relict of British colonial policies and is one of the reasons why we can talk about the development of an Anglo-Malay maddhab in former British colonies in Southeast Asia. In the case of Singapore, this phrase means that decisions from Malaysia are of particular importance, as they elucidate variations in Malay custom.

The case of *Zainoon binte Ibrahim v Mohamed Zain bin Ismail*[65] illustrates this point. In this case, it was held for the first time that the principle of *harta sepencarian* (matrimonial property, jointly acquired property during marriage) was applicable in independent Singapore. Using section 35(3) of the AMLA of 1966 (Singapore), counsel successfully argued that *harta sepencarian* was indeed part of Malay custom and should be recognized in Singapore for that reason. Reference was made to cases decided by Malaysian courts, including *Roberts alias Kamarulzaman v Ummi Kalthom*[66] and *Mohamed v Commissioner of Lands and Mines, Terengganu & Anor*.[67] The court held that, while these cases were not binding, they are highly persuasive. Furthermore, it argued that Malay custom in Singapore is *Adat Temenggong*, which 'is much the same as that found in the States of Malaya', thus allowing for the principle of *harta sepencarian* to be applied. This was a noteworthy departure from previous precedents, as existing Straits Settlements cases did not allow for this principle to be applied.[68]

The importance of these Malaysian cases is also evident in situations when they are not followed. If cases from the Anglo-Malay maddhab are not followed, the Singaporean Syariah courts are very careful in explaining their reasons for not applying them. The case of *Mohd Rashid bin Mohd Hussein*[69] is particularly interesting with regard to several common law techniques that were adopted. The husband had pronounced a triple *talak*[70] to his wife over the telephone by saying, 'I divorce you with a triple *talak*'. Subsequently, the husband applied to the *kadi* (judge) for a divorce, declaring that he had used the word 'triple' intentionally, so as not to reconcile with his wife. As per statute, the case was referred to the Syariah Court where the husband confirmed his intention to utter of a triple talak. He later regretted the divorce and appealed the Syariah Court's decision granting a divorce by triple talak. On appeal, the husband

64 M. B. Hooker, *Accommodating Islam in Singapore* (Unpublished Paper, on file with the author), 3.

65 *Zainoon v Mohamed Zain* [1981] 2 MLJ 111.

66 *Roberts alias Kamarulzaman v Ummi Kalthom* [1965] 3 LNS 1, [1966] 1 MLJ 163.

67 *Mohamed v Commissioner of Lands and Mines, Terengganu & Anor* [1968] 1 LNS81, [1968] 1 MLJ 227.

68 See, for example, *Bongh v Mat Din* (1937) 15/1 JMBRAS 16 or *Tijah Mat Alli* (1937) 15/1 JMBRAS 15.

69 *Mohd Rashid bin Mohd Hussein*, Appeal Case No. 01/1988.

70 *Talak* is a divorce initiated by the husband when he pronounces the word *talak, I divorce you*. The issue is how a triple *talak* is viewed by the different schools of legal thought, as the consequence might be that the husband and wife could not reconcile if they later changed their minds.

argued that he was consumed by anger at the time of pronouncing the triple talak and had not been aware of the consequences.

The Appeal Board disagreed and rejected the husband's arguments out of hand but had to entertain the notion whether the husband's maddhab—the Hanafi school of legal thought—allowed for a triple talak to take place. What followed was a discussion of various sources, Sayid Sabiq and his *Fiqh-al-Sunnah* and two texts from Saudi Arabia, that supported the position that a triple talak was indeed permissible and irrevocable. The Board also supported this with its own precedent by which it felt bound. In the case *In re Assim Amat*,[71] the court had held that if a husband pronounced triple talak with the intention of effecting triple talak, then a triple talak was effected.

In the end, the Appeal Board came to the conclusion in *Mohd Rashid bin Mohd Hussein* that, while they were not convinced that the Hanafi school of legal thought prohibited a triple talak, the appellant had not produced sufficient evidence to show that he belonged to that particular Islamic school. In other words, the Appeal Board stated that they were not convinced that a particular foreign law had been proven in substance and, moreover, sufficient evidence was not provided that a particular law should be applied.

In addition, the Appeal Board used the common law technique of distinguishing between cases on the grounds of facts and legislative context. The Appeal Board referred to the Malaysian case of *Re Mohd Hussin bin Abdul Ghani and Anor*,[72] where a husband claimed to be of the Hanafi school of legal thought and had uttered a triple talak. Ibrahim, a judge of the deciding Syariah Appeal Board of Kuala Lumpur in that case, held that he was convinced that the husband did, in fact, belong to this maddhab, and moreover, that this maddhab did not allow for a triple talak to take place at the same time. Interestingly, Ibrahim referred back to Singapore and the case in which a man had pronounced a triple talak at the same time and place. According to Ibrahim, the Syariah Court in Singapore had considered this to be just one talak. Unfortunately, the Syariah Appeal Beard in Kuala Lumpur did not provide further details of the Singaporean case. Moreover, the Singaporean Appeal Board in *Mohd Rashid bin Mohd Hussein* referred to its own precedents that stated otherwise.

Distinguishing the cases at hand, the Singapore Appeal Board in our case of *Mohd Rashid bin Mohd Hussein* stated that the Kuala Lumpur Syariah Appeal Board was influenced by the fact that the husband's wife had been pregnant at the time of the divorce and that the Malaysian Islamic Family Law, No. 303 of 1984 (Federal Territories) in sections 47(3), 54, and 124 prohibited a divorce by *talak* outside the court. Based on the different legislation applicable in Singapore and Malaysia and the different circumstances of the cases—the wife in the Singaporean case was not pregnant—the court argued that this would provide sufficient grounds not to follow Malaysian precedent but basically the Singaporean one and considered the uttered divorce a valid triple talak.

In Malaysia, foreign cases can be constructed in two ways—they can be understood as cases from foreign countries, that is, extraterritorial cases, and also as cases from

[71] *In re Assim Amat*, Appeal Case No. 14/1986.
[72] *Re Mohd Hussin bin Abdul Ghani and Anor* [1990] 2 MLJ 125.

within Malaysia but from another state.[73] Referring to these extraterritorial cases, Ahmad Ibrahim criticized the fact that Syariah courts' decisions generally lacked references to cases from other countries.[74] A few years later, Horowitz commented that this has been changing and judges are starting to develop 'a body of law for which they are collectively responsible'.[75] In the case of the Syariah courts this is changing as they are starting to refer to cases within Malaysia. In creating this body of law, other Syariah court decisions are being utilized in a similar way to the practice of Singapore's courts—that is, to illustrate a point[76] or to lend support to an argument.[77] For instance, in the case of *K v S*,[78] the Syariah Board of Appeal (Kuala Lumpur) referred to the case law from Selangor[79] and Kelantan[80] to argue and support their position that the welfare of a child is the paramount consideration when deciding custody of a child. In the case of *Mohd Zuhdi bin Mohd Nawawi v Norsharifah binti Sharif*,[81] the 'precedent' of other Malaysian states was mentioned by the parties, and perhaps because of this, the court stated that it did not feel bound by it. Despite this, reference to extraterritorial Syariah court cases are still rare in Malaysia.

However, Malaysian cases appear to be very popular sources for the other Syariah courts. Syariah courts in Brunei, as in Singapore, are using them to give more credibility and support to their decisions. In the case of *Kamaluddin bin Hj Mohd Sum v Ajijah binti Ibrahim*,[82] the Bruneian court had to determine the amount of child maintenance that a father had to pay. The court referred to the Malaysian case of *Hayati binti Othman v Ayob bin Zainal*,[83] in which the same issue was to be decided. In the Malaysian case, Ahmad Ibrahim, delivering the verdict, stated that the obligation to provide 'clothing and maintenance must be borne by the father in a fair way...No mother shall be made to suffer harm on the account of her child, nor any father on account of his.' As is often done in Malaysian cases, a reference to Islamic law—this time, the Qur'an, surah *Al-Baqara*, verse 2: 233—was used in support of this argument.

Malaysian cases appear to be commonly cited by Syariah courts in both Singapore and Brunei. Malaysia's Syariah courts venture less frequently out of their national jurisdiction, although they more frequently cite one another. In the long-term, this will further cement the Anglo-Malay maddhab. This maddhab will, however, most likely develop under the 'leadership' of Malaysian Syariah courts, making it a very different

[73] As briefly mentioned earlier, Islam is a matter for the individual states in Malaysia, meaning that the decisions from other Syariah courts in other Malaysian states are not part of the case law of a different state as they fall outside its jurisdiction.

[74] A. Ibrahim, 'The Shariah Courts and Its Place in the Judicial System', Shariah Law Journal, 5(1) (1989) as cited in D. Horowitz, 'The Qur'an and the Common Law: Islamic Law Reform and the Theory of Legal Change: Part 1', American Journal of Comparative Law, 42 (1994), 233–93, 237.

[75] Horowitz, 'The Qur'an and the Common Law', 237.

[76] *Mejar Mohammed Sultan bin Ismail Dan Saodah binti Hj Abdul Kadir* [1991] 8(1) JH 266.

[77] *Rojmah binti Abdul Kadir v Mohsin bin Ahmad* [1991] 3 MLJ 30.

[78] *K v S* [1990] MLJ 1x.

[79] *Nooranita binte Kamarudin bin Yeop* [1990] 7(1) JH 52.

[80] *Wan Abdul Aziz v Siti Aishah* [1975] 1(1) JH 47, [1977] 1 JH 50.

[81] *Mohd Zuhdi bin Mohd Nawawi v Norsharifah binti Sharif* [2003] 16(1) JH 85.

[82] *Kamaluddin bin Hj Mohd Sum v Ajijah binti Ibrahim*, Unreported Civil Appeal, Case No. MTS/R/BM/4/02.

[83] *Hayati binti Othman v Ayob bin Zainal* [1991] 7(2) JH 246.

Anglo-Malay maddhab indeed to the one initially developed under British colonial influence.

III. Conclusion

This chapter set out to discuss the use of comparative law with regard to the sources and techniques employed by judges in selected Southeast Asian Malay Muslim communities to assess whether they are grounded in common law or Islamic law.

Regarding sources of law, legal transplant or borrowing is frequently used in the area of Islamic law in Singapore, Malaysia, and Brunei with regard to all three different types of 'foreign' law—that is, primary Islamic sources, classical Islamic schools of legal thought, and the Anglo-Malay maddhab as enunciated in other Malay Muslim countries. Classical Islamic sources, whether primary or the different classical Islamic schools of thought, are used to greatly varying degrees by the different Syariah courts. The frequency of use, and the manner in which they are used, depends very much on the local circumstances. In Singapore, the vast majority of references to Islamic law are from the Qur'an, but just as frequent, if not more so, are references to case law from Singapore and Malaysia.[84] In Brunei, reference to classical Islamic law is made in order to support existing legislation, providing it with additional authority. In Malaysia, Islamic law has found its strongest supporter in the regional Syariah courts.

This may explain why Malaysian cases are also more frequently cited by the Syariah courts in Singapore and Brunei than the other way around; the Malaysian cases thus appear to be more grounded in what is perceived as Islamic legal tradition. Watson described a similar phenomenon when he stated that a legal transfer bias exists, caused by 'the general high standing of the donor system, the general high prestige, apart from its law, of the donor state; a shared legal tradition of the donor and borrower; and the accessibility—for instance, in writing or in a code—of the law to be borrowed.'[85]

This partially answers the secondary question of how much of the colonial legacy is still evident in the Syariah courts of Singapore, Malaysia, and Brunei. The initial creation of the Anglo-Malay maddhab as such is a colonial product. However, the post-colonial independent states have taken very different approaches to how Islam is to be accommodated in their systems. Singapore followed the well-trodden path of carefully policing Islam, while Malaysia and Brunei followed a more integrated approach, making Islamic thought part of the political landscape. This, of course, will eventually affect how appropriate it may be in the future to refer to each other's cases—but this is still far away.

On the question of whether the style of the Syariah court decisions is based in the common law or the Islamic legal tradition, the answer is that they are neither. Rather, the Syariah courts are an eclectic mix. Providing written judgments is a testament to the common law tradition—and this is increasing in Singapore, Malaysia, and Brunei, where the states are starting to provide compilations of written judgments and

[84] Lindsey and Steiner, *Islam, Law and the State in Singapore*, 209.
[85] Watson, 'Legal Change', 1147.

compilations of legislation that are more easily accessible by the public.[86] The general formula of the court's decisions reveals adherence to the common law tradition as well. Yet common law tradition is not always followed in other matters. Perhaps being an eclectic hybrid is also a sign of the Anglo-Malay maddhab.

In general, one could wish for more rigour in the arguments of the courts. This can be said for other jurisdictions, too, and is not a weakness exclusive to the decisions of the Syariah courts. Addressing this issue would require an overhaul of the training of the legal profession.

Moreover, addressing this eclectic hybridization would require an engagement with the question as to what the appropriate techniques and methods are for judges when deciding a case in the modern Syariah courts. It is not just Syariah court judges in Southeast Asian countries that were once British colonies facing this problem. It is a common problem among judges in modern nation Syariah courts all around the world where colonial policies once dictated the accommodation of Islamic law.

[86] In Singapore, one of the latest initiatives is the launch of the Singapore Syariah Appeals Report in 2012, a compilation of written decisions by the Board of Appeal. Malaysia has established an e-Syariah portal where legislation applicable to Muslims is easily available nowadays and a website where the *fatwa*, both federal and state, are available online.

PART VII

USING COMPARATIVE LAW: CASE STUDIES

33

'Liaison Magistrates'

Their Role in International Judicial Cooperation and Comparative Law

Bernard Rabatel and Olivier Deparis***

I. Introduction

Until relatively recently, it was not common practice for a domestic judge to consult the legislation or the jurisprudence of foreign countries before giving his decision, though he might well have been given the opportunity to find out about the legal system of a foreign country, more or less distant from his own in geographical, cultural, and linguistic terms, during the course of his legal studies.

This interest in foreign law now appears to be one of the elements forming part of the training of young lawyers. The large number of requests for internships which are received by French embassies confirms this and suggests that future judges may well adopt a different approach from that of their predecessors towards foreign legislation.

The *Ecole Nationale de la Magistrature*, which has ensured the initial and continuing training of French judges for over 50 years, has developed programmes with the primary objective of raising awareness of the legal systems of other countries. However, there is a difference between, on the one hand, initiation in the law of other countries and, on the other hand, the concrete and practical use which judges are able to make of such knowledge when they must give judgment in cases where the issues are not confined to the domestic sphere.

The development of Community law and the jurisprudence of the European Court of Human Rights, and the accompanying consequences, have profoundly changed the way in which judges have, up until now, viewed the operation of their legal systems.

Equally, the arrival of the Internet in courts means that judges now have access to the law of foreign jurisdictions by means of a simple click.

Times are changing.

It could therefore be thought that the majority of barriers which discouraged judges from being inspired by, or indeed from borrowing, legal concepts or solutions from their neighbours, have fallen. That would, however, be a somewhat premature conclusion. In reality, even with the assistance of technology, obstacles remain and such

* Bernard Rabatel was the French liaison magistrate in the United Kingdom from January 2002 until April 2007. In November 1996, he was the first liaison magistrate to be posted to the United States of America, and he undertook this role in Washington DC until December 2001. He is currently the 'Procureur général' in Martinique.

** Olivier Deparis was French liaison magistrate in the United Kingdom until February 2014. He is currently 'Président de chambre' at the Douai Court of Appeal.

obstacles go beyond simple questions of linguistics. A desire to resolve a legal problem by comparing solutions already adopted in other jurisdictions can come up against the problems caused by a greater or lesser understanding of the real meaning of foreign legislation and case law. A lack of knowledge of the local context of a country's laws and jurisprudence can lead to misunderstanding, which does not assist the reasoning of a judge curious to know how a foreign colleague would respond to a question which is similar to the one before him.

For a little over 20 years now, judges have been able to receive assistance from certain colleagues if they wish to find out the solution adopted by foreign jurisdictions towards a novel problem. In March 1993, the first appointment of a French judge to a post in the Italian judicial authorities was made, in Rome, with the primary mission of improving mutual judicial assistance between France and Italy. This first appointment was followed by the appointment of another French judge, this time in Holland. Several other posts for so-called 'liaison magistrates' have been created within the judicial authorities in America, Spain, Germany, the United Kingdom, Czech Republic, Canada, and Morocco. More recently, posts for liaison magistrates have been created in North Africa (Algeria, Tunisia), Turkey, the Middle East (Qatar), and South America (Brazil). It shows the will of the French Ministry of Justice to improve judicial cooperation throughout the world and especially in economically emerging countries. Reciprocal posts for 'liaison magistrates' have been created in France at the Ministry of Justice in Paris. These appointments, made with the common objective of improving, in a general manner, judicial cooperation between countries, have encouraged other countries to embark upon this route. The process was formalized by a Joint Action of the European Union of 22 April 1996.

The activities undertaken by liaison magistrates fall into four broad categories:

- mutual assistance in the sphere of international criminal law;
- mutual assistance in the sphere of civil law;
- comparative law;
- the forging of links between judicial authorities.

II. Liaison magistrates and mutual assistance in matters of international crime

Due to their knowledge of the law and procedure of both their own country and of their host country, liaison magistrates tend to be in a position to remove the principal obstacle which a domestic judge is likely to encounter when he considers that it would be useful to consult the law of another country: the misunderstanding, created by the real or imagined differences between the legal systems. In the sphere of bilateral cooperation in criminal law, an imperfect understanding of another country's legal system can still lead all too often to a form of self-censorship. Thus, for example, the French 'juge d'instruction' who wishes to hear evidence from a witness who is abroad or wishes to collect evidence (bank documents, DNA samples, etc) may well hesitate to send an international letter rogatory, fearing that a response is by no means certain. On the other hand, if such a judge is able to request assistance from a colleague posted in the relevant country, he is able to direct his request, taking into account the requirements which are particular to the procedure applied in that other country.

An increasingly large number of 'juges d'instruction' in France now send to the liaison magistrate, by fax or by email, letters rogatory which they wish to send to the authorities of that country. Their colleague in the foreign post will accordingly be led to clarify certain points, such as in the capacity in which a person is to give evidence (as a witness or as a suspect), to provide the evidence required for a search warrant, or to have telephone numbers identified. This advisory, indeed expert, work, carried out prior to the transmission of the request for mutual assistance in the criminal sphere, can pre-empt the need for the foreign authorities to make a request for further information, which would otherwise delay the execution of the letters rogatory. In an urgent case, the proximity of the liaison magistrate to his colleagues in the host country enables him to draw their attention to the need to respond to the request for judicial assistance as quickly as possible.

Similarly, liaison magistrates are able to provide information to their foreign colleagues on the requirements of French law and on the rules of procedure applicable in their country of origin. This explanation is rendered easier by their presence in the workplace of their foreign colleagues. Even in the era of the Internet, nothing quite compares to a direct exchange, face-to-face, between two people who know each other, and meet regularly.

Equally, the judge who has made the request for mutual assistance can, with the help of his colleague posted to the relevant member state, follow the execution of his request and so will not receive the impression that his request has fallen into a black hole, a reproach heard all too often in the area of cooperation in international crime. Moreover, should difficulties arise in the execution of the request, the judge can swiftly be informed of the reasons for the problem. Such information is particularly useful if one or more of the people being investigated are being held in detention. How often is it heard that a 'juge d'instruction' cannot finish his dossier since he is still waiting for the response to his international letter rogatory!

The formation of joint inquiry teams between two or more countries—a form of cooperation which is now indispensable in order to combat more effectively the new types of international organized crime—has caused liaison magistrates to play increasingly the role of facilitator and interpreter of legal systems. Even though the rules applicable in a country are often no more than the specific enunciation of common principles, the intervention of liaison magistrates means that a rapid response can be provided to the everyday, practical problems of cooperation: changing the letter of the law is not enough unless there is also a simultaneous change of mentality. Mutual assistance must be founded on a great degree of confidence between operators, based on common standards which guarantee the respect of the rights and liberties of those participating in a criminal trial.

For some 20 years now, liaison magistrates have thus intervened as real 'legal adapters' between different systems. Since they are integrated within the workplace of their foreign colleagues, liaison magistrates are also regularly consulted by the judicial authorities of their host country when members of such authorities have an interest in the legislation, the jurisprudence, or, more generally, the operation of the French legal system.

This role of facilitator between the procedures of different countries also encompasses extradition procedures (which underwent profound change in 2004 with the entry into force of the European arrest warrant). In 2014, it must be acknowledged that, despite the European texts related to the arrest warrant procedure which is applicable between countries of the EU, there remain significant differences between countries of common law and continental law systems. Which should take priority: a provisional arrest request or an extradition request? The answer may differ according to the country in question. The compilation of a dossier must also take into account the avenues of appeal available in the country in question: for example, the opening of a dossier of extradition to the United Kingdom is directly dependent on habeus corpus appeals and judicial review, exercised against the decisions of the judge sitting at Bow Street in London and of the executive power (the Home Secretary). The liaison magistrate must thus play his role of adapter between two systems which are even further apart.

The same goes for matters concerning the transfer of people who have been sentenced to imprisonment and who wish to carry out their sentence in the country of which they are a citizen.

III. Liaison magistrates and mutual assistance in civil matters

Liaison magistrates also participate in the handling of bilateral cases, such as those concerning the international abduction of children by a parent (The Hague Convention of 1980). Liaison magistrates ensure that the two parties who are claiming custody of the child do not take advantage of the different legal systems in order either to deprive one of them of the exercise of their rights as a parent of the child, or to render impossible any amicable agreement: liaison magistrates aim to fill the gaps between the legal systems which might otherwise present problems to one or other of the parents when they have to make submissions to the foreign judiciary.

Moreover, the creation of the European Judicial Network in civil and commercial matters, in which liaison magistrates are included, has contributed to facilitating the execution of judicial decisions from one country to another, preventing parties from 'choosing' their judges.

The implementation of measures to protect those under guardianship increasingly gives rise to the intervention of liaison magistrates as soon as those under guardianship move from one place to another, thus presenting difficulties for the administration of their possessions.

The execution of letters rogatory in civil matters therefore means that the liaison magistrate's sphere of competence is not limited to matters of criminal law.

IV. Liaison magistrates and comparative law

Initially, liaison magistrates were involved in comparative law for our domestic courts. Nowadays, comparative law is the most important part of their work: indeed, in the law-making process, impact studies must be carried out and must include comparative law studies.

An area in which liaison magistrates are increasingly involved is that of the dissemination of foreign law, when a national court is called to pronounce upon a new legal question.

In the absence of any relevant legislative provision or case law precedent, it is tempting and even advisable, for the domestic judge to try to find out what answer has been given to the question by a foreign legislature or court. This situation can often arise in the sphere of so-called 'social problems'. In France, one can cite the legal problems raised by, for example: a couple's use of a surrogate mother; an application for adoption made by a same-sex couple; the case of involuntary manslaughter of a fœtus; the principle of whether compensation should be granted to children who are born handicapped, where the mother had been denied the option of abortion due to a clinical error. Each time they have been consulted, liaison magistrates have informed their colleagues of the response, or absence of a response, made by the foreign legislature or courts to these sorts of fundamental questions which confront our society.

Even in more so-called 'classic' cases, bearing on, for example, the right to respect for private life, liaison magistrates are invited to inform the court of the approach adopted by the courts in their country of origin. Obviously, it is not simply a matter of copying another judge's decision, made in the context of a different legal system. However, the knowledge of the law applicable in another country and of its interpretation by one of that country's judges undoubtedly provides valuable assistance in reaching a decision. Liaison magistrates do not content themselves with simply providing a copy of the relevant judgment, which could prove to be of limited use to a foreign court. Rather, they accompany their response with personal commentary, enriched by their knowledge of the legal system of their host country.

Thus, the era, not so long ago, when it was considered to be an admission of a lack of serious argument for a lawyer to cite foreign legislation or case law, appears to be consigned to history. This can only be welcomed.

Recently, the French legislator considered that all significant projects of law must first be the subject of an impact study in order to evaluate its consequences on the financial costs that may be incurred, while taking into account the dispositions in force in the world's democratic states, especially in European countries.

In that context, it is the work of the liaison magistrate to ensure a good analysis of comparative law and explain the current context and the law in his host country.

And so the question of same-sex marriages was discussed before Parliament and the *Assemblée Nationale* at the same time. At the time, it was required of the liaison magistrate to underline the specificities of the question in the United Kingdom where some religious authorities were able to validly celebrate unions without having a registrar present. It was also required of the liaison magistrate to explain the current legislation allowing same-sex couples to adopt children or to use the methods of IVF or surrogate mothers.

Actually, these points that had been mentioned and contested during the discussion at the French Parliament had already been resolved in 2005 in the Parliament of Westminster.

Each year, the liaison magistrate must draft around 50 comparative law studies on various topics of criminal law, criminal procedure rules, such as, for example, the question of investigative powers or the specificity of military offences in common law or the sentencing system in common law. He must also address questions on civil law and commercial law. Comparative law has therefore become one of the main activities of the liaison magistrate.

At their modest level, liaison magistrates thus participate in the growing convergence of legal cultures.

V. The 'rapprochement' of judicial authorities

Knowledge of the particular characteristics of a foreign legal system can assist in preventing misunderstandings, assuaging anxieties borne of ignorance, and facilitating exchanges between those participating in the civil and criminal systems.

Each year, internships are organized in order to allow lawyers, judges, or public prosecutors to discover or to deepen their knowledge of the operation of justice in other countries. Evidently in those countries where there is a liaison magistrate, the latter will intervene directly, both in the setting-up of the internship and in the choice of the programme. Liaison magistrates benefit in this from the valuable assistance provided by organizations which forge links with different legal cultures, such as associations of lawyers, schools, universities, or training institutions. In addition to such institutions, an important role is played by the goodwill shown by many lawyers in welcoming their foreign colleagues and in helping them to get to know their legal system.

Liaison magistrates also participate in the preparation of bilateral negotiations concerning, for example, the implementation of a convention on mutual judicial assistance in criminal matters (such as that signed between France and the United States of America) with a view to forging links between the positions of the countries in question. During the elaboration of these new texts, liaison magistrates are asked to shed light on the difficulties that they have observed in the course of their everyday work, enabling the implementation of concrete and useful solutions.

At the point at which linguistic and textual barriers disappear, the barrier which exists too often in the minds of those participating in the legal systems must also be removed, in order to give way to confidence: in their own way, liaison magistrates are dedicated to achieving this aim.

34

Comparative Law in Consumer Litigation

Geraint Howells and Jonathon Watson***

I. Introduction

Comparative law is frequently used in legislative reform. Indeed at the European level there is an abundance of comparative surveys that have preceded and contributed to the justification of Commission legislative initiatives that intend to harmonize consumer law.[1] This chapter concerns the use of comparative law in consumer litigation. Our examples are taken primarily from the English jurisdiction, though we also consider the role of the Court of Justice of the European Union (CJEU) and possible ways in which comparative materials can be made more readily available. In this essay we restrict our discussion to the way English courts use civilian European laws in consumer litigation. Different issues arise when they look at other common law jurisdictions applying the same or similar principles. Indeed this family of law tradition is evident within Europe with definable families of French, Germanic, and Nordic origin happily sharing jurisprudence.[2] A key issue will be whether within the scope of the *ius commune* there is a sufficient commonality of legal order for legal systems to borrow in the same way and, even if there is, whether the barriers in terms of access to and comprehension of other legal systems make this practical and desirable.

Researching comparative law arguments may involve considerable time and use of resources. Invoking comparative law is very expensive, if one moves beyond relying on textbooks, and there may be good reasons why parties will not simply accept secondary sources. It may also be risky as to costs for even if one wins one might not recover all or any of the costs relating to comparative research when costs are assessed. Recent reforms to costs law in England and Wales may make it even more difficult to justify extensive comparative research.[3] The combination of these factors in part explains the rarity of comparative law discussion in the courts. This is also of course due to the reluctance of courts to entertain such arguments, which may be viewed as too speculative. As is well known, consumer cases are rarely litigated as often the amounts

* Dean of the School of Law and Chair Professor of Commercial Law, City University of Hong Kong.
** Westfälische Wilhelms-Universität Münster, Germany.

[1] For example, Commission, 'Proposal for a Council Directive on unfair terms in consumer contracts' COM (90) 322 final, p. 12 et seq.; Reiner Schulze and Hans Schulte-Nölke, *Analysis of National Fairness Laws Aimed at Protecting Consumers in Relation to Commercial Practices* (2003).

[2] See Thomas Wilhelmsson, 'Free Movement of Legal Sources: The Use of Foreign Sources in Private Law in Europe' in Kai Purnhagen and Peter Rott (eds.), *Varieties of European Economic Law and Regulation* (Springer 2014) 185.

[3] See The Legal Aid, Sentencing and Punishment of Offenders Act 2012, Chapter 10, Part 2 (litigation and funding costs); Civil Procedure (Amendment No. 4) Rules 2014, SI 2014/867 and Practice Direction 3E—Costs Management.

involved do not justify litigating or are dealt with in small claims procedures or 'Alternative Dispute Resolution' (ADR) procedures. The fact we have anything to discuss is due to the rare consumer cases where large sums were involved and also due to regulator involvement in litigation.

A distinction can be drawn between comparative law used as a policy tool and its use as an interpretative tool. The line between policy and interpretation is of course porous as acts of interpretation may be underpinned by policy choices. However, when we draw this distinction we make a more radical distinction by seeing policy choices as being situations where the courts are overtly seeking to develop a new approach and use comparative law to support it. We treat *White v Jones*[4] as a consumer case and use that as an example of such an approach as well as *Fairchild v Glenhaven Funeral Services*.[5] We consider this use of comparative law first before moving on to look at comparative law as an interpretive guide to EU law.

It is not to be overlooked that although national law has in the past responded to protect the interests of consumers, a broad range of modern national consumer protection legislation has its origins in EU law.[6] Accordingly, a main use of comparative law has been to interpret EU law. European law requires an autonomous interpretation and represents a common legislative basis across the EU.[7] However, it does contain concepts that may have been inspired by some Member State approaches, thus creating the need to refer to civilian jurisdictions as a basis for comparison rather than drawing upon developments in other common law jurisdictions outside of the European Union.

We look at selected UK cases on product liability, unfair terms, and unfair commercial practices to assess the extent and nature of the use of comparative law in the context of consumer litigation. We then briefly review how the CJEU has used comparative law in some of its decisions. Finally, we consider the tools available to make comparative law available to practitioners. This essentially involves databases and we remain sceptical as to the extent they will actually assist in the use of comparative law in the courtroom. The role of academics in this process is then analysed through various forms of publications to see if they can provide a means to develop the law in a consistent and principled manner.

II. Comparative law and judicial policy development: *White v Jones* and *Fairchild v Glenhaven Funeral Services*

White v Jones concerned the conceptually difficult question of how, if at all, any remedy could be obtained by an intended beneficiary under a will when a solicitor had negligently failed to fulfil the intentions of the testator. Contractual claims were

[4] [1995] 2 AC 207. [5] [2003] 1 AC 32.

[6] Recent examples include The Consumer Protection from Unfair Trading Regulations 2008, SI 2008/1277; The Consumer Credit (EU Directive) Regulations 2010, SI 2010/1010; The Timeshare, Holiday Products, Resale and Exchange Contracts Regulations 2010, SI 2010/2960; The Consumer Contracts (Information, Cancellation and Additional Charges) Regulations 2013, SI 2013/3134.

[7] Case C-75/63 *Mrs M.K.H. Hoekstra (née Unger) v Bestuur der Bedrijfsvereniging voor Detailhandel en Ambachten (Administration of the Industrial Board for Retail Trades and Businesses)* [1964] ECR 177.

problematic because of privity issues, whereas tortious claims faced the problem of recovery for economic loss/expectation loss/liability for omissions. Liability was eventually established either on the basis of an extension of negligence principles (by the Court of Appeal and one House of Lords' judge) or by an extension of the *Hedley Byrne v Heller*[8] principle by two of the three judges in the majority in the House of Lords. The use of comparative law was interesting. Commonwealth, US, German, French, and Dutch cases were all cited, the majority of which had found a way to impose liability in such circumstances. The impact of these seems to have at least bolstered the confidence of the judges to find a way to impose liability. As Lord Goff stated 'the effect of the special characteristics of any particular system of law is likely to be ... not so much that no remedy is recognized, but rather that the system in question will choose its own special means for granting a remedy notwithstanding the doctrinal difficulties involved.'[9] Indeed he specifically rejected the German conceptual solutions of 'contracts with protective effects for third parties' (*Verträge mit Schutzwirkung zugunsten Dritte*) and 'transferred loss' (*Schadensverlagerung*) as being an illegitimate circumvention of long-established doctrines that can only be introduced by Parliament and not by the courts.

Lord Goff's approach to comparative law was interesting. He said:

> I hesitate to embark in an opinion such as this upon a comparison, however brief, with a civil law system; because experience has taught me how very difficult, and indeed potentially misleading, such an exercise can be. Exceptionally however, in the present case, thanks to material published in our language by distinguished comparatists, German as well as English, we have direct access to publications which should sufficiently dispel our ignorance of German law and so by comparison illuminate our understanding of our own.[10]

There are several points that can be drawn from this. First, it is clear that the use of comparative law is exceptional. The reason the reluctance to use comparative law is overcome is due to the availability of material written by academics seemingly all in the English language. Only English language publications are cited and references to cases are said to be from the academic sources. It also seemed important that the academics were recognized as being distinguished. So this is a limited exception where there is academic material published in English. But is this a valid approach? Academics sometimes use materials to make provocative arguments they may or may not believe in to different degrees. Certainly in the German system it is well known that academics draw strands from jurisprudence to develop a thesis they hope the courts will then adopt. It is also not unknown for academics to get things wrong or at least for their interpretation to be questioned. This reliance on secondary sources carries risks. These risks are not so pronounced when the material is used as in *White v Jones* to assess policy choices. There the real value of the comparative law approach is in its persuasiveness in the market for ideas so that the best solution can be adopted for the national legal system. Where interpretation is at stake there is still a potential role for comparative law, but there may be a far greater need for accurate assessment of what has been

[8] [1964] AC 465. [9] [1995] 2 AC 207, 263. [10] [1995] 2 AC 207, 263.

decided by other courts and reliance on academic commentaries of the traditional type may not be sufficient.

Fairchild v Glenhaven Funeral Services[11] is another House of Lords case in which comparative law, including European sources, was surveyed. This case involved asbestos and the problem of attributing causation where there were several tortfeasors, who were potentially liable but would not be liable on the balance of probabilities using the 'but-for' test. This time the survey was by Lord Bingham, who said a survey of other jurisdictions was necessary, however, superficially.[12] In fact it again seems that English language sources were used and the ius commune casebook on tort law[13] figured prominently. As with *White v Jones* the rationale for using comparative law seems to have been to identify the need for a novel solution based on the experiences of others, rather than finding a common solution by adopting a civilian solution. This is evident from the following passage:

> The law must be developed coherently, in accordance with principle, so as to serve, even-handedly, the ends of justice. If, however, a decision is given in this country which offends one's basic sense of justice, and if consideration of international sources suggests that a different and more acceptable decision would be given in most other jurisdictions, whatever their legal tradition, this must prompt anxious review of the decision in question. In a shrinking world (in which the employees of asbestos companies may work for those companies in any one or more of several countries) there must be some virtue in uniformity of outcome whatever the diversity of approach in reaching that outcome.[14]

Lord Bingham noted that Lord Rodger referred to Roman law in much the same way to highlight the need for a policy solution. This seems relatively unproblematic. The rest of this chapter turns to the more nuanced question of how the use of comparative law within the EU Member States can help address the interpretation of law of European origin. Here the policy choice has in principle already been made by the legislature and it is a matter of interpreting the wording used. Admittedly, interpretation has a policy dimension underpinning it, but here comparative law is not being used to highlight the need for a solution, but rather to confirm what the solution is.

III. Comparative law in the European Union law context

The European legislator—as well as the European courts—have for more than 30 years been very active in drafting and giving guidance on the interpretation of EU consumer protection legislation. Although the legislation is mostly targeted at regulating specific aspects of consumer protection, of which product liability,[15] unfair contract terms,[16]

[11] [2003] 1 AC 32. [12] [2003] 1 AC 32, 58.

[13] Walter van Gerven, Pierre Larouche, Jeremey Lever (eds.), *Cases, Materials and Text on National, Supranational and International Tort Law* (Hart 2000).

[14] [2003] 1 AC 32, 66.

[15] Council Directive 85/374/EEC of 25 July 1985 on the approximation of the laws, regulations and administrative provisions of the Member States concerning liability for defective products [1985] OJ L 210/29.

[16] Council Directive 93/13/EEC of 5 April 1993 on unfair terms in consumer contracts [1993] OJ L 95/29.

and unfair commercial practices[17] are a part, it has had wide-reaching implications for the foundations of national legal systems. Litigation is often the mechanism that highlights the extent of the impact of EU law in practice. The effect of the transposition of EU legislation of course has an impact on the domestic legal system. Such effect may be particularly profound within the common law system due to the duality between statute and common law and the strong influence of continental traditions on the rule development at European level; this is particularly true in the areas of unfair terms and unfair commercial practices where the German legal tradition is very evident. The transposition of EU directives by Parliament may not only introduce new terminology and concepts to existing regimes (e.g. new remedies for non-conforming consumer goods),[18] or even previously non-existing legal areas (e.g. package travel)[19] but it can accentuate the interpretative use of comparisons to civilian jurisdictions on semantic and substantive levels. The areas of product liability, unfair contract terms, and unfair commercial practices reflect three such areas in which the interpretation of European law not only highlights the interaction between EU and national laws but also different degrees of restraint when comparative law arguments are made in litigation. We will review case law in these areas. Of course with the move to maximal harmonization (as with unfair commercial practices) the impact of a common approach will be more keenly felt than in areas governed by minimal harmonization directives (such as unfair terms) or directives that, although maximal in character, allow parallel regimes (such as product liability). Regimes that permit national deviations do not force courts in all circumstances to find a solution four square within the directive.

1. Product liability

A v National Blood Authority[20] is in many ways an outstanding example of a national court undertaking comparative research to assist it in interpreting a directive. What is notable in contrast to the two previous cases (*White v Jones* and *Fairchild v Glenhaven Funeral Services*) is the willingness of the judge to engage with foreign language materials. Most of the discussion surrounded academic works, where again the point can be made that the court may not always be aware of the (legitimate) agendas of authors seeking to influence the development of the law. The reference to different language versions of the Product Liability Directive is entirely appropriate as all language versions have equal weight.[21] It is interesting to review what the judge said about his use of comparative European case law:

[17] Directive 2005/29/EC of the European Parliament and of the Council of 11 May 2005 concerning unfair business-to-consumer commercial practices in the internal market [2005] OJ L 149/22.

[18] Repair, replacement, price reduction and termination in Art. 3 Consumer Sales Directive 1999/44/EC ([1999] OJ L 171/12) introduced into the Sale of Goods Act 1979 as Part 5A.

[19] Prior to the Package Travel Directive 90/314/EEC ([1990] OJ L 158/59) there were no specific and exclusive laws in the UK which governed the rights and duties of the parties to a contract for travel package, Commission, 'Proposal for a Council Directive on package travel, including package holidays and package tours' COM (88) 41 final, p. 10.

[20] [2001] 3 All ER 289.

[21] Case C-283/81 *Srl CILFIT and Lanificio di Gavardo SpA v Ministry of Health* [1982] ECR 3415, para 18.

> I turn to consider the few court decisions in Europe in which the Directive, or these issues under the Directive, have been considered or touched upon. As indicated above, these have not been many, notwithstanding the fact that the Directive and implementing legislation within the Community countries (save in France, which delayed its implementation, although its own local laws were and remained in some respects more stringent) have been in force for ten to fifteen years. Leaving aside any English decisions, to which the ordinary rules of precedent would apply, so far as relevant, I would of course pay particular attention to any European decisions, not because they are binding upon me, but because not only does respect have to be paid, on the usual principles of comity, to reasoned decisions of competent foreign courts considering the same or similar issues, whatever the nature of the legislation, but particularly so where Community courts are applying the Directive. In such a case, even though Community courts are entitled to come to different views, particularly on the facts, by reference to national and local conditions, and even though the European Court can resolve and give a final opinion upon issues where different views have been taken in different Community countries on the same legislation, nevertheless harmony is desirable, particularly where it can be said that an autonomous or Community approach or meaning is required.[22]

The *A v National Blood* case is of particular interest, not only because it used so much comparative law, but also because the legal actors (counsel for claimants and defendants and the judge) explained their view of the case in a fascinating paper.[23] The claimants' leading counsel who drafted the main part of the article described their research process. This involved looking at the German law prior to the adoption of the Product Liability Directive, the *travaux préparatoires*, consulting the retired draftsman of the Directive (Dr Hans Taschner), research into other Member States' law and in the United States, research at the Max Planck Institute in Hamburg, and collecting all language versions of the Directive.[24] Our focus is on the last three, i.e. where comparative law research is undertaken on directives and their implementation, but brief comments will be made on the first three as they highlight issues of costs and principle.

German law prior to the Product Liability Directive was used to show a pattern that underpinned the new approach taken in the Directive; the *travaux préparatoires* were used to show concerns raised by defendants were stated, examined, and not accepted by the drafters. It was accepted that the Commission official's view on how the Directive should be interpreted could not be evidenced; in the end he did not even testify to the history of the Directive's evolution though both aspects seem to have been included by reference to his written work. It is surely right that a Commission official's view on the meaning of the Directive is not given any special status. In this instance (unusually) the same official stayed with the measure for several years, but in any event it is the court which is the arbiter of the meaning of laws and any official status given to the views of officials on controversial issues risks undermining the rule of law. That is not to say that

22 [2001] 3 All ER 289 at para 44.

23 See Chapter 36 of this work; Michael Brooke and Ian Forrester, 'The Use of Comparative Law in A & Others v National Blood Authority', postscript by N. Underhill and afterword by Mr Justice Burton, in Duncan Fairgrieve (ed), *Product Liability in Comparative Perspective* (CUP 2005).

24 Brooke and Forrester, ibid., pp. 18–22.

officials cannot usefully explain laws to interested parties, but the utility of their explanation stops where one side disputes their interpretation. Defence counsel Underhill QC noted that the official was actually a protagonist in the debate over the meaning of the Directive and it would be wrong to draw from his intentions as to the effect of the Directive any 'collective intention'.[25] Equally we tend to agree with the defence counsel's view that *travaux préparatoires* must at best be used sparingly and with caution because they conceal a deal of horse trading. The research on the evolution of German product liability law is fascinating, the present authors have themselves enjoyed a very illuminating time in German libraries researching the case law.[26] It doubtless had an influence on the debate, especially given the Commission official was himself a German professor of law. But equally the same claim might be made for the French law, which if anything had evolved in an even more dramatic manner.[27] Moreover, there is a risk that European laws become too aligned with those states where the principles originated; whereas they should be treated as creating autonomous European concepts.[28] This is more of a risk in the area of unfair terms and unfair commercial practices as strict product liability (in this form at least) was new to all states. One of the general points is the cost of comparative research. Underhill QC has an opinion on this connected to the amount of work that went into these and other comparative law efforts that were not deployed and the majority of whose useful points could have been derived from other sources.[29] Our point is that given the other considerations surrounding these first three sources it would be better to focus those resources that are available on those sources which deal directly with the law and case law of the Member States.[30]

Fascination with US cases in product liability is obvious given the rich jurisprudence in the field compared to the dearth of European material.[31] However, given the differences in content between US and EU product liability laws we believe it is better to focus on comparison with the admittedly thinner vein of European jurisprudence. European case law is developing now; but at the time of litigation in *A v National Blood Authority* only two product liability cases had reached the CJEU,[32] and one lower court judgment from the Netherlands involving blood was unearthed. But the laws of Germany,[33] France, Spain, The Netherlands, Belgium, Italy, and Portugal were researched. However, the means of doing this was to rely on friendly members of the bar in those countries to unearth cases and academic writings. This was at best haphazard and ran the obvious risk of selectivity and bias. Fortunately this was

[25] Brooke and Forrester, ibid., pp. 35–6.

[26] See Geraint Howells, *Comparative Product Liability* (Dartmouth 1993), pp. 123–44.

[27] Howells, ibid., pp. 101–18.

[28] *Srl CILFIT and Lanificio di Gavardo SpA v Ministry of Health* at para 19 (n 21).

[29] Brooke and Forrester (n 23), pp. 35 and 37.

[30] The amount of consumer litigation varies from state to state. We note there is therefore a risk that litigation from a particular Member State with a more extensive and accessible court system could exert a greater influence on the interpretation of EU law than others.

[31] See Jane Stapleton, *Product Liability* (Butterworths 1994), pp. 20–36; Duncan Fairgrieve and Richard Goldberg, *Product Liability* (3rd edn, OUP forthcoming).

[32] Case C-300/95 *Commission v United Kingdom* [1997] ECR I-2649; Case C-203/99 *Henning Veedfald v Århus Amtskommune* [2000] ECR I-3569.

[33] This was not listed but is evident from other statements that it was researched.

supplemented by visits to the Max Planck Institute in Hamburg where works in German, Swedish, Italian, Portuguese, and English were consulted. How many cases could justify such research trips one might wonder?

The judge spoke French comfortably and several other European languages adequately;[34] indeed he was said to be the only one to attempt the Greek version of the Directive and even he did not attempt the Finnish version.[35] All counsel spoke French and some spoke moderate German and Italian. Three judgments were translated in full (two of the *Bundesgerichtshof* and one of Arnhem district court) with the Swedish *travaux préparatoires* being also translated. Full texts of academic commentaries were made available with translations made of sentences or paragraphs of particular relevance.[36] The Livenote translators included linguists able to type accurately in German, French, Italian, or Spanish.[37] However, the lawyers still had to rely on one another at times to give fair translations and even with the obvious trust and respect there was between the lawyers, Underhill QC noted 'though the passage of arms about the significance of the use of the subjunctive in one sentence in the Italian version of the Advocate General's Opinion in *Commission v UK* possibly tested the parties' mutual confidence.'[38]

This case involved 50 court days (49 for hearing and one for judgment) and produced over 100 files, several of them full of comparative and academic literature. It is evident that claimant counsel and the judge were more captivated with the comparative law aspects than was the defence leading counsel. All parties seemed to acknowledge this procedure was a luxury one.[39] It was paid for by the legal aid board (on the claimant side). That source has effectively disappeared for such claims. It is unlikely that lawyers would do such comparative work as readily on a conditional fee, or that under the new Jackson fee regime judges would be overly keen to allow such expenses. Of concern is that even in this Rolls-Royce system the collection of data was haphazard, relying to some extent on informal contacts of fortuitous expertise and reliability and upon the chance of the exceptional linguistic skills of those participating in the process. The judge had raised the notion of having, but then agreed he should not have, an assessor to help him wade through the materials. Discussion of our possible solutions follows.

2. Unfair contract terms

The notion of protecting consumers against unfair contract terms serves as an ideal example of the how the use of comparative law may be impeded by the lack of sufficient commonality between various legal systems. The main focus of this section concerns the concepts of (un)fairness, but also the overlap between other underlying open-textured values such as good faith which are present in this area of contract law. The decision in *Director General of Fair Trading v First National Bank*[40] represented the

[34] See Brooke and Forrester (n 23), p. 22.
[35] Brooke and Forrester, ibid., p. 28.
[36] Brooke and Forrester, ibid., p. 22.
[37] Brooke and Forrester, ibid., p. 28.
[38] Brooke and Forrester, ibid., p. 39.
[39] Brooke and Forrester, ibid., p. 33.
[40] [2001] 1 AC 481.

first instance in which the House of Lords had to determine the meaning of 'unfair' within the context of the Unfair Terms in Consumer Contract Regulations 1994,[41] which transposed the European Unfair Contract Terms Directive 93/13/EEC. This area of law has implications for the heart of contracting, the principle of freedom of contract; the importance of this area of law was acknowledged on appeal to the House of Lords.[42] At first instance, Evans-Loombe J remarked that the 'words "*good faith*" are not to be construed in the English law sense of absence of dishonesty but rather in the continental "*Civil law*" sense'[43] and opted to follow Lord Bingham's summarizing explanation in *Interfoto*[44] and academic commentary rather than seeking clarification from the CJEU in determining the fairness of the term.[45]

During litigation the disputed contract term not only raised questions of fairness of the term itself but also its categorization as a 'core' term of the contract—the fairness test not being applicable to such core terms.[46] Comparative arguments were used before the Court of Appeal[47] to support the proposition that it would be in the interests of achieving uniformity—as an underlying objective of the Unfair Terms Directive—to follow the same approach as in other Member States in determining the core nature of the term:

> [The Respondent] submits that the Regulations should be read, if possible, in a way which avoids an anomaly between the position in England and that in Scotland and that the obvious way to do this is to treat the relevant term as conferring a single unbroken right to interest at the contractual rate and so as a core term... Lord Goodhart [for the respondent] argued that an aim of the Directive was to harmonise the position in Member States of the European Union and he suggested that harmonisation towards the Scottish and French position by recognising a provision for post-judgment interest as a core term was desirable.[48]

In addition to Scots and French laws, Irish and German laws were consulted in order to ascertain how such contract terms at issue are to be categorized. However, the limited comparisons in this instance seemingly appear to have not made a fruitful contribution to the outcome. As stated by Gibson LJ: 'We do not know what the laws of other Member States provide. On the material before us we find it impossible to say that the Directive encourages harmonisation to accord with the Scottish and French model rather than the English or some other model.'[49]

The comment is particularly interesting from a comparative perspective. Taken by itself it suggests that further, more extensive, comparative research on the law of other Member States could have exerted greater influence on the Court's judgment. Of course, in light of the variation apparent from the selected jurisdictions, greater use of comparative law might have ultimately led merely to changing 'impossible' to

[41] SI 1994/3159. The 1994 Regulations ('UTCCR 1994') were revoked by The Unfair Terms in Consumer Contracts Regulations 1999, SI 1999/2083.

[42] [2001] 1 AC 481, 498.

[43] [2000] 1 WLR 98, 109.

[44] *Interfoto Picture Library Ltd v Stiletto Visual Programmes Ltd* [1989] QB 433, 439.

[45] M. Dean, 'Defining Unfair Terms in Consumer Contracts. Crystal Ball Gazing? Director General of Fair Trading v First National Bank plc' (2002) 65 MLR 773, 779.

[46] UTCCR 1994, reg 3(2); Council Dir 93/13, Art. 7(2).

[47] [2000] QB 672.

[48] [2000] QB 672, 685.

[49] [2000] QB 672, 685.

'difficult', but it is nonetheless an indication of the weight a comparative argument could have in a European context. Furthermore, it may also be inferred from the statement that the use of comparative law in matters of a European flavour may require a broader approach, which, in light of the continually increasing number of EU Member States accompanied by the greater variation in legal culture, may require more comparisons in order to have greater interpretative value. With 28 Member States, such a task greatly emphasizes the importance of the need to develop an effective and accessible network to facilitate the exchange of information.

Gibson LJ also comments on the meaning of good faith, but his observation is more precise than the remark made at first instance by Evans-Loombe J. Gibson LJ goes beyond the general conceptual basis of the meaning of good faith and delves deeper into the history of the Directive and the role played by German law:

> 'Good faith' has a special meaning in the Regulations, having its conceptual roots in civil law systems. The German Standard Contract Terms Act, providing for the avoidance of a term which is unreasonably disadvantageous to a party 'contrary to the requirements of good faith'... appears to have had a significant influence on the Directive.[50]

As at first instance, references are made to academic commentary on the subject and *Interfoto*. On appeal, the House of Lords approached the issue of the test of good faith contained within the Directive, and accordingly within the UK Regulations. Their Lordships emphasized—citing academic literature—that a common concept of good faith or fairness is not to be found in the Member States,[51] implying that even if a broader comparative net were to be cast the lack of commonality would certainly impede the effective use of comparative law as an interpretative instrument in the matter at hand. However, despite the absence of express comparisons concerning the fairness in accordance with the law of other jurisdictions, the judgments highlight the role and the contribution of academic research on comparative law. References were made by the House to the commentary on the Principles of European Contract Law (PECL),[52] principles which were developed in the 1980s and 1990s on the basis of extensive comparative research of the national laws of European countries. The PECL represent a 'common core of solutions to problems of contract law'.[53] Although such principles were not designed specifically for consumer contracts, Lord Steyn refers to the purpose of the requirement of good faith and fair dealing noted by the PECL and that such requirement is also true for consumer transactions. However, it appears that within the context of good faith, Lord Hope indicates that a comparative interpretation would be unnecessary: 'But in the present context there is no need to explore this topic in any depth. The directive provides all the guidance that it needed as to its application.'[54] This may have been due to the considerable differences across the Member States and the open-textured nature of the concepts of good faith and fair dealing may be an

[50] [2000] QB 672, 686.

[51] [2001] 1 AC 481, 494.

[52] Ole Lando and Hugh Beale (eds.), *Principles of European Contract Law, Parts I and II* (Kluwer Law International 1999).

[53] Lando and Beale, ibid., p. xxii.

[54] [2001] 1 AC 481, 502.

obstacle to convincing comparative argumentation. It also demonstrates how the effective use of comparative law could, paradoxically, be reduced due to the greater diversity of the results. Of course part of the problem was that comparative law in this context was looking at the pre-existing traditions of the Member States and there was always the risk that this impacted on national decisions interpreting the Directive. The position is easier when a comparison is made of national systems' interpretation of the Directive's concepts and the more so when these are not tied to existing national ways of legal thinking, which is of course not the case with good faith in civilian regimes.

The use of comparisons can be more fruitful when seeking to define not only the scope of the protection afforded to consumers, but also how the concept of a consumer is to be understood in a broad sense. From a comparative perspective, the decision in *Khatun & Others v London Borough of Newham*—both at first instance[55] and on appeal[56]—is of particular interest as it highlights how comparative law cannot only work on both a substantive and semantic level but also as a tool of policy and interpretation. The disputed subject-matter concerned the terms contained within a tenancy agreement. There were, inter alia, two issues which arose: firstly, whether the tenants were to be considered 'consumers', and the local authority 'suppliers' for the purposes of the application of the legislation; secondly, whether the legislation on unfair contract terms extends to cover terms contained within contracts relating to land.

One particular aspect of the decision centred on the distinction between moveable and immoveable property. In coming to the decision that the Unfair Contract Terms Directive does in fact include contracts relating to land, at first instance Newman J not only referred to different language versions of the Directive (French, Italian, Spanish, and Portuguese) but also to the French Civil Code and the European Convention on Human Rights in determining that the language used in these versions of the Directive does encompass both moveable and immoveable property.[57] More significantly, references were made to CLAB database entries from Austria, Spain, the Netherlands, and Belgium which each supported the inclusion of contracts for land. Although used with caution, the entries were regarded nonetheless as 'a pointer towards the proper fulfilment of the Directive's purpose'.[58] The Court of Appeal confirmed the High Court's decision on the application of the Directive to contracts relating to land and in so doing Laws LJ used comparative arguments to dismiss various points made by the appellant. Firstly, concerning the weight of linguistic comparisons in interpreting the scope of application he noted:

> First, Mr Underwood's seemingly strong point on the language—that 'goods and services' does not include land—is effectively demolished by the impact of the other language texts. 'Biens' and its cognates in Italian, Spanish and Portuguese refer to immovables as readily as movables. This alone undercuts a good deal of what Mr Underwood had to say.[59]

Secondly, the European context of the legislation requires contemplation of the underlying policy and whether the typical features of national law are suitable for

[55] [2003] EWHC 2326 (Admin). [56] [2005] QB 37. [57] [2003] EWHC 2326 (Admin) [58].
[58] [2003] EWHC 2326 (Admin) [65]. [59] [2005] QB 37, 68.

achieving the European policy considerations. Comparing the law at European level therefore may not just extend to comparisons with the Member States but also to comparing the functionality of instruments of national law with European objectives:

> But more than this: I think, with respect to Mr Underwood, that other aspects of his submissions on this part of the case place an implicit but illegitimate reliance on the large divide in the law of England between real and personal property... In our domestic law these distinctions have a long history and a present utility. In the context of a Europe-wide scheme of consumer protection, they could be nothing but an embarrassing eccentricity.[60]

Thirdly, the comparisons of substantive law during the legislative process can also serve as an indication whether the European legislator has intended a distinction at national level:

> There is then the absence from the Explanatory Memorandum of any reference either to the *exclusion* of land transactions from the British consumer protection legislation, or to their *inclusion* in the German legislation. That, as it seems to me, sits alongside the fact that in paragraph 2.2.2 of the ECOSOC Opinion the laws of Germany and the United Kingdom (and seven other Member States) are, if I may use the phrase, lumped together for all the world as if there were no significant differences between them; and in my judgment, from the perspective of the Community legislator there were not.[61]

Finally, and most importantly, the judge considered that the general weight of comparative arguments can play a decisive role in determining the direction of the decision in the absence of binding authority: 'And while there is plainly no authority, domestic or European, which binds this court to conclude in Mr Green's favour, the learning such as it is points in that direction.'[62]

Where unfair contract terms are concerned, the decisions in *Director General of Fair Trading v First National Bank* and *Khatun & Others v London Borough of Newham* can be said to not only demonstrate the different roles that comparative law can play in the judicial process but also the impact of European consumer protection policy on the national legal system. On the one hand, the paradox of refraining from in-depth comparisons due to the extent and sensitivity of the diversity can send a clear policy signal that the issue will have to be solved using, as far as possible, domestic legal doctrine and consideration of the framework of the relevant directive. On the other hand, European consumer policy considerations may necessitate comparisons where the legal concepts present in the national legal system do not achieve the desired result in order to support fundamental changes to key principles of English law.

3. Unfair commercial practices

Of the three areas of consumer law that are discussed in this chapter, it is the regulation of unfair commercial practices that has been subject to more recent European

60 [2005] QB 37, 68. 61 [2005] QB 37, 69. 62 [2005] QB 37, 69.

legislation. The Unfair Commercial Practices Directive is, in contrast to the Unfair Contract Terms Directive, an instrument of maximal harmonization. Its maximal harmonization approach is stricter than in the Product Liability Directive, which expressly allowed certain existing forms of liability to be retained. It thus strives to obtain the same level of consumer protection with respect to unfair commercial practices legislation in each Member State. As noted earlier, it was argued by the respondents in *Director General of Fair Trading v First National Bank* that the harmonization of national law should require the interpretation of the respective directive in line with other legal systems; with respect to unfair commercial practices a similar point was raised in *Office of Fair Trading v Purely Creative Ltd & Others.*[63]

The case itself concerned the various practices of informing consumers that they had won a prize, but claiming the prize required the consumer to incur costs, for example through calling a premium rate telephone number; though there was the option of merely posting a response, most consumers chose in practice a more expensive option. Briggs J made some observations on the use of comparative law in relation to a maximal harmonization directive such as the Unfair Commercial Practices Directive. There was common ground between the counsel and judge that the interpretation of the underlying Directive is 'independent of the member state's national law and, for that matter, independent of any other member state's national law'.[64] The focus instead lies on seeking (non-binding) assistance from the decisions of other national courts, if no (binding) CJEU jurisprudence is available: 'The national court may also obtain assistance from, but is not bound by, guidance issued by the Commission, and by the decisions of other national courts as to the meaning of the relevant Directive.'[65]

There was a dispute between counsel as to whether it is legitimate to have recourse to differences in the manner in which a maximum harmonization directive has been implemented by the national regulations of different Member States, as opposed to the decisions of the courts of Member States about the meaning of the governing directive.[66] In the absence of authority on the matter, Briggs J concluded that the 'recourse to differences of implementation of a directive intended to have uniform effect throughout the EU is likely to prove a time-consuming and ultimately fruitless exercise'.[67] One might think that such reviews might be helpful where an implementing law is shown to be in the clear minority. However, the example of the deduction of 500 Euro from property damage claims in the Product Liability Directive (Art. 9(b)) shows the dangers of such an approach, as whilst the UK solution of treating the 500 Euro as a threshold rather than a deductible is the minority approach, it is arguably best suited to the policy objective of avoiding litigation over small amounts.

On appeal[68] the Chancellor of the High Court, Sir Andrew Morritt, agreed with Briggs J on the lack of benefit of referring to national implementing measures, although he noted that 'the different approaches of Member States may well be important to the

[63] [2011] EWHC 106 (Ch).
[64] [2011] EWHC 106 (Ch) [40].
[65] [2011] EWHC 106 (Ch) [40].
[66] [2011] EWHC 106 (Ch) [40].
[67] [2011] EWHC 106 (Ch) [41].
[68] [2011] EWCA Civ 920.

exercise of this court's discretion whether to refer questions of interpretation of the Directive to the Court of Justice of the European Union.'[69]

The matter was ultimately referred to the CJEU,[70] but the reference by the Court of Appeal was based on the absence of clear interpretative guidance from other national courts and divergences in the translated national implementing measures indicating doubt as to the true meaning. However, only the Republic of Ireland's implementing law was cited in the judgment and it is otherwise not clear from the decision which other Member States' laws were used as a point of reference. Nonetheless, the Chancellor's statement illustrates that the use of comparative law can serve a further function in order to determine the absence of guidance justifying a reference to the CJEU. This absence of insight from comparative law may be of real importance in justifying a reference that removes uncertainty and has the potential to shape the direction of the law and commercial practices across Europe. One of the main conclusions from this case is that there are thus considerable policy implications concerning the need to seek guidance from the CJEU arising from the absence of clear interpretative guidance from other Member States, especially when the underlying European legislation aims at maximal harmonization across the EU. It does indeed pose the question whether genuine consistency of EU measures can occur and how comparative approaches can contribute to this objective in the form of a 'bottom-up' harmonization.

IV. European Court case law

A survey of the CJEU case law on product liability shows that there has been no use of comparative law on the face of the judgments. This may be explained by most of the litigation being about the correct implementation, maximal harmonization nature, or links with procedural law. There have been few substantive law questions raised, and when they have, as in *Commission v United Kingdom*[71] and *Henning Veedfald v Århus Amtskommune*,[72] there was probably limited national case law to rely on.

It is perhaps more surprising that national comparative case law has not been used more frequently in the fields of unfair terms and unfair commercial practices where previous national traditions could be referred to. That it has not been is probably due in part to the nature of the litigation that has taken place: in the unfair terms context this has for the most part revolved around ensuring national procedural laws provide effective redress for unfair terms in consumer contracts, whereas in the unfair commercial practices context it has mainly been about the extent of harmonization and its impact on per se national prohibitions. However, it may also reflect deeper values about the nature of European law and the CJEU's role.

When considering general principles of law the Court has referred to the principles common to the Member States,[73] but where substantive European law has been

[69] [2011] EWCA Civ 920 [10].

[70] Case C-428/11 *Purely Creative Ltd and Others v Office of Fair Trading* [2012] ECR nyr.

[71] Case C-300/95 [1997] ECR I-2649. [72] Case C-203/99 [2001] ECR I-3569.

[73] E.g. Case C-11/70 *Internationale Handelsgesellschaft mbH v Einfuhr und Vorratsstelle für Getreide und Futtermittel* [1970] ECR 1125, para 4; Case C-4/73 *J. Nold, Kohlen- und Baustoffgroßhandlung v Commission of the European Communities* [1974] ECR 491, para 13.

enacted it is probably right that the Court is not seen as drawing on existing Member States' traditions, but rather is recognized to be adopting an autonomous European interpretation. In the fundamental rights contexts the Court is using common principles to develop EU legal principles, whereas in the consumer law context the EU legislator has already provided the rules. A less positive analysis might be that the judges of the Court tend to have a more constitutional law background and so are at ease with such surveys of fundamental rights in a way they are not with private law comparative jurisprudence.[74] It may also simply be that the issues at stake justify such comparisons when making fundamental law, but not when detailed interpretations of specific laws are proposed.

However, the CJEU seems to go further at times in disengaging itself from questions of substantive justice in the private law context. Indeed in *Freiburger Kommunalbauten GmbH Baugesellschaft & Co KG v Hofstetter*[75] the Court expressly left it to national courts to apply the law and seemed not to want to get involved in substantive discussions around the concept of fairness. The lack of engagement with the experiences of national courts when struggling to interpret substantive EU private law rules is puzzling; this is particularly striking in the unfair terms context, as the Commission has itself sponsored the CLAB database which might provide some tools for comparative analysis.

In passing it might be mentioned that in *Mediaprint Zeitungs- und Zeitschriftenverlag GmbH & Co. KG v 'Österreich'-Zeitungsverlag*[76] Advocate General Trstenjak made reference in a footnote to the Draft Common Frame of Reference,[77] which was prepared by an international network of academics for the European Commission.[78] This may be significant for our thesis that judges may feel comfortable if they are able to refer to texts that have some status within the European legal order.

V. Comparative law in courts

National courts are under an obligation to interpret national law implementing EU law in line with EU law.[79] There is no obligation to follow decisions of other Member States' courts, but Mr Justice Burton in *A v National Blood* seemed to adopt the right spirit of comity by seeking wherever possible to promote harmony by comparative reference. Unlike the traditional role of comparative law, which is to give inspiration to find the best legal solution, the exercise in this context is concerned with finding the best interpretation of the European legal principles. Doubtless that gives some scope for policy choice where the EU law is ambiguous. Equally we have seen the lack of case law

[74] Wolfgang Wurmnest and Christian Heinze, 'General Principles of Tort Law in the Jurisprudence of the European Court of Justice' in Reiner Schulze (ed), *Compensation of Private Losses: The Evolution of Torts in European Business Law* (Sellier 2011), p. 62.

[75] Case C-237/02 [2004] ECR I-3403. [76] Case C-540/08 [2010] ECR I-10909.

[77] Study Group on a European Civil Code, Research Group on the Existing EC Private Law (Acquis Group), *Draft Common Frame of Reference (DCFR) Outline Edition* (Sellier 2009).

[78] Commission, 'A More Coherent European Contract Law—An Action Plan', COM (2003) 68 final, p. 16.

[79] Case C-14/83 *Von Colson* [1984] ECR 1891.

or divergent approaches might be relevant to the decision whether a national court makes a preliminary reference to the CJEU.

How can this comparative input best be done? In considering this question we have to find a solution that suits all states. Member States have varying court structures. We have focused on the English courts where litigation is infamously expensive; with highly experienced judges and the oral tradition of adversarial advocacy dominant. Within the Union there are a wide variety of courts with different infrastructures and resources. Even within states there are of course hierarchies and it may be sensible to expect comparative analysis to be more likely to be conducted in only those courts used to dealing with more complex litigation—but as European law applies in all courts, probably the comparative approach should not be formally excluded in any context. Indeed arguments may need to be run in first instance courts for them to be picked up on appeal.

Even in the UK system—which participants themselves describe as a Rolls-Royce system—we find the use of comparative law can impose a strain. *A v National Blood* lasted 50 days in part due to the comparative law deployed. Even in the UK it is unlikely that such extensive use of comparative law will be affordable in the future in many consumer cases. The heady days of generous legal aid are past and the new Jackson costs regime is likely to make it harder to recover costs for comparative research. Trips to the Max Planck Institutes by practitioners are likely to be a thing of the past. But even under the Rolls Royce conditions there were problems: it depended on the chance of the linguistic skills of the lawyers, judge, and court note takers; not all materials were translated and there was reliance on academic literature. As academics we believe our works are valuable, but they do run the risk of inaccuracy or being slanted towards suiting the author's thesis. In some cases (such as *White v Jones* and *Fairchild v Glenhaven Funeral Services*) the works relied upon were by some of the most distinguished comparatists; but, whilst that probably reduces the risk of inaccuracies, it does not exclude the capacity for individual interpretations. In *A v National Blood*, as the Product Liability Directive was new, Mr Justice Burton used a wider range of sources, including from some junior academics. It is a lesson from comparative law that one needs to act with caution when reading secondary sources, especially as in some jurisdictions the role of the academic is to develop a core meaning from a patchwork of jurisprudence that has no inherent biding authority.

So our first conclusion is that systems that rely on the participants undertaking their own comparative research is inherently flawed. A system like that operating in Switzerland where comparative research can be sought by the courts from the Comparative Law Institute in Lausanne is an option,[80] but it can be expensive and would need changes to national procedural law and a far more extensive comparative law research infrastructure.

[80] The institute was established in 1978 by a Federal Act (AS 1979 56). According to Art. 3(1)(c) of the Act, the institute shall provide information and reports to courts, administrative bodies, attorneys and other interested parties.

Databases such as CLAB, the Commission-sponsored but no longer functioning database on unfair terms, might seem to be a way forward.[81] However, we view them as being of limited use directly to practitioners and as more of a research tool to assist a broader process. This broader process would not in our opinion be manageable if it relied solely on individual research. The same is true of the British Institute's Product Liability Database, which is a useful research tool, but also suffers from lack of funding to ensure full coverage and has limited access rights.[82] The European Commission occasionally moots developing more extensive databases[83] and it has a model to build on in the work of the 2008 EU Consumer Law Compendium,[84] which covered eight consumer directives. Our view is that these are useful research tools, but the case of *Khatun & Ors v London Borough of Newham* is unusual in referring to the database as normally courts might require an original source.

The role of regulatory bodies in litigation raises the question of the extent to which cross-border co-operation with regulatory bodies or consumer protection organizations in other Member States takes place. Such co-operation is currently provided for in Regulation 2006/2004/EC,[85] although under this Regulation the provision of mutual assistance is limited to 'intra-community infringements', i.e. where there is harm, or likely to be harm, to the collective interests of consumers residing in another Member State.[86] As the European Union has already provided for such a network to be implemented, the exchange and access to information could be facilitated even further by expanding upon the structure currently in place, such as with longer secondments and exchanges.[87] Again, these could help facilitate the exchange of information, which might feed into databases, and promote a common understanding, but will not be of direct relevance to what happens in courtrooms.

Some books might come to be treated as authoritative. For instance, the ius commune casebook on consumer law[88] draws upon the experience of several scholars from different states, but it is not exhaustive in coverage of states or material and is aimed at being a teaching tool. The EU Compendium, though only covering eight directives, is more promising as a potential reference for courts as it also had the quasi-official imprint of the Commission because it resulted from a Commission study. However, updates to the Compendium are required in light of recent legislative developments.

81 See for a balanced critique, Hans-Werner Micklitz and Malek Radeideh, 'CLAB Europa—The European Database on Unfair Terms in Consumer Contracts' (2005) 28 JCP 325.

82 See <http://www.biicl.org/plf/database>.

83 For proposals on the future development of databases see Regulation (EU) No 254/2014 of the European Parliament and of the Council of 26 February 2014 on a multiannual consumer programme for the years 2014–20 [2014] OJ L 84/42, Annex I. See also Commission, 'Proposal for a Regulation of the European Parliament and of the Council on a Common European Sales Law', COM (2011) 635 final, p. 10.

84 Hans Schulte-Nölke, Christian Twigg-Flesner, and Martin Ebers (eds.), *EC Consumer Law Compendium* (Sellier 2008).

85 Regulation (EC) No 2006/2004 of the European Parliament and of the Council of 27 October 2004 on cooperation between national authorities responsible for the enforcement of consumer protection laws [2006] OJ L 364/1.

86 Council Reg 2006/2004, Art. 2(1).

87 Biennial Report of the UK Member State on the Application of the Regulation of Consumer Protection Cooperation (EC) 2006/2004 (2011), p. 24.

88 Hans-Werner Micklitz, Jules Stuyck, and Evelyne Terryn (eds.), *Cases, Materials and Text on Consumer Law: Ius Commune Casebooks for a Common Law of Europe* (Hart 2010).

In addition, the value of model rules based upon comparative research ought not to be underestimated. References to model rules such as the Principles of European Contract Law may be useful in gaining an insight into continental legal thinking—the commentary to the Draft Common Frame of Reference[89] offers an in-depth overview of the position in the Member States and extends beyond the realms of contract law. Although the authoritative nature of these academic works is lower when compared to the legislation and jurisprudence from other Member States, they do have value as a signpost along a comparative path. Indeed a decision of the Swedish Supreme Court, which suggested the Draft Common Frame of Reference may even be used as a 'gap-filler' for national law,[90] certainly raises the credibility of academic research on comparative law and its contribution to furthering national law.

In our view the expansion of the academic function in providing an extra-judicial mechanism for developing the law could be built on possibly through the medium of the recently founded European Law Institute (ELI).[91] Like its US counterpart, the American Law Institute (ALI),[92] it could produce restatements of European law not only based on EU legislation, but also on how it had been interpreted in Member States' courts. This would be one cheap and easily accessible point of reference for all lawyers and courts in Europe. A national court would not be bound by the Restatement, but one would expect them to have good reasons to deviate from it. The drafting of Restatements would involve some interpretation of jurisprudence and choices to be made where there are competing decisions or decisions which are considered simply wrong, but at least the Restatement would be voted on by a body with some standing. Though of course its rules would not be binding. There need not be any explicit reference to the European Law Institute Restatements in the Constitution, though that would be ideal; the CJEU could give these instruments status by referring to them and encouraging national courts to do the same.

The extent to which law moves beyond the national and uses the tools of comparative law depends upon the mentality of the national lawyers. Changes in legal education will slowly produce an increase in lawyers with experience of other legal systems, but this needs to be enhanced by the training given to practising lawyers and most importantly judges. However, once they are open to the use of comparative law they need systems that are simple and easy to use. All courts at all levels across the Union should have access to such assistance. Restatements are one way of creating a level playing field.

[89] Christian von Bar and Eric Clive (eds.), *Draft Common Frame of Reference (DCFR) Full Edition* (Sellier 2009).

[90] Mateusz Grochowski, 'The practical potential of the DCFR Judgment of the Swedish Supreme Court (Högstadomstolen) of 3 November 2009, Case T 3-08' (2013) 9 ERCL 96.

[91] Information about the ELI is available under <http://www.europeanlawinstitute.eu>.

[92] <http://www.ali.org>.

VI. Conclusion

There is far more use of comparative law than ever before in the English courts. Comparative law has been used to either provide possible solutions or to highlight considerable conceptual diversity.

Consumer law is an area in which EU law has had a major impact and comparative law can be used to find solutions or decide that a reference is needed to the CJEU, especially in instances in which a comparative analysis shows that a uniform approach is not apparent across the Member States. Yet the result of case law does cause one to question whether true harmonization can be achieved. Nonetheless, comparative arguments can contribute to this objective.

To date the invocation of comparative law has been due to the whim of particular lawyers or judges. It has been ad hoc and often relied upon chance knowledge or connections. We believe that if lawyers in all Member States are to use comparative law in a systematic and even manner, there need to be some procedures for developing common and acknowledged sources that can be relied upon. The Commission's Proposal for a Common European Sales Law[93] foresees the development of a database of national or European judgments relating to the Regulation, which may assist in the interpretation of the overlaps between this instrument and national law transposing EU directives. Nevertheless, a database of the final outcomes of court decisions in this context requires the use of reliable comparative law sources. Courts, however, also need a synthesis of the mass of decisions which are likely to be reported from across the Union. We see the European Law Institute potentially performing this function, but that is a fledgling institution and the position needs to be monitored.

[93] COM (2011) 635 final (n 83).

35

The Use of Comparative Law by Courts in Birth-Related Tort Cases

*Romain M. Lorentz**

The recent development of birth-related torts is due to the combination of scientific and medical progress—*i.e.* the advancement of procreation and contraception techniques, as well as genetic testing methods—and the enactment of legal tools allowing for the management of procreation and pregnancy—primarily the legalization of abortion.[1] Thus, in the past few decades, various new heads of damages have appeared before the courts, both in common law and civil law systems.[2] The main question raised by those various situations is whether the birth of a child may be considered a legal injury, which the law may compensate.

The very wording of the latter question is undoubtedly rather shocking, or, at the very least, much more disturbing than the issues that other situations may raise. For instance, the question whether a broken leg is a compensable injury seems to be much more 'normal' and much easier to answer. Indeed, the question of the injurious nature of the birth of a child has more dimensions than that of the compensable character of a physical injury. In addition to strictly legal considerations, courts need to weigh ethical, moral, and economic aspects.

Due to the inherent complexity of the issues, courts seem to be more inclined to examine foreign decisions, in order to understand how courts in other jurisdictions dealt with similar questions when presented with them. Of course, such foreign rulings may only be used as persuasive authorities, but their influence may be quite strong.

In this chapter, we shall primarily address decisions from the United Kingdom, the United States, and France, even though we shall discuss cases from other jurisdictions, such as Canada and Australia.

Before focusing on the extent to which courts resort to comparative law in birth-related tort cases (section II) and its influence on the rulings (section III), it is

* Participating Adjunct Professor, University of St Thomas Opus College of Business, St Paul, Minnesota (USA). Maîtrise (Université d'Orléans, France); DEA (Universités Paris I Panthéon-Sorbonne & Paris II Panthéon Assas); Doctorat (Université Paris II Panthéon-Assas).

[1] In the United Kingdom, termination of pregnancy by registered medical practitioners was allowed by the Abortion Act 1967. In France, abortion was legalized by Law 75-17 of 17 January1975 (the Veil law, named after Simone Veil, who initiated the law), as amended by Law 2001-588 of 4 July 2001, authorizing voluntary termination of pregnancy. In the United States, abortion was legalized by the Supreme Court in *Roe v Wade*, 410 US 113 93 S Ct 705 (1973).

[2] For a comparative overview, see G. Demme and R. Lorentz, 'Responsabilité civile et naissance d'un enfant. Aperçu comparatif' (2005), 57 (1) RIDC 103 et seq. See also B. Steiniger, 'Wrongful Birth and Wrongful Life: Basic Questions' (2010), 1 JETL, no. 2, 125 et seq.; A. Ruda, '"I Didn't Ask to be Born": Wrongful Life from a Comparative Perspective' (2010), 1 JETL, no. 2, 204 et seq.

necessary, in a preliminary section (section I), to give a comparative overview of this area of the law.

I. Birth related torts—a comparative perspective

Birth-related torts began to develop in the 1960s. This area of the law encompasses primarily four causes of action. Two types of claims must be distinguished, based on whether the child was born healthy or with birth defects. The factual scenarios upon which such claims may arise are thus different. Before examining the current state of the law in the various legal systems covered by this chapter (section I.2), it is critical to specify and explain the terminology that will be used in the latter (section I.1).

1. Terminology

This chapter will address four types of actions related to the birth of a child. It must be noted at the outset that there is no consensus as to the meaning given to the expressions used across the jurisdictions considered. Courts and commentators give the expressions used different meanings depending on the legal system in question. Therefore, it is necessary to clearly define the various causes of action (a), in order to avoid confusion (b).

a) Definitions

The first distinction that must be drawn is whether the child was born healthy (i) or with defects (ii).

i. Child born healthy

This first type of claim is brought by the parents of a healthy, but unwanted child for damage caused to them by the birth of their child. Two categories of situations exist. In the first one—known as wrongful pregnancy[3]—a pregnant woman was wrongfully told by her physician that she was not pregnant. This, in particular, prevented her from being given the opportunity to choose whether or not she would keep the child or resort to terminating the pregnancy within the deadline imposed by the law.[4] Such cases are rather rare.

The second category—known as wrongful conception—is more common. The birth of a healthy child is the result of either a failed contraception method or a failed sterilization procedure. For instance, in order to limit the size of his family, a man decides to undergo a vasectomy surgery. After performing the required tests to ensure that the operation was successful, the physician tells the patient that he and his wife no longer need contraceptive precautions. Nevertheless, the wife becomes pregnant again

[3] See, in gen., D. Kerrane, 'Damages for Wrongful Pregnancy' (2000), 11 Journal of Contemporary Legal Issues 467.

[4] See on this topic A. Holder, 'Physician's Failure to Diagnose Pregnancy' 7 Am. Jur. Proof of Facts 2d 579.

and gives birth to a healthy child. Another example would be a woman who decides to undergo a tubal ligation procedure. During the surgery, the physician found and ligated only one of the plaintiff's two fallopian tubes and then failed to inform her of the unsuccessful outcome of the operation. She thus remained fertile, took no birth-control precautions, and conceived a child, who was born as a normal, healthy baby.[5]

In both situations, the question is whether the birth of a healthy, but unwanted child may constitute a compensable damage for the parents. Furthermore, in order for the tort to be established, the birth must be the result of a mistake made by the physician, pharmacist, or laboratory. If the conception is simply due to the margin of error associated with any contraception method or sterilization procedure, there are, of course, no grounds for liability.

ii. Child born impaired

This second type of claim stands on different grounds. Unlike in the previous situations, the child was not unwanted, but was born severely handicapped due to an error made in the performance of a genetic test or the reading of its results.

The child's disability is either the result of an act or an omission of the physician, or due to the defendant's failure to diagnose or discover a genetic defect in the proper timeframe for the parents to make an informed decision as to whether to continue the pregnancy.

In other words, an expectant mother decides to undergo genetic testing, such as an amniocentesis, in order to determine what the risk of giving birth to a child with birth defects is. In the event the test results are positive, the parents will terminate the pregnancy. Due to an error made by the physician or laboratory in the conduct of the testing procedure or the interpretation of its results, the parents are mistakenly told that there is no issue. However, the child suffers serious birth defects, like, for instance, *spina bifida*.[6] Because of the aforesaid error, the parents were deprived of their right to terminate the pregnancy. Therefore, such claims may only be allowed in jurisdictions where abortion is legal.[7] Furthermore, it has even been said that the mere existence of a law authorizing abortion was sufficient to introduce a duty on the part of the defendant physician.[8]

This type of claim is similarly divided into two categories, both based on the same factual scenario. The distinction between the two lies in who the plaintiff is. On the one hand, the action may be brought by the child's family—primarily his parents, but the action could also be brought by his siblings[9]—in which case the action is said to be of

[5] *Lovelace Medical Center v Mendez*, 111 NM 336, 805 P2d 603 (1991) at 604.

[6] 'A major birth defect and a type of neural tube defect that involves an opening in the vertebral column caused by the failure of the neural tube to close properly during embryonic development. (The neural tube is the structure in the developing embryo that gives rise to the brain and spinal cord.) Because of the defect in the spine, part of the spinal cord is exposed and protrudes as a meningomyelocele. People with *spina bifida* often have neurological deficits below the level of the lesion and can suffer from bladder and bowel incontinence, limited mobility (due to paralysis of the legs), and learning problems', Webster's New World Medical Dictionary, <http://www.medterms.com/script/main/art.asp?articlekey=5526>.

[7] A. Holder, 'Physician's Failure to Diagnose Pregnancy' (n 4).

[8] *Rand v East Dorset Health Authority*, 56 BMLR 39, [2000] Lloyd's Rep Med 181.

[9] See *e.g. Cox v Stretton*, 77 Misc 2d 155, 352 NYS2d 834, dismissing such an action.

wrongful birth.[10] On the other hand, the action may be brought by the child himself—or rather on his behalf by his guardian—in which case the action is said to be of wrongful life.[11]

Even though both types of actions are based on similar facts, the consequences associated with the party bringing the action differ greatly. 'The distinction drawn between the two types of claim is that while one (the child's claim for "wrongful life") would require a court to determine the worth—or lack thereof—of a human existence, the other (the parents' claim for . . . "wrongful birth") merely requires it to make a financial assessment of the costs associated with child-rearing.'[12]

'Wrongful birth actions are brought by parents to recover for the birth of an unhealthy child. The parents' right to recover is based on the defendant's negligent deprivation of the parents' right not to conceive the child or to prevent the child's birth.'[13] Unlike wrongful conception or pregnancy actions, wrongful birth claims may only be brought when the child is born with a defect. The parents claim that they would have avoided conception or terminated the pregnancy had they been properly informed.[14]

Wrongful life is a much more controversial cause of action.[15] Unlike wrongful birth, the wrongful life action is brought by or on behalf of the child, claiming that, but for the physician's mistake, the child would not have been born.[16] In practice, the wrongful life and wrongful birth actions are brought simultaneously,[17] which has been described as illogical.[18] The root of the controversy lies in the fact that the issue is whether an impaired child would be better off not having been born at all.[19]

Even though this chapter will be using the foregoing definitions, a certain confusion exists amongst courts and commentators across the jurisdictions considered.[20]

[10] See in gen. C. Palo, 'Cause of Action for Wrongful Birth or Wrongful Life' (2005), 23 COA 2d 55.

[11] See in gen. J. Botkin, 'The Legal Concept of Wrongful Life' (1988), 259 JAMA 1541; M. Kelly, 'The Rightful Position in "Wrongful Life" Actions' (1991), 42 Hastings L. J. 505.

[12] M. Fordham, 'Blessing or Burden? Recent Developments in Actions for Wrongful Conception and Wrongful Birth in the U.K. and Australia' (2004), Sing. J. Legal Stud. 462 at 463.

[13] C. Palo, 'Cause of Action for Wrongful Birth or Wrongful Life' (n 10).

[14] M. Sullivan, 'Note: Wrongful Birth and Wrongful Conception: A Parent's Need for a Cause of Action' (2000, 2001), 15 J.L. & Health 105, 108.

[15] See, *e.g.*, K. Gallagher, 'Wrongful Life: Should the Action Be Allowed?' (1986–1987), 47 La. L. Rev. 1319 (1986–1987); R. Hughes, 'Recognition of Wrongful Life Actions: Trend or Aberration?' (1986–1987), 22 Tort & Ins. L.J. 585.

[16] See, *e.g.*, I. Saltz, 'Better Off Never Born?' (1986), 72 ABAJ 46; S. Human and L. Mills, 'The Immeasurable Wrongfulness of Being: The Denial of the Claim for Wrongful Life' (2010), Stell LR (1) 67.

[17] See, *e.g.*, *Harbeson v Parke-Davis*, 88 WN 2d 460, 656 P2d 483 (1983), in which the Supreme Court of the State of Washington recognized both claims.

[18] J. Bopp, D. McKinney, and B. Bostrom, 'The "Rights" And "Wrongs" of Wrongful Birth and Wrongful Life: A Jurisprudential Analysis of Birth Related Torts' (1989), 27 Duq. L. Rev. 461, 483.

[19] It must be noted that the first wrongful life action had not been brought on behalf of a child born with defects, but by a child who was born from unmarried parents in order to be compensated for the negative consequences of being born illegitimate. *Zepeda v Zepeda*, 190 NE 2d 849 (Ill. 1963).

[20] See, *e.g.*, T. Foutz, 'Comment, "Wrongful Life": The Right Not to be Born' (1980), 54 Tulane L. Rev. 480, 483–5; P. Lavette, '*Boone v. Mullendore*: Confusion of Actions in Wrongful Life, Wrongful Birth, and Wrongful Pregnancy' (1984), 35 Ala. L. Rev. 179.

b) Lack of consistency among jurisdictions

'"[W]rongful life", "wrongful birth" and other expressions canvassed by courts and commentators are potentially a source of considerable confusion.'[21] For quite a number of courts and authors, primarily in the United Kingdom and other common law systems, including certain US states, wrongful birth actions are those initiated by the parents of an unintended child, whether the latter was born impaired or not, and wrongful life actions are those brought by the child for the damage caused to him by its own birth.[22] In other instances, wrongful birth refers to actions brought by the parents of a healthy, but unwanted child, whereas wrongful life refers to claims brought by either the parents or the child, when the latter was born with defects. In order to avoid such confusion, we shall use the distinction adopted by most of the US jurisdictions and commentators. Thus, in this chapter, wrongful birth shall only refer to claims brought by parents of an impaired child, and wrongful life to actions brought by the child himself. Actions initiated by the parents of a healthy, but unwanted child shall be referred to as either wrongful conception or wrongful pregnancy, depending on whether the pregnancy had been misdiagnosed or resulted from a failed sterilization procedure. A lack of consistency exists about this distinction as well. Indeed, some courts and commentators do not distinguish between wrongful pregnancy and wrongful conception, and use the term 'wrongful pregnancy' for both situations.[23] However, the outcomes in both types of case are identical.

After exposing the forgoing elements of terminology, focus should be thrown onto the current state of the law in the various jurisdictions considered.

2. Current state of the law

We shall first explore the current state of the law as to the birth of a healthy—but unwanted—child (a), before examining the status of claims associated with the birth of a handicapped child (b).

a) Child born healthy

When presented with such cases, the question that courts have to answer is whether the birth of a healthy child may be considered a compensable injury for the parents. From a comparative perspective, the solutions given by the various legal systems range from no liability at all[24] to a full compensation of the parents' injury, *i.e.* the compensation for both the infliction of nervous shock and the financial consequences for the rearing and education of the child until the latter reaches the age of majority,[25] or even past the

[21] H. Teff, 'The Action for "Wrongful Life" in England and the United States' (1985), 34 Int'l & Comp. L.Q. 423, 425.

[22] *Turpin v Sortini*, 31 Cal. 3d 220 (1982) 225.

[23] See, *e.g.*, T. Foutz (n 20) at 483.

[24] That is the solution adopted in France, Civ. 1ère 25 juin 1991, *D.* 1991, Jur. p. 566, n. P. Le Tourneau J.C.P. 1992, II, 21784, n. Barbieri, Jean-François.

[25] *Lovelace Medical Center v Mendez,* 111 NM 336, 805 P2d 603 (1991); *Zehr v Haugen,* 871 P2d 1006 (Oregon, 1994); *Marciniak v Lundborg,* 450 NW.2d 243 (Wisconsin, 1990).

child's majority.[26] Some jurisdictions choose a median way by recognizing the parents' injury, but by limiting the defendant's liability to the pain and suffering that the parents sustained by having to go through pregnancy and birth.[27] In *McFarlane*, Lord Slynn of Hadley stated:

> [T]he wife, if there was negligence, is entitled by way of general damages to be compensated for the pain and discomfort and inconvenience of the unwanted pregnancy and birth, and she is also entitled to special damages associated with both extra medical expenses, clothes for herself and equipment on the birth of the baby. Whether the parents should be entitled as a matter of principle to recover for the costs of maintaining the child is a much more difficult question.[28]

Courts' refusal to recognize an injury is primarily based on moral considerations.[29] 'That a child can be considered as an injury offends fundamental concepts attached to human life'.[30] The French *Cour de cassation* ruled that 'the birth of a child may not, in itself, constitute an injury'.[31] However, courts allowing the action—in the United Kingdom[32] and at least 35 of the United States[33]—base their decisions on notions of justice and fairness. For those courts, the recognition of the defendant's liability constitutes a mere application of medical malpractice rules. In addition, granting physicians immunity from liability because the result of their malpractice is the birth of a child would be highly unfair. As Justice Leibson put it in his dissent, '[t]he physician who undertakes to provide medical treatment in the form of sterilization should not be afforded immunity from the major consequences of his negligence'.[34]

The second type of claim arises out of the birth of a handicapped child.

[26] *Fincham v Levin*, 155 So. 2d 883 (Florida, 1963); *Matter of Estate of Glass*, 175 Kan 246, 262 P2d 934 (1953); *Williams v West*, 258 SW2d 468 (Kentucky 1953); *Lieberman v Lieberman*, 517 SW2d 478 (Missouri, 1974); *Kruvant v Kruvant*, 100 NJ Super. 107, 241 A2d 259 (New Jersey, 1968); *Sayne v Sayne*, 39 Tenn. App. 422, 284 SW2d 309 (Tennessee, 1955); *Commonwealth v Shepard*, 212 Va 843, 188 SE2d 99 (Virginia, 1972); *Phillips v United States*, 575 F Supp. 1309 (DC 1983).

[27] *McFarlane and another v Tayside Health Board* [1999] 4 All ER 961.

[28] *McFarlane* (n 27) 970.

[29] *Schork v Huber*, 648 SW2d 861 (Kentucky, 1983).

[30] *Schork v Huber* (n 29) 862.

[31] Cass. Civ. 1ère 25 juin 1991 (n 24).

[32] *McFarlane and another v Tayside Health Board* (n 27).

[33] *Boone v Mullendore*, 416 So2d 718 (Alabama, 1982); *University of Ariz. Health Sciences Ctr. v Superior Court*, 667 P2d 1294 (Arizona, 1983); *Wilbur v Kerr*, 628 SW2d 568 (Arkansas, 1982); *Stills v Gratton*, 127 Cal. Rptr. 652 (California, 1976); *Ochs v Borelli*, 445 A2d 883 (Connecticut, 1982); *Garrison v Medical Ctr. of Del., Inc.*, 571 A2d 786 (Delaware, 1989); *Flowers v District of Columbia*, 478 A2d 1073 (D.C., 1984); *Fassoulas v Ramey*, 450 So2d 822 (Florida, 1984); *Fulton-DeKalb Hosp. Auth. v Graves*, 314 SE2d 653 (Georgia, 1984); *Cockrum v Baumgartner*, 447 NE2d 385 (Illinois, 1983); *Garrison v. Foy*, 486 NE2d 5 (Indiana, 1985); *Nanke v Napier*, 346 NW2d 520 (Iowa, 1984); *Byrd v Wesley Medical Ctr.*, 699 P2d 459 (Kansas, 1985); *Macomber v Dillman*, 505 A2d 810 (Maine, 1986); *Jones v Malinowski*, 473 A2d 429 (Maryland, 1984); *Burke v Rivo*, 551 NE2d 1 (Massachusetts, 1990); *Rinard v Biczak*, 441 NW2d 441 (Michigan, 1989); *Sherlock v Stillwater Clinic*, 260 NW2d 169 (Minnesota, 1977); *Girdley v Coats*, 825 SW2d 295 (Missouri, 1992); *Kingsbury v Smith*, 442 A2d 1003 (New Hampshire, 1982); *P. v Portadin*, 432 A2d 556 (New Jersey, 1981); *O'Toole v Greenberg*, 477 NE2d 445 (New York, 1985); *Jackson v Baumgardner*, 347 SE2d 743 (North Carolina, 1986); *Lovelace Medical Ctr. v Mendez*, 805 P2d 603 (New Mexico, 1991); *Johnson v University Hosps. of Cleveland*, 540 NE2d 1370 (Ohio, 1989); *Morris v Sanchez*, 746 P2d 184 (Oklahoma, 1987); *Mason v Western Pa. Hosp.*, 453 A2d 974 (Pennsylvania, 1982); *Smith v Gore*, 728 SW2d 738 (Tennessee, 1987); *Terrell v Garcia*, 496 SW2d 124 (Texas, 1973); *C.S. v Nielson*, 767 P2d 504 (Utah, 1988); *Miller v Johnson*, 343 SE2d 301 (Virginia; 1986); *McKernan v Aasheim*, 102 Wash.2d 411, 687 P2d 850 (Washington, 1984); *James G. v Caserta*, 332 SE2d 872 (West Virginia, 1985); *Marciniak v Lundborg*, 450 NW2d 243 (Wisconsin, 1990); *Beardsley v Wierdsma*, 650 P2d 288 (Wyoming, 1982).

[34] *Schork v Huber* (n 29) at 867.

b) Child born disabled

i. Wrongful birth

Even though wrongful birth claims encountered some opposition,[35] such actions are quite widely recognized across the jurisdictions considered. Only four jurisdictions—four US states—judicially rejected the action,[36] and a few more did so legislatively,[37] the issue being, for some, 'a question best left for legislative address'.[38] Some courts asserted that the physician was not responsible for the child's handicap—his genes were. As Justice Mitchell of the Supreme Court of North Carolina put it in *Azzolino v Dingfelder*, '[t]he disorder is genetic and not the result of any injury negligently inflicted by the doctor. In addition, it is incurable and was incurable from the moment of conception.'[39]

The wrongful birth action has been admitted in the majority of US states,[40] in the UK,[41] Canada,[42] Australia,[43] and France, both by the *Conseil d'État*[44]—the highest administrative court—and the *Cour de cassation*.[45] The courts considered the issue to be one of malpractice. Even though the physician's error did not cause the child's handicap, it caused the frustration of 'the intended exercise [by the parents] of the[ir] legal right [to terminate the pregnancy or not to conceive]'.[46] Not holding the physician

[35] M. Sullivan (n 14) at 116.

[36] *Azzolino v Dingfelder*, 337 SE2d 528 (North Carolina, 1985); on this ruling, see D. Peck, 'Survey of Developments in North Carolina Law, 1984: Xiii. Torts: *Azzolino v Dingfelder*: North Carolina Court of Appeals Recognizes Wrongful Birth and Wrongful Life Claims' (1985), 63 NCL. Rev. 1329; *Atlanta Obstetrics and Gynecology Group v Abelson*, 398 SE2d 557 (Georgia, 1990); *Grubbs v Barbourville Family Health Center*, 120 SW3d 682 (Kentucky, 2003); on this decision, see J. Frantz, 'The Ramifications of Rejecting Wrongful Birth: A Closer Look at *Grubbs v. Barbourville Family Health Center*' (2004–2005), 93 Ky. L.J. 507; *Taylor v Kurapati*, 600 NW2d 670 (Michigan, 1999); on this decision, see M. Croon, 'Notes and Comment: Case Note: *Taylor v. Kurapati*, the Court of Appeals of Michigan's Decision of Refusing to Recognize the Tort of Wrongful Birth' (2002), 5 DePaul J. Health Care L. 317.

[37] See, *e.g.*, Idaho Code § 5-334 (Idaho); Minn. Stat. Ann. § 145.424 (Minnesota); Mo. Rev. Stat. § 188.130 (Missouri); 42 Pa. Cons. Stat. § 8305 (Pennsylvania); S.D. Codified Laws § 21-55-2 (South Dakota); Utah Code Ann. § 78-11-23 à 25 (Utah).

[38] *Becker v Schwartz*, 386 NE2d 807 (1978) 814.

[39] *Azzolino v Dingfelder* (n 36) 536.

[40] *Keel v Banach*, 624 So2d 1022 (Alabama, 1993); *Walker ex rel Pizano v Mart*, 790 P2d 735 (Arizona, 1990); *Andalon v Superior Court*, 208 Cal. Rptr. 899 (California, 1984); *Lininger v Eisenbaum*, 764 P2d 1202 (Colorado, 1988); *Garrison v Medical Center of Delaware*, 581 A2d 286 (Delavare, 1989); *Haymon v Wilkerson*, 535 A2d 880 (D.C. 1987); *Kush v Lloyd*, 616 So2d 415 (Florida, 1992); *Goldberg v Ruskin*, 499 NE2d 406 (Illinois, 1984); *Bader v Johnson*, 675 NE2d 1119 (Indiana, 1997); *Arche v United States Dept. of Army*, 798 P2d 477 (Kansas, 1990); *Pitre v Opelousas General Hosp.*, 519 So2d 105 (Louisiana, 1987); *Reed v Campagnolo*, 630 A2d 1145 (Maryland, 1993); *Viccaro v Milunsky*, 551 NE2d 8 (Massachusetts, 1990); *Proffitt v Bartolo*, 412 NW2d 232 (Michigan, 1987); *Greco v US*, 111 Nev. 405 (Nevada, 1995); *Smith v Cote*, 513 A2d 341 (New Hampshire, 1986); *Berman v Allan*, 404 A2d 8 (New Jersey, 1979); *Becker v Schwartz*, 386 NE2d 807 (New York, 1978); *Flanagan v Williams*, 87 Ohio App3d 768 (Ohio, 1993); *Jacobs v Theimer*, 519 SW2d 846 (Texas, 1975); *Naccash v Burger*, 290 SE2d 825 (Virginie, 1982); *James G. v Caserta*, 332 SE2d 872 (West Virginia, 1985); *Harbeson v Parke-Davis, Inc.*, 656 P2d 483 (Washington, 1983); *Dumer v St. Michael's Hosp.*, 233 NW2d 372 (Wisconsin, 1975).

[41] *Rand v East Dorset Health Authority* (2000) 56 BMLR 39; *Hardman v Amin* (2000) 59 BMLR 58 (QBD).

[42] E. Nelson, and G. Robertson, 'Liability for Wrongful Birth and Wrongful Life' (2001), 2:2 ISUMA: Canadian Journal of Policy Research 102, 103–4.

[43] P. Watson, 'Case Note: *Edwards v Blomeley*; *Harriton v Stephens*; *Waller v James*: Wrongful Life Actions in Australia' (2002), 26 Melbourne U. LR 736.

[44] C.E. Ass. 2 juil. 1982, Delle. R., Rec. P. 260; R. D. San. et soc. 1983, p. 95. Concl. Pinault, Michel.

[45] Cass. Civ. 1ère 26 mars 1996 (1ère espèce), D. 1997, jurisp., p. 36.

[46] *Becker v Schwartz*, 386 NE2d 807 (New York, 1978) 815.

liable because the result of his negligence was the birth of a child would result in granting immunity to a class of defendants. There is 'no reason why a physician who performs such surgery [sterilization] should be held to a lesser standard of care than a physician or surgeon who performs any other surgical procedure.'[47]

The French *Cour de cassation*, while precluding parents from recovery in the event of the unwanted birth of a healthy child,[48] specified that this rule applied 'in the absence of a specific damage, which, added to the normal expenses associated with maternity, would have entitled the mother to seek compensation'.[49] This wording created an exception to the general prohibition rule, in particular when the child is born handicapped, like in the 1996 case. However, the extent of the compensation awarded to the parents varies between jurisdictions, from compensation limited to the parents' pain and suffering,[50] to the full coverage of their expenses to raise, educate, and care for their child[51] because '[t]he claimant should be placed in a position in which she can take care of her disabled son's reasonable needs during the duration of their joint life span.'[52]

ii. Wrongful life

As already mentioned, wrongful life is a much more complex and controversial cause of action. Very few jurisdictions in the United States have allowed the action in wrongful life,[53] and those have been in a limited manner. Those jurisdictions have indeed awarded the plaintiff with special damages, in order for the child to receive financial support for his care needs. However, they have always refused to award the plaintiff with general damages, which would have meant that his life itself was to be considered a compensable injury. In *Turpin v Sortini*, the child plaintiff was born with hereditary deafness. She brought a 'wrongful life' action against the defendants, namely the doctor, hospital, and others, who had misdiagnosed the hereditary defect in her sister, which deprived her parents of the choice to conceive her. The Court held that the plaintiff should be entitled to special damages, if her special medical needs were proximately caused by the defendants' error.[54] As we pointed out earlier, wrongful birth and wrongful life claims are generally initiated at the same time. Both the parents and the child bring an action seeking compensation for the same situation. In order to

[47] *C.S. v Nielson*, 767 P2d 504, (Utah, 1988) 506.

[48] Cass. Civ. 1ère 25 juin 1991, D. 1991, Jur. p. 566, n. P.Le Tourneau, J.C.P. 1992, II, 21784, n. Barbieri, Jean-François.

[49] Ibid. '[en] l'absence de dommage particulier qui ajouté aux charges normales de la maternité aurait été de nature à permettre à la mère de réclamer une indemnité.'

[50] *Sherlock v Stillwater Clinic*, 260 NW2d 169, at. 175: 'the parents of an unplanned child should at least be entitled to recover all damages immediately incident to pregnancy and birth. The allowance of these damages, we believe, is wholly consistent with the elementary principle of compensatory damages which seeks to place injured plaintiffs in the position that they would have been in had no wrong occurred.'

[51] In the UK, *Rand v East Dorset Health Authority* (2000) 56 BMLR 39; in the US, *Lovelace Medical Center v Mendez*, 111 NM 336, 805 P2d 603 (New Mexico, 1991); *Zehr v Haugen*, 871 P2d 1006 (Oregon, 1994); *Marciniak v Lundborg*, 450 NW2d 243 (Wisconsin, 1990). See, on this question, Jennifer Mee, 'Wrongful Conception: The Emergence of a Full Recovery Rule' (1992), 70 Wash. U. L.Q. 887.

[52] *Hardman v Amin* (2000) 59 BMLR 58 (Q.B.D.).

[53] *Turpin v Sortini*, 643 P2d 954 (California, 1982); *Procanik by Procanik v Cillo*, 97 NJ 339 (New Jersey, 1984); *Harbeson v Parke-Davis, Inc.*, 98 Wash 2d 460 (Washington, 1983). On *Turpin v Sortini*, see, Saltz and Irwin, 'Better Off Never Born?' (1986), 72 ABAJ 46; K. Kearl, '*Turpin v Sortini*: Recognizing the Unsupportable Cause of Action for Wrongful Life' (1983), 71 Cal. L. Rev. 1278.

[54] *Turpin v Sortini*, 643 P2d 954 (n 53).

avoid a situation in which the physician would have to pay damages twice for the same injury, the Supreme Court of the state of Washington specified after allowing the child's action:

> We hold, accordingly, that a child may maintain an action for wrongful life in order to recover the extraordinary expenses to be incurred during the child's lifetime, as a result of the child's congenital defect. Of course, the costs of such care for the child's minority may be recovered only once. Wooldridge v Woolett, 96 Wn.2d 659, 666, 638 P.2d 566 (1981). If the parents recover such costs for the child's minority in a wrongful birth action, the child will be limited to the costs to be incurred during his majority.[55]

It must be noted that, even though three jurisdictions in the United States have allowed the action, the extent of compensation has been limited to special damages, as opposed to general damages. Had the latter been awarded, it would have meant that the child was to be compensated for emotional distress or for an impaired childhood.[56] Rather, courts have awarded special damages, in order to cover the extraordinary expenses incurred during the child's majority 'as they were reasonably certain, readily calculable, and of a kind daily determined by judges and juries.'[57] Courts reject the general damage claim because 'man does not know whether non-life would have been preferable to an impaired life.'[58] The Supreme Court of New Jersey, while allowing the action, found that 'the infant's claim for pain and suffering and for a diminished childhood presents insurmountable problems. The philosophical problem of finding that such a defective life is worth less than no life at all has perplexed... distinguished members of [the] Court.'[59] The Court concluded:

> We need not become preoccupied, however, with these metaphysical considerations. Our decision to allow the recovery of extraordinary medical expenses is not premised on the concept that non-life is preferable to an impaired life, but is predicated on the needs of the living. We seek only to respond to the call of the living for help in bearing the burden of their affliction.[60]

In 2000, the French *Cour de cassation* allowed the action in the well-known *Perruche* decision.[61] In this case, a child was born with severe defects because of the rubella that his mother had while pregnant. After noticing a rash, a pregnant woman got tested for rubella. She specified that, in case there was a risk for the child, she would terminate her

[55] *Harbeson v Parke-Davis, Inc.*, 98 Wash2d 460 (Washington, 1983) (n 53) at 479–80.

[56] *Procanik by Procanik v Cillo*, 97 N.J. 339 (Opinion by Justice Pollock) (n 53) at 353.

[57] *Procanik* (n 53) at 352 (Opinion by Justice Pollock).

[58] *Procanik* (n 53) at 369 (Justice Schreiber's dissent).

[59] *Prokanik* (n 53) at 353. [60] *Prokanik* (n 53) at 353.

[61] Cass. plén. 17 nov. 2000, *Gaz. Pal.* 25 janv. 2001, pp. 26 et seq., note J. Guigue. Amongst the vast literature on the topic, see *e.g.*, L. Aynès, 'Le préjudice de l'enfant né handicapé (ou la plainte de Job devant la Cour de cassation)—A propos de Cass. plén.', 17 novembre 2000, *D.* 2001, p. 492; P. Delmas Saint-Hilaire, 'Le handicap prévu et le droit de ne pas naître' (décembre 2000), Personnes et famille, 19 et seq.; F. Dreifuss-Netter, 'Observations hétérodoxes sur la question du préjudice de l'enfant victime d'un handicap congénital non décelé pendant la grossesse' (janvier 2001) Médecine et droit, 1 et seq.; B. Edelman, 'L'arrêt Perruche: une liberté pour la mort?' (2002), Droits, vol. 35, p. 151 et seq.; P-Y.Gautier, 'Notes autour de l'affaire P...' (2002), Droits, vol. 35, pp. 147 et seq.; M. Gobert, 'La Cour de cassation méritait-elle le pilori?' (8 décembre 2000), Pet. aff. n°245, 4 et seq.; J. Hauser, 'Le préjudice d'être né, question de principe' (janvier 2001), Droit et patrimoine, 6 et seq.

pregnancy. The tests were erroneously performed and the mother was told that she was immune to rubella. When her child was born, he was severely handicapped. The *Cour de cassation*, using a legal reasoning 'trick', asserted that the physician's error caused the child's handicap, which, therefore, had to be compensated. The following year,[62] the Court confirmed this view and specified that the damage suffered by the child was not constituted by the loss of a chance, but by the handicap itself. This assertion stirred debate among the legal community.[63] Indeed, the physician's error did not cause the handicap. Had the physician not made a mistake in the tests, the defect would still have been present, but the parents would have decided to terminate the pregnancy. The birth defect could not have been avoided—the birth itself could have. In 2002, the legislator intervened to preclude children from seeking compensation 'solely because of his/her birth'.[64] This Act was later partially invalidated by the European Court of Human Rights (ECtHR), but only because it applied to pending claims.[65] This retroactivity was deemed to constitute a deprivation of property under Art. 1 of the First Protocol to the European Convention on Human Rights. Both the *Cour de cassation*[66] and the *Conseil d'État*[67] later ruled in compliance with the ECtHR decisions. Thus, wrongful life actions are no longer allowed in France.

The vast majority of jurisdictions that have addressed the wrongful life issue have rejected the claim, either judicially[68] or by statute.[69] The claim raises questions that

[62] Cass. plén., 13 juil. 2001, cases No. 478, 479 and 480, B.I.C.C. 542; D. 2001, p. 2325, note P. Jourdain; Gaz. Pal., 7–8 sept. 2001, n. J. Guigue; *J.C.P.* 2001, II, 10601, concl. J. Sainte-Rose, n. F. Chabas; RGDA, 2001, n° 3, p. 751, note L. Mayaux,; Cass. plén., 28 nov. 2001, case No. 486; J.C.P. 2002, II, 10018.

[63] F. Chabas, 'Note sous Cass. plén., 13 juil. 2001' J.C.P. 2001, II, 10601; L. Mayaux, 'Note sous Cass. plén., 13 juil. 2001', RGDA 2001, n° 3, pp. 751 et seq.; L. Aynès, 'Un droit à naître sans handicap?', Les cahiers du C.C.N.E., n° 29, oct. 2001, p. 12; G. Loiseau, 'Chronique d'une vie non désirée : le droit de ne pas naître de l'enfant handicapé', Droit et patrimoine, n° 98, nov. 2001, p. 101; A. Sériaux, 'Morales sur Perruche', Droits, vol. 35, 2002, pp. 134 et seq.

[64] Law No. 2002-303 on the Rights of the Sick and the Quality of the Health System (Kouchner Act), Gaz. Pal., Bull. Leg. 2002, p. 113; J.O. 5 mars 2002, p. 4118. For a comment, see *e.g.* C. Bou, 'Les apports de la loi du 4 mars 2002 concernant l'indemnisation des accidents médicaux', Gaz. Pal., 4 juin 2003, pp. 2 et seq. This provision was codified in 2005 in Art. L. 114-5 of the *Code de l'action sociale et des familles [Code of Social Action and Families]*.

[65] *Draon v France* (App no 1513/03) ECHR 6 October 2005 and, *Maurice v France* (no 11810/03) ECHR, 6 October 2005.

[66] Cass. civ. 1ère, 24 janv. 2006 (3 decisions), cases No. 02-13.775, 02-12.260 and 01-16.684, J.C.P. 2006, éd. G, IV, 1331, 1332 et 1333.; *D.*, 2006, IR p. 325, n. I. Gallmeister; Gaz. Pal., 14 fév. 2006, avis J. Sainte-Rose; *Resp. civ. et assur.*, mars 2006, comm. 94, n. C. Radé.

[67] C.E., 24 févr. 2006, J.C.P., 2006, éd. A, 1074.

[68] *Elliot v Brown*, 361 So2d 546 (Alabama, 1978); *Walker v Mart*, 790 P2d 735 (Arizona, 1990); *Willis v Wu*, 607 SE2d 63 (South Carolina, 2004); *Lininger v Eisenbaum*, 764 P2d 1202 (Colorado, 1988); *Garrison v Medical Ctr. of Del., Inc.*, 581 A2d 288 (Delaware, 1990); *Haymon v Wilkerson*, 535 A2d 880 (D.C., 1987); *Kush v Lloyd*, 616 So2d 415 (Florida, 1992); *Atlanta Obstetrics v Abelson*, 398 SE2d 557 (Georgia, 1990); *Siemieniec v Lutheran Gen. Hosp.*, 512 NE2d 691 (Illinois, 1987); *Bruggeman v Schimke*, 718 P2d 635 (Kansas, 1986); *Pitre v Opelousas Gen. Hosp.*, 530 So2d 1151 (Louisiana, 1988); *Viccaro v Milunsky*, 551 NE2d 8 (Massachusetts, 1990); *Proffit v Bartolo*, 412 NW2d 232 (Michigan, 1987); *Smith v Cote*, 513 A2d 341 (New Hampshire, 1986); *Becker v Schwartz*, 386 NE2d 807 (New York, 1978); *Flanagan v Williams*, 623 NE2d 185 (Ohio, 1993); *Nelson v Krusen*, 678 SW2d 918 (Texas, 1984); *James G. v Caserta*, 332 SE2d 872 (West Virginia, 1985); *Dumer v St. Michael's Hosp.*, 233 NW2d 372 (Wisconsin, 1975); *Beardsley v Weirdsma*, 650 P2d 288 (Wyoming, 1982).

[69] In the United States: Idaho Code § 5-334(1) (Idaho); Burns Ind. Code Ann. § 34-12-1-1 (Indiana, 2004); Minn. Stat. Ann. §§ 145.424 (1), (2) (Minnesota, 1997); Mo. Rev. Stat. § 188.130(2) (Missouri, 1997); N.C. Gen. Stat. § 14.45.1(e) (North Carolina, 1997); N.D. Cent. Code § 32.03-43 (North Dakota, 1997); 42

may not be answered by law. May one be compensated for the mere fact of having been born? Is impaired life worse than non-life? In addition, from a causation standpoint, the physician or laboratory's error did not cause the child's disability, but rather, it deprived the parents from their right to make an informed choice as to either conceiving, terminating, or pursuing the pregnancy. The child's handicap could not have been avoided. That is one of the reasons why the British legislator, in the Congenital Disabilities (Civil Liability) Act 1976, allows the child's action only when the birth defect has been caused by the physician's act, which excludes the situation in which the disability is the result of a genetic defect.[70] This was confirmed in *McKay v Essex Area Health Authority and Another*,[71] in which the Court of Appeal rejected the claim initiated by a child who was born deformed due to the rubella that her mother contracted in the early stages of her pregnancy. The claim was rejected because, even though a child has the right not to be injured before birth, in this case, her handicap was due to her mother's rubella, not the physician's act.[72]

That duty may be owed to the mother, but it cannot be owed to the child.

To impose such a duty towards the child would, in my opinion, make a further inroad on the sanctity of human life which would be contrary to public policy. It would mean regarding the life of a handicapped child as not only less valuable than the life of a normal child, but so much less valuable that it was not worth preserving, and it would even mean that a doctor would be obliged to pay damages to a child infected with rubella before birth who was in fact born with some mercifully trivial abnormality.[73]

The assessment of the injury is another reason that courts have put forward, in order to dismiss such claims. '[T]he most compelling reason to reject this cause of action is the intolerable and insoluble problem it would create in the assessment of damage.'[74]

In the Canadian decision *Lacroix v Dominique*, the parents of a child born severely impaired claimed that they had not been informed of the risks associated with a medication that had been prescribed to the wife to treat her epilepsy. Their child was born with physical anomalies and was diagnosed as being developmentally delayed and retarded.[75] After reviewing the various arguments at stake, which have already been addressed, the judge concluded he was 'unable to accept that an action for wrongful life should be recognized in Canada'.

It appears that Courts use comparative law when they are to decide birth-related cases.

Pa. Cons. Stat. § 8305(a) (Pennsylvania, 1993); S.D. Codified Laws Ann. §§ 21-55-1 à -2 (South Dakota, 1997); Utah Code Ann. § 78-11-24 (Utah, 1997); in the United Kingdom: Congenital Disabilities (Civil Liability) Act 1976; in France: Law No. 2002-303 on the Rights of the Sick and the Quality of the Health System (Kouchner Act), Gaz. Pal., Bull. Leg. 2002, p. 113; J.O. 5 mars 2002, p. 4118.

70 I. Guisen, 'The Use and Influence of Comparative Law in "Wrongful Life" Cases' (2012), 8 Utrecht L. Rev. 35, 39.

71 [1982] 2 All ER 771, QB 1166.

72 M. Redmond, 'Casebook' (1982), 72–3 Law & Just.—Christian L. Rev. 60, 61.

73 *McKay v Essex Area Health Authority and Another* [1982] QB 1166 at 1180.

74 *McKay* (n 73) 1190 (Griffiths, LJ).

75 *Lacroix v Dominique*, 2001 MBCA 122.

II. The use of comparative law by courts—reasons and extent

When presented with birth-related tort cases, courts—across the jurisdictions considered—seem to be more inclined to use comparative law than when they review less complex issues. We shall explore the reasons thereof (section II.1) before examining the extent to which courts resort to comparative law in their own decisions (section II.2).

1. Reasons for the use of comparative law by courts

As evoked above, the issues raised by birth-related torts are highly complex. This is due in part to the fact that these questions are not merely of a legal nature, but they have extra-legal dimensions, in particular, ethical, moral, and economic. That is why, more than in other areas of the law, courts need to draw their inspiration from jurisdictions which have already decided similar matters. Thus, before reviewing the state of the law as to wrongful life in other jurisdictions, Justice Crennan stated:

> Decisions from overseas jurisdictions where the same issue and identical questions have arisen may assist, despite not being binding, because determining, as a matter of law, whether a duty of care exists or not falls to be considered at a 'higher level of abstraction'[Shirt v Wyong Shire Council [1978] 1 NSWLR 631 at 639] than, for example, factual questions of breach, turning on local normative standards, and causation.[76]

By using foreign examples and comparative law, in order to elaborate their own decisions, courts show the usefulness of the discipline, which is often confined to a secondary purely intellectual role—'an unnecessary course for eggheads',[77] a 'marginalised area of the law curriculum'.[78] The need to use comparative law was impeccably stated by Lord Steyn in the landmark decision *McFarlane and another v Tayside Health Board*:[79]

> My Lords, the discipline of comparative law does not aim at a poll of the solutions adopted in different countries. It has the different and inestimable value of sharpening our focus on the weight of competing considerations. And it reminds us that the law is part of the world of competing ideas markedly influenced by cultural differences.[80]

Scholars have also emphasized the need for the use of foreign decisions by courts in birth-related tort cases. In his analysis of the *Perruche* case, Sir Basil Markesinis asserted that using comparative law is:

> highly desirable when arises a novel and important question which has been solved by another legal system, but not by that which is faced with the issue for the first time.

[76] *Harriton v Stephens* [2006] HCA 15.

[77] M. Waxman, 'Teaching Comparative Law in the 21st Century: Beyond the Civil/Common Law Dichotomy' (2001), 51 J. Legal Educ. 305, 305.

[78] B. Markesinis and J. Fedtke, 'The Judge as Comparatist' (2005), 80 Tul. L. Rev. 11, 15.

[79] [1999] 3 WLR 1301, 52 BMLR 1 (1999).

[80] *McFarlane and another v Tayside Health Board* [1999] 4 All ER 961, at 976.

> There is little doubt that the *Perruche* case belongs to this category, and few will doubt that German and American laws are richer on this issue than French law – and this despite the fact that the issue has often been subject to litigation in France.[81]

Thus, comparative law must be used as an enlightening tool by judges, in order for them to rule in a more rational and critical manner on complex topics.

Let's examine the extent to which courts use comparative law.

2. Extent of the use of comparative law by courts

It is a well-known fact that the form of rulings issued by common law courts is quite different from that of civil law courts' decisions. Judicial style is one of the most striking differences between the two legal traditions.[82] Common law rulings are generally lengthy with a clear description of the facts and reasons for the decision, whereas civil law decisions (especially those issued by the highest courts, like the French *Cour de cassation*) are traditionally, very short, concise, and often understandable by jurists only.

Because of the foregoing, the manner in which comparative law is used by courts varies widely between both legal traditions, comparative considerations being part of the decision itself in the common law world (a), whereas those will only be included in pre-ruling judicial reports or *conclusions* in the civil law world (b).

a) Common law rulings

When faced with wrongful conception, wrongful birth, or wrongful life issues, common law courts seem to not be reluctant to explore foreign decisions, in order to make their own. Thus, in the landmark case *McFarlane v Tayside Health Board*, the House of Lords examined how foreign courts addressed the question, using 'a valuable *tour d'horizon* of comparative jurisprudence'[83] initiated in the *Emeh* case.[84] Like a number of other common law decisions, the House of Lords referred primarily to rulings issued in other common law systems, including the United States,[85] Canada,[86] Australia,[87] and New Zealand.[88] The Court also referred to civil law jurisprudence, in particular that of Germany[89] and France.[90] Lord Steyn's survey of foreign decisions led him to conclude that, even though some jurisdictions allowed the parents' claim for full

[81] B. Markesinis, 'Réflexions d'un comparatiste anglais sur et à partir de l'arrêt Perruche' (2001) R.T.D. Civ., 2001, p. 77, 98.

[82] See, *e.g.*, F. H. Lawson, 'Comparative Judicial Style' (1977), 25 Am. J. Comp. L. 364; J-L. Goutal, 'Characterstics of Judicial Style in France, Britain and the USA' (1976), 24 Am. J. Comp. L. 43.

[83] *McFarlane* (n 80) 975–6.

[84] *Emeh v Kensington and Chelsea and Westminster Area Health Authority* [1984] 3 All ER 1044, [1985] QB 1012.

[85] *Johnson v University Hospitals of Cleveland* (1989) 540 NE2d 1370.

[86] *Kealey v Berezowski* (1996) 136 DLR (4th) 708.

[87] *CES v Superclinics (Australia) Pty Ltd* (1995) 38 NSWLR 47.

[88] *Re Z* (1982) 3 NZAR 279; *XY v Accident Compensation Corp* (1984) 4 NZAR 219.

[89] *Bundesgerichtshof* (Federal Court of Justice), 6th Chamber, 18 March 1980, BGHZ 76, p. 249.

[90] Cass. Civ 1ère, 25 June 1991, D 1991, 566.

compensation for the financial consequences of the birth of their healthy child, courts generally reject such claims.[91]

In its 2006 decision *Harriton v Stephens*, the High Court of Australia reviewed quite extensively the 'position elsewhere',[92] emphasizing British and US cases and mentioning those of other jurisdictions, namely Canada,[93] Israel,[94] Germany,[95] France,[96] and the Netherlands.[97]

In *Lacroix v Dominique*, the Court of Appeal of Manitoba simply evoked the decisions of courts in a few states of the US, but relied quite strongly on *McKay*, which it cited at length, to reject the child's claim.[98]

b) *Civil law rulings*

As already mentioned, decisions issued by supreme courts in the civil law world are very concise, generally no more than a few paragraphs. They do not include a lot of details, nor do they contain any explanations of the reasons ('*motivation*') why the courts chose to interpret the law in one way and not the other.[99] Based on the foregoing, one may understand the total absence of references to foreign decisions in the decisions. Guy Canivet, former *Premier président* of the *Cour de cassation*, underlined that the *Cour de cassation* and, more generally, the other French courts, are structurally forced—because of the very style of the decisions which makes it impossible to give an interpretative explanation of the rule—to not expressly refer to foreign laws in the body of the rulings.[100]

However, one may find enlightening elements in some of the courts' working documents, such as—in the case of France—preliminary reports and the Advocate General's *conclusions*.

Thus, in Pierre Sargos' preliminary report to the *Perruche* decision, brief references to foreign decisions were made at the very end of the document. The report underlined that no supreme court equivalent to the *Cour de cassation* had ever clearly rejected or allowed the action. It indicated that, on the one hand, *McKay* and most US decisions rejecting the child's claim did so because of a statute barring recovery in such cases. On the other hand, it underlined that the US courts which allowed the action did so in a limited manner by only awarding special damages. In his preliminary report to the three decisions of 13 July 2001, which confirmed the ruling adopted by the

91 *McFarlane* (n 80) 976.

92 *Harriton v Stephens* (n 76) 78.

93 See, *e.g.*, *Lacroix v Dominique* (2001) 202 DLR (4th) 121. Generally, see E. Nelson and G. Robertson, 'Liability for Wrongful Birth and Wrongful Life' (n 42).

94 See, *e.g.*, *Zeitsov v Katz* (1986) 40(2) PD 85, as discussed in D. Heyd, 'Are "Wrongful Life" Claims Philosophically Valid? A Critical Analysis of a Recent Court Decision' (1986), 21 Israel Law Review 574.

95 Bundesgerichtshof, 18 January 1983, *Juristenzietung* (1983), p. 450.

96 The Court cites the *Perruche* case.

97 *Leids Universitair Medisch Centrum v Kelly Molenaar*, Hoge Raad 18 maart 2005, RvdW 2005, 42.

98 *Lacroix v Dominique*, 2001 MBCA 122, discussed in section I.2.b.ii.

99 J-F. Weber, 'Comprendre un arrêt de la Cour de cassation rendu en matière civile' (2009), BICC, No. 702, 15/05/2009, <http://www.courdecassation.fr/publications_cour_26/bulletin_information_cour_cassation_27/bulletins_information_2009_2866/n_702_3151/>.

100 G. Canivet, 'Le juge entre progrès scientifique et mondialisation' (2005), R.T.D.Civ., 33, 45.

Perruche court,[101] Henri Blondet simply referred to the comparative law section in Pierre Sargos' report to the *Perruche* decision.[102]

In her *Conclusions* to the 1997 *Conseil d'État* decision,[103] Valérie Pécresse, *Commissaire du Gouvernement*, mentioned the McKay case, as well as the usual US decisions, in order to support her recommendation to the *Conseil* to reject the child's claim.

To what extent does comparative law influence courts?

III. The influence of comparative law on judicial decisions

Even though it appears that courts do use comparative law in birth-related tort cases, the extent of its influence is uncertain.

The differences evoked earlier pertaining to judicial style in the civil law and the common law world will affect the role of comparative law on the decision-making process, or, at least, the perception that one may have thereof. Indeed, measuring the influence of foreign decisions on national rulings is easier in common law rulings than in civil law ones.

As already mentioned, the section devoted to comparative law in the Advocate General's conclusions in the *Perruche* case is rather concise. The foreign decisions referred to were not thoroughly explored.

Although there has been a trend—at least from a theoretical standpoint—towards a wider opening of French courts to comparative law, it is unlikely that the examination of foreign decisions influenced the court.

It appears that the reason why both Sargos and Pécresse referred to comparative law was more to justify and support their positions than to actually use foreign decisions as a basis for reflection. In the *Perruche* preliminary report, instead of using comparative law a priori, prior to making a choice as to what direction to take, foreign rulings were used a posteriori, to show that the stance the French court was about to take was novel and that the *Cour de cassation* was a pioneer in that area of the law.

French legal culture has been said to be 'rather inward looking',[104] and the same could be said about the United States. Generally, very few references to foreign decisions are made. Because of the federal structure of the system, US courts often refer to rulings issued by other US state courts, which is—to a lesser scale—a form of comparative law, but very rarely refer to foreign cases.

Justification seems to be the primary role of the use of comparative law by courts—an a posteriori use. As a scholar put it, 'a justification based on foreign sources is not essentially a free-standing justification, but rather it gives additional support to arguments that can be based on existing domestic law sources by showing that they illustrate a principle or value shared by a number of other legal systems.'[105]

[101] Cass. plén., 13 juil. 2001, No. 478, 479 and 480, B.I.C.C. 542; *D.* 2001, p. 2325, n. P. Jourdain.

[102] H. Blondet, Rapport, Cass. plén., 13 juil. 2001, Ibid.

[103] C.E., 14 Févr. 1997, *Centre hospitalier régional de Nice c/Epoux Q...*, *RFD adm.* 13 (2), mars-avr. 1997, p. 374, conclusions Valérie Pécresse, commissaire du Gouvernement, n. Bertrand Mathieu.

[104] I. Giesen, 'The Use and Influence of Comparative Law in "Wrongful Life" Cases' (2012), 8 Utrecht L. Rev. 35, 49.

[105] J. Bell, 'The Argumentative Status of Foreign Legal Arguments' (2012), 8 Utrecht L. Rev. 8, 8.

The Canadian case *Lacroix v Dominique* is interesting as it is one of the only decisions in which the influence of comparative law may truly be assessed. Indeed, the judge mentioned that a few US courts had allowed the child's claim, but 'their reasons for doing so d[id] not persuade [him]'. However, after reviewing and citing *McKay* at length, the judge concluded:

> Despite a valiant attempt by the plaintiffs' counsel to persuade me otherwise, I am unable to accept that an action for wrongful life should be recognized in Canada. I find the reasoning of the judges in McKay v. Essex Area Health Authority . . . too compelling to do otherwise and I am unaware of any Canadian circumstances which would cause judges here to think differently.[106]

Prior to the *Harriton* case in Australia, a decision by the New South Wales Supreme Court—*Edwards v Blomeley*[107]—relied also to a large extent on *McKay*, as the court was faced with a case of first impression Justice Studdert explained:

> No other Australian authority directly in point has come to the attention of the Court. The absence of other authority in Australia suggests an acceptance in this country hitherto of the decision of the Court of Appeal in McKay v Essex Area Health Authority, and I shall now turn to a consideration of that case.[108]

McKay has therefore been influential on the reasoning of both Canadian and Australian courts.[109] Even though the influence of a foreign decision in those two systems is clear, one could wonder, however, if, due to the fact that both Canada and Australia are Commonwealth countries, this influence could not be relativized.

These Canadian and Australian decisions are the rulings in which comparative law seems to have had the strongest influence. More than just being used as justification to support the judge's decision, the foreign cases cited seemed to have actually driven the decision-making process, or, at the very least, was part of the basis for the decision.

IV. Conclusion

Birth-related torts constitute a field of choice for comparative law to be part of judicial reasoning. Courts may find in foreign decisions the arguments, ideas, and justifications they need to resolve issues that are not only novel, but also extremely complex and multi-dimensional. This chapter showed that courts across the legal systems considered do include comparative law in the judicial decision-making process. Whether the case examined was issued by a common law court or a civil law one will affect the extent to which comparative law was used. Nonetheless, even if references to foreign decisions do not appear in the decisions themselves, judges in civil law systems do rely on comparative law.

106 *Lacroix v Dominique*, 2001 MBCA 122, discussed in section I.2.b.ii.

107 [2002] NSWSC 461, available at <http://www.vrlaw.com.au/cases/pdfs/200403010931370.blomeley.pdf>.

108 *Edwards v Blomeley*, ibid.

109 M. Bagaric and P. Dimopoulos, 'The High Court and Wrongful Life Claims: How Should it Decide?' (2005), 1 High Ct. Q. Rev. 173, 176.

Even though comparative law is used by courts, its actual influence on the rulings is much more complicated to assess. It appears that most courts use comparative law to justify and support their reasoning. In those situations, foreign decisions are simply used as examples, not as persuasive authorities. In a few decisions, in particular in Canada and Australia, the influence of comparative law—a British case—seemed to be quite strong. However, comparative law arguments are not the predominant factors in the decision-making process. The area of birth-related torts is strongly attached to the culture—not only legal—of a country and it would be erroneous to believe that such complex issues could be determined by primarily relying on foreign decisions,[110] even within common law-based legal systems. As Jane Stapleton put it:

> The cultures, legal cultures and legislative environments within which tort law operates are not equivalent and such differences, though not necessarily apparent, may profoundly influence how tort principles are shaped, applied and perceived: the concerns of tort law are culturally and historically contingent.[111]

Local politics, the national government's stance on abortion, the readiness of the legal system to take a clear position on such an ethically charged issue, and the place of religion in society, are among the factors that will influence courts.

Even though the role of comparative law is, generally, more to justify and support than to persuade, and theoretically 'the role of the court of final appeal is to "judge," not provide some intellectual survey of world law',[112] the fact that courts seem to be willing to use, examine, and rely on—at least to some extent—foreign cases, is a step towards a broader recognition of the merits and usefulness of comparative law.

[110] See I. Giesen (n 104) 52 et seq.

[111] J. Stapleton, 'Benefits of Comparative Tort Reasoning: Lost in Translation' (2007), 1 Journal of Tort Law, No. 3, p. 1 et seq.,15; Reprinted in M. Andenas and D. Fairgrieve (eds.), *Tom Bingham and the Transformation of the Law: A Liber Amicorum for Lord Bingham* (Oxford University Press, 2009), p. 773 et seq.

[112] Stapleton, ibid., 18.

36

The Use of Comparative Law in *A & Others v National Blood Authority*

His Honour Judge Michael Brooke QC and Ian Forrester QC***

I. Introduction

The editors of this publication have invited two of the claimants' advocates instructed in the important case of *A & Others v National Blood Authority*[1] presenting both comparative law and Community law questions to describe how the case came to judicial attention, and the legal and factual challenges presented by arguing broad principle-driven doctrines before an English court during a trial lasting 49 court days. We represented 112 individuals who were infected with hepatitis C as a result of blood transfusions in England. This chapter, written with the consent of the claimants' solicitors, is extended with a postscript by counsel for the defendant and completed by an afterword from the trial judge. The claimants were successful, but it was a 'close-run thing'.

The problem of contaminated blood transfusions is not new to medicine or to litigation, especially in the United States. The United Kingdom avoided the excesses of the United States by having a non-commercial blood bank system. The claimants had certainly been injured but it was questionable whether they had a good cause of action under conventional negligence principles. It is intrinsically difficult to establish liability on the part of a public authority performing a valuable public service. A case based on negligence would need to demonstrate considerable levels of breach of duty. While the HIV Haemophiliac Litigation (HHL)[2] in England was brought to an acceptable conclusion for the plaintiffs infected with HIV from blood products, the difficulty of pursuing such a case in negligence against government departments and agencies raising arguments of immunity and 'non-justiciability' and at the very least challenging the plaintiffs to establish 'Wednesbury negligence'[3] were only too daunting.

For the victims of infection with the Hepatitis C virus through blood transfusions, a case based on Community law appeared more promising, precisely because it was intended to remove the need to prove negligence or knowledge on the part of the blood

* The editors sadly record Michael's passing away in 2014 before the publication of the second edition.

** White and Case LLP. QC at the Scots Bar.

[1] *A & Others v NBA* [2001] 3 All ER 289; [2001] Lloyd's Rep Med 187. Hereafter references to the reported judgment will be by paragraph number thus: Para.

[2] Where the Plaintiffs' cause of action was negligence.

[3] For non-English lawyers, liability of the public authority by reason of its manifestly gross or unreasonable misconduct.

authorities. However, as of the late 1990s, although the EU Product Liability Directive[4] had been in force for some 15 years (and had been under discussion for years before that), it had been little commented upon by courts in the UK or indeed elsewhere in the Common Market. The Newcastle solicitors who represented the majority of the potential claimants had already instructed barristers specializing in common law clinical negligence and product liability to review their clients' chances. One was also a member of the Paris Bar, with a network of professional colleagues and professional acquaintances in France and elsewhere. Counsel advised the potential claimants they had a sustainable case under the Consumer Protection Act 1987 (CPA) upon the basis that blood infected with the hepatitis C virus was defective upon a proper construction of the CPA.

The point being novel and not straightforward, the Legal Aid Board authorized the solicitors to seek a second opinion from further counsel, based in Brussels, a member of a London chambers, working with colleagues of different nationalities.

The latter's opinion on the application of the Directive was first sought in 1997. In March 1997, he gave the opinion that it was reasonable to presume that patients and others would expect to receive uncontaminated blood in a transfusion, and would correspondingly regard as 'defective' blood which might infect them with a serious illness. As we will describe further below, the Directive presented a number of questions: would the public at large be entitled to regard as 'defective' a blood transfusion which might transmit hepatitis C, and would the various defences contemplated by the Directive avail the defendant blood authority? On this basis, questions of whether the potential defendants had followed good practice with respect to epidemiological probabilities appeared relevant not so much for whether the blood was defective under the Directive but rather whether a defence might be available based upon the patient's acceptance of the risk or the defendant's unawareness of the risk. The opinion noted that there were surprisingly few judicial decisions applying the Directive, although there was a large quantity of material commenting on the proposal to have a Directive, the dangers and uncertainties of the Directive, and its implications for domestic product liability law. Particular attention in counsel's opinion was given to the writings of the European Commission official charged with drafting the Directive who, from the early 1970s, had been responsible for shepherding the proposal through the process of inter-governmental and intra-institutional negotiation to a conclusion in the form of the promulgation of Directive 85/374/EEC.

The two leading counsel thus separately reached the conclusion that an action based upon the Directive would indeed have a reasonable prospect of success. A number of supplementary opinions were dispatched, on the strength of which the solicitors were able to persuade the legal aid authorities in England that the case was maintainable. (The Scottish legal aid authorities apparently rejected a parallel claim for help in Scotland, on the grounds that the case was not winnable.)

[4] Council Directive 85/374/EEC on the approximation of the laws, regulations and administrative provisions of the Member States concerning liability for defective products.

II. The medicine

It is necessary to give a brief outline of what the scientific case was about.

Hepatitis is an inflammation of the liver, which can be caused by various viral infections. Once the hepatitis A virus and the hepatitis B virus had been identified in the early 1970s, it was then appreciated that post-blood-transfusion viral hepatitis continued to occur due to infection with other (as yet unidentified) viruses and NonA NonB Hepatitis (NANBH) was the description applied to this viral hepatitis. It was particularly noted because people were regularly seen to develop symptoms of hepatitis after receiving blood transfusions. At first, there was no direct screening test to identify donors as carrying the virus, but there were practical procedures for excluding blood from donors at increased risk of carrying the virus. These were called 'surrogate' tests and the most useful one was to carry out a blood test to check the levels of an enzyme produced in the liver (ALT). High levels of ALT in the blood were suggestive that the person might have some abnormality of liver function, and one possible cause for this was that the donor was a carrier of the NANBH virus. This surrogate testing of blood donors had been routine in Germany since the 1960s, it was made routine in the USA in 1986, and in France by 1988. Routine ALT screening of blood donors was considered in the UK but was never introduced.

In May 1988 came a breakthrough when the Chiron Corporation of America announced the identification of the hepatitis C virus and the development of a prototype screening test. The first version of the test (the Ortho Elisa) became commercially available in late 1989 (when a licence for the export of the test from the USA was first obtained) and it was soon used in programmes for the routine screening of blood donors in Japan and in France. In May 1990 the US Food and Drugs Administration (FDA) gave approval for use of this test within the USA and so it went into routine use for screening there, as well as in a number of other countries.

There were concerns about the accuracy of this 'first generation' test, both as to its sensitivity (not detecting all it should, i.e. false negatives) and its specificity (detecting those it should not, i.e. false positives). A further concern was the lack of a confirmatory or supplementary test to verify positive results and identify some of the false positives. Nevertheless the relevant Department of Health committee (UK Advisory Committee on Virological Safety of Blood: ACVSB) advised, in principle, as early as November 1989 that the Ortho Elisa should be used for routine screening subject to three conditions[5]. In May 1990 a confirmatory test (RIBA 1) became available. In July and November 1990 the ACVSB recommended that screening of blood donors should be started, subject to the holding of various trials. Second generation Elisa tests became available by April 1991. Routine screening of blood for hepatitis C was introduced throughout England and Wales on 1 September 1991.

NANBH had been a proxy in the HIV Haemophiliac Litigation (HHL) for the AIDS virus emerging in the 1980s, the argument being that the precautions, which could and should by then have been taken against the contamination of blood products with

[5] Satisfactory pilot tests, FDA approval, and availability of a confirmatory test.

NANBH, would also have avoided their contamination with the yet to be identified HIV.[6]

Near the end of the HHL, Mr Justice Ognall allowed for the plaintiffs' lawyers to act in the forthcoming Hepatitis Litigation, using the knowledge acquired when acting in the HHL, particularly resulting from the disclosure provided by the various defendants. In the Hepatitis Litigation NANBH, no longer the proxy, was the target itself.

III. The English legal principles

The Product Liability Directive (1985/374) came into effect on 25 July 1985 after a very lengthy process of drafting, lobbying, discussion, and negotiation, including intergovernmental and parliamentary discussion. The UK[7] implemented the Directive by passing the Consumer Protection Act 1987 (CPA), which came into effect on 1 March 1988. A claimant's cause of action under the CPA is made out where damage is caused to the claimant by a defect in a product taken[8] to have been produced by the defendant. Section 4(1)(e) of the CPA provides that a defendant may escape liability by showing: 'That the state of scientific and technical knowledge at the relevant time was not such that a producer of products of the same description as the product in question might be expected to have discovered the defect if it had existed in his products while they were under his control.'

The litigation therefore turned on the rights of patients infected due to transfusions after 1 March 1988.

Most[9] of the claimants in the Hepatitis Litigation relied on the CPA cause of action, although argument in the litigation essentially focused on the Directive, whose words, by common consent, prevailed in case of doubt, and it is that cause of action which is the subject of Mr Justice Burton's judgment in *A & Others v NBA*.

IV. Preparation of the case

The Directive is framed in the civil law tradition, expressed very tersely with questions of general principle set forth in a few words. The 50[10] days in court turned on the proper construction[11] of fewer than 100 words. A respectable case could be made that the reasonable expectation of the public at large should reflect the intrinsic characteristics of transfused blood in a bag: having come from another person's body, it could not fail to contain the qualities of the blood of the donor. It would be strange, the defendants would say, if liability could exist despite the defendants having taken every, or every reasonable, or every practical precaution against the transmission of

[6] The keystone of the argument was the Scottish decision by the House of Lords in *Hughes v Lord Advocate* [1963] AC 837.

[7] One of the early states to do so.

[8] i.e. the producer or the own brander or the importer or the supplier unable to identify the producer.

[9] There were a small number relying on clinical negligence.

[10] Forty-nine days trying the case and one day delivering the reserved judgment.

[11] Legal argument as to that proper construction took place on no less than 13 days in the course of the trial.

contaminated blood. If it were proved that no method (or no sufficiently reliable method) existed of catching infective bags of blood, was the ordinary citizen entitled to hope that the transfusion service would never deliver an infective bag of blood? Could society regard as 'defective' what science could not prevent?

Setting the purpose of the legislation in context would be essential. The preparations fell into different categories: (1) research on German civil law under Article 823 of the *Burgerliches Gesetzbuch* (BGB, the German Civil Code) until the adoption of the Directive; (2) gathering *travaux préparatoires*; (3) consulting the now-retired drafter of the Directive; (4) research in other EC Member States and in the United States concerning relevant writings and judicial experience; (5) carrying out research at the Max Planck Institute; and (6) collecting all language versions of the legislation and selecting those portions of other authorities in foreign languages which required translation in whole or in part into English.

1. German law

The *Bundesgerichtshof* (BGH, Germany's supreme civil court) rendered a series of judgments from 1956 concerning product liability. In each case, undoubted injury was done due to the failure of a product: the fork of a bicycle broke and injured the rider; a mineral water bottle exploded, injuring a child; a consignment of vaccine infected a flock of chickens with fowl pest. In each case, the supplier said that the product had been manufactured according to the highest possible standards, under the strictest conditions of supervision, and with all due diligence. In the 1956 case, the BGH found for the manufacturer, stating that the injury was one of the *Lebensrisiko*, one of the risks of life, and that without demonstrable fault on the part of the manufacturer, the victim could not be compensated. The victim almost always would lack the capacity to show how the fault had occurred (particularly without a doctrine like *res ipsa loquitur*), and anyway, the manufacturer could show it had done all in its power to prevent rogue products reaching the market. The climate of opinion changed in the late 1960s/early 1970s due to the Thalidomide tragedy (*Contergan* was its name in Germany) when children were born with unforeseen defects (late 1960s/early 1970s), and was further influenced by the legal consequences of compensating victims of the crash of a Turkish aircraft in Paris in 1974 because of a badly designed cargo-hold door. The BGH decided to reverse its previous positions and found for the claimant in an exploding mineral water bottle case in 1995. Translations of these judgments (which are by English standards quite brief) were prepared; and copies of the relevant portions of the BGB, were compiled both in German and in English translation.

2. *Travaux préparatoires*

The Secretary General of the European Council was requested to furnish copies of the *travaux préparatoires* from the Council's archives pertinent to the drafting, review, modification, and final adoption of the Directive. After some weeks, the Secretariat General supplied a large mass of documents dating back to the earliest days (late 1960s/early 1970s) when notions of a European Directive on product liability were first canvassed. Included were memoranda prepared within the context of a Council of Europe experts' committee, the first working drafts of a possible Directive prepared within the Commission, submissions by a wide range of parties concerning the merits of the draft Directive, and, most interestingly, the minutes of the many meetings of the EU Council Working Group at which the proposed Directive moved through its successive stages to final adoption in 1985. Most of the latter documents were in French and indicated the identities and theories of the Member States requesting particular modifications during the drafting process. The *travaux préparatoires* could be relied on, the claimants thought, to demonstrate that most of the arguments to be considered in the litigation had been reviewed and debated extensively during the drafting process; quite how far they would be useful was uncertain.

3. Consulting the retired draftsman of the Directive

Commission officials generally rotate between positions every three to five years. The Product Liability Directive was so controversial and so sensitive that the official in question[12] had the rare privilege of seeing it through from initial conception in about 1970 to ultimate adoption by the Council in 1985. He had written an excellent book in German on the subject[13] and was a teacher of law at German universities. He quite relished the opportunity to see how a case concerning the Directive was prepared and was happy to give his personal comments on the history of the Directive, and a statement was framed recording his recollection of its drafting. There was debate between opposing counsel concerning the admissibility of such testimony, since part of it would consist of recording familiar institutional and procedural facts about how directives are drafted, revised, debated, and adopted. Community law (it was said) is a matter for argument, not evidence. The learned doctor could not testify to the proposition that a former Commission official considered the Directive should be interpreted in a particular way, but his insights were plainly useful to a full understanding of the history and the purposes of the Directive. After discussion with the Bench and between counsel, it was agreed that he would not submit testimony and that the procedural history to which he could speak would be adopted as part of the submissions by the claimants on the history of the Directive.

4. Research in other EC Member States and in the United States concerning relevant writings and judicial experience

As already noted, although the implications of the adoption of the Directive had been widely debated, and indeed colourfully debated, actual decisions applying the Directive appeared to be rare. Judgments in all civil law countries are brief by comparison to English standards. The reasoning of the French *Cour de Cassation* may be one short sentence, a phenomenon that has so far survived scrutiny by the European Court of

[12] Professor Doctor Hans Claudius Taschner.

[13] Hans Claudius Taschner, *Produkthaftungsgesetz und EG-Produkthaftungsrichtlinie* (München, 1990).

Human Rights. There is generally speaking no principle of *stare decisis* in civil law jurisdictions, although the significance of that difference can be exaggerated.

It was therefore decided to research the implementation of the Directive in France, Spain, the Netherlands, Belgium, Italy, and Portugal. Accordingly, friendly members of the bar in those countries were consulted and requested to report on significant academic writing or judicial decisions concerning the Directive, particularly in the context of medical practice. It turned out that there was a remarkable dearth of judicial authority and a moderate level of academic commentary during the period after the adoption of the Directive. Two cases had reached the European Court, one of which had been decided. One lower court judgment emerged: a district court in the Netherlands made a finding partially favourable to the claimants and partially unfavourable (that the blood was a defective product but that the hospital could not be blamed for having delivered it to the patient, since the defect could not have been screened out). There were a number of French cases reflecting more the distinctive and painful history of contaminated blood in France than the Directive in particular. Apart from the German cases before the *Landgericht*, *Oberlandesgericht*, and *Bundesgerichtshof*, referred to earlier, there were few other judgments of obvious relevance, but the academic commentary was fairly copious, and would in due course be relied upon both in argument and in the judgment. The professional colleagues in other countries were extremely interested and helpful in suggesting lines of approach and relevant sources of academic literature.

Advice on the American experience was sought from an American friend, Professor Shael Herman, who taught at the Tulane University of Louisiana and at the Sorbonne. He synthesized the complex and inconsistent American history of how blood transfusion infection cases have been handled judicially and legislatively.

5. Carrying out research at the Max Planck Institute

Academic writing is a stronger source of legal authority in the civil law tradition than in England. In the absence of judgments of higher courts (with the notable exception of Germany) it was necessary to review the available literature. For this purpose, the best-equipped law library in Europe was the Max Planck Institute in Hamburg. The Institute staff were hospitable and welcoming. Works from a number of authors of different nationalities in German, Swedish, Spanish, Italian, Portuguese, and English were consulted. One curiosity was that Belgian authors wrote on German law, German authors wrote on French law, and Australian authors wrote on English and Australian law. The claimants were thus able to produce at least 25 books and articles published outside the UK relevant to the fundamental questions presented by the litigation: Was blood capable of being regarded as a product? Was it the reasonable expectation of the public that a blood transfusion would not contain hepatitis C virus? Was the public entitled to regard as defective a contaminated transfusion? What was the relevance of the precautions which could in theory be taken or had in fact been taken? Did it make a difference if the unwanted characteristics of the transfused blood were incapable of being eliminated by skill and diligence? What was the relevance of the prescribing doctor's knowledge of the risk of infection? Of what relevance was the so-called 'state-of-the-art defence'? Was the public entitled to have an expectation about the quality of transfused blood, which was technically unattainable in the circumstances?

6. Collecting all language versions of the legislation and preparing translations of other material

The parties were greatly helped by the fact that the judge having the conduct of the litigation, Mr Justice Burton, was known to speak French comfortably and, as it turned out, other European languages very adequately. It was not necessary to go to the expense of preparing translations of all the material in various foreign languages. This was particularly convenient as to French, the language of most of the *travaux préparatoires*. However, translations of the entirety of two of the judgments of the BGH were prepared, as well as translations of the Arnhem district court judgment and Swedish *travaux préparatoires* which accompanied the promulgation in Swedish law of the Directive. The full texts of the academic commentators relied upon were made available and translations prepared of sentences or paragraphs which seemed particularly relevant. (All counsel spoke French, and some spoke moderate German and Italian.)

V. The request for a reference in 1999

In October 1999, the claimants invited the judge to make a preliminary reference to the European Court of Justice on a number of questions as to the true and proper construction to be placed on the Directive. This application was rejected. His order indicated that he felt the request was premature in that it was not yet certain what questions would turn out to be the relevant ones. A year later the trial started before the same judge. By then the scene had been set for a very full comparative analysis of how the Directive should be construed and applied to the facts relating to the claimants' infection through blood transfusions with the hepatitis C virus.

VI. The non-issues

Three points of general importance hovered in the wings of the trial but did not in the end arise for decision. They are worth mentioning in passing and may crop up in future cases.

1. Product

On the generic pleadings the claimants' allegation that blood and *Blood products* were 'products' within the meaning of the CPA was not admitted by the defendant. The defendant's position on the pleadings had support from one of the leading academic writers in the field, Professor Jane Stapleton in *Product Liability*,[14] but in the event it was conceded by the time of trial that blood and *Blood products* were 'products'.

[14] Jane Stapleton, *Product Liability* (Butterworths, 1994). Professor Stapleton is Research Professor, Research School of Social Sciences, Australian National University; Ernest E Smith Professor, University of Texas School of Law; Statutory Visiting Professor of Law at Oxford University.

2. Producer

The defendant admitted that it was responsible for the liabilities of its predecessors in the National Blood Transfusion Service and the Bio Products Laboratory[15] and in effect accepted that they were the producers within the meaning of the CPA. During the course of the trial it was submitted by the defendant that in approaching the question of the consumer's legitimate expectation as to the safety of blood, the court should put in the defendant's favour the fact that, unlike a purely commercial producer, the defendant had no alternative but to continue supplying blood to hospitals and patients, as a service to society. Burton J rejected this argument in paragraph 42 of his judgment: noting that the defendants did not put forward a defence under Article 7(d) 'that the defect is due to compliance of the product with mandatory regulations issued by the public authorities', he concluded that there was no necessary reason why a public authority or a non-profit-making organization should be in any different position from a commercial undertaking if the product is unsafe. He also noted that that was the opinion expressed by the Advocate General (Colomer) in the *Danish Kidney* case.[16] This was before the ECJ gave its judgment in the case[17] on various questions referred to it by the Højesteret (Danish Supreme Court).

3. Consumer Protection Act versus Directive

There are significant differences between the wording not merely of Article 7(e) and section 4(1)(e) CPA but also between Article 6 and section 3 in the definition of defect. The differences between Article 7(e) and section 4(1)(e) were considered by the European Court of Justice in the enforcement proceedings brought by the Commission against the UK[18] to challenge the adequacy of the UK's implementation of the Directive. As the pleadings developed, a pattern emerged of the claimants sticking resolutely to the wording of the Directive, while the defendant stuck to the wording of the CPA. By the time of the trial, however it was accepted on both sides that the dominant provision was the Directive and that insofar as the CPA's wording differed from the wording of the Directive, the CPA should not be construed differently from the Directive. As Burton J. said: 'and consequently the practical course was to go straight to the fount, the Directive itself'.[19] The clash of the Statutes, feared by the Commission in its challenge to the UK's implementation of the Directive and an issue

[15] The Regional Health Authorities and the Central Blood Laboratories Authority.

[16] *Henning Veedfald v Århus Amstkommune* Case C-203/99, para. 27.

[17] Holding that Art 7(c) 'the product was neither manufactured by him for sale or any form of distribution for economic purpose nor manufactured or distributed by him in the course of his business' did not furnish a defence where the defective product is used in the course of a medical service financed entirely from public funds and for which the patient is not required to pay any consideration. The Court also addresses some interesting questions directed to whether the damage suffered in the case (loss of a harvested kidney through contamination prior to transplant into the plaintiff) was within Article 9 of the Directive.

[18] *Commission v UK* Case C-300/95 [1997] All ER (EC) 481.

[19] Para. 2.

on our pleadings[20] did not in fact take place, although a great deal of time was spent analysing *Commission v UK*, in at least three language versions.

VII. The core issues

The two fundamental issues were:

(a) Is the infection of blood with hepatitis C virus a defect within the meaning of Article 6?

(b) If so, was the state of scientific and technical knowledge such that the existence of the defect could not be discovered as provided by Article 7(e)?

Article 6(1) provides:

> A product is defective when it does not provide the safety which a person is entitled to expect, taking all the circumstances into account, including:
> i. the presentation of the product;
> ii. the use to which it could reasonably be expected that the product would be put;
> iii. the time when the product was put into circulation.

The main points of common ground were that:[21]

(a) liability under the CPA is 'defect-based' not 'fault-based' (Recitals 2 and 6 of the Directive);

(b) the question to be resolved is the degree or level of safety or safeness which persons generally are entitled to expect;

(c) the expectation is that of the public at large;

(d) the expectation is not the *actual* expectation of persons generally, but what they are *entitled* to expect. 'Legitimate expectation' became the common formulation of the expectation, which was consistent with other language versions of the Directive, e.g. '*la sécurité à laquelle on peut légitimement s'attendre*';

(e) the court decides what the public is entitled to expect.

Against that common background:

(a) The claimants' primary case on defect was that:
   i. the legitimate expectation of people generally throughout the relevant period[22] was that transfused blood would not infect patients with hepatitis C;
   ii. the conduct of the producer is irrelevant and questions of avoidability of the defect, practicability of its avoidance, and economic feasibility thereof are all irrelevant.

[20] Despite the terms of section 1(1) CPA: 'This Part [of the Act] shall have effect for the purpose of making such provision as is necessary in order to comply with the product liability Directive and shall be construed accordingly.'

[21] See Para. 31, where Burton J lists in detail a number of points of common ground.

[22] From 1 March 1988.

(b) The defendant's case on defect was that:
   i. the risk of infection with hepatitis C was known to the treating doctors, for whom it was a risk worth running for the sake of the patient in need of a transfusion;
   ii. avoidability or unavoidability is a circumstance for the purpose of Article 6;
   iii. the legitimate expectation of people generally was not that blood would be 100 per cent clean but that all legitimately expectable (reasonably available) precautions had been taken;
   iv. it would therefore be necessary to investigate whether the producers had taken all legitimately expectable steps to avoid the risk of the product being defective.

(c) The claimants' fall-back case on defect, in consequence, was:
   i. that the defendant's case is contrary to the intention of the Directive as revealed by the *travaux préparatoires*, the Recitals, and the observations of the Advocate General and the European Court of Justice in *Commission v UK*, requiring as it did an investigation of fault in all but name;
   ii. that nevertheless, the investigation required by the defendant's case in fact reveals that throughout the relevant period the producers *had* failed to take all legitimately expectable steps to avoid the risk of the product being defective: (1) from 1 March 1988 in failing to perform routine surrogate testing of blood donors; and (2) from 1 January 1990 in failing to perform anti-hepatitis C Elisa testing of blood donations.

Article 7 (e) provides: 'The producer shall not be liable as a result of this Directive if he proves . . . that the state of scientific and technical knowledge at the time when he put the product into circulation was not such as to enable the existence of the defect to be discovered.'

(a) The defendant's case on Article 7(e) was that in the then state of scientific and technical knowledge, the defect in the particular product could not be discovered, given the shortcomings of both surrogate testing and anti-hepatitis C Elisa 1st generation tests. In other words, the defect has to be discoverable in the blood in the bag in question.

(b) The claimants' case on Article 7(e) was that the defence is not available once the risk of the product being defective was known (which had been the case since the 1970s), whether or not the defect can be discovered in a particular product. In other words, the existence of the defect in the population of products in general has to be undiscoverable for the defence to arise.

VIII. Comparative law features of the oral argument

Once the trial began, the European law case was opened by referring to the adoption of the BGB in 1896, and the evolving interpretation of Article 823, which is the basis for establishing liability due to fault under German law. German law in the 1950s and 1960s found against plaintiffs who had unquestionably been injured but were unable to demonstrate fault as against a diligent manufacturer who could show the existence of all possible precautions. Thereafter the law changed, reflecting what English lawyers would call a decision to shift the burden of proof, concluding with the celebrated case of the child injured by the exploding mineral water bottle. This case concerned a young claimant injured by an exploding mineral water bottle resulting from a very fine hairline crack, not discovered despite what was found to be a technical and supervisory procedure in the defendant's factory in accordance with the very latest technology. Both the Court of Appeal of Hamm and the BGH had experienced little difficulty in concluding that the bottle was a defective product under Article 6 of the Directive, categorizing the bottle as an Ausreisser, as a rogue product or sub-standard product. The battlefield in the German courts was Article 7(e) and the young claimant was the victor in the BGH. German law was thus presented as an example of legal evolution in accordance with the principles ultimately espoused by the Product Liability Directive. There was then a very thorough examination of the *travaux préparatoires* over a period of about 15 years, from which, so argued the claimants, one could observe that many of the arguments advanced by the defendants had been voiced, examined, and not accepted by the drafters of the Directive. The claimants of course had to concede that it was the words of the Directive which should prevail, and that the *travaux préparatoires* could not supply principles which were not present in the adopted text. It was interesting to observe that the *travaux préparatoires* contained submissions from chambers of commerce, memoranda from governments, and reports by successive chairmen of the Council Working Group charged with the responsibility of reaching a consensus among the Member States. The books and articles published by those involved in the drafting process, especially Professor Taschner, were particularly relied on.

The claimants also referred to English and Scottish cases such as *Smedleys v Breed* [1974] AC 839 (the factory produced 3,500,000 cans of peas a year successfully but was convicted when four caterpillars of the same colour, shape, and density as the peas escaped detection in its food preparation processes and were discovered in a can of peas), and *Donoghue v Stevenson* [1932] AC 562[23] (concerning the alleged snail in the bottle of ginger beer) was invoked as authority for the proposition that what manufacturers claimed was ridiculously severe nonetheless could make good law. There had been two recent English decisions under the CPA,[24] which the trial judge considered. The conclusion of the BGH was echoed[25] (albeit *obiter*) by Ian Kennedy J in *Richardson*:[26]

[23] It should be recorded that, despite its absence from the lists of authorities in both the Lloyd's Rep Med and the All ER reports of *A v NBA*, the great case of *Donoghue v Stevenson* was referred to in argument on at least 10 occasions! Reading the dissenting speeches in *Donoghue v Stevenson* was a salutary reminder that famous cases were not foregone conclusions; Mrs Donoghue was fortunate in having a dogged solicitor who believed he could change the law.

[24] *Iman Abouzaid v Mothercare (UK) Ltd* (Court of Appeal, 21 December 2000); *Richardson v LRC Products Ltd* [2000] Lloyd's Rep Med 280, a decision at first instance in respect of a failed condom which Ian Kennedy J held not to be defective.

[25] Ian Kennedy J cleaves to the CPA in the course of his judgment and does not mention the Directive at all. While counsel had referred him to *Commission v UK* and the Article 7(e)/Section 4(1)(e) linguistic discrepancy, he was not apparently referred to the BGH decision.

[26] Para. 285.

> This provision [Article 7(e)] is, to my mind, not apt to protect a defendant in the case of a defect of a known character merely because there is no test which is able to reveal its existence in every case.

A certain amount of time was devoted to the United States, where the commercialization of the blood industry led to a high incidence of infection and a corresponding number of lawsuits, to which a number of legislatures had reacted by enacting so-called shield laws immunizing blood banks from liability in certain circumstances. Indeed, New Jersey and Illinois judgments were duly cited in the judgment.

An Australian case[27] of toxic[28] oysters was considered, but the wording of the Australian statute's equivalent of Article 7(e) was subtly different, alluding to the discoverability of the defect in 'the action goods'. This, it was held, provided a defence, since the presence of hepatitis A virus in any given oyster could not be discovered.

The language of Articles 1, 4, 6, and 7 of the Directive as well as its Recitals was reviewed at length. Of the nine European Union languages, the judge was the only person who attempted the modern Greek texts, and the Finnish text was not consulted. Most attention was given to the English, French, German, Italian, and Portuguese texts. The Livenote transcribers of the shorthand record of the hearings included linguists[29] who were able to produce accurately typed German, French, Italian, or Spanish in the transcript delivered to the judge and counsel at the end of the day. Emphasis was placed on the fact that the explanatory memoranda adopted by other Member States usually made recitals of certain principles relevant to the construction of the Directive. Much time was also devoted to the opinion of Advocate General Tesauro and the judgment in *Commission v UK*.[30]

IX. The judgment

The resolution of these issues as to the true and proper construction of the Directive, having entailed wide-ranging comparative arguments, led to a judgment which refers to authorities from eight[31] jurisdictions and numerous learned books and papers.[32]

The learned judge directed himself that he should approach the *travaux préparatoires* with caution.[33] Bearing in mind that he should be alive to there being an 'autonomous' or Community meaning or construction for harmonizing pan-European legislation, the judge welcomed the guidance to be obtained from considering the official different language versions of the Directive and was tentatively prepared to look at how the Directive had been implemented and judicially applied in other Community countries;[34] a little later in his judgment he shows more enthusiasm for judicial decisions elsewhere in Europe for reasons both of comity and harmony, in

[27] *Graham Barclay Oysters v Ryan* [2000] FCA 1099.

[28] They were contaminated with the hepatitis A virus.

[29] Assisted by one counsel's polyglot son. [30] Case C-300/95 [1997] All ER (EC) 481.

[31] England, ECJ, New Jersey, Illinois, Germany, Holland, France, and Australia.

[32] The reader should know that the judgment, even by English standards, is long: as handed down it is 170 pages long containing 284 paragraphs (105 pages in Lloyd's Law Reports, Medical containing 283 paragraphs).

[33] Para. 15.i. [34] Para. 15.ii.

approaching this piece of common legislation.[35] The judge attached great importance to the Directive's recitals as aids to its construction, listing the significant ones at an early stage.[36]

The judgment makes many citations from the academic literature in respect of both Article 6 and Article 7(e). In part this is because of the dearth of previous judicial decisions, particularly on Article 6, but it also demonstrates a willingness by the judge to adopt a broad and purposive approach to the task of construction that faced him. The judge, in formulating his conclusions on Article 6, underpins them at the outset by reference to European academic literature.[37]

The court decisions that carried most weight with the judge and clearly gave him most assistance were *Commission v UK* and the decision of the BGH in the mineral water bottle case, both cases directed at Article 7(e) but both offering some assistance on Article 6. It is interesting to observe that the opinion of Advocate General Tesauro (in *Commission v UK*) needed to be consulted in its original Italian to see that at one point he had used the subjunctive, which had not been carried over into the official English translation.[38] The judge took on the task of analysing the BGH's very dense judgment in the mineral water bottle case and came to the conclusion that: 'What the BGH was primarily saying is that if the risks are known, unavoidability of the defect in the particular product is no answer.'[39]

Burton J's conclusions on Article 6 may be summarized thus:

(a) The words *all the circumstances* are not exclusive; neither are they unlimited. They are not to be subjected to a restricted construction *eiusdem generis* to the specific examples given in Article 6. Having regard to other language versions,[40] in particular the French where '*notamment*' (≅ 'notably') is used rather than 'including', the specific examples given in Article 6 are intended to be the most significant circumstances. *All the circumstances* are to be construed as all *relevant* circumstances.

(b) *Avoidability* (i.e. the defendant's case on Article 6) is not one of the *circumstances* to be taken into account within Article 6.[41] It is not a relevant circumstance, being outwith the purpose of the Directive,[42] which was to relieve consumers not merely of the need to prove fault or negligence, but also of the need to show that the producer had taken all legitimately expectable steps. Furthermore, had *avoidability* been relevant, it would have been a significant

[35] Para. 44. [36] Para. 14. [37] Para. 55. [38] Para. 53.i.a. [39] Para. 53.ii.

[40] In Para. 34.ii. the judge observes: '[a possibility is] that they ["all circumstances"] are to be construed as the most significant examples of the circumstances. There was some support for this proposition, both by way of some exemplars in European legislation—from which it could be suggested that European draftsmen had considered that the matters actually set out as examples were the ones most worthy of mention—and also by reference to the French language version of Article 6, which used the word, before the list of the circumstances, "notamment", and the German, which used "insbesondere", both of which I take to mean "in particular" or "especially"—although other language versions use phraseology more similar to the English "including".'

[41] Para. 63.

[42] Having regard, in particular, to the recitals of the Directive, recitals 2 and 6 being most apposite.

circumstance departing from the purpose of the Directive and as such would have been mentioned specifically in Article 6.

(c) The first step is to identify the harmful characteristic which caused the injury. The next step is to conclude whether the product is standard or non-standard. If the respect in which it differs from the series includes the harmful characteristic, then for the purpose of Article 6 it is non-standard. The judge preferred this approach to that taken in the United States[43] of categorizing product defects as design, manufacturing, or labelling[44] defects, which approach has commonly been adopted by academic writers. The judge saw[45] no reason to take this approach (he was not invited to do so by either party) and observed both that the Directive made no attempt to categorize defects and that the attempt to fit any particular situation into one of these 'boxes' in fact gave no assistance in carrying out the task of deciding under Article 6 whether the product is defective. Materials in the *travaux préparatoires* deflected the judge from taking the 'risk/utility' approach to defect favoured by the US Second Restatement on Torts (1965).[46] He was encouraged in his course of preferring 'standard/non-standard' as part of the test of defectiveness by the fact that both Italy and Spain by express legislation had provided that non-standard products would automatically be defective within Article 6 of the Directive, an example of implementing legislation in other Community countries feeding our debate.[47]

(d) In the case of non-standard products it will be relevant to compare them with other products on the market and to consider whether the public at large accepted the non-standard nature of the product, but that is not the end of the matter, as the court has to decide the question what is the *legitimate* expectation as to safety of the product, which may be higher or lower than the public expectation.

(e) If the unsafe product is standard for the purpose of Article 6, then the judge acknowledged that the process may be more difficult,[48] though questions of *avoidability* would remain irrelevant and social acceptability would only arise through knowledge of the unsafeness.[49]

(f) The judge proceeded to hold:
    i. that blood infected with hepatitis C was non-standard;[50]
    ii. that the public had not taken it to be socially acceptable for non-standard units of blood to infect patients with hepatitis C,[51] the knowledge of the medical profession being irrelevant to that consideration;[52]
    iii. that the public at large were entitled to expect that the blood transfused to them would be free from infection;[53]

[43] See the American Law Institute's Third Restatement of the Law of Torts 1998, Cap 1, Section 2 Categories of Product Defect.
[44] Instructions and warnings. [45] Paras. 39 to 41. [46] Para. 35.i. [47] Para. 36.
[48] Para. 73. [49] Para. 65.ii. [50] Para. 73. [51] Para. 65.ii.
[52] Para. 80. [53] Para. 80.

iv. that the blood, which infected each of the claimants, was defective for the purpose of Article 6.

(g) Burton J went on to address the defendant's case on defect and, having heard a large body of factual and expert evidence, having made a number of findings of fact, having taken into account:
   i. all the *circumstances* on the defendant's construction of Article 6;
   ii. the fact that the precautions of the introduction of surrogate testing and earlier introduction of routine screening were not taken,

he came to the conclusion[54] that 'such blood so infected on and after 1 March 1988 did not provide the safety which persons generally are entitled to expect.'

Burton J's conclusions[55] on Article 7(e) may be summarized thus:

(a) Article 7(e) derogates from the purpose of the Directive and should be construed strictly for that reason.[56] The judge had already used the very restrictedness of the Article 7(e) defence as an aid to construction when considering Article 6.[57]

(b) The *existence of the defect* means the existence of the generic defect, not the defect in the particular product.[58]

(c) Article 7(e) protects the producer in respect of the unknown generic defect; its purpose is to protect the producer against liability for the '*inconnu*' not to provide a defence in the case of damage caused by a known but undetectable generic defect.[59] In his analysis of Article 7(e) the judge acknowledges the guidance of *Commission v UK* and suggests that his conclusions are in line with the decision of the BGH and the majority of academic writers. When encapsulating the *travaux préparatoires* for the purpose of Article 7(e),[60] the judge records that originally the intention of the Commission was that the Directive should impose liability even for the '*inconnu*', meaning the inclusion of liability for true development risks; the outcome of the legislative process was the opposite and became Article 7(e). This was a further reason for concluding as the judge did in respect of Article 7(e): 'Hence it protects the producer in respect of the unknown (*inconnu*).'[61]

(d) Accordingly non-standard products may qualify under Article 7(e); 'However once the problem is *known* by virtue of accessible information, then the non-standard product can no longer qualify for protection under Article 7(e).'[62]

(e) Throughout the relevant period the generic defect of blood sometimes being infected with hepatitis C[63] was well known and the defendant could not therefore establish a defence under Article 7(e).

[54] Para. 173. [55] Paras. 74 to 77.

[56] Para. 75. Note that in the Danish Kidney case the ECJ said much the same in relation to Article 7(a) treating it as a given but going through a similar thought process (see paragraph 15 of the judgment).

[57] Para. 64. [58] Para. 74.iii. [59] Para. 76. [60] Para. 52.

[61] Para. 76. [62] Para. 77. [63] Or NANB.

Burton J also addressed the consequence had the defendant's construction of Article 7(e) been accepted[64] and resolved several causation issues and a number of damages issues. It is not proposed to discuss those matters here.

X. Envoi

Participating as advocates in the case was a great honour. No other European country would devote so much care and resources by so many specialized lawyers to settling a question of product liability for personal injuries. The judge can have handled little else for about six months. The courtroom was filled with medical and legal authorities who came and went. The atmosphere was quiet, orderly, courteous, *confraternelle*, and intense, qualities that are not necessarily found in every Member State. The Legal Aid authorities in England are to be commended for making enough money available to permit a good job to be done. As advocates, we had the privilege of very thoroughly prepared written pleadings, the loose rein but firm grip of very experienced instructing solicitors, a broad and deep survey of the academic literature in at least 12 countries, excellent professional relations with our opponents (throughout the case), and the undistracted attention of an interested and talented member of the judiciary with a gift for languages and an interest in the development of the law.[65] The quality of the judgment, its thoroughness and comprehensiveness, reflect the amount of money and time, which the legal system in our country traditionally affords to the resolution of important matters affecting ordinary people. By continental European standards this was luxury justice.

Recently Mr Justice Lightman gave an interesting lecture.[66] Without dissenting from many of his observations (e.g. about the value of good preparation and pre-trial resources), we respectfully but firmly disagree with his suggestion that a continental European approach to civil litigation would deliver a better *quality* of civil justice than is provided by the systems we enjoy in the UK. We have each of us had the privilege of pleading both in the UK and in its civil law neighbours across the channel. It may be worth concluding by recording some differences. The English tradition used to give greater weight to oral pleading. Written arguments—so-called 'Skeletons'—were matchstick-thin, and in the old days were often not used at all. Today, skeletons have become fleshy, and the oral portion has become more focussed. But the oral portion is still a highly demanding exchange of views with a well-prepared judge. Counsel expects to be thoroughly cross-examined. That which is not relevant is rebuffed. The judge advances several theories to test the argument.

The French approach is quite different. Commonly the oral argument is heard in total judicial silence: counsel have no inkling whether they are being relevant,

[64] Paras. 181 to 187.

[65] And, also in accordance with the traditions of the English Bar, all the barristers and the judge had a dinner together, and the menu for the dinner contained such dubious delicacies as *Potage Générique*, *Agneau Réformé pas Directive*, *Fromage résolumment anglais sans référence aux normes européennes*, capped with *Café de l'avenir* (the which beverage was named in the (ill-founded) expectation that an appeal was inevitable).

[66] 6th Edward Bramley Memorial Lecture, University of Sheffield.

persuasive, or tedious. The judgment is usually short, sometimes very short (French Cour de Cassation judgments may have one sentence of reasoning). The written pleadings (customarily two for and two against) are pieces of advocacy, more carefully polished than an English skeleton, closely responding to the arguments of the adversary.

We would submit, as our personal and no doubt idiosyncratic conclusion, that the relative weights accorded to written and oral submissions are reversed between England and France. The care given to crafting individual judgments is higher in England than in France and consequently, a French judgment is 'only' a decision about the case-in-hand. England takes more care with a single judgment than France, and individual English judgments can be major sources of new legal principle. It is very unlikely that in France 120 infected patients advancing novel legal theories would have received such a thorough examination of their claims. It is very rare that one first instance French or Belgian judgment would shape the flow of future legal developments. We can be proud that the English legal system could deliver high quality justice to people of modest means pursuing a case with a difficult legal theory and complex scientific facts.

Postscript by Nicholas Underhill QC*

I am grateful to have been given the opportunity to comment briefly on Michael Brooke and Ian Forrester's lucid and fair-minded account of the *Hepatitis C* litigation. I need not argue the toss on the (very) few points where I disagree with their exposition of the issues and the submissions, still less argue whether the decision was correct. The area of interest for readers of this journal is the extensive use made in the course of the trial of comparative law materials. The authors clearly explain how central the use of such materials was to their presentation of the claimants' case. If I had more space I should be inclined to argue that it does not follow that they were central to the determination of the decisive issues. The parties agreed on most of the points of principle: see the section of the judgment headed 'Common Ground', which contains a valuable summary of the correct approach to the Act.[67] Although the Judge referred at some points in that summary to comparative law materials, there was nothing that could not have been clearly derived from the terms of the Directive and the Act themselves. The only fundamental difference of principle as regards Article 6—whether so-called 'avoidability' was a relevant circumstance—was one on which the authorities and academic materials hardly touched.

However, there is no opportunity here to develop this provocative thesis. I will confine myself to drawing attention to three specific points, which may not clearly emerge from the authors' account.

First, the authors write feelingly of the assistance which they received from Dr Taschner, the Commission official who had had primary responsibility for the

* Nicholas Underhill QC was the defendants' leading counsel. He is now a member of the Court of Appeal of England and Wales.

[67] See Para. 31, where Burton J lists in detail a number of points of common ground.

Directive from its genesis through to its final adoption. As they say, it was their original intention to call Dr Taschner as a witness. His witness statement not only gave a factual account of the prolonged gestation of the Directive but also expressed strong views about the intended meaning and effect of the relevant provisions. The Defendants opposed the admission of this evidence in principle. In relation to English legislation it would of course be wholly improper to adduce the evidence of the promoter or the draftsman of a piece of legislation as to what he intended it to mean. The Defendants argued that the position should be no different in relation to EU legislation. Indeed the objections here were *a fortiori*. The genesis of the Directive was bitterly contested. Different Member States took widely different views as to just how strict the new strict liability regime should be. The result is generally acknowledged to have been a political compromise. It would be extremely dangerous for a Court to entertain evidence from one of the protagonists in that debate since his intention as to the effect of the Directive could not be taken to represent the eventual (and largely notional) 'collective intention'. Although the authors may be formally correct to say that it was eventually 'agreed' that they would not seek to rely on Dr Taschner's evidence, that agreement was only reached after the Judge had made it plain that he accepted the validity of the Defendants' objection. The point seems to me important because it is sometimes thought, or assumed, that familiar domestic rules as to the admissibility of evidence can be ignored when 'Euro-issues' are in play. That may be so where the rules are purely local and technical; but where, as here, they reflect legitimate objections of principle they should apply equally whatever the source of law being relied on.

My second point is not dissimilar. The authors explain that they obtained from the archive of the European Commission a mass of minutes and associated materials showing the formal progress of the draft Directive. These went far beyond the drafts which appeared in the Official Journal and the other formal *travaux préparatoires* which are sometimes relied on. The Defendants objected to the admission of these materials—partly because of their sheer untranslated dullness, but also as a matter of principle. The trouble with such materials is that they can give the illusion of completeness but in fact only tell part of the story. In this case, for example, the minutes largely ceased at the crucial moment when the Directive entered the black hole of consideration by the Council of Ministers. It was impossible to find out from them what considerations—if what was no doubt largely a matter of political horse-trading can be so dignified—influenced the final form of the Directive. Again, there was no formal ruling; but the Claimants agreed to a short summary of the legislative history based almost wholly on materials from the Official Journal, and virtually none of the minutes were referred to in Court. Again, the moral is that the introduction of Euro-issues is not *carte blanche* for unrestricted reference to the legislative history.

My third point is somewhat different. Our prolonged discussion during the trial of a variety of comparative law materials often left me with the feeling that we were skating—enjoyably and with a fine display of linguistic talent (my own lagging behind that of the Claimants' counsel)—on very thin ice. At any point we might fall though the surface and discover ourselves seriously out of our depth. Comparative law materials are not easy to use properly. If they are not in English they have to be translated: even when translated, unfamiliar terminology, concepts, and procedures have to be explained if basic misunderstandings are to be avoided. There is no expert available to the Court, which is accordingly dependent on counsel. In our case Mr Forrester was as fair as he was learned, and when he offered the Court a translation of an untranslated passage in an article, or in the parallel text of the Directive, it could be accepted without reserve—though the passage of arms about the significance of the use of the subjunctive in one sentence in the Italian version of the Advocate General's Opinion in *Commission v UK* possibly tested the parties' mutual confidence. But it is dangerous in principle to be thus reliant. Without a sure and impartial guide it is very easy to go astray.

Superficiality is a risk in other ways as well. The Claimants' counsel, as they have explained, had done extensive research in the library of the Max Planck Institute. The Defendants' counsel had in turn had great assistance from Professor Stapleton[68] in mining the very thick seam of product liability law in the US (and the narrow but rich seam of the *Oysters* litigation in Australia). But it was not realistic to draw the Court's attention to any but a very small proportion of this material. Hundreds of pages of copied materials—from both sides—were not in the end deployed. I hope we were intelligently selective. The Judge in any event showed himself keenly able to identify points of principle out of a wide variety of disparate materials. But the fact is that English lawyers cannot hope to educate either themselves or the Court to a full understanding of the subtleties of foreign legal systems. Comparative law materials are best used to illustrate or illuminate broad points of principle: even the most learned cannot become good German or US lawyers in the space of a single trial.

This postscript is intended as a counter-balance to the main article and has accordingly focused on qualifications to the authors' main thesis. But I would not want it to be thought that the comparative law materials deployed in the *Hepatitis C* case were of little value, still less that they were of little interest. Anyone reading Burton J's formidable judgment will see how deeply they penetrated the argument—and also with what vigour counsel and the Court debated them.

Afterword by Mr Justice Burton*

A number of reflections occur to me in relation to the *Hepatitis C* litigation, by reference to the need for consideration of comparative law and its relevance to the decision:

1. Although the decisions of foreign courts are, in the English courts, strictly speaking only a part of the evidence, because evidence of foreign law is at English law to be treated as evidence of fact, nevertheless our modern systems now enable us to dispense with any problems with admissibility: hence the cases and the relevant academic works, whether extracts from textbooks, learned treatises or articles from journals, are collected together and bundled, and, in a long case, delivered to the judge before the trial starts.
2. In this case such 'foreign law' authorities and the academic articles were efficiently copied, indexed, and paginated into files which rendered it easy for me to

[68] See n 14. * The trial judge.

be able to underline and 'sticker up', with colour-coded tabs (essential in a case such as this where in the end there were not far off 100 files, including more than 10 containing comparative law authorities and written submissions). This could be done both during the process of speed reading prior to the hearing, before I was fully understanding what all the issues consisted of, and then again during the hearing as they were given more detailed consideration and explanation. I was given some time for pre-reading all the documents prior to the trial starting. With the modern system of 'skeletons' (very often, at any rate in a long case, a misnomer for the lengthy written submissions which are delivered) supplied by way of exposition of each party's case, a judge can obtain a relatively informed grasp in advance by reading the submissions with care, and by speed-reading particularly those documents or, in the case of these comparative law questions, authorities and articles, which are specifically referred, or cross-referred, to in the submissions. Not only did we look at authorities from more than a dozen different jurisdictions (cases which became familiar friends, such as the '*German Bottle case*'[69] and the '*Danish Kidney case*'[70]) but we considered learned contributions from academic writers from the UK, US, Australia, Germany, Italy, and France.

3. The decisions of other national courts in Europe are of course of great interest, but they are normally at best persuasive. However where they are decisions seeking to construe or enforce the same European Directive, and we all ought together to be aspiring towards a common or 'autonomous' meaning of that Directive, then such comparative study becomes the more essential. Of course, unless and until there is a definitive conclusion by the European Court binding on all the national courts, we may nevertheless each be arriving at our own different result.
4. It is in my experience very rare, short of the House of Lords, for a court to have the opportunity to look at so much foreign law and academic authority as we did in the *Hepatitis C* case. This was not just because of the importance of the case and the time which had been set aside for the hearing, but I think largely because of the novelty of the issues and arguments, at any rate in an English Court. There has been a considerable jurisprudence developed in the United States which, on analysis, did not appear to be of great assistance in the interpretation of the somewhat differently drafted European Directive, but, that apart, there was little jurisprudence throughout the world, and certainly very little in England and Wales. In attempting to arrive at the correct solutions, an English judge in those circumstances had to look abroad, at any rate for his starting point, and the parties gave me that opportunity.
5. The same novelty meant that whereas, on some occasions, in a long case it may be possible, as the proceedings continue, for a judge to be reaching provisional conclusions, or even provisionally drafting parts of his judgment in advance, this was not possible for me. Indeed I had an entirely open mind and was very much

[69] BGH 9/5/95. [70] See n 17.

swayed first one way and then the other as the argument and evidence continued and developed. This meant that, once the case finished, I was able with a blank sheet of paper to re-read not only my notes but, more importantly and more accurately, the transcripts of the 49 days of evidence and argument, and in particular to reconsider the bundles, including the comparative law. I was given some five weeks 'time-off' to write the judgment, and I just about managed it in the deadline, working the sort of hours which I had thought I had left behind at the Bar!

6. The full and detailed oral argument was in my view essential to ensure both proper investigation of the issues and to put me in a position to arrive at an informed and reasoned decision. Bad ideas (whether coming from Counsel or from the Judge) can be tested and discarded. Good ideas can actually emerge in the course of discussion, but in any event can be tested and developed. Misunderstandings can be eliminated. Difficult arguments can be explained and reiterated. The need for oral argument, both in respect of the legal submissions and in due course by reference to the factual disputes, the time necessary for exploration and assimilation of the documents, and above all the need for examination and cross-examination of the considerable number of important witnesses, both factual and expert, meant that it took a great deal of co-operation, hard work, and case management to achieve a situation in which everything that any one wished said or read was completed in 49 days of hearing.

7. It is certainly right that my judgment ended up very much longer—perhaps at least 10 times longer—than any of the cases which we had been considering, at any rate in European jurisdictions. Perhaps it is right to suggest that the traditional English legal proceedings are a luxury. But it is certainly the case that it is expected of the judge to give full reasons, analysing all the evidence and law before him or her, and in a case such as *Hepatitis C*, by reference to the British system, after a three-month trial, this inevitably meant a long judgment. One of the authors of this article, Ian Forrester QC, has told me that in conversation with some European judges he has found them astonished that our judgments are of the length they are, and he says (although I am not sure I believe him!) that they wish they were permitted or encouraged to follow suit. The time when this kind of detailed analysis, giving proper credit to the arguments, both of law and fact, put before the judge during the course of the hearing, is of particular importance is, naturally, at the ground-breaking stage. *Hepatitis C* was the first case in England and Wales in which any detailed consideration had been given to all the relevant aspects of the European Directive, and there were very full and thorough arguments by very able counsel to be resolved. It may be that the very setting out in detail of my reasoning, which had to be given in the judgment, contributed to a decision not to appeal.

8. Perhaps the most important matter to emphasize, from the judge's point of view, under our system, is of course the fact that our procedure is adversarial. Absent a case in which a judge happens to be familiar with an authority of which none of the parties in front of him had previous knowledge, in which case he would draw

it to their attention and give them an opportunity to make submissions on it, the judge depends upon being 'fed' with information and authorities from the various parties in front of him. We are not expected to do our own research and we do not have any system of researchers or clerks to do any original work for us. It is therefore interesting to me to read in this article how it came about that the various documents were collected and put before me. But I made my decision solely on the basis of those documents and authorities. At one stage prior to trial I asked the parties whether they thought it would be a good idea if I were accompanied by an expert assessor (as is now occasionally the case in our courts), who would have no part to play in the decision-making, but could assist the judge in relation to reading and assimilating the documentation, particularly on medical matters. The parties were both strenuously opposed to the idea, and I did not pursue it, because in fact I agreed with them. There is clearly a risk in the appointment of an assessor that the judge will find himself delegating either some part of his understanding or possibly some part of his decision-making to someone else: and at least the parties knew who it was that they were in the process of educating and then persuading during the hearing. But the result of this fact, that it is the judge who is being educated by the parties, and not carrying out his own independent research, is that sometimes outsiders do not understand why points are not dealt with by the judge. Indeed such an experience occurred to me in this case. Professor Stapleton, the leading expert in the field of consumer law, to whom reference has been made,[71] was kind enough to take me out to lunch some months after the judgment and, from her deep understanding of the law, she belaboured me over points that I did not seem to have taken into account. I was able to indicate that, so far as I could see, such points, even if otherwise available to either of the parties on the particular facts, had not in fact been put before me. This means that perhaps the *Hepatitis C* case, notwithstanding that it was not appealed, will not be the last word on the subject![72]

[71] See n 16.

[72] Postscript (2015): The author notes that now, almost a decade later, the case does seem to remain the last word!

37

What Europeans Can Learn from an Untold Story of Transjudicial Communication

The Swiss/Turkish Experience

*Erdem Büyüksagis**

I. Introduction

The role of the use of foreign law in the courts is shaped by the legal context in which it takes place, and by the structure of the legal system it serves. Swiss courts have considered foreign law on numerous occasions when filling a gap in the current domestic law, or when interpreting existing domestic rules. A study based upon 1,541 instances has shown that slightly more than 10 per cent of the decisions refer to foreign law (notably to German, but also to French, Austrian, Italian, British, American, Belgian, Dutch, and even to Swedish and Turkish law).[1] In the same way, Swiss law is a source of inspiration for foreign legislatures and courts.[2] The accessibility of Swiss private law to ordinary citizens, its solutions, which are pragmatic rather than conceptual, and the wide discretion given to judges as well as some additional historical facts and circumstances played a key role in the adoption by the Turkish legislature of the Swiss civil codes[3] and, to some extent, of the Swiss rules of international arbitration.[4]

* Dr. iur. habil., LL.M. (Georgetown). Priv.-Doz. Dr. at the University of Fribourg in Switzerland, and Full-tenured Aggregate Professor at Antalya International University in Turkey. I wish to express my gratitude to Franz Werro (Fribourg University and Georgetown University), Emre Cumalıoğlu (Yaşar University, Izmir), and Kevin Lerch (Attorney at law in Tucson, Arizona) for our fruitful discussions and their astute comments on the manuscript.

1 Alexandra Gerber, 'Der Einfluss des ausländischen Rechts in der Rechtsprechung des Bundesgerichts', in Institut Suisse de Droit Comparé (Ed.), *Perméabilité des ordres juridiques* (Zurich, 1992), 142.

2 See e.g. 5Ob148/07m; 4Ob62/07g; 13Os109/07i; 1Ob253/06x; 4Ob28/06f; 6Ob91/05h; 6Ob90/05m; 6Ob112/05x; 6Ob93/05b; 6Ob92/05f; 6Ob89/05i; 9Ob12/05p; 8Ob135/04t; 6Ob330/04d; 6Ob342/04v; 6Ob333/04w; 6Ob298/04y; 4Ob191/03x; 6Ob239/03w; 6Ob309/01m; 7Ob47/02s; 6Ob267/01k; 4Ob255/01f; 4Ob166/00s; 3Ob59/00y; 3Ob324/98p (Austria); P010274N; C010322N 8 (Belgium); *Regina v Adrian Reed* (England); 07-80412; 05-16586; 05-18855; 04-17639; 03-12342; 98-19232; 00-45629 (France); BGH 7.4.2004, FamRZ 2004, 1023; BGH 5.12.2006, BGHZ 170, 115; BGH 15.11.2006, NJW 2007, 2394; BGH 28.11.2007, NJW 2008, 1531 (Germany); Hoge Raad, 01984/07CW; Hoge Raad, R06/096HR; Hoge Raad, R05/083HR; Hoge Raad, 02967/03; Hoge Raad, 02966/03; Hoge Raad, 02960/03; Hoge Raad, 01060/01; Hoge Raad 01439/01; Hoge Raad, 03237/06U (Netherlands). The cases are quoted by Martin Gelter/Mathias Siems, 'Cross-Citations between Supreme Courts in Europe'—dataset available at http://cross-citations.blogspot.ch; see also M. Gelter and M. Siems, 'Networks, Dialogue or One-Way Traffic?', Chapter 11 of this collection.

3 E. Büyüksagis, *Le nouveau droit turc des obligations, Perspective comparative avec les droits suisse et européen* (Basel, 2014), 9.

4 UNCITRAL Model Law was another source of inspiration for the Turkish Arbitration Act of 2001.

Since the Turkish legal establishments did not only adopt the Swiss statutory rules, but progressively the academic opinion on their interpretation as well, Turkish courts have not hesitated to rely, among others, on Swiss case law and Swiss academic knowledge in their own judgments.[5] At the same time, however, cultural differences between the two countries as well as their different needs, priorities, and socio-economic realities inevitably entailed some differences in their case law.[6] As a result, while comparing the judge-made law of these two countries, one might observe that there are not just two parallel paths in the application of the law, but a wide road with several lanes, offering mostly similar but also sometimes different solutions, which have been shaped by the legal cultures of these countries.[7] While differences between the two systems based on very similar rules demonstrate the growing importance of the courts' law-making power, the references to foreign sources show the influence of comparative law in courts' practice.

In my opinion, the role of courts in the evolution of the Swiss/Turkish transplant may provide us with some useful insights into the future direction of private law in Europe, and particularly into the relevance of the possible methods aimed at harmonizing private law in the EU. Indeed, at EU level, there is a current debate as to whether harmonization should come about by the mere drafting and enacting of 'Model rules' (top-down approach) or by courts deciding in an organic way, while taking into account the cultural background of the given legal system (bottom-up approach).[8] The argument that I will make in this chapter is that, in light of the Swiss/Turkish experience, European legal harmonization in some particular areas might result in the emergence of a spontaneous order that does not have so much to do with the model rules and idealized conceptions, but much more to do with the evolution of each given legal system's case law.

I will start by presenting the legal westernization process in Turkey, particularly the reception of Swiss private law at the beginning of the last century (section II). I will then try to draw a picture of the courts' role in the organic evolution of judicial comparativism in Switzerland and Turkey to show the practical differences between these two systems based on very similar rules. This will allow me to argue that the similarity between the statutory provisions of different countries is not enough to confirm the similarity of their law (section III). I will then ask in what general ways the appreciation of a foreign system illuminates the interpretation done by Swiss and Turkish courts, and try to find out whether comparative reasoning flourishes better in contexts which are bound by deep legal connections (section IV). Finally, I will compare my key findings with the organic development of private law in Europe (section V).

[5] For some examples in tort law for instance see E. Büyüksagis, 'The New Turkish Tort Law', JETL 2012, 44ff.

[6] E. Büyüksagis, n 3 at 12.

[7] On the idea that the recognition of difference should play the key role in comparative analysis between different systems, see Pierre Legrand, *Le Droit Comparé* (3rd ed. Paris, 2009), 107.

[8] R. Zimmermann, 'The Present State of European Private Law', AJCL 2009, 479ff; Mathias Reimann and Daniel Halberstam, 'Top-Down or Bottom-Up? A Look at the Unification of Private Law in Federal Systems', in Roger Brownsword, Hans-W Micklitz, Leone Niglia, and Stephen Weatherill (Eds.), *The Foundations of European Private Law* (Oxford, 2011), 363ff.

II. The global reception of Swiss private law in Turkey

In Turkey, the westernization process began 200 years ago—during the Ottoman Empire era[9]—well before the adoption of the Swiss codes. The transfer of some Western—mainly French—commercial rules and their implementation in the Ottoman judicial system in the mid-19th century created some incentives for local businesses to change, and thus smoothed the transition from a non-western legal culture based on a partially divinely ordained system, to a western legal culture based on rules of reason and evidence.[10] The transition from Empire to Republic accelerated this process. Comprehensive and rapid changes took place in the Turkish legal system following the proclamation of the Republic in 1923. Indeed, in 1926, with the deliberate adoption of the modern Swiss Civil Code and Code of Obligations, the legislature put aside the relatively complex Ottoman code—which was mainly based on obligations—in favour of an easily understandable legislation based not only on obligations but also on rights.

The debate boils down to these straightforward questions: why, in 1926, did the Turkish legislature not develop an original law based on the social realities of the country at the time? Why did it choose the Swiss codes as a model? And how were the adopted Swiss codes, with only a few minor modifications made by the Turkish legislature, applied until today? A commission established just after the proclamation of the Republic was charged to study different legal systems in order to assess various alternatives. The French *Code Civil* of 1804, already more than a century old at that time, was not modern enough. Although newer, the German *Bürgerliches Gesetzbuch* (BGB) was not appropriate either because, at that time, the German language was not very popular among Turkish judges and lawyers. Moreover, according to some Turkish scholars, the BGB's detailed provisions based on an extreme conceptualism would be useless in the hands of a layperson.[11]

The Swiss codes offered an intermediate solution between the French and German codes and were at that time the most recent and the most successfully implemented legislative work in Europe.[12] In addition, the Swiss codes had already proved that they could be applied successfully to different ethnic communities with different linguistic, religious, and cultural traditions.[13] Moreover, even if some of their solutions are not necessarily easy to apply because of their extremely fragmentary character, such as those concerning the time-limits or the legal effects of a breach of contract, the

[9] G. Plagemann, *Gesetz und Gesetzgebung im Osmanischen Reich und der Republik* Türkei (Berlin, 2009), 83ff.

[10] B. Lewis, *The Emergence of Modern Turkey* (3rd ed. New York, 2002), 272.

[11] Sabri Ş. Ansay and Hukuk Bilimine Başlangıç, *Introduction to Legal Science* (7th ed. Ankara, 1958), 78. On this point, see recently O. Moréteau, 'A Summary Reflection on the Future of Civil Codes in Europe', in P. Apathy, R. Bollenberger, P. Bydlinski, G. Iro, E. Karner, and M. Karollus (eds.), *FS für Helmut Koziol* (Vienna, 2010), 1450.

[12] Norman J. Singer, 'The Reception of the Swiss Civil Code in Modern Turkey', in P. Tercier, M. Amstutz, A. Koller, and H. Stöckli (eds.), *FS für Peter Gauch, Gauchs Welt: Recht, Vertragsrecht und Baurecht* (Zurich, 2004), 267; Heinrich Honsell, '100 Jahre Schweizerisches Obligationenrecht', ZSR/RDS 2011/II, 103.

[13] P. Pichonnaz, 'Le centenaire du Code des obligations, Un code toujours plus hors du code', ZSR/RDS 2011/II, 121ff.

simplicity and clarity of most dispositions of the Swiss codes made it possible for laymen to understand them.[14]

Another advantage of the Swiss codes is the considerable discretion granted to the courts on the basis of the rules of equity, as well as the possibility for courts to intervene in the contract or even decide in accordance with the rule that they would make as legislature in the absence of a provision applicable to the legal issue.[15] Thus, the transplantation of the Swiss codes offered the Turkish judges tools granting them certain flexibility in the intermediate period between the abandonment of the old Ottoman system and the establishment of the new one.[16] It gave them a chance to find new solutions corresponding to the needs of a rapidly evolving society.[17] Besides, the new law facilitated the establishment of democracy and the westernization process of the country, thanks to an autonomous legal system whose administration does not depend on a privileged group but on professional lawyers working independently of the authority imposing the rule.

In addition to the reception of the Swiss Civil Code and the Code of Obligations, in 1956, the Turkish legislature enacted the first systematic Commercial Code, which had been prepared by the German-born, Turkish-naturalized law Professor Ernst E. Hirsch on the basis of Swiss law.[18] The adoption of the Commercial Code as well as that of the Swiss codes in 1926 deeply affected the life of every Turkish citizen and played a very significant role in the westernization of the country.

In order to bring solutions better adapted to the social sensibilities of the new century, in 2012, the Turkish legislature revised the Commercial Code as well as the Code of Obligations. The legislature nevertheless did not change the general structure of the previous codes modelled on Swiss legislation. The new statutory dispositions such as those governing the new corporate audit mechanism, the legal effects of the transactions which exceeded the scope of corporate policy, new types of squeeze-out procedures, judicial control of standard terms, the moment of the transfer of benefit and risk in sale contracts, and the adaptation of contracts in view of changing circumstances, were formulated on the basis of the provisions and principles set out by EU directives and other similar regulatory schemes.[19] Actually, some of these changes have their roots in standards already established by the Turkish courts.

III. The role of courts in the law-making process

The introductory chapter of the Swiss and Turkish Civil Codes opens with a statement that, in cases where the Code does not provide applicable provisions, the judge should decide according to customary law, or, if there were no applicable customary law,

[14] E. Bucher, 'The Position of the Civil Law of Turkey in the Western Civilization', in *Atatürk and Modern Turkey* (Ankara, 1999), 222.

[15] Article 1(2) of the Civil Code. See also Esin Örücü, 'The Role of Judicial Creativity and Equity in the Developments of Turkish Law and Its Covert Hybridity', Tul. Eur. & Civ. L. F. 2014, 217ff.

[16] Şerif Mardin, *Religion, Society, and Modernity in Turkey* (New York, 2006), 266.

[17] A. Oğuz, 'The Role of Comparative Law in the Development of Turkish Civil Law', Pace Int'l L. Rev. 2005, 380ff.

[18] E. Hirsch, 'Der Einfluss des schweizerischen Rechts auf das neue türkische Handelsgesetzbuch', SJZ 1956, 325ff.

[19] E. Büyüksagis, *Comparative Reflections on Commercial and Social Expectations in New Turkish Contract Law* (forthcoming).

according to the rule which he himself would formulate were he the legislature (Article 1(2) of the Civil Code). In the latter case the judge should follow established doctrine and case law (Article 1(3)).[20]

According to this hierarchical structure, although the judge is not given the main task of creating the law, by way of interpreting existing statutory provisions he can, and does, find creative solutions to complex problems.[21] Indeed, Article 1 of the Swiss and Turkish Civil Codes offers the judge a democratic mandate to have the final say, a solution which found a positive echo even among American judges. Benjamin Cardozo noted that 'the tone and temper in which the modern judge should set about his task are well expressed in the first Article of the Swiss Civil Code of 1907'.[22] In a dissenting opinion in *State Tax Commission v Aldrich*, Justice Jackson referred to Article 1 as a 'candid recognition of what necessarily is the practice' of courts.[23]

This point of view is particularly suited to Turkish case law where, on the basis of the Turkish version of Article 1, courts soften the legal consequences of possibly too rigid or simply unsatisfactory application of the statutory dispositions without waiting for a legislative intervention. A case deserves note in this vein.[24] In the aftermath of the 1999 earthquake in Gölcük, people who had suffered personal injuries as well as economic harm as a result of the collapse of their houses claimed compensation from the builders. Although most of the damaged buildings had been constructed before the 1980s, the Turkish Supreme Court accepted that there was no reason for the injured persons to bring an action at the time of the (faulty) construction, and held that the ten-year time limit began to run only when the claimants discovered the damage—in other words from the date of the earthquake.[25] The Court overruled the pleas of statute of limitation filed by the contractors on the basis of contractual as well as extra-contractual time limits, which, according to the first instance judgments, had both expired. The Supreme Court held that if the claim was not yet actionable, it would not be fair for the ten-year time limit to start running from the date the act was committed. Until the judgments of the Supreme Court, the rule was, in conformity with the Code of obligations, that the time limits begin when harmful conduct occurs, and not when the plaintiff learned about the damage he had suffered.

The Turkish Supreme Court's solution to latent damage cases shows its ability to diverge from the text of the codes to find new solutions corresponding to the needs of

[20] For an analysis see Paul-Henri Steinauer, 'Le Titre préliminaire du Code civil', in Pierre Tercier (Ed.), *Traité de droit privé suisse*, V. II/1, Basel 2009; Franz Werro, 'Article 1 CC', in Pascal Pichonnaz and Bénédict Foëx (eds.), Commentaire romand, Code civil I, Basel 2010, no 38.

[21] Franz Werro, n 20, no 42ff; Marc Amstutz, 'Der Text des Gesetzes: Genealogie und Evolution von Art. 1 ZGB', ZSR/RDS 2007/II, 252; Peter Gauch, 'Was zählt, ist einzig, was man gerade weiss', in Alexandra Rumo-Jungo, Pascal Pichonnaz, Bettina Hürlimann-Kaup, and Christiana Fountoulakis (eds.), *Mélanges en l'honneur de Paul-Henri Steinauer* (Bern, 2013), 15: 'Am Gesetzestext kann das Gericht zwar nichts ändern; was es stattdessen aber tun kann, ist, den Text zu interpretieren'.

[22] Benjamin N. Cardozo, *The Nature of the Judicial Process* (New Haven, 1921), 140.

[23] 316 U.S. 174 (1942).

[24] Y4.HD, 3.2.2005T, 2004/7039E, 2005/746K.

[25] Ibid. See also Y4.HD, 30.6.2004T, 2004/2110E, 2004/8595K; YHGK, 4.6.2003T, 2003/4-400E, 2003/393K; Y4.HD, 18.12.2002T, 2002/13842E, 2002/14290K. For a similar approach in bodily injury cases, see Y4.HD, 30.01.2009T, 2008/5440E, 2009/1354K (stating that the time limit begins when the plaintiff is aware of his bodily injury and not when the traffic accident occurred).

an evolving society, where—unlike in Switzerland—the compulsory insurance has not yet been developed.[26] This solution has nevertheless been subject to criticism from the literature. It has been argued that, according to Article 1 of the Civil Code, judicial interpretation shouldn't be the primary vehicle of change.

Although Swiss judges sometimes adapt the law to the needs of new situations using notably the teleological method,[27] unlike their Turkish counterparts, they are, in general, reluctant to go beyond the solutions imposed by statutory provisions. I will quote a case with similar facts that raised similar issues before the Turkish Supreme Court. From 1965 to 1978, the plaintiff was exposed to asbestos dust in the course of his activities. In 2004 he was diagnosed with cancer caused by exposure to asbestos. In 2005 he applied to the courts seeking an award from his employer in respect of pecuniary and non-pecuniary damage, arguing that his employer had failed in his obligations by failing to take the necessary measures to protect employees. On the basis of the very same statutory test as in Turkey, unlike the Turkish Supreme Court, the Swiss Federal Supreme Court held in a judgment of 29 January 2010 that the plaintiff's claim had lapsed, on the grounds that the absolute time limit of ten years from the date of the occurrence of the damage had expired.[28] The Swiss Federal Supreme Court found that the limitation period began running from the date on which the damage had occurred, irrespective of when it had become apparent. Moreover, the Court denied the plaintiff's claim that such an interpretation would violate the European Convention on Human Rights, in particular Article 6 which protects the right to a fair trial.[29]

One might argue that, in general, Swiss judges prefer not to (or, for some, may not) assume the responsibility of acting *modo legislatoris*.[30] However, this is debatable, since there are also cases where Swiss judges seem willing to engage in developing substantive law.[31] Thus, for example, before the 2011 amendment to the Swiss Unfair Competition Act,[32] which aims to bring Swiss law in line with the Unfair Terms Directive (93/13/EEC), the Swiss Federal Supreme Court had already broadened the scope of the judicial control of standard terms (incorporation control) to include content verification of contractual clauses.[33] In finding normative solutions, the Swiss High Court

[26] A comparative overview is offered by Erdem Büyüksagis, 'Le nouveau CO turc est-il toujours attaché à ses racines suisses? Analysée à la lumière du principe européen d'effectivité, une réponse particulièrement intéressante en matière de prescription extinctive', HAVE/REAS 2012, 45.

[27] For an analysis see Thomas Probst, *Die Änderung der Rechtsprechung* (Basel, 1993), 198ff; Marc Amstutz, n 21 at 259; Kathrin Klett, 'Der Einfluss des europäischen Rechts auf die schweizerische Rechtsprechung im Vertragsrecht', recht 2008, 234. See also BGE 121 III 219, para. 1d.aa.

[28] BGE 137 III 16, para. 2.4. For a critical comment, see Benoît Chappuis and Franz Werro, 'Délais de prescription et dommages différés: réflexions sur l'ATF 137 III 16 et la motion parlementaire 07.3763', HAVE/REAS 2011, 139ff.

[29] This decision was subject to review by the European Court of Human Rights (ECtHR) which, in its 11 March 2014 judgment, found that there had been a violation of the right of access to a court (*Howald Moor v Switzerland*, 11.3.2014, nos 52067/10 and 41072/11, para. 78).

[30] Arthur Meier-Hayoz, 'Der Richter als Gesetzgeber', in Max Kummer and Hans U. Walder (eds.), *FS Max Guldener* (Zurich, 1973), 197.

[31] Franz Werro, n 20, no 49; Pierre Moor, 'De la pratique du juriste à la théorie du droit, plädoyer' 2007/4, 54.

[32] For more information on the amendment, see Hubert Stöckli, *UWG 8: neues Recht gegen unfaire Verträge, Schweizerische Baurechtstagung* (Fribourg, 2013), 171ff.

[33] BGE 135 III 1, para. 2.2; Thomas Koller, 'Einmal mehr: das Bundesgericht und seine verdeckte AGB-Inhaltskontrolle', AJP/PJA 2008, 943ff.

sometimes goes further than the Turkish Supreme Court, which sporadically takes a conservative stance. In a wrongful birth case where a healthy but unplanned child born as a result of clinical negligence, for instance, after examining (and criticizing) different court decisions adopted in other European countries, the Swiss Federal Supreme Court held that the parents should recover for the maintenance costs of the negligently born child.[34] Yet the general view in Turkey is that if parents suffer any loss, this economic loss is outweighed by the blessings of having a healthy child.[35]

Consequently, although, in many areas, one can notice a convergence between Swiss and Turkish law due to the reception of Swiss private law by Turkey, the different application of some of their very same provisions, such as those governing time limit and damages, reveals the fact that the similarity between their statutory rules does not entail a similarity between their laws. There is nothing surprising about that. As the former President of the Austrian Supreme Court stated, 'judges do not act in a vacuum; they do not live in an ivory tower; their thinking is shaped by their cultural environment and by their training, by their role models, be it at law school or at court'.[36] This observation, which goes beyond the bounds of written rules set forth in a given time and under given circumstances, calls for a deeper consideration of the concrete claims judges have to deal with.[37]

IV. The importance of comparative law and its impact on judicial assessment

Within the factual approach described, turning the whole process into an even more creative and dynamic enterprise, there is one more element which plays a significant role in law making: comparative judicial analysis.[38] It has been gaining in importance, although its role remains controversial.[39] According to one author, in the 19th and 20th centuries, '[comparative law] was distinct because it was constructed as separate from law itself, and as something which followed it (like the cigarette after sex, in the old movies). It was marginal because people are more interested in the real action than in that which follows it.'[40] This sterile vision, which reduces the function of

[34] BGE 132 III 359, para. 4. This judgment was cited by the Austrian Supreme Court in its decision of 11 December 2007 (5Ob148/07m).

[35] Erdem Büyüksagis and Yeni Sosyo-Ekonomik Boyutuyla Maddi Zarar Kavramı [The Concept of Damage in Its New Socio-Economic Dimension] (Istanbul, 2007), 381.

[36] Irmgard Griss, 'How Judges Think: Judicial Reasoning in Tort Cases from a Comparative Perspective', JETL 2013, 248. See also Aharon Barak, *The Judge in a Democracy* (Princeton, 2006), 107ff.

[37] Geoffrey Samuel, 'Taking Methods Seriously (Part Two)', J. Comp. L. 2007, 229; Ole Lando, 'Judicial Activism', in Peter Mankowski and Wolfgang Wurmnest (eds.), *FS für Ulrich Magnus zum 70. Geburtstag* (Munich, 2014), 693ff.

[38] On the increasing role of comparative law before courts, see Guy Canivet, Mads Andenas, and Duncan Fairgrieve (eds.), *Comparative Law Before the Courts* (London, 2004); Basil Markesinis and Jörg Fedtke (eds.), *Engaging with Foreign Law* (Oxford, 2009); Michal Bobek, *Comparative Reasoning in European Supreme Courts* (Oxford, 2013).

[39] Mads Andenas and Duncan Fairgrieve, '"There is A World Elsewhere" – Lord Bingham and Comparative Law', in Mads Andenas and Duncan Fairgrieve (eds.), *Tom Bingham and the Transformation of the Law: A Liber Amicorum* (Oxford, 2009), 831.

[40] H. Patrick Glenn, 'Com-paring', in Esin Örücü and David Nelken (eds.), *Comparative Law: A Handbook* (Oxford, 2007), 91.

comparative reasoning to mere ornament, probably results from the fact that in many judgments foreign law was, at that time, used only as supporting material. Today evidence suggests that the time of the old nation-state as the great forum has passed, and the interaction between different systems is more subtle and complex than may have been assumed in the last century.[41] The fundamental issues arising from the interplay between national and international law as well as the duty to implement into national law international norms and standards such as the European humanitarian law and the new European regulatory policies, which tend to strengthen the role of (international) non-governmental actors, challenge traditional judicial approaches.[42]

It is arguable that this phenomenon has created an increased need for more horizontal dialogue between courts, a dialogue that goes beyond the mere citation of foreign information. The Swiss and Turkish jurisdictions are no exception. Judges in these countries are provided with effective tools to cite a foreign court's decision when dealing with uncertainties in domestic law. As the Swiss[43] and Turkish Supreme Courts[44] made it clear in their rulings, Article 1 of their Civil Code, which itself found its roots in a foreign (French) source,[45] allows judges to turn to comparative law, as does the legislature when preparing a new statute. As an example, in its judgment of 20 December 2005, after stating that the recoverability of the financial damages of a healthy but unplanned child's birth as a result of clinical negligence had not yet been discussed by the Swiss Federal Supreme Court, the latter first examined how German, Dutch, Austrian, and UK courts addressed the issue.[46] The Swiss High Court then criticized the position of the House of Lords in *Rees v Darlington Memorial Hospital NHS Trust*[47] as well as the 25 May 1999 ruling of the Austrian Supreme Court[48] as unconvincing. Citing in total about 20 times German[49] and Dutch[50] case law

[41] Basil Markesinis and Jörg Fedtke, 'The Judge as Comparatist', Tul. L. Rev. 2005–2006, 11ff; Aharon Barak, n 36 at 197ff; Joxerramon Bengoetxea, 'The Eurocrises and What Socio-legal Studies Could Do about Them, or: Comparing European Pluralisms from Legal Cultural Approaches', in Maurice Adams and Dirk Heirbaut (eds.), *The Method and Culture of Comparative Law: Essays in Honour of Mark Van Hoecke* (Oxford, 2014), 266.

[42] Kal Raustiala, 'The Architecture of International Cooperation: Transgovernmental Networks and the Future of International Law', Va. J. Int'l. L. 2002, 1; Anne-Marie Slaughter, *A New World Order* (Princeton, 2004), 65ff; Malcolm N. Shaw, *International Law* (7th ed. Cambridge, 2014), 33–34.

[43] BGE 124 III 266, para. 4: 'bei der Auslegung [sind] alle herkömmlichen Auslegungselemente zu berücksichtigen . . . ; auch rechtsvergleichende'. See also Eugen Bucher, Rechtsüberlieferung und heutiges Recht, ZEuP 2000, 486.

[44] YHGK, 15.1.2014T, 2013/11-1138E, 2014/16K. In this case, the owner of a registered trademark sued an Internet service provider for infringement based on the sale of products that contain unauthorized reproductions. The Turkish Supreme Court noted that, if there is a gap in the statutory provisions, the lower court would be able to take foreign law into account.

[45] François Gény, *Méthode d'interprétation et sources en droit privé positif*, Vol. II (2nd ed. Paris, 1919), 326. Article 1 of the Swiss Civil Code of 1907 finds its roots in the first edition of this book published in 1889 and, for some authors, even in Aristotle's philosophical reflections (The Athenian Constitution, 9.2). See Henri Torrione, 'Les articles 1, 2 al. 2 et 4 du Titre préliminaire du Code civil, et la philosophie du droit', in Alexandra Rumo-Jungo, Pascal Pichonnaz, Bettina Hürlimann-Kaup, and Christiana Fountoulakis (eds.), n 21 at 67; Franz Werro, n 20, no 4.

[46] BGE 132 III 359, para. 3.2.

[47] *Rees v Darlington Memorial Hospital NHS Trust* [2003/UKHL 52].

[48] OGH, 25 May 1999, JBl 121/1999, 593ff.

[49] BGH, 18 Mars 1980, NJW 1980, 1450ff.

[50] Hoge Raad, 21 February 1997, JZ 18/1997, 893ff.

as substantive evidence along with the Swiss academic literature,[51] the Swiss High Court arrived at the conclusion that there is damage, as the parents' legal duty to provide needed care to their children certainly reduces their financial assets. Hence the use of the comparative method enabled Swiss judges, on the one hand, to gain inspiration from the German and Dutch case law in which a seemingly satisfactory solution to the wrongful birth issue had been found and, on the other hand, to distance themselves from the Austrian and British judge-made law, which they found unpersuasive. This aspect of the judgment undermines the argument that courts cite foreign systems only when and where this seems appropriate to promote the judge's own cause (the cherry-picking argument).

In Turkey, courts also consider foreign law or international law, but then occasionally—although not often—reject it as they find it inappropriate to national conditions. The 18 June 2011 ruling of the Turkish Supreme Court illustrates the manner in which the High Court cites domestically implemented international human rights norms, even if they differ from the norms Turkish judges preferred.[52] The plaintiff argued that the refusal by the lower courts to allow her to bear only her maiden name had unjustifiably interfered with her private life. In its judgment, the Turkish Supreme Court first cited a decision from the European Court of Human Rights (ECtHR), which had found that the obligation imposed on married women, in the interests of family unity, to bear their husband's surname—even if they could put their maiden name in front of it—had no objective and reasonable justification.[53] The Turkish High Court then saw an inconsistency between the ECtHR's ruling and Turkish law, stating that the existing domestic rules and principles governing this issue stem from a tradition designed to reflect family unity by having the same name. However, in its judgment of 19 December 2013, based upon the legal doctrines developed by the ECtHR, the Turkish Constitutional Court allowed the plaintiff to bear only her maiden name and thus put an end to the debate.[54]

Cases in which, after discussing and comparing different options, judges explain why they prefer applying the existing domestic solution and not the foreign one are of particular interest to academics, even though the reference to foreign sources is unproductive in the context of a courtroom. As a recent empirical study has shown, the frequency with which a court cites foreign law is not necessarily evidence of the extent to which it actually considers foreign law.[55] Particularly in public legal matters, courts seem less amenable to other perspectives or other methods of reasoning, albeit they cite foreign law.[56] That is one of the reasons why, particularly in foreign

[51] See e.g. Franz Werro, Article 41 CO, in Luc Thévenoz and Franz Werro (eds.), *Commentaire romand, Code des Obligations* I (Geneva/Basel, 2003), no 27f.

[52] YHGK, 18.6.2011T, 2011/7737E, 2012/16695K, YKD 2012, 1475f.

[53] ECtHR, *Ünal Tekeli v Turkey*, 16.11.2004, no 29865/96, para. 66.

[54] AYM, 19.12.2013T, 2013/2187, Resmi Gazete (Turkish Official Gazette) 7 January 2014, no 28875.

[55] David S. Law and Wen-Chen Chang, 'The Limits of Global Judicial Dialogue', Wash. L. Rev. 2011, 523ff.

[56] Otto Kahn-Freund, 'On Uses and Misuses of Comparative Law', Mod. L. Rev 1974, 17. Recently see Carlos F. Rosenkrantz, 'Against Borrowing and Other Non-authoritative Uses of Foreign Law', Int'l. J. Const. L. 2003, 282–3.

investment, arbitration has become a preferred dispute resolution.[57] In the traditional view, courts can more easily turn to foreign law materials in private contractual legal matters.[58] In the relationships between individuals, the adaptation of the rigid statutory language to particular factual settings through the use of flexible foreign solutions often does not violate public order.

When filling gaps in private legal matters or interpreting the law, Turkish courts often refer to Swiss judgments and academic literature approvingly. Thus, for example, during the economic crisis at the beginning of the 1980s, the Turkish Supreme Court had to deal with the effects of fluctuation in the values of currencies in the circumstances that the parties could not reasonably have foreseen at the time of the conclusion of the contract. In general, the stability of contractual relationships requires that the judge does not adjust or terminate the obligation if the debtor assumed the risk of the change of circumstances, or if the circumstances are such that the debtor can reasonably be regarded as having assumed the risk of the change. Taking into account Swiss judge-made law, in a 1982 decision, the Turkish Supreme Court set forth the conditions for a party to be released from its obligations by supervening events which make the performance much more onerous than anticipated.[59]

References to Swiss law by the Turkish Supreme Court can be found in tort law as well. An example is the Turkish Supreme Court's 2002 ruling,[60] where it referred to some decisions of the Swiss Federal Supreme Court[61] in order to determine the legal grounds for an action to recover damages for injuries suffered by a third party as a result of a defective product.

There are instances that are, from an academic point of view, just as interesting as the previous judgments of the Turkish Supreme Court, and these include cases where judges make use of the same foreign sources, and then reach different conclusions. For example, on an issue concerning a real estate transaction, for which the law requires a strict adherence to certain forms, the majority judges of the Turkish Supreme Court cited Swiss law and refused to invalidate some transactions because of the violation of form requirements. They argued that, in some circumstances mentioned by the Swiss Supreme Court, the invalidation of a contract for the sale of the separate parts of a building would be against the principle of good faith.[62] The dissenting judges cited the same Swiss law in their reasoning which arrived at an opposite conclusion. Since judicial interpretation is a subjective science moulded by the personal discretion of

[57] Turkey and Switzerland are party to the Convention on the Settlement of Investment Disputes between States and Nationals of Other States (ICSID Convention) as well as the United Nations Convention on the Recognition and Enforcement of Foreign Arbitral Awards (New York Convention).

[58] Michel Rosenfeld and András Sajó, 'Introduction', in Michel Rosenfeld and András Sajó (eds.), *The Oxford Handbook of Comparative Constitutional Law* (Oxford, 2012), 2.

[59] Y13.HD, 26.11.1982T, 1982/6186E, 1982/7199K. It is worth noting that, unlike the previous Code, the new Turkish Code of Obligations, which entered into force in 2012, contains a specific statutory rule governing this issue.

[60] YHGK, 13.2.2002T, 2002/4-114E, 2002/84K.

[61] BGE 64 II 260; BGE 66 II 117, BGE 79 II 69, BGE 80 III 59.

[62] YİBGK, 30.9.1988T, 1987/2E, 1988/2K.

judges, the reason for this difference is perhaps that, to support his position, each judge relies on a different interpretation he finds persuasive.

Such situations, which may lead to inconsistencies, are nevertheless rare in the application of EU law. Indeed, accession negotiations with the EU made an important breakthrough in the use of comparative law by Turkish courts. In October 2005, negotiations started with the so-called screening process, which aims at determining to what extent Turkey meets the EU's rules and regulations known as the *acquis communautaire*. The Turkish Supreme Court then started citing the case law of the European Court of Justice (ECJ) more frequently, while still referring to Swiss law. In a judgment handed down on 27 November 2012, to define the conditions for the transfer of an entity, and in particular to determine whether any direct contractual relationship between the transferor and the transferee is needed in certain labour-intensive sectors, the Turkish Supreme Court referred to the judgments of the ECJ[63] and in a more general way mentioned the position of the Swiss Supreme Court without expressly quoting any of its judgments.[64]

Numerous other references to European and Swiss judge-made law and academic literature can be found in Turkish case law. Without giving further examples, let me simply say that, over the 88 years since the reception of Swiss private law in Turkey, cooperation between their academic institutions has been promoted, thanks to numerous projects, and much work has been and is being done to enhance a mutual legal understanding. A comparison between Swiss and Turkish judge-made law will nevertheless reveal an asymmetrical pattern. Mainly because of the language barriers, the references to Turkish case law and academic works in decisions by Swiss courts are extremely rare, if not absent. However, this does not mean that Swiss courts do not cite the case law of other jurisdictions.

First, in the absence of a statutory rule or a generally accepted principle, Article 7 of the Swiss Law on Maritime Navigation directs the judge to consider law and custom, doctrine and case law of seafaring countries. Furthermore, Swiss courts apply the relevant *acquis* under bilateral and sectoral agreements concluded with the EU. Moreover, Swiss courts consider ECJ case law, particularly when interpreting a rule that purports to implement EU law.[65] Finally, the Swiss Federal Court makes use of judgments by other national courts, and quotes them explicitly.[66] Since the acknowledgement of comparative law sources requires a level of immersion in foreign law,[67] the overwhelming majority of them are derived from the continental European tradition and written in languages in which Swiss judges have competency.[68]

[63] C-13/95, [1997] ECR I-1259; C-24/85, [1986] ECR 1119.

[64] Y9.HD, 27.11.2012T, 2011/51419E, 2012/39553K.

[65] BGE 128 I 295, para. 4c.bb.

[66] BGE 126 III 129, para. 4; Jörg Schmid, Alexander H. E. Morawa, and Lukas Heckendorn Urscheler (eds.), *Die Rechtsvergleichung in der Rechtsprechung* (Zurich/Basel/Geneva, 2014).

[67] Daniel Jutras, 'Énoncer l'indicible: le droit entre langues et traditions', RIDC 2000, 781ff; Pierre Legrand, 'Friendship, Language, and the Invention of Foreign Law', Fribourg 2013, 1ff (text distributed during the conference celebrating the 250th anniversary of the Faculty of Law, which was held on 7 November 2013 in Fribourg).

[68] Alexandra Gerber, n 1 at 141ff.

Setting aside the references to the case law of the ECJ[69] and ECtHR,[70] whose number has been increasing over the last years, German case law is the most important foreign source of the Swiss Supreme Court.[71] References to German judgments range from a mere citation as supporting information to a genuine attempt to take advantage of the German experience in order to implement the best possible solution. Besides, in the absence of a ruling from the ECJ, the Swiss Supreme Court sometimes looks at German developments to interpret national law adopted pursuant to an EU directive. Consider this example. The Swiss Product Liability Act is largely based on the Product Liability Directive (85/374/EEC), and just like the latter it fails to distinguish between different types of defects, with all types lumped together and defined in terms of the 'consumer expectation test'.[72] In a groundbreaking decision of 19 December 2006,[73] in order to define manufacturing defect, in addition to the Swiss literature,[74] the Swiss Supreme Court referred to the 9 May 1995 judgment of the German Supreme Court, which had distinguished between major product defect types and attached different legal consequences to each type.[75]

Swiss judges also look at other foreign sources besides German law. In a judgment handed down on 28 November 2006, for instance, the Swiss Supreme Court sought to apply the legal principles limiting the scope of damages for breach of contract, and to this end referred to French law.[76] According to Article 208 of the Swiss code of obligations, where a defect leads to the rescission of the sale, the purchaser is entitled to recovery of the contract price and to the payment of damages for all losses which have been *directly caused* as a result of the defective goods. Fault is not required to establish the seller's liability for such losses. In addition, the seller is liable for any *indirect loss* (e.g. lost profit) caused by the defective goods, unless he proves that he did not commit any fault.[77] In order to draw a distinction between direct and indirect damage, the Swiss Supreme Court drew inspiration from Article 1150 of the

[69] See e.g. BGer 2C_628/2013 (concerning the place of value added tax on services provided by the World Economic Forum) referring to C-155/12, [2013] All ER (D) 115 (Jul); C-218/10, [2012] ECR I-0000; C-114/05, [2006] ECR I-2427; C-452/03, [2005] ECR I-3947; C-327/94, [1996] ECR I-4595 and BGE 125 I 21 (concerning positive action in gender equality) referring to C-409/95, [1997] ECR I-6363. For more information see Franz Werro and Thomas Probst, 'La jurisprudence de la CJCE en matière de droit privé et son influence sur la pratique du droit suisse', Annuaire Suisse de droit européen 2005/2006, 453ff.

[70] Approximately 11–13 per cent of the decisions of the Swiss Federal Supreme Court refer to the ECtHR. See Hansjörg Seiler, 'Einfluss des europäischen Rechts und der europäischen Rechtsprechung auf die schweizerische Rechtspflege', ZBJV 2014, 348.

[71] Lukas Heckendorn Urscheler, 'Gedanken zur Methode der richterlichen Rechtsvergleichung im Bereich des Zivilrechts', in Jörg Schmid, Alexander H. E. Morawa, and Lukas Heckendorn Urscheler (eds.), n 66 at 106.

[72] For a critical comment, see Erdem Büyüksagis, *La notion de défaut dans la responsabilité du fait des produits défectueux, th. Fribourg* (Zurich/Basel/Geneva, 2005), 258ff.

[73] BGE 133 III 81, para. 3.2.

[74] Erdem Büyüksagis, n 72 at 248–50.

[75] BGH, 9 May 1995, NJW 1995, 2162; Gerhard Wagner, '§ 3 ProdHaftG', in *Münchener Kommentar zum Bürgerlichen Gesetzbuch*, V. V/3 (6th ed. Munich, 2013), no 29ff (the author points out that, in German case law, the risk-utility test is used to determine whether a product's design is defective, whereas this is not the case for manufacturing defects).

[76] BGE 133 III 257. For an analysis see Pascal Pichonnaz, 'Defective Goods and Consequential Loss', RabelsZ 2012, 819ff.

[77] Marie-Noël Zen-Ruffinen and Silvio Venturi, 'Article 208 CO', in Luc Thévenoz and Franz Werro (eds.), *Commentaire romand, Code des obligations I* (2nd ed. Geneva/Basel, 2012).

French Civil Code as well as Pothier's *Treatise on the Law Obligations*,[78] which influenced the development of the English common law of contract as well (see *Hadley v Baxendale*).[79]

As these extracts show, comparative law is not a separate or ring-fenced area of legal studies.[80] It is rather a dynamic practice, which is part of a deeper critique of law itself.[81] Indeed, judges keep an eye on what other legal systems are doing. Besides, they can and do go beyond that, using comparative arguments in their rulings. In Switzerland and Turkey, while some of the foreign references are used as '*garniture d'appoint*' to solutions courts seem to have already reached by traditional ways of reasoning,[82] others seek to enlarge the domestic interpretative options courts have at their disposal. Such a transnational judicial interaction not only enables courts to overcome their relative institutional isolation while allowing them to benefit from better solutions, but it also makes these solutions known to a broader audience.

V. Similar observations in the EU context

Observations similar to those I have presented may be made about the EU where, as in Switzerland and Turkey, there coexist more or less similar statutory dispositions. Even though, in many areas, the statutory provisions of the Member States seem almost identical as a result of their duty to meticulously implement directives into national legislation, the degree of the actual convergence or divergence between these provisions indeed depends on their judicial interpretation and application. In fact, as an author explains:

> harmonization projects, like legal transplants, tend to focus principally on the 'formal' institutions of the law. They are, therefore, vulnerable to situations where informal institutions on which the formal institutions rely are missing in the receiving jurisdiction, and even more so to situations where the transplanted rule conflicts with informal institutions in the receiving jurisdiction.[83]

The scope of the judicial control over potentially unfair terms in (consumer) contracts, which varies from jurisdiction to jurisdiction, illustrates this dynamic viewpoint. At first glance the dispositions of the UK Unfair Terms in Consumer Contracts Regulations (1999) and §§305–310 of the German BGB seem rather similar: they both exclude

78 BGE 133 III 257, para. 2.5.2.

79 (1854) 9 Ex 341; Tom Bingham, *Widening Horizons: The Influence of Comparative Law and International Law on Domestic Law* (Cambridge, 2010), 5.

80 For a general observation in this sense see Mads Andenas and Duncan Fairgrieve, n 39 at 864.

81 Marie-Claire Ponthoreau, 'Le droit comparé en question(s) entre pragmatisme et outil épistémologique', RIDC 2005, 23; Peer C. Zumbansen, 'Comparative Law's Coming of Age? Twenty Years after Critical Comparisons', in Russel A. Miller and Peer C. Zumbansen (eds.), *Comparative Law as Transnational Law* (Oxford, 2012), 124.

82 Franz Werro, *La jurisprudence et le droit comparé, in Institut Suisse de Droit Comparé* (Ed.), n 1 at 166; Peter V. Kunz, *Einführung zur Rechtsvergleichung in der Schweiz*, recht 2006, 44.

83 T. T. Arvind, 'The "Transplant Effect" in Harmonization', ICLQ 2010, 79.

individually negotiated terms from the fairness test.[84] However, closer judicial scrutiny of these statutes, which are both based on the EU Unfair Terms Directive (93/13/EEC), reveals a difference between their scopes and thus the degree of protection for weaker parties. According to the German *Bundesgerichtshof* (BGH, Federal Supreme Court), individual negotiation implies that the parties have been given a chance to influence the content of the terms.[85] Yet 'individually negotiated' seems to have a narrower meaning in UK case law. In a decision rendered in February 2010 (*UK Housing Alliance Ltd v Francis*), the High Court of England and Wales stated that 'the fact that a consumer or his legal representative has had the opportunity of considering the terms of an agreement does not mean that any individual term has been individually negotiated. The supplier must prove that the relevant term was individually negotiated'.[86] So, identical or nearly identical provisions can be implemented in ways that cause diametrically opposed results, where the burden of pleading and/or proof is allocated differently. The devil is always in the details!

The disharmony is even more pronounced in tort law.[87] Thus, for example, since the adoption of the Product Liability Directive (85/374/EEC), which sought to harmonize a no-fault liability regime for defective products across the EU, different interpretations as to the meaning of some key notions have accumulated. In the so-called *Mineralwasser* case, which was cited by the Swiss Supreme Court as well,[88] the German *Bundesgerichtshof* held that the development risks defence applies exclusively to design defects, but is not available for manufacturing defects.[89] In the English *Blood Transfusion* case, the High Court of England and Wales considered the German solution and questioned whether the German Federal Supreme Court interpreted the Directive correctly and applied it appropriately. Unlike its German counterpart, the English Court then came to the conclusion that there is no need to adopt different approaches for different types of defects.[90]

The comparison of different cases draws attention to a crucial feature of the EU legislation, which is often the result of a compromise carrying with it some degree of ambiguity. The EU law simultaneously promotes convergence and divergence. Superficially similar terms will be interpreted differently in different countries, because they are broad (vague) and therefore subject to manipulation (re-definition) by courts in different jurisdictions.[91] Differences in the cultural values, legal needs, judicial organizations play a role in the judicial interpretation of abstract statutory rules as well as of doctrinal notions, and consequently in the creation of legal meaning ('jurisgenesis'). It is then

[84] For a critical comment, see Erdem Büyüksagis, 'La bonne foi dans l'article 8 LCD: un remède à l'impuissance des consommateurs face aux clauses générales "soi-disant" négociées?', AJP/PJA 2012, 1393ff.

[85] BGH, 19 May 2005, NJW 2005, 2543.

[86] *UK Housing Alliance (North West) Ltd v Francis* [2010] EWCA Civ 117.

[87] For an analysis see Franz Werro and Erdem Büyüksagis, 'The Bounds between Negligence and Strict Liability', in Mauro Bussani and Anthony J. Sebok (eds.), *Comparative Tort Law: Global Perspectives* (Cheltenham, 2015), Chapter 10.

[88] BGE 133 III 81, para. 3.2.

[89] BGH, 9 May 1995, NJW 1995, 2162.

[90] *A & Others v The National Blood Authority* [2001] 3 All ER 289. See also Duncan Fairgrieve, Geraint Howells, and Marcus Pilgerstorfer, 'The Product Liability Directive: Time to get Soft?', JETL 2013, 32.

[91] Robert M. Cover, 'Nomos and Narrative', Harv. L. Rev. 1983, 4; Rodolfo Sacco, 'Legal Formants: A Dynamic Approach to Comparative Law', AJCL 1991, 27.

legitimate to inquire into the appropriateness of the ever burgeoning 'unification' required by Brussels or suggested by some legal scholarship through principles, definitions, and model rules—with little or no attention to case law.

However that may be, at EU level, international judicial interaction based upon comparative research is gaining importance.[92] This, in turn, helps to create, step by step, a common language in some areas while promoting a bottom-up approach to Europeanization. A simple example will help to clarify what is being argued here. Consider some of the most important advances in the field of non-pecuniary damages. In *Leitner v TUI Deutschland GmbH*, the *Landesgericht* Linz had first studied German law, which requires compensation for loss of enjoyment of the holidays as a form of non-pecuniary damage.[93] The Austrian Court then requested the ECJ to provide a clarification on the general concept of damage used in the Package Travel Directive (90/314/EEC). When the ECJ ruled on this issue, it referred to various national laws, which award damages to compensate the injured person for the frustration caused by 'spoiled holidays'.[94] As such this decision contributed to the gradual internalization of common values by the domestic legal systems. In the light of the ECJ's case law, one may conclude that the rulings of the Court play an important role in the finding of common ground between different legal systems. As one author observed, 'the European Court is . . . concerned about the constitutional autonomy and authority of EU law and of the Court itself.'[95]

VI. Conclusions

I started with a study of the reception of Swiss private law in Turkey, and described the commonality between their civil codes. By expanding the range of studied materials beyond the statutory instances, I then analysed the organic development of case law in both countries. My research led to two main observations. Firstly, it appeared that, particularly in Turkey—but occasionally in Switzerland as well—through the application of Article 1 of the Civil Code, judges go beyond the mere interpretation of the statutory provisions. That is why some of the very same provisions have been interpreted differently by Swiss and Turkish courts. Indeed, there is often more than a single meaning for a provision which operates simultaneously in two countries with different languages and cultural backgrounds. Secondly, my analysis revealed that comparative reasoning plays a very significant role in the judicial law-making process. When determining what a new statute actually entails,[96] interpreting an existing statutory

[92] A similar point in the literature can be found in Thomas Kadner Graziano, 'Est-il légitime et utile pour le juge de comparer?', in Marianne Faure-Abbad and Michel Boudot (eds.), *Obligations, procès et droit savant: Mélanges en l'honneur de Jean Beauchard* (Paris, 2013), 77ff. Besides, the European Parliament and the Commission agree on the importance of supporting the improved availability of national databases on national court rulings concerning Community law. See the European Parliament resolution of 9 July 2008 (2007/2027(INI)).

[93] C-168/00, [2002] ECR I-2631. For a comment, see Franz Werro, 'Comparative Studies in Private Law: A European Point of View', in Mauro Bussani and Ugo Mattei (eds.), *The Cambridge Companion to Comparative Law* (Cambridge, 2012), 126.

[94] C-168/00, [2002] ECR I-2631, para. 18.

[95] Gráinne de Búrca, 'International Law before the Courts: The European Union and the United States Compared', 2014 (available at SSRN: <http://ssrn.com/abstract=2487361>), 34.

[96] See the Swiss product liability case in n 73.

provision[97] or filling in a legislative gap,[98] Swiss judges do not hesitate to seek guidance in foreign rules and judgments, and Turkish judges refer to Swiss judgments and academic literature as a source of authority. That is one of the reasons why, despite some differences in their positions on certain issues, Swiss and Turkish courts often reach similar conclusions in similar circumstances. Combining these observations, I conclude that the mere reading of the codes and statutes is not enough to understand a legal system. Such a reading should be completed with many other discourses that are produced in and around the legal system being studied. In this context, particular attention should be paid to the case law surrounding the statutory dispositions.[99] Indeed, law is the end product of the process of judicial reasoning, a process in which judges—particularly Supreme Court judges—are influenced by many variables. Some of the most noticeable among these are foreign sources.

The court's role in finding normative solutions, when the authority points towards an answer that seems inappropriate or unclear, is gaining importance in other European jurisdictions as well. Even in countries in which the person finding and applying the law is seen as seeking the single correct solution for a case, there are signs of a change in the courts' role.[100] In a hotly debated article, a former president of Germany's highest appeals court (*Bundesgerichtshof*) wrote that 'the judge is a pianist who interprets the compositions of the legislature with artistic freedom'.[101] My brief study of the case law of different European countries as well as that of the ECJ goes even further and shows that the judge should be seen as an active element in decision-making, and that the use of comparative analysis is one of the most precious components of this process. The Swiss/Turkish experience illustrates how comparative law in the courts is indeed an effective catalyst for possible innovations. There are other examples which seem to be similar to the Swiss/Turkish experience. The American example reveals that the various states of the Union refer to the case law of other states. Likewise, comparative law could also play a role in judicial coordination in Europe, provided that judges are educated on the utility of judgments from the courts of foreign countries. When this condition is satisfied, comparative law stops being a mere academic exercise of exploring similarities and differences between legal systems, and becomes elevated to a legitimate source of law. As such it would be considered alongside constitutions, laws, precedents, traditions, and policy as a tool for determining the outcomes of cases.

[97] See the cases where the Swiss Supreme Court had to deal with a wrongful birth (see above, n 46) or the distinction between direct and indirect damage (see above, n 76).

[98] See the Turkish case concerning the transfer of an entity in n 64.

[99] For a similar point, see Mitchel Lasser, 'The Question of Understanding', in Pierre Legrand and Roderick Munday (eds.), *Comparative Legal Studies: Traditions and Transitions* (Cambridge, 2003), 203ff.

[100] Thomas Lundmark, 'Legal Science and European Harmonisation', LQR 2014, 71.

[101] Günter Hirsch, *Zwischenruf—Der Richter wird's schon richten,* ZRP 2006, 161.

38

The Draft Common Frame of Reference in the Courts

The Remaking of Comparative Law

*Galateia Kalouta**

I. Introduction

The Draft Common Frame of Reference (DCFR)[1] is not only a series of books. It is a thorough academic work containing principles,[2] definitions,[3] and model rules[4] of important areas of European private law, such as contract law, the law of obligations, unjustified enrichment etc., which are meticulously commented and followed by notes.[5] The Notes refer to the various legal acts either of the Member States or of the EU from which the model rules of the DCFR derive. Ergo, DCFR is simultaneously a legal anthology, a codification, a commentary, and a European legal melting pot.

The DCFR was originally conceived as the preparatory work for the upcoming Common Frame of Reference (CFR). The latter was announced by the European Commission, within its 'Action Plan on a more Coherent European Contract Law' in February 2003. Its principal goal was to develop a CFR which could then be used by the Commission when reviewing already existing European private contract law (*acquis*) as well as when drafting new legislation.[6] In a further paper of the Commission in October

* LL.M. Munich, Legal Researcher Osnabrück—ex cathedra Prof. Dr. h.c. mult. Christian von Bar, FBA.

1 The DCFR contains the results of the work of the Study Group on a European Civil Code (Study Group) and the Research Group on existing Community law in the area of general contract law (Acquis Group). The former Commission on European Contract Law (Lando Commission) provided the basis for much of Books II and III, since it was on their Principles of European Contract Law (PECL) that the Study Group and the Acquis Group built; Christian von Bar and Eric Clive (eds.), *Definitions and Model Rules of European Private Law. Draft Common Frame of Reference (DCFR)* (Full Edition, Sellier European Law Publishers 2009) Intr. 1 p. 1 marginal no. 1.

2 Namely rules of a more general nature, such as freedom of contract of good faith. Also underlying principles in the whole of the DCFR are the following: freedom, security, justice, and efficiency.

3 The internal coherent to the model rules definitions are mainly found in Book I. Thereto DCFR I-1:108; 'The definitions in the list of definitions apply for all the purposes of these rules unless the context otherwise requires'. This expressly incorporates the list of terminology as part of the DCFR; *Definitions and Model Rules of European Private Law*, n 1, Intr. 22 p. 10 marginal no. 23.

4 Model rules, with comments and notes, bring together rules derived from the legal systems of the Member States and the over-arching Community law. Principles explain the main underlying value judgements. Definitions bring to the defined terms and concepts the shared experience and ideas of jurists from 30 different jurisdictions; *Definitions and Model Rules of European Private Law*, n 1, Intr. 1 p. 1 marginal no. 1.

5 At least the full edition of the DCFR is commented. In contrast to its Outline Edition, which, apart from the Introduction and the principles, is comprised of the uncommented model rules.

6 Action Plan para. 72.

2004, titled 'European Contract Law and the revision of the *acquis*: the way forward', it was once again proposed that the CFR should provide 'fundamental principles, definitions and model rules' which could then assist in the improvement of the existing *acquis communautaire*, and which also might form the basis of an optional instrument. The model rules would therefore form the bulk for the CFR, its main purpose being to serve as a kind of legislators' guide or 'tool box'.[7]

For these reasons, a group of legal researchers from all around Europe and under the guidance of well-respected professors were brought together in order to provide in-depth information about the various European legal systems on certain legal matters. Their ultimate work was tremendous in content. It not only compared the different legal families, but it also presented and examined in detail the specific laws of the various Member States in search of the 'best solution'.[8] Numerous criteria, as well as the political reasons behind each legislation, were scrutinized, in order to determine any common ground within the various laws of the different European legal systems, which, after thorough comparative examination, did not seem that different after all.

But since the political legitimation for a more coherent EC private law by a European body still remains omitted, the DCFR stands on its own, as an academic work,[9] which promotes comparative knowledge of private law in the various jurisdictions of the EU. Moreover, the DCFR aims to prove the existence of a European private law, since the different jurisdictions of the Member States, consciously or unconsciously, often tend to coincide when resolving common problems. Another key purpose of the DCFR is to serve as a source of inspiration for higher national or European courts or other official bodies, or even beyond the EU itself. It is in this way that the DCFR both prepares a modernization of the law of contract and significantly contributes to an informal harmonization of private law.[10] The DCFR model rules, lacking in normative force, act as soft law rules, such as the ones found in the PECL, which aim to improve the coherence of contract law within the European legal *status quo*.

These being the goals set by the DCFR, the following chapter aims to illustrate the impact of the DCFR before European courts, by presenting cases of the European Court of Justice (ECJ) as well as Supreme Court decisions of various European countries. Even though the DCFR is not a legally binding document, it is still applied by courts throughout Europe when in need of support for their legal arguments, and is often used in parallel or analogically to the national legislation, when it happens to coincide with DCFR provisions. Sometimes the DCFR is even applied directly by the courts in order to amend legislative loopholes, thereby keeping the law up-to-date. The following, almost 30, illustrative cases try to depict the whole applicability range of the DCFR. The reason why these cases are portrayed in a detailed manner is that this way they might serve as a possible source of inspiration for cases to come. However, since the DCFR resumes the general rules of European civil law, one can

[7] *Definitions and Model Rules of European Private Law*, n 1, Intr. 50 p. 19 marginal no. 49.

[8] The 'best solution approach' was used when comparing the different national laws.

[9] Since the scope of the DCFR is thus considerably broader than what the European Commission seemed to have had in mind for the coverage of the CFR; *Definitions and Model Rules of European Private Law*, n 1, Intr. 30 p. 11 marginal no. 30.

[10] *Definitions and Model Rules of European Private Law*, n 1, Intr. 7 p. 4 marginal no. 8.

easily understand that its content is quite immense. Therefore, for reasons of coherence, but also so that the reader may acquire an overview of the DCFR itself, this chapter follows the structure of the DCFR.

II. How the DCFR has been applied by the courts

1. DCFR applied by national courts

a) Book I—General provisions

i. I a. Art. I.-1:103(2) DCFR; Good faith and fair dealing

The question of good faith and fair dealing within a contractual agreement is most essential in itself and therefore this particular issue emerges rather frequently in the case law of the various European countries. This is illustrated by the case filed before the Spanish Supreme Court on 3 December 2010.[11] The Court had to determine whether a party that was claiming payment several years after the deadline of a contractual loan (but where its limitation period had not been reached), was acting dutifully or whether this party had committed an abuse of process. Of importance in this matter is the continued accumulation of interest on the debt, which would then have required a very large sum to be paid.

The Supreme Court noted that the appellant bank had correctly filed its payment claim when it was informed that the debtor had increased his assets. However, the delay was still substantial and therefore unfair. The Court based its decision on the doctrine of good faith, as it is found in art. I.-1:103(2) DCFR. There it is stated that it is, in particular, contrary to good faith and fair dealing for a first party to act inconsistently in regards to its prior statements or conduct when the second party has reasonably relied on the first party to its own detriment. A party is therefore lacking good faith, when the right holder behaves in contradiction to the legitimate trust he had given his counterparty through his conduct over an extended period of time.

The Court then accordingly explained that a delay may be forfeited as unfair when: (a) an amount of time has passed without the claim being issued; (b) the exercise of the claim was unsuccessful; and (c) the other party was led to believe that the claim wouldn't be issued.[12]

Consequently, the Court concluded that the respondent was led to legitimately trust that the bank would no longer issue a claim against him. Since a large amount of time had elapsed and an enormous amount of default interest had been accumulated, a legal process would have led to the respondent's detriment. For these reasons the Court found the delay unfair and contradictory to good faith.

The case filed before the Spanish Supreme Court on 12 December 2011,[13] in which the Court faced a similar question—concerning a mortgage due on a loan

[11] Tribunal Supremo (TS) 769/2010 Sala 1. de lo Civil on 3 December 2010. [12] Ibid., par. 4.

[13] TS 872/2011, Sala 1. de lo Civil on 12 December 2011, at <http://www.poderjudicial.es/search/doAction?action=contentpdf&databasematch=TS&reference=6223450&links=%221830/2008%22&optimize=20120102&publicinterface=true>. Also Sentencia Nr. 95/2011 on 9 May 2011, Juzgado de lo Mercantil Nr. 1 in Las Palmas de Gran Canaria.

agreement—provides a further example. The respondent bank had ordered a wage garnishment 18 years after the agreed date of payment and the appellants issued a claim against the bank's legal action, claiming compensation for damages. Since the initial claim by the Bank had ended with the dation in payment, the Court concluded that the process was carried out with an unfair delay. The Court stated that, according to art. I.-1:103(2) DCFR, a subjective right cannot be exercised, or a claim cannot be issued, if the right holder did not enforce it for a substantial period of time. This negligent behaviour by the right holder leads his counterparty to be confident that no claim will be issued.[14]

Moreover, the Court clarified the distinction between an unfair delay in the execution of judicial power and the statute of limitation. Although, as the Court declared, both of the above require that a claim against the debtor be held for a long period of time, in order to stipulate an unfair delay, however, the right holder must have caused the debtor to be confident that no claim will be made against him. In order to conclude that the claim has been waived, the right holder is then required to make evident that he will not make a claim against the debtor. Therefore, for such cases the rule of good faith is of great importance. Similarly, the Spanish Supreme Court prefers the provision of good faith as it pertains in art. I.-1:103(2) DCFR.[15]

Therefore, the Court rejected the compensation claim for damages. It found that in order for the delay to have been unfair, the respondent must have acted either maliciously or with gross negligence, neither of which could be confirmed in this case.

b) Book II—Contracts and other juridical acts

i. II a. Interpretation of contracts

Concerning the admissibility of evidence of pre-contractual negotiations, it is interesting to note that supporters of their admissibility in the English legal system refer also to the DCFR article, in order to substantiate that preliminary negotiations should be included to the relevant matters, when it comes to contract interpretation. In the case of *Chartbrook v Persimmon Homes*,[16] the Lords decided to allow evidence of the pre-contract negotiations, as they could not find the conceptual limits between what should be regarded as background or as pre-contractual negotiation. For this reason they exercised common sense and corrected a mistake, which was evident that it was amiss. The House of Lords hereby deviated a little from a long tradition regarding admissibility. By doing so, the House of Lords did not change the rule of English law on not admitting evidence of negotiations. However, a less strict application of the exclusionary rule was preferred and thereby the House of Lords opted to use common sense instead. For this reason they tried to find support on the fact that many other European legal systems do accept preliminary negotiations in contract interpretation. Their

[14] As the first of the above, par. 3.

[15] Art. I.-1:103(2) DCFR: It is, in particular, contrary to good faith and fair dealing for a party to act inconsistently with the party's prior statements or conduct when the other party has reasonably relied on them to that other party's detriment.

[16] *Chartbrook Ltd v Persimmon Homes Ltd and others* [2009] UKHL 38, Lord Hoffmann par. 39 p. 15–16.

Lordships therefore cited various other sources such as the UNIDROIT Principles of International Commercial Contracts and the Principles of European Contract Law (PECL). This common ground of the continental law is, however, also depicted in art. II.-8:102 DCFR.

On 25 May 2009,[17] the Spanish Supreme Court was confronted with the question of whether a private distribution agreement *inter vivos* should be declared void or not. This particular issue centred on the question of how the private agreement should be interpreted. The private agreement was found to be a partition's agreement by the Court of first instance. Instead the Court of Appeal found it to be an atypical contract.

In Spain, with the sole exception of Catalonia, it is not compulsory for such a distribution agreement *inter vivos* to have a standard form nor to bear a specific title or name. According to the Court, the general contract rules as found in the Spanish Civil Code and in the DCFR also apply analogically to contracts without a standard form. The Court then decided in favour of the particular contract, since art. II.-8:106 DCFR[18] prefers the interpretation which is most favourable to the effectiveness of the contract.[19] As explained in the DCFR Comment, if a term is ambiguous and could be interpreted in one way which would make it invalid or in another which would make it valid, the latter interpretation should prevail (*favor negotii*).[20]

ii. II b. Contents and effects of contracts

The Swedish Supreme Court was confronted on 23 September 2011[21] with the question of whether dental expenses can be claimed before the corrective treatment is performed. Although the errors in dental treatment were not in dispute, however, the parties disagreed on when the patient should pay. The clinic referred to its general terms and conditions, which stipulated payment before the corrective treatment is performed, whereas the patient refused to pay before the corrective treatment, instead expecting to pay afterwards.

Both the Court of Appeal as well as the Supreme Court found that the Swedish Consumer Services Act does not apply in such a case, since this Act does not cover health care services. In absence of another directly applicable law, the Supreme Court turned to precedent cases as well as to art. II.-9:103(1) DCFR, in order to decide, whether the patient was bound to the general terms and conditions (GTC) of the university hospital.

The hospital claimed that the patient was bound by its GTC from the moment he entered the clinic and received treatment. According to its GTC, various amounts were also expected to be paid in advance, during the course of a treatment, in the form of a warranty.

But according to art. II-9:103 (1) and (3a), a term supplied by one party is not individually negotiated if the other party has not been able to influence its content,

[17] TS 366/2009, Sala 1. de lo Civil on 25 May 2009, RAJ 2009 Nr. 2417 p. 5963–5.

[18] Article II.-8:106 DCFR: Preference for interpretation which renders the terms of the contract lawful, or effective, is to be preferred to one which would not.

[19] Supremo Tribunal on 25 May 2009, par. 5.

[20] *Definitions and Model Rules of European Private Law*, n 1, Book II Art. II.-8:106 p. 569.

[21] Swedish Supreme Court Judgment on 23 September 2011, Case No. T 4062-09, NJA 2011 p. 600 (NJA 2011:59).

in particular because it has been drafted in advance, whether or not as part of standard terms. Therefore, if a party has not taken appropriate steps to bring the terms to the other party's attention the contract is treated as having been made without the terms, if the other party wishes this to be the case.[22]

The Supreme Court ruled that standard GTC must be made known to the other party before the conclusion of the contract in order that they become part of the binding contract. Thus, the conclusion was reached that the clinic had failed to inform the other party in a timely manner about this general rule.[23] The patient was, therefore, not aware of the hospital's general principle on liability, which also applies before the performance of the service. The Court referred mainly to art. II–9:103(1) DCFR[24] and it consequently decided that since the patient had not been properly informed beforehand, he could not be bound by the hospital's GTC. Consequently, the patient could not be held liable, until the treatment had been fully performed.

In an additional example, the Dutch Supreme Court, in its decision on 11 May 2012,[25] decided whether GTC are part of the binding contract. The main question was: to what extent were the GTC of the plaintiff part of the contract, since the GTC stipulated limitation of liability in favour of the plaintiff. The Court, in its verdict, refers to the different rules in various legal systems in order to substantiate whether or not GTC should be included in the contract. But due to the theoretical dispute on this matter, the Court turned to art. II.-9:103 DCFR[26] and rejected the GTC from being part of the negotiated, and therefore binding, contract.

c) Book III—Obligations and corresponding rights

i. III a. Remedies for non-performance

The Swedish Supreme Court dealt with a liability claim for liquidated damages in its verdict on 11 October 2012.[27] According to this case, the plaintiff, along with other sub-contractors, entered into a concession contract, with the final aim of constructing power plants. The performance contract[28] regulated certain tasks[29] which were to be carried out by each of the sub-contractors. Moreover, it regulated that the contractor was liable for the execution of the contract. However, the completion of the contract was delayed, which prevented the power plant from operating on the set date. In the

[22] *Definitions and Model Rules of European Private Law*, n 1, Book II Art. II.-9:103 p. 589, 591.

[23] Supreme Court T 4062-09 p. 6.

[24] Article II.-9:103: Terms not individually negotiated. (1) Terms supplied by one party and not individually negotiated may be invoked against the other party only if the other party was aware of them, or if the party supplying the terms took reasonable steps to draw the other party's attention to them, before or when the contract was concluded... (3) For the purposes of this Article (a) 'not individually negotiated' has the meaning given by II.-1:110 (Terms 'not individually negotiated'); and (b) terms are not sufficiently brought to the other party's attention by a mere reference to them in a contract document, even if that party signs the document.

[25] HR Verdict on 11.5.2012, LJN: BW0730, NJ 2012 Nr. 318.

[26] The same rule can also be found in Art. 2:104 PECL as well as in Art. 70 CESL.

[27] Supreme Court Judgment Case no. T 5670-10, announced in Stockholm, 11 October 2012, NJA 2012 p. 597 (NJA 2012:60), *Ann-Sophie Greberg*, Commentary Info Torg Juridik published 20 November 2012.

[28] AB 92—General requirements for the construction and installation contracts.

[29] In particular the supply and installation of the plant's generator.

construction contract a certain amount had been agreed upon as a penalty for each week of delay. The main problem, however, focuses on the fact that the assignment would have been hampered nonetheless, since another sub-contractor was also delayed in his assignment.[30] This meant that the commission would have still been delayed even if the main contractor had completed its part of the assignment on time.

The Court could not base its decision entirely on the wording of the penalty clause in the concession agreement, since it could be interpreted both ways. Therefore, it examined the doctrine on the remedies matter in case of non-performance, with special reference[31] to art. III.-3:101 DCFR.[32] Thus, it concluded that although the delay in the fulfillment of the project was not only caused by the respondent, the latter was, however, liable to pay liquidated damages. The reasoning was that in cases such as this, when two wrongful events cause the same damage within the same period of time, both events entail liability.[33] Hence, the Court adjudicated joint liability[34] for liquidated damages caused by the delay, in order to avoid overcompensation of the victim.[35]

ii. III b. Termination effects

In another case before the Spanish Supreme Court[36] the appellant had entered into a contract with the respondent, in which one party provided certain telephone lines and the other party acted as a service provider, providing premium rate services[37] to callers. In summary, the appellant considered the respondent to be in a breach of contract, whereas the respondent sought termination of the contract *ex tunc* and unjust enrichment.

The Court based its decision on the incorrect access code and acknowledged wrongful gain in favour of the respondent. Moreover, according to the written agreement the respondent could terminate the contract if the appellant was in a breach of contract. The Court then concluded that the appellant was in fact in a breach of contract, since he had been using the access code that was incorrect for this type of service. As per the Court's decision, the cancellation of the contract was reciprocal.

When it comes to the effects of a contract cancellation, the Spanish Supreme Court refers to art. III.-3:509 and 3:510 DCFR, according to which there are two types of effect: namely the termination of the obligation, and restitution. Since the obligations of the parties under the contract had ended and since both parties were in a breach of contract, the obligation to restitute the benefits received by performance was reciprocal.

[30] Namely, the delivery and installation of the plant's generator was also delayed.

[31] Swedish Supreme Court Judgment (HD) 11.10.2012 Case No. T 5670-10 NJA 2012 p. 597 (NJA 2012:60) announced in Stockholm, p. 5.

[32] Article III.-3:101: Remedies available. (1) If an obligation is not performed by the debtor and the non-performance is not excused, the creditor may resort to any of the remedies set out in this chapter. (2) If the debtor's non-performance is excused, the creditor may resort to any of those remedies except enforcing specific performance and damages. (3) The creditor may not resort to any of those remedies to the extent that the creditor caused the debtor's non-performance.

[33] Ibid., p. 9. [34] Ibid., par. 16.

[35] This approach corresponds to the principle that the injured party, in case of damages, should not be placed afterwards in a better financial situation than the one in which it was prior to the harmful event. Ibid., par. 15.

[36] STS 4714/2010 on 22 June 2010. Appeal No.: 363/2006 Resolution No.: 380/2010.

[37] This actually being fortune telling by reading the tarot cards.

The Court then had to decide if the termination effects should apply from the moment the breach occurred onward. The Court explained that since restitution affects third parties (customers), who could not be restituted, the termination effects should pertain as soon as the termination occurs. Therefore the Court ruled a breach of contract for both parties, therefore the restitution of the benefits was reciprocal and the termination effects applied *ex nunc.*

Furthermore, in various other cases[38] before the Spanish Supreme Court, the appellants had bought certain tourist apartments from the respondent firm within a certain resort. The local administration, however, later withdrew its licence, with the result that the whole resort could not be used as a tourist resort.

Both previous instances found that the constructor was in a breach of contract. The Supreme Court, however, held that it was rather a revocation or a cancellation of contract instead. Therefore the provisions cited in both previous instances had not been applied correctly.[39] The Court substantiated its decision by referring to previous Spanish jurisprudence as well as by explicitly citing art. III.-3:510(5) DCFR,[40] according to which, the reimbursement obligation extends to all natural and civil fruits. Therefore, the Court concluded that the effects of the contract's termination should not apply from the time of its cancellation. Instead, the termination's effects should apply retroactively, from the moment of the contract's completion. The intention was to return back to the previous legal status. That, of course, entails that each party has to restore objects or benefits that may have been received due to the terminated contract.[41] As per the Spanish Supreme Court, the reason for this rule determining the cancellation of all contractual effects is to balance the consequences from the loss of the contract between the parties.

iii. III c. Damages and interest

A landmark case is the ruling of the Swedish Supreme Court in Case No. T 5926:11,[42] where, following a train accident, the plaintiff claimed compensation for rescue costs. The plaintiff had a transportation agreement with the respondent to transport chlorine gas on behalf of the plaintiff. The parties had agreed that the Uniform Rules concerning the Contract of International Carriage of Passengers by Rail (also known as CIM)[43] is applicable regarding the transportation in question, and they both claimed compensation for the costs made during the rescue operation. In Sweden, there is no precedent

[38] TS 99/2012, Sala 1 de lo Civil, on 29 February 2012 and TS 103/2012 Sala 1. de lo Civil on 1 March 2012.

[39] Ibid., par. 5–6.

[40] Article III.-3:510 (5) DCFR: Restitution of benefits received by performance. (5) The obligation to return a benefit extends to any natural or legal fruits received from the benefit.

[41] Ibid., par. 6.

[42] HD 4 February 2013 Case No. T 5926-11, *Anne Hansen* Commentary to T 5926-11 Info Torg Juridik, published on 6 February 2013.

[43] In 1980 a treaty concerning International Carriage by Rail (COTIF) has been signed. This treaty primarily regulates the international transport of goods and passengers, and includes rules of both civil and public law. It consists of the Constitutive Act, followed by two appendixes; CIV—the Uniform Rules concerning the Contract of International Carriage of Passengers by Rail and CIM—the Uniform Rules concerning the Contract of International Carriage of Goods by Rail. The revised text of the Convention in 1999 has not yet been ratified by Sweden.

case which would serve as an example. Moreover, the issues raised in this particular case had never been tried before in any other Court within the whole Convention Area.

The Supreme Court was confronted with the question of whether the costs borne by the customer, to limit the effects from the breach of contract on behalf of the carrier, can be recoverable or not. However, the CIM, as well as other transportation law treaties, contain no explicit regulation for compensation rights for damages that are caused when the transportation customer takes certain measures in order to limit certain damages.[44] In other words, the CIM does not regulate the case of damages due to damage limitation measures, as it determines reimbursement only for damaged or delayed goods.

Due to the regulatory loophole as well as the lack of precedent in this matter within the whole Convention Area, the Swedish Supreme Court turned to the general principles of contract law and in particular to art. III.-3:705 DCFR.[45] The right to compensation was thereafter linked to an obligation foreseen under the general rules of contract law, according to which the injured party must take reasonable steps to limit the harmful effects in the case of default of the counterparty.[46] Moreover, one can be entitled to compensation by the general contract rules, when the measures taken were reasonable, regardless of whether or not the measures were successful, or even if they eventually led to an even greater injury. The purpose of this general contract rule is to encourage the injured party to take active measures in order to reduce the damage. Furthermore, it is in the best interest of the party that is allegedly in breach of contract that the injured party be encouraged to take any reasonable measures needed to reduce the damage. The injured party is usually in a better position to limit the damage.[47]

In summary, here the Supreme Court dealt with the question of whether the parties of a transportation contract are obliged to take reasonable steps in order to limit the damage by a breach of contract or if the carriage contract should constitute an exception to the rules of general contract law.[48] Considering the lack of explicit regulation of this obligation by the CIM and other carriage contracts, and the rather sparse case law on this matter, the Court then concluded that such legislative gaps can be filled by applying the general rules of contract law, as they are represented in DCFR.[49]

Furthermore the Court substantiated its ruling with the argument that, otherwise, the lack of action by the travel customer would be rewarded. This would then mean that transport customers would receive economic gains by allowing goods to be lost, instead of incurring any further costs in order to limit the damage.[50] Such a result would not be reasonable, both from a general point of view and from an economic perspective.

[44] Ibid., par. 3.8 and 3.9.

[45] Article III.-3:705 DCFR—Reduction of loss (1); The debtor is not liable for loss suffered by the creditor to the extent that the creditor could have reduced the loss by taking reasonable steps. (2) The creditor is entitled to recover any expenses reasonably incurred in attempting to reduce the loss.

[46] Ibid., par. 3.3–3.5, with reference to *Definitions and Model Rules of European Private Law*, n 1, vol. I, p. 939 f.

[47] Ibid., par. 3.6. [48] Ibid., par. 3.12. [49] Ibid., par. 3.13. [50] Ibid., par. 3.11.

iv. III d. Stipulated payment for non-performance

In Case No. T 4728:08[51] before the Swedish Supreme Court, the main question concerned a lost master key. The Court had to elaborate if the penalty in the Annex of the Acknowledgement agreement should be considered to be a liability limitation clause and if this particular clause pertained against the Insurance Company.

In the Court's opinion, in standardized contracts or in contracts about construction supplies, it is common that the penalty is a comprehensive settlement of the obligation to pay compensation for delaying the main performance, unless the contract is terminated.

The Scandinavian literature is, however, divided on this matter. It remains rather disputed in Sweden whether the aggrieved party can choose compensation instead of demanding action or if it should exclusively demand action when the meaning of the agreement is not clear. The Court then turned to the literature from other European nations, only to find out that this topic is also rather controversial in the whole of Europe. The question still remained whether compensation should be paid in addition to an agreed penalty or if liquidated damages should be deemed the exclusive remedy when the contract is not cancelled. The latter, however, corresponds to art. III.-3:712[52] DCFR.[53] Therefore, the Court interpreted the wording of the Annex in accordance with art. III.-3:712 DCFR and it concluded that the agreement between the owner and subcontractor meant that the penalty constituted the exclusive provision of compensation. Consequently, the Court ruled in favour of the subcontractor, who perceived the penalty clause as the final settlement in case of loss of the key.[54]

v. III e. When different types of obligation arise

In another case,[55] the Spanish Supreme Court was confronted with a question about liability regarding a car accident during an organized trip. The plaintiffs had booked a trip in a third country through a travel agency (retailer) domiciled in their own country. The trip, however, was organized by another firm (wholesaler). During the trip the plaintiffs suffered a severe car accident with the bus that had been hired by the wholesaler. The question centred on whether only one of the organizing parties should be therefore liable or whether they both shared liability and should accordingly pay for damages.

[51] Case No. T 4728-08 Högsta Domstolens Dom p. 1–26 and *Richard Byström,* Vitesavtal begränsar skadeståndet för borttappad nickel, InforTorg Juridik on 27.12.2010.

[52] Article III.-3:712: Stipulated payment for non-performance. (1) Where the terms regulating an obligation provide that a debtor who fails to perform an obligation is to pay a specified sum to the creditor for such non-performance, the creditor is entitled to that sum irrespective of the actual loss. (2) However, despite any provision to the contrary, the sum so specified in a contract or other judicial act may be reduced to a reasonable amount where it is grossly excessive in relation to the loss resulting from the non-performance and the other circumstances.

[53] *Definitions and Model Rules of European Private Law,* n 1, vol. I p. 964 on Article III.-3:712.

[54] Case No. T 4728-08 Högsta Domstolens Dom marginal no.:11. The Court refers further on to *Definitions and Model Rules of European Private Law,* n 1, Vol. I, p. 964 f. concerning, art. III.-3:712.

[55] TS 870/2009, Sala 1 de lo Civil on 20 January 2010.

The main problem, however, was that the pertaining Directive in this case[56] does not establish whether or not, in such cases, liability should be shared between the organizer (wholesaler) and the retailer. Instead, this particular issue has been left to be freely decided upon by every Member State. This means that every Member State can establish the liability issue by opting in when implementing the Directive in its own legal system. Since the Spanish legislator implemented the Directive as such, and in the absence of any precedent, the Court reviewed the various solutions given by other European Member States,[57] as well as seeking guidance from the Model Rules of European Private Law in DCFR.

Therefore the Court referred to art. III.-4:103(2) DCFR, according to which, if the terms of the obligation do not determine the question, the liability of two or more debtors to perform the same obligation is solidary. In particular, liability is solidary when two or more persons are liable for the same damage. Hence, the Court decided in favour of joint liability, shared between the retailer and the trip organizer. According to the same Court, this decision strengthens consumer protection.

A similar case of a different type of obligation was brought before the Spanish Supreme Court. In this case,[58] the buyer of nine air conditioning units had sued the seller as well as the supplying company, demanding: (a) termination of the purchase contract; (b) cancellation of the settlement agreement; and (c) compensation for the price paid and for damages with the appropriate interest.

The subsequent settlement agreement was concluded only between the applicant and the second defendant (supplier). The first defendant (seller) therefore denied being in a breach of contract, since he had not participated in this second agreement. But the Court still held the first defendant liable due to the sale contract. According to its ruling, the subsequent settlement agreement between the buyer and the supplier fell within the manufacturer's warranty and therefore did not exclude any possible claims against the seller for selling defected or malfunctioning equipment.[59]

The main problem with such cases is that the seller usually acts as an intermediary, whereas the supplier is the one who directly responds to the buyer in case of defective products. However, the Court has an established judicial practice in this matter, which fully complies with art. III.-4:103 DCFR. According to par. II of this article, if the contractual terms do not determine whether an obligation is solidary or not, the liability of two or more debtors to perform the same obligation is solidary. Liability is solidary in particular where two or more persons are liable for the same damage.

Applying the rule of solidary liability, the Court found both the seller as well as the supplier jointly liable in fulfilling the obligation. In cases in which the exact cause of the obligation might not be the same, the Court finds it important to provide greater assurance to the purchaser.[60] Due to joint liability, as found in art. III.-4:103 DCFR, the counterclaim of the first defendant had been dismissed.

[56] Directive 90/314/EEC.

[57] Such as Austria, England, Italy, and France. In addition, the Supremo Tribunal reviewed Norwegian law.

[58] TS 597/2010 Sala 1. de lo Civil on 8 October.

[59] Ibid., par. 6.

[60] Ibid., par. 6.

vi. III f. Prescription

There have been a number of cases concerning the prescription of claims in which the DCFR has been referred to. This was the main topic in Case No. E 265:11[61] before the Swedish Supreme Court. The appellant argued that his debt towards the Swedish Social Insurance Agency for the reimbursement of child support fees had already been barred. Therefore the enforcement of the reimbursement claim should be precluded.

According to Swedish law,[62] the general period of prescription is five years after the end of the calendar year, within which the claim becomes due. Excluding cases concerning child support fees, the reimbursement is due ten days after the notification of the debtor. Hence the Court considered if, in this case, the prescription period should then begin when the debtor had been notified of the reimbursement decision, without regarding the time that had elapsed between the decision itself and the notification of the debtor—which in this case was almost 12 years.

In order to answer this question, the Court had to distinguish between the maximum length of a prescription period and a short-term prescription period. Whereas the first goes into effect as soon as a claim arises, a short-term prescription period begins from its due date, or, in other words, from as soon as there is an order. As the Court noted, the main objective of such a short-term prescription period is to be able to provide a debt settlement as soon as possible.

The Court then concluded that it is possible to combine these two types of prescription by following the example set in DCFR. In the DCFR, a short-term general prescription period is provided in art. III.-7:201,[63] whereas the maximum length of a prescription period is set in art. III.-7:307.[64] Accordingly, the Court decided to combine the two types of prescription period that are applicable in this case, meaning that the Swedish provisions on prescription are to be interpreted in agreement with the DCFR prescription model. Therefore, the reimbursement obligation in this case could be claimed until ten days after notification of the debtor but, at the very most, within five years after the claim has been made. In this case, since 12 years had elapsed since the claim was filled, the reimbursement claim was found to have expired.

d) Book IV—Specific contract and the rights and obligations arising from them

i. IV a. Contracts covered

A case appeared before the Dutch Supreme Court[65] of whether the law concerning the sale of goods is also applicable to software programs.[66] The Court tried to classify

[61] Case No. E 265-11 on 20.06.2012. NJA 2012 p. 452 (NJA 2012:46).

[62] Applicable to this case is Article 3 par. 1 Act (1982:188) concerning taxes, prescriptions etc.

[63] Article III.-7:201 DCFR: General period—The general period of prescription is three years.

[64] Article III.-7:307 DCFR: Maximum length of period—The period of prescription cannot be extended, by suspension of its running or postponement of its expiry under this chapter, to more than ten years or, in case of rights to damages for personal injuries, to more than 30 years. This does not apply to suspension under III.-7:302 (Suspension in case of judicial and other proceedings).

[65] Hoge Raad (HR) Verdict on 27.4.2012, LJN: BV1301, NJ 2012 Nr.293.

[66] The obligations and remedies of the parties to a sales contract were also contemplated at an all European level in *Lloyds TSB Foundation for Scotland v Lloyds Banking Group PLC* [2011] CSIH 87; 2012 SC 259, par. 29.

standard software from a legal perspective, referring to the DCFR in order to understand how standard software is regulated within other European countries.[67] Therefore, the Court explicitly referred to art. IV.A.-1:101 DCFR, which specifies the various contracts for the sale of goods. Art. IV.A.-1:101(2)(d) DCFR specifically stipulates software as a possible object of a sale contract. As a result, the Court concluded that software can be an item within a purchase agreement. Hence, the sale of goods law is also applicable for software.

ii. IV b. Causation

Moreover the Swedish Supreme Court in its ruling of 17 April 2014[68] has actually once again recognized the DCFR. In the trial of whether an auditor acting negligently, since he deviated from generally accepted auditing principles (GAAP), should be held liable for damages to a shareholder, the Swedish Supreme Court revoked the lower court's decision by actually following the exact wording of the DCFR art. IV.C.-7:109[69] on Causation. According to the rule within the DCFR article, the Swedish Supreme Court decided that the claimant would have acted in the same manner, as he would have acquired shares in the company, even if the auditor had not deviated from the GAAP. Therefore, the chain of causation could not be established.[70]

iii. IV c. Termination of contractual relationships

In Case No. T 3:08,[71] the Swedish Supreme Court had to decide what a reasonable period is for the requisition of a resale contract. The particular case caused great uproar within the Swedish legal community, since in Sweden there is no specific legislation regarding reselling agreements.

In this case, however, the whole business relationship was based on an oral agreement and a fixed term for the nature of this particular business connection had not been agreed upon. After seven years of consistent cooperation, the supplying baker terminated the agreement with immediate effect.

The Court stated that the relationship in question was a resale agreement. Moreover, the case referred to the matter of whether a notice within reasonable time is then needed. Thus, if such a notice is needed, what time limit is to be considered reasonable? Furthermore, in case of a failure of such notice, would this comprise a breach of

[67] HR Verdict on 27.4.2012, LJN: BV1301, NJ 2012 Nr.293, par. 3.10.2 (Conclusie).

[68] HD 17.04.2014, NJA 2014 p. 272 (NJA 2014:26), at <http://://www.notisum.se/rnp/domar/hd/HD014272.htm>.

[69] Art. IV.C.-7:109: Causation. 'If the provider knows or could reasonably be expected to know that a subsequent decision will be based on the information to be provided, and if the client makes such a decision and suffers loss as a result, any non-performance of an obligation under the contract by the provider is presumed to have caused the loss if the client proves that, if the provider had provided all information required, it would have been reasonable for the client to have seriously considered making an alternative decision.'

[70] More on this ruling in the International Law Office (ILO) Newsletter, *Bo Thomaeus* Draft Common Frame of Reference and the Supreme Court, 13 October 2014, at <http://www.internationallawoffice.com/Newsletters/Detail.aspx?g=03f6ce44-450c-4c9d-bc7a-6e71ad76d802&l=7M69R9A>.

[71] Supreme Court Judgment of 03.11.2009 (Case No. T 3-08) NJA 2009 p. 672, Supreme Court Judgment NJA 1989 A 7, *Svante O. Johansson*, Avtalsrätt published on 20 November 2009, *Christina Ramberg*, The Supreme Court's silent coup, published on 3 July 2009.

contract? These particular issues were of substantial significance, as resale agreements are not regulated within Swedish law. According to the Court, a notice is definitely required and the reasonable time in case of resale agreements was determined to be three months. This particular case is considered to be a great landmark, as it directly opposes previous judgments by the same Court on the very same matter.[72] With this decision the Court made new case law by directly applying new legal source material, which is none other than the DCFR and in particular art. IV.E.-2:302 and IV.E.-2:305.

In contrast to both previous instances the Supreme Court did not linger on the true nature of the parties' agreement. Instead, it stated laconically: 'The distributor bought bread from the supplier and then sold it under his own name, so there is no question of whether it is a commission agreement or a trade agency, as it is a resale.' The short explanation by the Court regarding the nature of the agreement has been criticized in the literature as being rather abrupt. Although not elegantly stated, it still is acknowledged for clearly creating a new precedent.[73] Rather than following its own previous case law, which actually only acknowledged the legal loophole, the Supreme Court chose to directly apply art. IV.E.-2:302 and IV.E.-2:305 DCFR instead. According to these articles as they have been implemented by the Court, in case of resale agreements, either party may terminate the contract by giving notice within reasonable time, without having to pay for any damages. Whether a notice period is considered reasonable depends, along with other factors, on (a) the duration of the contractual relationship that has been terminated; (b) the investments that have been made; (c) the time needed in order to find a reasonable alternative; and (d) commercial use.

In summary, the Court decided that the party terminating the resale agreement is required to comply with a reasonable notice. Agreements on reasonable notice, other than those that may be deemed as reasonable by the Court, may be subjected to an adjustment by following the recommendations of the DCFR. The Court then concluded that a reasonable period of notice in this case was three months.

iv. IV d. Amount of indemnity

The Dutch Supreme Court[74] had to define the possible compensation amount in the case of an agency agreement. The case revolved around an agent representative agreement, which included a clause on exclusive arbitration. Under this agreement the plaintiff hired an agency (the respondent) to act on its behalf on an exclusive basis. The plaintiff, however, terminated the contract after three years. The respondent, in return, claimed payment of certain outstanding sums, based on still-pending commission fees for arbitration activities. The exact amount to be paid was particularly litigious in this case. The Supreme Court repealed the verdict of the Court of Appeal and sent the case back to it, ordering the Court of Appeal to specify, under which circumstances and to what extent, fees for agent services[75] are to be compensated. Once again, the Court referred to the DCFR while attempting to determine the standard approaches of a framework on this matter that refers to all of the European Union.[76] Even though the

[72] *Contra:* NJA 1989 A 7. [73] *Svante O. Johansson*, Avtalsrätt published on 20 November 2009.
[74] In its case HR on 2.11.2012, LJN: BW 9865, NJB 2012, 2307. [75] Such as promoting clients.
[76] HR on 2.11.2012 par. 2.35 Conclusie, LJN: BW 9865, NJB 2012, 2307.

Court recognizes that the DCFR has no official status, it compared art. IV.E.-3:312 DCFR[77] to Art. 7:442 of the Dutch Civil Code,[78] before applying it.

v. IV e. Dependent personal security

In the case already discussed concerning the lost master key,[79] the Swedish Supreme Court[80] further concluded that prior to payment, the security service must inquire if the other party has any objections which could be raised against the creditor when claiming payment from another party due to right of recourse. Otherwise, the right of recourse is void. At this point the Court pointed out that this solution corresponds also with art. IV.G.-2:112 DCFR.[81]

vi. IV f. Rights of the donor to revoke

The Spanish Supreme Court had to evaluate what constitutes ingratitude on the part of the donee. The defendant in this case[82] applied for the revocation of the donation due to ingratitude, claiming that the respondent's accusations to the public prosecutor against the appellant constitute a form of ingratitude.

Since the Spanish school of thought on this matter is rather controversial, the Court reviewed the relevant Articles in other Civil Codes and also turned to art. IV.H.-4:201 DCFR. According to par. 1, the donation contract may be revoked if the donee is guilty of gross ingratitude by intentionally committing a serious wrong against the donor. Therefore, the Court contemplated whether making accusations about the donor to the public prosecutor constituted a serious wrongdoing against the donor. The claim then was dismissed with the argument that the donee cannot conduct criminal investigations against the donor himself, since these are conducted only *ex officio*, namely from the public prosecutor. However, informing or making accusations about the donor to the public prosecutor was considered not to be a serious wrongdoing against the

[77] Art. IV.E.-3:312 dDCFR: Amount of Indemnity—(1) The commercial agent is entitled to an indemnity for goodwill on the basis of IV.E.-2:305 (Indemnity for goodwill) amounting to: (a) the average commission on contracts with new clients and on the increased volume of business with existing clients calculated for the last 12 months, multiplied by: (b) the number of years the principal is likely to continue to derive benefits from these contracts in the future. (2) The resulting indemnity must be amended to take account of: (a) the problem attrition of clients, based on the average rate of migration in the commercial agent's territory; and (b) the discount required for early payment, based on average interest rates. (3) In any case, the indemnity must not exceed one year's remuneration, calculated over the preceding five years or, if the contractual relationship has been in existence less than five years, from the average during the period in question. (4) The parties may not, to the detriment of the commercial agent, exclude the application of this Article or derogate from or vary its effects.

[78] Burgerlijk Wetboek (BW). [79] Reference no.: 44 f.

[80] In its Decision T 4728:08 Högsta Domstolens Dom p. 1–26 and *Richard Byström*, Vitesavtal begränsar skadeståndet för borttappad nickel, InforTorg Juridik on 27.12.2010.

[81] Art. IV.G.-2:212 DCFR: Notification and request by security provider before performance—(1) Before performance to the creditor, the security provider is required to notify the debtor and request information about the outstanding amount of secured obligation and any defences or counterclaims against it. (2) If the security provider fails to comply with the requirements in paragraph (1) or neglects to raise defences communicated by the debtor or known to the security provider for other sources, the security provider's right to recover from the debtor under IV.G.-2:113 (Security provider's rights after performance) are reduced by the extent necessary to prevent loss to the debtor as a result of such failure or neglect. (3) The security provider's rights against the creditor remain unaffected.

[82] TS 261/2010, Sala 1. de lo Civil on 13 May 2010.

donor. Consequently, the ingratitude was not major enough and, therefore, the donation could not be revoked.

2. DCFR applied by the ECJ

In a preliminary question towards the Advocate General about the interpretation of the Directive provisions concerning unfair business-to-consumer commercial practices in the internal market, art. II.-3:102 DCFR was pertained, since the model of Directive 2005/29/EC art. 7(4) remains rather unclear. Advocate General Trstenjak referred to this DCFR article, because it imposes specific duties on businesses marketing to consumers to provide information as regards the main characteristics of the goods and services acquired.[83] The businesses are thereupon obliged not to give misleading information when goods, other assets, or services are being marketed to consumers. Moreover, it was sought that art. II-3:102(2) DCFR, which contains the so-called 'completeness rule' for commercial communication, would improve and amend the Directive mentioned.[84] The Advocate General supports her decision on the DCFR article, since the wording of the Directive failed to bring clarity upon this certain matter.

In another case, Advocate General Trstenjak had to decide whether or not a contract had even taken place. Art. II.-4:101 DCFR was then applied, in order to establish the conclusion of the contract. As per this article, the basic requirements for the conclusion of a contract are when the parties intend to enter into a binding legal relationship or bring about some other legal effect and reach a sufficient agreement. Therefore, the offer and the acceptance have to be verified. For this reason, art. II.-4:201 and II.-4:204 DCFR were employed, according to which an offer becomes a contract provided that the general requirements for concluding a contract are met. The offer must (a) show an intention that a contract is to result if that is the case; and (b) contain terms which are sufficiently definite. Before the offer can be effective it must also be communicated to one or more specific persons or to the public.[85] Any form of statement or conduct by the offeree is an acceptance if it indicates assent to the offer.[86] The Advocate General then continued that the question of whether an offer has been made must be determined from the standpoint of the offeree. The intention of a party to enter into a binding legal relationship is to be determined from the party's statements or conduct as they could reasonably be expected to be understood by the other party[87] (art. II.-4:102).[88]

[83] Opinion of Advocate General Trstenjak delivered on 24.3.2010, Case C-540/08par. 33 ft. 7, Mediaprint Zeitungs- und Zeitschriftenverlag p. I-10922.

[84] *Definitions and Model Rules of European Private Law*, n 1, Book II Art. II.-3:102 p. 206.

[85] *Definitions and Model Rules of European Private Law*, n 1, Book II Art. II.-4:201 p. 292.

[86] Opinion of Advocate General Trstenjak delivered on 11 September 2008, Case C-180/06 *Renate Ilsinger v Martin Dreschers* (administrator in the insolvency of Schlank & Schick GmbH) par. 49 ft. no. 45–48.

[87] *Definitions and Model Rules of European Private Law*, n 1, Book II Art. II.-4:204 p. 310.

[88] As above, par. 51 ft. 52. The same point of view is also mentioned in *Chartbrook Ltd v Persimmon Homes Ltd and others* [2009] UKHL 38, Lord Hoffmann.

In another occasion concerning a withdrawn distance sell, compensation was claimed for diminution in value, which occurred due to inspection and testing of the goods. Advocate General Trstenjak applied art. II.-5:201(1) along with art. II.-5:201(4), according to which, in a distance-selling situation, the consumers have the right to withdraw within the basic withdrawal period of 14 days—the same withdrawal period as pertains across the whole of Europe. The withdrawal right of the DCFR is nevertheless broader than the ones found in the Directives on doorstep and distance selling, as it includes particular situations in its scope, which are not covered by the Directives.[89] The scope of the Directives was rather restrictive in contrast to the laws of several Member States. Therefore, the DCFR meets the requirements of the Member States and broadens the scope of the Directives mentioned. Furthermore, the effects of withdrawal are set in art. II.-5:105(4). Its main function is to secure repayment at the latest within 30 days and to exclude a right to withhold performance against the withdrawing party.[90] The compensation claim was overruled, since the diminution in value, when caused by reasonable and appropriate inspection and testing of the goods, excludes liability (art. II.-5:105(4)). What can be considered to be reasonable care may vary depending on the circumstances. One of these circumstances is whether the entitled party was informed of the existence of a right of withdrawal.[91] If the consumer is not at all or is not properly informed of his right of withdrawal, the consumer will not be held liable for diminishing the value of the product, even if the diminution of value occurred due to normal use (art. II.-5:105(5)).[92] Moreover, Advocate General Trestnjak came to the conclusion that by applying the DCFR, the obligation to produce evidence and the burden of proof should lay by the seller.[93]

Hence, Advocate General Trestnjak concluded that the trader must return to the consumer the amount already paid, by applying art. II.-5:105, which *inter alia* provides that any payment made by the withdrawing party must be returned without undue delay, and in any case not later than 30 days after the withdrawal becomes effective.[94]

(a) Book II

i. II d. Contracts infringing fundamental principles

In another case concerning the distinction between nullity and voidability of a contract infringing fundamental principles, Advocate General Trestnjak once again resorted to the DCFR and in particular to art. II.-7:301. According to this article, a contract is void

[89] Such as the supply of goods, other assets, and services on public streets and spaces. More on its broader scope: *Definitions and Model Rules of European Private Law*, n 1, Book II Art. II.-5:201 p. 388.

[90] *Definitions and Model Rules of European Private Law*, n 1, Book II Art. II.-5:105(3) p. 374.

[91] As the right of withdrawal is meant to enable the entitled party to make an informed choice, there should be no disincentive to inspecting and testing the goods; *Definitions and Model Rules of European Private Law*, n 1, Book II Art. II.-5:105(3) p. 375.

[92] More to it; *Definitions and Model Rules of European Private Law*, n 1, Book II Art. II.-5:105(3) p. 375–6.

[93] Opinion of Advocate General Trstenjak delivered on 18 February 2009, Case C-489/07 *Pia Messner v Firma Stefan Krüger*, par. 85 ft. no. 74, 78–80.

[94] Opinion of Advocate General Ms Trstenjak delivered on 8 February 2009, Case C-215/08 par. 69 ft. no. 62.

when (a) it infringes a principle recognized as fundamental to the laws of the Member States of the European Union; and (b) nullity is required to give effect to that principle. Such a contract is to be given no effect at all. Intentions and knowledge of the parties are irrelevant.[95] The Advocate General then continued that, as per the DCFR, contracts are void in cases where, for example, there is a mistake (as in art. II.-7:201), fraud (as in art. II.-7:205), coercion, or in case of a threat (as in art. II.-7:206) at the time of the conclusion of the contract.[96]

ii. II e. Interpretation of contracts

Moreover, Advocate General Cruz Villalón elaborated the argument that the jurisdiction of the European Union judicature to order compensation for any damage which may ultimately arise not from a breach of contract but from any conduct constituting a tortious act is in accordance with the general principles common to the laws of the Member States. Especially in regard to the relevant circumstances which are to be taken into consideration in cases of interpretation of agreements, the Advocate General[97] pertained art. II.-8:102 DCFR, which particularly gives a non-exhaustive list of matters which are relevant in contract interpretation. The pre-contractual negotiations are explicitly mentioned under I(a). The interpreter may consider the preliminary negotiations between the parties, unless an individually negotiated clause prohibits the parties from including anterior negotiations even for contract interpretation purposes.[98]

a) Book III—Obligations and corresponding rights

i. III a. Interest on late payments

The main question presented in Case C-275/07 of the *Commission v Italy* was, if there is an obligation to pay default interest for the delay in sending the proof to the office of departure that the goods had arrived at the office of destination.[99] Particularly decisive was whether the Member State of the customs office, which has an obligation to enter the Community's entitlement to own resources on the accounts, must pay default interest from the date on which that obligation arose until the date on which the presumption of a customs debt was rebutted.[100] The Advocate General found himself in a dead-end, since the principles deriving from the concurrent Regulations[101]—as well as the relevant case law of the same Court[102]—are applicable only when customs

[95] *Definitions and Model Rules of European Private Law*, n 1, Book II Art. II.-7:301 p. 535–7.

[96] Opinion of Advocate General Trstenjak delivered on 7 May 2009, Case C-227/08 *Eva Martín Martín v EDP Editores*, S.L. par. 51 ft no. 40–44.

[97] Opinion of Advocate General Cruz Villalón delivered on 15 November 2012 on Case C-103/11 P, *European Commission v Systran SA and Systran Luxembourg SA*, par. 73 & ft no. 24.

[98] *Definitions and Model Rules of European Private Law*, n 1, Book II Art. II.-8:102 p. 561.

[99] Case C-275/07 *Commission of the European Communities v Italian Republic*, par. 91.

[100] Ibid., par. 79.

[101] Article 11 of Regulation No. 1552/89 and article 11 of Regulation No. 1150/2000.

[102] See Case C-275/07 *Commission of the European Communities v Italian Republic*, Marginal No.: 80, Case C-96/89 *Commission v Netherlands*, par. 38; Case C-104/02 *Commission v Germany*, par. 45; and Case C-392/02 *Commission v Denmark*, par. 67.

debt actually does exist or at least whilst the debt can still be presumed. Moreover, any precedent[103] could not be transposed to the present case, since there is an essential difference between situations in which a customs debt exists but the Member State cannot recover it due to errors by its customs offices, and situations where the customs debt did not exist in the first place.[104]

For these reasons Advocate General Trstenjak turned to secondary Community legislation, but also to the DCFR, which standardizes European law. The DCFR recognizes the principle of the ancillary nature of interest. Thereupon, the Advocate General explicitly referred to art. III.–3:708(1)[105] DCFR,[106] which actually provides that the debtor must pay default interest only if he is late in payment. On the contrary, neither DCFR nor secondary Community legislation[107] acknowledge that the creditor should be entitled to default interest where there is no longer an obligation to pay the sum owed.[108]

The Advocate General concluded that there is a legal loophole regarding the punishment in case of failure in fulfilling the Member States' obligation to credit own resources. Thereupon it was stated that it would be contrary to the very nature of default interest if such interest were to be used as a substitute for the lack of an effective penalty system in cases of infringement of Community legislation.[109]

Moreover, the Advocate General recommended that the Commission should propose an amendment to the existing Community legislation, which will set an effective penalty for the above infringements and which should be independent from the payment of default interest. It would be contrary to the very nature of default interest if such interest were to be used as a substitute for the lack of an effective penalty system in cases of infringement of Community legislation.[110] Further on, it was noted that the principles of civil law as stated in art. III.-3:708(2) DCFR do not preclude the creditor from claiming further compensation from his debtor, when unconnected with the payment of default interest.[111] Thereupon the Advocate General recommended that the Commission should base its amendment on the civil law principle, stated in art. III.-3:708(2) DCFR.[112]

[103] *De Haan Beheer* Case C-61/98 [1999] ECR I-5003.

[104] Case C-275/07 *Commission of the European Communities v Italian Republic*, par. 84.

[105] Article III.-3:708 (1) DCFR: Interest on late payments—If payment of a sum of money is delayed, whether or not the non-performance is excused, the creditor is entitled to interest on that sum from the time when payment is due to the time of payment at the average commercial bank short-term lending rate to prime borrowers prevailing for the currency of payment at the place where the payment is due.

[106] With reference to Christian von Bar and others (eds.), *Principles, Definitions and Model Rules of European Private Law. Draft Common Frame of Reference (DCFR)* (Interim Outline Edition, Sellier Munich 2008) p. 170.

[107] Nor does Article 4.507 (1) of the Principles of European Contract Law.

[108] Ibid., par. 90.

[109] Ibid., par. 93.

[110] Ibid., par. 93.

[111] Ibid., par. 94.

[112] Article III.-3:708: Interest on late payments; (2) The creditor may in addition recover damages for any further loss. Consequently the Advocate General assessed that the Member State does not have an obligation to pay default interest from the day on which the State was obliged to credit such resources to the Community's account until the date on which the presumption as to the existence of the customs debt was rebutted; Case C-275/07 *Commission of the European Communities v Italian Republic*, par. 95.

b) Book VI—Non-contractual liability arising out of damage caused to another

i. VI a. Prevention; Liability for loss in preventing damage

But the DCFR is applied also in cases other than merely contract law cases. Furthermore, its scope of applicability extends to cases of non-contractual liability. For instance, Advocate General Mengozzi referred to art. VI.-6:302 DCFR in his effort to establish compensation for expenses, when such expenses had occurred reasonably, in order to prevent anticipated damage or in order to limit its seriousness.[113] Thereupon, Advocate General Mengozzi constructed his legal analogy. According to which, since negligence, in certain circumstances, can break the causal link between the unlawful conduct and the damage: that should also pertain in the case when the same person was diligent. Therefore, due to his diligent behaviour, the damage incurred by his previously unlawful conduct, will be different or maybe even lesser than the recoverable damage which otherwise would have derived from the same unlawful behaviour.[114]

III. Assessment of the approaches taken by the ECJ and the national courts

First and foremost, one can rather easily understand that national courts of certain European countries have a much more liberal approach when seeking the relevant legal rule in a given legal matter, while others are definitely more reluctant to do so. The same could also be said for Advocate Generals. Some are certainly keener to consider other legal sources than others. This detailed list of DCFR cases in the courts shows a distinct pattern, however. Both the ECJ and the national courts tend to resort to the DCFR either in cases of legal loopholes and absence of precedence, or in order to justify their decisions, by pointing out that the relevant national laws do comply with the model rules of the DCFR. Through its compliance with the DCFR, the applied law seems to gain in validity and authenticity. This therefore displays that the DCFR is already established within the EU and it is recognized as a work which depicts and promotes the general rules and principles of a unified European private law.

Both the ECJ and the national courts apply the DCFR mostly per legal analogy, when, for instance, the existing laws do not cover a certain legal matter, or when the wording of either a legal text or of a contract is unclear, or the scope of a legal source is considered as too narrow, so that it contradicts existing legal situations in the Member States. In such cases the DCFR is applied in order to correct eventual flaws in the legal texts. Therefore, DCFR is already well accepted as a work which determines the standard legal approaches within Europe. Both the ECJ as well as the national courts refer to DCFR when existing laws fail to provide an answer to a certain legal question or when a topic is controversial as a whole. But moreover and most of the time, courts use DCFR as a source for legal definitions and principles which apply in the whole of Europe. However, national courts seem to be somehow keener to apply the DCFR rules in order to interpret conflicting (national) laws.

113 Opinion of Advocate General Mengozzi delivered on 11 January 2007, Case C-282/05 p. I-2970 ft. 58.

114 Ibid., p. I-2969–I-2970 par. 115.

Out of all the DCFR cases, however, one is of particular significance. In order to cover a legal loophole, the Swedish Supreme Court first overviewed the legislation on resale agreements in other European countries and after establishing that, with the sole exception of Belgium, no other European country had a definitive legislation on resale agreements, it then directly applied the DCFR rules in its decision. This particular case is stated in the national legal literature as an example of the Court's eagerness to create a modern property law.[115] This decision triggered great controversy within the local legal community, especially about the source status of the DCFR within the legislation. DCFR is acknowledged by the legal community as a great asset, but scepticism prevailed as to whether its rules could be applied directly. According to prevailing opinion, DCFR would better be considered as a range of recommendations.[116] The European legal community certainly appreciates the DCFR as a common legal basis, but in its current form it is rather difficult to justify direct applicability of its rules. However, this particular case made it obvious that the DCFR is of great importance to the Swedish Supreme Court, so much so, that it willingly opposed its own previous judgments.[117] The Supreme Court, by directly implementing the DCFR, in order to fill the legal gap, did set a totally new precedent.

This analysis of DCFR case law also reveals the tendency of the courts to refer to the DCFR mainly when contract law issues have to be resolved, with the exception of Advocate General Mengozzi's Opinion[118] on non-contractual liability deriving from damage caused to another. Although the DCFR promotes knowledge on all private law topics, it is, however, used by both national and community courts mainly for issues relating to the law of contract. It does so to such an extent, that DCFR in the courts certainly contributes to a harmonious and informal modernization and homogenization of at least private contract law.

IV. Closing remarks

From the case law overview regarding the DCFR in legal practice, it becomes rather clear how much the DCFR can contribute to the development of EU private law. One can't see how the DCFR has a broad potential application in terms of its extensive content and general adaptability. This is not only the case because tort law and contract law cases are both represented within the European case law concerning the DCFR, but also because the DCFR is applied by the ECJ as well as by Supreme Courts of various European countries. Even though it is mostly acknowledged for offering guidance, as some kind of Ariadne's thread, helping to determine general legal standards in the labyrinth of the many different legal systems within the whole of Europe, however, on several occasions, both the Advocate General and European Supreme Courts have taken the leap and applied the DCFR provisions directly to their cases. The latter has

[115] *Christina Ramberg*, The Supreme Court's silent coup, published 3 July 2009.

[116] Supreme Court Judgment of 3 November 2009, NJA 2009 p. 672, *Svante O. Johansson*, Avtalsrätt published on 20 November 2009.

[117] *Svante O. Johansson*, Avtalsrätt published on 20 November 2009.

[118] Opinion of Advocate General Mengozzi delivered on 11 January 2007, Case C-282/05 p. I-2970 ft. 58.

occurred primarily when a legislative gap was determined by the court in the relevant legal text, which was then amended by directly applying the DCFR provisions. In such instances, the DCFR can actually shape national and community law and can be used as an instrument for law reform.

A direct application of the DCFR within a certain legal issue before a court of a Member State is by no means simple. Precisely because the DCFR is not a legislative act, one could argue that it therefore lacks legitimacy, or even that the courts have exceeded their own jurisdiction. By doing this, the distinction to the legislative power has become even narrower. However, it is also generally acknowledged that the courts are usually the first that have to react to any new ways of thinking, or to new institutions within a society. Therefore, as the courts try to keep up and adapt to the various changes, they often tend to modernize the law, thereby compelling the legislator to also adjust.

On the other hand, however, the DCFR has repeatedly proven to be of great assistance, especially to the ECJ. The ECJ itself acknowledges that as long as there is no uniform European Civil Law, the ECJ shall continue to be dependent on the information provided by the national courts on the points of national law arising in any given domestic case. However, the ECJ explicitly states that in the alternative, it turns to codification models developed by European academics, and especially to the DCFR, in order to find appropriate solutions to disputes concerning the civil law. Furthermore, the ECJ recognizes that the DCFR, which formulates the common European rules of contract law, is capable of providing the Court with the criteria necessary to carry out a more robust review of contractual terms on a European scale.[119] Moreover, the ECJ, through Advocate General Opinions, has also made direct recommendations towards the Commission of the EU, not only to take an example from DCFR but furthermore to implement its provisions, when trying to rectify loopholes in EU legislation.

At the time of writing, apart from the ECJ, it is primarily the Dutch, Estonian, Spanish, and Swedish Supreme Courts that have applied DCFR provisions within their rulings. DCFR has, however, also interested English[120] and Scottish[121] courts. As per Italy, court rulings of other European countries, which directly apply DCFR, are considered as sensational and are set as examples in Italian legal journals.[122] However, it would not be particularly daring to predict that the tendency concerning the application of DCFR provisions in both national and EU courts is constantly rising. Since, for instance, the new Catalan and the new Hungarian Civil Codes, the new Belgian security laws, the upcoming review of the Scottish contract law, and the upcoming new Czech Civil Code have incorporated DCFR articles within their own provisions, one can say that we currently stand on the brink of a breakthrough and

[119] Opinion of Advocate General Trstenjak delivered on 6 July 2010—Case C-137/08 par. 96 footnote no. 54.

[120] *Chartbrook Ltd v Persimmon Homes Ltd* [2009] UKHL 38.

[121] e.g. *Lloyds TSB Foundation for Scotland v Lloyds Banking Group plc* [2011] CSIH 87; 2012 SC 259.

[122] *Alessandra De Marco*, Alcune riflessione a margine della sentenza 3 novembre 2009 della Corte Suprema di Svezia: un primo esempio applicativo del Draft Common Frame of Reference in Il diritto del commercio internazionale 2012 p. 236–47.

great change within European law as a whole. Moreover, the law reform induced by the DCFR seems to have already exceeded the confining boundaries of the European region, as supported by, for example, the Australian Attorney General's observation of its possibility to inspire,[123] and the fact that DCFR is already translated into Korean, Japanese, and Russian.

DCFR will certainly remain a safeguard and a compendium of contemporary European contract law in general and it will, of course, continue to be applied as such. Already now, due to the fact that some courts are applying DCFR, law practitioners are being advised not to disregard DCFR.[124] The difference, however, lies in the fact that it is not only innovative court decisions that will in the future directly apply it. Instead, its provisions already constitute part of the legislation of various Member States, and this is certainly going to affect the case law accordingly.

[123] Australian Government—Attorney General's Department, Improving Australia's Law and Justice Framework: A discussion paper to explore the scope for reforming Australian contract law, 22 March 2012 par. 5.1 ff.

[124] Eric Clive, 'The Draft Common Frame of Reference in the Swedish Supreme Court' in European Private Law News, 14 October 2014, at <http://www.epln.law.ed.ac.uk/2014/10/14/the-draft-common-frame-of-reference-in-the-swedish-supreme-court> and *Bo Thomaeus* Draft Common Frame of Reference and the Supreme Court, in ILO (International Law Office), 13 October 2014, at <http://www.internationallawoffice.com/Newsletters/Detail.aspx?g=03f6ce44-450c-4c9d-bc7a-6e71ad76d802&l=7M69R9A>.

Index

References such as '178–9' indicate (not necessarily continuous) discussion of a topic across a range of pages. Wherever possible in the case of topics with many references, these have either been divided into sub-topics or only the most significant discussions of the topic are listed. Because the entire work is about the 'comparative law', the use of this term (and certain others which occur constantly throughout the book) as an entry point has been minimized. Information will be found under the corresponding detailed topics.